Mastering Modern CAD Drawings with SOLIDWORKS 2026

AF694517

Lani Tran, CSWE

SDC
PUBLICATIONS

SDC Publications
P.O. Box 1334
Mission, KS 66222
913-262-2664
www.SDCpublications.com

Copyright 2026 Lani Tran

The lessons and exercises in this textbook are the sole property of the author. The material is to be used for learning purposes only and not to be used in any way deleterious to the interest of the author.

This textbook is copyrighted, and the author reserves all rights. No part of this publication may be reproduced, transmitted, transcribed, stored in a retrieval system, or translated into any language or computer language, in any form or by any means, electronic, mechanical, magnetic, optical, chemical, manual, or otherwise, without the prior written permission from the author.

It is a violation of United States copyright laws to make copies in any form or media of the contents of this book for commercial or educational purposes without written permission.

Examination Copies
Books received as examination copies are for review purposes only and may not be made available for student use. Resale of examination copies is prohibited.

Electronic Files
Any electronic files associated with this book are licensed to the original user only. These files may not be transferred to any other party.

Trademarks
SOLIDWORKS is a registered trademark of Dassault Systems. Microsoft Excel / Word are registered trademarks of Microsoft Corporation. All other brand names or trademarks belong to their respective companies.

Disclaimer
The author makes a sincere effort to ensure the accuracy of the material described herein; however, the author makes no warranty, expressed or implied, with respect to the quality, correctness, reliability, currency, accuracy, or freedom from error of this document or the products it describes.

The author disclaims all liability for any direct, indirect, incidental, or consequential, special, or exemplary damages resulting from the use of the information in this document or from the use of any products described
in this document. Data used in examples and sample data files are intended to be fictional.

Download all needed model files from the SDC Publication website (www.SDCpublications.com/downloads/978-1-63057-786-5).

ISBN-13: 978-1-63057-786-5

ISBN-10: 1-63057-786-3

Printed and bound in the United States of America.

Acknowledgments

Thanks as always to my dad, Paul Tran, a semi-retired sr. design engineer, for always being there and providing support and honest feedback on all the lessons in the textbook.

Also, I would like to thank you, our readers, for your continued support. It is with your consistent feedback that we were able to create the lessons in this book with more detailed and useful information.

Preface

My SOLIDWORKS journey began in my youth, while observing my dad operate his engineering company. As I developed my career, I became more involved in different facets of the software, from design work to project management. After nearly two decades of exposure to SOLIDWORKS, I found myself working through distinctive projects, where hundreds of components are considered small assemblies.

Throughout this time I've had the opportunity to focus on reoccurring challenges and develop unique solutions. One such challenge I faced on a daily basis was the need to quickly create efficient models to print for testing. In a deadline driven work environment, it is crucial to create accurate and manufacturable designs.

The lessons in this manual reflect much of what I do at work. I wanted to share the techniques I have developed to create various models, assemblies, and drawings. I hope you will find this manual useful and that you can apply these lessons to grow your own skills.

TABLE OF CONTENTS

Lesson 1:	**INTRODUCTION TO CAD DRAWINGS**	**1-1**
	Manual vs. Computer Aided Drawings	1-1
	Technical drawings	1-1
	Sketching	1-1
	Manual drawings	1-2
	Computer Aided Design	1-3
	Limitations of 2D CAD	1-5
	Benefits of 3D CAD	1-5
	SOLIDWORKS – The industry standard	1-6
	Which industries use SOLIDWORKS	1-7
	Why companies use SOLIDWORKS	1-8
	SOLIDWORKS drawings	1-8
	System Options & Document Properties	1-11
Lesson 2:	**DETAILING A MACHINED PART**	**2-1**
	Stainless Steel Flange	2-1
	Opening a part document	2-1
	Setting the drawing properties	2-2
	Creating an engineering drawing	2-3
	Changing the scale of the drawing Views	2-5
	Rearranging the drawing Views	2-6
	Modifying the sheet scale	2-7
	Creating a section view	2-8
	Modifying the crosshatch properties	2-9
	Adding the centerlines	2-10
	Changing the Font Size	2-10
	Changing the drawing paper size	2-12
	Inserting the model dimensions	2-14
	Moving dimensions	2-15
	Removing dimension overlaps with Break-Lines	2-16
	Inserting other dimensions	2-17
	Adding callouts	2-18
	Adding additional callouts	2-19
	Adding datums	2-21
	Adding the General Notes	2-23
	Adding the Revision Table	2-24
	Filling out the Title Block	2-26
	Switching back to the Sheet	2-27
	Exercise: Detailing a Machined Part	2-29

Lesson 3: **UNDERSTANDING TOLERANCE, PRECISION, & GD&T** **3-1**
Using GD&T in a Drawing 3-1
What is GD&T? 3-2
Rule #1 and #2 3-3
Terminology used in GD&T 3-4
Maximum material condition 3-6
Least material condition 3-7
Size, location, orientation, Form 3-8
Types of GD&T Tolerances 3-9
Material modifier 3-10
Straightness 3-11
Flatness – Surface 3-12
Flatness – FOS/DMP 3-13
Circularity 3-14
Cylindricity 3-15
Line profile 3-16
Surface profile 3-17
Parallelism – FOS 3-18
Parallelism – Surface 3-19
Perpendicularity – Surface 3-20
Perpendicularity – FOS 3-21
Angularity 3-22
Runout 3-23
Total runout 3-24
Position 3-25
Concentricity 3-26
Symmetry 3-27
GD&T in a nut shell 3-28
What are the advantages of GD&T 3-28

Lesson 4: **USING TOLERANCE, PRECISON, and GD&T** **4-1**
Stainless steel flange 4-1
Opening a drawing document 4-1
Adding a symmetric tolerance 4-2
Adding a bilateral tolerance 4-3
Adding a limit tolerance 4-4
Adding a basic dimension 4-5
Adding a unilateral tolerance 4-7
Adding a true position tolerance 4-9
Bonus tolerance formular 4-10
Adding a concentricity control 4-11

	Exercise: Detailing a machined part	4-13
	Creating the drawing views	4-14
	Adding dimensions	4-15
	Adding tolerance and precision	4-16
	Adding the general notes	4-17
	Adding a revision block	4-18
	Filling out the title block	4-19
	Exercise: Detailing a machined part	4-21
	Transferring to a drawing	4-21
	Creating the drawing views	4-22
	Adding the model dimensions	4-23
	Adding the General Notes	4-24
	Filling out the Title Block	4-24
Lesson 5:	**DETAILING PLASTIC PARTS**	**5-1**
	Plastic Gear	5-1
	Opening a part document	5-1
	Transferring to drawing	5-2
	Creating the drawing views	5-3
	Creating a section view	5-4
	Changing the hatch pattern	5-5
	Creating a detail view	5-6
	Adding centerlines automatically	5-7
	Adding centerlines manually	5-7
	Inserting the model dimensions	5-8
	Moving the dimensions	5-9
	Moving and Hiding dimensions	5-10
	Adding the missing dimensions	5-11
	Adding datums	5-14
	Adding Geometric tolerance	5-14
	Adding the general notes	5-16
	Adding the revision block	5-17
	Filling out the title block	5-18
	Exercise 1: Detailing a Plastic Part 1	5-20
	Creating the drawing views	5-21
	Making a section view	5-22
	Modifying the hatch pattern	5-23
	Adding the detail views	5-24
	Creating a crop view	5-25
	Breaking the view alignment	5-26
	Adding dimensions	5-26

	Adding the general notes	5-28
	Filling out the title block information	5-29
	Exercise 2: Detailing a Plastic Part 2	5-31
	Exercise 3: Detailing a Plastic Part 3	5-35
Lesson 6:	**DETAILING SHEET METAL PARTS**	**6-1**
	Detailing a Sheet Metal Part	6-1
	Opening a part document	6-1
	Setting up the drawing sheet	6-2
	Creating the drawing views	6-3
	Creating an auxiliary view	6-4
	Creating a crop view	6-5
	Inserting the model dimensions	6-6
	Rearranging and adding the dimensions	6-7
	Adding the general notes	6-8
	Filling out the title block	6-9
	Adding the isometric flat pattern	6-10
	Exercise: Detailing a Sheet Metal Part	6-12
	Transferring to a drawing	6-12
	Creating the drawing views	6-13
	Adding centerlines and center marks	6-14
	Inserting the model dimensions	6-14
	Rearranging and modifying Dimensions	6-15
	Adding the general notes	6-16
	Filling out the title block	6-17
	Exercise: Detailing a Sheet Metal Part	6-19
	Exercise: Adding Dimensions to a Spline	6-25
Lesson 7:	**DETAILING CASTINGS AND FORGINGS**	**7-1**
	Detailing a Casted Part	7-1
	Opening a part document	7-1
	Drawings overview	7-2
	Adding a 2nd sheet	7-3
	Creating the casted drawing	7-3
	Inserting the model dimensions	7-4
	Creating the general notes	7-6
	Filling out the title block information	7-7
	Creating the machined drawing	7-8

Inserting the model dimensions 7-9
Adding datums 7-12
Adding geometric tolerances 7-13
Filling out the title block 7-14

Exercise: Detailing a casted part 1 7-16
Exercise: Detailing a casted part 2 7-35
Exercise: Detailing a casted part 3 7-39

Lesson 8: **ASSEMBLY DRAWINGS** **8-1**
Detailing an assembly drawing 8-1
Opening an assembly document 8-1
Making a drawing from assembly 8-2
Creating the drawing views 8-3
Adding balloons 8-4
Adding the number of instances 8-6
Inserting a bill of materials 8-7
Adjusting the BOM 8-9
Filling out the BOM manually 8-10
Filling out the title block information 8-11

Exercise: Detailing an assembly drawing 8-13
Transferring to a drawing 8-13
Creating the drawing views 8-14
Adding balloons and instance counts 8-15
Inserting the bill of materials 8-16
Changing the custom properties 8-17
Filling out the title block information 8-18

Exercise: Detailing an assembly drawing 8-21

Lesson 9: **CUSTOM PROPERTIES** **9-1**
Creating the custom properties – Part 1 9-1
Opening an assembly document 9-1
Opening a part from an assembly 9-2
Creating the custom properties 9-2
Entering the custom property information 9-3
Making a drawing from assembly 9-5
Creating the drawing views 9-6
Adding balloons 9-7
Inserting the bill of materials 9-8

	Switching the custom properties	9-9
	Filling out the title block information	9-10
	Part 2: Using the Property Tab Builder	9-12
	Starting a new drawing	9-12
	Accessing the custom properties tab	9-13
	Switching the Template type	9-14
	Modifying the Groupbox	9-14
	Adding a textbox field	9-15
	Adding a list field	9-15
	Adding another Textbox field	9-16
	Saving the Property Tab template	9-17
	Testing the DRW Properties Template	9-17
	Adding a Textbox field	9-18
	Saving the Property Tab Template	9-19
	Testing out the Part Properties Template	9-20
	Creating a sample part	9-20
	Making drawing from part	9-21
Lesson 10:	**CONFIGURATIONS AND DESIGN**	**10-1**
	Creating a Design Table using MS-Excel	10-1
	Opening a part document	10-1
	Renaming the dimensions	10-2
	Inserting an Excel-based design table	10-3
	Adding new configurations in Excel	10-4
	Adding new features to the design table	10-5
	Assigning the feature's states	10-6
	Switching back to SOLIDWORKS application	10-7
	Viewing the new configurations	10-8
	Adjusting the rows and columns	10-9
	Making a drawing from part	10-10
	Inserting the design table	10-11
	Adjusting the table header in Excel	10-12
	Switching back to the drawing	10-13
	Filling out the title block information	10-14
	Creating a tabulated table	10-15
	Exercise: Design Table - Creating a tabulated table	10-18

Lesson 11:	**ADDITIONAL DRAWING TOOLS**	**11-1**
	Detailing the base mount block	11-1
	Opening a part document	11-1
	Adding the standard drawing views	11-2
	Creating an auxiliary view	11-3
	Breaking the view alignment	11-4
	Creating a broken-out section view	11-5
	Modifying the hatch pattern	11-6
	Creating a detail view	11-7
	Adding centerlines and center marks	11-8
	Inserting the model dimensions	11-9
	Rearranging dimensions	11-10
	Moving dimensions	11-11
	Reviewing the drawing	11-12
	Changing the color of a dimension	11-13
	Showing a sketch from the model	11-14
	Inserting the pattern instances	11-15
	Creating a parametric note	11-16
	Changing the number of pattern instances	11-17
	SOLIDWORKS DrawCompare	11-19
	Comparing the drawings	11-20
	Viewing the differences	11-21
	SOLIDWORKS Pack and Go	11-23
	Opening an assembly document	11-23
	Launching the Pack and Go utility	11-24
	Exercise: Detailing the aluminum block	11-25
	Opening a part document	11-25
	Creating the additional drawing views	11-26
	Inserting the model dimensions	11-27
	Adding the instance callouts	11-28
	Filling out the title block	11-29
	Exercise: Other options in assembly drawings	11-31
	Adding the explode lines	11-32
	Collapsing the assembly	11-35
	Making drawing from assembly	11-36
	Inserting the drawing views	11-37
	Adding balloons	11-38
	Inserting a bill of materials	11-39
	Formatting the BOM	11-40

	Changing the custom properties	11-41
	Hiding components	11-43
	Other display options	11-46
Lesson 12:	**SOLIDWORKS MBD - Model Based Definition**	**12-1**
	Part 1: Model Based Definition – Prismatic parts	12-1
	Opening a part document	12-1
	Understanding the types of parts	12-2
	Understanding the DimXpert tool	12-2
	Setting up the DimXpert options	12-3
	Adding datums	12-5
	Showing tolerance status	12-8
	Opening another part document	12-9
	Adding datums	12-9
	Adding the size dimensions	12-10
	Checking the constraint status	12-11
	Showing all annotations	12-12
	Part 2: Model Based Definition – Turned parts	12-13
	Opening a part document	12-13
	Adding datums	12-14
	Rearranging the annotations	12-16
	Recreating the basic dimensions	12-17
	Opening another part document	12-19
	Using the plus and minus tolerances	12-19
	Using polar	12-20
	Part 3: Model Based Definition – Capturing 3D Views	12-22
	Switching to 3D View tab	12-23
	Capturing the Front Views	12-24
	Capturing the orthographic views	12-25
	Creating a zonal section view	12-26
	Capturing the zonal section view	12-27
	Testing the 3D views	12-28
	Publishing to 3D-PDF document	12-29
	Saving the 3D-PDF	12-31
	Publishing to eDrawing	12-32
	Viewing the animation	12-33

Lesson 13: CSWP-Drawing Tools Exam Preparation Material 13-1

Challenge 1 – Part Drawings:
View Creation & Projected Dimensions 13-3
Opening an existing drawing 13-3
Adding the Front drawing view 13-3
Adding dimensions 13-4
Creating the 1st section view 13-5
Measuring the perimeter 13-6
Creating the 2nd section view 13-7
Measuring the perimeter 13-8

Challenge 2 – Assembly Drawings:
View Creation & Measurements 13-9
Opening an assembly document 13-9
Changing the orientation 13-9
Finding the angle 13-10
Entering the angle for Arrow Key rotation 13-11
Rotating the model 13-12
Updating the standard views 13-13
Making a drawing 13-15
Adding a drawing view 13-17
Moving the drawing view 13-18
Lock View Focus vs. Lock Sheet Focus 13-19
Lock Sheet Focus 13-20
Finding the angle 13-21
Sketching a reference line 13-22
Adding another reference line 13-23
Finding the distance 13-24
Creating an Auxiliary View 13-25
Creating an Alternate Position View 13-26
Finding the angle 13-27

Challenge 3 – Assembly Drawings:
Drawing & BOM Creation 13-29
Opening an assembly document 13-29
Making a drawing 13-30
Creating a Bill of Materials 13-31
Finding the quantity of a component 13-32
Switching the Custom Properties 13-33
Finding the Item Number of a component 13-34
Switching the BOM Type 13-35
Finding the Total Cost 13-36
Adding a Note 13-41

Challenge 4 – Assembly Drawings:
Hide and Show Components 13-43
Opening an assembly document 13-43
Finding the hidden components 13-44
Measuring the angle 13-45
Saving the drawing 13-46

Challenge 5 – Part Drawings:
Broken Out Section & Insert Model Items 13-47
Opening a drawing document 13-47
Creating a Broken Out Section view 13-48
Measuring the perimeter 13-50
Inserting the Model Dimensions 13-51
Saving the drawing 13-52

Challenge 6 – Part Drawings:
View Creation & Feature Measurement 13-53
Opening a drawing document 13-53
Creating a custom drawing view 13-54
Saving the custom view 13-56
Inserting the custom view 13-57
Creating a section view 13-58
Saving your drawing 13-59

Index and Glossary

Model library

The models and drawings used in this textbook were created by the author using SOLIDWORKS.
All rights reserved.

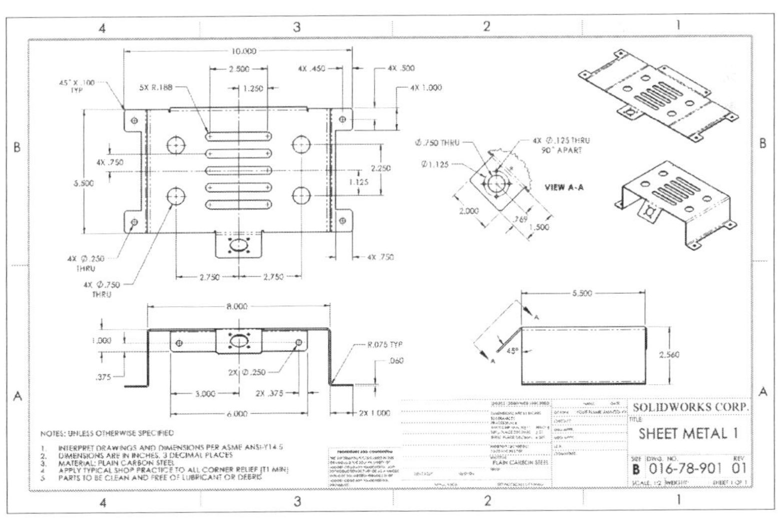

Notes:

CHAPTER 1: INTRODUCTION TO CAD DRAWINGS

Manual Vs. Computer Aided Drawings (CAD)

Creating technical drawings is a time-honored art form which is used in all fields of engineering (mechanical, civil, architectural, electrical, aerospace, etc.).

The main purpose of technical drawings is to communicate specific information to other technical people (i.e., engineers, designers, inspectors, machinists, etc.).

Technical drawings give all of the information needed to make a product and being accurate in that information is the main goal. In engineering, one must be very particular and detail oriented when creating drawings.

Technical drawing is the act and discipline of composing drawings that visually communicate how a manufactured good functions or is constructed.

Technical drawing is essential for communicating ideas in industry and engineering. To make the drawings easier to understand, people use familiar symbols, perspectives, units of measurement, notation systems, visual styles, and page layout. Together, such conventions constitute a visual language and help to ensure that the drawing is clear and relatively easy to understand. Many of the symbols and principles of technical drawing are codified in an international standard called ISO 128.

The need for precise communication in the preparation of a functional document distinguishes technical drawings from the expressive drawings of the visual arts. Artistic drawings are subjectively interpreted; their meanings are multiply determined.

Technical drawings are understood to have one intended meaning.
A drafter, or draftsperson, is a person who makes a drawing (technical or expressive).
A professional drafter who makes technical drawings is sometimes called a drafting technician.

Sketching

A sketch is a quickly executed, freehand drawing that is usually not intended as a finished work. In general, sketching is a quick way to record an idea for later use. An engineering sketch, for example, is a kind of diagram. These sketches, like metaphors, are used by engineers as a means of communication in aiding design collaboration. This tool helps engineers to abstract attributes of hypothetical provisional design solutions and summarize their complex patterns, thereby enhancing the design process.

Manual Drawing

The basic drafting procedure is to place a piece of paper (or other material) on a smooth surface with right-angle corners and straight sides—typically a drawing board. A sliding straightedge known as a T-square is then placed on one of the sides, allowing it to slide across the side of the table, and over the surface of the paper.

"Parallel lines" can be drawn simply by moving the T-square and running a pencil or technical pen along the T-square's edge. The T-square is used to hold other devices such as set squares or triangles. In this case, the drafter places one or more triangles of known angles on the T-square—which is itself at right angles to the edge of the table—and can then draw lines at any chosen angle to others on the page. Modern drafting tables come equipped with a drafting machine that is supported on both sides of the table to slide over a large piece of paper. Because it is secured on both sides, lines drawn along the edge are guaranteed to be parallel.

In addition, the drafter uses several technical drawing tools to draw curves and circles. Primary among these are the compasses, used for drawing simple arcs and circles, and the French curve, for drawing curves. A spline is a rubber coated articulated metal that can be manually bent to most curves.

This basic drafting system requires an accurate table and constant attention to the positioning of the tools. A common error is to allow the triangles to push the top of the T-square down slightly, thereby throwing off all angles. Even tasks as simple as drawing two angled lines meeting at a point require a number of moves of the T-square and triangles, and in general, drafting can be a time-consuming process.

A solution to these problems was the introduction of the mechanical "drafting machine", an application of the pantograph (sometimes referred to incorrectly as a "pentagraph" in these situations) which allowed the drafter to have an accurate right angle at any point on the page quite quickly. These machines often included the ability to change the angle, thereby removing the need for the triangles as well.

In addition to the mastery of the mechanics of drawing lines, arcs, and circles (and text) onto a piece of paper—with respect to the detailing of physical objects—the drafting effort requires a thorough understanding of geometry, trigonometry, and spatial comprehension, and in all cases demands precision and accuracy, and attention to detail of high order.

Although drafting is sometimes accomplished by a project engineer, shop personnel (such as a machinist), and skilled drafters (and/or designers) usually accomplish the task and are always in demand to some degree.

Computer Aided Design (CAD)

An example of a design created in CAD systems such as SOLIDWORKS or Catia replaces the paper drawing discipline. The lines, circles, arcs, and curves are created within the software. It is down to the technical drawing skill of the user to produce the drawing.

There is still much scope for error in the drawing when producing first and third angle orthographic projections, auxiliary projections and cross-section views. A 2D CAD system is merely an electronic drawing board. Its greatest strength over direct to paper technical drawing is in the making of revisions. Whereas in a conventional hand drawn technical drawing, if a mistake is found, or a modification is required, a new drawing must be made from scratch, the 2D CAD system allows a copy of the original to be modified, saving considerable time.

2D CAD systems can be used to create plans for large projects such as buildings and aircraft but provide no way to check the various components will fit together.

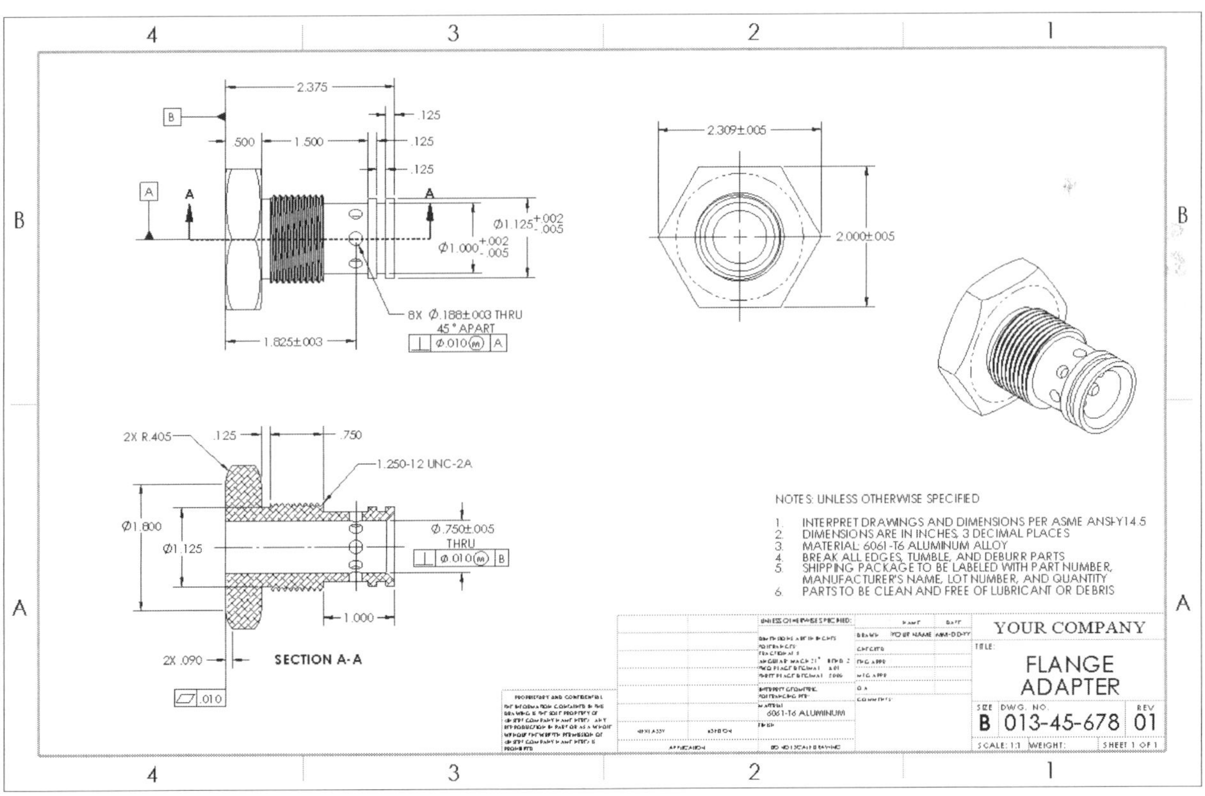

A 3D CAD system (such as SOLIDWORKS) first produces the geometry of the part; the technical drawing comes from user defined views of that geometry.

Any orthographic, projected, or sectioned view is created by the software. There is no scope for error in the production of these views. The main scope for error comes in setting the parameter of first or third angle projection and displaying the relevant symbol on the technical drawing.

3D CAD allows individual parts to be assembled together to represent the final product. Buildings, aircraft, ships, and cars are modeled, assembled, and checked in 3D before technical drawings are released for manufacture.

Both 2D and 3D CAD systems can be used to produce technical drawings for any discipline. The various disciplines (electrical, electronic, pneumatic, hydraulic, etc.) have industry recognized symbols to represent common components.

ANSI and ISO produce standards to show recommended practices but it is up to individuals to produce the drawings to a standard. There is no definitive standard for layout or style. The only standard across engineering workshop drawings is in the creation of orthographic projections and cross-section views.

In representing complex, three-dimensional objects in two-dimensional drawings, the objects can be described by at least one view plus a material thickness note, and 2, 3 or as many views and sections as needed to show all features of an object.

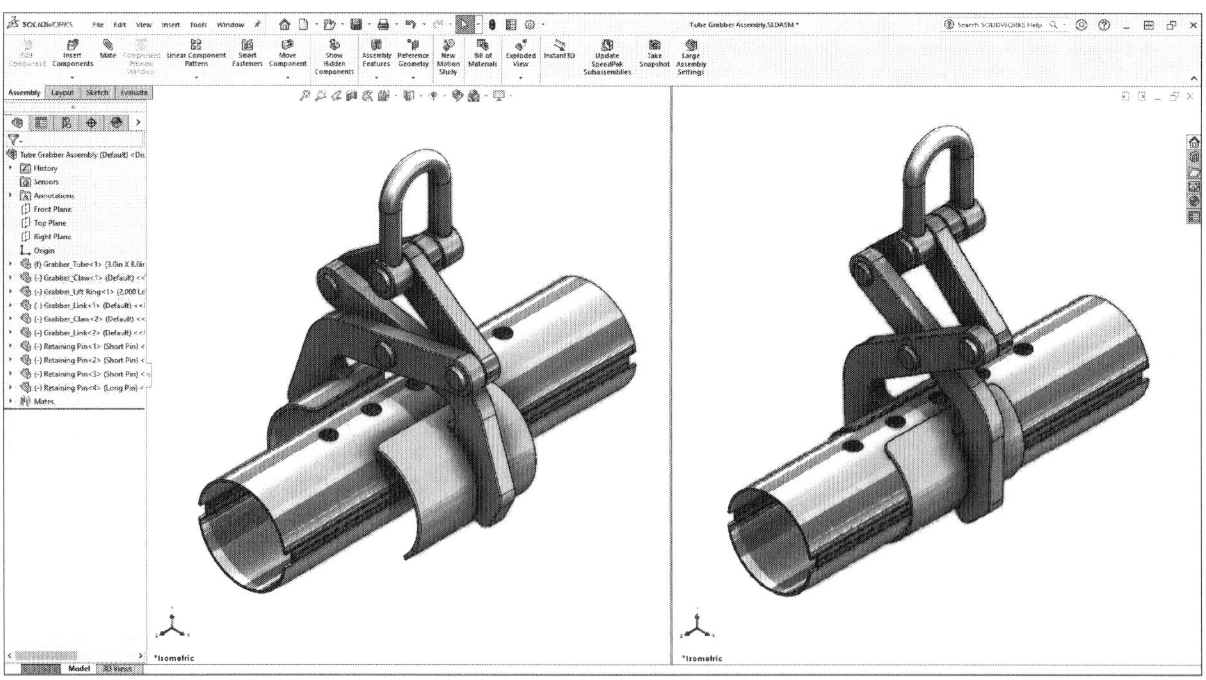

CAD is quick to learn and easy to use, allowing engineers and designers to work faster and more effectively than ever before. While hand-drawing models can be rewarding, it is often a slow and laborious process. Thanks to CAD software, organizations can produce high-quality designs quickly without compromising on precision.

3D CAD modeling makes better use of the designer resources by taking away the manual and tedious part of designs. It also helps the designer visualize all components in 3D during the initial design stage.

Limitations of 2D CAD

- Complicates Checking Processes
- 2D Design Requires Prototypes
- Design Changes are Difficult
- Utilizes New Product Design Technologies like 3D Printing
- Speed Up Approvals
- Makes Design Changes Quick and Easy
- Visualization
- Photorealistic Renderings and Animations

Benefits of 3D CAD

- 3D CAD Allows for More Effective Design Communication
- Avoid Costly Mistakes
- Increased Efficiency and Productivity
- Better Visualization
- Collaboration
- Decreased Manufacturing Time
- Product Lifecycle Management (PLM)

With 2D programs, drawing is fast and easy. But the output is still a 2D drawing, which does not readily work with downstream systems like purchasing and manufacturing.

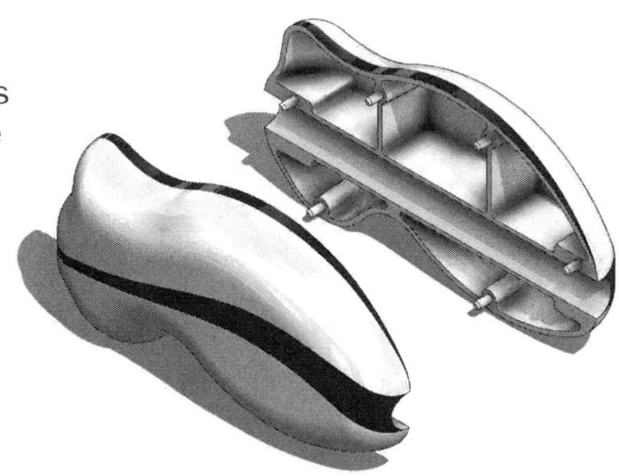

These 2D drawings do not contain all the information needed to develop a three-dimensional product. It is usually during the manufacturing stage that problems arise, particularly with material or matching and mating assemblies.

Most 3D CAD systems generate dimensioned 2D drawings almost automatically, but they also include a virtual prototype that offers unambiguous data for subsequent processes. Viewing 3D models on screen helps identify errors early. These systems also promote innovation; recognition of good ideas is fast.

Converting from 2D to 3D programs is easier with hybrid 2D-3D systems. When budgets permit, engineering departments can convert to pure 3D CAD systems. The newer versions are affordable, Windows based, and support component as well as assembly modeling.

In addition, many 3D CAD packages include features specific to cooperative situations, such as data management, revision status tracking, change order management, and bill of materials data to name a few.

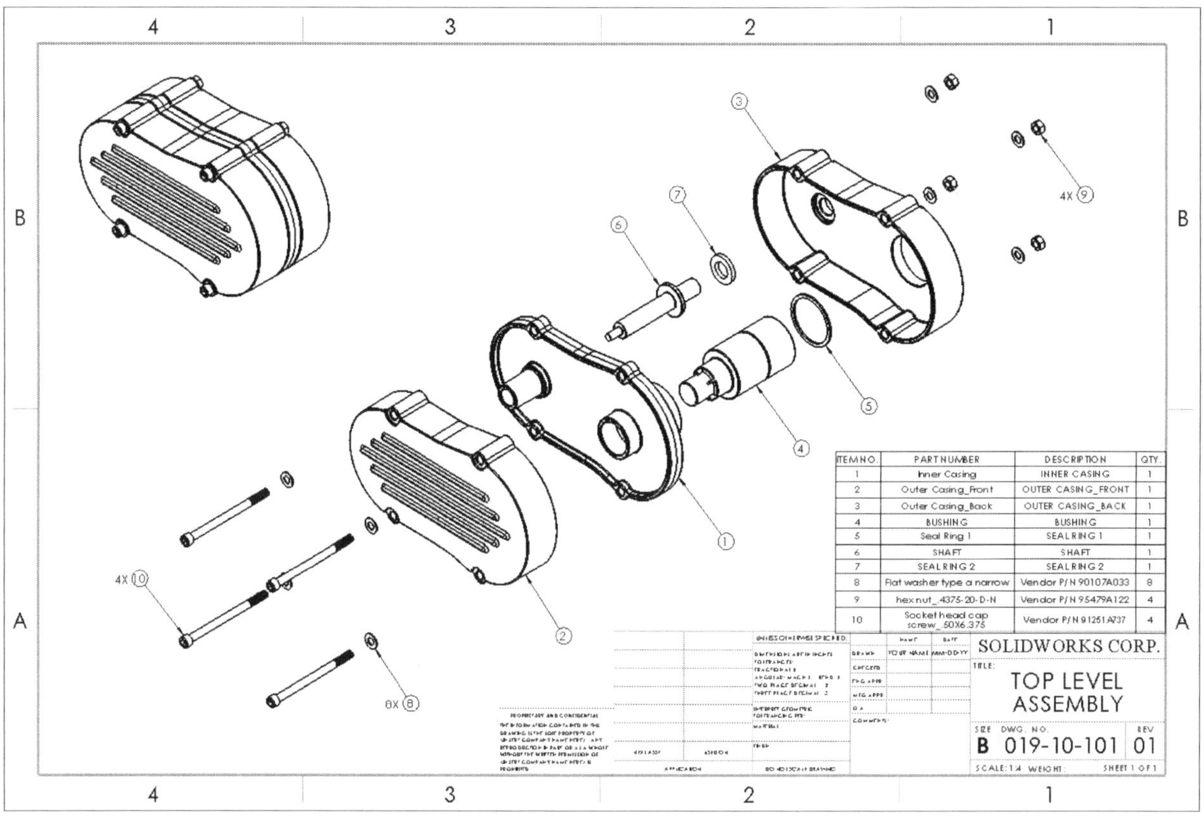

SOLIDWORKS - The Industry Standard

SOLIDWORKS, a solid modeling computer-aided design and computer-aided engineering program, is one of the most popular software options for mechatronics engineers.

SOLIDWORKS was developed by MIT graduate Jon Hirschtick in 1993 and introduced to the public in 1995. The company was acquired by Dassault Systems in 1997. The software now encompasses a number of programs that can be used for both 2D and 3D design.

SOLIDWORKS is used to develop mechatronics systems from beginning to end. At the initial stage, the software is used for planning, visual ideation, modeling, feasibility assessment, prototyping, and project management. The software is then used for design and building mechanical, electrical, and software elements.
Finally, the software can be used for management, including device management, analytics, data automation, and cloud services.

SOLIDWORKS is used heavily in mechanical engineering and other design industries. It is the industry standard for product development.

The software offers quick and simple solutions to share designs in 2D or 3D formats, meaning you can get instant feedback and continue to work on your designs. Designs can even be shared as 3D animations, which allows you to accurately demonstrate new products and features.

SOLIDWORKS drawings also help to detect inconsistencies and allow the designer to make changes to models and sketches before they are finished. This cuts down manufacturing time and enhances the process, making it more cost-effective and allowing companies to adhere to tight deadlines.

SOLIDWORKS helps in the quick generation of 3D models from 2D data as part of product development or mechanical design. DWG files can be imported into SOLIDWORKS 3D CAD software and View Folding can automate 3D model development with tweaks to imported 2D drawings.

Which industries use SOLIDWORKS

Mechanical Parts & Assembly Design	SOLIDWORKS
Automotive Design & Engineering	SOLIDWORKS
Aerospace Design & Engineering	SOLIDWORKS
Manufacturing Firms	SOLIDWORKS
Industrial Engineering	SOLIDWORKS
Mechanical and Electrical Engineering	SOLIDWORKS
Architectural & Construction Design	AutoCAD or Others
Civil & Structural Engineering	AutoCAD or Others

Today, SOLIDWORKS is available in 110 countries throughout the world and available in the following languages:

* English
* Chinese-Simplified
* Chinese-Traditional
* Czech
* French
* German
* Italian
* Japanese
* Portuguese-Brazilian
* Korean
* Polish
* Russian
* Spanish
* Turkish

Why companies use SOLIDWORKS

It is parametric 3D modeling software, meaning that it operates on dimension value. When the dimensions are modified, the 3D model changes its shape. SOLIDWORKS has powerful tools, including Simulation, the ability to draw using either parts or assemblies, rendering tools, and others.

Some highlights of SOLIDWORKS software:

Short learning curve
Cost effective
Intuitive interface
2D innovative drafting tools
Top of the line 3D parametric modeling features
Manages large assemblies
Excellent 3D rendering and animation
Enhanced Collaboration
Analysis tools to reduce errors
Integration with Product Lifecycle Management (PLM)
Create multiple configurations of parts or assemblies using MS-Excel
Flexible assemblies and sub-assemblies

SOLIDWORKS Drawings

With SOLIDWORKS you can create 2D drawings of the 3D solid parts and assemblies you design. Parts, assemblies, and drawings are parametrically linked documents; any changes that you make to the part or assembly will update the drawing document.

Generally, a drawing consists of several views generated from the model. Views can also be created from existing views. For example, a section view is created from an existing drawing view.

You can generate drawings in SOLIDWORKS the same way you would generate them in any other 2D CAD systems.

In SOLIDWORKS, the 3D models and assemblies are created first and the drawings are generated after. This method has many advantages such as:

* Designing models is faster than drawing lines.
* SOLIDWORKS creates drawings from models, so the process is efficient.
* You can review models in 3D and check for correct geometry and design issues before generating drawings, so the drawings are more likely to be free of design errors.
* You can insert dimensions and annotations from model sketches and features into drawings automatically, so you do not have to create them manually in drawings.
* Parameters and relations of models are retained in drawings, so drawings reflect the design intent of the model.
* Changes in models or in drawings are reflected in their related documents, so making changes is easier and drawings are more accurate.

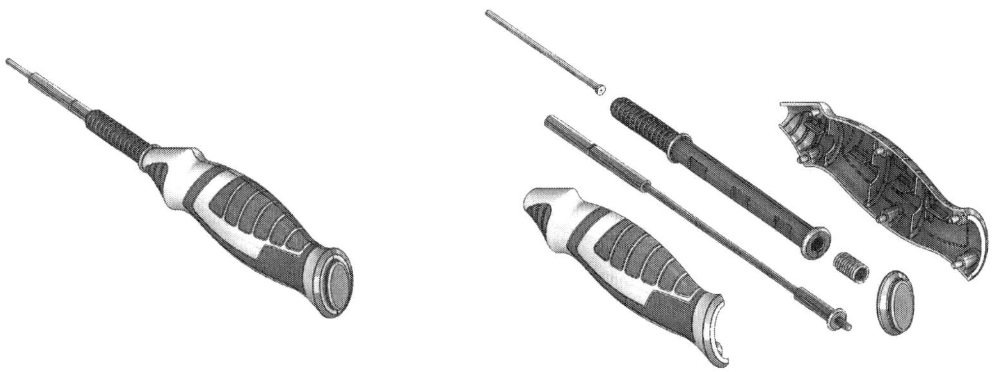

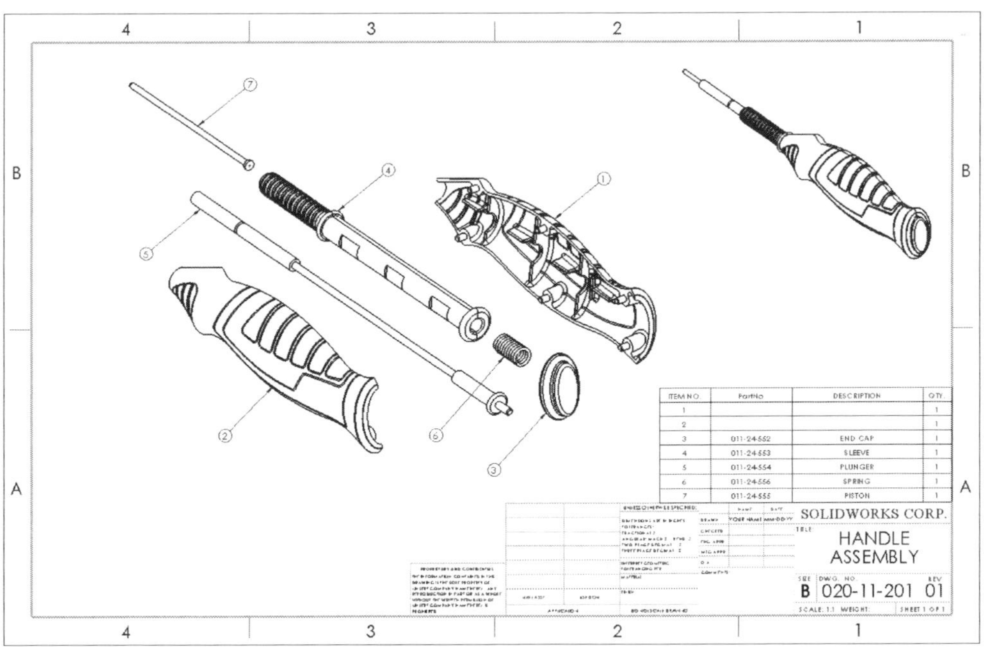

In the process of design development, technical drawings are used to explain the details of the design and also to communicate between the designer and the manufacturer.

During this stage, changes in previous designs take a long time because the drawings have to be produced again. Computer-aided drawing is a technique where engineering drawings are produced with the assistance of a computer and, as with manual drawing, is only the graphical means of representing a design.

Computer-aided design, however, is a technique where the attributes of the computer and those of the designer are blended together into a problem-solving team. When the term CAD is used to mean computer-aided design it normally refers to a graphical system where components and assemblies can be modeled in three dimensions.

The term design, however, also covers those functions attributed to the areas of modeling and analysis. The acronym CAD is more commonly used nowadays and stands for computer-aided drafting and design; a CAD package is one which is able to provide all drafting facilities and some or all of those required for the design process.

This textbook was uniquely put together to teach us how to use SOLIDWORKS drawing functionalities to produce engineering drawings precisely and in a timely manner.

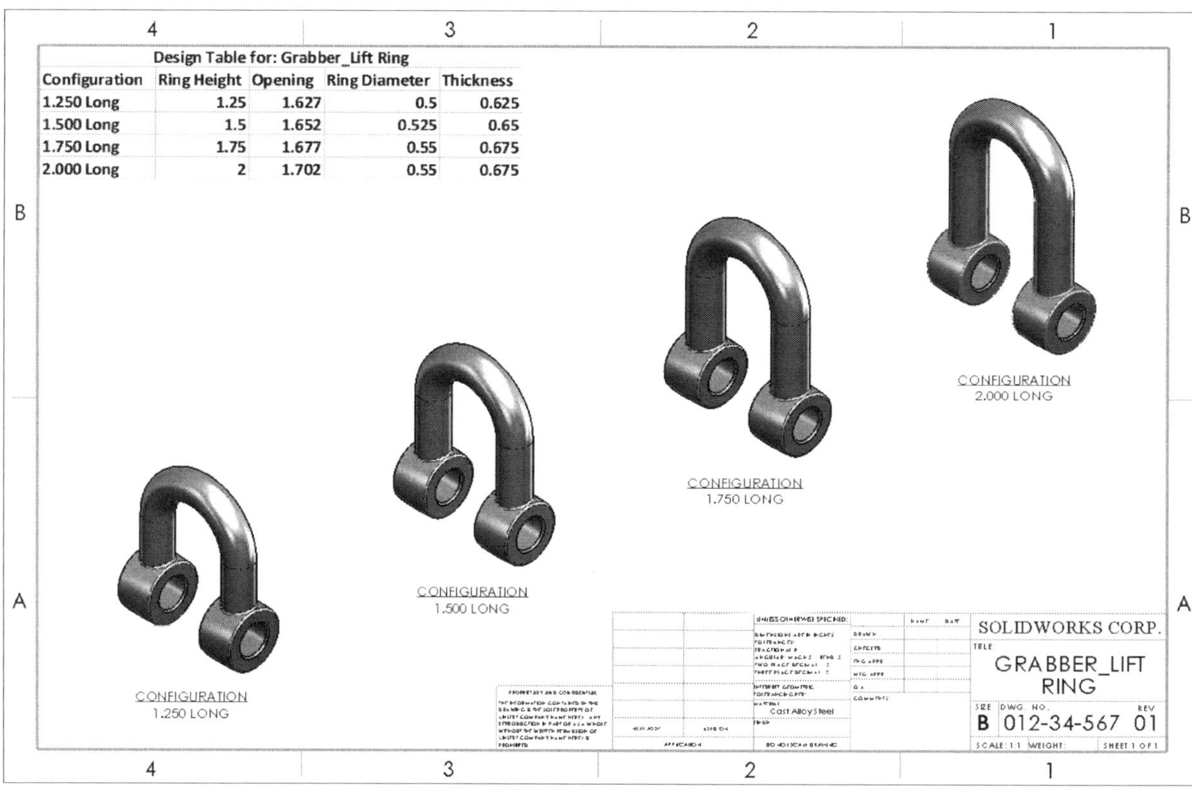

SOLIDWORKS 2026
System Options & Document Properties

There are 2 types of settings available in SOLIDWORKS to help you work more efficiently:

1. System Options:
The system options are stored in the registry and are not part of the documents. Therefore, these changes affect all documents, current and future.

2. Document Properties:
The document properties apply only to the current document, and the Document Properties tab is available only when a document is open. New documents get their document settings (such as Units, Image Quality, and so on) from the document properties of the template used to create the document. Use the Document Properties tab when you set up document templates.

We will take a look at some of the parameters that we need to create and save prior to going through the lessons in this textbook.

Let us start with a new B-Size drawing.

System Options

Click **File, New, Drawing, B-Size.**

Select **Tools, Options.**

General:

Specify general system options such as enabling the number of recent documents, confirmation corner, technical alerts, etc.

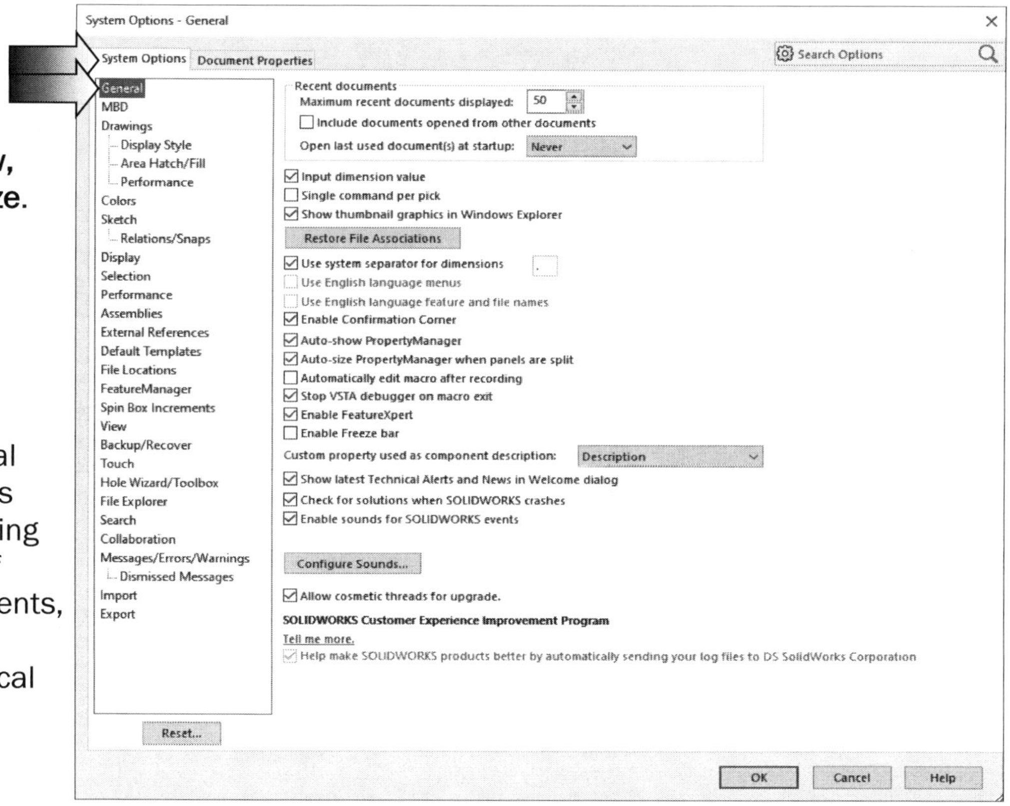

Drawings:

Set the options for drawings such as eliminate duplicate dimensions, auto-scale new drawing views, auto-populate View Palette views, and so on.

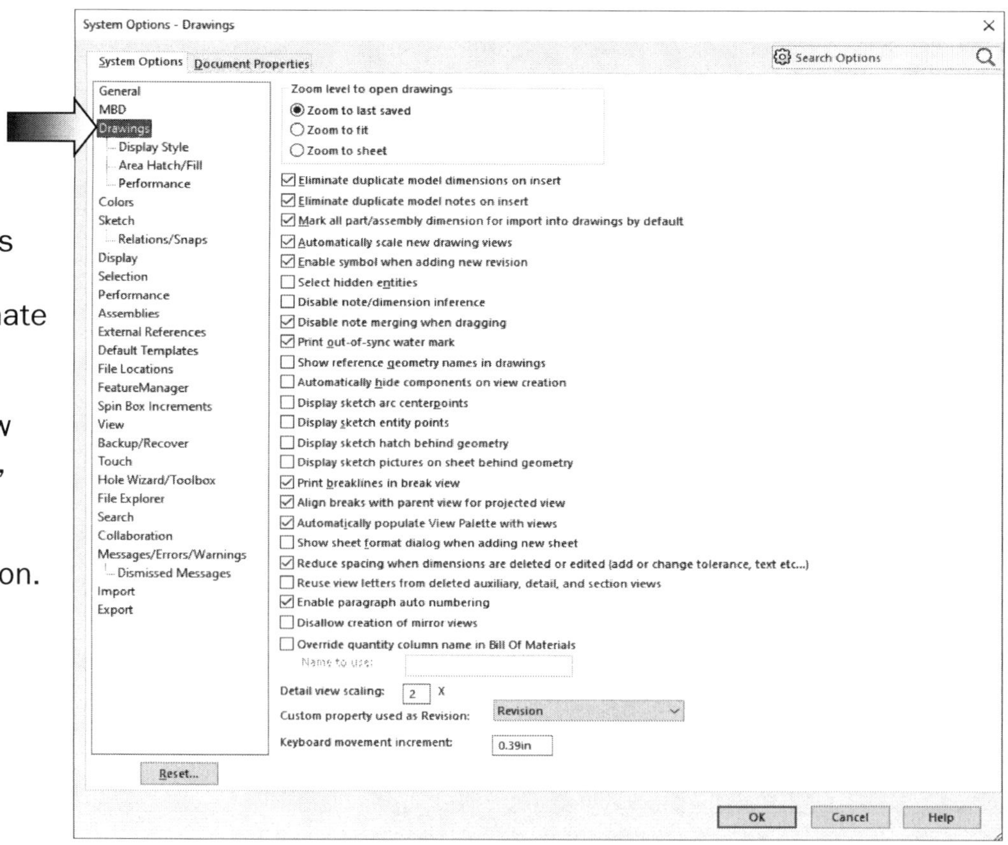

Display Style:

Set options for the default display of edges in all drawing documents.

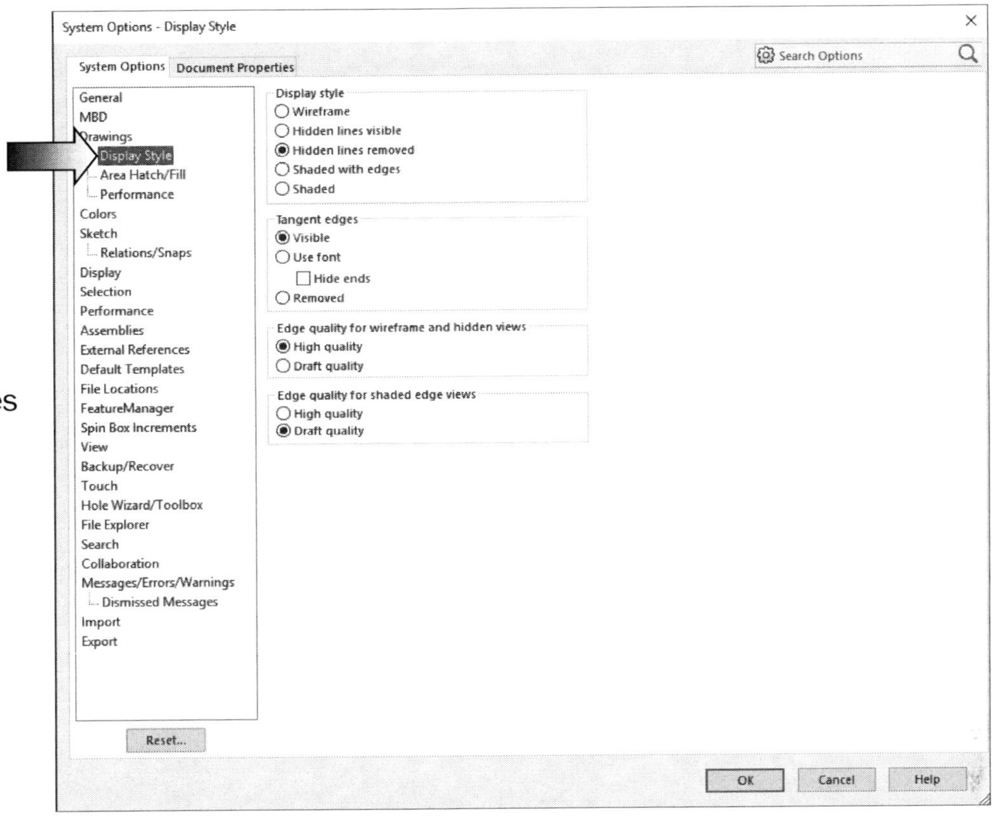

Area Hatch/Fill:

Set the hatch or fill options for any area hatch that you apply to a face or to a closed loop of a sketch entity, in a drawing.

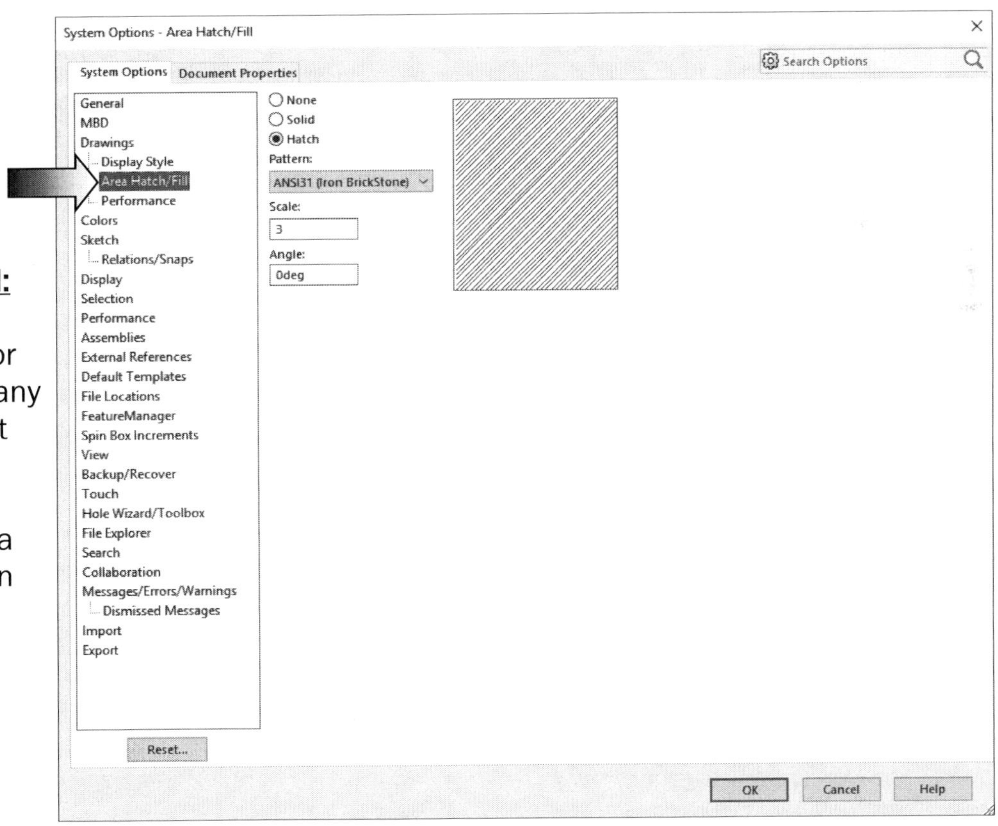

Sketch:

Sets the default system options for sketching such as: Auto-rotate view, display entity points, enable spline tangency.

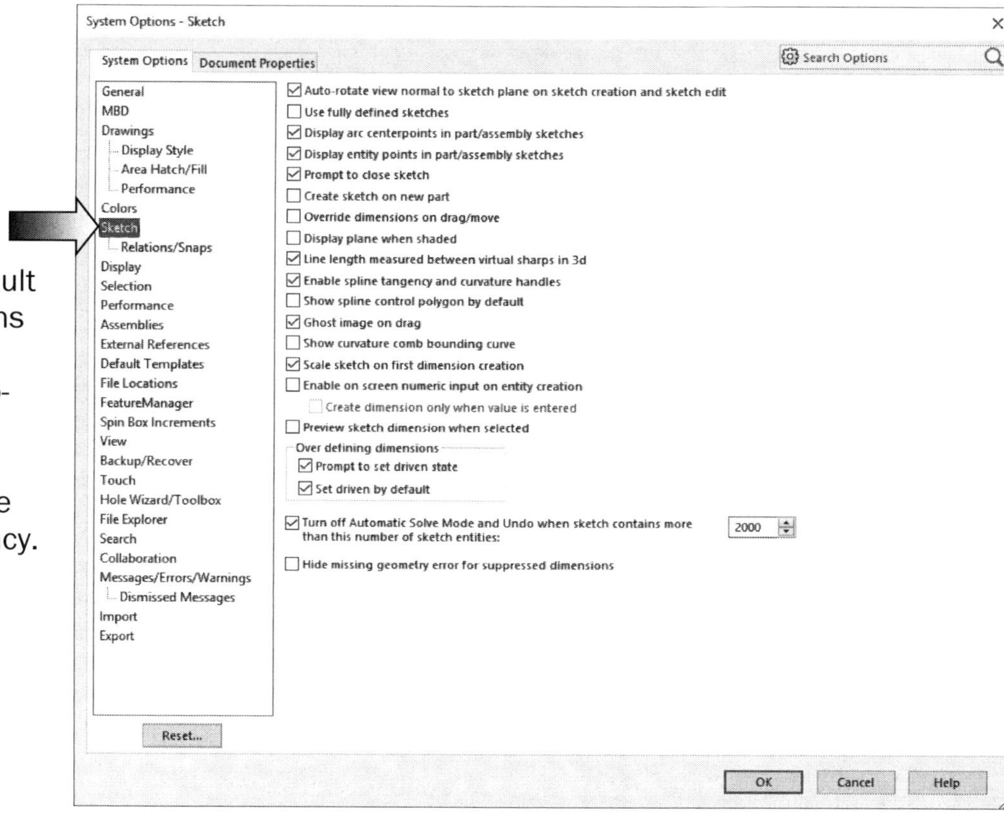

Relations/Snap:

Clear or select all the types of Sketch Snaps.

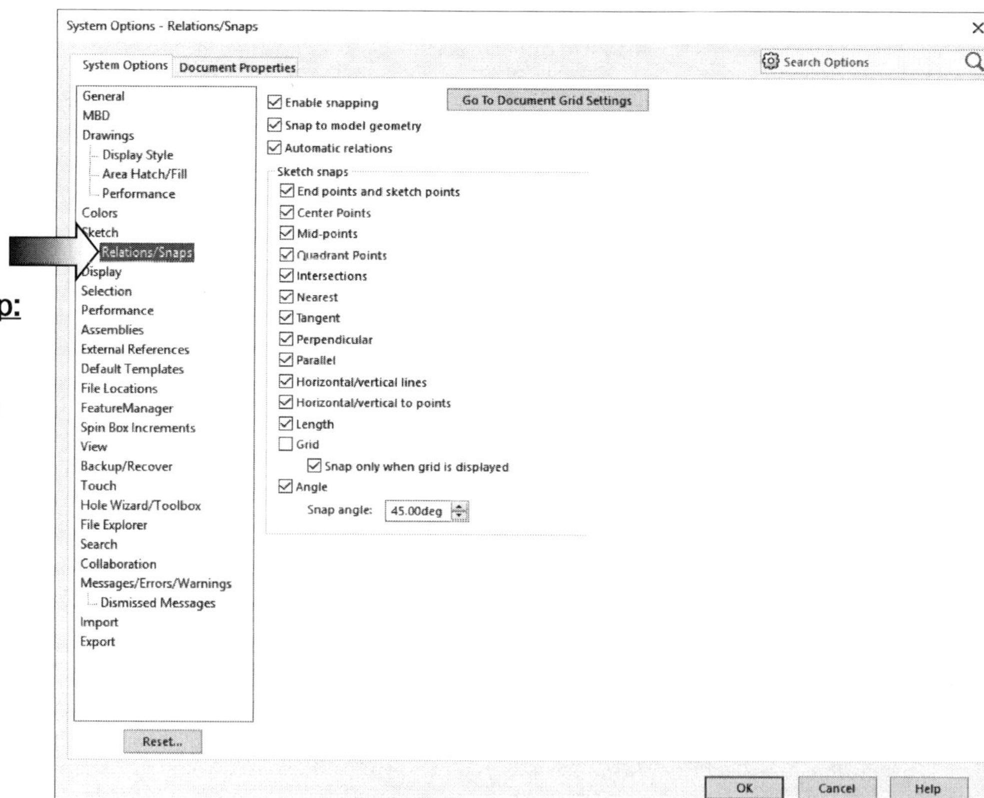

Display:

Specify options for the display of edges, planes, and so on.

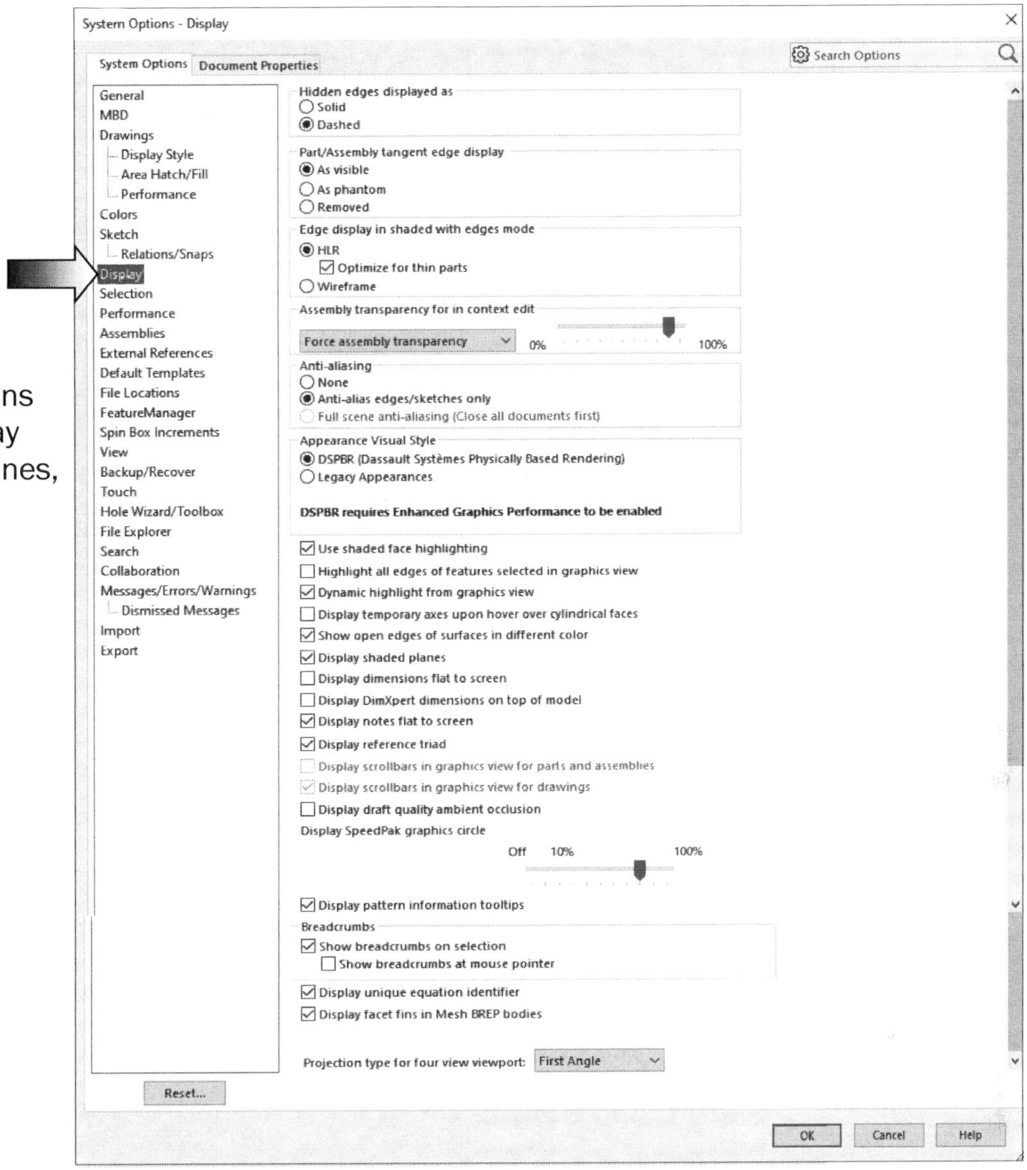

Selection:

Specify options for the selection of edges, planes, and so on.

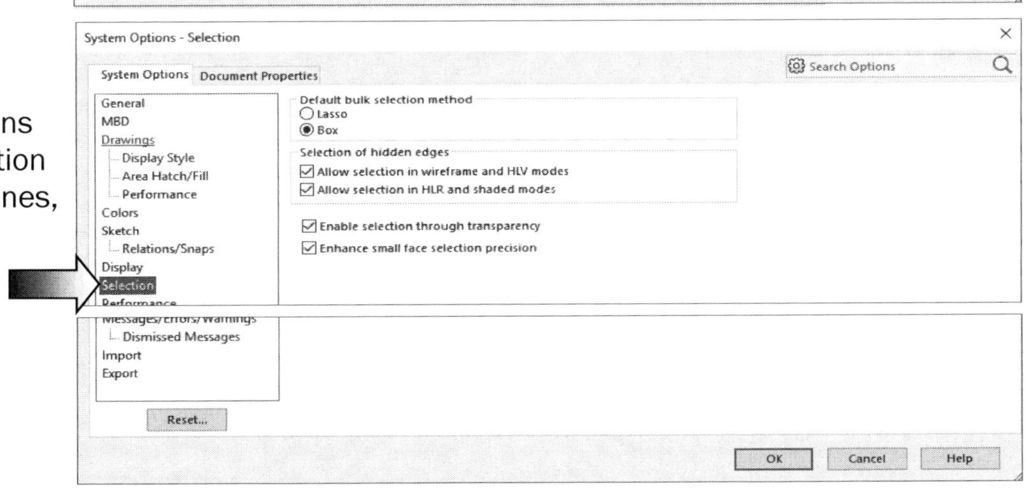

Default Templates:

Specify the default templates to use for creating new part, drawing, and assembly documents.

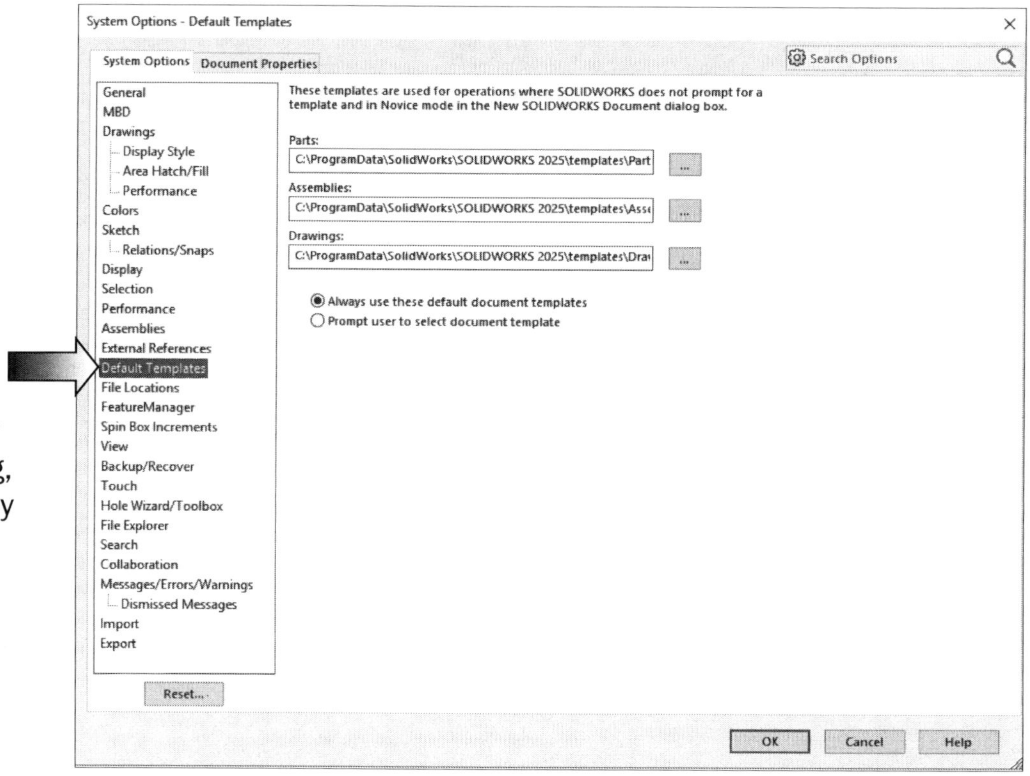

File Location:

Specify folders to search for different types of documents.

Folders are searched in the order in which they are listed.

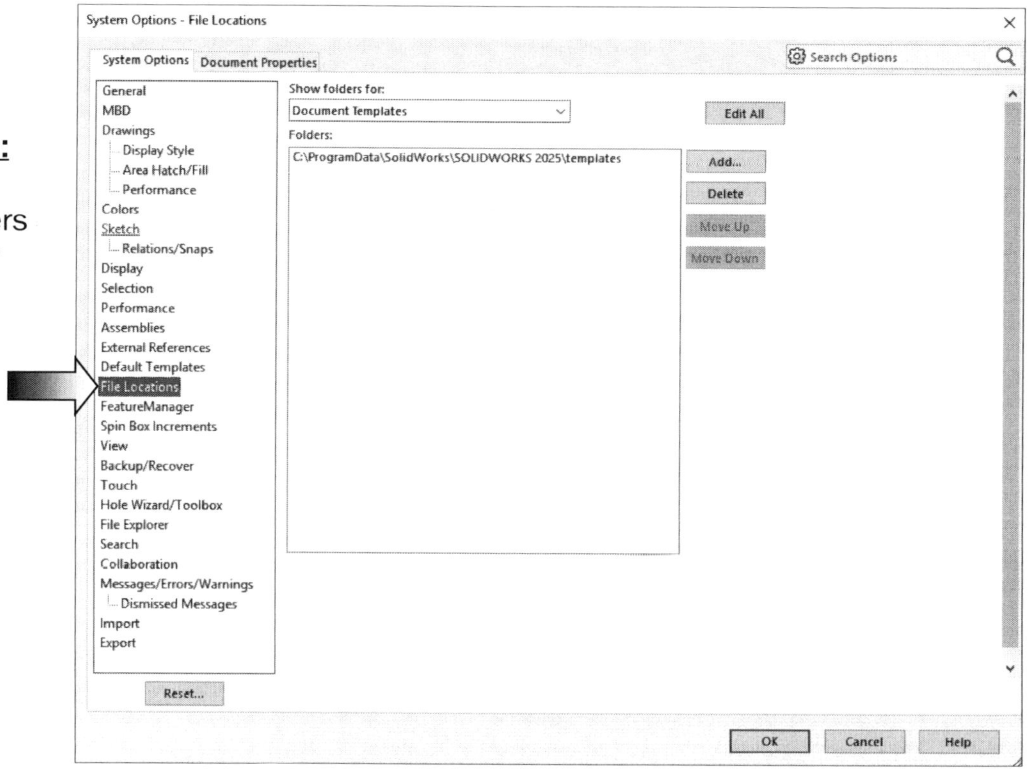

FeatureManager:

Specify the options that appear on the Feature Manager design tree.

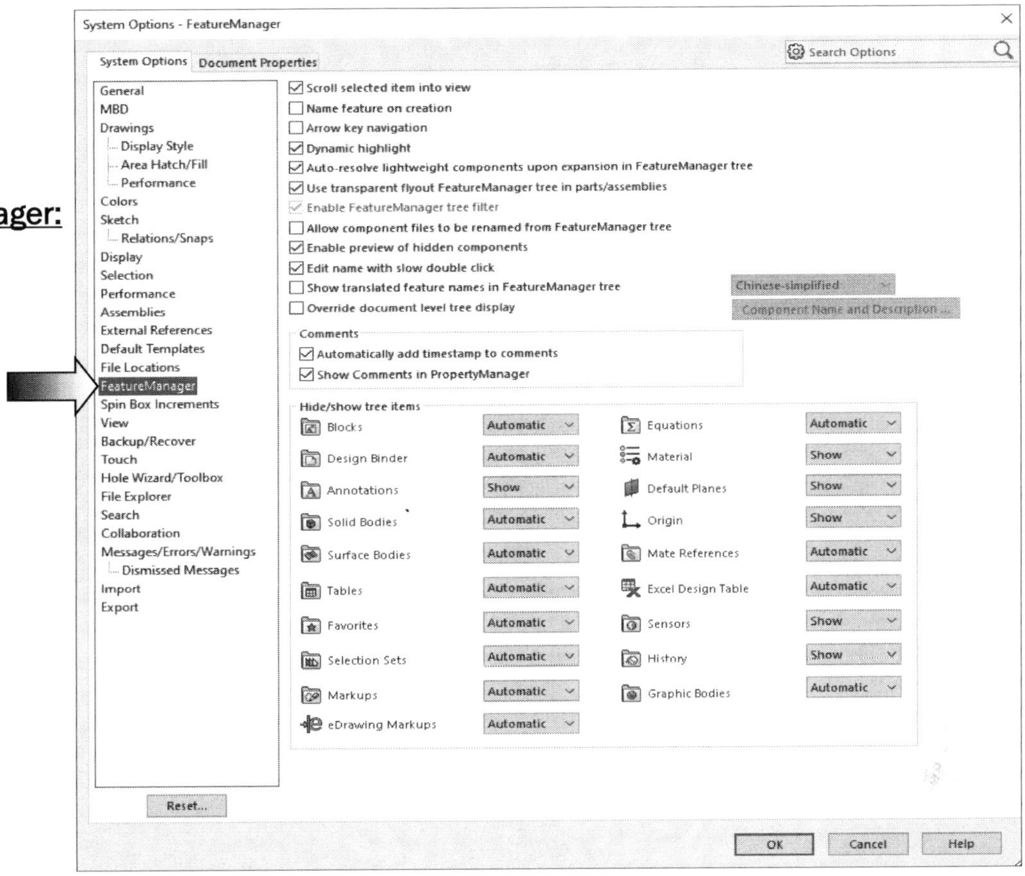

Backup/Recover:

Specify the frequency and folders for auto-recovery, backup, and save notifications.

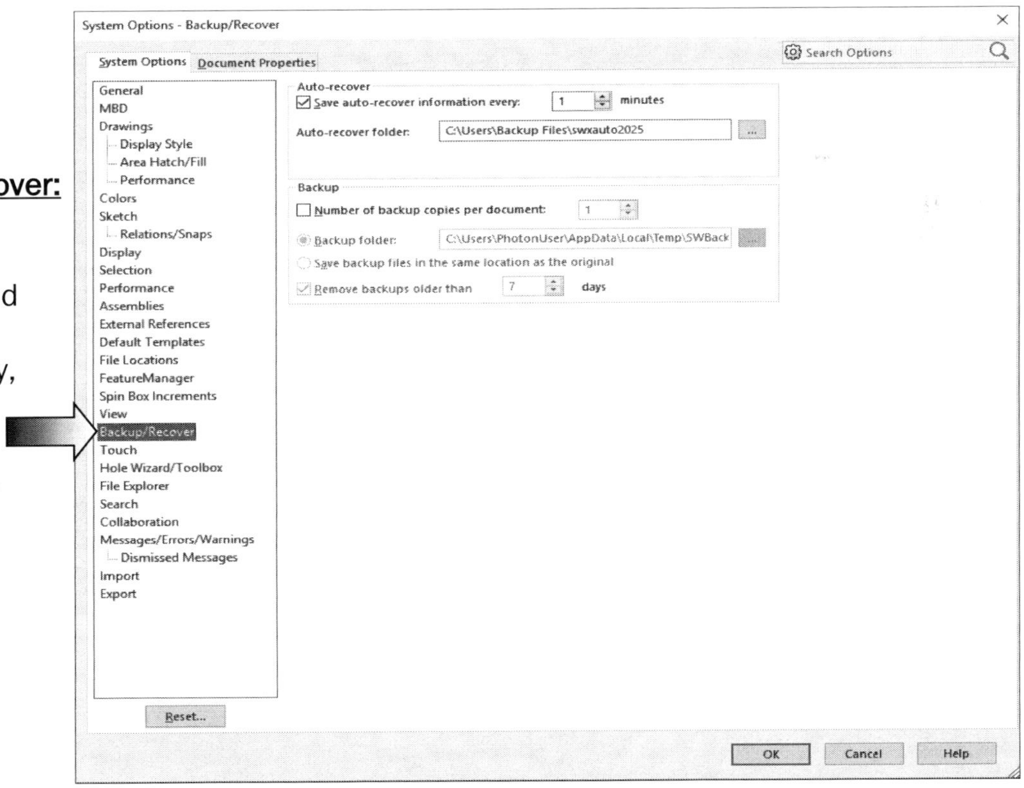

Document Properties

Click the **Document Properties** tab.

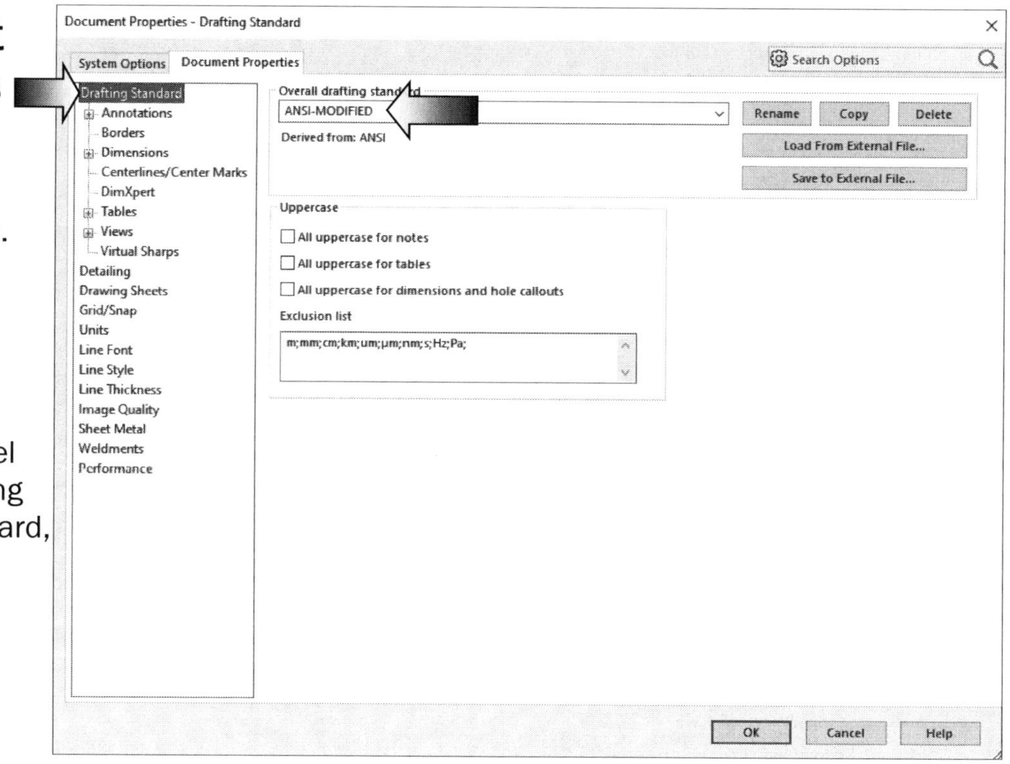

Drafting Standard:

Specify the document-level overall detailing drafting standard, and load or saved custom drafting standards.

Annotations:

Specify document-level drafting settings for all annotations. Available for all document types.

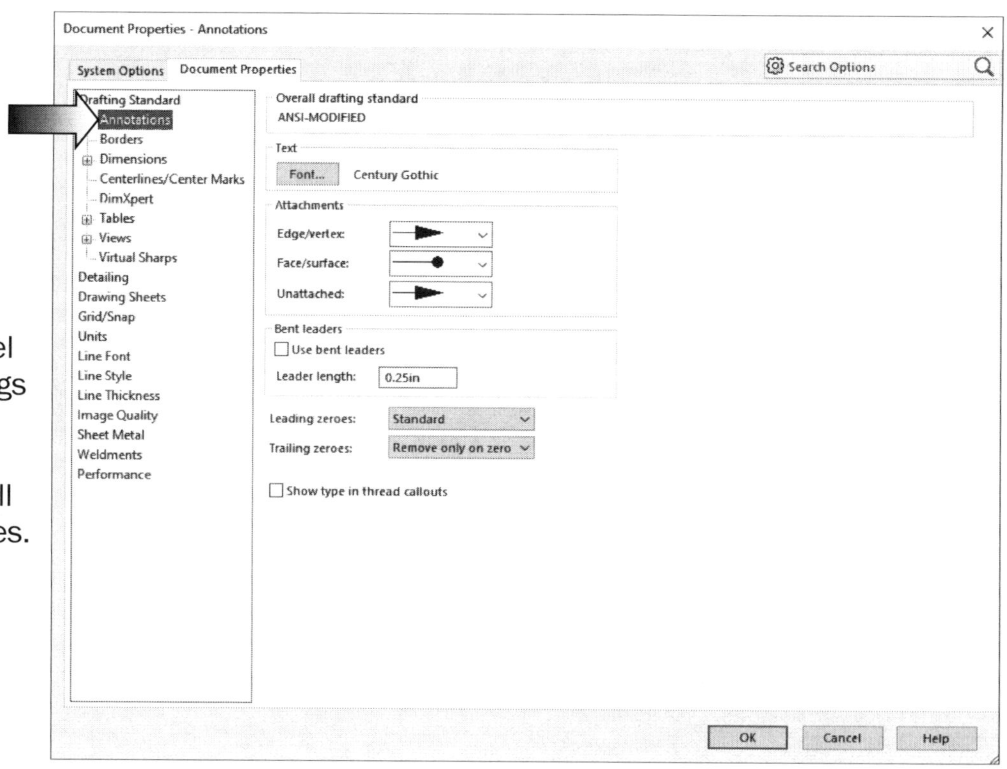

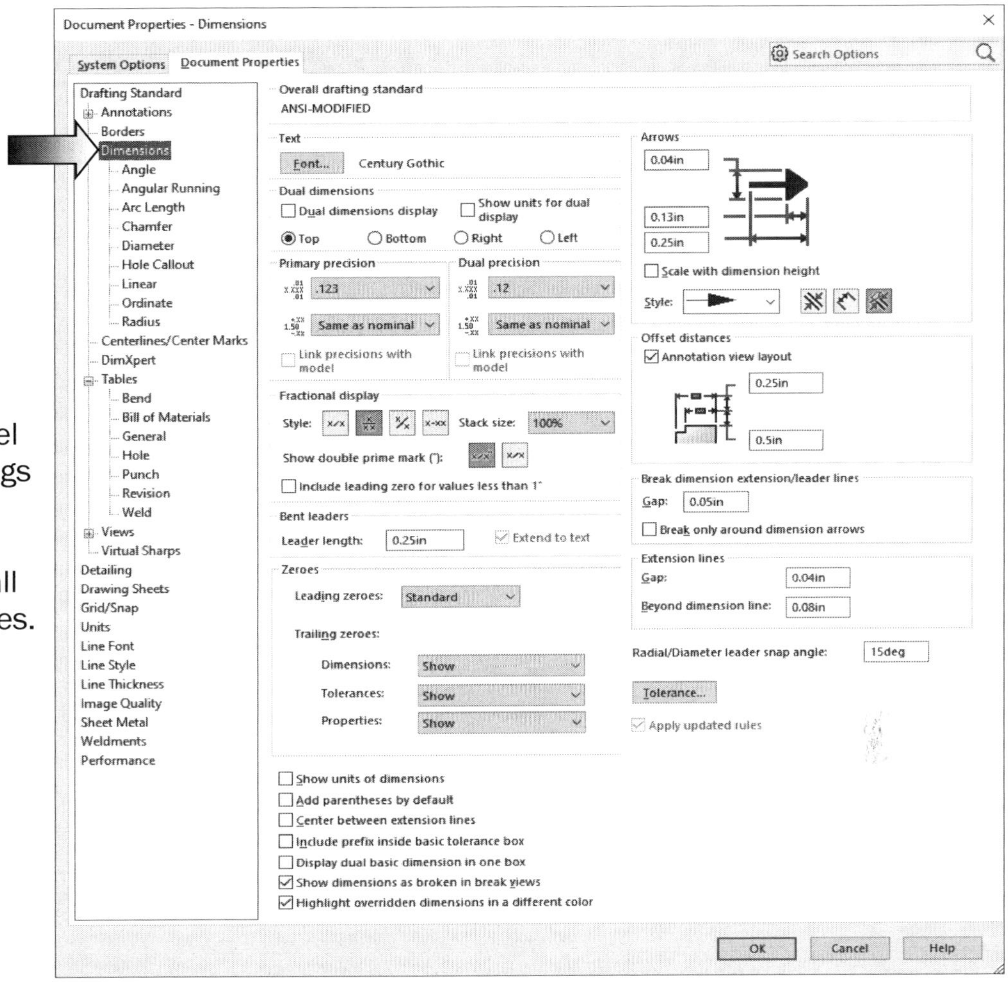

Dimensions:

Specify document-level drafting settings for all dimensions. Available for all document types.

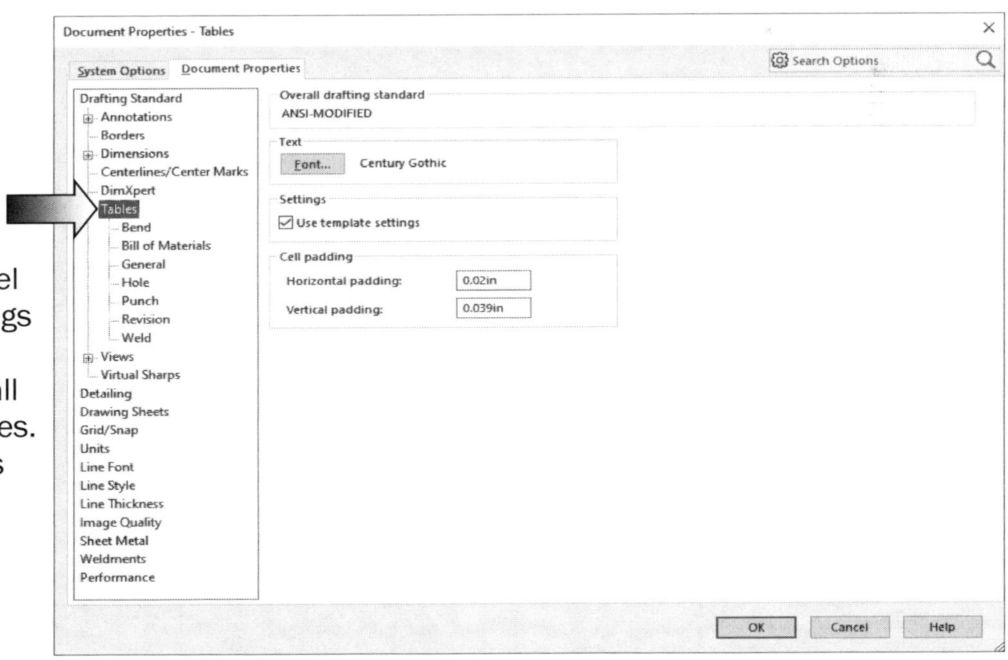

Tables:

Specify document-level drafting settings for all tables. Available for all document types. Some settings are only available for drawings.

Views:

Specify document-level drafting settings for all view labels. Available for drawings only.

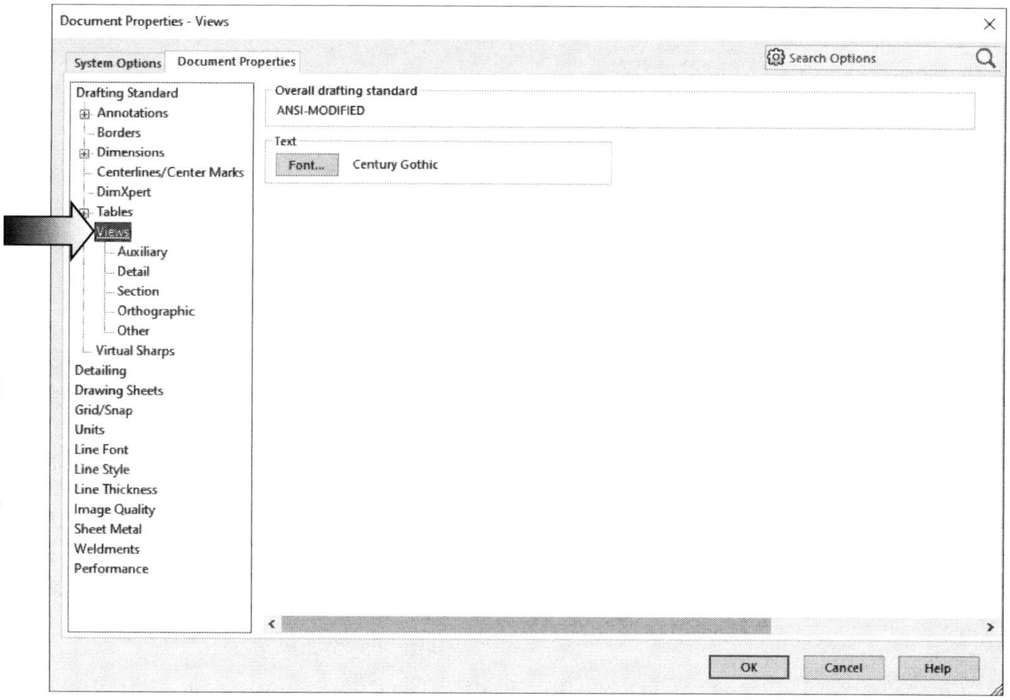

Detailing:

Specify document-level drafting settings for detailing options. Available for all document types.

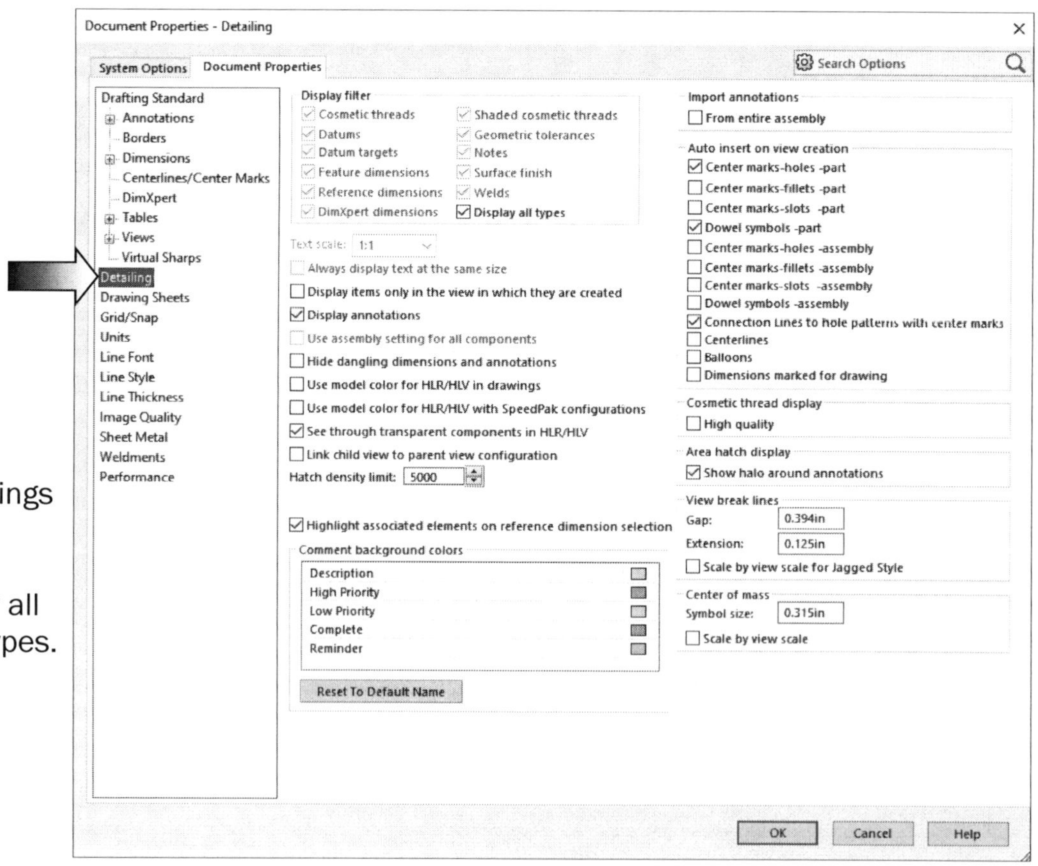

Units:

Specify the properties of document-level units. Available for all document types.

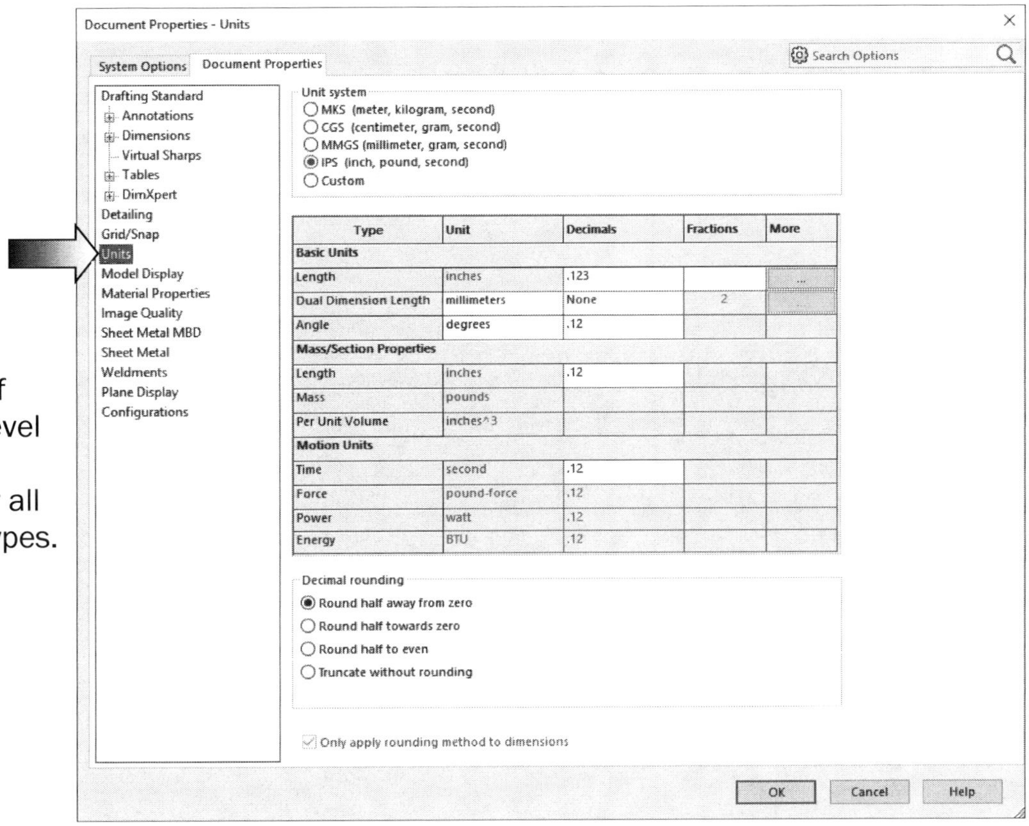

Line Font:

Set the style and weight of lines for various kinds of edges. Available for drawings only.

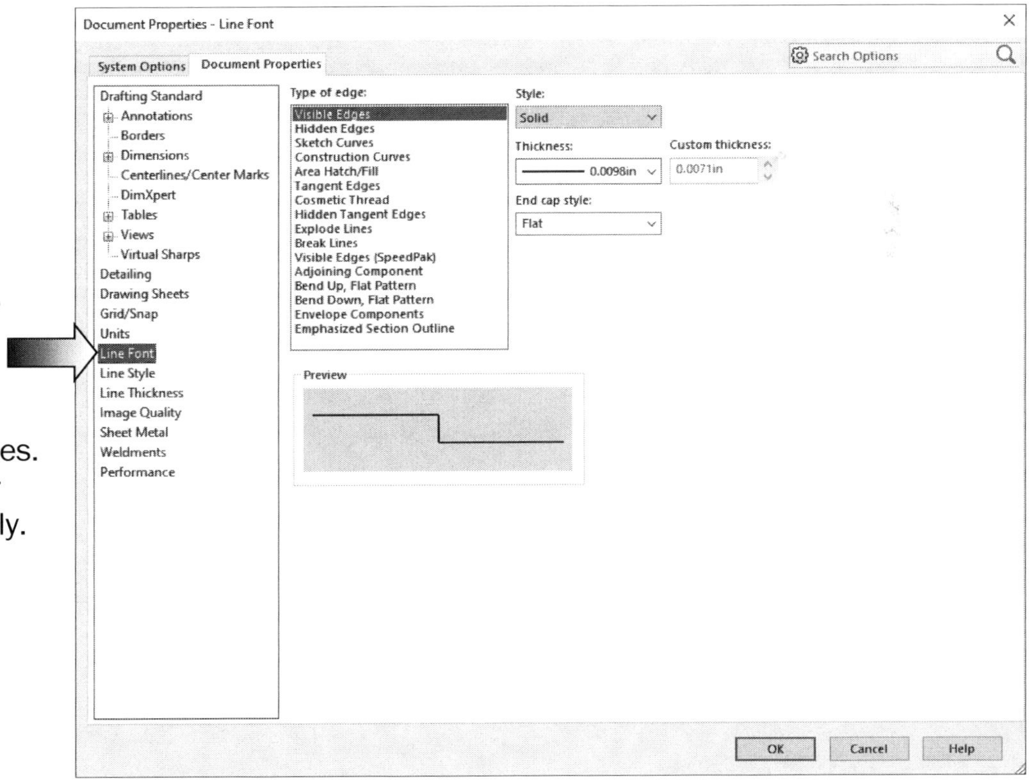

Line Style:

Create custom line styles and apply them to edges. Available for drawings only.

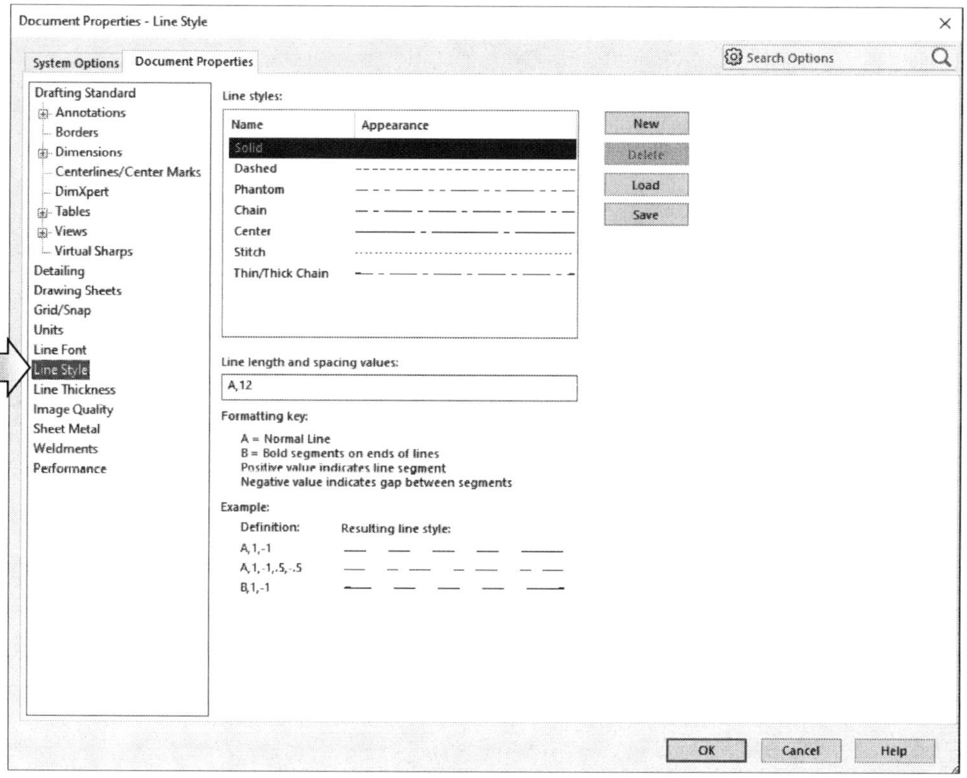

Line Thickness:

Set the line weights in an active document that work best with your printer. Available for drawings only.

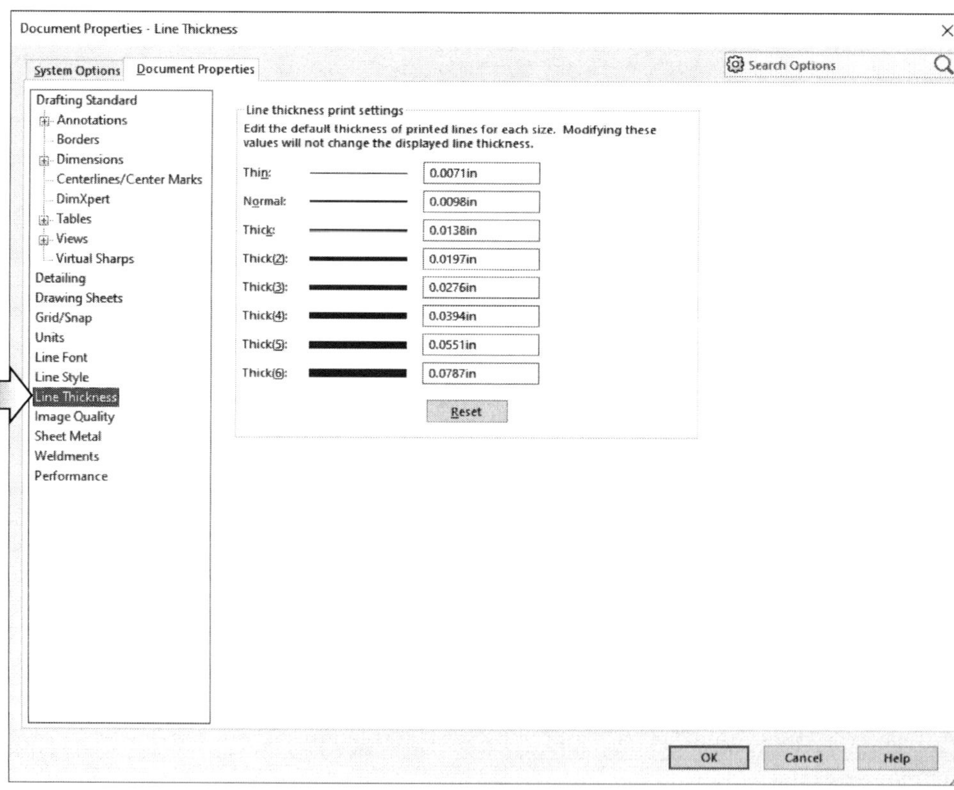

Image Quality:

Specify quality options for image display. Available for all document types.

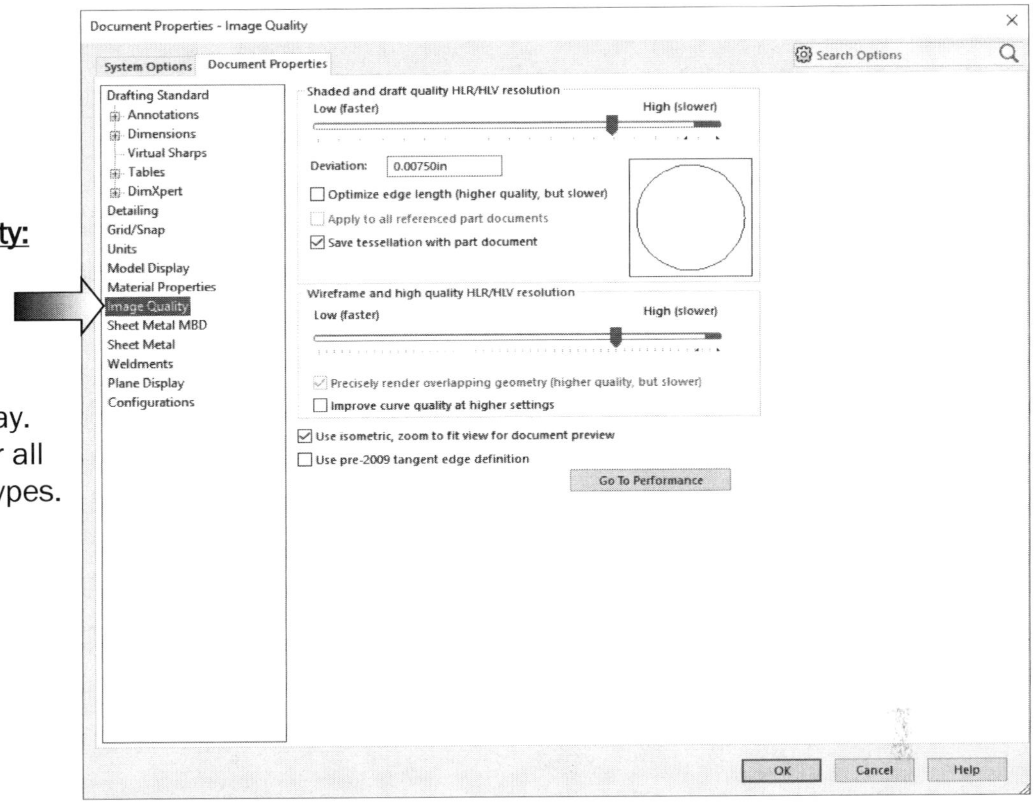

Sheet Metal:

Specify sheet metal options. Available for all document types. Options vary depending on whether you are working with a part, assembly, or drawing.

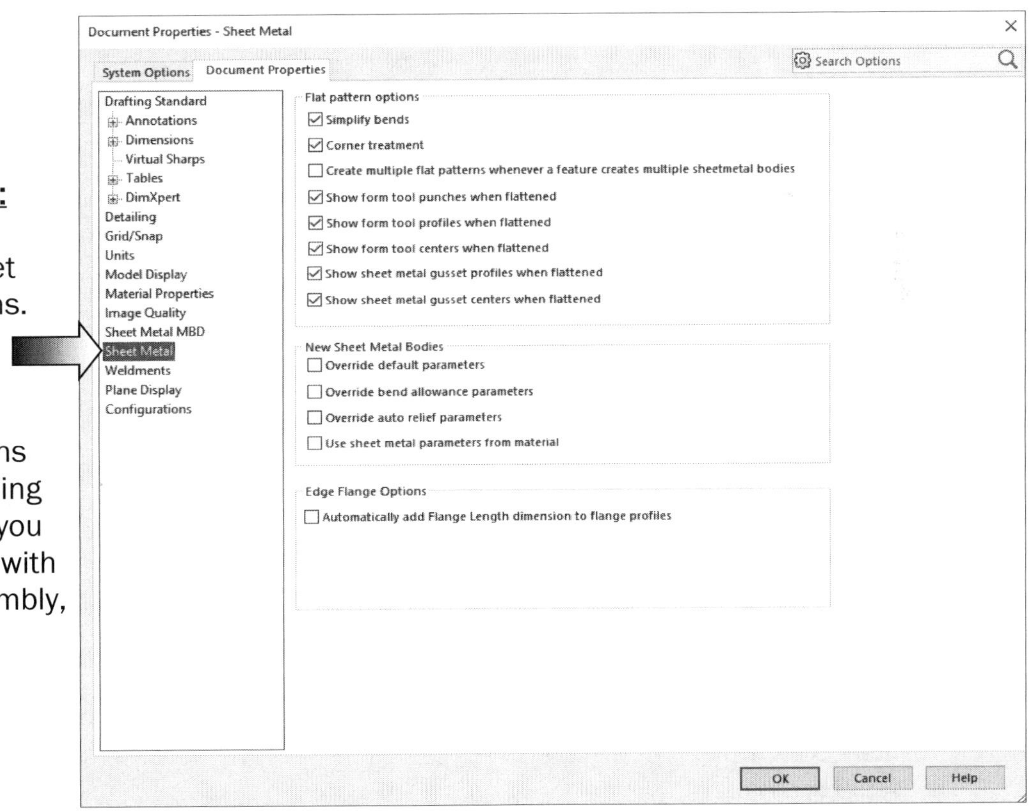

Weldments:

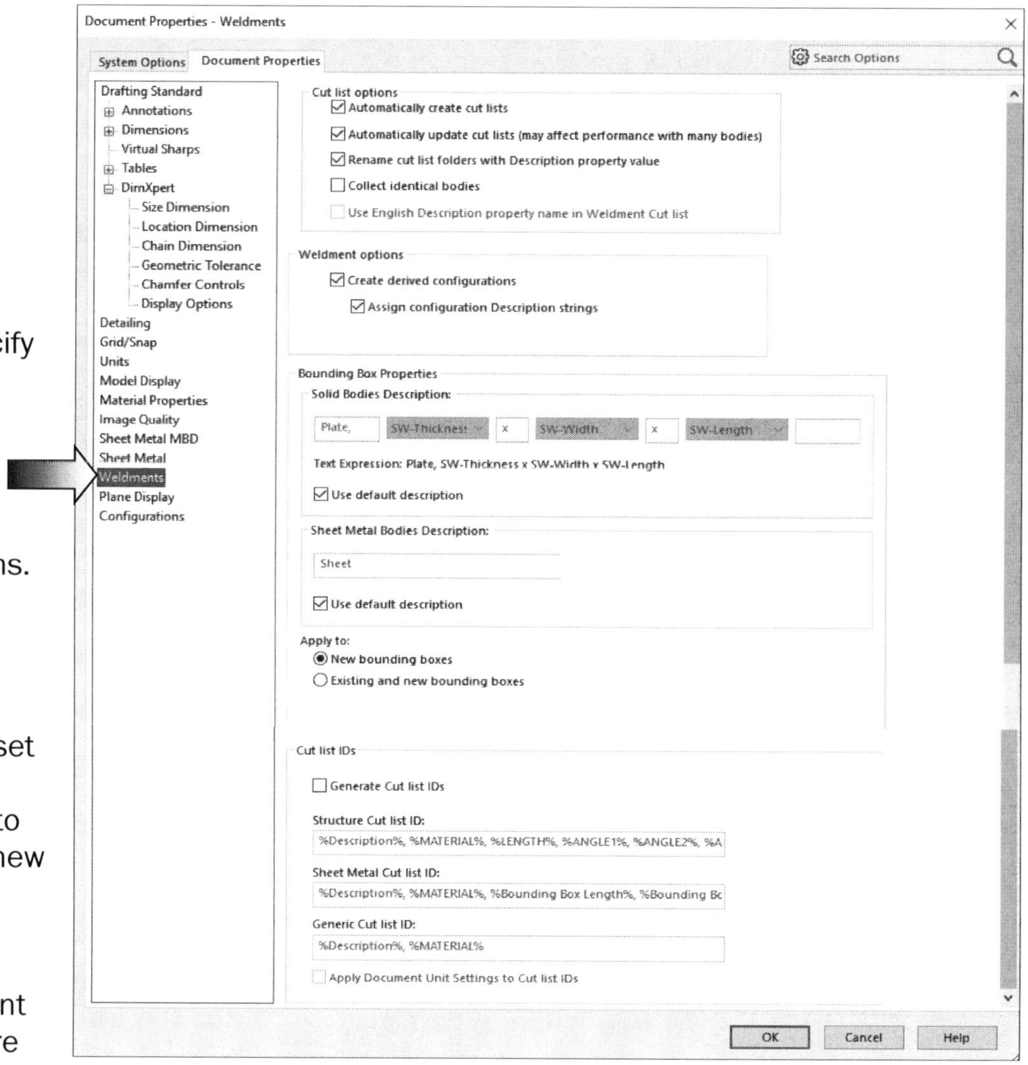

On a per-document basis, use the Document Properties, Weldments page to specify how the weldment software creates cut lists and configurations.

Summary:

The System Options are set and save as parameters to use with all new and existing documents.

The Document Properties are parameters to use with new documents only. These settings are often saved in a template, and you can have as many templates as needed for different requirements on different projects.

Saving your settings to a template:

Select: **File, Save As.**

For Save As Type, **Select Drawing Template**.

Enter: **B-Size ANSI Drawing.slddrw** for the file name.

Click **Save.** This template can now be used to create drawings from the lessons in this textbook.

CHAPTER 2: DETAILING A MACHINED PART

Stainless Steel Flange

Machined parts are parts manufactured using material removal such as a lathe, a mill, or a router for machining operation.

Machining parts is an excellent alternative to other manufacturing operations such as molding, casting, extrusion, etc.

Machined parts do have some advantages compared to 3D printed, injection molded, or casted parts such as:

* They do not require any special tooling; you just need to clamp down the work piece and start machining.

* Unlike injection molded or sheet metal parts, machined parts can have different wall thickness and can be flipped and cut from different sides as needed.

* Machined parts can hold tighter tolerance and can produce higher accuracy and precision.

A wider variety of material options are also available for machined parts.

This chapter discusses the process of creating an engineering drawing for the machined flange.

1. Opening a part document:

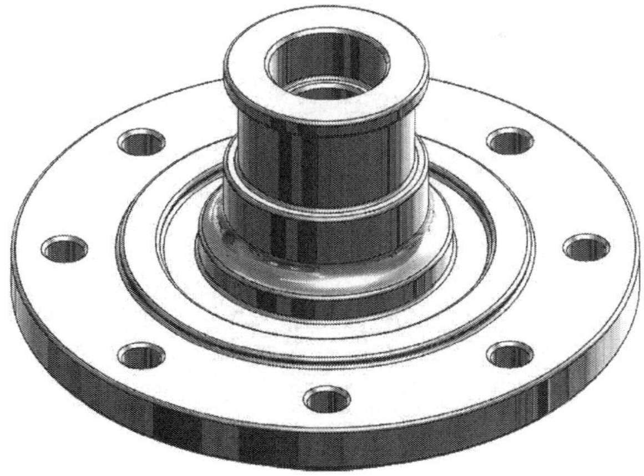

Select: **File, Open.**

Browse to the training folder and open the part document named: **Flange.sldprt.**

The material **AISI 304** has already been assigned to the part. AISI stands for American Iron and Steel Institute. This material is the most common stainless steel used in the industry.

2. Setting the drawing properties:

A part, or a 3D model, is designed and created in a 3D environment and a detailed drawing is created on a sheet of paper, in a 2D environment.

To generate a drawing from a part, first we have to transfer the part to a drawing sheet.

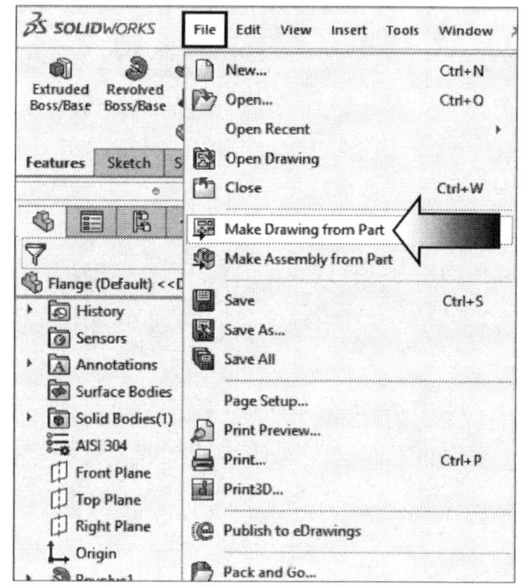

Select: **File, Make Drawing From Part** (arrow).

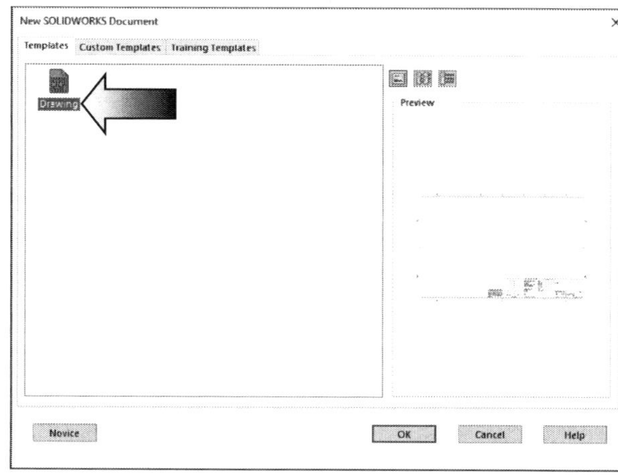

Select **Drawing** (or Draw) template from the New SOLIDWORKS Document dialog box.

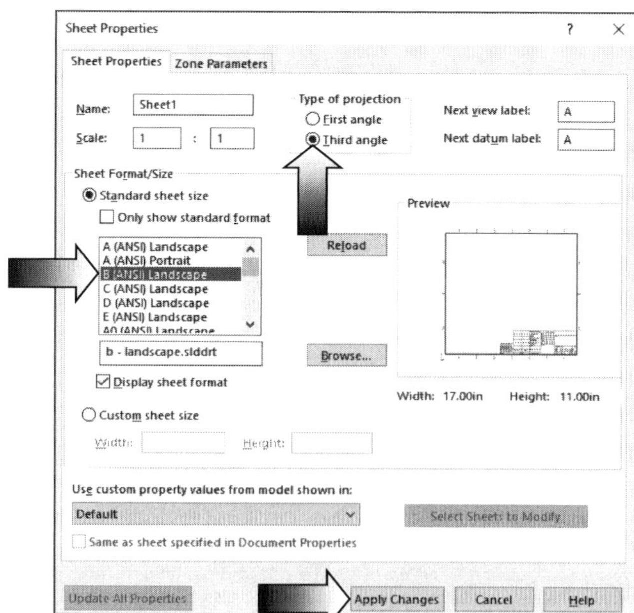

In the Sheet Properties dialog box, select the following:

* Scale: **1:1**

* Type Of Projection: **Third Angle**

* Sheet Format/Size: **B (ANSI) Landscape**

* Next View Label: **A**

* Next Datum Label: **A**

* Display Sheet Format: **Enabled**

Click **Apply Changes**.

The **B (ANSI) Landscape** drawing template is opened (the paper size is 11" x 17").

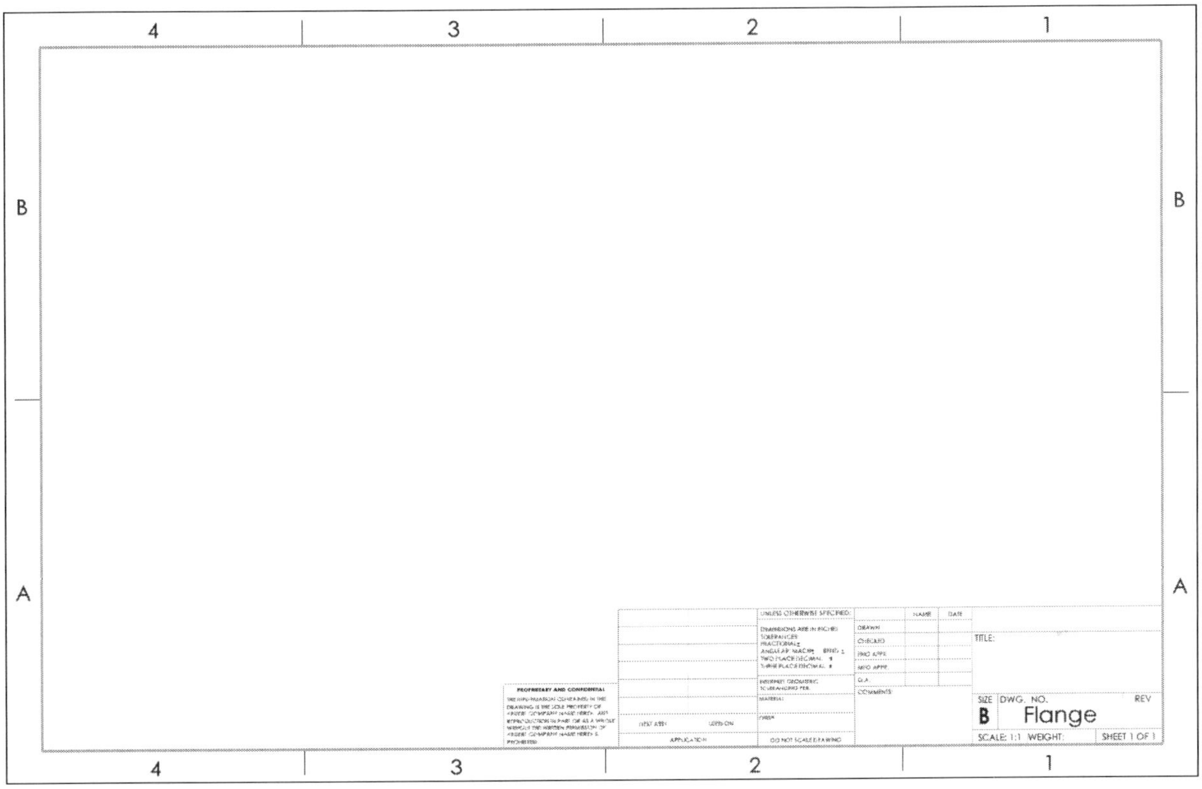

3. Creating an engineering drawing:

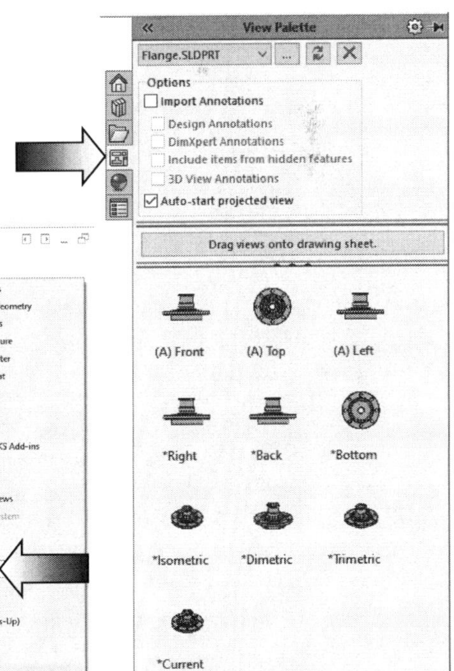

SOLIDWORKS offers several options to create the drawing views. We will take a look at the **View Palette** option first.

If the Task Pane is not visible on the upper right side of the screen, right-click the document name (Flange-Sheet1) on top of the screen and select: **Toolbars, Task Pane**.

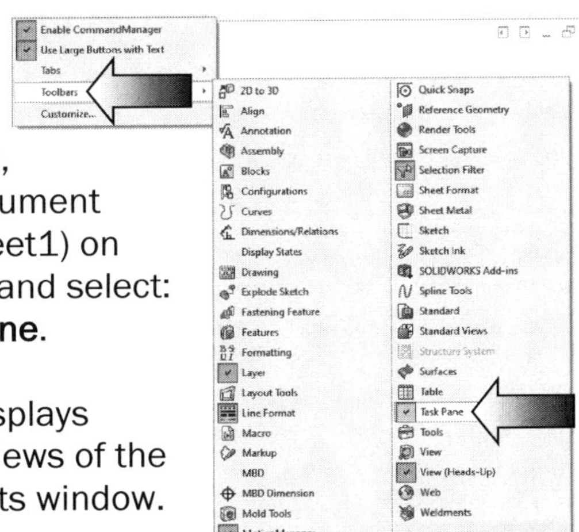

The Task Pane displays several drawing views of the current model in its window.

In the Task Pane, under Options, enable only one checkbox: **Auto-Start Projected View** and clear all other checkboxes.

Locate the **Front** drawing view and drag/drop it onto the drawing as shown below.

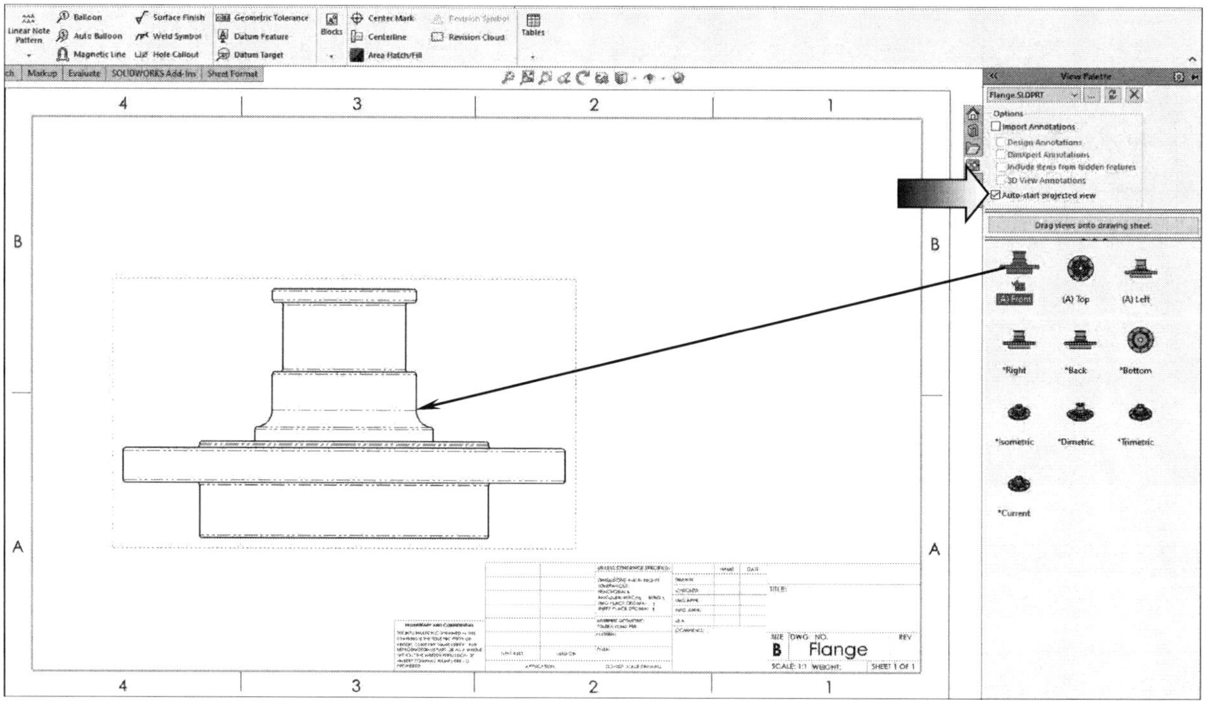

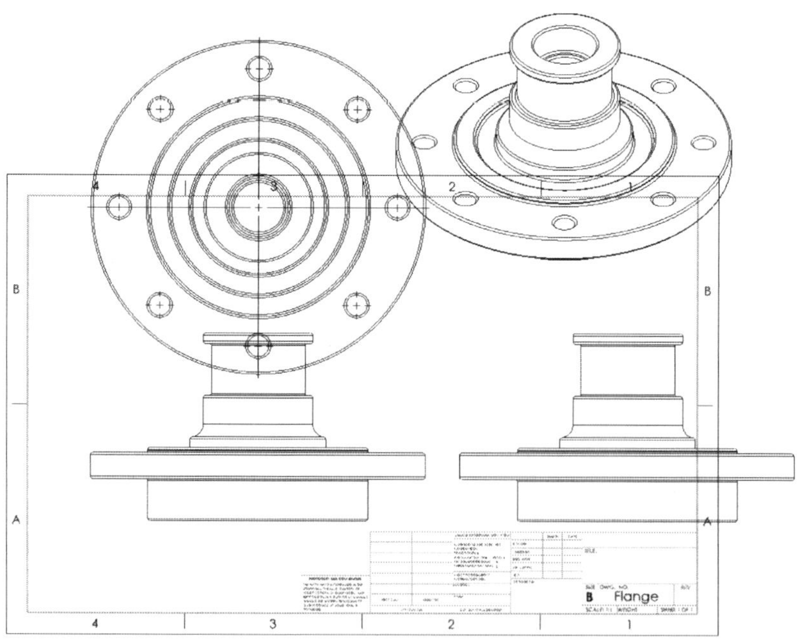

The **Projected View** command is activated automatically to allow for more views to be created.

Move the mouse pointer upwards; when the preview of the **Top** drawing view appears, click the mouse to make the Top drawing view.

Also add the **Right** and the **Isometric** views.

4. Changing the scale of the drawing Views:

The Front drawing view was added to the drawing first; therefore, it is considered the parent view. Changing the scale of the parent view will also update the other drawing views as well.

Click the dotted border of the **Front** drawing view (or click any where inside the Front drawing view) to access the scale options.

In the **Scale** section, select the **Use Custom Scale** option.

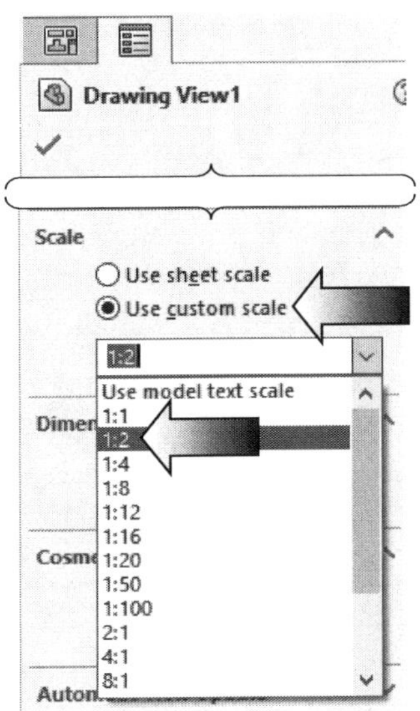

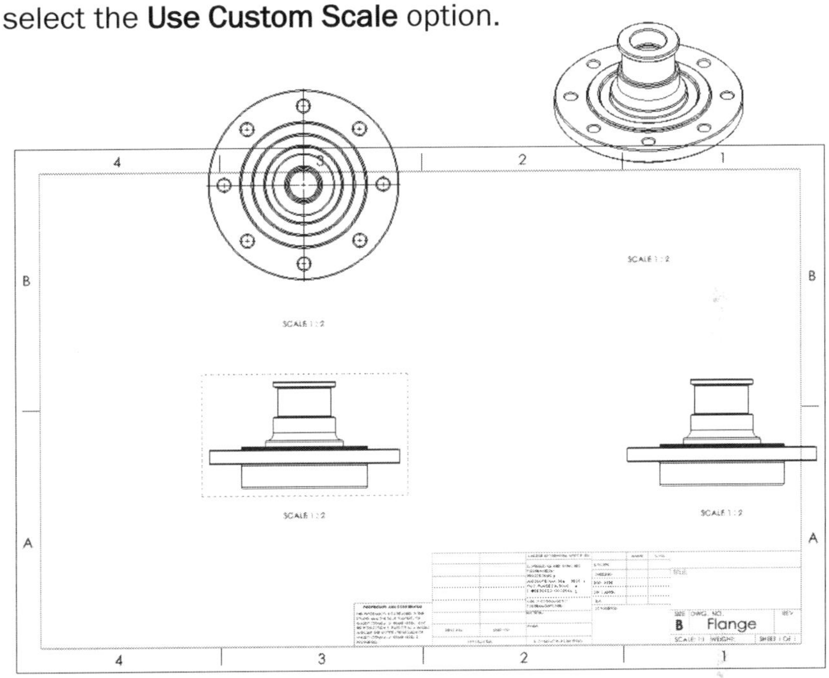

Expand the **Scale** drop-down arrow and select: **1:2** (one-half scale).

Click **OK**.

The scale of the Front drawing view and the others are changed to one-half the actual size.

The scale option only resizes the drawing views so that they will fit in the current B-size drawing, the dimensions remain at 1 to 1, or full size.

5. Rearranging the drawing Views:

Drag the dotted border of each drawing view to rearrange them.

Move the drawing views to the approximate locations as shown below.

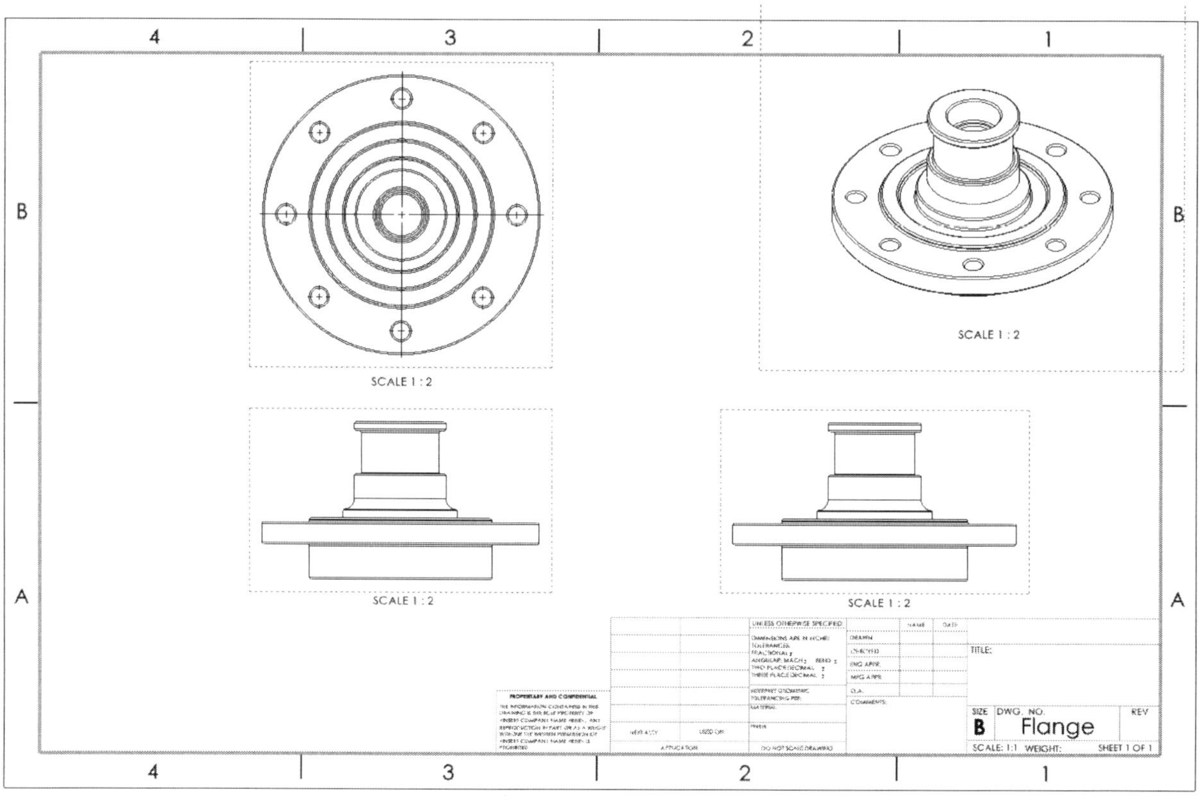

<u>Delete</u> the **Right** drawing view; we will replace it with a section view in the next couple steps.

Also, <u>delete</u> the scale callout "**Scale 1:2**" below each drawing view. We will change the main Sheet Scale in the next step.

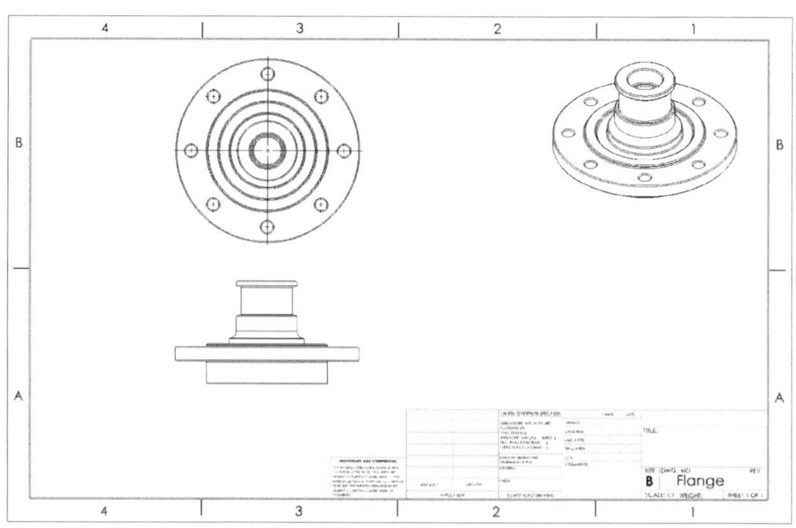

6. Modifying the sheet scale:

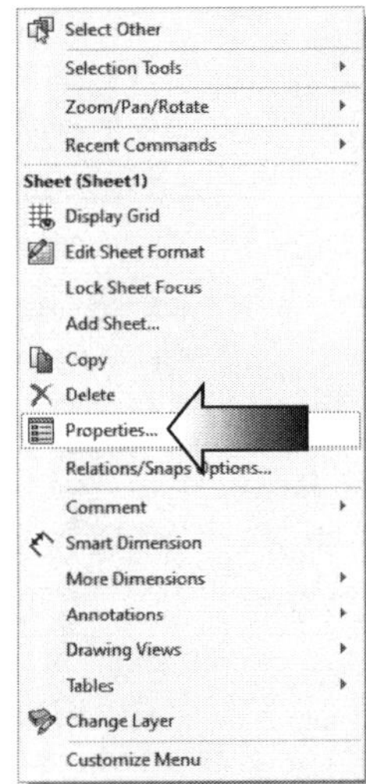

The Sheet Scale that was entered in step 2 is the default scale for all new drawing views. The user can change the scale of any drawing views by accessing the Scale Properties on the FeatureManager tree and entering the custom scales.

Right-click anywhere inside the drawing and select **Properties.**

Change the Sheet Scale to **1:2** and click **Apply Changes.**

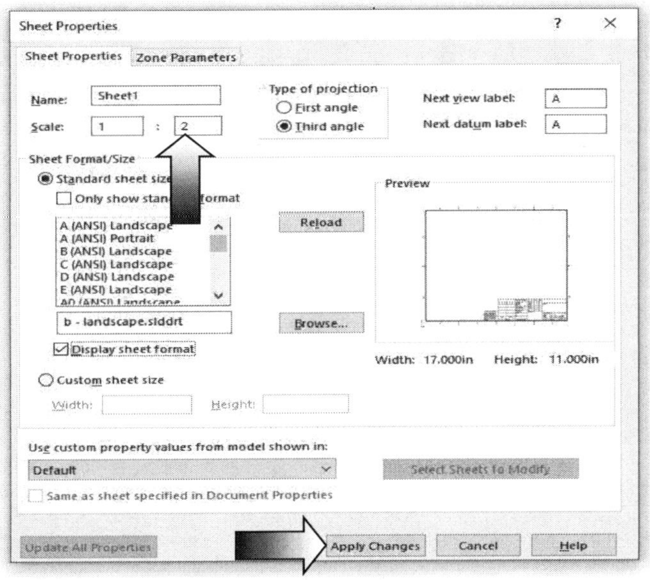

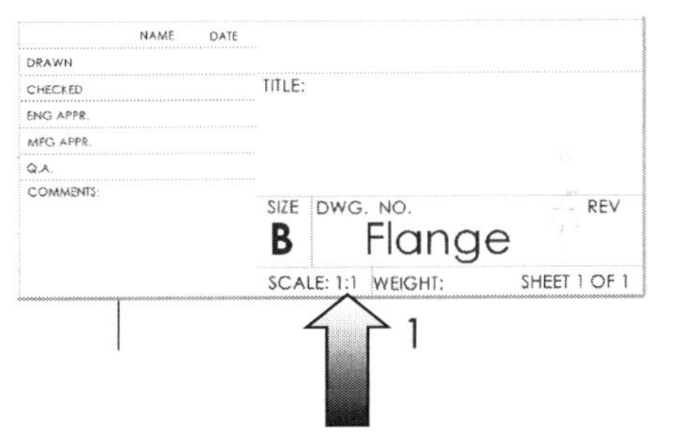

The Sheet Scale is updated in the Title Block.

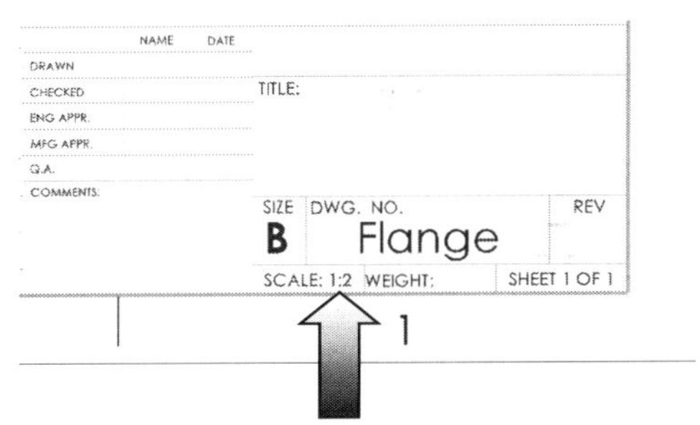

The status bar at the bottom right displays a pop-up to select a list of commonly used scales. If you needed a custom scale, it requires going into the Sheet Properties (above), where the scale values can be input.

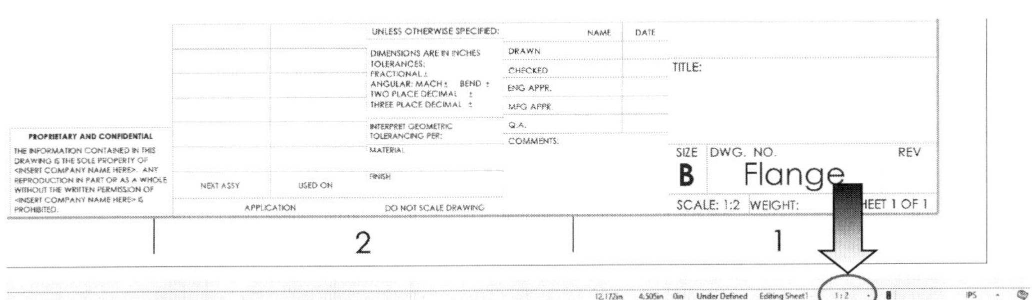

7. Creating a section view:

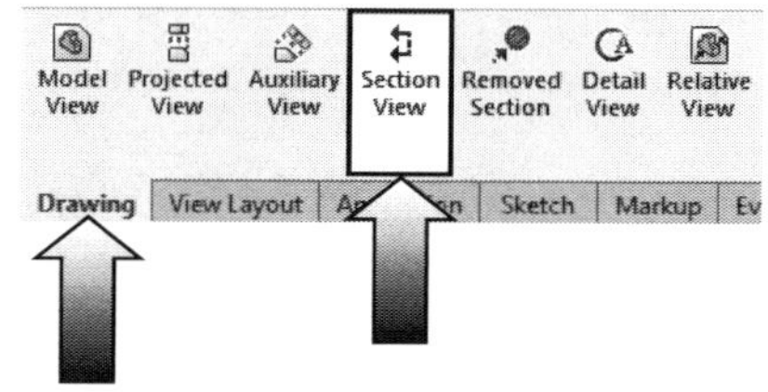

Section Views are used to clarify the interior construction of a part that cannot be clearly described by hidden lines in exterior views. By taking an imaginary cut through the object and removing a portion, the inside features may be seen more clearly.

Select the dotted border of the **Front** drawing view.

Switch to the **Drawing** tab and click **Section View.**

For Cutting Line, select the **Vertical** option.

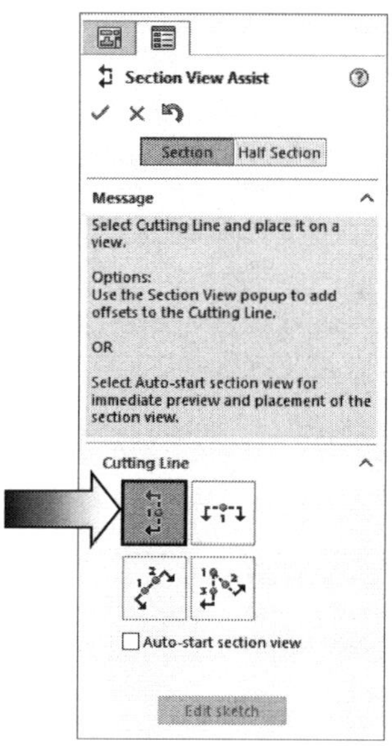

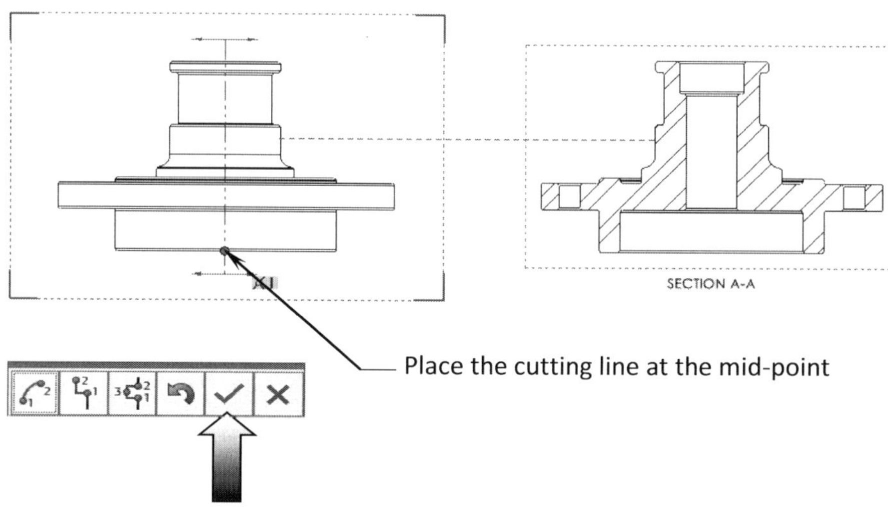

Hover the mouse pointer over the bottom **horizontal edge** and click the mouse when the **mid-point** pops up.

Click the **green check** to accept the placement of the cutting line.

Place the section view on the right side of front drawing view.

Click **OK.** (The material crosshatch will be discussed in the next step.)

8. Modifying the crosshatch properties:

In a section view, the crosshatch lines represent the cutting surface(s) and the material of the part. They should be clear, easy to see and not to be mistaken with other object lines. One way to achieve that is to increase the density of the crosshatch.

Click inside the crosshatch area to access the **Area Hatch/Fill** options.

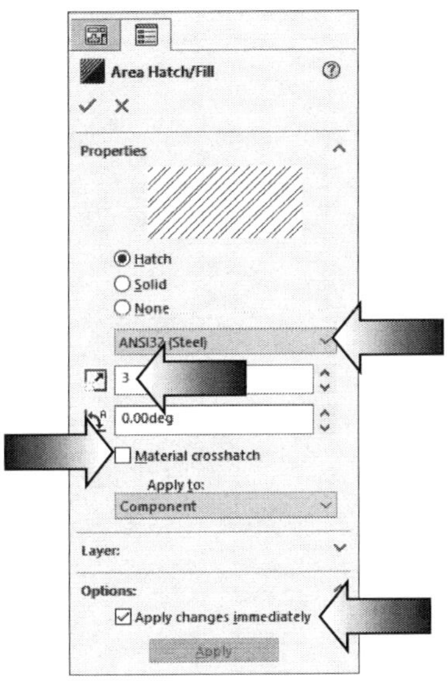

<u>Clear</u> the **Material Crosshatch** checkbox.

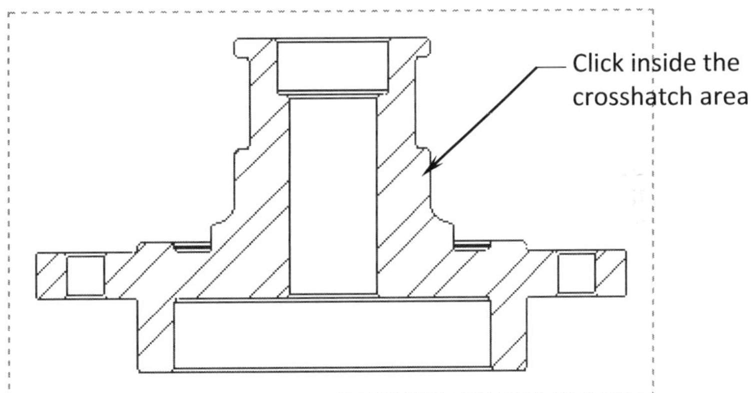

SECTION A-A

For Hatch Pattern, select **ANSI 32 (Steel).**

For Hatch Pattern Scale, change it to **3**.

In the Options section, enable the checkbox: **Apply Changes Immediately.**

Click **OK.**

The crosshatch lines are more dense.
It is now much easier to see the sectioned areas than before.

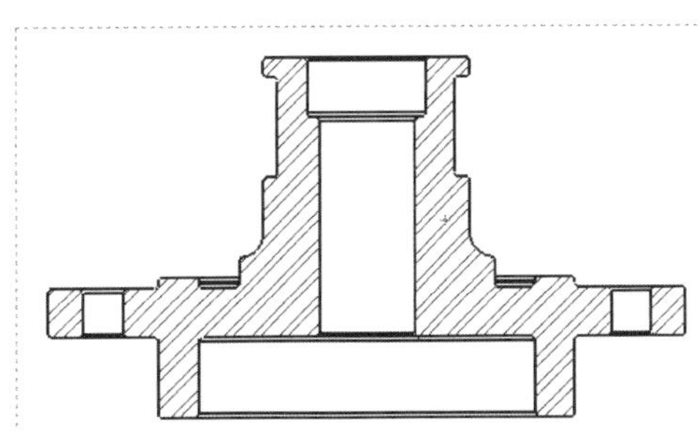

SECTION A-A

9. Adding the centerlines:

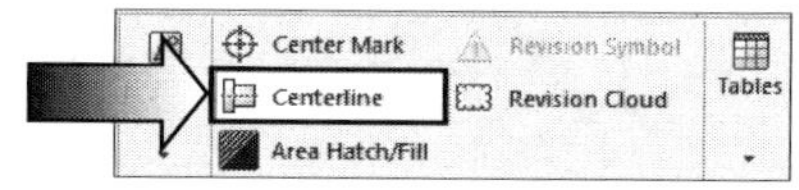

Depending on the Document Property settings, both Centerlines and Center Marks can be added automatically to the drawing views. In this case, only the center marks were added to the Top drawing view but the centerlines were not. We will add them manually to the section view.

Switch to the **Annotation** tab and click **Centerline**.

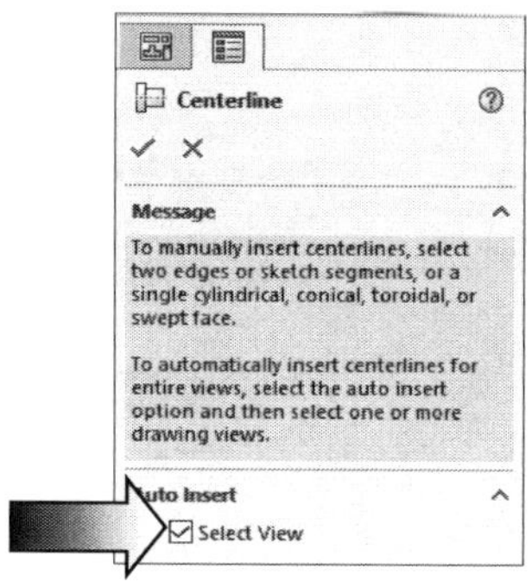

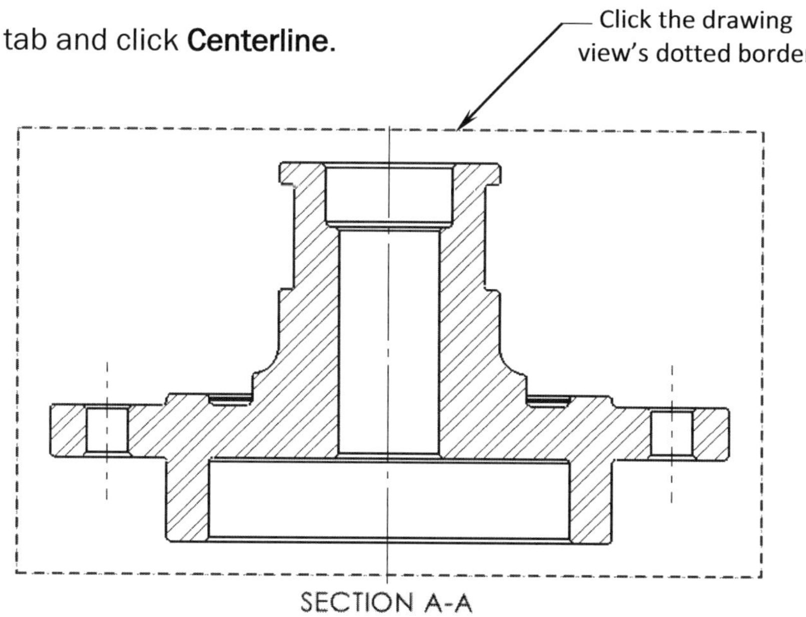

Enable the **Select View** checkbox.

Click the **dotted border** of the section view. Centerlines are automatically added to all holes.

Click **OK**.

10. Changing the Font Size:

For clarity, the view label such as Section A-A, View B, etc., should be changed to a larger font size than the other annotations, so that they can be seen more easily.

The current font size is 12 points; we will change it to 14 points, and Bold.

Select the view label "**A**" as noted below.

From the FeatureManager tree, under the Cutting Line section, <u>clear</u> the checkbox for **Document Font**, and click the **Font** button (arrow).

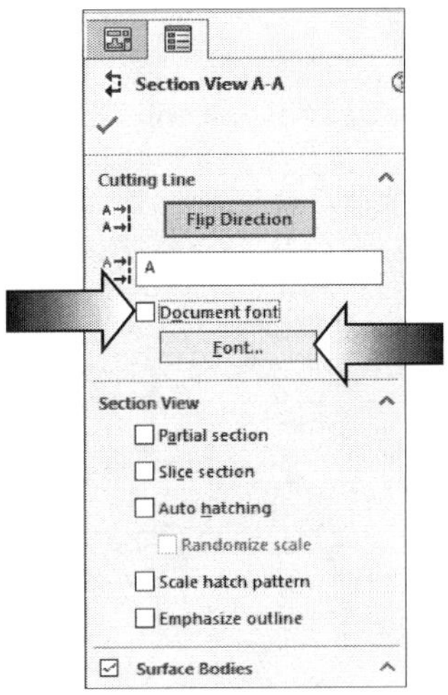

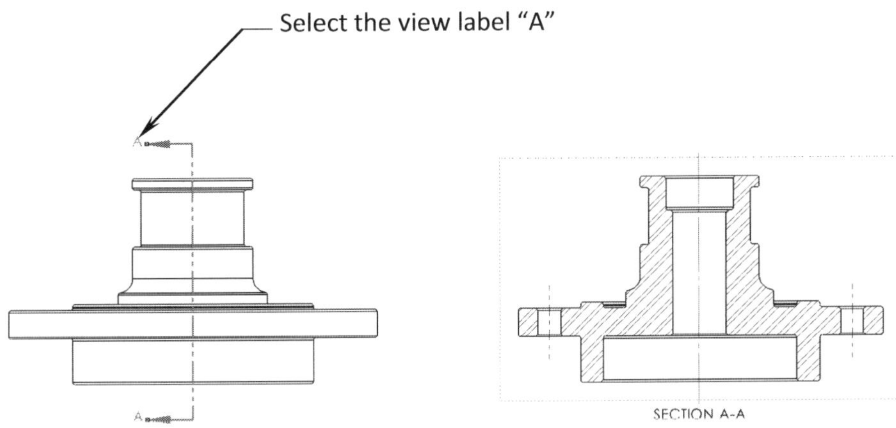

Select the following: **Bold, Points, 14 points** and click **OK.**

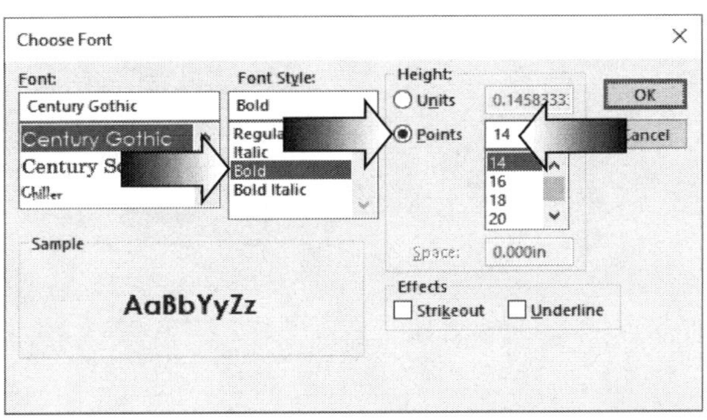

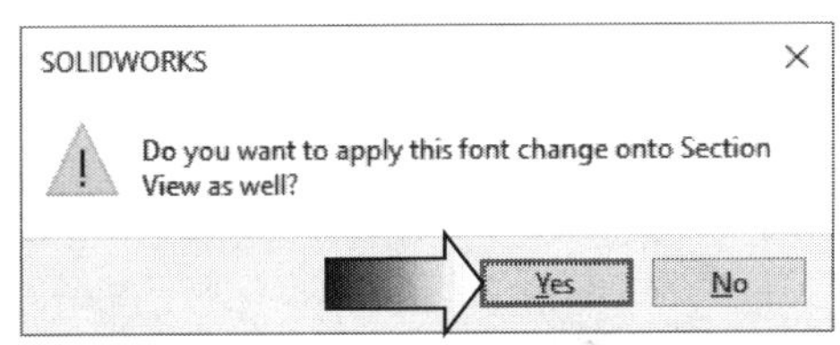

Click **YES** to also change the font of the section view label.

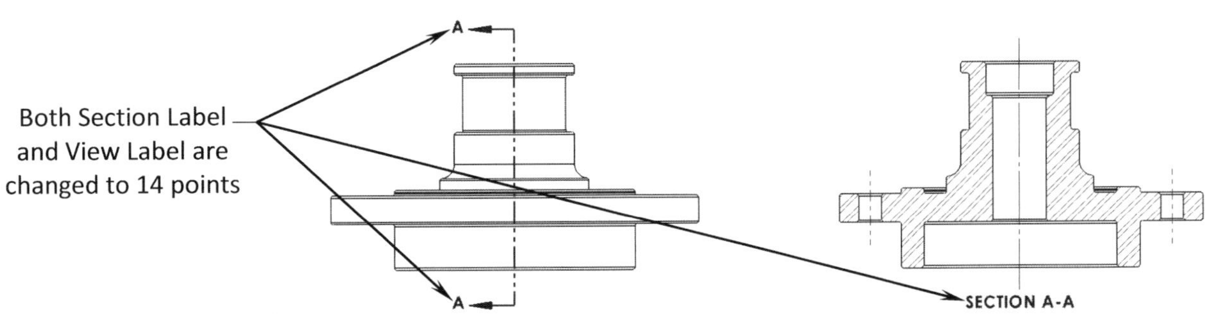

11. Changing the drawing paper size:

It seems we may not have enough room to add dimensions and annotations. We do not want to make the drawing views scale any smaller as it will make small features in the part more difficult to see. Instead, we will change the size of the drawing paper to the next size up, the C-Size 22" X 17".

Right-click anywhere inside the drawing and select **Properties**.

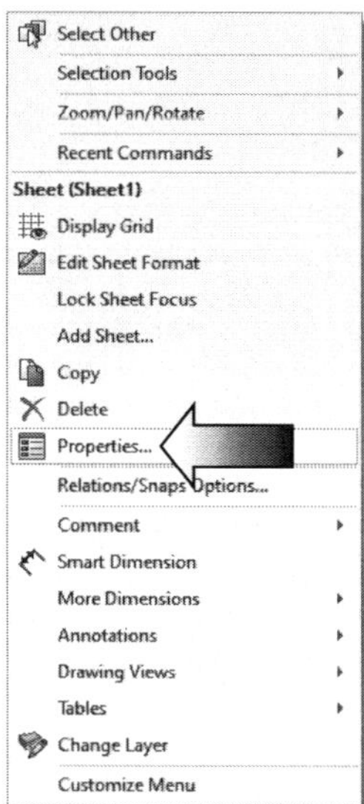

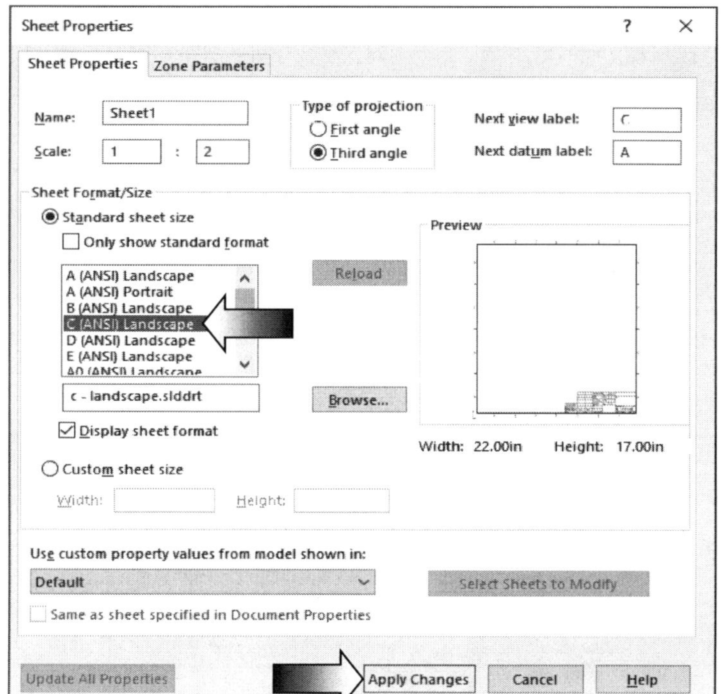

Under the Sheet Format/ Size, select: **C (ANSI) Landscape**. (the paper size is 22.0" x 17.0").

Click **Apply Changes.**

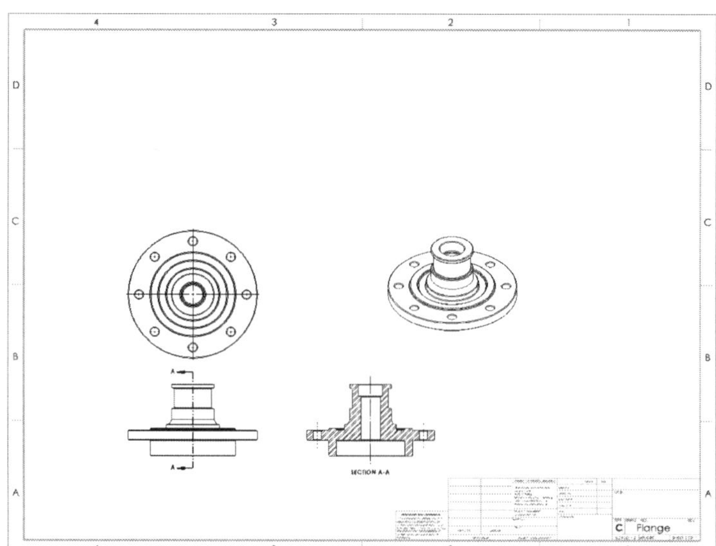

The C-Size drawing format is loaded. We now have a lot of extra room to add dimensions and annotations.

But first, let us rearrange the drawing views.

Move the drawing views by dragging their dotted borders.

Space them out similar to the image shown below. There should be plenty of room to allow for dimensions and annotations to be added.

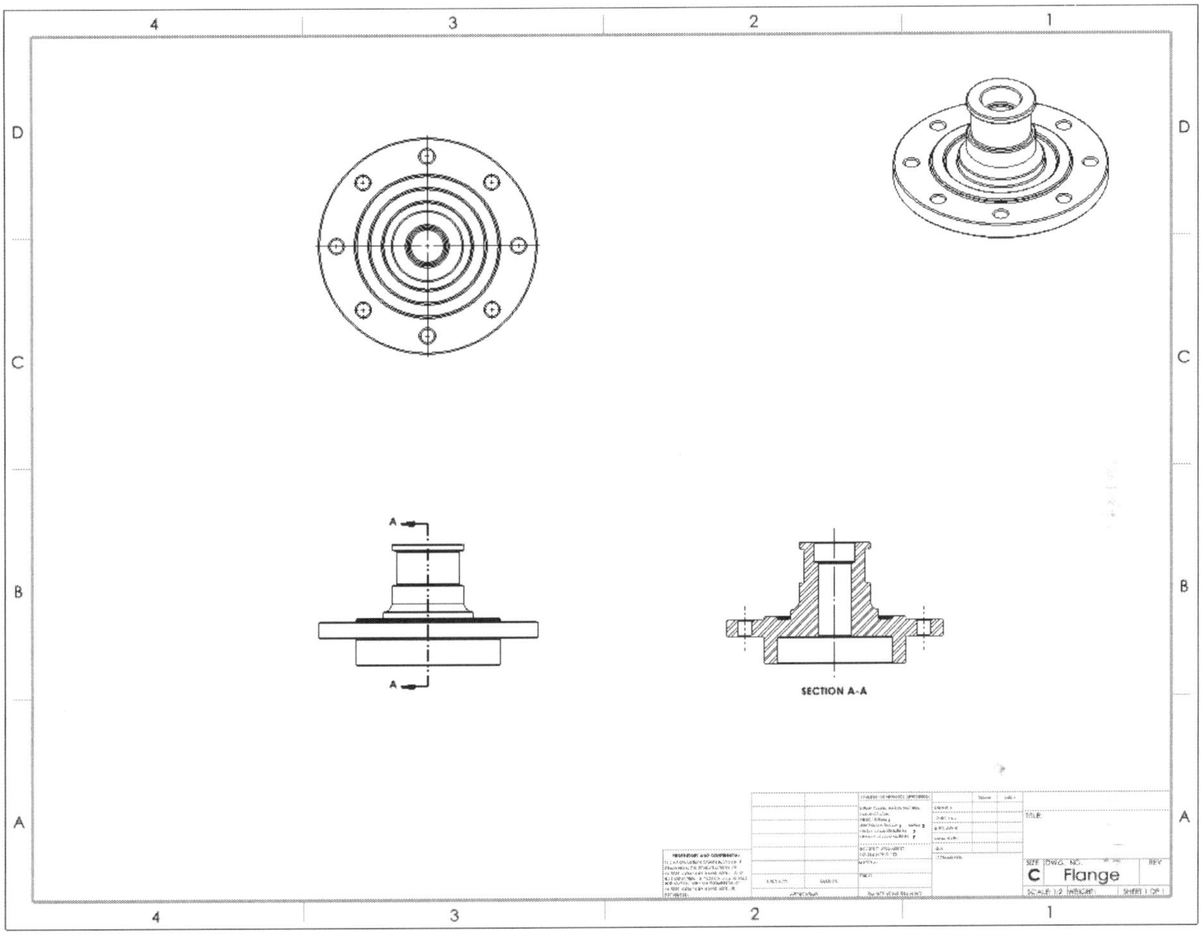

For training and learning purposes, it would be easier to focus on one topic at a time such as creating the drawing views, inserting the model dimensions, and adding the datums and tolerances.

We will add the General Notes, the Revision Block, and fill out the information in the Title Block towards the completion of this drawing.

Remember to save your work every once in a while.

12. Inserting the model dimensions:

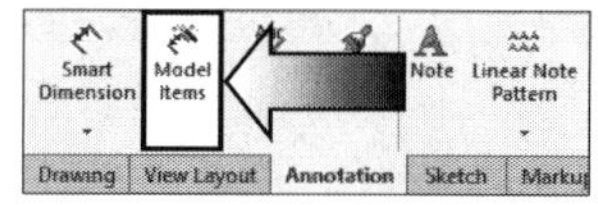

To maintain the parametric relationship between the 2D drawing and the 3D model, the driving dimensions in the model should be inserted into the drawing views. This way, any changes done to the model will be populated to the drawing automatically.

Select the dotted border of the **Front** drawing view.

Switch to the **Annotation** tab and click **Model Items**.

For Source, select **Entire Model**.

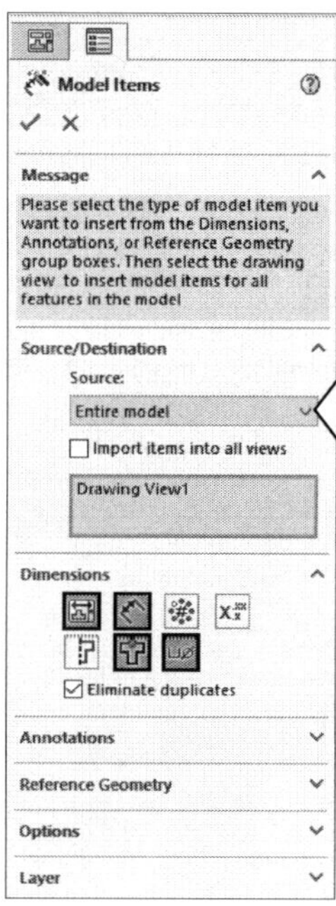

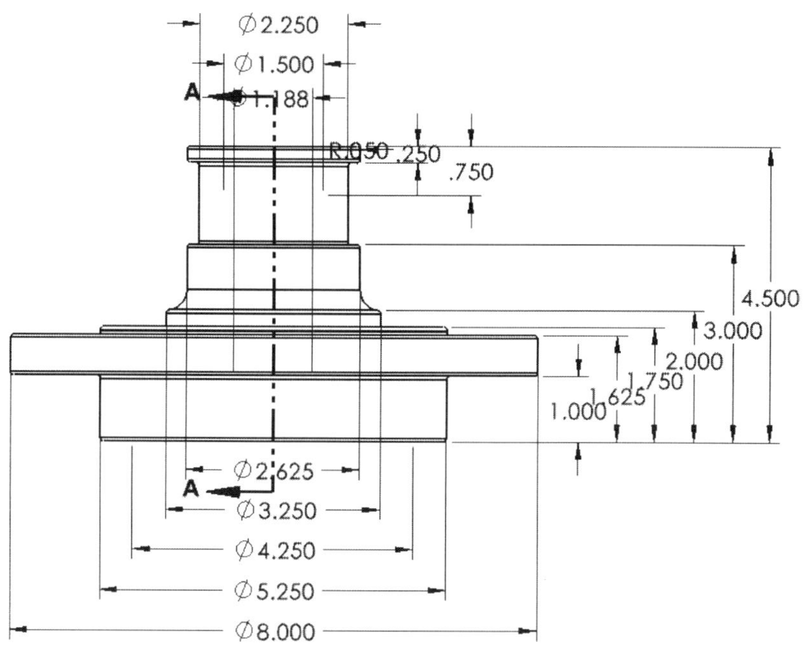

For Dimensions, select:

* Marked For Drawing
* Not Marked For Drawing
* Hole Wizard Locations
* Hole Callout

Click **OK** to export the model dimensions into the selected drawing view.

13. Moving dimensions:

Dimensions can be moved from one drawing view to another and still maintain their associations to the model.

Hold the **Control** key and select 3 dimensions: **Ø1.500**, **Ø 1.188**, and **Ø 4.250**.

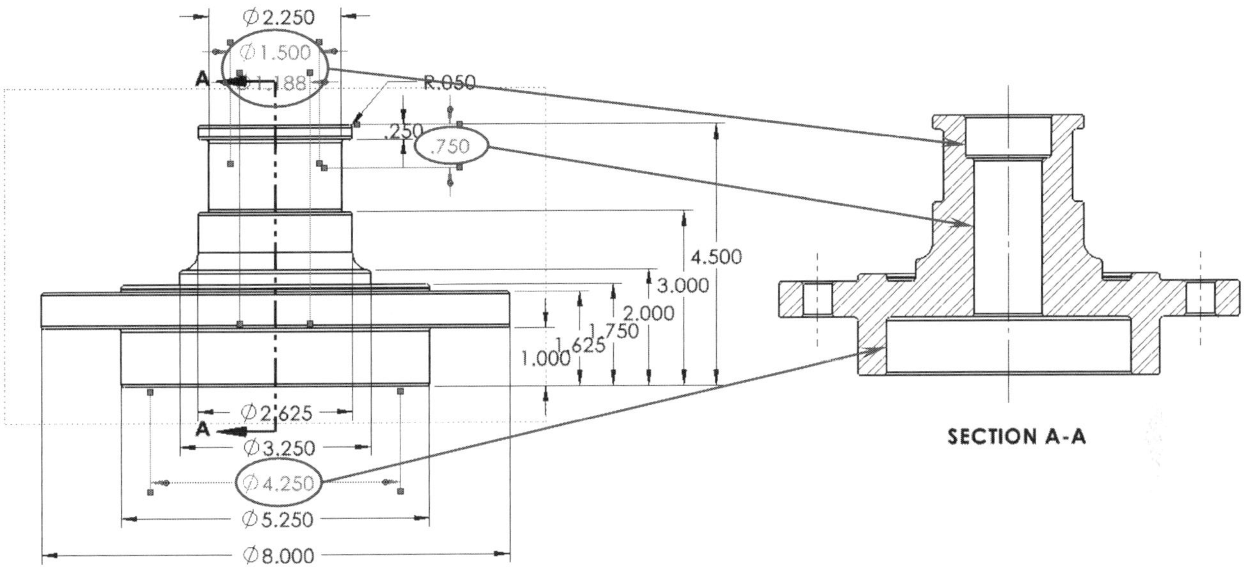

Now hold the **Shift** key and drag/drop the 3 selected dimensions to anywhere inside the **section view**.

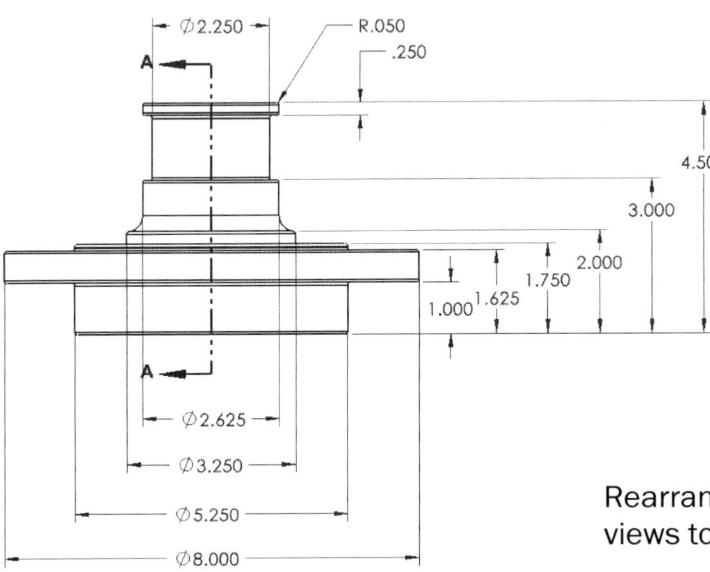

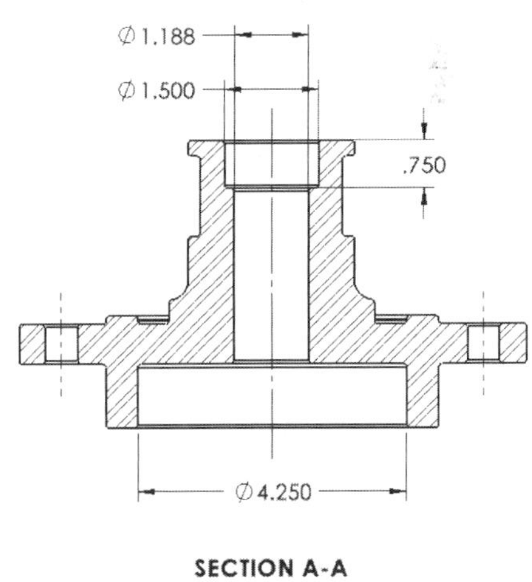

Rearrange the dimensions in both drawing views to look similar to the images above.

14. Removing dimension overlaps with Break-Lines:

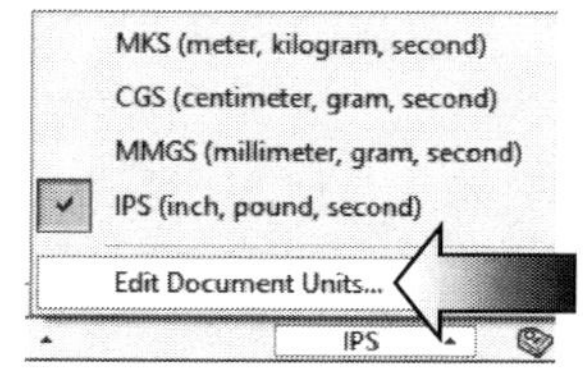

To further enhance the clarity of a drawing, the overlaps between the dimension leader lines should be replaced with small gaps. This can be done quite easily with a couple simple steps.

Click the small arrow at the bottom right corner of the screen, next to the IPS units, and select: **Edit Document Units.**

On the left pane, select the **Dimensions** option.

On the right pane, <u>clear</u> the checkbox for **Break Only Around Dimension Arrow.**

Click **OK.**

Select the dimension **Ø1.188** and click the **Leaders** tab.

Enable the **Break Lines** checkbox and click **OK.**

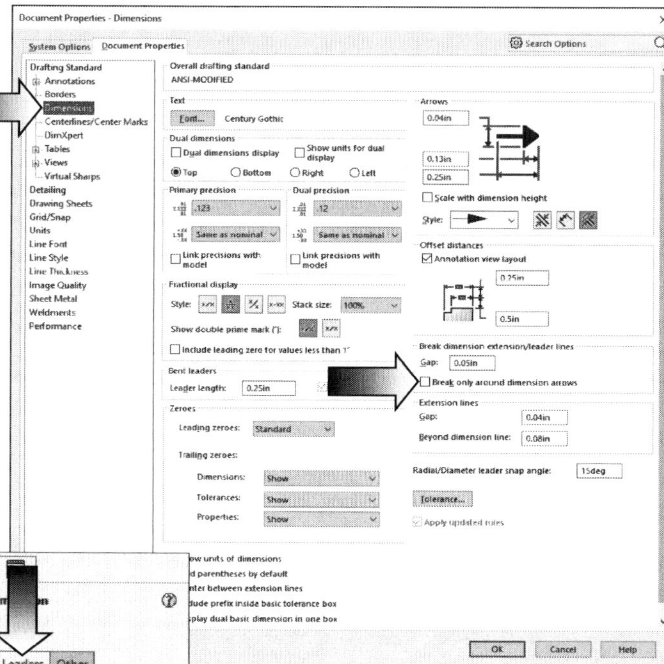

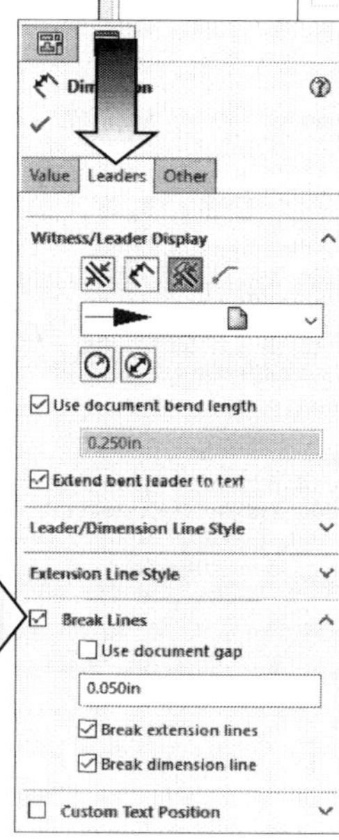

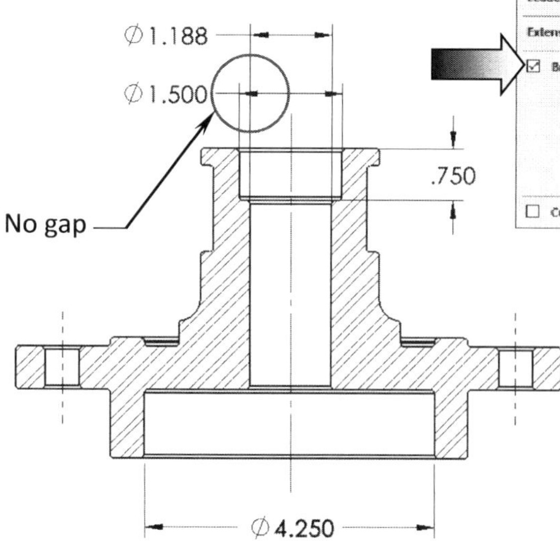

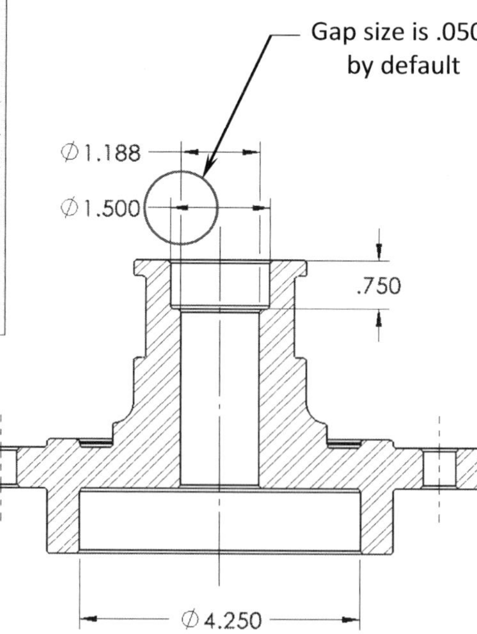

15. Inserting other dimensions:

Zoom in on the **Top** drawing view and select its dotted border.

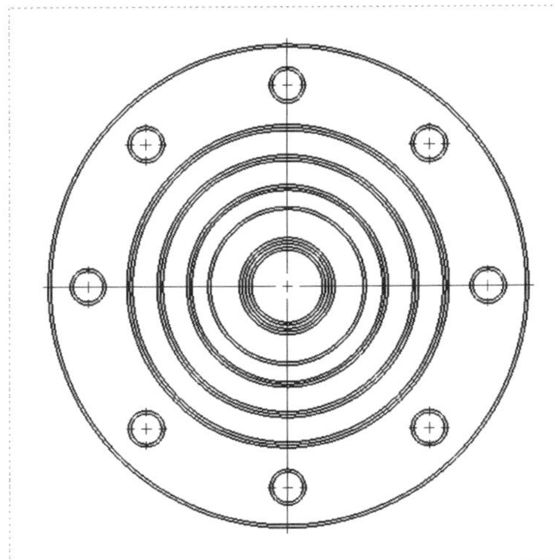

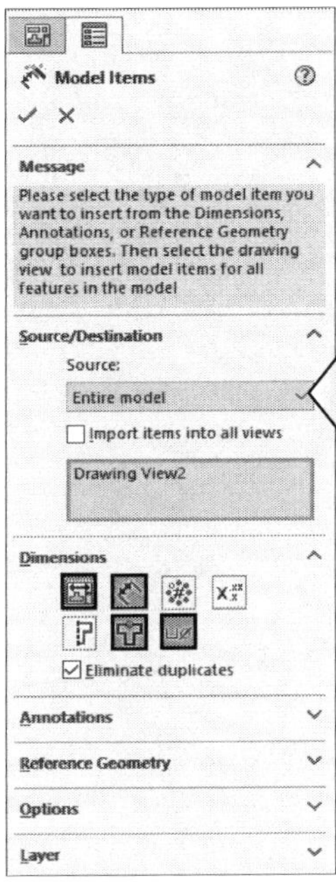

Click **Model Items** on the **Annotation** tab.

The options that were selected from the previous step should still be active.

Click **OK**.

Three dimensions were added, but the Ø6.650 must be attached to the Bolt-Circle of the hole Pattern.

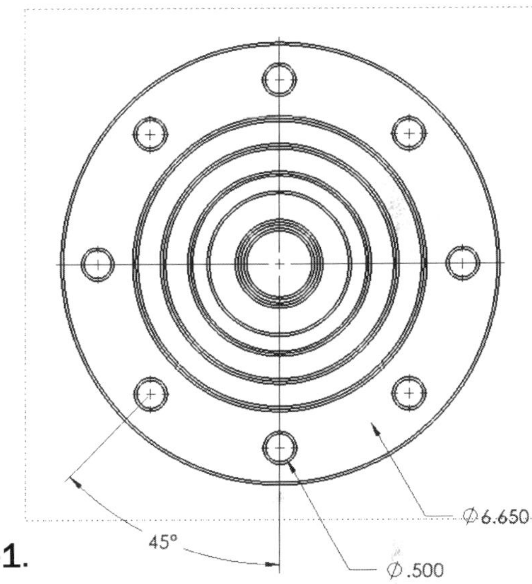

Make sure the dotted border of the **Top** drawing view is still selected.

Click the **DrawingManager Tree** tab (arrow); expand the **Drawing View2** (Top view). Also expand the part **Flange** and the **Cut-Extrude1**.

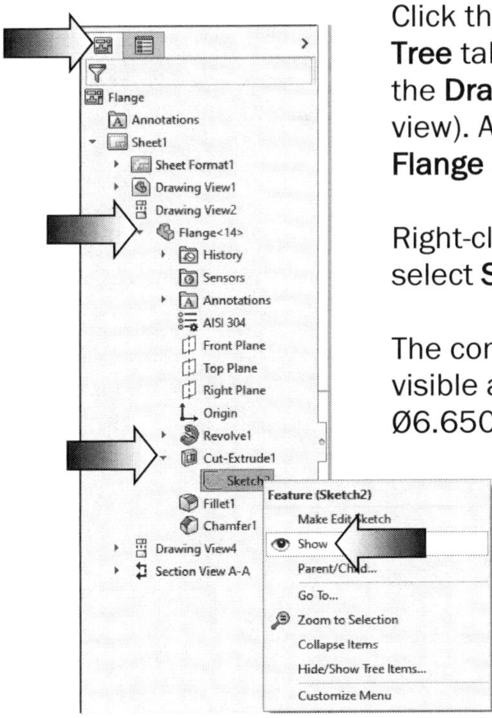

Right-click **Sketch-2** and select **Show**.

The contruction circle is now visible and the dimension Ø6.650 is attaching to it.

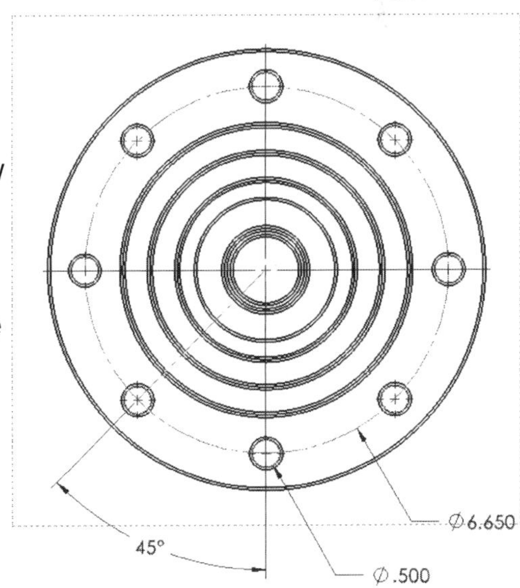

Click on the name **Drawing View 2** and press: **Shift+C** to collapse the tree.

16. Adding callouts:

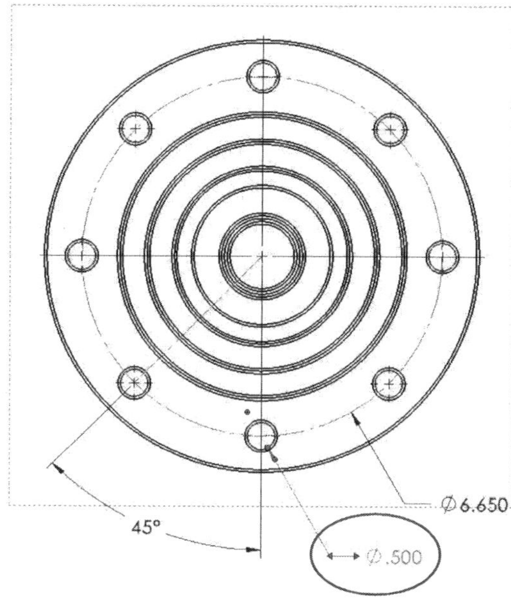

Callouts such as Depth and Number of Instances will be added at this time.

Select the dimension **Ø.500** in the Top drawing view.

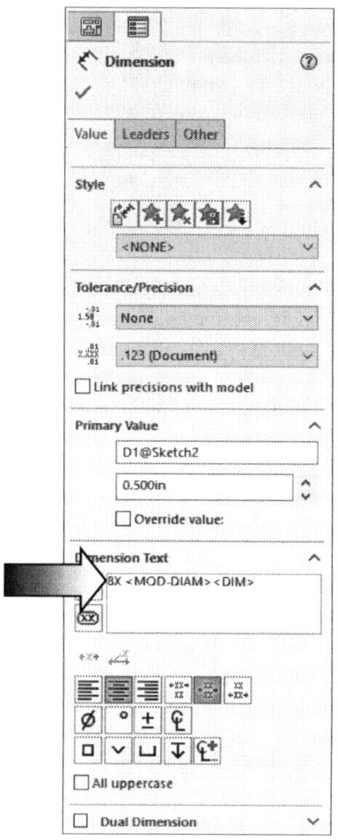

Locate the **Dimension Text** section and place the mouse cursor before the <MOD-DIAM><DIM> and Enter: **8X**.

Do not click OK just yet.

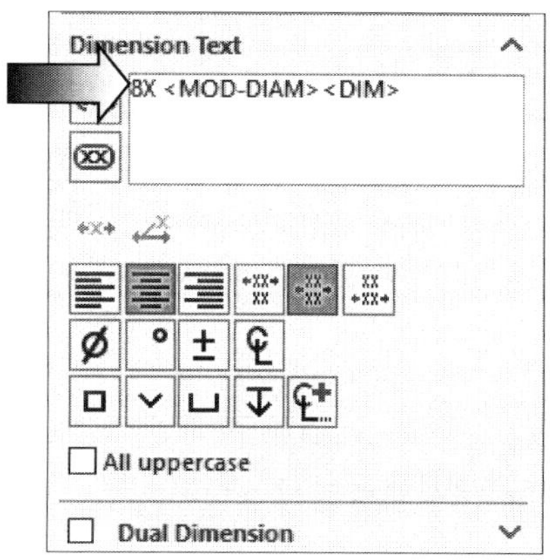

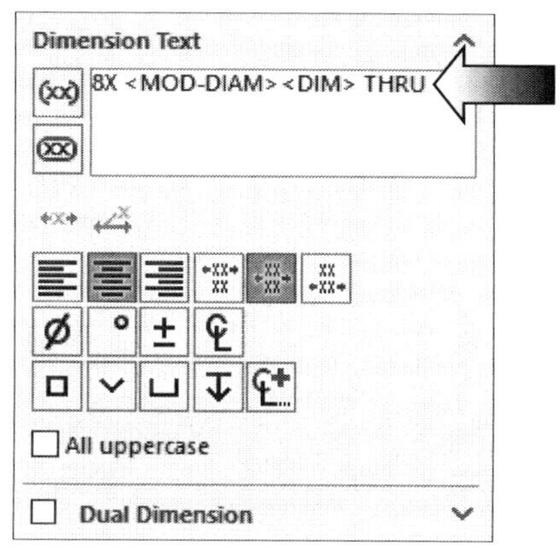

Next, click to place the mouse cursor after the <DIM> and enter: (space) **THRU**.

Repeat the last step and update the following callouts:

8X 45°
EQUALLY SPACED

Ø6.650 BOLT CIRCLE

Click **OK**.

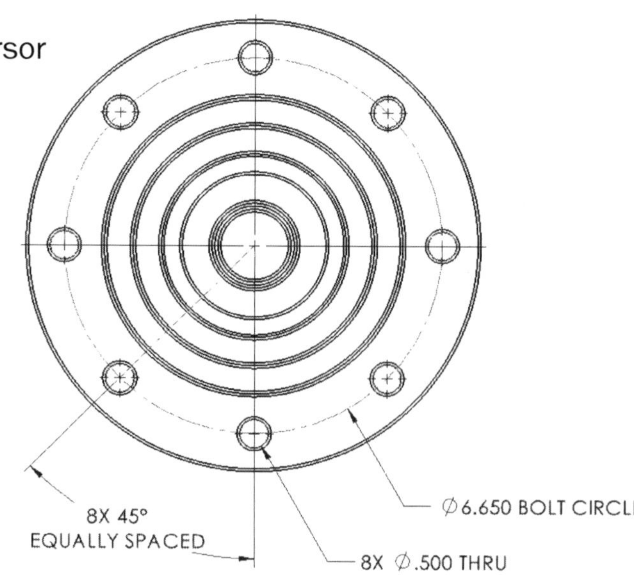

17. Adding additional callouts:

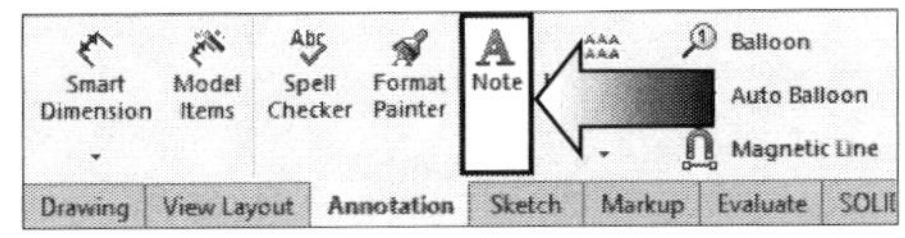

Sometimes the chamfer dimensions do not get exported properly, and even if they did, they may appear at some odd locations. To overcome this issue, we will use a note to callout the chamfer dimensions instead.

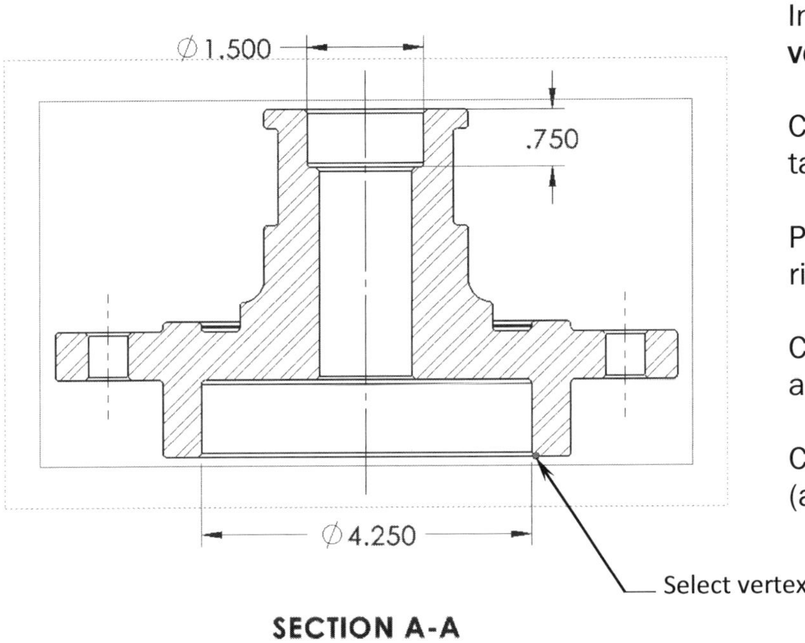

In the section view, select the **vertex** as indicated below.

Click **Note** on the **Annotation** tab.

Place the note on the lower right side and enter: **45**

Click the **Add Symbol** button and select the **Degree** symbol

Continue to type: **X 050 TYP** (after the degree symbol).

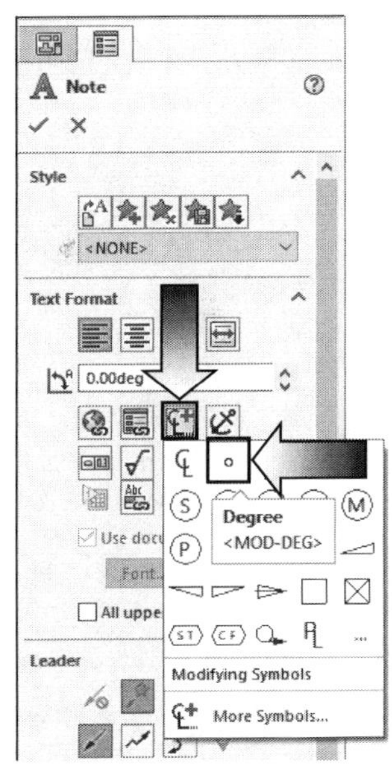

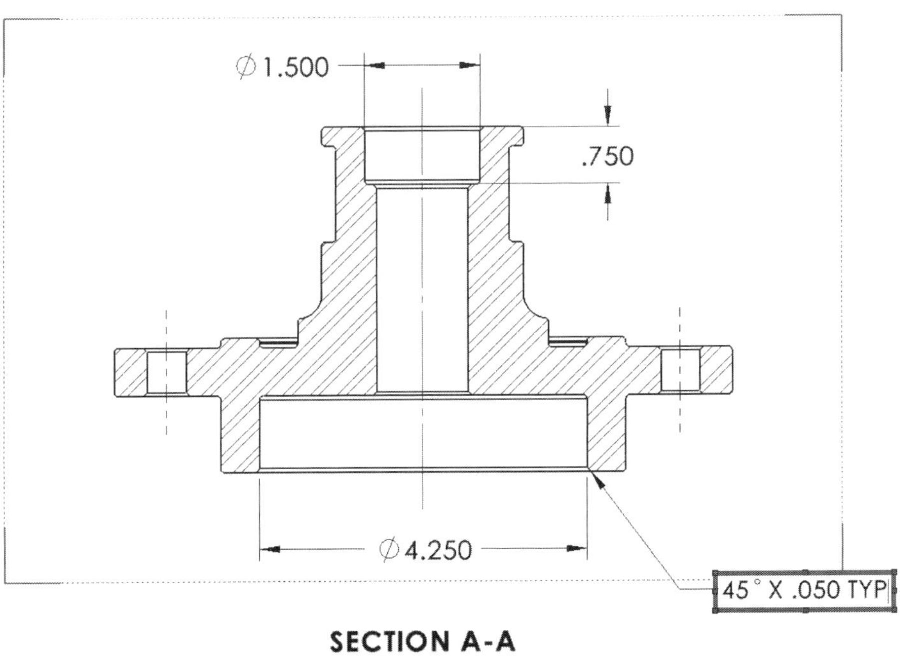

Click **OK**.

Check your note against the one shown here.

Select the **Smart Dimension** tool on the **Annotation** tab.

Add the **radius** dimension as shown in the image on the right.

Click the **round handle** to flip the dimension arrow outward.

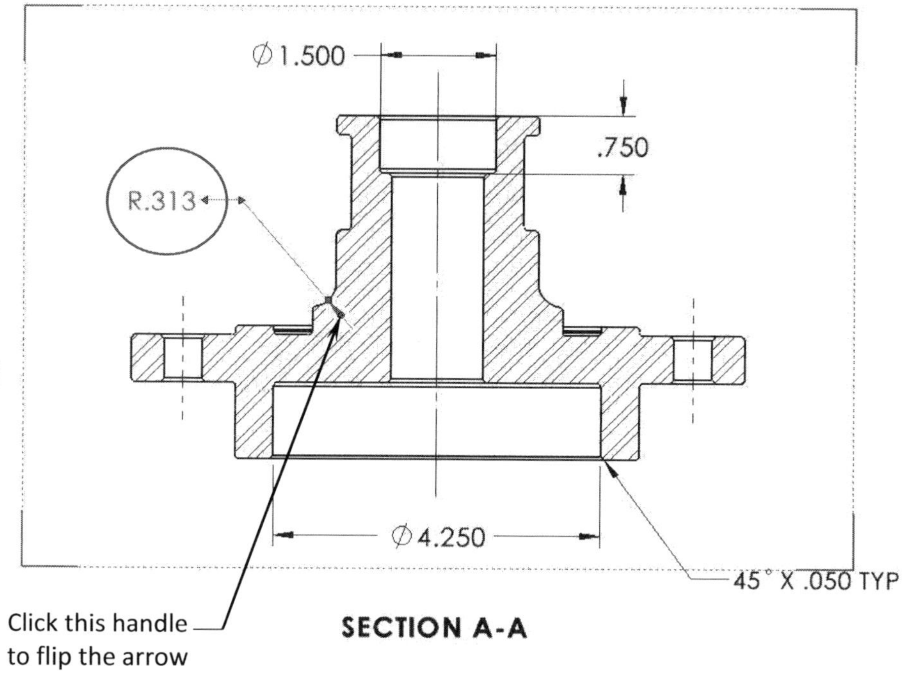

Add the text **"THRU"** under the dimensions **Ø1.188** (circled) and select the **Top Justify** button (arrow) to align the callout to the top.

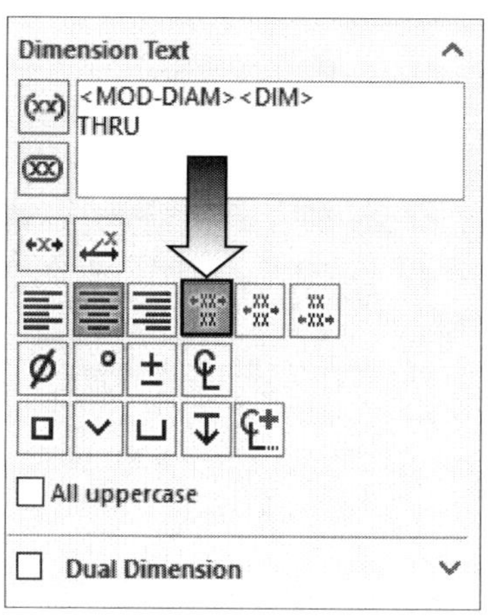

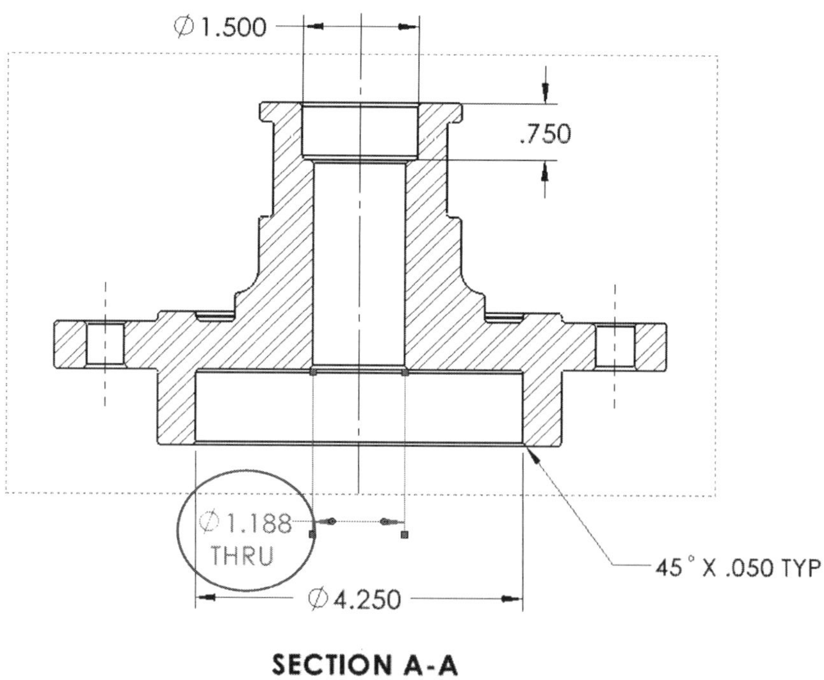

Click **OK**.

18. Adding datums:

In an engineering drawing, datums are used with geometric dimensioning and tolerancing on an object used to create a reference system for measurement.

In short, a datum is used as a reference point, surface, or axis on an object against which measurements are made.

Switch to the **Annotation** tab and click: **Datum Feature**.

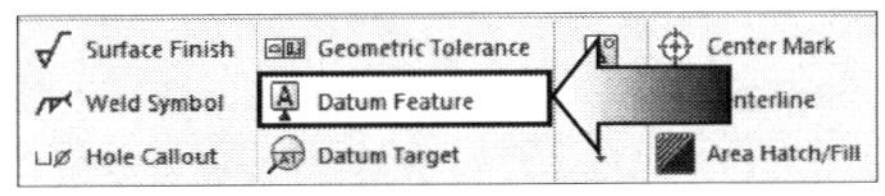

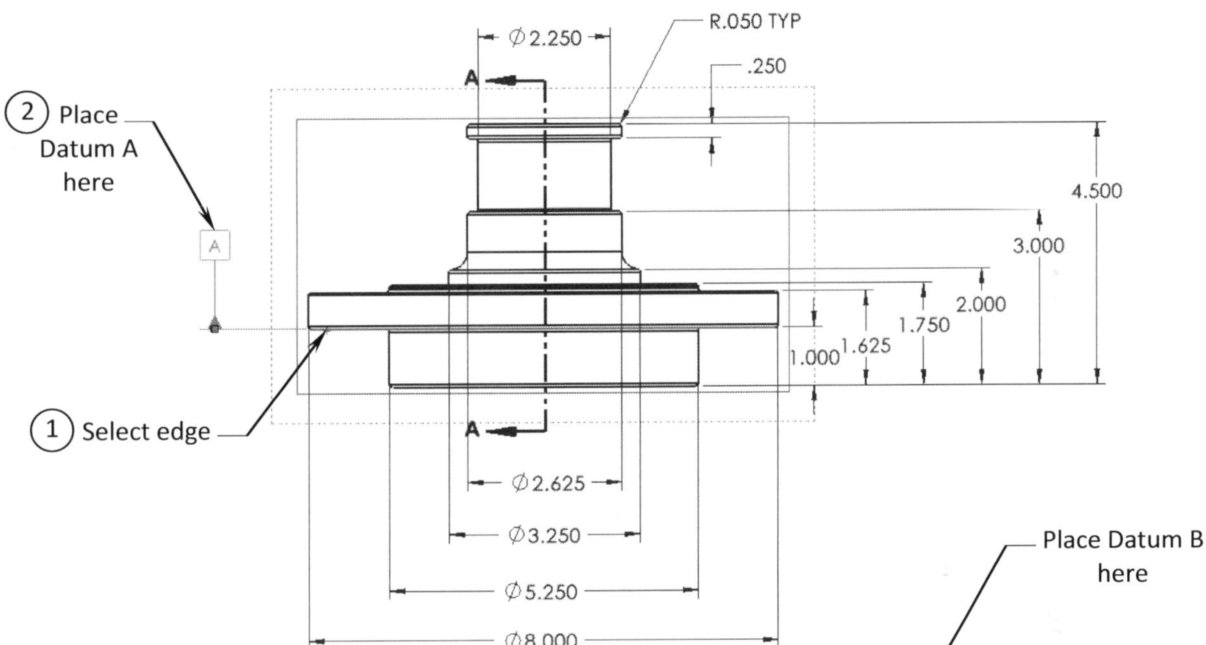

For **Datum A,** (click 1) select the <u>bottom edge</u> of the flange in the **Front** drawing view.

Move the cursor outwards and click (click 2) to place Datum A as shown in the image above.

For **Datum B**, select the <u>centerline</u> in the middle of the section view.

Place Datum B as noted in the image.

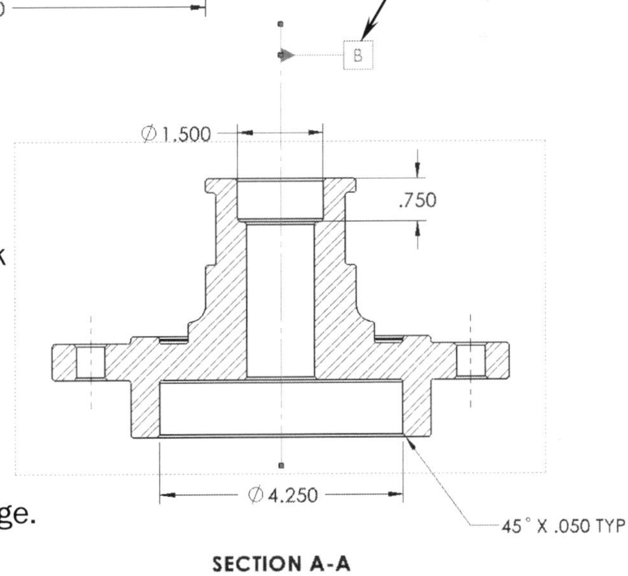

Your drawing should look similar to the one shown below. Make any corrections as needed.

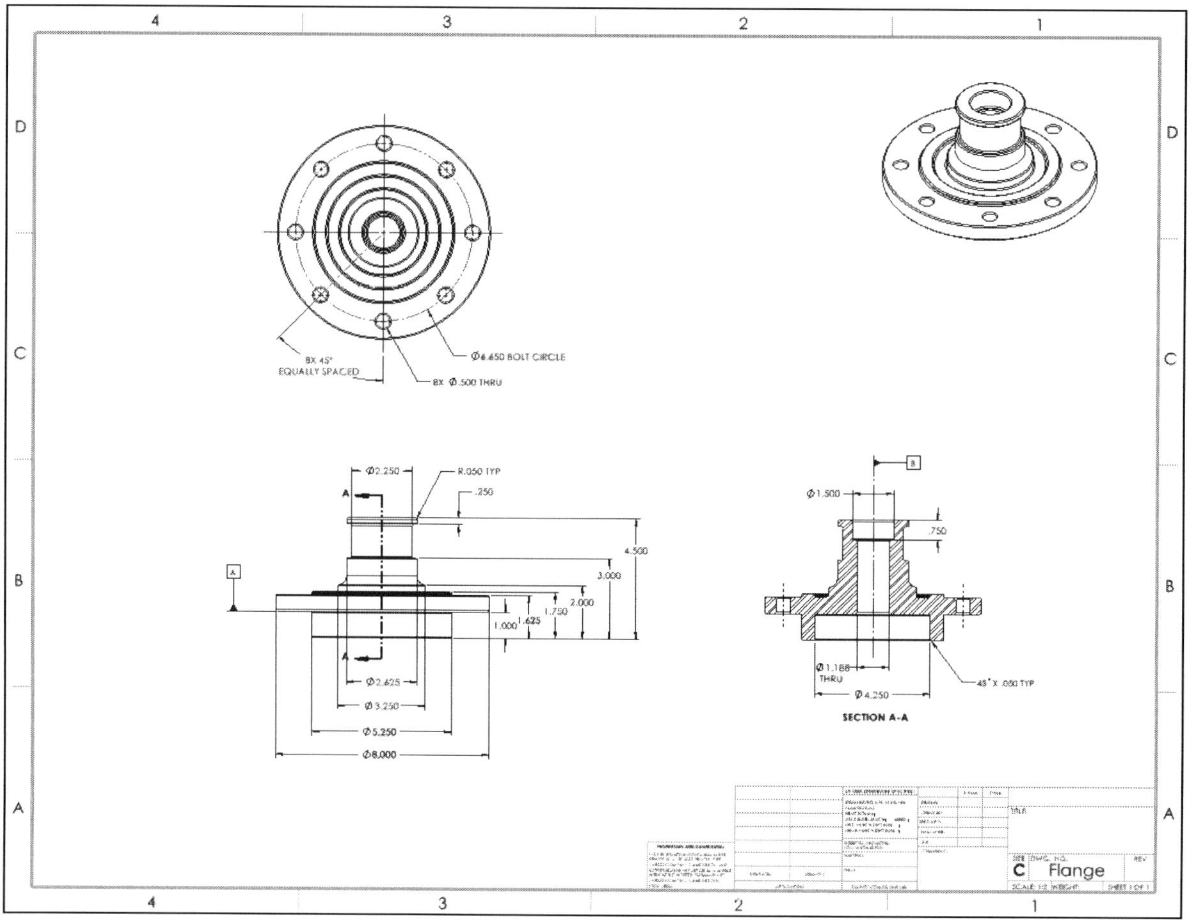

Remember to save your work every once in a while.

We will create the General Notes, the Revision Block, and fill out the Title Block information at this time.

The Tolerance and precision topics will be discussed and added to the drawing in the next chapter.

19. Adding the General Notes:

General notes provide information and direction to the manufacturers by clarifying design details or construction practices.

The general and specific notes should not be confused with the information found in the bill of materials, title block, revision chart, or the drawing specifications. The general notes are usually located in the upper left corner of the drawing.

Switch to the **Annotation** tab and click **Note**.

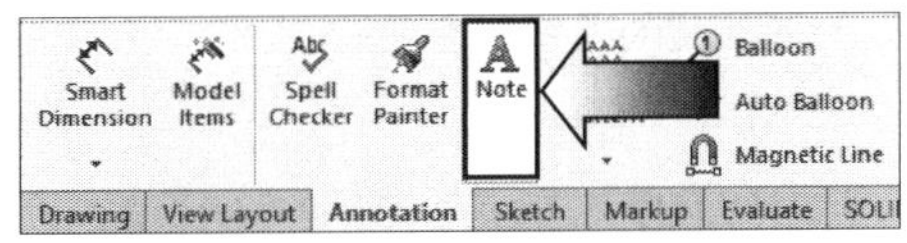

Zoom in closer to the upper left corner of the drawing.

Place the note here

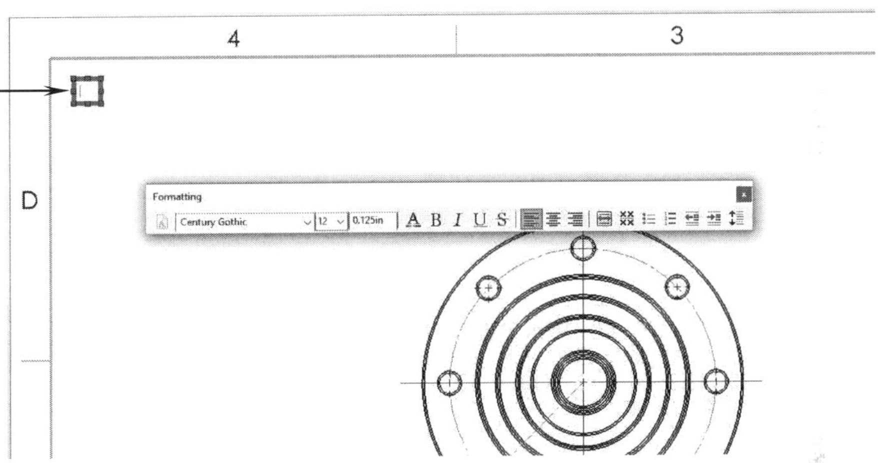

Place the note near the upper corner of the drawing and enter the note shown below:

NOTES: UNLESS OTHERWISE SPECIFIED
1. INTERPRET DRAWINGS AND DIMENSIONS PER ASME ANSI-Y14.5
2. DIMENSIONS ARE IN INCHES, 3 DECIMAL PLACES
3. MATERIAL: STAINLESS STEEL 304 OR EQUIVALENT
4. BREAK ALL EDGES, TUMBLE, AND DEBURR PARTS
5. SHIPPING PACKAGE TO BE LABELED WITH PART NUMBER, MANUFACTURER'S NAME, LOT NUMBER, AND QUANTITY
6. PARTS TO BE CLEAN AND FREE OF LUBRICANT OR DEBRIS

Click **OK**.

20. Adding the Revision Table:

The Revision Table or revision block, located in the upper right corner of the drawing, shows details about the changes that were made to roll the revision.

The Revision Table includes the revision, the description of what changes were made, the date of the revision, and approval of the revision.

Zoom in closer to the upper right corner of the drawing.

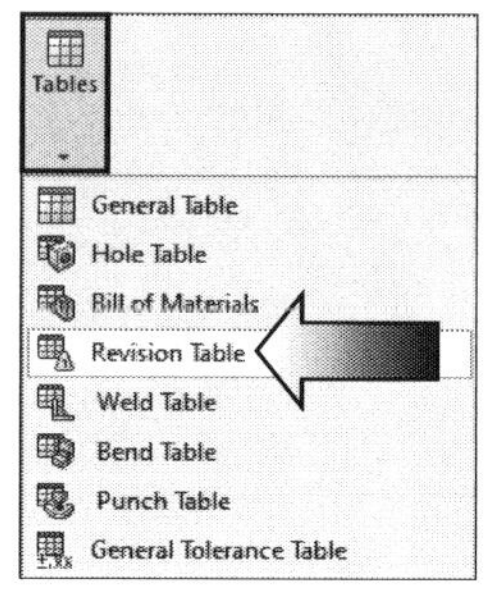

Switch to the **Annotation** tab, expand the **Tables** drop-down list and select: **Revision Table** (arrow).

For Table Template, use the default **Standard Revision Block**, which can be found in the C:\Program Files\SolidWorks Corp\SolidWorks 20XX\Lang\English.

Enable the checkbox for **Attached to Anchor Point.** This option will snap/lock the Revision Table to the upper right corner of the drawing automatically.

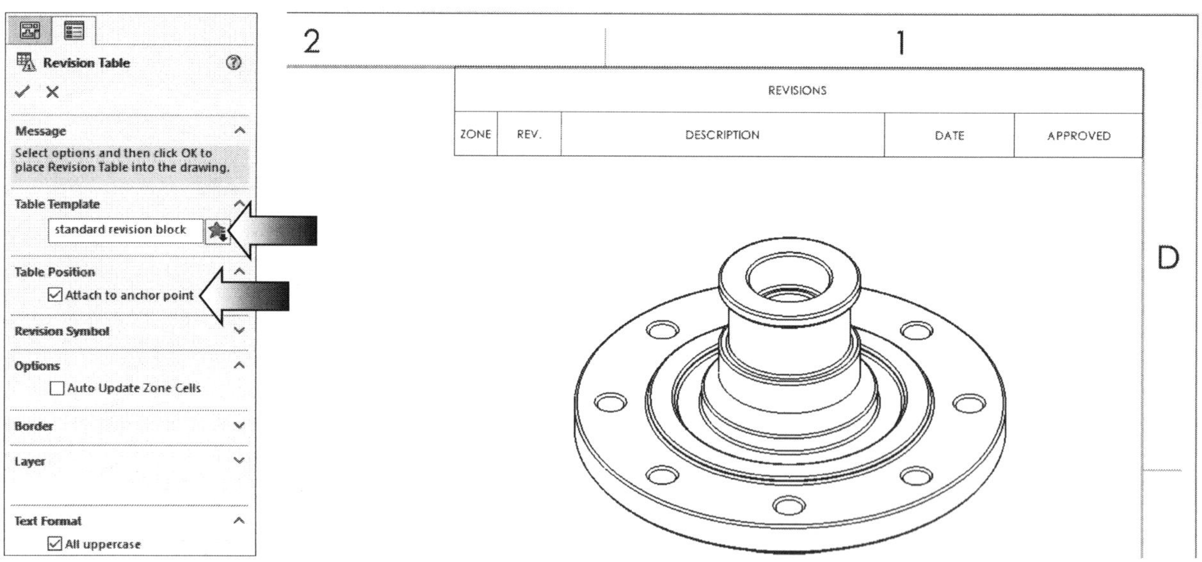

Click **OK.**

Hover the mouse pointer over the Revision Table and click square ↳B at the lower left corner, to add a new row.

A	B	C	D	E
REVISIONS				
ZONE	REV.	DESCRIPTION	DATE	APPROVED
	A		5/7/2023	

Click this symbol to add a new row

Double-click the letter **A** and change it to **01**.

Double-click in the **Description** field and enter: **RELEASED FOR REVIEW ONLY.**

Double-click in the **Date** field and enter today's date.

Double-click in the **Approved** field and enter your name there.

A	B	C	D	E
REVISIONS				
ZONE	REV.	DESCRIPTION	DATE	APPROVED
	01	RELEASED FOR REVIEW ONLY	DD/MM/YY	YOUR NAME HERE

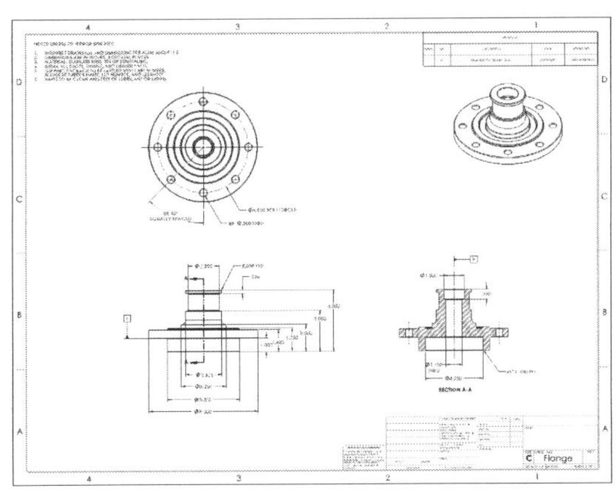

Zoom-To-Sheet (or press F) and rearrange the drawing views so that they look more presentable and easy to read.

The Isometric view should be kept at the upper right corner of the drawing to comply with ANSI standards.

We will now take a look at how to fill out the information in the Title Block.

21. Filling out the Title Block:

By default, every SOLIDWORKS drawing will have 2 layers to start with; more layers can be added at any time during the creation of the drawing.

The “Front Layer” is called the **Sheet**, and the “Back layer” is called the **Sheet Format.**

The Sheet is where drawing views, dimensions and annotations are created, and the Sheet Format is where the information that belongs to the Title Block is kept.

We will need to edit the Sheet Format in order to fill out the information in the Title Block.

From the FeatureManager tree, expand **Sheet1** and double-click the **Sheet-Format1** to activate the back layer.

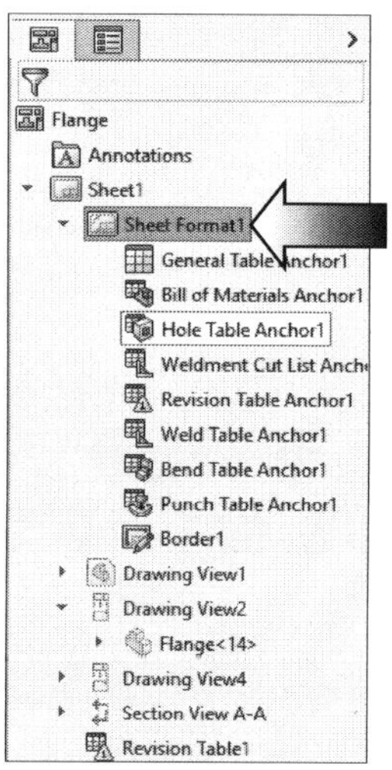

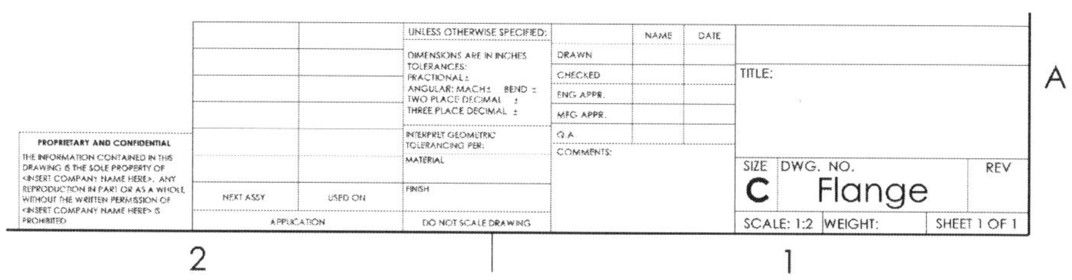

The Sheet Format is activated. The lines and text in the Title Block can be modified at this time.

Hover the mouse cursor over the middle of the Company field until the symbol appears. This is the symbol of a blank note; there is a blank note in every field by default.

Double-click this blank note and enter the name of your company (or school) here.

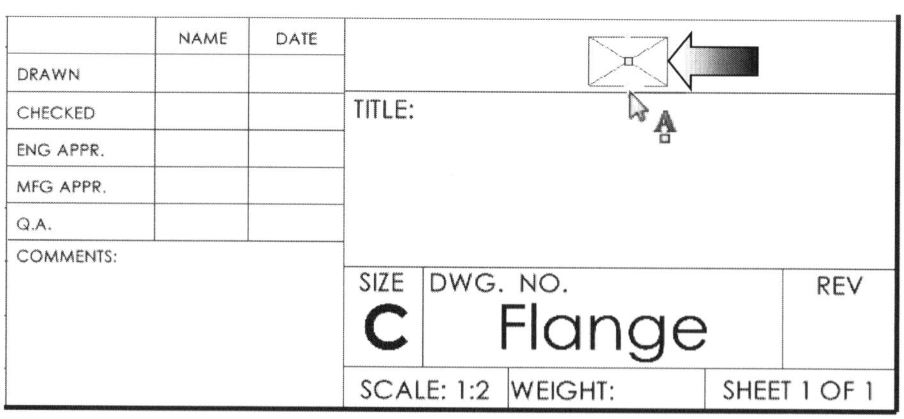

Continue adding or modifying the information in the Title Block as shown below.

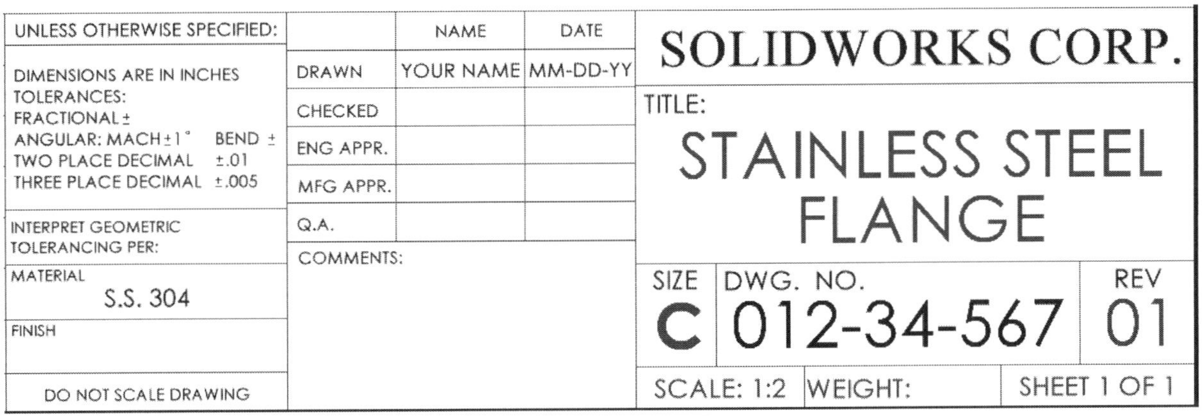

Note: The information provided in this lesson is intended for training and learning purposes only.

22. Switching back to the Sheet:

After the Title Block is filled out, we should go back to the Sheet (the Front Layer) prior to saving the drawing.

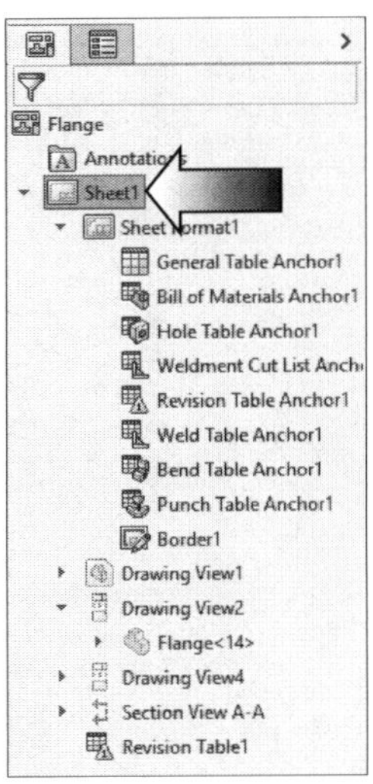

From the FeatureManager tree, double-click **Sheet1** to activate it.

When the Sheet layer is active, the information in the Title Block is no longer editable.

If you need to edit the Sheet Format again, simply double-click Sheet Format1 on the FeatureManager tree.

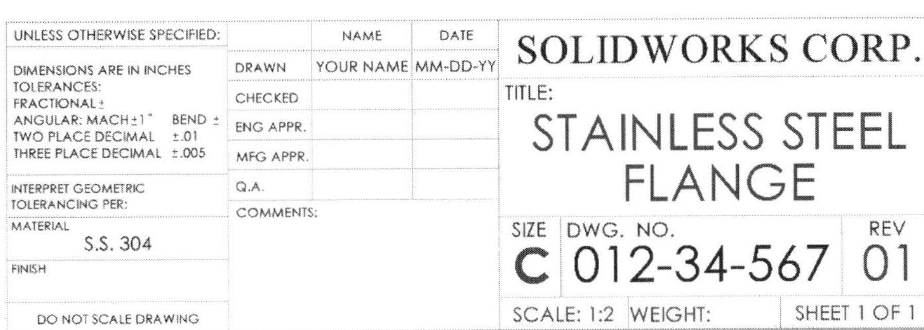

The 1st half of the lesson is completed. Let us save our work at this time.

23. Saving your work:

Select: **File, Save As**.

Enter: **Detailing a Machined Part.slddrw** for the file name.

Click **Save**.

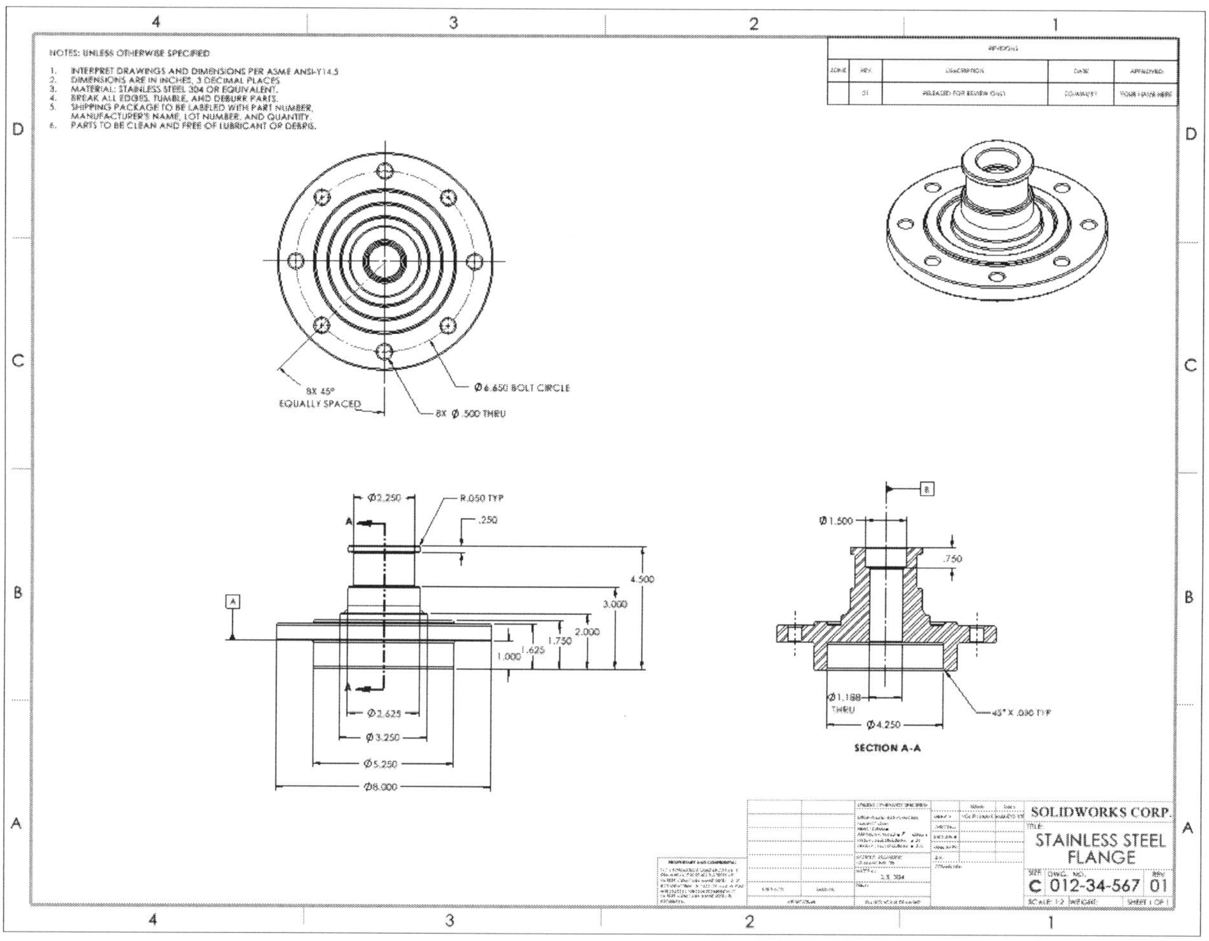

Close all documents.

The Tolerance and precision topics (GD&T) will be discussed and added to the same drawing, in the next chapter.

Exercise: Detailing a Machined Part

Base Block Drawing

The exercises are intended to help you apply what you have learned from the previous lessons. They come with some instructions, but they are not as detailed as the lessons. The purpose is to give you an opportunity to explore and create drawings on your own, at your own pace.

1. Opening a part document:

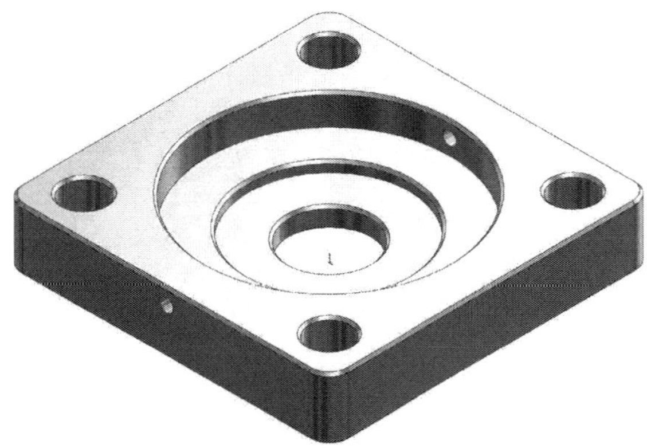

Select **File, Open.**

Browse to the Training Folder and open the part document named: **Machined Part_EXE.sldprt.**

The material Aluminum **5052-H32** has already been assigned to the part.

2. Transferring to a drawing:

Create a drawing from the model using the following:

* **B (ANSI) Landscape**
* **3rd Angle Projection**
* **Scale: 1:2**
* Add the **Front, Top,** and **Isometric** views from the **View Palette.**

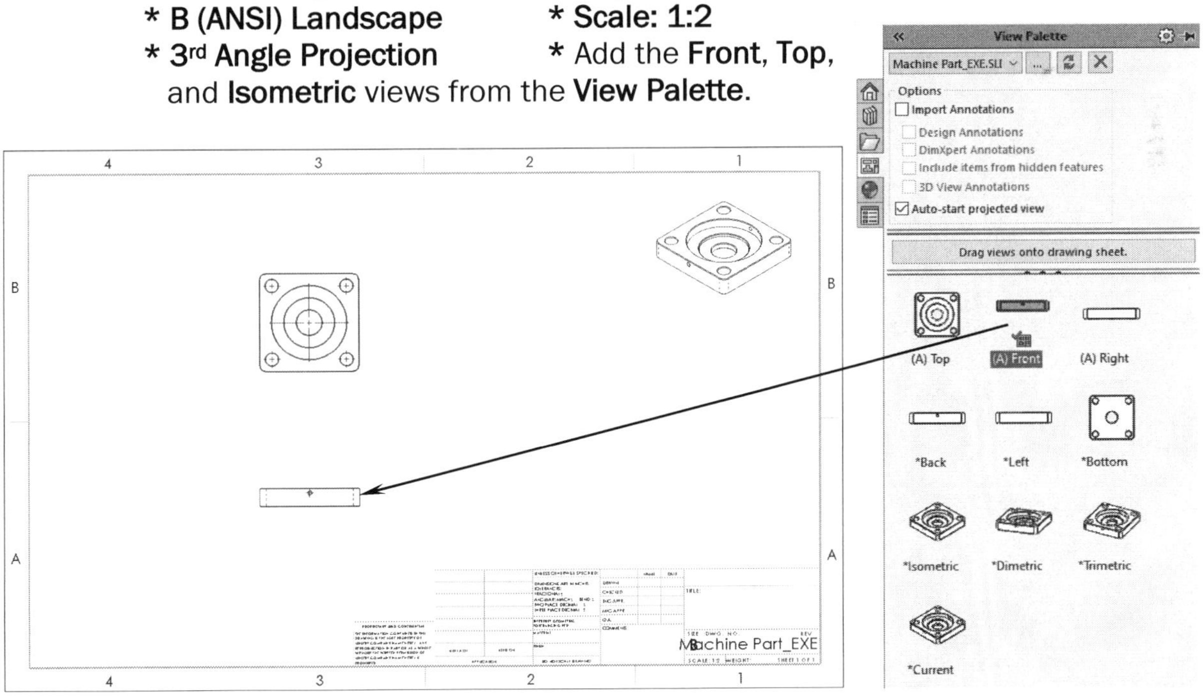

3. Adding a Section View:

Switch to the **Drawing** tab and click **Section View.**

Select the **Vertical Cutting Line** and place the line on the center of the hole.

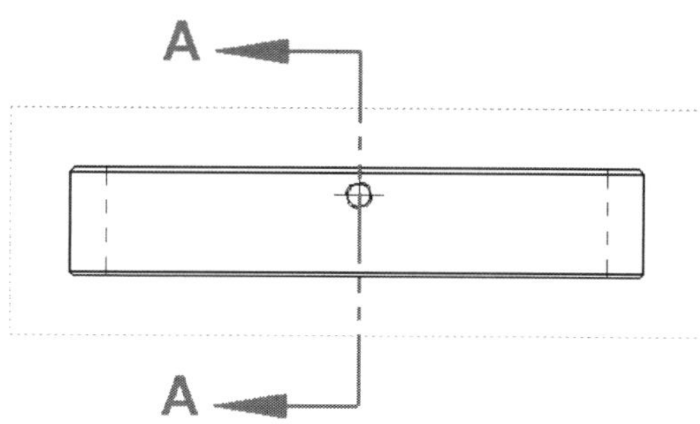

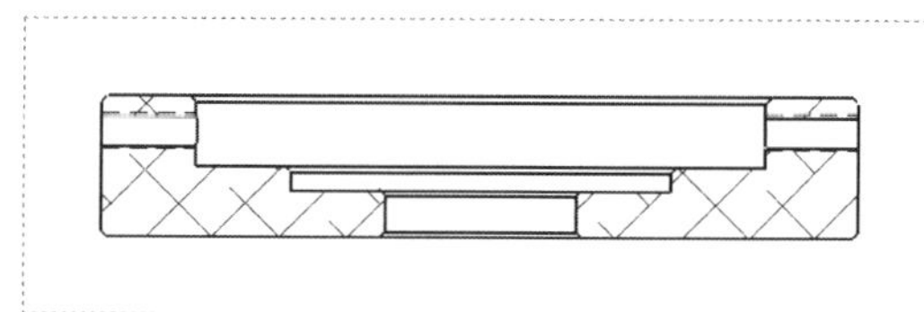

SECTION A-A

Place the Section View on the right side of the Front view. Verify that the section arrows are pointing to the left as shown in the image above.

4. Modifying the Hatch Pattern:

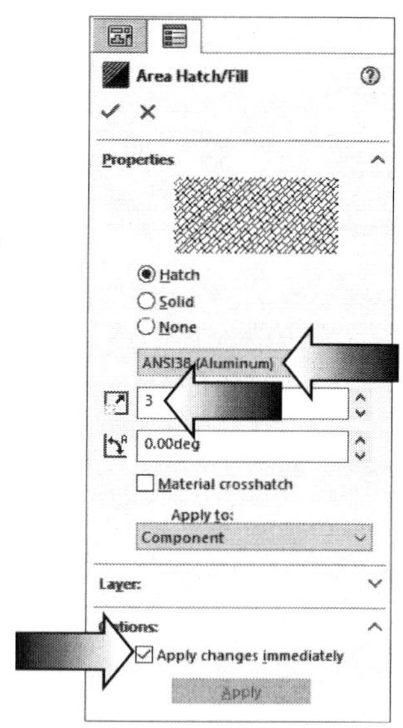

Click inside the hatch area to access the **Hatch Properties.**

For Hatch Pattern, select **ANSI38 (Aluminum).**

For Scale, enter **3.**

Enable the checkbox **Apply Changes Immediately.**

Click **OK.**

Compare your hatch pattern against the image shown on the right.

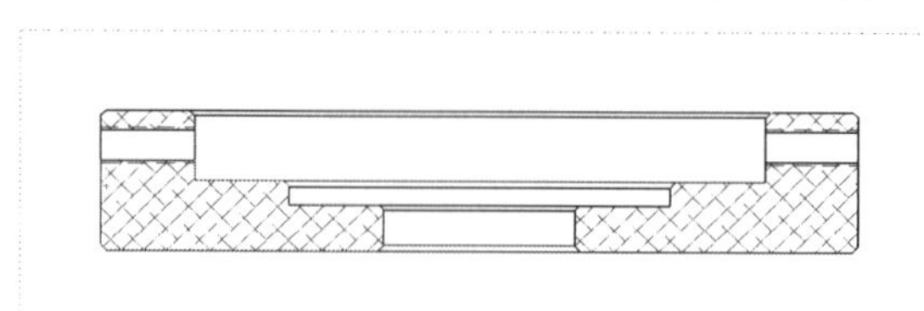

SECTION A-A

5. Adding Centerlines:

Switch to the **Annotation** tab and click **Centerline**.

Add the **3 centerlines** shown in the image below to the section view.

Adjust the length of the centerlines by dragging the handles at the ends, if needed.

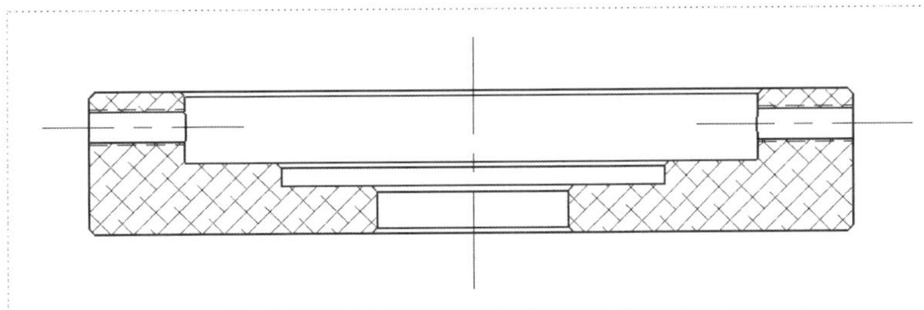

SECTION A-A

6. Adding the Model Dimensions:

Click **Model Items** on the **Annotation** tab.

Select the options shown in the dialog box on the right and click **OK**.

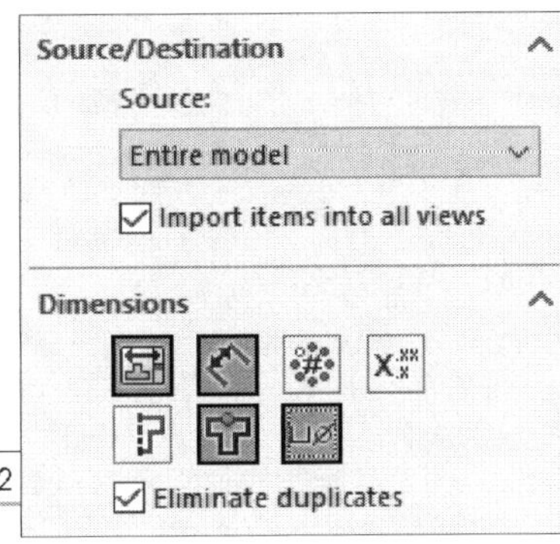

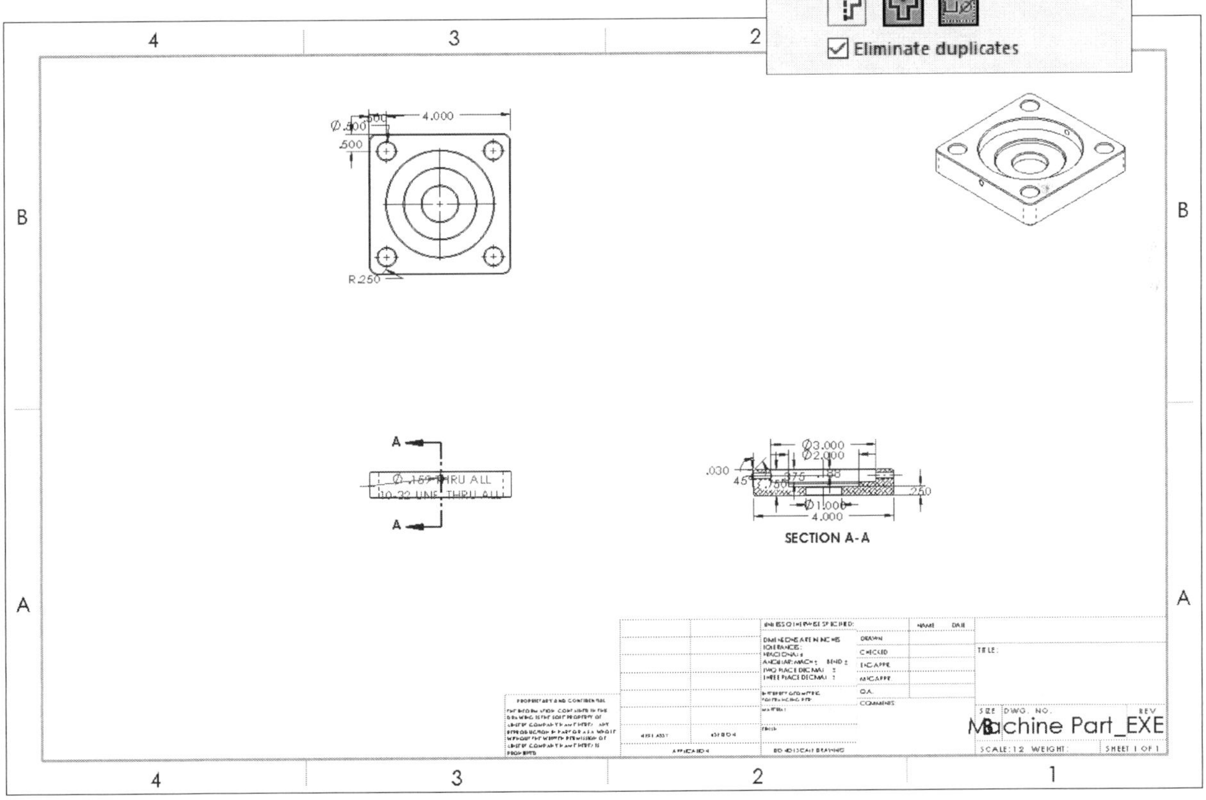

7. Rearranging dimensions:

Zoom in on each drawing view and rearrange the dimensions to look similar to the images shown below.

Starting with the **Top** drawing view, move the dimensions so that they are easier to read.

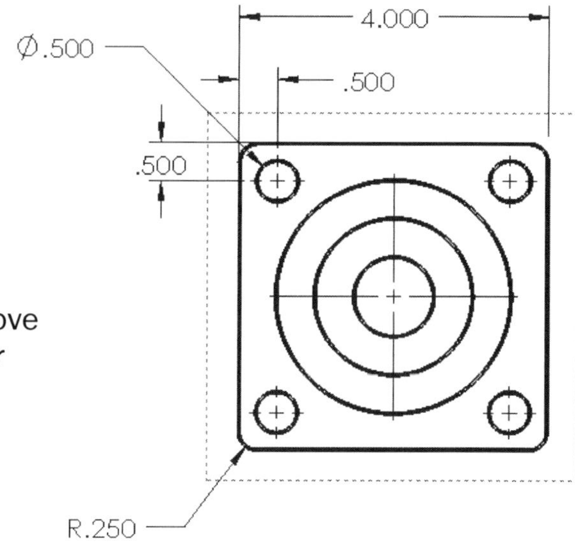

Next, zoom closer to the **Front** drawing view.

The hole callout will be modified in the next step.

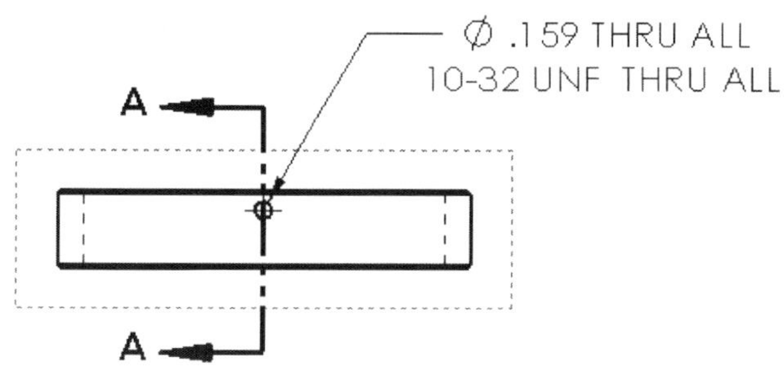

Zoom in on the **Section View**.

Rearrange the dimensions similar to the image shown on the right.

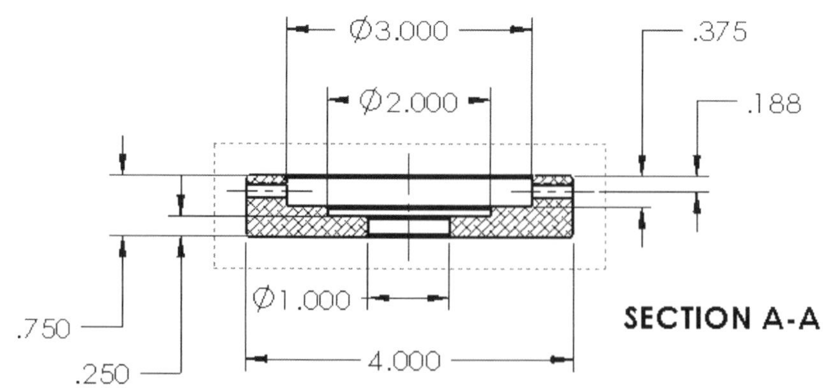

8. Modifying the dimensions:

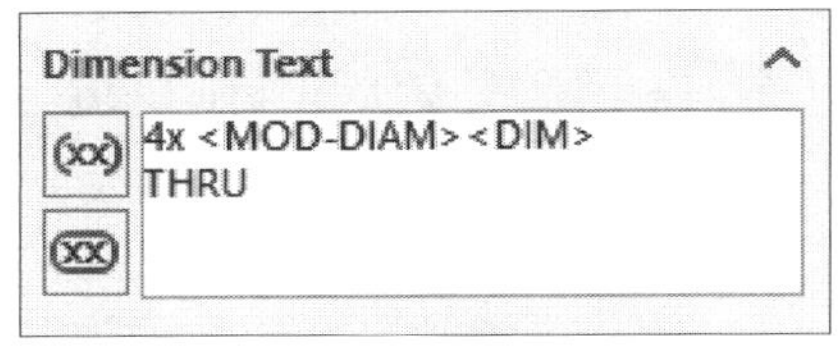

Add the number of instances to the dimensions using the **Dimension Text** box as shown here.

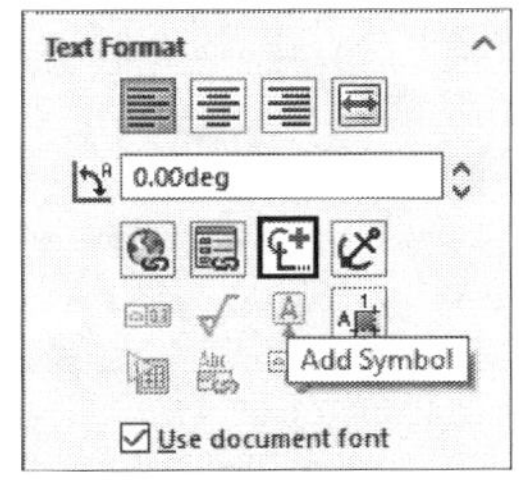

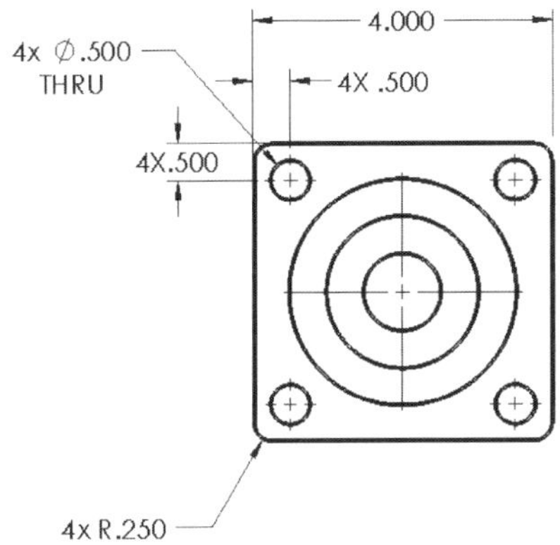

Add a note for the chamfer dimension (circled).

Click the Add Symbol button and select the degree symbol from the list.

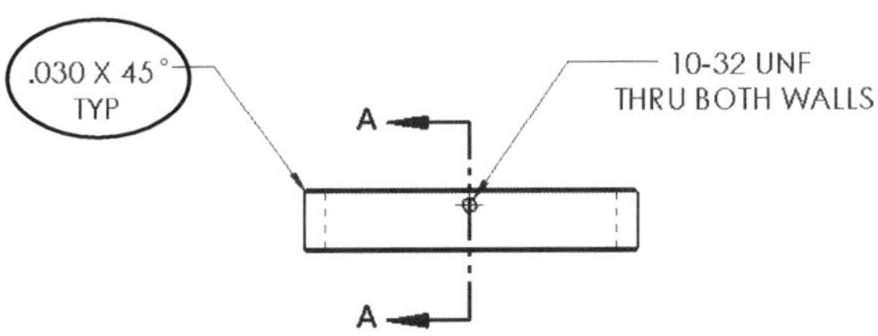

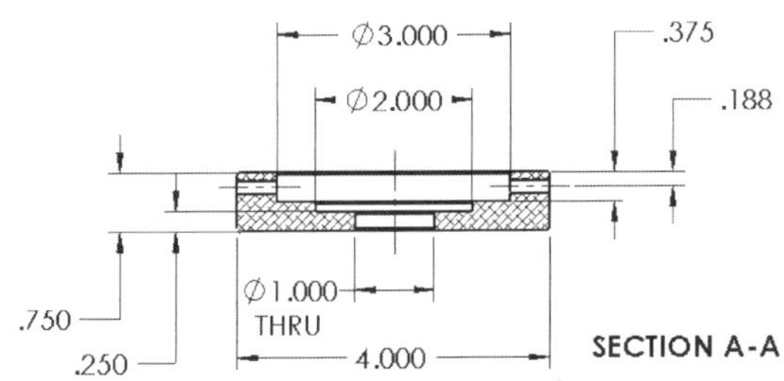

9. Adding the General Notes:

Click **Note** from the **Annotation** tab, and enter the notes below:

NOTES: UNLESS OTHERWISE SPECIFIED
1. INTERPRET DRAWINGS AND DIMENSIONS PER ASME ANSI-Y14.5
2. DIMENSIONS ARE IN INCHES, 3 DECIMAL PLACES
3. MATERIAL: ALUMINUM 5052-H32
4. BREAK ALL EDGES, TUMBLE, AND DEBURR PARTS
5. SHIPPING PACKAGE TO BE LABELED WITH PART NUMBER, MANUFACTURER'S NAME, LOT NUMBER, AND QUANTITY
6. PARTS TO BE CLEAN AND FREE OF LUBRICANT OR DEBRIS

Place the General Notes on the lower left corner of the drawing.

10. Filling out the Title Block:

From the FeatureManager tree, expand **Sheet1** and double-click the **Sheet-Format1** to activate the back layer.

Enter the information shown below, in each appropriate section.

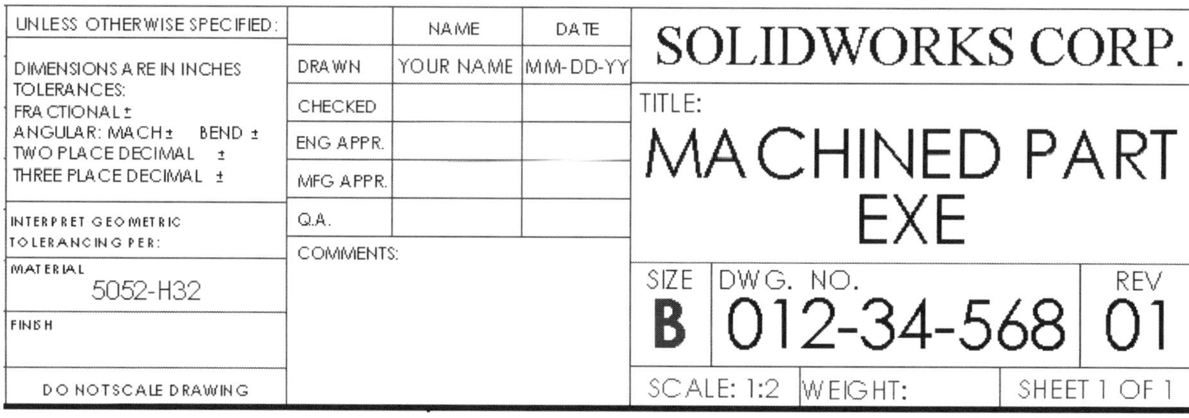

Double-click **Sheet1** on the FeatureManager tree to switch back to the Sheet.

11. Saving your work:

Make any corrections as needed prior to saving the drawing document.

Select **File, Save As.**

Enter **Machined Part_EXE.slddrw** for the file name.

Click **Save.**

Close the part and the drawing documents.

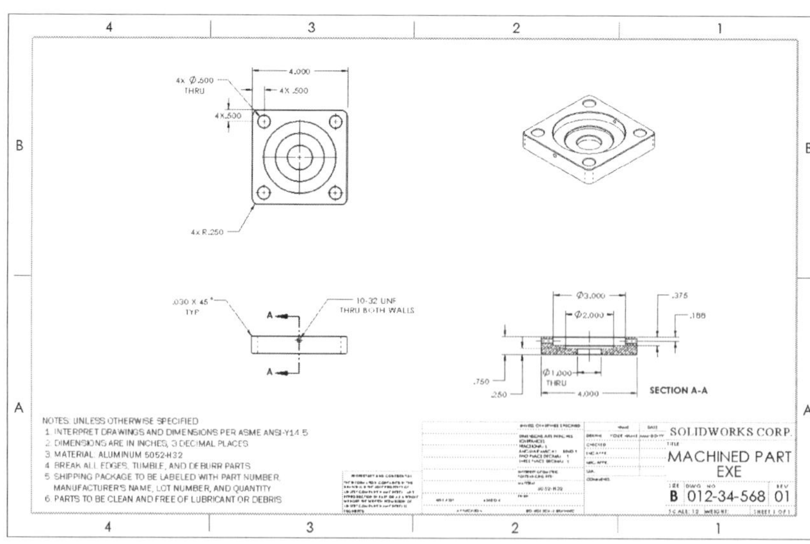

CHAPTER 3: UNDERSTANDING TOLERANCE, PRECISION, AND GD&T

Using GD&T in a Drawing

Tolerance is the total amount a dimension may vary and is the difference between the upper (maximum) and lower (minimum) limits.

Precision is defined as 'the quality of being exact' and refers to how close two or more measurements are to each other, regardless of whether those measurements are accurate or not.

GD&T, or Geometric Dimensioning & Tolerancing, is used to communicate the design intents between the designers and the manufacturing and/or inspection personnel.

GD&T provides a robust method to communicate all necessary information associated with a part which includes dimensions, tolerances, geometry, materials, finish, and all other pieces of information about a drawing such as revision, description, part number, etc.

To accommodate all of this, GD&T utilizes a set of standard symbols to describe the different features or requirements of a part. These symbols have been able to replace the traditional handwritten notes and ensure a standard approach to dimensioning and tolerancing that is friendly to the manufacturing & inspection world.

There are 4 different types of tolerances that are often used in the industries. They are **Limit Tolerance**, **Single Limit Tolerance**, **Bilateral Tolerance**, and **Unilateral Tolerance**. The examples of these 4 types are shown below:

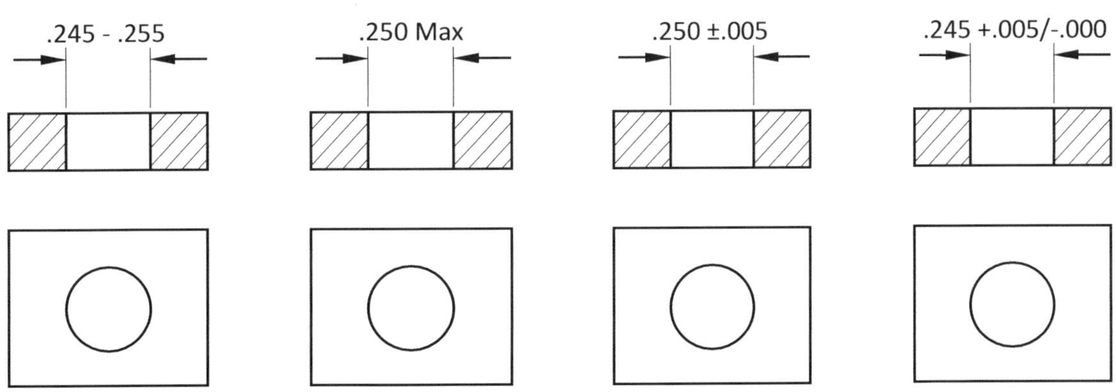

Limit Tolerance | **Single Limit Tolerance** | **Bilateral Tolerance** | **Unilateral Tolerance**

As shown in the previous image, the **Limit Tolerance** shows both a maximum and minumum dimension allowable for the feature.

A **Single Limit Tolerance** only defines one limit dimension, normally either the maximum or minimum value for a feature.

The **Bilateral Tolerance** shows the nominal dimension .250 and the allowable tolerance in either direction ±.005.

The **Unilateral Tolerance** shows the nominal dimension .245 and a tolerance in only one direction +.005.

What is GD&T?

The primary goal of GD&T is to design, fabricate and inspect the part so that the design intent is accurately communicated.

GD&T has several advantages, and the focus is always on function throughout design, manufacturing, and inspection.

Geometric control can provide detail and requirements that cannot be done in other ways without lots of notes and confusion.

Since GD&T is a universal way of communicating function from design to manufacturing, to inspection, it allows an easy way for production to give feedback on the manufacturability of a design and find alternative ways to save cost or cycle time.

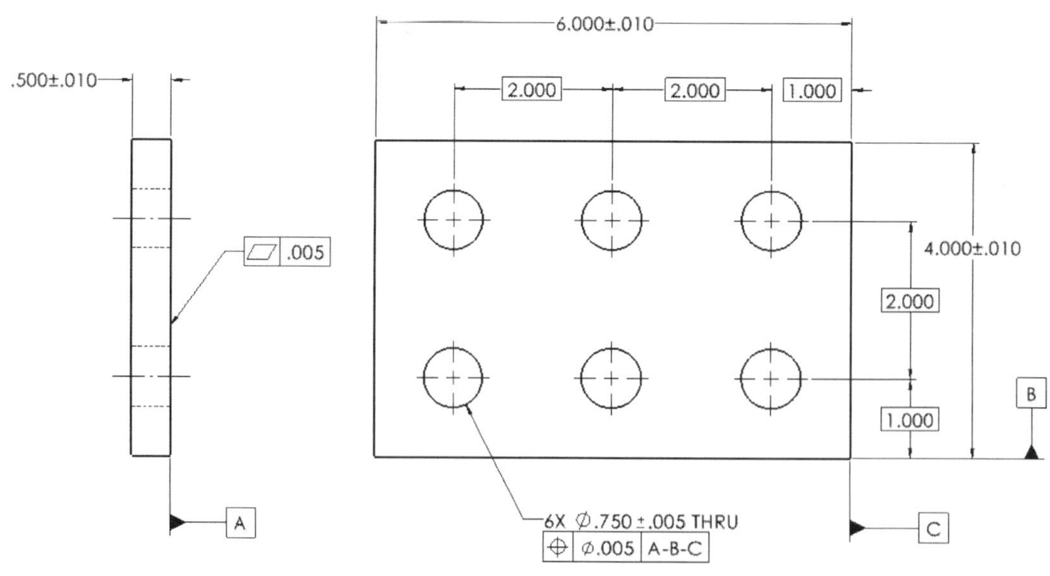

Rules #1, #2, and #2a

There are 2 fundamental rules of GD&T:

Rule #1 is referred to as the "**Individual Feature of Size Rule**".
It is a key concept in geometric tolerancing. Rule #1 is a dimensioning rule used to ensure that Features of Size (FOS) will assemble with one another. When Rule #1 applies, the maximum boundary (or envelope) for an external FOS is its MMC. The minimum envelope for an internal FOS is its MMC. To determine if two features of size will assemble, the designer can then compare the MMCs of the features of size.

Rule #2 is RFS (Regardless of Feature Size). RFS applies with respect to the individual tolerance, datum reference, or both, where no modifying symbol is specified. MMC or LMC must be specified on the drawing where required. Certain geometric tolerances always apply RFS and cannot be modified to MMC or LMC. Where a geometric tolerance is applied on an RFS basis, the tolerance is limited to the specified value regardless of the actual size of the feature.

Rule #2a is an alternative practice of Rule #2. **Rule #2a** states that, for a tolerance of position, RFS may be specified in feature control frames if desired and applicable. In this case, the RFS symbol would be the symbol from the 1982 version of Y14.5.

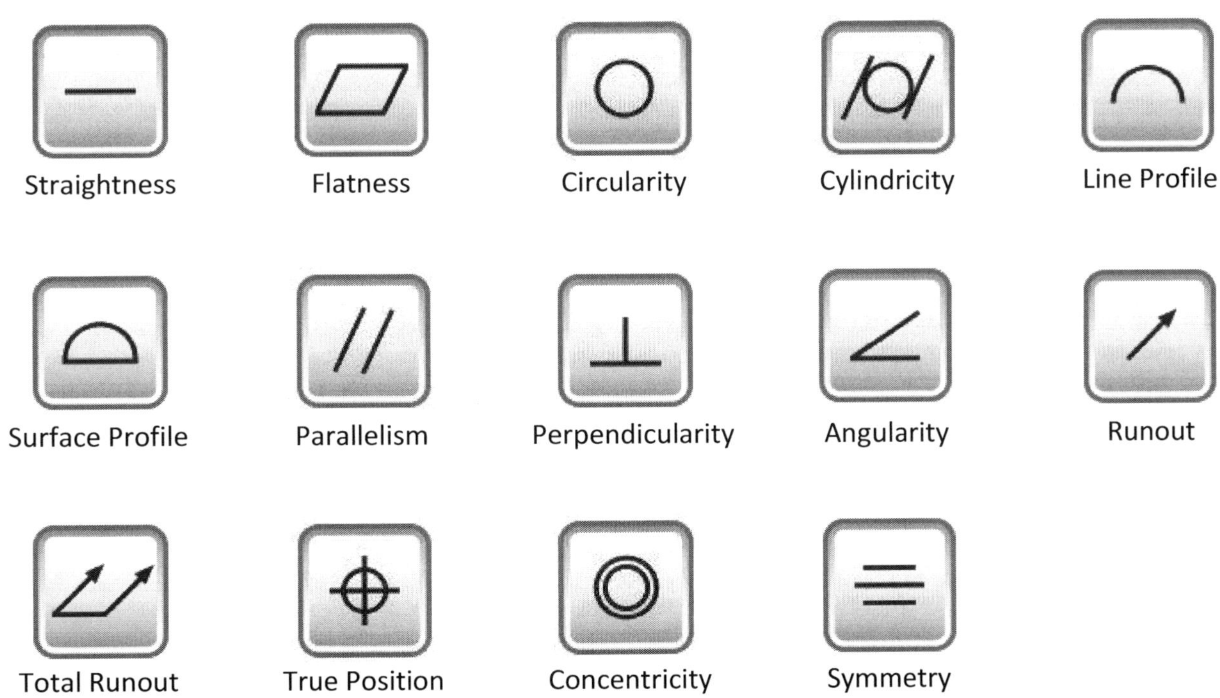

Terminology used in GD&T

- The **Feature Control Frame** is the method to communicate GD&T on an engineering drawing.

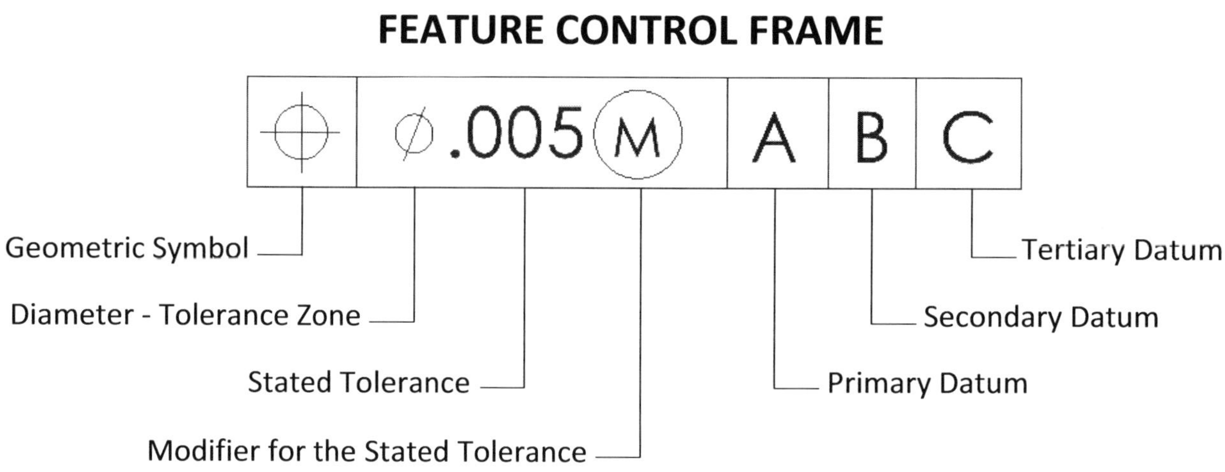

- The **Feature** refers to the surface, plane, axis, or derived elements that the GD&T symbol is controlling on the drawing.

- **Geometric Tolerance** is the variation or tolerance on the Form, Orientation, Location, Profile, or Runout of a part.

- A **Size** or **Dimensional Tolerance** is a tolerance of Size that is placed on a feature that has a size dimension. This can be diameter, thickness, depth, width, height, radius, size or angle dimension.

- **Basic Dimensions** are defined as theoretically exact dimensions. They do not have a dimensional tolerance and are used to set the perfect location of the exact or true profile, position, angle, or measurement location.

- **Tolerance Zone** is the area in space within which the entire referenced feature must be controlled.

- **Surface Features** require the Feature Control Frame to be pointing to the surface, placed directly on the surface or extended from the surface using an extension line.

- **Features of Size** requires the Feature Control Frame to be directly next to the size dimension text or pointing to the size dimension arrows with an extension line.

- **Modifiers** allow you to further specify the geometric control and establish special conditions.

- **Max Material Condition** (MMC) is the dimension where the most amount of material exists.

- **Least Material Condition** (LMC) is the dimension where the least amount of material exists.

- **Regardless of Feature Size** is the default condition of all geometric tolerances by rule #2 of GD&T and requires no callout. Regardless of feature size simply means that whatever GD&T callout you make, it is controlled independently of the size dimension of the part.

- **Size** is the physical size of the feature.

- **Form** is the overall shape of the feature.

- **Location** is the location in 3D space of the feature.

- **Orientation** is the orientation in 3D space of the feature.

- **Datum** is a theoretical reference point on a part. Datum features control orientation, profile, location, or runout of part features.

- **Datum Targets** are often used with parts of complex geometry or do not require the use of a complete surface.

Maximum Material Condition Ⓜ

This on drawing

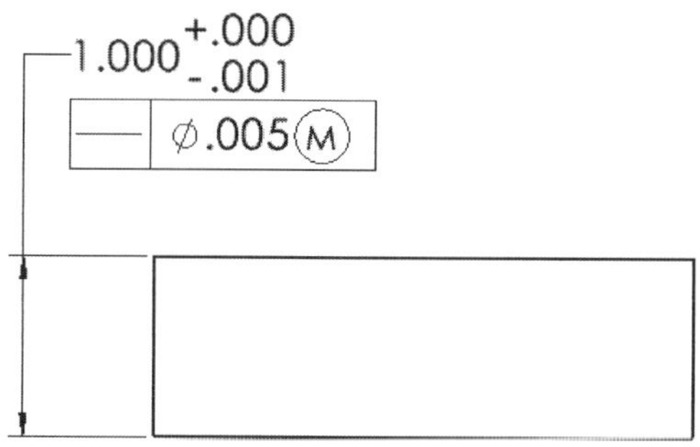

External Feature – Virtual Condition

Means this

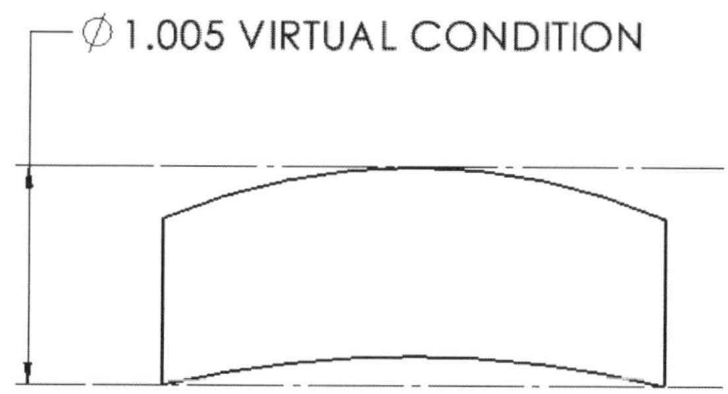

Internal Feature – Virtual Condition

- Maximum Material Condition (MMC) is a material modifier which specifies a conditional geometric tolerance, based on the size of the part. For MMC, you are specifying the geometric tolerance when the feature is in its maximum material condition (largest external feature, smallest internal feature).

- As the size of your part deviates away from MMC toward LMC, your geometric tolerance increases by the same amount. This is known informally as bonus tolerance.

- The combination effect of the geometric tolerance and the size tolerance creates what is called the virtual condition of the part. Based on this effect, no point on the feature is allowed to extend beyond this boundary.

- Your part must still be within its size tolerance for any two-point measurement. You cannot gain “bonus” size tolerance.

- Material Modifiers like MMC can only apply to certain symbols: Straightness, Flatness, Parallelism, Perpendicularity, Angularity and Position.

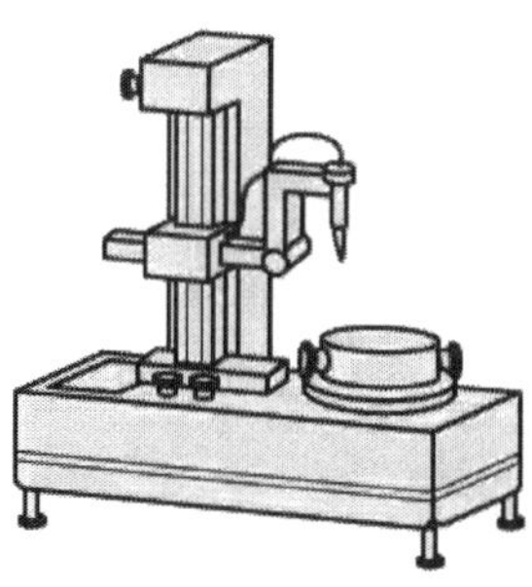

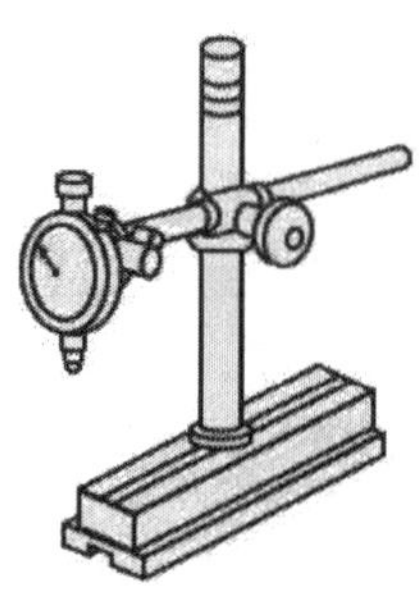

Least Material Condition (L)

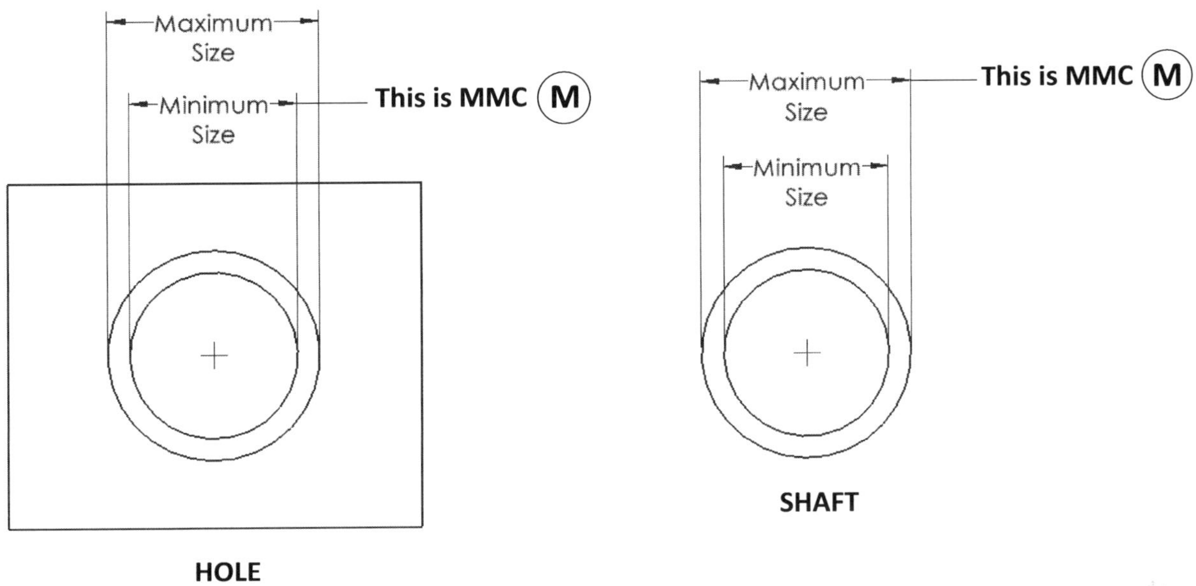

- Least Material Condition (LMC) is a material modifier which specifies a conditional geometric tolerance based on the size of the part. For LMC, you specify the geometric tolerance when the feature is in its least material condition (smallest external feature, largest internal feature).

- The effect of LMC is opposite from MMC - As the size of your part deviates away from LMC toward MMC, your geometric tolerance increases by the same amount. This is known informally as bonus tolerance.

- LMC can apply to: Straightness, Flatness, Parallelism, Perpendicularity, Angularity and Position. However, in the real world, it is almost always used with Position to control the minimum wall thickness of an internal feature, like a hole or slot.

- LMC is not as common as MMC, because you cannot guarantee 100% assembly and interchangeability with your parts.

- Common applications for the LMC modifier are for internal features not designed to mate with other parts, such as weight reduction holes and fluid channels. You can use it anytime the wall thickness is more critical than assembly.

Size, Location, Orientation, & Form (SLOF)

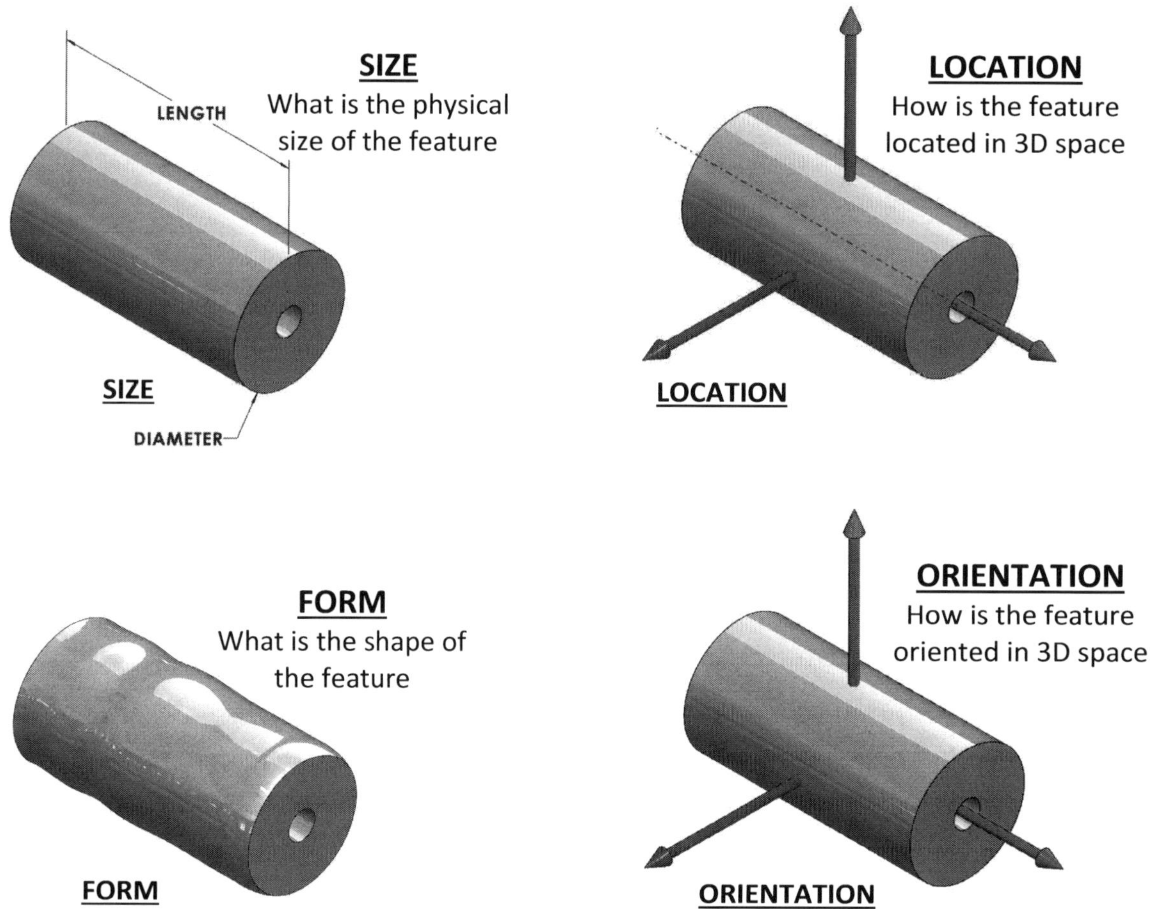

- Every feature on your drawing must have **Size, Location, Orientation, and Form Control (SLOF).**
- In the ASME-ANSI Y14.5, your Size automatically controls your Form (Rule #1), and your Location can automatically control your Orientation, when used with datums.
- Location is the most commonly missed symbol in GD&T on a drawing – All features should be precisely located, and fully defined.
- Primary datum surfaces can benefit from form control to stabilize a part more accurately for measurement. Secondary and Tertiary datums can apply an Orientation control, to ensure that the datums are properly oriented to each other.
- Make your tolerances as loose as your function (and Factor of Safety) will allow. The parts will be easier to fabricate, and cost less, too.

Types of GD&T Tolerances

TYPE OF TOLERANCE	CHARACTERISTIC	SYMBOL
FORM	STRAIGHTNESS	⏤
	FLATNESS	⏥
	CIRCULARITY	○
	CYLINDRICITY	⌭
PROFILE	PROFILE OF A LINE	⌒
	PROFILE OF A SURFACE	⌓
ORIENTATION	ANGULARITY	∠
	PERPENDICULARITY	⊥
	PARALLELISM	∥
LOCATION	POSITION	⌖
	CONCENTRICITY	◎
	SYMMETRY	⌯
RUNOUT	CIRCULAR RUNOUT	↗
	TOTAL RUNOUT	⌰

FORM CONTROLS

- ⏥ Flatness
- ⏤ Straightness
- ○ Circularity
- ⌭ Cylindricity

PROFILE CONTROLS

- ⌒ Profile of a line
- ⌓ Profile of a surface

ORIENTATION CONTROLS

- ∥ Parallelism
- ⊥ Perpendicularity
- ∠ Angularity

LOCATION CONTROLS

- ⌖ Position
- ◎ Concentricity
- ⌯ Symmetry

RUNNOUT CONTROLS

- ↗ Circular Runnout
- ⌰ Total Runout

Rule # 2 and Material Modifiers

- RFS – Stands for Regardless of Feature Size - it is the default condition in GD&T that sets the Geometric Tolerance Independent of the size tolerance.
- Rule #2 states that all GD&T symbols are RFS by default. You must use a modifier symbol to state otherwise.
- RFS is one of the three material conditions on a part – the other two being Max Material Condition (MMC) and Least Material Condition (LMC).
- Adding the Material Modifiers negates Rule #1 and Rule #2 allowing you to specify the geometric tolerance at a certain material condition. Your part envelope is now your Virtual Condition.
- All symbols are RFS by default. However, Circularity, Cylindricity, Profile of a Surface and Line, Runout, Total Runout, Symmetry and Concentricity are always RFS.

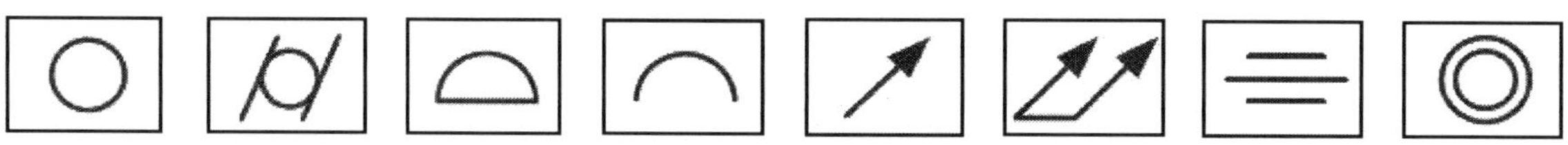

- Material Modifiers have many benefits over simply using RFS alone. In most situations, manufacturing a part's feature RFS is more expensive than using MMC or LMC, since you cannot benefit from bonus tolerance.

RULE #2

RFS is the default for tolerance and datum references.

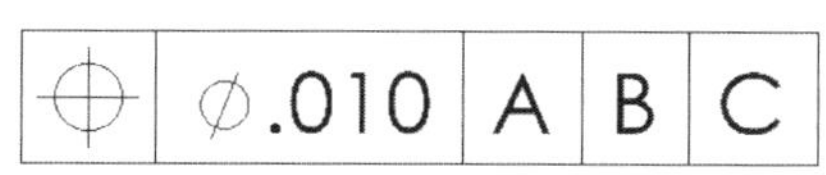

(F) (Free State) Applies only when part is otherwise restrained

(S) (Free State) Means the part is not constrained
S is now a discontinued practice in 1994 standards.

RULE #2a

For a tolerance of position, RFS may be stated for the tolerance and datum references.

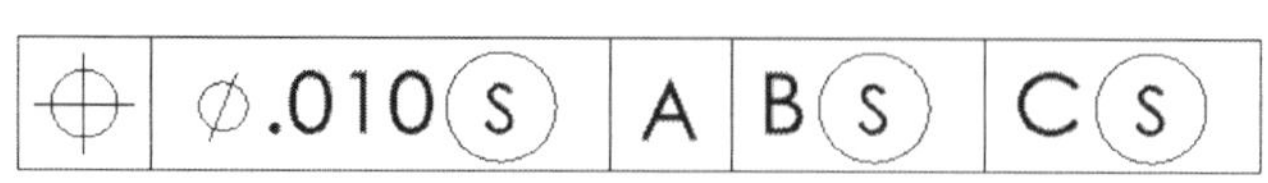

Straightness (Surface)

- **Straightness** is a 2D tolerance zone that only controls the form of a feature.
- No Datums are used in the callout.
- Straightness can be called with Max Material Condition (MMC).
- The entire referenced surface must lie between two parallel lines set apart at the straightness tolerance. However, the orientation and location of these lines is not controlled.
- Straightness is most commonly measured with a CMM.
- It is mainly used when surface contact or sealing contact with another mating part is required.
- Rule #1 still applies, so the tolerance must be less than the size dimension tolerance.
- Straightness should only be used as a specific refinement due to being controlled by both Rule #1 and several other geometric controls.

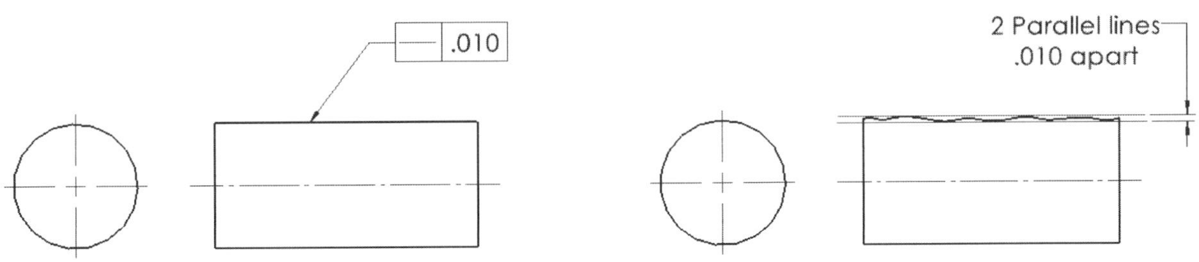

STRAIGHTNESS (SURFACE)

Flatness (Surface)

- **Flatness** is a <u>3D tolerance</u> zone that only controls the <u>form</u> of a feature, not size, location, or orientation.
- No Datums are ever used in the flatness feature control frame.
- The entire referenced surface must lie within two parallel planes that are not held to any orientation or location.
- It can be gauged only if the surface is held perfectly parallel to the measurement device. However, flatness is usually surface mapped with a CMM.
- It is mainly used when datum surface refinement is required.
- Flatness allows you to control a surface without modifying (or tightening) any size tolerances.
- Rule #1 still applies to the size of the part. This also means the flatness tolerance must be less than the size dimension tolerance (only for surface flatness).
- Flatness controls straightness of a planar surface. Flatness is automatically controlled by orientation, profile of a surface, and any size dimension applied to a planar feature (due to Rule #1).

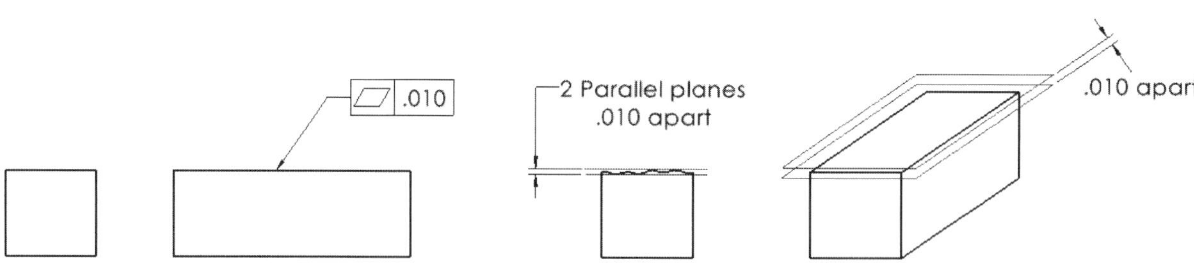

FLATTNESS (SURFACE)

Flatness – FOS/DMP ⏥ Ⓜ
(Feature of Size / Derived Median Plane)

- **Flatness** on a **Feature of Size** is a <u>3D tolerance zone</u> that only controls the <u>form</u> of the derived median plane (not the perfect midplane).

- No datums are allowed in the Feature Control Frame callout.

- Flatness of a Feature of Size (FOS) is usually called out with Max Material Condition (MMC) to allow use of functional gauging.

- The entire Derived Median Plane (DMP) must lie between two parallel planes set apart by Flatness tolerance. However, the orientation and location of these planes are not controlled.

- DMP Flatness is most commonly measured using a fixed functional gauge (such as two parallel planar gauge blocks) set apart by the virtual condition of the part size. The part can also be measured with a CMM, but with less efficiency.

- DMP Flatness is mainly used when the entire form of a feature of size is required to be flat, such as with a washer or a critical sealing square slot.

- Rule #1 is no longer applicable with DMP Flatness, so the tolerance may or may not be less than the size dimension tolerance

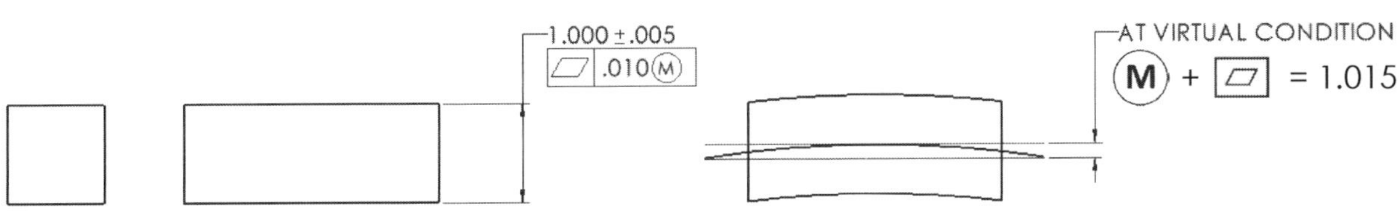

FLATNESS (Derived Median Plane with Ⓜ)

Circularity

- **Circularity** is a <u>2D tolerance zone</u> that only controls how close the <u>form</u> of a feature adheres to a perfectly circular shape.
- No Datums are used in the callout.
- The cross section of the feature's surface has to lie between two concentric circles spaced at the specified circularity tolerance.
- Circularity is usually measured with a Digital Polar Probe on a rotating spindle or a CMM (Coordinate Measuring Machine).
- It is mainly used on bearing surfaces, rotating parts, and round sealing surfaces.
- It allows you to control how round a surface is without modifying the diameter tolerance.
- Circularity is also commonly used to control the form of a sphere.
- Rule #1 still applies to the part, so the tolerance must be less than the size tolerance and the part envelope can never be exceeded.

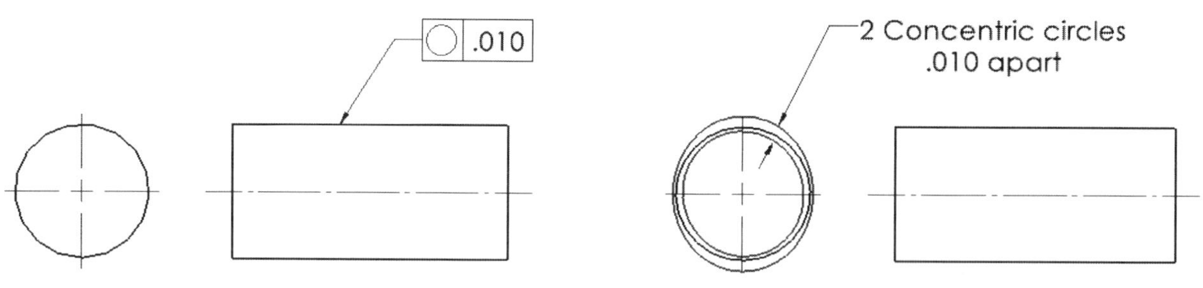

CIRCULARITY ○

Cylindricity

- **Cylindricity** is a 3D tolerance zone that only controls the form of a cylindrical feature.
- No Datums are ever used in the feature control frame.
- The entire referenced surface must lie between two coaxial cylinders set apart by the cylindricity tolerance. However, the orientation and location of these cylinders are not controlled.
- Cylindricity is most commonly measured with a digital probe on a special spindle or with a CMM.
- It is mainly used when surface contact or sealing contact with another mating part is required or when the taper of a cylinder needs to be controlled.
- Rule #1 still applies to the part, so the tolerance must be less than the size dimension tolerance.
- Cylindricity should only be used as a specific refinement because it is controlled by both Rule #1 and several other geometric controls.

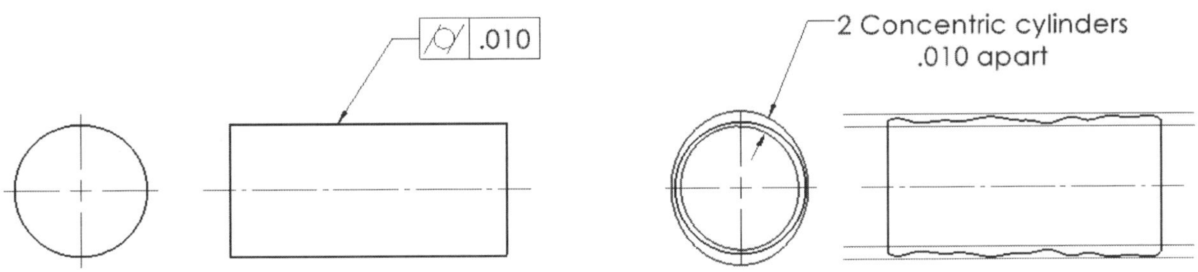

CYLINDRICITY ⌭

Profile

- **Line Profile** is a 2D tolerance zone that applies to the full length of the part over the indicated feature in the given view.
- Datums are optional – they may or may not be called out.
- The MMC and LMC modifiers are not allowed in the tolerance zone block of the Feature Control Frame.
- The Line Profile can control size, location, orientation, and form (SLOF) of surface line elements, depending on datum structure.
- Unless otherwise specified, the tolerance zone is equally disposed about the true profile and applies normal-to the surface at any given point.
- The most common specifications will be as a Surface Profile refinement. Line Profile can also be used to check the Profile of an extruded shape, or anywhere Surface Profile would be difficult or unnecessary.
- When Profile of a Line is used as a refinement of Surface Profile, the tolerance must be less than the Surface Profile tolerance. If only a form refinement (no datums), the tolerance zone for Line Profile is allowed to float within the larger Surface Profile control.

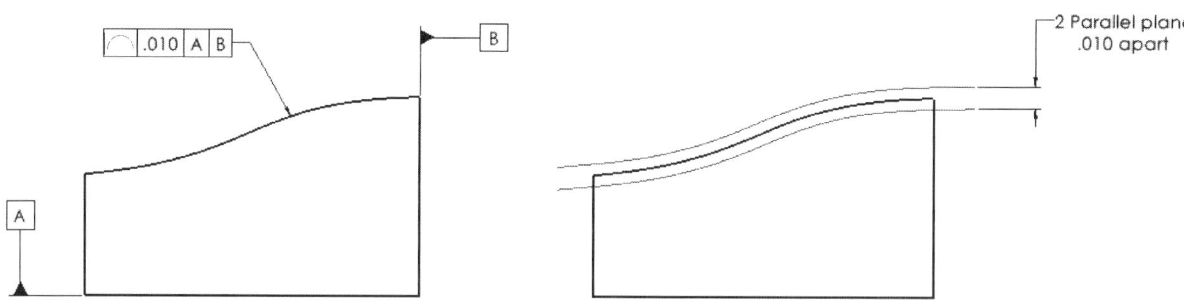

PROFILE OF A LINE ⌒

Surface Profile

- **Surface Profile** is a 3D tolerance zone that applies to the full width, length, and depth of the part over the indicated feature.

- Datums are optional – they may or may not be called out depending on functional requirements.

- The MMC and LMC modifiers are not allowed in the tolerance zone block of the Feature Control Frame.

- Unless otherwise specified, the tolerance zone is equally disposed about the true profile and applies normal-to the surface at any given point. It is always a total tolerance.

- Surface Profile can control size, location, orientation, and form (SL OF) of surfaces depending on datum structure.

- Additionally, Surface Profile can control the co-planarity between two or more separate surfaces, as well as the offset between them.

- Profile is the universal symbol in GD&T. If you cannot control it with any other symbol, use Profile.

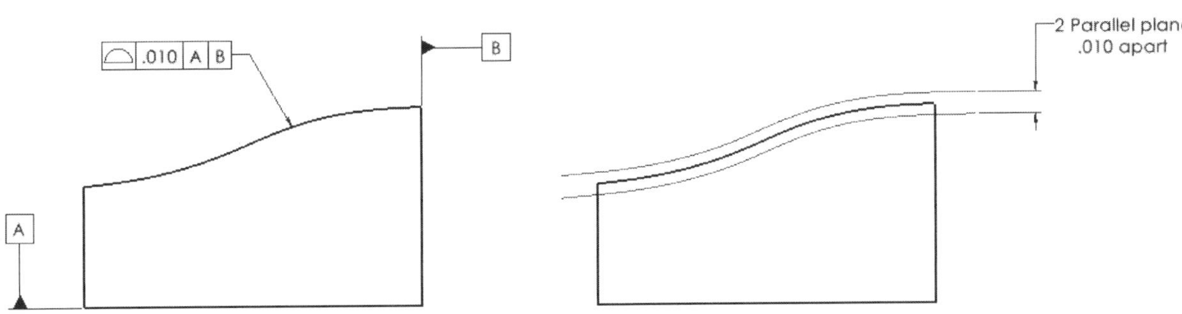

PROFILE OF A SURFACE

Parallelism (Feature of Size)

- **Parallelism** Feature of Size (FOS) is a 3D tolerance zone that controls the orientation of a dimensioned feature. It cannot control the location.
- The drawing callout must reference at least one datum.
- The shape of the tolerance zone can vary depending on whether you are controlling an axis or a flat feature. For a cylindrical tolerance zone controlling an axis, the diameter symbol (Ø) must be used.
- Parallelism is most commonly measured with a CMM to determine the orientation of a central axis or midplane of a feature. Parallelism can also be controlled with Max Material Condition (but this is somewhat rare).
- Since Parallelism cannot control location, it is most often used as a refinement of a Position tolerance. It is also used to control the orientation for holes in high speed applications, such as piston rods and rocker arms.

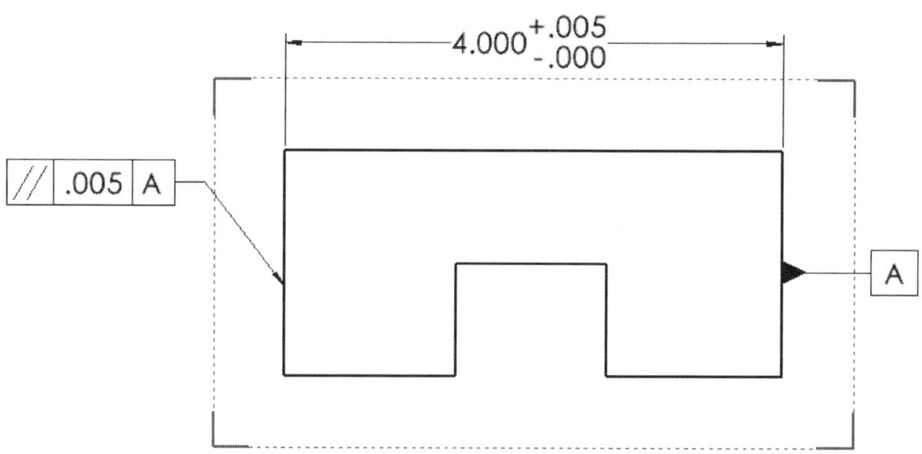

PARALLELISM (Feature Of Size FOS //)

Parallelism (Surface)

- **Parallelism** is a 2D or 3D tolerance zone that controls the orientation of features.

- It is important to distinguish between **Surface Parallelism** and **Feature Of Size Parallelism.** Both use the same symbol, but they control two very different types of features.

- A datum is always required in the Feature Control Frame. No diameter symbol (Ø) is allowed in the Feature Control Frame for the Surface version of Parallelism.

- The tolerance zone for the surface version is defined by two parallel planes set parallel to a datum, where the entire surface of the referenced feature must lie within.

- Parallelism is most commonly measured with a dial indicator/height gauge as it is set parallel to a datum simulator like a granite table. It can also be measured with a CMM.

- Parallelism is commonly used for press parts like die fixtures. It can also be used for parts that need to maintain parallel contact during rotation like washers.

- Parallelism orients relative to a datum.

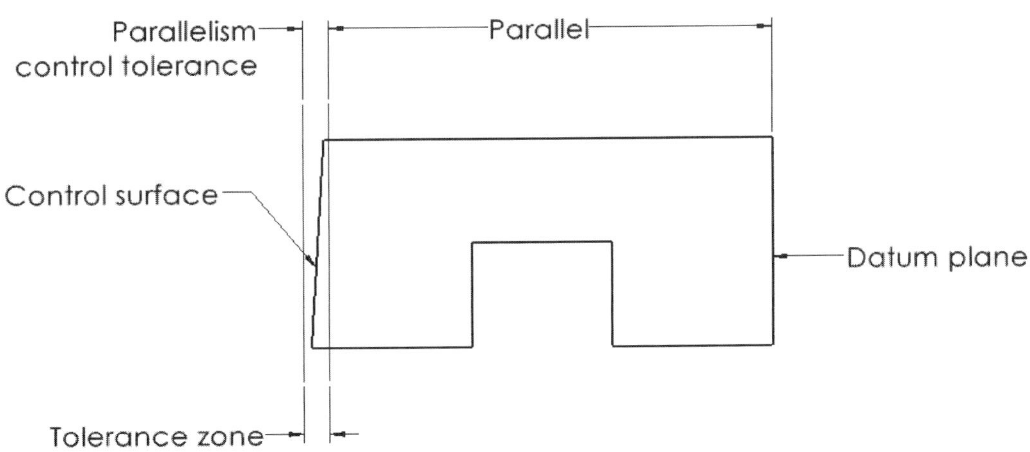

PARALLELISM (Surface //)

Perpendicularity (Surface)

- **Surface Perpendicularity** is a 2D or 3D tolerance zone that controls the orientation of features to 90°.

- It is important to distinguish between **Surface Perpendicularity** and **Feature Of Size Perpendicularity**. Both use the same symbol, but they control two very different types of features.

- A datum is always required in the Feature Control Frame. No diameter symbol (Ø) is allowed in the Feature Control Frame for the Surface version of Perpendicularity.

- The tolerance zone for the surface version is defined by two parallel planes set perpendicular to a datum plane or axis, where the entire surface of the referenced feature must lie between.

- Perpendicularity is most commonly measured with a dial indicator/height gauge as it is set perpendicular to a datum simulator. It can also be measured with a CMM.

- Surface Perpendicularity is commonly used when two surfaces must be controlled at 90° for function. It is commonly seen in a title block to establish a general tolerance. It also is used to orient one datum to another for establishing an accurate datum reference frame.

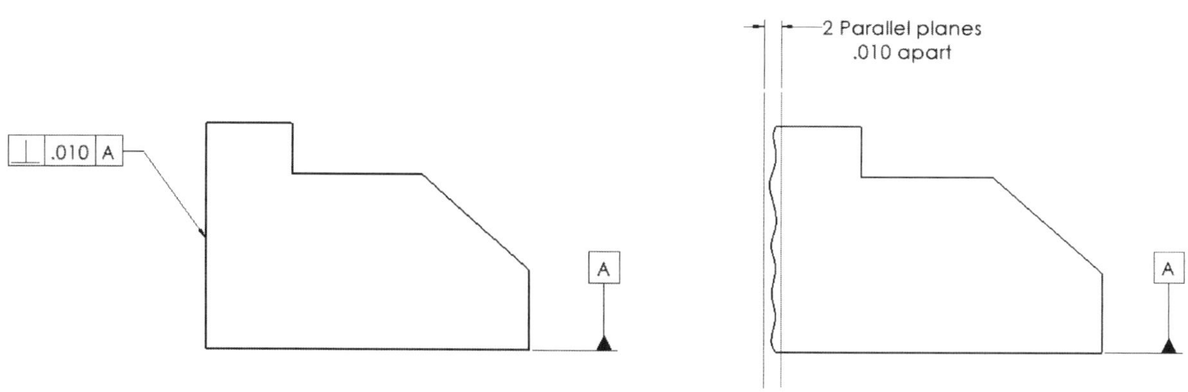

PERPENDICULARITY (Surface ⊥)

Perpendicularity (FOS)

- **Feature of Size Perpendicularity** is a 3D tolerance zone that controls the orientation of a dimensioned feature.
- The drawing callout must reference at least one datum.
- The shape of the tolerance zone can vary depending on whether you are controlling an axis or a flat feature. For a cylindrical tolerance zone controlling an axis, the diameter Ø symbol must be used.
- Perpendicularity is most commonly measured with a CMM to determine the orientation of a central axis or midplane of a feature.
- Perpendicularity can apply to any feature of size where orientation is critical such as a precision hole or pin. However, since Perpendicularity cannot control location, it is most often used as a refinement of a Position tolerance.
- Perpendicularity can be used with Max Material Condition when applied to a feature of size. This allows the use of functional gauging to control the orientation and size of a feature.

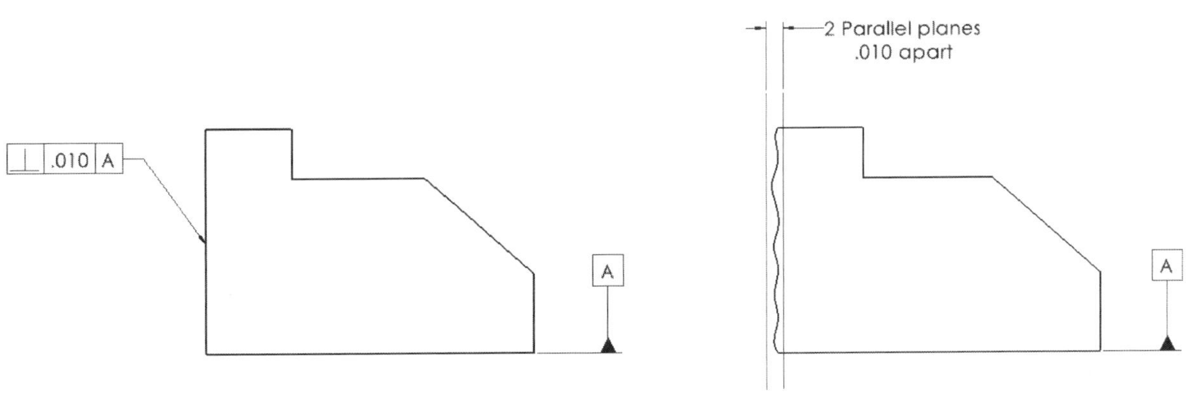

PERPENDICULARITY (Feature Of Size ⊥)

Angularity ∠

- **Angularity** is a <u>2D or 3D tolerance zone</u> that controls the <u>orientation</u> of surface features or features of size at a given basic angle.

- A datum is always required in the Feature Control Frame for either surface or Feature Of Size Angularity.

- Angularity only indirectly controls the angle of the two features. The units for angularity are in distance units (mm/in) not in degrees (°).

- The tolerance zone is the distance between two lines, planes or within a cylinder (the diameter Ø symbol required).

- Surface Angularity is most commonly measured with a dial indicator/height gauge when placed on a sine bar set at the basic angle. Angularity on a feature of size is commonly measured with a CMM to accurately determine the angle of the axis or mid-plane.

- Angularity is used predominantly when a controlled angle is required, and a feature needs to be functionally located relative to a datum. Applications include detailed fixtures and piston bores.

- Angularity can be used in place of Perpendicularity and Parallelism. This can eliminate the need to specify several different callouts of one feature relative to several datums.

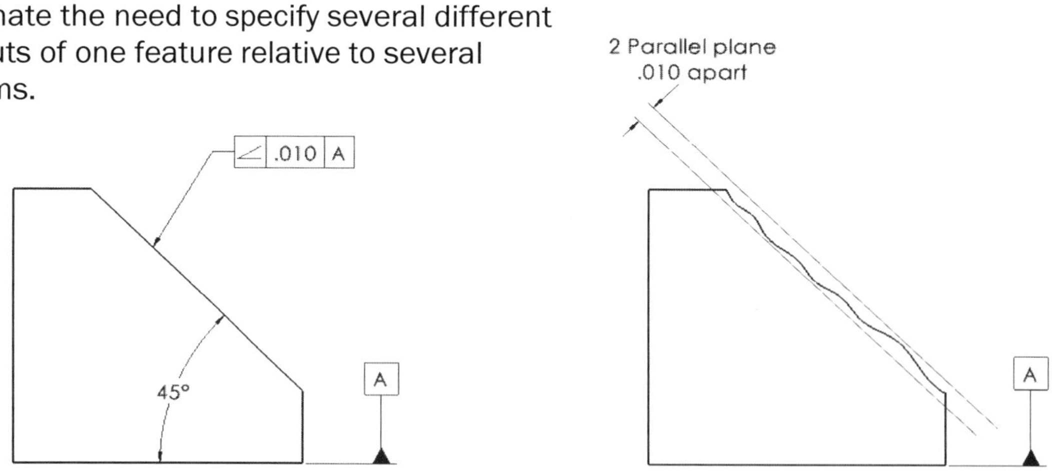

ANGULARITY ∠

Runout

- **Runout** (or Circular Runout to distinguish it from Total Runout) is a combination control that controls the <u>location</u>, <u>orientation</u>, and <u>form</u> of an axial feature.

- Runout must be specified with respect to at least one datum reference at all times. If a single datum is used, it must be of sufficient length, or an additional datum or dual coaxial datum setup is required.

- The cross section of the feature's surface has to lie between two concentric circles spaced at the specified Runout tolerance and located coaxially to the datum axis. This is the "located" version of Circularity.

- Runout tolerances are evaluated using a dial indicator that measures the "Full Indicator Movement" (FIM) of a 360° turn while constraining the datum feature(s).

- Runout inherently controls Circularity and Concentricity because the total variations of these two geometric errors contribute to the total amount of indicator movement.

- Runout is usually applied to parts with circular cross sections that must be assembled such as drill bits, segmented shafts, or machine tool components. Runout helps to limit the axis offset of two parts to ensure they can spin and wear evenly.

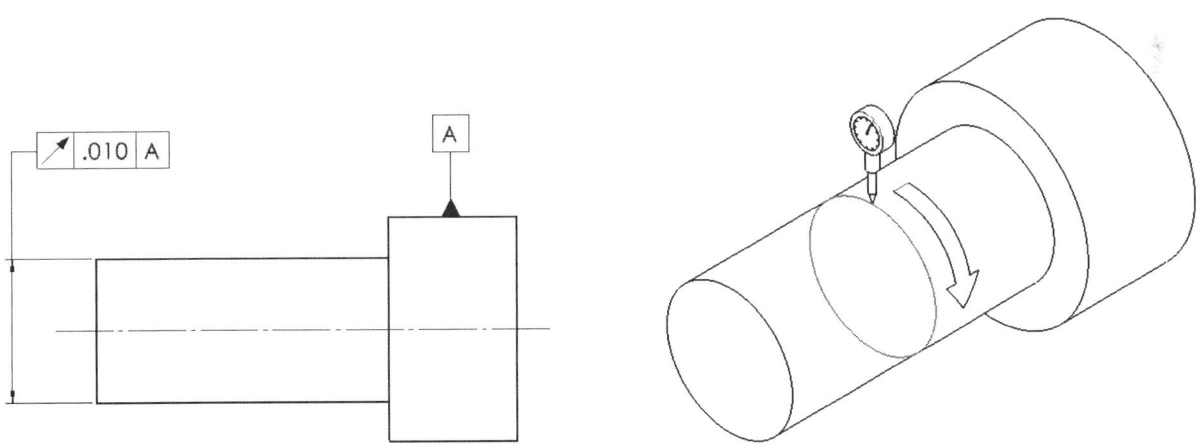

RUNOUT ↗

Total Runout

- **Total Runout** is a combination control that controls the location, orientation, and form of a cylindrical or axial feature.

- Total runout is different than runout because it applies to the entire surface simultaneously instead of individual circular elements.

- The entire feature's surface has to lie between two concentric cylinders spaced at the specified Total Runout tolerance and located coaxially to the datum axis.

- Total Runout must be specified with respect to at least one datum reference at all times. If a single datum is used, it must be of sufficient length. Otherwise, a perpendicular face or dual coaxial datum setup is required.

- Runout tolerances are evaluated using a dial indicator that measures the "Full Indicator Movement" (FIM) of a 360° turn while constraining the datum feature(s). For Total Runout, these dial indicators determine the FIM applied around and across the entire surface. They are never reset.

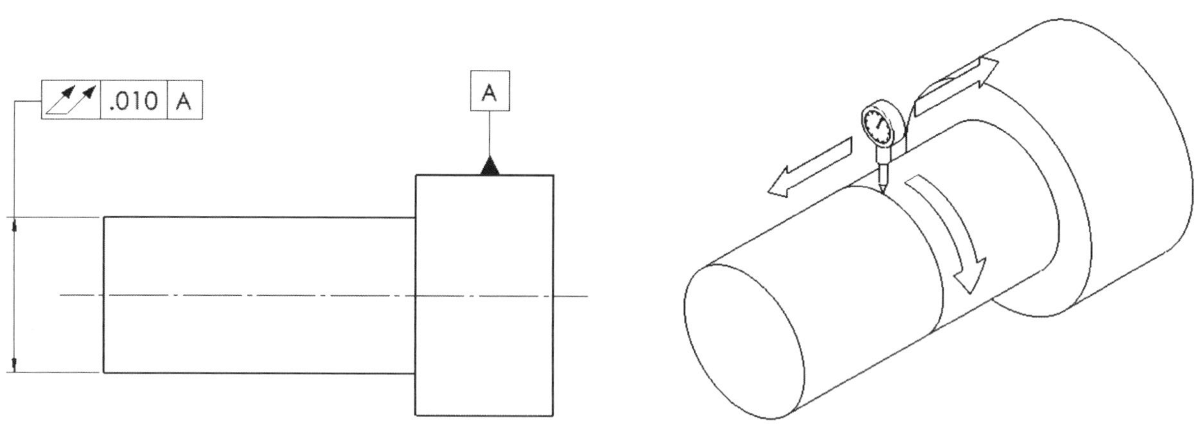

TOTAL RUNOUT

Position

- **Position** (also called "True Position") is the main location tolerance in GD&T. It specifies how far away a feature's center plane, point or axis can deviate from a theoretically perfect location (i.e., its "true" position).

- Basic dimensions are mandatory with Position, in order to identify the exact point in space that is the center of the Position tolerance.

- The tolerance zone for Position depends on whether you are controlling an axial or planar feature and which datums are used.

- When an axial feature is controlled, the diameter symbol (Ø) must be used, since it is a cylindrical tolerance zone. The axis of the part must lie within this zone. For a planar feature, the tolerance zone is a set of two parallel planes centered on the datum plane. The midplane of the controlled feature must lie within this planar zone.

- Position used with Maximum Material Condition becomes a very useful control. Position when paired with the size tolerance of that feature can control the location, orientation, form, and the size of the feature all at once.

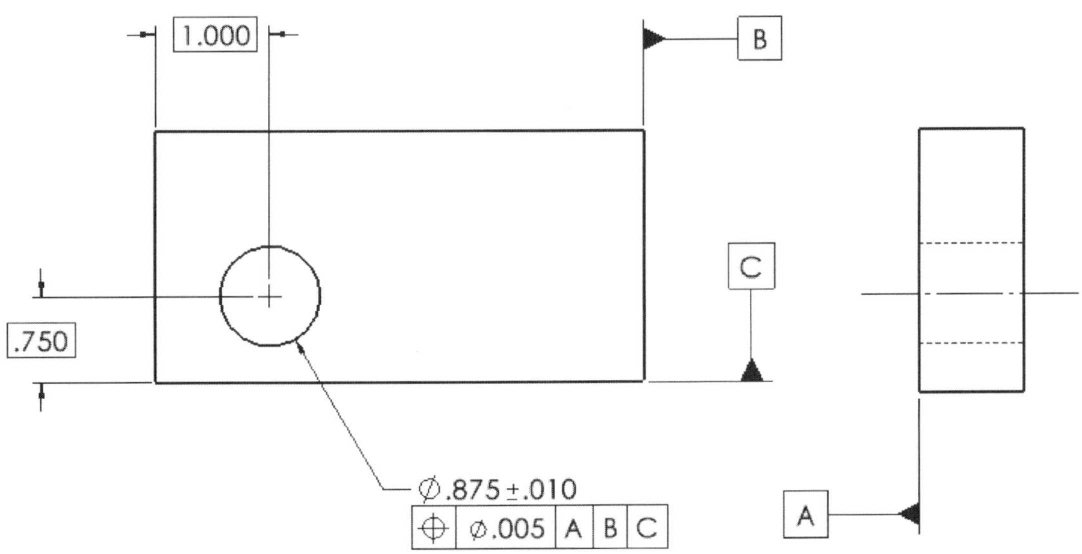

POSITION (True Position ⌖)

Concentricity

- **Concentricity** is a 3D tolerance zone that controls the location of a feature relative to a datum axis and the distribution of form error of the feature's surface.
- A datum is always required and modifiers such as MMC & LMC are not allowed. (The exception to this is with ISO Standards.)
- The derived median points of all diametrically opposed surface elements on the controlled diameter must lie within the tolerance zone.
- Concentricity allows the designer to control mass distribution for a rotating part, to prevent lobing or maintain an equal wall thickness.
- Inspection for Concentricity control is fairly difficult. Consider using Position or a Runout tolerance first – it is more likely to fit your functional requirements.

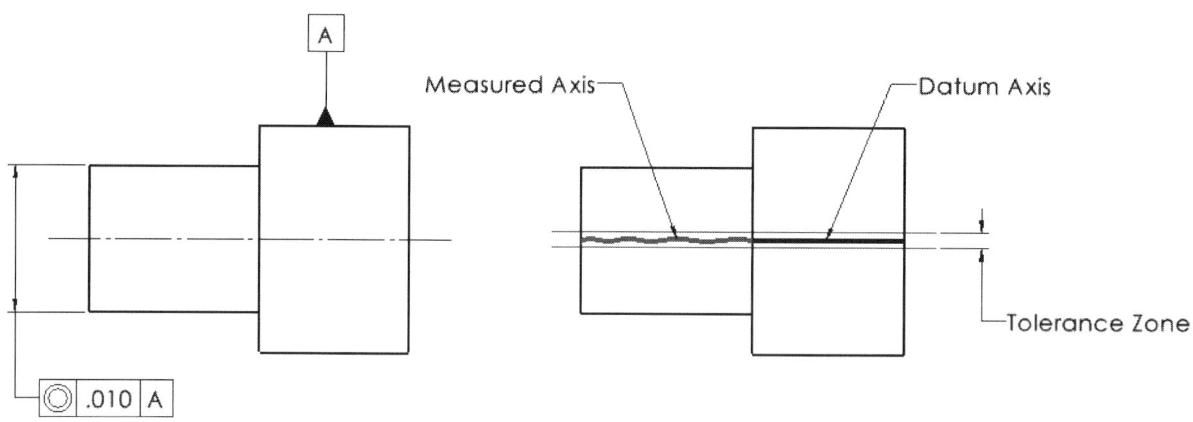

CONCENTRICITY ◎

Symmetry

- **Symmetry** is a 3D tolerance zone that controls the median points of a tolerance feature of size.
- A datum is always required to use Symmetry – the midplane of this datum feature locates and orients the planar tolerance zone.
- All median points of the dimensioned feature must lie within the tolerance zone of two planes, located and oriented at the center of the datum feature. Your tolerance zone is spaced apart by the amount of the Symmetry tolerance.
- Because it involves controlling the distribution of mass and an extensive measuring process, Symmetry requirements are difficult and expensive to produce and inspect.
- Symmetry is rarely used and should be substituted by a Position tolerance in most circumstances.
- Symmetry should only be used with parts requiring a precise balance, equal mass distribution, or equal mass wall thickness. If this is not a requirement then avoid using Symmetry!

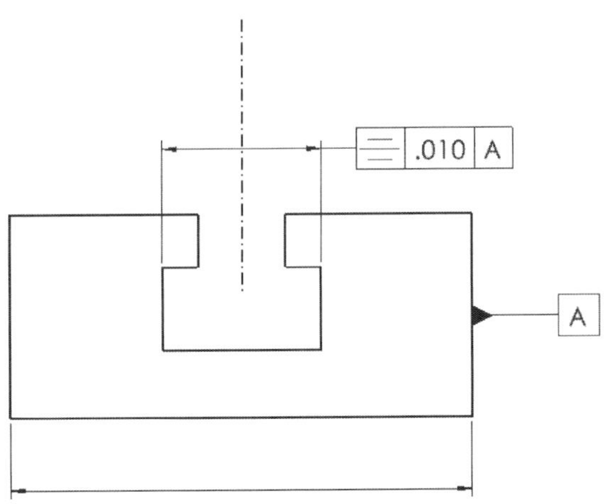

SYMMETRY ⌯

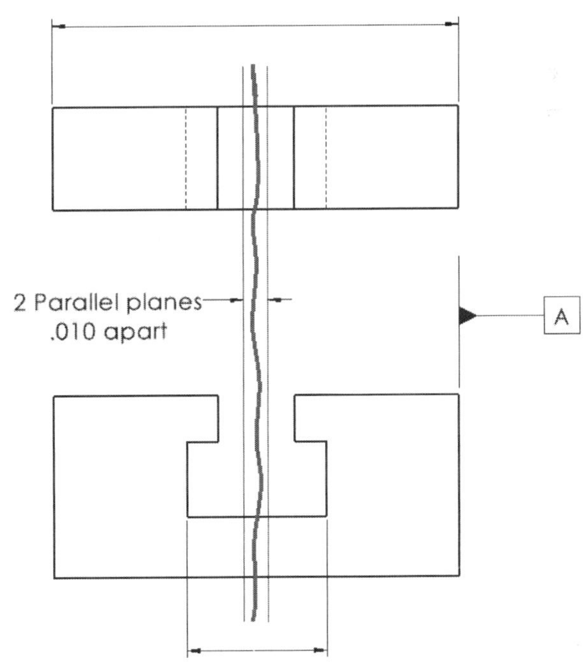

GD&T – Geometric Dimensioning & Tolerancing in a Nutshell

Geometric dimensioning and tolerancing (GD&T) is a system of symbols used on engineering drawings to communicate information from the designer to the manufacturer through engineering drawings. GD&T tells the manufacturer the degree of accuracy and precision needed for each controlled feature of the part.

What are the advantages of GD&T?

GD&T comes with many advantages, the most important of which is that sometimes the exact information is needed for manufacturers who may not understand the intent of the design. Manufacturers have to know how a part will be used to produce the best version of that component.

Here are some of the main advantages of the GD&T process:

- **Cost reduction:** GD&T enhances the accuracy of your designs, allowing for appropriate tolerances that optimize production.

- **Optimized functionality:** Explicitly stating all design requirements guarantees the accurate fulfillment of dimensional and tolerance specifications related to a part's functionality.

- **Uniformity and convenience:** GD&T is a consistent language among manufacturers. Using it reduces guesswork and misinterpreting designs, which ensures consistent geometries.

- **Accurate communication:** Translating intricate designs into physical parts requires accurate and reliable communication. GD&T enables designers, manufacturers, and quality teams to communicate clearly with one another, saving time and money in the process.

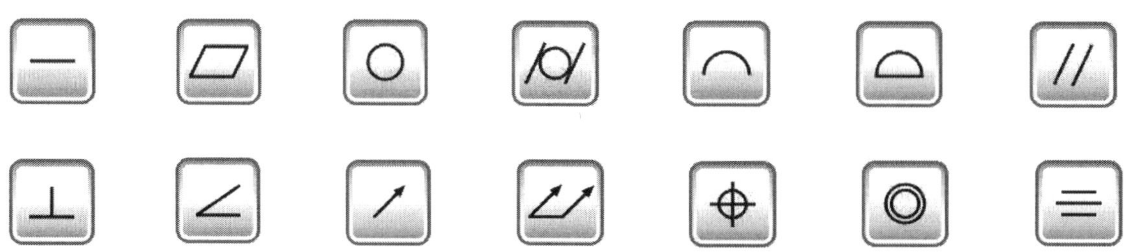

CHAPTER 4: USING TOLERANCE, PRECISION, AND GD&T

Stainless Steel Flange

Geometric dimensioning and tolerancing (GD&T) is a system of 14 symbols used on engineering drawings to communicate information from the designers to the manufacturers through engineering drawings.
Note: Concentric and Symmetric symbols have been removed in ASME Y14.5-2018 due to their controversial and complicated nature but are still being used in many companies.

By employing GD&T to functional features on engineering drawings, designers are able to communicate to the manufacturer how much geometrical imperfection is tolerable before compromising the function of the component. Where the fit or function of a component is related to the size of a functional feature, the tolerance zone for that feature can be made flexible if appropriate.

Controlling the functional features this way and allowing greater dimensional flexibility elsewhere on the component eases the manufacturing process and consequently reduces the cost of manufacture. The likelihood of producing scrap product is also reduced which leads to further cost saving.

Let us take a look at how to incorporate the GD&T functionality into the drawing that we made earlier.

1. Opening an existing drawing:

Select: **File, Open**.

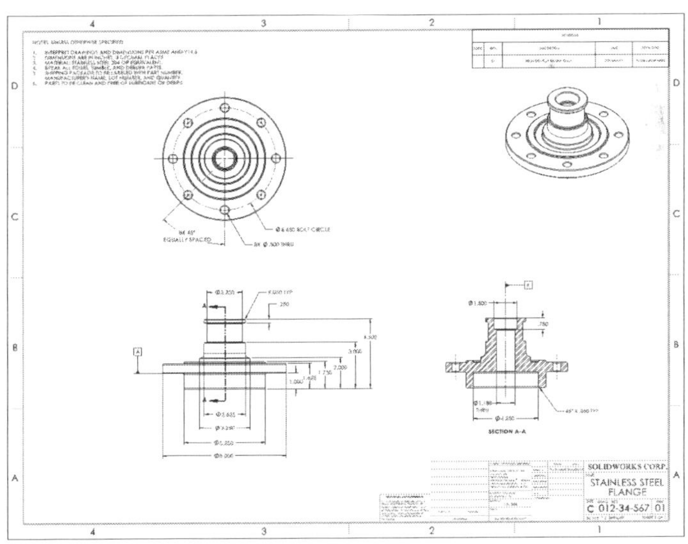

Locate the drawing that was created in Chapter 2 called **Detailing a Machined Part** and open it.

This drawing was generated from a 3D model, and the dimensions were also exported from the same model to maintain their associativities.

The next step is to add some tolerances and precisons to the drawing to increase accuracy, reduce manufacturing confusions, and increase cost effectiveness.

2. Adding a Symmetric tolerance:

A Symmetric tolerance sets the same value in either direction (plus or minus) under the nominal dimension.

Zoom in on the **Top** drawing view and select the dimension **8X Ø.500 THRU** (circle).

From the FeatureManager tree, under the Tolerance and Precision section, select: **Symmetric** from the drop-down list (arrow).

For Maximum/Minimum variation enter: **.010in**.

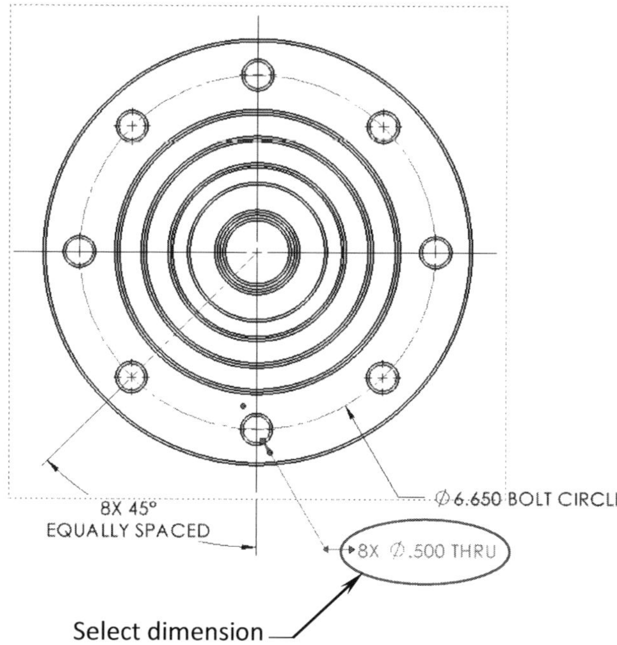

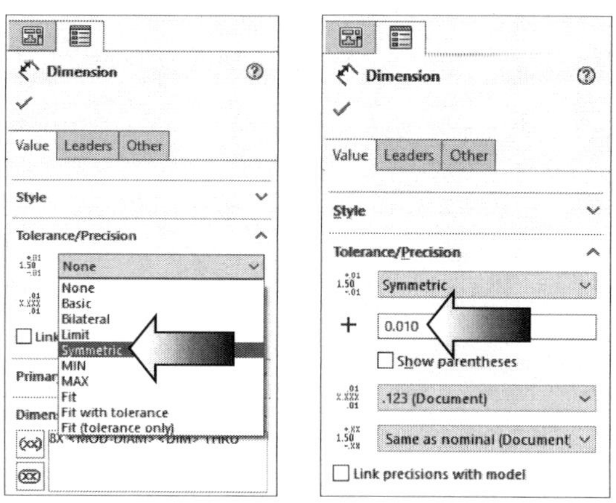

Click **OK**.

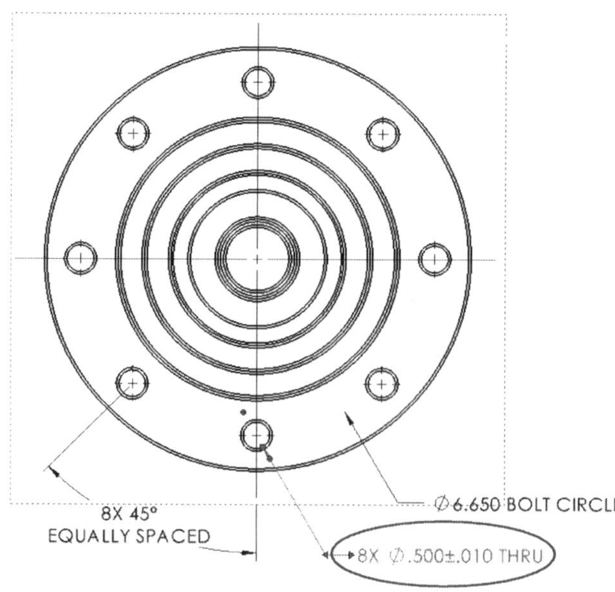

3. Adding a Bilateral tolerance:

In general, it is recommended to apply tolerances logically and consistently, avoiding unnecessary or contradictory tolerances. For example, you should not use both limit dimensions and plus/minus dimensions for the same feature or use a tolerance that is larger than the fit allowance.

However, if you have different features that require different tolerances, then it is acceptable to use different types of tolerances in the same drawing.

For learning purposes, we will try out different tolerance types to see how they can be added to dimensions.

Zoom in on the **Front** drawing view and select the dimension **Ø2.250**.

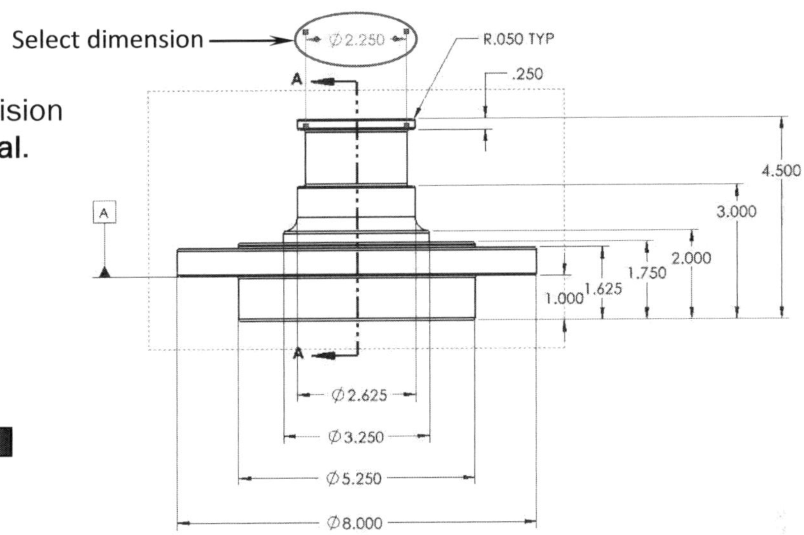

In the Tolerance/Precision section, select **Bilateral**.

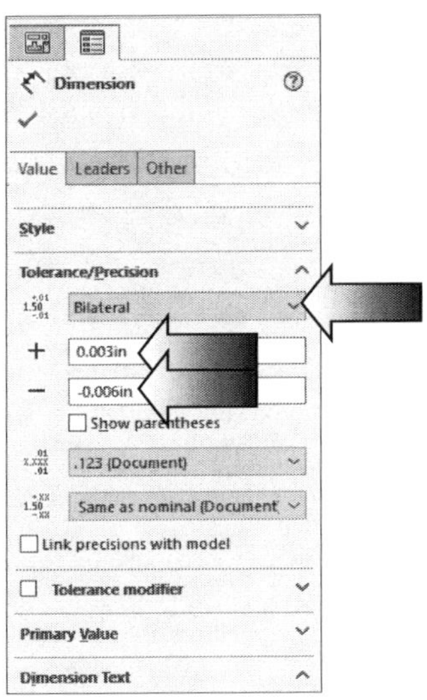

For Maximum Variation, enter **.003in**.

For Minimum Variation, enter **.006in**.

Click **OK**.

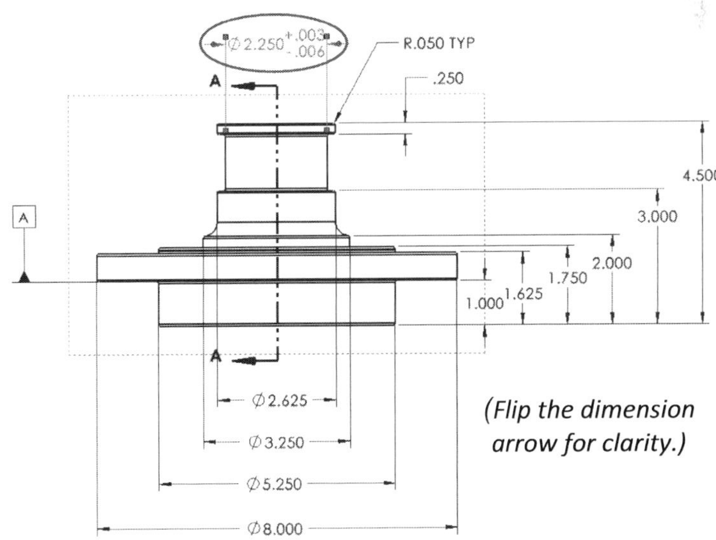

(Flip the dimension arrow for clarity.)

4. Adding a Limit tolerance:

A Limit tolerance is a form of dimensional tolerancing that specifies a tolerance range for a specific feature. Limit tolerances are also known as limit dimensioning and are an effective way to specify requirements on a drawing. They clearly identify the tolerance range without requiring additional calculations by the reader.

Select the dimension **1.000** in the **Front** drawing view.

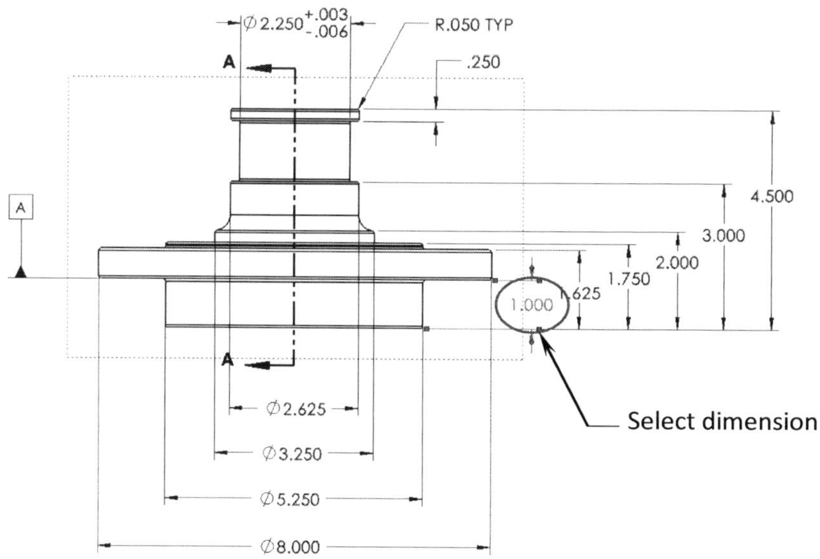

Select **Limit** under Tolerance/Precision.

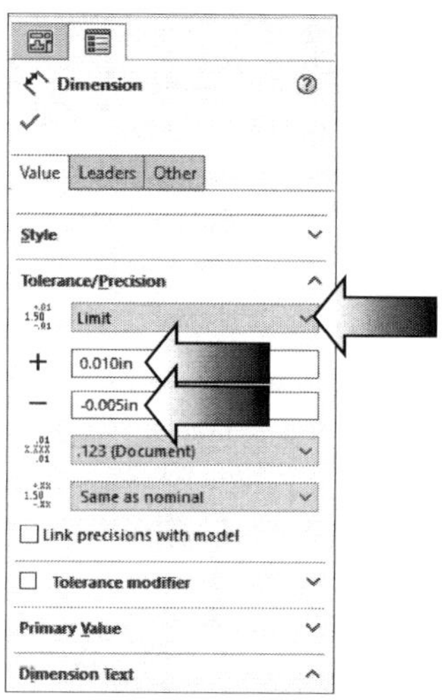

For Maximum Variation enter: **.010in.**

For Minimum Variation, enter: **.005in.**

Click **OK.**

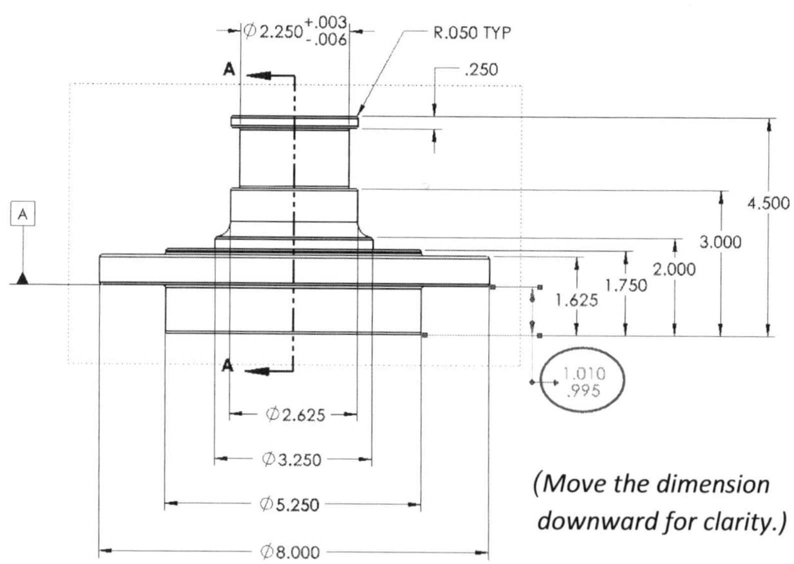

(Move the dimension downward for clarity.)

5. Adding a Basic dimension:

A Basic dimension is a theoretically exact size or location. It is enclosed in a rectangular box. Basic dimensions do not have tolerance applied to them; this includes any general tolerance blocks. An example of this would be a true position callout for a hole or group of holes.

The basic dimension(s) specify the location of the hole.

Zoom in on the **Top** drawing view and select the **Ø6.650 Bolt Circle** dimension.

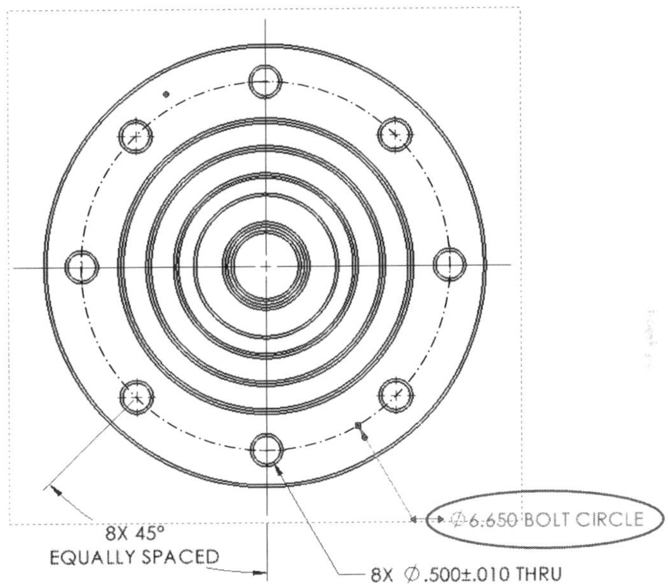

In the Dimension Text section, highlight the text: **<MOD-DIA><DIM>**

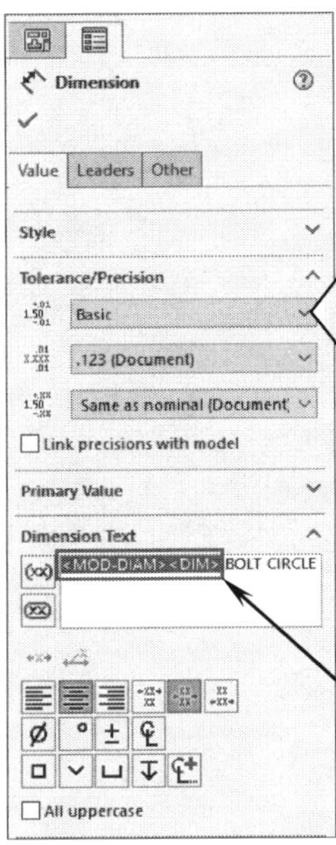

Highlight <MOD-DIA> <DIM>

In the Tolerance/Precision section, select: **Basic**

A rectangular box is added around the highlighted text.

Click **OK**.

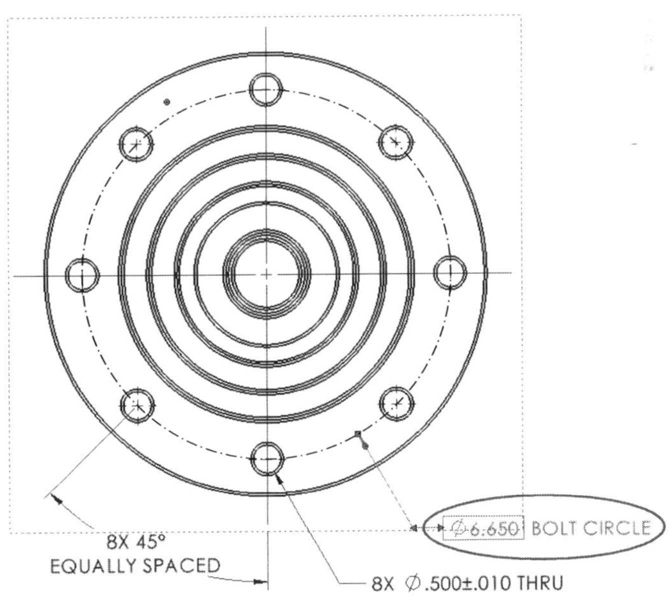

Select the dimension **8X 45°** also in the **Top** drawing view.

In the Dimension Text section, highlight the text: **<DIM>**.

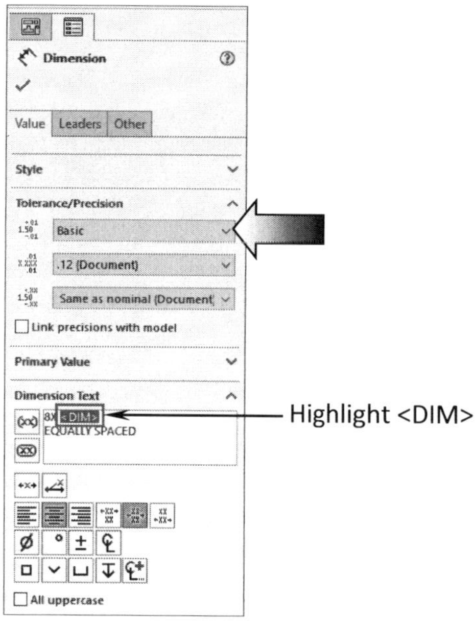

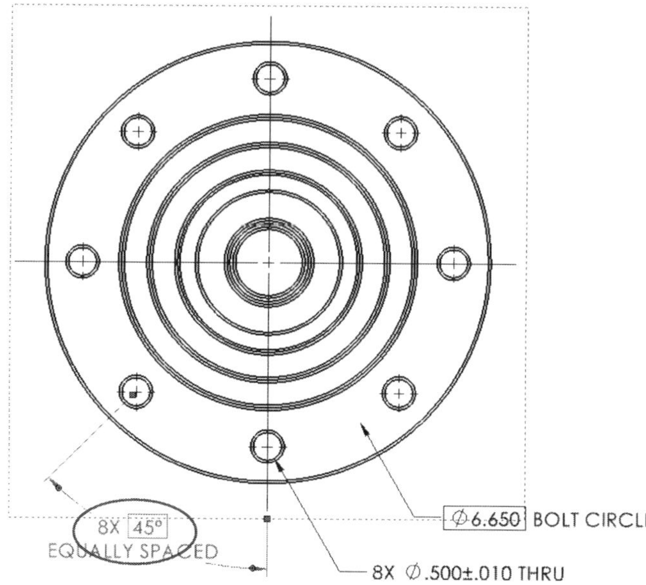

Select **Basic** under the Tolerance/Precision section.

A rectangular box is added around the highlighted text.

Click **OK**.

Inspect your Basic dimensions against the image shown on the right.

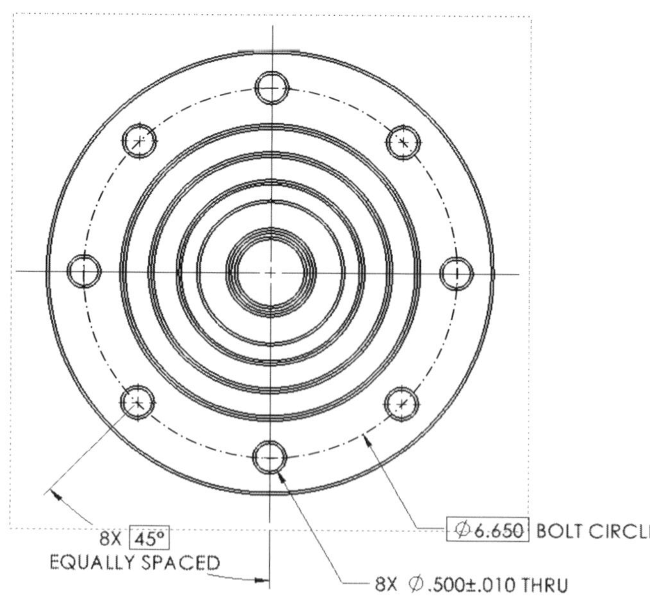

6. Adding a Unilateral tolerance:

Unilateral tolerances are often used to specify dimensions that require a specific fit with a mating part.

Basically, unilateral tolerance is a type of tolerance that is only allowed in one direction. Either an all plus tolerance or an all minus tolerance.

Per ASME Y14.5, the notation for a unilateral tolerance is to show a plus or a minus tolerance associated with a nominal dimension. It is acceptable for one of the specified tolerances to be zero.

Zoom in on the **Section view** and select the dimension **Ø4.250**.

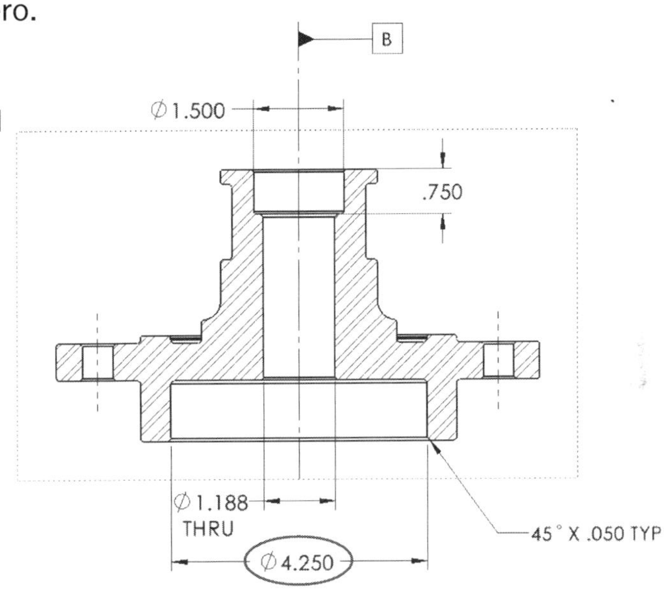

SECTION A-A

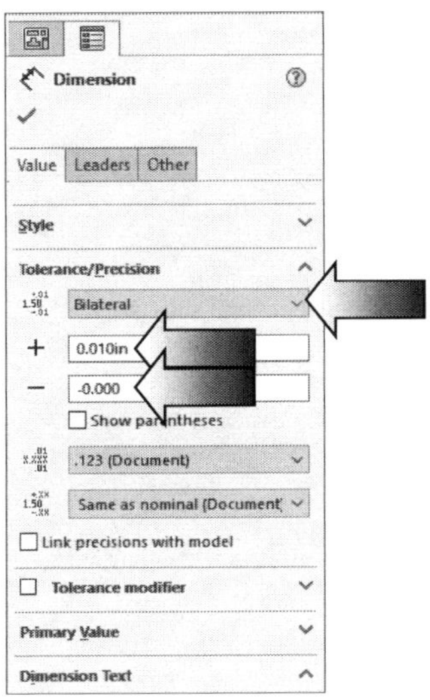

Select **Bilateral** under the Tolerance/ Precision section.

For Maximum Variation,
Enter: **.010in**.

For Minimum Variation,
Enter: **.000in**.

Click **OK**.

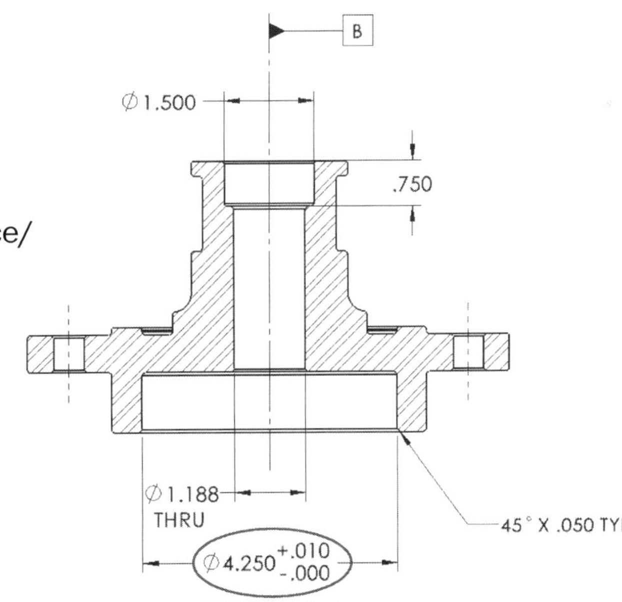

SECTION A-A

Also, add a Symmetric tolerance to the dimension **Ø1.188**.

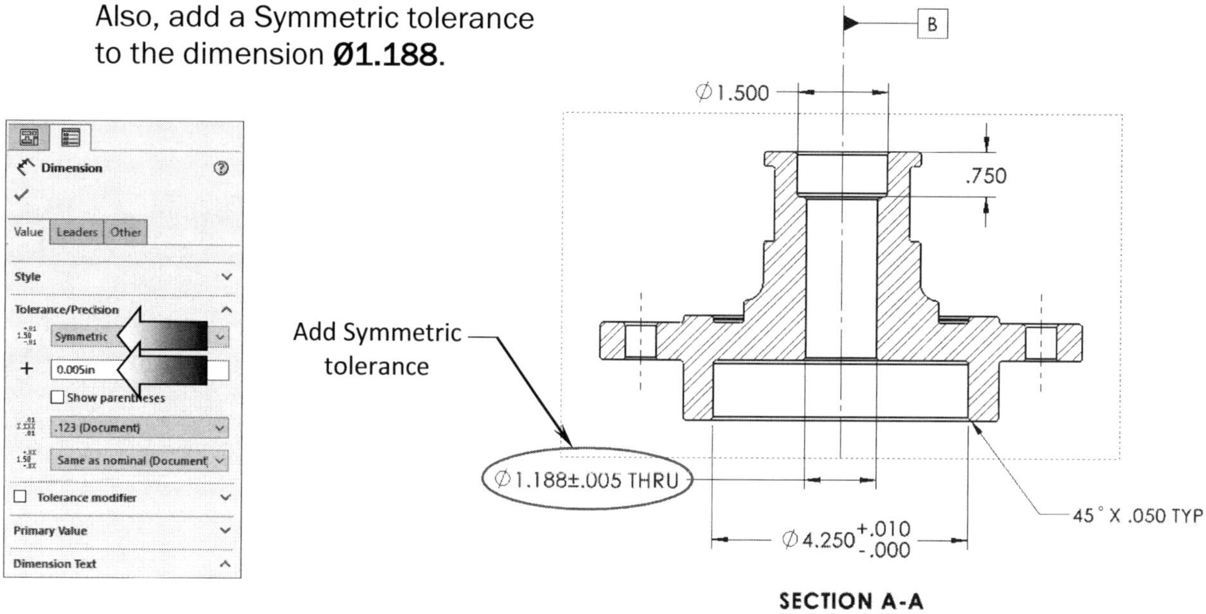

Remember to save your work every once in a while.

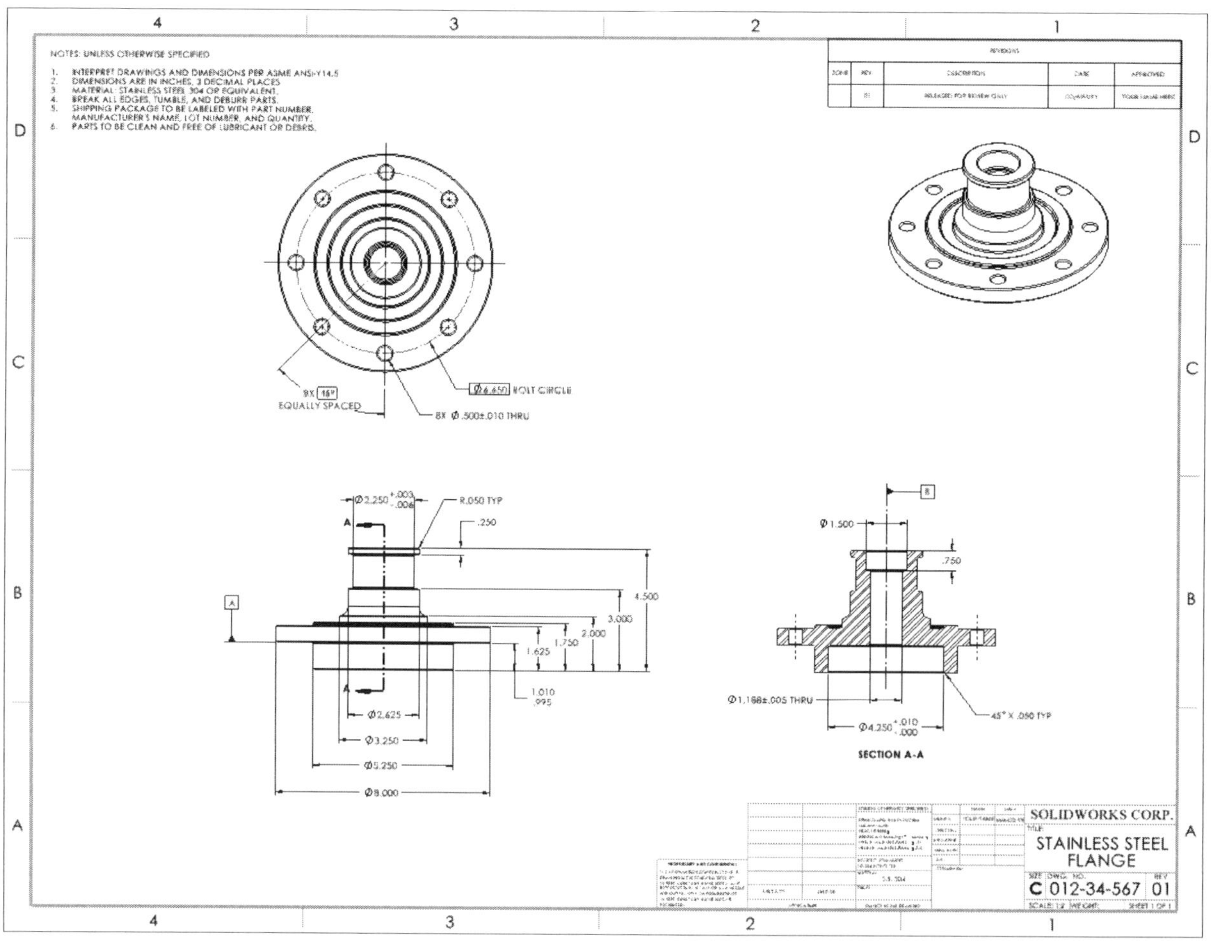

7. Adding a True Position tolerance:

True Position is a Location tolerance usually set at the center of the feature being toleranced. For example, for a hole, the true position is set at the hole's axis.

Location tolerance determines the location (true position) of the feature in relation to a reference. A datum is always necessary to indicate location tolerance.

Select the dimension **Ø1.188** in the section view.

Switch to the **Annotation** tab and click **Geometric Tolerance.**

A square appears below the Dimension; **click the square** to display the Tolerance dialog box.

Select the **Position** symbol.

Click the **Diameter** symbol and enter **.010.**

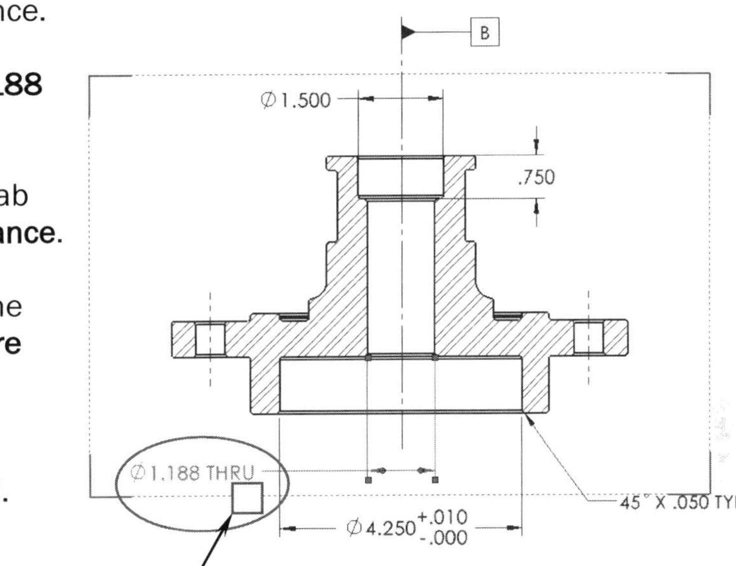

SECTION A-A

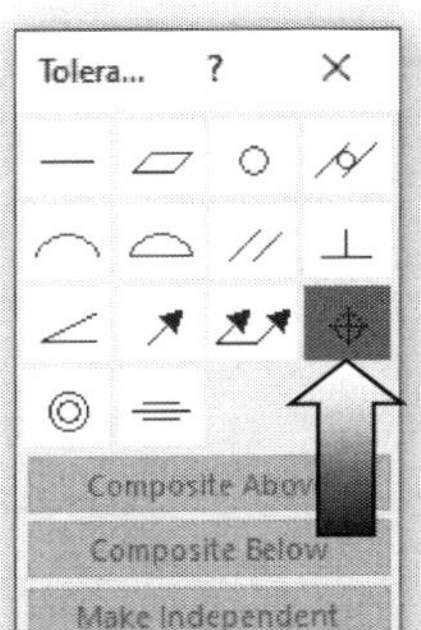

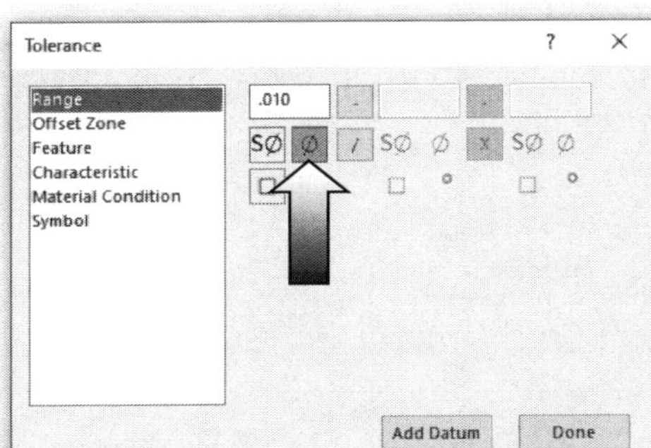

Click **Material Condition** on the left pane and select Ⓜ

Click the **Add Datum** button and enter: **A.**

Click the **Add New** button and enter: **B.**

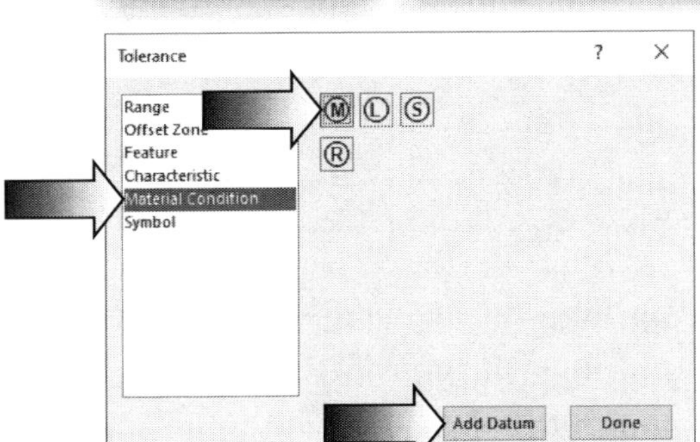

Click **Done.**

Your Position tolerance should look like the one shown below.

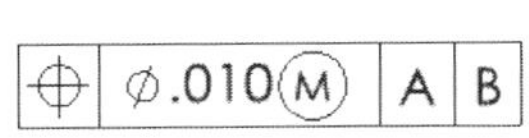

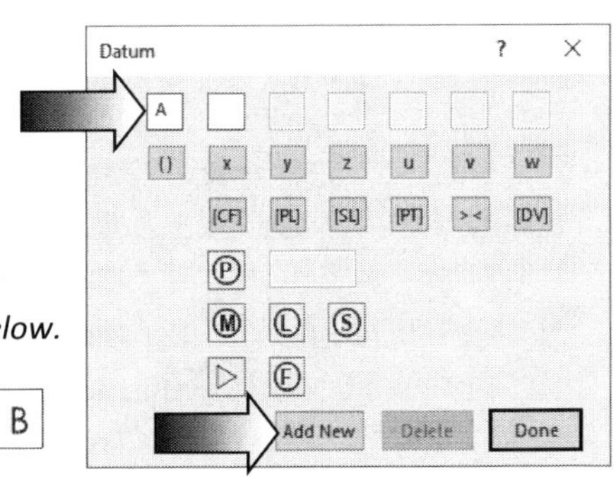

The MMC (M) modifier when used with Position control gives a bonus tolerance to the part feature.

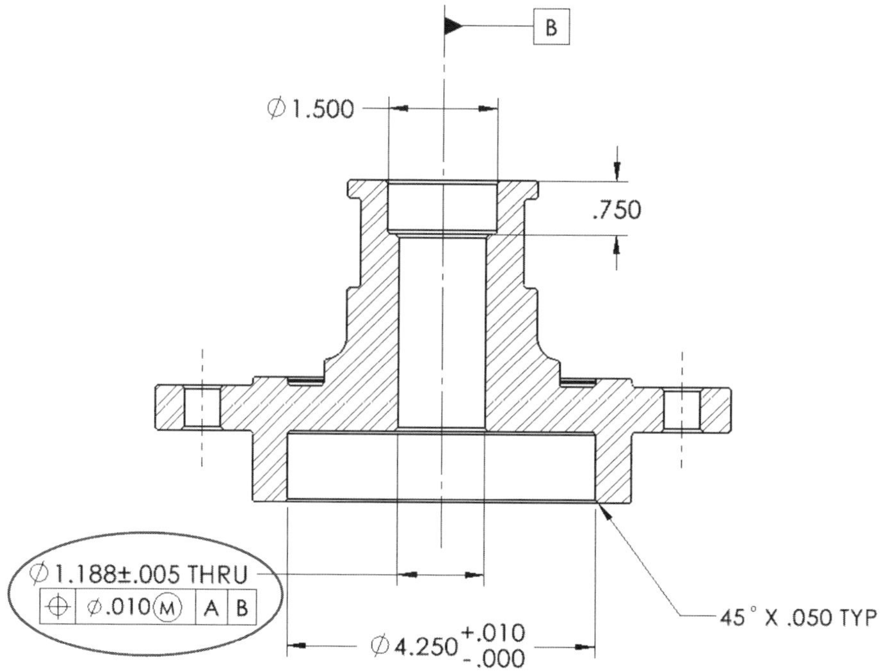

SECTION A-A

<u>**Bonus Tolerance Formular:**</u>

Bonus tolerance (for hole)**:** Feature actual size ***minus*** Feature size at MMC

Total Allowable Tolerance: Position tolerance ***plus*** Bonus tolerance

<u>**Example:**</u> The hole diameter is **Ø1.188**, or **1.183** at **MMC**, or **1.193** at **LMC**

Feature Diameter	Position Tolerance	Bonus Tolerance	Total Tolerance
Ø1.183 (at MMC)	.010	0	.010
Ø1.188 (at MMC)	.010	.005	.017
Ø 1.193 (at MMC)	.010	.010	.020

The Bonus tolerance and Position tolerance can be added if the feature size is below MMC. The GD&T Position control tolerance with the MMC tolerance zone is equal to the sum of Position control tolerance and Bonus tolerance.

8. Adding a Concentricity control:

Concentricity is a tolerance that controls the central derived median points of the referenced feature, to a datum axis. In reality, concentricity is a very complex feature because it relies on measurements from derived median points as opposed to a surface or feature's axis.

Select the dimension **Ø1.500** in the section view.

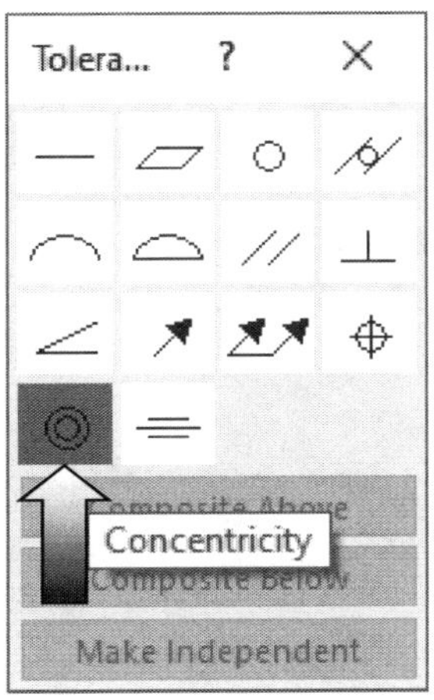

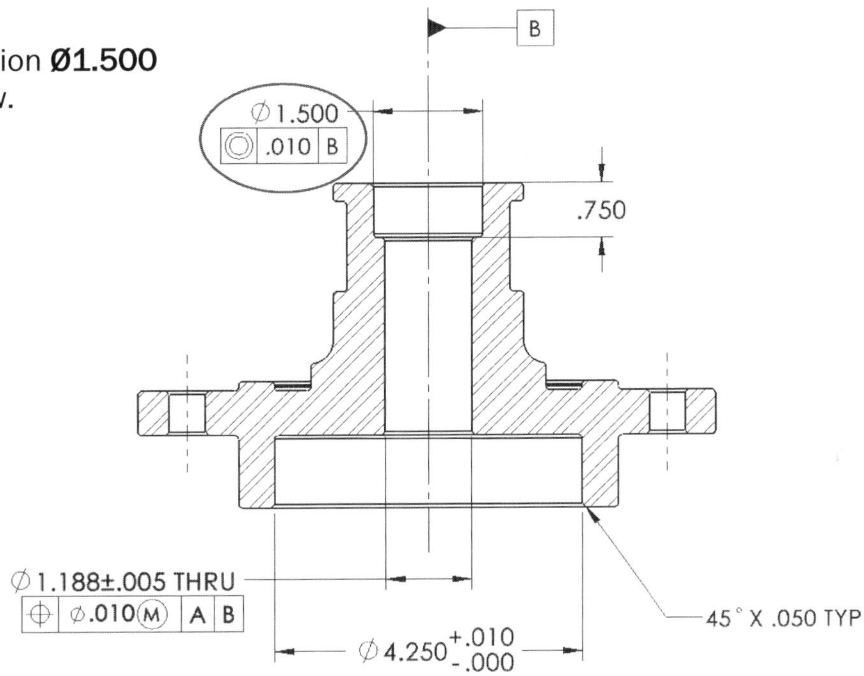

SECTION A-A

Select **Geometric Tolerance** and click the square below the dimension Ø1.500 to activate the Tolerance dialog box.

Select the **Concenteric** button and enter **.010** for variation.

Click **Add Datum** and enter **B.**

Click **OK.**

Your Concentric control frame should look like the one shown on the right.

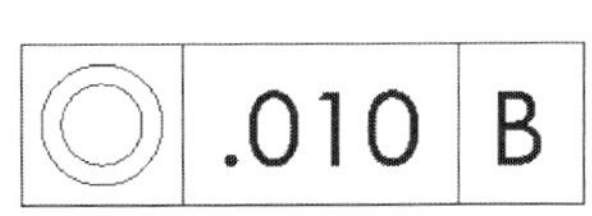

9. Saving your work:

Select **File, Save As.**

Enter **Flange with Tolerance & Precision.slddrw** for the file name.

Click **Save.**

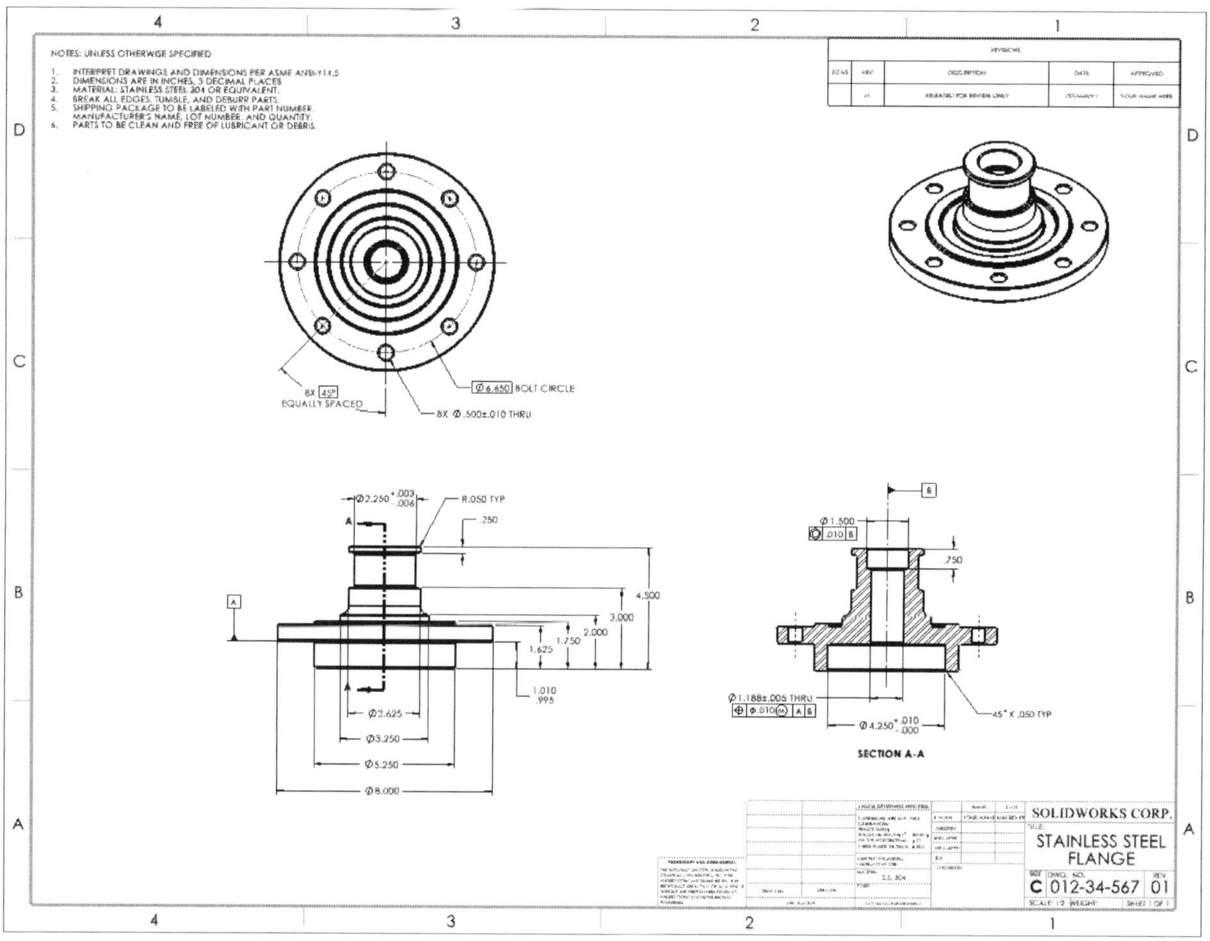

Exercise: Tolerance & Precision

Detailing a Machined Part

The exercises are designed to help you apply what you have learned from the previous lessons. They come with some instructions but not as detailed as the lessons, to give you an opportunity to explore and to try and create the drawings on your own, at your own pace.

1. Opening a part document:

Select **File, Open**.

Browse to the Training Folder and open the part document named: **Machined Part 2.sldprt**.

The material **6061-T6** has already been assigned to the part.

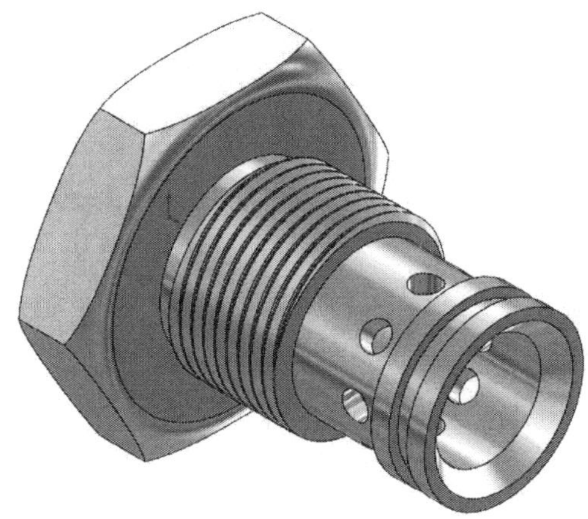

2. Transferring to a drawing:

Select **File, Make Drawing from Part.**

Select the **B-Size** drawing paper.

Set the Type-Of-Projection to: **3rd Angle**.

Keep all other parameters at their default.

Click **OK**.

This is SOLIDWORKS B-Size drawing.

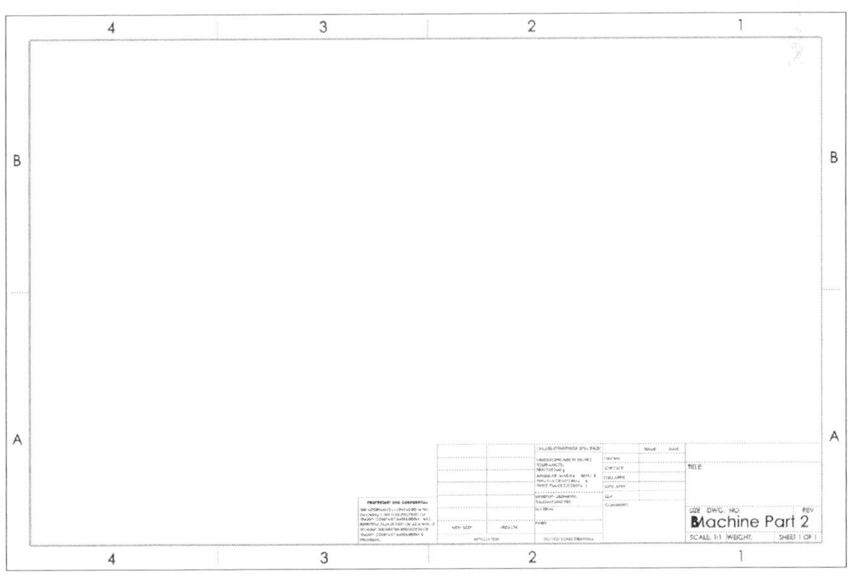

3. Creating the drawing views:

Use the View Palette and the tools in the Drawing tab to create the 4 drawing views shown below: The Front drawing view, Right view, Isometric view, and a section view.

Use the default scale **1:1**. *Note: The section view is placed below the Front view.*

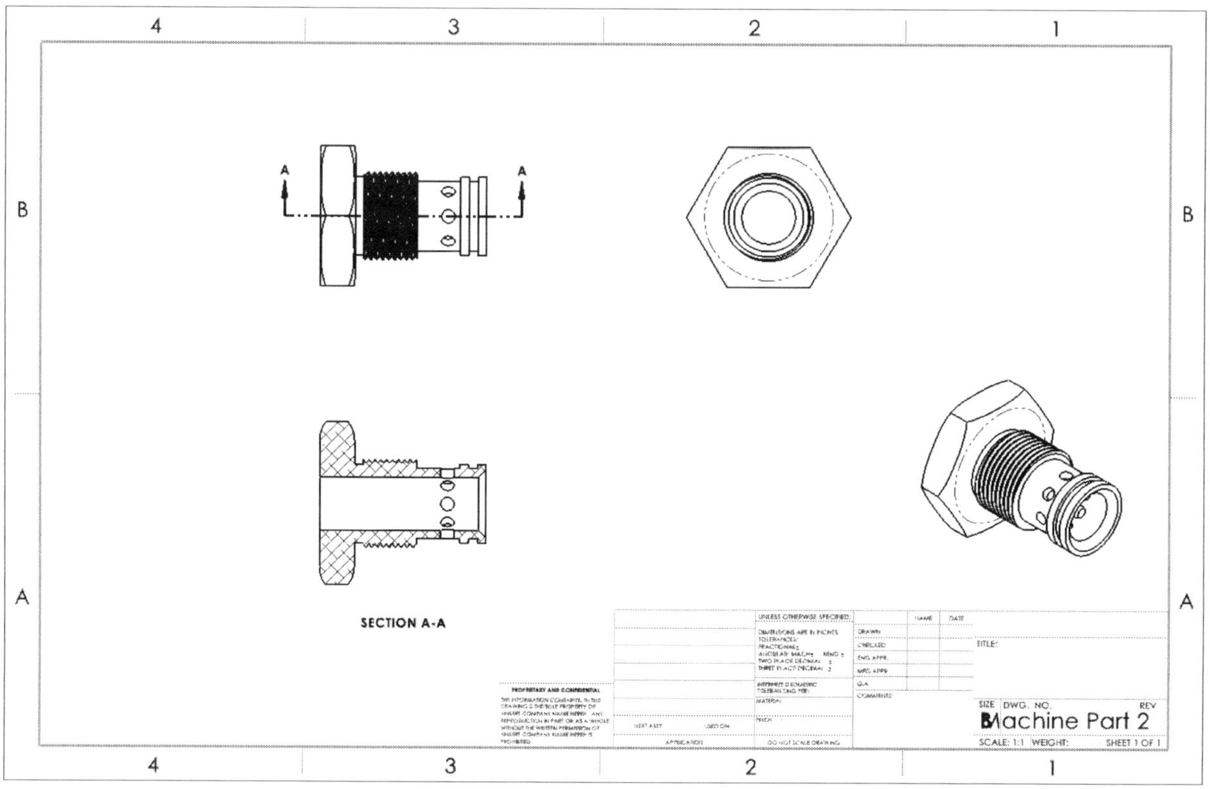

The crosshatch should be set to **ANSI38 Aluminum.**

Be sure to set your Drafting-Standard to **ANSI** and **Units** is **IPS, 3 Decimals** *(Tools, Options, System Options, Document Properties).*

Arrange the drawing views similar to the image above. We need to have enough room in each view to add dimensions and annotations.

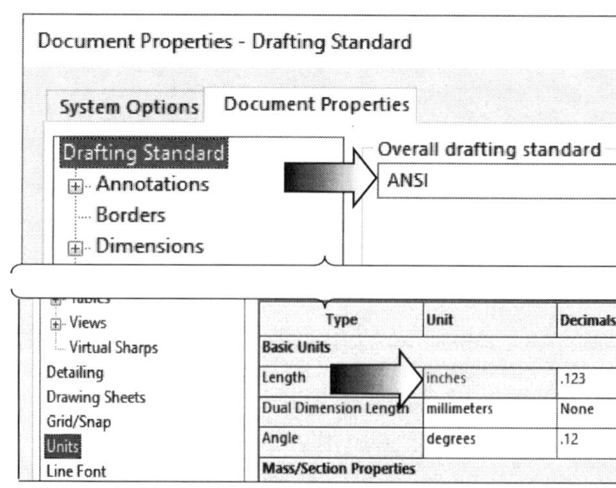

4. Adding dimensions:

Use the tools in the **Annotation** tab to detail the drawing views.

The recommended tools are:

Model Items

Smart Dimension

Geometric Tolerance

Datum Feature

Notes

Centerline

Center Mark, etc.

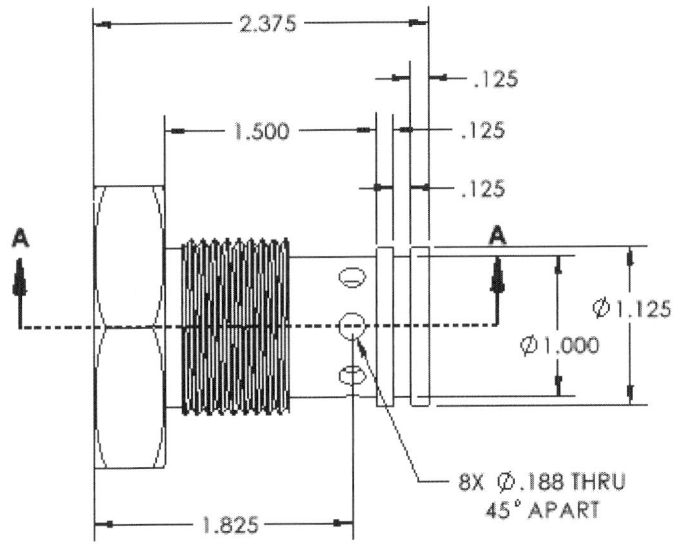

Depending on how the features were created in the model, some of the dimensions can be inserted into the drawing views automatically, some will have to be added manually, and sometimes with features like Chamfers and Threads, the Note tool may need to be used to indicate their details.

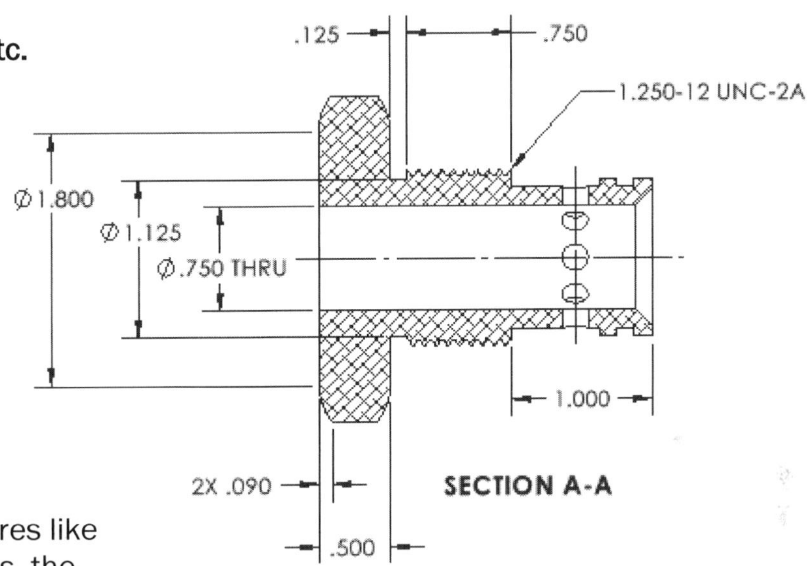

Add dimensions to each drawing view as shown.

Add the instance numbers as well as the centerlines and center marks.

Round off the number of decimals to 3 places where needed.

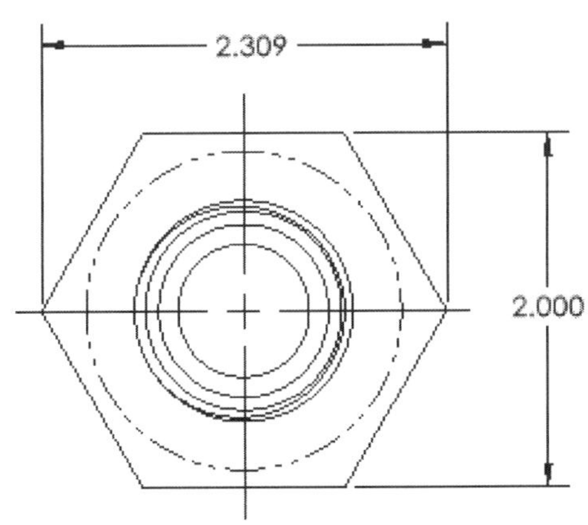

5. Adding tolerance & precision:

GD&T enhances design accuracy by allowing for appropriate tolerances that maximize production.
For some projects, the GD&T process provides extra or bonus tolerances, further increasing cost effectiveness.

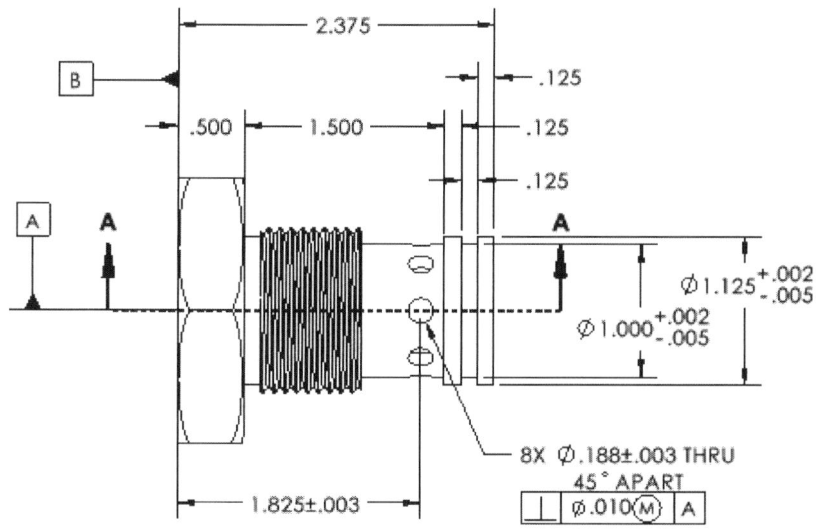

Add Datums **A** and **B** as shown in the **Top** drawing view.

Add the **Bilateral** tolerances to the three dimensions in the **Top** drawing view. Also, add a **Symmetric** tolerance to the hole pattern.

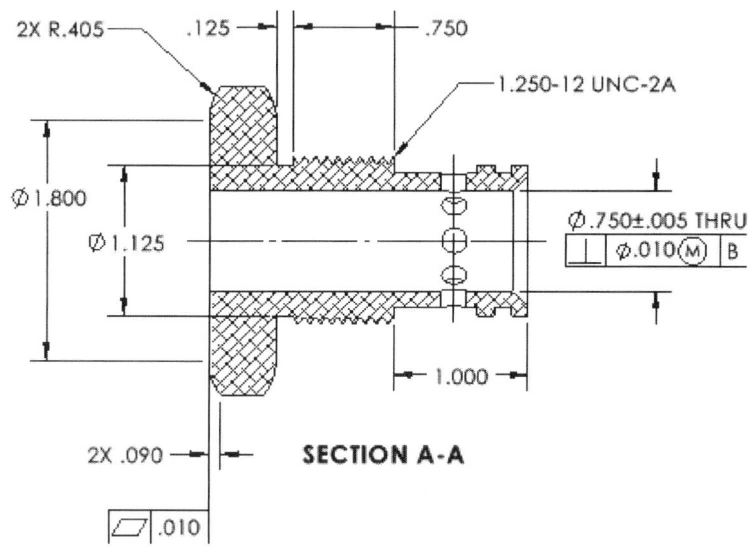

Add the **Flatness**, and the **Perpendicular** controls to the **Top** and the **Section** views.

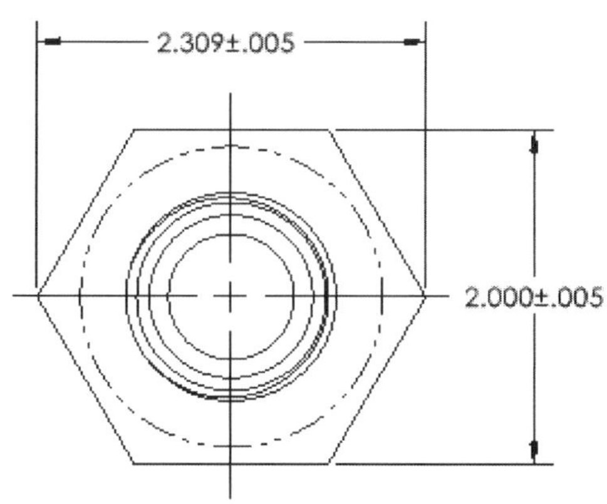

Add the **Symmetric** tolerances to the two dimensions shown in the **Right** drawing view. Use 3 decimal places for all dimensions and tolerances.

6. Adding the General Notes:

Engineering drawings are graphical representations of technical objects, systems, or processes that convey important information such as dimensions, tolerances, materials, or specifications. Notes are textual elements that complement the graphical elements and provide additional details, instructions, or references.

General Notes are usually placed on the upper corner of the drawing, or lower corner when the drawing is getting too busy.

Switch to the **Annotation** tab and click **Note.**

Enter the notes below, all in uppercase letters:

NOTES: UNLESS OTHERWISE SPECIFIED

1. INTERPRET DRAWINGS AND DIMENSIONS PER ASME ANSI-Y14.5
2. DIMENSIONS ARE IN INCHES, 3 DECIMAL PLACES
3. MATERIAL: 6061-T6 ALUMINUM ALLOY
4. BREAK ALL EDGES, TUMBLE, AND DEBURR PARTS
5. SHIPPING PACKAGE TO BE LABELED WITH PART NUMBER, MANUFACTURER'S NAME, LOT NUMBER, AND QUANTITY
6. PARTS TO BE CLEAN AND FREE OF LUBRICANT OR DEBRIS

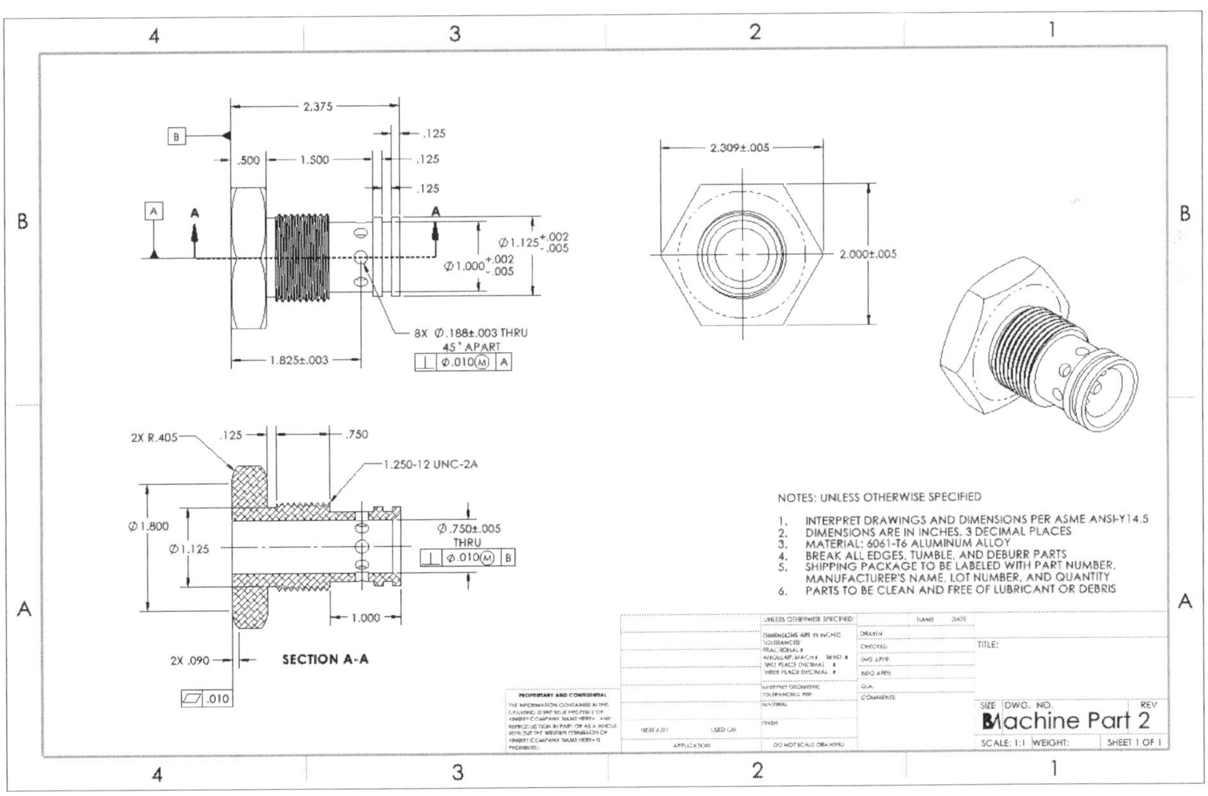

7. Adding a Revision Block:

When a drawing is released for review, it is called revision zero, or 01, and the revision block is empty. As each revision is made to the drawing, an entry is placed in the revision block. This entry will provide the revision number, a description, the date of the revision, and the person that created the changes.

From the **Annotation** tab, expand the **Tables** drop-down menu and select: **Revision Table**.

Create a Revision Table and fill out the information shown below.

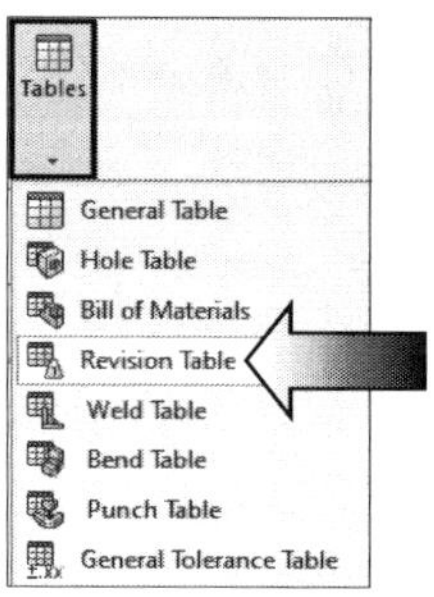

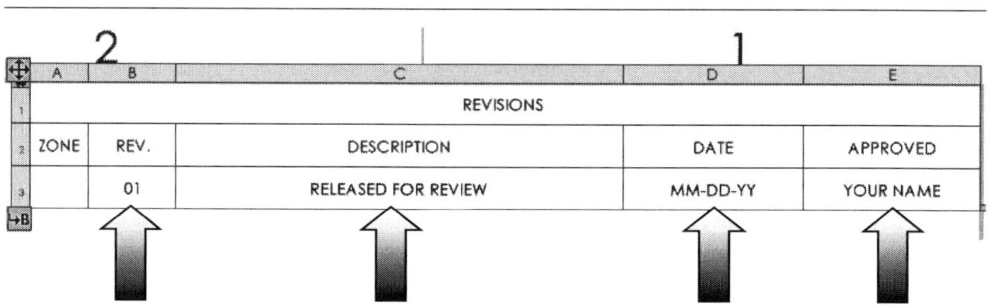

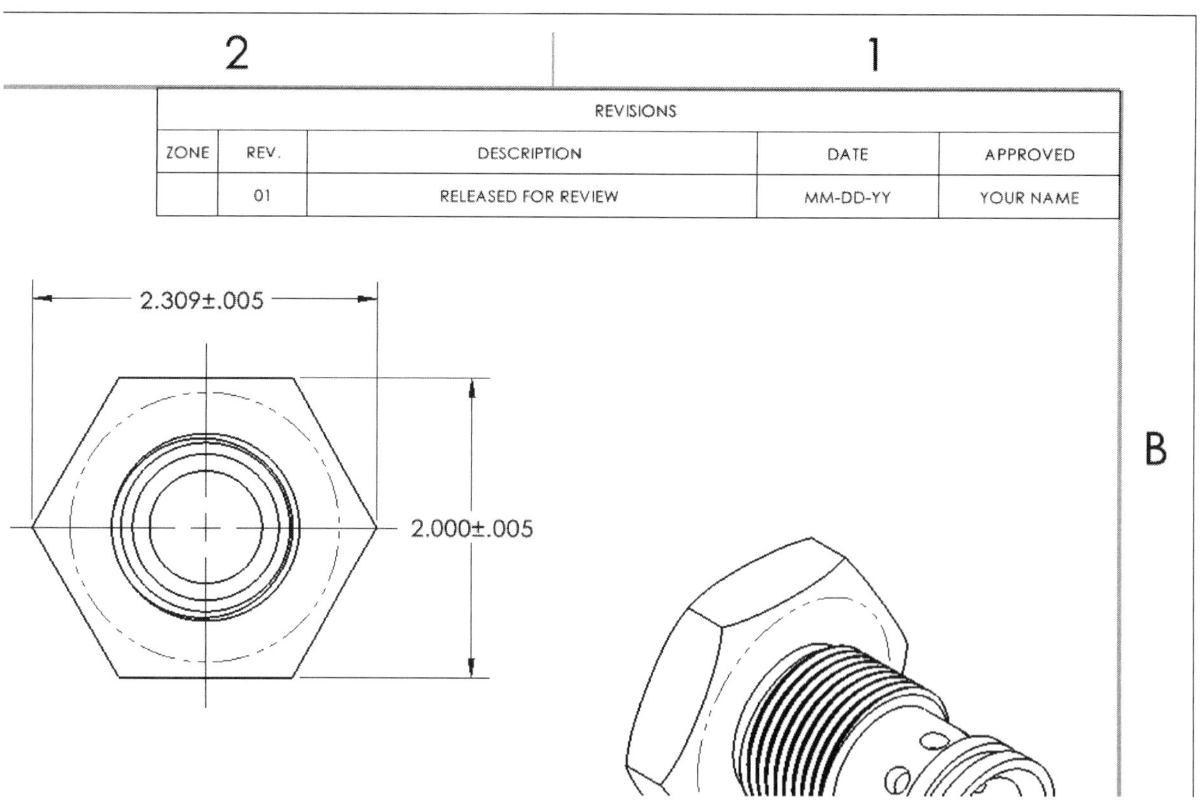

8. Filling out the Title Block information:

Title blocks are used to record all important information necessary for the working drawings. They contain general as well as specific information such as Drawing Title, Drawing Number, Revision, Material, Finish, Drawn Date, Approved Date, etc.

From the FeatureManager tree, expand **Sheet1** and double-click **Sheet Format1** to activate the Format layer.

Fill out the information shown below.

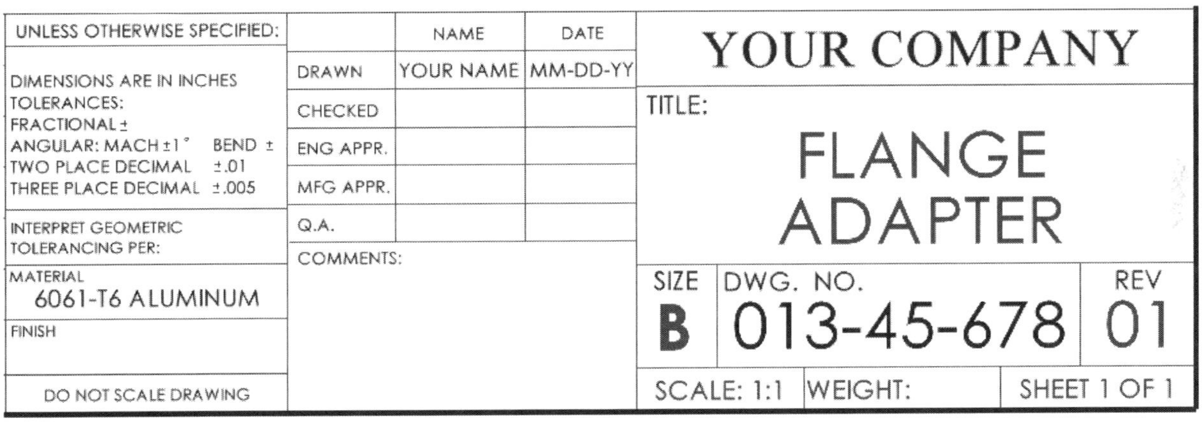

When finished, double-click **Sheet1** on the Feature-Manager tree to activate the Sheet layer.

Rearrange the drawing views and the General Notes to look similar to the image shown here.

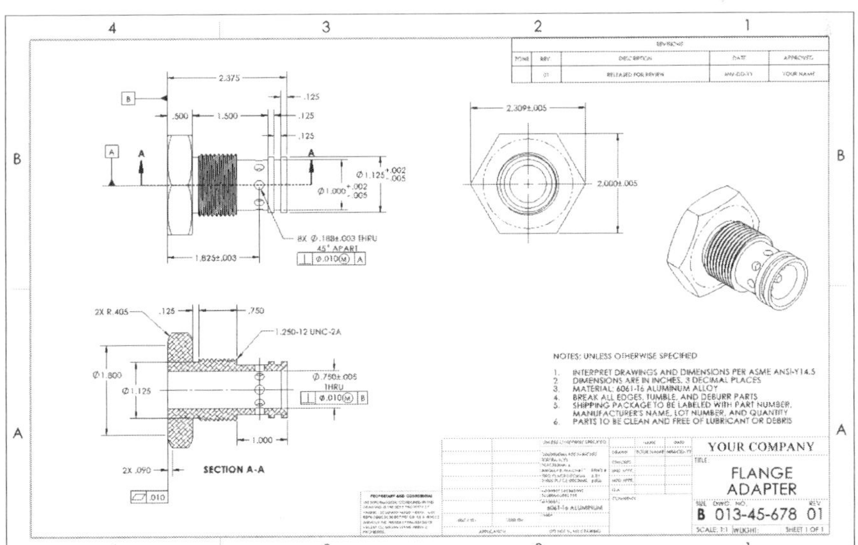

9. Saving your work:

Select **File, Save As.**

Enter: **Machine Part 2.slddrw** for the file name.

Click **Save.**

Close all documents.

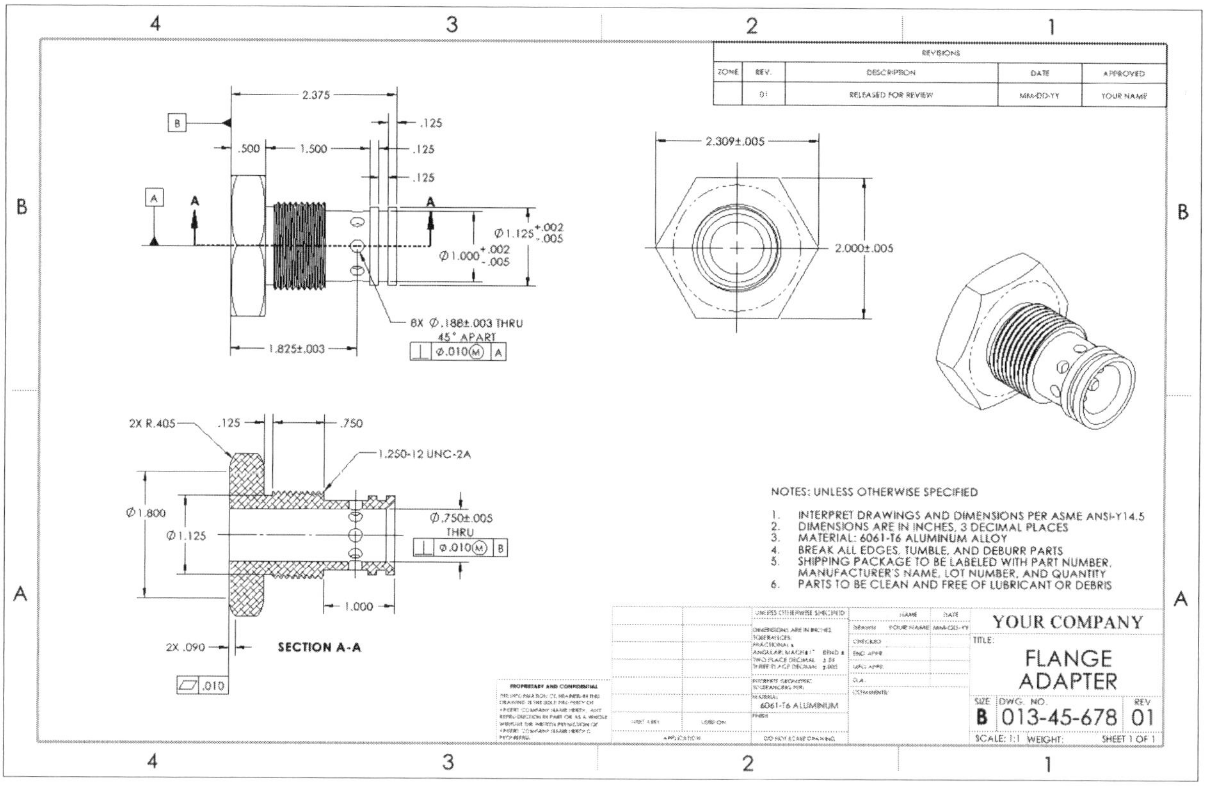

Exercise: Tolerance & Precision

Detailing a Machined Part

The exercises are designed to help you apply what you have learned from the previous lessons. They come with some instructions but not as detailed as the lessons, to give you an opportunity to explore and to try and create the drawings on your own, at your own pace.

1. Opening a part document:

Select **File, Open**.

Browse to the Training Folder and open the part document named: **Threaded Coupling.sldprt**.

The material **AISI 304** has already been assigned to the part.

2. Transferring to a drawing:

Select **File, Make Drawing from Part.**

Select the **B-Size** drawing paper.

Set the Type-Of-Projection to: **3rd Angle**.

Set the Scale to **1:1** (Full size).

Click **OK**.

The B (ANSI) Landscape template is loaded.

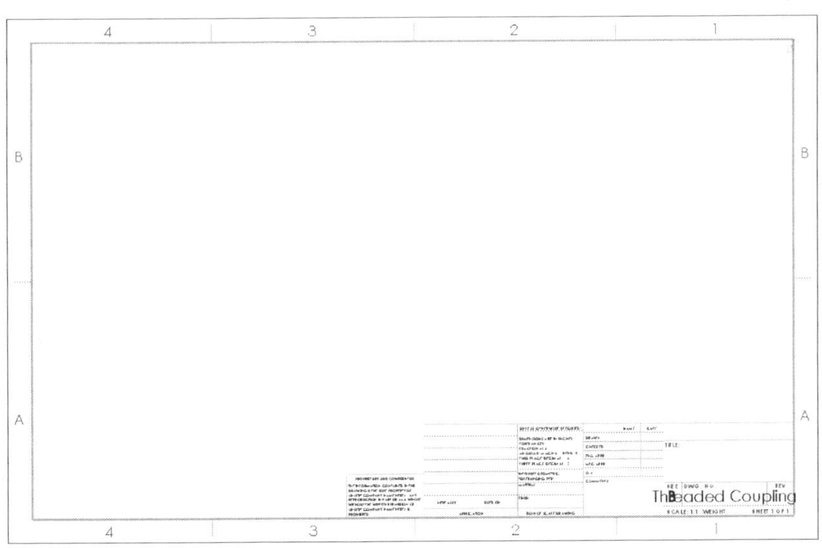

3. Creating the drawing views:

Using the **View Palette**, drag & drop the **Front** and **Isometric** drawing views onto the drawing.

Create a **Section View** as shown below.

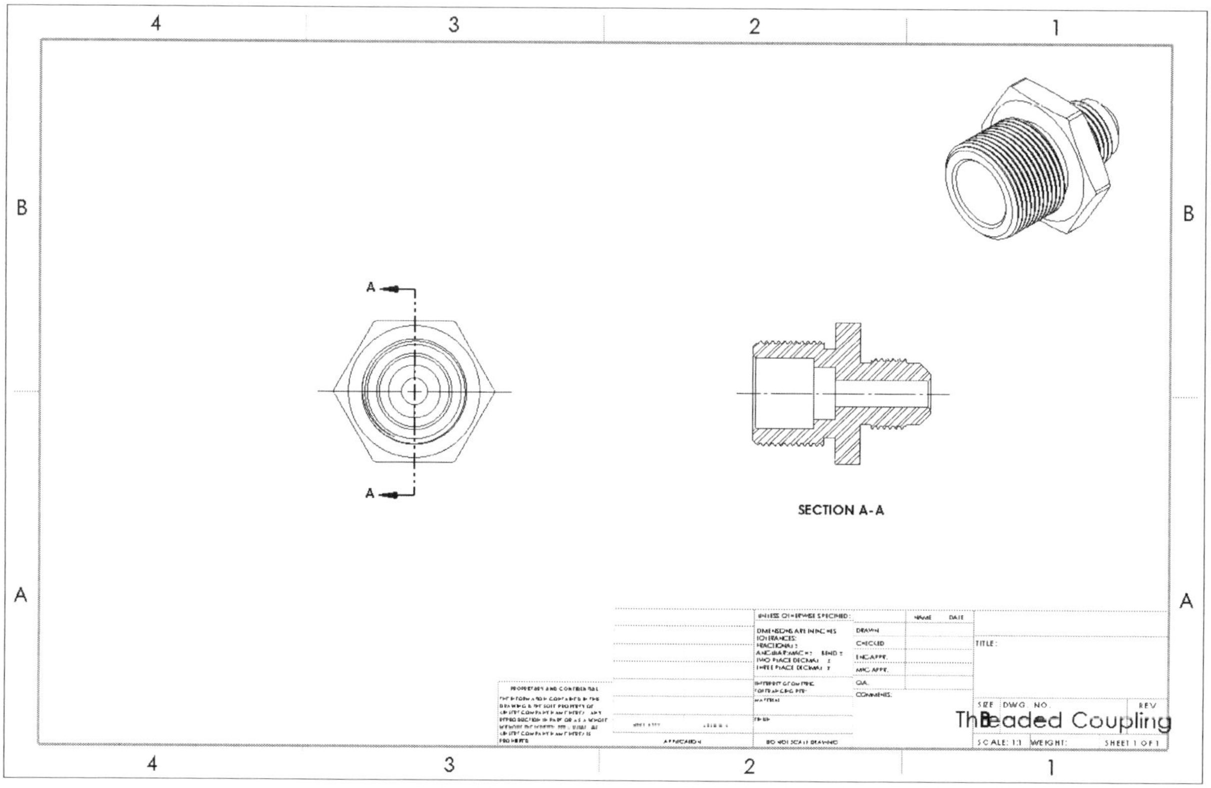

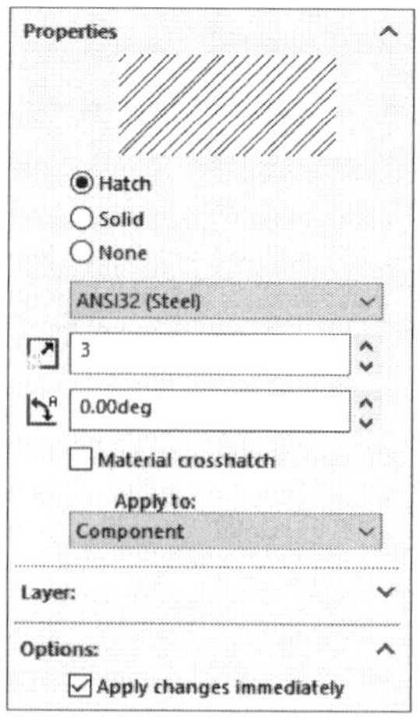

Ensure that the section arrows are pointing to the left side, and the section view is placed on the right as shown in the image above.

Click inside the hatch area to access the hatch Properties.

Change the Hatch Pattern to **ANSI32 (Steel)** and the Scale to **3**.

4. Adding the model dimensions:

Insert the **Model Items** and modify the dimensions to look like the ones shown in the drawing views below.

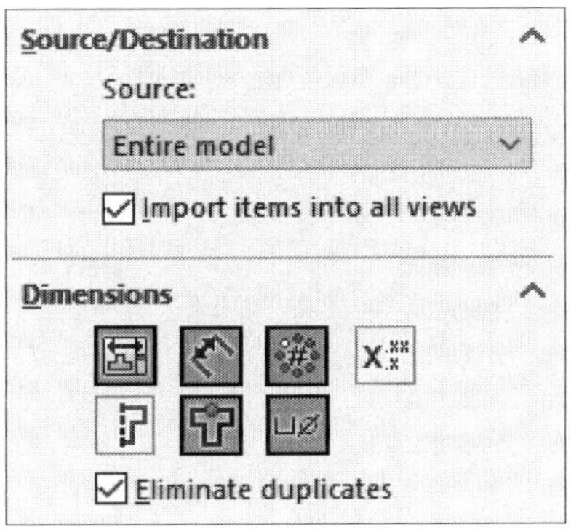

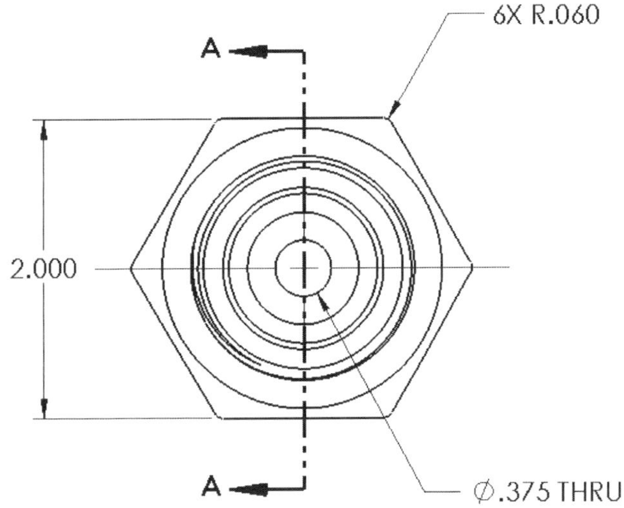

Note: Use the Note tool to call out the threads.

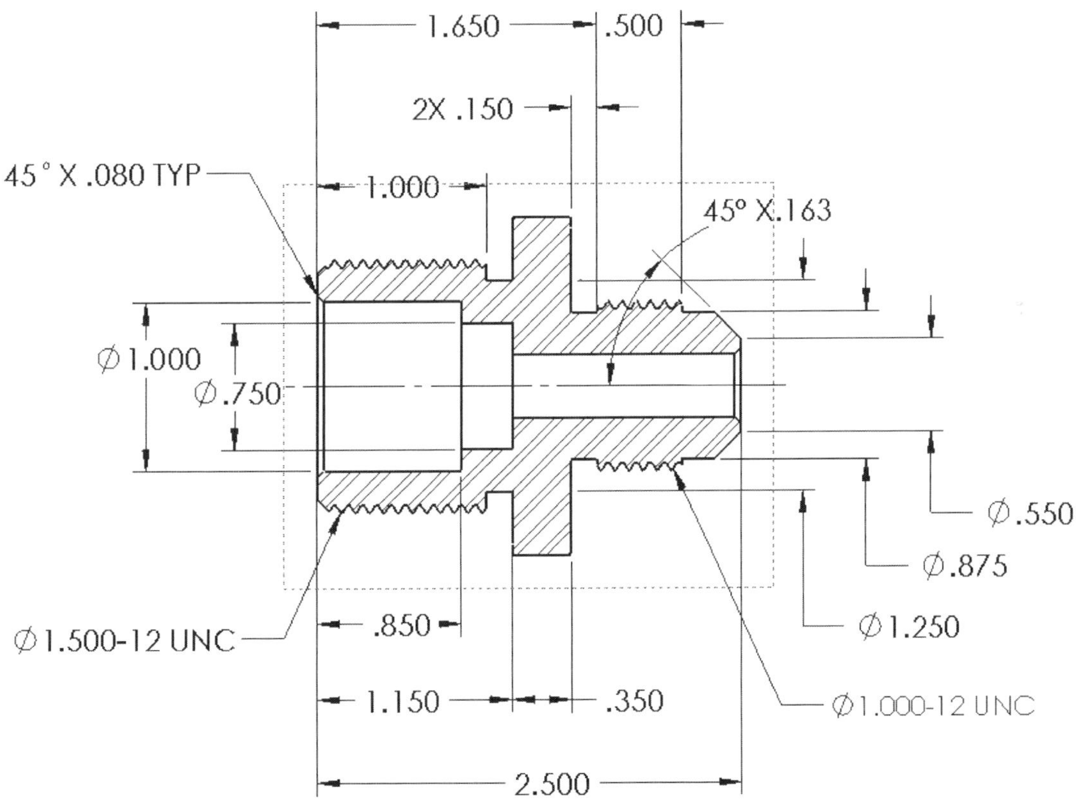

SECTION A-A

5. Adding the General Notes:

Click **Note**.

Enter the **General Notes** shown below:

NOTES: UNLESS OTHERWISE SPECIFIED

1. INTERPRET DRAWINGS AND DIMENSIONS PER ASME ANSI-Y14.5
2. DIMENSIONS ARE IN INCHES, 3 DECIMAL PLACES
3. MATERIAL: STAINLESS STEEL 304
4. BREAK ALL EDGES, TUMBLE, AND DEBURR PARTS
5. SHIPPING PACKAGE TO BE LABELED WITH PART NUMBER, MANUFACTURER'S NAME, LOT NUMBER, AND QUANTITY
6. PARTS TO BE CLEAN AND FREE OF LUBRICANT OR DEBRIS

6. Filling out the Title Block:

From the FeatureManager tree, expand **Sheet1** and double-click **Sheet Format** to activate the Format layer.

Enter the information shown below:

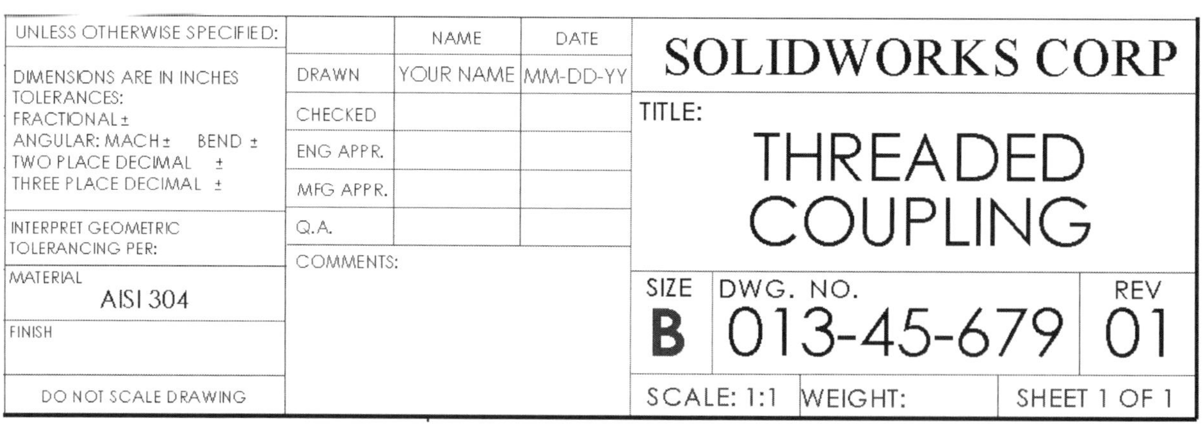

When finished, double-click **Sheet1** to activate the Sheet layer.

7. Saving your work:

Select **File, Save As**.

Enter **Threaded Coupling.slddrw** for the file name.

Click **Save**.

Close all documents.

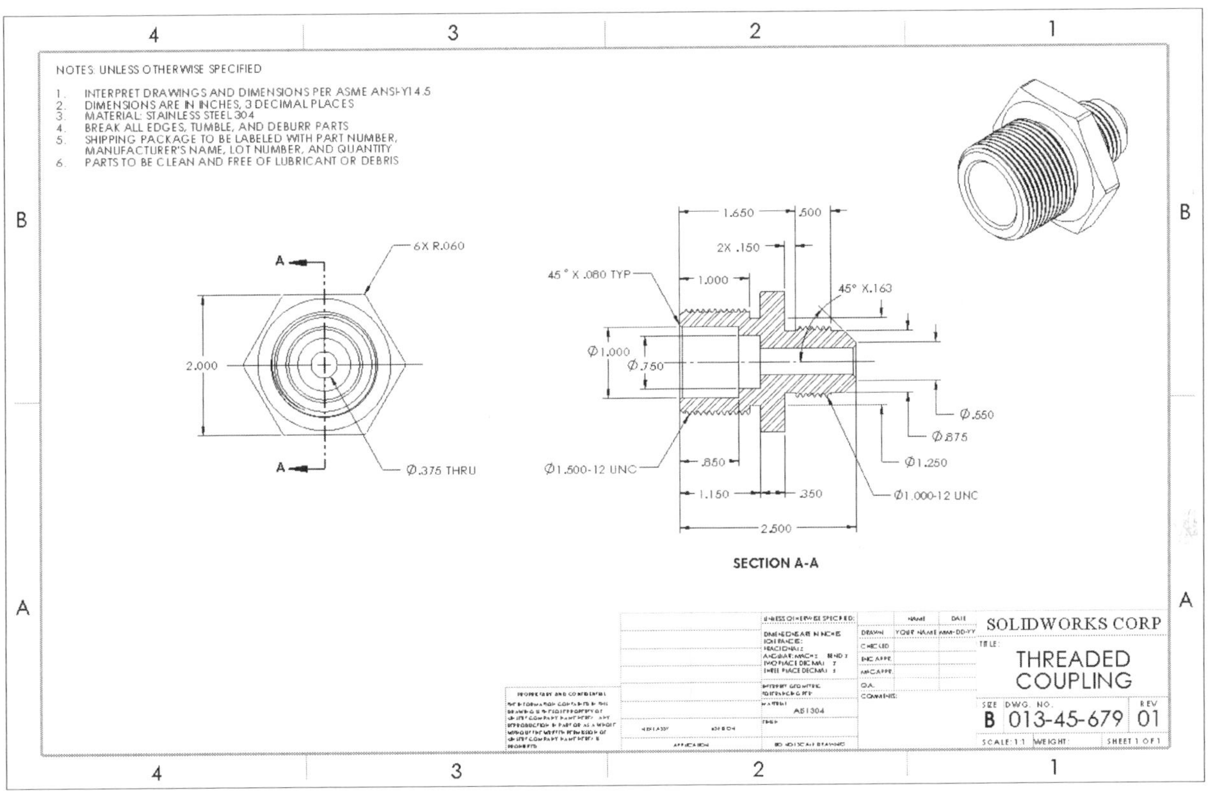

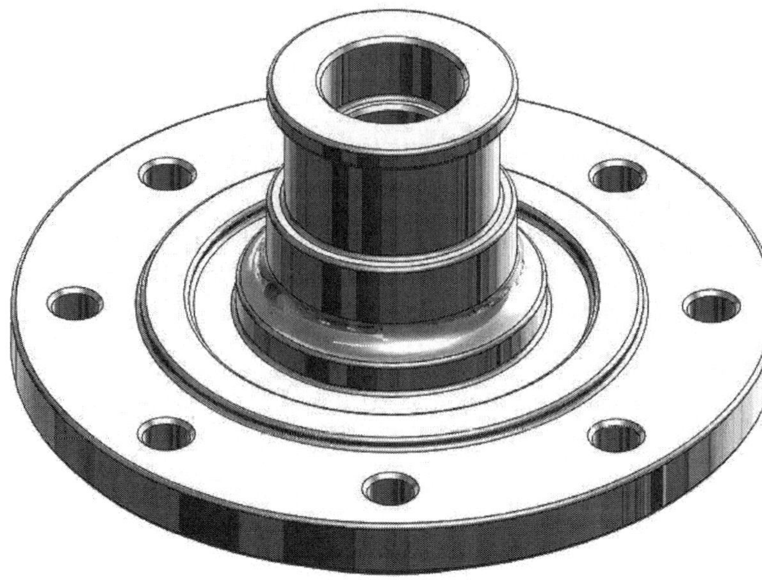

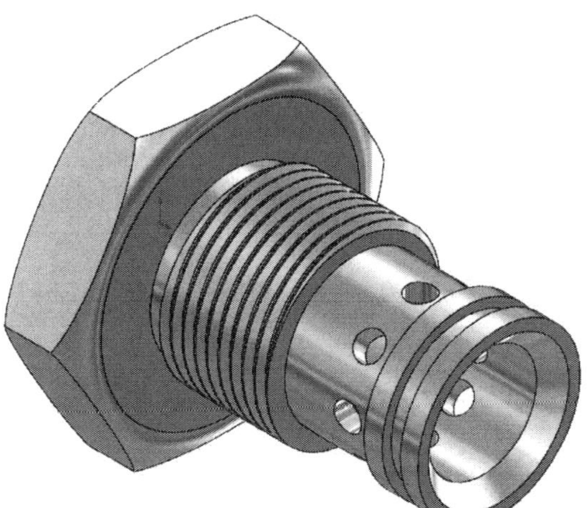

CHAPTER 5: DETAILING PLASTIC PARTS

Plastic Gear

Plastic parts are a little more involved to design than machine parts. There are several factors to consider when designing plastic parts to meet your design goals, and also to ensure a successful production process.

Some of the key factors are constant wall thickness, generous fillets, adequate draft angles, support ribs, material, and mold shrinkage, etc.

This chapter and its exercise will walk you through the process of creating engineering drawings for a couple of plastic parts.

1. Opening a part document:

Select **File, Open**.

Browse to the Training Folder and open the part document named: **Plastic Gear.sldprt.**

The material **POM Acetal Copolymer** has already been assigned to the part. It is an engineering thermoplastic used in precision parts that require low friction, high stiffness, and excellent dimensional stability.

A properly packed-out acetal part produced at the correct mold temperature will exhibit continued shrinkage of about 0.001 in./in. between the time the part reaches room temperature and the time that it is truly stable.

This value may increase if the nominal wall is very thick, and the areas that have the most material in this part are the teeth; they are .500” thick. This may result in internal stress.

2. Transferring to a drawing:

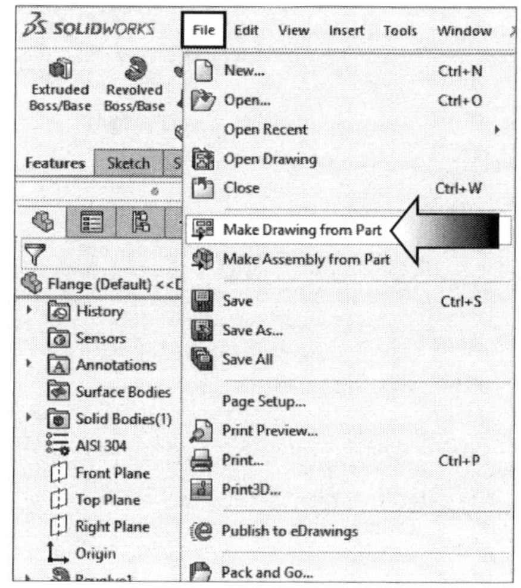

In SOLIDWORKS, the design is done in the 3D environment and a drawing is generated after the fact to capture the design intents and also to document the details of the design.

It is strongly recommended that changes or corrections should be done to the 3D model and populated to the drawing.

Select: **File, Make Drawing From Part** (arrow).

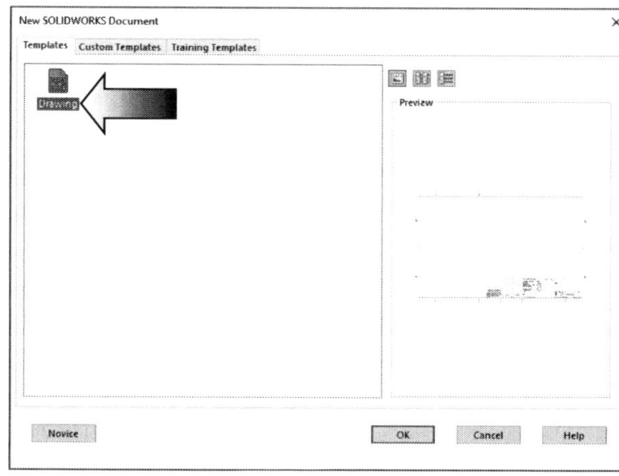

Select **Drawing** (or Draw) template from the New SOLIDWORKS Document dialog box.

In the Sheet Properties dialog box, select the following:

* Scale: **1:1**

* Type Of Projection: **Third Angle**

* Sheet Format/Size: **B (ANSI) Landscape**

* Next View Label: **A**

* Next Datum Label: **A**

* Display Sheet Format: **Enabled**

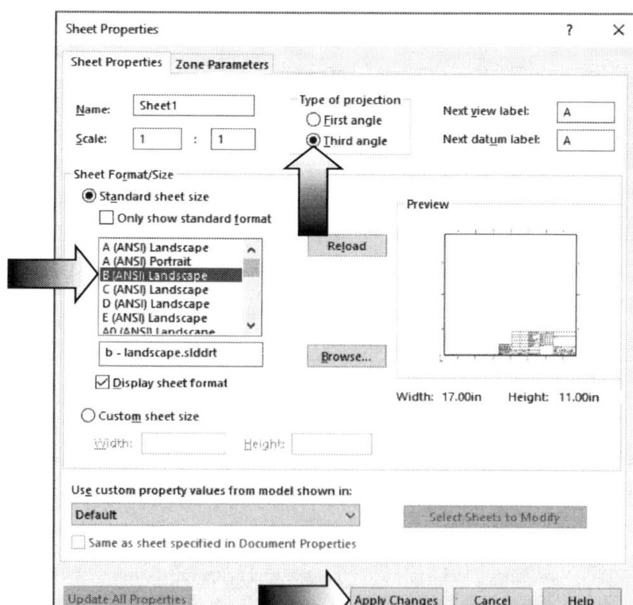

Click **Apply Changes**.

The B-Size landscape drawing template (17" x 11") is loaded into the graphics.

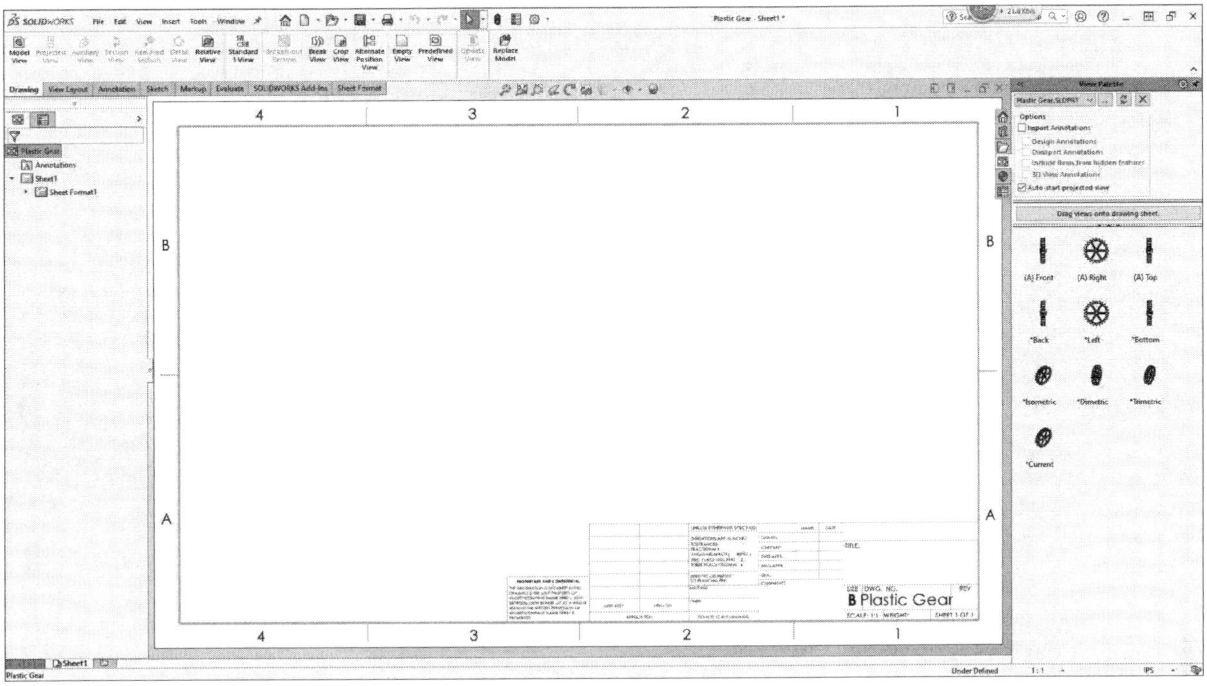

3. Creating the drawing views:

Expand the **View Palette** and enable the checkbox for **Auto-Start Projected View.**

Drag/drop the **Front**, **Right**, and **Isometric** view as shown.

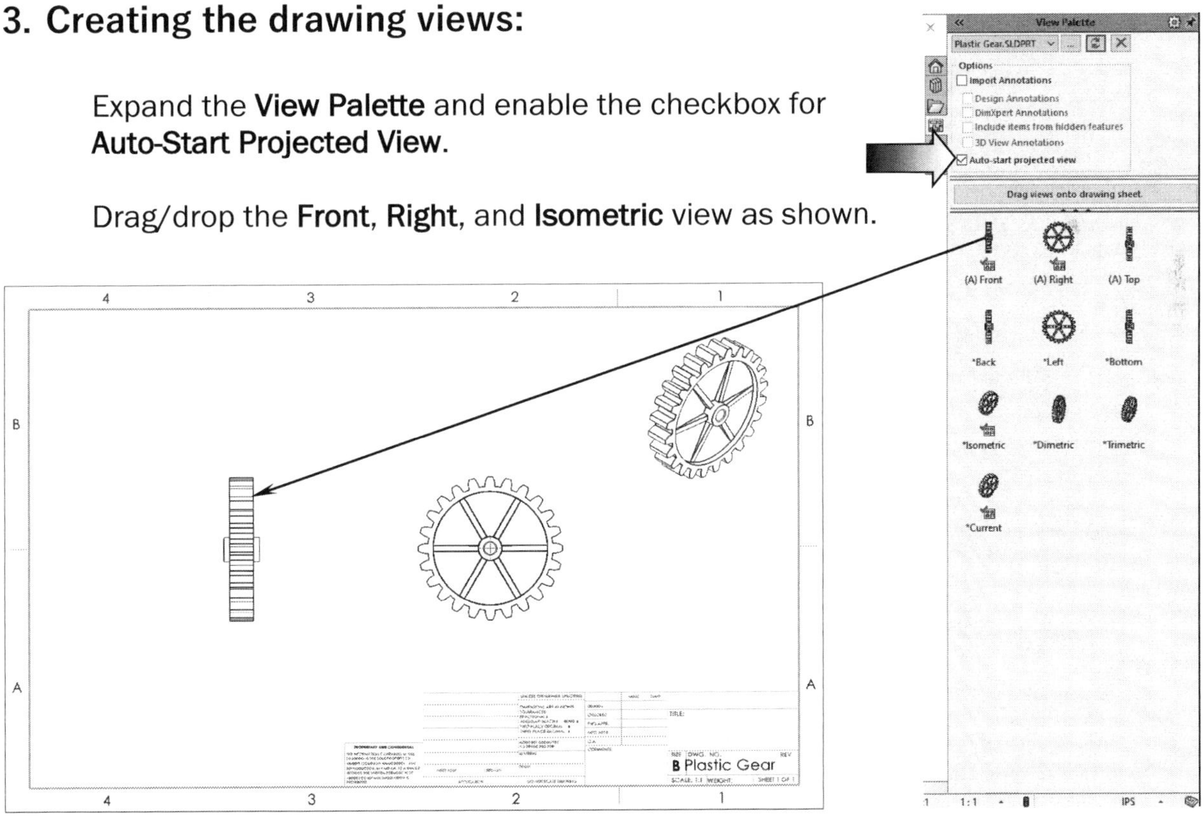

4. Creating a section view:

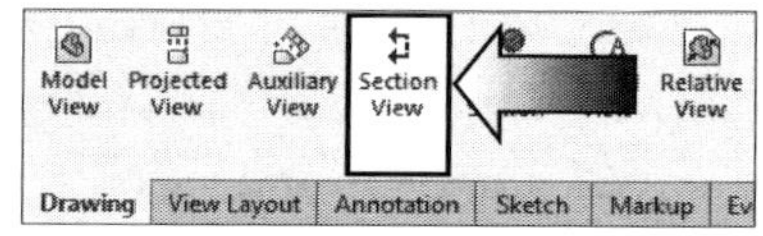

Section views are used to clarify the interior construction of a part that cannot be clearly described by hidden lines in exterior views.

Switch to the **Drawing** tab and click **Section View**.

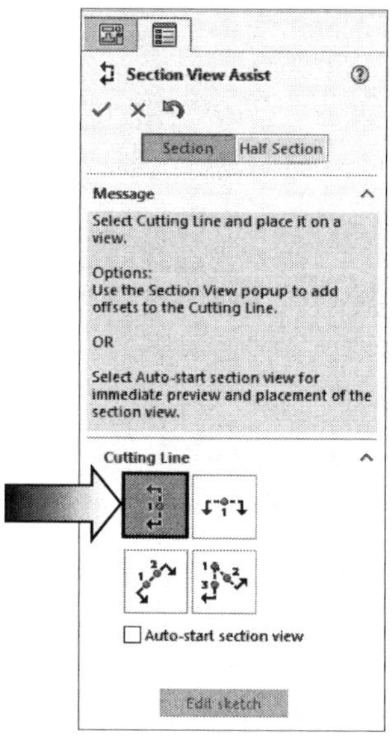

Place the Cutting Line in the center

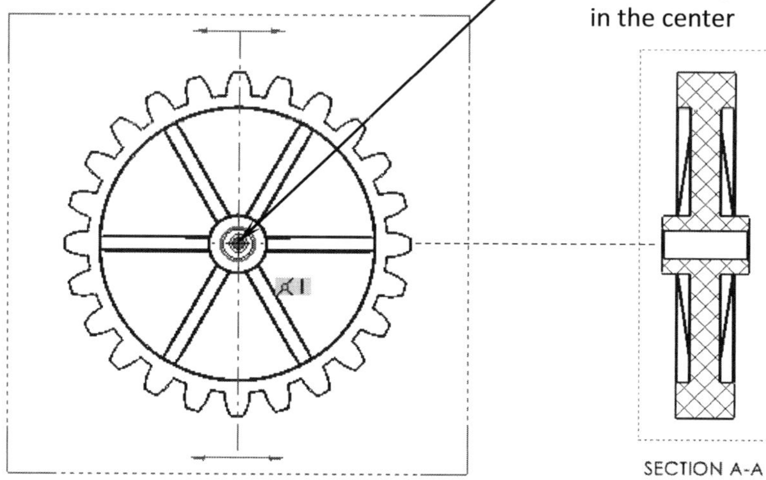

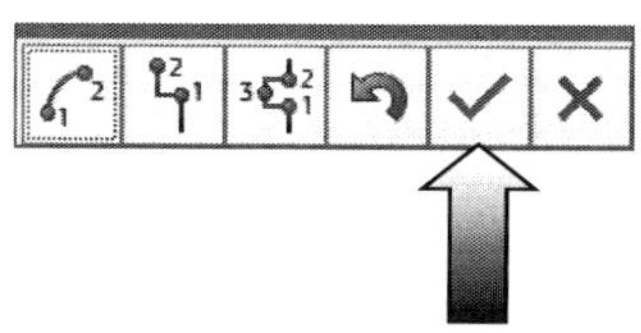

For Cutting Line, select the **Vertical** option.

Place the cutting line on the **center of the part** and click the **green check** to accept the line placement.

Place the section view on the right side of the right drawing view.

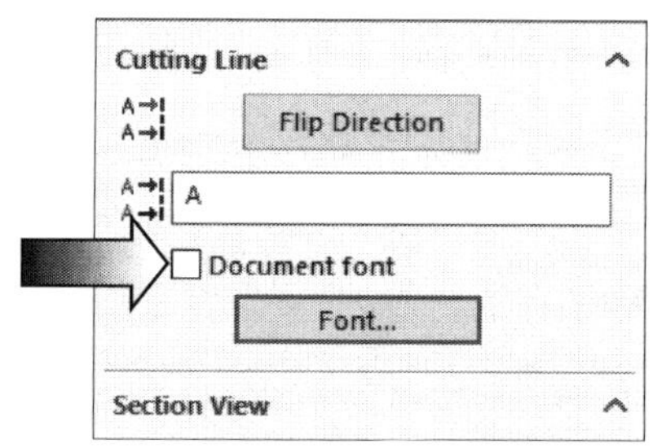

<u>Clear</u> the **Document Font** checkbox, click the **Font** button and select:

Bold, Points, 14

Click **OK**, and **OK** again to change the Font size of both, the Section view and the View Label to 14 points, Bold.

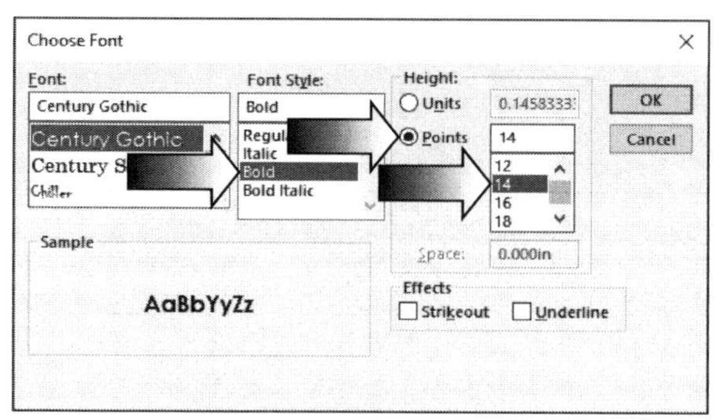

5. Changing the Hatch Pattern:

The hatch, or crosshatch, is used to display the areas that are being cut by the section tool, and the hatch pattern represents the material of the part.

Click anywhere inside the hatch area to activate the **Area Hatch/Fill** options.

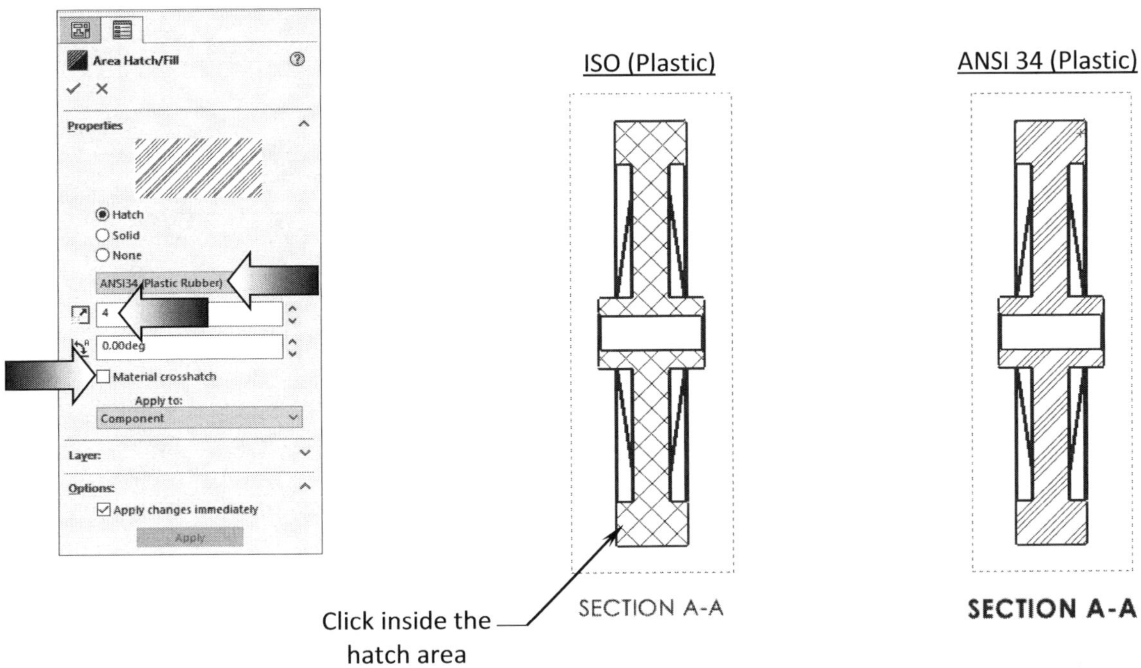

Clear the **Material Crosshatch** checkbox.

Change the Hatch Pattern to **ANSI34** (Plastic Rubber).

Increase the Hatch Scale to **4**.

In the **Options** section, enable the checkbox **Apply Changes Immediately**.

Click **OK**.

6. Creating a Detail View:

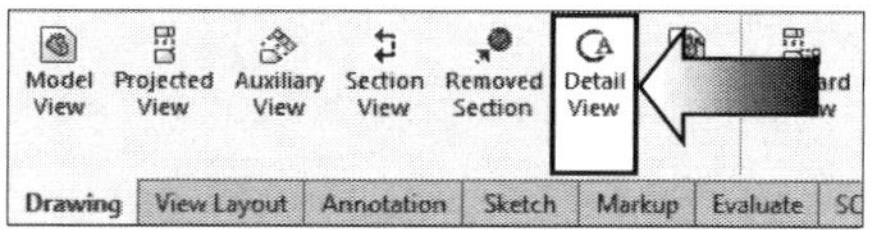

A detail view is an enlarged drawing view used to clarify specific areas of a drawing.
The scale of the detail view must be at least 2 times larger than the parent view.

Switch to the **Drawing** tab and click:
Detail View.

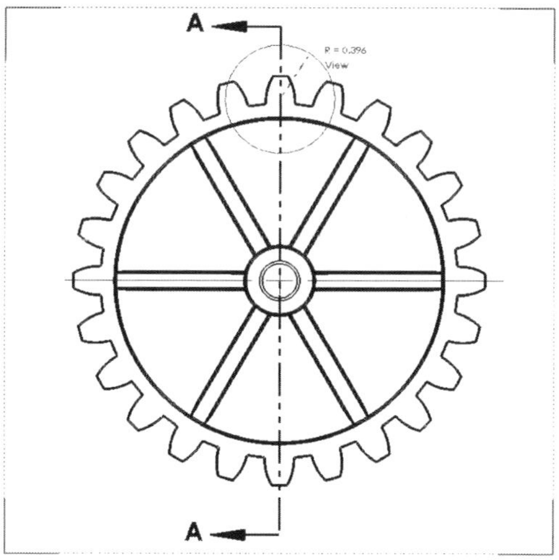

The **Circle** tool is activated automatically. Sketch a <u>circle</u> approximately as shown in the image on the right.

Place the Detail View <u>below</u> the parent view and select the following from the Feature-Manager tree:

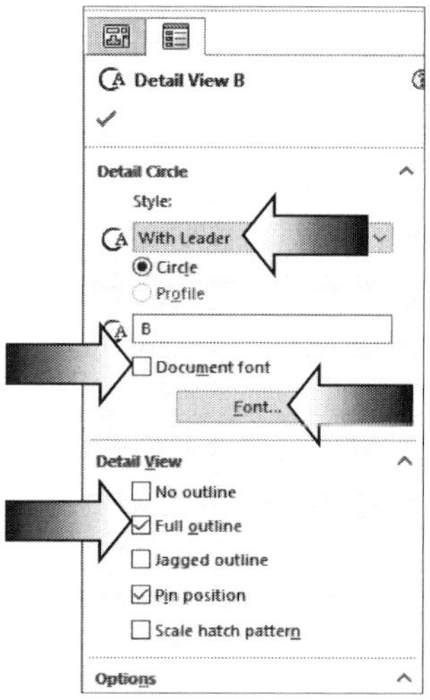

Style: **With Leader**

<u>Clear</u> the **Document Font** checkbox and select the **Font** button and:
Points, 14, Bold

Full Outline: **Enabled**

Keep all other checkboxes at their default values.

Click **OK.**

<u>NOTE</u>: Your company may choose to go with different styles such as Per Standard, Connected, Broken Circle, etc.

Select the Style that you prefer to use.

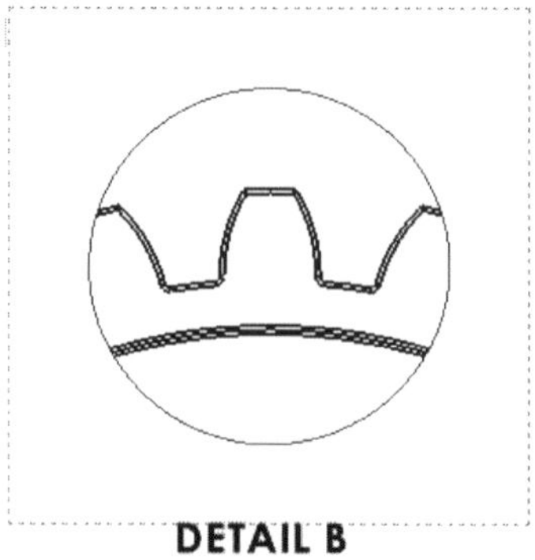

DETAIL B
SCALE 2 : 1

7. Adding centerlines automatically:

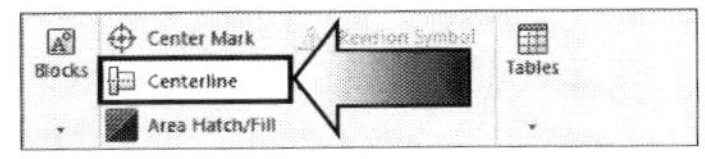

Centerlines are one of the most frequently used tools in engineering drawing. Their basic purpose is used to indicate the centers of holes, arcs, and symmetrical features.

In a SOLIDWORKS drawing, centerlines can be added either automatically or manually.

First, let us take a look at the automatic option to add the centerlines.

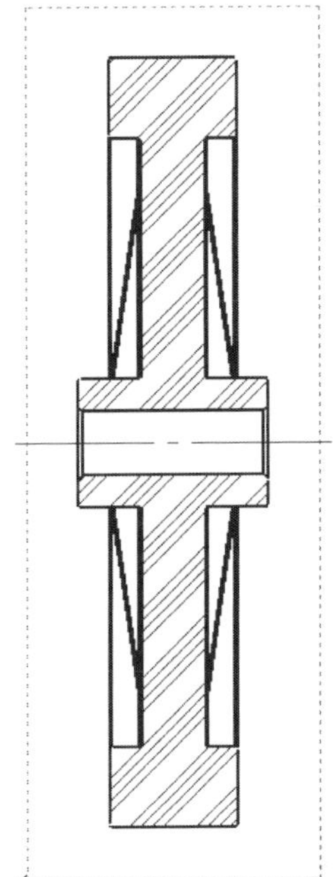

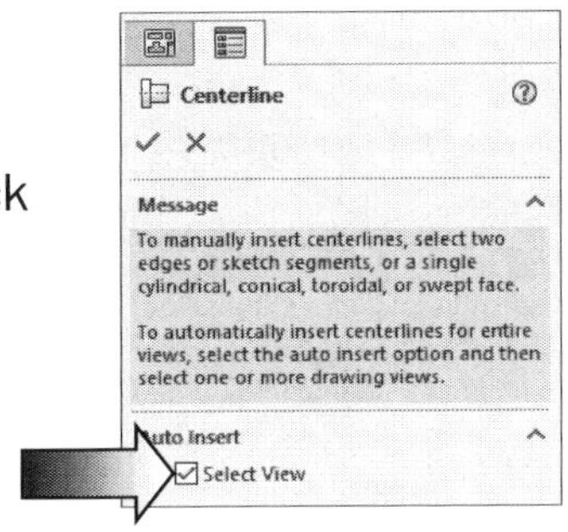

Zoom in on the Section view and click **Centerline** on the **Annotation** tab.

From the FeatureManager tree, under the Auto Insert section, enable the checkbox: **Select View.**

Click the dotted border of the Section view. A centerline is added to the center of the part.

Click **OK**.

8. Adding centerlines manually:

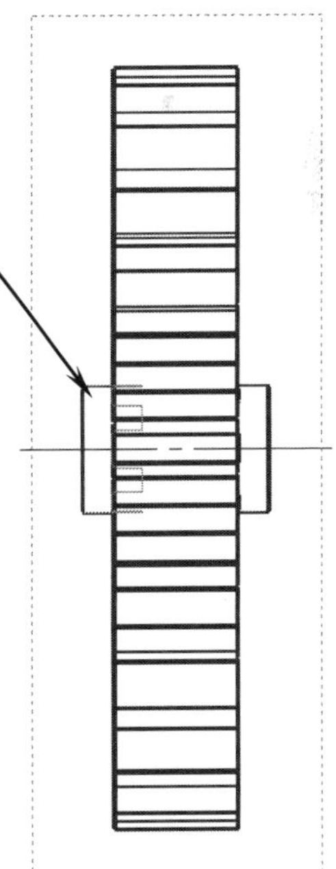

Select the **Centerline** tool again.

Next, for manual centerline, clear the **Select View** checkbox.

Click the **cylindrical face** of the boss, as indicated.

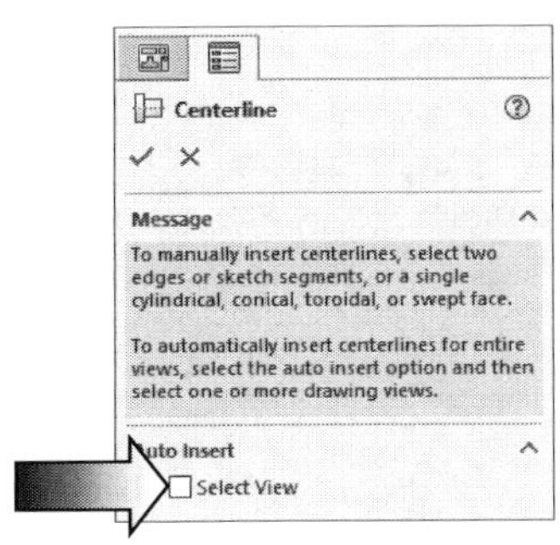

A centerline is added to the center of the selected feature.

Click **OK**.

9. Inserting the Model Dimensions:

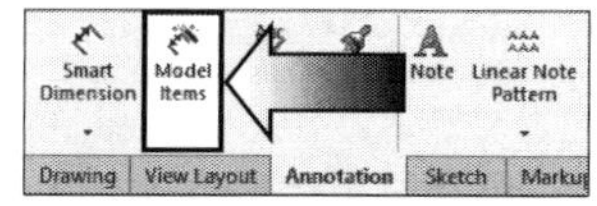

When it comes to adding dimensions to the drawing views, it is strongly recommended that the dimensions should be imported from the model so that if changes are done to the model, the drawing will be updated automatically.

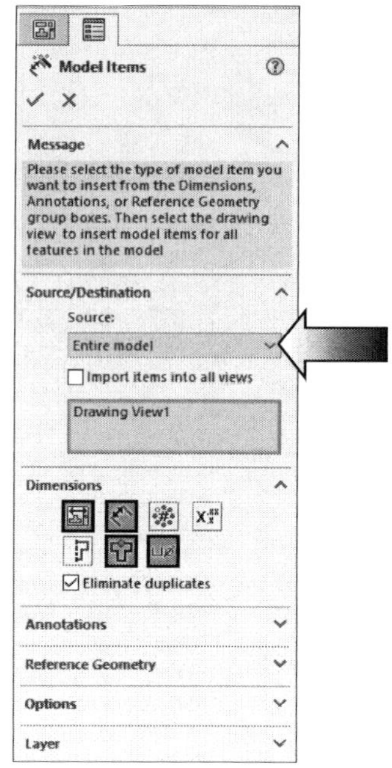

From the **Annotation** tab, click **Model Items.**

For Source/Destination, select: **Entire Model.**

For Dimensions, select:

Marked For Drawing
Not marked for Drawing
Hole Wizard Locations
Hole Callout

Click **OK.**

It looks a bit messy, but we will clean it up in the next step.

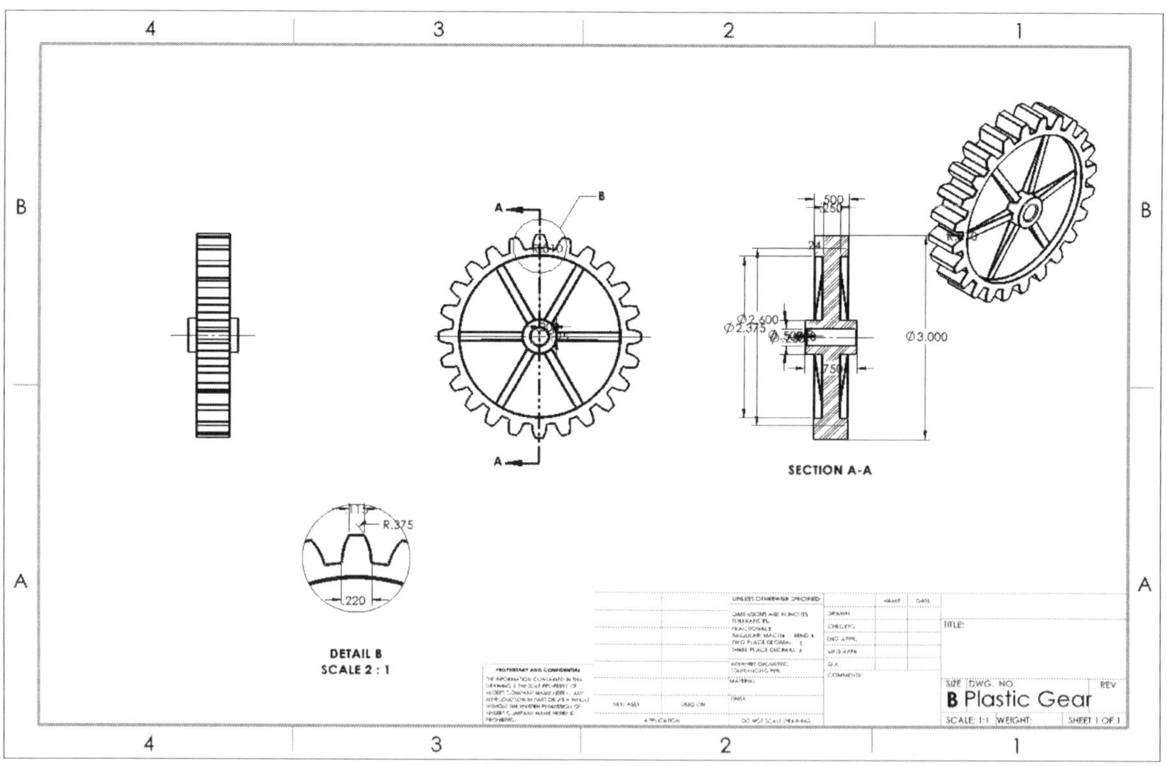

10. Moving the dimensions:

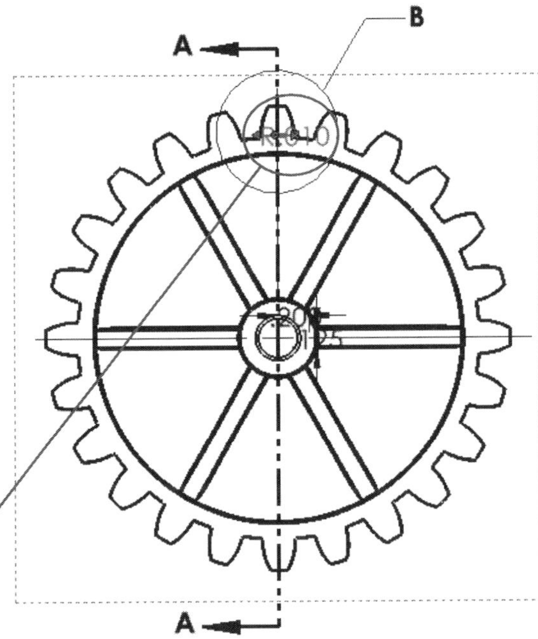

To move dimensions from one drawing view to another, simply hold the Shift key while dragging one or more dimensions and dropping inside of another view.

Zoom in closer between the **Right** view and the **Detail** view.

Hold down the **Shift** key, drag the dimension **R.010** from the Right view and drop it anywhere **inside** of the Detail view.

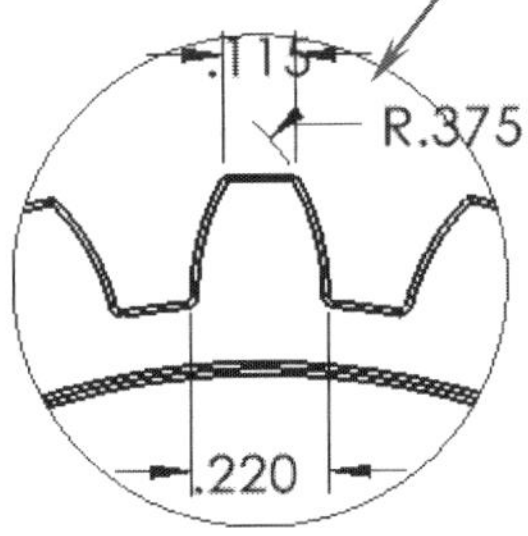

DETAIL B
SCALE 2 : 1

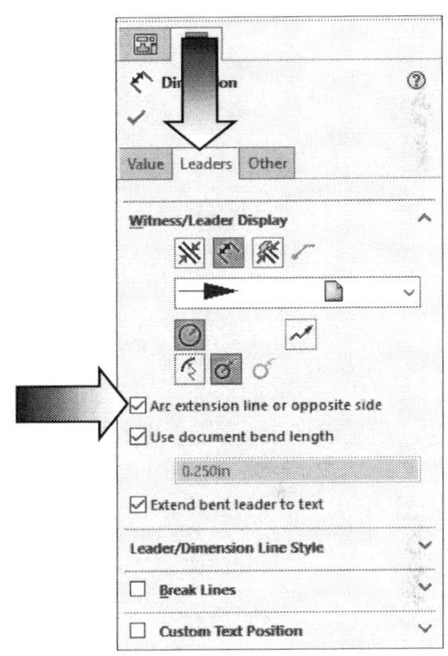

Rearrange the dimensions to look similar to the image shown at the lower right.

Select the dimension **R.010** and flip the dimension arrow by clicking on the **Circular Arrowhead Handle.**

To attach the arrowhead to a right spot, toggle on or off the checkbox: **Arc Ext. Line or Opposite Side**, under the **Leaders** tab.

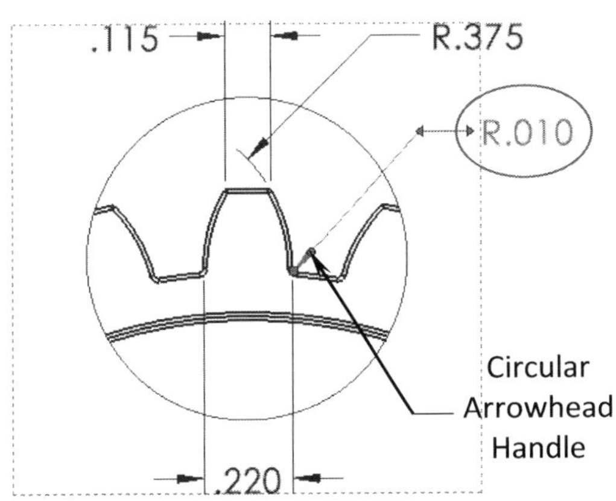

11. Moving and Hiding dimensions:

Dimensions like pattern instances, chamfer depths, symmetric or double dimensions that were used when creating the model are quite confusing in the drawing. Let us hide them.

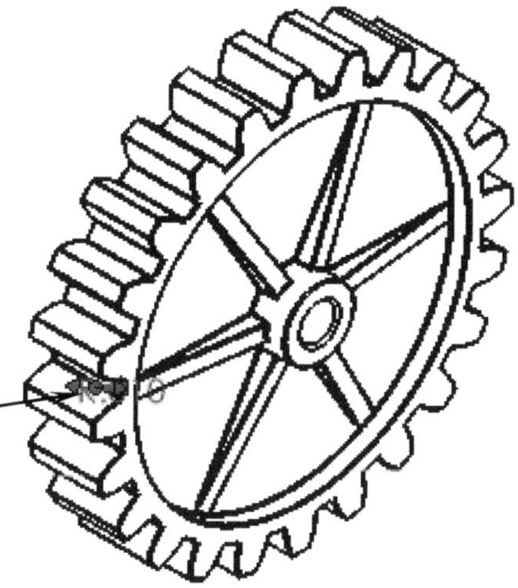

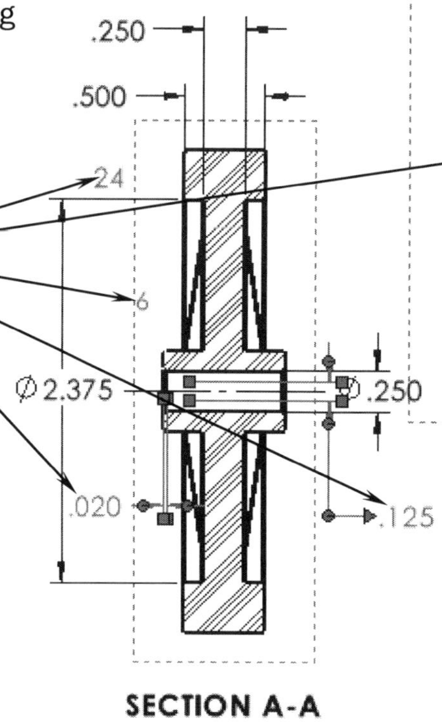

Hold the **Control** key and select the dimensions shown here.

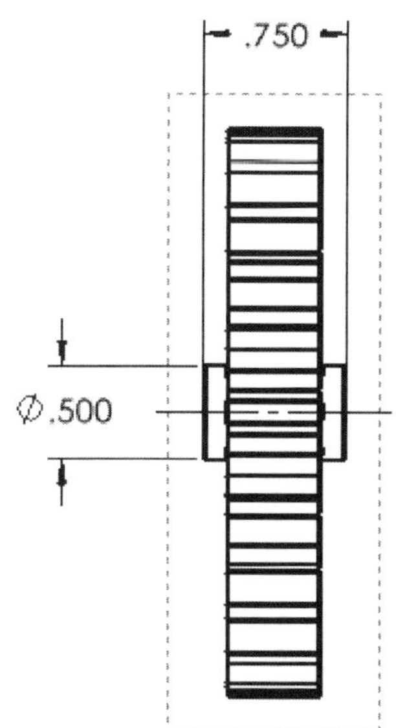

Right-click one of the highlighted dimensions and select **Hide**.

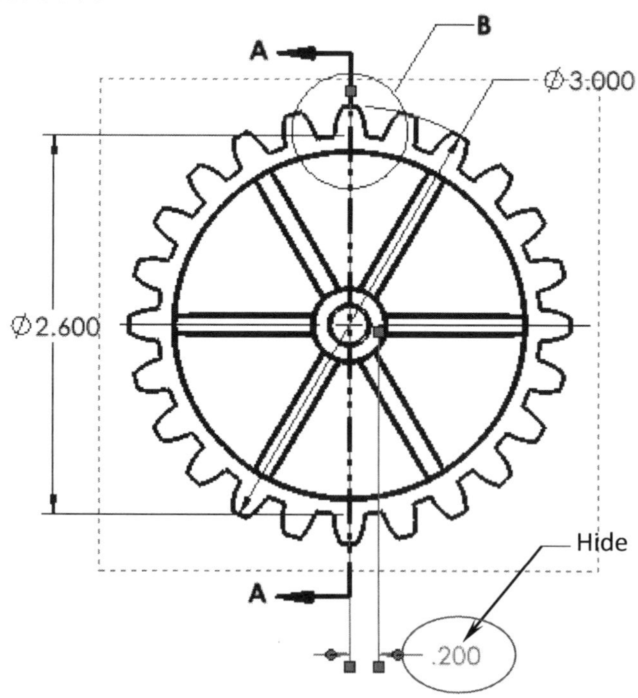

Move the other Dimensions to the drawing views as shown in each view above.

Check your drawing against the one shown below. Make any corrections as needed before going forward to the next step.

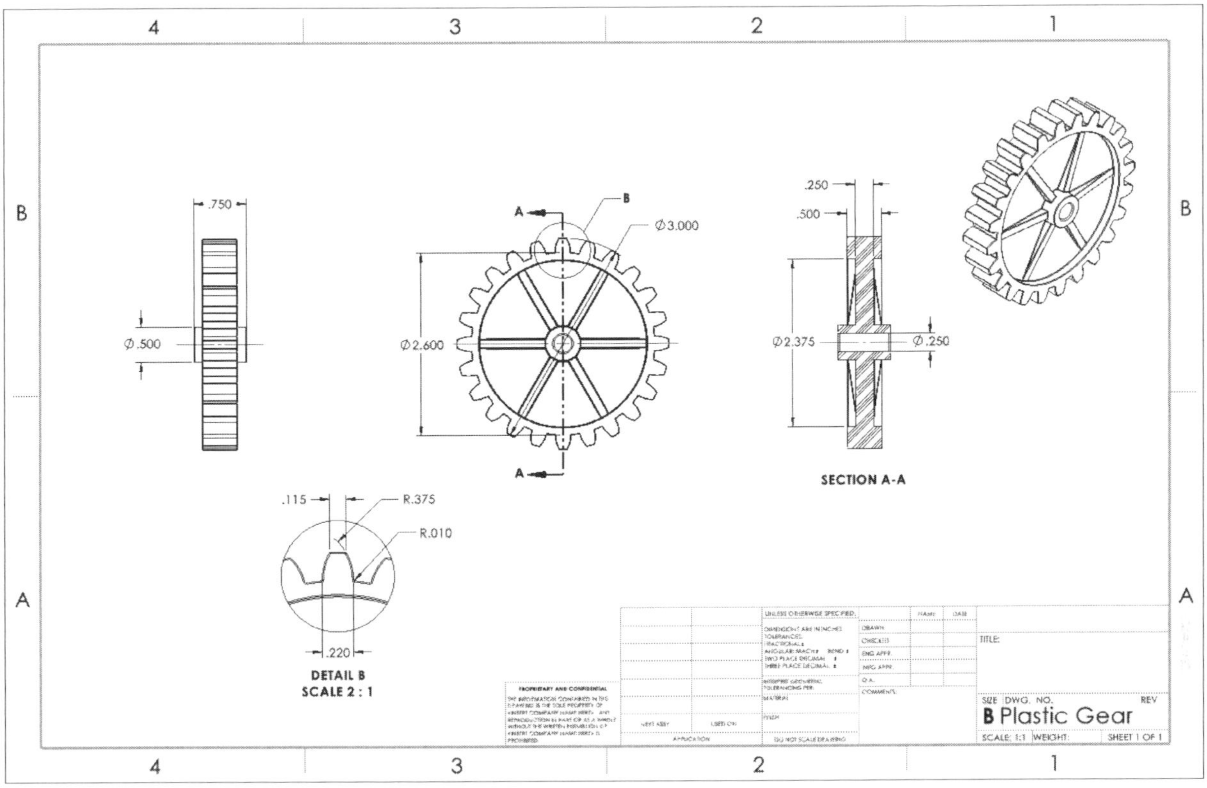

Remember to save your work every once in a while.

12. Adding the missing dimensions:

We need to add a centerline in the middle of one of the ribs so that an angular dimension can be added to locate the ribs.

Switch to the **Sketch** tab.

Expand the **Line** tool and select the **Centerline** command.

Sketch a **Centerline** from the center of the hole to the mid-point of one of the teeth.

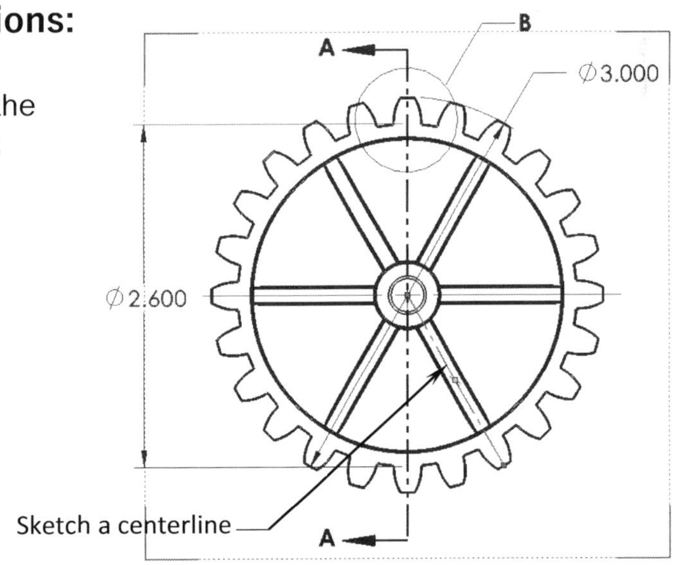

Add an **angular dimension** between the 2 centerlines as shown below.

Modify the dimension (circled) in the **Dimension Text** box, to match the text shown in the images below.

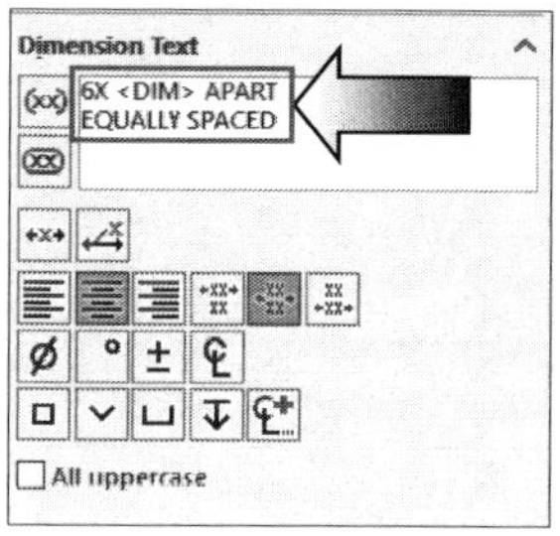

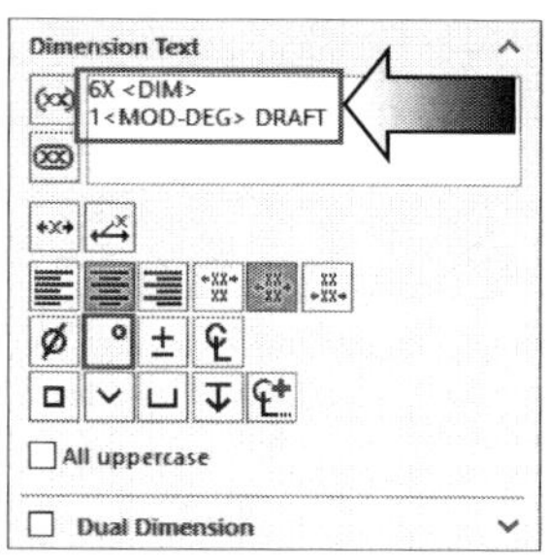

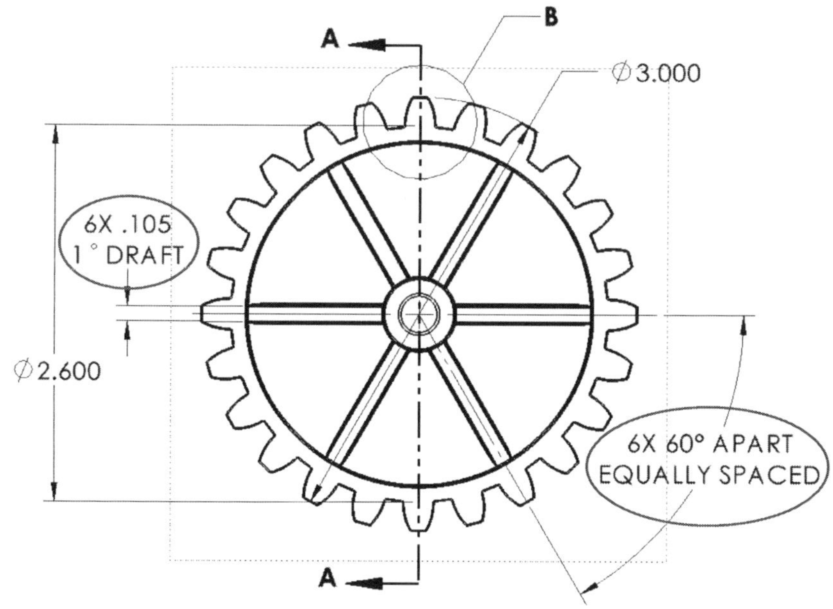

Use the **degree symbol** under the Dimension Text box when needed.

Zoom in on the **Section** view.

Add the word **THRU** after the dimension **Ø.250**.

Add the **6X** before the two **.118** dimensions.

Rearrange the dimensions to look similar to the images shown here.

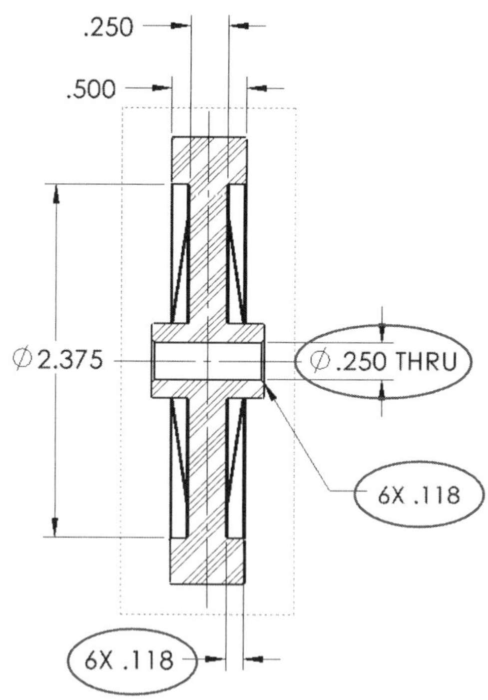

SECTION A-A

Zoom in on the **Detail** view.

Add the instance count **24X** before the two dimensions **.115** and **.220**.

Add the text **TYP** after the two dimensions **R.375** and **R.010**.

Rearrange the dimensions to look similar to the image shown here.

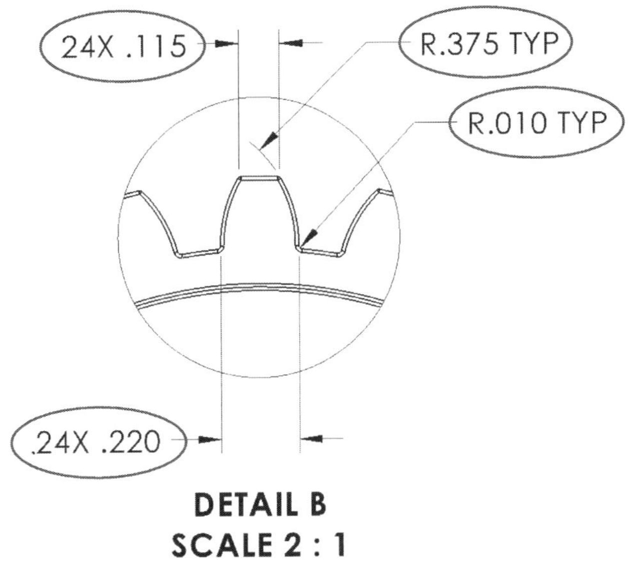

Check your drawing against the one shown below. Make any corrections as needed.

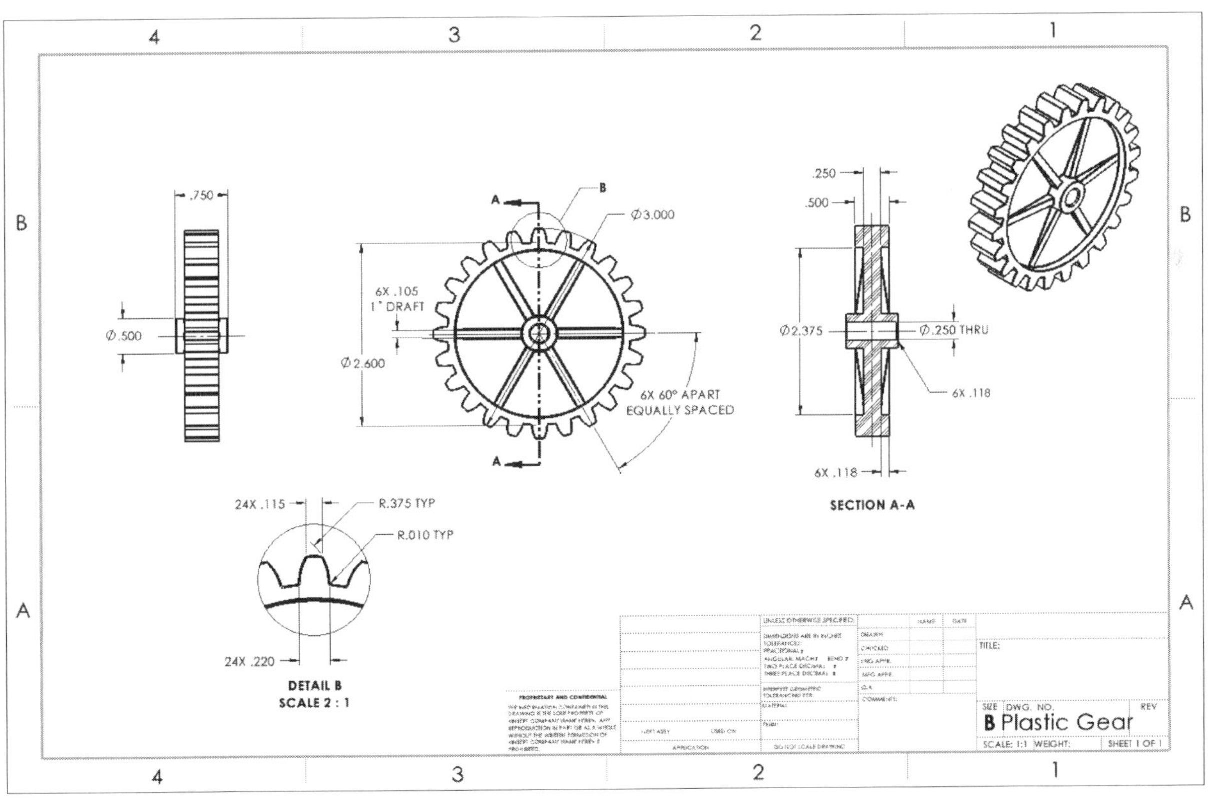

13. Adding Datums:

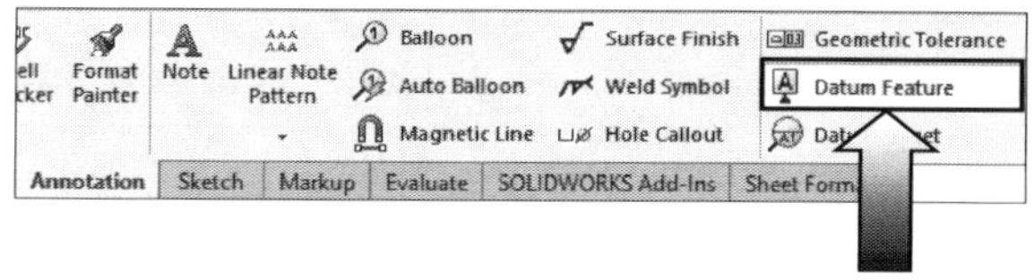

A datum is a reference point, surface, or axis on an object against which measurements are made.

Zoom in on the **Front** drawing view.

Switch to the **Annotation** tab.

Click **Datum Feature.**

Place **Datum A** on the horizontal **centerline** in the middle of the part.

Place **Datum B** on the vertical **edge,** on the right side of the part, as shown in the image.

Click **OK.**

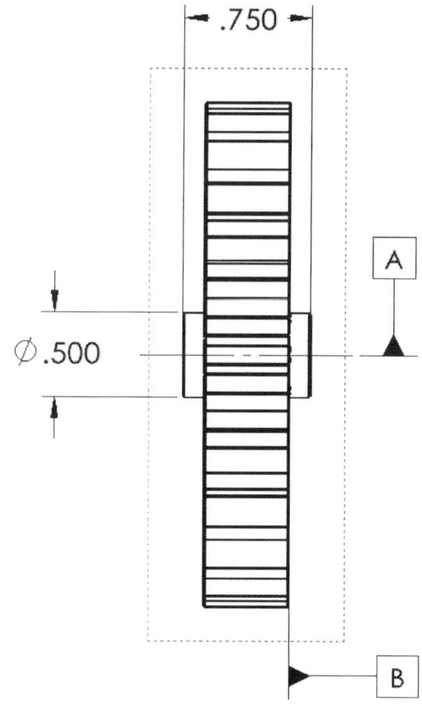

14. Adding Geometric Tolerance:

Geometric Dimensioning and Tolerancing (GD&T) is a system of 14 symbols used for defining and communicating design intent and engineering tolerances that help engineers and manufacturers optimally control variations in manufacturing processes.

Select the <u>outer edge</u> of the **Front** drawing view and click **Geometric Tolerance** on the **Annotation** tab.

Select the **Perpendicular** symbol and enter **.015.**

Click **Add Datum** and enter the letter **A.**

Click **Done** and **OK.**

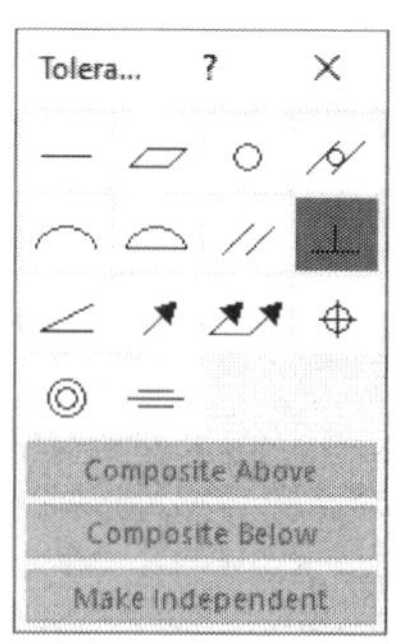

Move the control frame as shown.

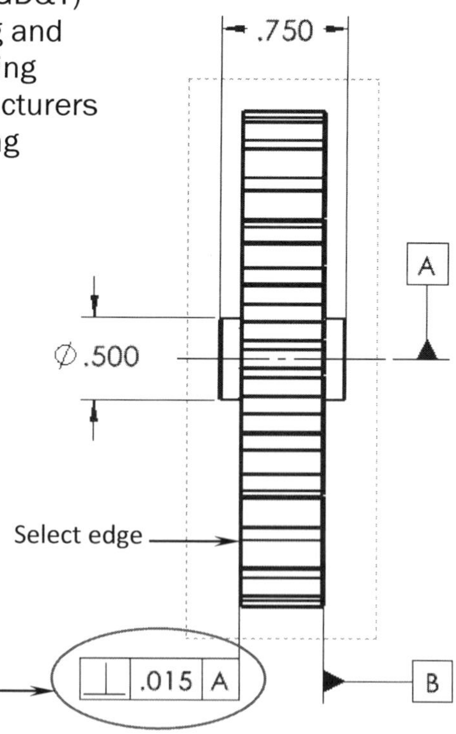

Zoom in on the **Section** view.

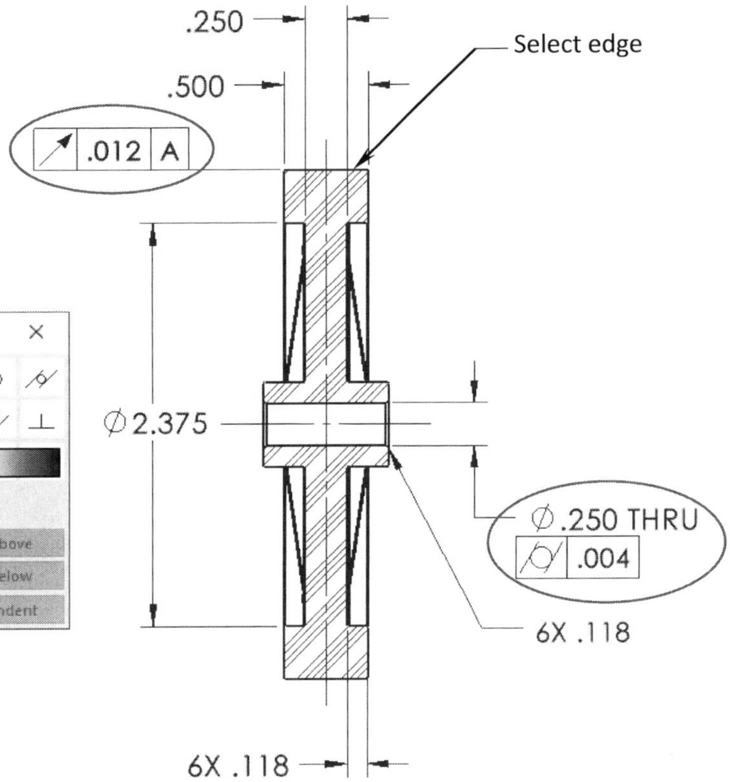

SECTION A-A

Select the upper edge of the section view and click **Geometric Tolerance**.

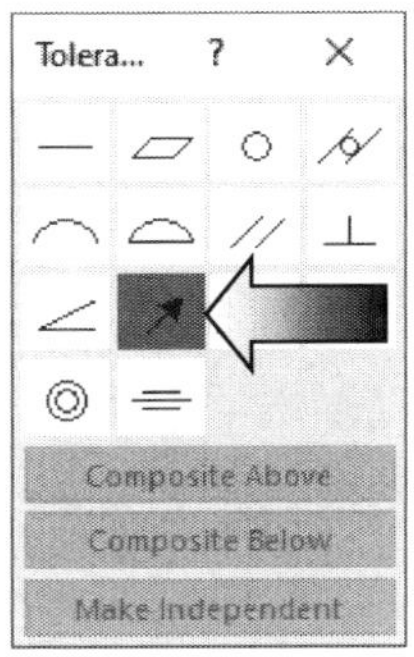

Select the **Runout** symbol and enter **.012**.

Click **Add Datum** and enter **A.**

Click **Done** and **OK.**

Select the dimension **Ø.250 THRU** and click **Geometric Tolerance** again.

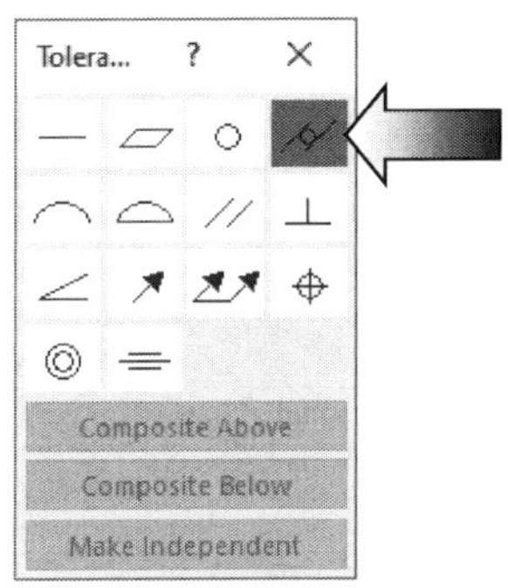

For Symbol, select the **Cylindricity** button.

For Tolerance, enter **.004**.

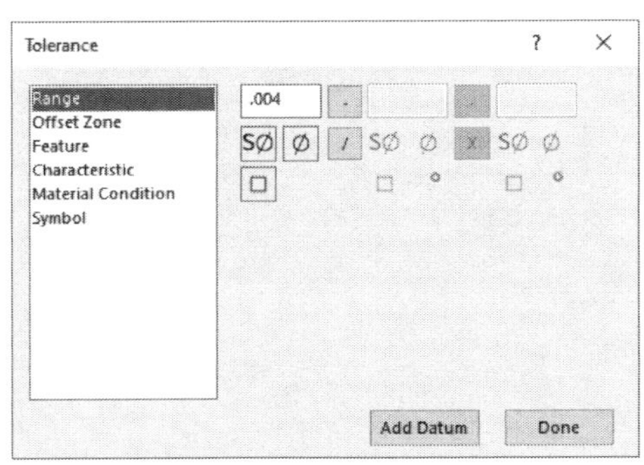

Click **Done** and **OK.**

The next step is to add the General Notes.

15. Adding the General Notes:

To save time, copy and paste the General Notes from the previous drawing and modify the text to match the notes below.

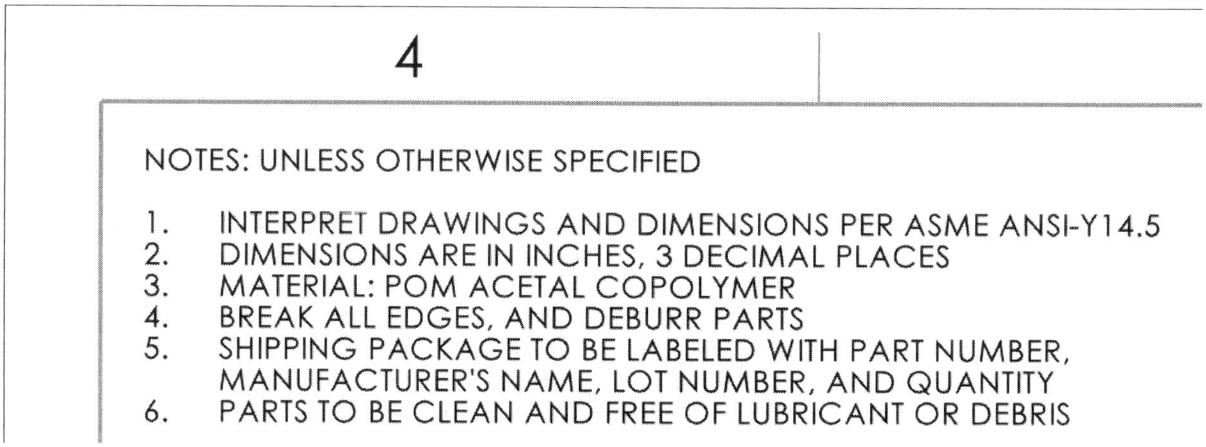

To prevent the General Notes from shifting around, it should be locked in place.

Select the General Notes and click **Lock Note** from the FeatureManager tree.

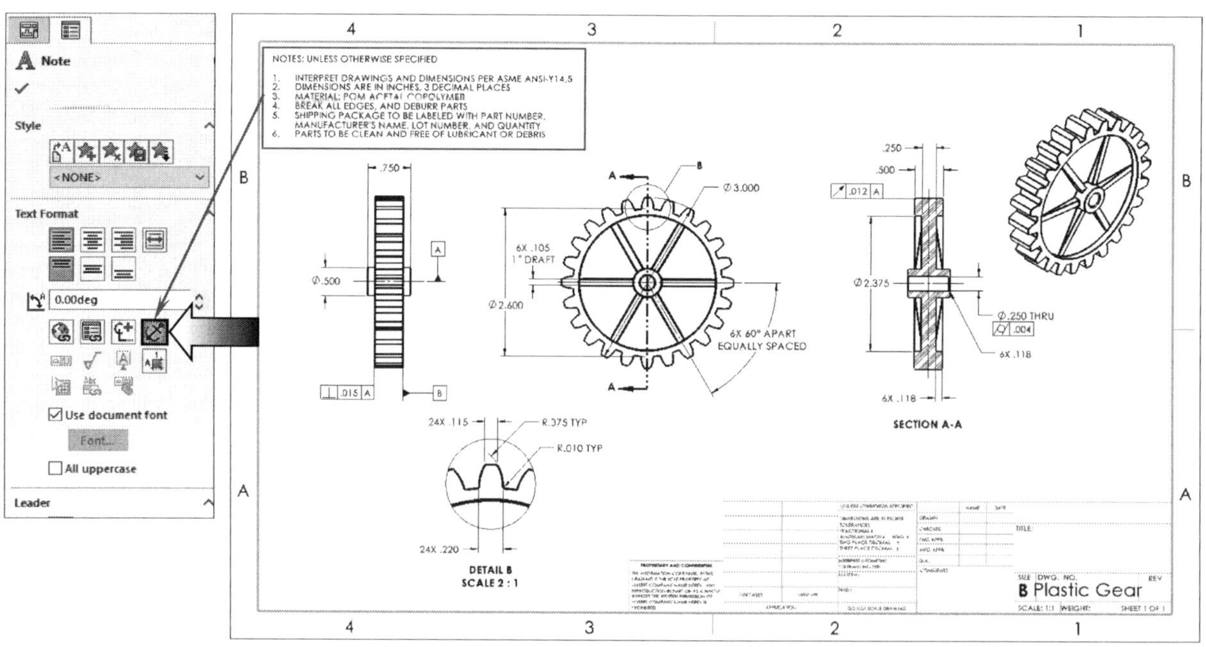

16. Adding the Revision Block:

As each revision is made to the drawing, an entry is placed in the revision block. This entry will provide the revision number, a description of the revision, the date of the revision, and the approval of the revision.

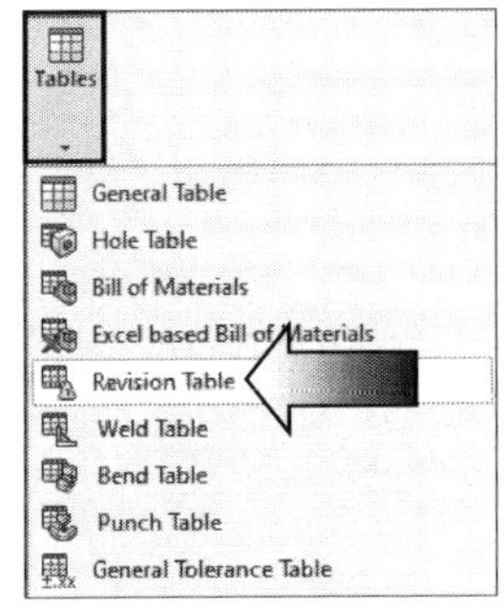

From the **Annotation** tab, expand the **Tables** drop-down list and select **Revision Table.**

For Table Template, use the default template:
Standard Revision Block.

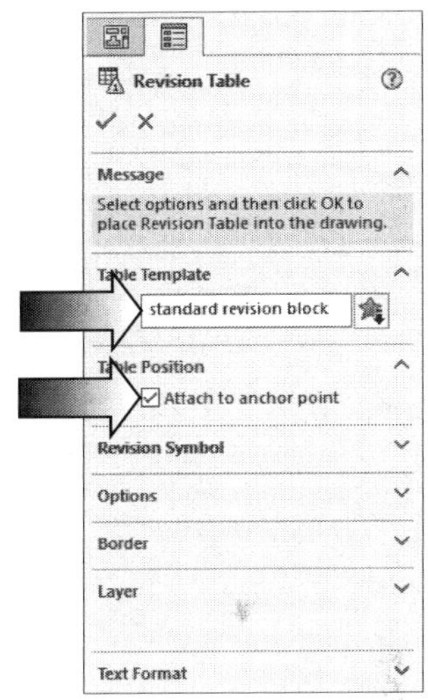

For Table Position, enable the checkbox:
Attach To Anchor Point.

Click **OK.**

Click the square at the lower left corner to add a new row.
Double-click each field and enter the information below.

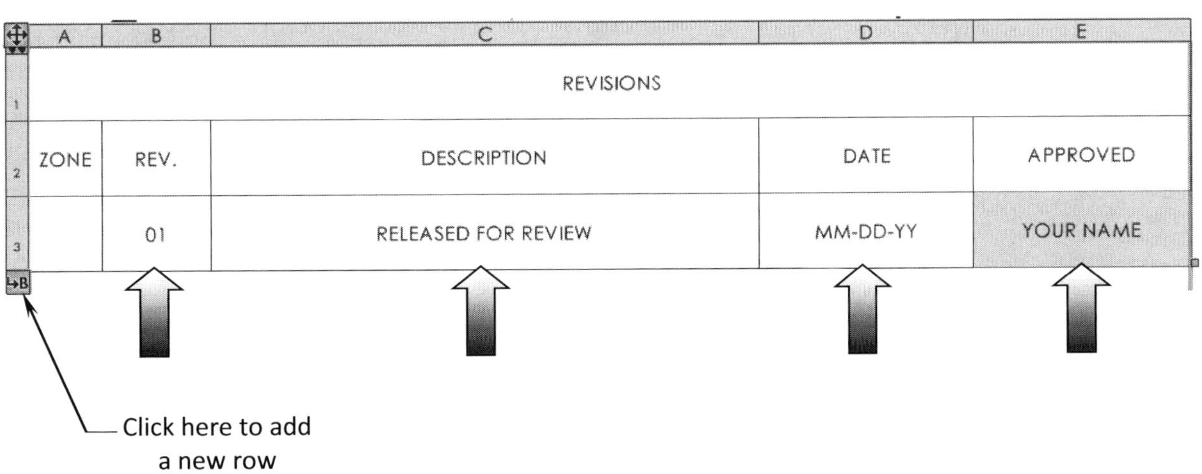

17. Filling out the Title Block:

From the FeatureManager tree, expand **Sheet1** and double-click **Sheet Format1** to activate the back layer.

There is a blank note in the middle of each field. Hover the pointer over the center until the note symbol appears . Double-click each note and fill out the information shown below.

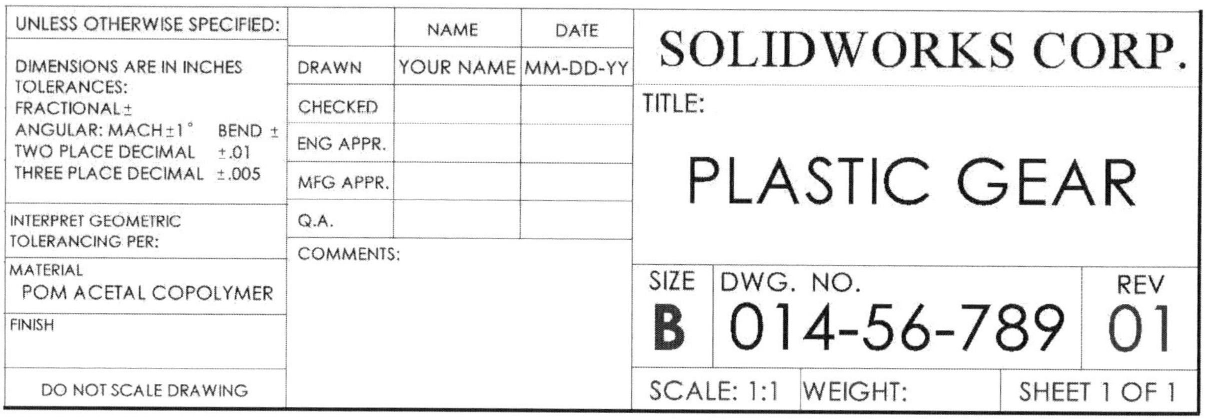

When finished, double-click **Sheet1** to deactivate the Sheet Format layer.

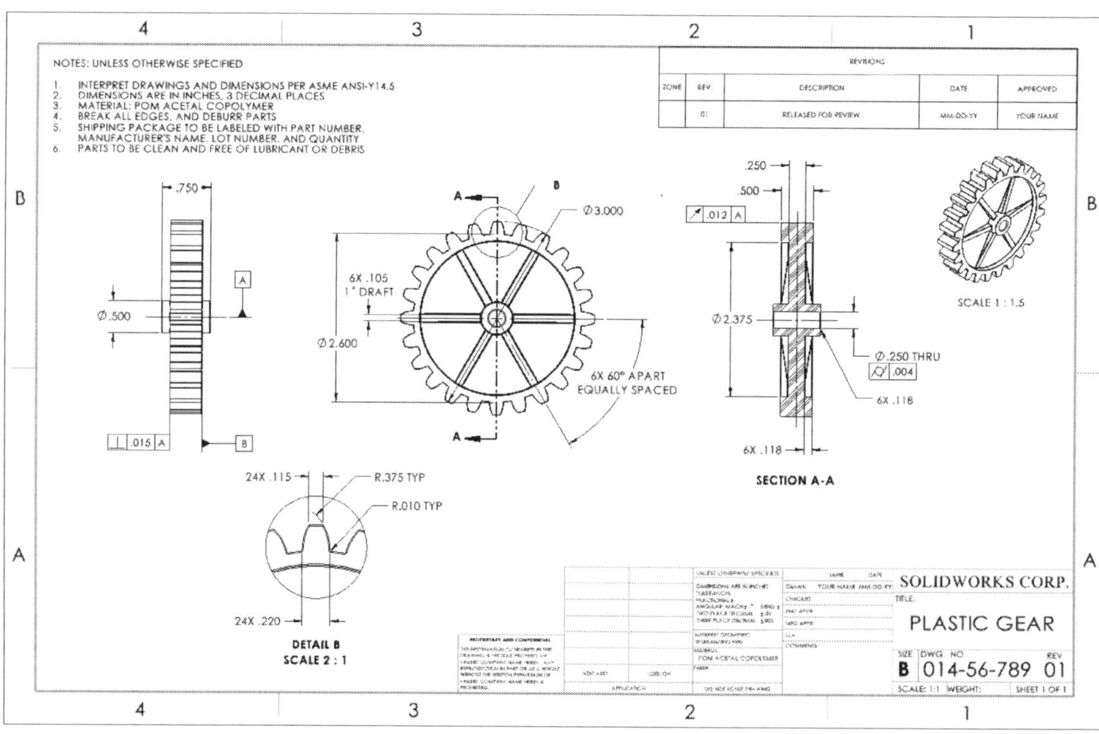

18. Saving your work:

Select **Files, Save**.

Enter **Plastic Gear.slddrw** for the file name.

Click **Save**.

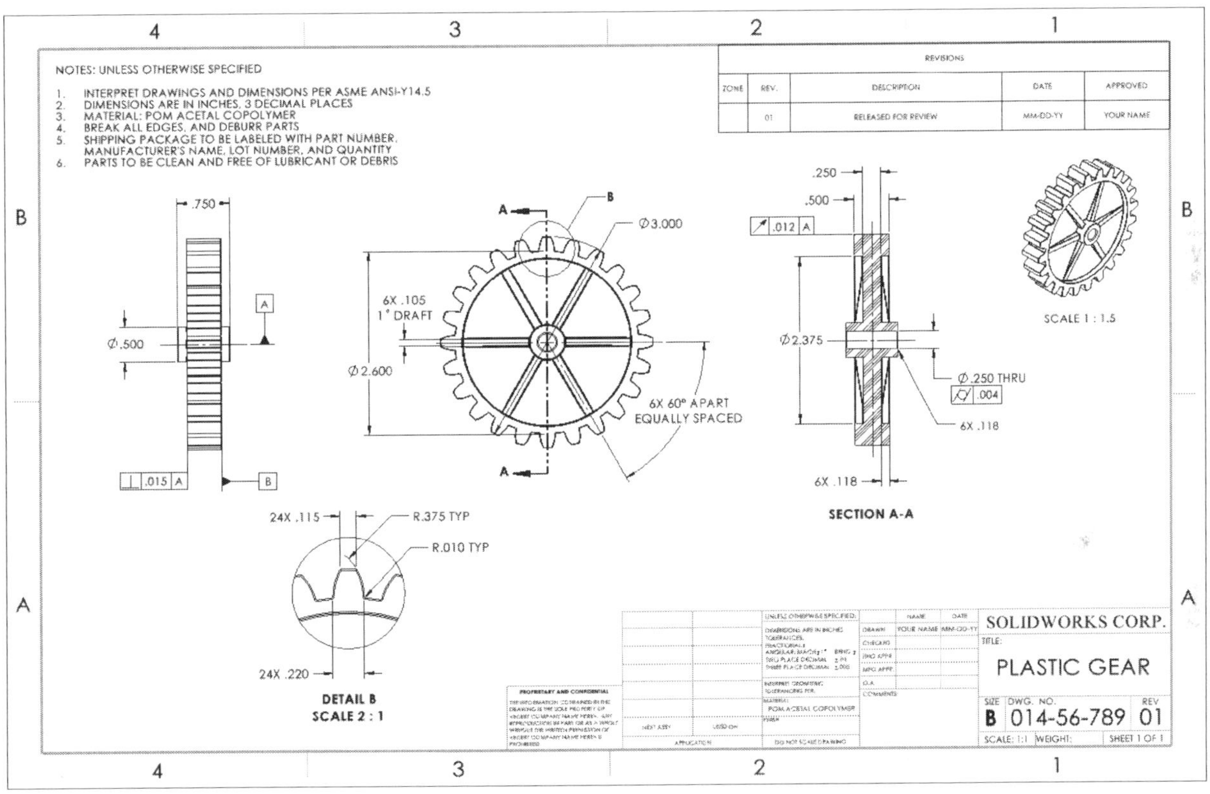

Close all documents.

Exercise: Plastic Parts

Detailing a Plastic Part 1

The exercises are designed to help you apply what you have learned from the previous lessons. They come with some instructions but not as detailed as the lessons, to give you an opportunity to explore and to try and create the drawings on your own, at your own pace.

1. Opening a part document:

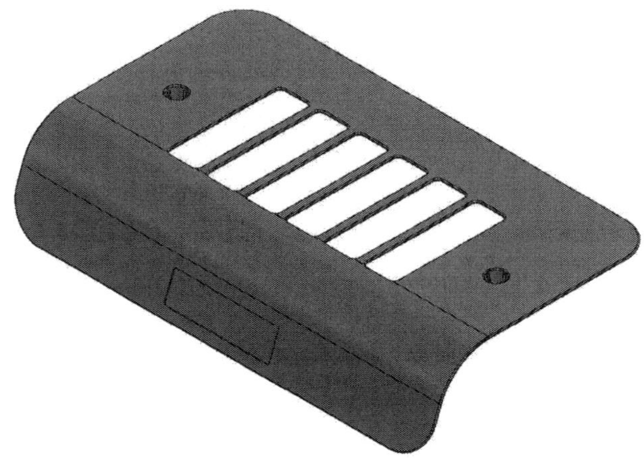

Select **File, Open**.

Browse to the Training Folder and open the part document named: **Plastic Part 2.sldprt.**

The material **ABS** has already been assigned to the part.

2. Transferring to a drawing:

Select **File, Make Drawing from Part.**

Select the **B-Size** drawing paper.

Set the Type-Of-Projection to: **3rd Angle.**

Keep all other parameters at their default.

Click **OK.**

SOLIDWORKS B-Size drawing is loaded.

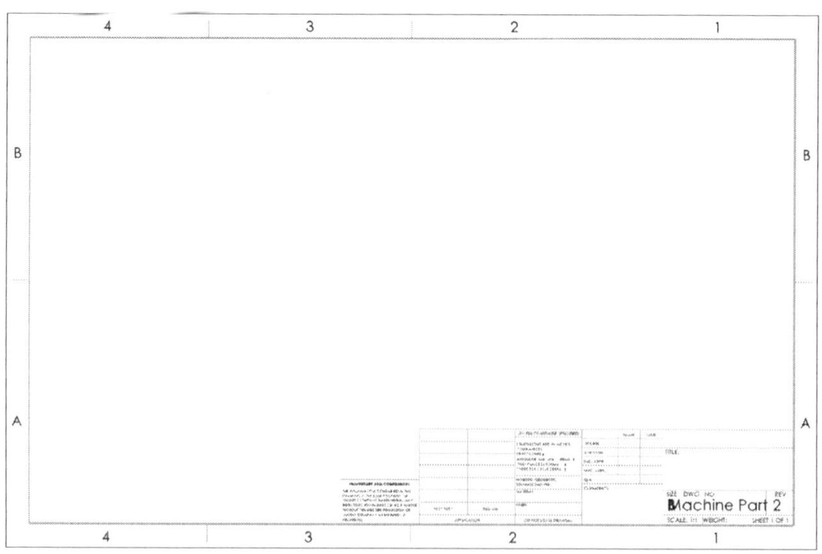

3. Creating the drawing views:

Expand the **View Palette** and enable the checkbox **Auto Start Projected View.**

Drag and drop 3 drawing views; start with the **Front**, the **Top**, and then the **Isometric** view.

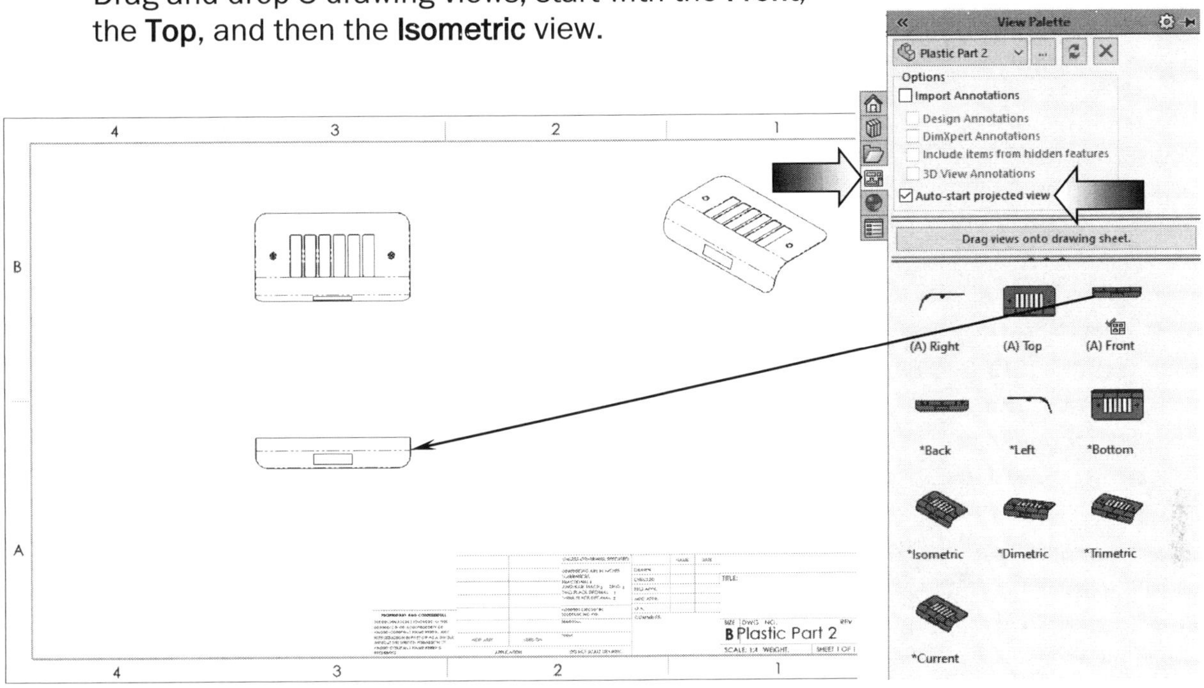

Select the **Front** drawing view and change the **Scale** to **1:3**.

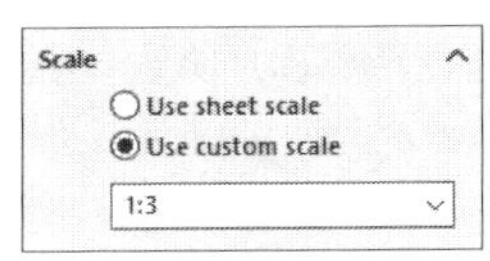

All 3 drawing views should be updated to the new scale.

Delete the **scale labels** in each view. The scale is preset in the Title Block.

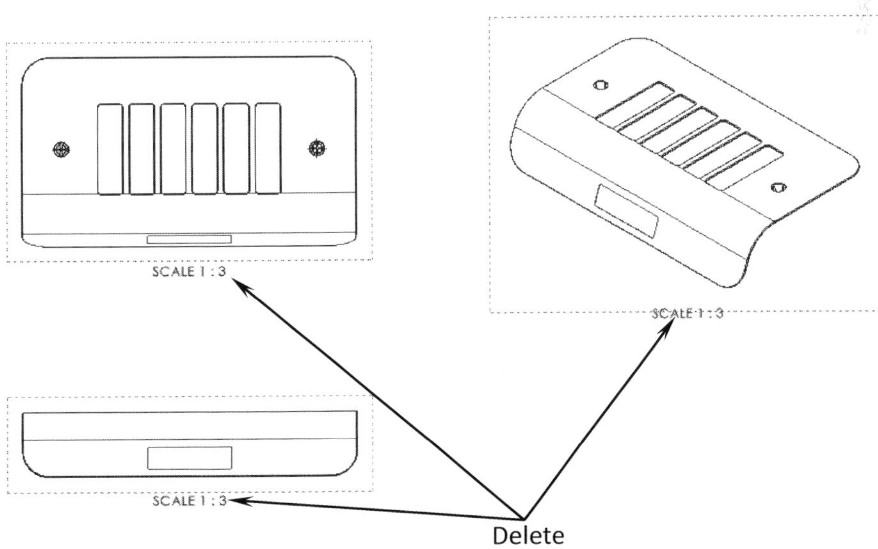

4. Making a section view:

Switch to the **Drawing** tab and click **Section View.**

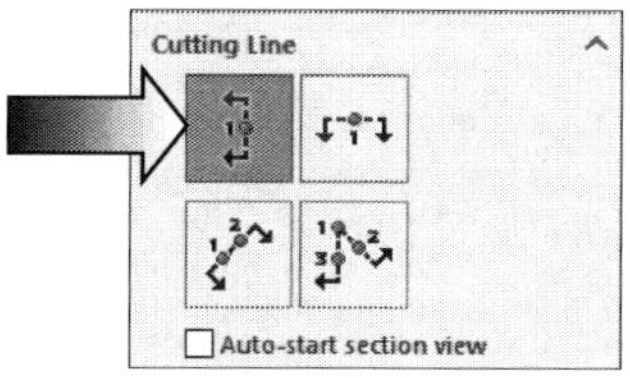

For Cutting Line, select the **Vertical** option.

Place the Cutting Line at the mid-point of the Front drawing view.

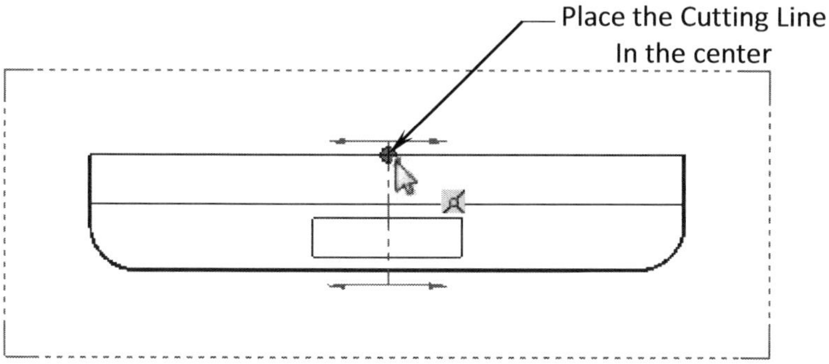

Click the green check-mark to accept the line placement.

Place the Section View on the **right side** of the Front drawing view.

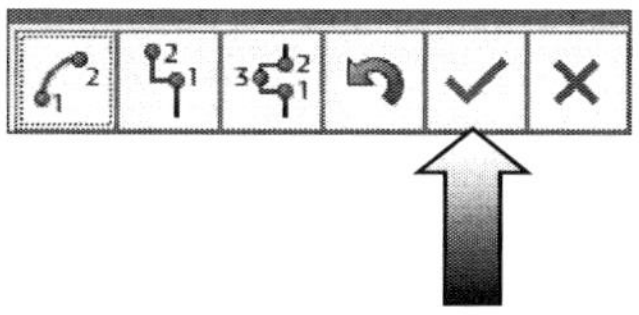

From the Feature Manager tree,
clear the Use **Document Font** checkbox and click the **Font** button.

Change the **Section Font** and the **Section View Label** to:

Bold
Points
14

The crosshatch pattern will be changed in the next step to comply with ANSI standards.

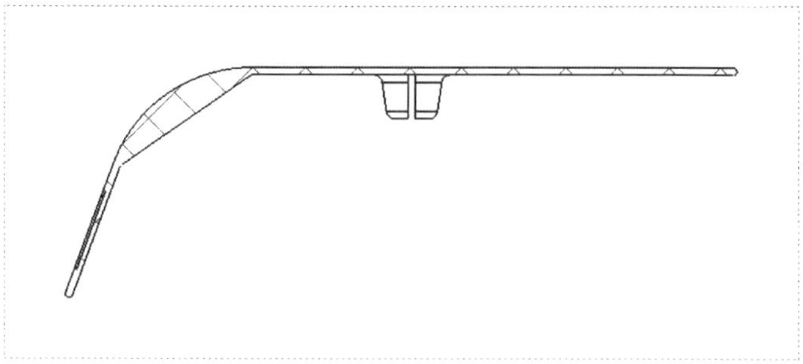

SECTION A-A
SCALE 1 : 3

5. Modifying the hatch pattern:

Zoom in closer on the Section View.

Click inside the crosshatch area to activate the **Area Hatch/Fill** options.

Clear the **Material Crosshatch** checkbox and select the options shown below:

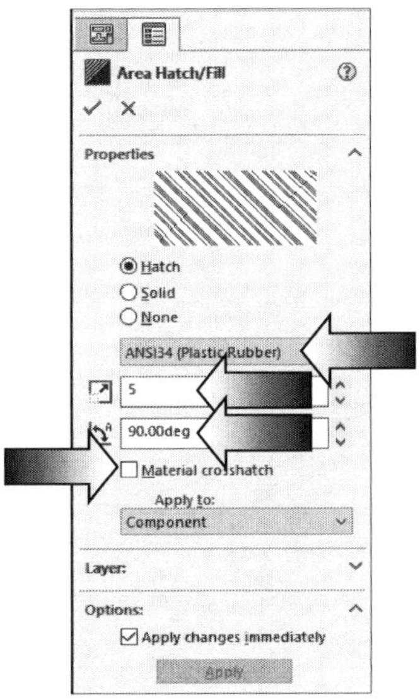

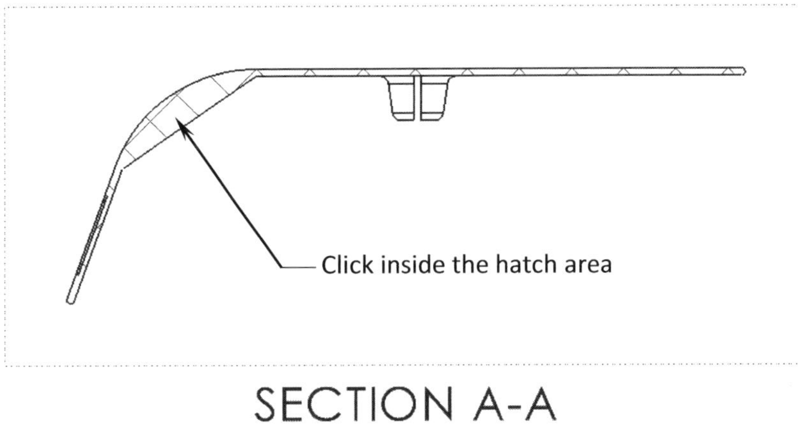

Pattern: **ANSI34 (Plastic/Rubber)**

Scale: **5**

Angle: **90**

Apply to: **Component**

Apply Changes Immediately: **Enabled**

Click **OK**.

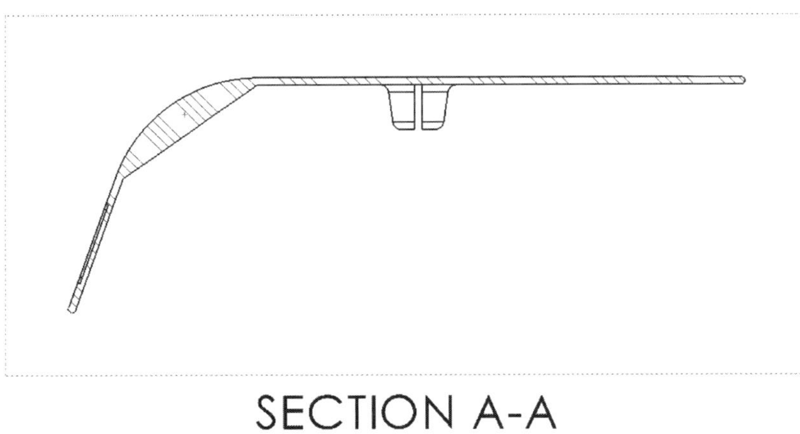

The crosshatch pattern is more visible now than before.

6. Adding the Detail Views:

Create **2 Detail Views B** and **C** as shown.

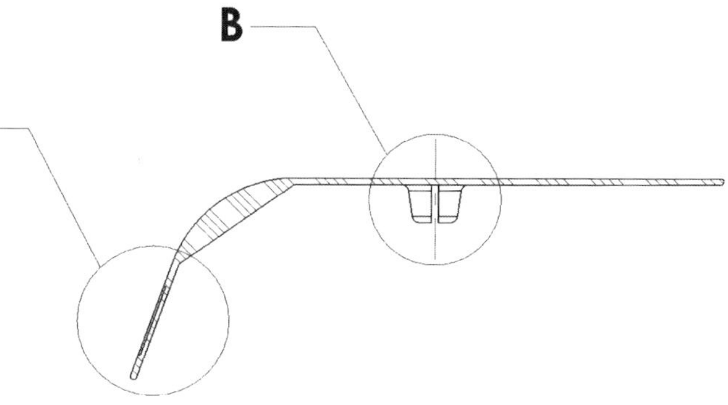

Change the scales of the 2 detail views to **1:1**.

Move the 2 detail views to above the section view.

SECTION A-A
SCALE 1 : 3

Add a **centerline** to the center of the circular boss (inside Detail B).

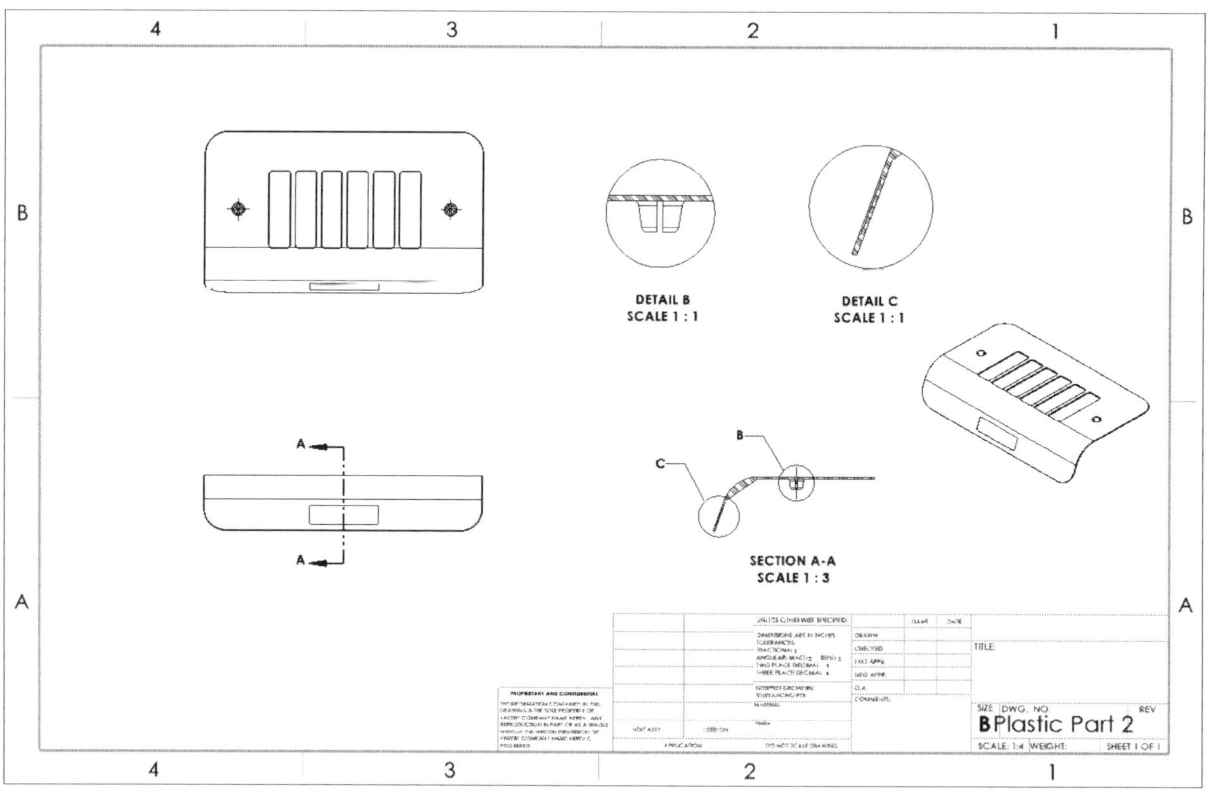

7. Creating a Crop View:

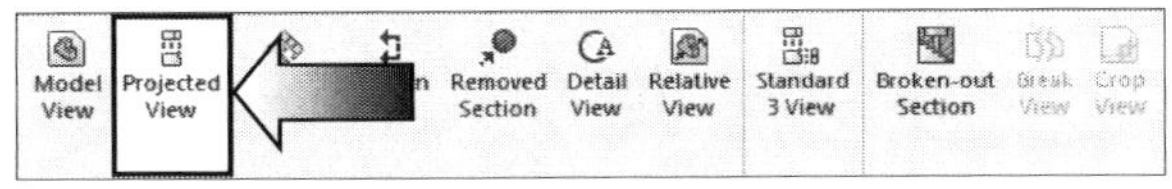

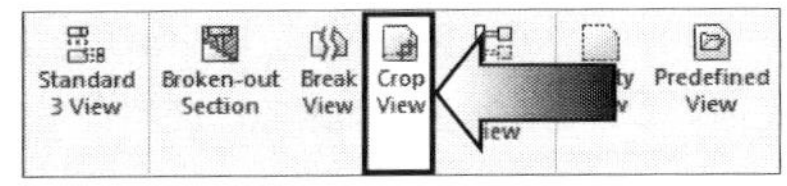

There are 3 ribs on the bottom of the part that need to be detailed.

We do not have enough room in the drawing to add a Bottom View, and instead of changing to a larger sheet size, there is an alternative option that we should take a look at.
It is called **Crop View**.

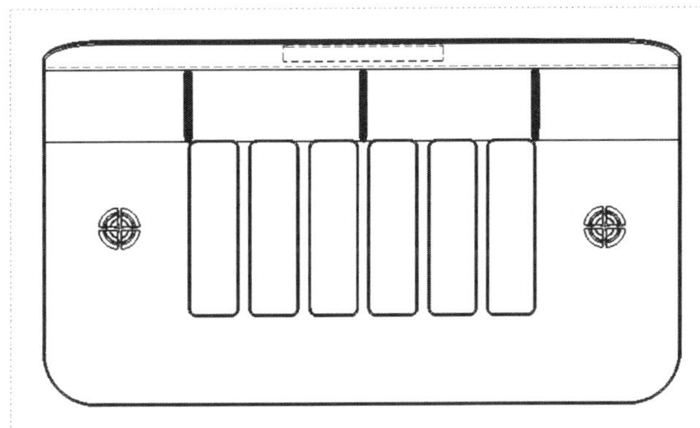

A crop view focuses on a portion of a drawing view by hiding all but a defined area. The uncropped portion is enclosed using a sketch, usually a circle, a spline or other closed contour.

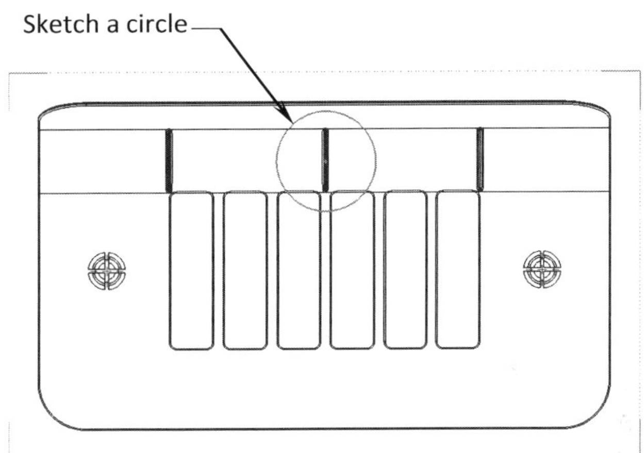

Select the **Front** drawing view and click **Projected View**.

Move the mouse pointer below the Front drawing view and click when the Bottom View appears. Click **OK**.

Switch to the **Sketch** tab and select the **Circle** tool.

Sketch a **Circle** around the rib in the middle as shown here.

Click **Crop View**.

The inner portion of the bottom view is kept and the outer portion is removed.

Enable the **Jagged Outline** checkbox as shown in the image on the right.

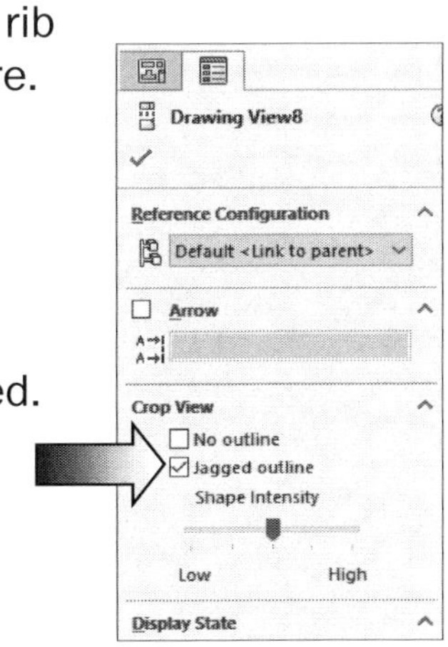

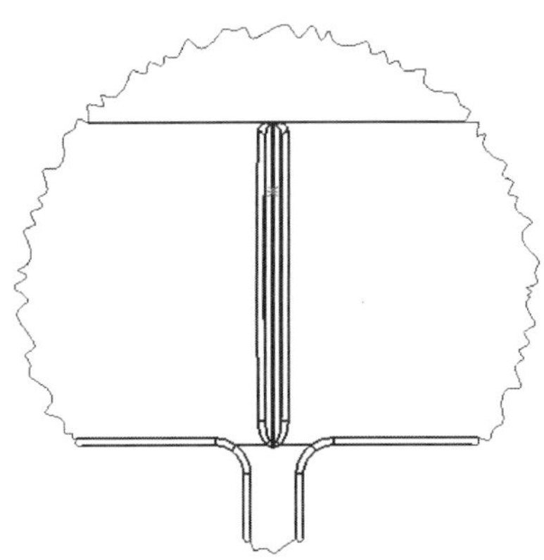

8. Breaking the view alignment:

The Crop view is aligned to the Front view by default. We need to break the alignment so that we can move the view to another spot.

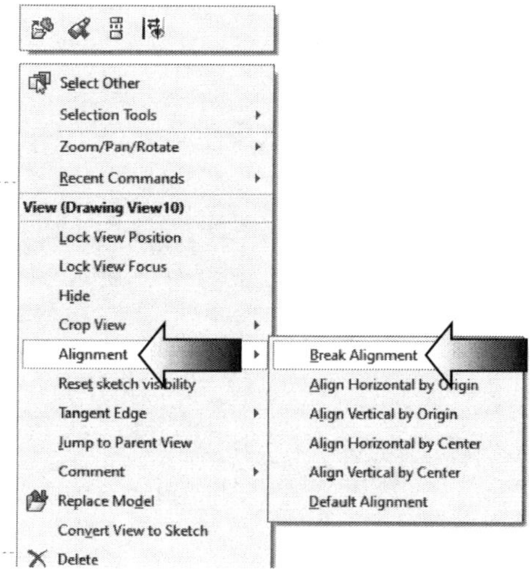

Right-click the dotted border of the **Crop** view and select: **Alignment, Break Alignment.**

Move the **Crop** view to the right side of the Section view.

9. Adding dimensions:

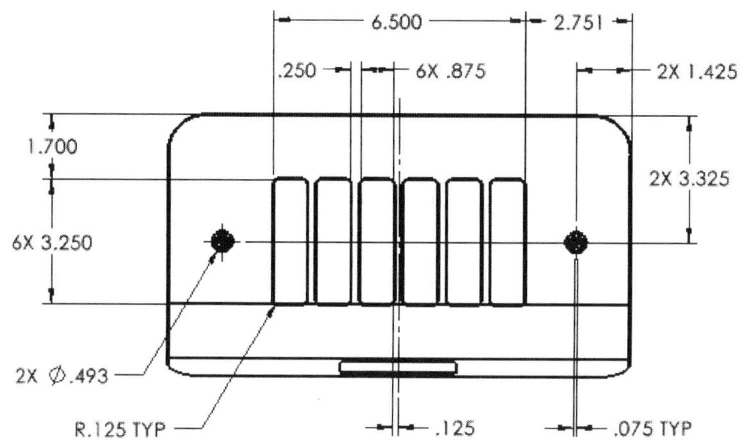

Use the following tools to add dimensions to the drawing views:

Model Items

Smart Dimensions

Start by inserting the dimensions from the model using the **Model Items** command.

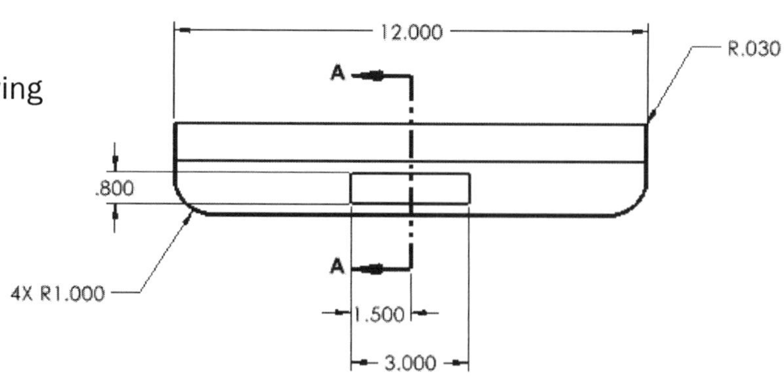

Add dimensions to the **Top** and the **Front** drawing views.

Add the **number of instances** where needed.

Continue with adding dimensions to the other drawing views.

Depending on the methods or techniques used when creating the model, some of the dimensions shown in the drawing views below will not be available when using the Model Items tool. For example: Some users would prefer to use relations or patterns to constrain the sketches rather than using dimensions.

To overcome this issue, simply add those missing dimensions using the **Smart Dimension** tool instead.

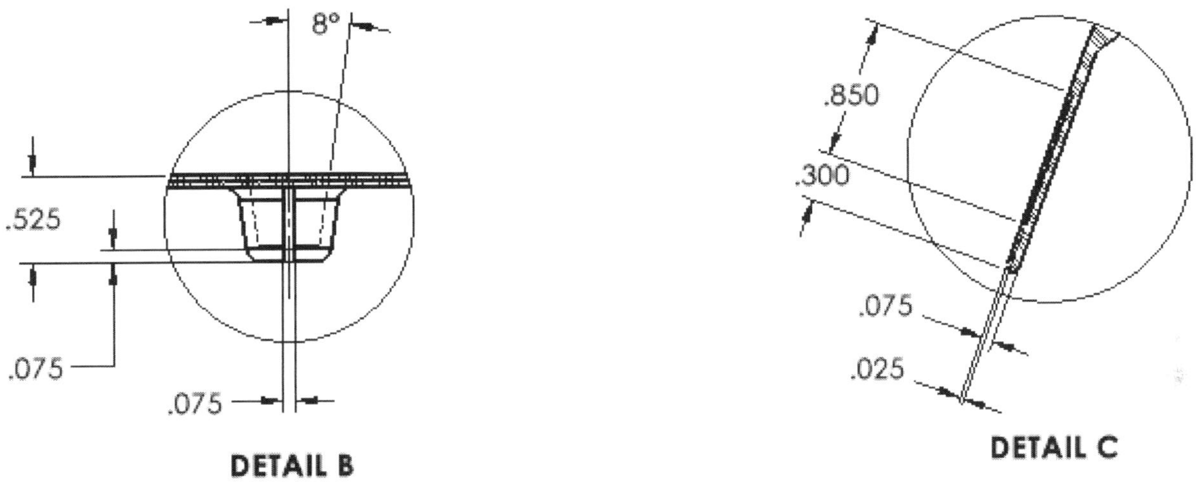

Add the number of instances where needed.

Also, modify the **Rib Thickness** dimension in the **Crop View** to include the spacing and the draft angle dimensions.

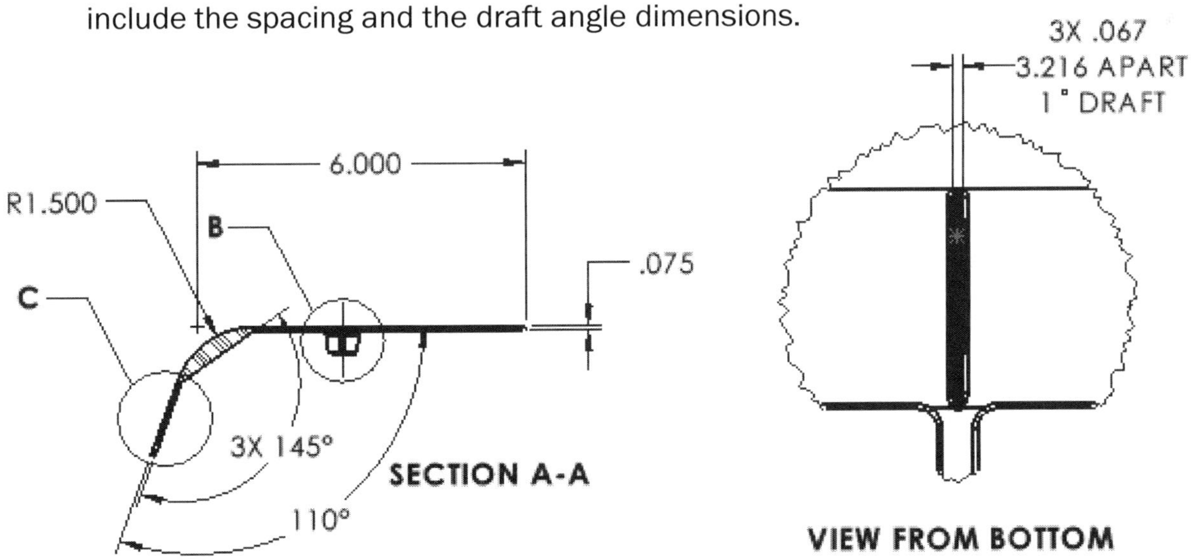

10. Adding the General Notes:

General Notes can be moved to different areas in the drawing when there is not enough space in the drawing.

Create the General Notes shown below and place it at the lower left corner of the drawing.

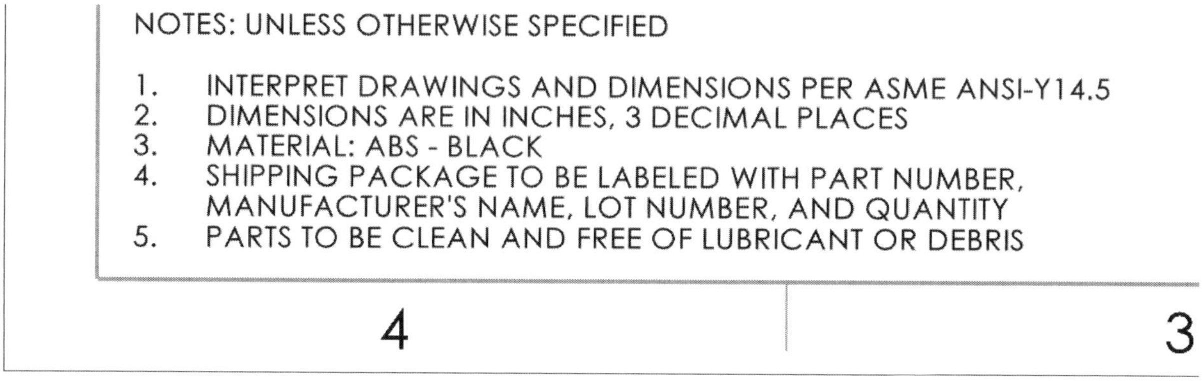

Remember to **lock** the General Notes so that it will not move.

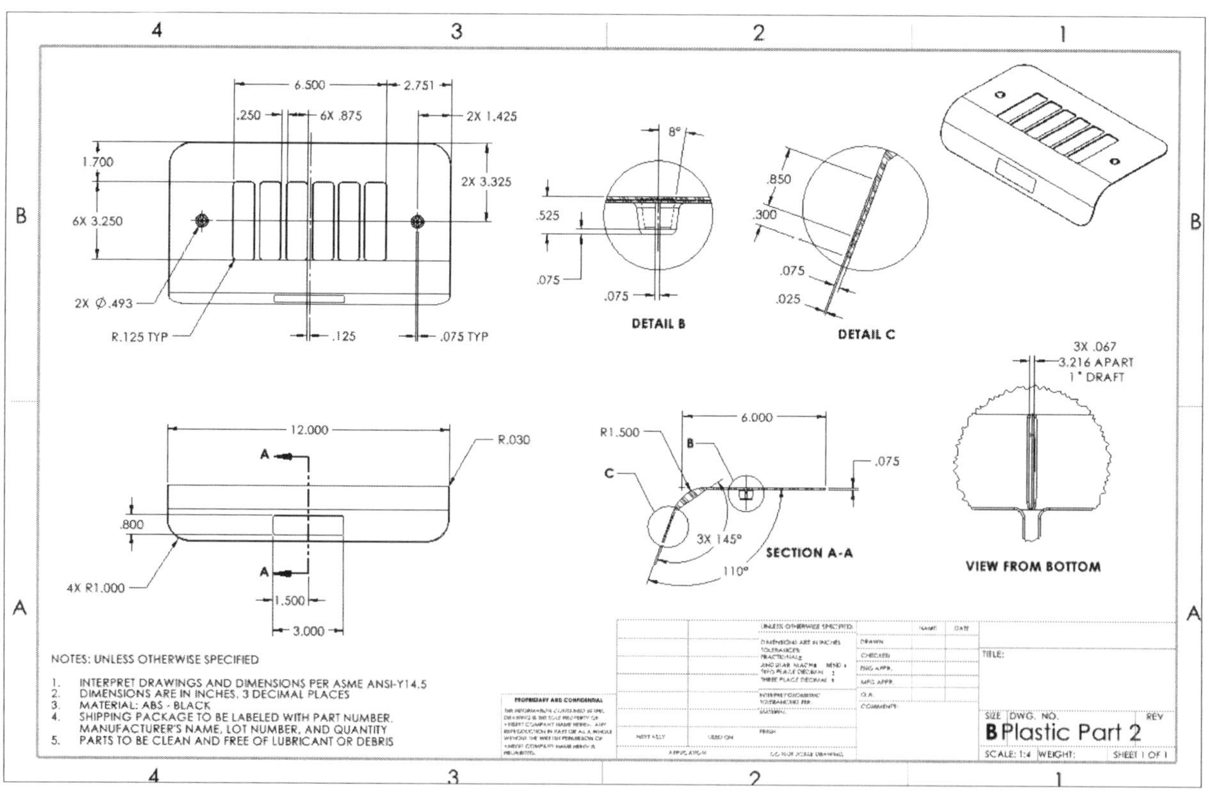

11. Filling out the Title Block information:

From the FeatureManager tree, expand **Sheet1** and double-click **Sheet Format1** to activate it.

Fill out the information shown below. Remember, you can either move the lines to increase the space where needed, or you can also change the font size so that your text can fit more properly.

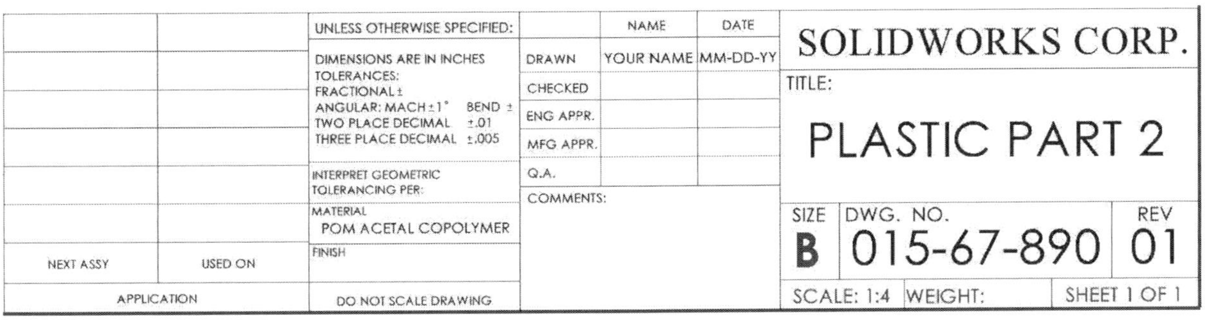

When you are done with filling out the Title Block, double-click **Sheet1** to bring the drawing layer back to the front.

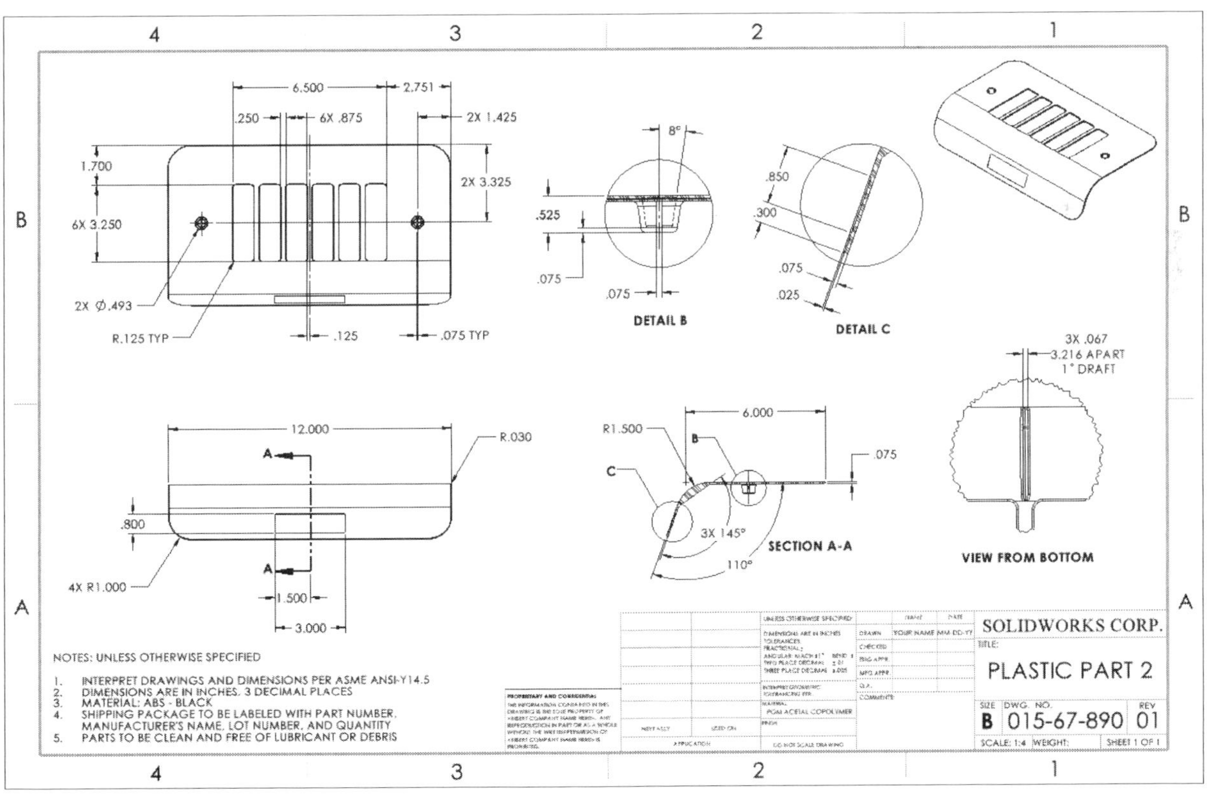

12. Saving your work:

Select **File, Save As.**

Enter: **Plastic Part 2.slddrw** for the name of the file.

Click **Save.**

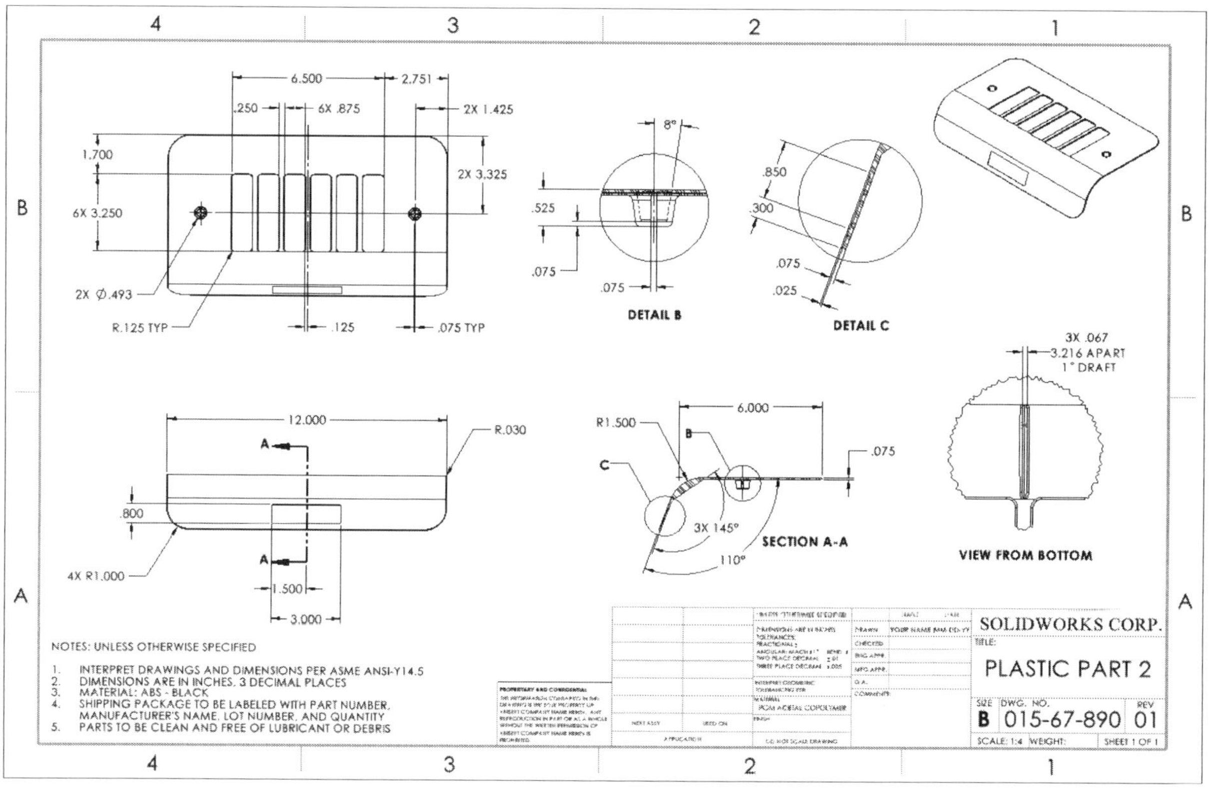

Close all documents.

Exercise: Plastic Parts

Detailing a Plastic Part 2

The exercises are designed to help you apply what you have learned from the previous lessons. They come with some instructions but not as detailed as the lessons, to give you an opportunity to explore and to try and create the drawings on your own, at your own pace.

1. Opening a part document:

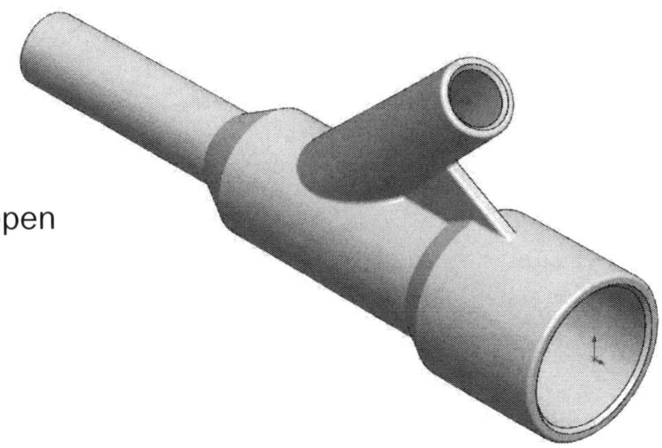

Select **File, Open**.

Browse to the Training Folder and open the part document named: **Plastic Parts_Connector.sldprt**.

2. Making a drawing:

Select **File, Make Drawing From Part**.

For paper size, use **B-ANSI Landscape**.

Set the Scale to **1.5:1**

Set the Type-Of-Projection to: **3rd Angle**.

Keep all other parameters at their default and click **OK**.

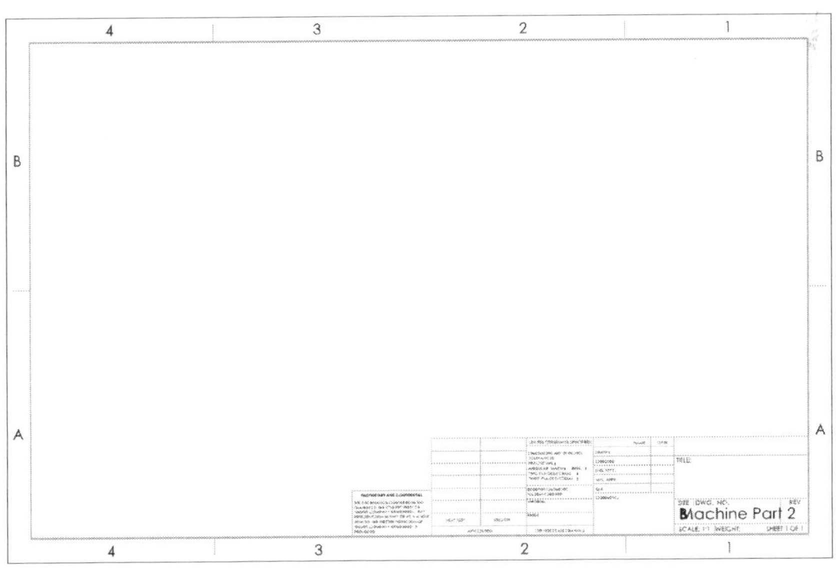

3. Creating the drawing views:

Using the **View Palette**, add the 4 drawing views shown below: a **Front** view, **Right** view, **Isometric** view, and a **Section** view.

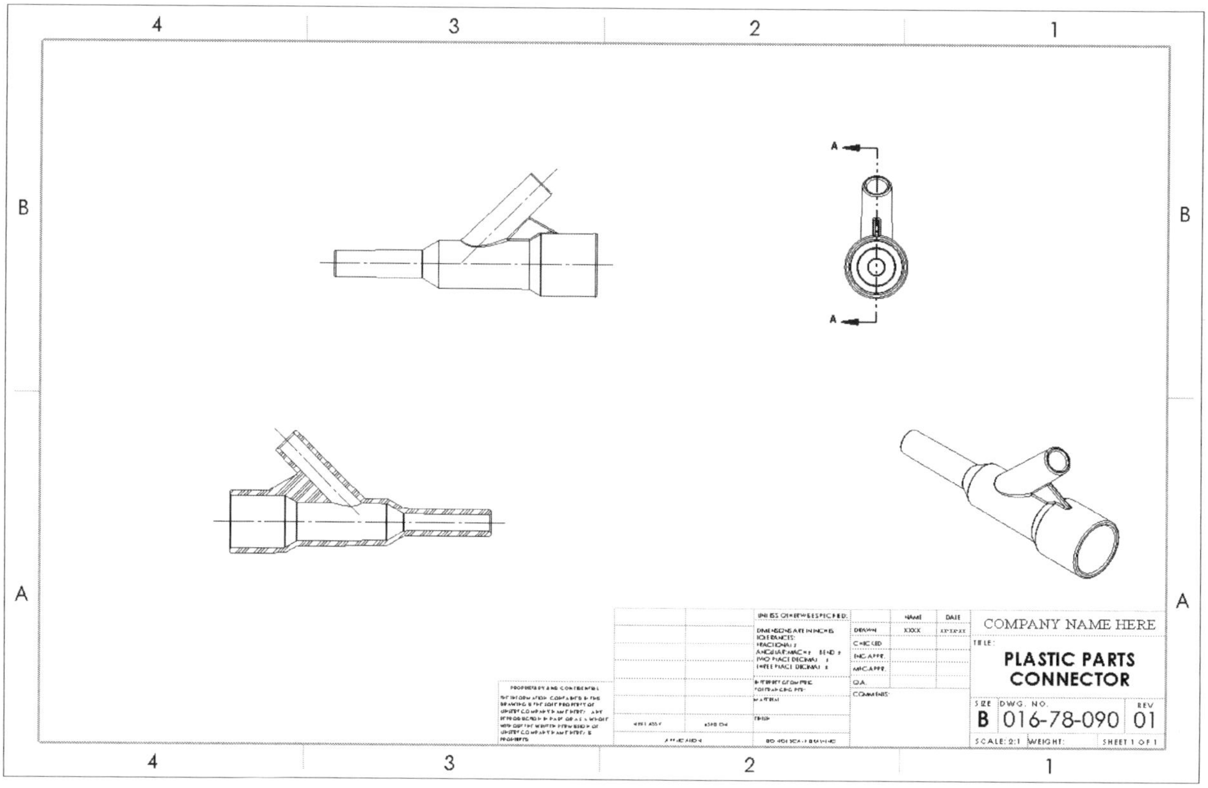

4. Adding dimensions:

Add the model dimensions to the **Front** drawing view.

Add/modify dimensions so that they look like the image shown here.

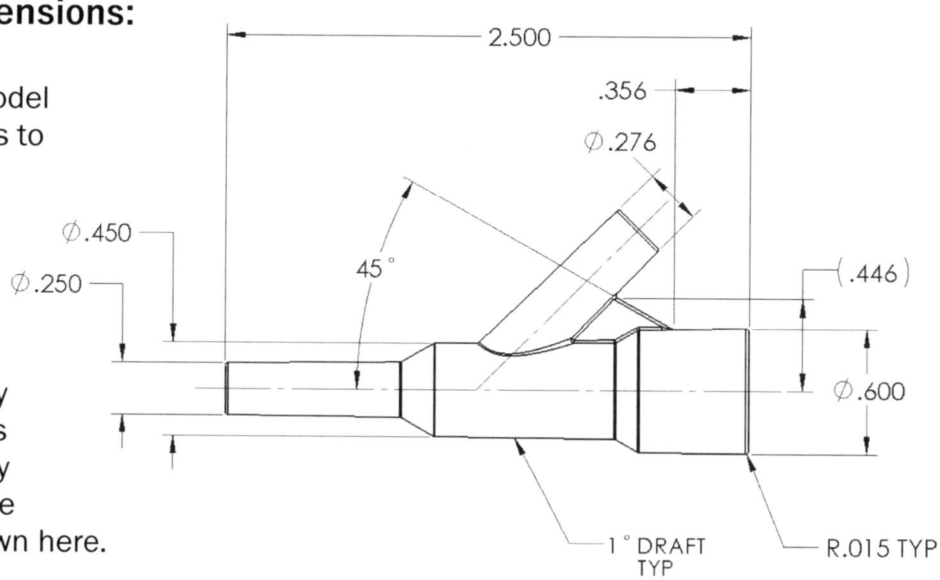

Add the width dimension to the **Rib** feature in the **Right** drawing view.

Zoom in on the **Section** view and add the model dimensions as shown below.

Add/modify dimensions so that they look like the ones in the image shown below.

Also, add the **number of instances** where applicable.

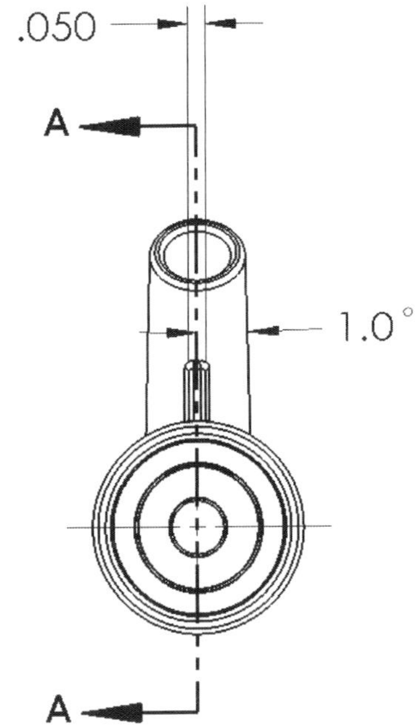

Modify the hatch pattern to include: **ANSI34 (Plastic/Rubber)** and the Hatch Pattern Scale of **4**.

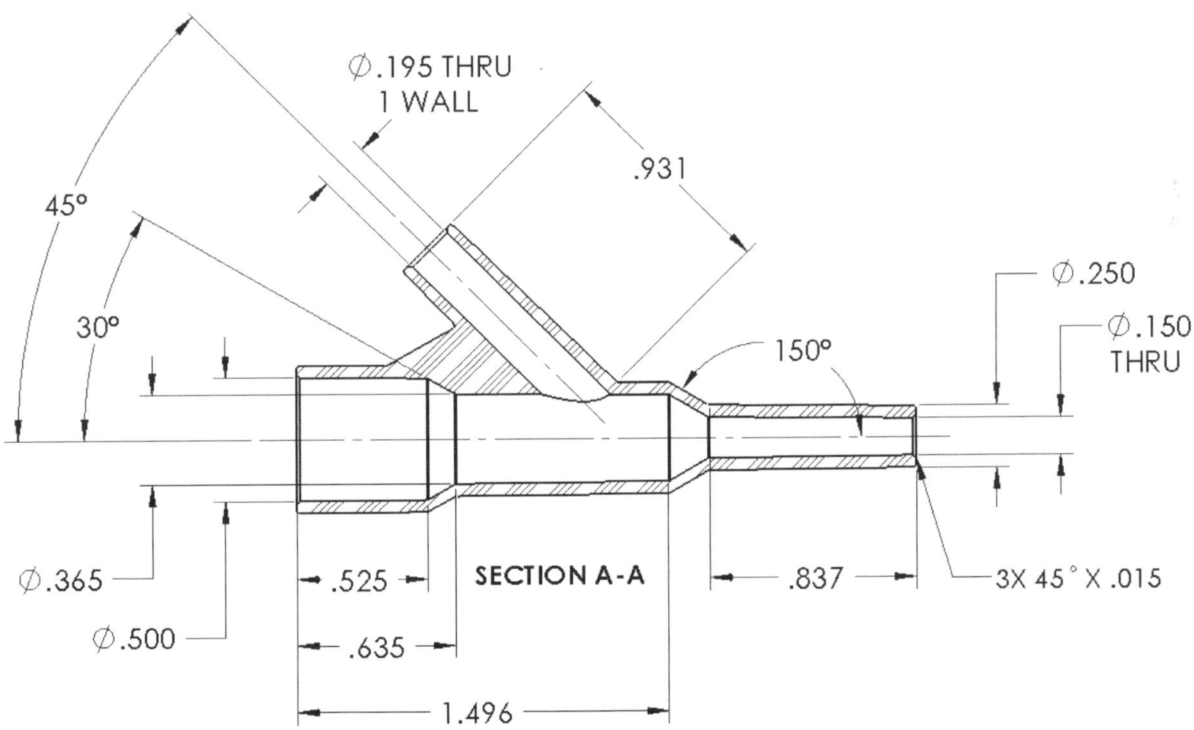

5. Filling out the title block information:

From the FeatureManager tree, expand Sheet1 and double-click on **Sheet-Format1** to activate it for editing.

Fill out the information shown in the image on the right.

Double-click on **Sheet1** to switch back to the Sheet layer.

6. Saving your work:

Save your work as: **Plastic Parts_Connector_Completed.sldprt**

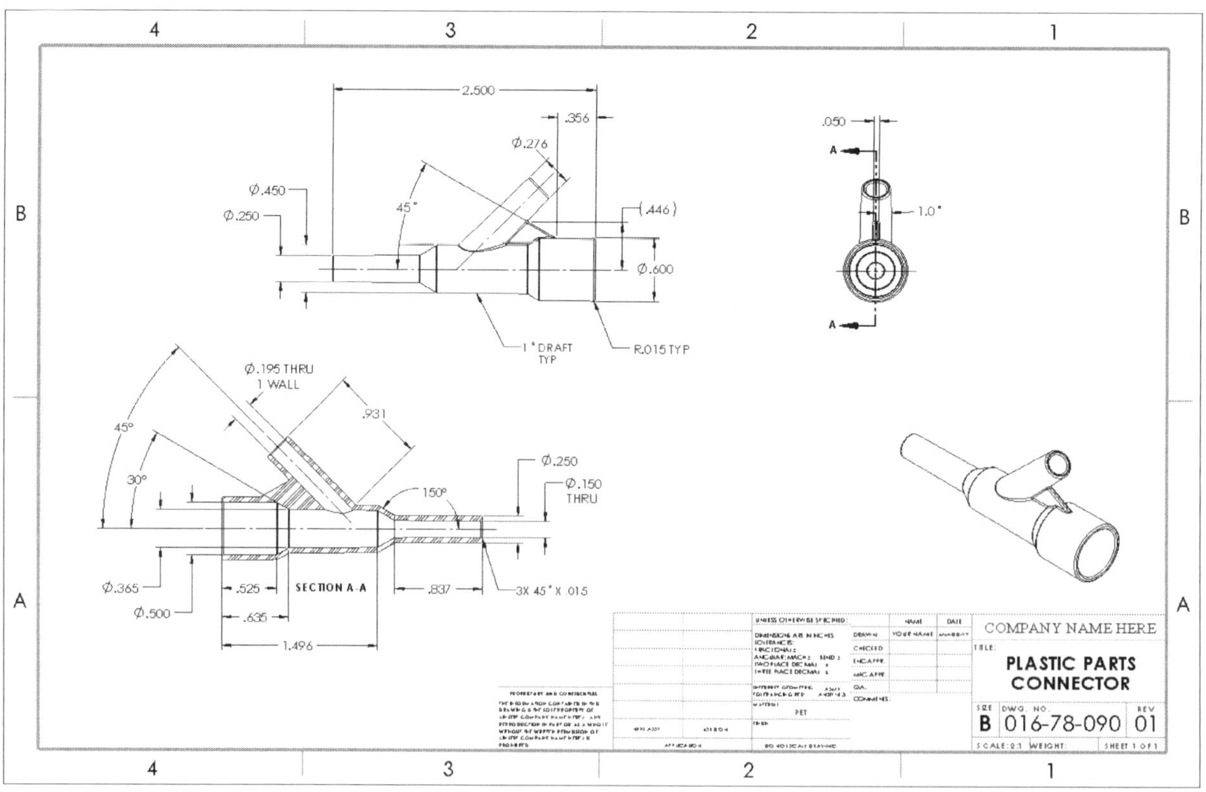

Exercise: Plastic Parts

Detailing a Plastic Part 3

The exercises are designed to help you apply what you have learned from the previous lessons. They come with some instructions but not as detailed as the lessons, to give you an opportunity to explore and to try and create the drawings on your own, at your own pace.

1. Opening a part document:

Select **File, Open**.

Browse to the Training Folder and open the part document named: **Plastic Parts_Upper Housing.sldprt**.

2. Making a drawing:

Select **File, Make Drawing From Part**.

For paper size, use **C-ANSI Landscape**.

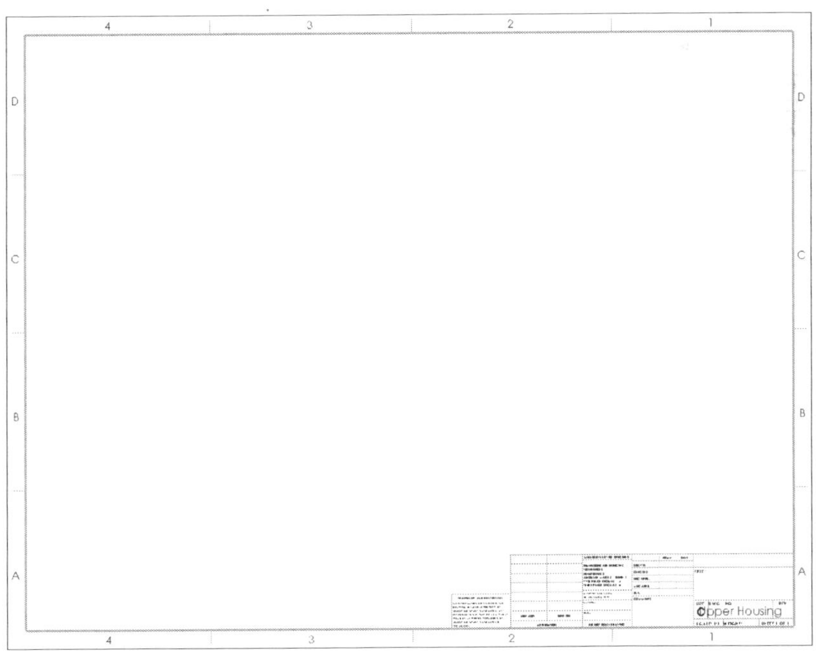

Set the Scale to **1:1**

Set the Type-Of-Projection to: **3rd Angle**.

Keep all other parameters at their default and click **OK**.

3. Adding the standard views:

Using the **View Palette**, add the **Front**, **Top**, and **Isometric** views to the drawing as show here.

We will create a section view to replace the right side view and to show the wall thickness and the height dimensions of the mounting bosses.

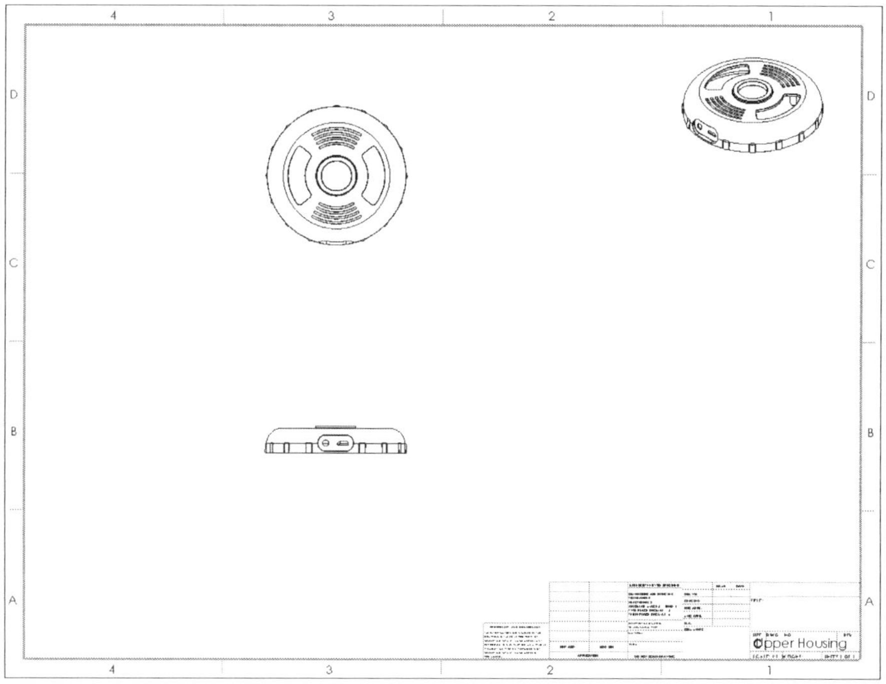

4. Creating an Aligned Section view:

Switch to the **Drawing** tab and select: **Section View**.

For Cutting Line, click **Aligned**.

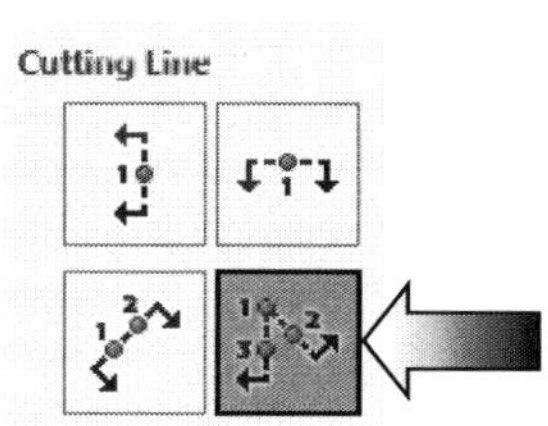

Click 1, 2, 3 to place the cutting line as shown.

Place the view and double-click the section line to flip the direction if needed.

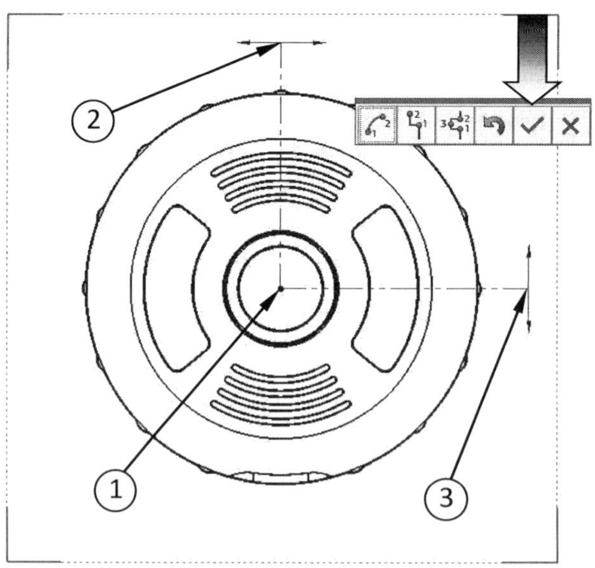

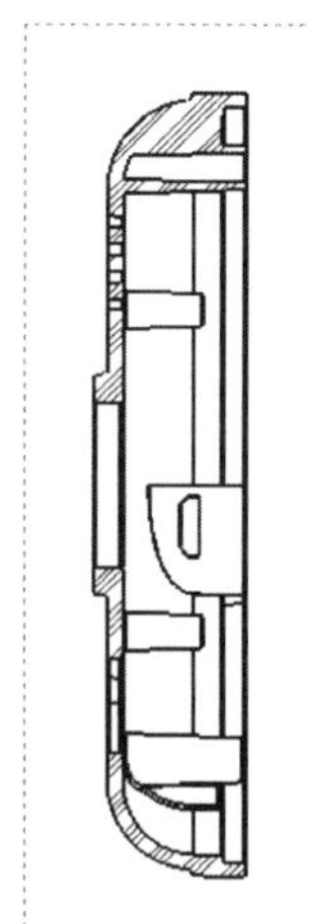

SECTION A-A

5. Rotating a drawing view:

Click the dotted border of the section view and select the **Rotate View** command on the View Heads-Up toolbar.

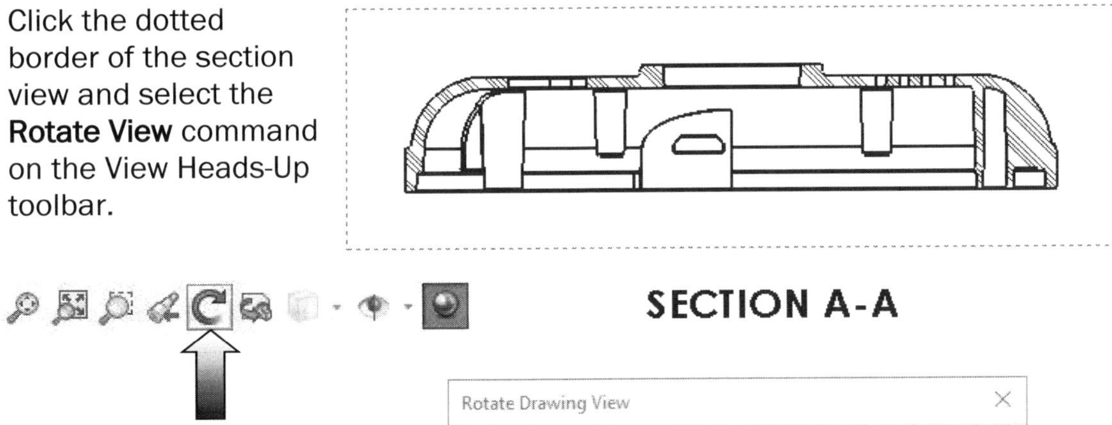

Enter **-90.00deg** for angle.

Click **Apply** and **Close**.

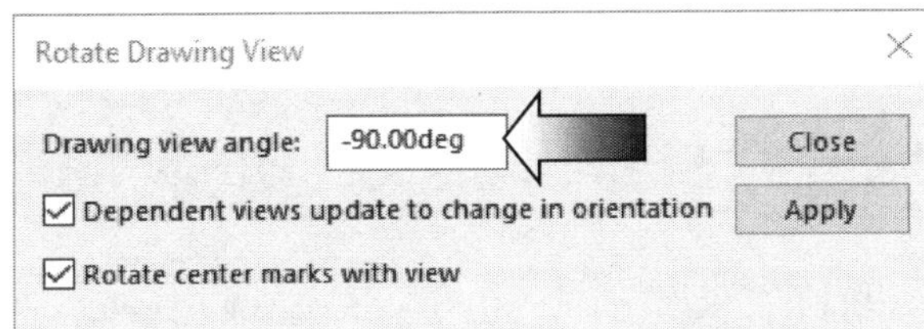

6. Breaking the view alignment:

The Section view should be aligned with the Front view, but first, we will need to break its default alignment.

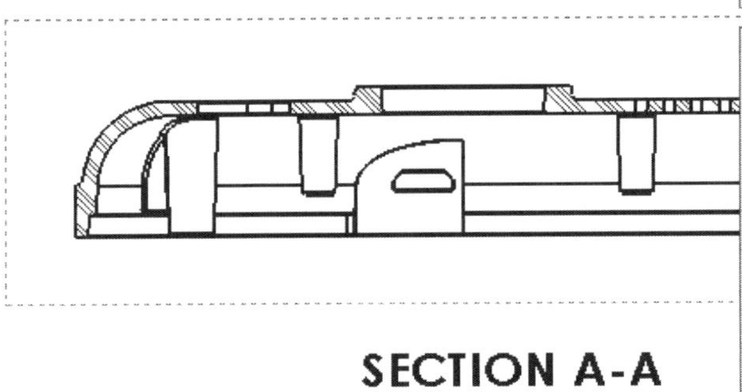

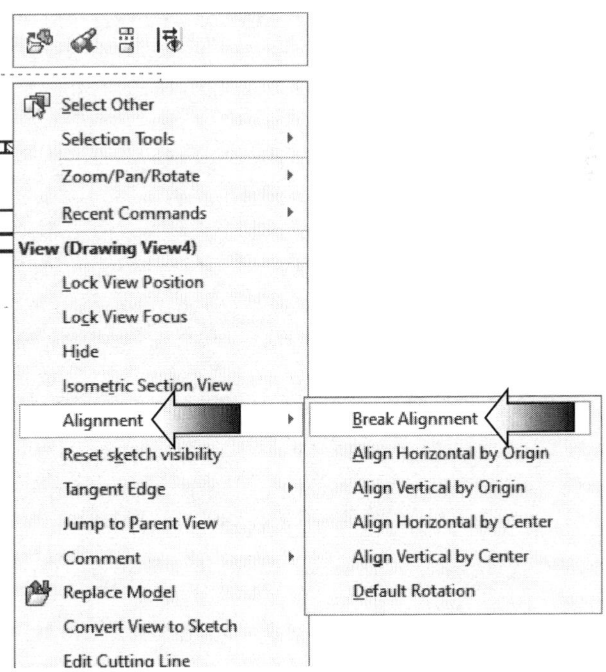

Right-click the dotted border of the Section view and select: **Alignment, Break Alignment**.

Move the Section view downward.

7. Aligning the drawing views:

Right-click the dotted border of the Section view and select:
Alignment, Align Horizontal By Origin.

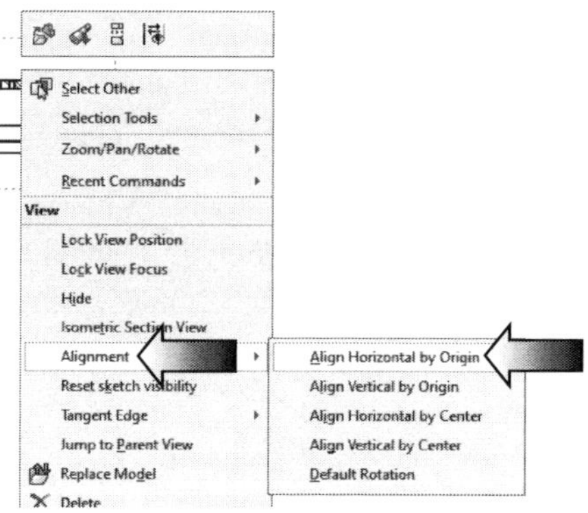

Click the dotted border of the **Front** view to align the Section view to it horizontally.

8. Adding the additional drawing views:

Add a **Detail** view and a **Bottom** view as shown below.

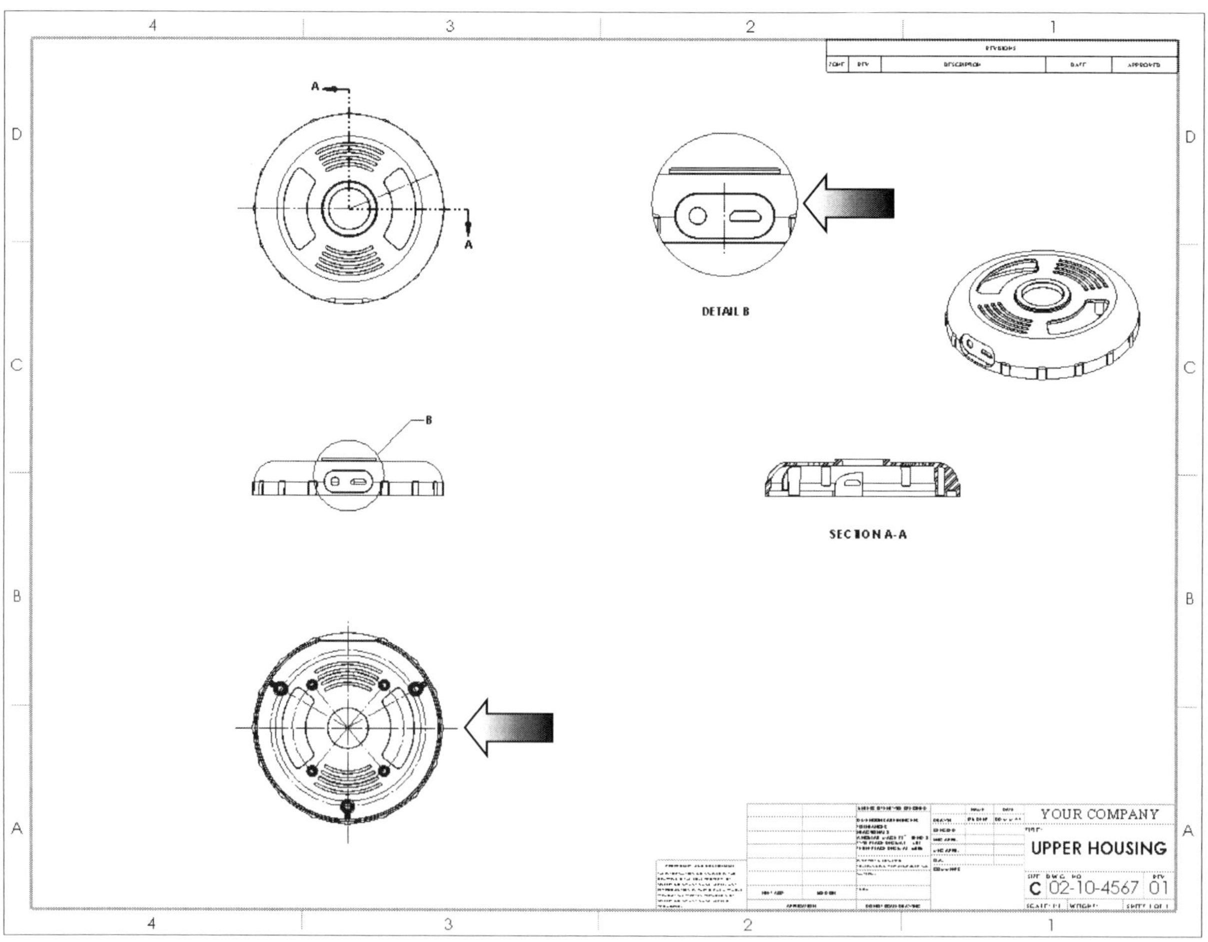

9. Adding dimensions:

Zoom in closer to the **Front** drawing view.

Add a **centerline** to the center of the drawing view.

Also add the **dimensions** shown in the view on the right.

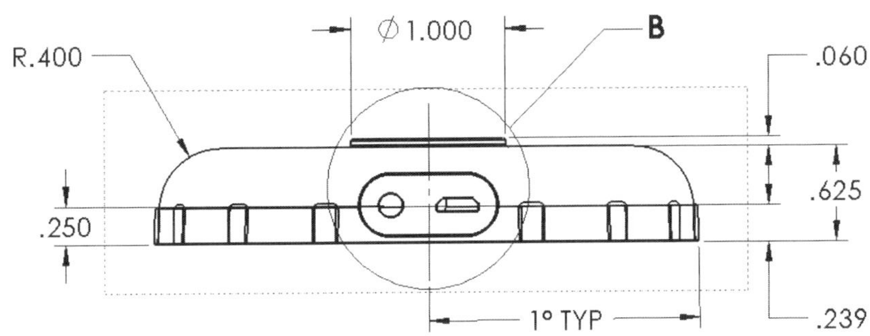

Zoom in on the **Top** drawing view.

Add **centerlines** that connect the center of the part to the centers of the curved slots; this will help with creating the angular dimensions more easily.

Add the **dimensions** and the **annotations** shown in the drawing view.

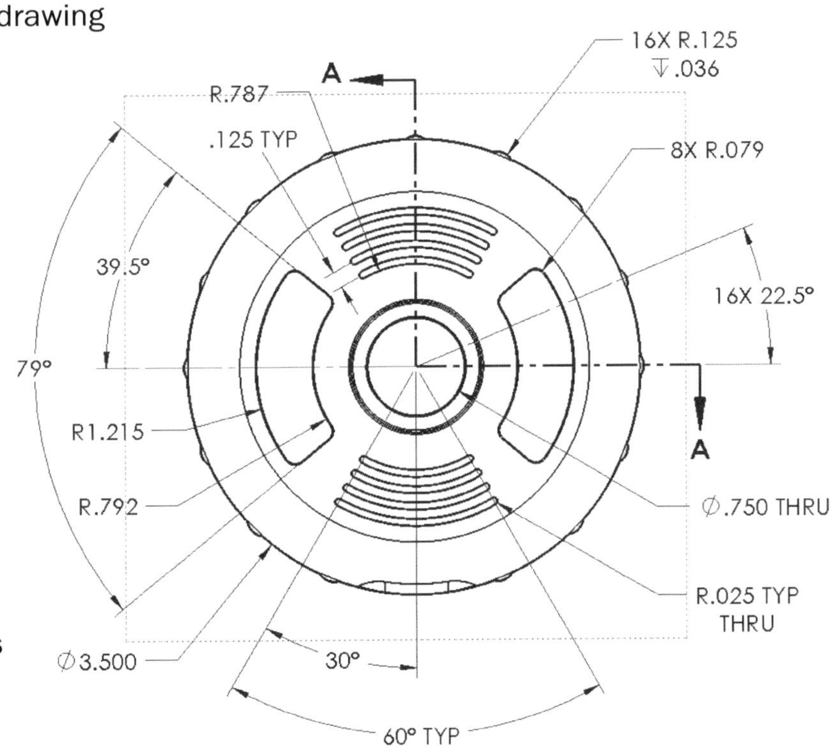

Zoom in on the **Bottom** drawing view.

Add the **centerlines** that connect the center of the part to the centers of all holes.

Also add the **construction circles** for the Bolt-Circle dimensions.

Add the **dimensions** and the number of **instances** shown in the drawing view.

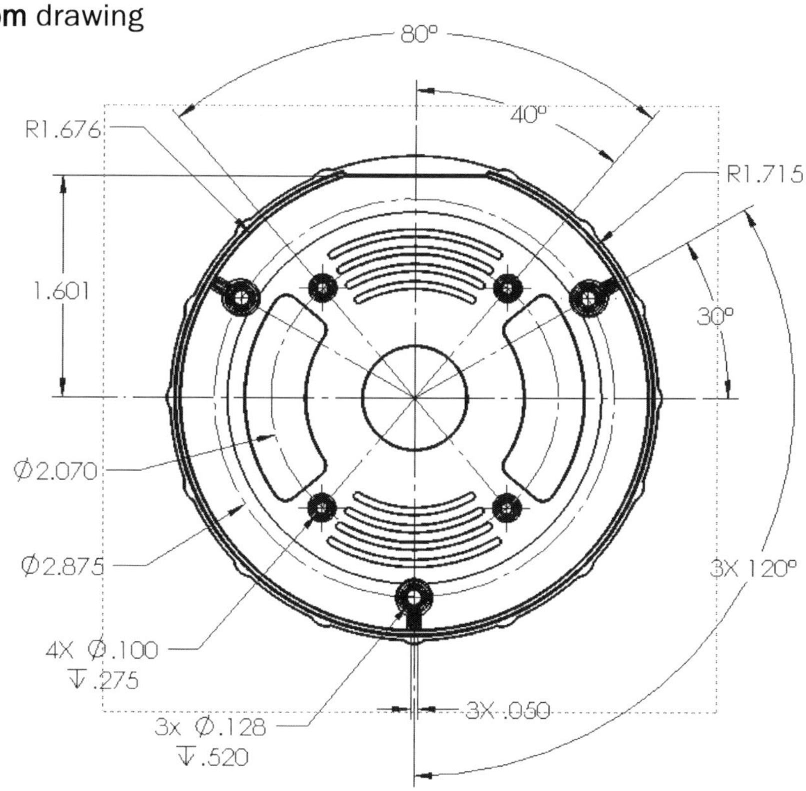

Zoom in on the **Detail** view.

Add a **centerline** to the center of the recess feature.

Add a **center mark** to the center of the hole.

Add the **dimensions** and annotations show here.

(Notes may be used in place of the fillet dimensions.)

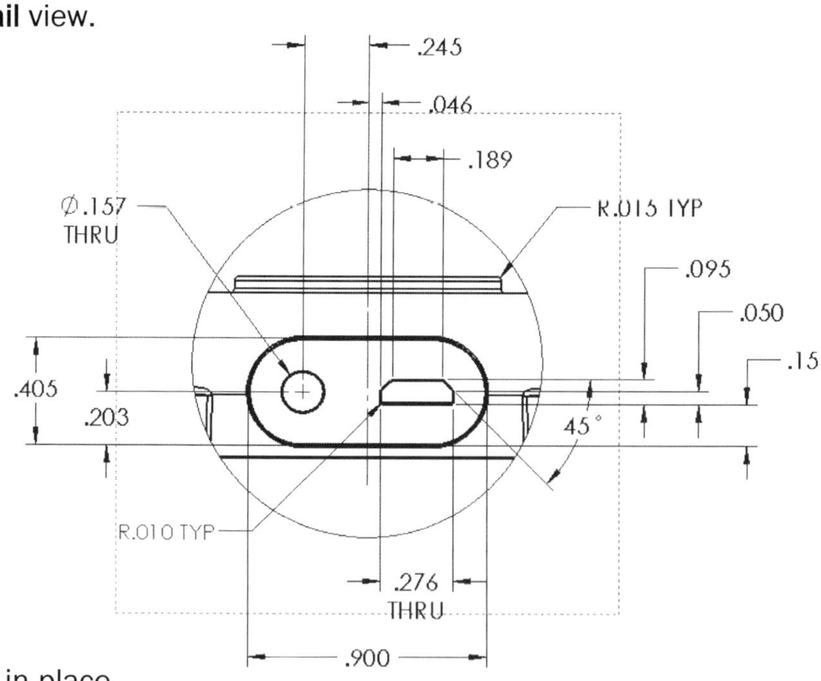

DETAIL B

Zoom in closer to the **Section** view.

Add **centerlines** to the holes and the mounting bosses.

Add the **dimensions** shown in the drawing view.

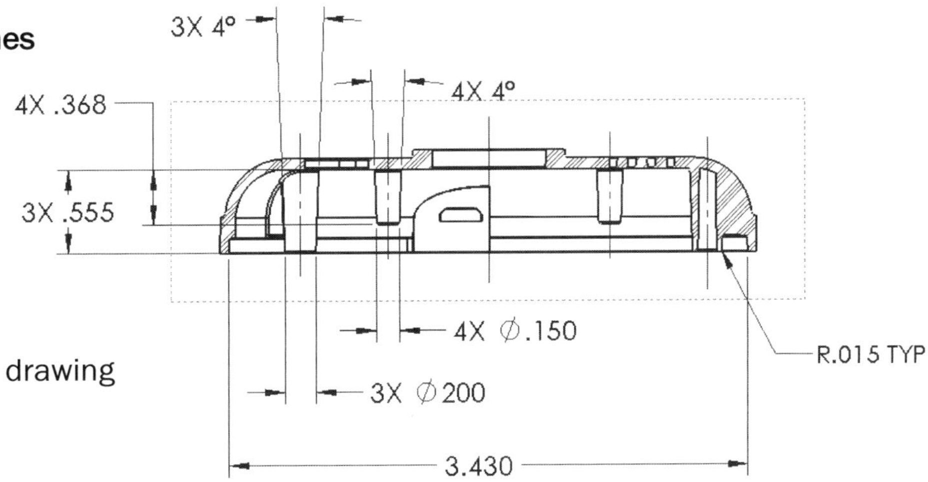

SECTION A-A

10. Adding the General Notes:

Since there is not much room available on the upper left and/or the lower left of the drawing, we will place the General Notes above the Title Block instead.

Switch to the **Annotation** tab and click **Note.**

Using all uppercase letters, enter the notes shown below:

NOTES: UNLESS OTHERWISE SPECIFIED
1. INTERPRET DRAWINGS AND DIMENSIONS PER ASME-ANSI 14.5
2. DIMENSIONS ARE IN INCHES, 3 DECIMAL PLACES
3. ADD CHAMFERS TO ALL HOLES .010 X 45°
4. UNSPECIFIED DRAFT ANGLE TO BE 1.0°

Place the notes above the Title Block.

11. Filling out the Title Block:

Edit the **Sheet Format** and fill out the information below.

UNLESS OTHERWISE SPECIFIED:		NAME	DATE	YOUR COMPANY		
DIMENSIONS ARE IN INCHES TOLERANCES: FRACTIONAL ± ANGULAR: MACH ±1° BEND ± TWO PLACE DECIMAL ±.01 THREE PLACE DECIMAL ±.005	DRAWN	STUDENT	DD-MM-YY	TITLE: **UPPER HOUSING**		
	CHECKED					
	ENG APPR.					
	MFG APPR.					
INTERPRET GEOMETRIC TOLERANCING PER: **ASME-ANSI Y14.5**	Q.A.					
MATERIAL ABC PC	COMMENTS:			SIZE C	DWG. NO. 02-10-4567	REV 01
FINISH						
DO NOT SCALE DRAWING				SCALE: 1:1	WEIGHT:	SHEET 1 OF 1

Save your work as: **Upper Housing_Completed.slddrw.**

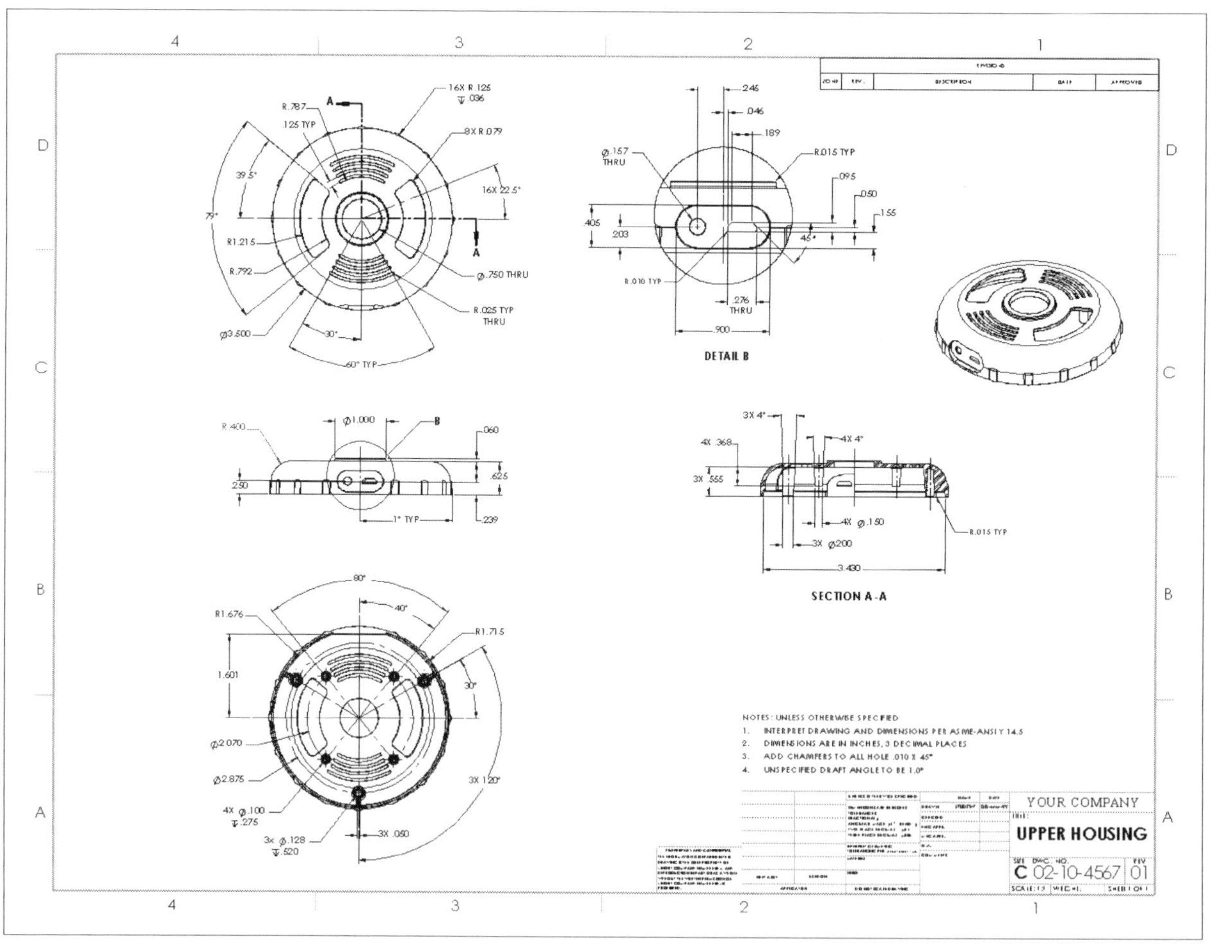

CHAPTER 6: DETAILING SHEET METAL PARTS

Detailing a Sheet Metal Part

Sheet metal parts are solid models that can be represented in either sheet metal form or as a flat model. These parts are of uniform thickness and can be modified by adding features. Features include walls, cuts, rips, bends, unbends, bend backs, forms, notches, punches, and relief.

Metals used in the sheet metal industry include cold rolled steel, mild steel, stainless steel, tin, nickel, titanium, aluminum, brass, and copper.

This lesson will teach us how drawings are made from sheet metal parts.

1. Opening a part document:

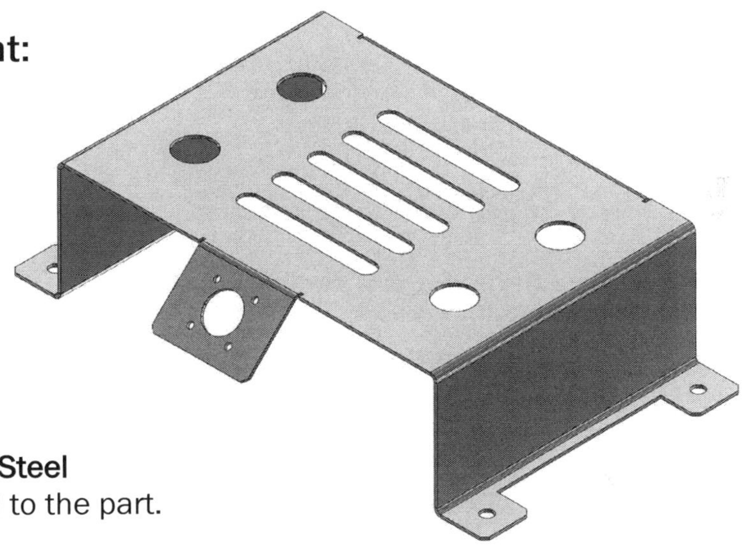

Select **File, Open**.

Browse to the Training Folder and open the part document named **Sheet Metal 1.sldprt**.

The material **Plain Carbon Steel** has already been assigned to the part.

When it comes to sheet metal drawings, we should show the finished, folded drawing views with dimensions for final inspection.

The flat patterns are not shown in the drawings unless requested by the manufacturing vendors, and the majority of the shops would do their own bend calculations instead of using the parameters that you entered while designing your sheet metal parts.

Sometimes the manufacturing vendors may ask you for a DXF flat pattern to get a headstart if your sheet metal parts have cuts that run across the bends.

2. Setting up a drawing sheet:

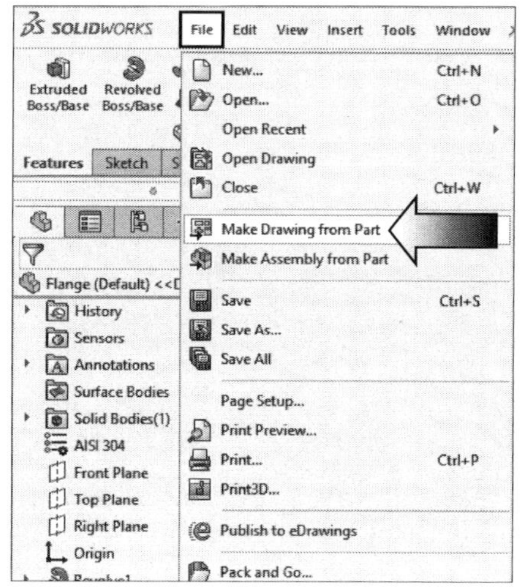

It is more common to use smaller size papers such as an A size (8.5” X 1.0”) or a B size (11.0” X 17.0”). Not only are they easier to manage, but the A or B size printer prices are more affordable than the other larger sizes.

We can add additional drawing sheets when the drawings get too busy or need more room.

Select: **File, Make Drawing From Part** (arrow).

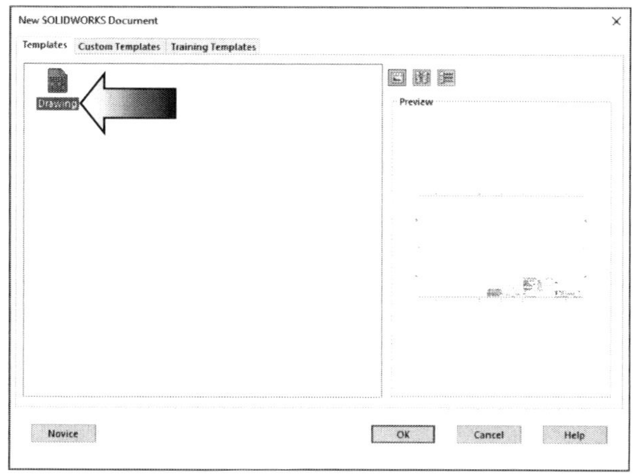

Select **Drawing** (or Draw) template from the New SOLIDWORKS Document dialog box.

In the Sheet Properties dialog box, select the following:

* Scale: **1:1**

* Type Of Projection: **Third Angle**

* Sheet Format/Size: **B (ANSI) Landscape**

* Next View Label: **A**

* Next Datum Label: **A**

* Display Sheet Format: **Enabled**

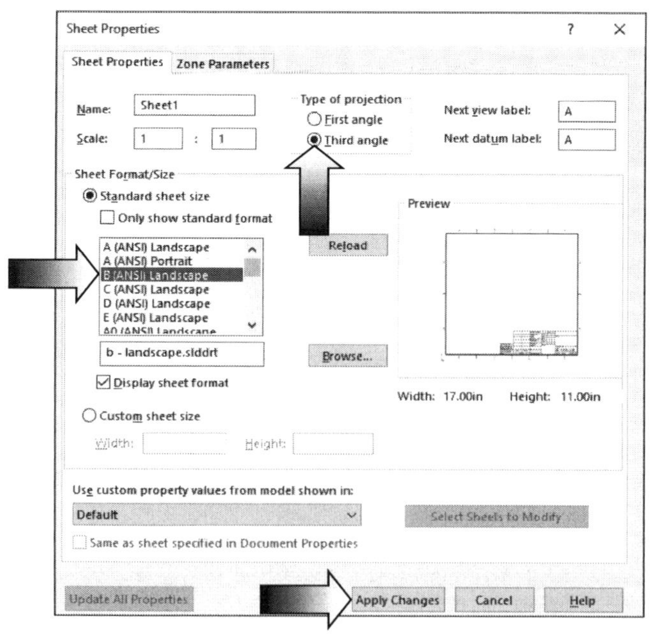

Click **Apply Changes**.

3. Creating the drawing views:

The **B Size** drawing paper (11.0” X 17.0”) is loaded into the graphics.

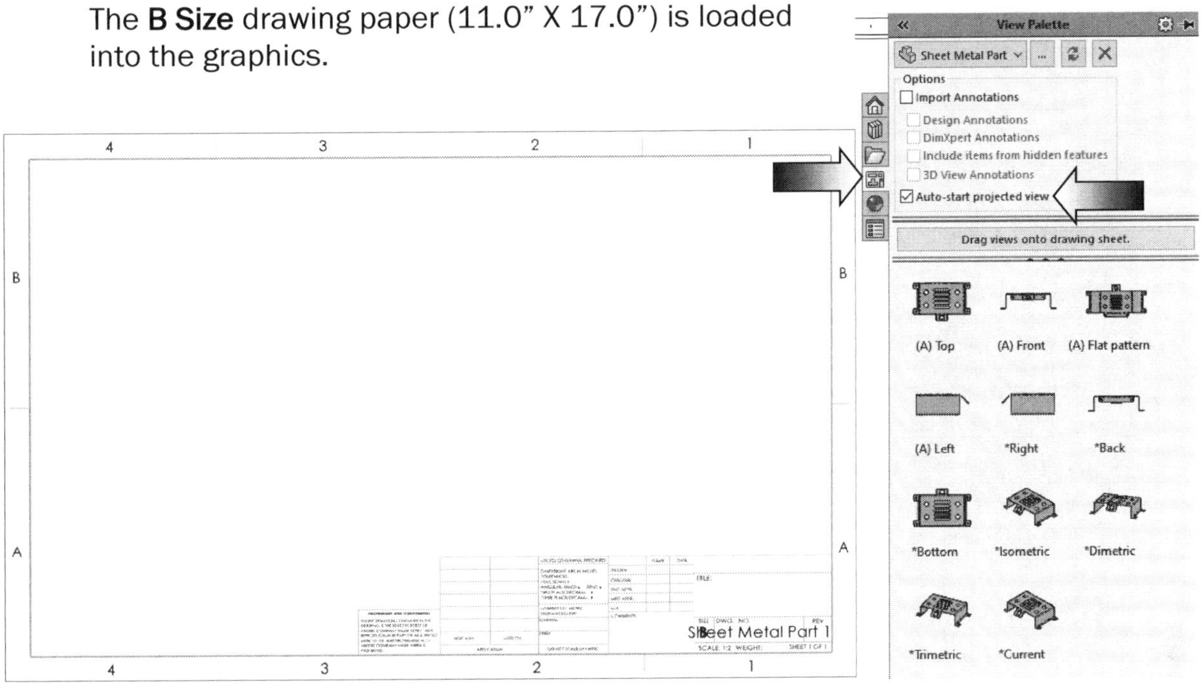

Expand the **View Palette** and enable only one option: **Auto-Start Projected View**, and clear all other checkboxes.

Drag and drop the **Front** drawing view first, and then the **Top**, the **Right**, and the **Isometric** view after.

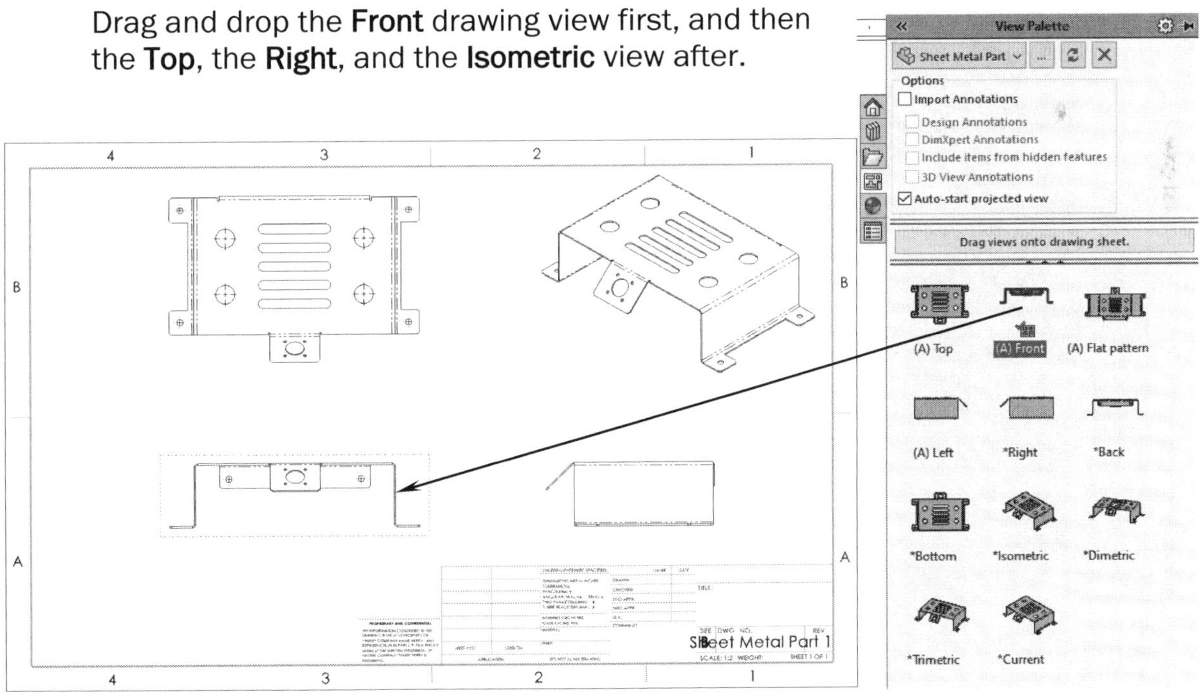

4. Creating an Auxiliary View:

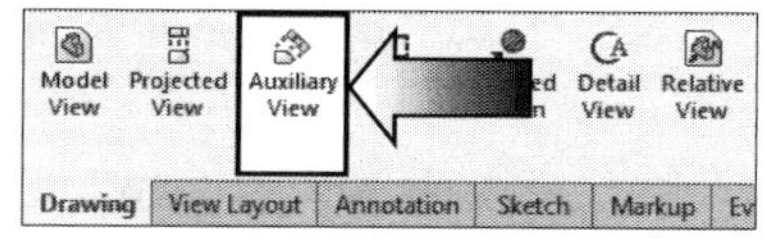

An Auxiliary View is similar to a Projected View, but it is unfolded normal to a reference edge in an existing view.

The tab in the front of the part needs to be shown normal to the view so that true dimensions and other callouts can be made to detail the features on the tab.

Zoom in on the Right drawing view and select the edge of the tab as indicated.

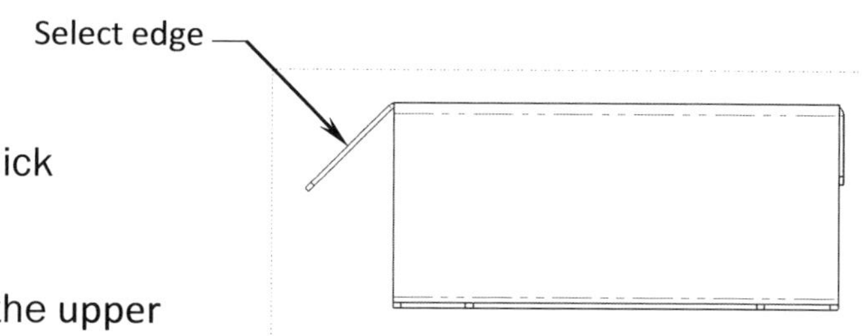

Switch to the **Drawing** tab and click **Auxiliary View**.

Place the new Auxiliary view on the upper left hand side of the Right drawing view.

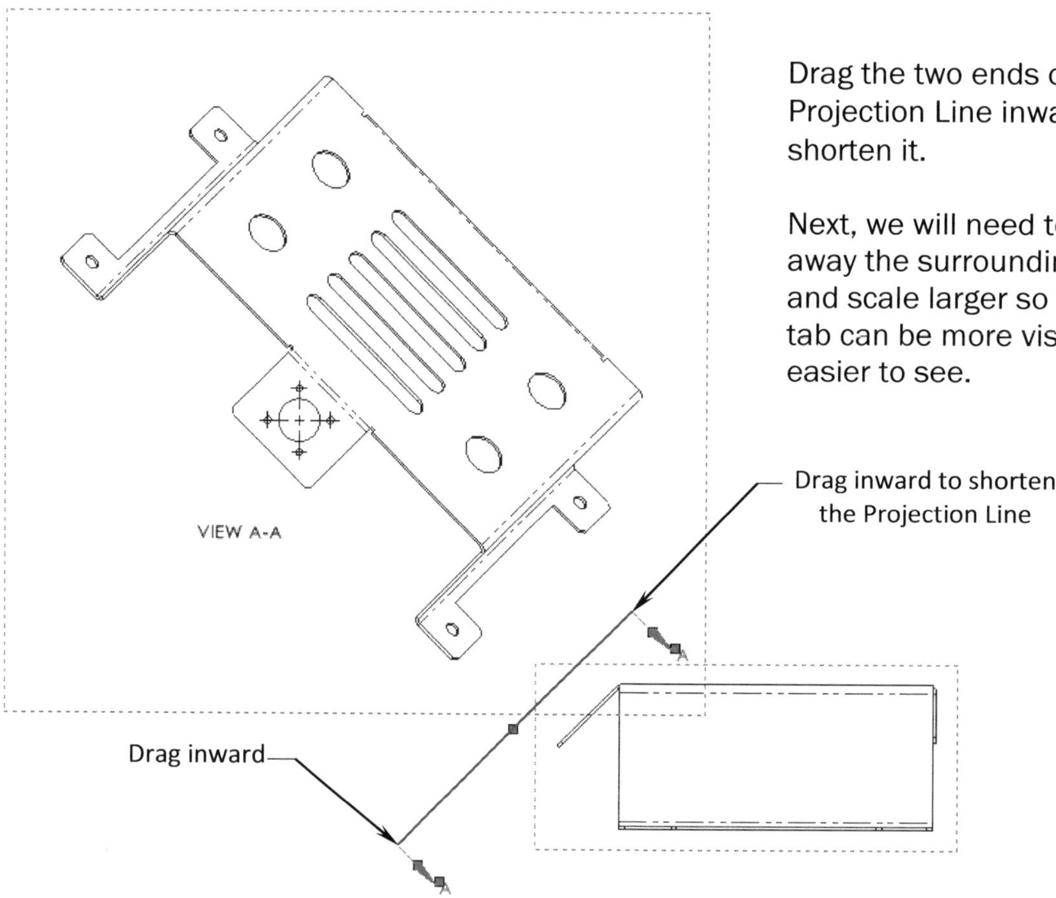

Drag the two ends of the Projection Line inwards to shorten it.

Next, we will need to trim away the surrounding areas and scale larger so that the tab can be more visible and easier to see.

5. Creating a Crop View:

A crop view focuses on a portion of a drawing view by hiding all but a defined area.

The uncropped portion is enclosed using a sketch, usually a spline or other closed contour.

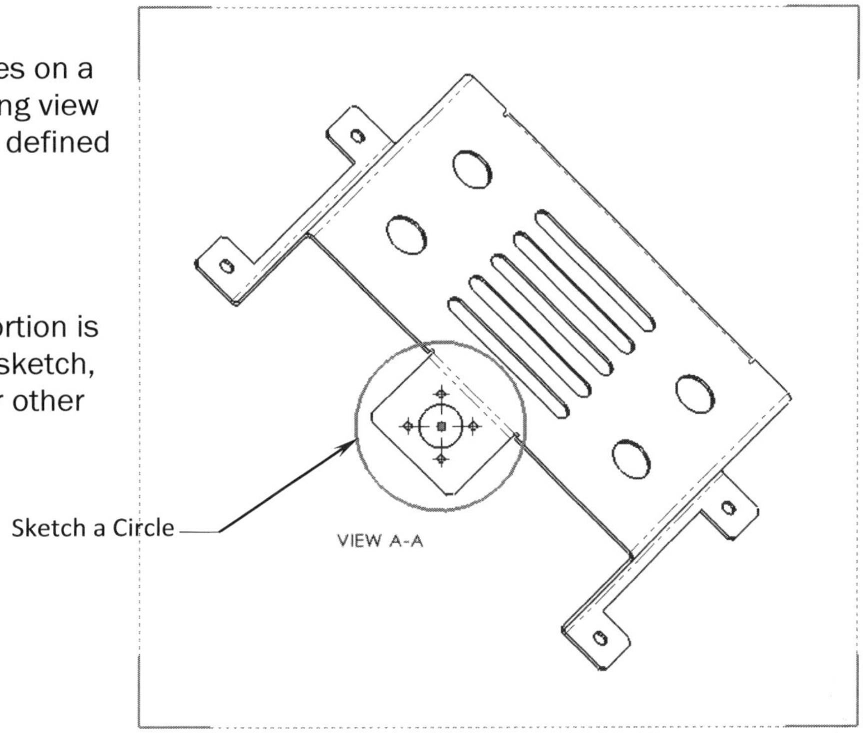

Switch to the **Sketch** tab and select the **Circle** tool.

While the sketch Circle is still highlighted, switch to the **Drawing** tab and click **Crop View**.

The details on the inside of the circle are kept but everything else on the outside of the circle is removed.

We will detail out this view in the next couple of steps.

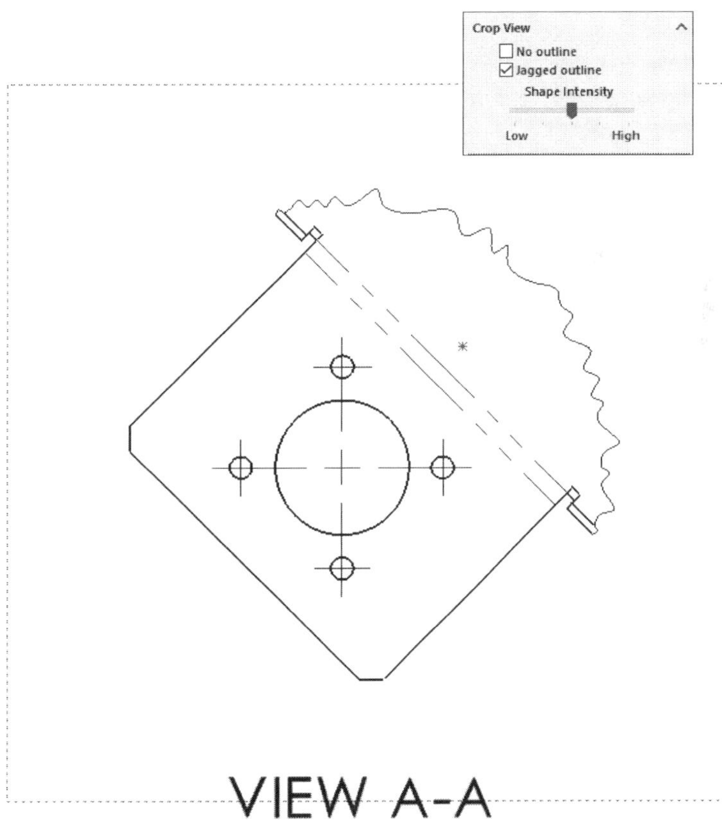

6. Inserting the model dimensions:

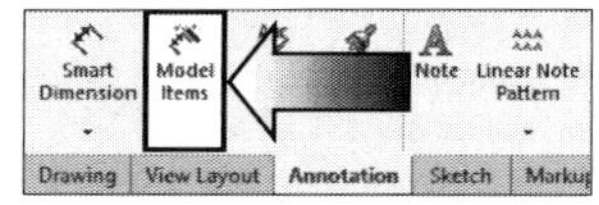

When designing sheet metal parts, we often focus on developing the geometry and the functionality of the features more than how the parts are going to be fabricated; and because of that, sometimes some of the dimensions may be missing, and they need to be added to the drawing.

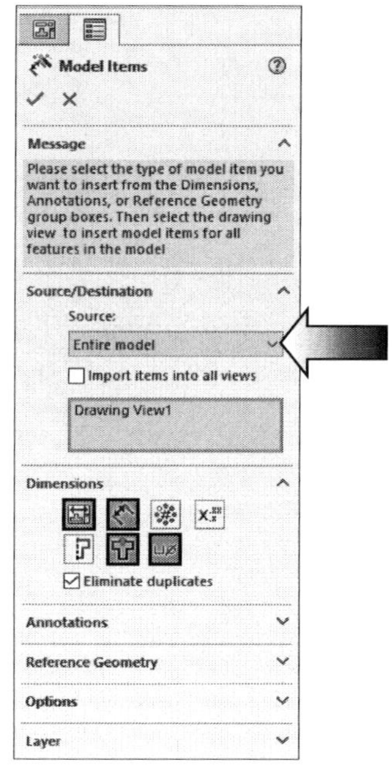

From the **Annotation** tab, click **Model Items.**

For Source/Destination, select: **Entire Model**.

For Dimensions, select:

Marked For Drawing
Not marked for Drawing
Hole Wizard Locations
Hole Callout

Click **OK.**

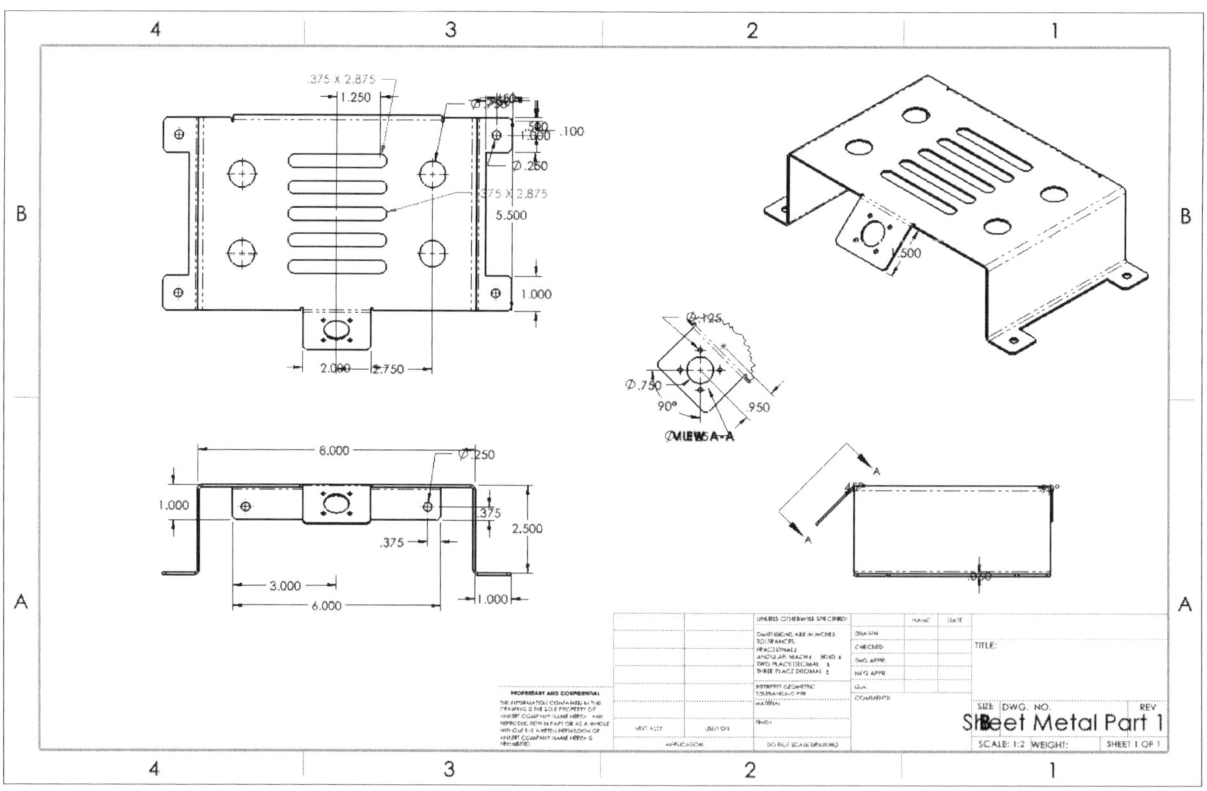

7. Rearranging and adding the dimensions:

Zoom in on the **Top** drawing view and rearrange the dimensions to look like the image on the right.

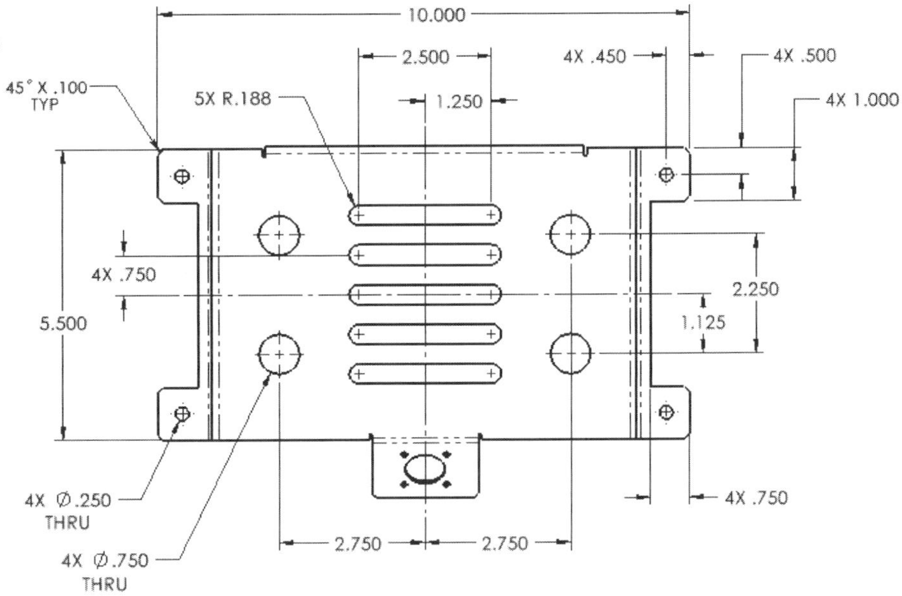

Modify the dimensions and add the number of instances as shown in each view.

Zoom in on the **Front** drawing view and rearrange the dimensions so that they look similar to the image shown on the right.

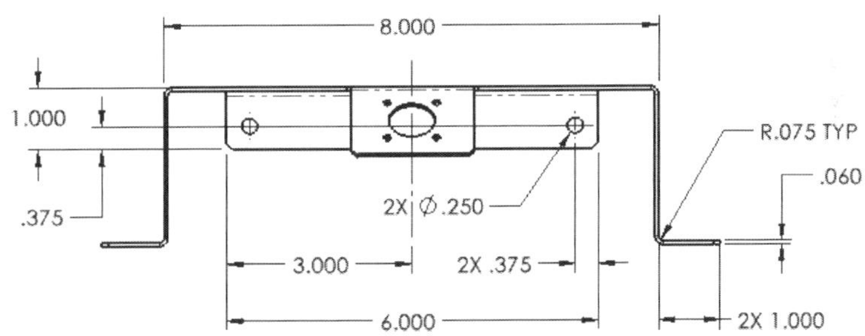

For the **Right** drawing view, add the angular dimension and the two overall height and width dimensions, (or move from the other drawing views).

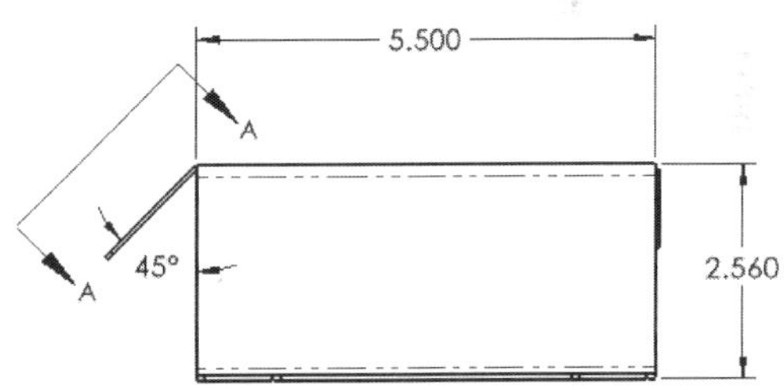

Zoom in on the **Crop** view and add or move the dimensions from other drawing views so that they look similar to the image shown on the right.

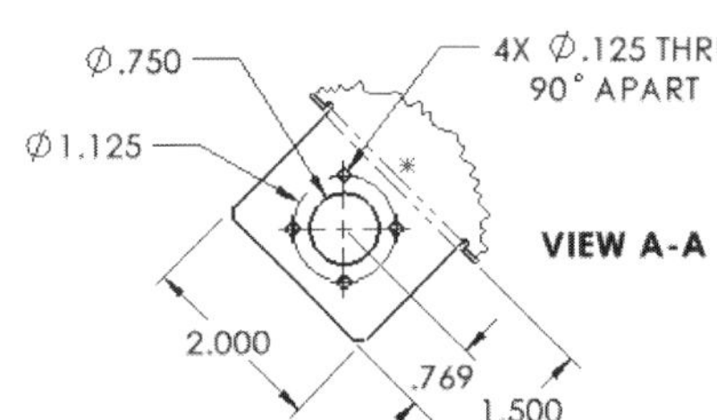

8. Adding the General Notes:

It seems that we do not have much room in the drawing for the general notes, We will have to place it in the lower left corner of the drawing, where we still have some room for it.

Switch to the **Annotation** tab and click **Note.**

Enter the notes shown below, all in uppercase letters.

NOTES: UNLESS OTHERWISE SPECIFIED

1. INTERPRET DRAWINGS AND DIMENSIONS PER ASME ANSI-Y14.5
2. DIMENSIONS ARE IN INCHES, 3 DECIMAL PLACES
3. MATERIAL: PLAIN CARBON STEEL
4. APPLY TYPICAL SHOP PRACTICE TO ALL CORNER RELIEF (T1 MIN)
5. PARTS TO BE CLEAN AND FREE OF LUBRICANT OR DEBRIS

(T1 = 1 thickness). When finished, select the notes, and click **Lock Note** to keep it from moving around.

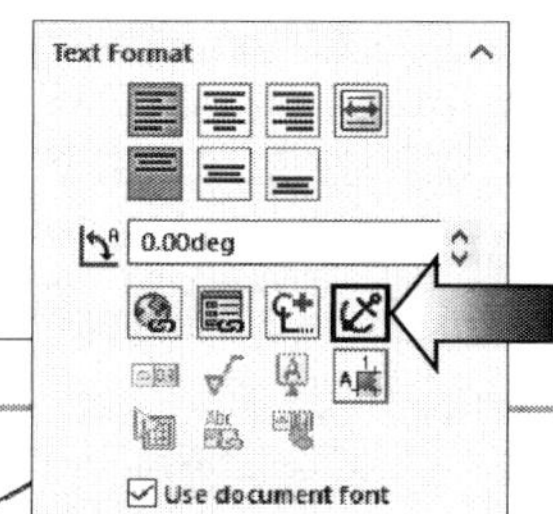

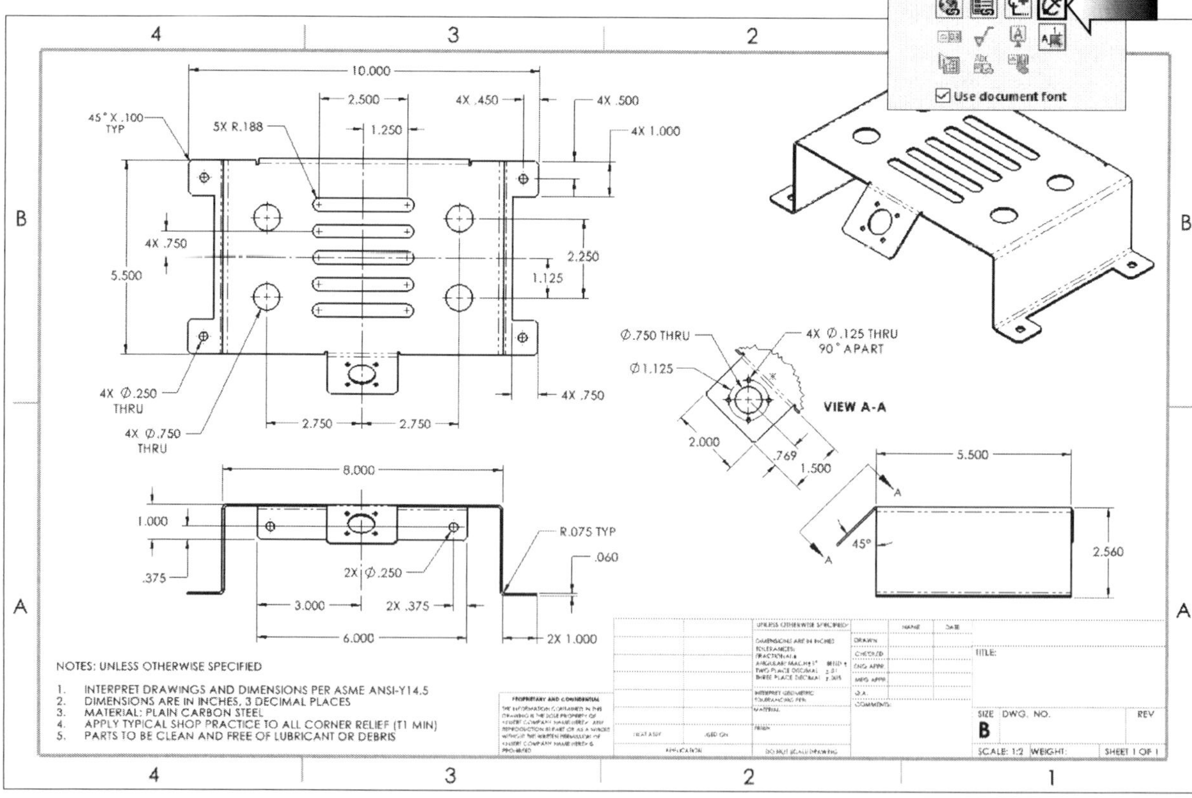

9. Filling out the Title Block:

From the FeatureManager tree, expand **Sheet1** and double-click **Sheet Format1** to activate the back layer for editing.

Zoom in closer to the Title Block area, double-click each blank note and fill out the information as shown below.

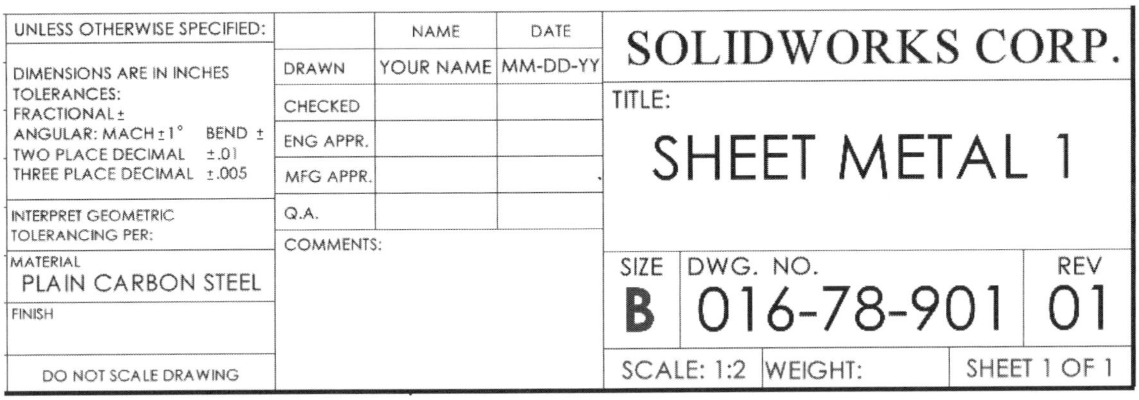

When finished, double-click **Sheet1** to bring the drawing layer back to the front.

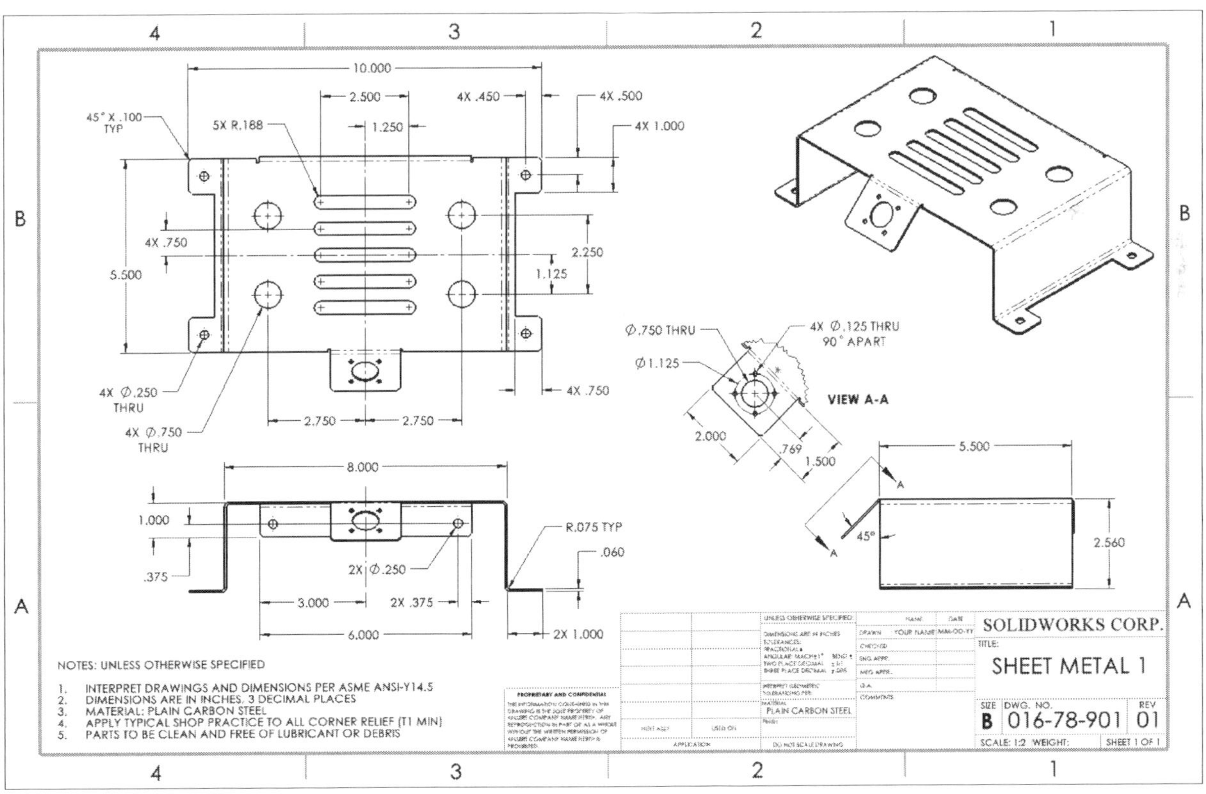

10. Adding the Isometric Flat Pattern:

The Flat Patterns are usually not necessary to be shown on a drawing unless requested by the manufacturing vendors.

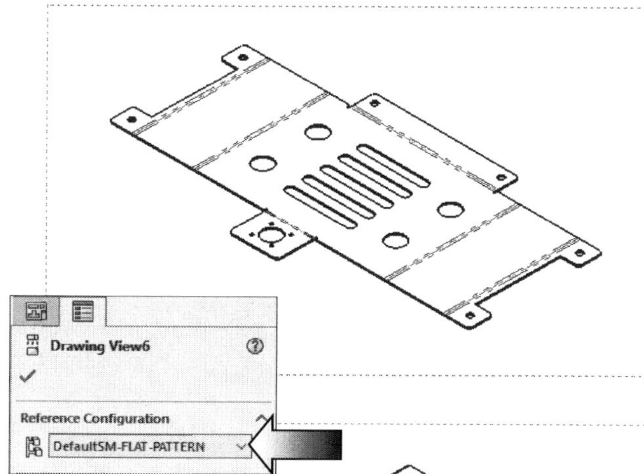

For learning purposes, we will go ahead and create a Flat Pattern drawing view and scale it down to fit in the drawing.

Drag and drop another instance of the **Isometric view** and place it above the first Isometric view.

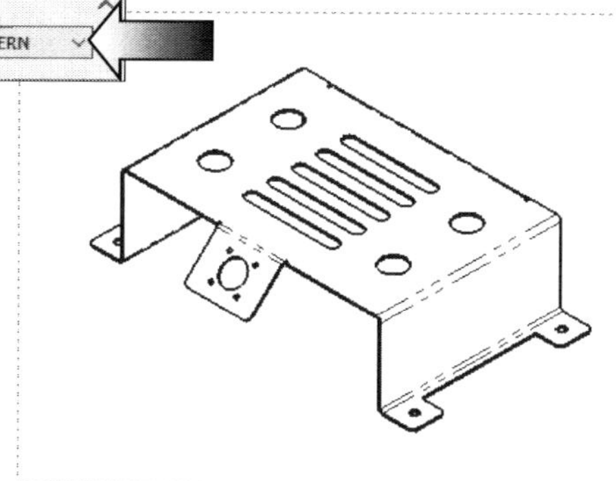

Locate the Reference Configuration section on the FeatureManager tree and select from the drop-down list: **Default SM-Flat-Pattern**.

Change the scale of the isometric views to **1:4**.

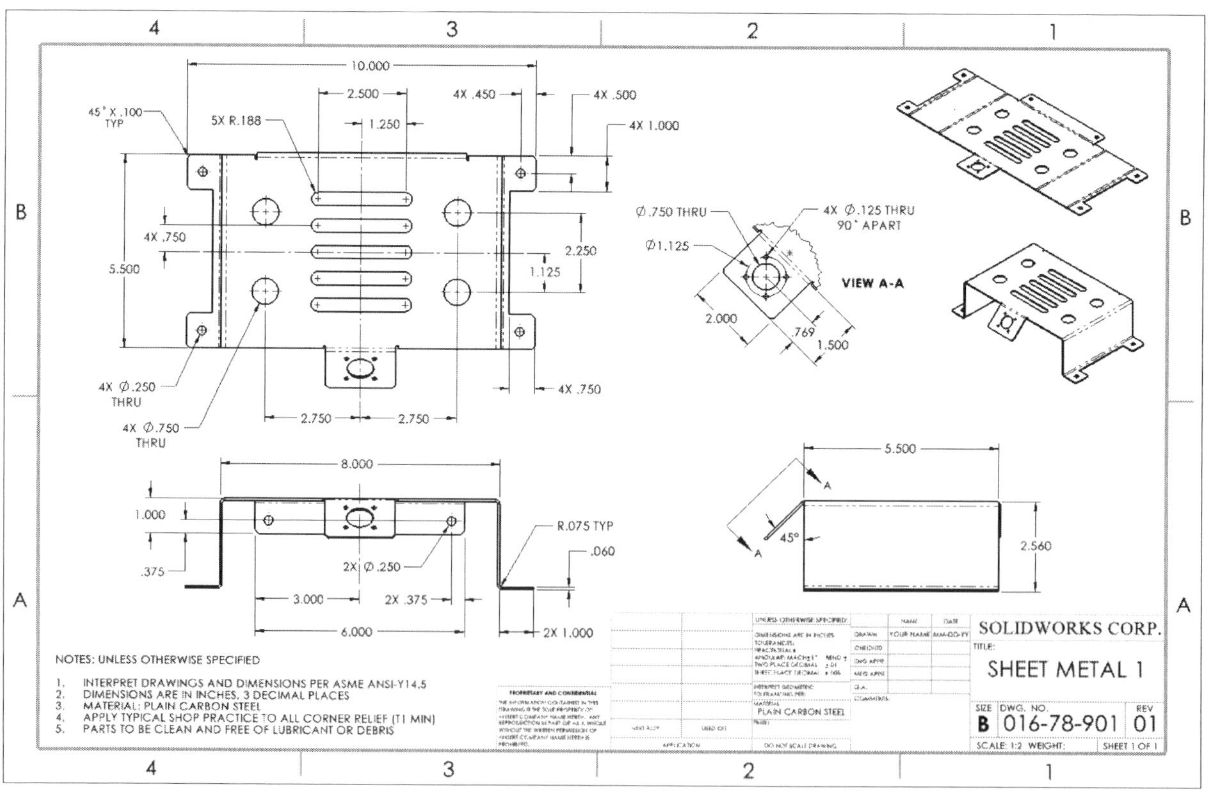

11. Saving your work:

Select **File, Save As.**

Enter: **Sheet Metal Part 1.slddrw** for the file name.

Click **Save**.

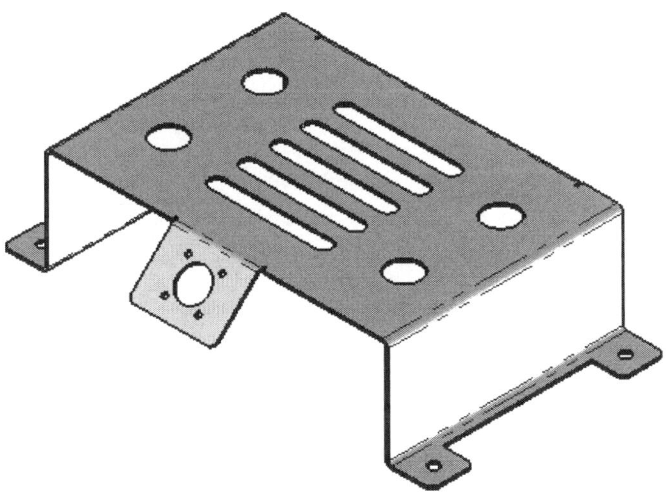

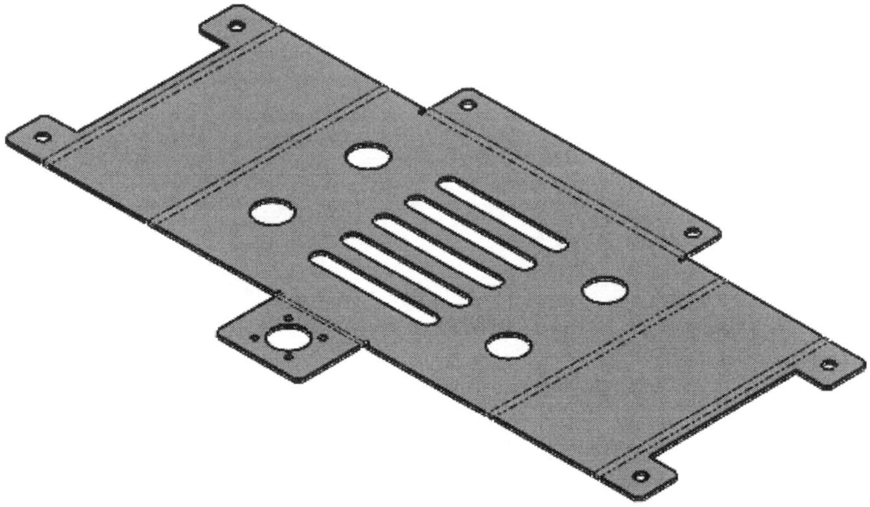

Exercise: Sheet Metal Parts

Detailing a Sheet Metal Part

The exercises are designed to help you apply what you have learned from the previous lessons. They come with some instructions but not as detailed as the lessons, to give you an opportunity to explore and to try and create the drawings on your own, at your own pace.

1. Opening a part document:

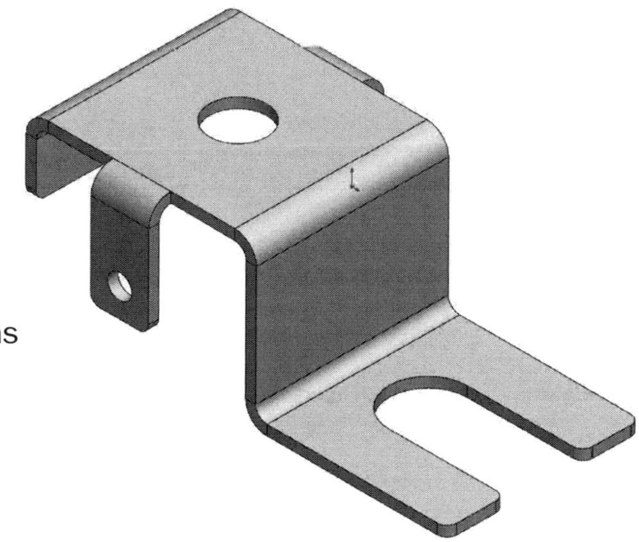

Select **File, Open**.

Browse to the Training Folder and open the part document named: **Sheet Metal Part 2.sldprt.**

The material **Plain Carbon Steel** has already been assigned to the part.

2. Transferring to a drawing:

Select **File, Make Drawing from Part.**

Select the **B-Size** drawing paper.

Set the Type-Of-Projection to: **3rd Angle.**

Keep all other parameters at their default.

Click **OK.**

The B-Size drawing is loaded.

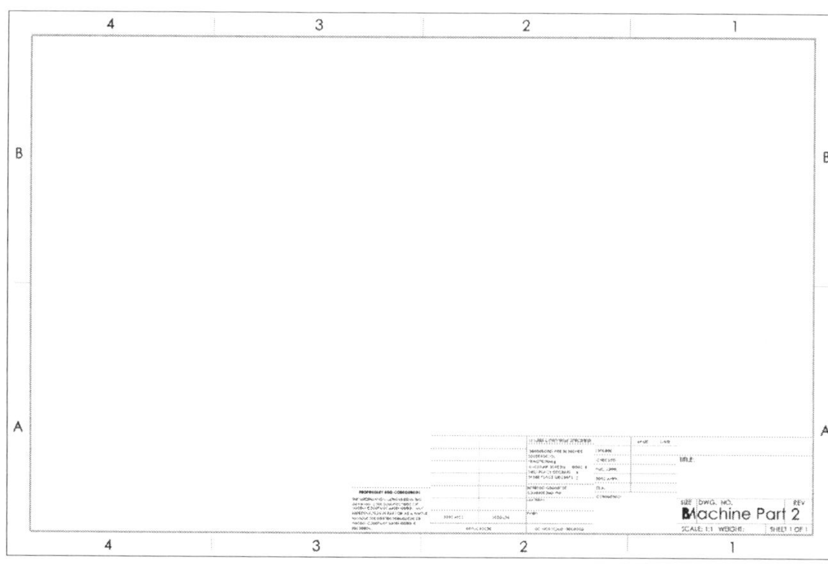

3. Creating the drawing views:

Using the View Palette, drag the **Front** drawing view and drop in the sheet, and then add the **Top**, the **Left**, and the **Isometric** view as shown below.

Move the Isometric view to the left-hand side of the drawing to use up the empty space, and make the drawing look more balanced.

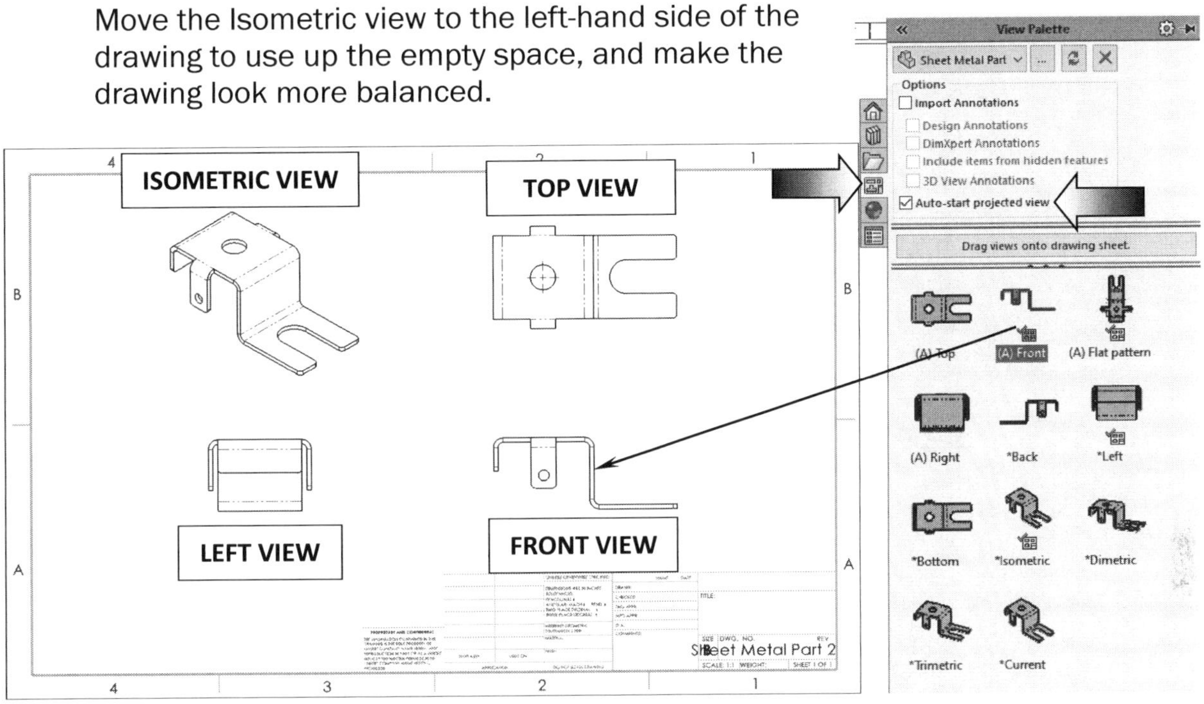

Change the scale of the Isometric view to **1:2** and change the other 3 drawing views to **1:1.5**.

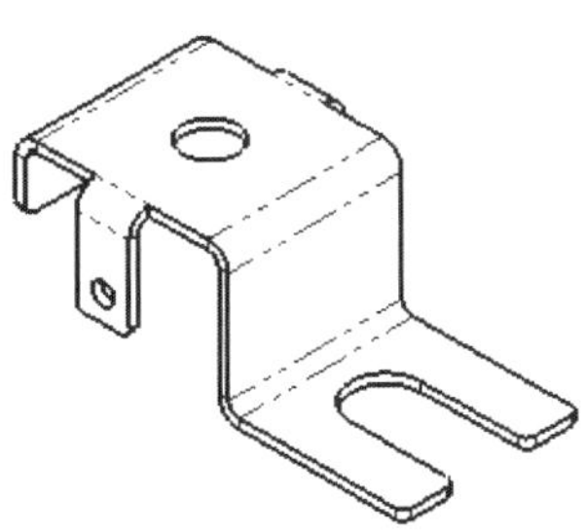

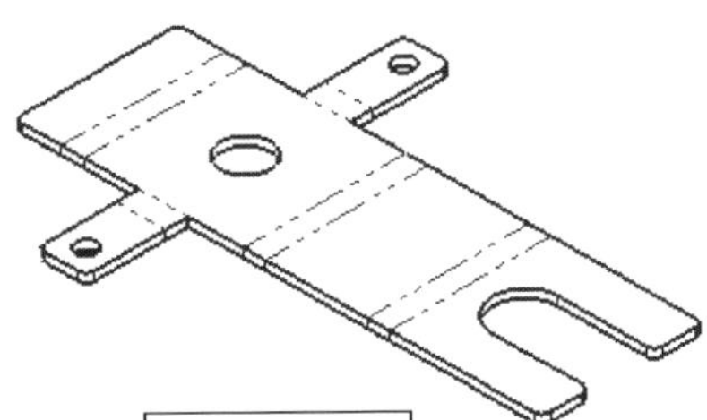

Scale: 1:2

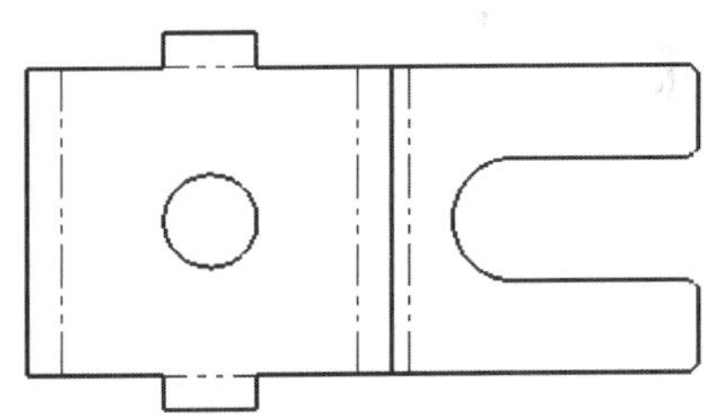

Scale: 1:1.5

Add another Isometric view and change it to the **Flat Pattern** configuration.

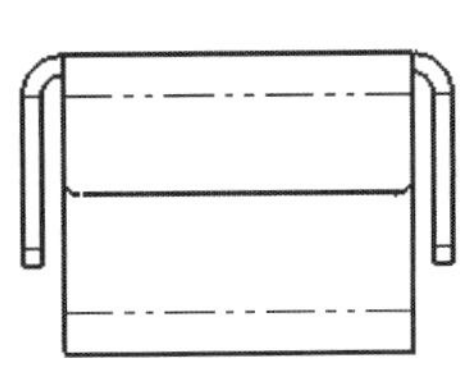

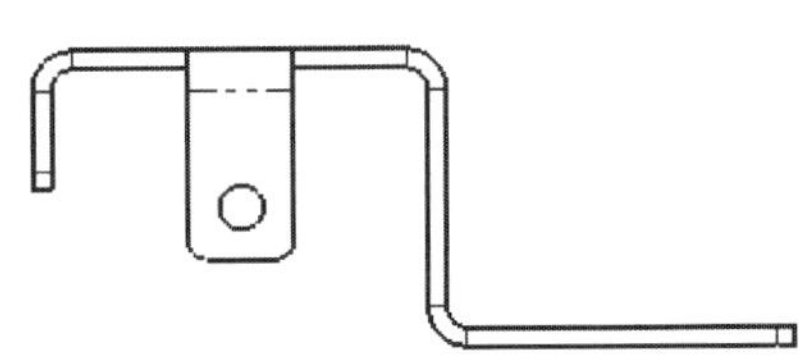

4. Adding Centerlines and Center Marks:

Use the **Centerline** and **Center Mark** tools on the **Annotation** tab to add the Centerlines and Center marks to the 3 drawing views shown below.

Drag the endpoint to lengthen them, where needed.

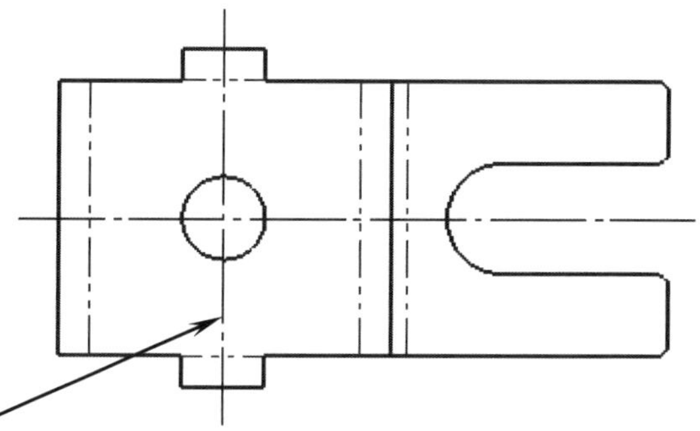

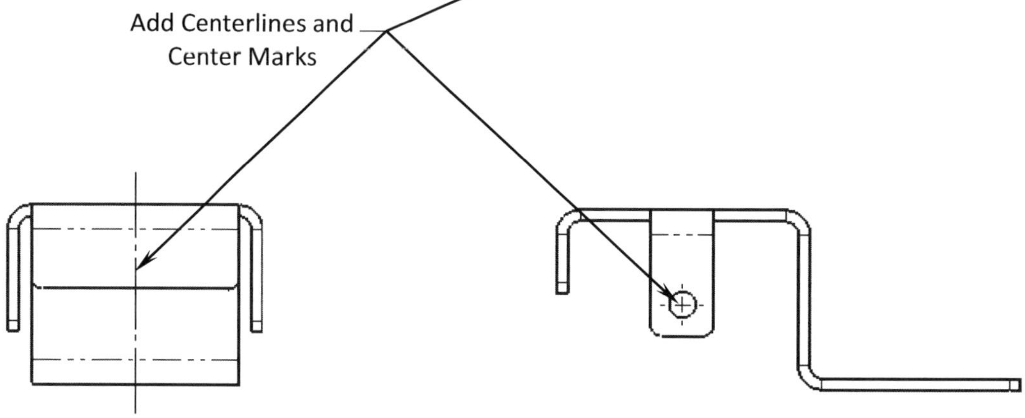

5. Inserting the Model Dimensions:

Insert the model dimensions to all drawing views using the settings below:

Marked For Drawing
Not marked for Drawing
Hole Wizard Locations
Hole Callout

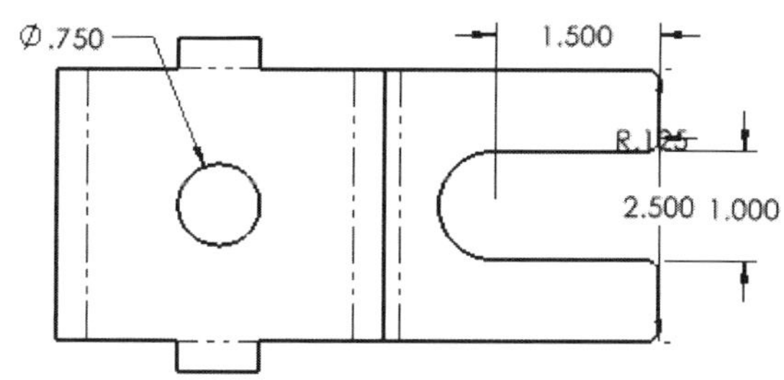

We will rearrange and modify the dimensions in the next step.

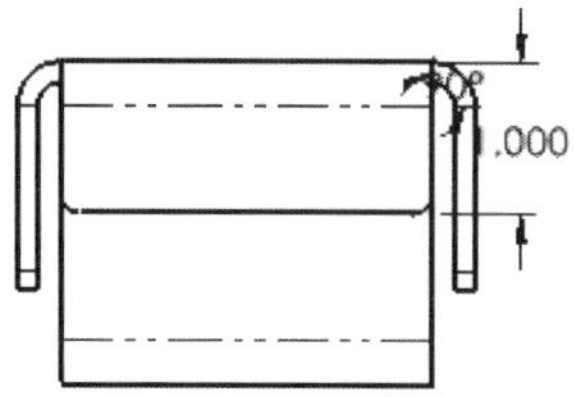

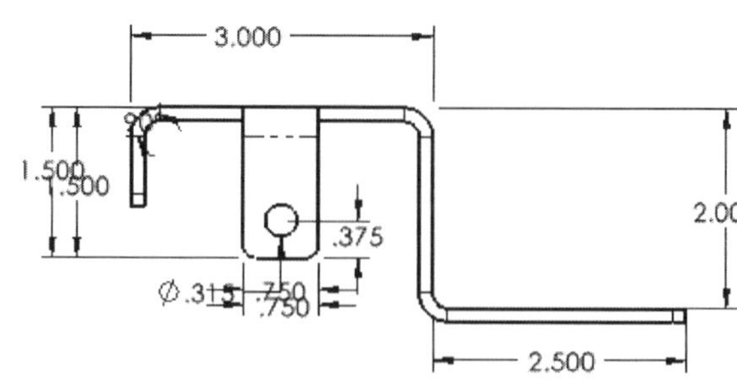

6. Rearranging and modifying Dimensions:

Zoom in on the **Top** drawing view and rearrange the dimensions to look similar to the image shown on the right.

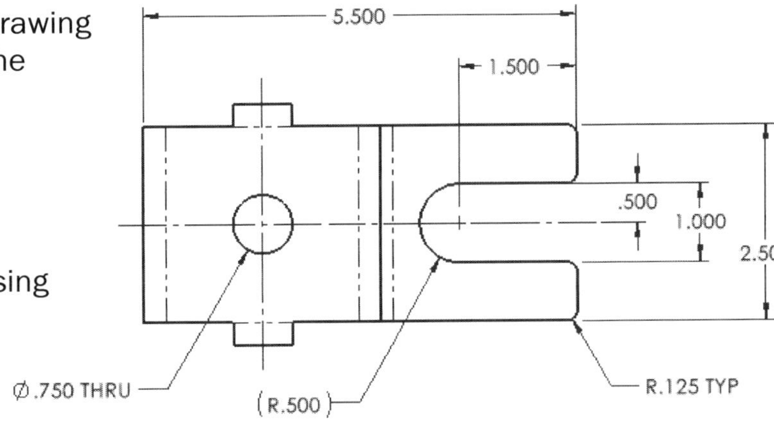

Add or move the missing dimensions where needed.

Select the **R.500** dimension and click **Add Parenthesis** to change it to a reference dimension.

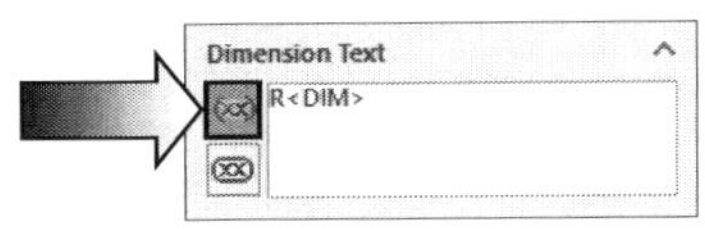

Zoom in on the **Front** drawing view.

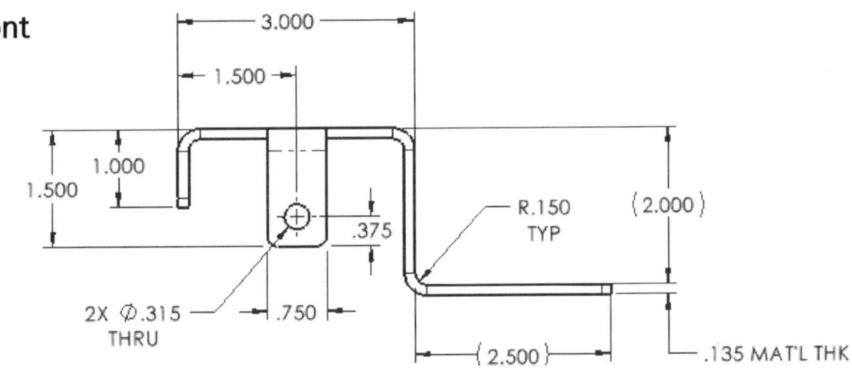

Add or move the missing dimensions to match the image shown here.

Make the dimension **2.000** a reference dimension.

Modify the dimensions and add the instance numbers as shown in each drawing view.

Zoom in on the **Right** drawing view.

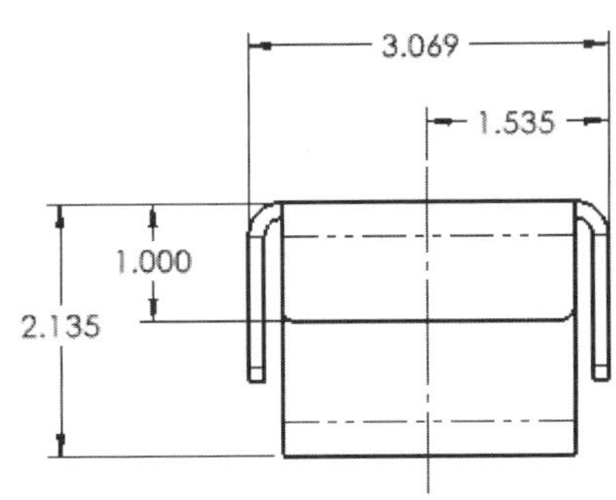

Add any missing dimensions or move them from the other drawing views, to look like the image shown on the right.

7. Adding the General Notes:

Switch to the **Annotation** tab and click **Note.**

Click near the lower left corner of the drawing to place the note, and enter the notes shown below:

NOTES: UNLESS OTHERWISE SPECIFIED

1. INTERPRET DRAWINGS AND DIMENSIONS PER ASME ANSI-Y14.5
2. DIMENSIONS ARE IN INCHES, 3 DECIMAL PLACES
3. MATERIAL: PLAIN CARBON STEEL
4. APPLY TYPICAL SHOP PRACTICE TO ALL CORNER RELIEF (T1 MIN)
5. PARTS TO BE CLEAN AND FREE OF LUBRICANT OR DEBRIS

Since the General Notes are used in almost every drawing, they are usually saved in the Template or saved as a block so that you can quickly insert it into a new drawing without having to recreate it every time.

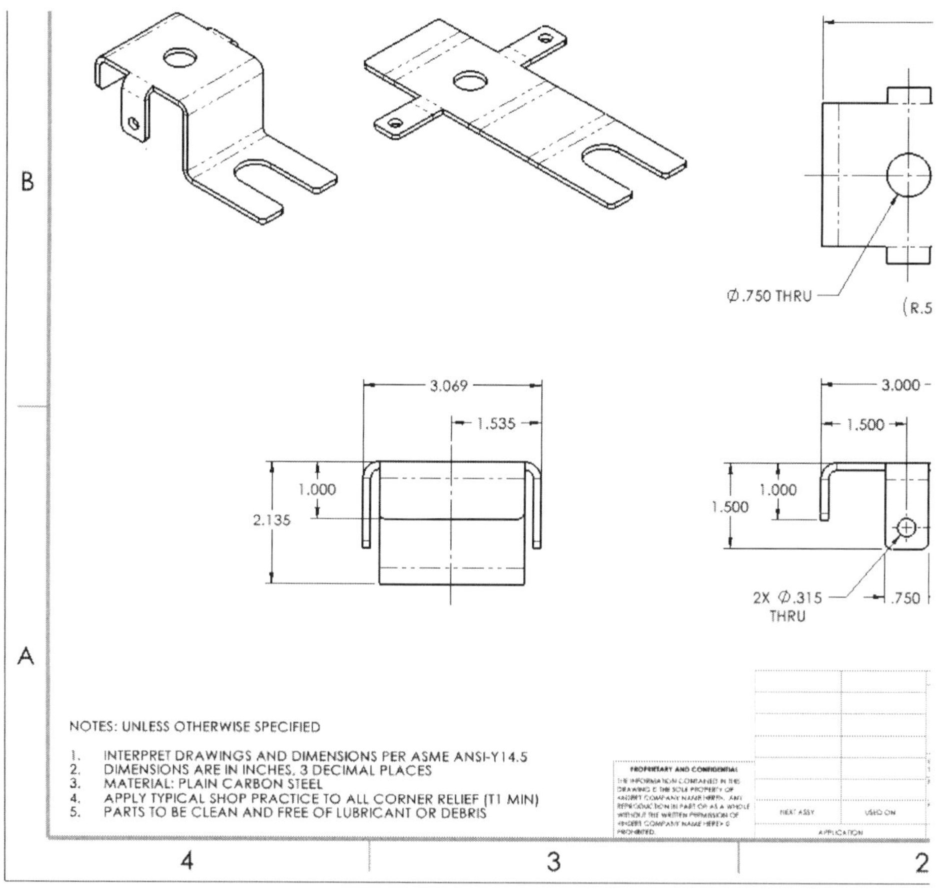

8. Filling out the Title Block:

From the FeatureManager tree, expand **Sheet1** and double-click **Sheet Format1** to activate it.

Fill out the information shown below. For the Name and Date areas, move the lines to increase the space, if needed.

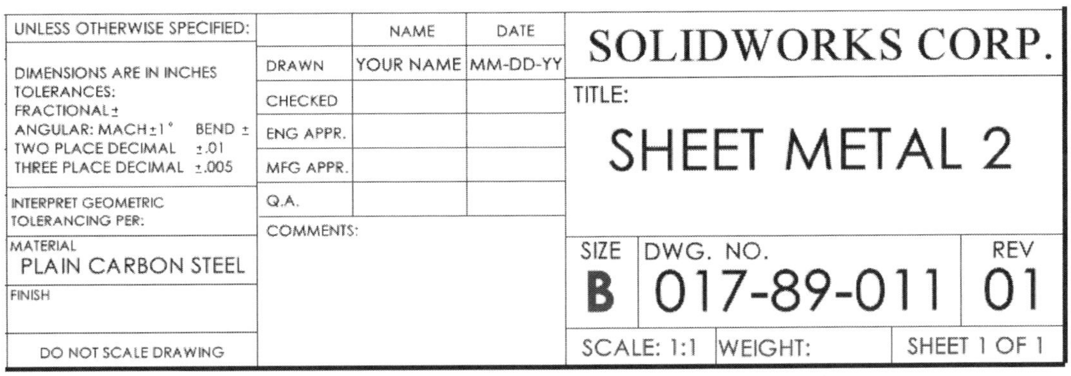

When finished, double-click **Sheet1** to bring the sheet layer back to the front.

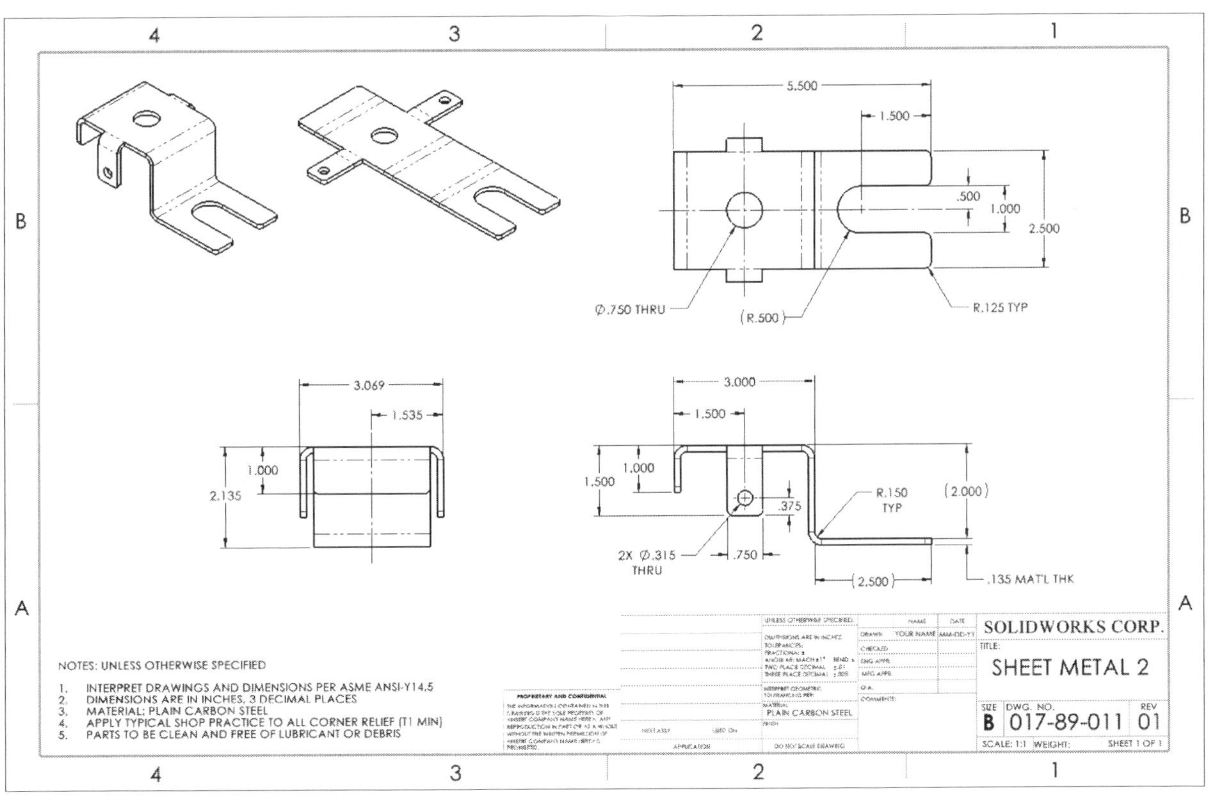

9. Saving your work:

Select **File, Save As.**

Enter: **Sheet Metal Part 2.slddrw** for the file name.

Click **Save.**

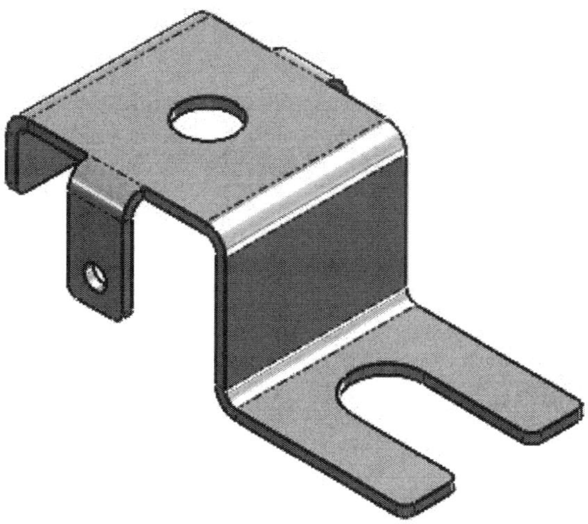

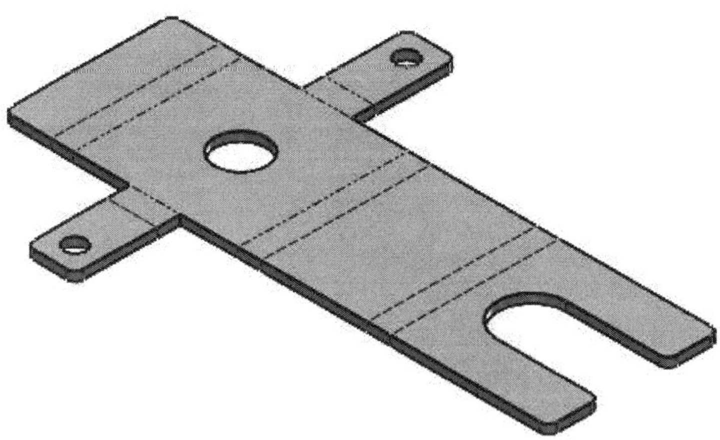

Exercise: Sheet Metal Parts

Detailing a Sheet Metal Part

The exercises are designed to help you apply what you have learned from the previous lessons. They come with some instructions but not as detailed as the lessons, to give you an opportunity to explore and to try and create the drawings on your own, at your own pace.

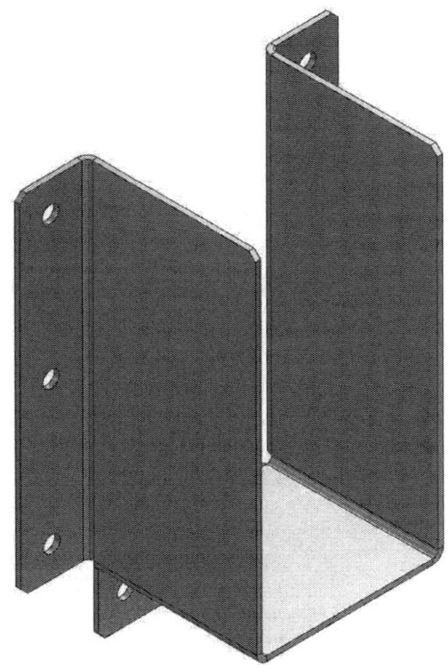

1. Opening a part document:

Select **File, Open**.

Browse to the Training Folder and open the part document named: **Sheet Metal Bracket.sldprt**.

The material **1060 Alloy** has already been assigned to the part.

2. Transferring to a drawing:

Select **File, Make Drawing from Part**.

Select the **B-Size** drawing paper.

Set the Type-Of-Projection to: **3rd Angle**.

Keep all other parameters at their default.

Click **OK**.

The B-Size drawing is loaded.

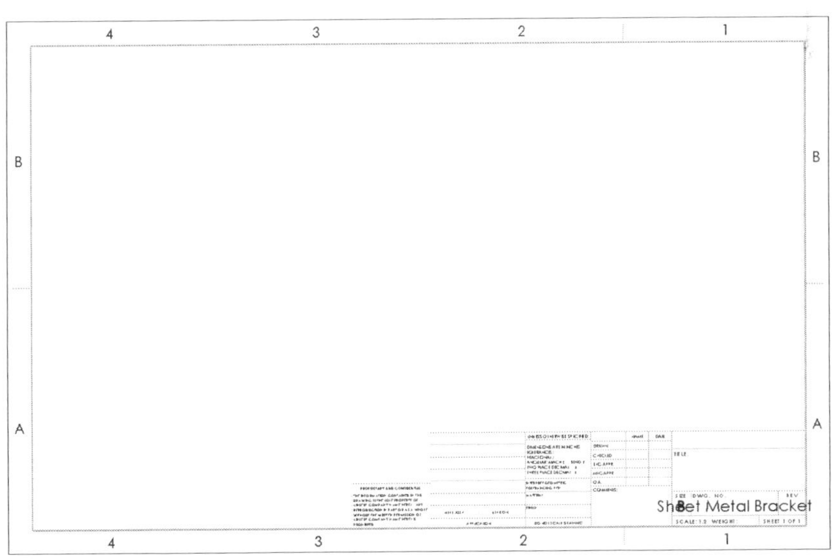

3. Creating the drawing views:

The Bend Notes should be disabled prior to creating the drawing views.

Select **Tools, Options**.

Select the **Sheet-Metal** option and clear the checkbox: **Display Sheet Metal Bend Notes** (arrow).

Using the View Palette, create the drawing views shown below, including the Flat-Pattern drawing view.

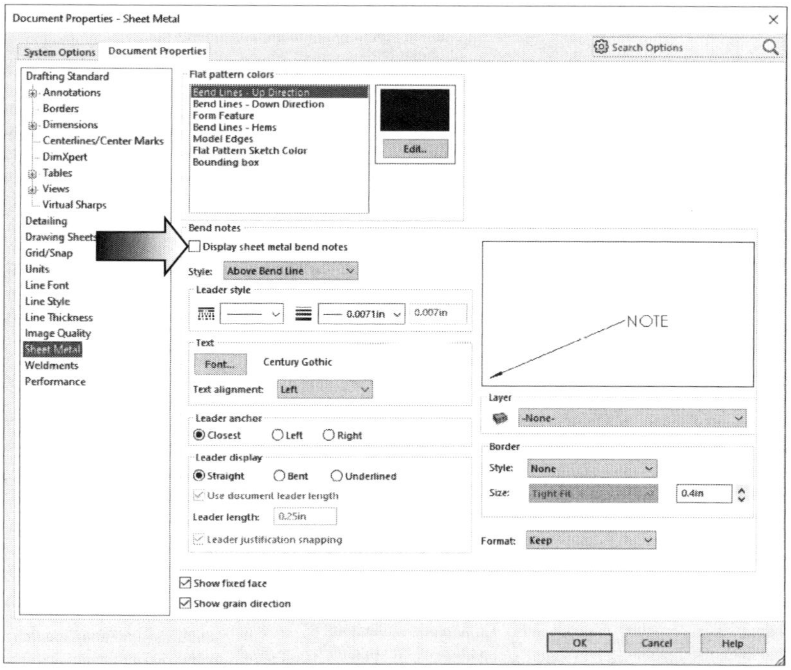

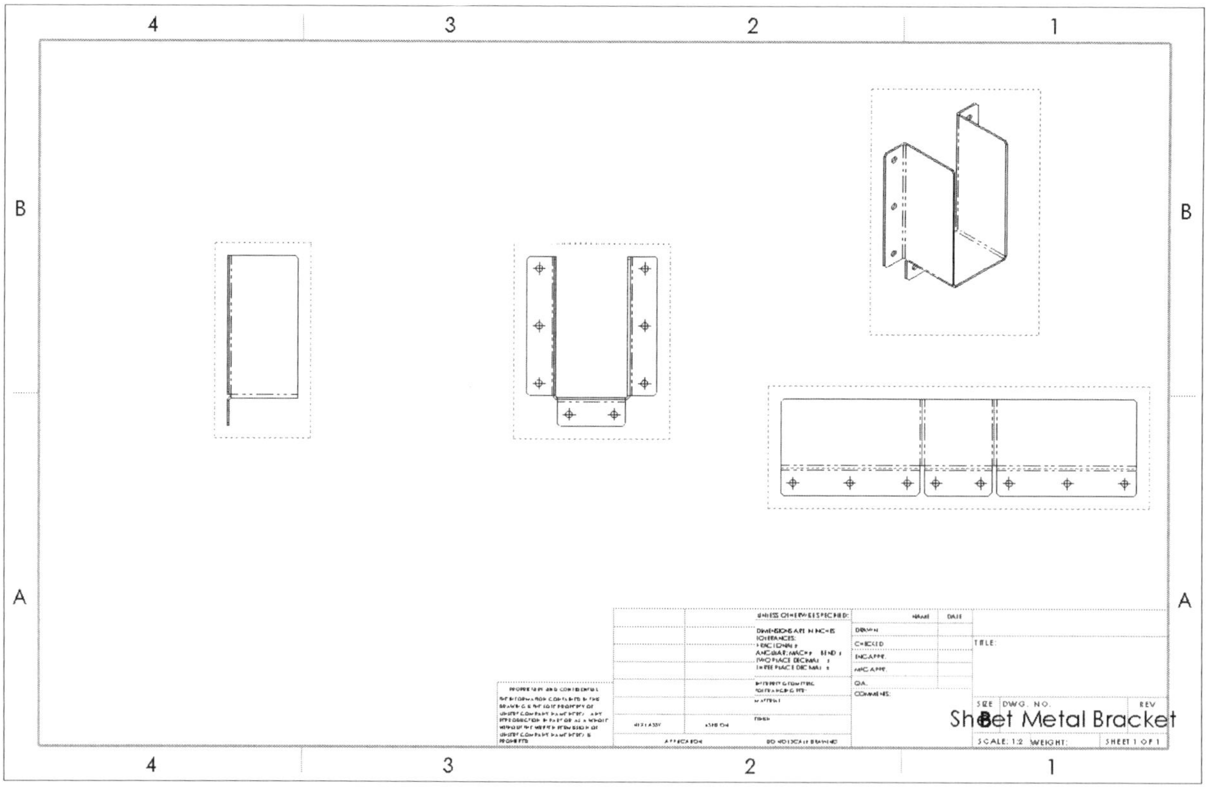

4. Inserting dimensions:

Switch to the **Annotation** tab and click **Model Items.**

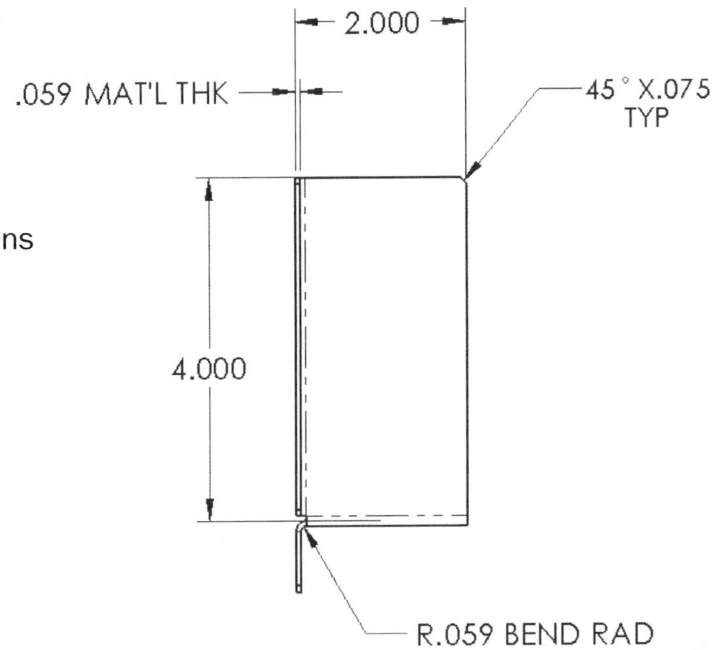

Select the options shown below to insert the dimensions from the model.

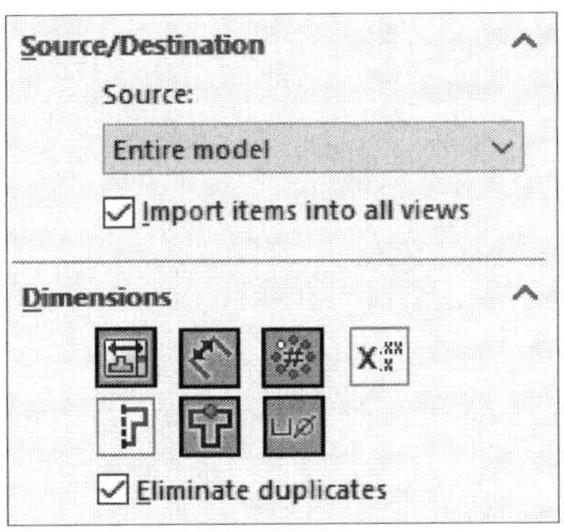

Rearrange the dimensions and add the missing ones.

Add the chamfer dimension as a note.

Using the options in the **Dimension Text** section and add the annotations and number of instances, where needed.

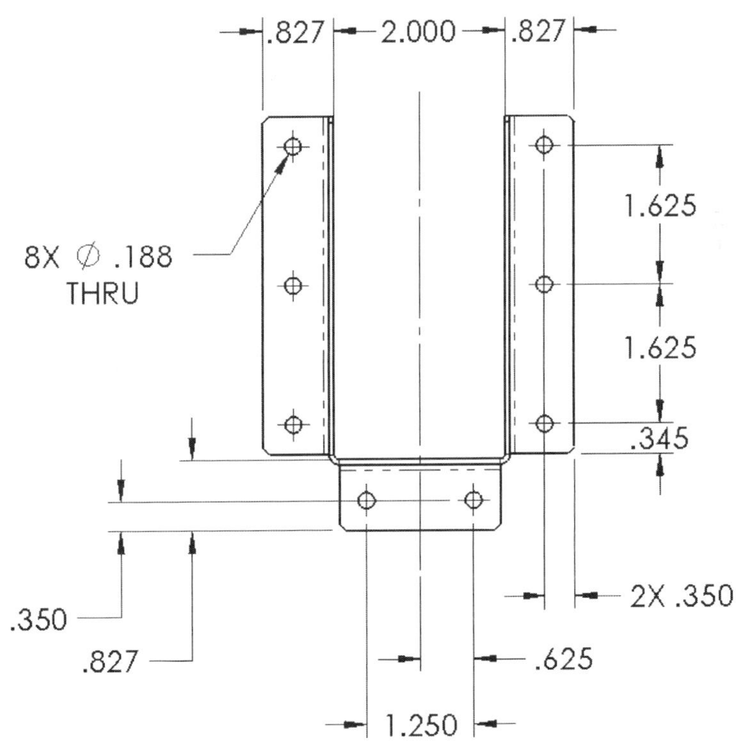

5. Adding the General Notes:

Switch to the **Annotation** tab and click **Note**.

Enter the notes shown below:

NOTES: UNLESS OTHERWISE SPECIFIED

1. INTERPRET DRAWINGS AND DIMENSIONS PER ASME ANSI-Y14.5
2. DIMENSIONS ARE IN INCHES, 3 DECIMAL PLACES
3. MATERIAL: 1060 ALLOY
4. APPLY TYPICAL SHOP PRACTICE TO ALL CORNER RELIEF (T1 MIN)
5. PARTS TO BE CLEAN AND FREE OF LUBRICANT OR DEBRIS

Place the note at the upper left corner of the drawing.

6. Filling out the Title Block information:

From the FeatureManager tree, expand **Sheet1** and double-click **Sheet Format** to activate the Format layer.

Fill out the information shown below in the appropriate sections.

UNLESS OTHERWISE SPECIFIED:		NAME	DATE	SOLIDWORKS CORP.		
DIMENSIONS ARE IN INCHES TOLERANCES: FRACTIONAL ± ANGULAR: MACH ± BEND ± TWO PLACE DECIMAL ± THREE PLACE DECIMAL ±	DRAWN	YOUR NAME	MM-DD-YY	TITLE: SHEET METAL BRACKET		
	CHECKED					
	ENG APPR.					
	MFG APPR.					
INTERPRET GEOMETRIC TOLERANCING PER:	Q.A.					
MATERIAL 1060 ALLOY	COMMENTS:			SIZE B	DWG. NO. 017-89-012	REV 01
FINISH						
DO NOT SCALE DRAWING				SCALE: 1:2	WEIGHT:	SHEET 1 OF 1

When finished, double-click **Sheet1** to return to the drawing.

7. Saving your work:

Select **File, Save As**.

Enter **Sheet Metal Bracket.slddrw** for the file name.

Click **Save**.

Close all documents.

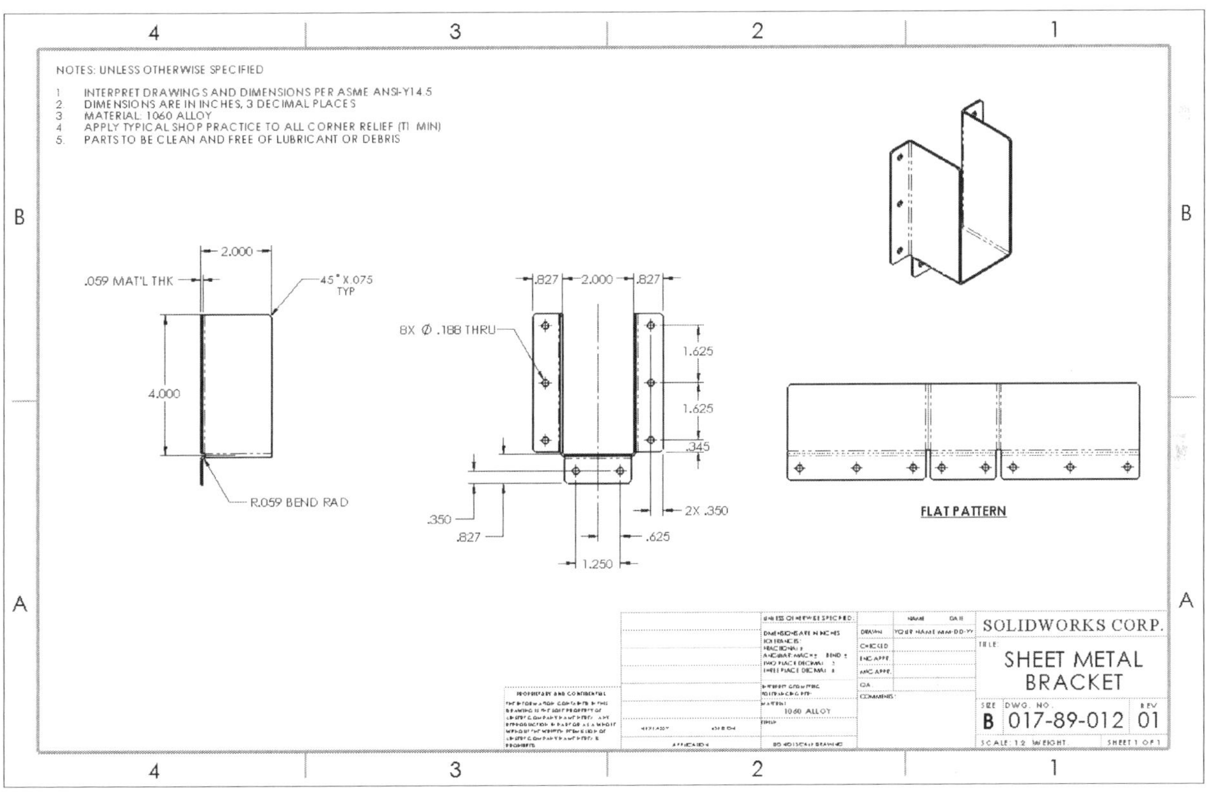

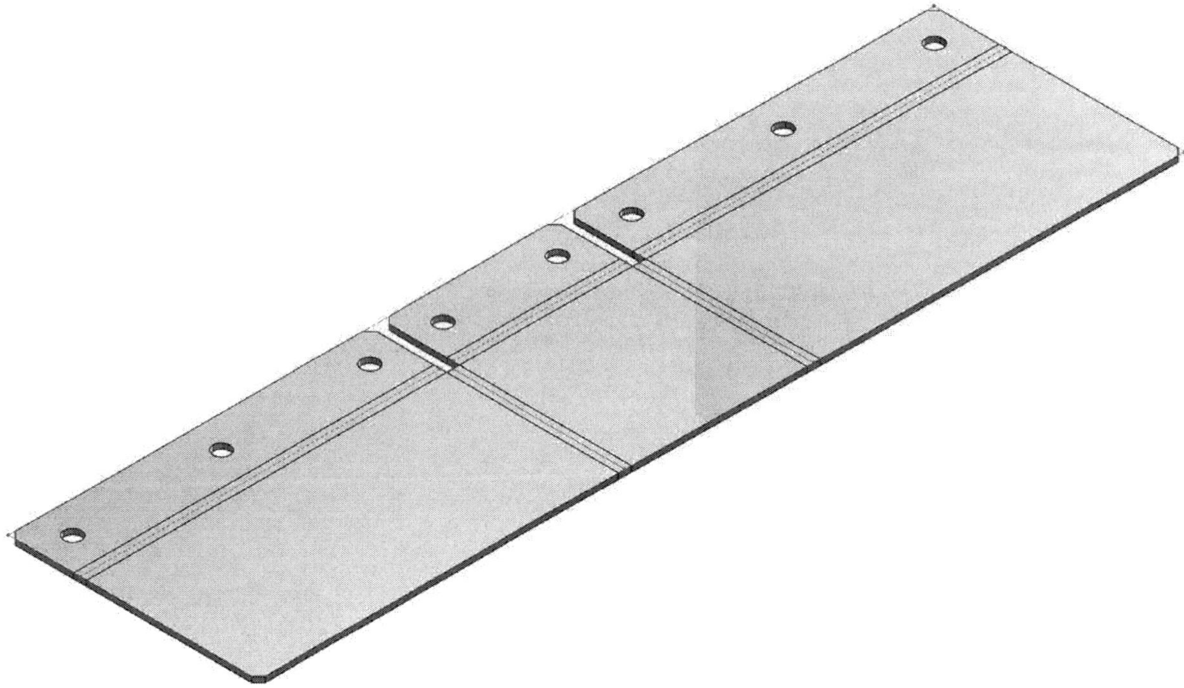

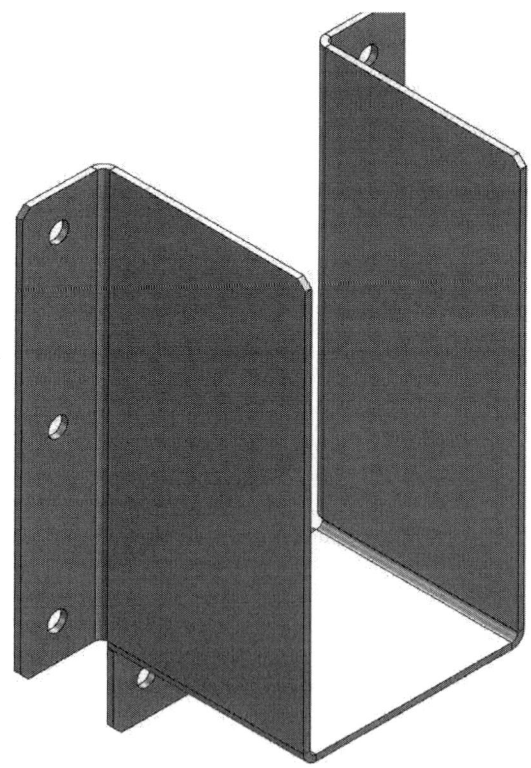

Exercise: Using the Segment Tool

Adding Dimensions to a Spline

Creating a precise curved spline is already a challenge; adding dimensions to the spline is even more challenging.

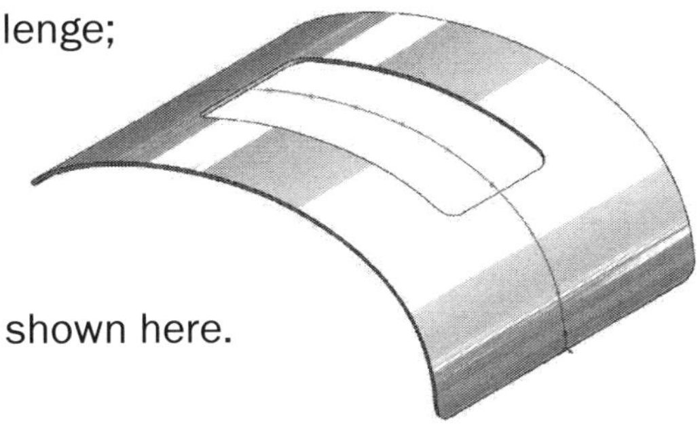

In this exercise, we will take a look at one of the methods that allow us to add dimensions more precisely to the curved spline in this model shown here.

1. Opening a part document:

Browse to the Training Folder and open a part document named: **Segments.sldprt**.

2. Converting the curved spline:

Select the **Front** plane from the FeatureManager tree and open a new sketch.

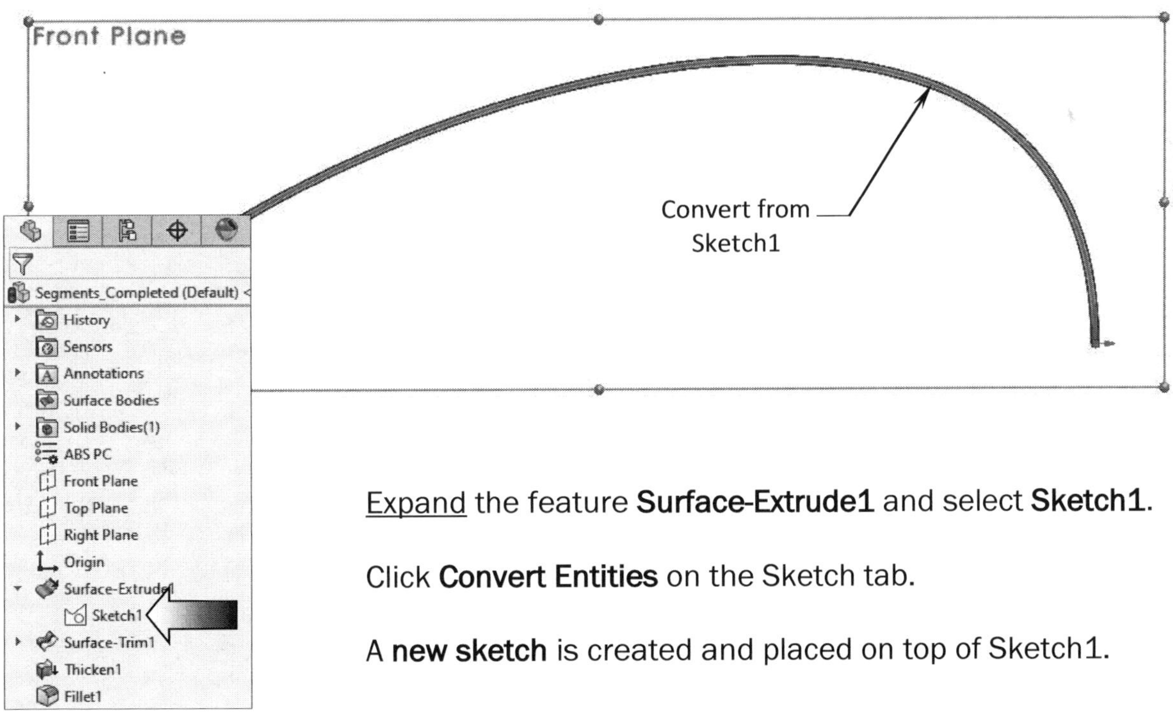

Expand the feature **Surface-Extrude1** and select **Sketch1**.

Click **Convert Entities** on the Sketch tab.

A **new sketch** is created and placed on top of Sketch1.

3. Adding the Sketch Points:

Select: **Tools, Sketch Tools, Segments**.

For Entity to Segment, select the **Converted Spline** from the graphics area.

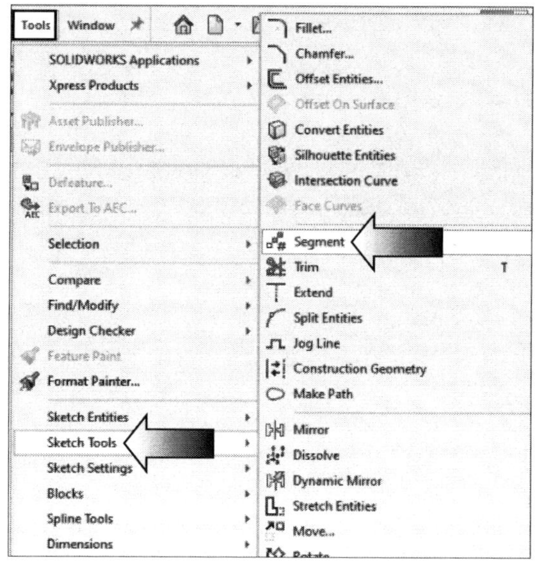

For Number of Points, enter: **10**.

Click the **Sketch Points** option.

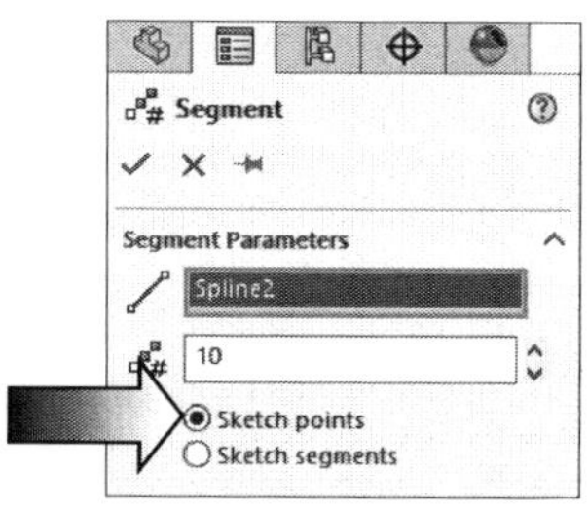

Click **OK**.

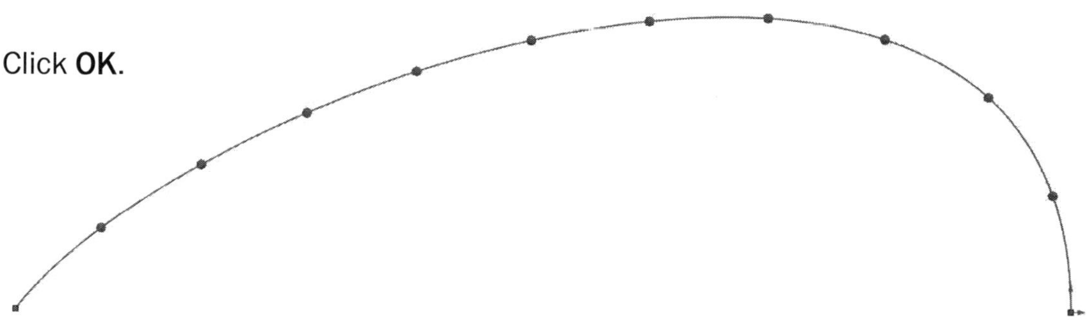

<u>Note</u>: *The more sketch points added to the spline the easier it will be to replicate the curve. But for this exercise, we will be using 10 additional sketch points to help speeds things up a little.*

4. Adding the Horizontal Ordinate dimensions:

For locations, Ordinate dimensions are used to specify the X and Y locations of each point.

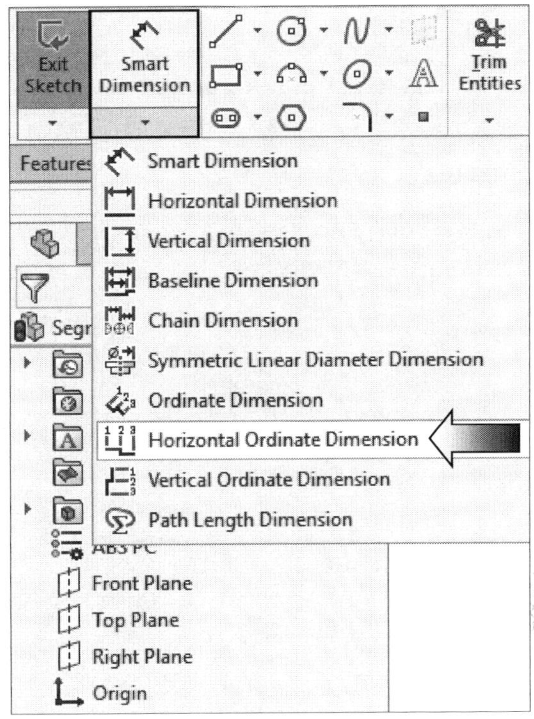

Expand the **Smart Dimension** tool and select **Horizontal Ordinate Dimension**.

Click the **Origin** point to place the **Zero** dimension.

Move towards the left and click **all** of the **segment points**.

The jog extensions are added to the dimensions that are too close to each other. Move the dimensions if needed.

The Vertical Ordinate Dimensions will be added next.

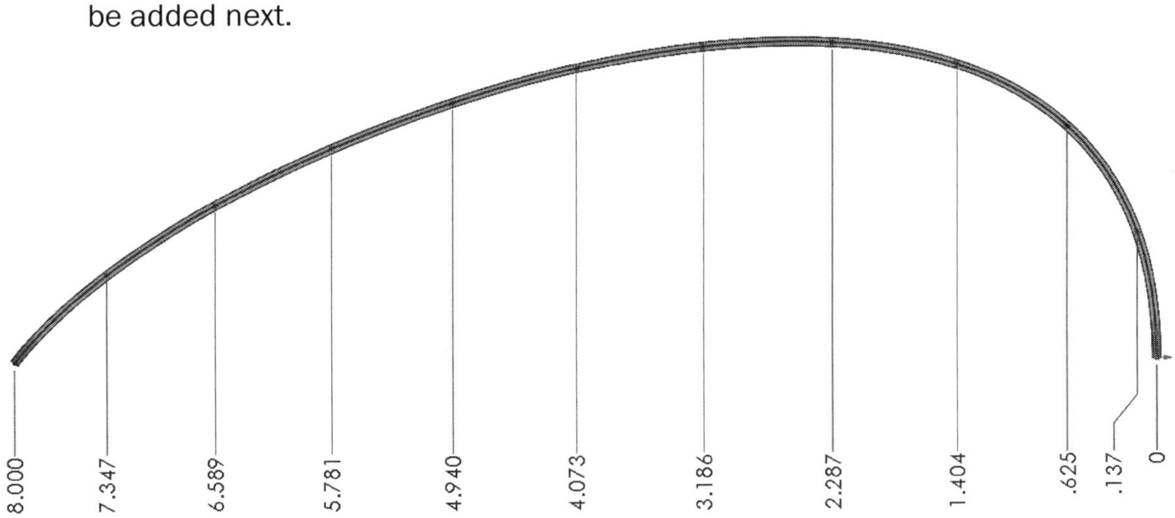

If a point is missing a dimension, right-click on the Zero dimension and select: Add To Ordinate, then select the point to add it to the group.

5. Adding the Vertical Ordinate dimensions:

Expand the Smart Dimension tool and select:
Vertical Ordinate Dimensions.

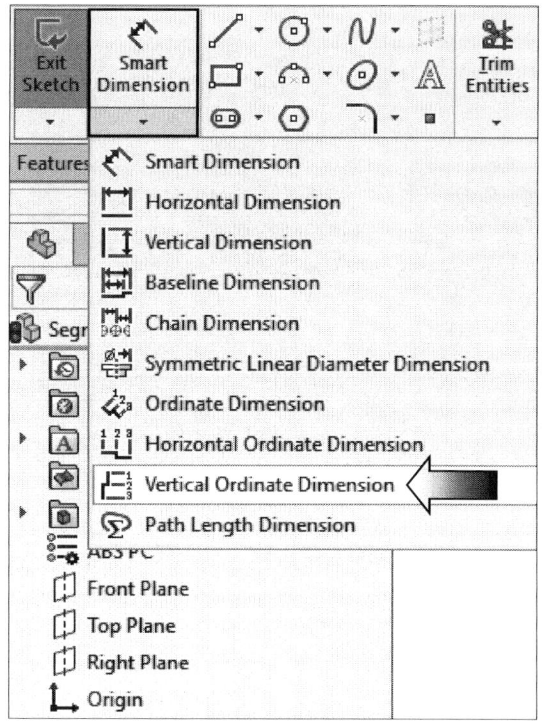

Start by clicking the **Origin** point to place the Zero dimension.

Move vertically and select all of the **segment points**.

<u>Note</u>: The last segment point is horizontal with the Origin; no vertical dimension is needed there.

Rearrange the dimensions so that they looked more evenly spaced, and easier to read.

Click **OK** to exit the dimension tool.

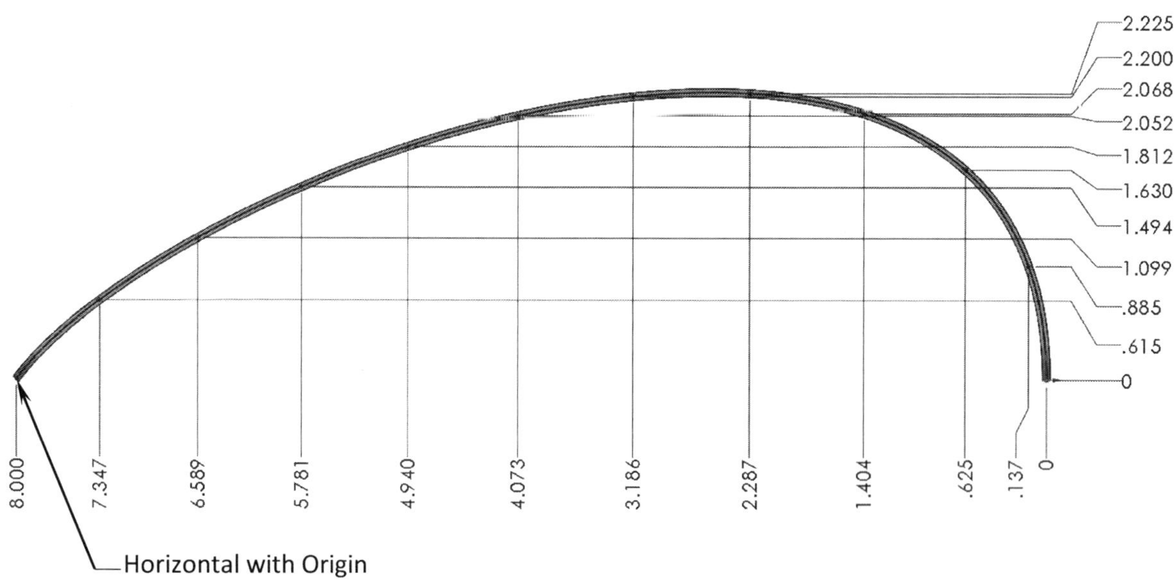

6. Saving your model:

Select **File, Save As**.

Enter: **Segments_Completed.sldprt**
for the file name.

Click **Save**.

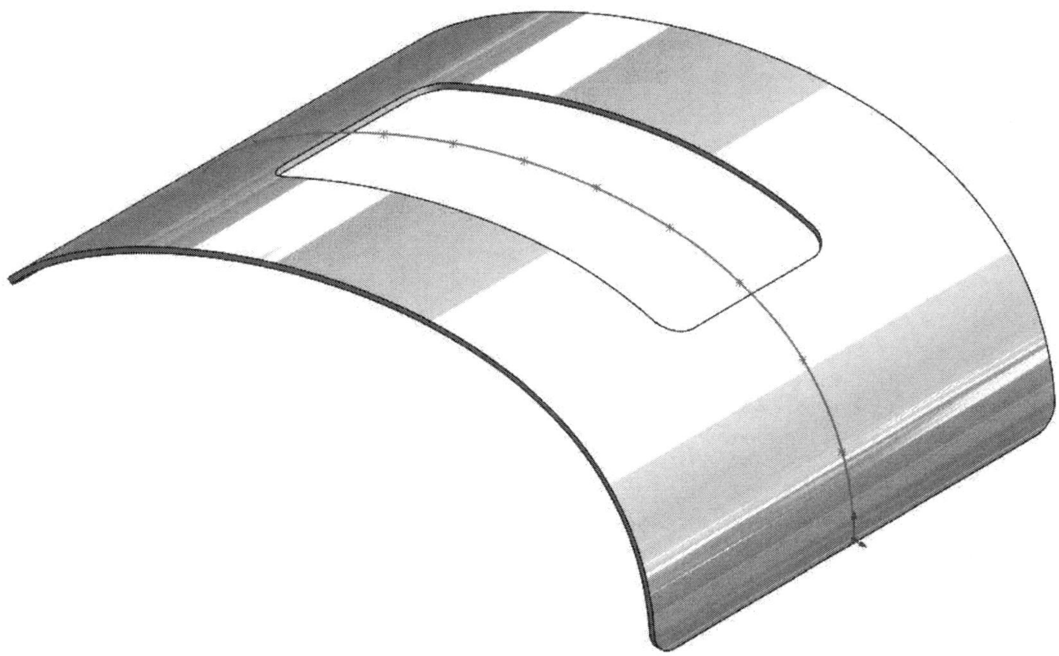

Hide the Converted Sketch; it is shown here for clarity only.

We will show this sketch again in the drawing when adding the annotations to the drawing view.

7. Making a drawing (Optional):

Create an engineering drawing from this model as shown below.

Use the following parameters:

B-Size ANSI Landscape

Third Angle Projection

Scale: 1:2

Show the Converted Sketch for the Front drawing view when adding dimensions.

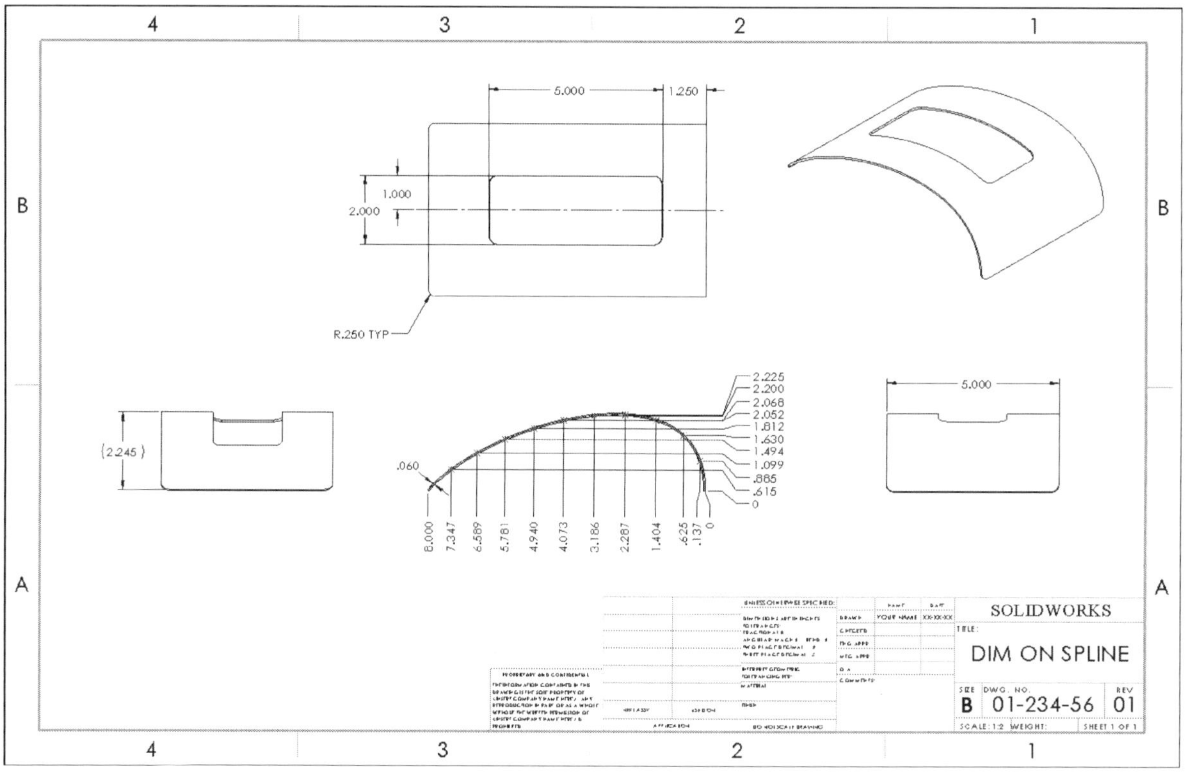

8. Saving your drawing:

Select **File, Save As**.

Enter: **Segments_Completed.slddrw** for the file name.

Click **Save**.

CHAPTER 7: DETAILING CASTINGS & FORGINGS

Detailing a Casted Part

Casting is a manufacturing process in which a liquid material is usually poured into a mold, which contains a hollow cavity of the desired shape, and then allowed to solidify. The solidified part is also known as casting, which is ejected or broken out of the mold to complete the process.

Casting materials are usually metals or various time setting materials that cure after mixing two or more components together. Casting is most often used for making complex shapes that would be otherwise difficult or uneconomical to make by other methods. Heavy equipment like machine tool beds, ships' propellers, etc. can be cast easily in the required size, rather than fabricating by joining several small pieces.

1. Opening a part document:

Select **File, Open.**

Browse to the Training Folder and open the part document named: **Casted Part 1.sldprt.**

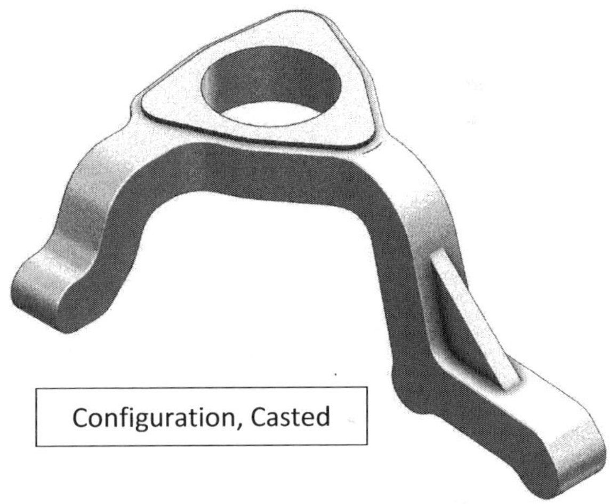

Configuration, Casted

The material **Cast Stainless Steel** has already been assigned to the part.

There are two configurations in this part, **Casted** and **Machined.**

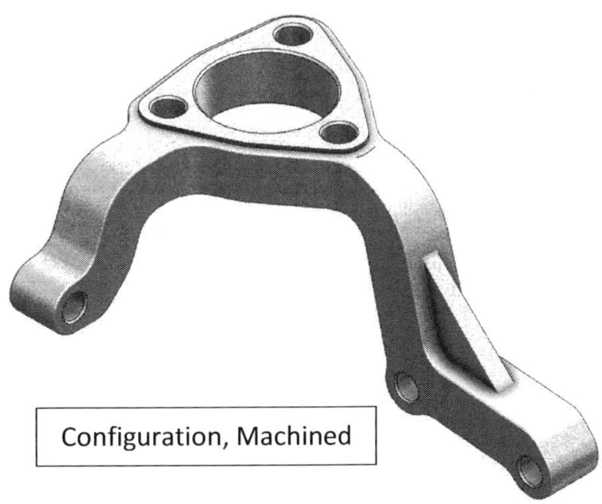

Configuration, Machined

The **Casted** configuration does not have the 6 small holes.

The **Machined** configuration has the 6 small holes, and the hole in the center is a little bit larger.

2. Drawing overview:

We will use 2 drawing sheets to detail both the Casted and Machined configurations of the part.

The 2 drawings shown below need to be created. The 1st sheet will be the drawing for the Casted configuration, and the 2nd sheet will be the Machined.

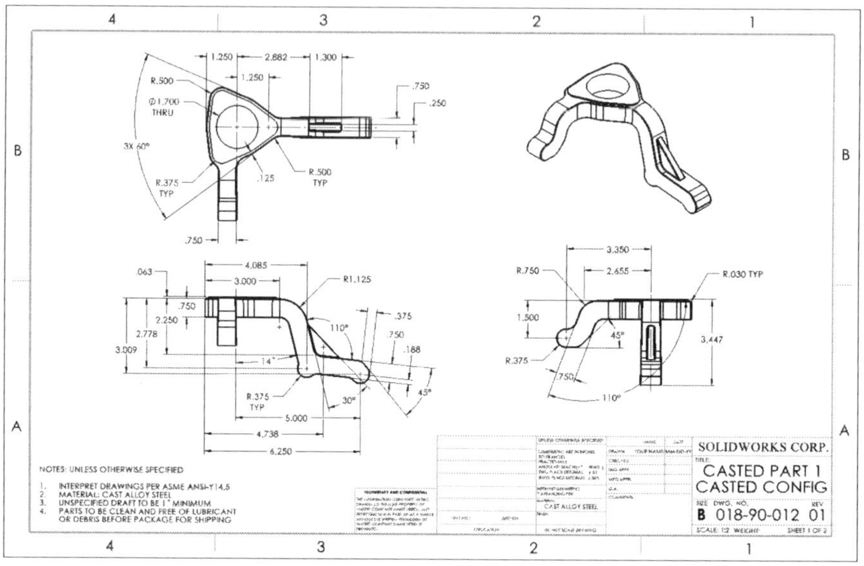

Casted Configuration

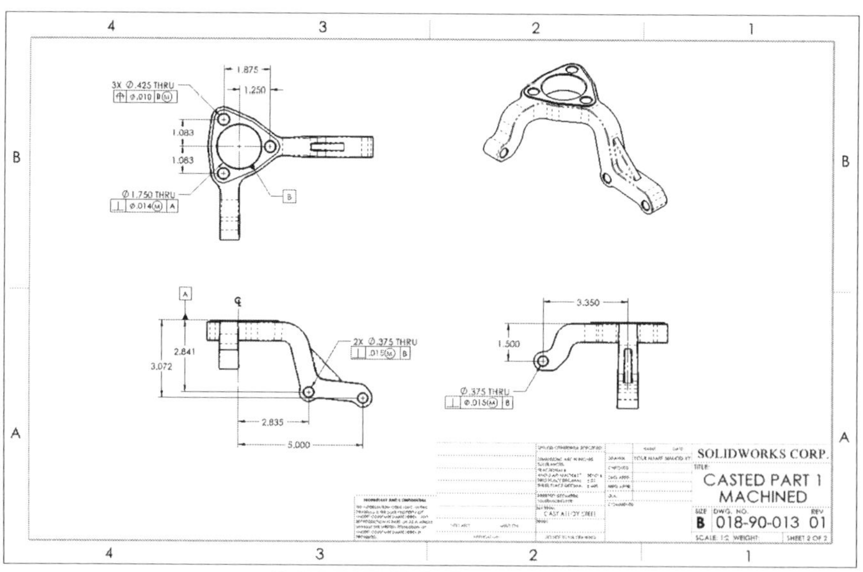

Machined Configuration

3. Adding a 2nd sheet:

At the bottom left corner of the screen, next to Sheet1, click the **Add Sheet** tab to add a new drawing sheet.

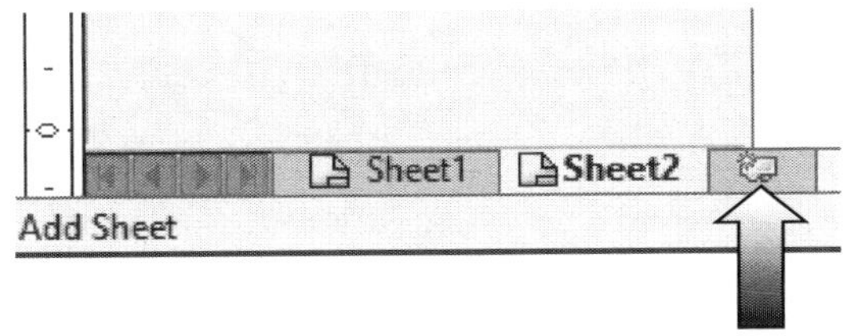

A new drawing sheet is added over Sheet1; it is automatically labeled as **Sheet2**. We will use Sheet2 to detail the Machined version of this part, but first, we will go back to Sheet1 and detail the Casted configuration.

Click **Sheet1** tab to change the sheet.

4. Creating the Casted drawing:

Expand the **View Palette** and enable only the checkbox: **Auto Start Projected View**; uncheck all other checkboxes.

Drag and drop the **Front** drawing view approximately as shown below, and then add the **Top**, the **Right**, and the **Isometric** view.

Change the scale of all views to **1:2**.

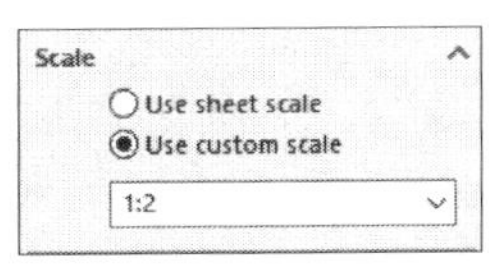

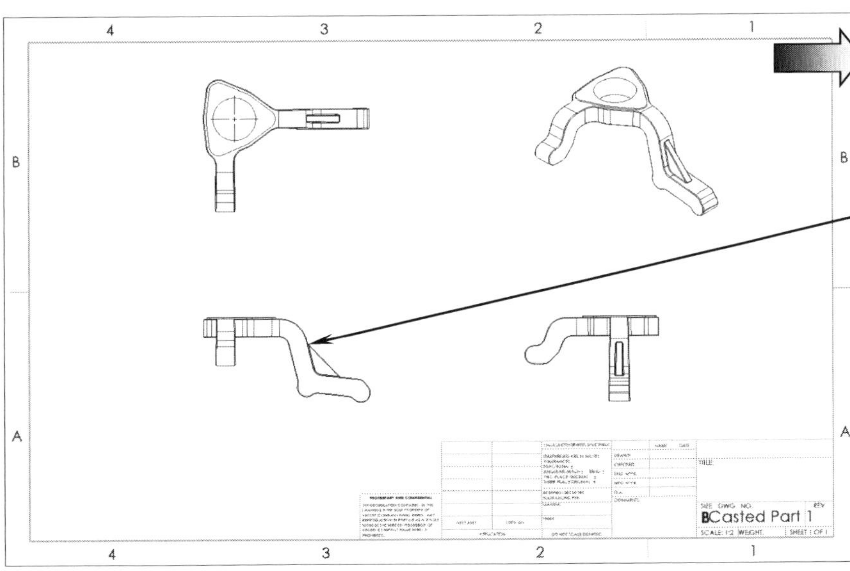

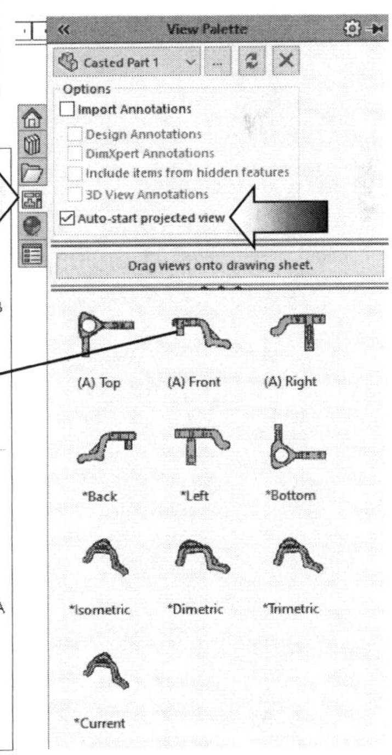

5. Inserting the model dimensions:

Switch to the Annotation tab and click **Model Items.**

Enable the options shown in the **Source** and the **Dimensions** sections.

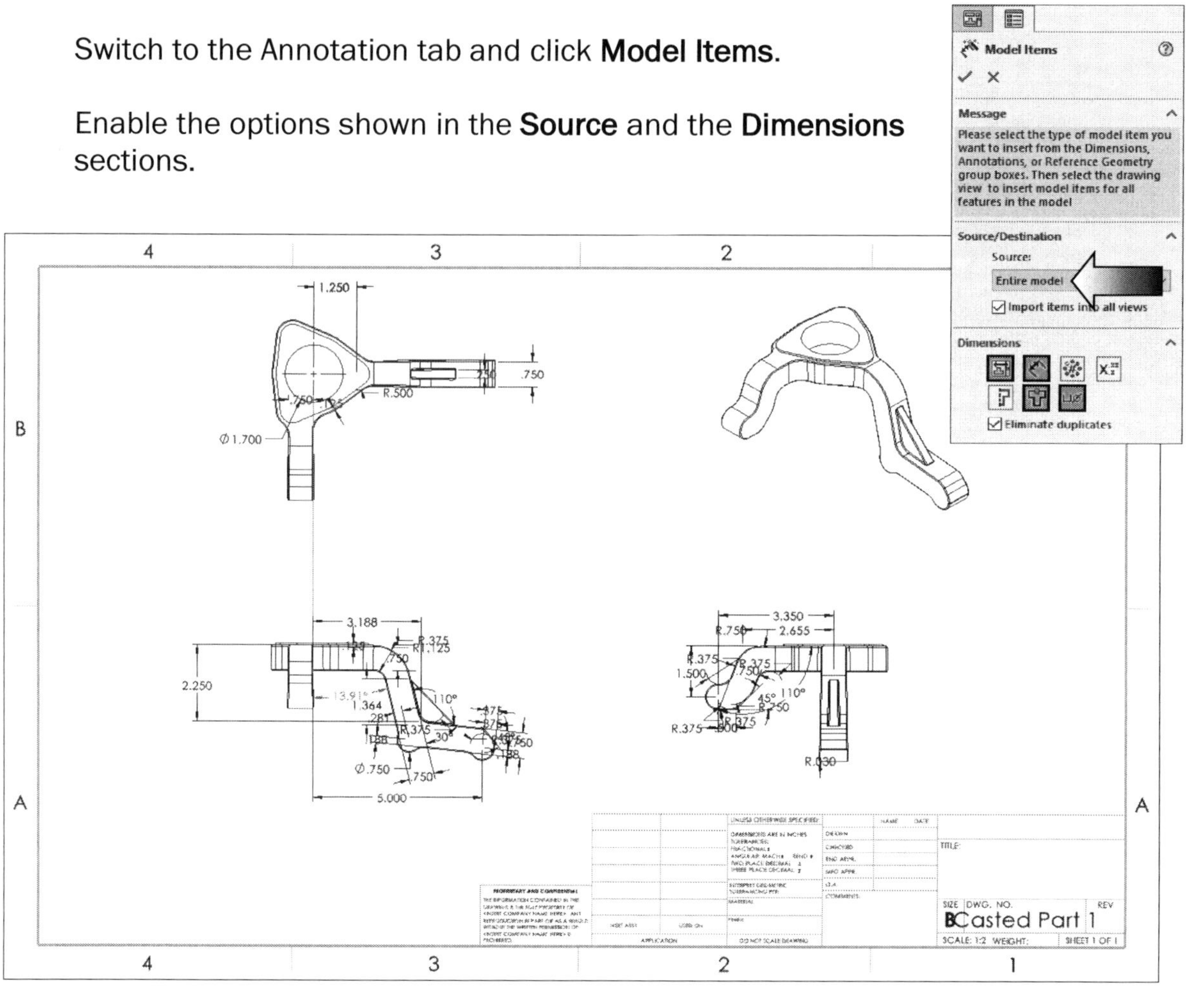

Zoom in on the **Top** drawing view, add the **Center Marks** and the **Centerlines** as shown.

Rearrange the dimensions and add the instances and additional dimensions where needed.

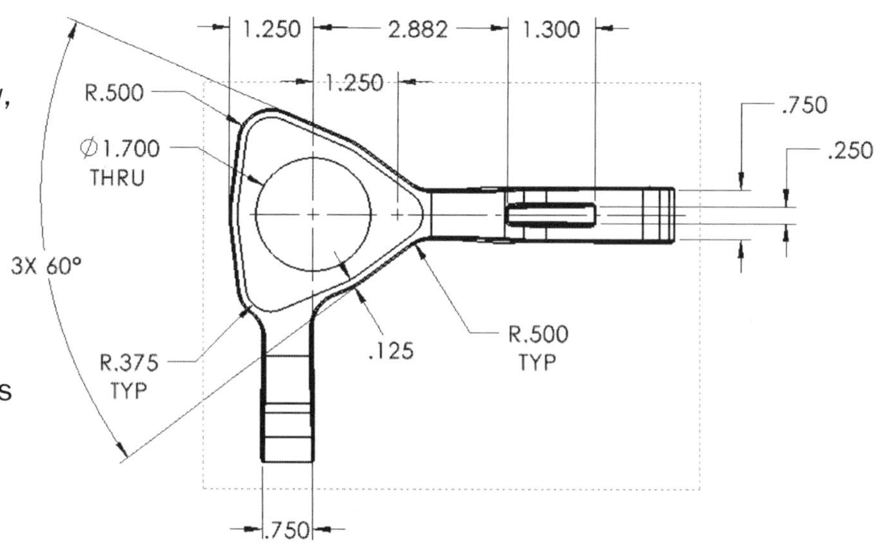

Zoom in on the **Front** drawing view.

Rearrange the dimensions to look similar to the image below.

Add **Center Marks, Centerlines,** and the additional dimensions where needed.

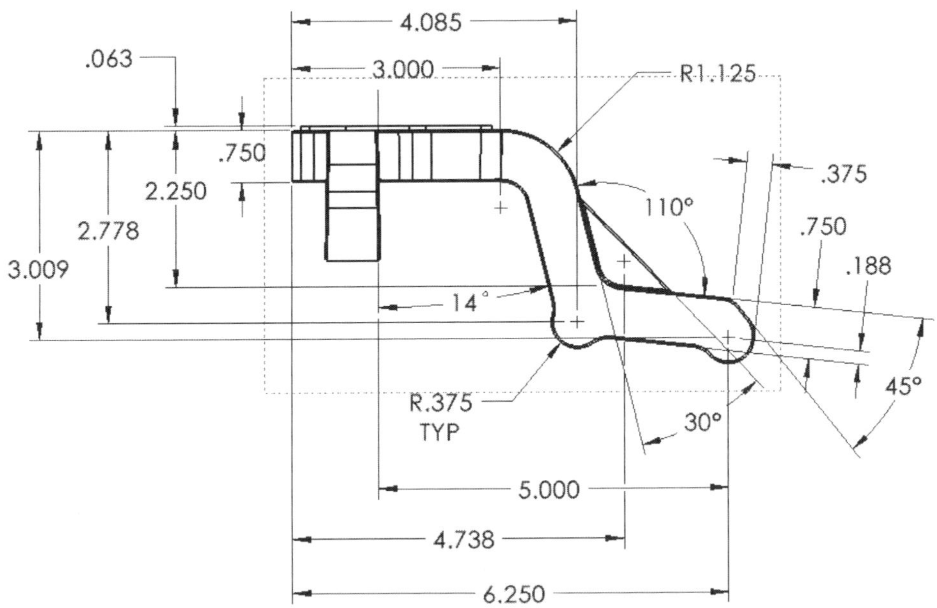

Zoom in on the **Right** drawing view.

Clean up the drawing view and make it look similar to the image shown below.

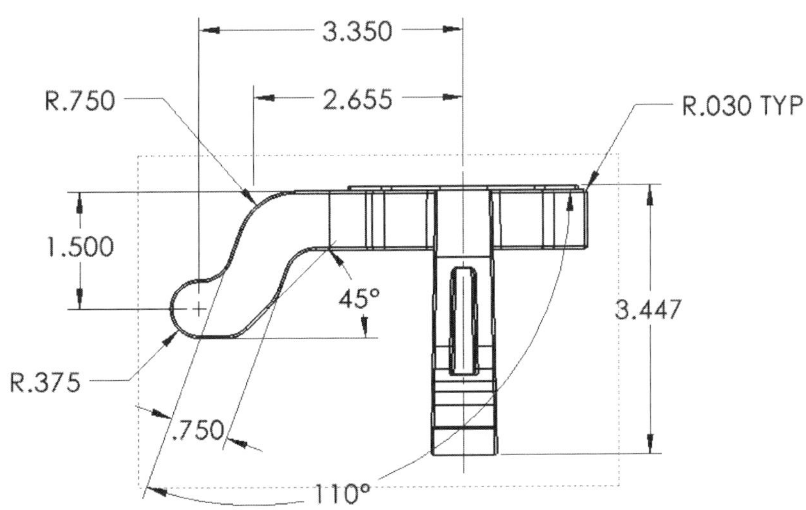

6. Creating the General Notes:

Zoom in on the lower left corner of the drawing.

Click **Note**, on the **Annotation** tab.

Enter the notes below using all uppercase letters.

NOTES: UNLESS OTHERWISE SPECIFIED
1. INTERPRET DRAWINGS AND DIMENSIONS PER ASME-ANSI 14.5
2. MATERIAL: CAST ALLOY STEEL
3. UNSPECIFIED DRAFT ANGLE TO BE 1° MINIMUM
4. PARTS TO BE CLEAN AND FREE OF LUBRICANT OR DEBRIS BEFORE PACKAGED FOR SHIPPING

When finished, select the notes, and click **Lock Note** to prevent it from moving around.

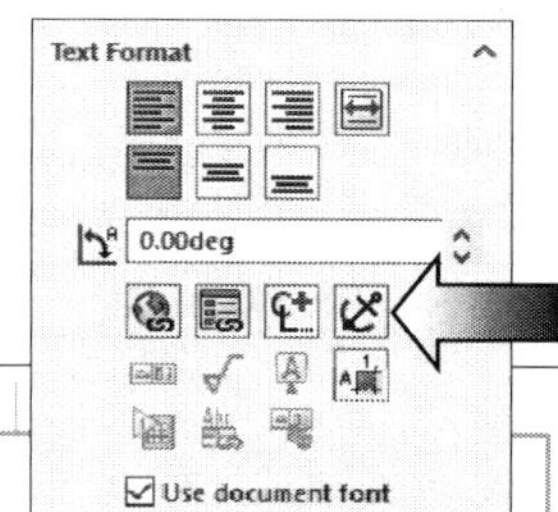

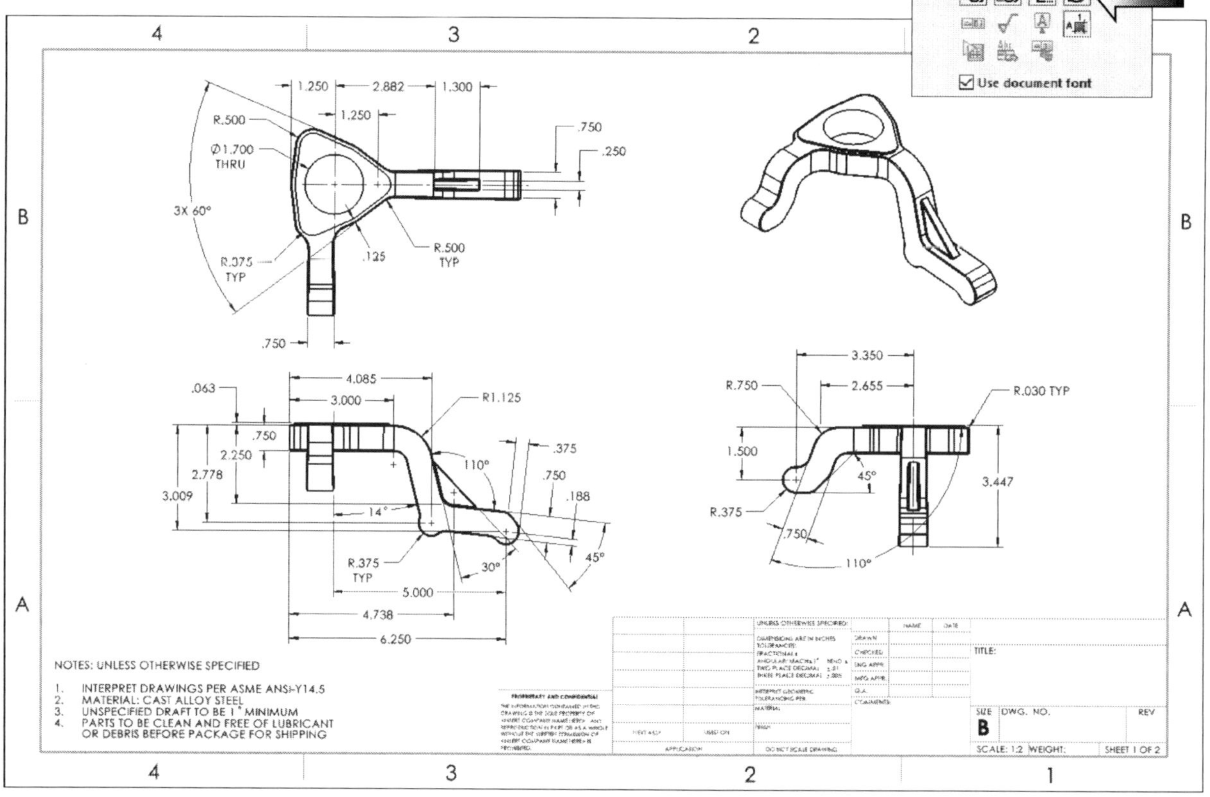

7. Filling out the Title Block information:

From the FeatureManager tree, expand **Sheet1** and double-click **Sheet Format1** to activate and bring the format layer to the front for editing.

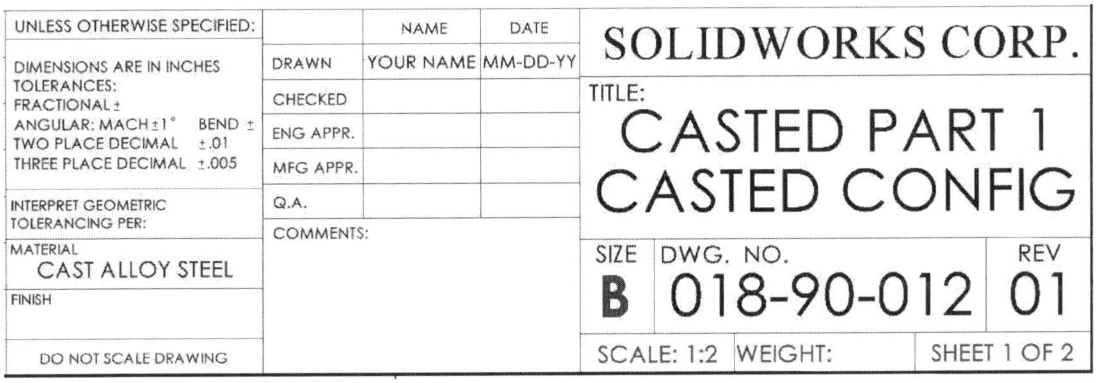

Double-click the blank notes inside of each field and fill out the information shown above.

When finished, double-click **Sheet1** to bring the drawing layer back to the front.

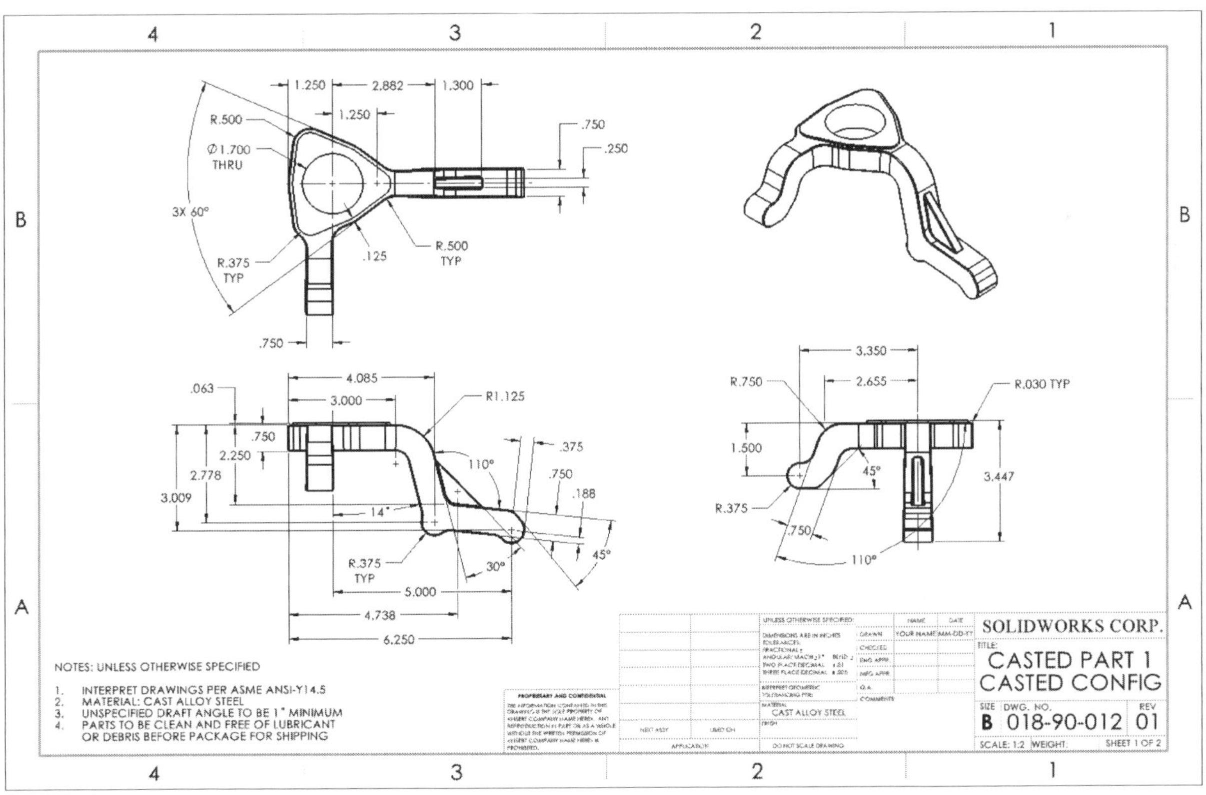

8. Creating the Machined drawing:

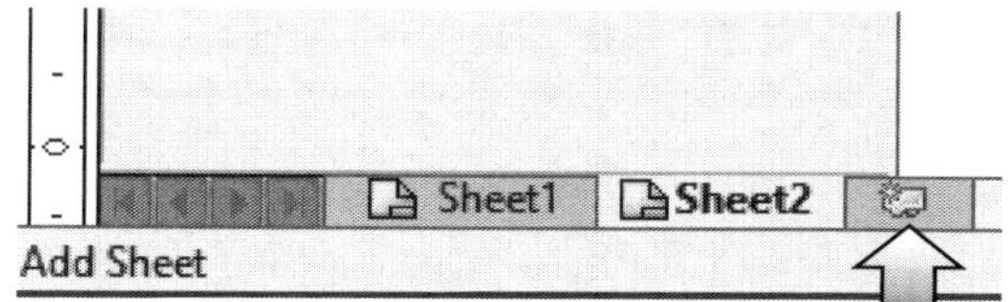

Next, we will create a drawing for the Machined configuration of the same part, on Sheet 2.

Click on the **Sheet 2** tab to activate Sheet 2.

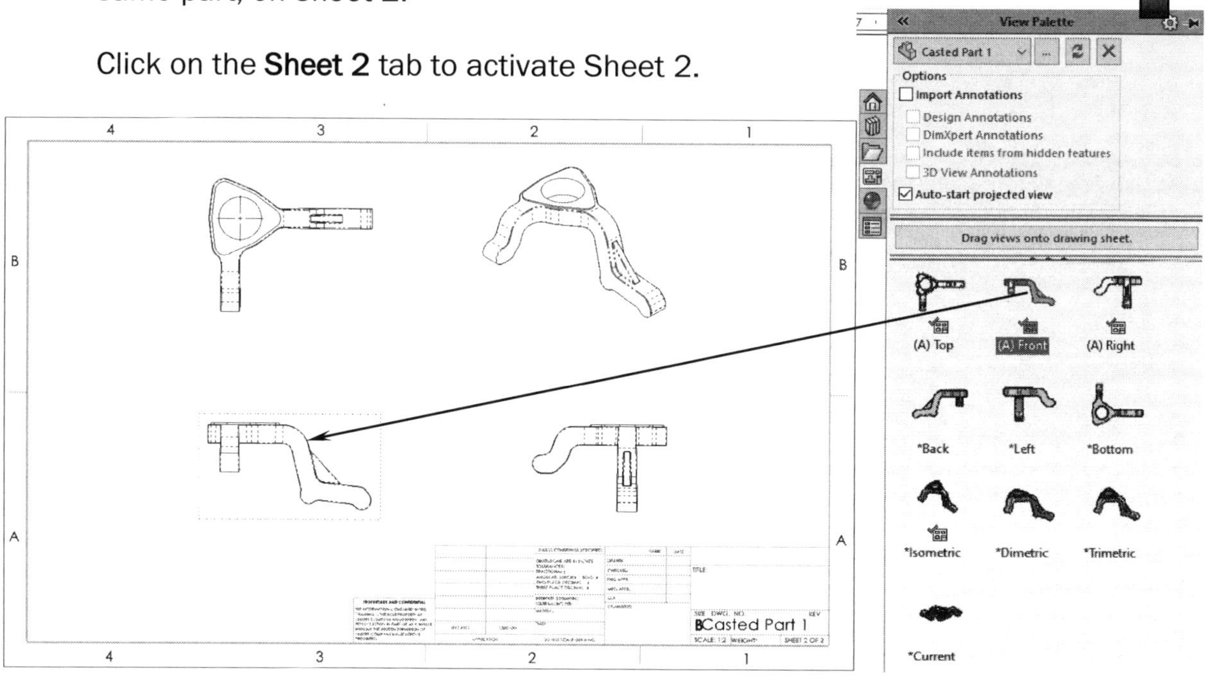

Using the **View Palette**, drag the **Front** drawing view into Sheet 2, and then add the **Top**, the **Right**, and the **Isometric** view as shown above.

The drawing views are still showing the Casted configuration; we will need to switch them to the Machined configuration.

Select the dotted border of the **Front** drawing view as noted below.

From the FeatureManager tree, expand **Reference Configuration** and select the **Machined** configuration.

Click **OK**.

All four drawing views are switched to the Machined configuration.

All the cut features are now visible in the drawing views.

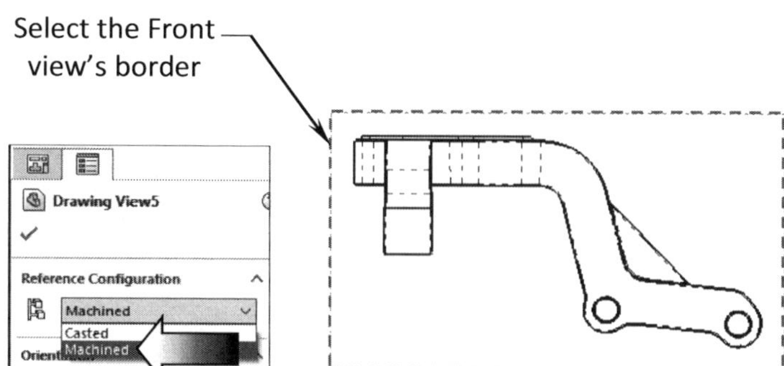

9. Inserting the model dimensions:

The dimensions of the machined features such as the holes and their locations will need to be inserted into the machined drawing views.

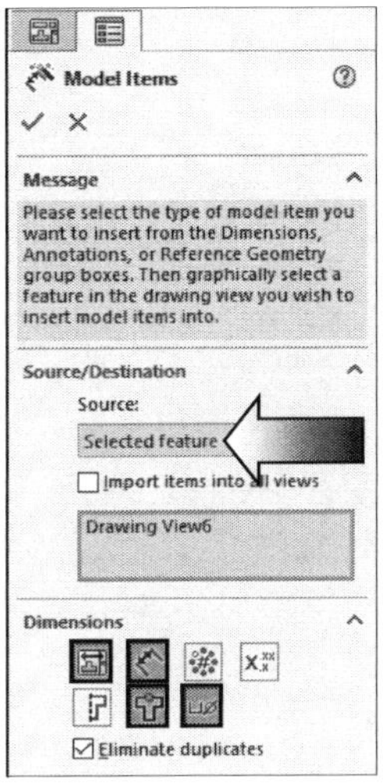

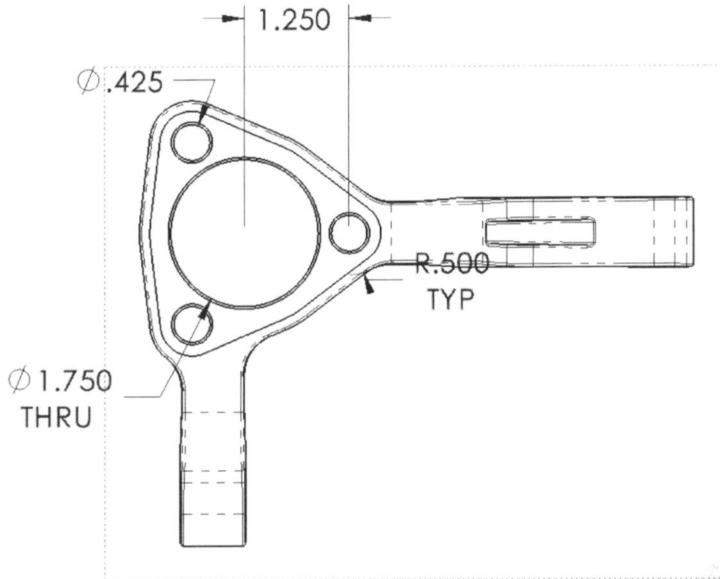

Select the **Top** drawing view, switch to the **Annotation** tab and click **Model Items.**

Enable the following options:

Source:
Selected Feature

Dimensions:
Marked for Drawing
Not Marked for Drawing
Hole Wizard Locations
Hole Callout

Click **OK.**

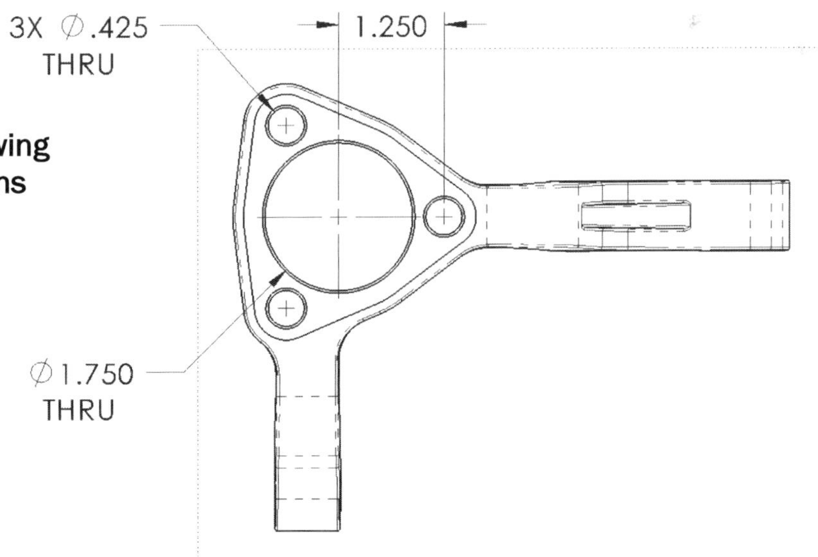

Rearrange the dimensions and add the instance call outs as shown.

Zoom in on the **Front** drawing view.

Select **Model Items** on the **Annotation** tab.

The parameters from the previous step should still be selected.

Click **OK**.

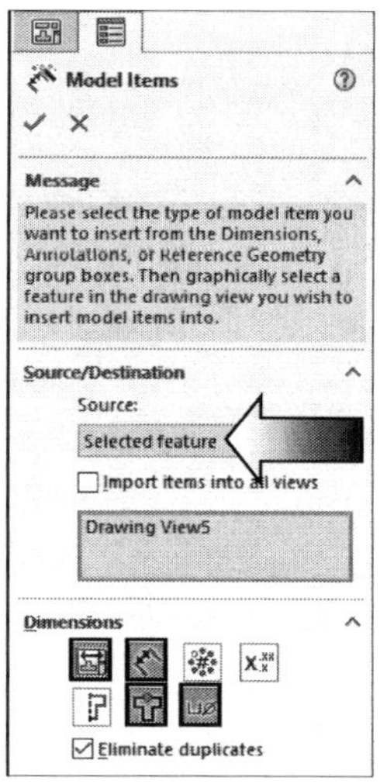

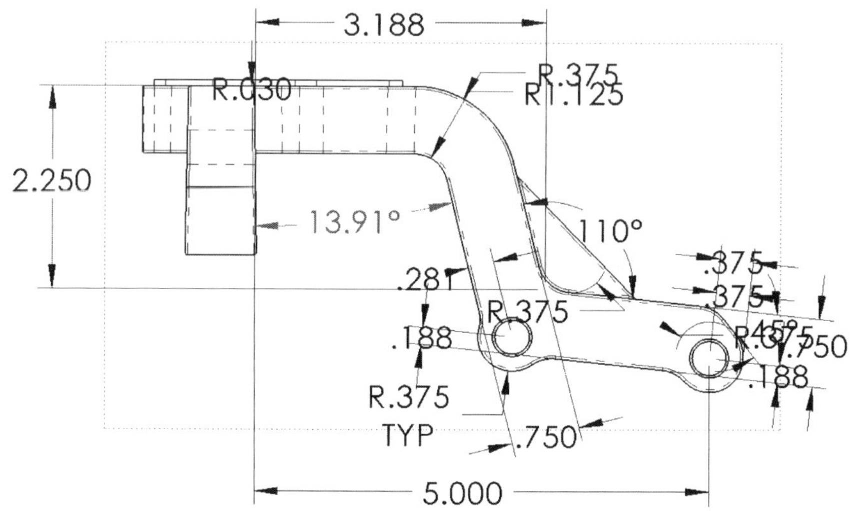

Add the **Centerline** and **Center Marks** as shown in the image below.

Click **Note** and add the Centerline symbol by accessing the **Add Symbol** button, under the **Text Format** section.

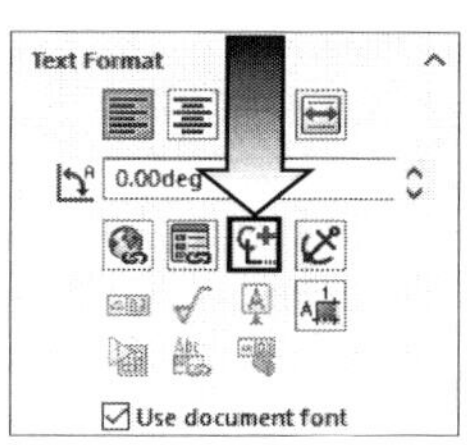

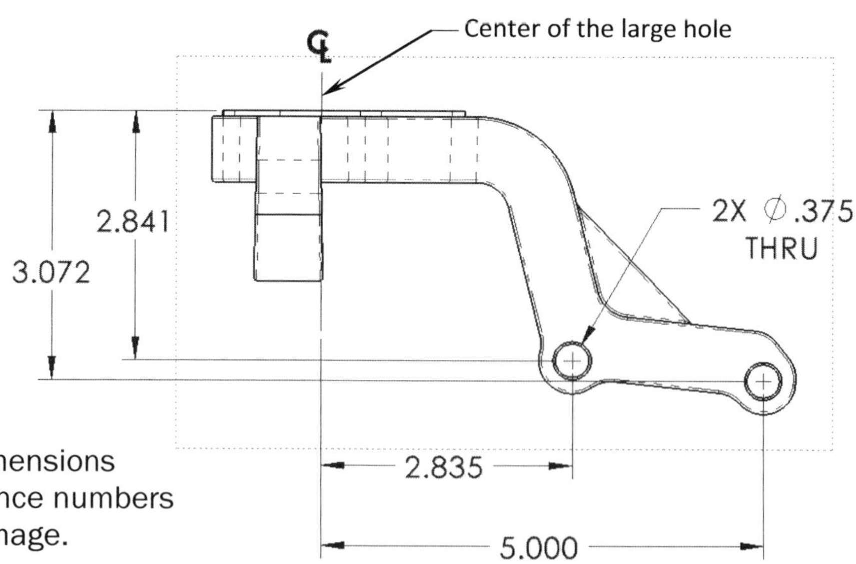

Rearrange the dimensions and add the instance numbers as shown in the image.

Zoom in on the **Right** drawing view.

Click **Model Items** from the **Annotation** tab.

Use the same parameters for the **Source** and **Dimensions** as the previous step.

Click **OK**.

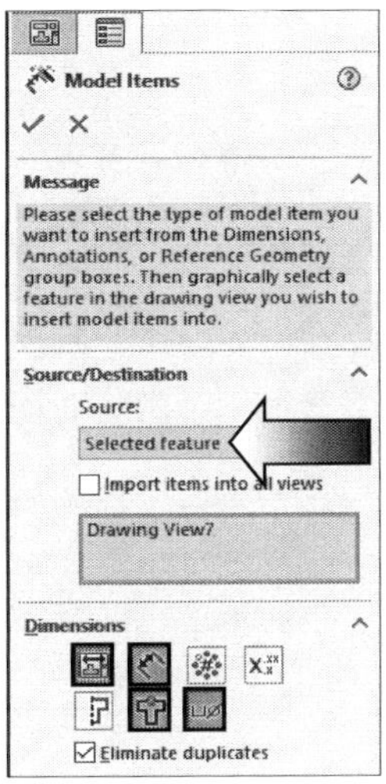

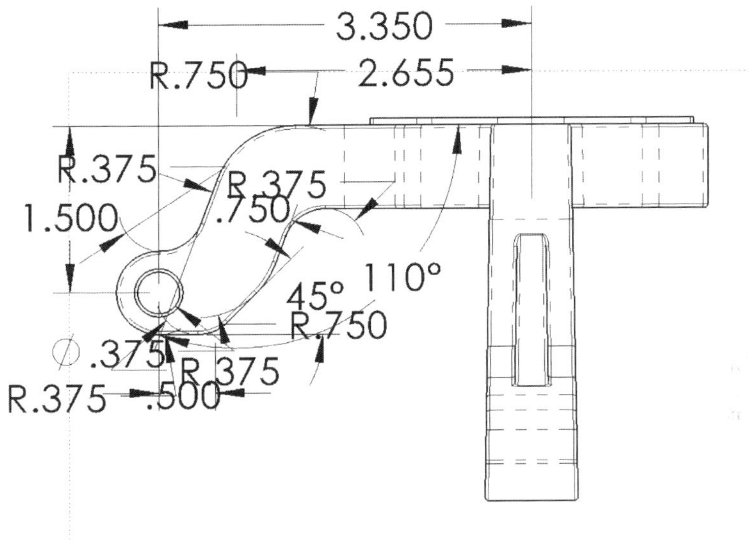

For this drawing view, we only need to show the dimensions for the hole.

Keep only the three dimensions shown here and delete the others.

Add a **Centerline** in the center of the rib.

Click **OK**.

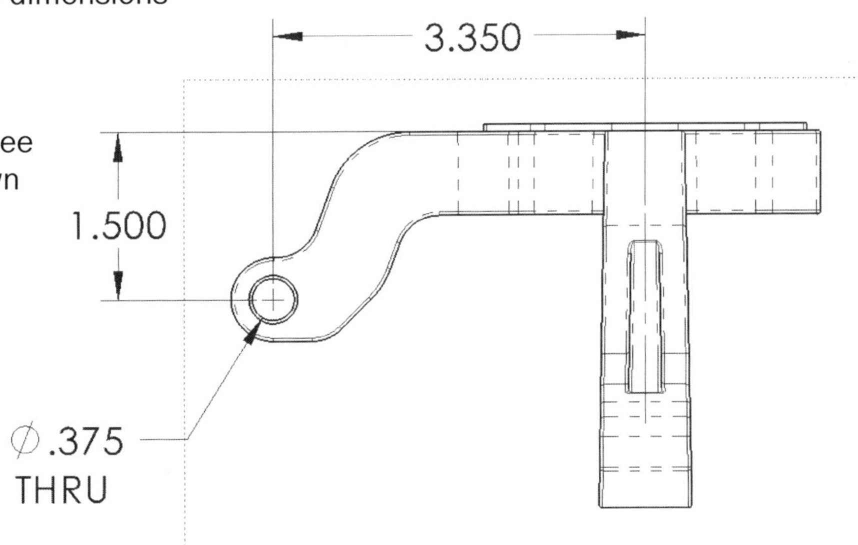

10. Adding Datums:

Datums are needed to be used with certain geometric tolerances. We will add Datum A to the top of the Front drawing view, and Datum B to the large hole.

Zoom in on the **Front** drawing view.

Click **Datum Feature** on the **Annotation** tab.

Click the top-most <u>edge</u> in the Front drawing view to attach **Datum A**.

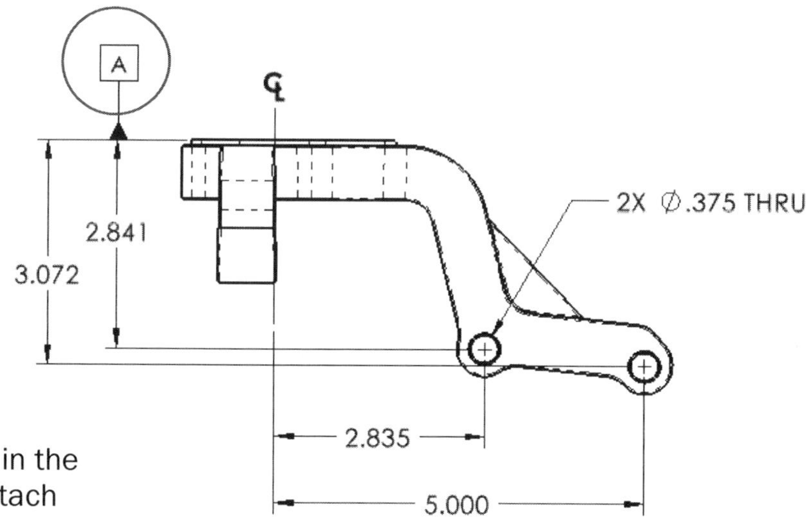

Zoom in on the **Top** drawing view.

Click the <u>circular edge</u> of the large hole to attach **Datum B**.

Move the two Datums out a little for clarity, and to see them easier.

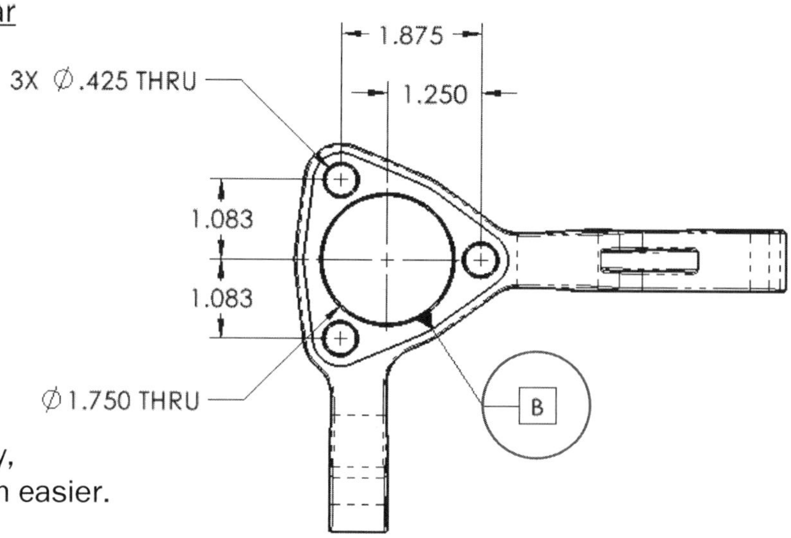

11. Adding Geometric Tolerances:

Zoom in on the **Top** drawing view.

Add a **Position** and a **Perpendicularity** geometric tolerances to the small and large holes, as shown in the image on the right.

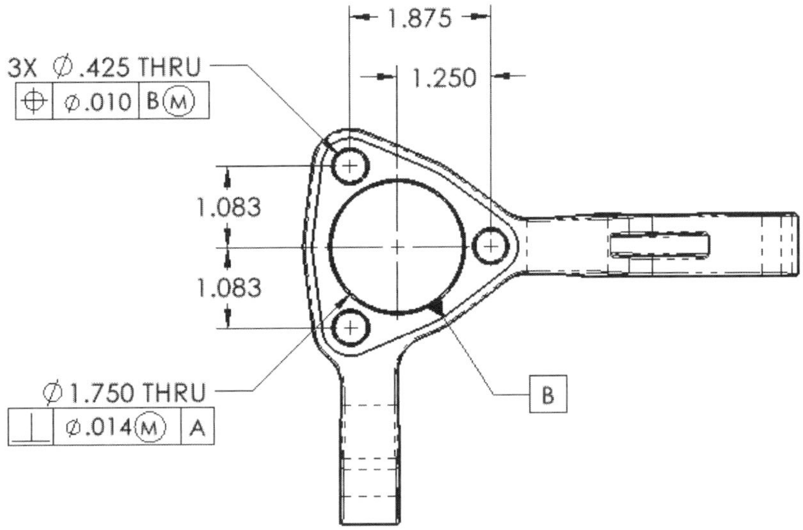

Zoom in on the **Front** drawing view.

Add a **Perpendicularity** geometric tolerance to the dimension **Ø.375**. It is the dimension of the two small holes.

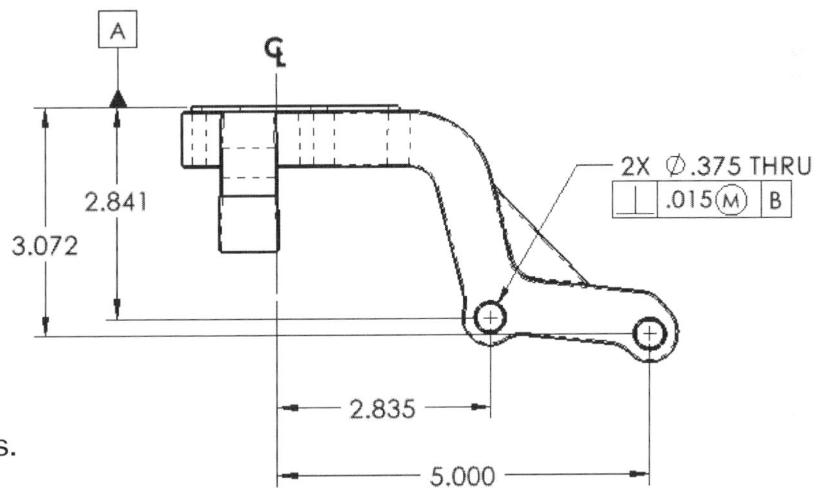

Zoom in on the **Right** drawing view.

Add a **Perpendicularity** control to the **Ø.375** dimension.

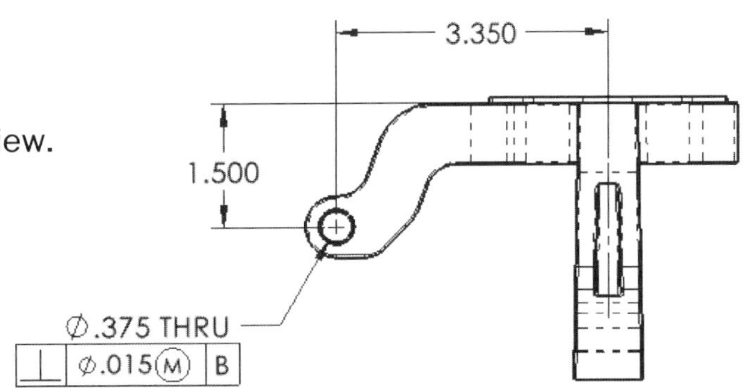

12. Filling out the Title Block:

From the FeatureManager tree, expand **Sheet1** and double-click **Sheet Format1** to activate the format layer to edit the Title Block.

Fill out the information shown below.

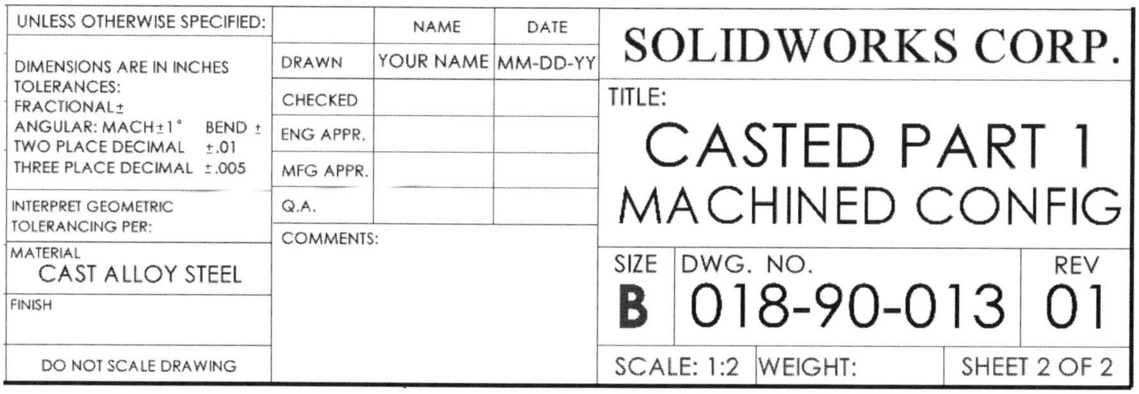

When finished, double-click **Sheet1** on the FeatureManager tree, to bring the sheet layer back to the front.

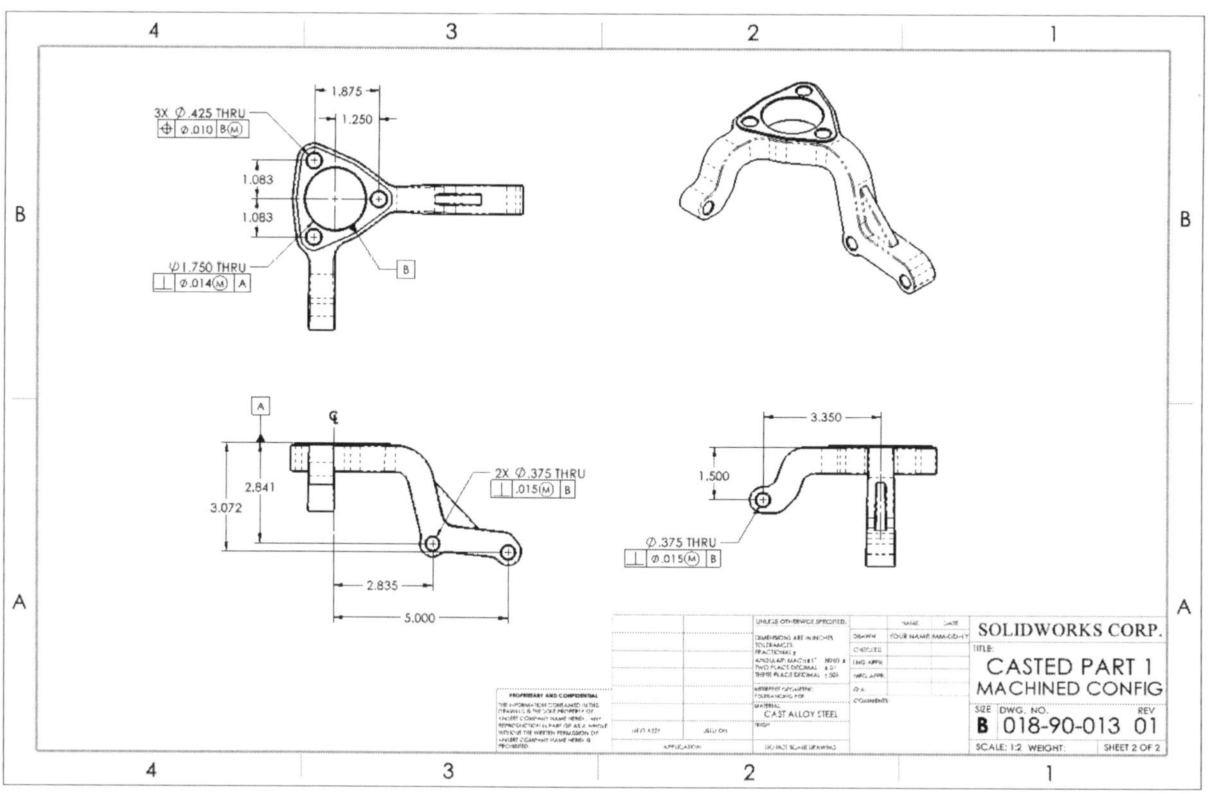

13. Saving your work:

Select **File, Save As.**

Enter: **Detailing a Casted Part.slddrw** for the file name.

Click **Save.**

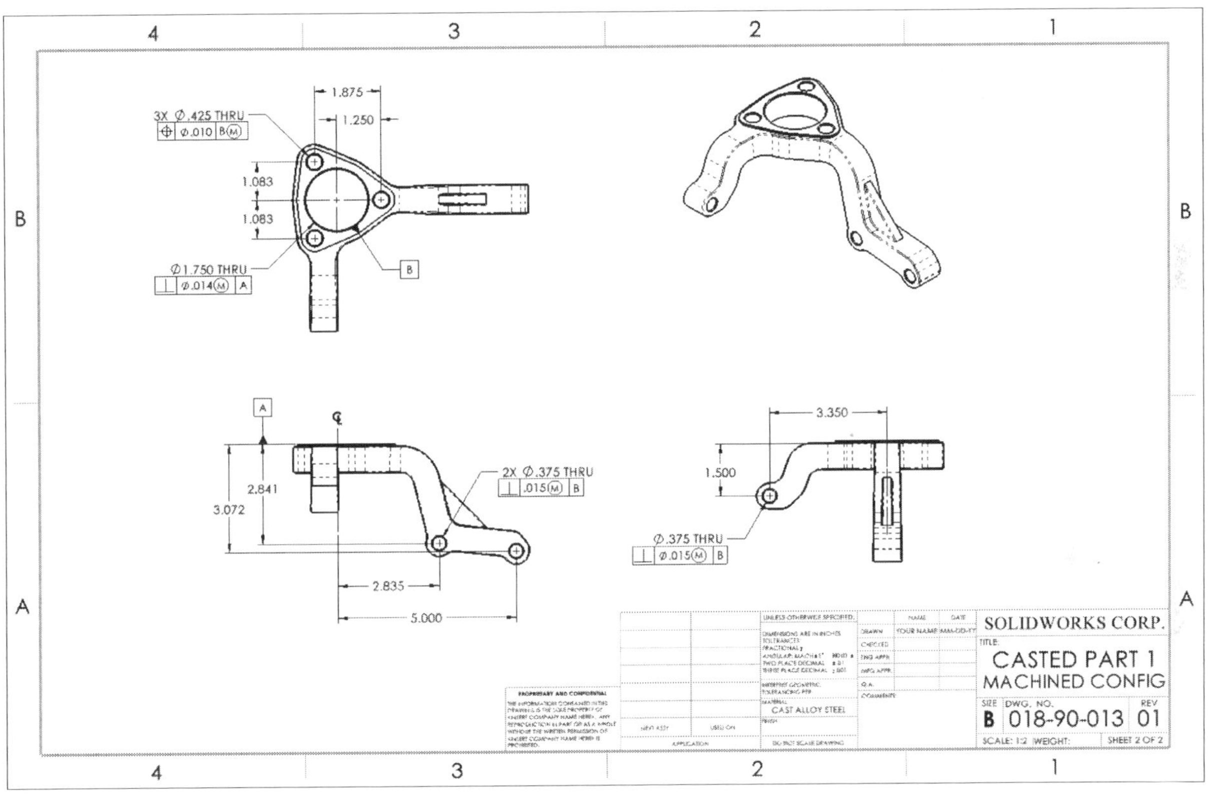

Close all documents.

Exercise: Castings & Forgings

Detailing a Casted Part 1

The exercises are designed to help you apply what you have learned from the previous lessons. They come with some instructions but not as detailed as the lessons, to give you an opportunity to explore and to try and create the drawings on your own, at your own pace.

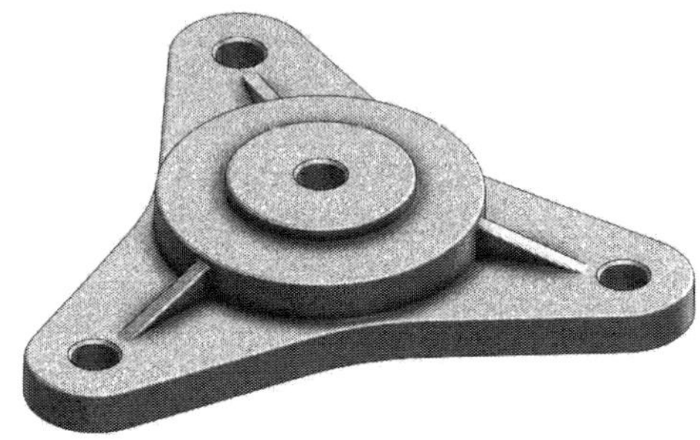

1. Opening a part document:

Select **File, Open**.

Browse to the Training Folder and open the part document named:
Casted Part 2.sldprt.

The material **Cast Alloy Steel** has already been assigned to the part.

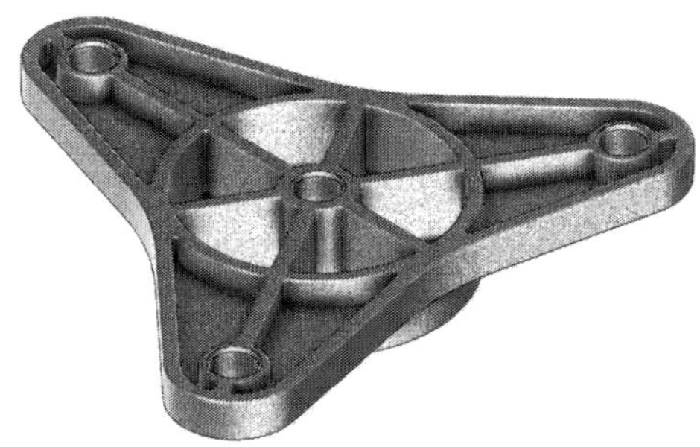

2. Transferring to a drawing:

Select **File, Make Drawing from Part.**

Select the **B-Size** drawing paper.

Set the Type-Of-Projection to:
3rd Angle.

Keep all other parameters at their default.

Click **OK.**

The B-Size landscape drawing is loaded.

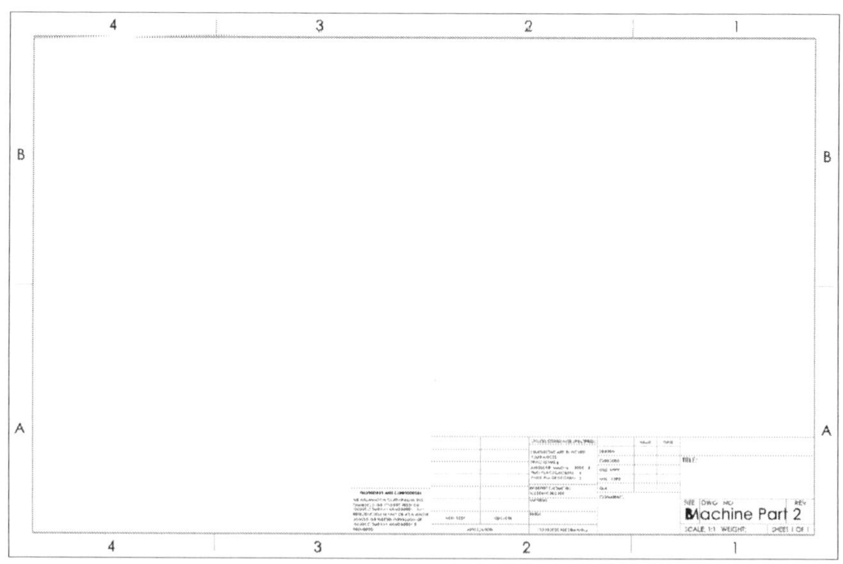

3. Drawing overview:

This part contains two configurations, a **Casted** and a **Machined** configuration. The only difference between the two configurations is the four drill holes.

We will use 2 sheets to detail the 2 configurations. The 1st sheet will be the details of the Casting, and the 2nd sheet will be the machining.

In the Casting drawing, we will detail all features in the part, but in the Machining drawing, we only need to show the details of the 4 holes. Some tolerance and precisions will also be added to the Machined drawing.

4. Creating the drawing views:

Expand the **View Palette** and enable only one option: **Auto-Start Projected View.**

Drag the **Front** drawing view into the drawing and drop it on the lower left-hand side.

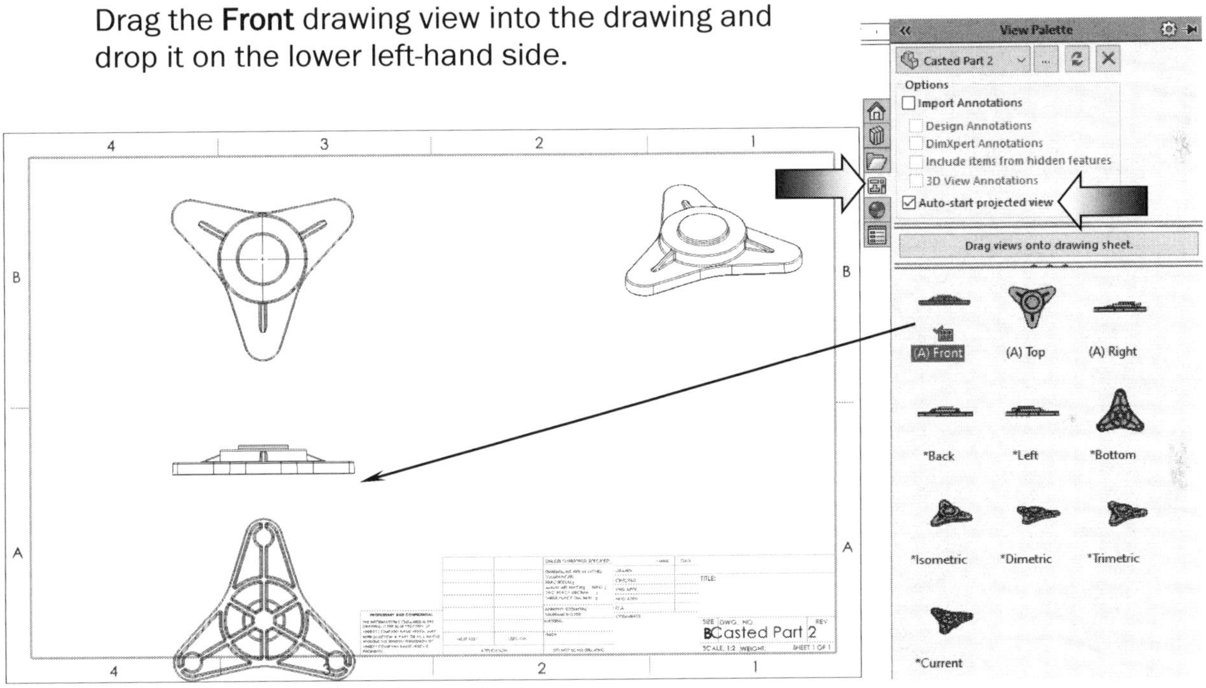

Auto Projection is started after the 1st view is created.

Add the **Top** drawing view, the **Bottom**, and the **Isometric** as shown above.

The Bottom view is automatically aligned vertically with the Front view. We will break the alignment and move the Bottom view to the right side of the drawing.

5. Breaking the view alignment:

Right-click over the dotted border of the Bottom drawing view and select: **Alignment, Break Alignment.**

The default vertical alignment of the view is removed; we can now move the Bottom view freely.

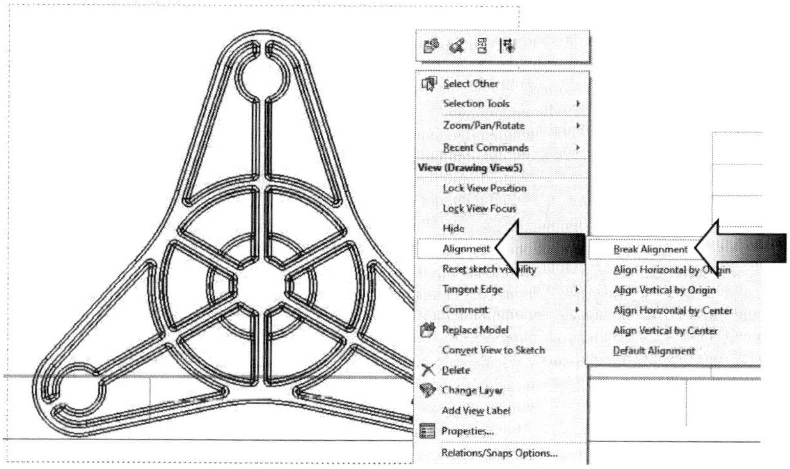

Drag the dotted border of the Bottom drawing view and move it to the right side of the drawing.

Move the other drawing views and create some extra room so that additional drawing views, dimensions, and annotations can be added.

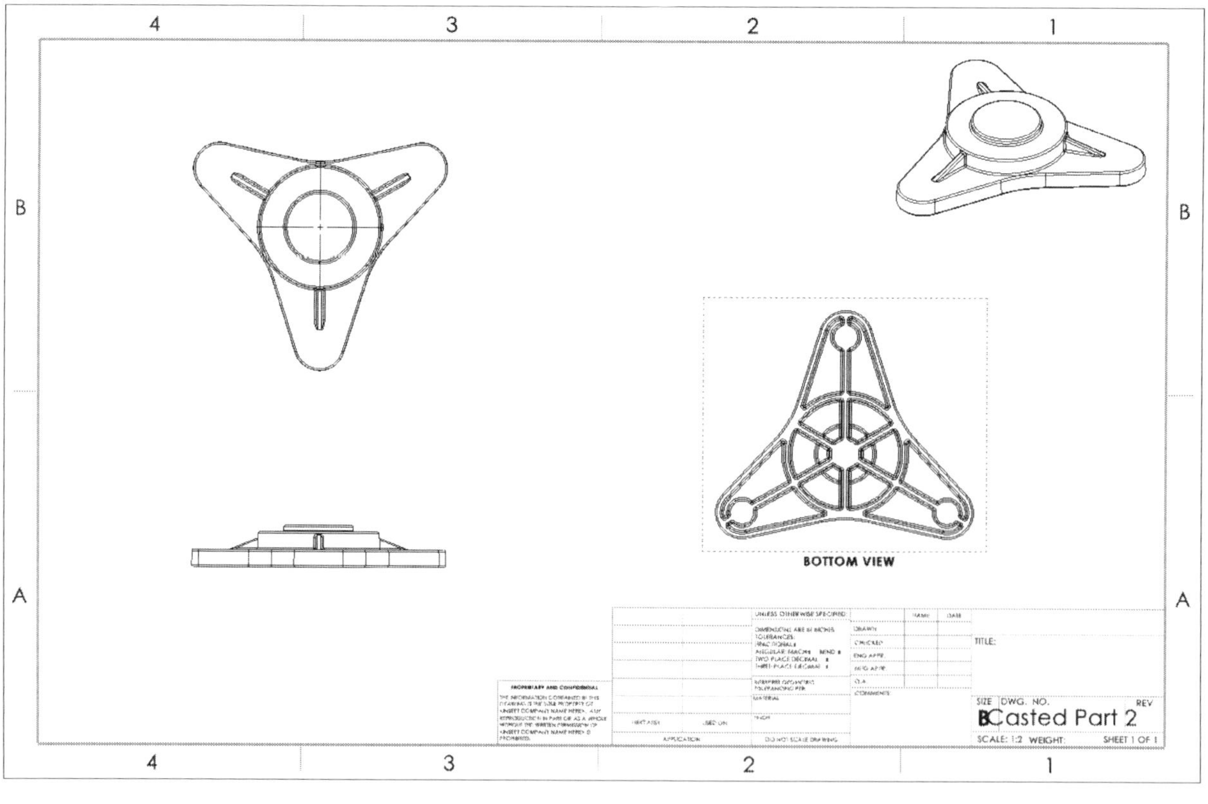

6. Creating a Section View:

Zoom in on the **Top** drawing view.

Click **Section View** on the **Drawing** tab.

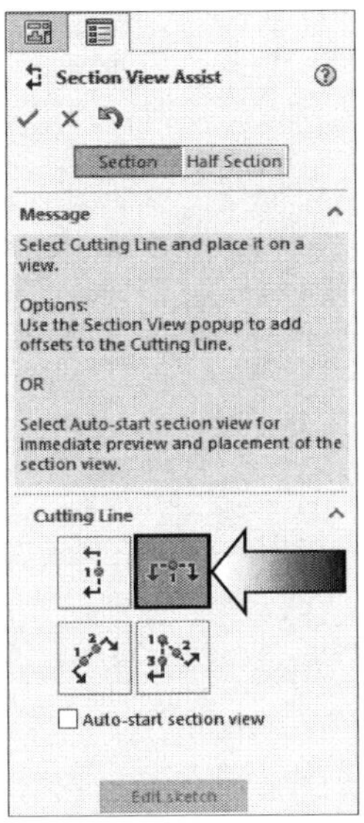

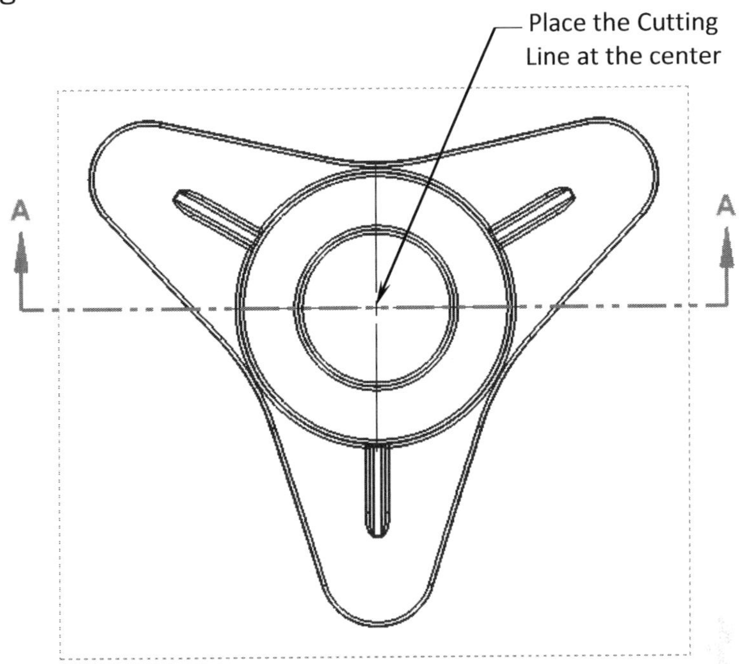

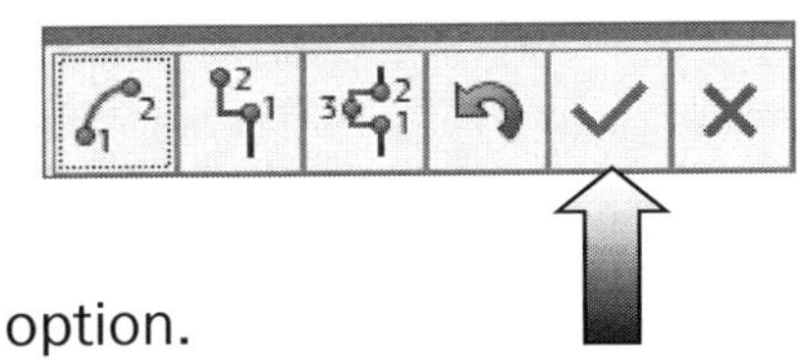

For Cutting Line, select the **Horizontal** option.

Place the Cutting Line at the <u>center</u> of the large hole.

Click the **green checkmark** on the pop-up toolbar to accept the Cutting Line placement.

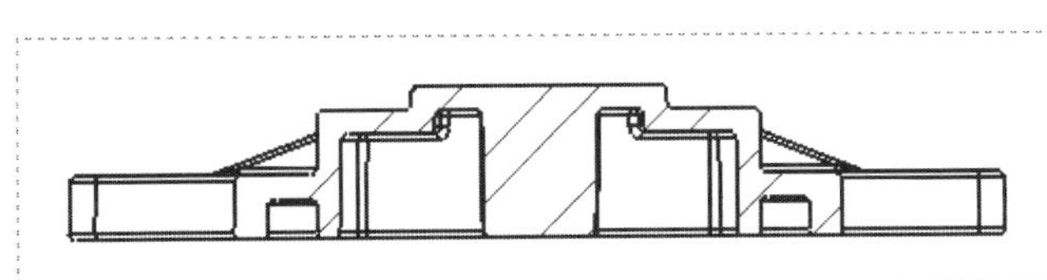

SECTION A-A

Place the Section View <u>below</u> the Top drawing view.

Click **OK**.

The view alignment needs to be broken so that it can be moved elsewhere.

7. Breaking the view alignment:

Right-click on the dotted border of the Section View and select: **Alignment, Break Alignment**.

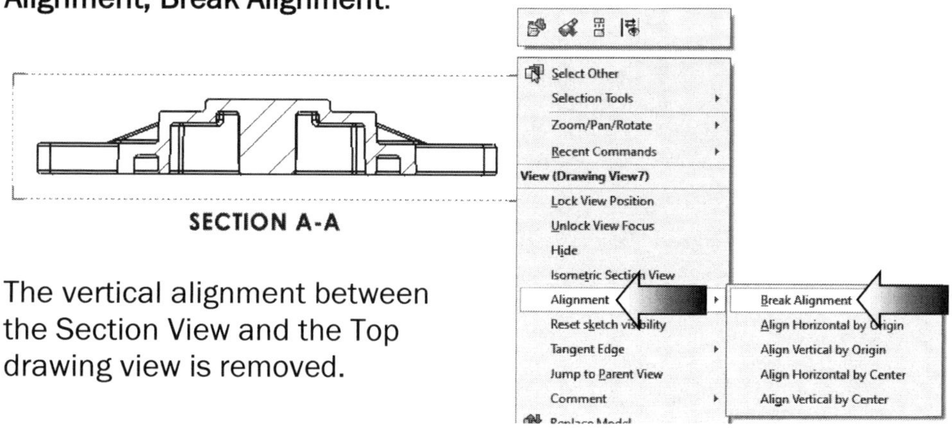

The vertical alignment between the Section View and the Top drawing view is removed.

The Section View can now be moved freely. Move the Section View to the right, between the Top drawing view and the Isometric view.

Add **Centerlines** and **Center marks** as shown in the drawing views below.

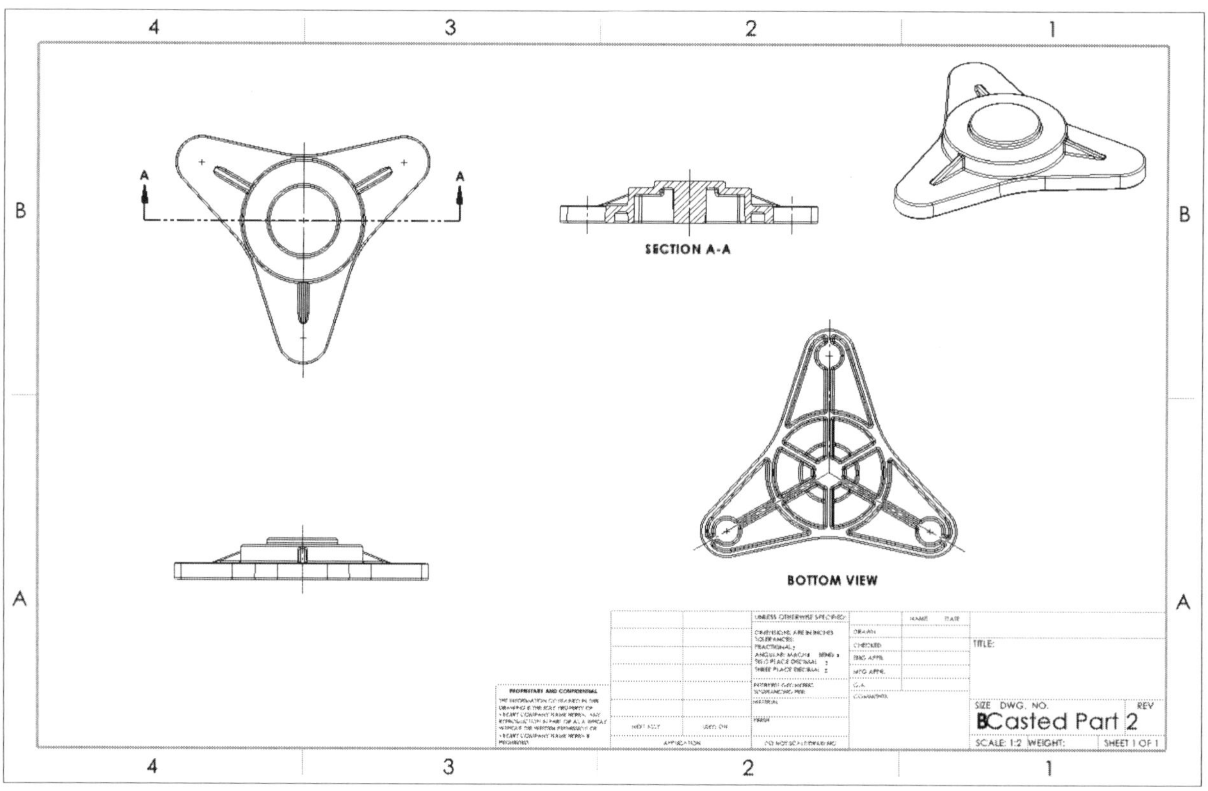

8. Modifying the Hatch Pattern:

Zoom in on the **Section View**.

Click <u>inside</u> the hatch area to access the hatch options.

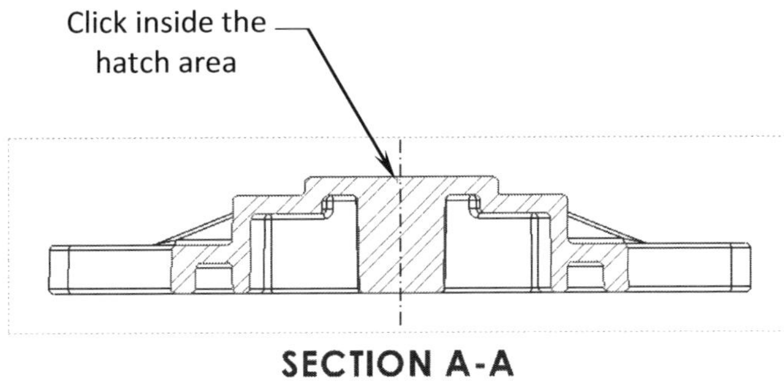

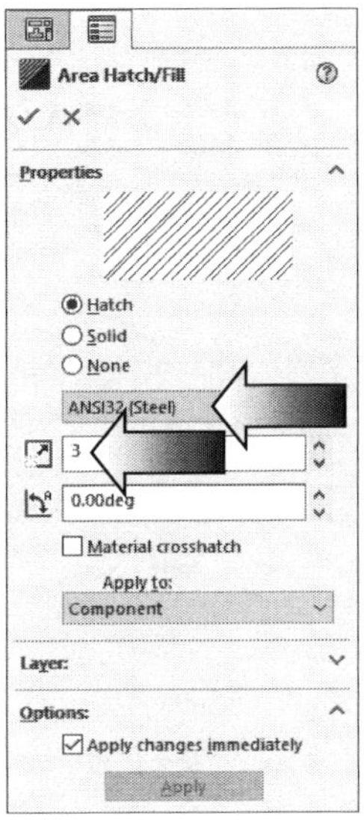

For Hatch Pattern, select **ANSI32 (Steel)** from the drop-down list.

For Scale, enter **3** to triple the hatch density.

Keep all other parameters at their default values.

Enable the checkbox: **Apply Changes Immediately.**

Click **OK.**

9. Inserting the Model Dimensions:

Switch to the **Annotation** tab and click **Model Items.**

Select the options shown below for **Source** and **Dimensions.**

Click **OK.**

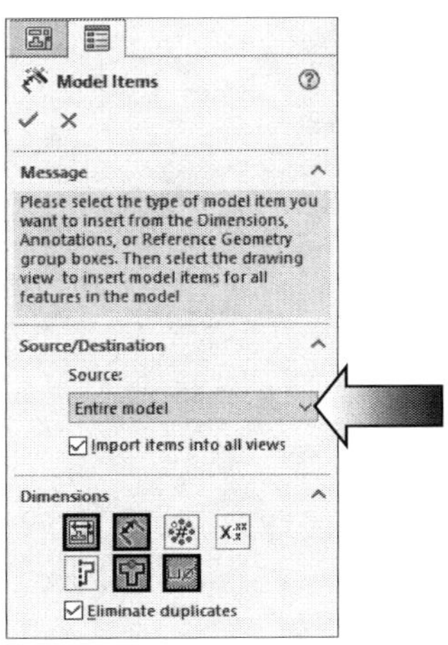

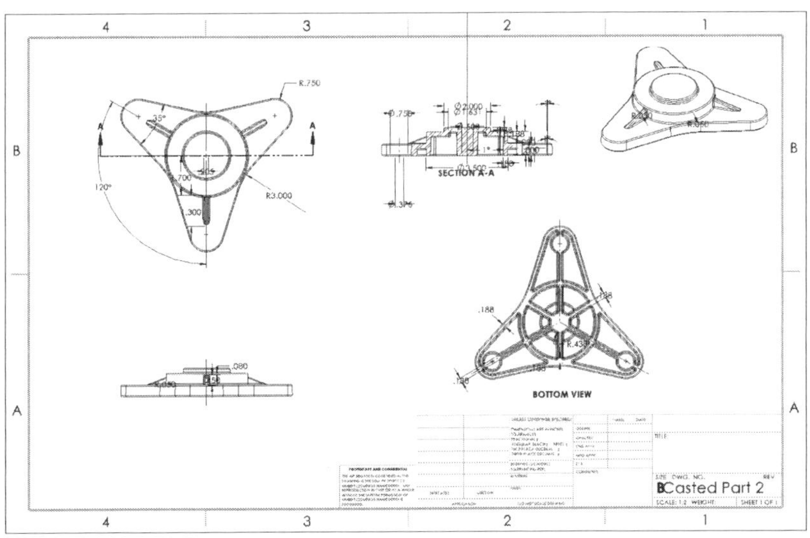

10. Rearranging dimensions:

Zoom in on the **Top** drawing view.

Rearrange the dimensions and add the additional ones as shown in the image on the right.

Add the **Construction Circle** to locate the locations of the 3 wings.

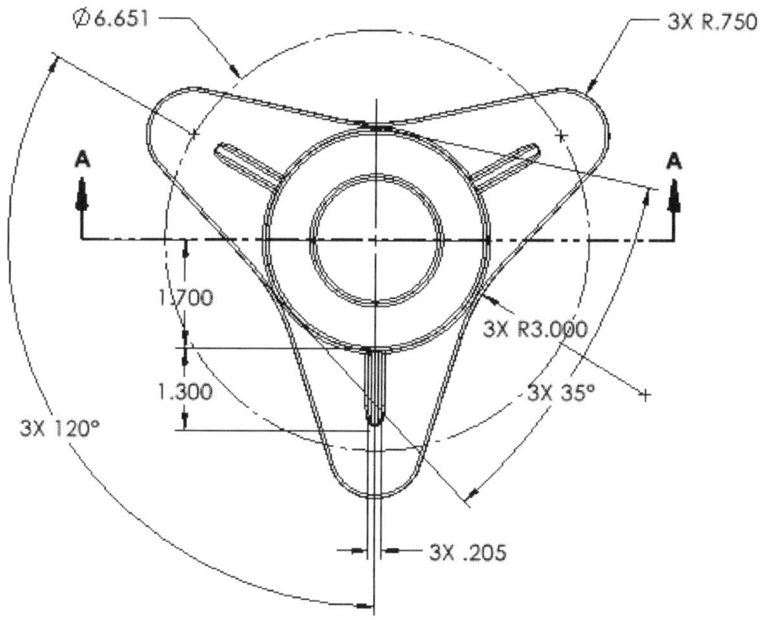

Zoom in on the **Front** drawing view.

Rearrange the dimensions and add the number of instances where needed. Also, add the 22° angular dimension as shown.

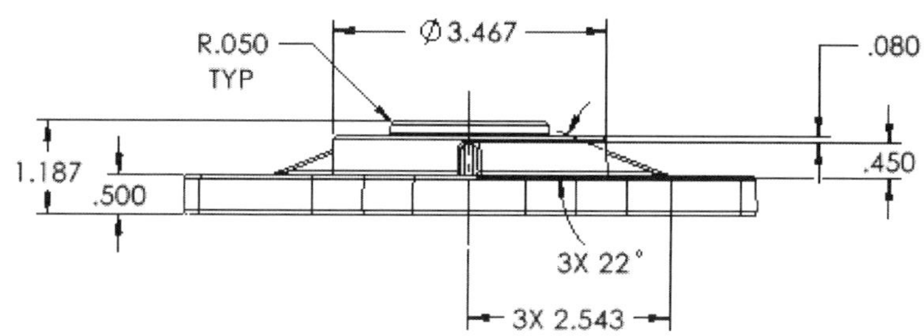

Zoom in on the **Section View** and the **Bottom View**. <u>Delete</u> the unwanted dimensions and <u>add</u> new dimensions and call outs to match the images below.

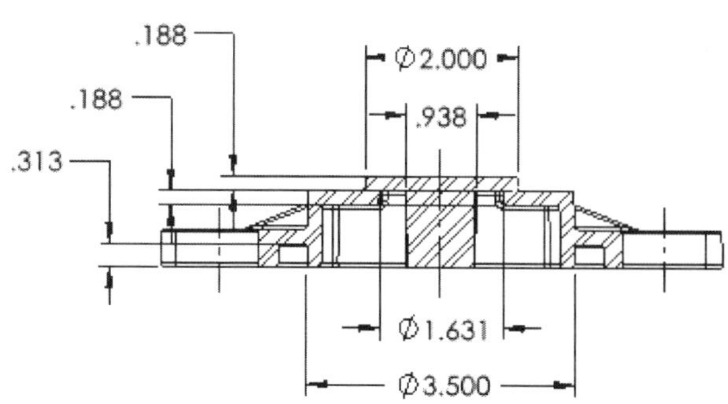

SECTION A-A

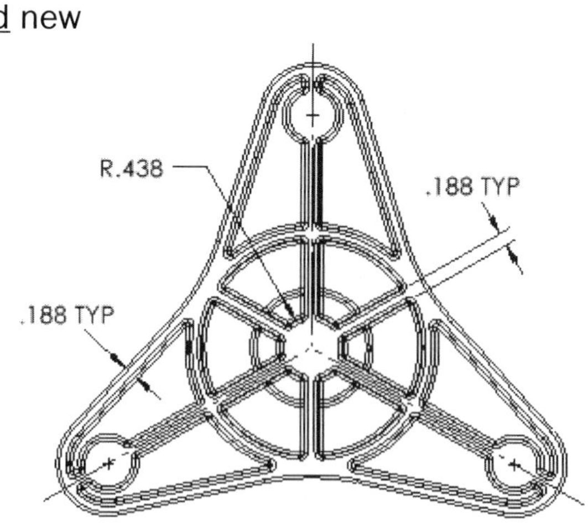

BOTTOM VIEW

11. Adding the General Notes:

Switch to the **Annotation** tab and click **Note**.

Enter the notes shown below. Place the General notes on the lower left corner of the drawing.

NOTES: UNLESS OTHERWISE SPECIFIED

1. INTERPRET DRAWINGS AND DIMENSIONS PER ASME-ANSI 14.5
2. MATERIAL: CAST ALLOY STEEL
3. UNSPECIFIED DRAFT ANGLE TO BE 1° MINIMUM
4. PARTS TO BE CLEAN AND FREE OF LUBRICANT OR DEBRIS BEFORE PACKAGED FOR SHIPPING

When finished, select the notes, and click **Lock Note** so that it stays fixed at the lower left corner of the drawing.

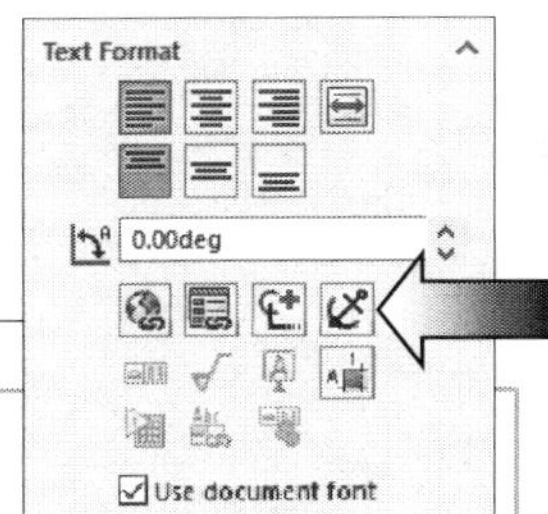

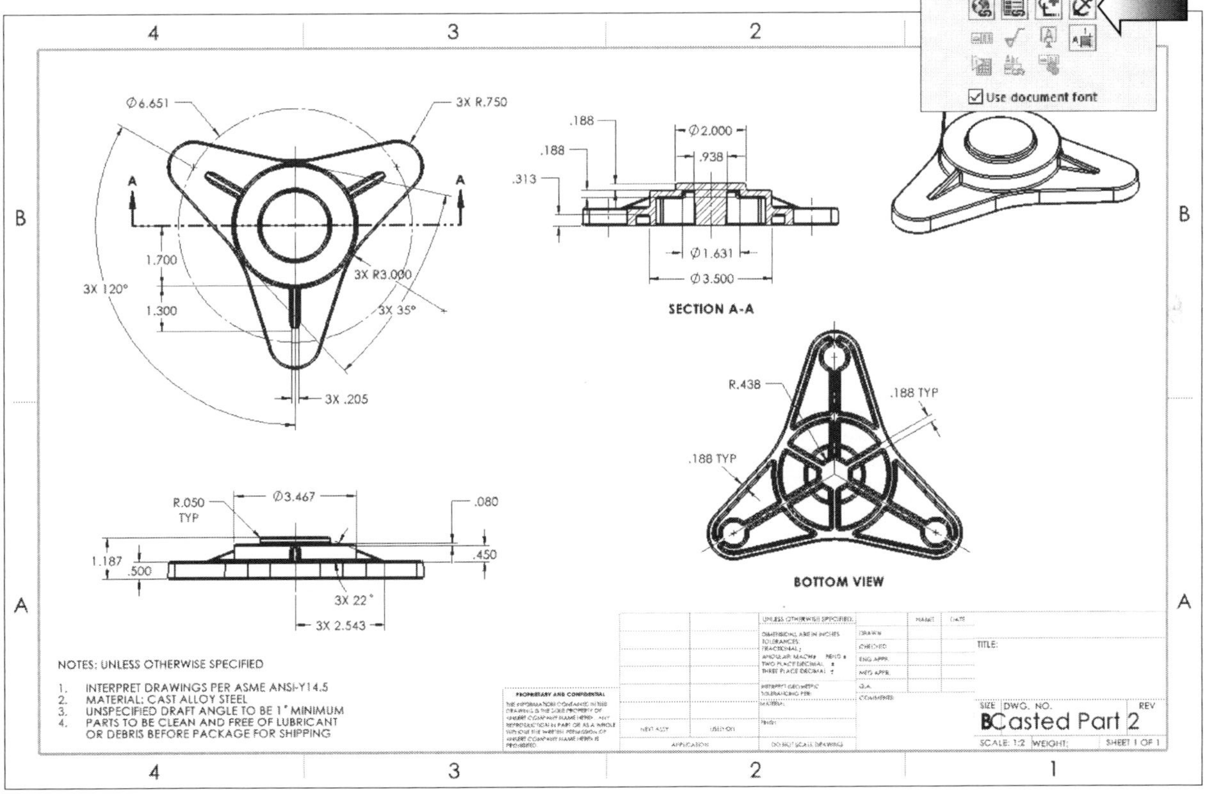

12. Filling out the Title Block:

From the FeatureManager tree, expand **Sheet1** and double-click **Sheet Format1** to activate it for editing.

Fill out the information shown below.

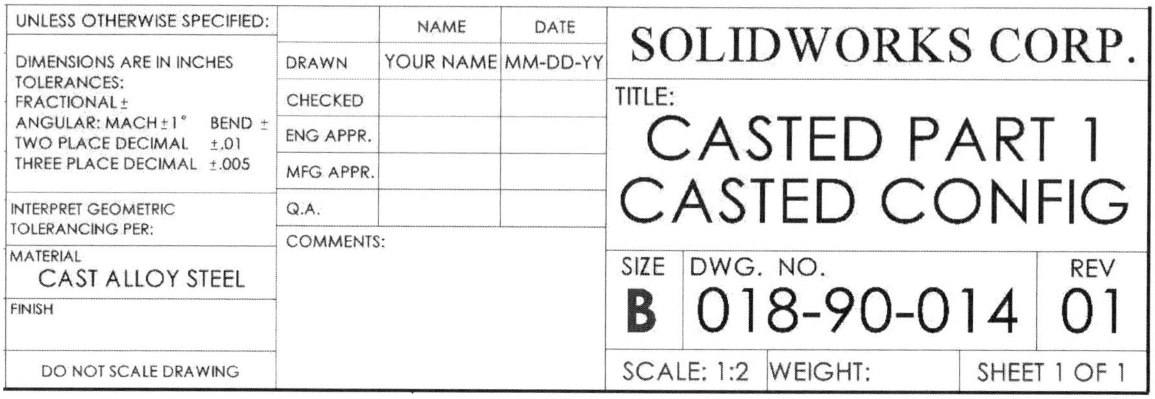

When finished, double-click **Sheet1** on the FeatureManager to bring the drawing layer back to the front.

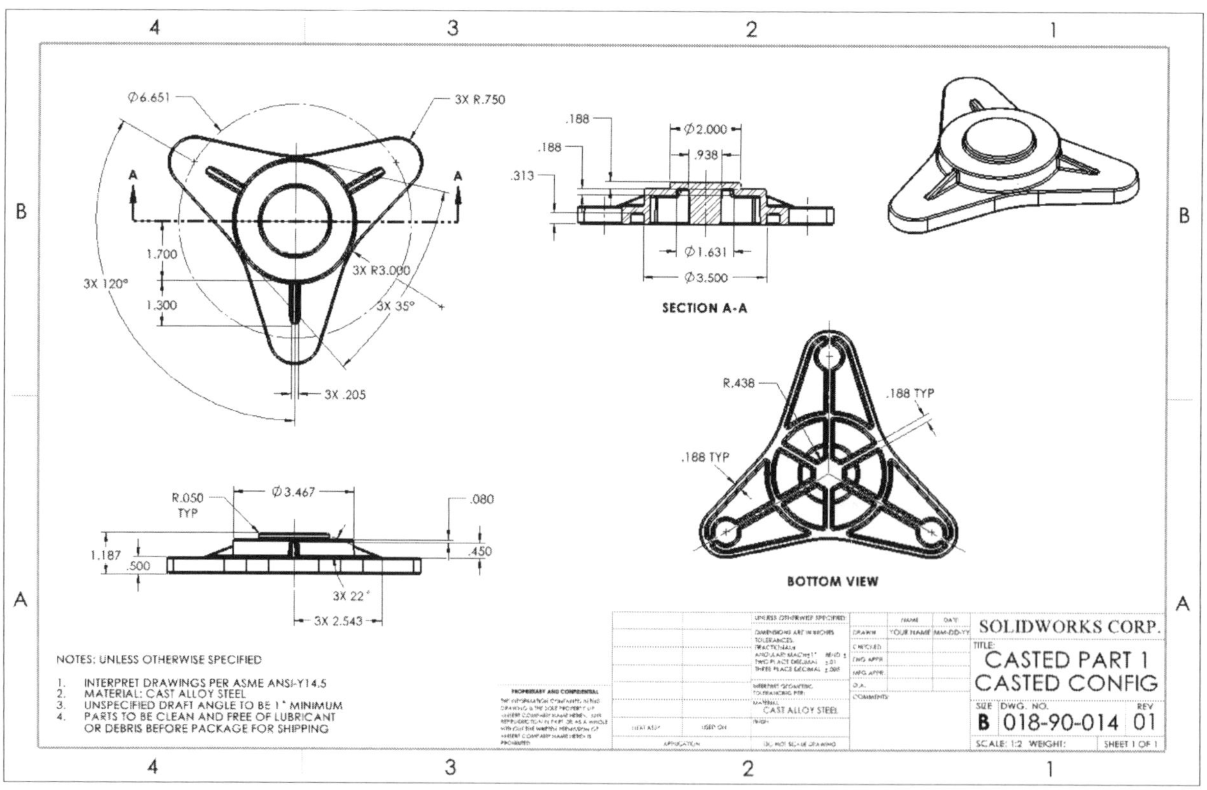

13. Adding a second sheet:

We will add sheet 2 to the drawing at this time and detail the Machined configuration of the same part.

From the lower left corner of the drawing, click the **small tab** next to Sheet1 to add a new sheet.

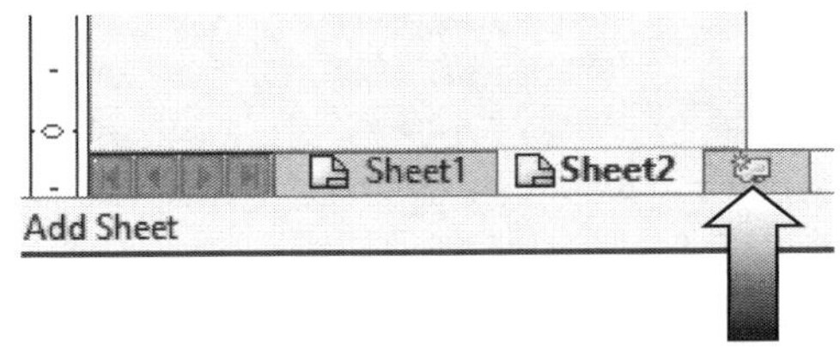

Expand the **View Palette** and enable only one checkbox: **Auto Start Projected View** and disable all other checkboxes.

Using the **View Palette**, drag the **Front** drawing view into Sheet 2, and then add the **Top**, and the **Isometric** view as shown below.

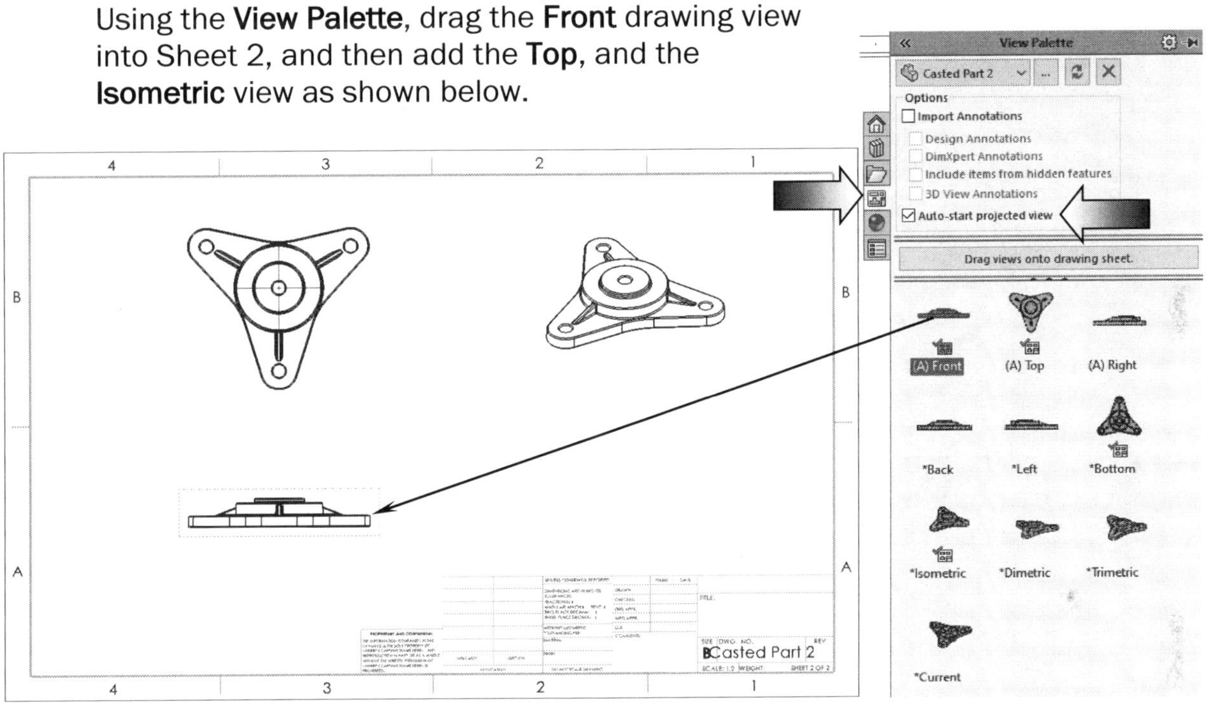

The drawing views are still showing the Casted configuration; we will need to switch them to the Machined configuration.

Select the dotted border of the **Front** drawing view as noted below.

From the FeatureManager tree, expand **Reference Configuration** and select the **Machined** configuration.

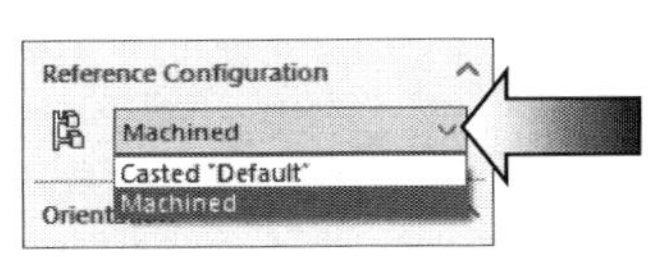

Click **OK**. All 3 drawing views are switched to the Machined configuration.

Rearrange the drawing views to look similar to the drawing shown above.

14. Creating an Aligned Section View:

The section line for an aligned section comprises two or more lines connected at an angle.

The aligned section rotates the cut into the plane of the selected segment.

Click **Section View.**

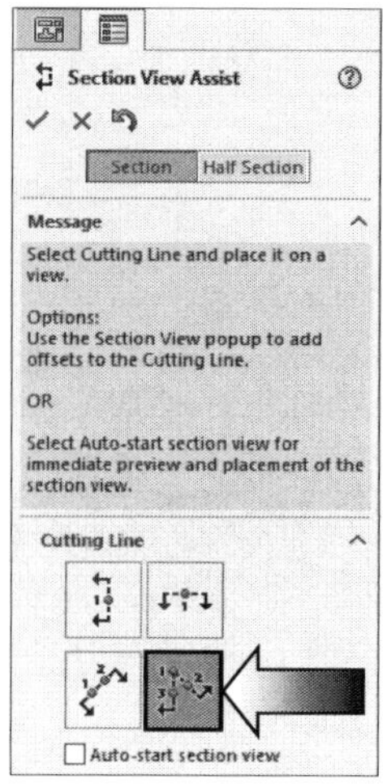

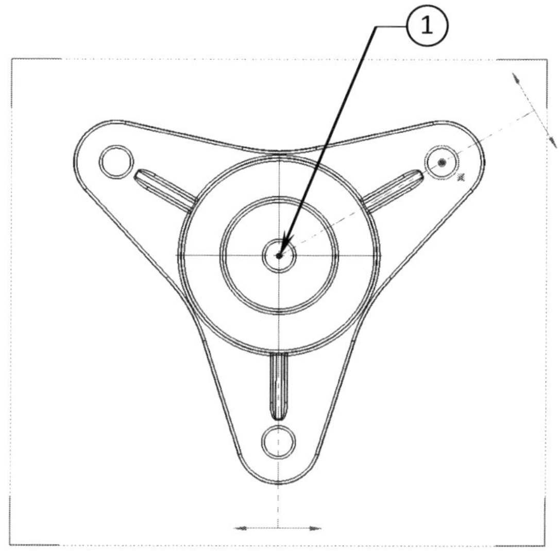

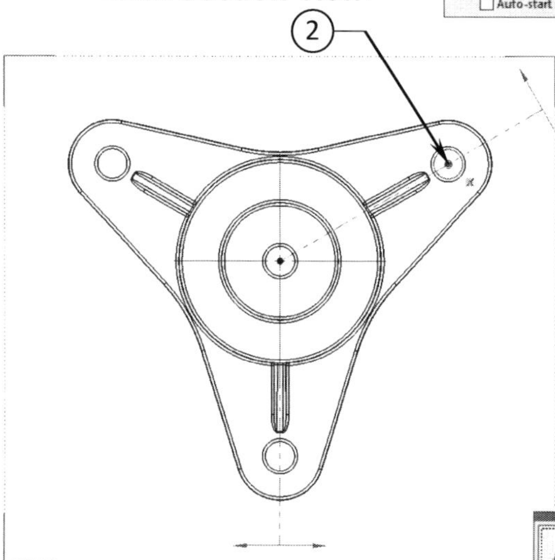

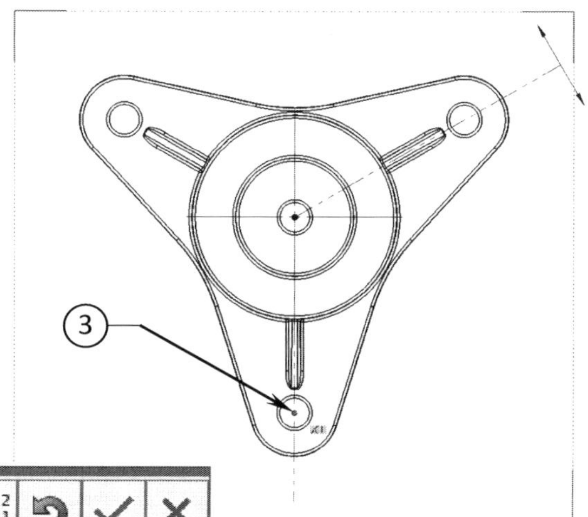

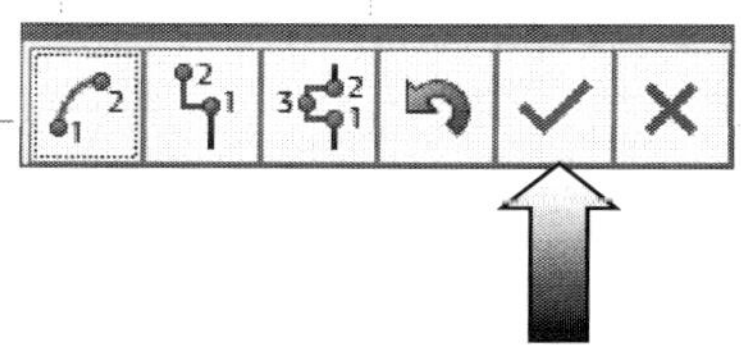

Select the **Align** option.

Click the **3 points** as noted in balloons 1, 2, and 3.

Click the **green checkmark** to accept the line locations.

Place the Aligned Section on the right side of the Top drawing view.

The crosshatch pattern will be edited in the next step.

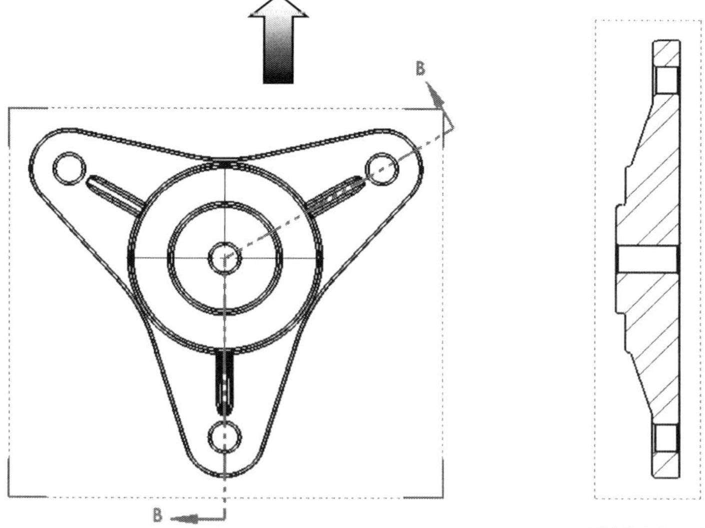

SECTION B-B

15. Modifying the hatch pattern:

The hatch pattern that was used in Sheet1 must be used again here to match.

Click inside the hatch area to enable the hatch options.

Change the Pattern to **ANSI32 (Steel)**.

Change the Scale to **3**.

Click **OK**.

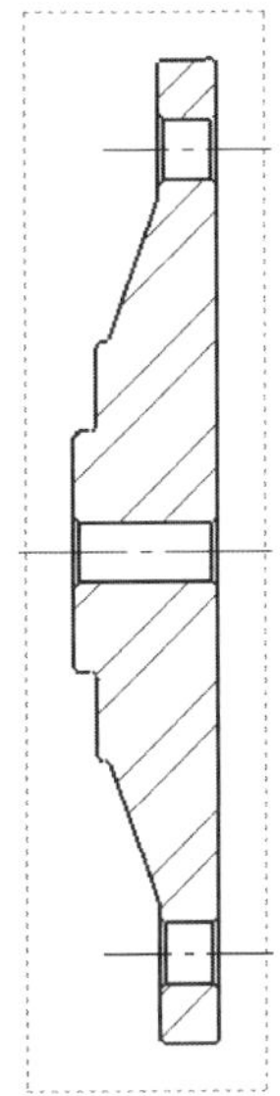

Pattern Scale of 1

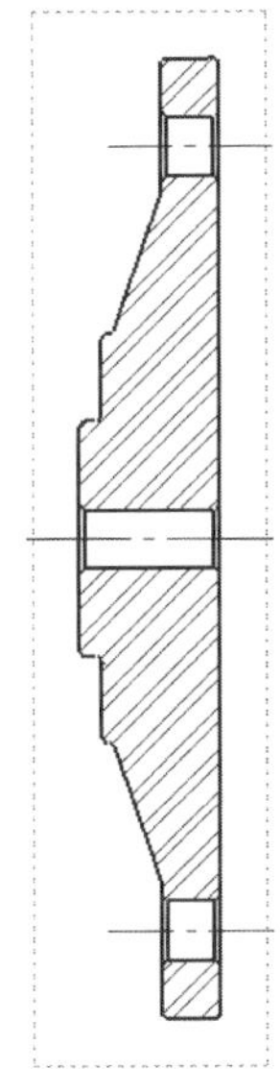

Pattern Scale of 3

Add **Centerlines** and **Center Marks** to all drawing views as shown below.

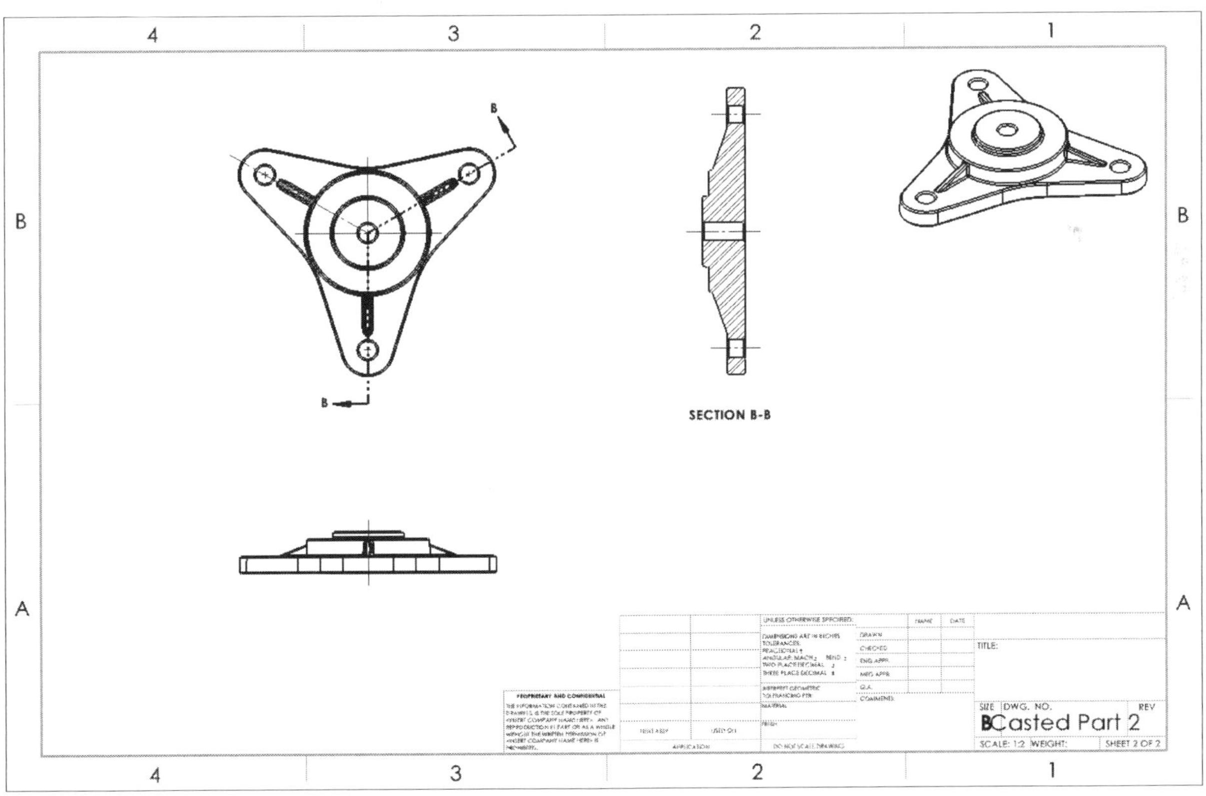

16. Inserting the Model Dimensions:

To fully maintain the associations between the drawing and the model, the dimensions from the model should be inserted into the drawing, instead of adding new dimensions in the drawings.

Switch to the **Annotation** tab and click **Model Items**.

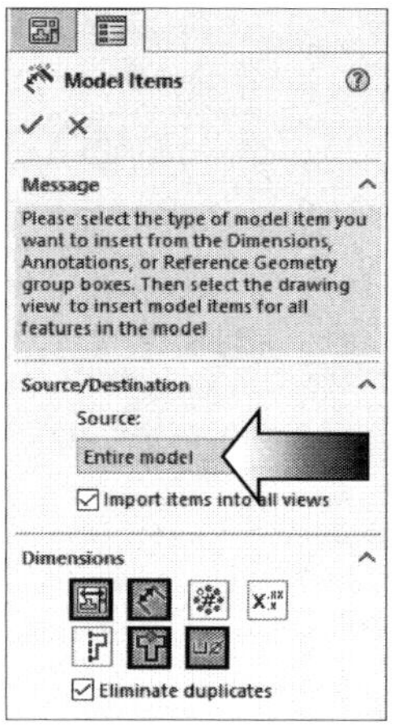

For Source, select **Entire Model**.

For Dimensions, select the **4 options** shown in the dialog box.

Click **OK**.

We will clean up the dimensions in the next step.

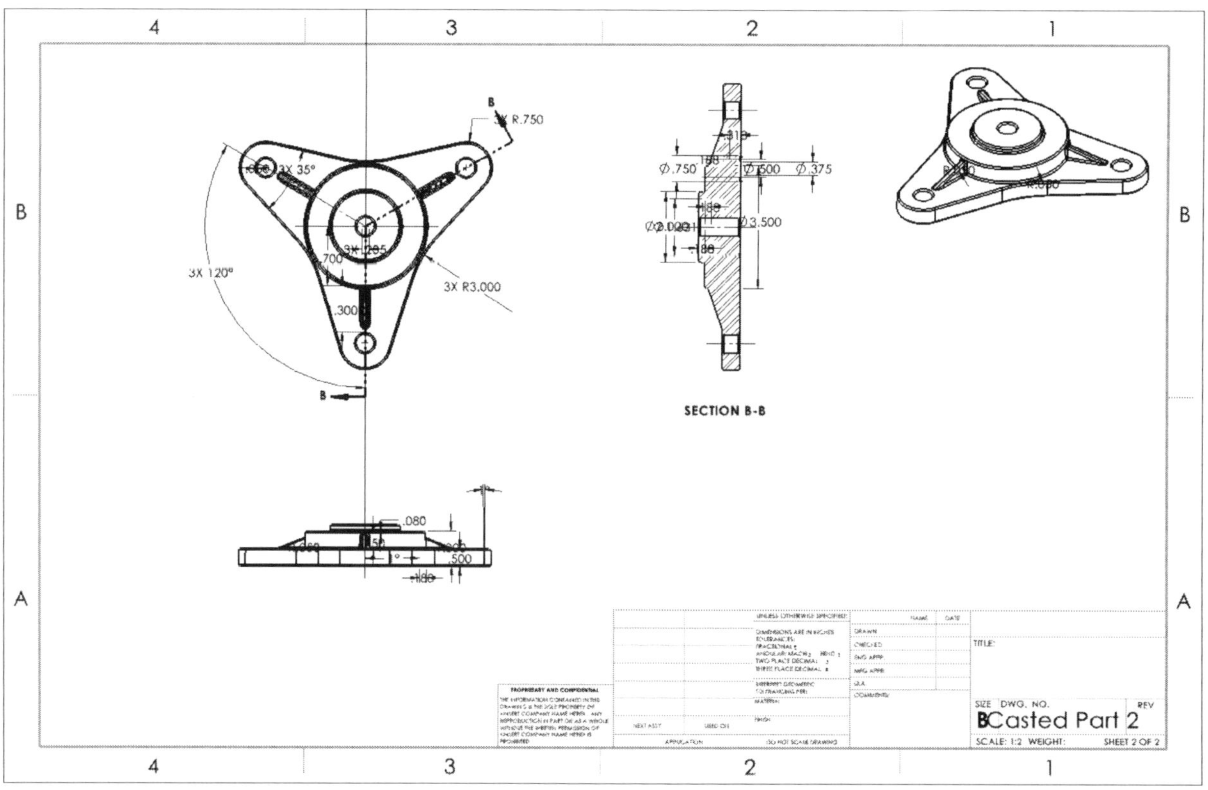

17. Cleaning up the dimensions:

Zoom in on the **Top** drawing view.

Sketch a **construction circle** to locate the 3 small holes.

Add the **2 diameter** dimensions shown in the image and delete the other dimensions.

Modify the Ø.500 dimensions and add the instance count.

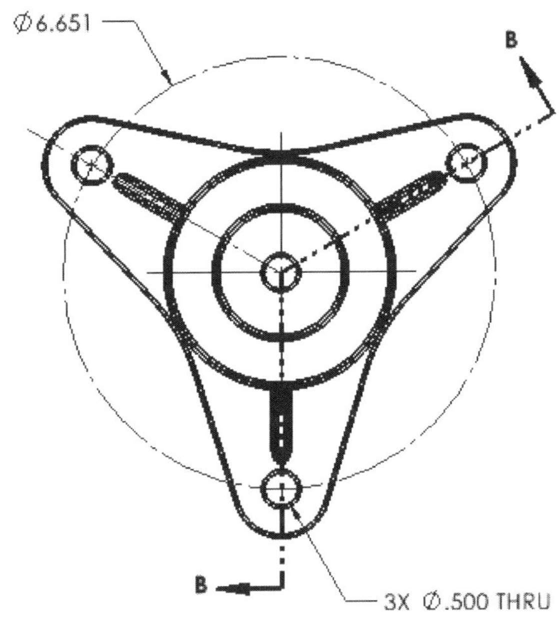

Zoom in on the **Section View**.

Delete all dimensions and keep only the **diameter dimension of the hole** in the center.

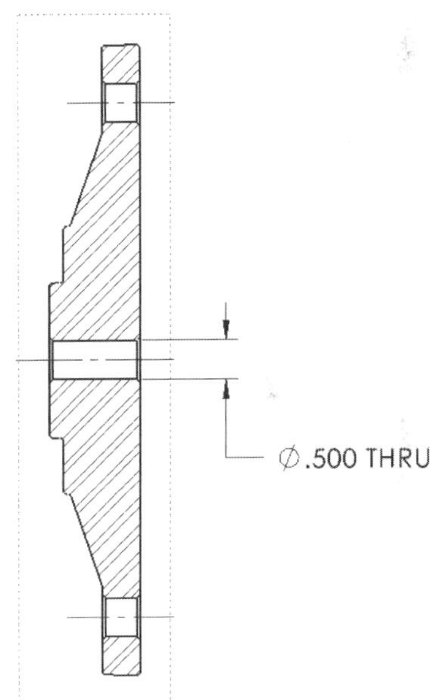

SECTION B-B

Zoom in on the **Front** drawing View.

Delete all dimensions and keep only the **overall height dimension**. This dimension can be added if missing from the view.

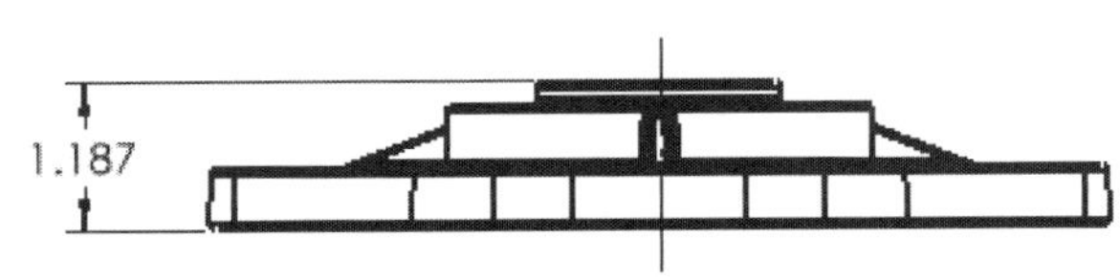

18. Adding Datums:

Datums are references used to inspect the accuracy of features.

We will add a couple of datums to help control the precisions of the drill holes.

Click **Datum Feature** on the **Annotation** tab.

Add **Datum A** to the bottom of the Front view, and **Datum B** to one of the small holes.

Click **OK**.

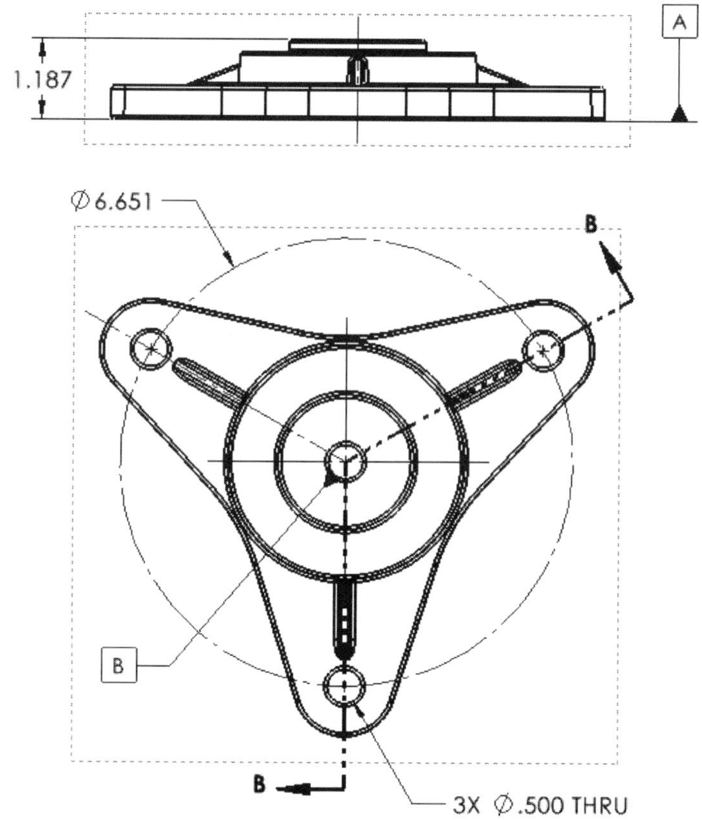

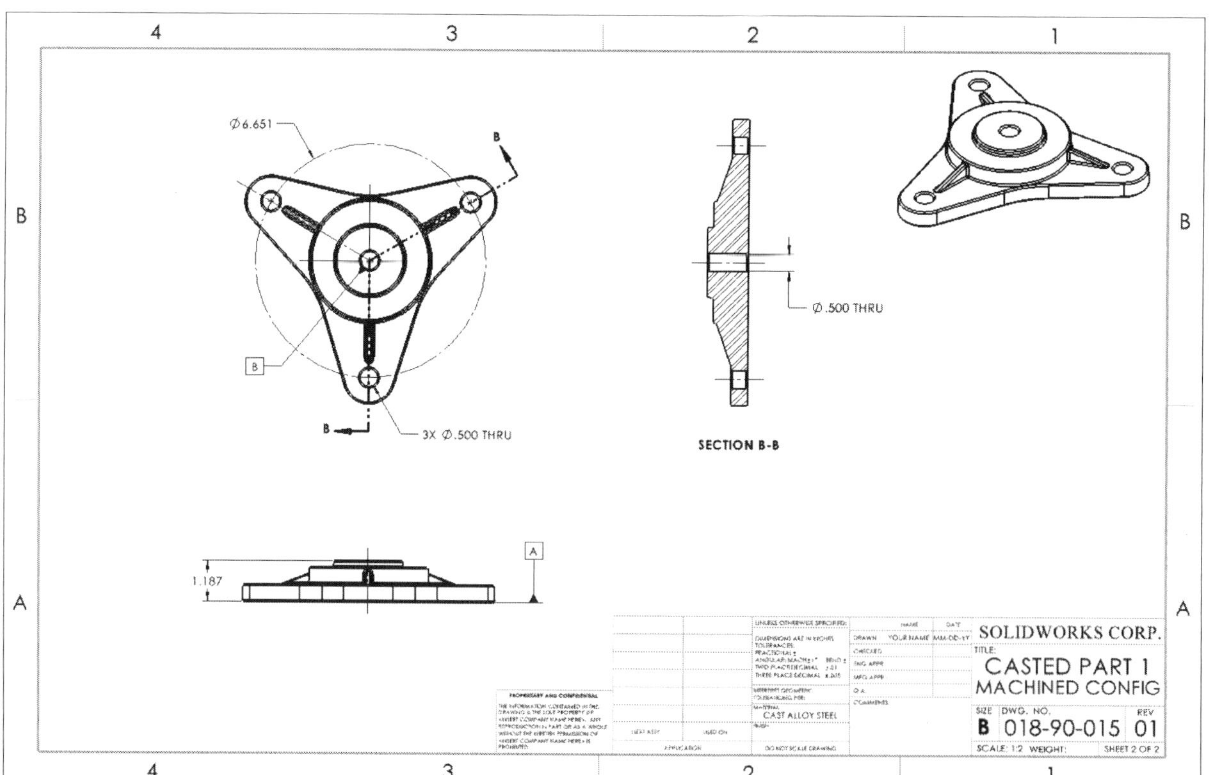

19. Adding Geometric Tolerances:

Geometric Tolerance is a system of 14 symbols for defining and communicating design intent and engineering tolerances that helps engineers and manufacturers optimally control variations in manufacturing processes.

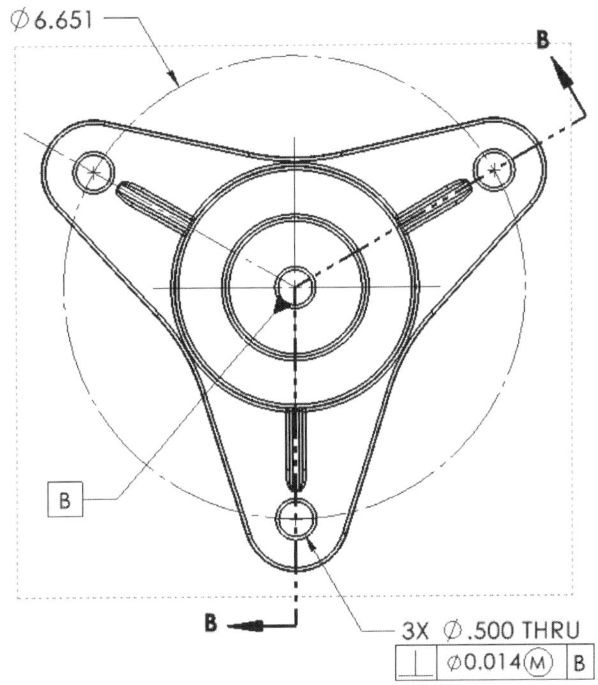

Zoom in on the **Top** drawing view.

Select the dimension **3X Ø.500** and click **Geometric Tolerance** on the **Annotation** tab.

Create a **Perpendicularity** tolerance as shown in the image on the right.

Click **OK**.

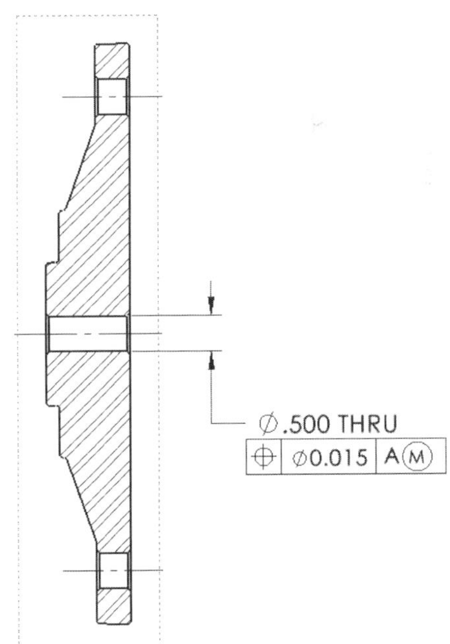

SECTION B-B

Zoom in on the **Section View**.

Select the dimension **Ø.500 THRU** and click **Geometric Tolerance** again.

Create a **Position** tolerance as shown in the image on the right.

Click **OK**.

Move either the dimensions to ensure the Control Frame is moved with it.

20. Filling out the Title Block:

From the FeatureManager tree, expand **Sheet1** and double-click **Sheet Format1** to activate it.

Enter the information shown below.

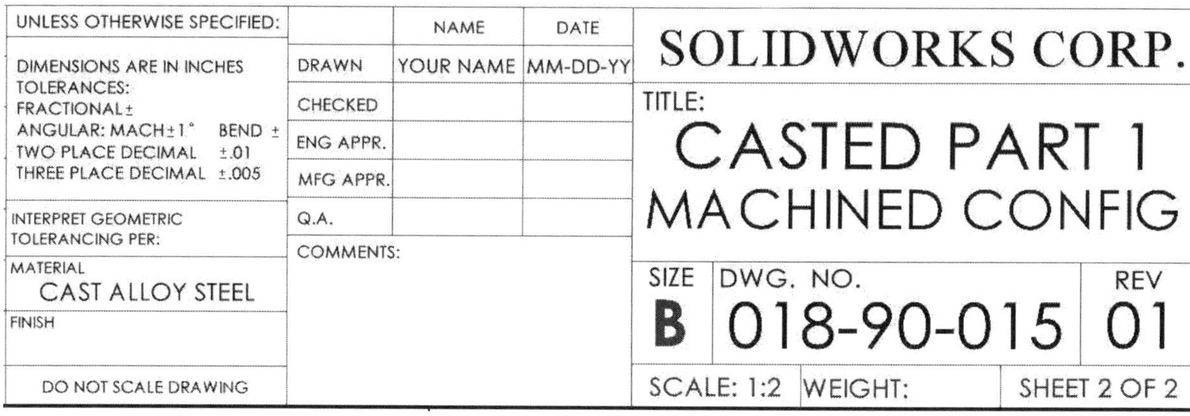

When finished, double-click **Sheet1** to bring the drawing layer back to the front.

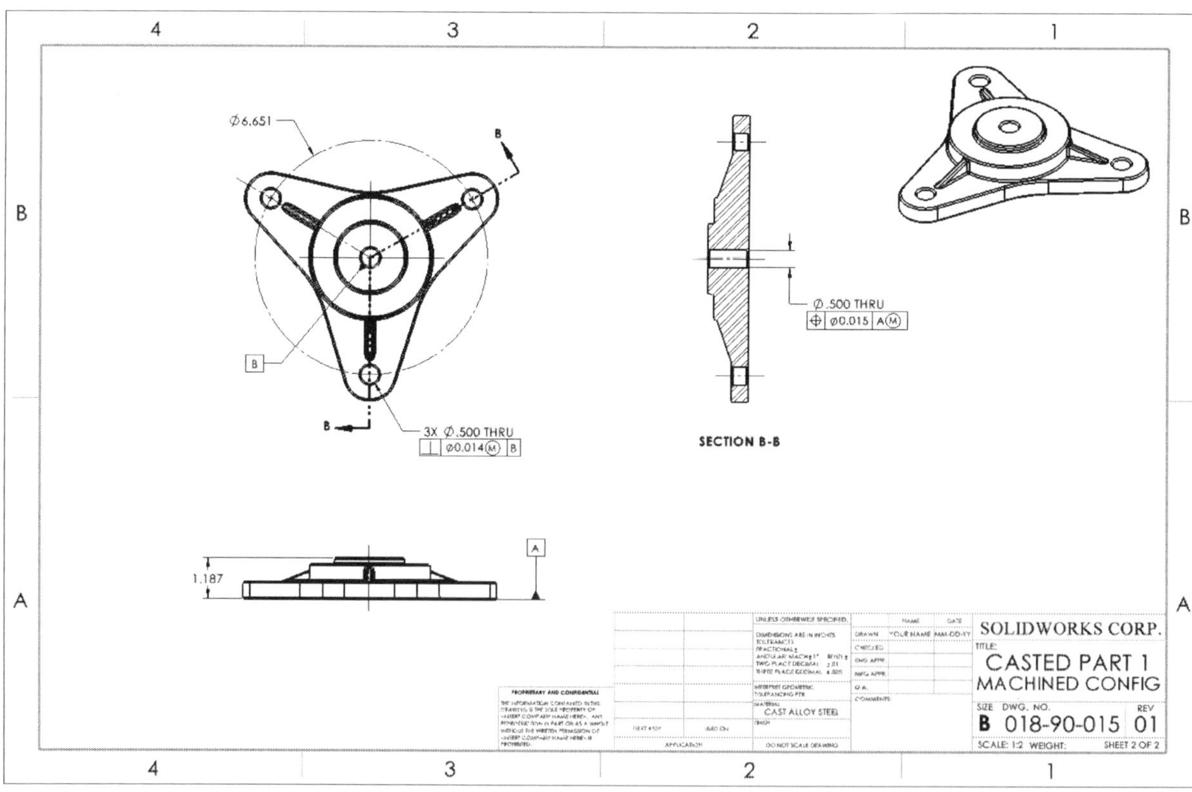

21. Saving your work:

Select **File, Save As.**

Enter: **Casted Part 2.slddrw** for the file name.

Click **Save.**

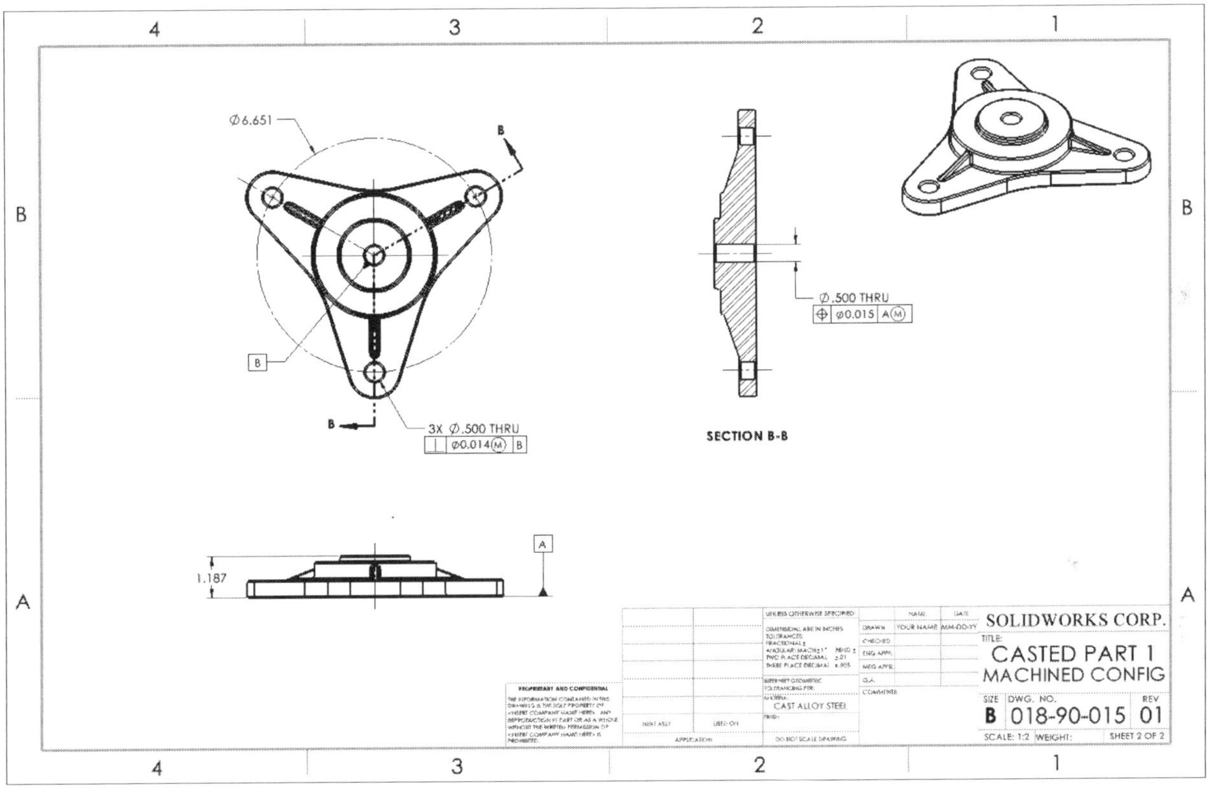

Close all documents.

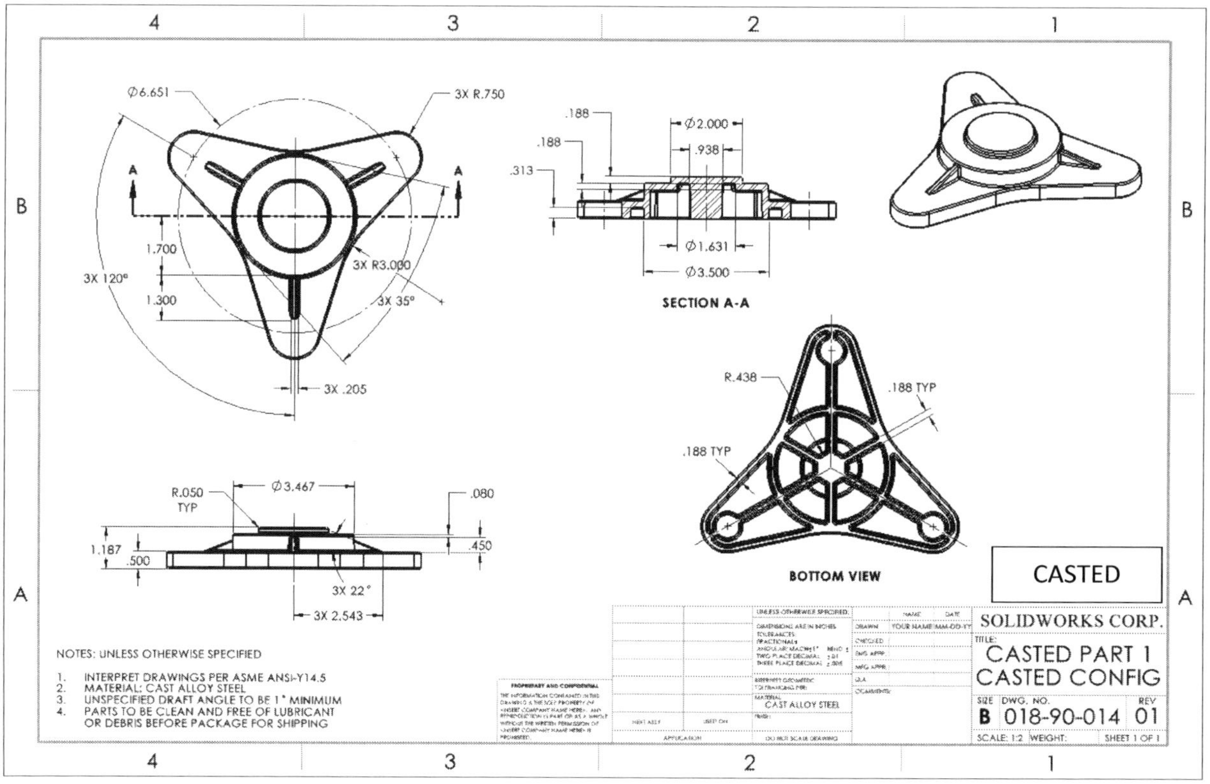

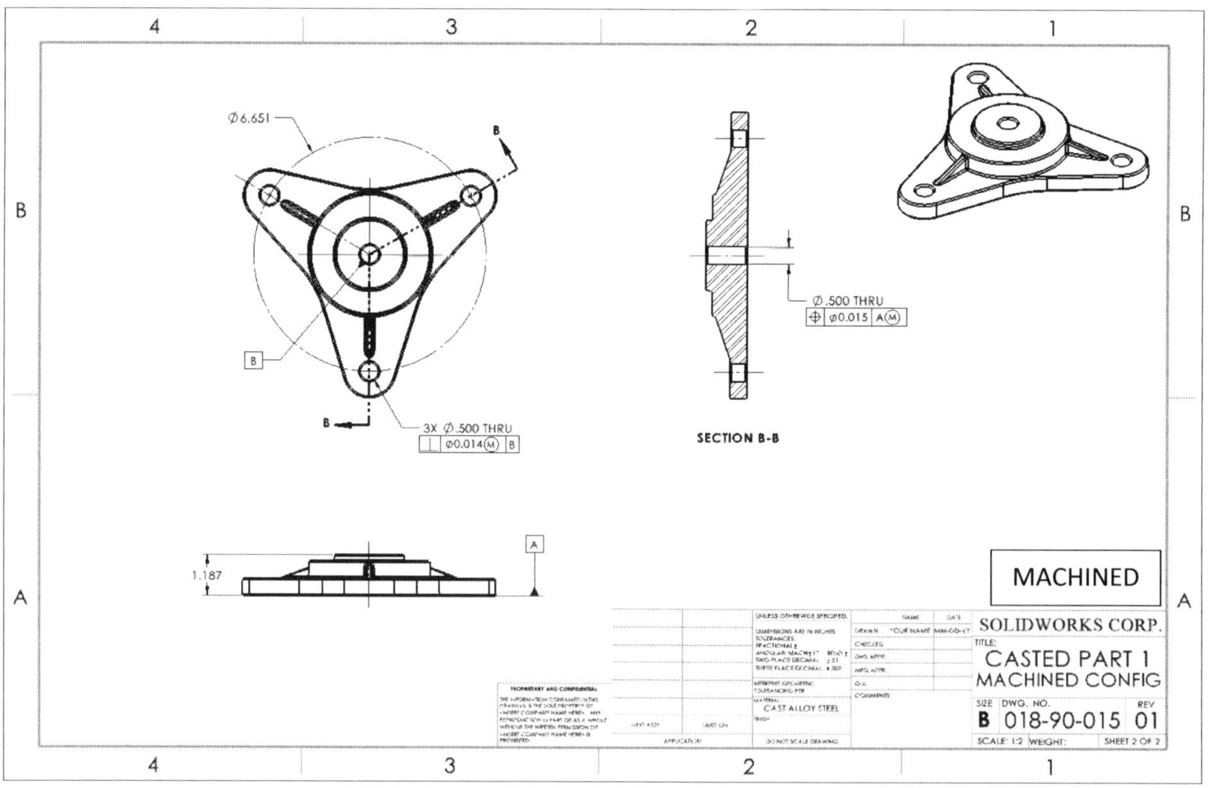

Exercise: Casted Parts

Detailing a Casted Part 2

The exercises are designed to help you apply what you have learned from the previous lessons. They come with some instructions but not as detailed as the lessons, to give you an opportunity to explore and to try and create the drawings on your own, at your own pace.

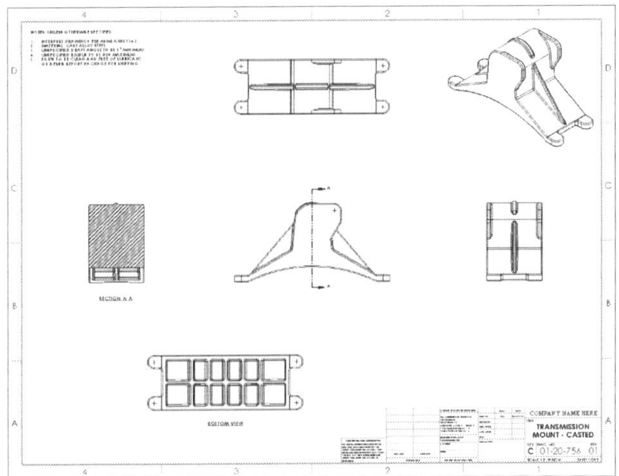

1. Opening a drawing document:

Click **File, Open.**

Browse to the Training Folder and open the drawing document named: **Casted Parts_Transmission Mount.slddrw**

This drawing document contains 2 sheets: sheet 1 is the Casted drawing, and sheet 2 is the Machined drawing. The model contains 2 configurations, Casted and Machined.

The drawings views have already been created for both sheets; you will need to add the dimensions and annotations as shown in the next section.

The Casted drawing contains the Front, Top, Right, Bottom, Isometric, and a Section view.

The Machined drawing contains the same drawing views plus a Detail view showing the height of the curved rib.

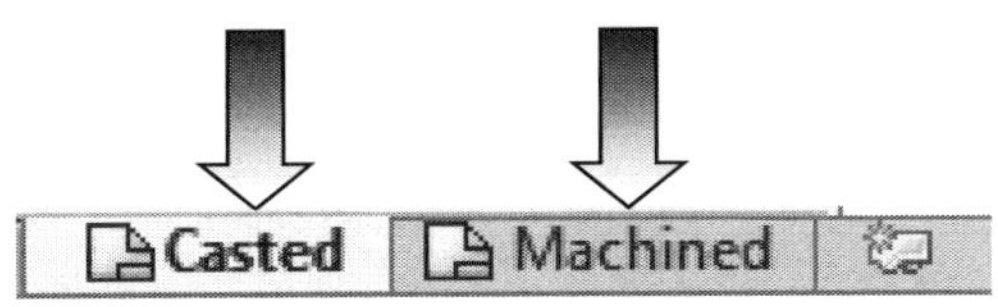

Click the Casted or Machined tabs at the lower left corner of the screen to toggle back and forth between the 2 sheets.

Sheet 1: **Casted**

Front view, Top view, Right view, Bottom view, Isometric view, and Section view.

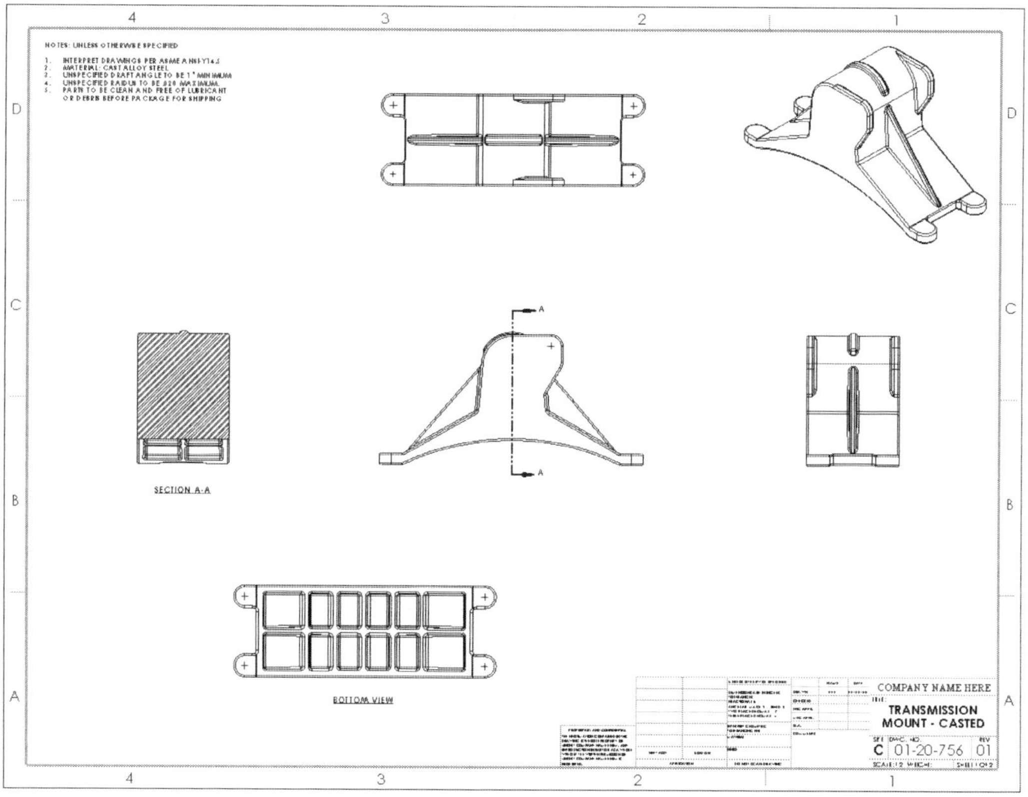

Sheet 2: **Machined**

Front view, Top view, Right view, Bottom view, Isometric view, Section view, and Detail view.

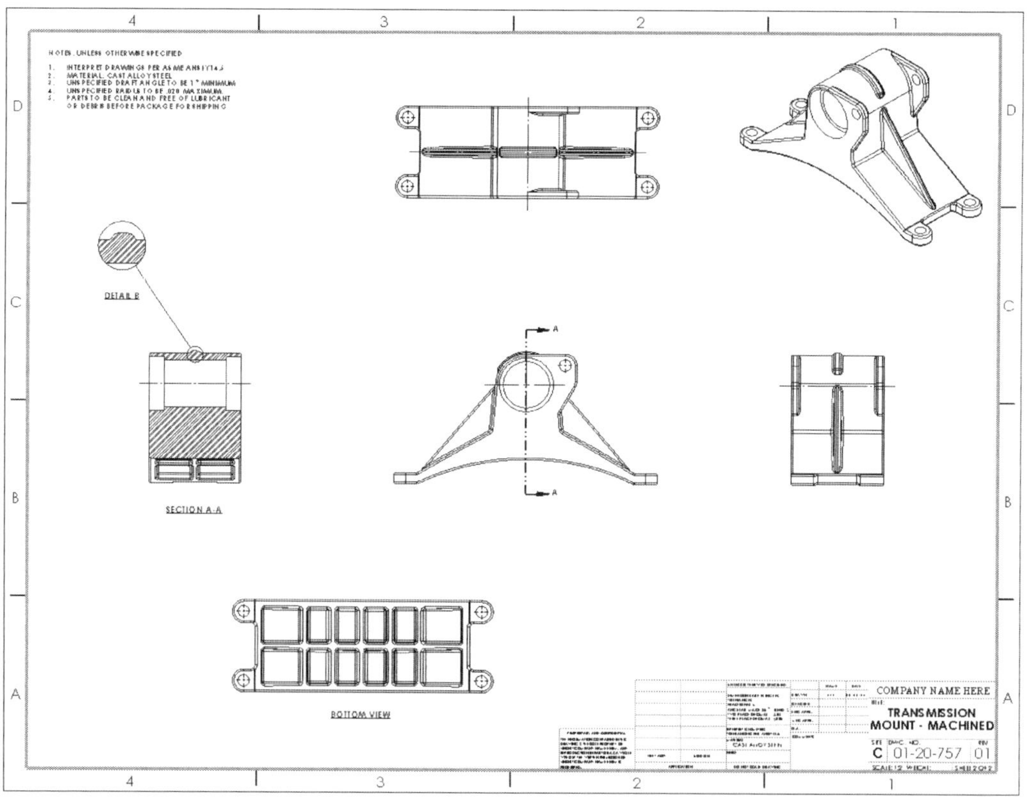

Sheet 1: **Casted Configuration**

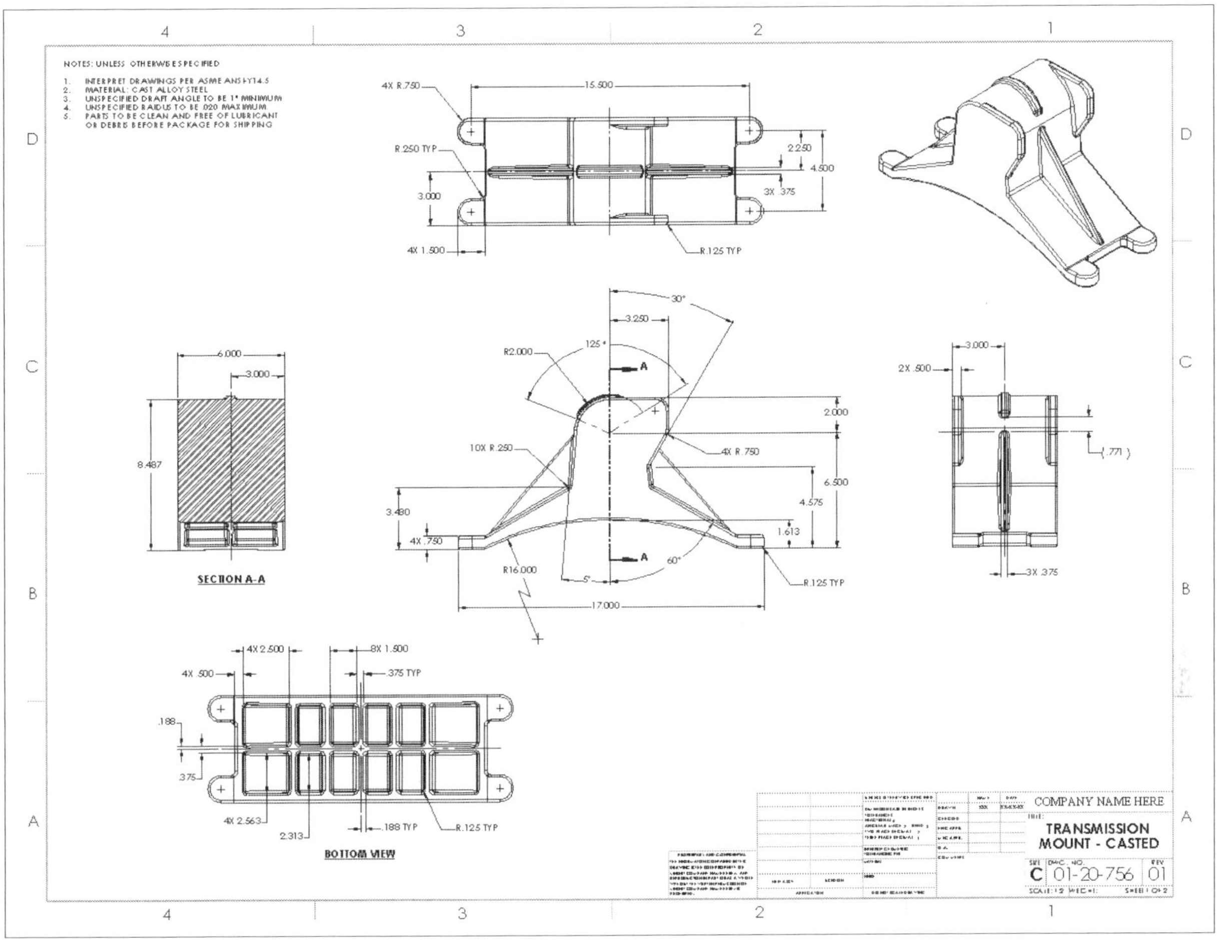

Switch back to Sheet 1 (Casted).

2. Detailing sheet 1:

Insert the model dimensions
Add centerlines and center marks
Add the annotations shown in the drawing
Add the number of instances where needed
Fill out the title block information

Sheet 2: **Machined Configuration**

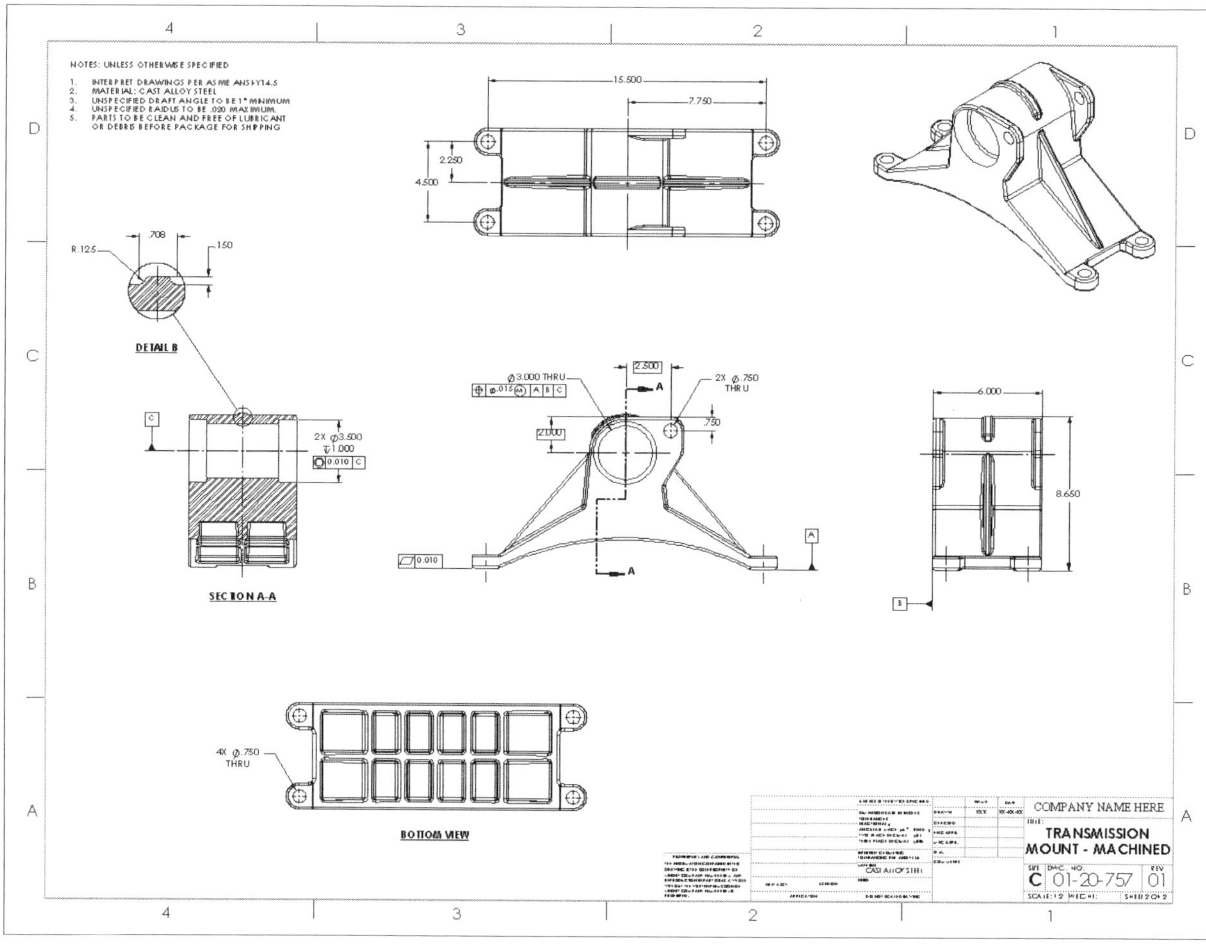

Switch to Sheet 2 (Machined).

3. Detailing sheet 2:

Insert the model dimensions
Add datums and geometric tolerances
Add centerlines and center marks
Add the annotations shown in the drawing
Add the number of instances where needed
Fill out the title block information

4. Saving your work:

Save your work as: **Casted Parts_Transmission Mount.slddrw**

Exercise: Casted Parts

Detailing a Casted Part 3

The exercises are designed to help you apply what you have learned from the previous lessons. They come with some instructions but not as detailed as the lessons, to give you an opportunity to explore and to try and create the drawings on your own, at your own pace.

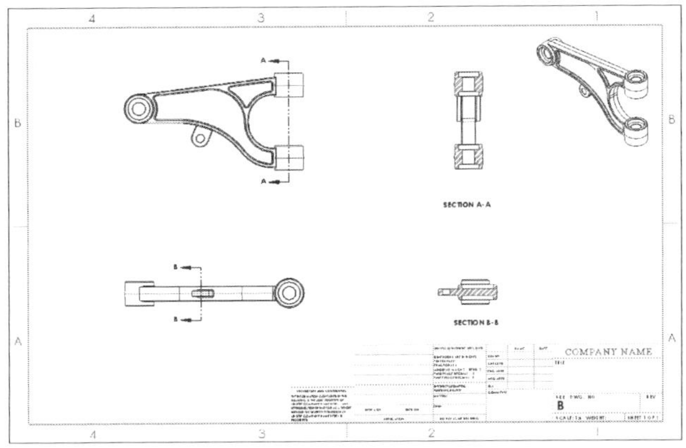

1. Opening a drawing document:

Click **File, Open**.

Browse to the Training Folder and open the drawing document named: **Casted Parts_Suspension.slddrw**

2. Adding centerlines and center marks:

Add centerlines and center marks to the holes and fillets as shown below.

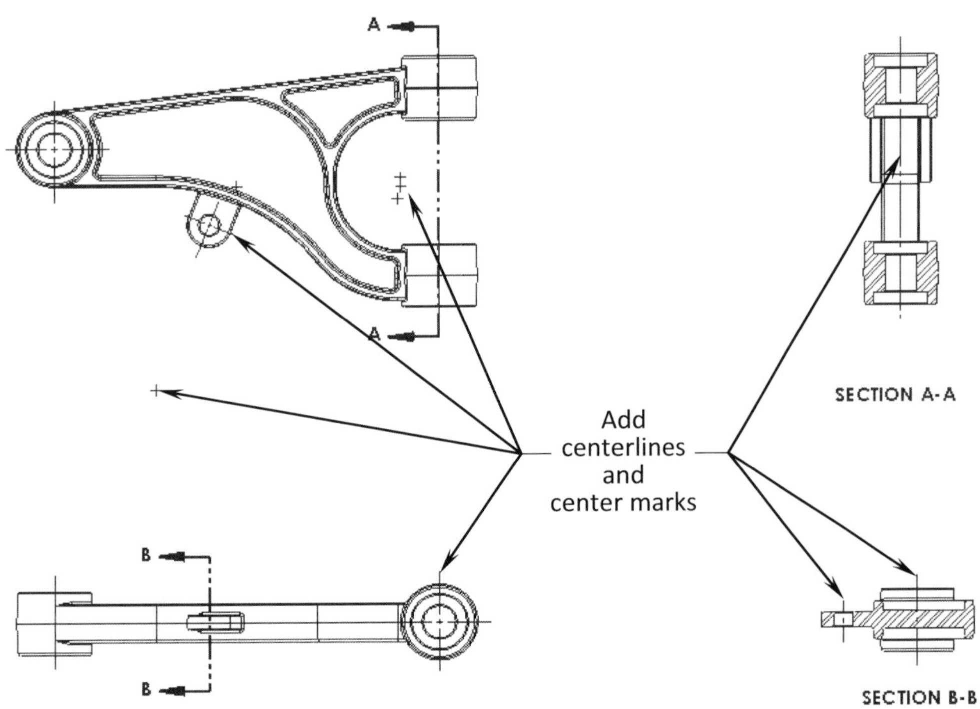

3. Inserting the model dimensions:

From the **Annotation** tab, use the **Model Item** command to insert the dimensions from the model to all drawing views.

<u>Note</u>: When creating the solid model, it is common to use commands like Convert Entities, Sketch (or Features) Patterns, Offset Entities, etc. to quickly create and define the geometry. This is often referred to as <u>Modeling Approach</u>, but when a drawing is made from these types of models, dimensions that are needed for manufacturing will be missing. Those dimensions need to be added to the drawings to fill in the gaps; this is often referred to as <u>Manufacturing Approach</u>.

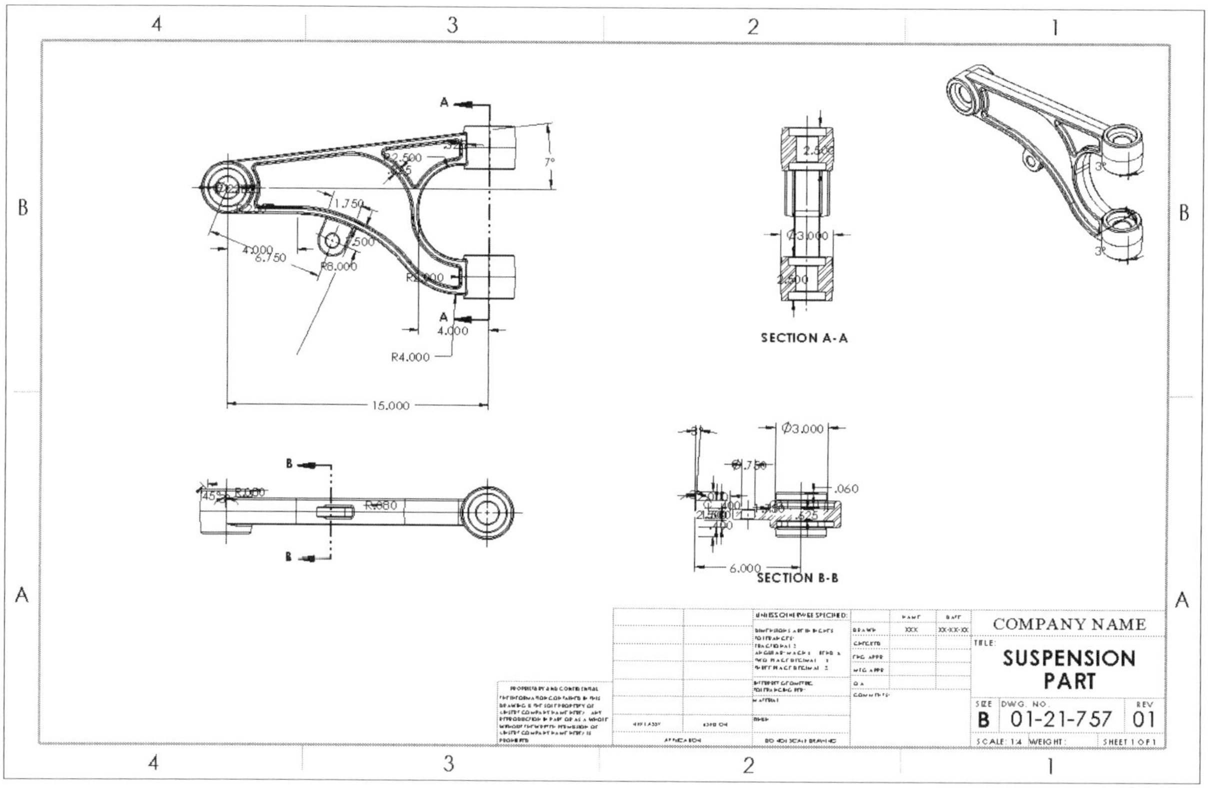

There are missing dimensions in every drawing view; we will add them manually to each view. This is not the best way to detail a drawing because these dimensions will be "driven dimensions" or "reference dimensions". Changes done to the model will update the reference dimensions in the drawing, but the reference dimensions in the drawing cannot be changed by themselves.

4. Rearranging dimensions:

Zoom in closer to the Top drawing view.

Rearrange the dimensions so that they are not crossing one another and add the missing dimensions and annotations that are shown in the image below.

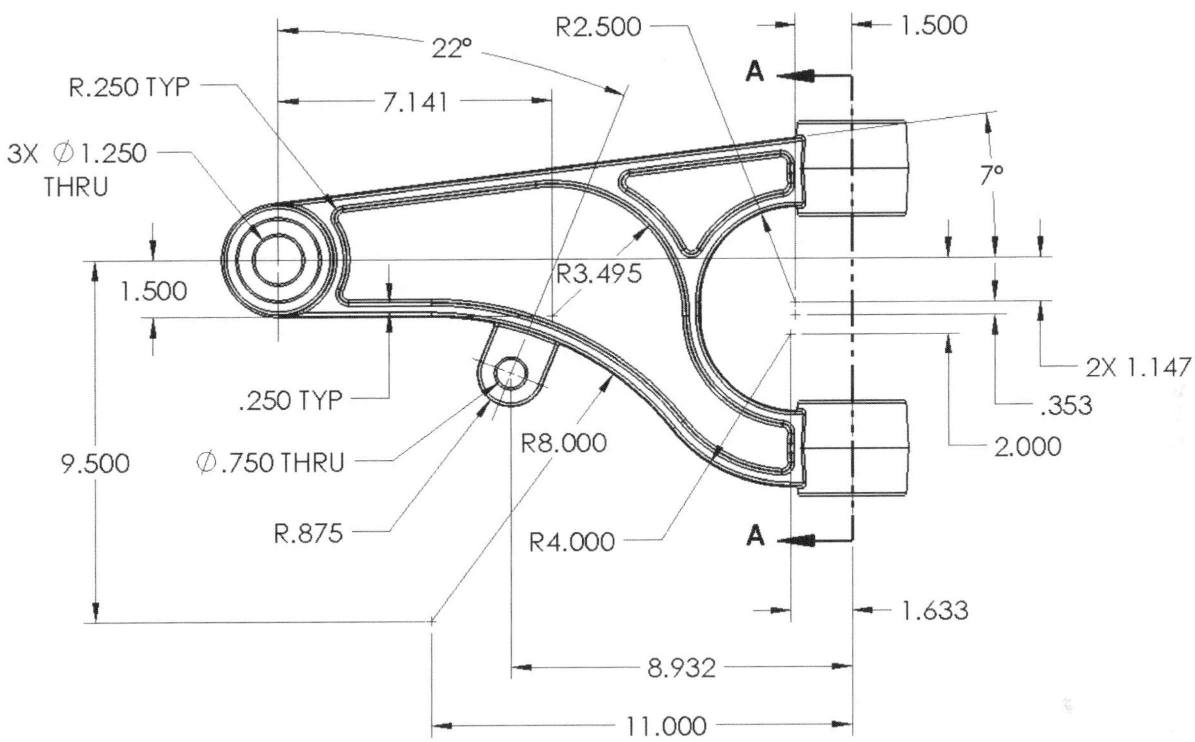

Add any missing dimensions to the Front drawing view as shown below.

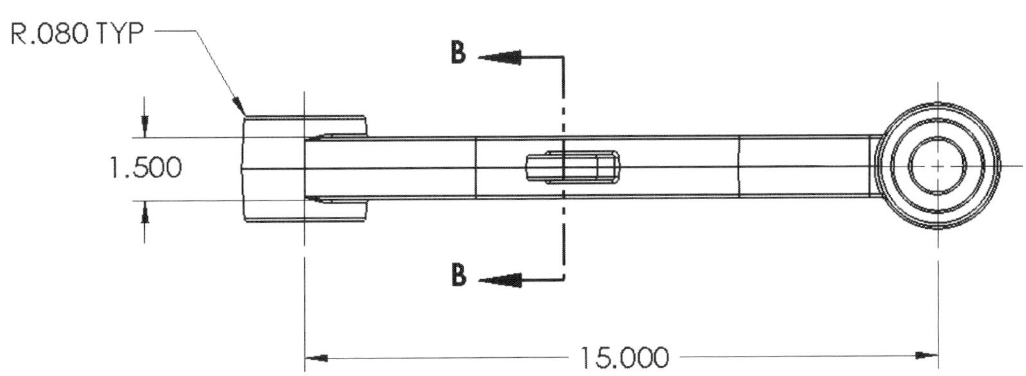

Zoom in closer to the Section A-A.

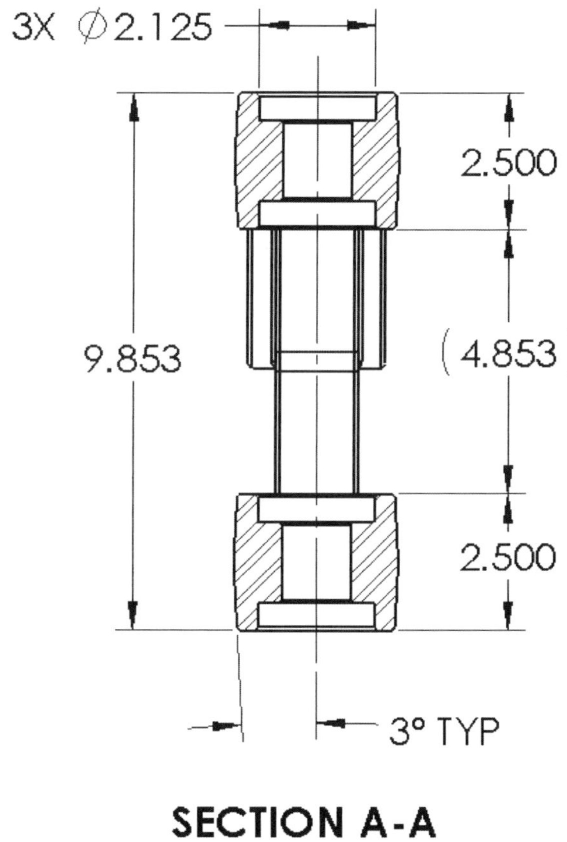

Move the dimensions and keep the spacing between each one as even as possible. This will make the drawing look very clear and easy to read.

Add the missing dimensions, if needed.

Clean up the dimensions in the Section B-B and add the missing dimensions as shown in the image below.

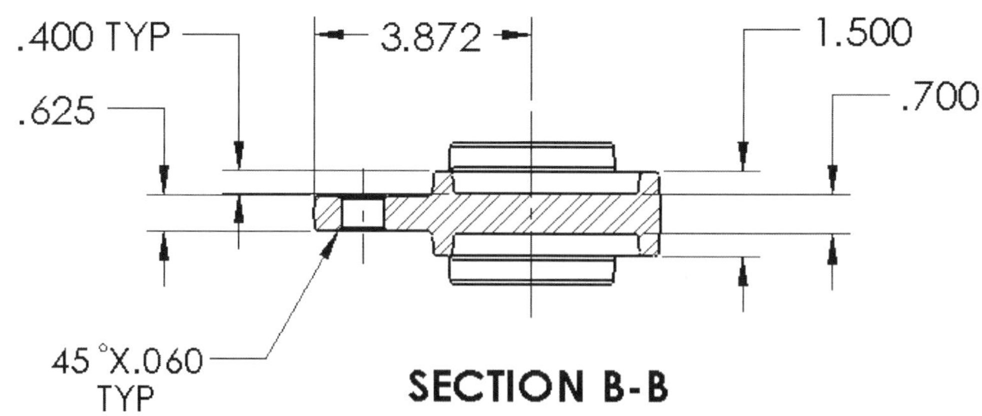

5. Adding the General Notes:

Using the **Note** command, type the notes below in uppercase letters:

NOTES: UNLESS OTHERWISE SPECIFIED
1. INTERPRET DRAWINGS AND DIMENSIONS PER ASME-ANSI 14.5
2. MATERIAL: CAST ALLOY STEEL
3. UNSPECIFIED DRAFT ANGLE TO BE 1° MINIMUM
4. PARTS TO BE CLEAN AND FREE OF LUBRICANT OR DEBRIS BEFORE PACKAGED FOR SHIPPING

Place the General Notes at the lower left corner of the drawing.

6. Filling out the Title Block information:

Right-click on the drawing sheet and select: **Edit Sheet Format.**

Fill out the information for:

* Company (or School) Name
* Drawing Number
* Drawn by
* Title
* Revision
* Drawn date

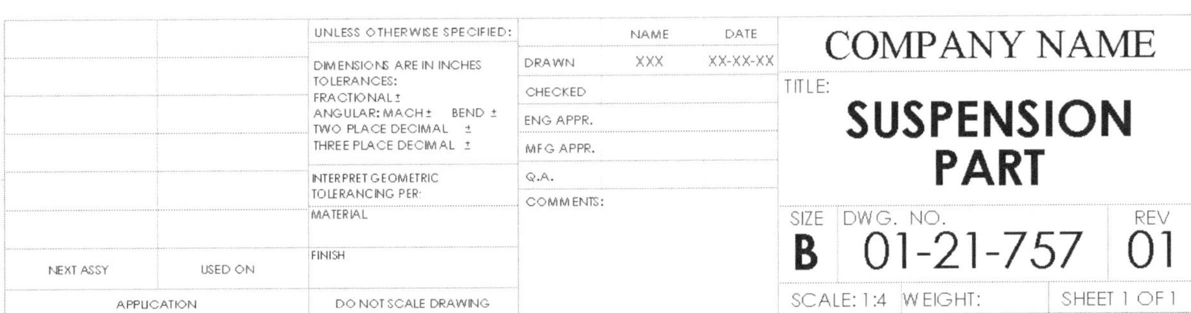

When finished, right-click inside the drawing sheet and select: **Edit Sheet** to return to the drawing.

7. Saving your work:

Select **File, Save As**.

Enter: **Casted Parts_Suspension_Completed.slddrw** for the file name.

Click **Save**.

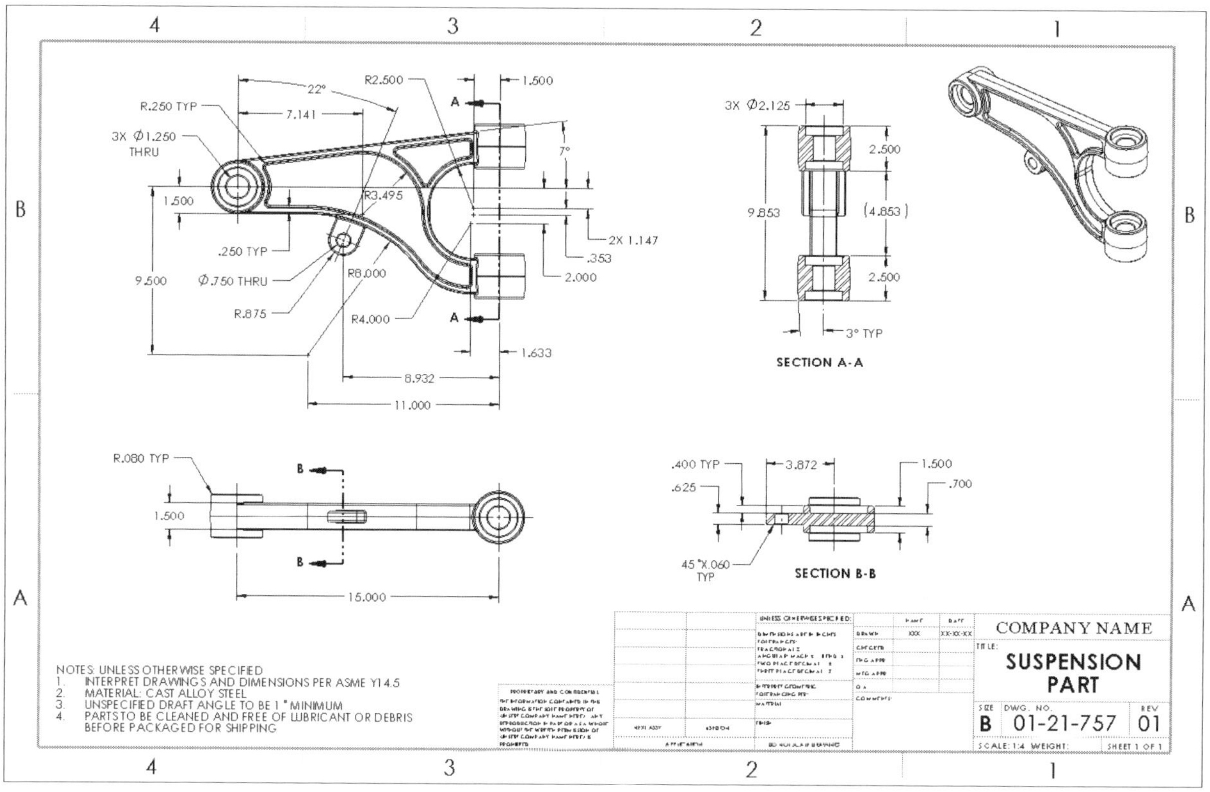

CHAPTER 8: ASSEMBLY DRAWINGS

Detailing an Assembly Drawing

There are three main parts in an Assembly Drawing:

1. The Drawing Views: an assembled **Isometric** drawing view to show how the components are put together, and an **exploded** drawing view to show the internal components.
2. The Balloons**:** to identify each component.
3. A Parts List (or Bill of materials): to display the information about the components.

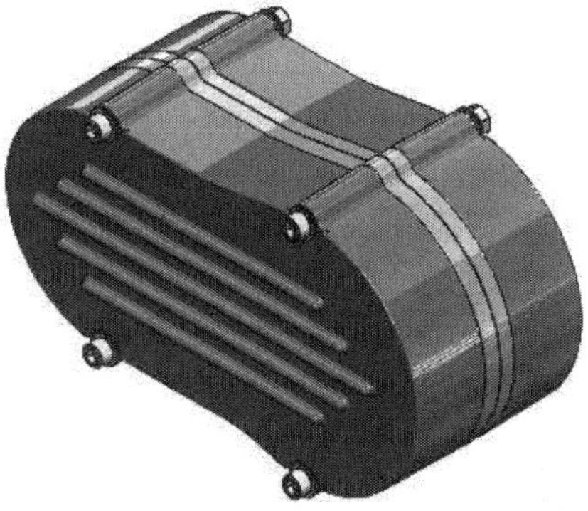

This chapter will teach us a quick and easy method to create an Assembly Drawing.

1. Opening an assembly document:

Select **File, Open**.

Browse to the Training Folder and open the assembly document named: **Top Level Assembly.sldasm**.

There are 2 configurations in this assembly document:

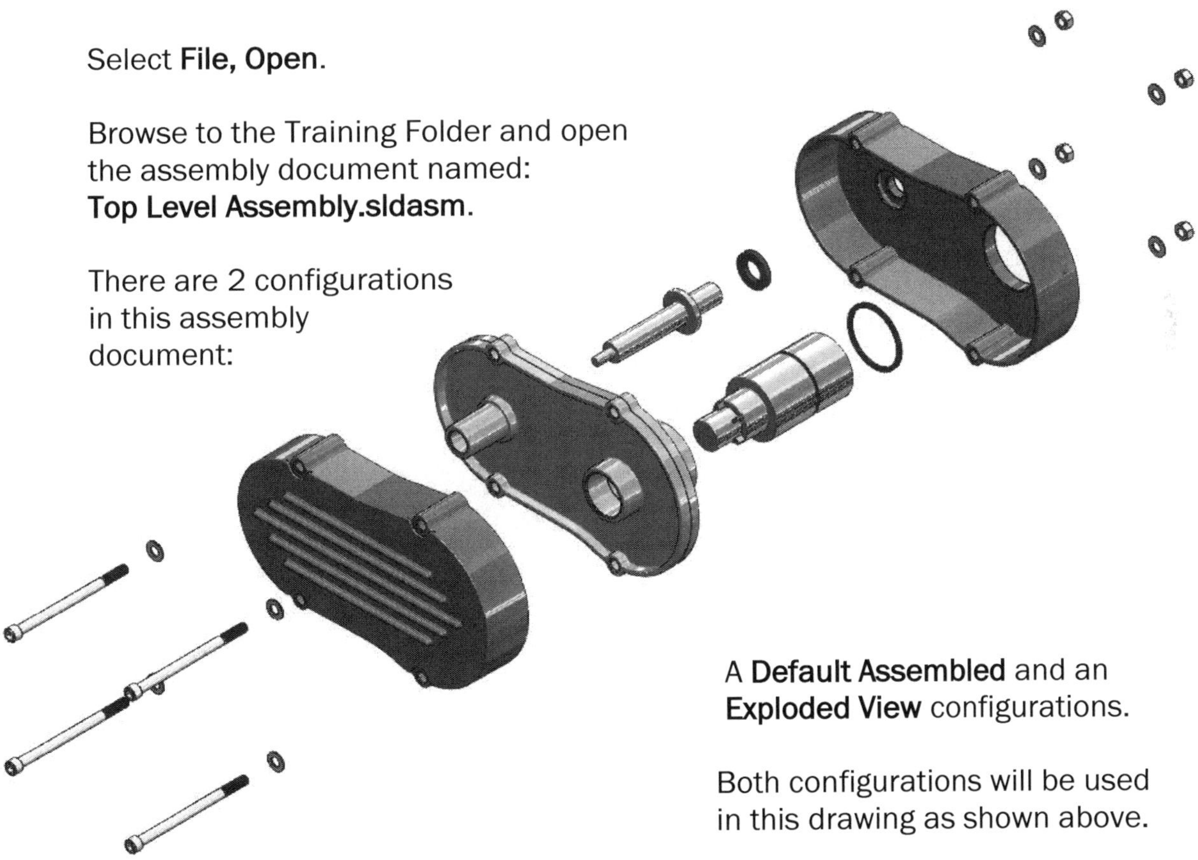

A **Default Assembled** and an **Exploded View** configurations.

Both configurations will be used in this drawing as shown above.

2. Making a drawing from assembly:

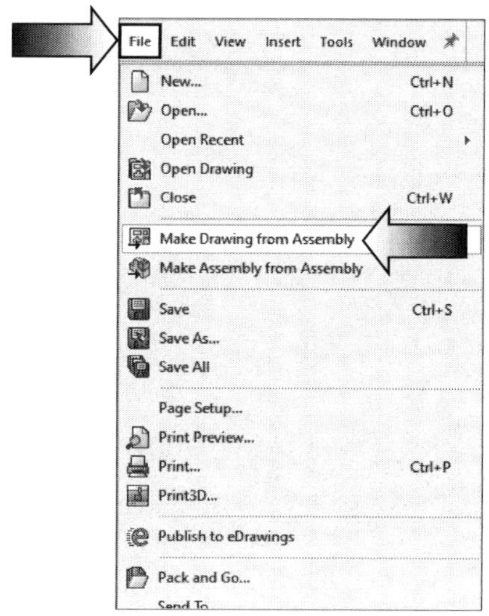

Assembly drawings are created very similar to part drawings, the same tools are used to create the drawing views and anotations.

Select **File, Make Drawing From Assembly**.

Select the **Assembly** template.

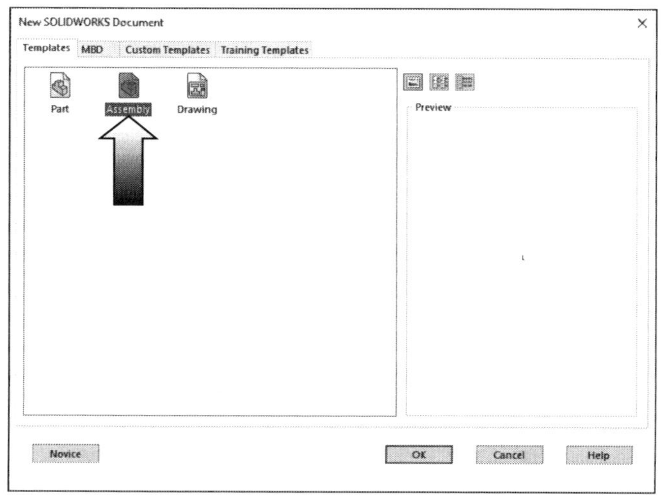

If the Sheet Properties dialog box does not pop-up automatically, right click inside the drawing and select: Properties.

In the **Sheet Properties** dialog box, select the following:

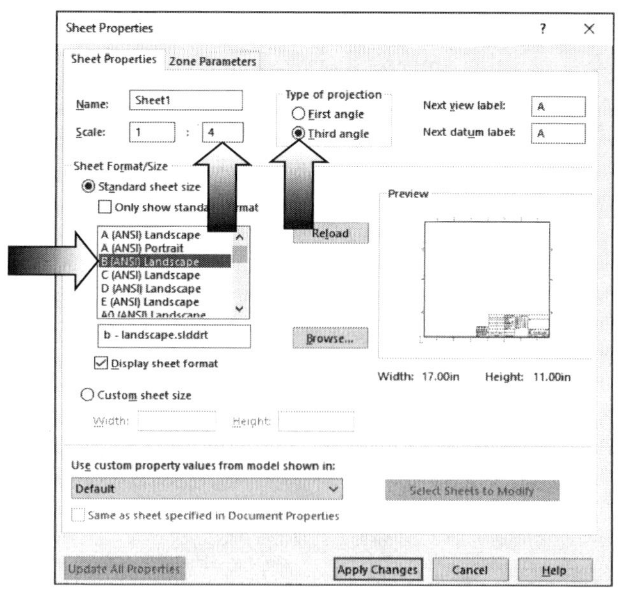

Scale: **1:4**

Type of Projection: **3rd Angle**

Sheet Format Size: **B (ANSI) Landscape**

Keep other parameters at their defaults.

Click **Apply Changes**.

3. Creating the drawing views:

Expand the **View Palette** on the right side of the screen.

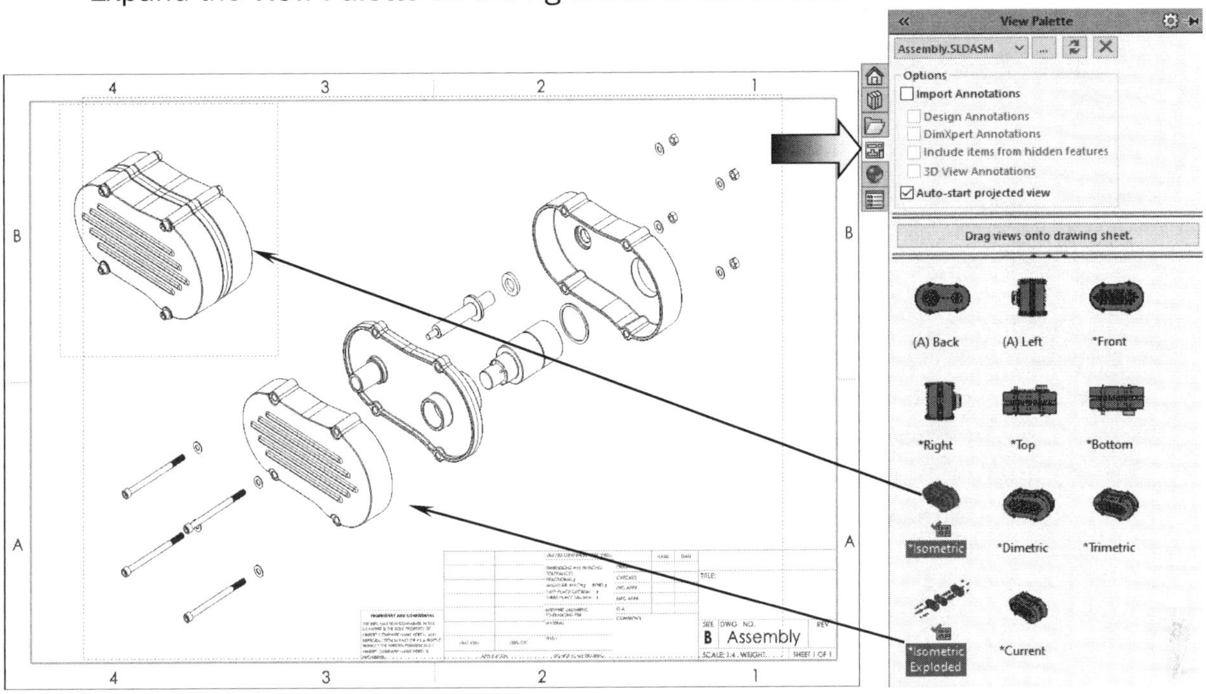

Drag and drop the **Isometric Exploded** view into the center of the drawing.

Also, drag and drop the **Isometric** view to the upper left corner of the drawing as shown above.

<u>Note</u>: *If the 2 drawing views are aligned to each other, right-click on the dotted border of the Isometric drawing view and select:* ***Alignment, Break Alignment.***

The Isometric view shows how the components are put together, and the Exploded Isometric view shows all interior components. They can now be labeled with balloons to identify them against the bill of materials.

The Exploded view has been created previously, but keep in mind when making the exploded views: all components should be fully exploded and avoid any overlaps so that they can easily be seen and recognized when balloons are added to them.

4. Adding Balloons:

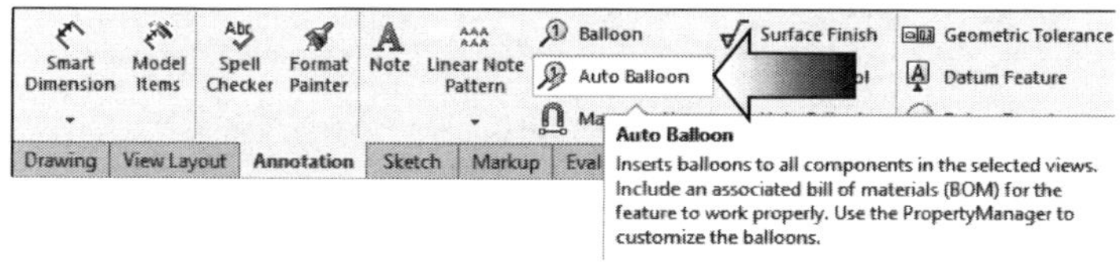

Balloons are used to label components with their item numbers from the bill of materials and reference notes in the drawing.

Balloons can be created one by one or all at once.

Switch to the **Annotation** tab and click **Auto Balloons**.

All unique components are labeled based on the order of the Assembly. The 1st component listed on the FeatureManager tree will receive balloon number 1, the 2nd component on the FeatureManger tree will receive balloon number 2, so on and so forth.

In the Balloon Layout section, select the **Square** layout and the size of **1 Character** as shown below.

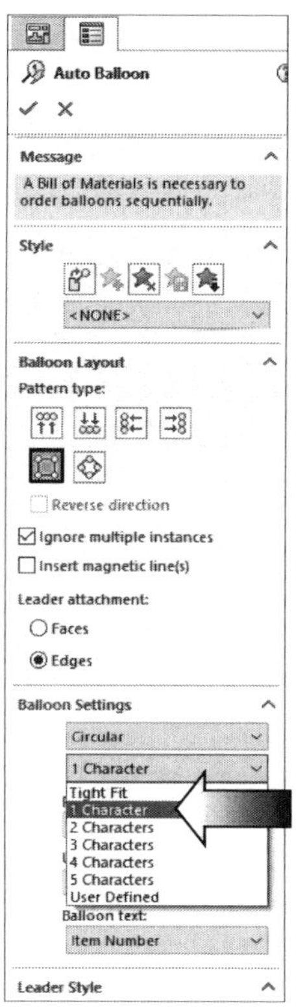

Click **OK**.

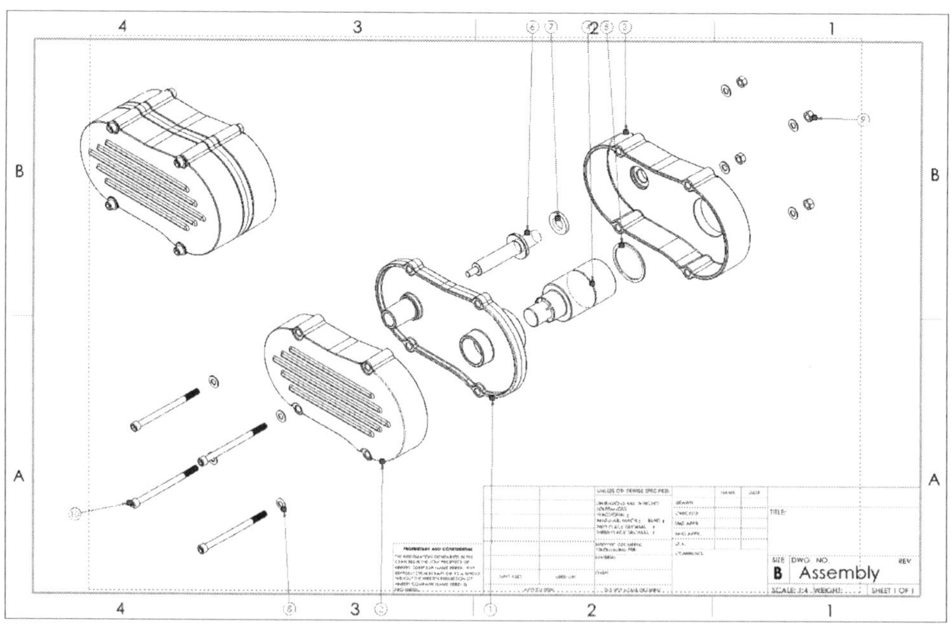

Rearrange the balloons to look similar to the ones shown in the drawing below.

It is best practice to keep the balloon's leader lines to about the same angle and length. They will help make the assembly drawing look cleaner and easier to read.

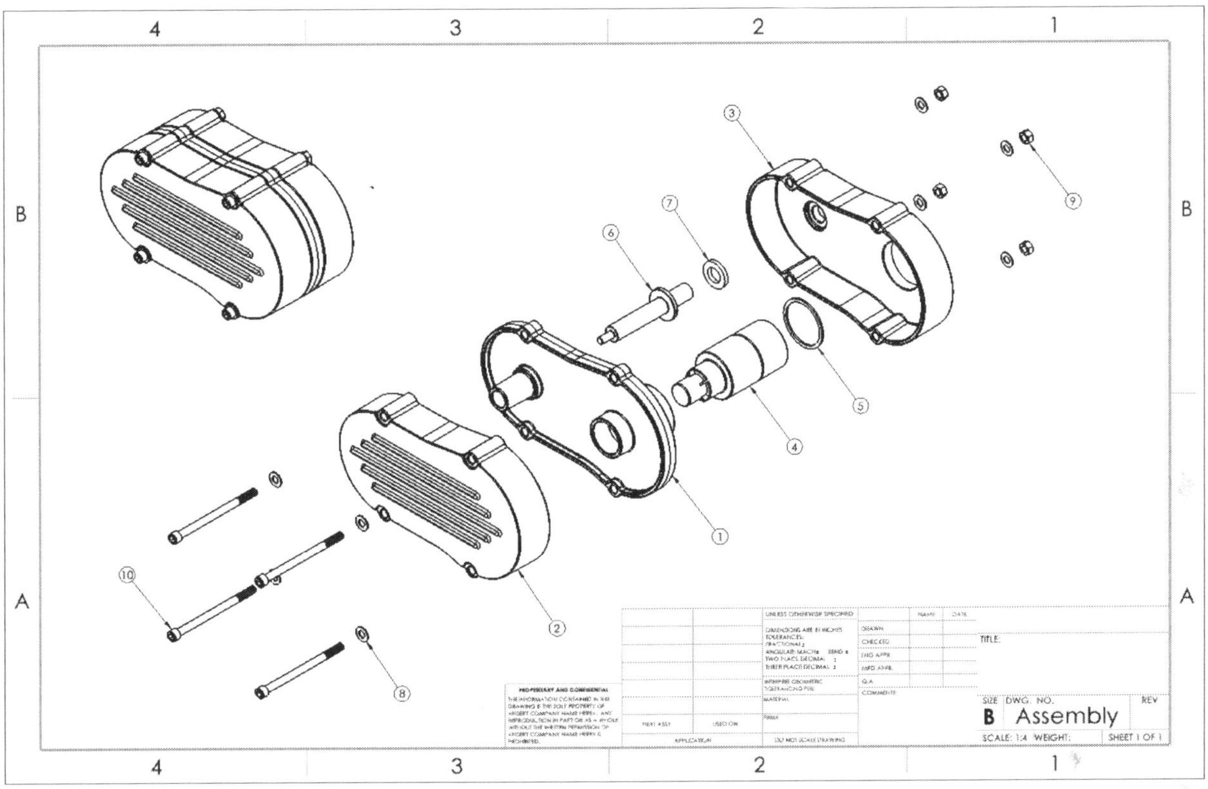

Since only the 1st instance will get a balloon, we will need to add the number of instances next to the balloons.

Depending on your company's standards, some companies preferred to use the **Circular Split Line** balloons (9/4), while some others would prefer to add the **Instance Call Out** (4X) next to the balloons.

We will be using the **Instance Call Out** for this drawing.

5. Adding the number of instances:

Hold the **Control** key and select the 3 balloons of the **Socket Head Cap Screw**, the **Washer,** and the **Hex Nut**.

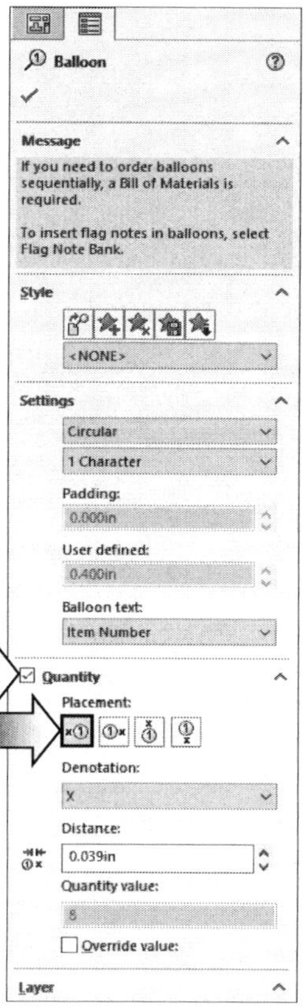

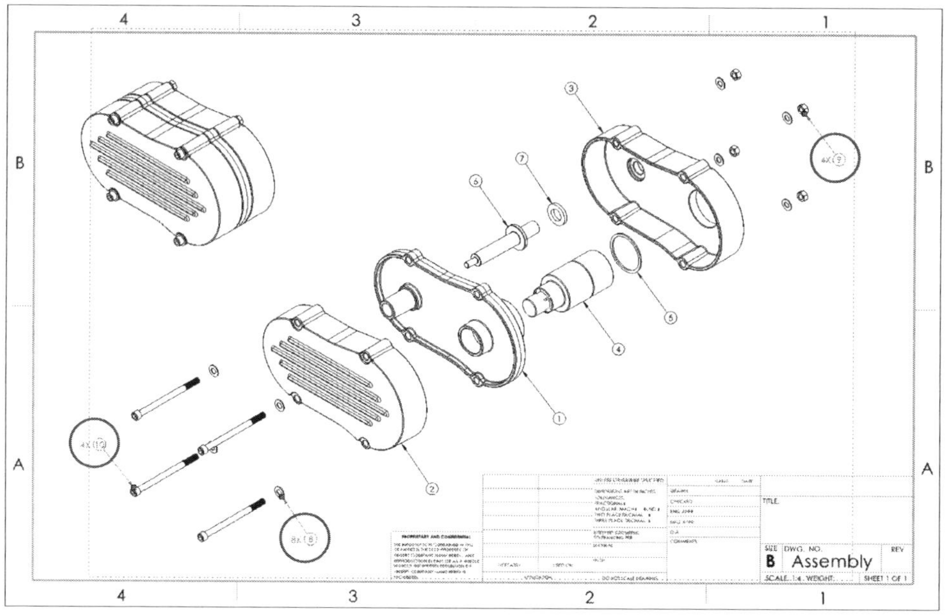

In the Balloons Properties tree, enable the **Quantity** checkbox and select the **Left Placement** option.

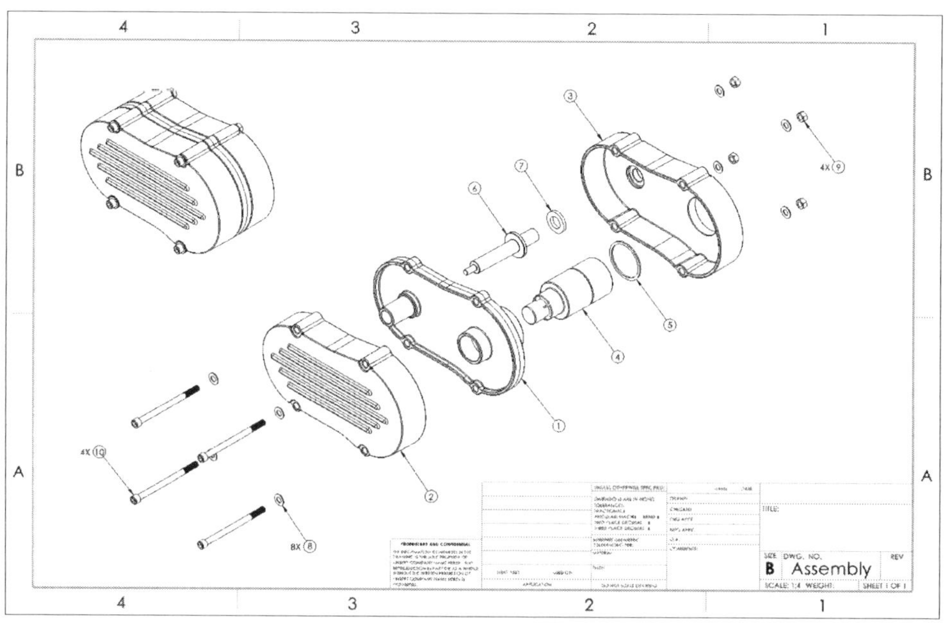

The three selected balloons now have the instance count placed on the left side of their balloons.

6. Inserting a Bill of Materials:

A Bill of Materials, or BOM, is a structured, comprehensive list of the materials, components and parts required to manufacture a product, as well as the quantities in which the materials are needed, and descriptions and costs.

There are two types of BOM in SOLIDWORKS, a **Table-Based** BOM and an **Excel-Based** BOM.

The **Table-based** Bill of Materials is based on SOLIDWORKS tables and includes

Templates
Anchors
Quantities for configurations
Whether to keep items that have been deleted from the assembly
Zero quantity display
Excluding assembly components
Following assembly order
Item number control
Ability to open parts and assemblies from the table.

The **Excel-based** Bill of materials offers more controls than the Table-Base such as:

Direct inputs using the MS-Excel application
Edit text and insert new parameters
Insert Part Number Column
Insert Custom Properties
Save the table as an Excel File
Create or manage configurations using Excel, etc.

The **Configuration tab** in the Bill of Materials Properties dialog box specifies basic display properties of a bill of materials. The other tabs available in the dialog box are Contents and Control. The software remembers your selections from session to session.

The **Contents tab** in the Bill of Materials Properties dialog box specifies which items appear in the bill of materials and allows you to reverse the order of the list. The other tabs available in the dialog box are Configuration and Control.

The **Control tab** in the Bill of Materials Properties dialog box specifies how row numbers are assigned, what happens when a component is deleted, and how to split long BOM tables. The other tabs available in the dialog box are Configuration and Contents.

The BOM must be linked to a drawing view. The exploded drawing view is the best one because it clearly shows all components in it.

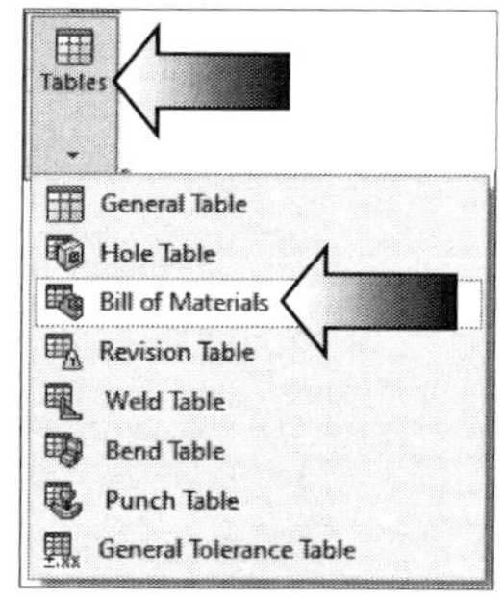

Click the dotted border of the exploded drawing view and select: **Tables, Bill of materials** from the **Annotation** tab.

Select the drawing view's border

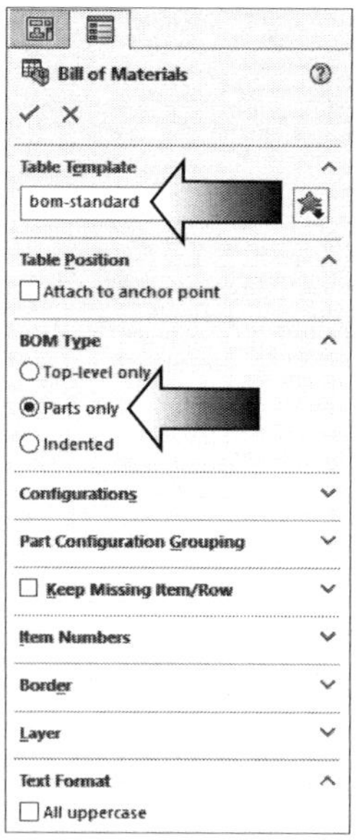

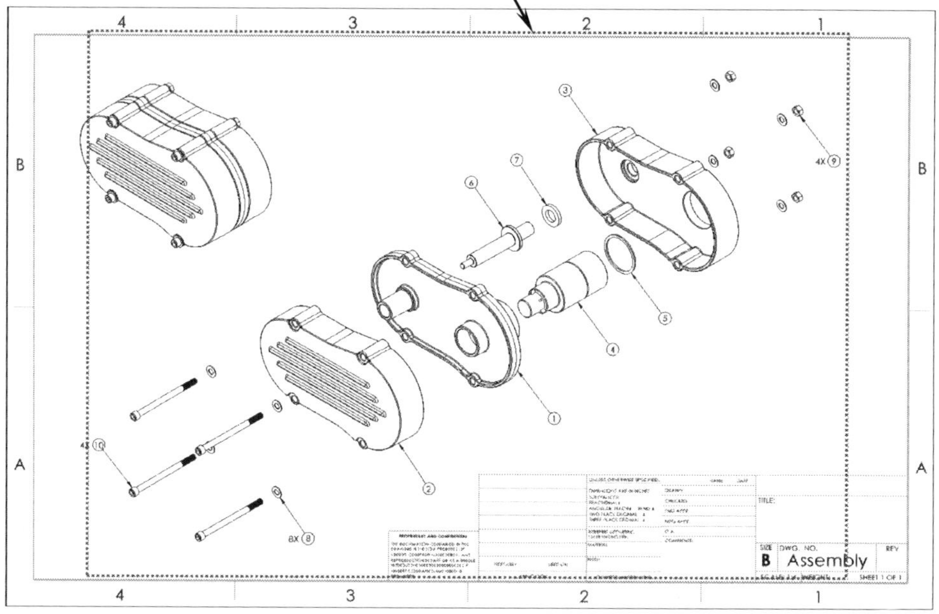

For Table Template, use the default **Bom-Standard.**

For Table Position, clear the **Attach to Anchor Point** checkbox.

For BOM Type, select **Parts Only**.

Click **OK**.

A BOM is created and attached to the mouse cursor.

Place the BOM on top of the Title Block as shown in the image on the right.

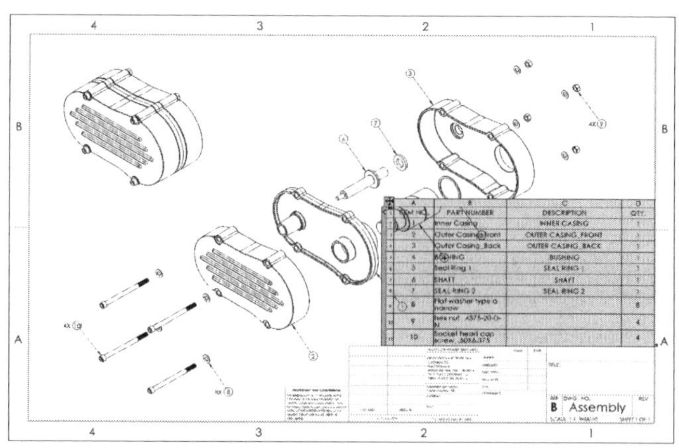

7. Adjusting the BOM:

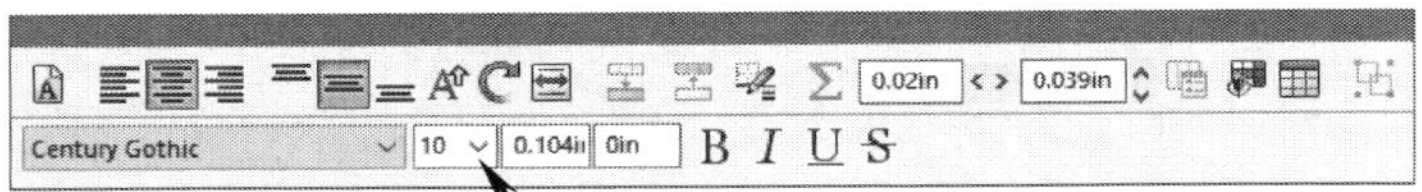

Formatting Toolbar

The BOM can be made smaller several ways:

Drag this handle to move the BOM

* Change to a smaller font size.

* Drag the corner handle to resize the BOM.

* Change the Row Height dimension.

	A	B	C	D
1	ITEM NO.	PART NUMBER	DESCRIPTION	QTY.
2	1	Inner Casing	INNER CASING	1
3	2	Outer Casing_Front	OUTER CASING_FRONT	1
4	3	Outer Casing_Back	OUTER CASING_BACK	1
5	4	BUSHING	BUSHING	1
6	5	Seal Ring 1	SEAL RING 1	1
7	6	SHAFT	SHAFT	1
8	7	SEAL RING 2	SEAL RING 2	1
9	8	Flat washer type a narrow		8
10	9	hex nut_.4375-20-D-N		4
11	10	Socket head cap screw_.50X6.375		4

Click inside the BOM to bring out the **Formatting Toolbar.**

Highlight all rows in the BOM and change the font size to **10 point.**

Drag the handle on the lower right corner to resize the table, and drag the 4-way handle at the upper left corner to move the BOM.

Drag this handle to resize the BOM

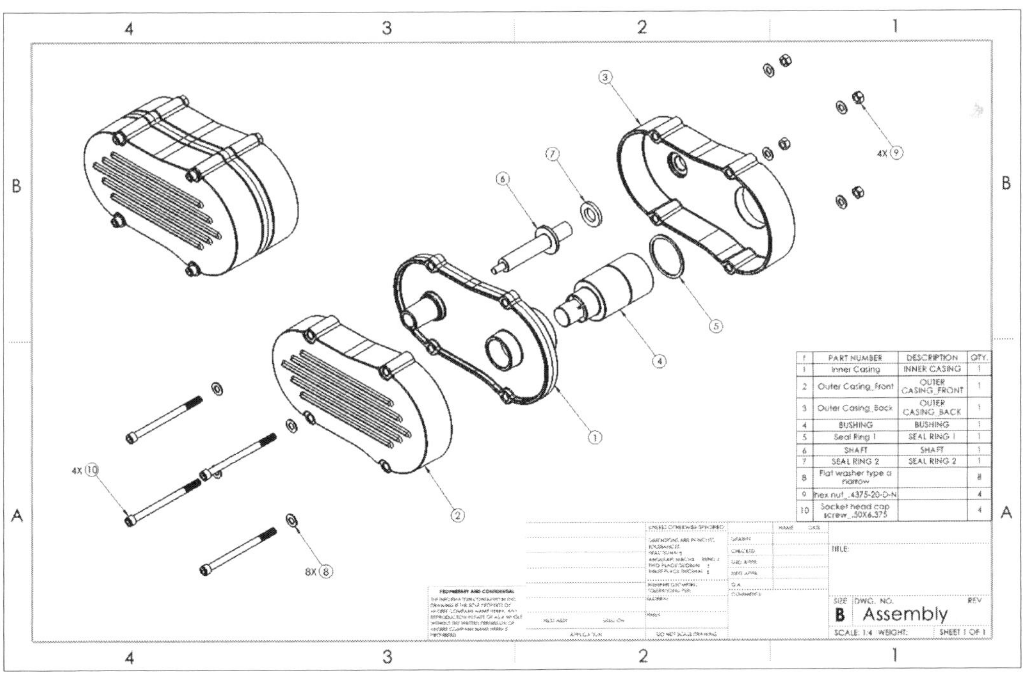

8. Filling out the BOM manually:

The information in the BOM should be filled out at the **Part-Level**, in the **File-Properties** section, so that they will be linked to the parts.

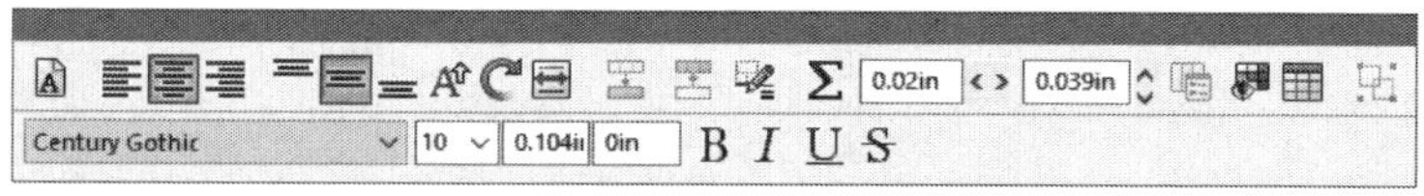

Any changes done to these Custom Properties will be populated to the BOM immediately.

Custom Properties will be discussed in a later chapter. We will go ahead and fill out the missing information manually at this time.

	A	B	C	D
1	f	PART NUMBER	DESCRIPTION	QTY.
2	1	Inner Casing	INNER CASING	1
3	2	Outer Casing_Front	OUTER CASING_FRONT	1
4	3	Outer Casing_Back	OUTER CASING_BACK	1
5	4	BUSHING	BUSHING	1
6	5	Seal Ring 1	SEAL RING 1	1
7	6	SHAFT	SHAFT	1
8	7	SEAL RING 2	SEAL RING 2	1
9	8	Flat washer type a narrow		8
10	9	hex nut_.4375-20-D-N		4
11	10	Socket head cap screw_.50X6.375		4

Zoom in closer to the BOM.

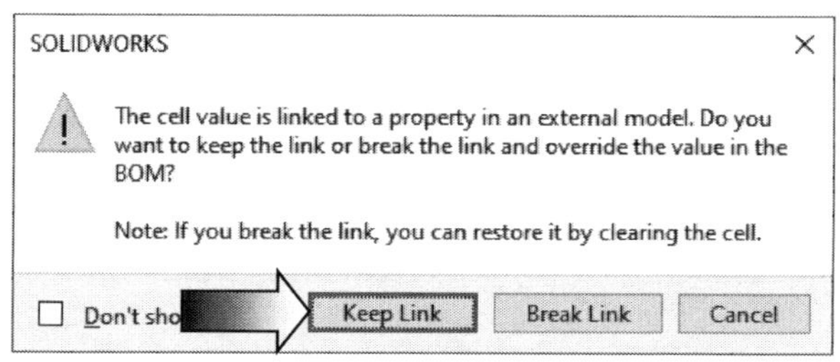

Double-click in cell **C9 Description** and select **Keep Link** from the pop-up dialog box.

Enter the text shown below and in the image on the right:

Vendor P/N:
90107A033
95479A122
91251A737

	A	B	C	D
1	ITEM NO.	PART NUMBER	DESCRIPTION	QTY.
2	1	Inner Casing	INNER CASING	1
3	2	Outer Casing_Front	OUTER CASING_FRONT	1
4	3	Outer Casing_Back	OUTER CASING_BACK	1
5	4	BUSHING	BUSHING	1
6	5	Seal Ring 1	SEAL RING 1	1
7	6	SHAFT	SHAFT	1
8	7	SEAL RING 2	SEAL RING 2	1
9	8	Flat washer type a narrow	Vendor P/N 90107A033	8
10	9	hex nut_.4375-20-D-N	Vendor P/N 95479A122	4
11	10	Socket head cap screw_.50X6.375	Vendor P/N 91251A737	4

9. Filling out the Title Block information:

From the FeatureManager tree, expand **Sheet1** and double-click **Sheet Format1** to activate it for editing.

Fill out the information shown below. The lines next to the **Name** and **Date** fields can be moved to fit the text if needed.

When finished, double-click on **Sheet1** to exit the Format layer and return to the Drawing layer.

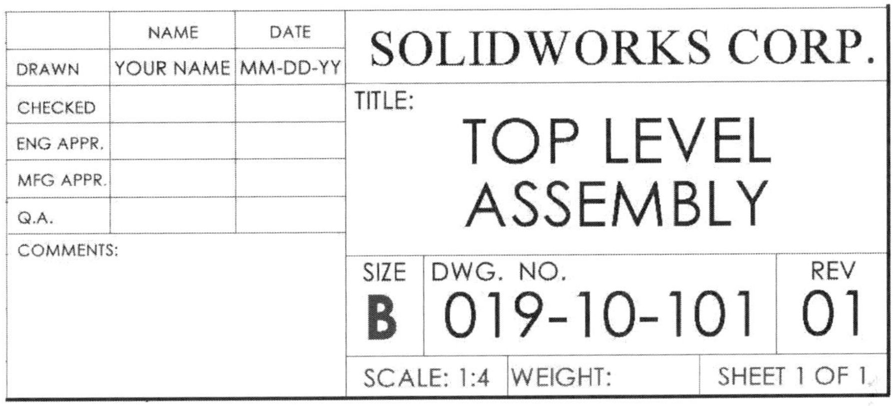

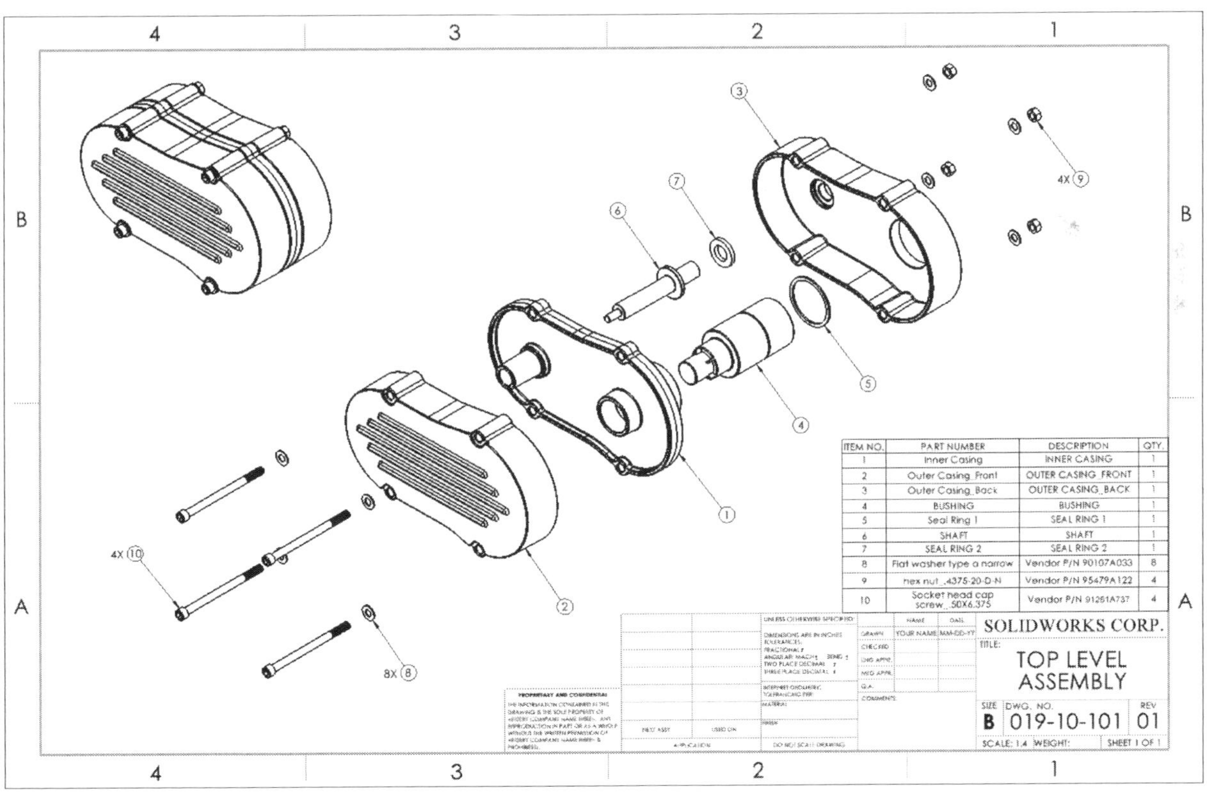

10. Saving your work:

Select **File, Save As.**

Enter: **Top Level Assembly.slddrw** for the file name.

Click **Save.**

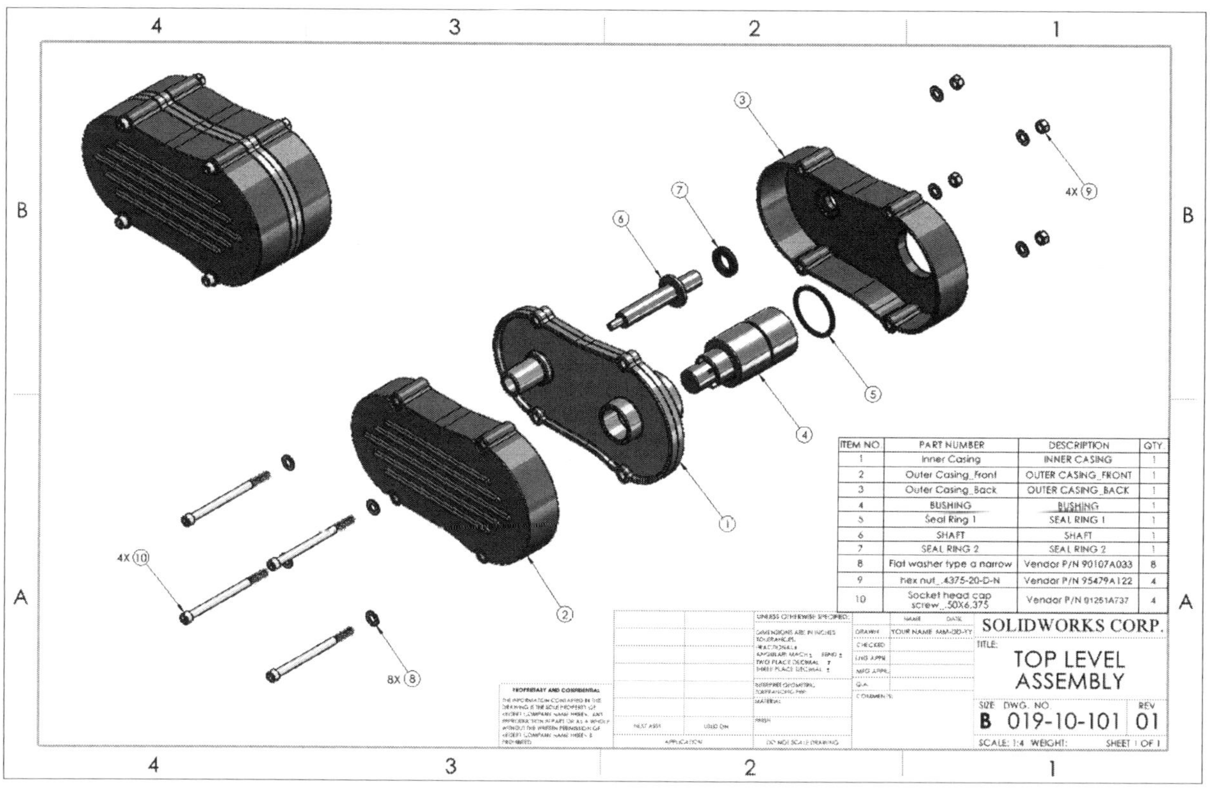

Exercise: Assembly Drawings

Detailing an Assembly Drawing 1

The exercises are designed to help you apply what you have learned from the previous lessons. They come with some instructions but not as detailed as the lessons, to give you an opportunity to explore and to try and create the drawings on your own, at your own pace.

1. Opening a part document:

Select **File, Open.**

Browse to the Training Folder and open a part document named: **4X4 Bracket Assembly.sldprt.**

The materials have already been assigned to each component.

2. Transferring to a drawing:

Select **File, Make Drawing from Assembly.**

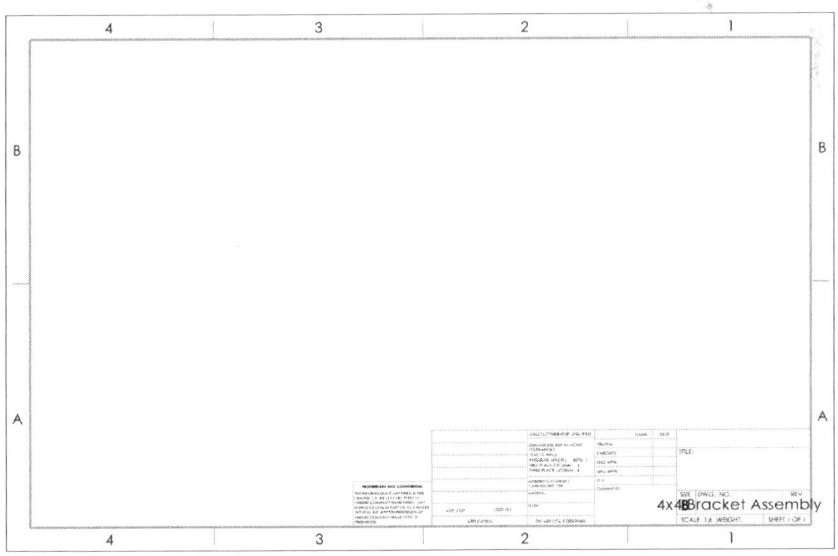

Select the **B-Size** drawing paper.

Set the Type-Of-Projection to: **3rd Angle.**

Set the Scale to **1:6**

Click **OK.**

The B-Size landscape drawing is loaded.

3. Creating the drawing views:

Expand the **View Palette** on the left side of the screen.

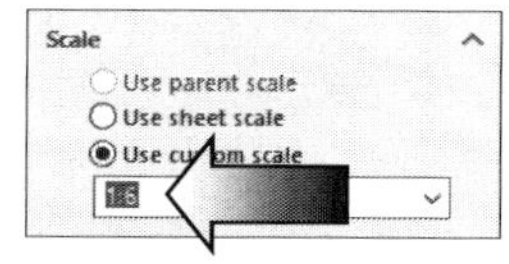

Drag and drop the **Isometric Exploded** view to the center of the drawing

Also drag and drop the **Isometric** view to the upper left corner of the drawing as shown below.

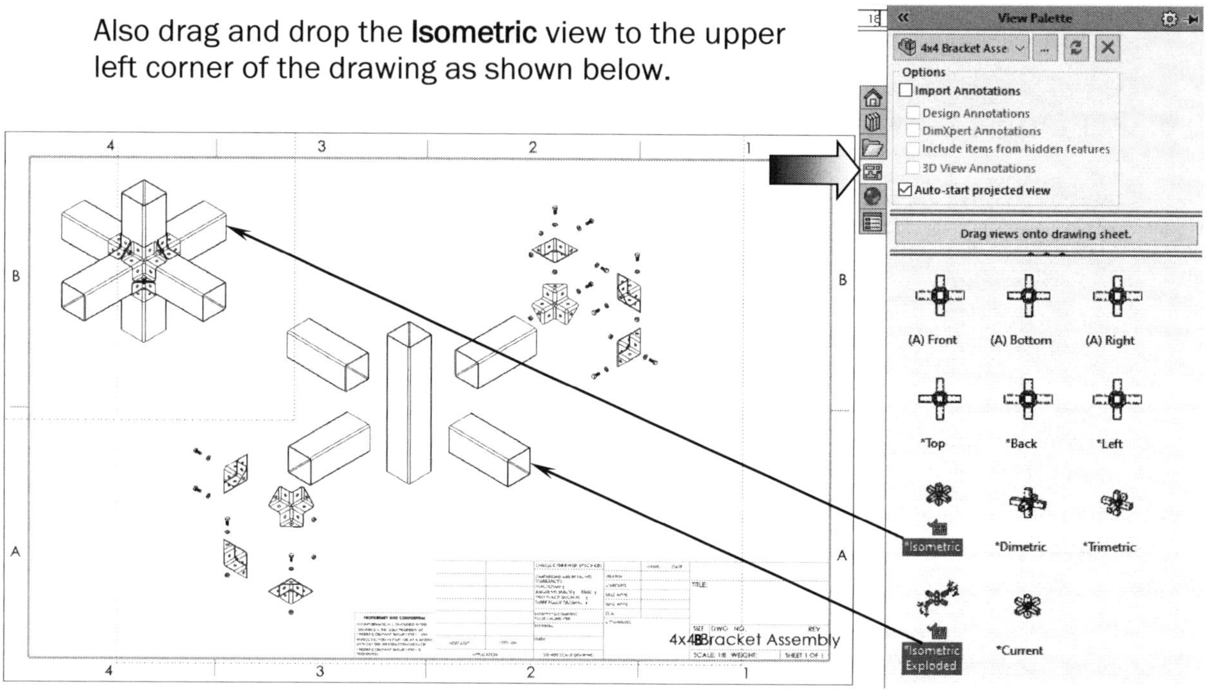

Check the scale of both drawing views to ensure that they are set to **1:6**.

Rearrange the drawing views to make room for the balloons and the BOM.

If the 2 drawing views are aligned and do not move freely, right-click the Isometric view and select: **Alignment, Break Alignment.**

The Tangent Edges are set to **Visible** by default. To change the Tangent Edges to the Phantom style, right-click a view, select: **Tangent Edges, Tangent Edges With Font.**

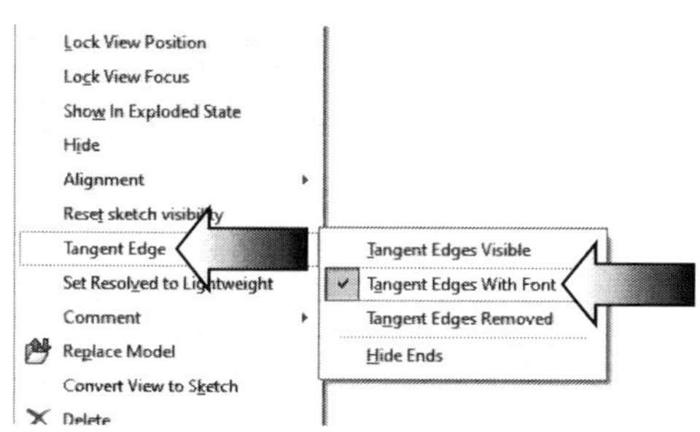

4. Adding balloons and instance counts:

Switch to the **Annotation** tab.

Click the dotted border of the **Isometric Exploded** view and select: **Auto Balloons.**

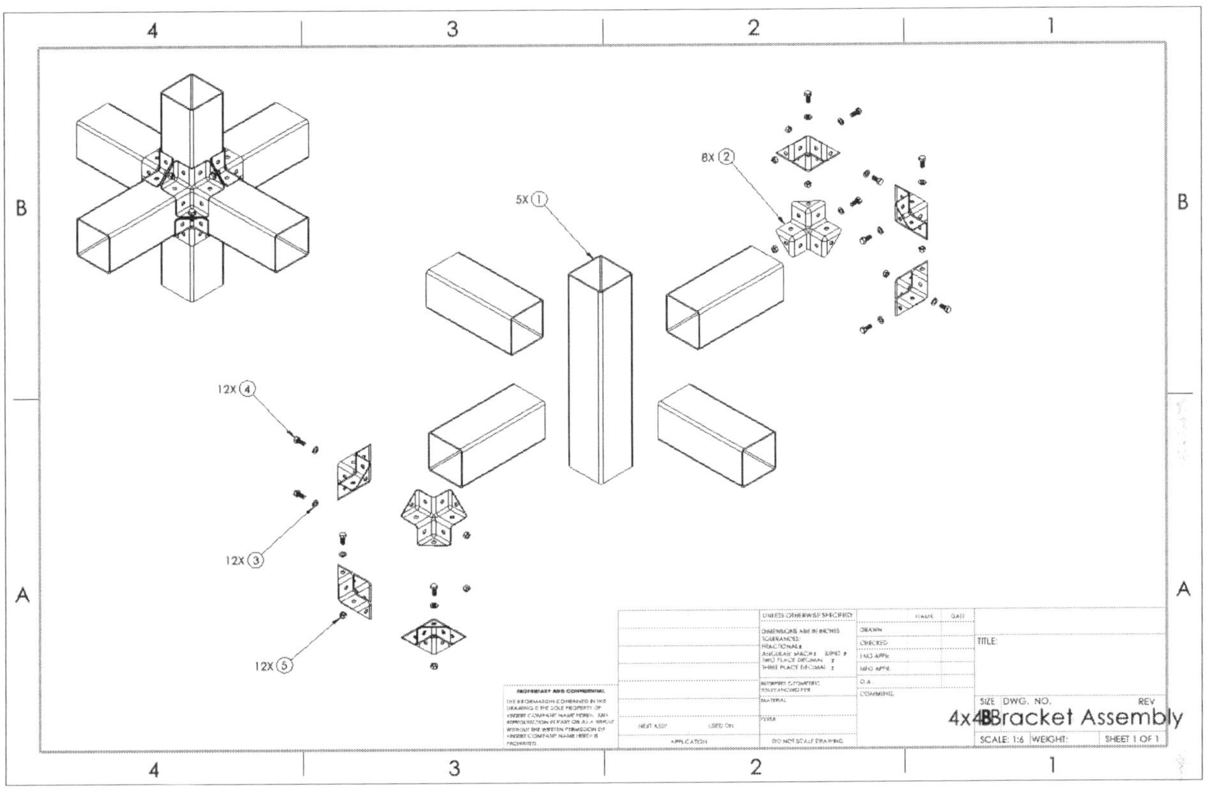

Add the number of instances to the following components:

* **3-Way Bracket**

* **Hex Bolt**

* **Hex Nut**

* **Flat Washer**

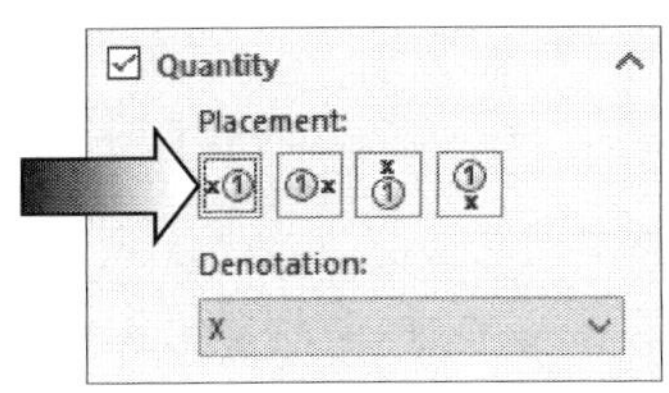

Move the instance numbers to the left side of the balloons.

5. Inserting the Bill of Materials:

The Bill of Materials must be linked to a drawing view.

Select the Isometric Exploded view and click: **Tables, Bill of materials.**

Use the default **BOM Standard** template and the **Parts Only** BOM type.

Click **OK.**

Change the Font Size to **10 point** and the **Row Width** to **.250in**.

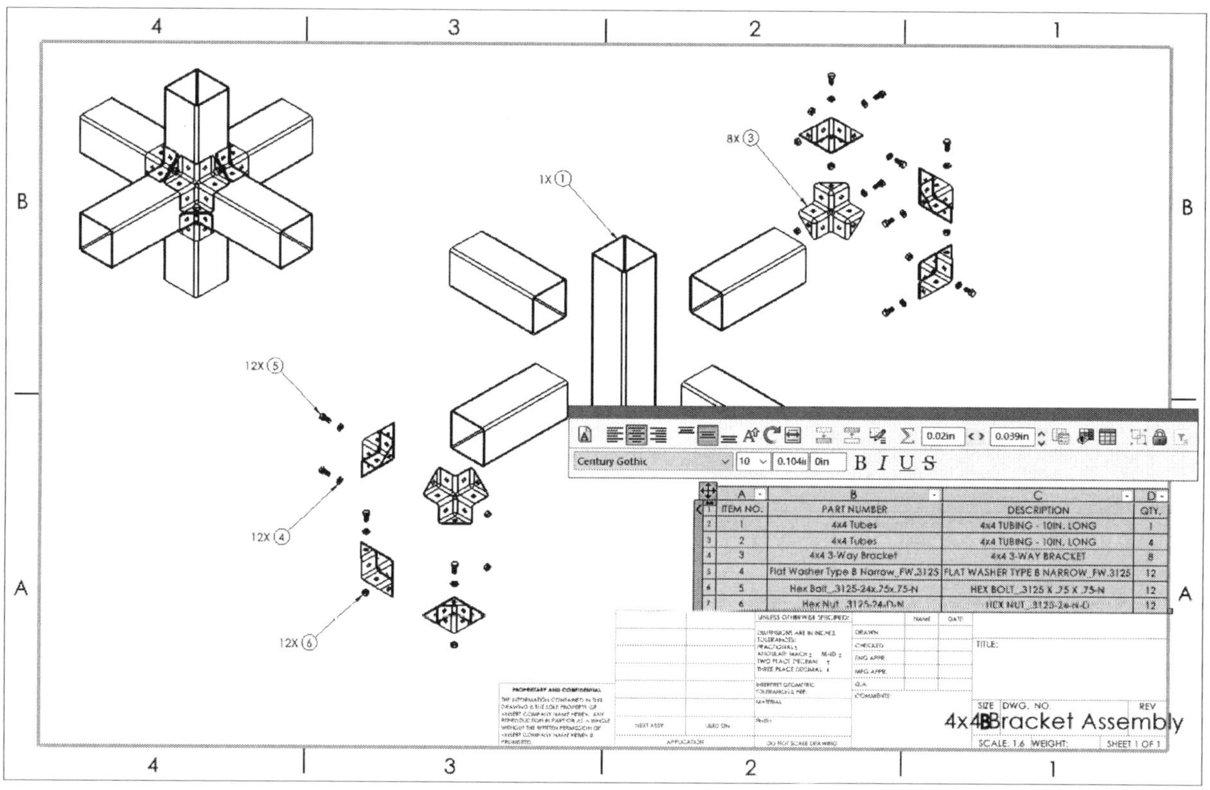

The information from each component populated all columns in the BOM, except for the Part Number column. It was supposed to display Numerical Values instead of Description.

The Custom Properties of each component will be discussed in the next chapter. For this particular exercise, we will change the column B to a Custom Property called Part Number and see how SOLIDWORKS populates the Part Numbers from the models to the Bill of Materials.

6. Changing the Custom Properties:

Zoom closer to the Bill of Materials.

Double-click the header "B"

Double-click the header **"B"** to activate the Custom Properties options.

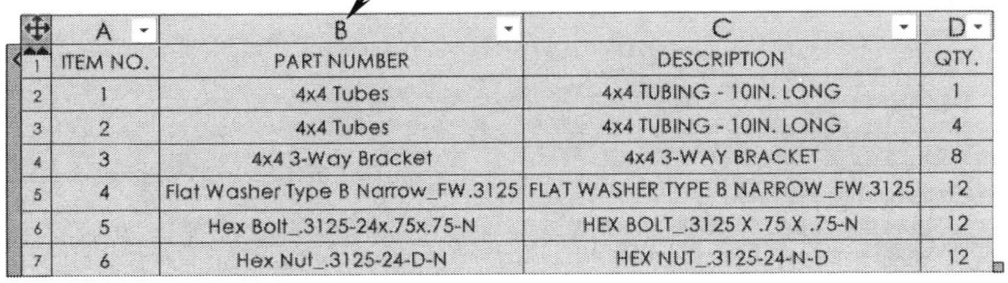

Expand the **Column Type** and select **Custom Properties** from the drop-down list.

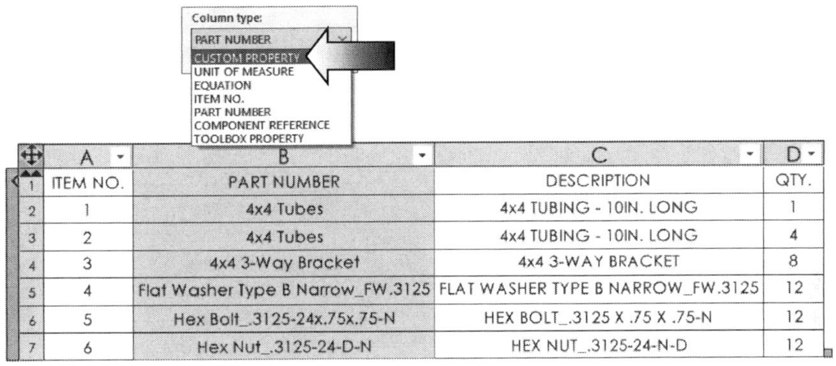

Expand the **Property Name** and select: **Part Number** from the list.

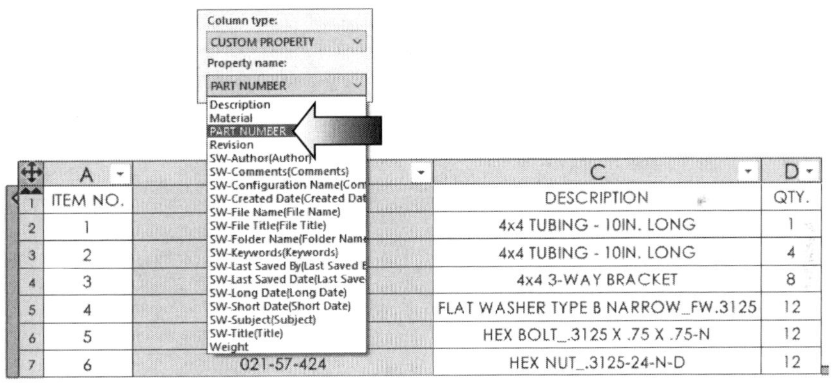

The Part Numbers from each component are populated to column B.

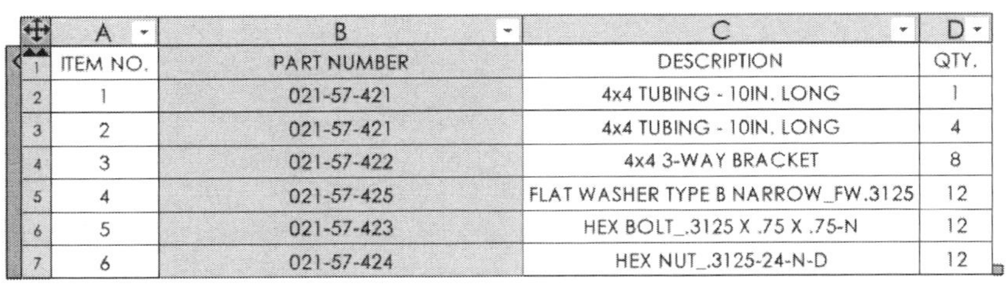

7. Filling out the Title Block information:

From the FeatureManager tree, expand **Sheet1** and double-click **Sheet-Format1** to activate it and bring the Format Layer to the front for editing.

Enter the information shown below.

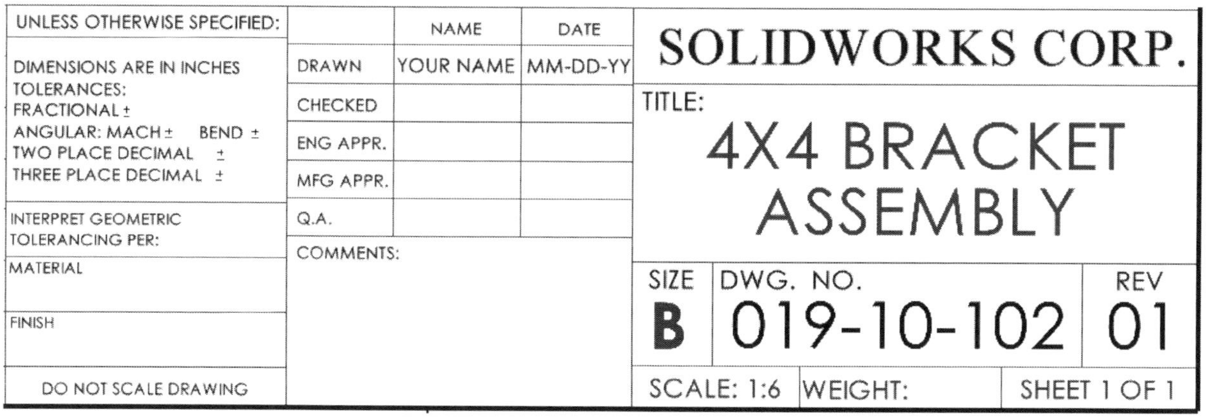

When finished, double-click Sheet1 to activate the Sheet and bring the Drawing Layer to the front.

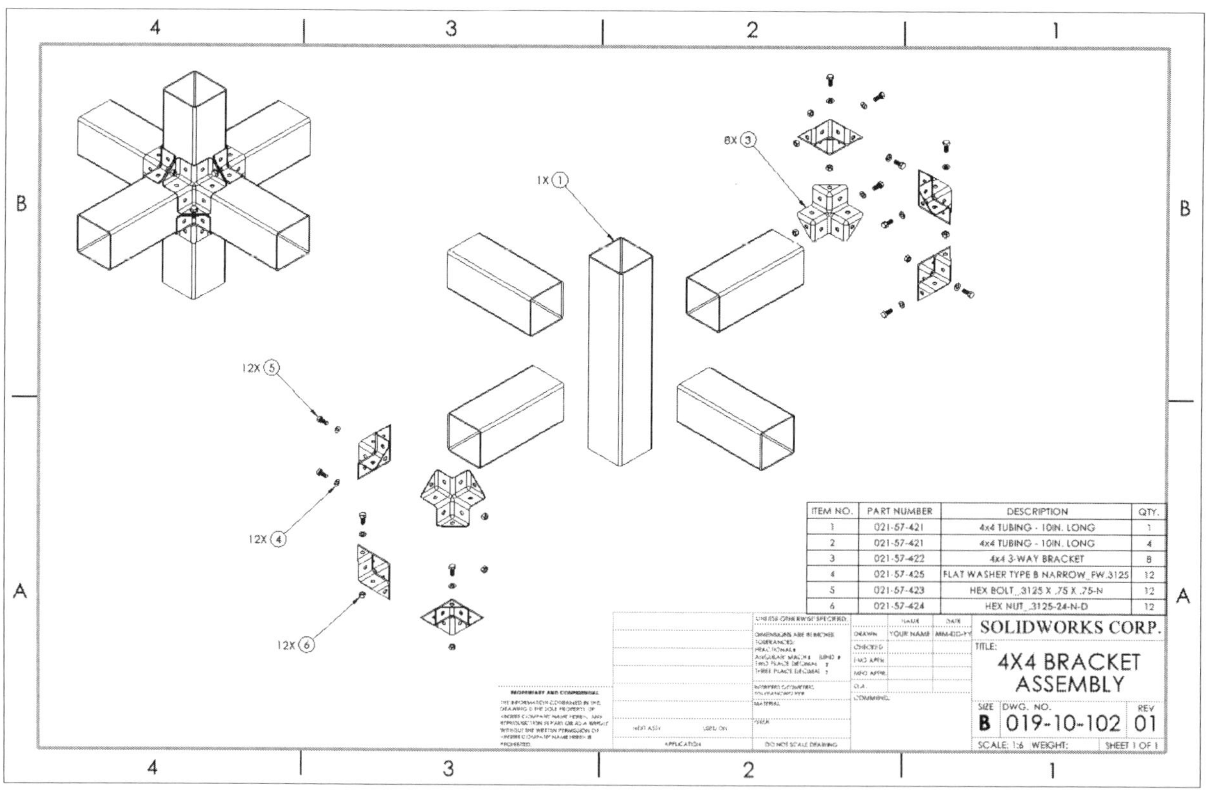

8. Saving your work:

Select **Files, Save As**.

Enter **4X4 Bracket Assembly.slddrw** for the file name.

Click **Save**.

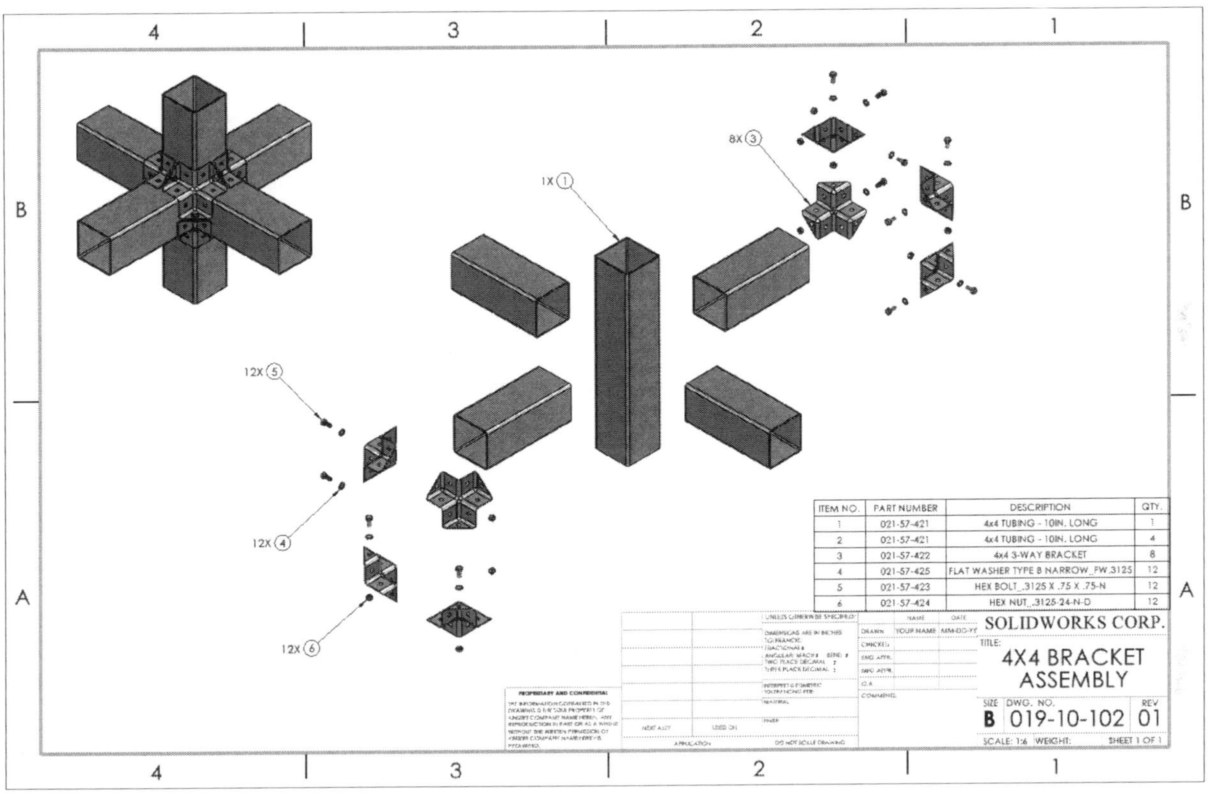

Close all documents.

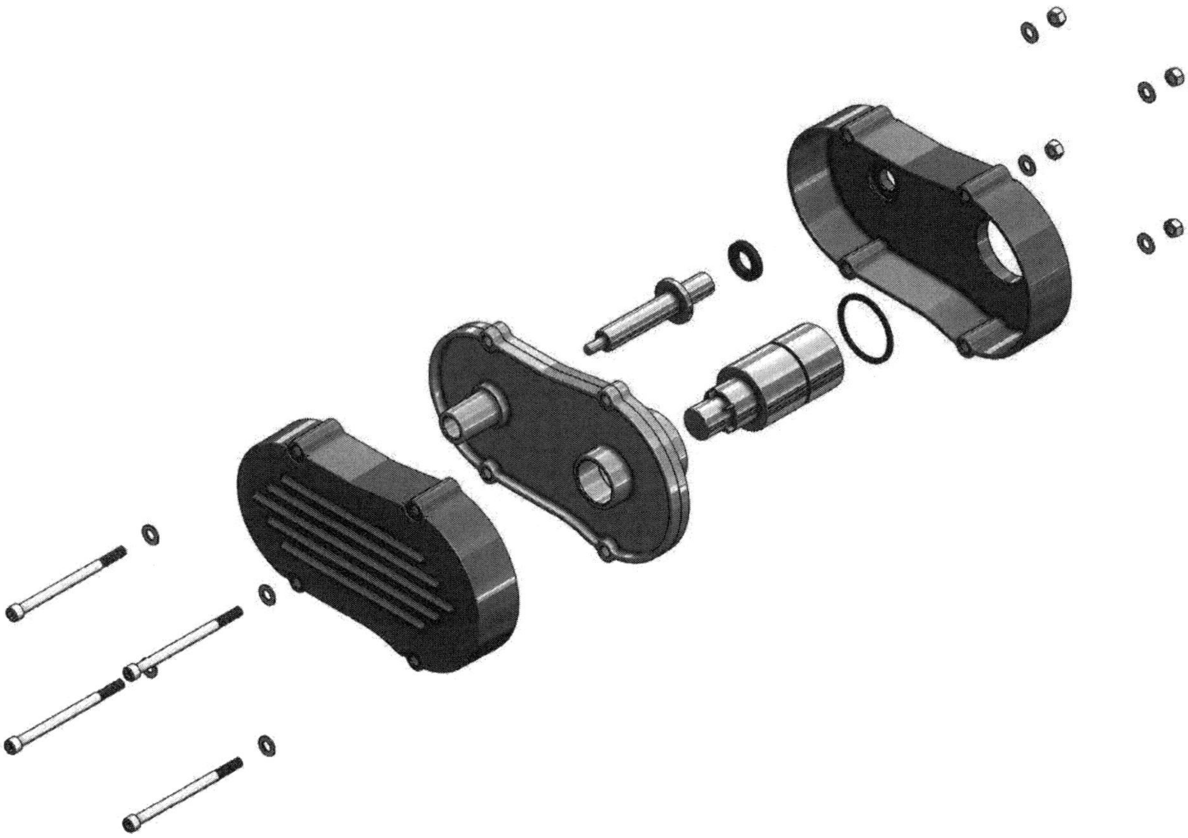

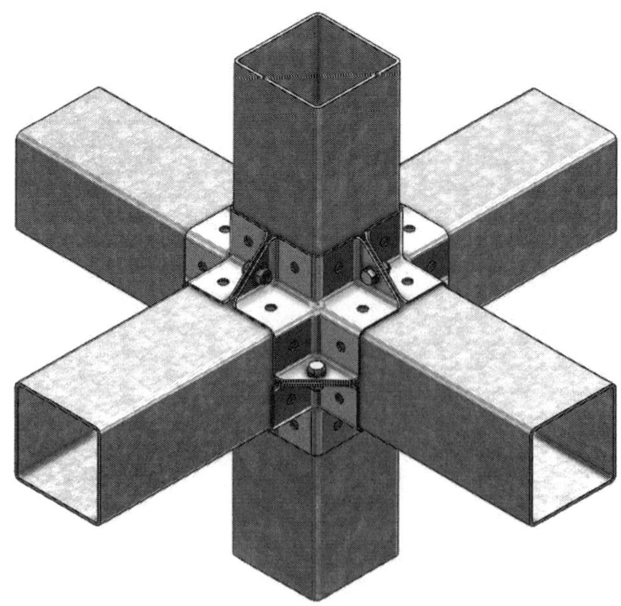

Exercise: Assembly Drawings

Detailing an Assembly Drawing 2

The exercises are designed to help you apply what you have learned from the previous lessons. They come with some instructions but not as detailed as the lessons, to give you an opportunity to explore and to try and create the drawings on your own, at your own pace.

1. Opening a part document:

Select **File, Open**.

Browse to the Training Folder and open a part document named: **Pulley Assembly.sldasm**.

The materials have already been assigned to each component.

2. Transferring to a drawing:

Select **File, Make Drawing from Assembly**.

Select the **B-Size** drawing paper.

Set the Type-Of-Projection to: **3rd Angle**.

Set the Scale to **1:4**

Click **OK**.

The B size (ANSI) drawing template is loaded.

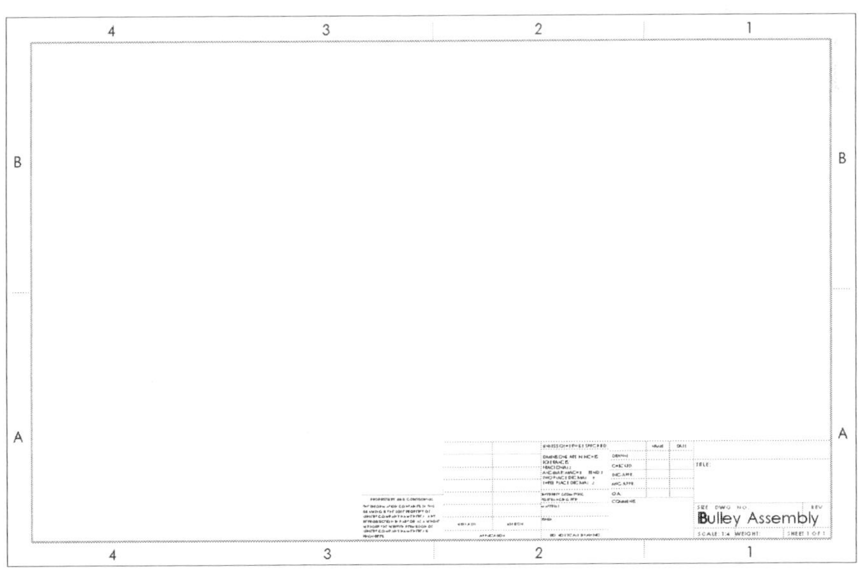

3. Creating the drawing views:

Using the **View Palette**, drag and drop the **Isometric** and **Isometric Exploded** Views onto the drawing.

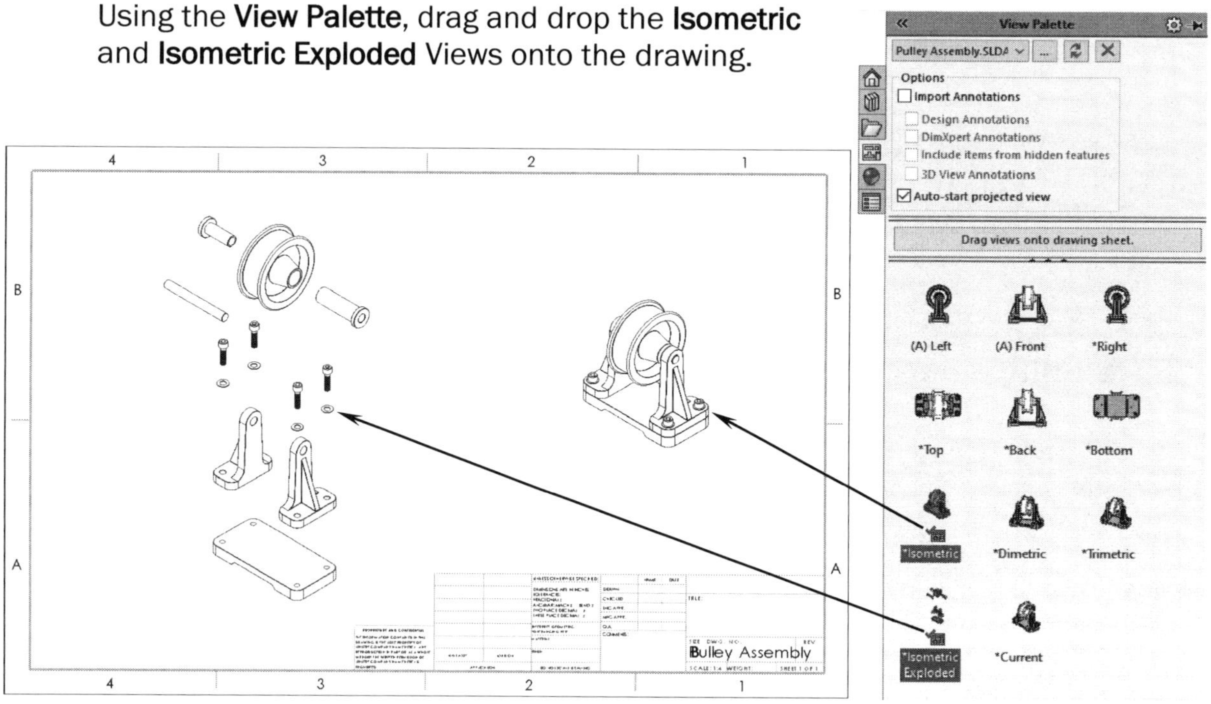

4. Adding balloons:

Click the dotted border of the **Exploded Isometric** drawing view to activate it.

Switch to the **Annotation** tab and click **Auto Balloons.**

For Style, select **Circular**.

For Size, select **1 character**.

Click **OK.**

Note: Only the 1st instance will get a balloon.

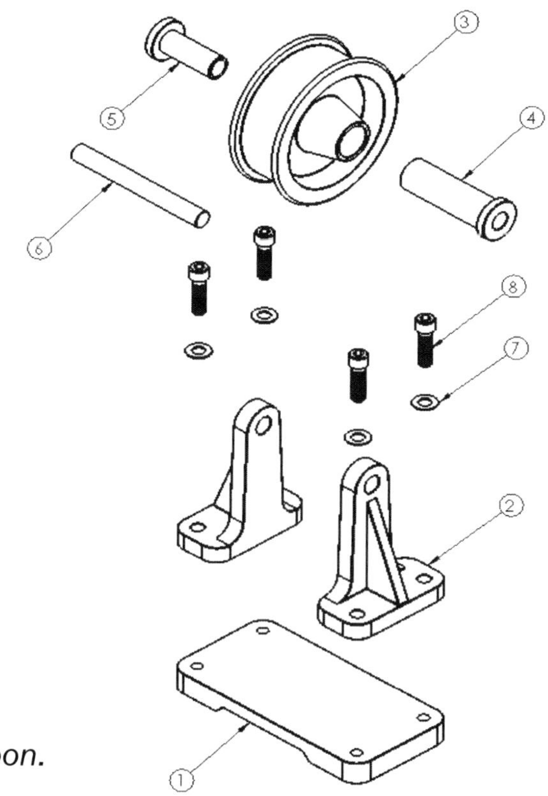

5. Inserting a Bill of Materials:

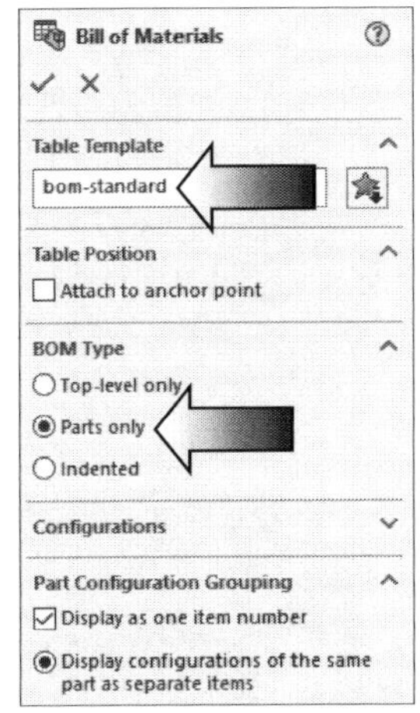

Click the dotted border of the **Exploded Isometric** drawing view to activate it once again.

Click **Table, Bill of Materials** from the **Annotation** tab.

For Table Template, use the **default Bom-Standard** template.

For BOM Type, select **Part Only** and click **OK**.

ITEM NO.	PartNo	DESCRIPTION	QTY.
1	019-10-103	BASE BLOCK	1
2	019-10-104	BRACKET	2
3	019-10-105	PULLEY	1
4	019-10-106	F-BUSHING	1
5	019-10-107	M-BUSHING	1
6	019-10-109	SHAFT	1
7	019-10-109	NARROW FW .50X.063	4
8	019-10-108	SOCKET HEAD CAP SCREW .50-20	4

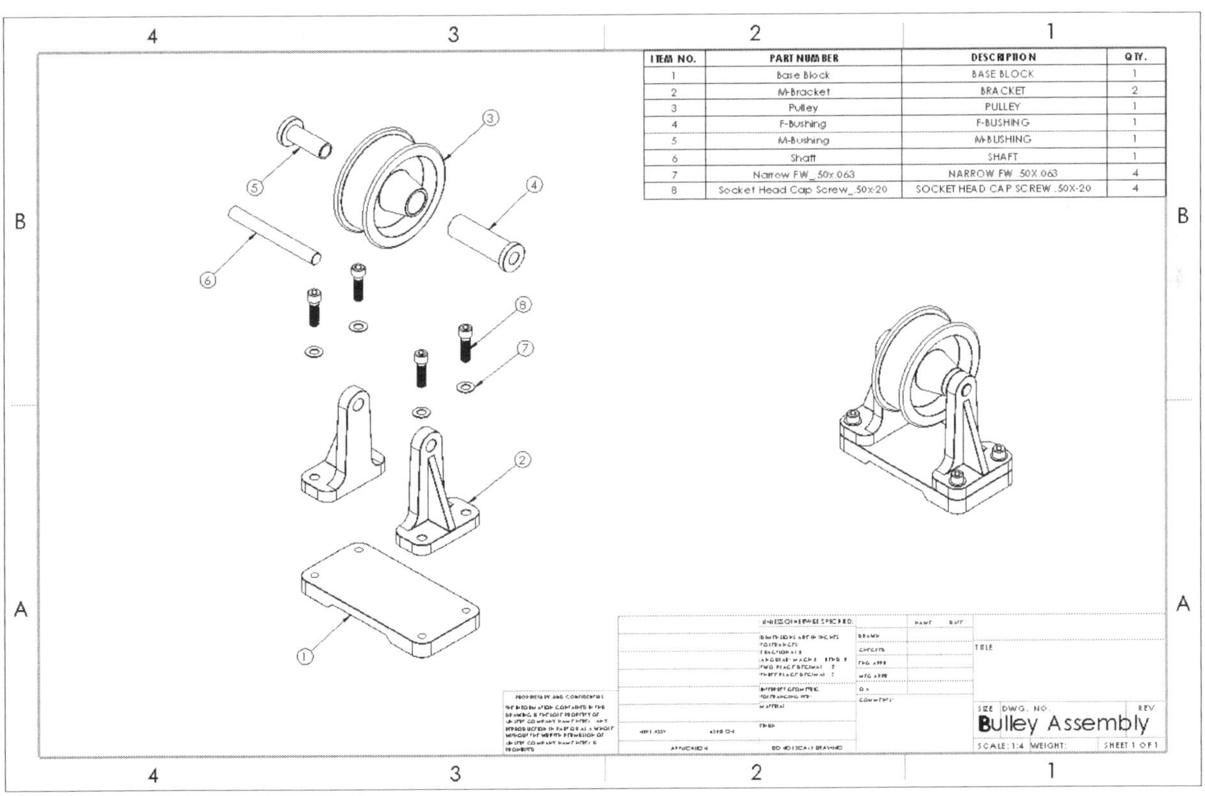

6. Changing the Custom Properties:

Column B should show **Part Numbers** instead of **Document Names.**

Double-click the header **"B"** and select **Custom Properties** for Column Type.

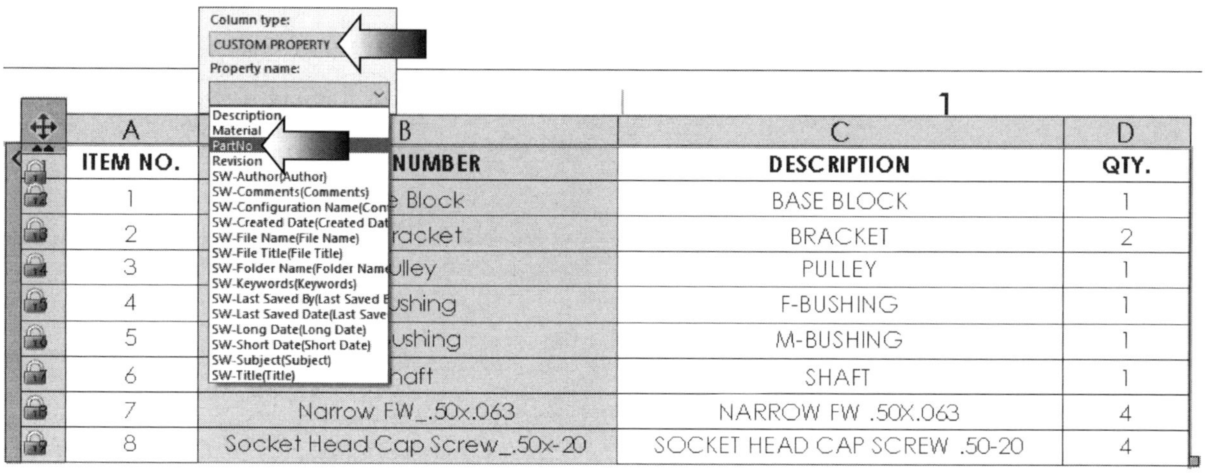

For Property name, select **PartNo** (arrow).

ITEM NO.	PART NUMBER	DESCRIPTION	QTY.
1	Base Block	BASE BLOCK	1
2	M-Bracket	BRACKET	2
3	Pulley	PULLEY	1
4	F-Bushing	F-BUSHING	1
5	M-Bushing	M-BUSHING	1
6	Shaft	SHAFT	1
7	Narrow FW_.50x.063	NARROW FW .50X.063	4
8	Socket Head Cap Screw_.50x-20	SOCKET HEAD CAP SCREW .50-20	4

Column B is now displaying the part number for each component, instead of the document name.

Compare your BOM against the one shown above. Make any corrections as needed to update the BOM.

7. Filling out the Title Block information:

From the FeatureManager tree, expand **Sheet1** and double-click **Sheet Format1** to activate the Format layer.

Fill out the information shown below for each section.

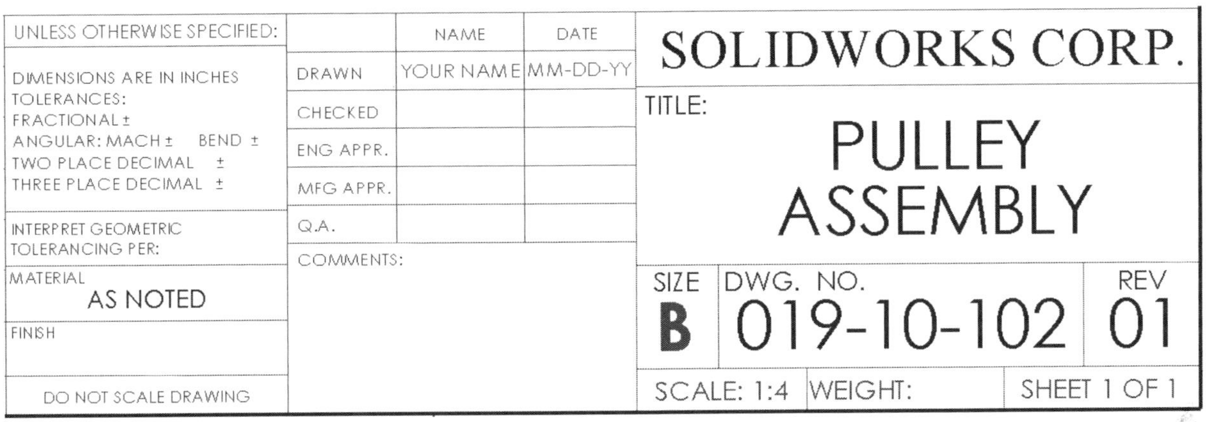

When finished, double-click **Sheet1** to return to the drawing.

<u>OPTIONAL</u>:

To add quantity to the balloons:

Select all balloons.

Enable the **Quantity** checkbox.

For Placement, select either Left, Right, Top, or Bottom.

Click **OK**.

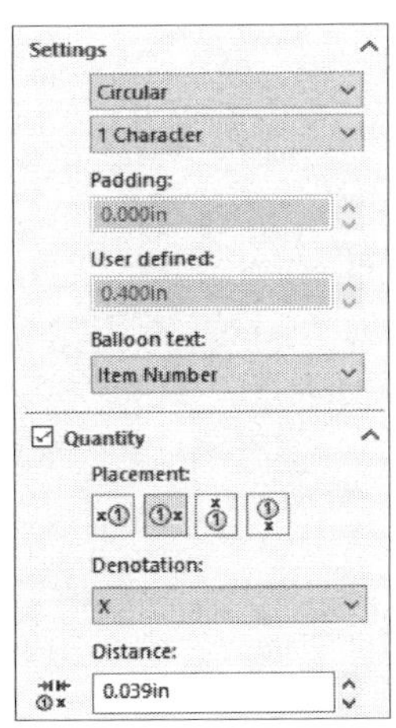

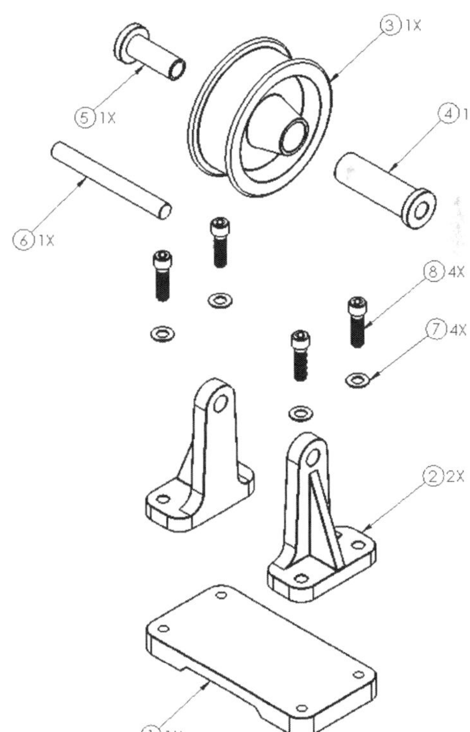

8. Saving your work:

Select **File, Save As.**

Enter: **Pulley Assembly.sldasm** for the file name.

Click **Save.**

Close all documents.

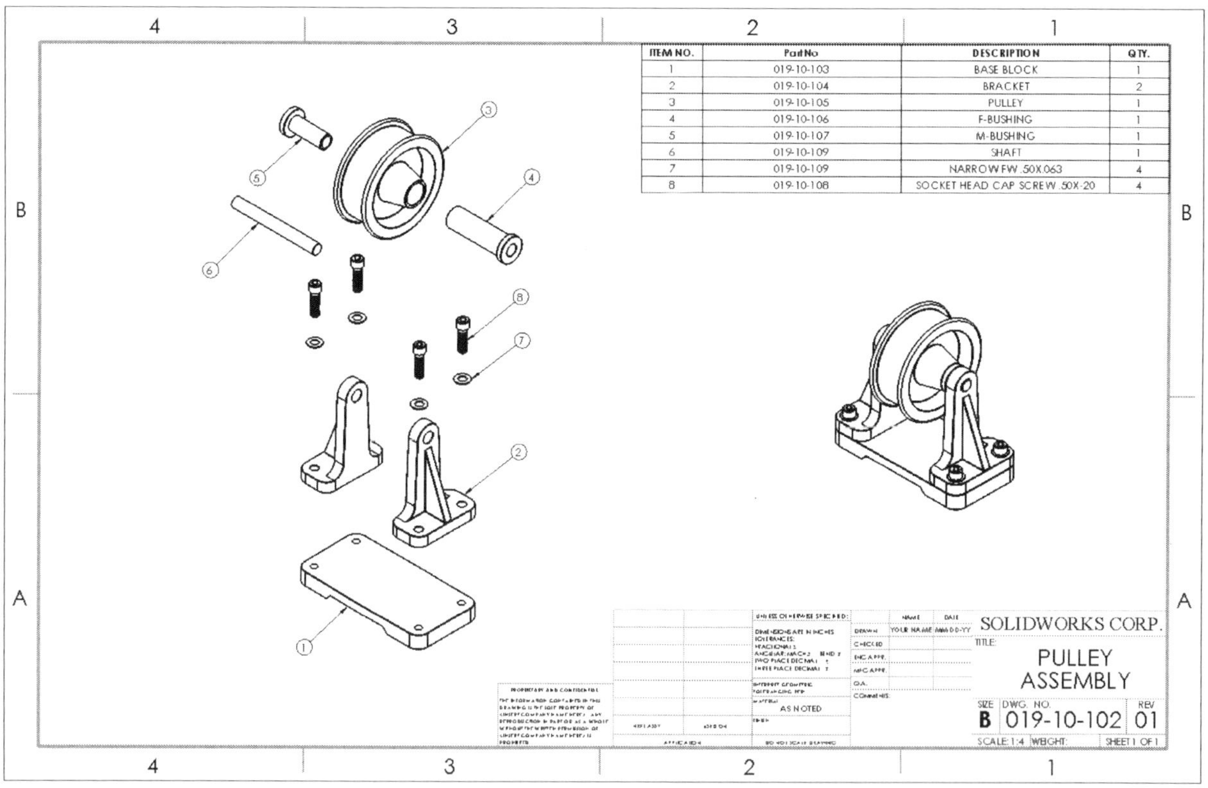

CHAPTER 9: CUSTOM PROPERTIES

Creating the Custom Properties – Part 1

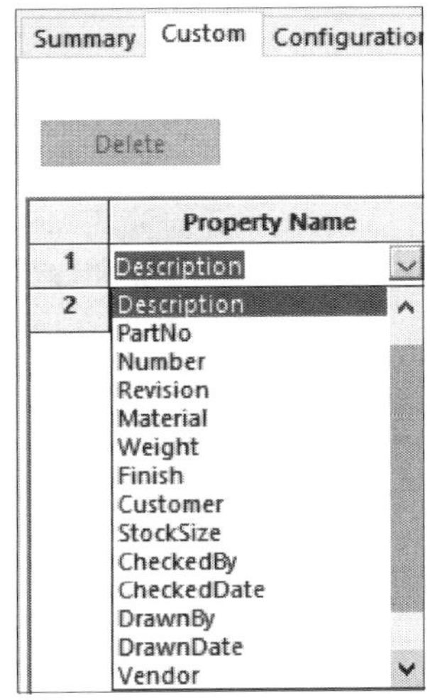

Custom properties are the metadata of your model, such as Description, Material, Part Number, Revision, Vendor, etc. You can use predefined properties or create your own.

When a Bill of Materials is inserted into an assembly drawing, the Custom Properties that were entered in each component will populate to the BOM automatically, maintaining the parametric link between the BOM and its components.

This chapter will teach us how to create the Custom Properties in the models and populate them into the assembly's BOM.

1. Opening an assembly document:

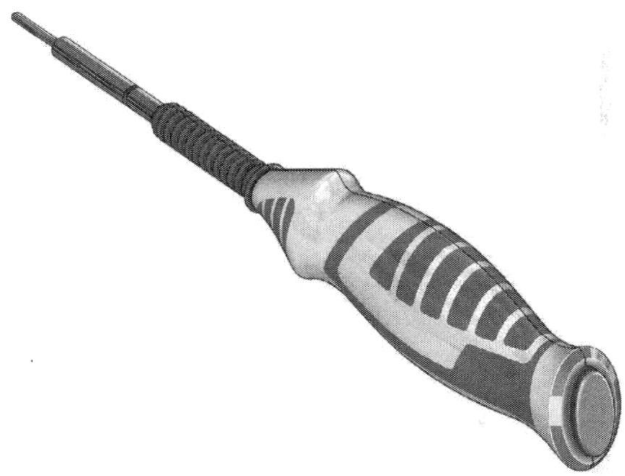

Select **File, Open**.

Browse to the Training Folder and open an assembly document named: **Handle Assembly.sldasm**.

The Custom Properties such as Description, Part Number, Revision, Material, Weight, Vendor, etc., have already been entered into the component file properties, except for the 2 handle halves.

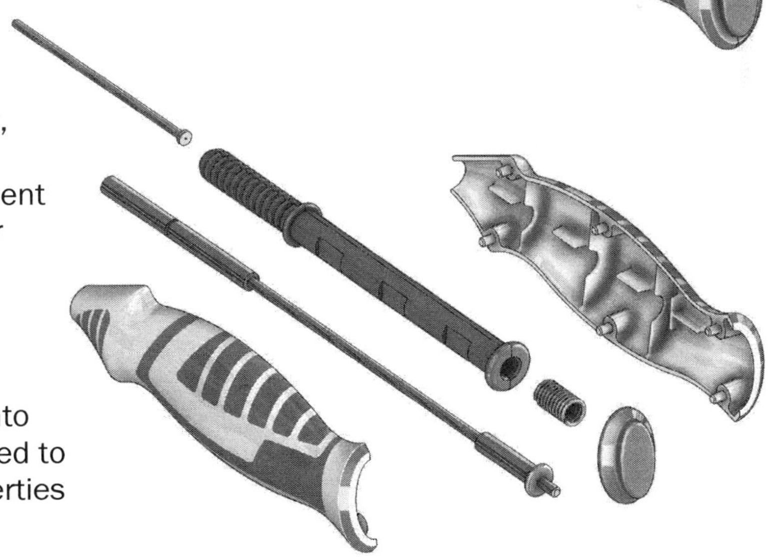

To help us focus on creating and populating the Custom Properties into the BOM, we will only need to create the Custom Properties for the 2 handle halves.

2. Opening a part from an assembly:

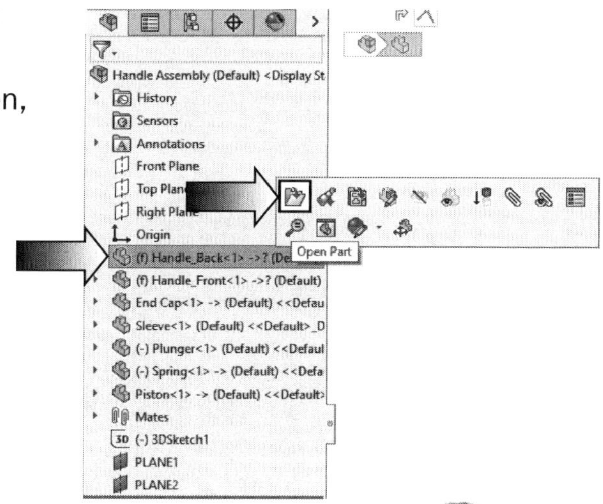

Custom Properties such as Description, Material, Part Number, Revision, etc., should be entered at the part level.

From the FeatureManager tree, click the part named **Handle_Back** and select **Open Part** from the pop-up toolbar.

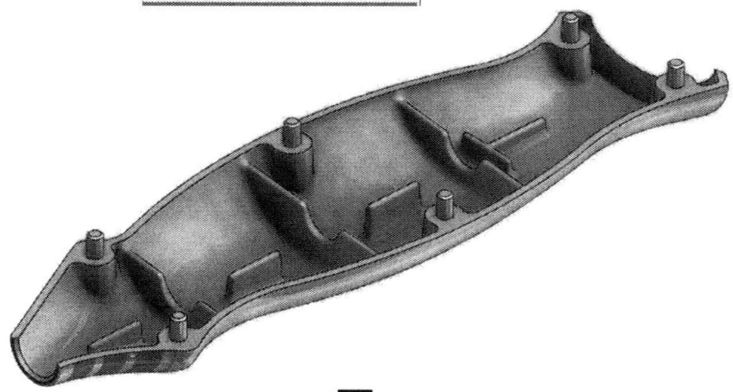

The Handle_Back component is opened in its own window.

3. Creating the Custom Properties:

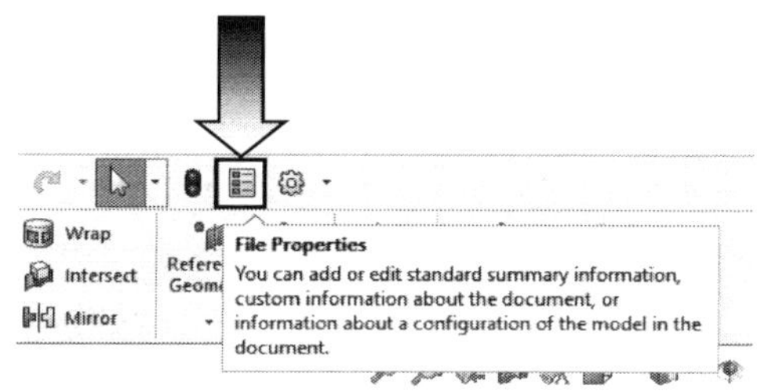

Click the **File Properties** button, next to the Rebuild stop light.

Click the **Custom** tab.

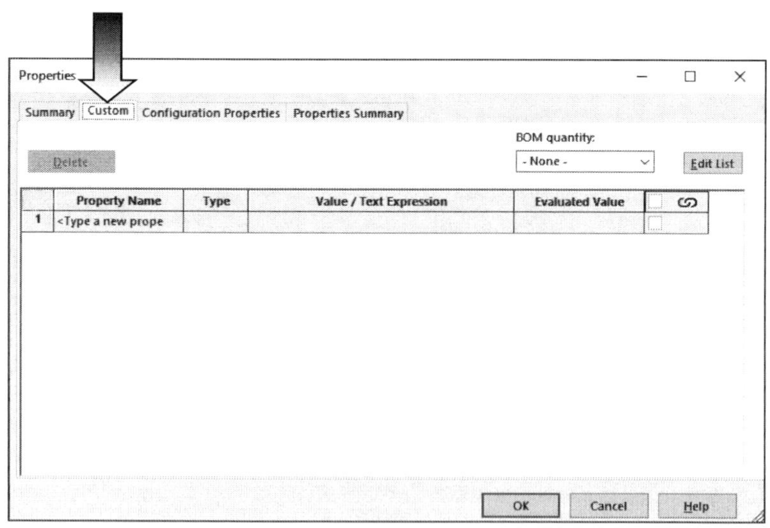

There is no Custom Properties available for this part document.

We will enter the information for Description, PartNo, Revision, Material, Weight, and Vendor.

4. Entering the Custom Property information:

Expand line number 1 below the Property Name column and select **Description**.

Click in the Value / Text Expression cell and enter: **HANDLE_BACK.**

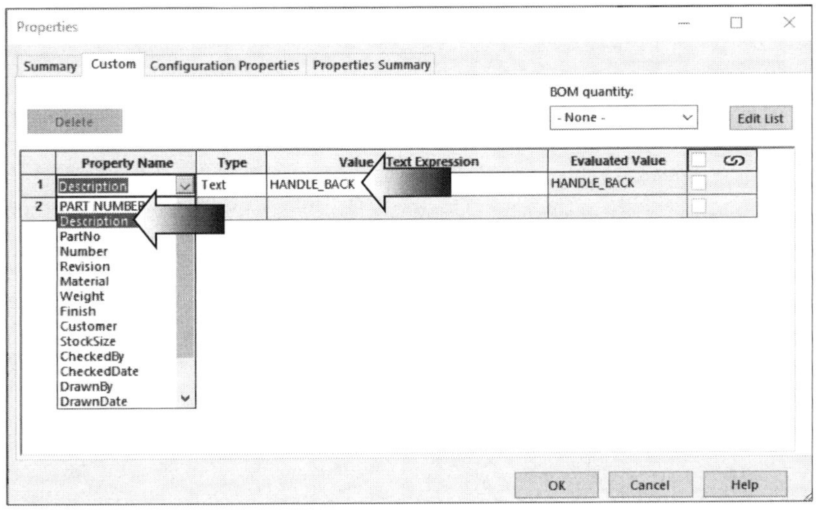

The 1st Custom Property is created.

Do not click OK just yet.

Expand line number 2, select **PartNo** from the list and enter: **011-024-550**

For Revision, enter: **01**.

For Material and Weight, select: **Material** and **Mass** from the drop-down list.

For Vendor, enter: **US-ABC**

Click **OK.**

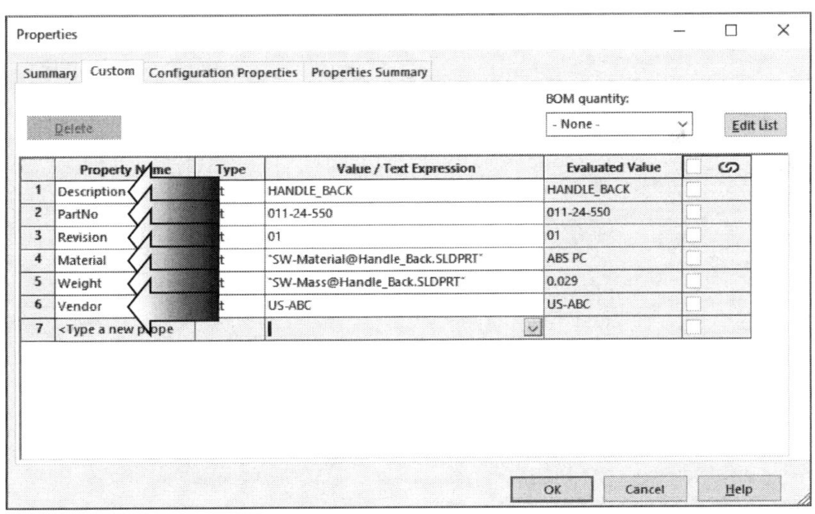

Any other Custom Properties that need to be displayed in the Bill of Materials should be entered into the Custom section at this time. The information will be parametrically linked between the BOM and its components.

5. Entering the Custom Properties for the 2nd component:

Save the **Handle_Back** before working on the next component.

Press **Control + Tab** to switch back to the Assembly document.

From the FeatureManager tree, click the part named **Handle_Front** and select **Open Part** from the pop-up toolbar.

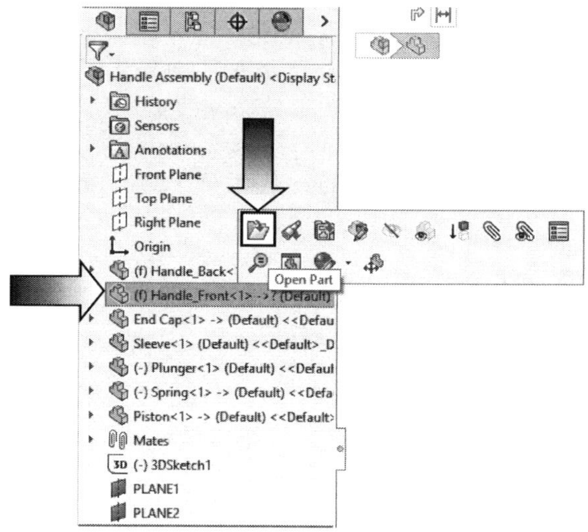

The Handle_Front component is opened in its own window.

Click the **File Properties** button.

Click the **Custom** tab.

Enter the following:

Description: **HANDLE_FRONT**

PartNo.: **011-24-551**

Revision: **01**

Material: Select **Material** from the drop-down list.

Weight: select **Mass** from the drop-down list.

Vendor, enter: **US-ABC**

Click **OK**.

Save the **Handle_ Front** using the same file name.

Overwrite the old file with this new version.

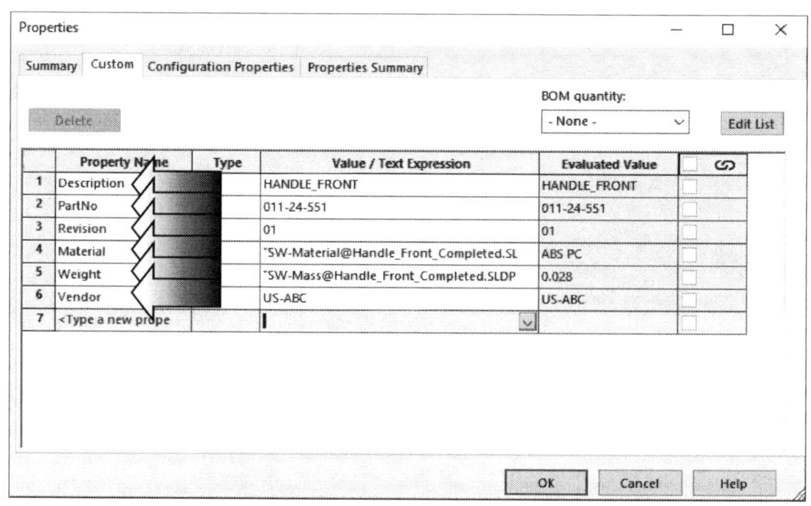

6. Making a drawing from assembly:

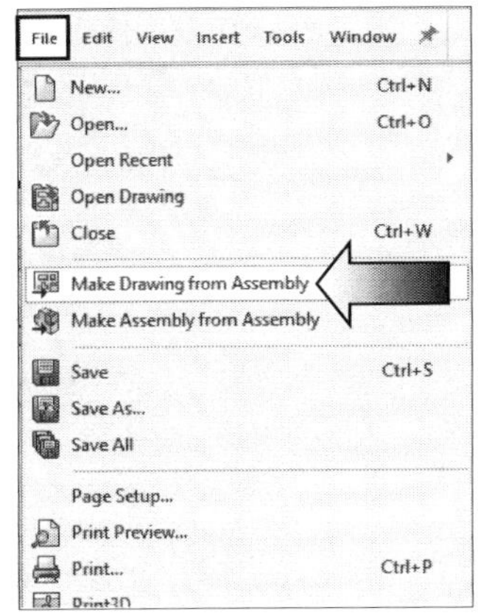

Press **Control + Tab** to switch back to the Assembly document.

Select **File, Make Drawing From Assembly**.

Select the **Drawing Template** from the New SOLIDWORKS Document dialog box.

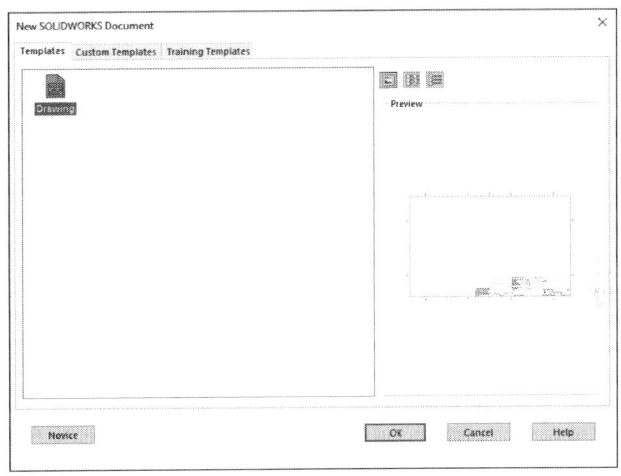

Right-click inside the drawing and select **Properties**:

Scale: **1:1**.

Angle of Projection: **3RD Angle**

Sheet Format Size: **B (ANSI) Landscape**

Click **Apply Changes**.

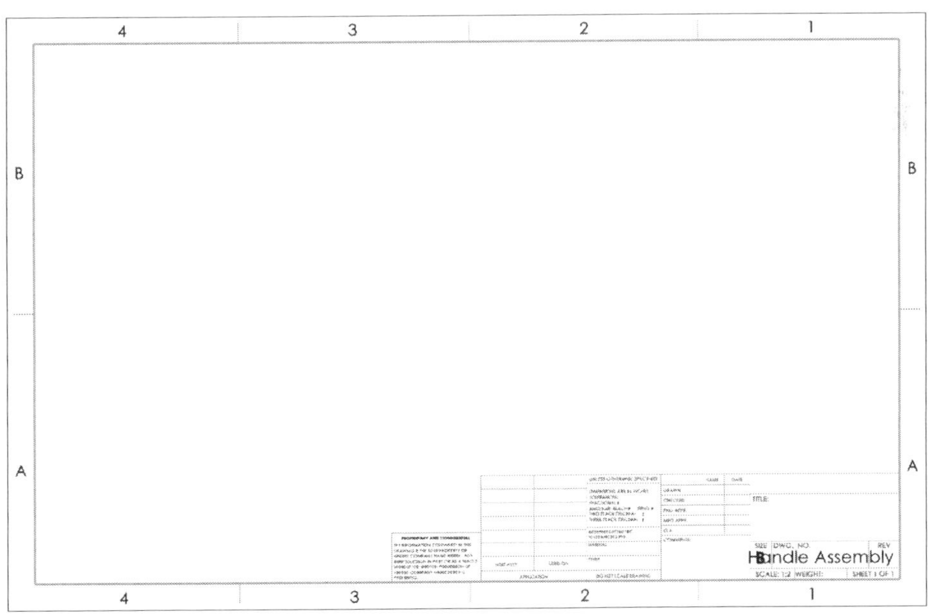

The B Size (ANSI) Drawing Template (11” x 17”) is loaded into the graphics area.

7. Creating the drawing views:

Expand the **View Palette** to access the drawing views.

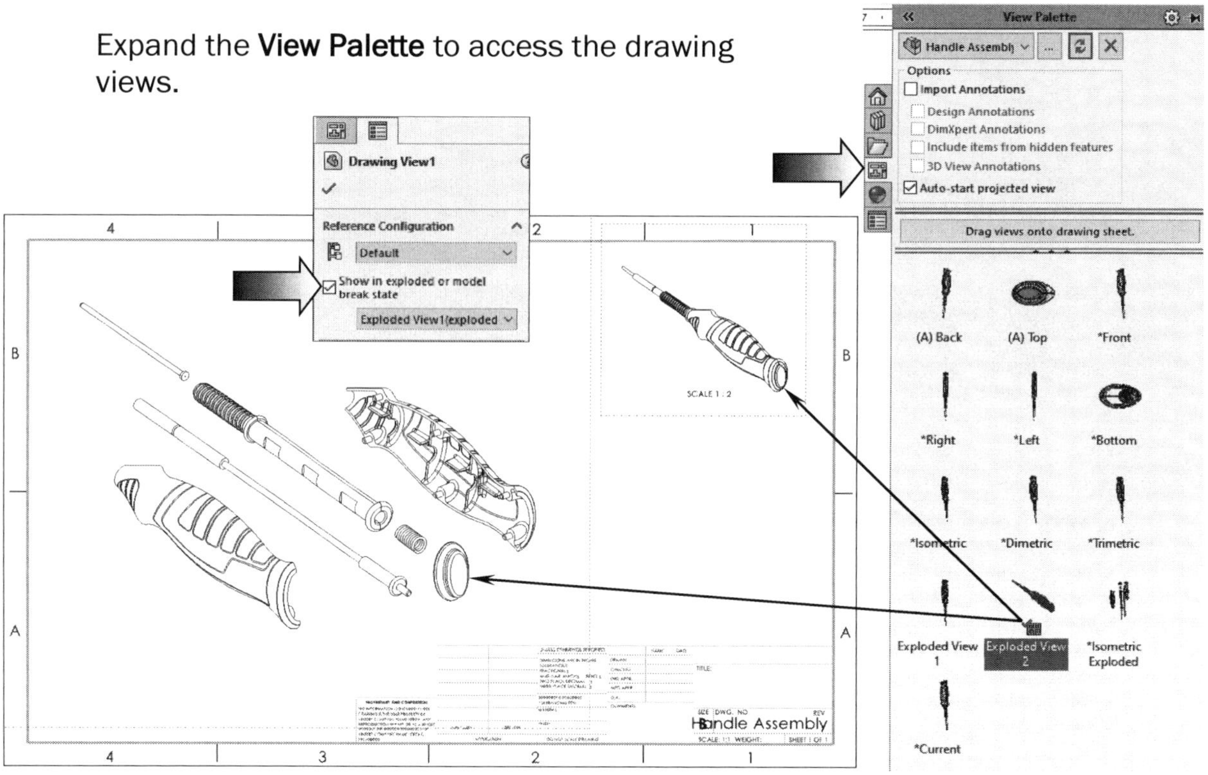

Drag the **Exploded View** and drop it on the left side of the drawing.

Enable the checkbox: **Show in Exploded or Model Break State** if the drawing view is not yet shown as exploded.

Add another instance of the same drawing view and place it on the upper right side of the drawing; keep this view collapsed.

Change the **Scale** of the **Isometric Exploded** drawing view to **1:1**.

Change the **Scale** of the **Isometric** drawing view to **1:2**.

Move the 2 drawing views similar to the image shown above to make room for the balloons and the Bill of Materials.

8. Adding Balloons:

Switch to the **Annotation** tab and click **Auto Balloons**.

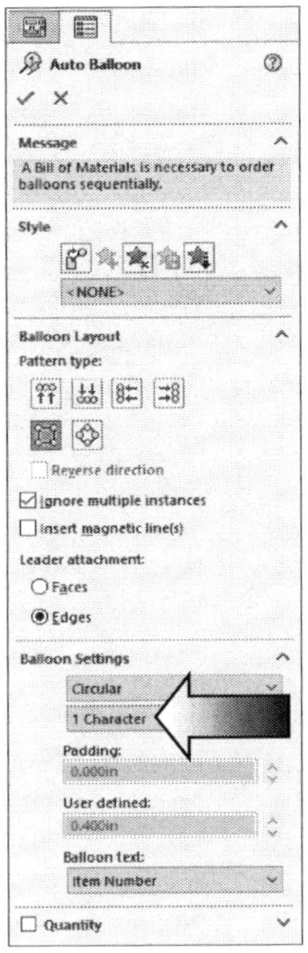

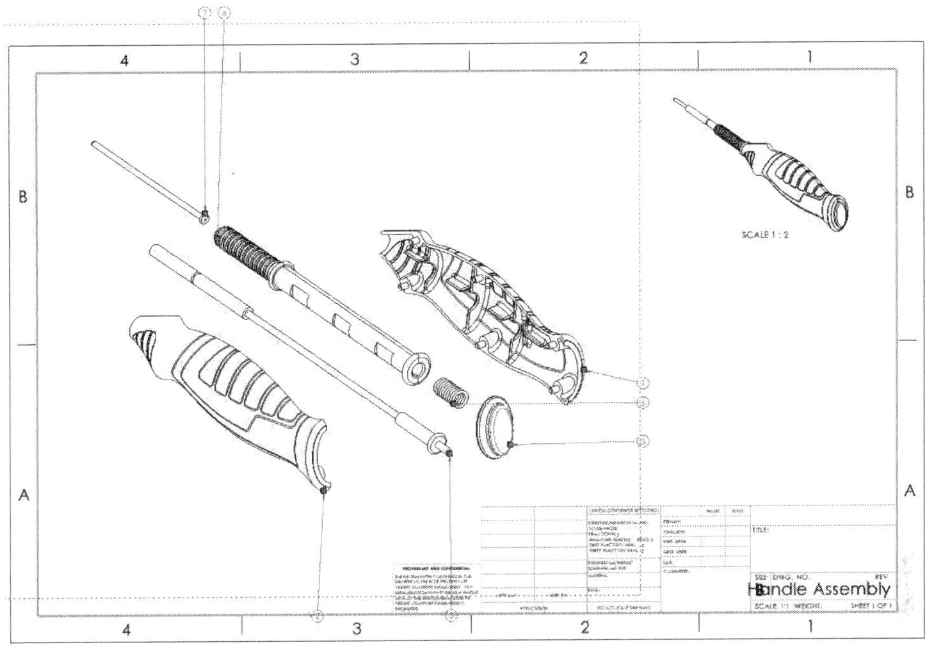

Use the **Square Pattern** and **Circular 1 Character** for size.

Rearrange the balloons so that they will fit inside the drawing, and the leader lines look nice and even in both angle and length.

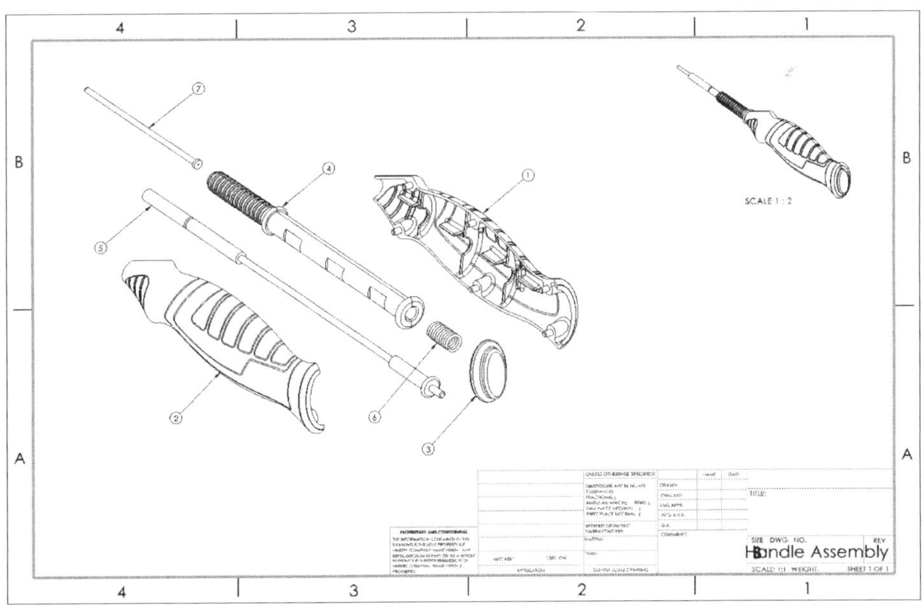

9. Inserting the Bill of Materials:

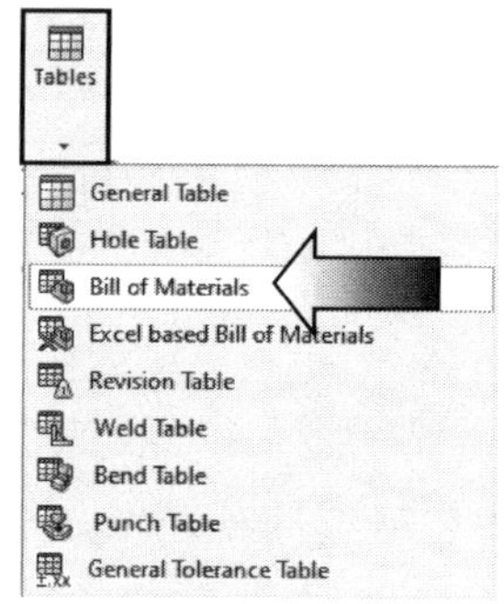

The Bill of Materials should always be linked to one of the drawing views, usually the Isometric Exploded view.

Click the dotted border of the **Isometric Exploded** view and select: **Tables, Bill of Materials** from the **Annotation** tab.

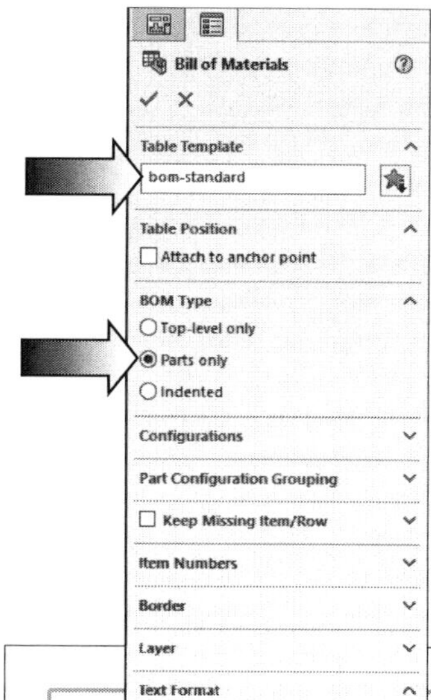

For Table Template, use the default **Bom-Standard.**

For BOM Type, select **Parts Only.**

Click **OK** and place the BOM above the Title Block.

Change the **Font Size** to **10 point.**

Change the **Row Height** to **.250in.** (right-click inside the BOM and select: Formatting, Row Height).

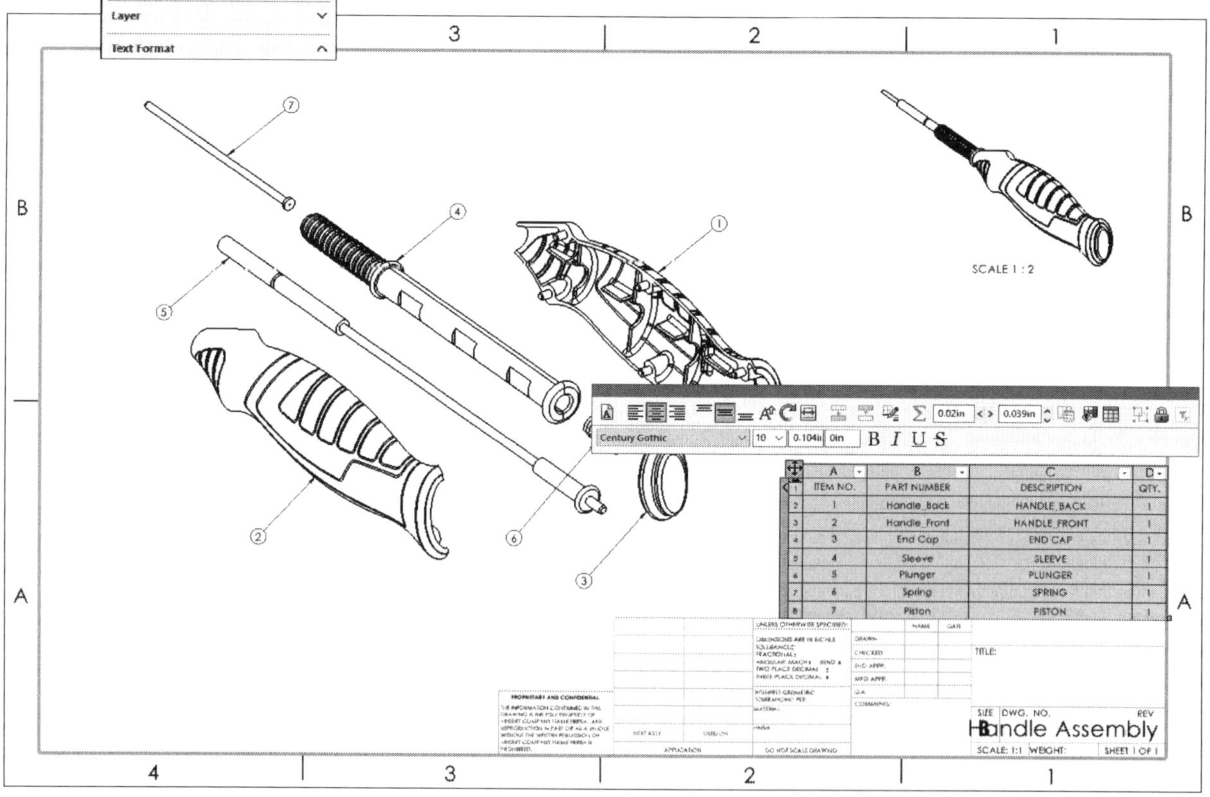

10. Switching the Custom Properties:

Zoom closer to the Bill of Materials table.

Column B is currently listing the <u>names</u> of the part files instead of the <u>Part Numbers</u>.

To correct this, double-click the column header "B" and select: **Custom Property** from the list.

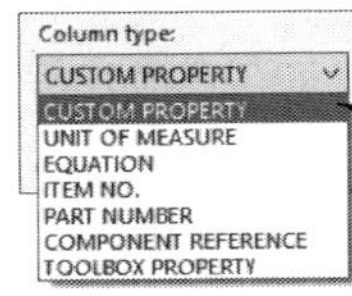

Double the header B, select Custom Property

	A	B	C	D
1	ITEM NO.	PART NUMBER	DESCRIPTION	QTY.
2	1	Handle_Back	HANDLE_BACK	1
3	2	Handle_Front	HANDLE_FRONT	1
4	3	End Cap	END CAP	1
5	4	Sleeve	SLEEVE	1
6	5	Plunger	PLUNGER	1
7	6	Spring	SPRING	1
8	7	Piston	PISTON	1

Expand the **Property Name** drop-down list and select: **PartNo**.

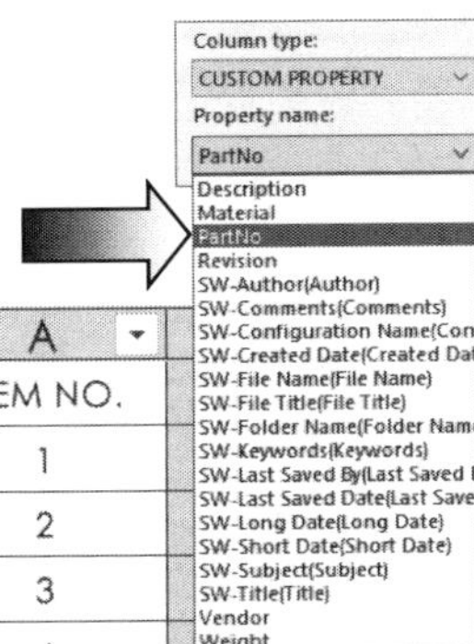

	A	B	C	D
1	ITEM NO.		DESCRIPTION	QTY.
2	1		HANDLE_BACK	1
3	2		HANDLE_FRONT	1
4	3		END CAP	1
5	4		SLEEVE	1
6	5	011-24-554	PLUNGER	1
7	6	011-24-556	SPRING	1
8	7	011-24-555	PISTON	1

The Part Numbers that were entered into each part's properties are populated to column B of the Bill of Materials.

	A	B	C	D
1	ITEM NO.	PartNo	DESCRIPTION	QTY.
2	1	011-24-550	HANDLE_BACK	1
3	2	011-24-551	HANDLE_FRONT	1
4	3	011-24-552	END CAP	1
5	4	011-24-553	SLEEVE	1
6	5	011-24-554	PLUNGER	1
7	6	011-24-556	SPRING	1
8	7	011-24-555	PISTON	1

11. Filling out the Title Block information:

From the FeatureManager tree, expand **Sheet1** and double-click **Sheet Format1** to activate it for editing.

Fill out the information shown below.

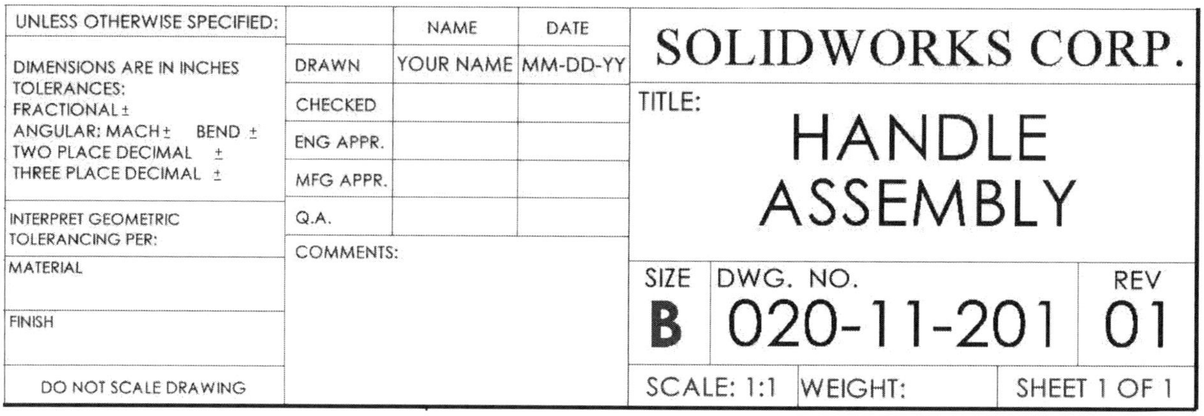

When finished, double-click **Sheet1** to bring the drawing layer back to the front.

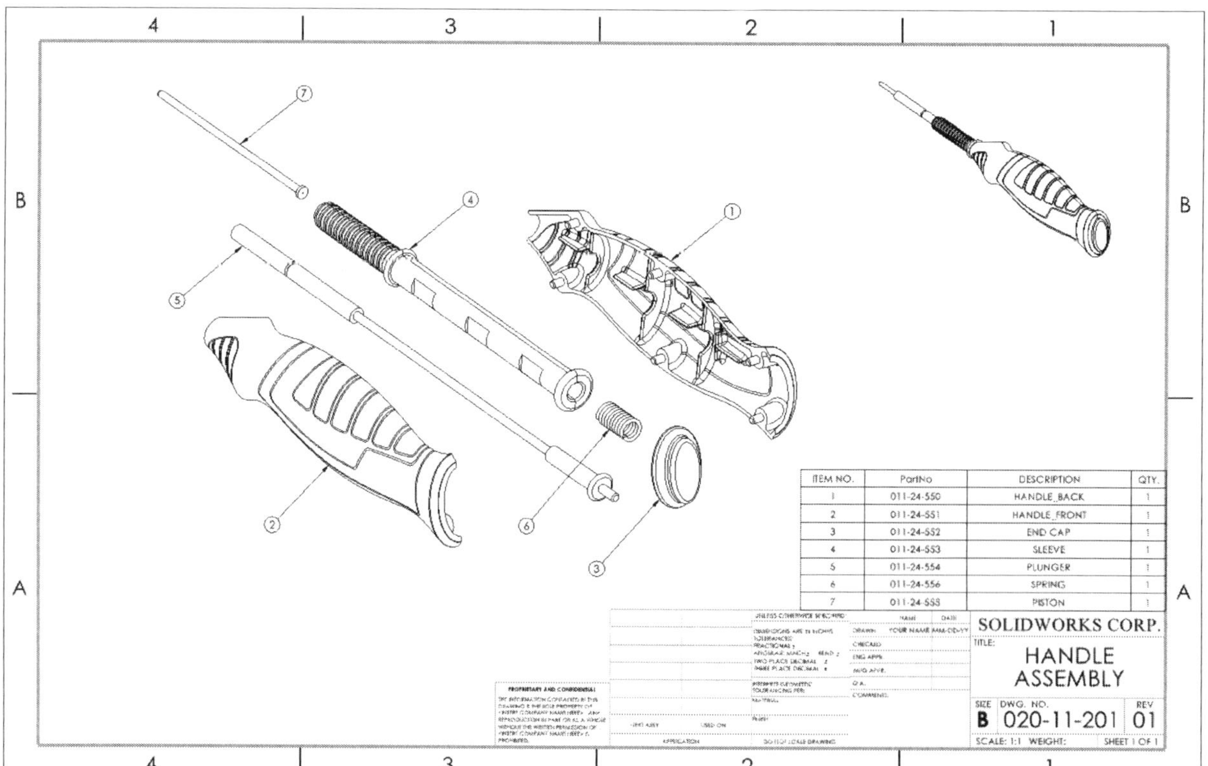

OPTIONAL:

Change the Isometric view to **Shaded**.

Delete the Scale note under the Isometric view.

12. Saving your work:

Select **File, Save As.**

Enter: **Handle Assembly.slddrw** for the file name.

Click **Save.**

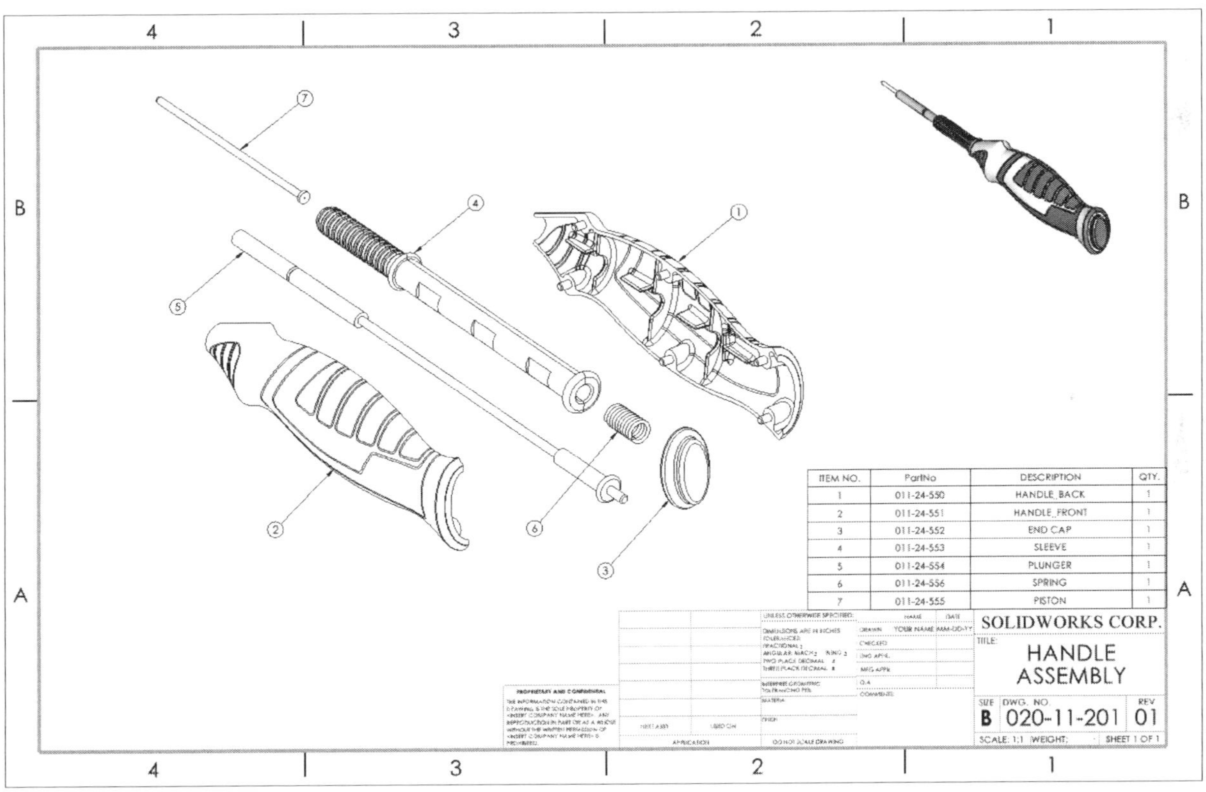

CHAPTER 9: CUSTOM PROPERTIES

Creating the Custom Properties – Part 2

Using the Property Tab Builder

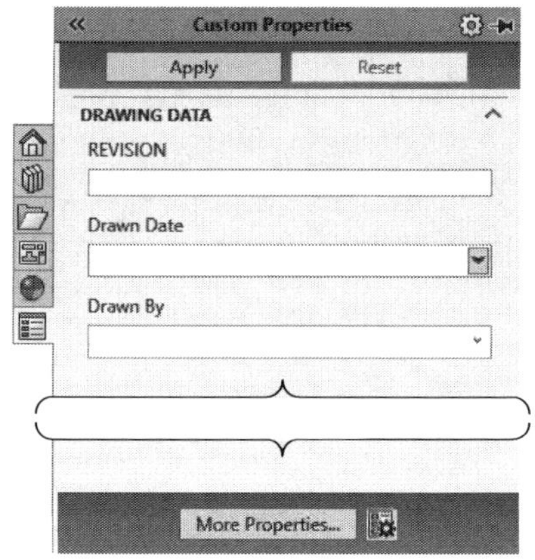

The Property Tab Builder is a stand-alone utility that you use to create a customized interface for entering properties into SOLIDWORKS files.

With the Property Tab Builder, you can enter properties on the Custom and Configuration Properties tabs in the Properties dialog box in SOLIDWORKS.

In a teamwork environment, an administrator creates customized tabs. Users will use these tabs to enter properties in SOLIDWORKS.

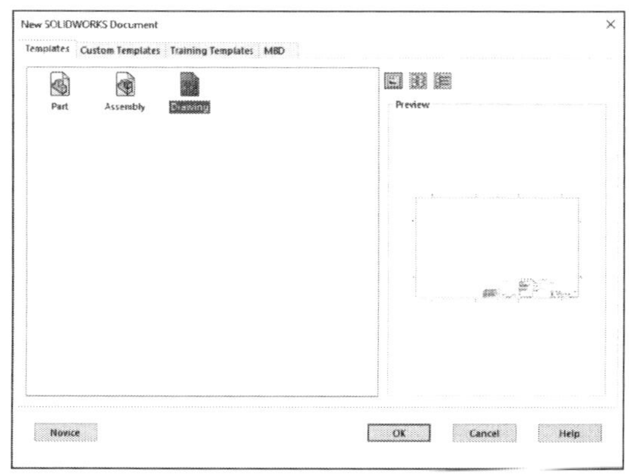

1. Starting a new drawing:

Click **File, New, Drawing.**

Select **B (ANSI) Landscape** template.

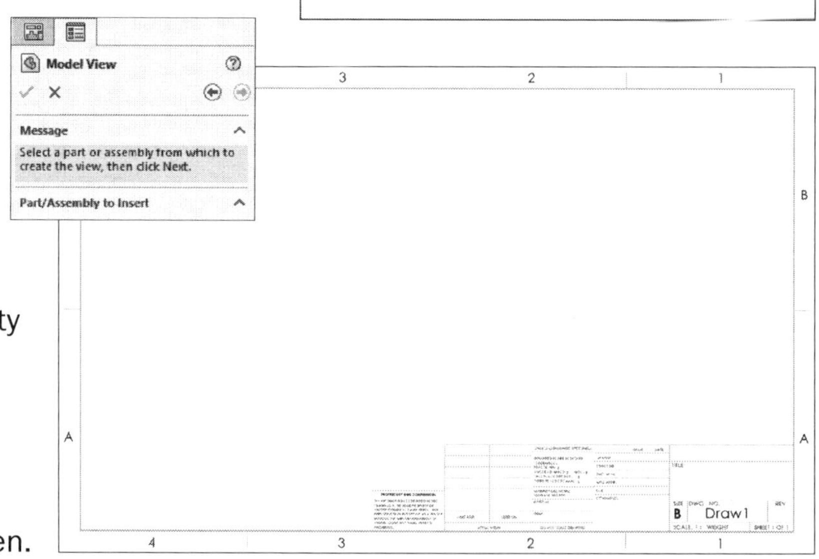

Click **Cancel** X to exit the Model View command.

This part of the chapter will teach us how to build a property tab template for a drawing custom properties.

Keep the drawing open.

2. Accessing the Custom Properties tab:

In the **Task Pane** on the upper left side of the screen, click **Custom Properties** .

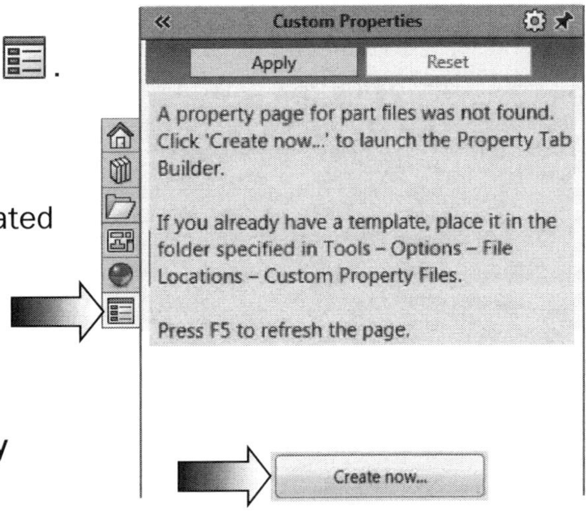

If there is no property tab template created previously, a yellow color message appeared to provide instructions on how to create them.

Click **Create Now** to launch the **Property Tab Builder**.

The Property Tab Builder window pops up.

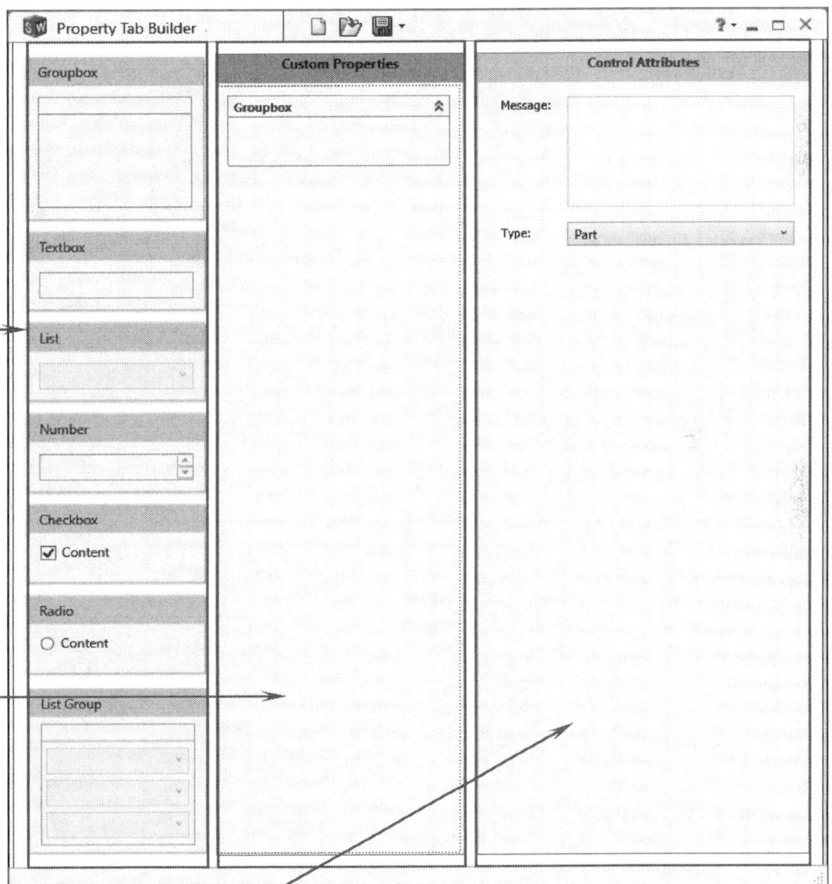

The left column is a list of properties that can be used.

Form Building Blocks

The middle column is what will be displayed in SOLIDWORKS when the property tab is ready.

Template Preview

The right column are the options for each parameter.

Form Control Options

Form Building Blocks:
Items from the left pane are added to the template preview pane by drag and drop.

Template Preview:
The middle pane shows a preview of the template.
The active items in the template preview are shown with a gray border.

Form Control Options:
Attributes and options for the active template items are available in the right pane.

3. Switching the Template type:

From the <u>right pane</u>, expand the **Type** drop-down list and select: **Drawing**.

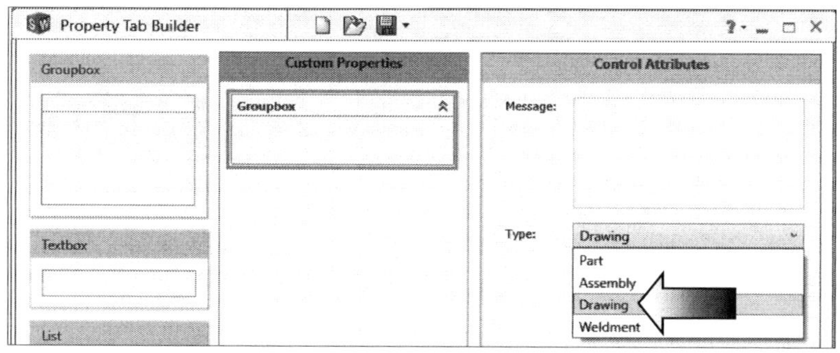

4. Modifying the Groupbox:

From the <u>middle pane</u>, click inside the Groupbox rectangle to access its attributes.

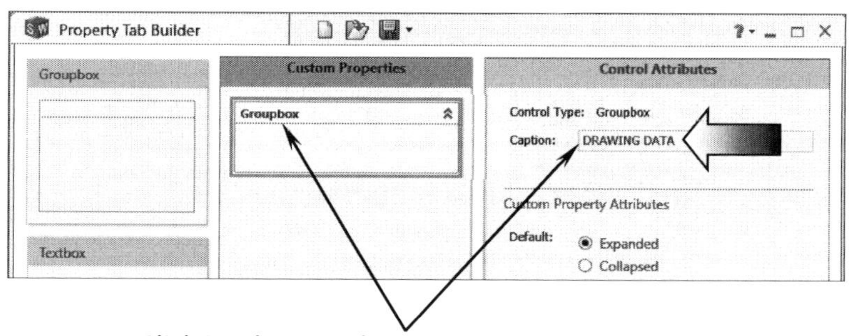

Click inside Groupbox to access the Caption

From the <u>right pane</u>, for Caption, enter: **DRAWING DATA.**

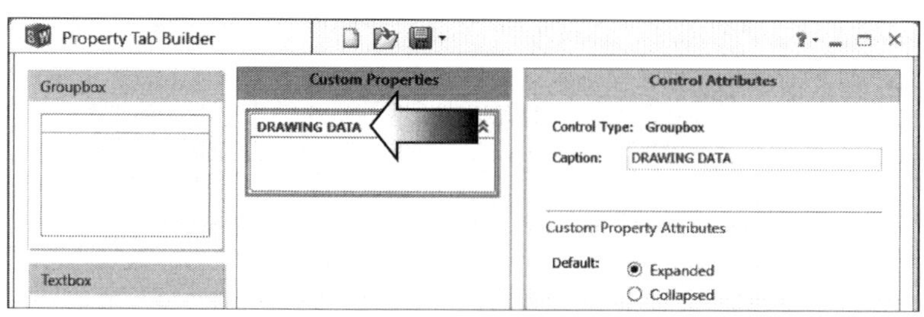

The 1st Groupbox is changed to DRAWING DATA.

5. Adding a Textbox field:

The Textbox Field controls the information that a user can enter in the field such as: Text, Dates, and Yes/No values.

You can leave the value blank, enter a value, or select a predefined value from the list. If you select a predefined value, you can enter text before and after the value to customize the string.

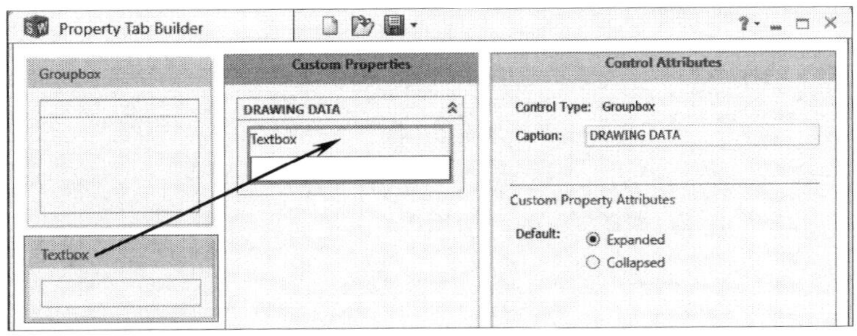

From the left pane, drag a **Textbox** into the DRAWING DATA groupbox.

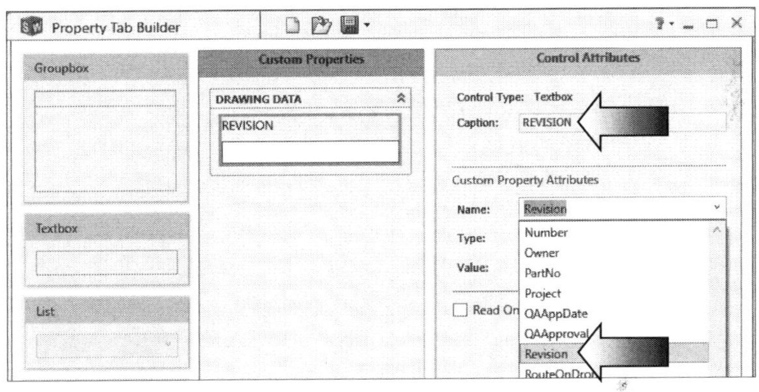

From the right pane, for **Caption**, enter: **REVISION**.

For Custom Properties Attributes, expand the **Name** field and select: **Revision**.

This field will populate in the Revision section of the Title Block.

6. Adding a List field:

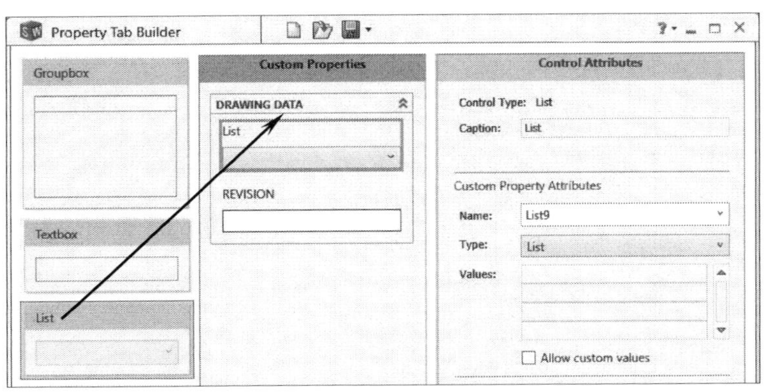

The List field controls the information that a user can enter into the field.

From the left pane, drag and drop a **List** into the DRAWING DATA groupbox.

In the <u>right pane</u>, for **Caption,** type: **DRAWN BY.**

For Custom Properties Attributes, expand the **Name** field and select: **DrawnBy.**

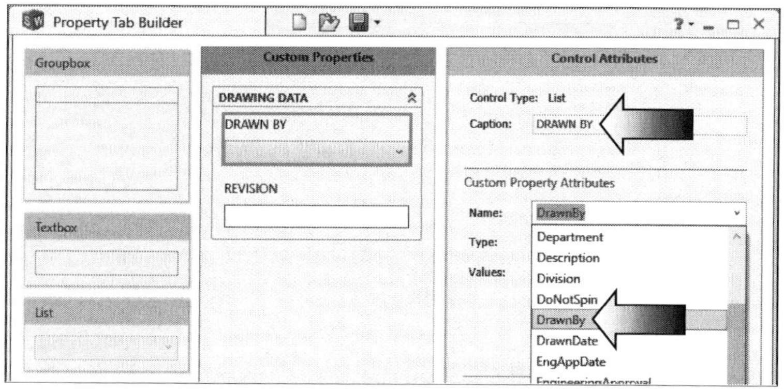

For **Values**, enter a <u>few names</u>, similar to what is shown in the image on the right.

Enable the checkbox: **Allow Custom Values.**

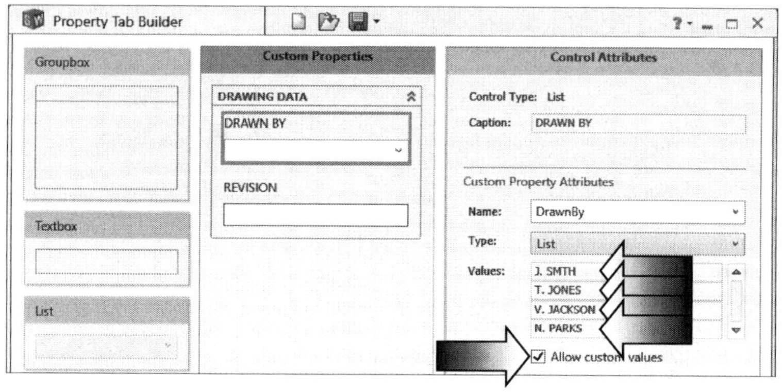

(The **Allow Custom Values** option allows users to manually enter text values into the box in SOLIDWORKS. When this option is cleared, users can only select values from the list.)

7. Adding another Textbox field:

From the <u>left pane</u>, drag and drop another **Textbox** into the DRAWING DATA groupbox.

For **Caption**, enter: **DRAWN DATE.**

For Custom Property Attributes, select:

Name = **DrawnDate**

Type = **Date**

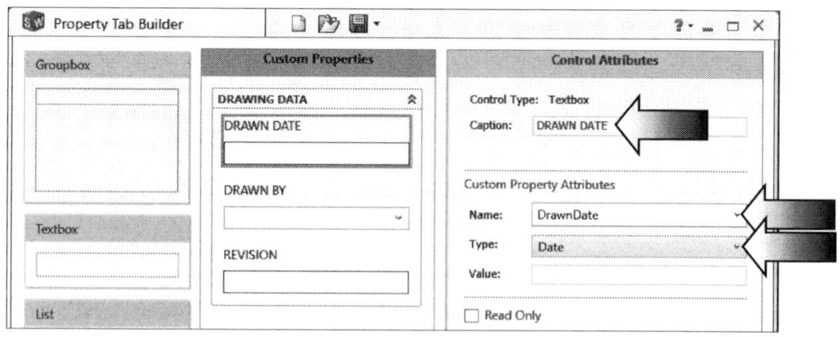

(The Date field will produce a calendar for users to select from.)

8. Saving the Property Tab Template:

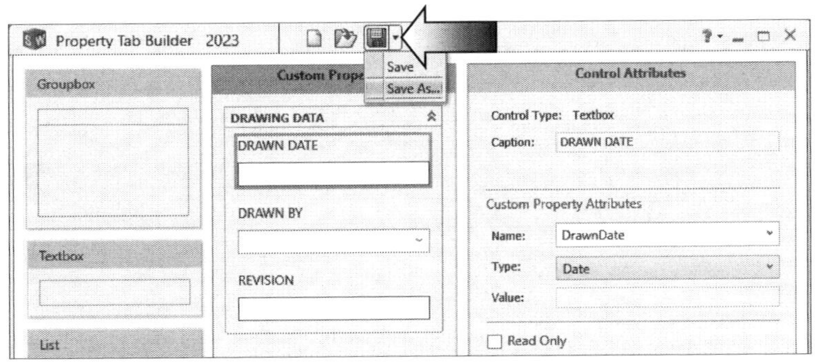

In the Property Builder Tab, expand the Save button and select: **Save As.**

For Location to save, browse to the Templates folder, in the following directories:

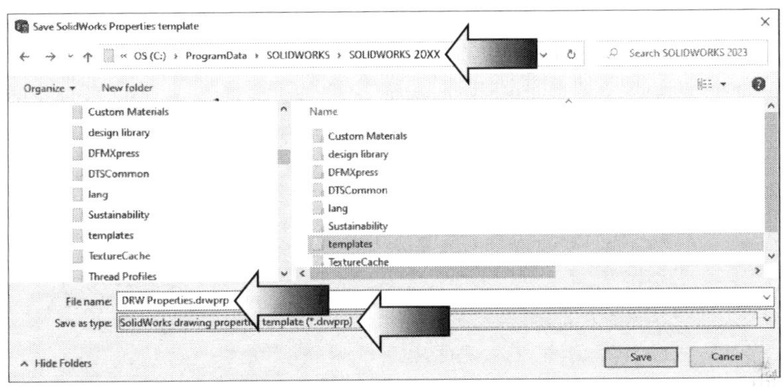

C: Program Data, SOLIDWORKS, SOLIDWORKS 20XX, Templates.

For File Name, enter: **DRW Properties.**

For Save As Type, select: **SolidWorks Drawing Properties Template** (*.drwprp).

Click **Save.**

9. Testing out the DRW Properties Template:

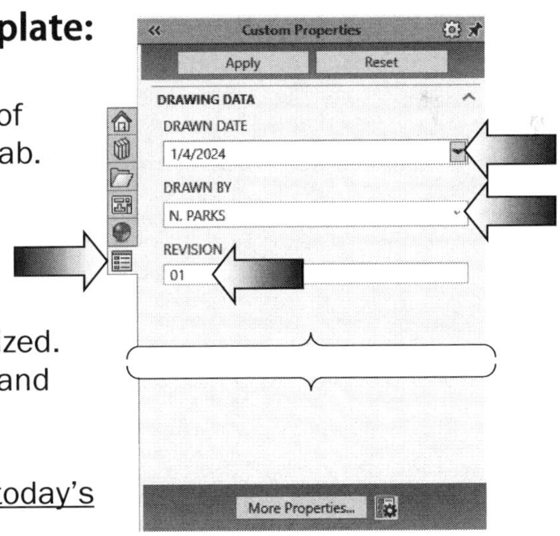

In the **Task Pane**, on the right-hand side of the screen, click the **Custom Properties** tab.

Push **F5** to refresh.

The text values and the names that were entered in the template are recognized. They are populated into the Drawn Date and the Name fields.

Expand the **Drawn Date** field and select today's date.

Expand the **Drawn By** field and select a name from the list.
The Custom Properties for a **Drawing Template** are now defined.

This time, let us create similar Custom Properties for a **Part Template.**

10. Adding a Textbox field:

From the left pane, drag a **Textbox** to the PART DATA groupbox.

Change Caption to: **PART DATA.**

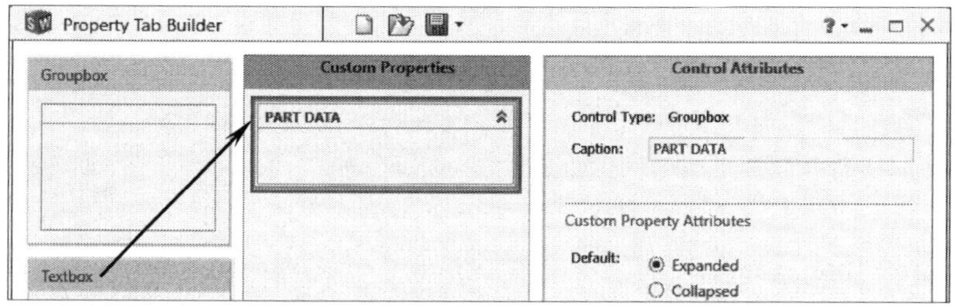

Drag a **List** field into the **PART DATA** groupbox.

Change Caption to: **DESCRIPTION** and select **Description** under the Name list. For Value, enter: **Custom Prop. for Part.**

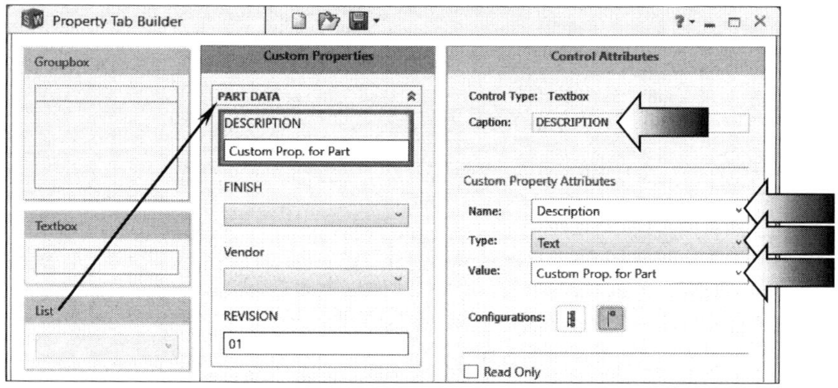

Drag and drop another **List** field into the **PART DATA** groupbox.

For Caption, enter: **Material**. Select **Material** for Name and enter a few materials for Values.

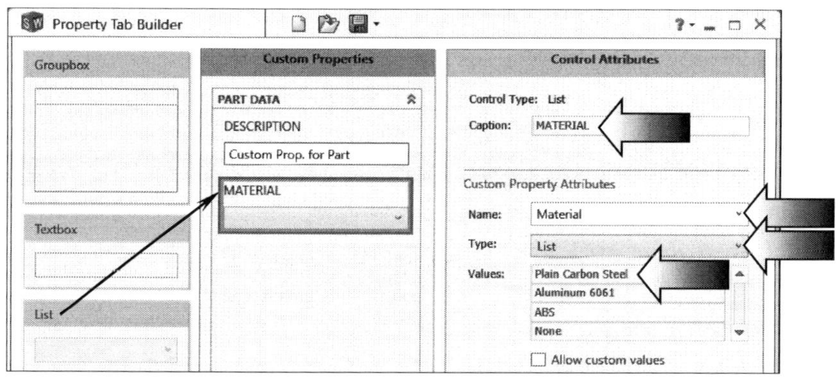

Add another **List** field for **Finish.**

For Caption, enter **FINISH**. For Name, select **Finish** from the drop-down list and enter: **Sand Blast, Paint**, and **None.**

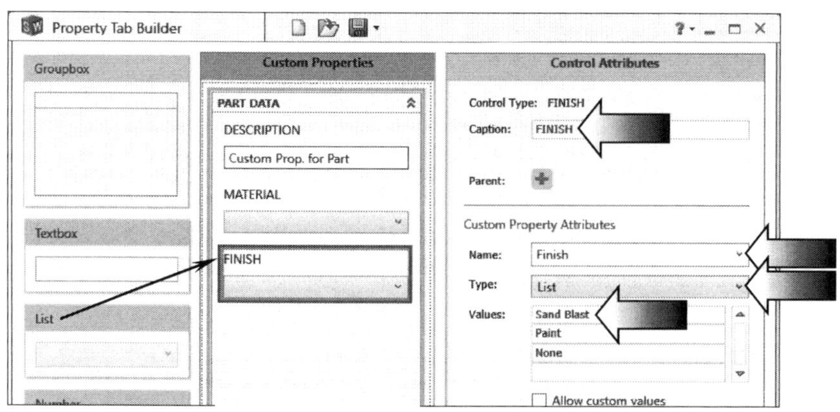

Drag and drop another **List** field into the **PART DATA** groupbox.

For Caption, enter: **Vendor**.

For Name, select: **Vendor** and enter a few names for Values.

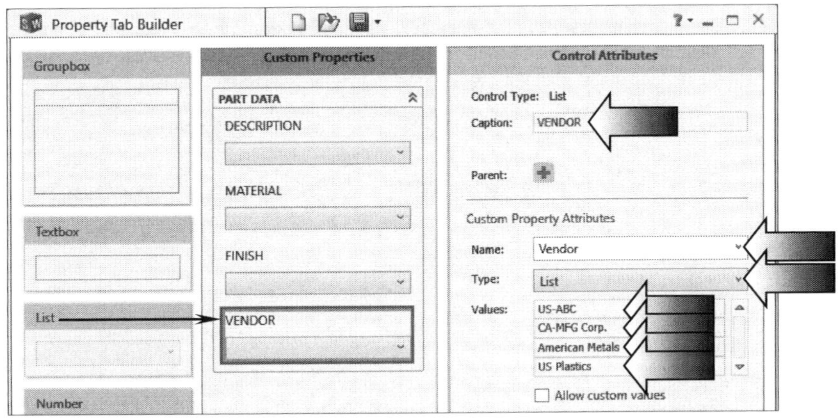

11. Saving the Property Tab Template:

In the Property Builder Tab, expand the Save button and select: **Save As**.

For Location to save, navigate to the Templates folder, in the following directories:

C: Program Data, SOLIDWORKS, SOLIDWORKS 20XX, Templates.

For File Name, enter: **PRT Properties.**

For Save As Type, select: **Custom Prop for Part** (*.prtprp).

Click **Save**.

The Custom Properties for a **Part Template** are now defined.

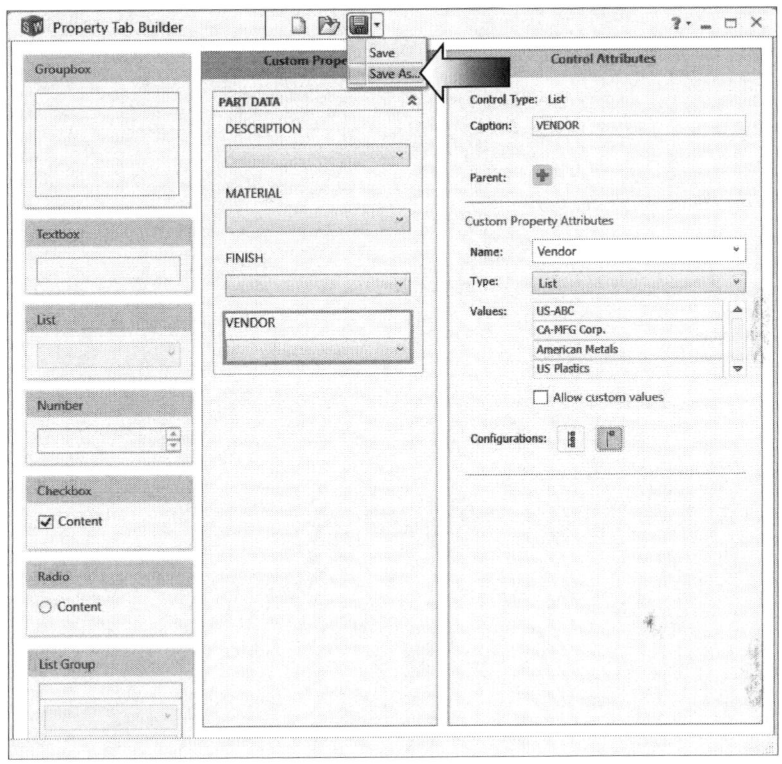

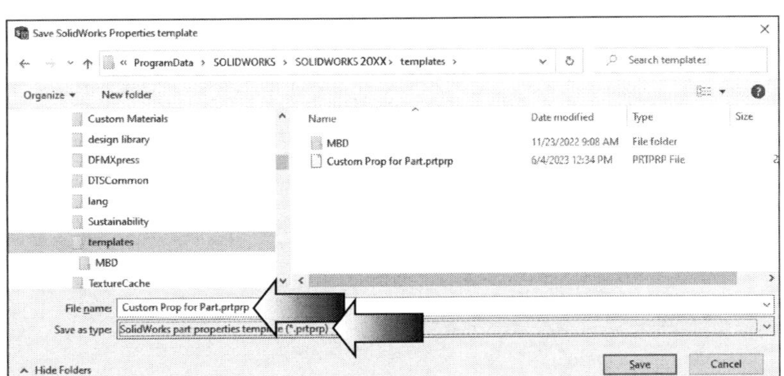

12. Testing out the Part Properties Template:

From the Training Folder, open a part document named: **Chapter 9_Sample Part.**

Currently, there are only 4 Customs Properties created for the Part Template: the Description, Material, Finish, and Vendor.

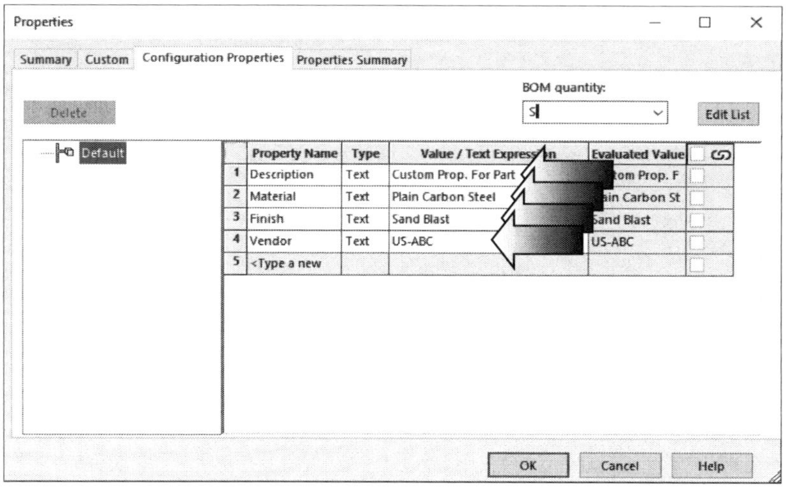

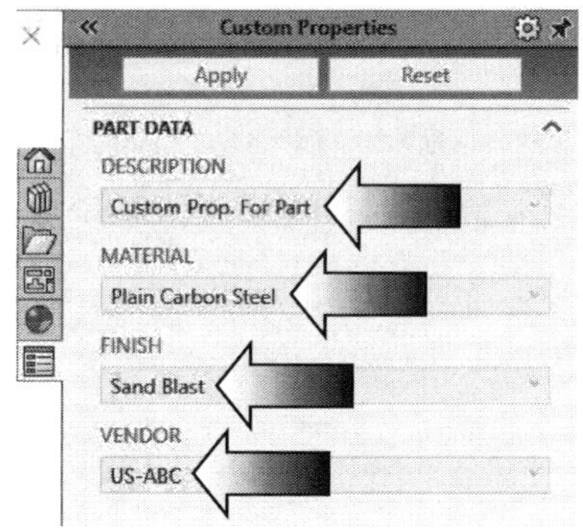

In the Task Pane, press F5 to refresh and populate the Custom Properties.

In SOLIDWORKS, click **File Properties** .
The 4 Custom Properties are recognized and populated automatically.

13. Creating a sample part:

To further test out the Part Custom Properties and see how they get populated from a model to a drawing, let us create a new part.

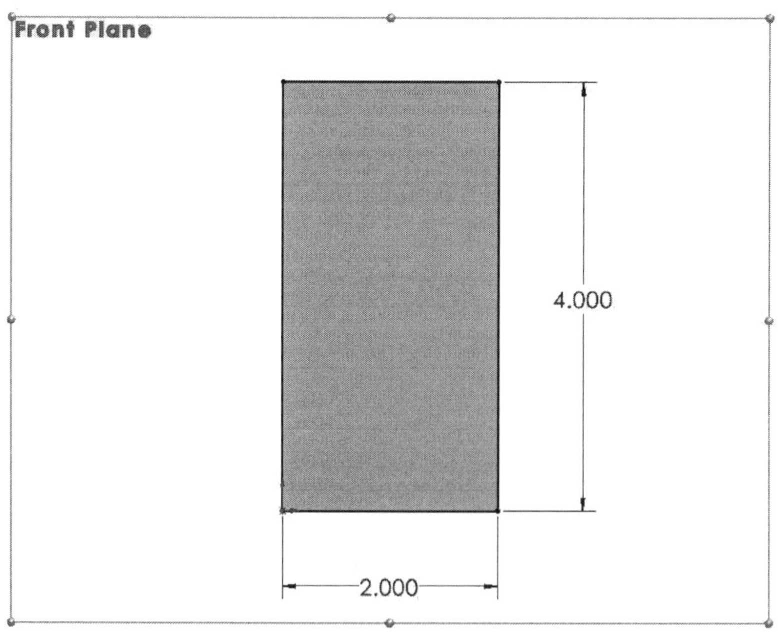

Using the existing Chapter 9_Sample Part, open a new sketch on the **Front** plane.

Sketch a **Rectangle** and add the height and width **dimensions** as shown.

Switch to the **Features** tab and click **Extruded Boss-Base**.

For Direction 1, use the default **Blind** type.

For Extrude Depth, enter **.500in**.

Click **OK**.

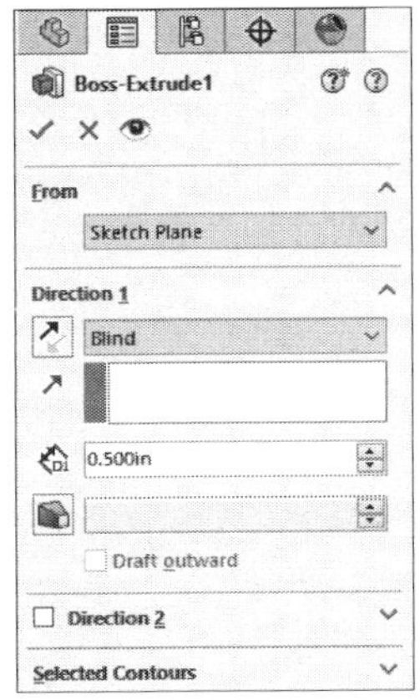

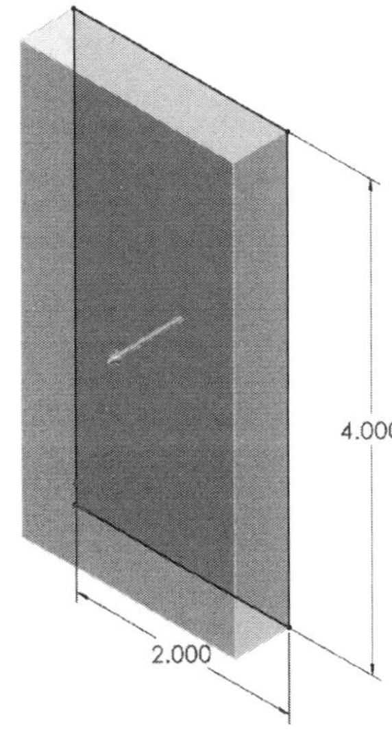

14. Making drawing from part:

Save the model using the same name (**Chapter 9_Sample Part**).

Click **File, Make Drawing From Part.**

Select **B (ANSI) Landscape** for sheet size. (Use any scale for this exercise.)

Using the **View Palette**, Drag/drop the **Isometric** view to the center of the drawing sheet.

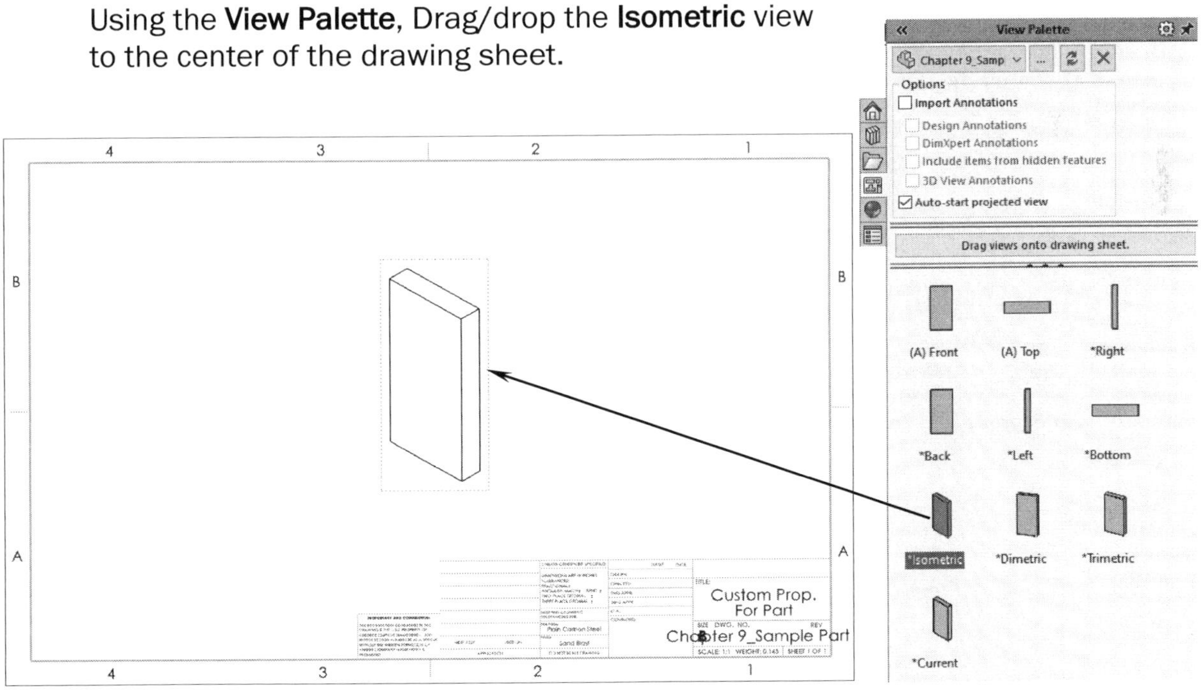

The Custom Properties that were created earlier are automatically populated into the Title (Description), the Material, and the Finish fields (arrows).

Other fields can also be customized by adding them to the Custom Property Tab Builder.

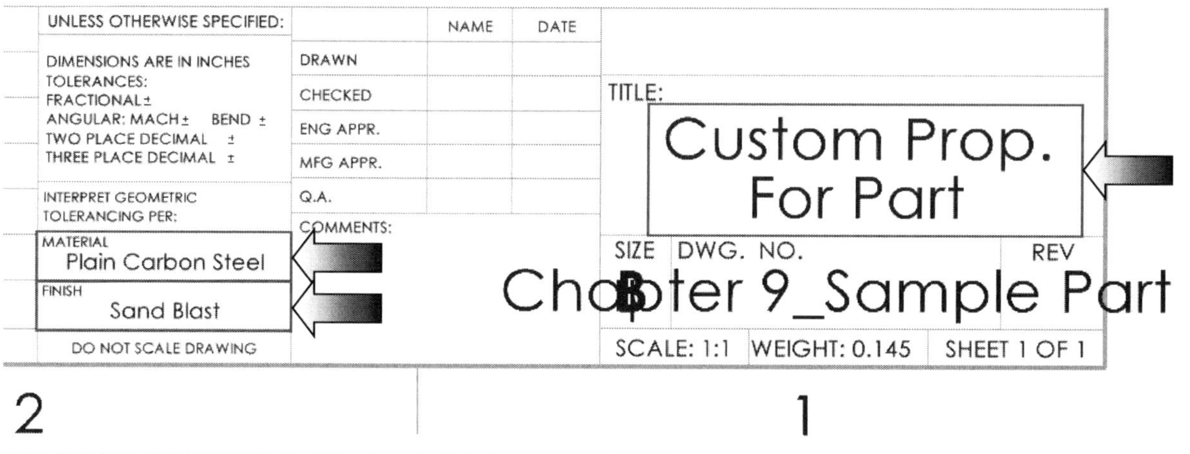

15. Saving your work:

Select **File, Save As.**

Enter **Chapter 9_Sample Part.slddrw** for thc file name.

Click **Save.**

Select **YES** to overwrite and replace the old document with the new one.

Close all documents.

CHAPTER 10: CONFIGURATIONS

Creating a Design Table using MS-Excel

In SOLIDWORKS, configurations allow you to create multiple variations of a part or assembly model within a single document. Configurations are a convenient way to develop and manage families of models with different dimensions, components, or other parameters.

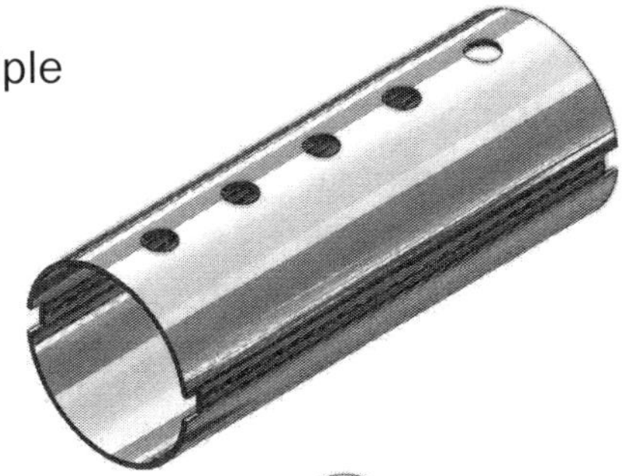

1. Opening a part document:

Select **File, Open.**

Browse to the Training Folder and open the part document named: **Grabber_Tube.sldprt.**

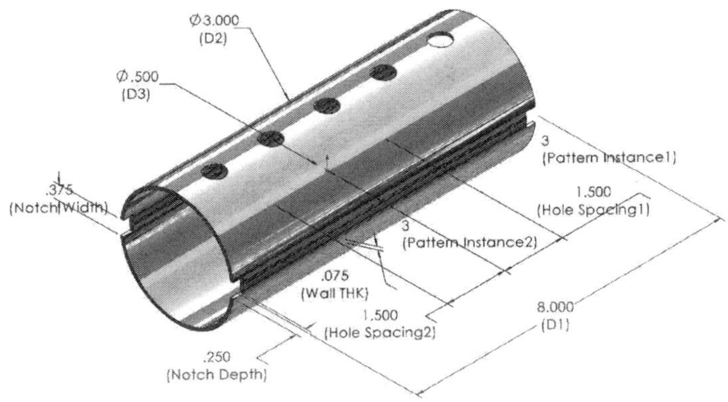

This model is part of an assembly named Tube Grabber as shown on the right.

We will use the model Grabber_Tube to create a family of tubes, with different lengths, thicknesses, with and without holes or notches.

Although there are 3 different methods for creating configurations (Manual Config., Configure Feature, and Design Table), we will focus on learning the most popular method called Design Table, where an Excel table will be used to create and manage the configurations.

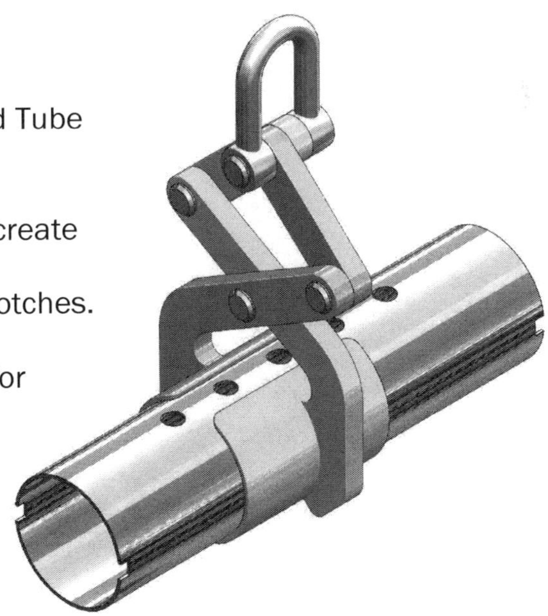

2. Renaming the dimensions:

You can create configurations manually, or you can use a design table to create multiple configurations simultaneously. Design tables provide a convenient way to create and manage configurations in a worksheet. You can use design tables in both part and assembly documents.

Regardless of which method you use to create the configurations, it is strongly recommended to name the dimensions to reflect what they are, so that when someone opens the Design Table, they will be able to recognize the configured dimensions and understand the design intents behind it all.

Select the dimension **12.00 (D1)**.

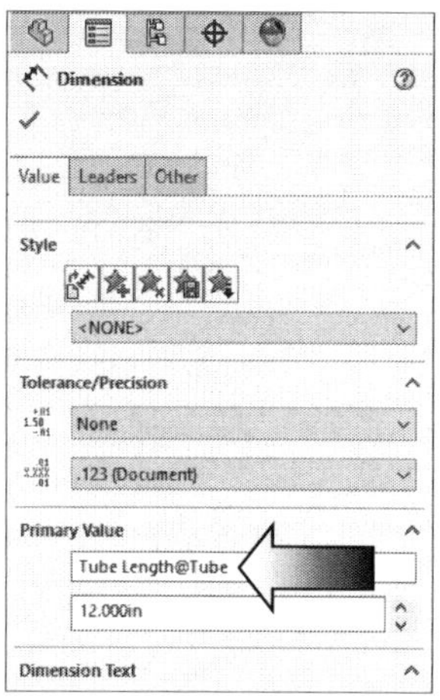

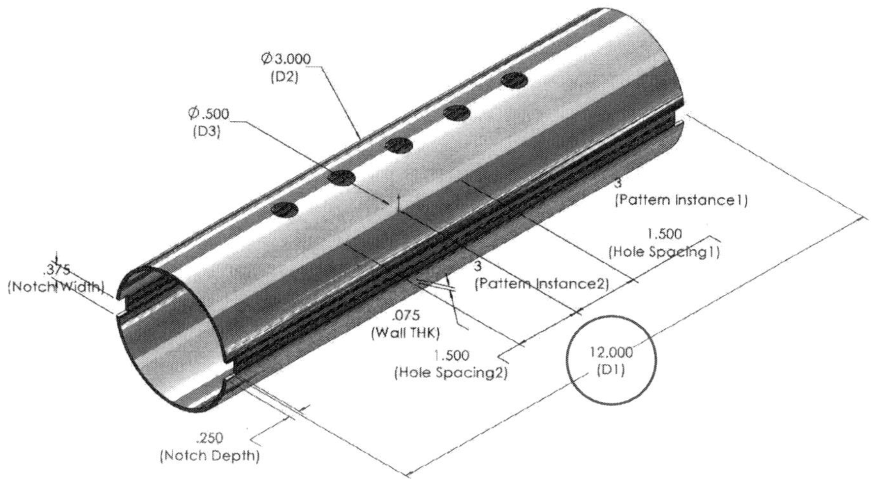

Using the FeatureManager tree, under the **Primary Value** section, change the name **D1** to **Tube Length**. <u>Do not</u> change the text **@Tube**; this is the actual link to the Sketch1 in the model.

Change the name of the dimension **Ø3.000 (D2)** to **Tube Diameter**.

Also, change the name of the dimension **Ø.500 (D3)** to **Hole Diameter** (circled in red).

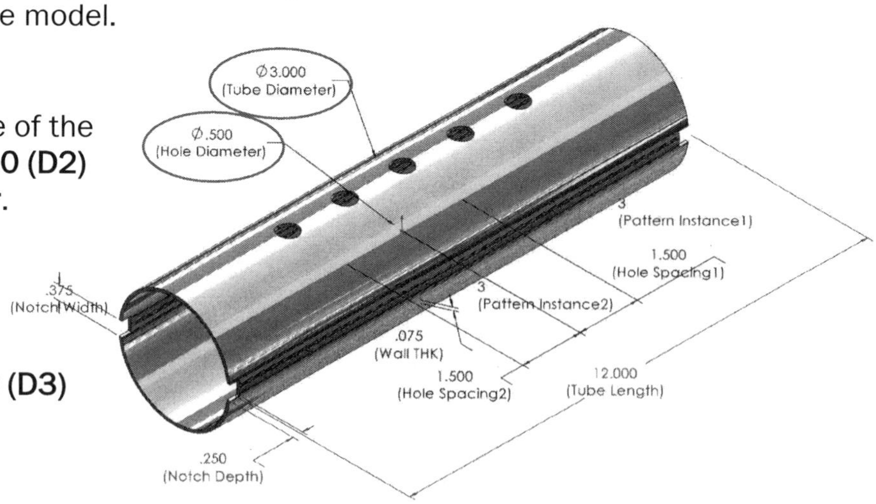

3. Inserting an Excel-Based Design Table:

To use the Design Table, you must have MS-Excel installed on your computer.

Select **Insert, Tables, Excel Design Table**.

Under the Source section, select the **Auto-Create** option.

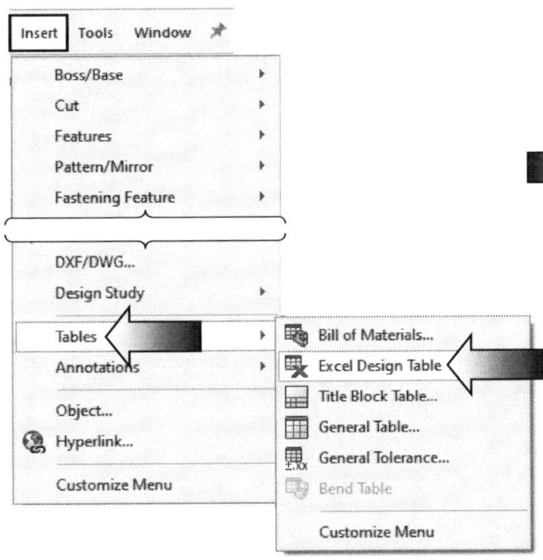

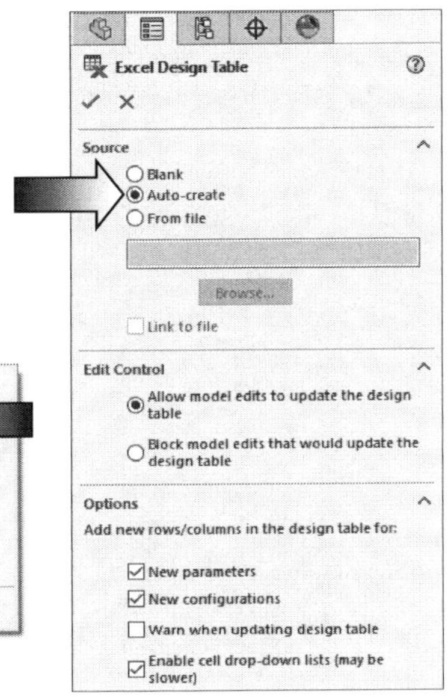

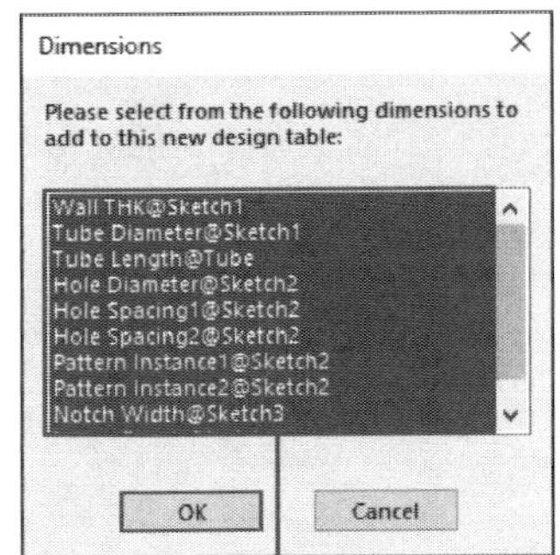

Select all dimensions to export to Excel

Click **OK**.

The MS-Excel application is being launched. A Dimensions dialog box pops up, asking which dimensions from the model to add to the Design Table; select all of them and click OK.

The selected dimensions are populated to the Excel worksheet.

Each dimension is placed in its own column and they are parametrically linked to the ones in the model.

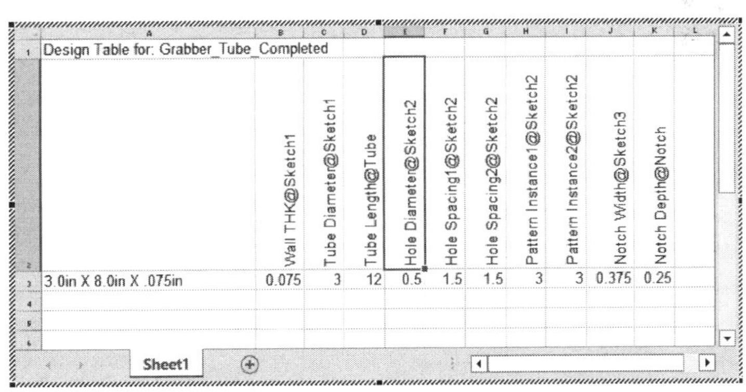

Both SOLIDWORKS and MS-Excel applications are running side by side at this time. Do not click in the background or Excel will be closed and you may need to start over again.

4. Adding new configurations in Excel:

Click inside <u>cell A4</u> and enter the name of the new configuration:
3.0 X 10.0in X .075in.

Click inside <u>cell D4</u> and enter **10** (10 inches) for the new Tube Length.

Click inside cell A5 and enter the name of the new configuration:
3.0 X 8.0in X .075in.

Click inside <u>cell D5</u> and enter **8** (8 inches) for the new Tube Length.

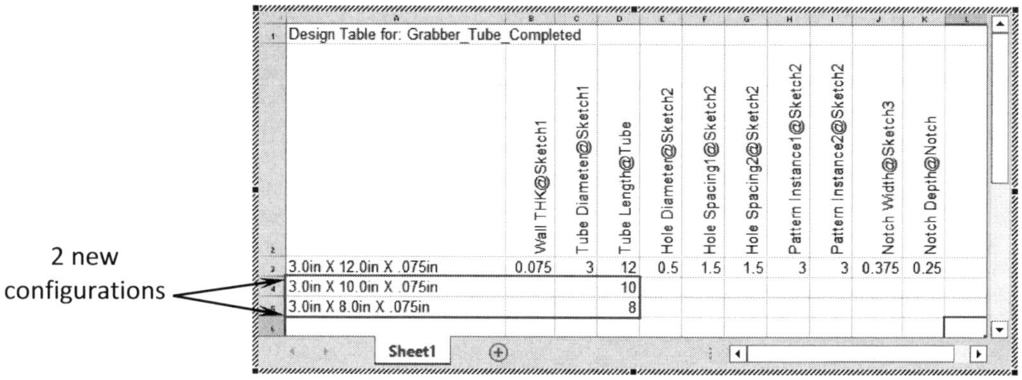

Drag the handle at the lower right corner of the table to increase the number of rows and columns.

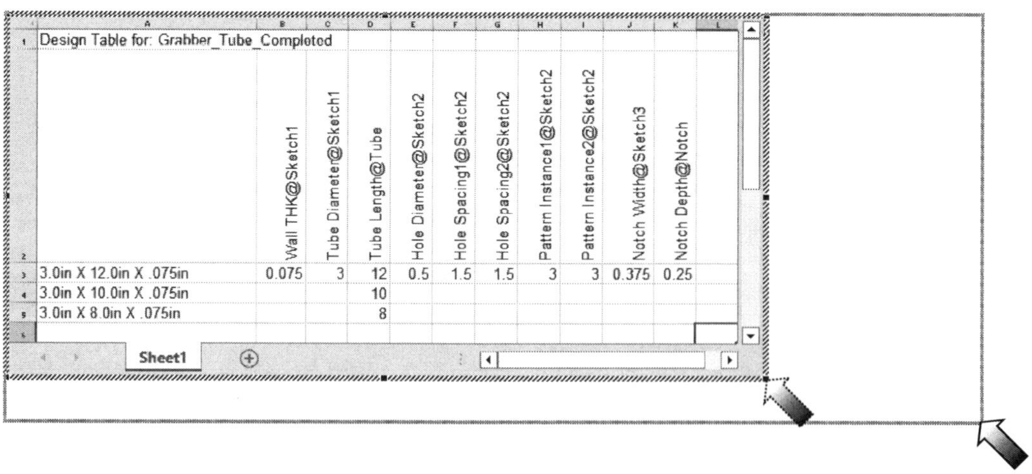

We will insert the Hole and the Notch features into the table, so that we can control their visibility (suppressed and unsuppressed) using the Design Table.

5. Adding new features to the Design Table:

Other features can be added to the Design Table very quickly and easily.

In Excel, click inside cell L2 to select it.

In SOLIDWORKS, double-click the name of the **Holes** feature.

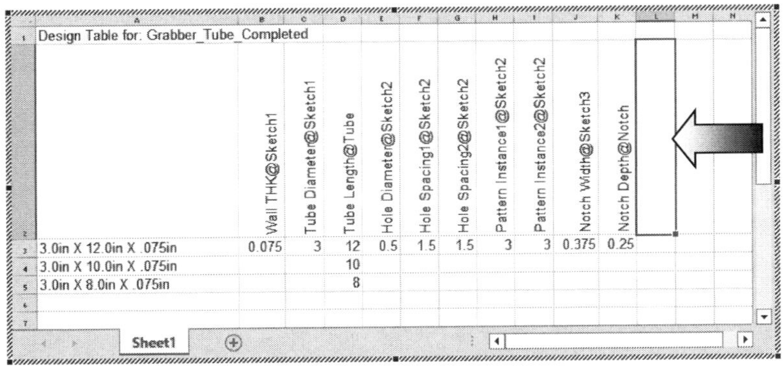

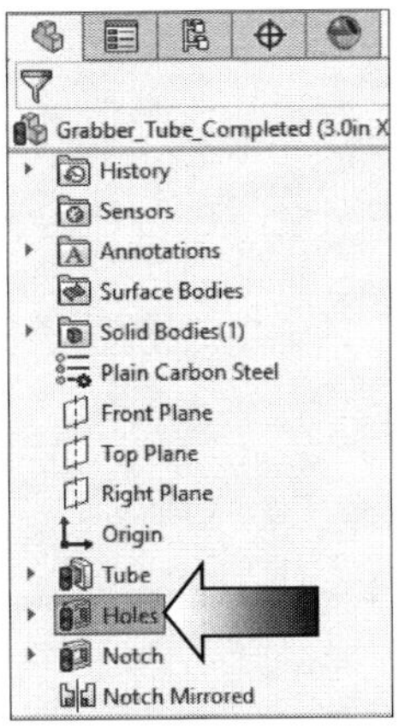

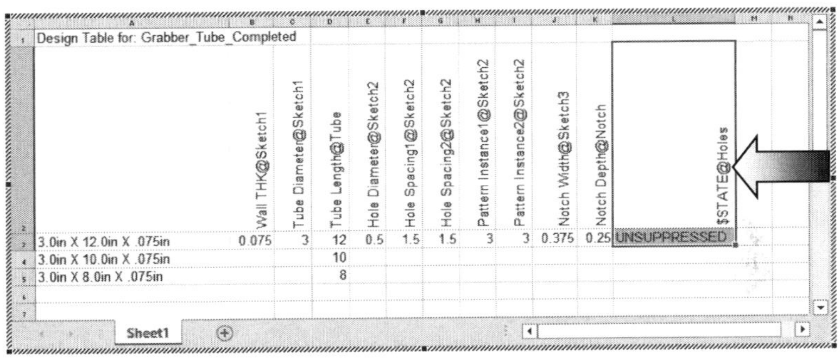

The hole feature is added to Cell L2, and the parameter Unsuppressed is added to the cell below because the actual feature is unsuppressed in the model itself.

Repeat the last step and add the **Notch** feature to the next column (cell M2).

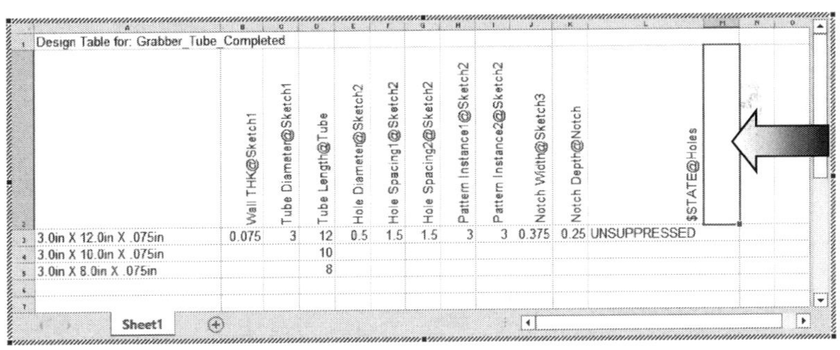

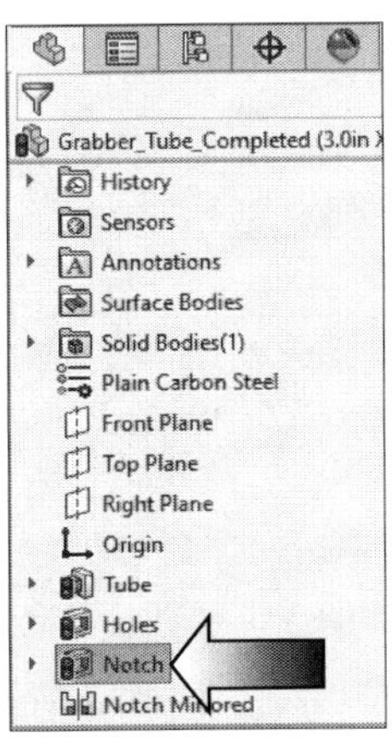

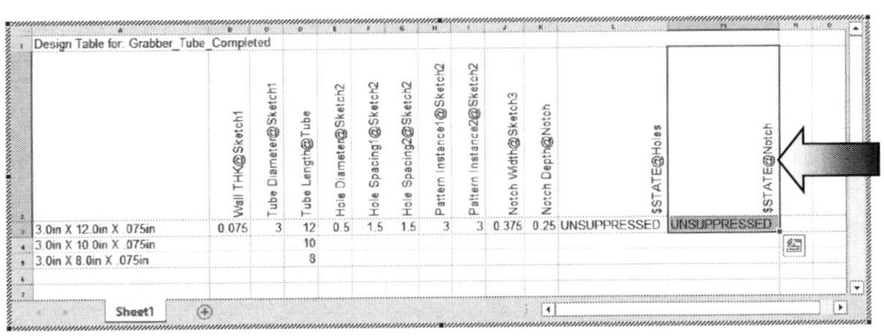

6. Assigning the features states:

The parameter "STATE" is used to either Suppressed or Unsuppressed a feature.
They can also be abbreviated with the letter "S" or "U", or "0" and "1".

Highlight the word **Unsuppressed** in <u>cell L3</u> (the **Hole** feature) and change it to **U**.

Assign the same letter **U** to the **Notch** feature.

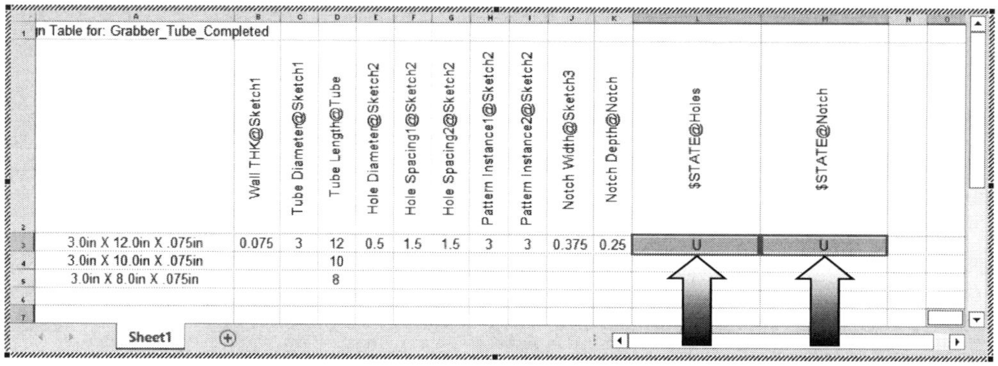

n Table for: Grabber_Tube_Completed

	Wall THK@Sketch1	Tube Diameter@Sketch1	Tube Length@Tube	Hole Diameter@Sketch2	Hole Spacing1@Sketch2	Hole Spacing2@Sketch2	Pattern Instance1@Sketch2	Pattern Instance2@Sketch2	Notch Width@Sketch3	Notch Depth@Notch	$STATE@Holes	$STATE@Notch
3.0in X 12.0in X .075in	0.075	3	12	0.5	1.5	1.5	3	3	0.375	0.25	U	U
3.0in X 10.0in X .075in			10									
3.0in X 8.0in X .075in			8									

Next, we will assign the Suppressed state to the 2nd configuration and Unsuppressed to the 3rd.

Click inside <u>cell L4</u> and type: **S** (suppressed) for both Hole and Notch features.

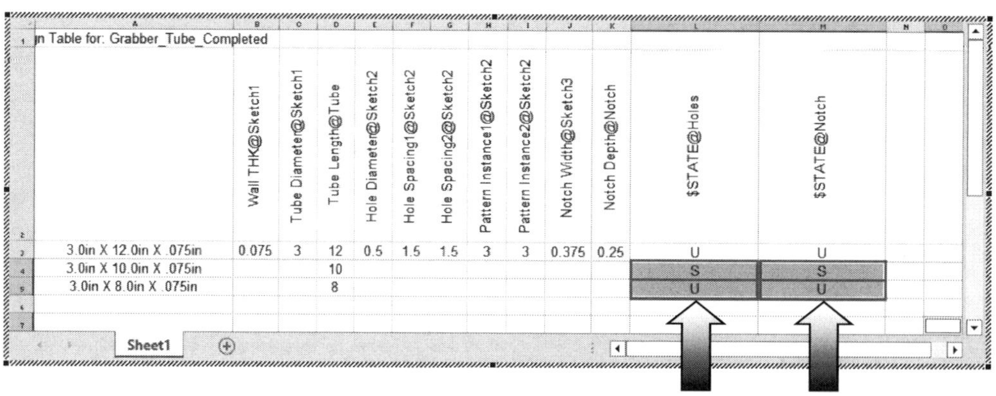

n Table for: Grabber_Tube_Completed

	Wall THK@Sketch1	Tube Diameter@Sketch1	Tube Length@Tube	Hole Diameter@Sketch2	Hole Spacing1@Sketch2	Hole Spacing2@Sketch2	Pattern Instance1@Sketch2	Pattern Instance2@Sketch2	Notch Width@Sketch3	Notch Depth@Notch	$STATE@Holes	$STATE@Notch
3.0in X 12.0in X .075in	0.075	3	12	0.5	1.5	1.5	3	3	0.375	0.25	U	U
3.0in X 10.0in X .075in			10								S	S
3.0in X 8.0in X .075in			8								U	U

There should be 3 configurations listed in the Design Table at this point.
The Hole and Notch features are Unsuppressed in the 1st and 3rd configurations but Suppressed in the 2nd configuration.

7. Switching back to the SOLIDWORKS application:

Either click the green checkmark on the upper right corner of the screen or click anywhere in the SOLIDWORKS background to switch back to the SOLIDWORKS application.

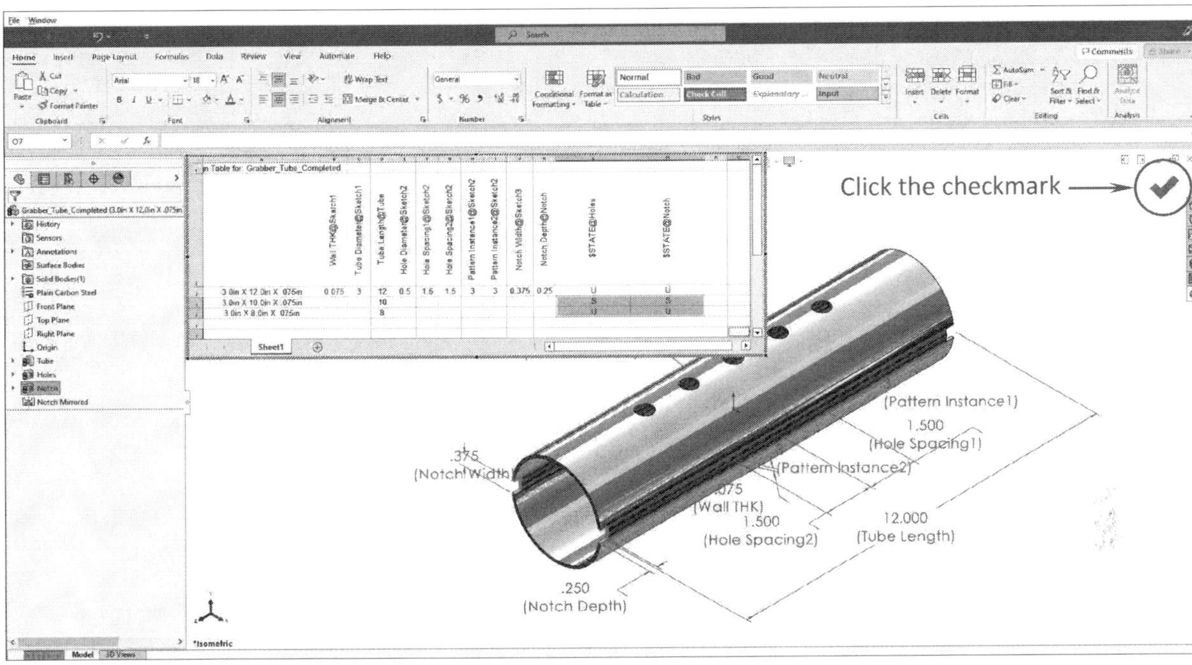

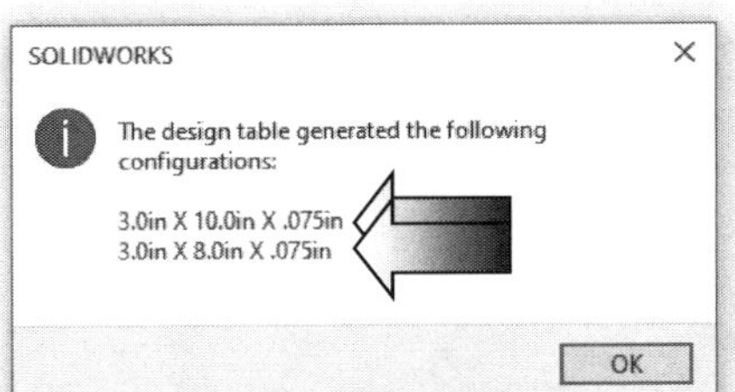

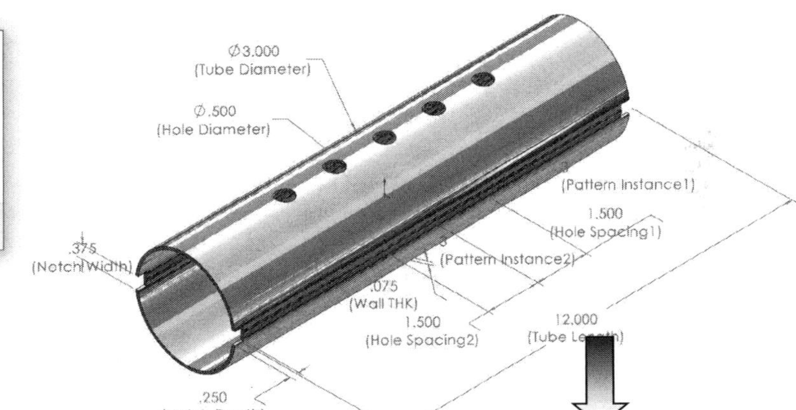

A message pops up indicating the Design Table has generated 2 new configurations.

Click **OK**.

Switch to the **ConfigurationManager** tree to see the new configurations. A Design Table is also added to the Tables folder.

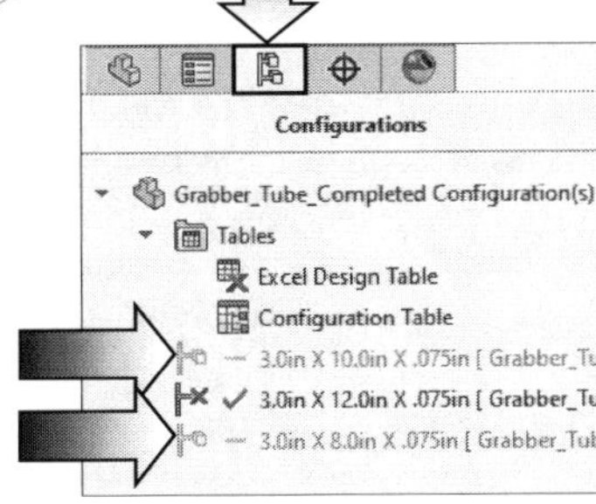

8. Viewing the new configurations:

The dimensions that were linked to the Design Table are changed to magenta (pink) color. Any changes made to those dimensions will populate the Design Table and vice versa.

Double-click on the configuration **3.0 X 8.0 X .075** (the shortest tube) to see the new part.

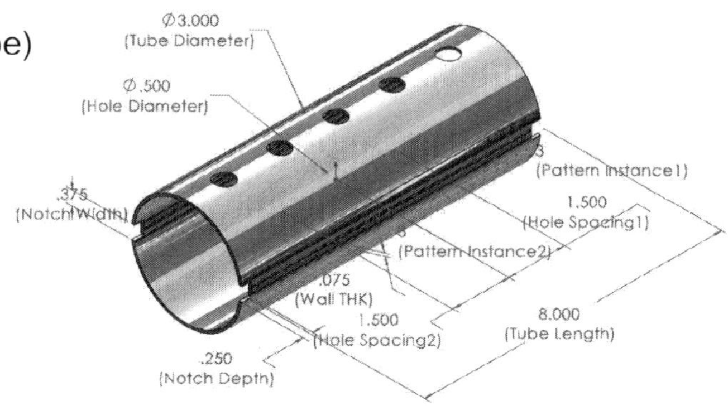

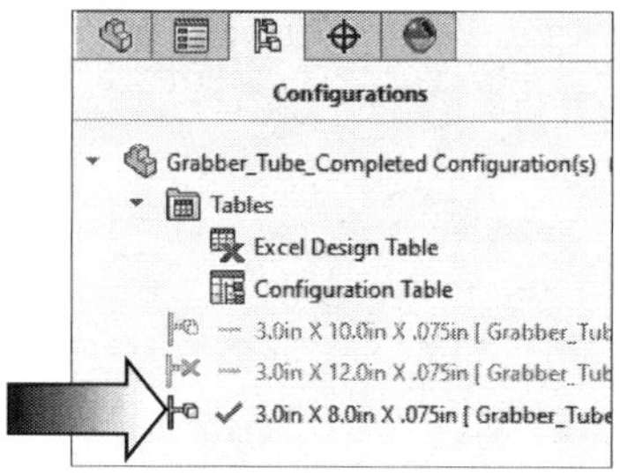

Double-click the configuration **3.0 X 10.0 X .075** (mid-size), the tube is longer and the holes and notches are suppressed.

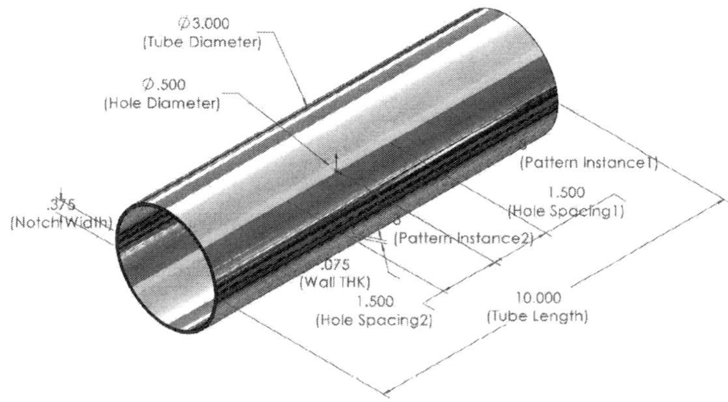

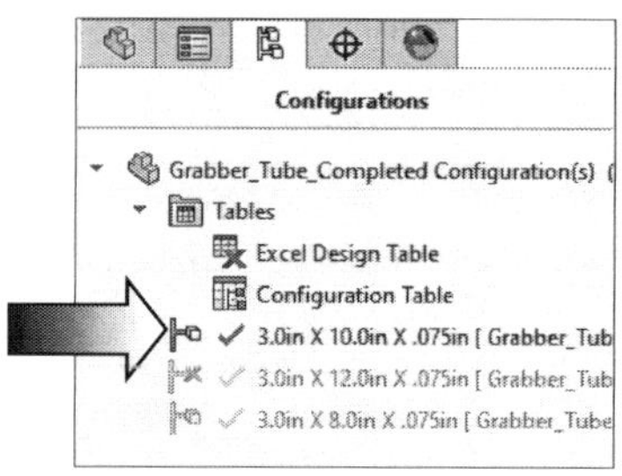

Double-click the configuration **3.0 X 12.0 X .075** (the longest); the tube is longer, the holes and notches are unsuppressed.

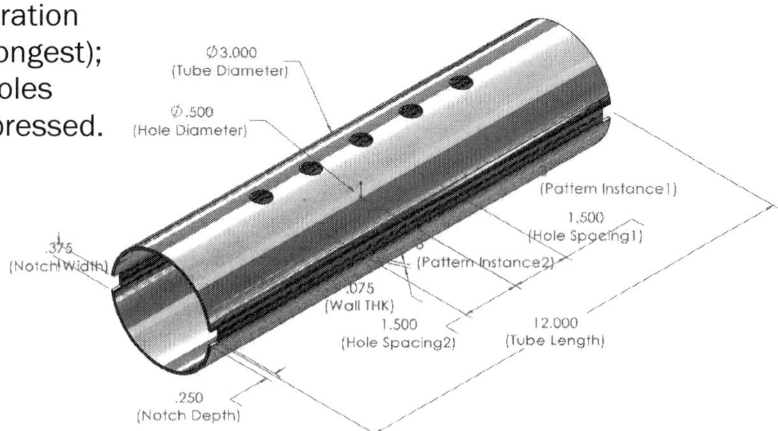

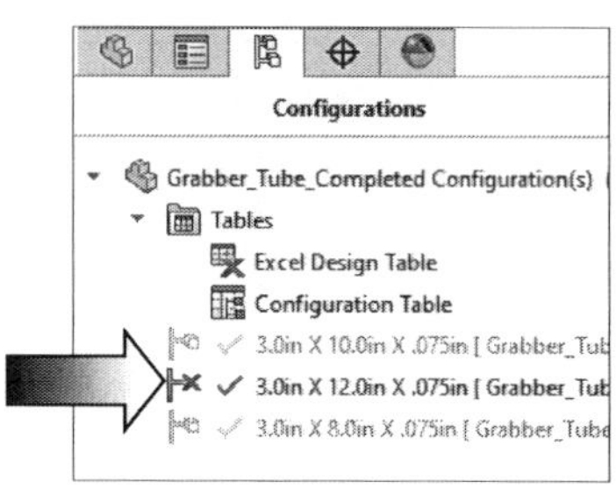

9. Adjusting the rows and columns:

Additional rows and columns will be displayed when the Design Table is inserted in the drawing. To eliminate confusion, we will edit the Design Table and remove the unwanted rows and columns, prior to making a drawing.

In the **ConfigurationManager** tree, right-click the Excel Design Table and select: **Edit Table**.

An Add Rows and Columns dialog box pops up indicating new parameters can still be added to the Design Table.

Click **OK**.

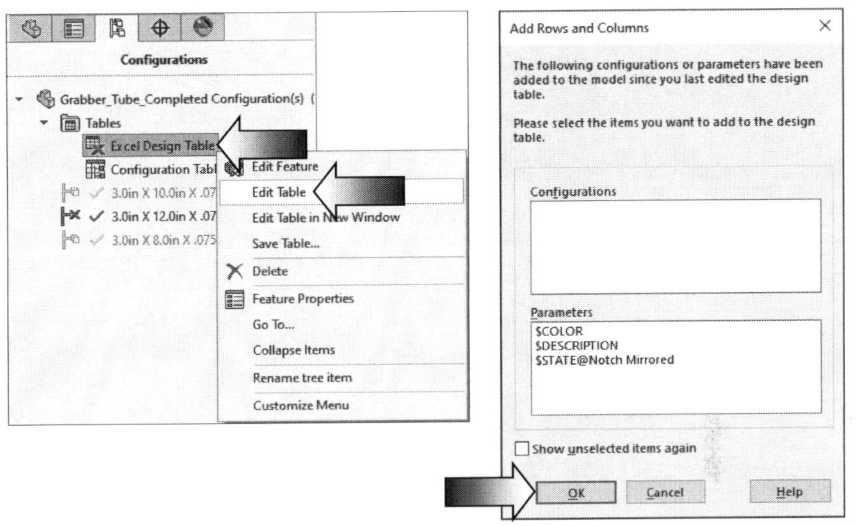

Drag the handle at the lower right corner <u>inwards</u>, to remove the extra rows and columns.

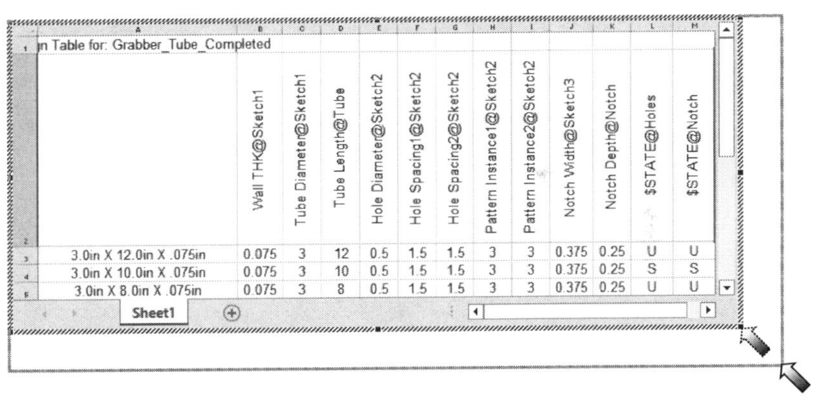

Make any adjustments needed so that the Design Table looks similar to the image shown on the right.

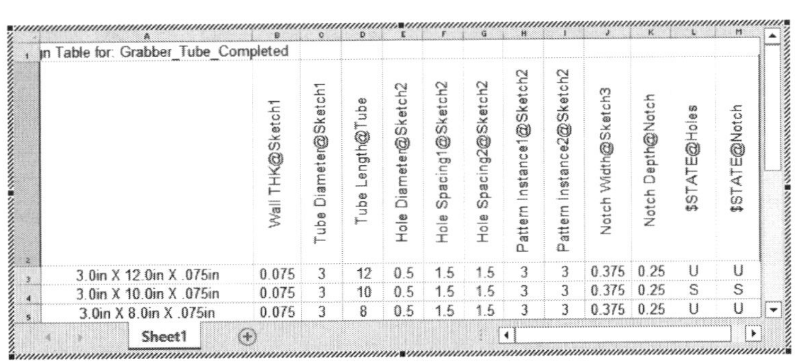

10. Making a drawing from part:

Let us create a drawing now to test out the new Design Table.

In SOLIDWORKS, select **Files, Make Drawing From Part.**

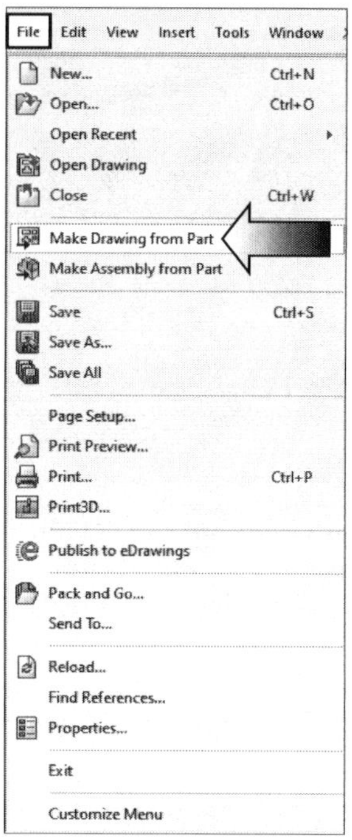

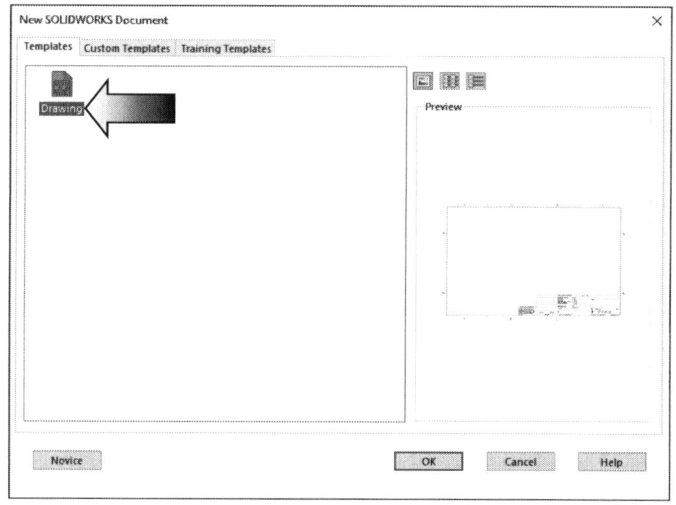

Select the default **Drawing Template** and set the sheet size to **B (ANSI) Landscape**, and the Scale to **1:2**.

Using the **View Palette**, drag the **Isometric view** and drop it in the middle of the sheet, similar to the image below.

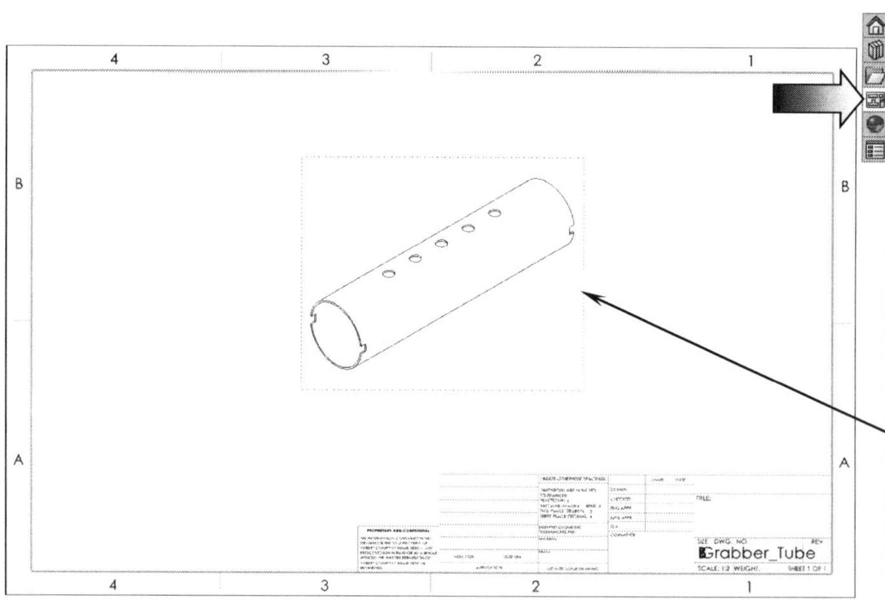

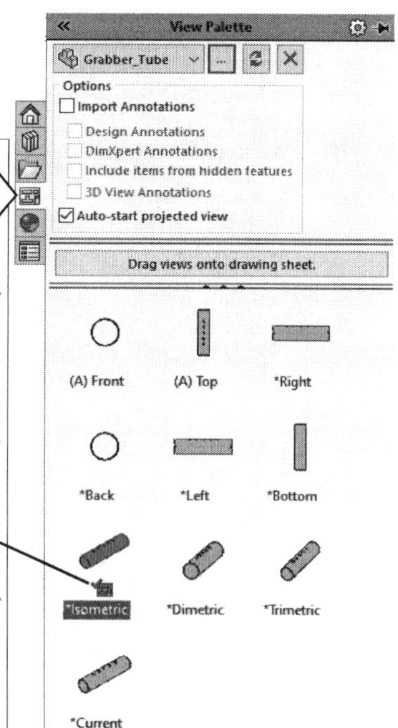

11. Inserting the Design Table:

Similar to the Bill of Materials, the table Design Table must be linked to a drawing view.

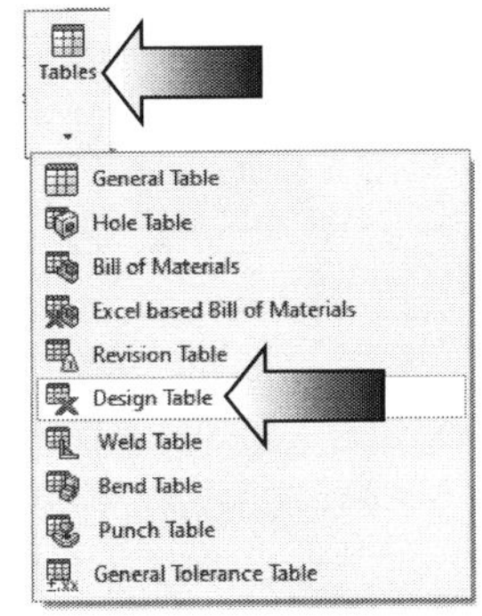

Click the dotted border of the **Isometric** view and switch to the **Annotation** tab.

Expand the **Tables** drop-down list and select **Design Table**.

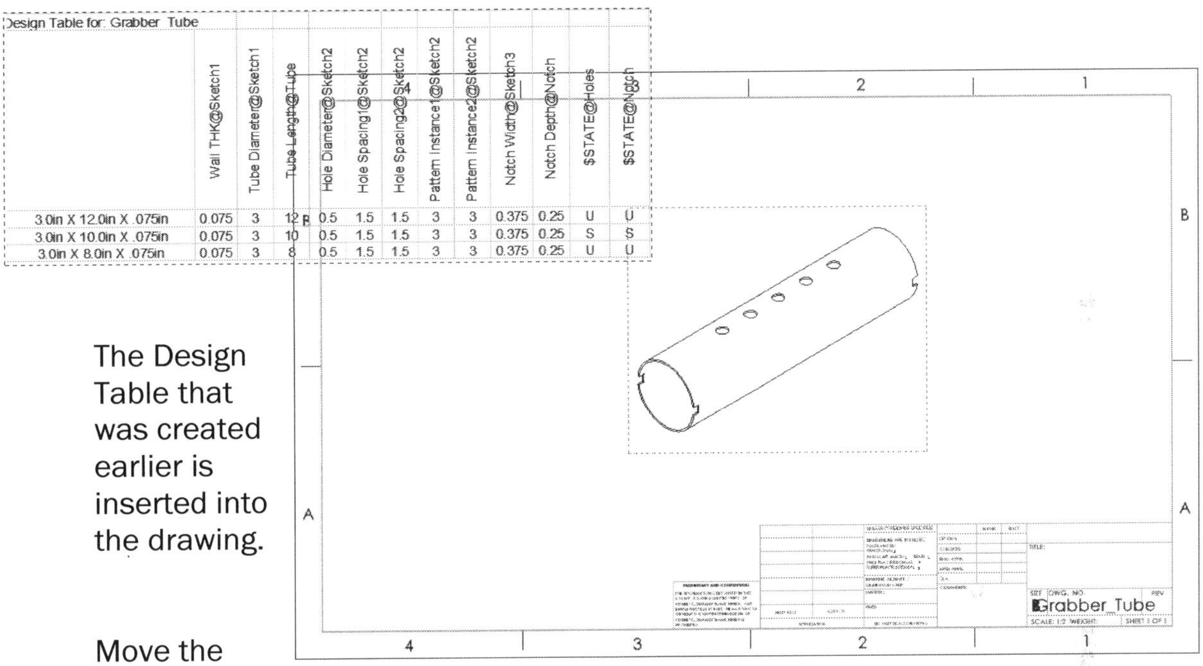

The Design Table that was created earlier is inserted into the drawing.

Move the Design Table inside the drawing and place it near the lower left corner of the drawing sheet.

Drag the handle at the upper left corner of the table to make it smaller.

Make any adjustments as needed so that your Design Table would look similar to the image shown on the right.

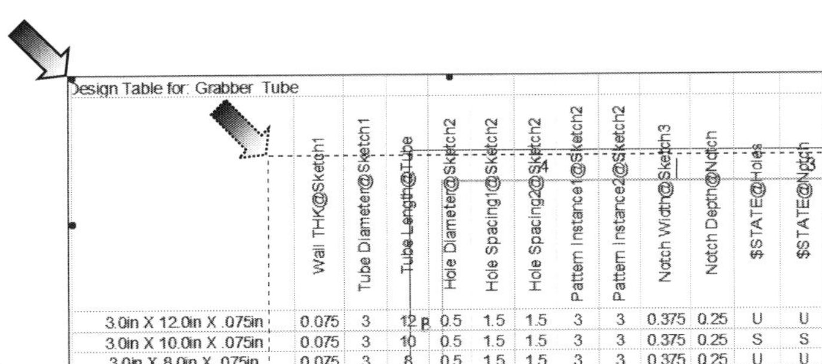

12. Adjusting the Table Header:

Resize and move the Design Table to the lower left corner of the drawing.

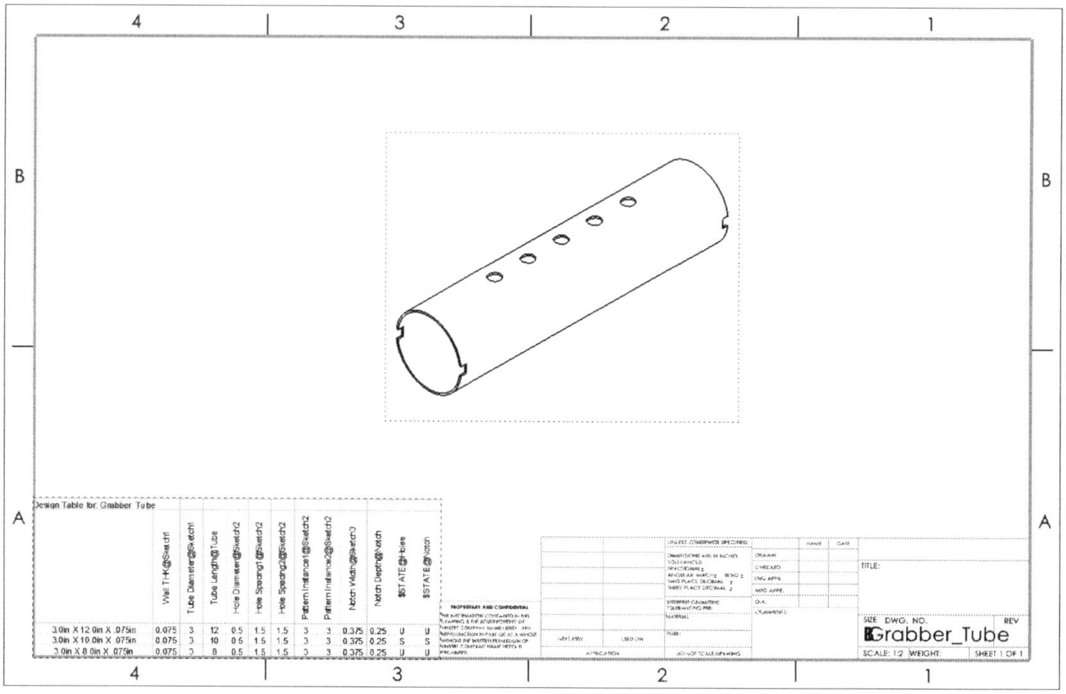

For clarity, the Header: **Design Table For: Grabber_Tube** needs to be centered in the 1st row.

Double-click inside the Design Table to launch MS-Excel for editing.

Highlight the entire <u>row 1</u> and right-click, select **Format Cells.**

Click the **Alignment** tab and select:
Text Alignment = **Center**
Text Control = **Wrap Text**
and **Merge Cell.**

Click **OK.**

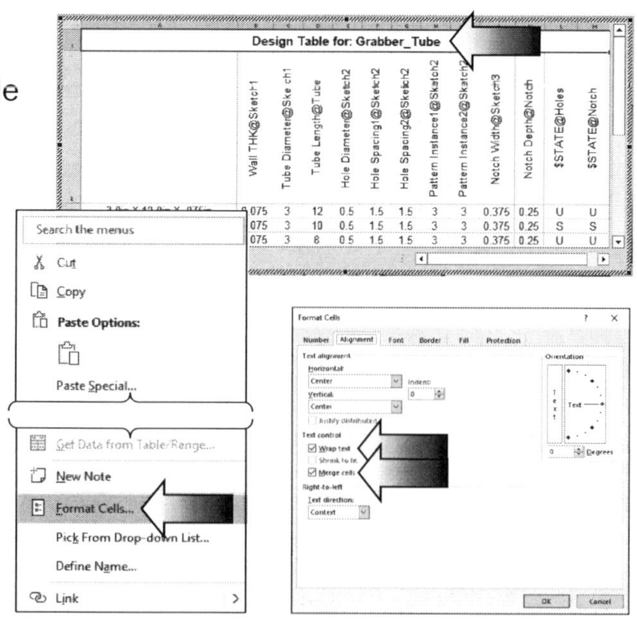

13. Switching back to the drawing:

It would be impractical if Row 2 were rotated and aligned horizontally; the Design Table will be too long to fit in a drawing. We will leave Row 2 the way it is for this exercise.

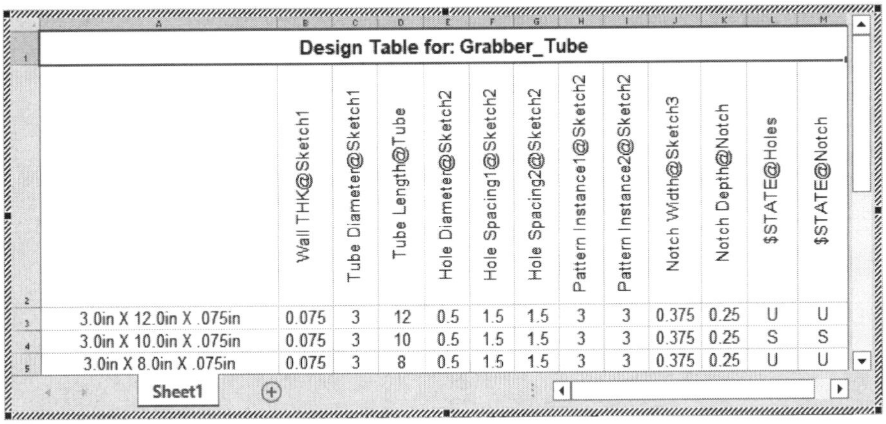

Design Table for: Grabber_Tube												
	Wall THK@Sketch1	Tube Diameter@Sketch1	Tube Length@Tube	Hole Diameter@Sketch2	Hole Spacing1@Sketch2	Hole Spacing2@Sketch2	Pattern Instance1@Sketch2	Pattern Instance2@Sketch2	Notch Width@Sketch3	Notch Depth@Notch	$STATE@Holes	$STATE@Notch
3.0in X 12.0in X .075in	0.075	3	12	0.5	1.5	1.5	3	3	0.375	0.25	U	U
3.0in X 10.0in X .075in	0.075	3	10	0.5	1.5	1.5	3	3	0.375	0.25	S	S
3.0in X 8.0in X .075in	0.075	3	8	0.5	1.5	1.5	3	3	0.375	0.25	U	U

Make any adjustments as needed to the Design Table before switching back to the drawing.

Click in the SOLIDWORKS background to bring the drawing back to the front.

Click **Rebuild** (or Control + B) to refresh and update the Design Table.

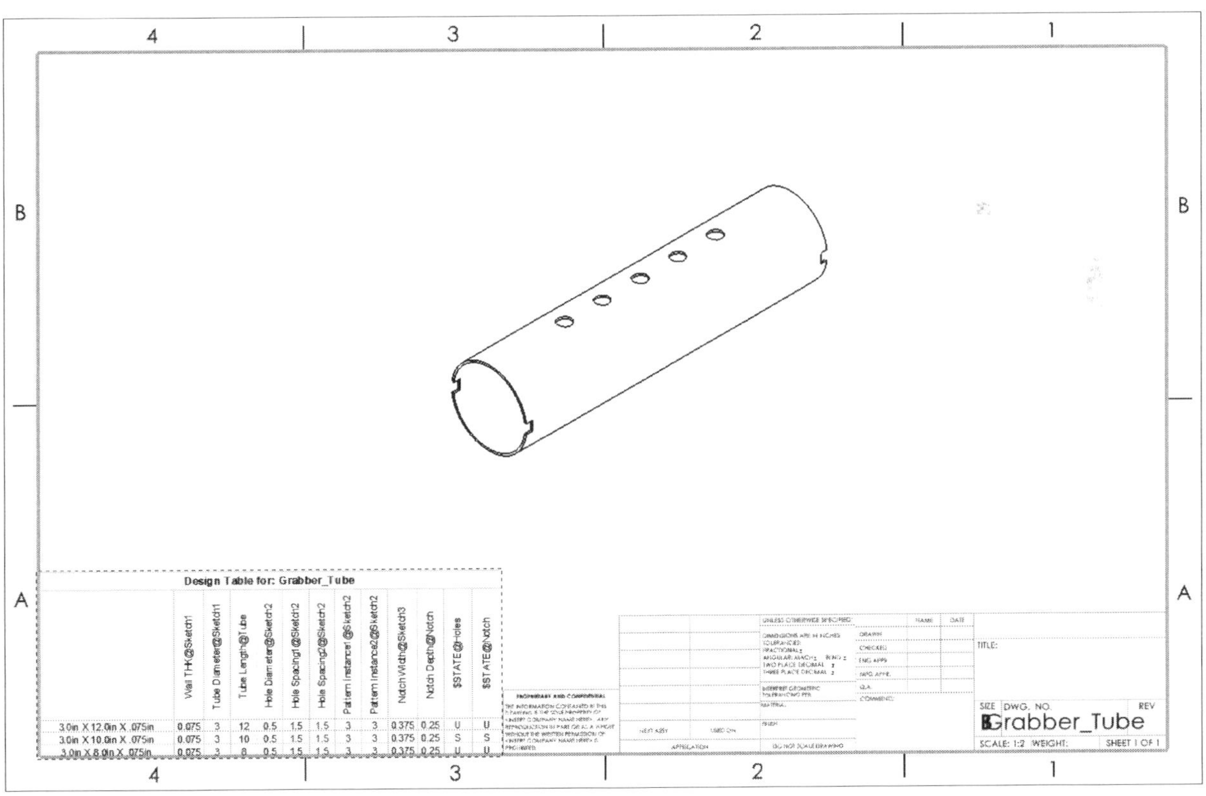

14. Filling out the Title Block information:

From the **FeatureManager** tree, expand **Sheet1** and double-click **Sheet Format1** to activate it for editing the Title Block.

Fill out the information shown below.

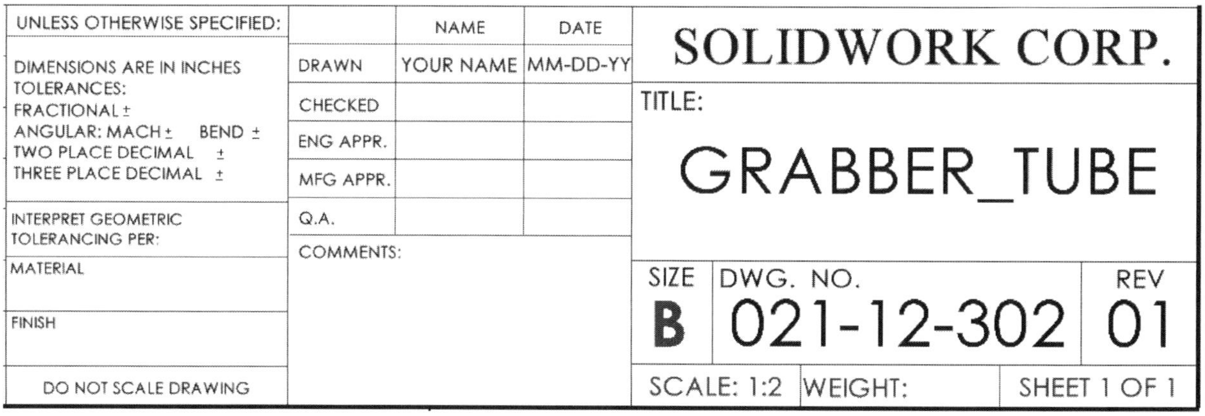

When finished, double-click on **Sheet1** to bring the drawing back to the front.

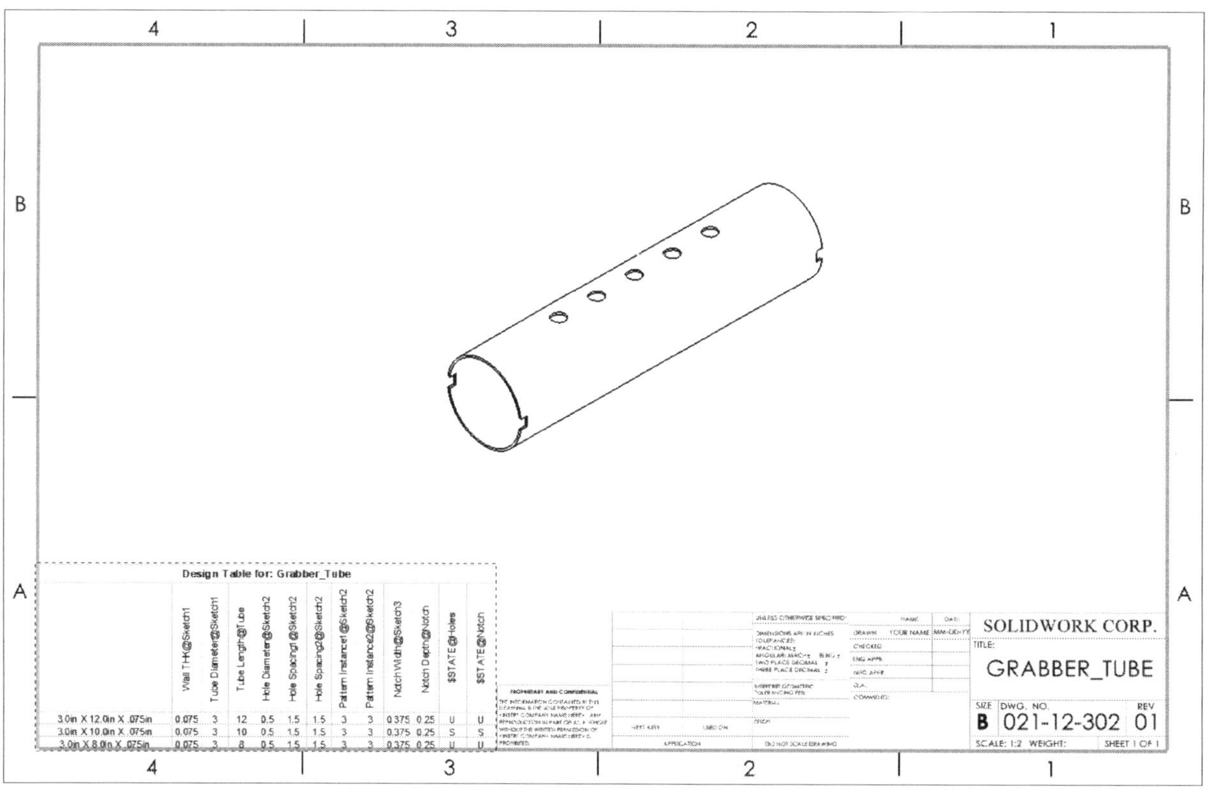

15. Creating a Tabulated Table:

Design Table is one of the great tools to create and manage configurations, but when displaying in a drawing, it needs to be made as clear as possible.

We will continue to customize the Design Table a little bit more so that it will be easier to read for everyone else.

Double-click inside the Design Table to launch MS-Excel again, for editing.

Right-click inside cell A2 and select **Insert** (arrow).

A new row is added. We will use this row to add the column headers.

Click inside the new row A2 and type: **Configuration**.

For row B2, enter: **Wall Thickness**.

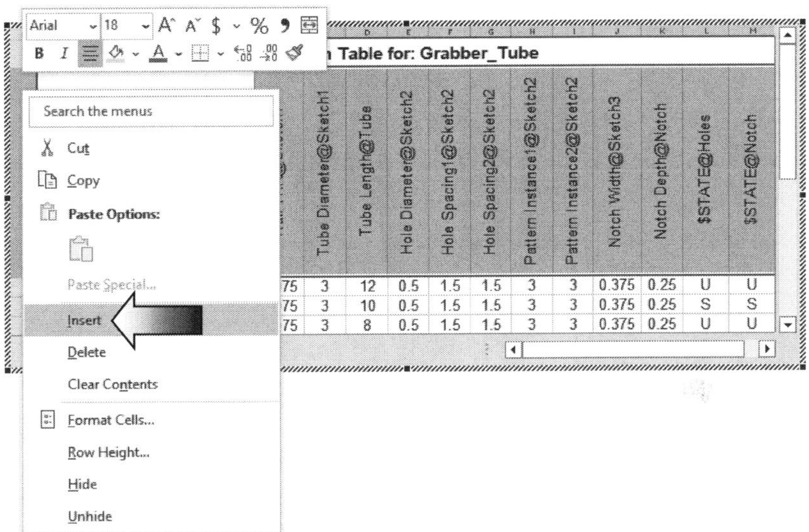

Repeat the step above to label the other columns:

C2 = Tube Diameter **D2 = Tube Length** **E2 = Hole Diameter**
F2 = Hole Spacing 1 **G2 = Hole Spacing 2** **H2 = Pattern Inst. 1**
I2 = Pattern Inst. 2
J2 = Notch Width
K2 = Notch Depth

Hide columns **L** and **H**

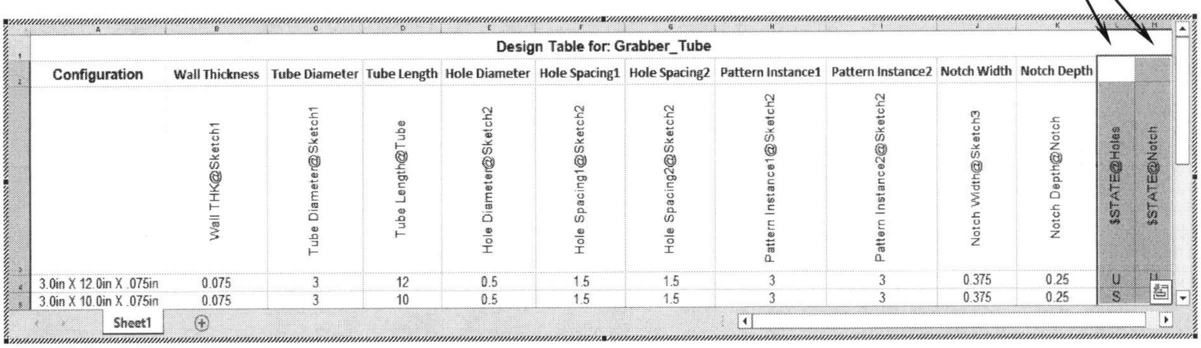

The previous row 2 (now row 3) is no longer needed. Right-click row 3 and select **Hide.**

Design Table for: Grabber_Tube										
Configuration	Wall Thickness	Tube Diameter	Tube Length	Hole Diameter	Hole Spacing1	Hole Spacing2	Pattern Instance1	Pattern Instance2	Notch Width	Notch Depth
3.0in X 12.0in X .075in	0.075	3	12	0.5	1.5	1.5	3	3	0.375	0.25
3.0in X 10.0in X .075in	0.075	3	10	0.5	1.5	1.5	3	3	0.375	0.25
3.0in X 8.0in X .075in	0.075	3	8	0.5	1.5	1.5	3	3	0.375	0.25

Sheet1

OPTIONAL: At this time, the table is called Tabulated Table, and it is much easier to read now than before. Colors and borders can also be added to further enhance the table's appearance and visibility.

Design Table for: Grabber_Tube										
Configuration	Wall Thickness	Tube Diameter	Tube Length	Hole Diameter	Hole Spacing1	Hole Spacing2	Pattern Instance1	Pattern Instance2	Notch Width	Notch Depth
3.0in X 12.0in X .075in	**0.075**	**3**	**12**	**0.5**	**1.5**	**1.5**	**3**	**3**	**0.375**	**0.25**
3.0in X 10.0in X .075in	**0.075**	**3**	**10**	**0.5**	**1.5**	**1.5**	**3**	**3**	**0.375**	**0.25**
3.0in X 8.0in X .075in	**0.075**	**3**	**8**	**0.5**	**1.5**	**1.5**	**3**	**3**	**0.375**	**0.25**

Sheet1

Switch back to the drawing and click **Rebuild** to update the Tabulated Table.

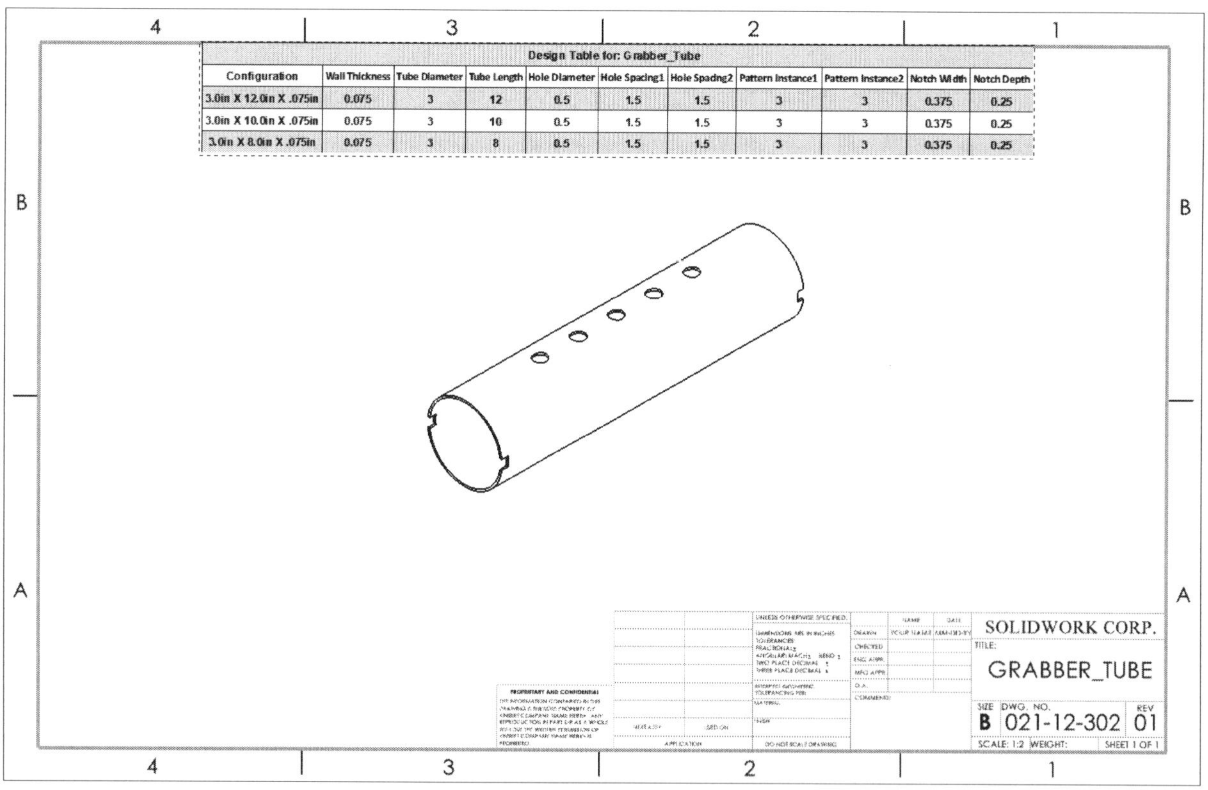

16. Saving your work:

Select **File, Save As**.

Enter: **Tube Grabber_Design Table.slddrw** for the file name.

Click **Save**.

Exercise: Design Tables

Creating a Tabulated Table

The exercises are designed to help you apply what you have learned from the previous lessons. They come with some instructions but not as detailed as the lessons, to give you an opportunity to explore and to try and create the drawings on your own, at your own pace.

1. Opening a part document:

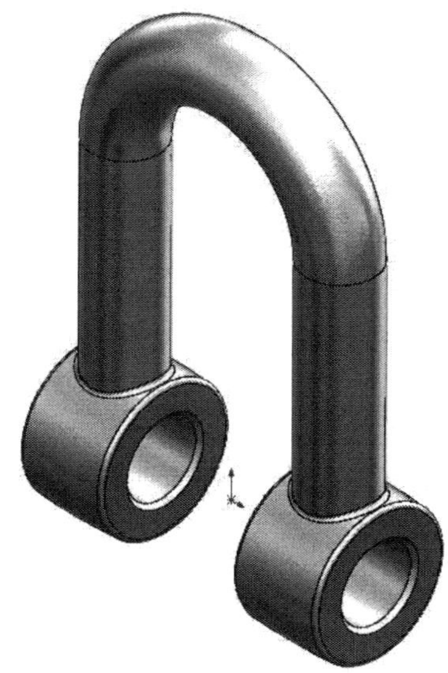

Select **File, Open.**

Browse to the Training Folder and open a part document named: **Lift Ring.sldprt.**

The part contains 4 configurations and the material **Cast Alloy Steel** has already been assigned to it.

2. Inserting a Design Table:

Select: **Insert, Tables, Excel Design Table.**

Click the **Auto-Create** button and click **OK.**

All existing configurations in the model are exported to the Excel worksheet.

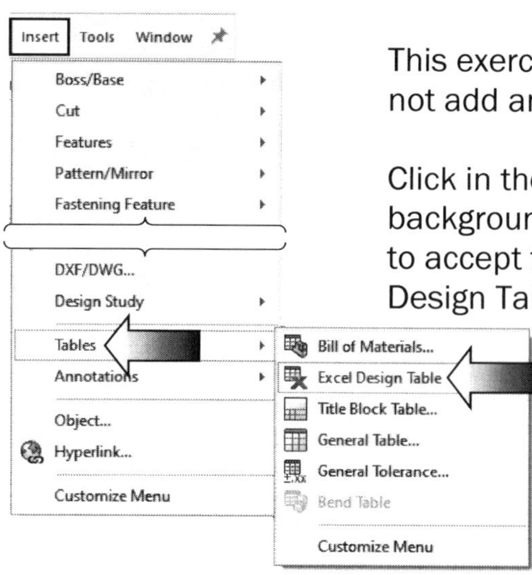

This exercise focuses on creating a Tabulated Table; we will not add any new configurations.

Click in the background to accept the Design Table.

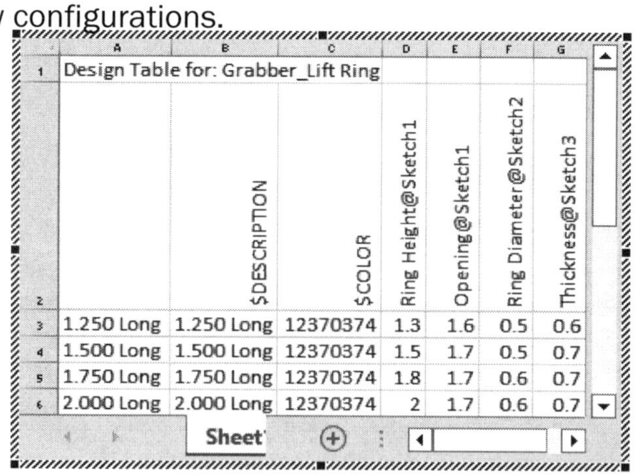

	A	B	C	D	E	F	G
1	Design Table for: Grabber_Lift Ring						
2		$DESCRIPTION	$COLOR	Ring Height@Sketch1	Opening@Sketch1	Ring Diameter@Sketch2	Thickness@Sketch3
3	1.250 Long	1.250 Long	12370374	1.3	1.6	0.5	0.6
4	1.500 Long	1.500 Long	12370374	1.5	1.7	0.5	0.7
5	1.750 Long	1.750 Long	12370374	1.8	1.7	0.6	0.7
6	2.000 Long	2.000 Long	12370374	2	1.7	0.6	0.7

The magenta (pink) color dimensions are the ones that have been linked to the Design Table. Changes can now be made bi-directionally.

Switch to the Configuration-Manager tree and expand the Tables folder to see the Design Table.

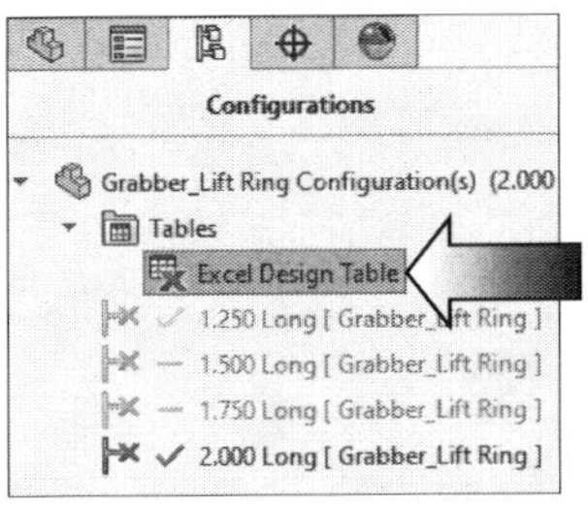

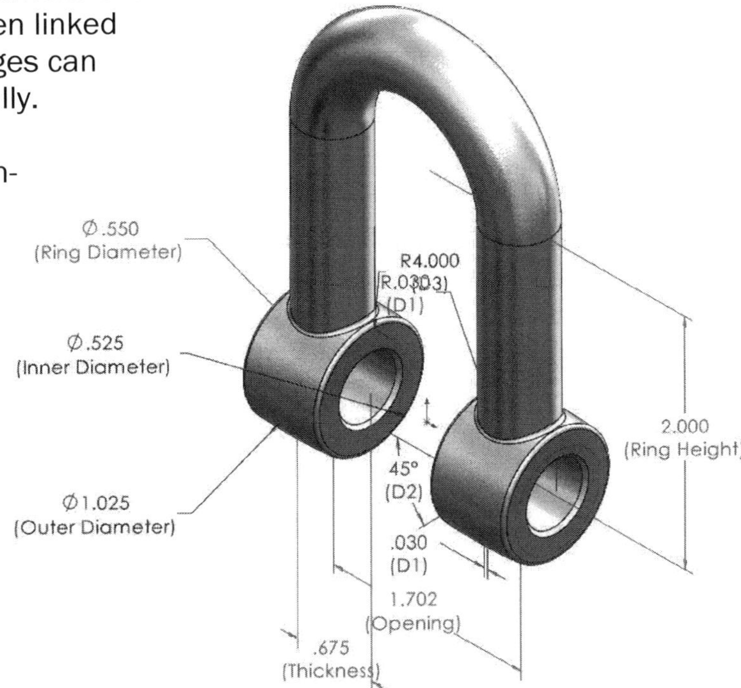

3. Transferring to a drawing:

Select **File, Make Drawing from Part.**

Select the **B (ANDSI) Landscape** drawing sheet.

Set the Type-Of-Projection to **3rd Angle**.

Set Scale to **1:1**.

Keep all other parameters at their defaults.

Click **OK**.

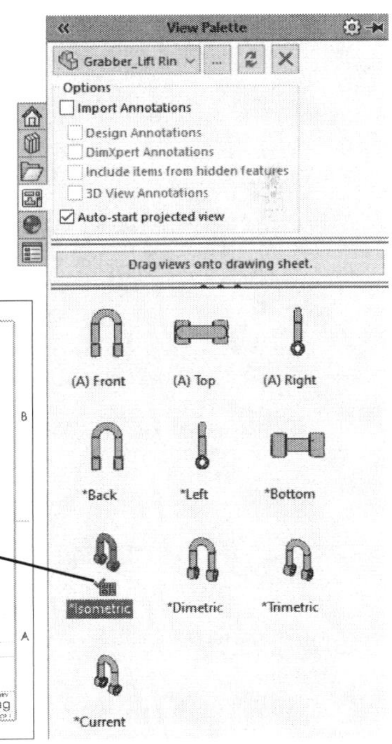

Drag and drop the Isometric view to the middle of the drawing as shown on the right.

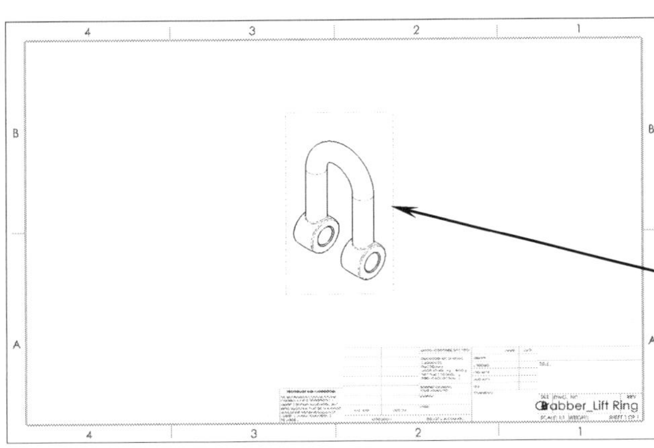

4. Inserting the Design Table:

Click the dotted border of the Isometric view and select:
Annotation, Tables, Design Table.

The Design Table from the model is inserted the way it was created in Excel. We will modify the table and make it look more like a Tabulated Table.

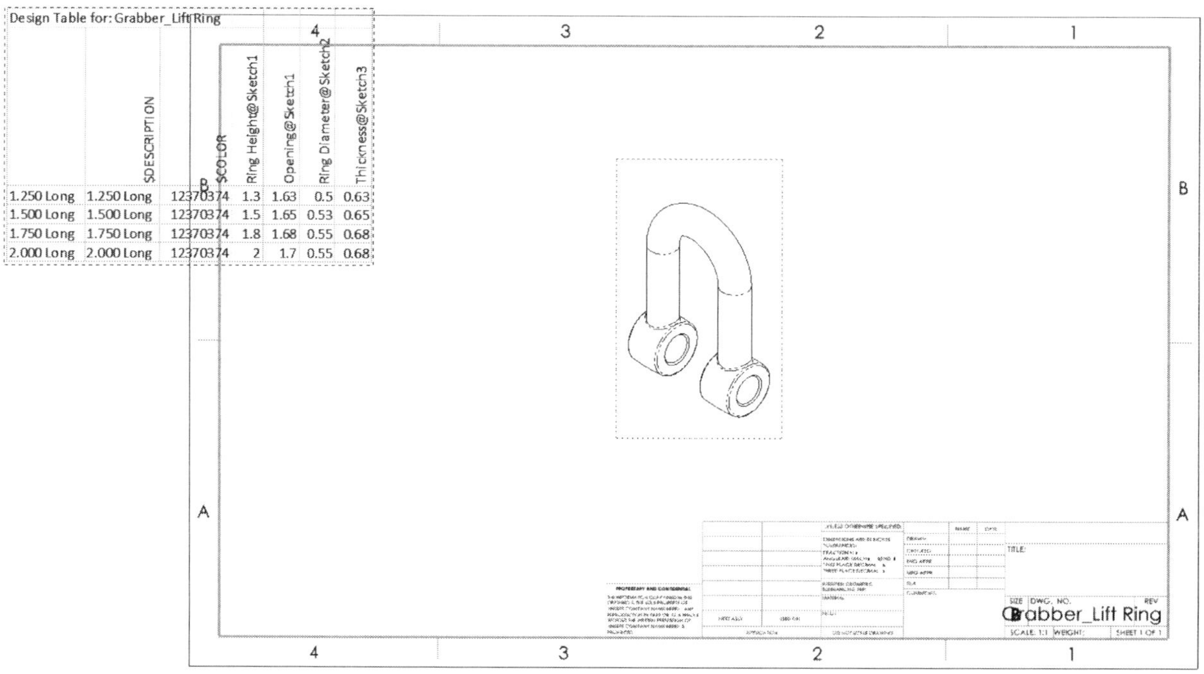

Double-click inside the table to launch the MS-Excel application for editing.

Modify the table to include the following:

*** Center the Row 1 header.**

*** Hide both columns: Color and the 2nd Configuration.**

*** Insert a new row above row 2 and add the column headers as shown.**

*** Hide row 3 (was row 2).**

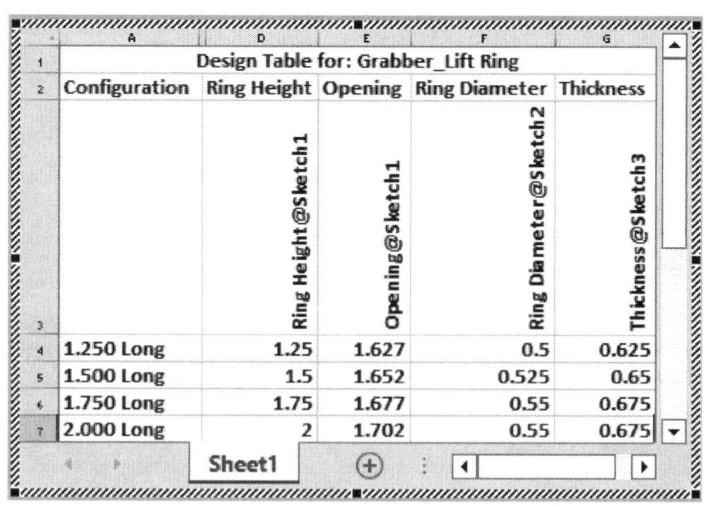

The revised table should look like the image shown on the right.

Click in the background to exit out of Excel and return to SOLIDWORKS.

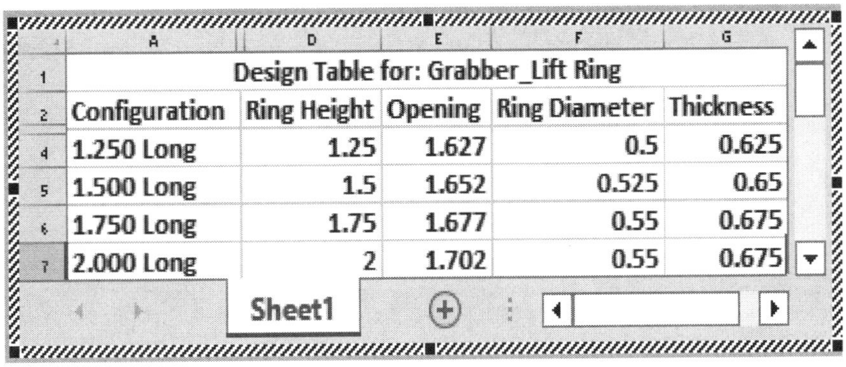

Design Table for: Grabber_Lift Ring				
Configuration	Ring Height	Opening	Ring Diameter	Thickness
1.250 Long	1.25	1.627	0.5	0.625
1.500 Long	1.5	1.652	0.525	0.65
1.750 Long	1.75	1.677	0.55	0.675
2.000 Long	2	1.702	0.55	0.675

5. Switching back to drawing:

Press **Control + Tab** to switch back to the drawing or click the Windows drop-down menu and select the current drawing from the list.

Click **Rebuild** to refresh the drawing and update the Tabulated table.

Move the Tabulated table to the upper left corner of the drawing.

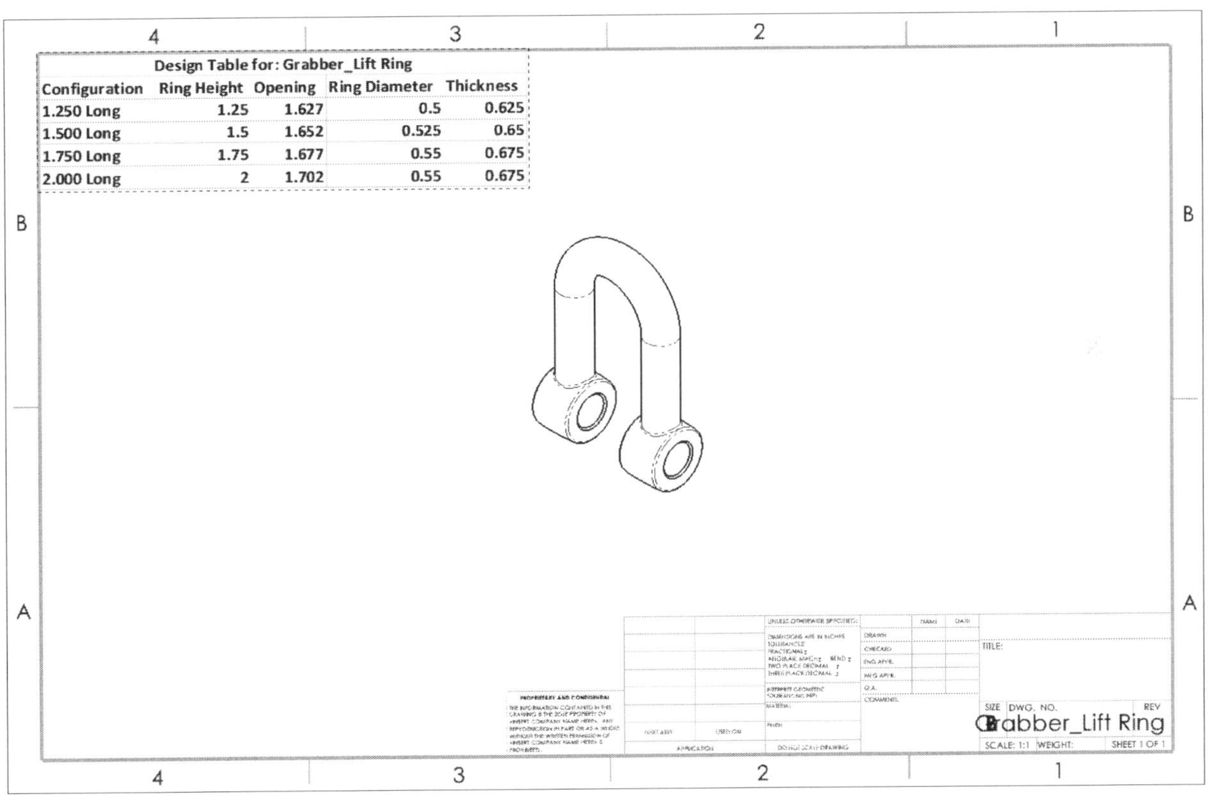

Design Table for: Grabber_Lift Ring				
Configuration	Ring Height	Opening	Ring Diameter	Thickness
1.250 Long	1.25	1.627	0.5	0.625
1.500 Long	1.5	1.652	0.525	0.65
1.750 Long	1.75	1.677	0.55	0.675
2.000 Long	2	1.702	0.55	0.675

Additional drawing views can be added to show other configurations if needed.

6. Saving your work:

Select **File, Save As.**

Enter **Grabber_Lift Ring.slddrw** for the file name.

Click **Save.**

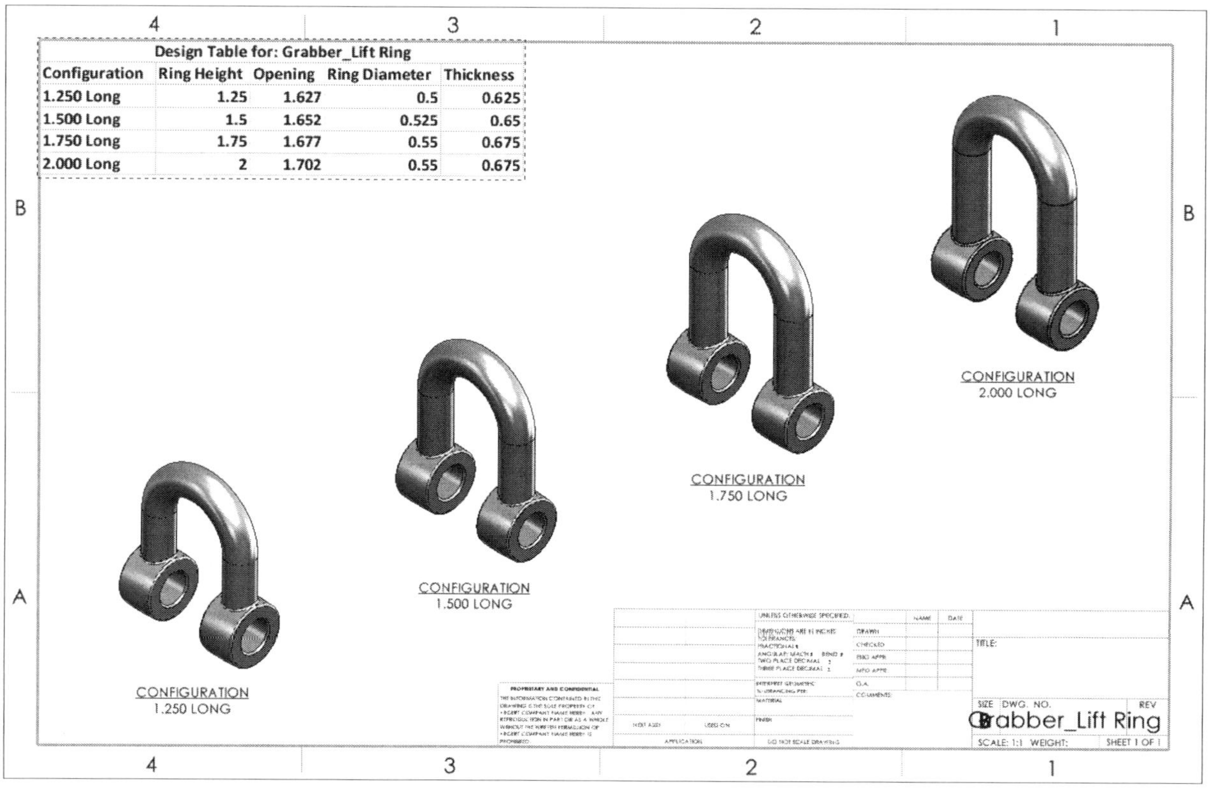

Close all documents.

CHAPTER 11: ADDITIONAL DRAWING TOOLS

Detailing the Base Mount Block

This chapter will teach us how to use the other drawing tools that are quite useful when detailing parts with patterned features and the unique drawing views such as Auxiliary View, Broken-Out Section View, Detail View, Parametric Notes, etc.
Other related tools like Hatch Patterns, Insert Model Items, Centerlines and Center marks are also reviewed throughout the chapter as well.

1. Opening a part document:

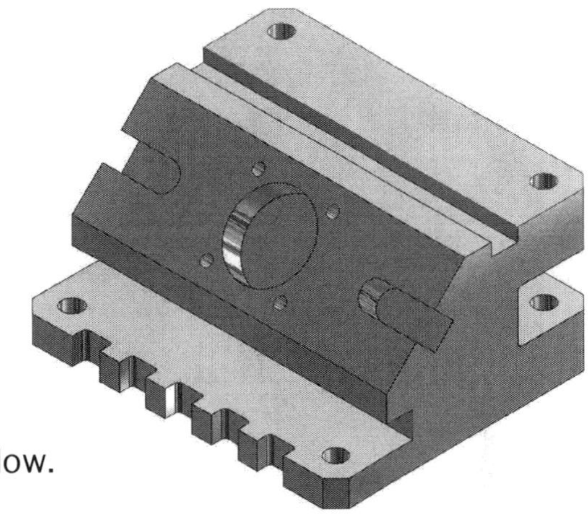

Select **File, Open**.

Navigate to the training folder and open the part document named: **Base Mount Block.sldprt**.

We will need to create an engineering drawing that looks like the one shown below.

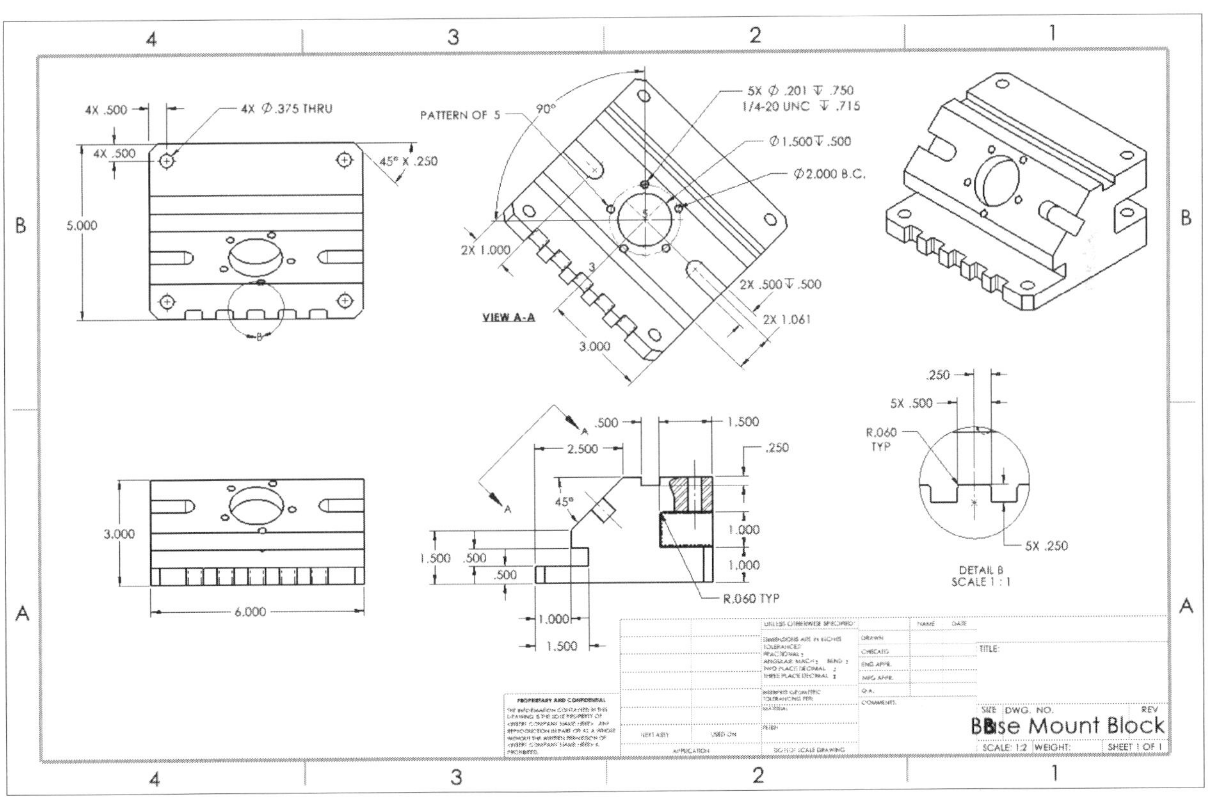

2. Adding the standard drawing views:

Start with the standard views such as the Front view, the Top, the Right, and the Isometric views, and then we can decide which other drawing views we may need to detail the other features.

Click the **View Palette** icon on the **Task Pane**. Select the part **Base Mount Block** from the drop-down list if the drawing views are not available.

Enable only the checkbox for **Auto-Start Projected View** and clear the others.

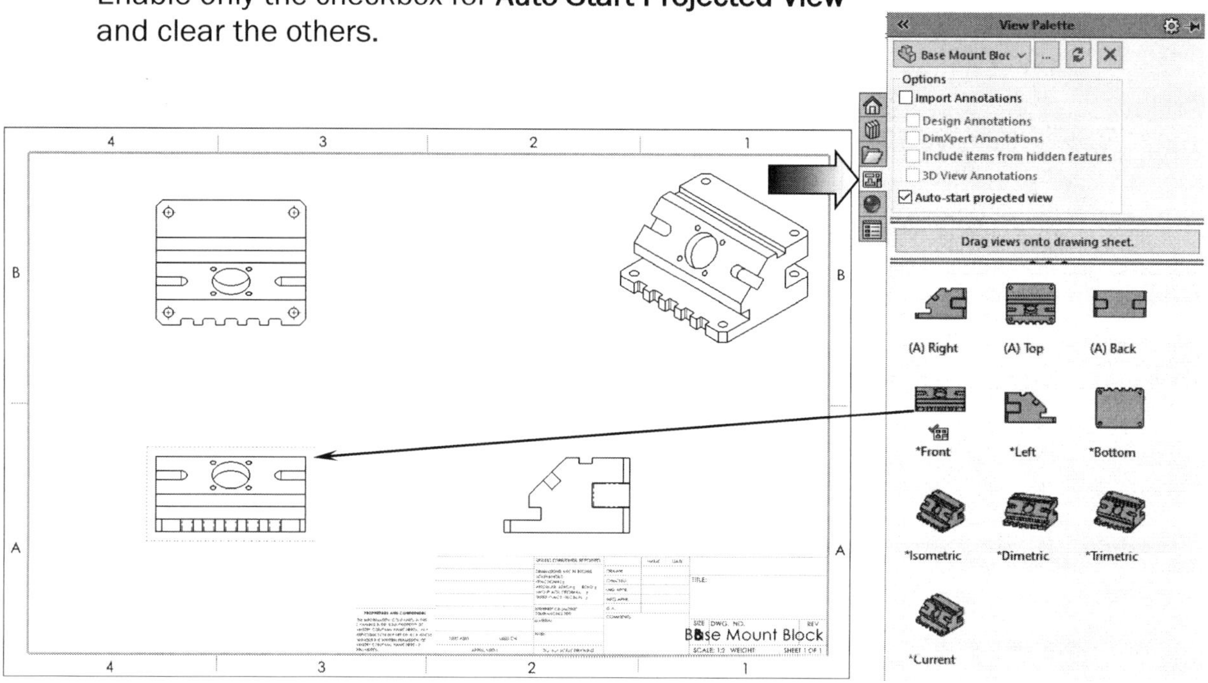

Drag the **Front** view into the drawing sheet first, and then the **Top** view, **Right** view, and the **Isometric** view after.

The Front, Top, and Right views are aligned with one another automatically. The Isometric view is free to move independently.

Move the Isometric view to the upper right corner of the sheet; we need to create some room for other drawing views, without having to create additional drawing sheets.

3. Creating an auxiliary view:

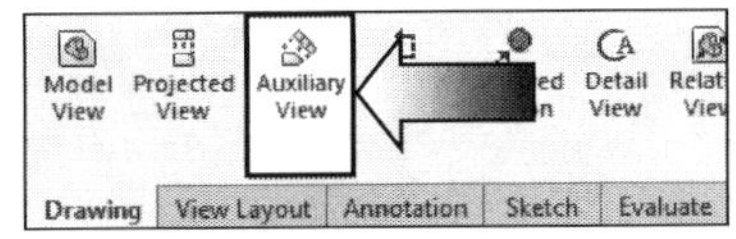

An Auxiliary view is used to project a view normal to a reference edge in an existing view.

Select the <u>angled edge</u> as indicated.

Switch to the **Drawing** tab and click: **Auxiliary**.

An Auxiliary drawing view is created normal to the selected edge. Place it on the <u>upper left side</u> of the Right drawing view.

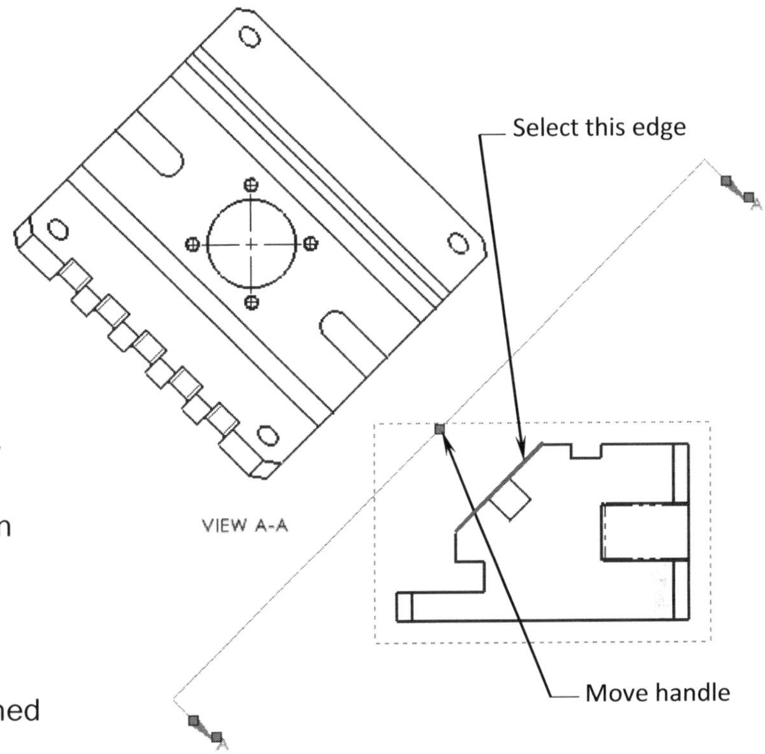

The Auxiliary view is aligned normal to the selected edge and can only be moved along the constrained direction. We will need to break this alignment so that the drawing view can be moved freely.

Drag the <u>square handle</u> as noted, to shorten the projection line (you can also hide it by unchecking the **Arrow** checkbox on the FeatureManager tree).

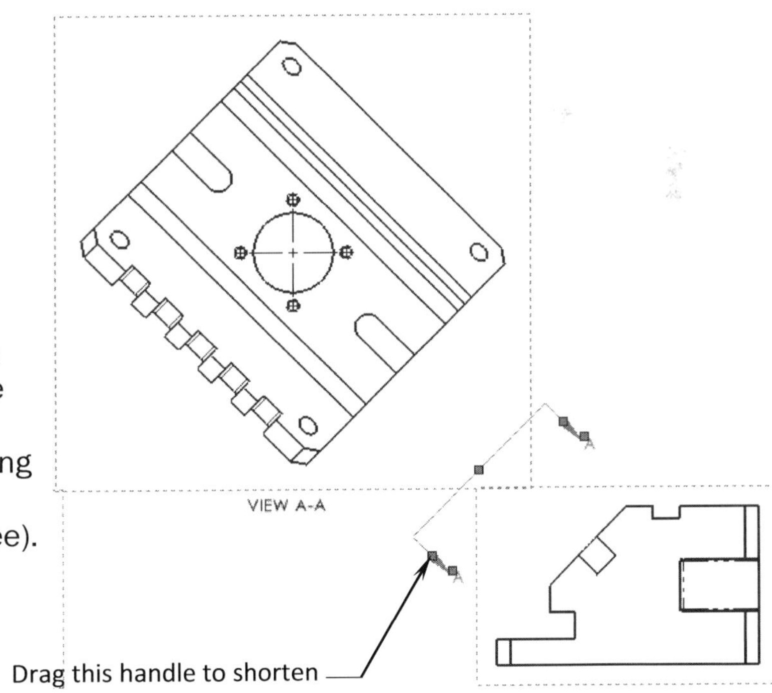

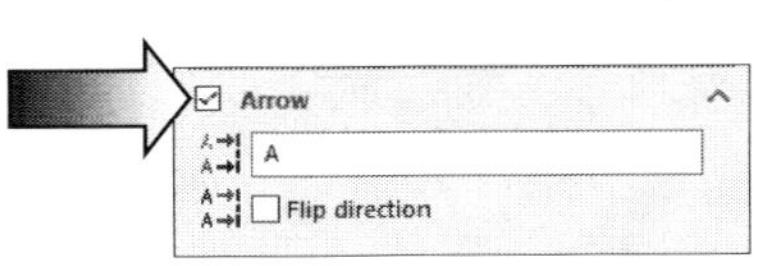

4. Breaking the view alignment:

Any drawing view's alignment can be broken or realigned at any time.

Right-click the dotted border of the Auxiliary drawing view and select: **Alignment, Break Alignment.**

Drag the dotted border of the Auxiliary view to test out its alignment. It should be able to move freely now.

Move the Auxiliary view approximately as shown in the drawing below.

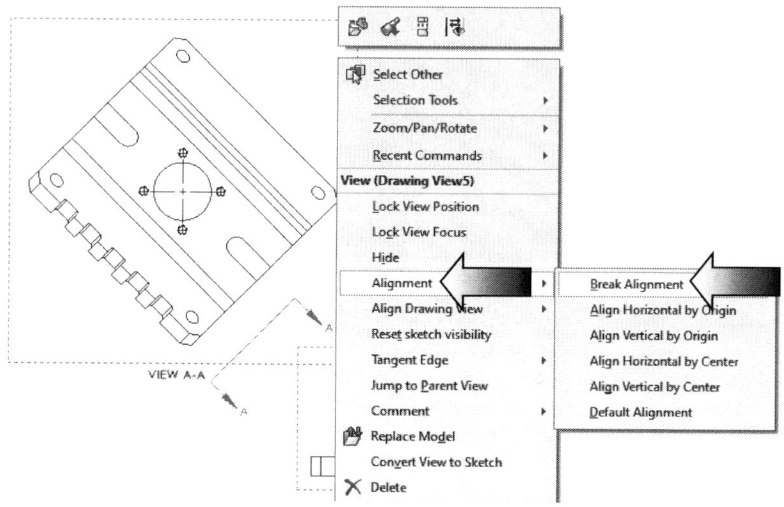

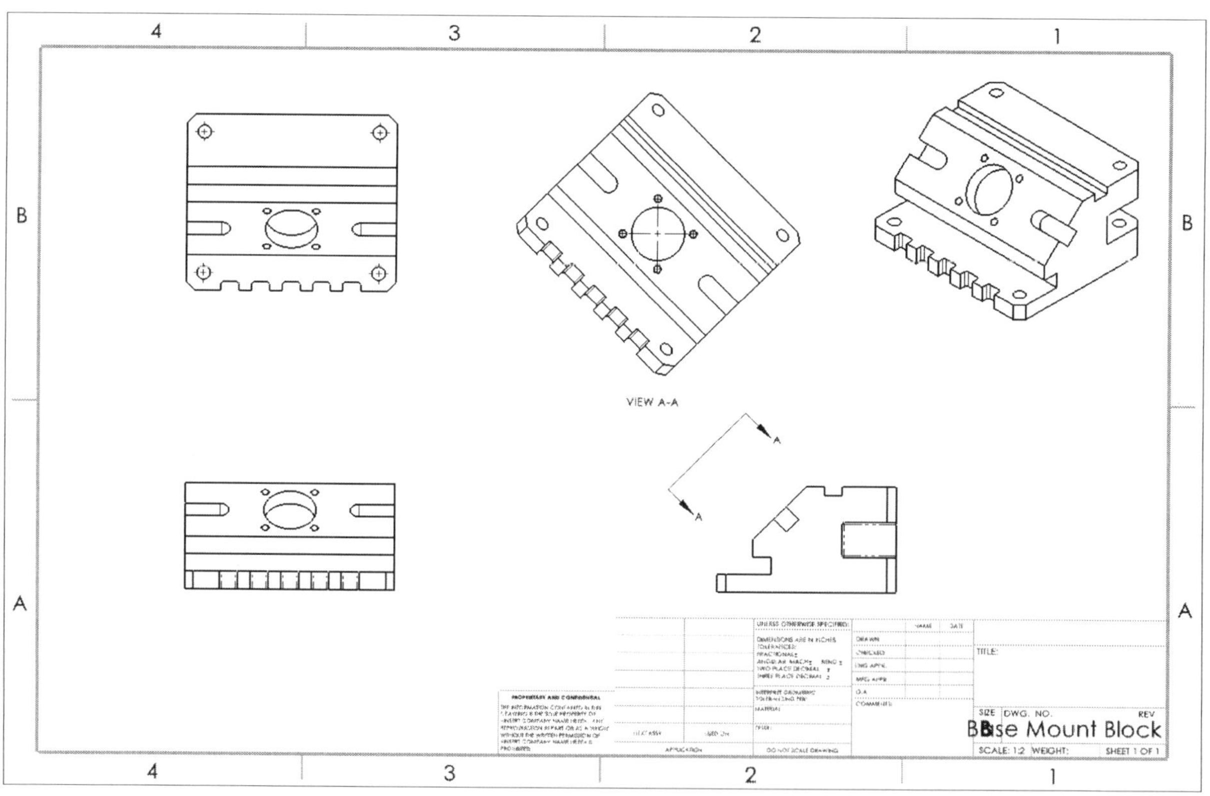

5. Creating a broken-out section:

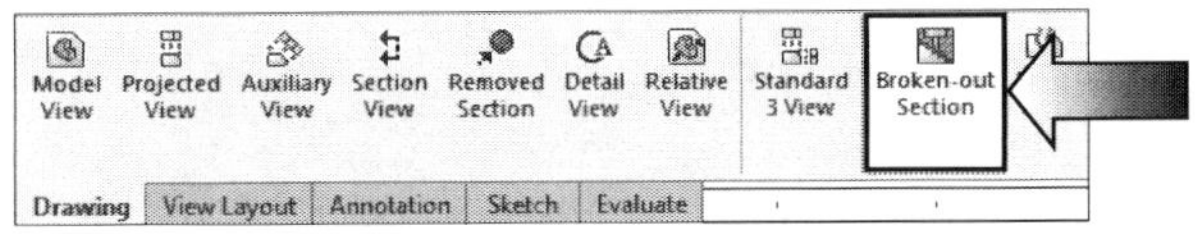

A broken-out section view cuts away a portion of a part in a drawing view to expose the inside details. Cross hatching is automatically generated on the sectioned faces.

A broken-out section is part of an existing drawing view, not a separate view.
A closed profile, usually a spline, defines the broken-out section. Material is removed to a specified depth to expose inner details. Specify the depth by setting a number or by selecting geometry in a drawing view.

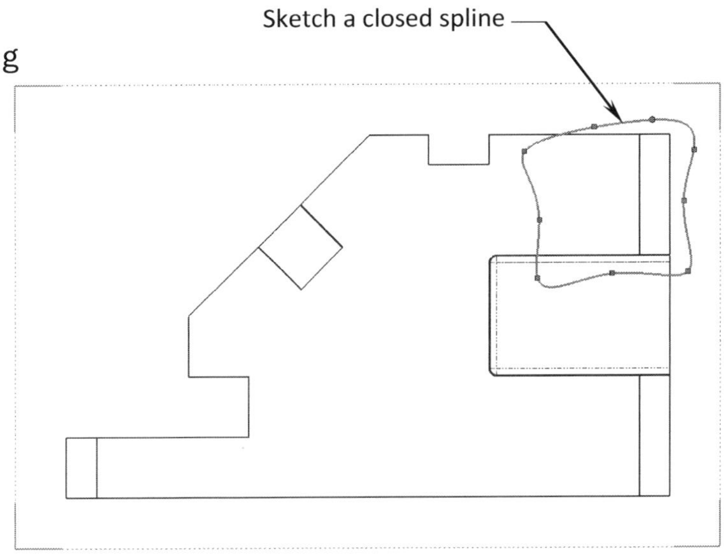

Click the dotted border of the **Right** view to activate it.

Switch to the **Sketch** tab and sketch a closed spline as shown above.

Switch to the **Drawing** tab and click **Broken-Out Section**.

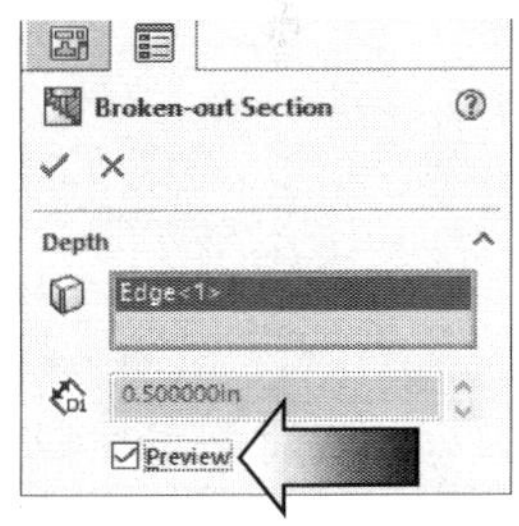

For Depth, select the circular edge of one of the holes as indicated.

Enable the **Preview** checkbox.

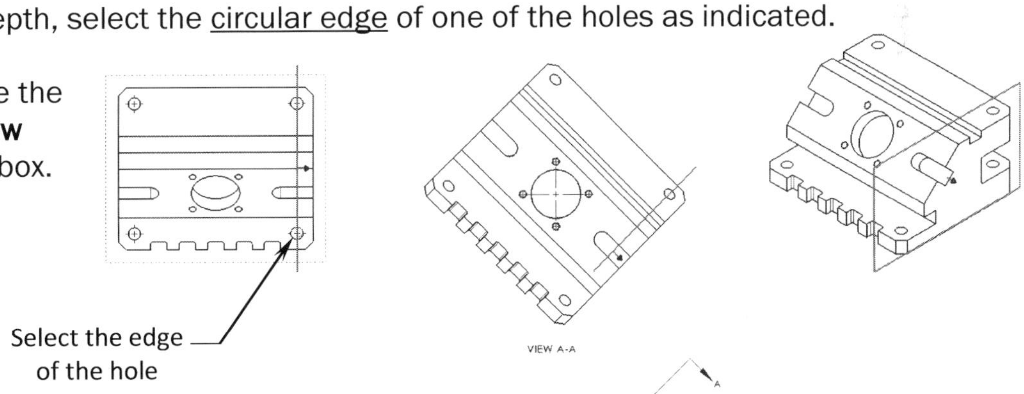

Click **OK**.

6. Modifying the hatch pattern:

The hatch pattern and crosshatch lines should be as clear as possible. One way to enhance the sectioned areas is to increase the scale of the hatch density.

Zoom in on the Right drawing view and click <u>inside</u> the hatch area to access the hatch options.

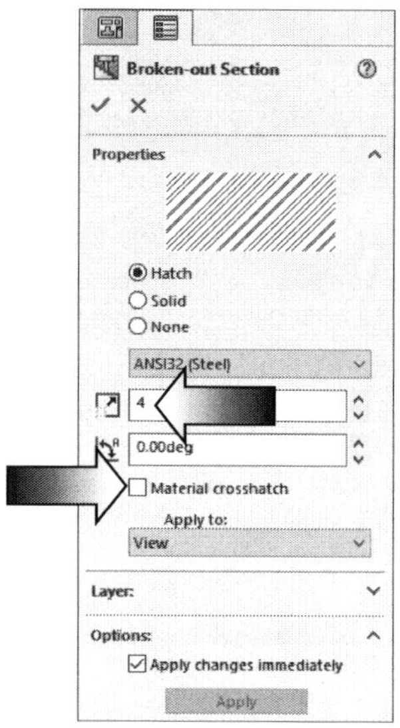

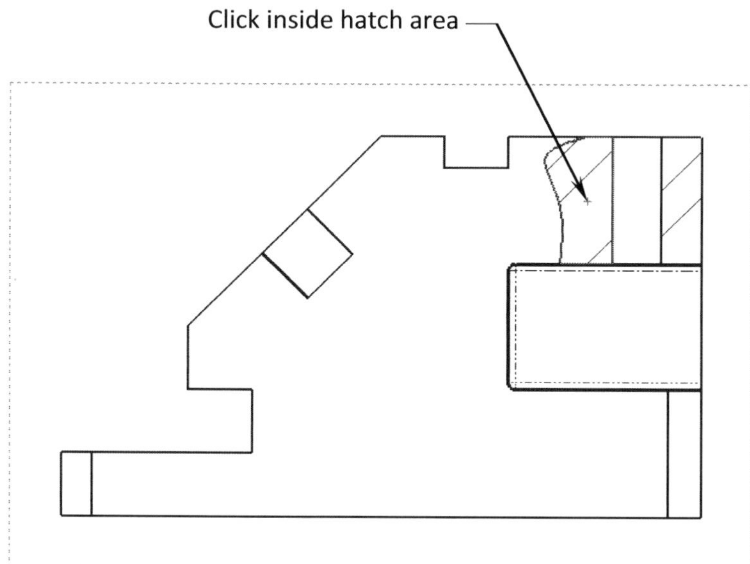

<u>Clear</u> the **Material Crosshatch** checkbox.

Change the Scale to **4**.

Click **OK**.

The Hatch Pattern is defaulted to **ANSI32 (Steel)** because the material was previously selected in the model.

The sectioned areas are much easier to see now.

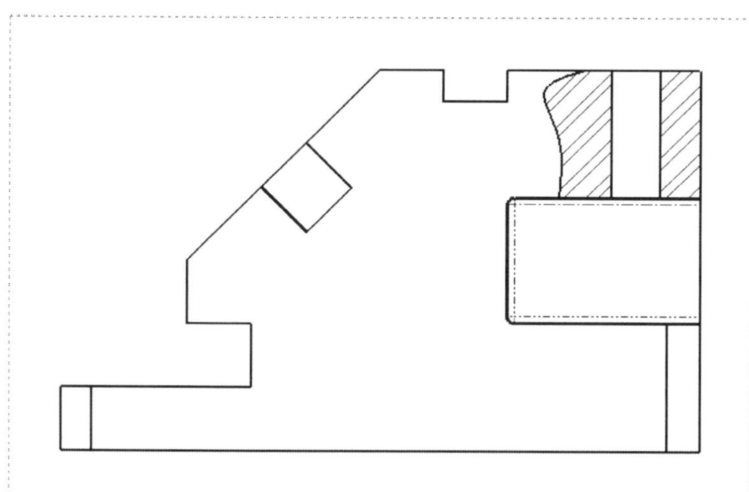

7. Creating a detail view:

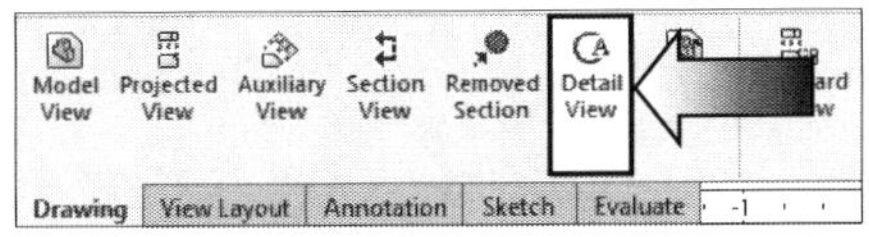

A detail view is created in a drawing to show a portion of a view at an enlarged scale, usually 2 times larger or more.

Click **Detail View** on the **Drawing** tab. The Circle tool is selected automatically.

Sketch a **circle** centered on the notch in the middle of Top drawing view, as shown in the image on the right.

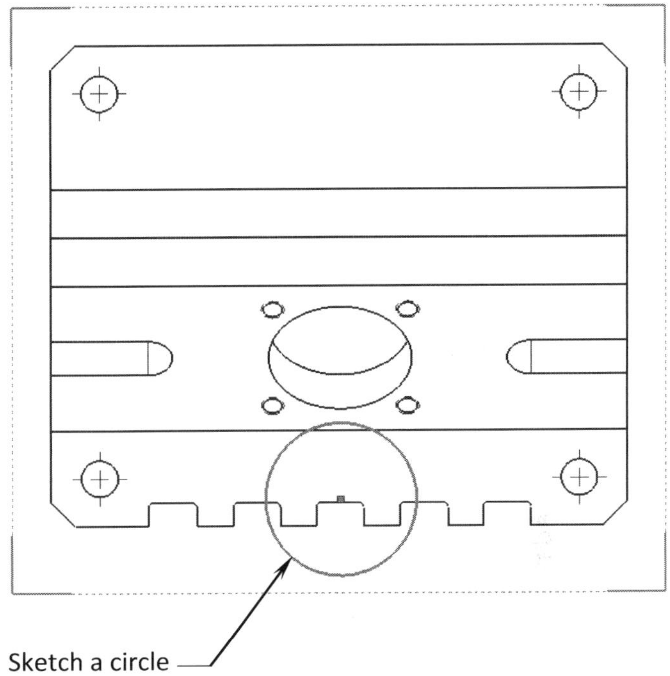

Place the Detail View on the lower right side of the drawing and enable the 2 options:

* **Per Standard**

* **Full Outline**

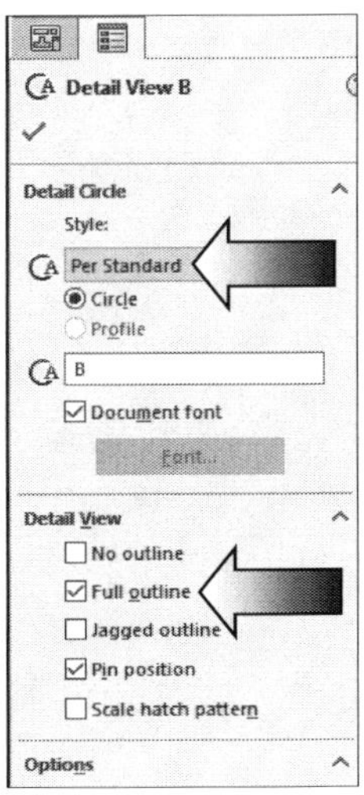

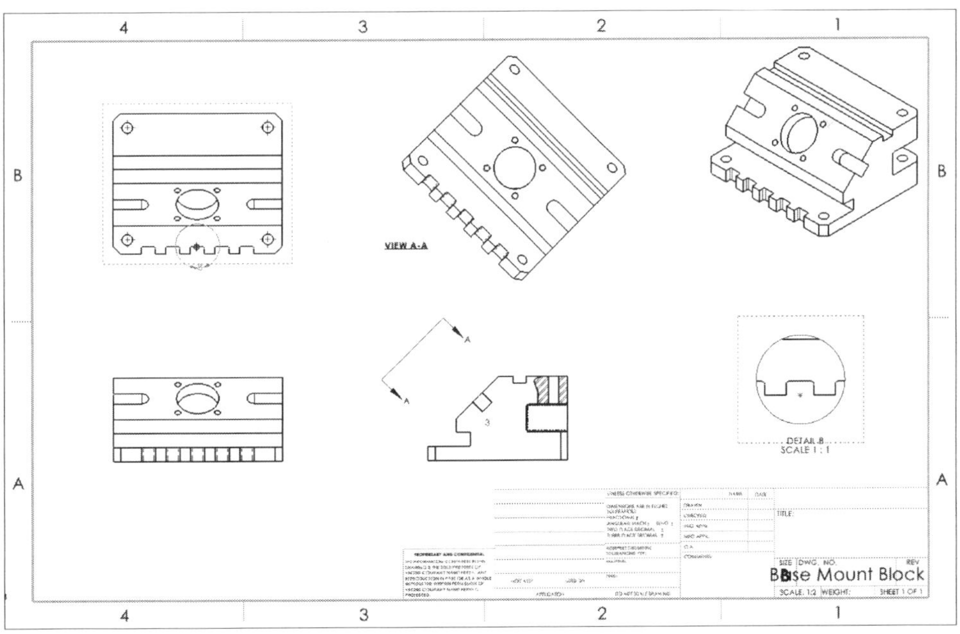

Click **OK**.

8. Adding centerlines and center marks:

Centerlines and Center Marks are annotations that mark the centers of circles or arc centers.

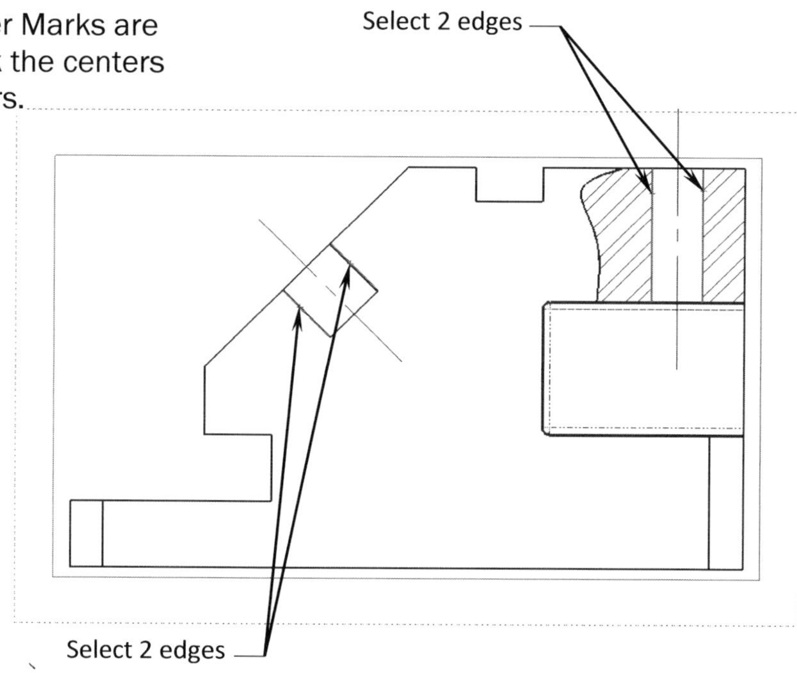

They are used to identify the hole locations in the model with dimensions.

Switch to the **Annotation** tab.

Click **Centerline**.

Select 2 edges that represent the hole feature. A centerline is added between the 2 selected lines.

Add center marks to other holes.

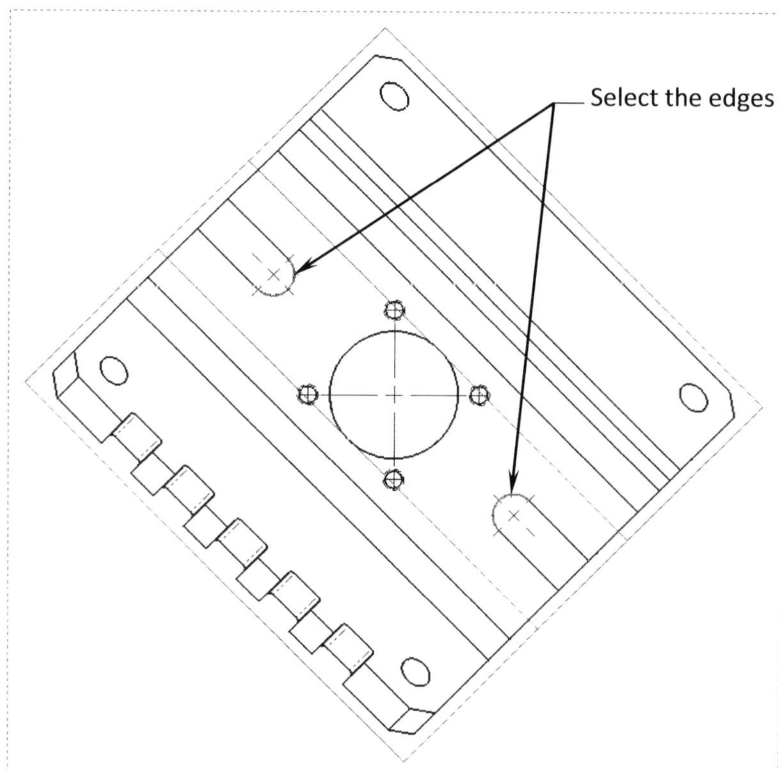

VIEW A-A

Zoom in on the **Auxiliary** view.

Click **Center Mark**.

Select the circular edges of all holes to add the center marks.

9. Inserting the model dimensions:

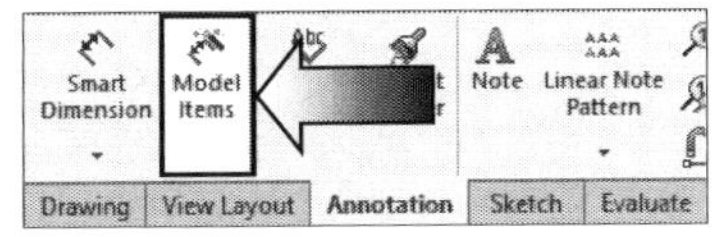

Dimensions in a drawing are associated with the model, and changes in the model are reflected in the drawing.

You would typically create dimensions as you create each feature in a part, then insert those dimensions into the various drawing views. Changing a dimension in the model updates the drawing, and changing an inserted dimension in a drawing changes the model.

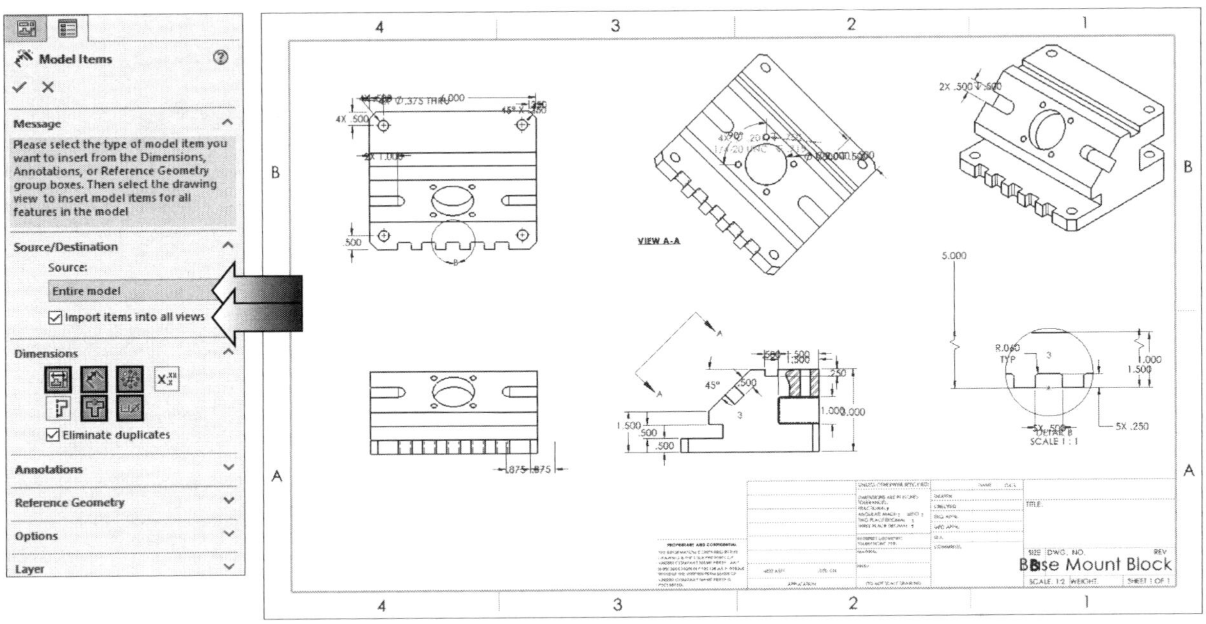

Switch to the **Annotation** tab and click **Model Items.**

For Source, select **Entire model** and <u>enable</u> **Import Items into All Views.**

For Dimensions, select:

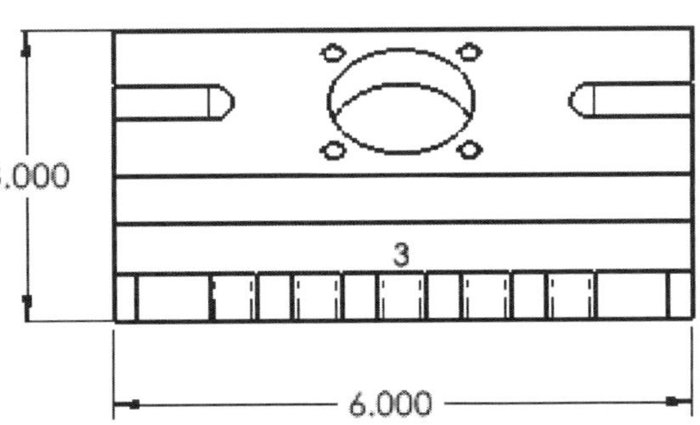

- **Marked for Drawing**
- **Not marked for Drawing**
- **Instance/Revolution Counts**
- **Hole Wizard Locations**
- **Hole Callout**

Click **OK.**

10. Rearranging dimensions:

Dimensions are imported to the drawing views the same way they were created in the model.

The Top plane (or right, or front plane) might have been used several times in the model to create various features. When the dimensions are exported to the drawing, they are all shown overlapping with one another, which can cause some confusion.

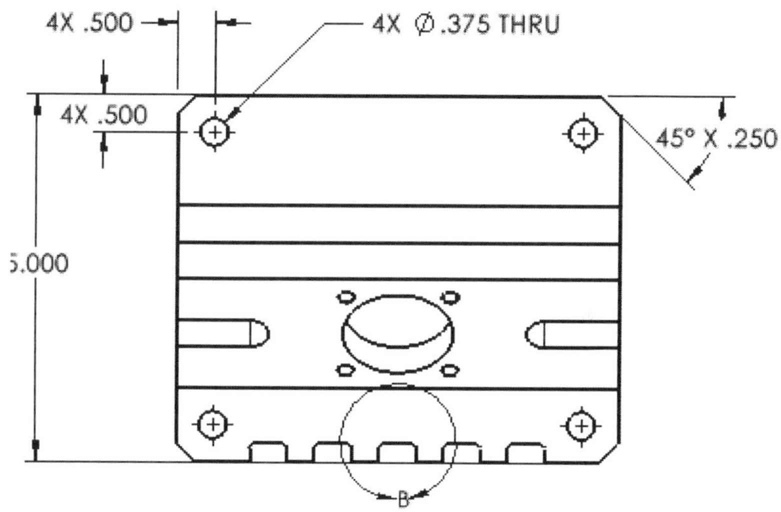

We will need to rearrange the dimensions or to move them to other drawing views to eliminate confusion and also to enhance the clarity of the drawing.

Hold the Shift key and drag the dimensions from one drawing view to another.

Add the instance counts to the dimensions that need it.

The gray color dimensions (the Hole Wizard) means they can only be edited in the model, not in a drawing.

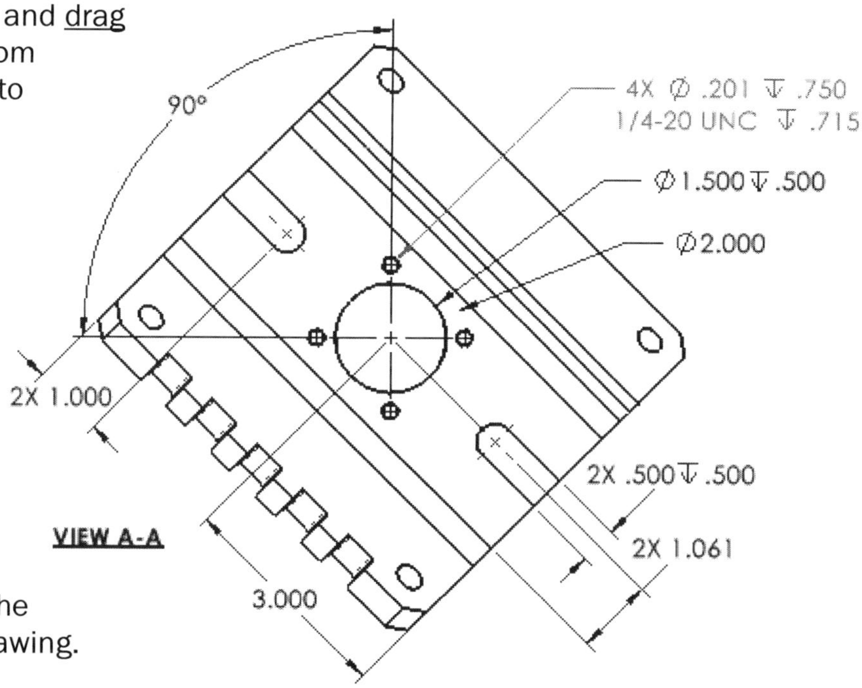

11. Moving dimensions:

Move the dimensions (Shift + drag) from other drawing views to the Right view and make it look similar to the image shown below.

Add any missing dimensions where needed.

Also add the callout **TYP** to the dimension **R.060**.

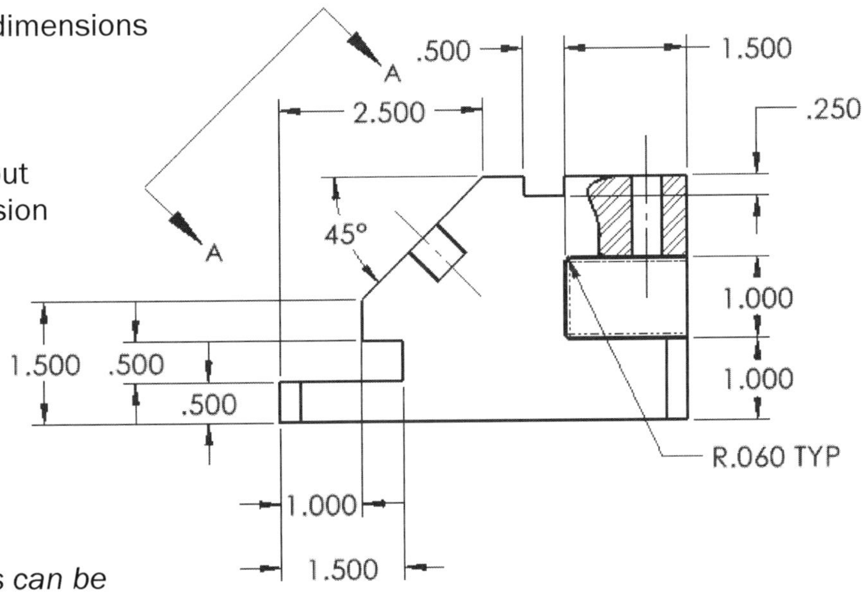

Note: Dimensions can be attached to other entities by dragging/dropping the square-handle at the tip of the arrowhead.

Zoom in on the Detail View.

Add a centerline to the middle of the notch and rearrange the dimensions to look similar to the image shown here.

Add the instance counts and the missing dimensions where needed.

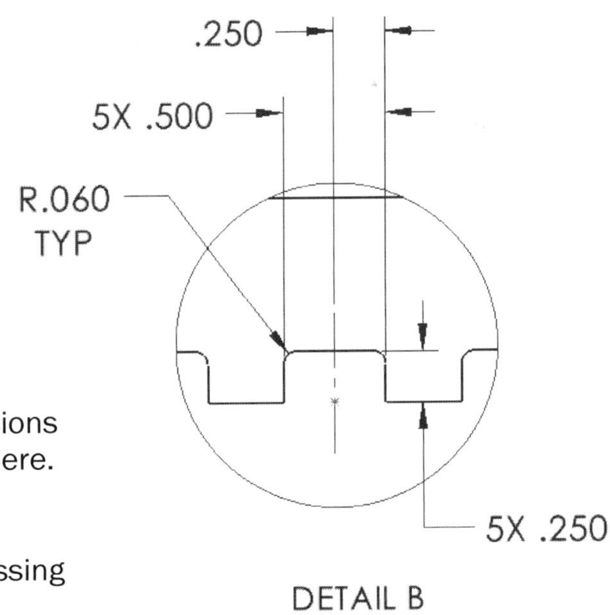

DETAIL B
SCALE 1 : 1

12. Reviewing the drawing:

Press the **F** key on the keyboard to zoom to fit.

Move the drawing views by dragging their dotted borders, and adjust the spacing of the dimensions if needed, so that everything will fit on the sheet.

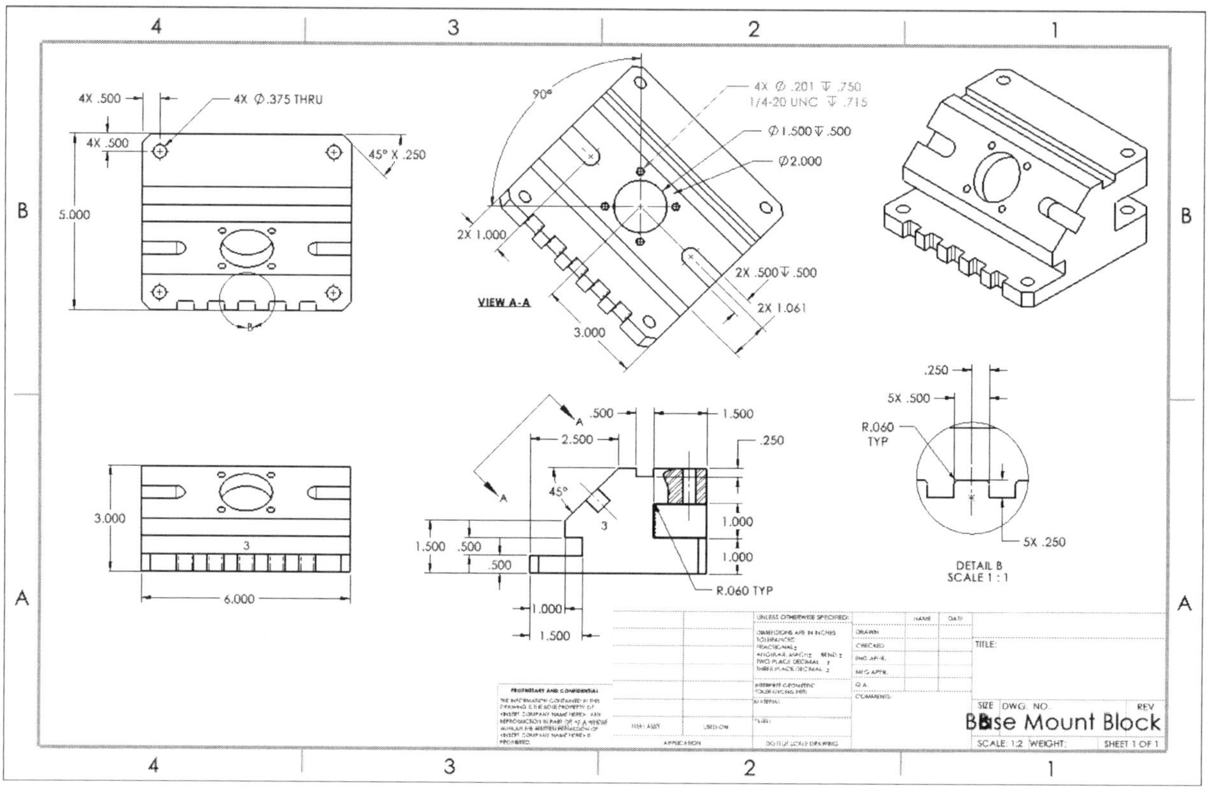

Compare your drawing with the one shown above and see if anything is missing before moving forward to the next step.

There is still more work that needs to be done to the drawing but remember to save your work every once in a while.

13. Changing the color of a dimension:

Although we do not really have to change the color of the Hole Wizard dimensions, changing them to black will make them look more consistent when we print out the drawing.

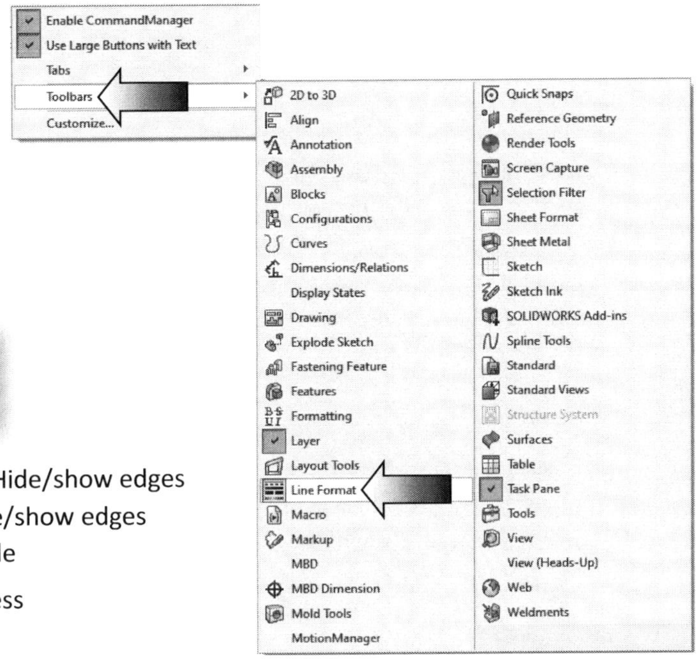

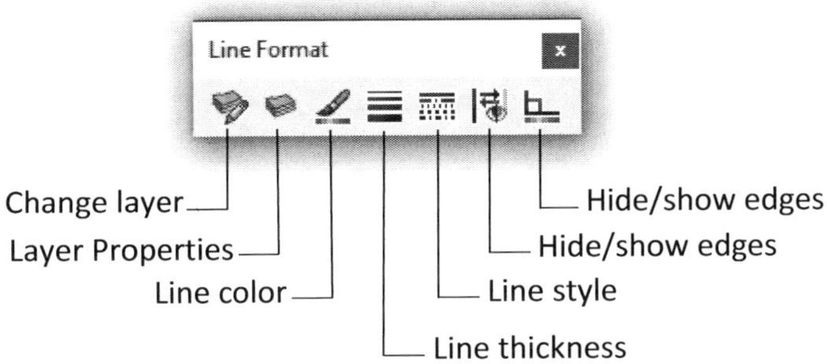

Click **View, Toolbars** and select **Line Format**.

Select the <u>gray</u> Hole Wizard dimension and click **Line Color**.

Select the **Black** color and click **OK**.

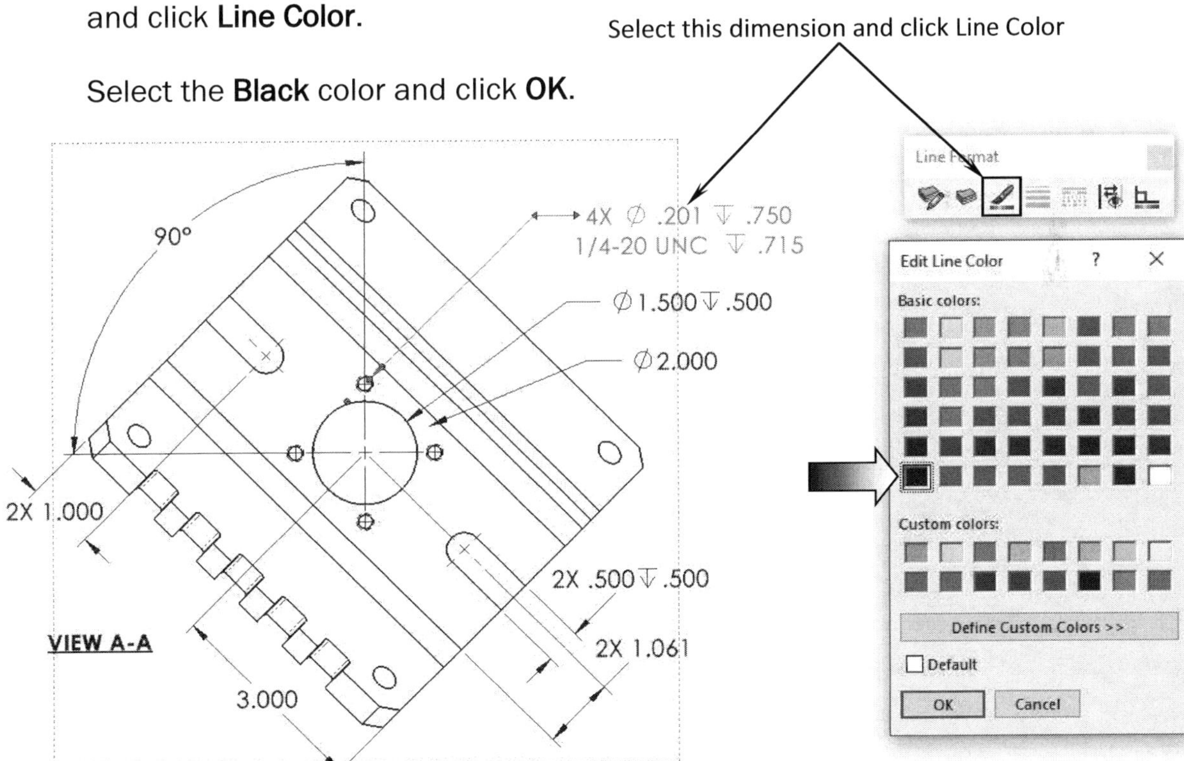

14. Showing a sketch from the model:

Zoom in on the **Auxiliary** drawing view.

The dimension Ø2.000 was supposed to attach to the construction circle that was created in the model. We need to make this circle visible in this drawing view.

From the FeatureManager tree, expand **Drawing View5**, and also expand the **Base Mount Block** and its **¼-20 Tapped Hole** feature.

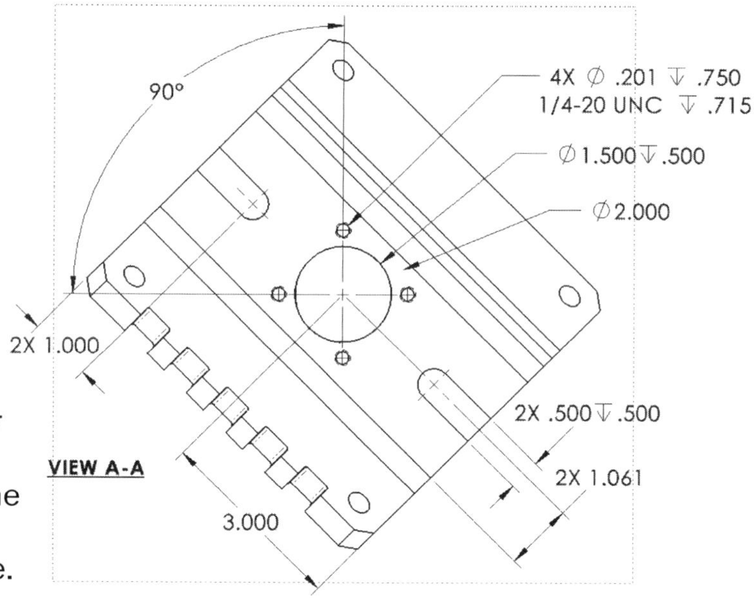

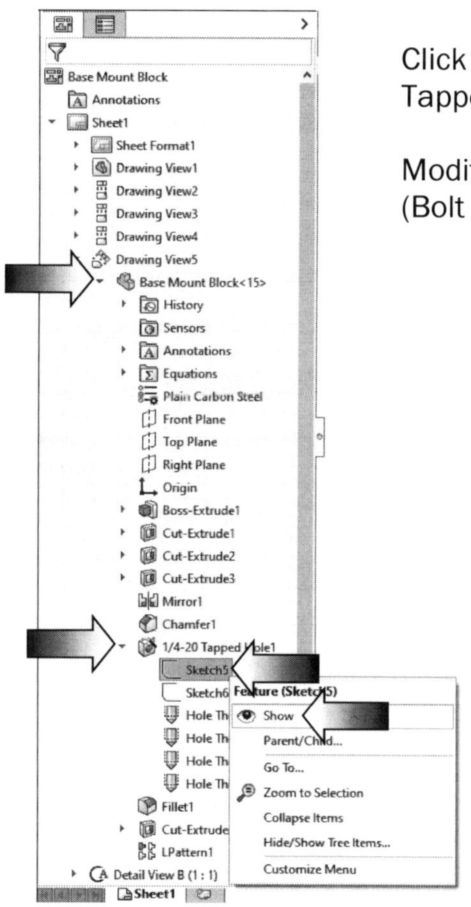

Click **Sketch5** (the construction circle) below the ¼-20 Tapped Hole feature and select **Show.**

Modify the dimension **Ø2.000** to include the text **B.C.** (Bolt Circle) as shown below.

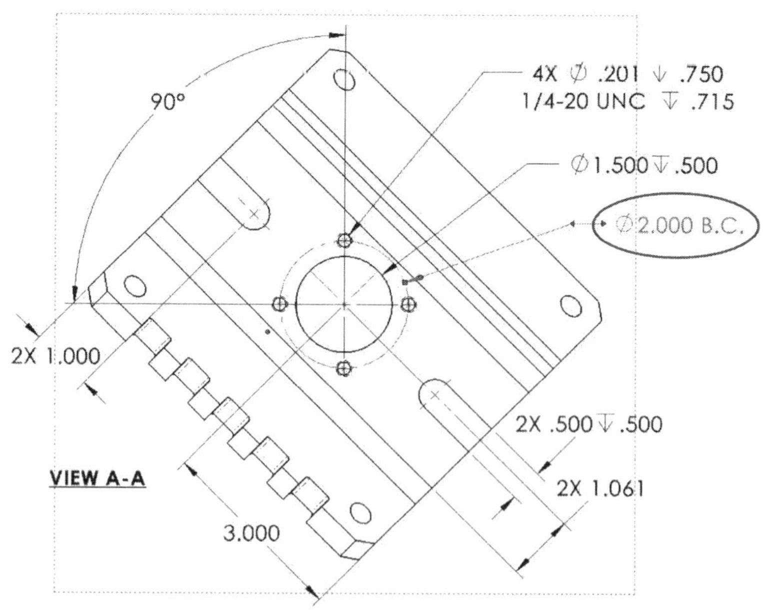

15. Inserting the pattern instances:

This step will demonstrate how a dimension or an instance count can be linked to a note.

Select the dotted border of the **Auxiliary** view.

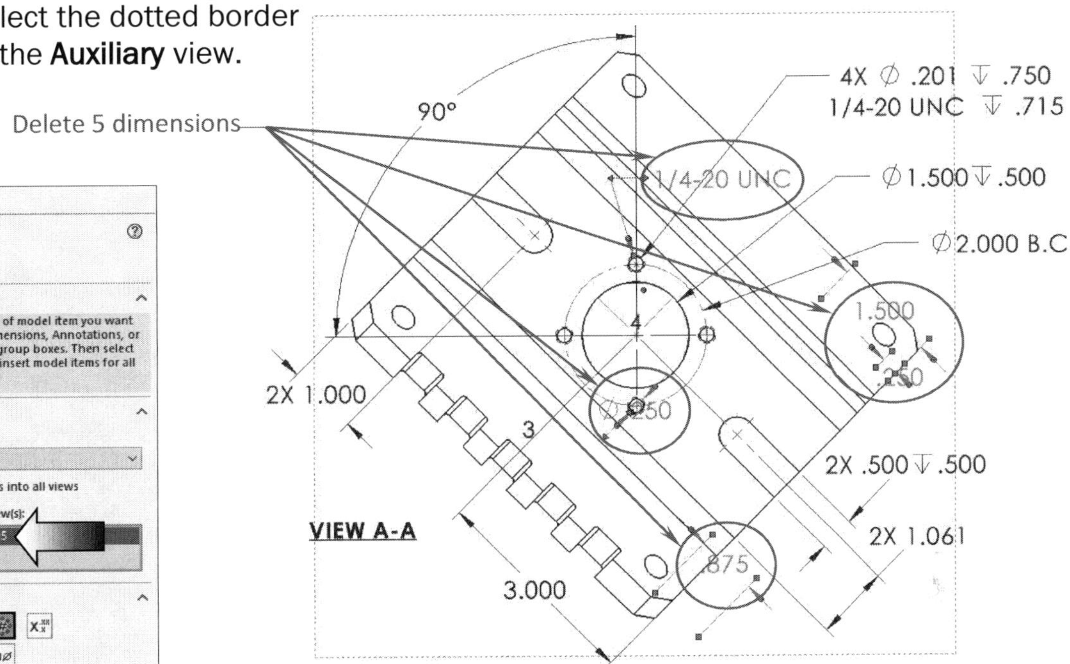

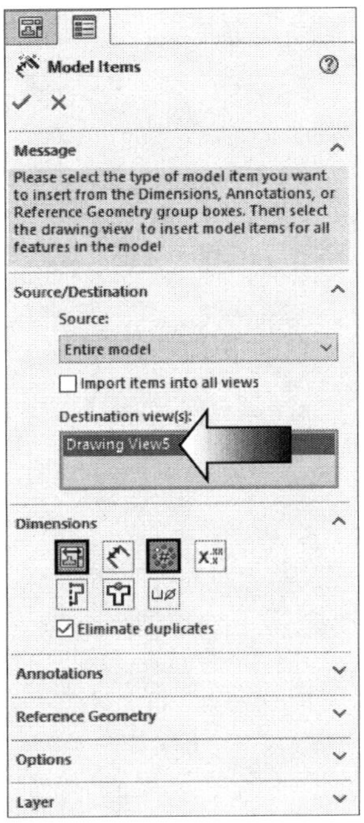

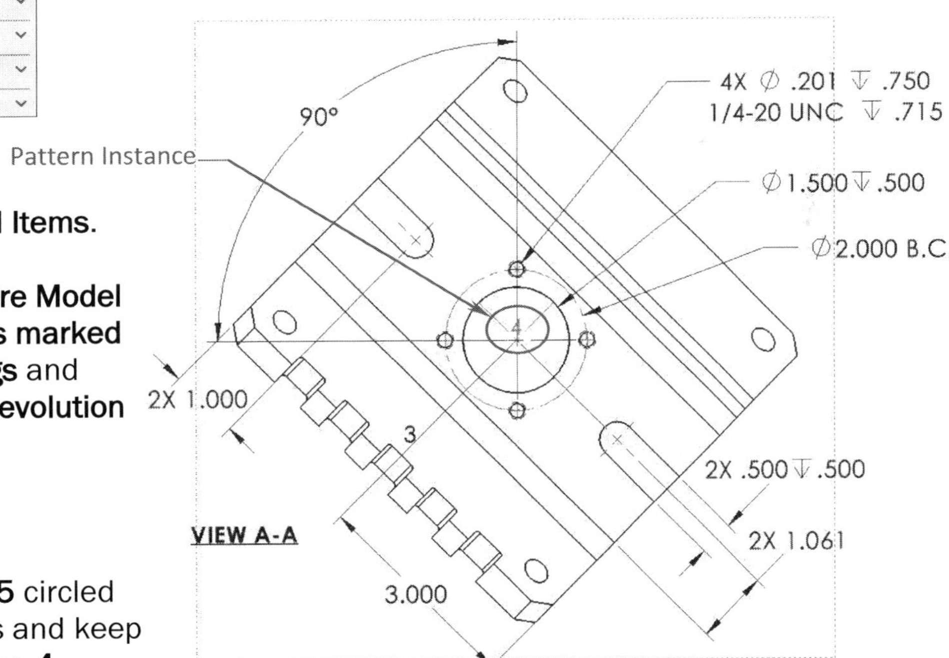

Click **Model Items.**

Select: **Entire Model Dimensions marked for Drawings** and **Instance/Revolution Counts**

Click **OK.**

Delete the **5** circled dimensions and keep only instance **4.**

16. Creating a parametric note:

Switch to the **Annotation** tab.

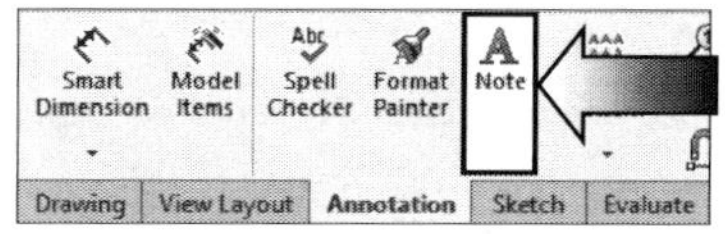

Click **Note**.

Select one of the circular edges of the Ø.201 holes to attach the note.

Type: **PATTERN OF** followed by a space.

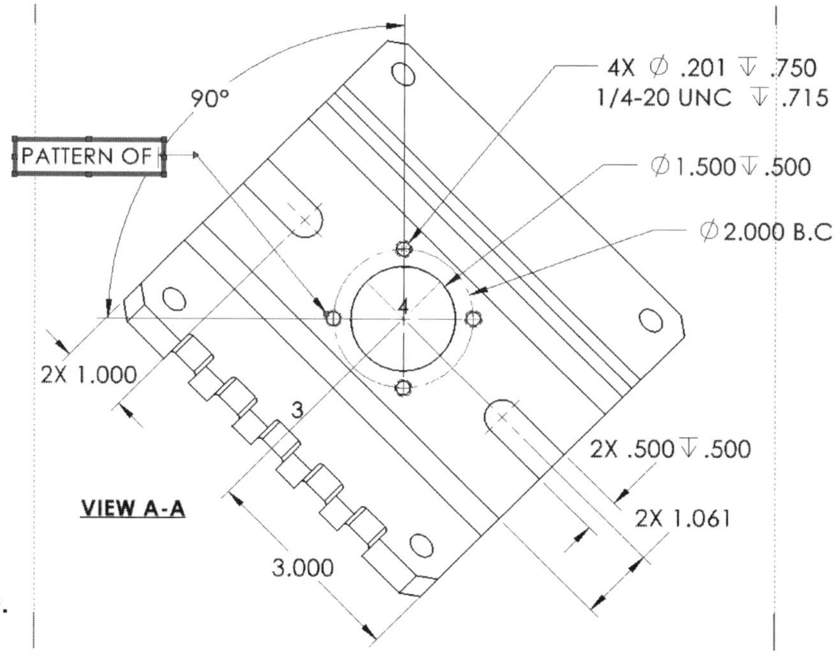

Click the instance **number 4** that was inserted from the previous step.

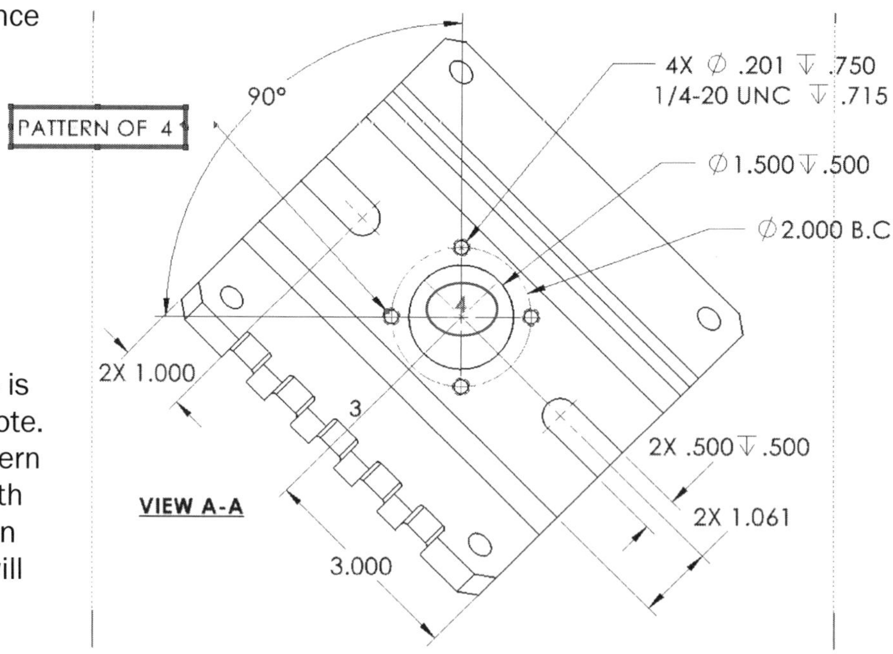

The instance 4 is linked to the note. If the hole pattern is changed, both the hole pattern and the note will be updated.

17. Changing the number of pattern instances:

Double-click the pattern instance number **4** and change it to **5**.

Press **Rebuild** (Control+B) to refresh and update the drawing views.

The note is updated and shows the Pattern of 5.

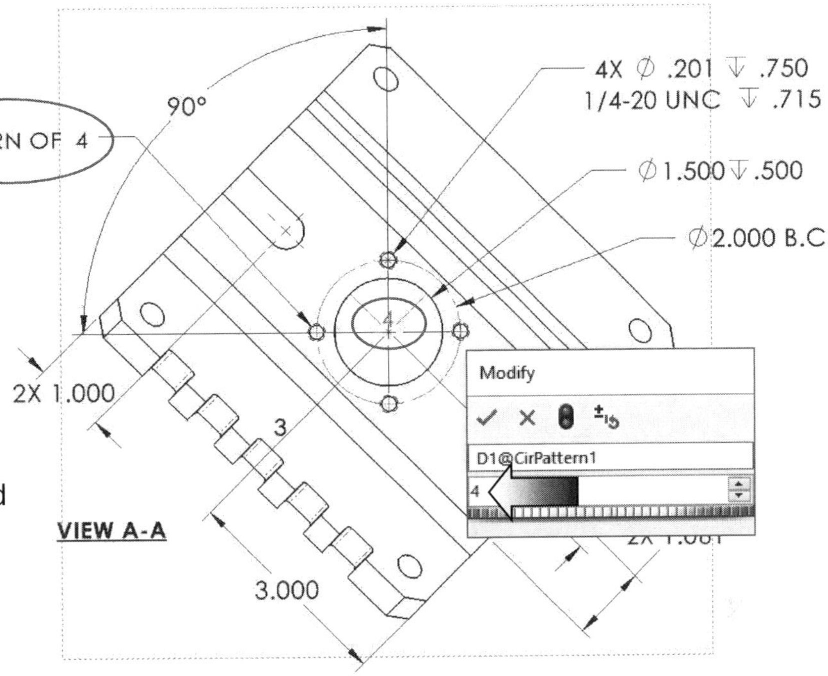

The drawing views are also refreshed and 5 holes are shown in all drawing views.

This change has also populated to the model. When the model is opened, the hole pattern will be displayed as a pattern of 5 holes.

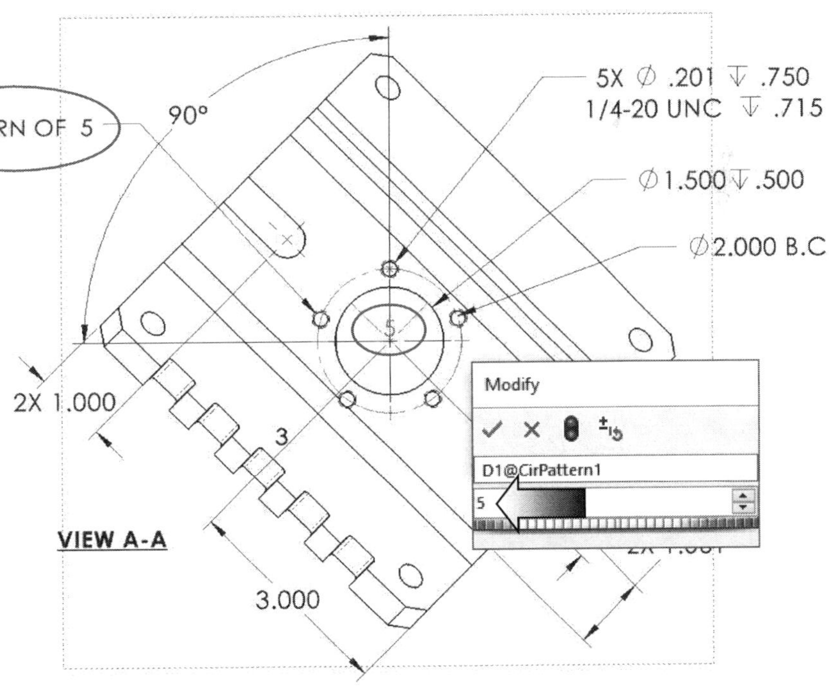

18. Saving your work:

Select **File, Save As.**

Enter **Base Mount Block.slddrw** for the file name.

Click **Save.**

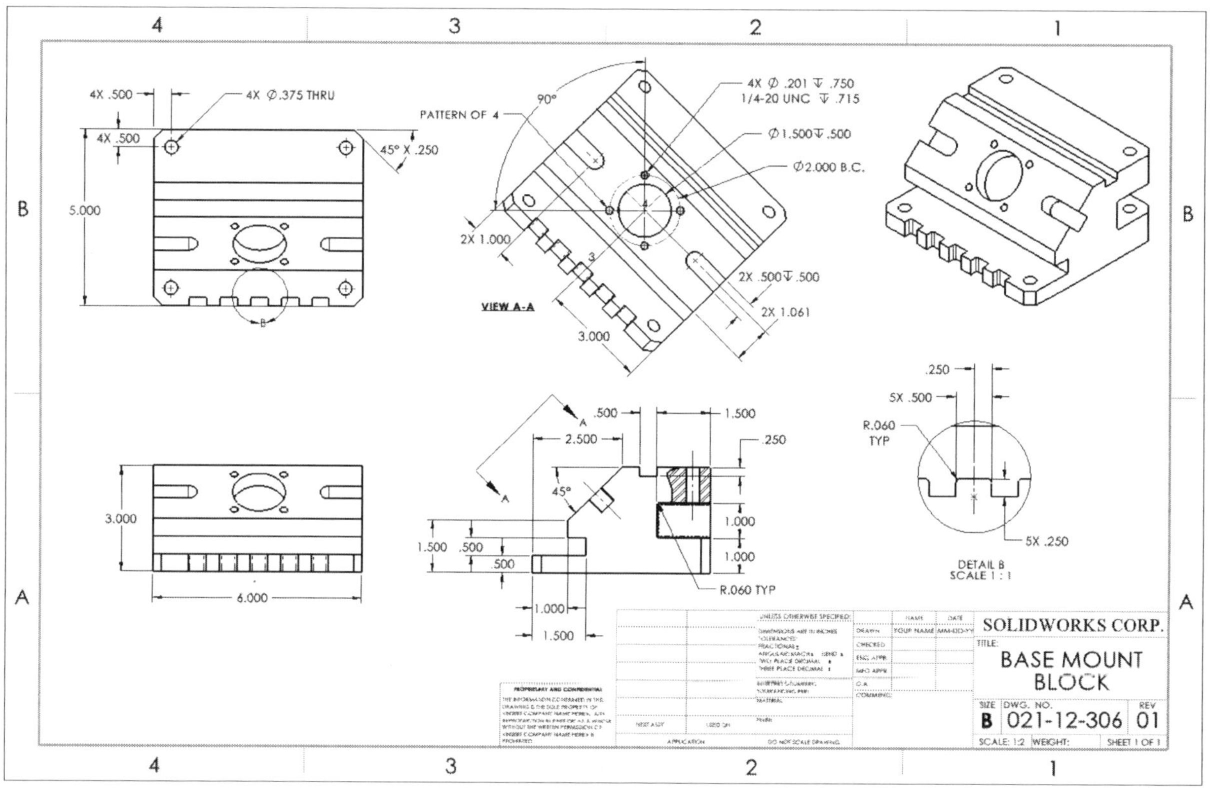

Close all documents.

Additional Drawing Tools

SOLIDWORKS DrawCompare

The SOLIDWORKS DrawCompare application compares all entities between two drawing documents. The differences between the drawings are displayed in color codes.

DrawCompare compares the bitmaps of two drawings at the bit level. Only visual changes are captured when the drawings are compared. For example, if you move a dimension to the other side of the drawing, this change is reflected in the comparison. Conversely, if you change a custom property such as the Description, this does not reflect in the comparison.

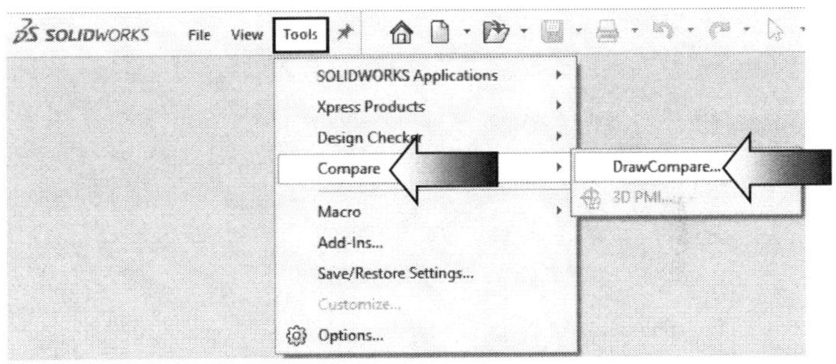

1. Enabling DrawCompare:

Select **Tools, Compare, DrawCompare**.

The DrawCompare application is opened in its own window.

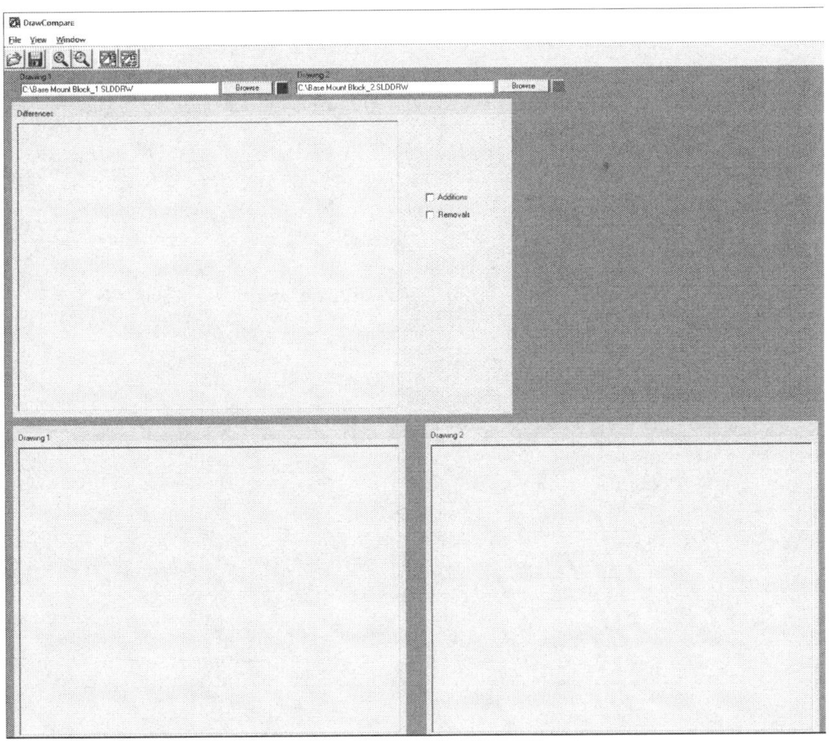

For Drawing 1, browse to the Training Folder and open the drawing named: **Base Mount Block _1.slddrw**.

For Drawing 2, open the drawing named: **Base Mount Block _2.slddrw** from the same location.

2. Comparing the drawings:

There are 2 types of drawing compare, DrawCompare for standard drawings and DrawCompare for detached drawings.

Click **Compare Drawings** (arrow).

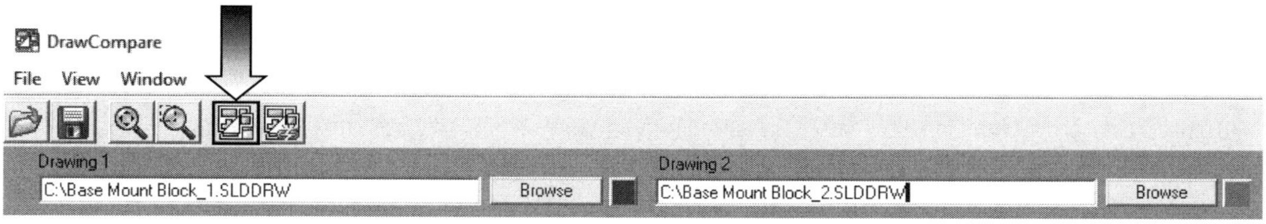

The Blue elements belong to the **Base Mount Block_1** drawing, and the Green elements belong to the **Base Mount Block_2** drawing.

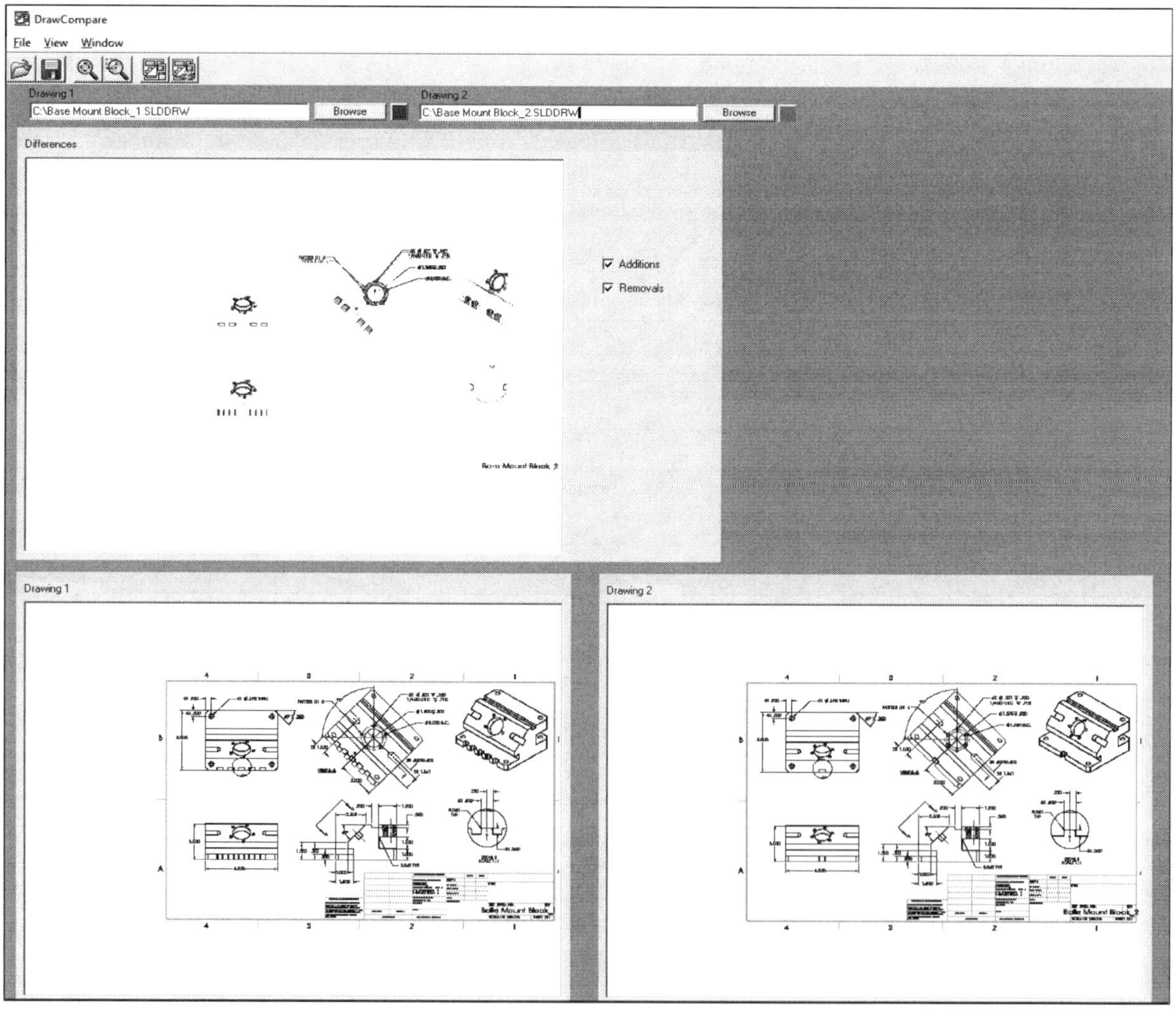

3. Viewing the differences:

Use the **Zoom To Area** tool  and zoom closer to the **Differences** window or select Window, Differences.

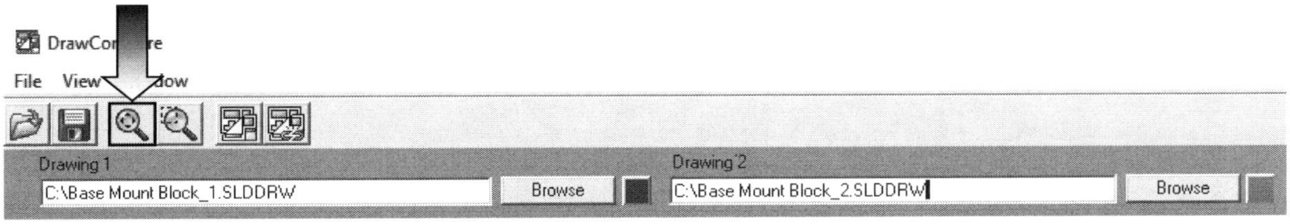

Since both options **Additions** and **Removals** are selected, the Blue elements are superimposed over the Green elements.

The major differences between the 2 drawings are:

*** A pattern of 5 small holes and 5 notches in drawing 1**

*** A pattern of 6 small holes and no notches in drawing 2**

*** Some of the annotations were moved or shifted in both drawings**

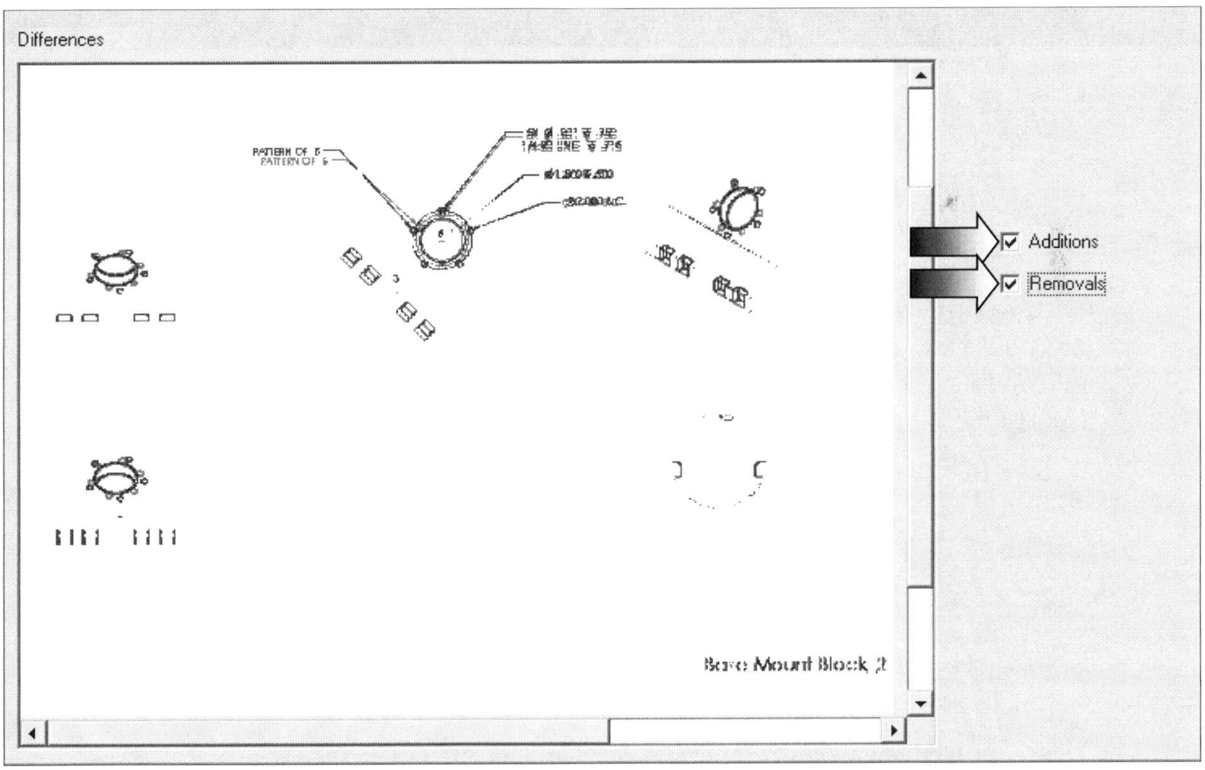

To be able to see the differences between the 2 drawings more clearly, let us toggle between the **Additions** and **Removals** options.

On the right side of the Differences window, clear the **Additions** checkbox to show only the Blue elements.

The Blue elements in drawing number 1.

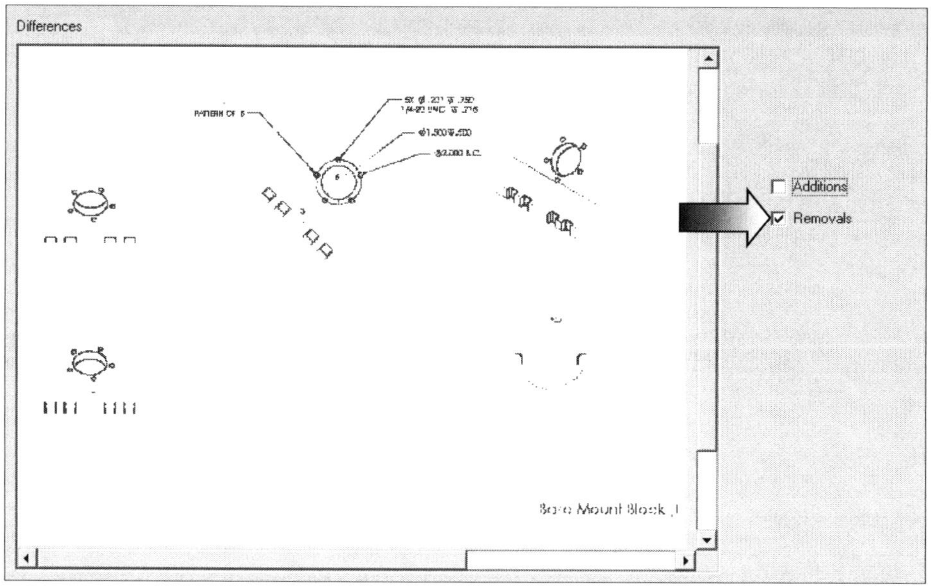

Now, enable the **Additions** and clear the Removals checkbox to see the Green elements.

The Green elements in drawing number 2.

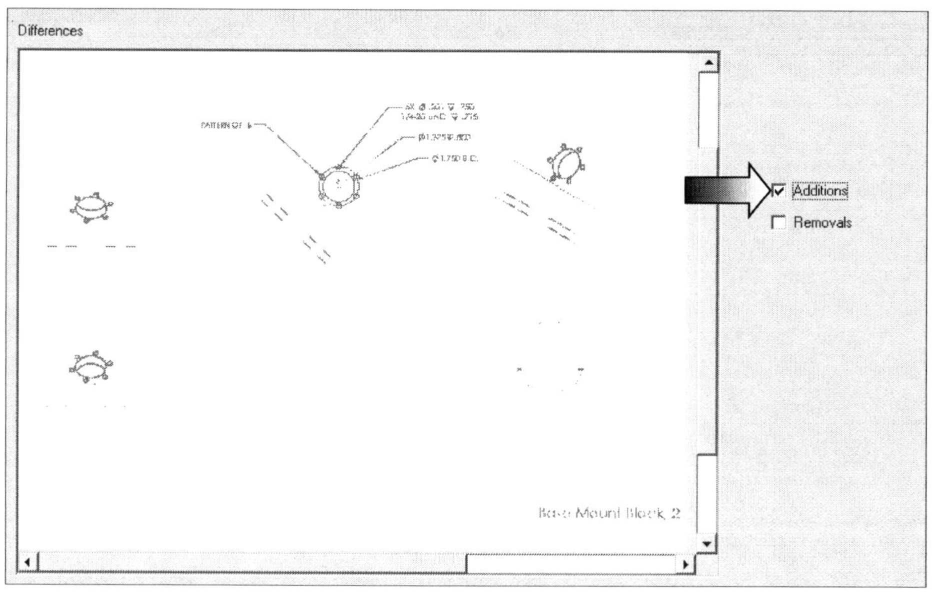

Exit the DrawCompare program.

Additional Drawing Tools

SOLIDWORKS Pack and Go

The SOLIDWORKS Pack and Go utility gathers all related files for a model design such as parts, assemblies, drawings, references, design tables, Design Binder content, decals, appearances, and scenes, and SOLIDWORKS Simulation results, into a folder or zip file.

The new files that are created by Pack and Go do not become the active documents in SOLIDWORKS. They are saved as copies to the selected location of your choice. Prefix or suffix can be added to all file names.

1. Opening an assembly document:

Select **File, Open**.

Browse to the Training Folder and open an assembly document named: **Tube Grabber Assembly.sldasm**.

This assembly document contains several parts and drawings.

By using Pack and Go you can copy and rename the files while ensuring the file references are retained.

If SOLIDWORKS Toolbox fasteners were used in the assembly, they can be quickly selected and included in the pack.

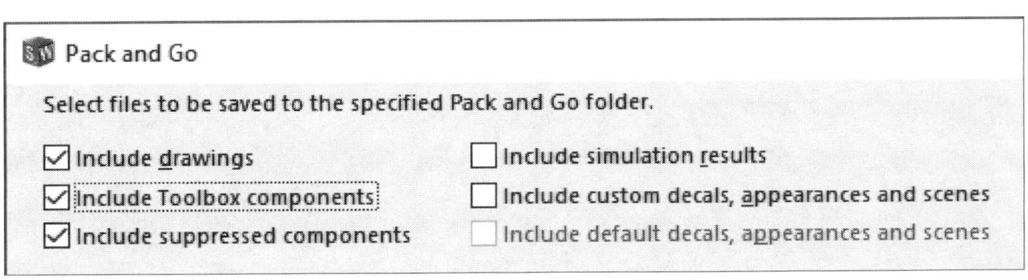

2. Launching the Pack and Go utility:

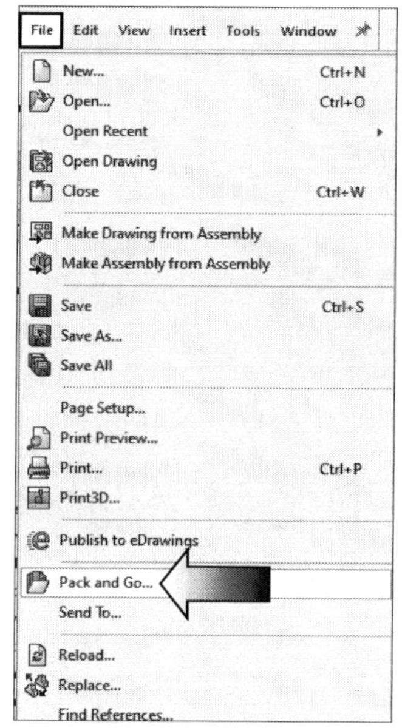

Select **File, Pack and Go.**

In the Pack and Go dialog box, select the following:

* **Include Drawings**

* **Include Suppressed Components**

* **Nested View**

* **Add Suffix** and enter: **-Bak**

The **Select / Replace** option searches columns in the Pack and Go list to select or clear items or replace text.

Select a location to save the backup files and click **Save.**

Exercise: Additional Drawing Tools

Detailing the Aluminum Block

The exercises are designed to help you apply what you have learned from the previous lessons. They come with some instructions but not as detailed as the lessons, to give you an opportunity to explore and to try and create the drawings on your own, at your own pace.

1. Opening a part document:

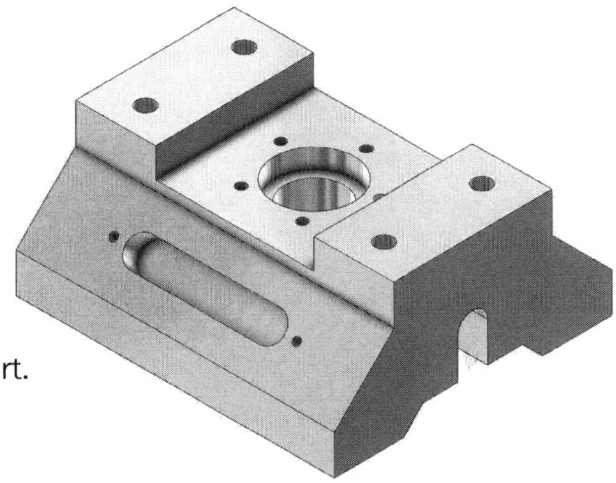

Select **File, Open**.

Navigate to the training folder and open a part document named: **Aluminum Block.sldprt.**

The material **6061 Aluminum Alloy** has already been assigned to the part.

2. Transferring to a drawing:

Select **File, Make Drawing from Part.**

Select the **B-Size** drawing paper.

Set the Type-Of-Projection to: **3rd Angle.**

Set Scale to **1:3**

Click **OK.**

Create 4 standard drawing views as shown, using the View Palette.

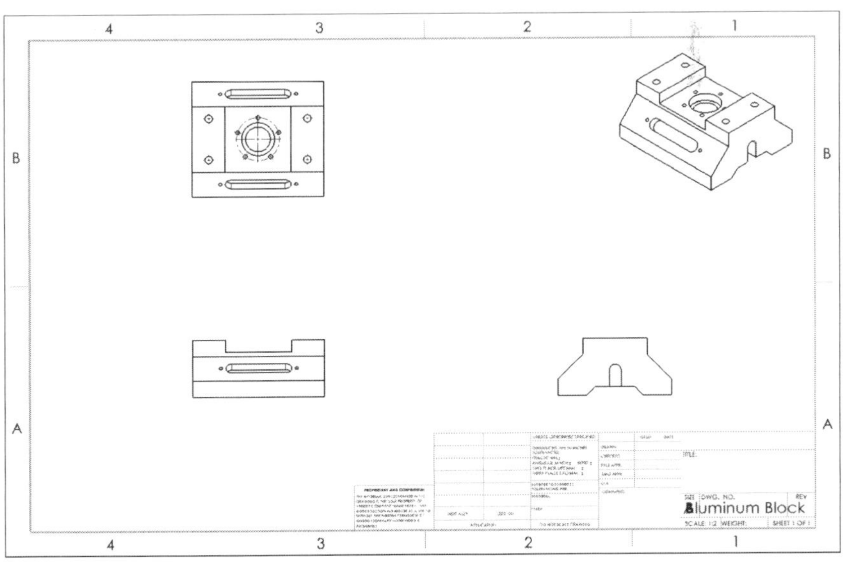

3. Creating the additional drawing views:

Use the drawing tools discussed earlier in this lesson and create two additional drawing views:

*** Auxiliary View**

*** Section View**

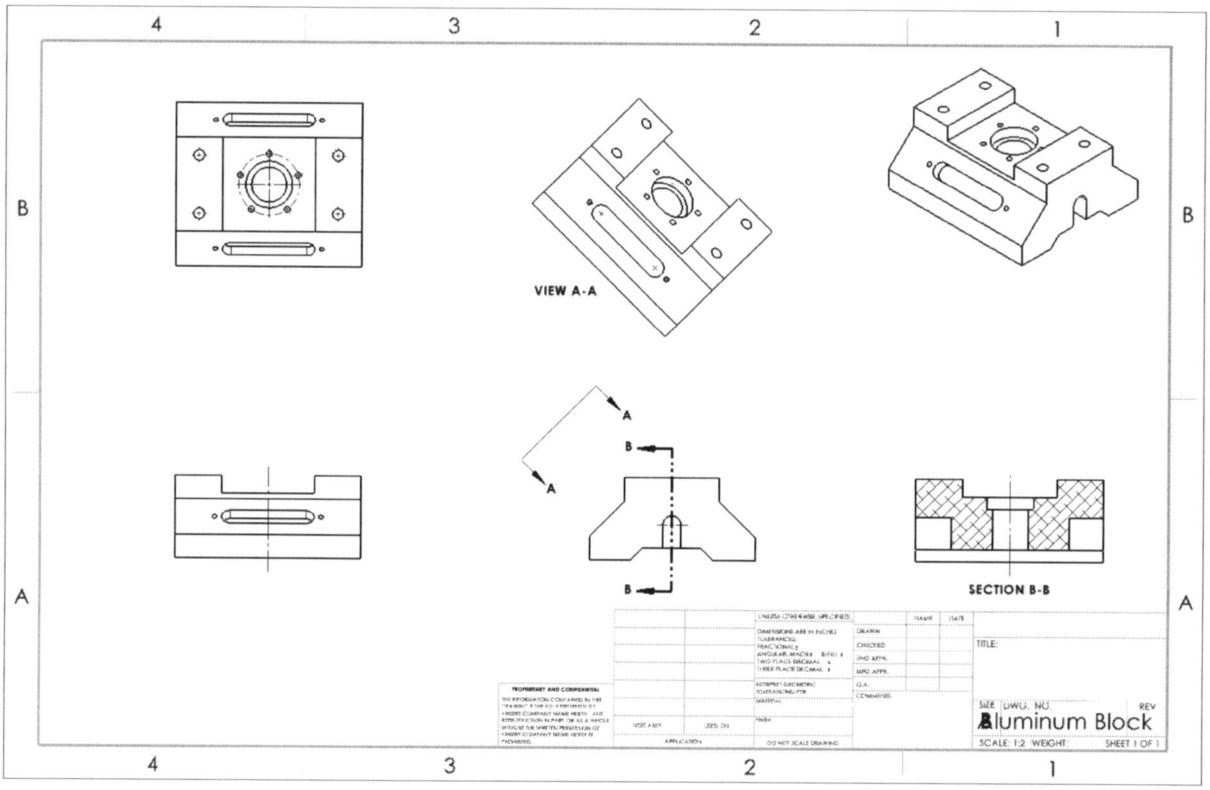

Break the alignment of the **Auxiliary view** and move it higher, as shown in the image above.

Shorten the **Auxiliary's Projection Line** to create room for dimensions and annotations.

Add **Centerlines** and **Center Marks** to all drawing views.

4. Inserting the Model Dimensions:

Insert the model dimensions and other annotations using the **Model Items** tool.

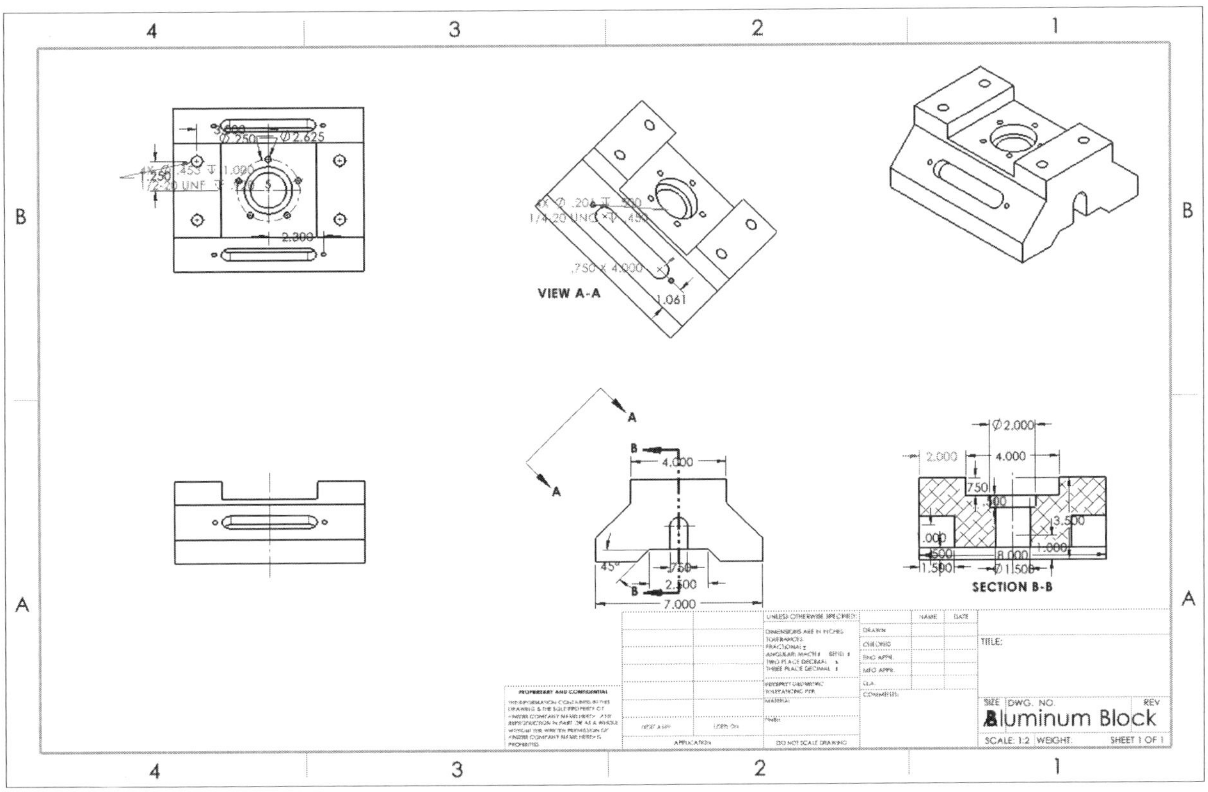

Start with the **Top** drawing view.

Rearrange the dimensions and move the missing ones from the other drawing views. Add dimensions where needed.

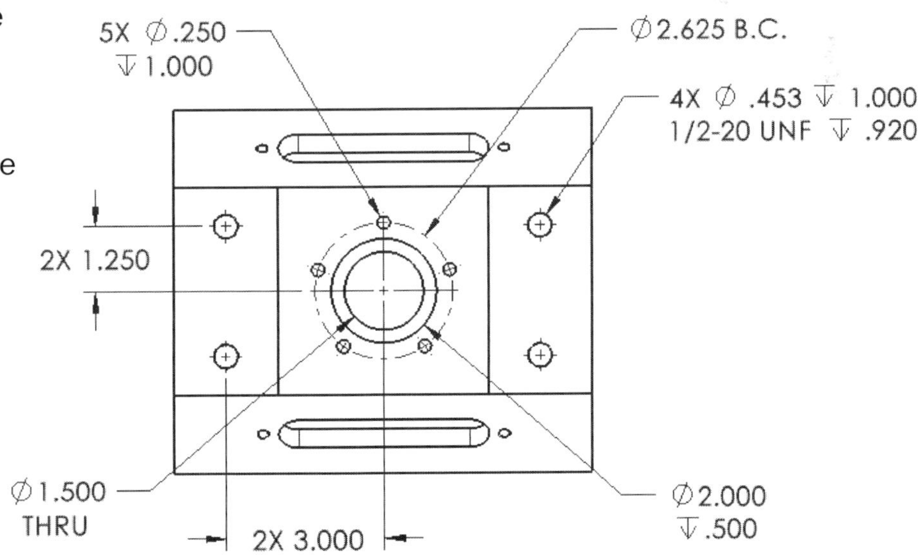

5. Adding the instance callouts:

Zoom in on the **Front** drawing view and add the height and width dimensions.

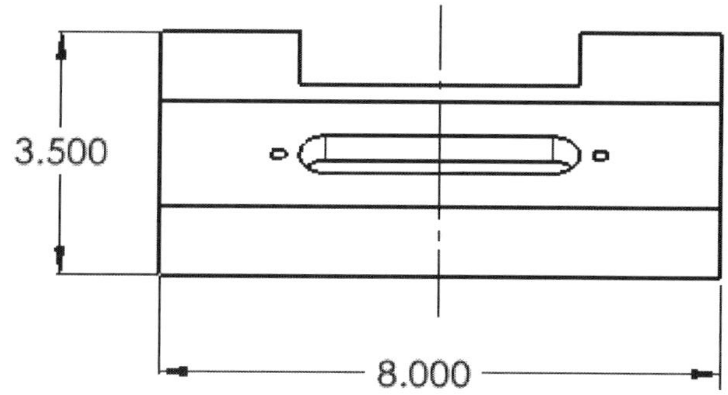

Move the dimensions (Shift + drag) from other drawing views if needed.

Zoom in on the **Auxiliary** drawing view.

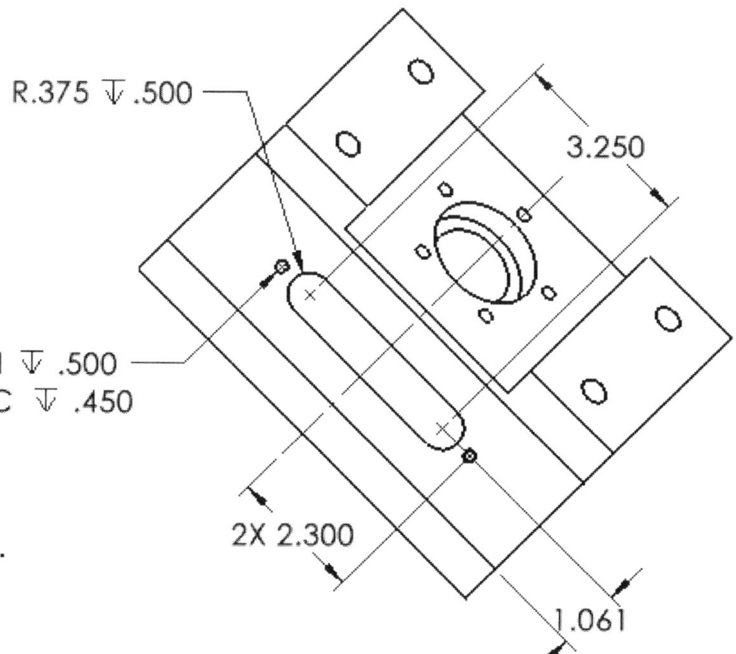

VIEW A-A

Add the instance counts to the dimensions that need them.

Most of the symbols needed can be found in the **Dimension Text** section.

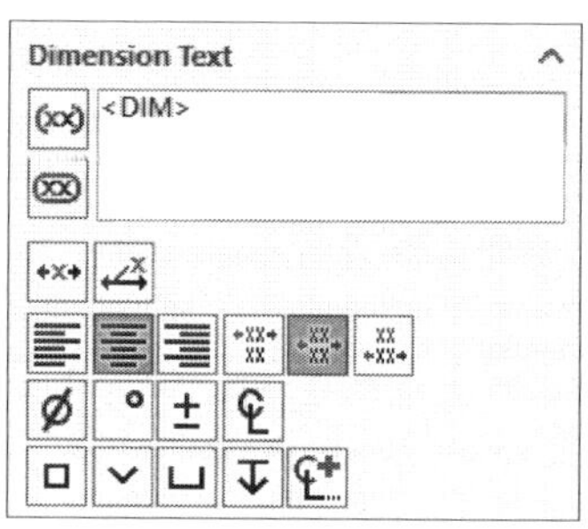

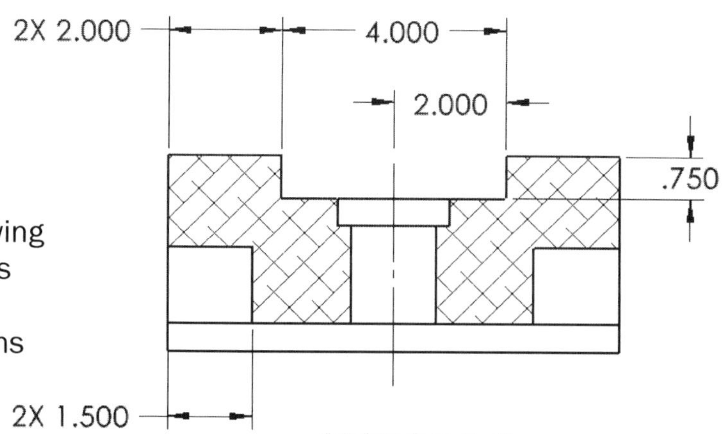

SECTION B-B

Zoom in on the **Section** drawing view and add the dimensions shown in the image on the right. Add new dimensions where needed.

Zoom in on the **Right** drawing view.

Add / move the dimensions from other drawing views to the Right drawing view to make it look similar to the image shown here.

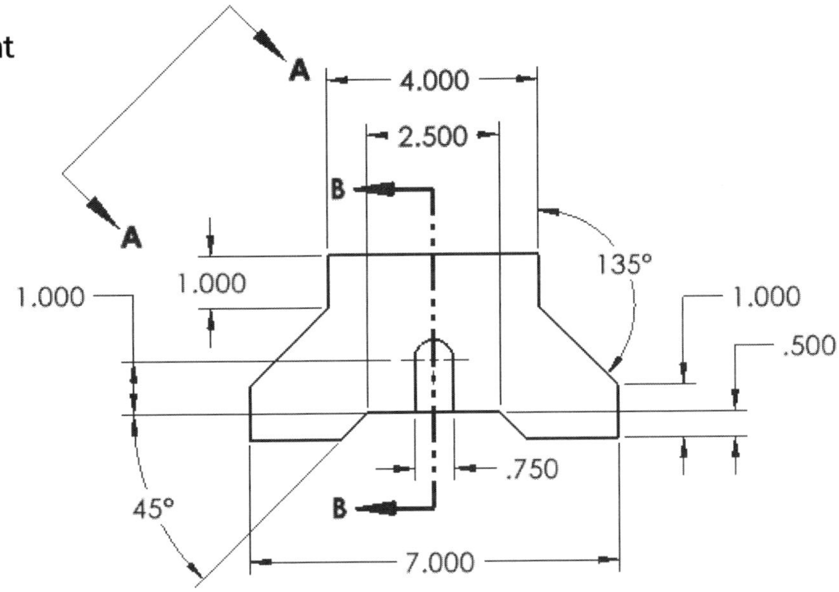

6. Filling out the Title Block:

From the FeatureManager tree, expand **Sheet1** and double-click **Sheet Format1** to activate it for editing.

Fill out the information shown here.

When finished, double-click **Sheet1** to bring the drawing layer back to the front and also to deactivate the Sheet Format layer.

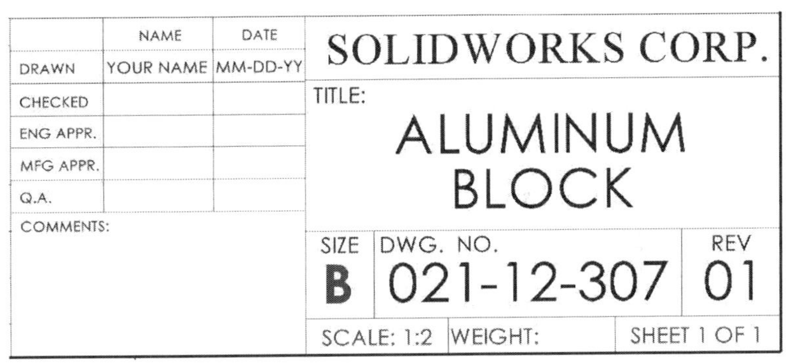

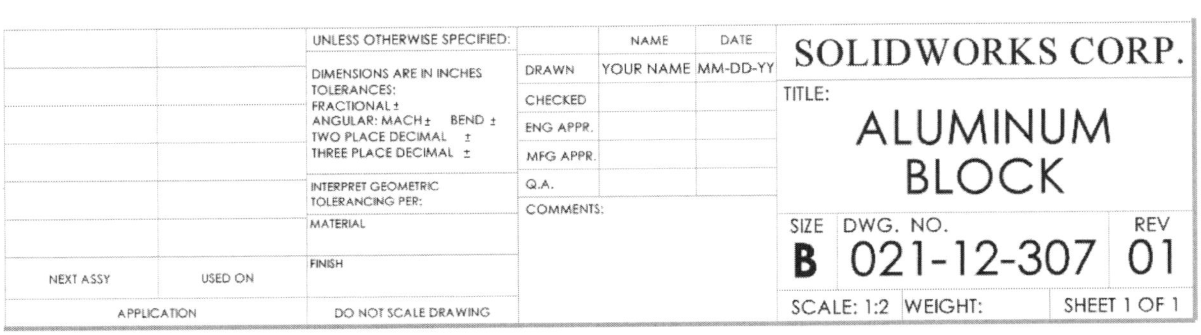

7. Saving your work:

Select **Files, Save As**.

Enter **Aluminum Block.slddrw** for the file name.

Click Save.

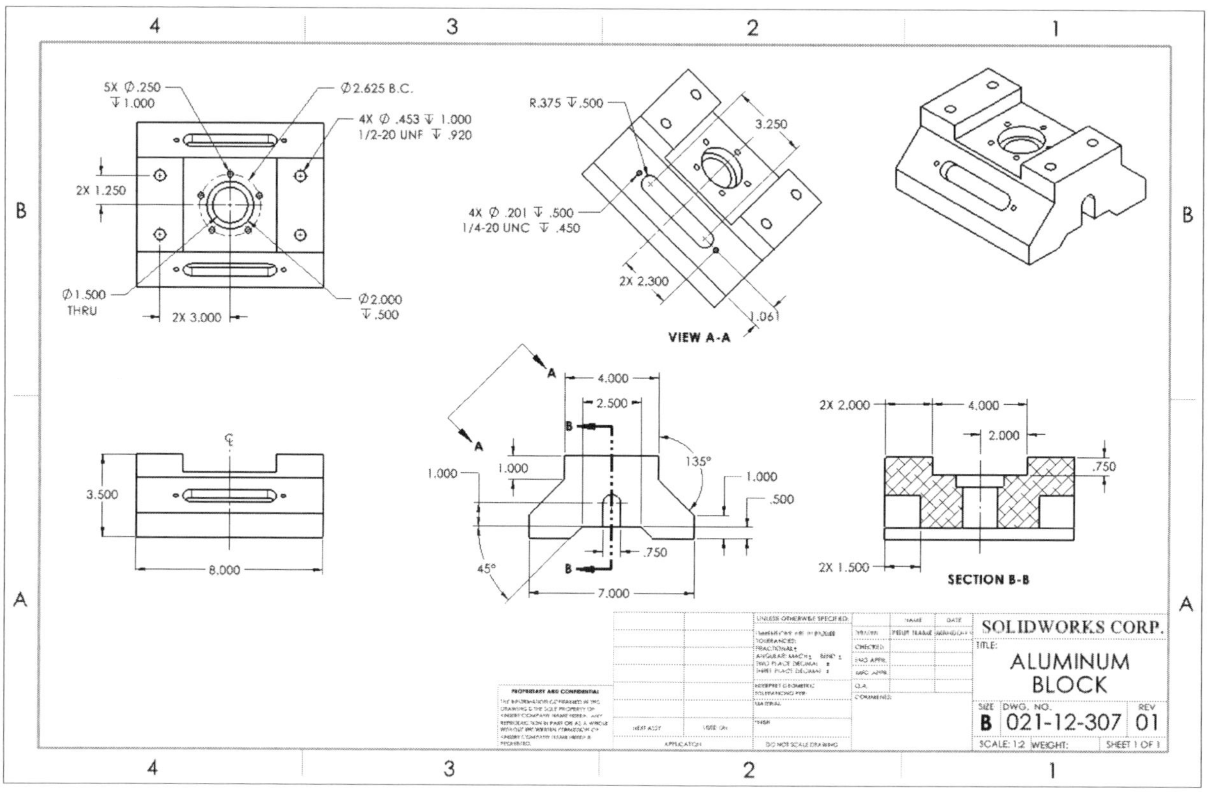

Close all documents.

Exercise: Additional Drawing Tools

Other options in Assembly Drawings

The exercises are designed to help you apply what you have learned from the previous lessons. They come with some instructions but not as detailed as the lessons, to give you an opportunity to explore and to try and create the drawings on your own, at your own pace.

1. Opening an assembly document:

Select **File, Open**.

Browse to the Training Folder and open an assembly document named: **Sliding Mechanism.sldasm**

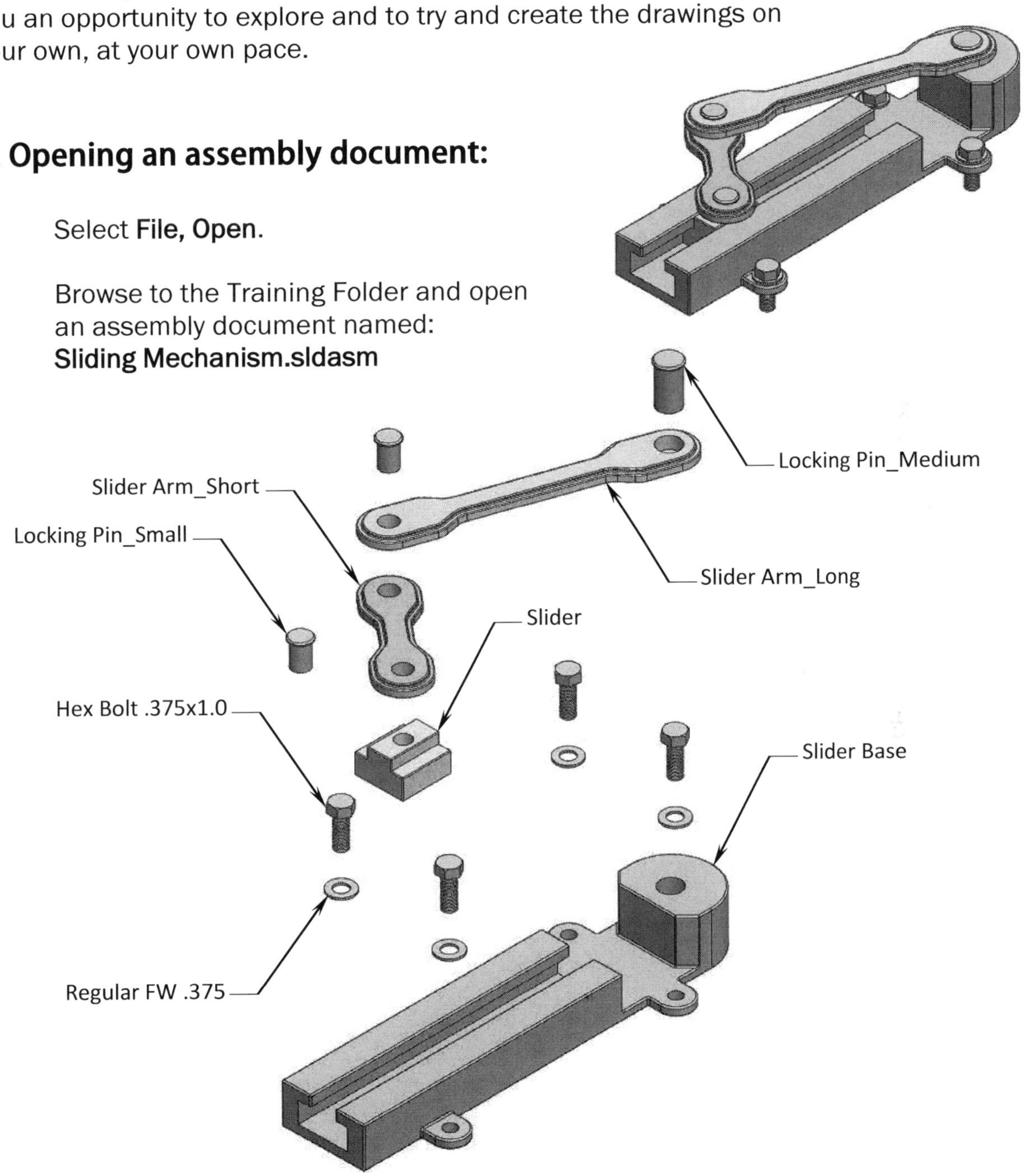

2. Adding the explode lines:

Switch to the **Configuration-Manager** tree.

Expand the **Default** configuration to see **Exploded View1**.

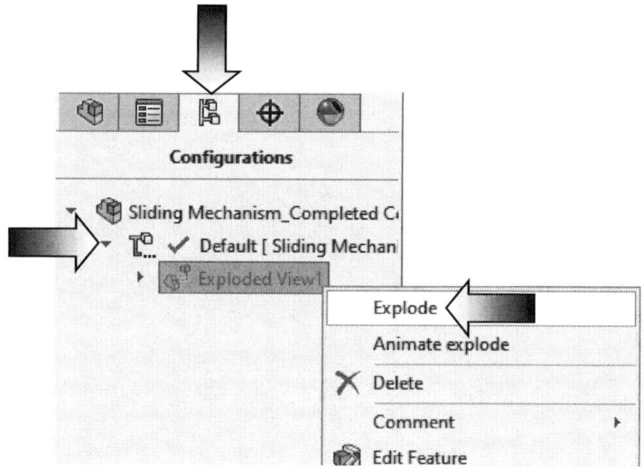

Right-click on **Exploded View1** and select **Explode** (arrow).

Switch back to the **Feature-Manager** tree and click the **Assembly** tab.

Expand the **Exploded View** drop-down list and select: **Explode Line Sketch**.

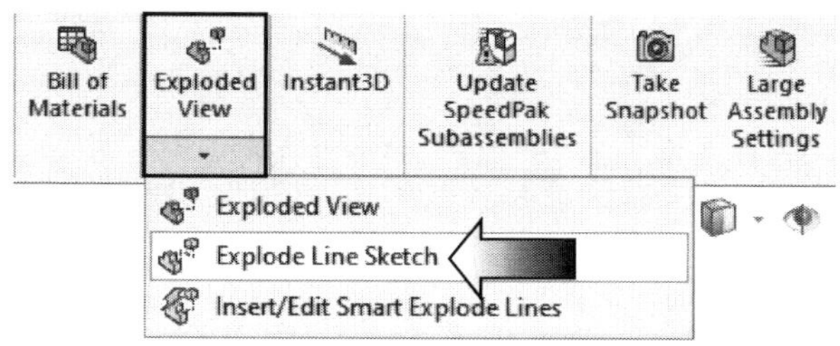

First, select the <u>body</u> of the **Locking Pin_ Medium** and click the **Reverse** arrow to connect to the Slider Base below.

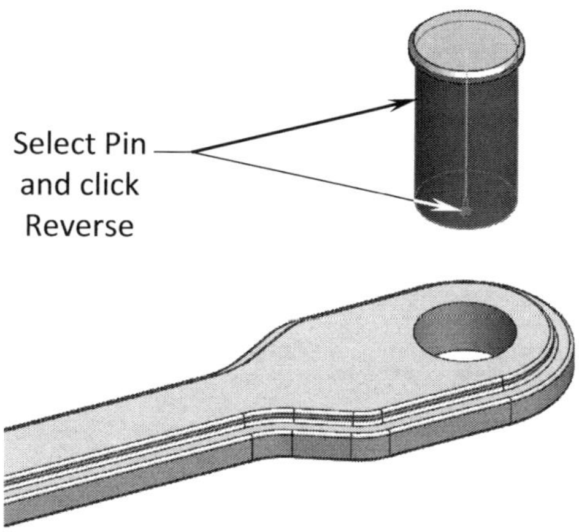

Second, select the <u>hole</u> on the right side of the **Slider Base**. An explode line sketch is added to connect the centers of the 2 selected features.

Click **OK** to accept the 1st exploded line sketch.

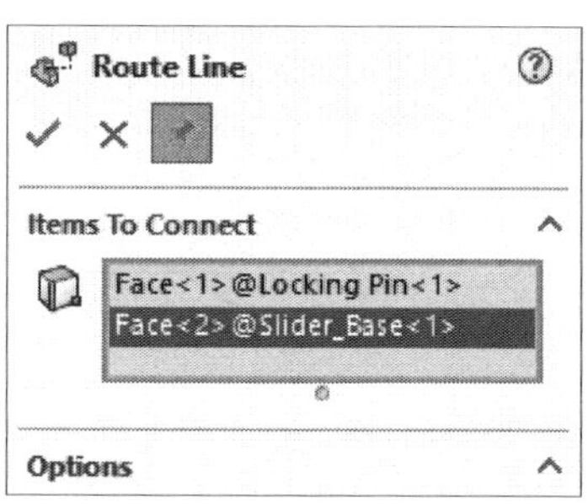

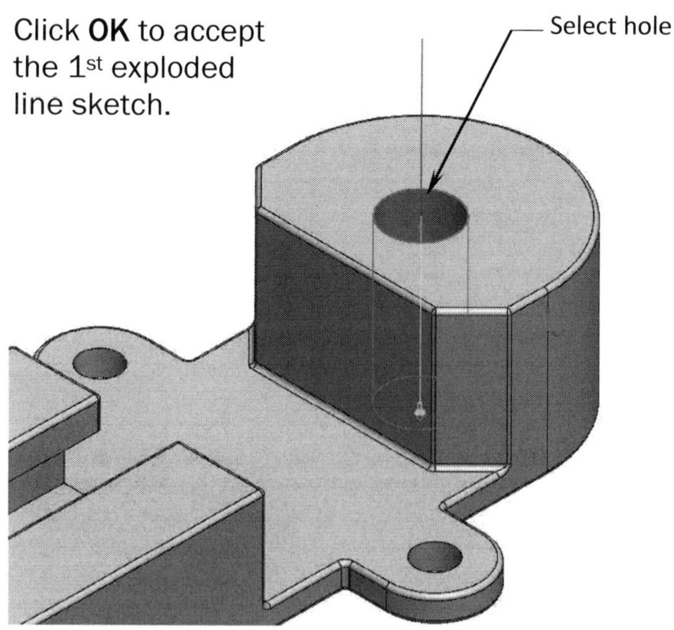

Next, we will connect the Locking Pin with the Slider Arm_Short.

Zoom in closer to the two components mentioned above.

Select the <u>body</u> of the **Locking Pin_Small** and the <u>hole</u> in the **Slider Arm_Short**. The direction arrow should be pointing downwards.

A new route line is created connecting the two selected features.

Click **OK**.

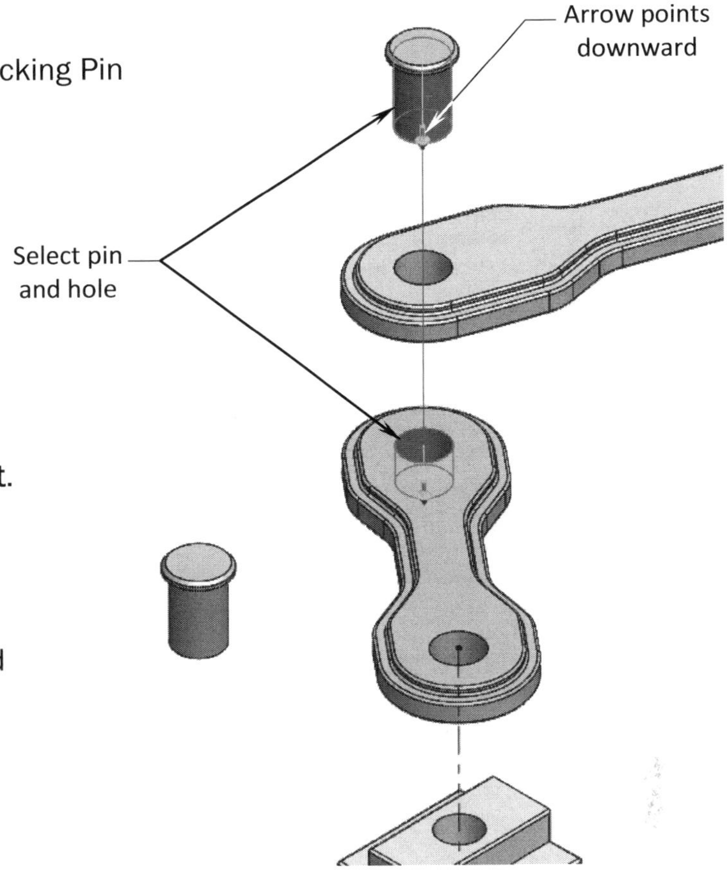

Zoom in closer between the Slider Arm_Short and the Slider.

Select the <u>hole</u> in the **Slider Arm_Short** and the <u>hole</u> in the **Slider**.

Make sure the direction arrow is also pointing downwards.

A new route line is created connecting the two selected features.

Click **OK**.

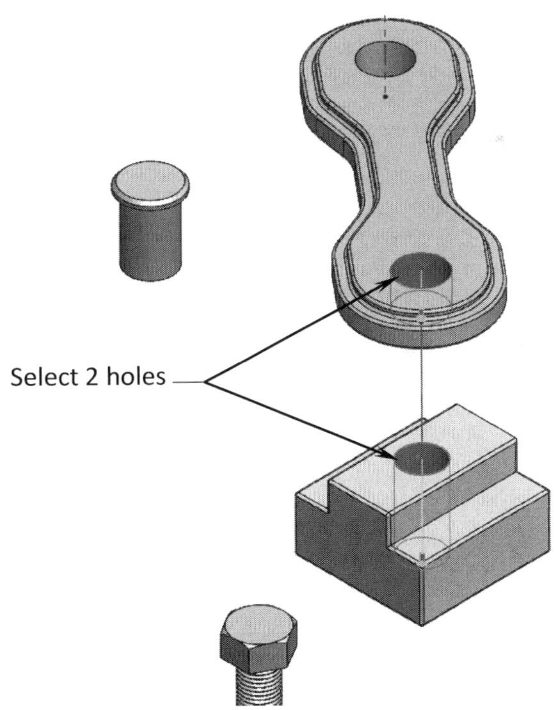

Zoom in closer to the Locking Pin_Small and the Slider Arm_Short.

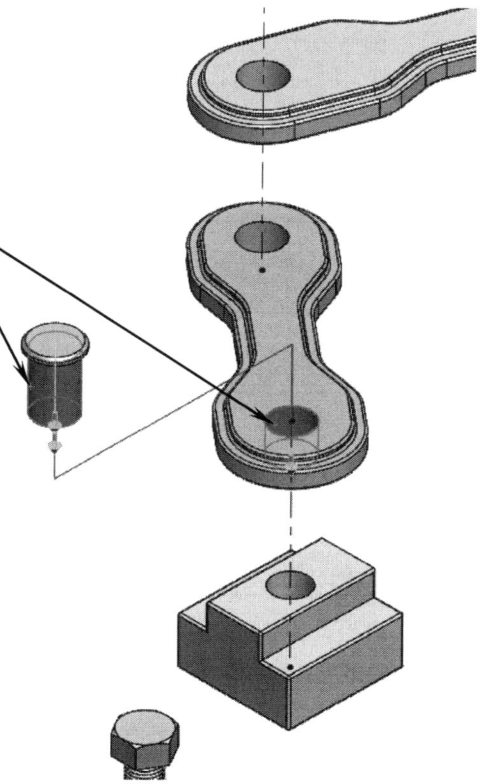

Select the body of the **Locking Pin_Small** and the hole in the **Slider Arm_Short.**

The direction arrow should be pointing downward; click Reverse if needed.

A new YZ route line is created to connect the two features.

Click **OK.**

Zoom in closer to one of the bolts and its mounting hole.

Select a circular edge in the **Bolt** and a hole in the **Slider Base.**

Click Reverse if needed to route the explode line downwards.

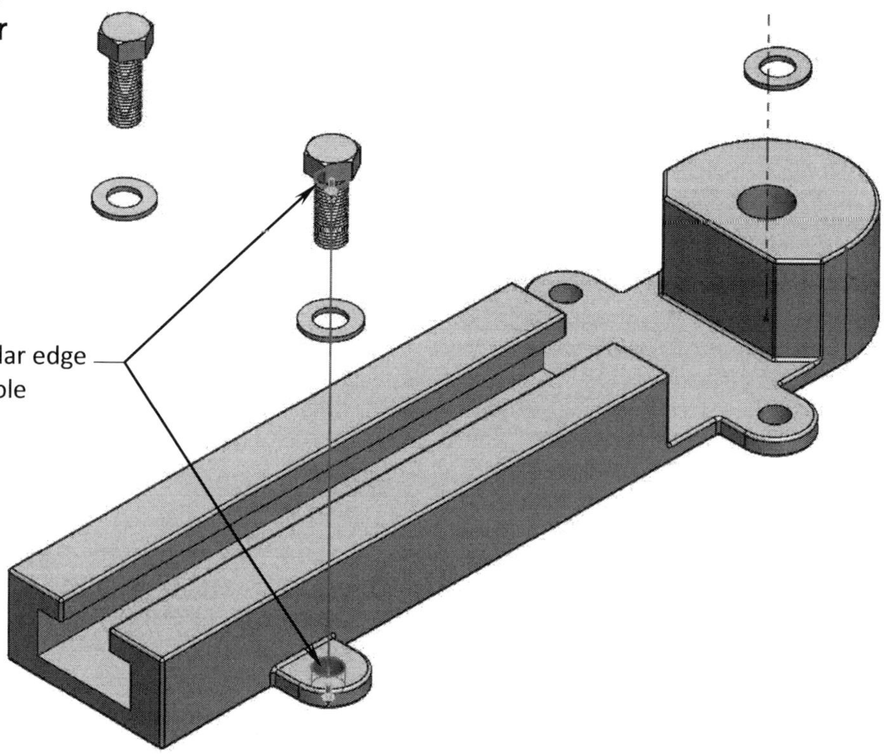

A new route line is created to connect the two components.

Click **OK.**

Continue with adding the route lines to connect the other components.

Use the image on the right as a reference to add the route lines.

Exit the sketch when finished.

A sketch called **3DExplode1** is added to the tree, below the Exploded View1. This sketch can be edited to modify the route lines.

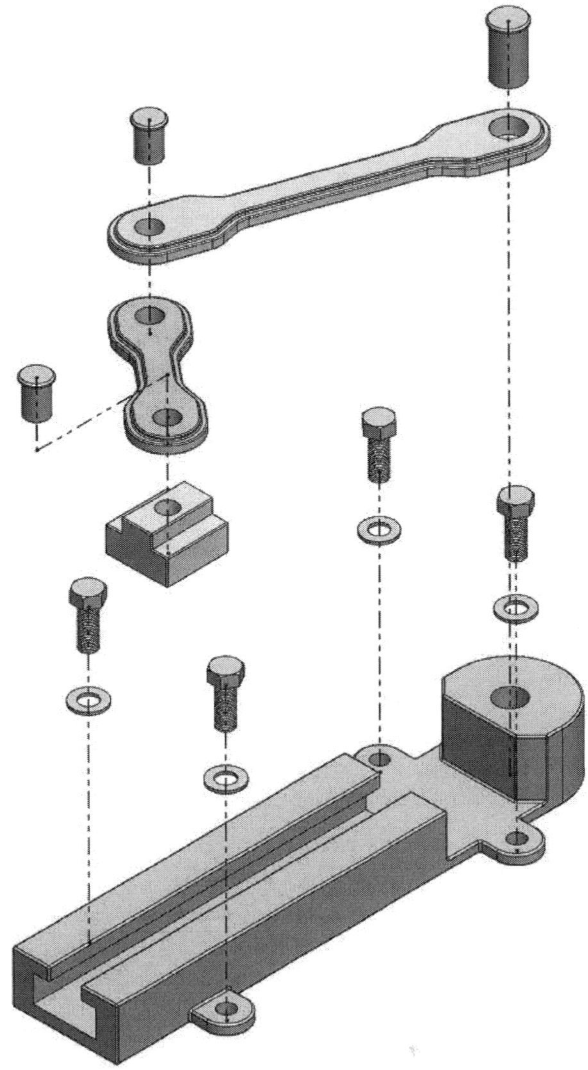

3. Collapsing the assembly:

The route lines are visible only when the view is exploded.

Right-click on **Exploded View1** and select **Collapse**.

The assembly is collapsed and the route lines are hidden.

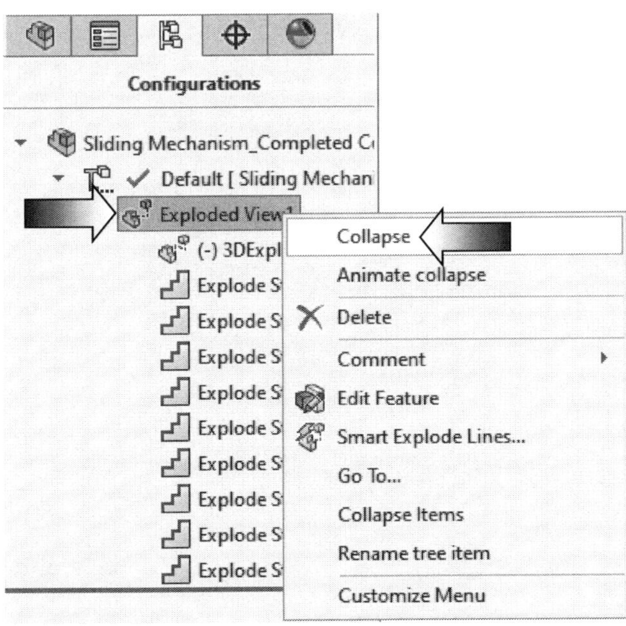

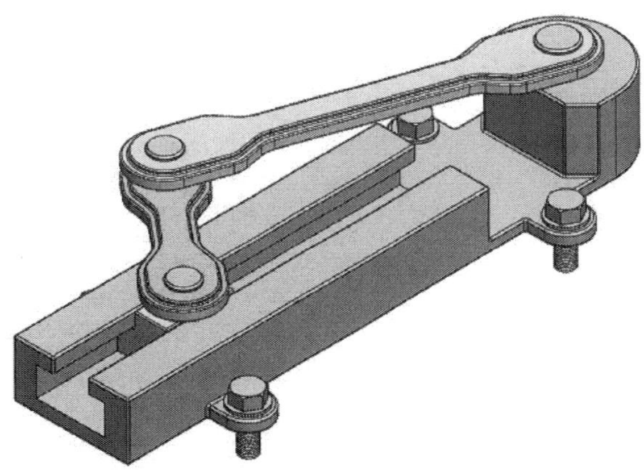

4. Making drawing from assembly:

Select **File, Make Drawing from Assembly**.

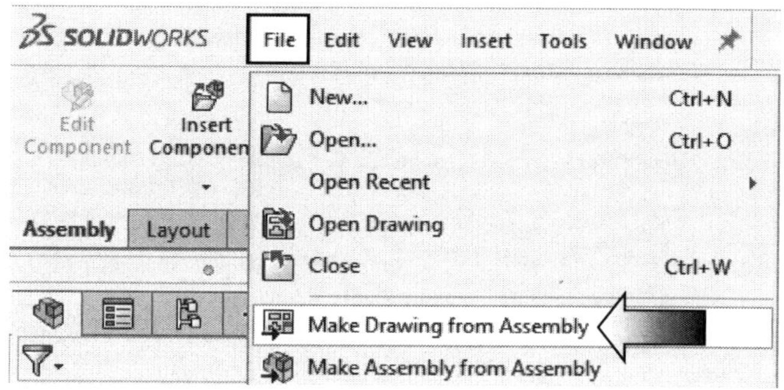

Select the following:

B (ANSI) Landscape

Third Angle

Scale: 1:2

Click **Apply Changes**.

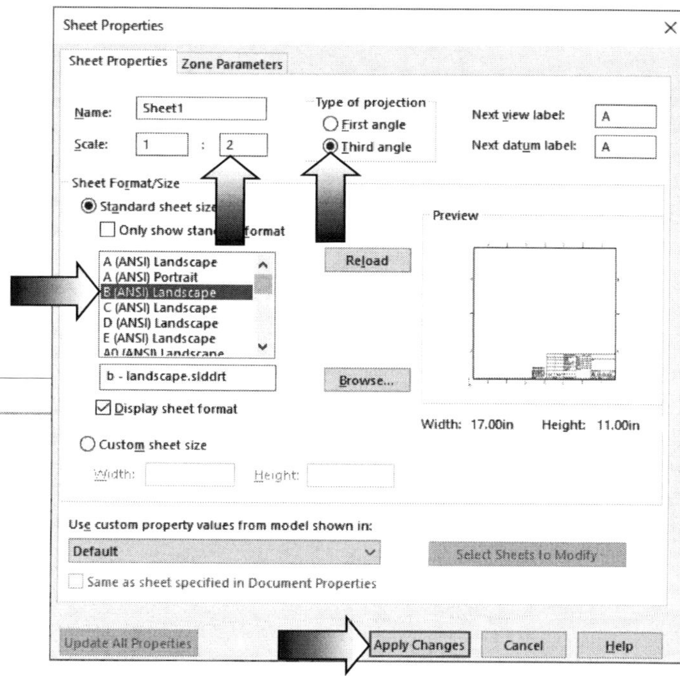

The B-Size drawing paper is loaded into the graphics area.

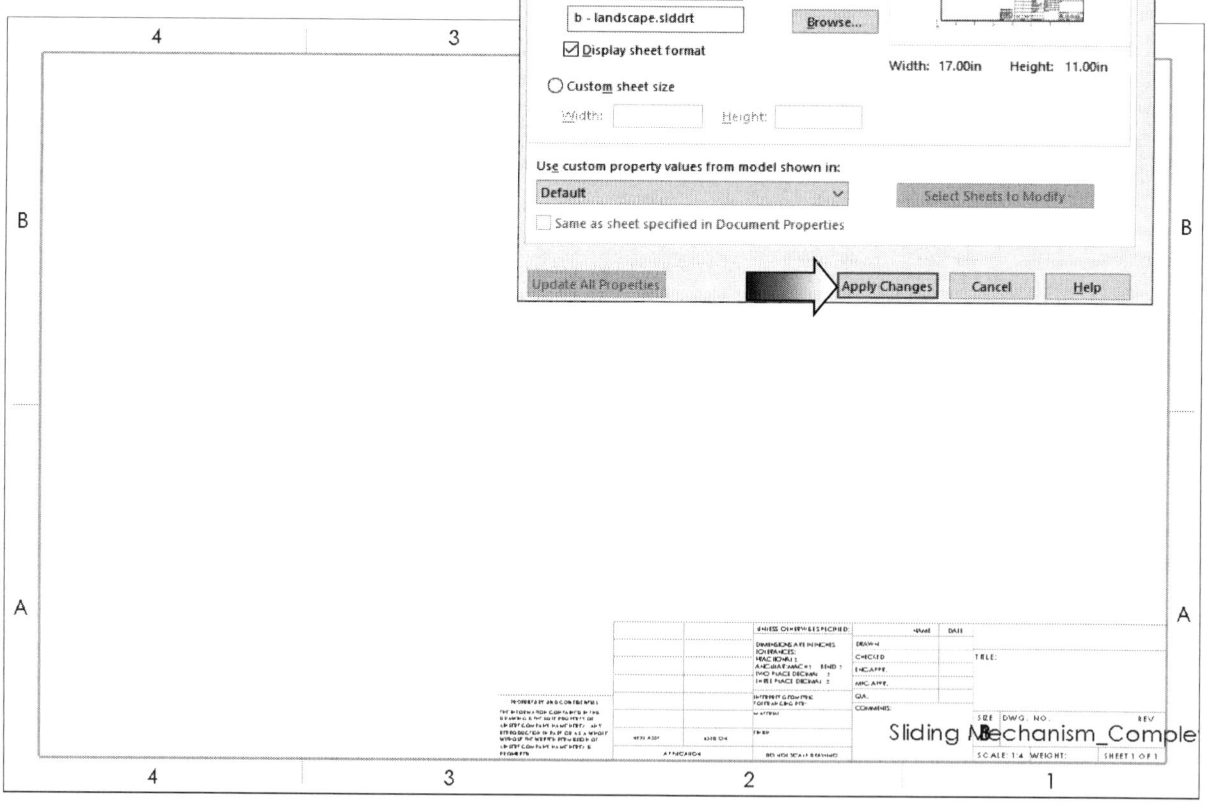

5. Inserting the drawing views:

Click the **View Palette** tab to see the drawing views.

Drag and drop the **Isometric** and the **Isometric Exploded** views to the drawing.

Position the drawing views similar to the image shown below.

The route lines should be visible in the Isometric Exploded view by default.

We will add the balloons in the next step.

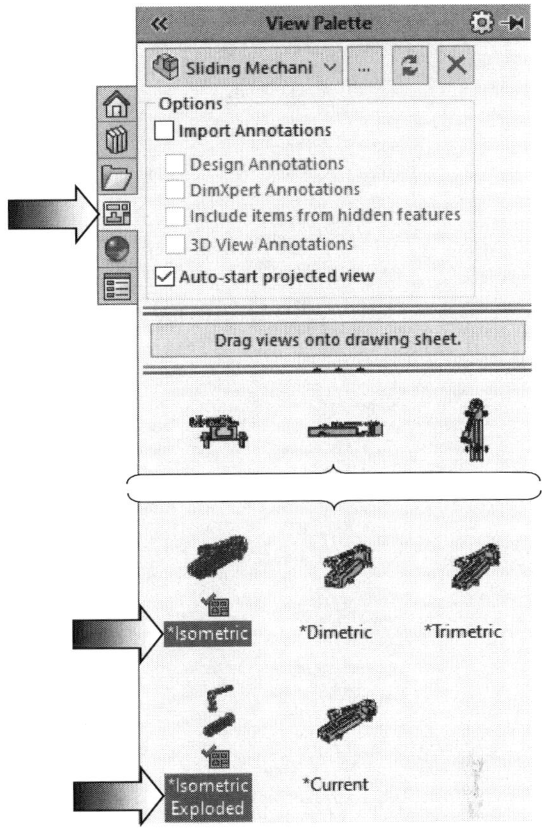

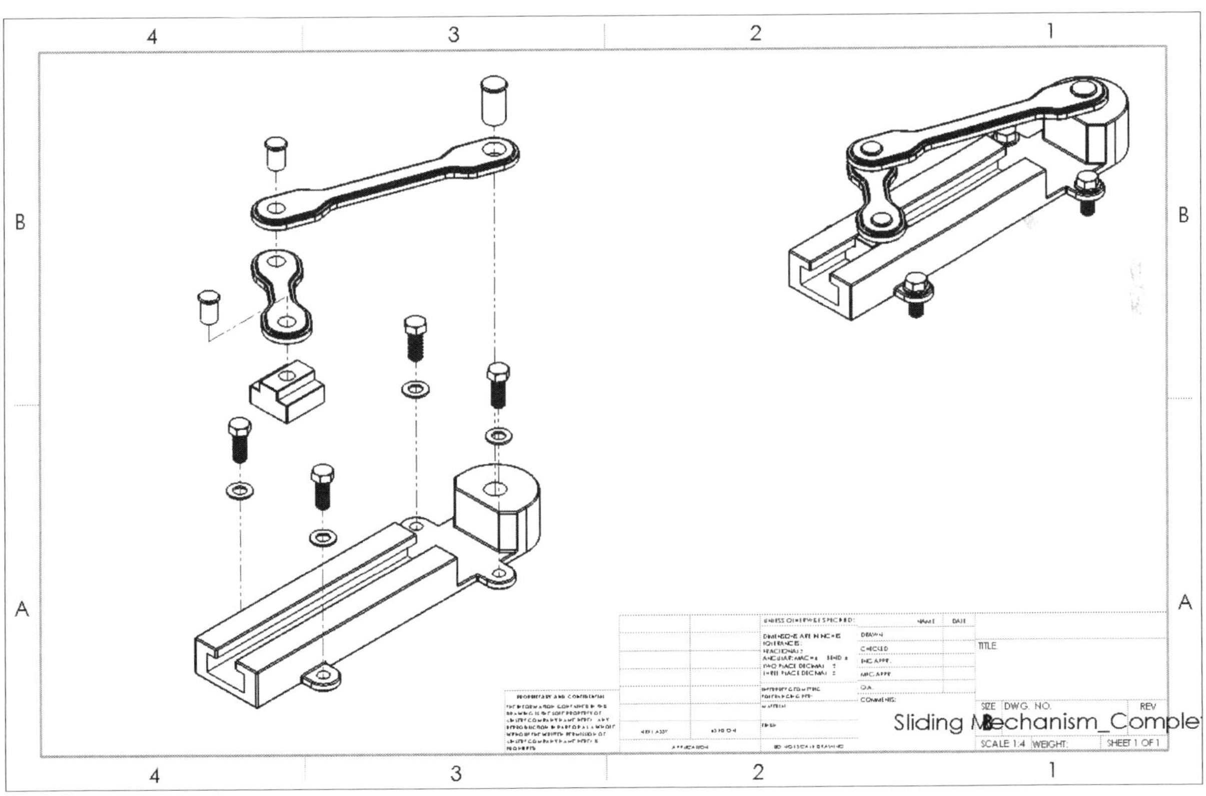

6. Adding Balloons:

Click the dotted border of the **Isometric Exploded** view to make it active.

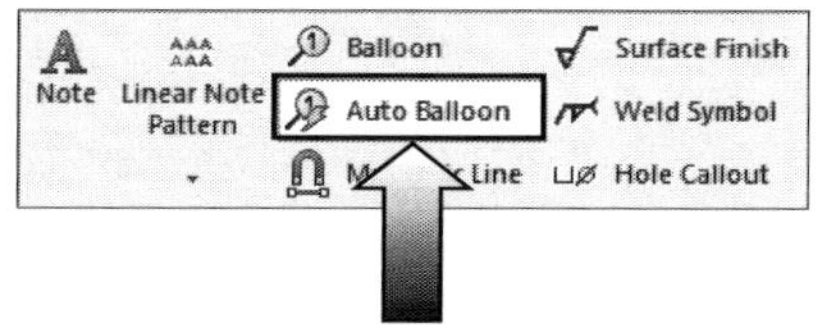

Switch to the **Annotation** tab and select the **Auto-Balloon** command.

Enable the **Quantity** checkbox to add the instance counts automatically.

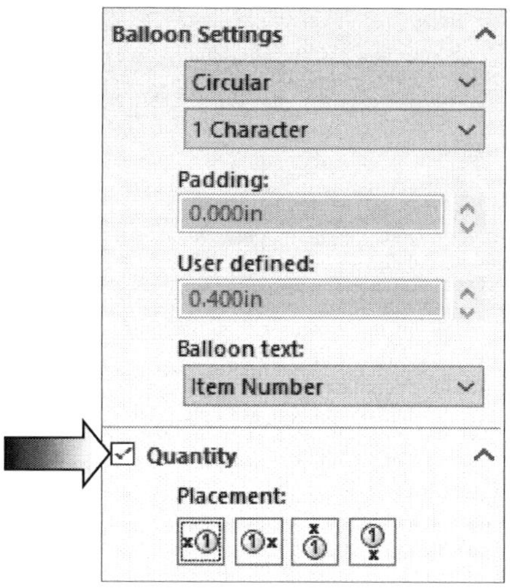

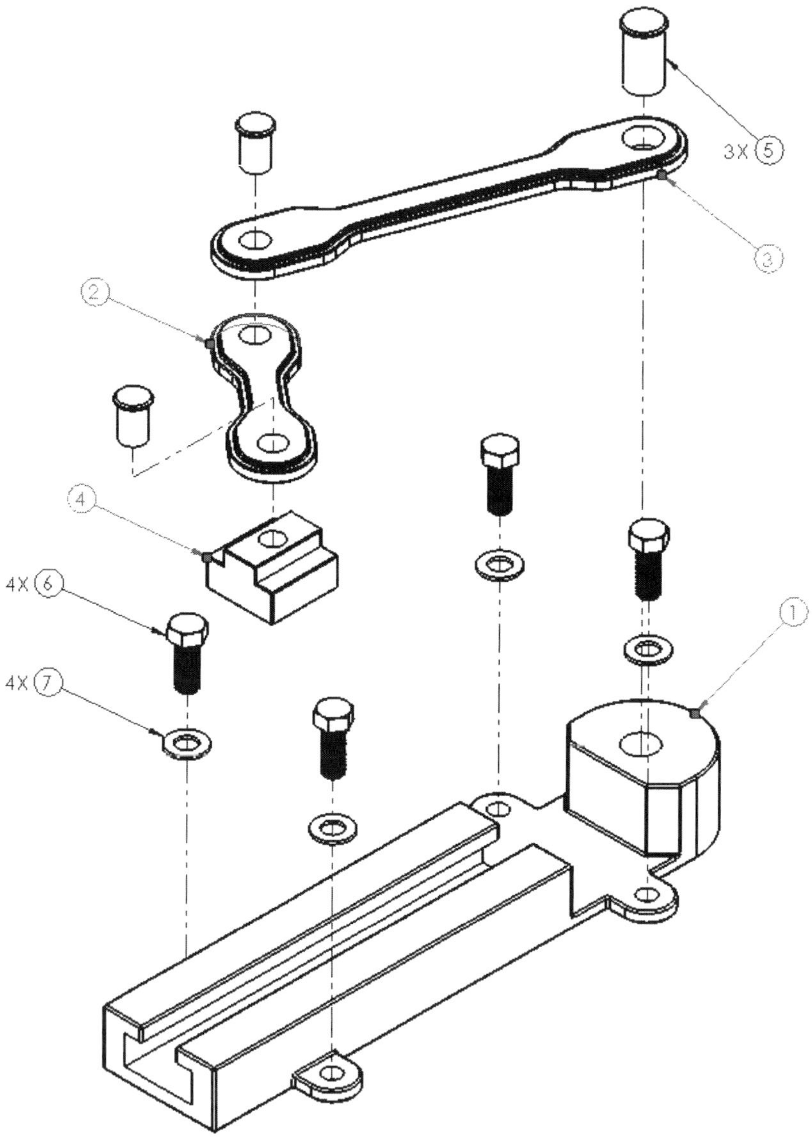

The components that are used only once should not have the instance count enabled.

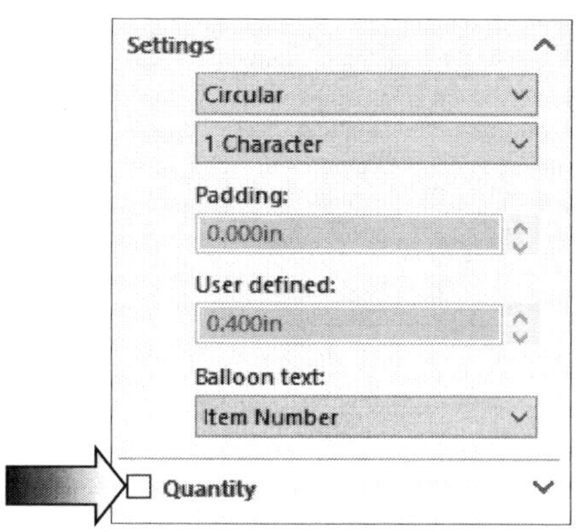

Control + select balloons **1, 2, 3, 4, 5** and <u>clear</u> the **Quantity** checkbox.

7. Inserting a Bill of Materials:

Select **Tables, Bill of Materials** from the **Annotation** tab.

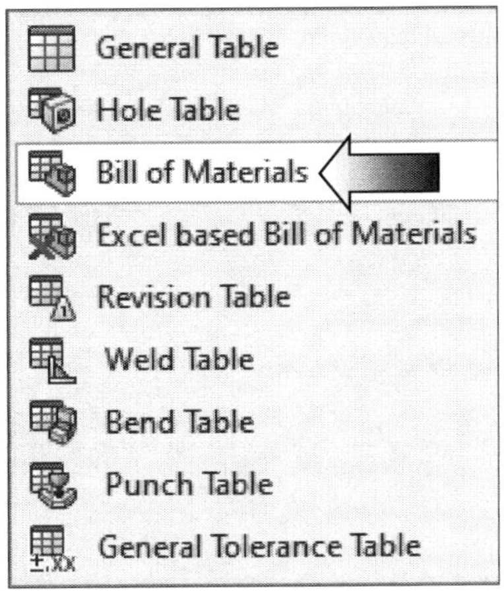

Select the following:

BOM-Standard
Parts Only

Click **OK**.

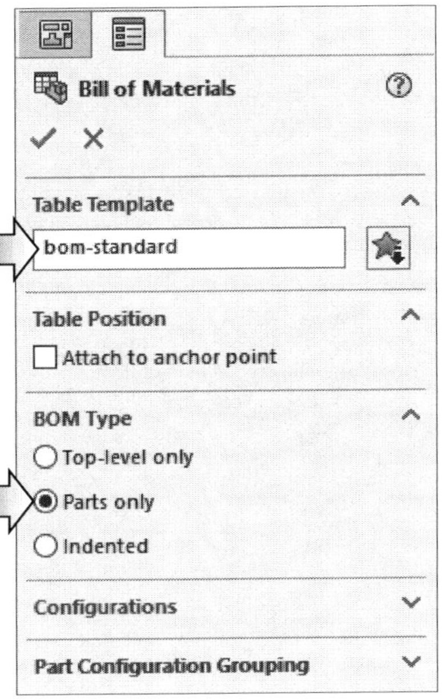

Place the Bill of Materials on top of the Title Block as shown below. We will format the BOM in the next step.

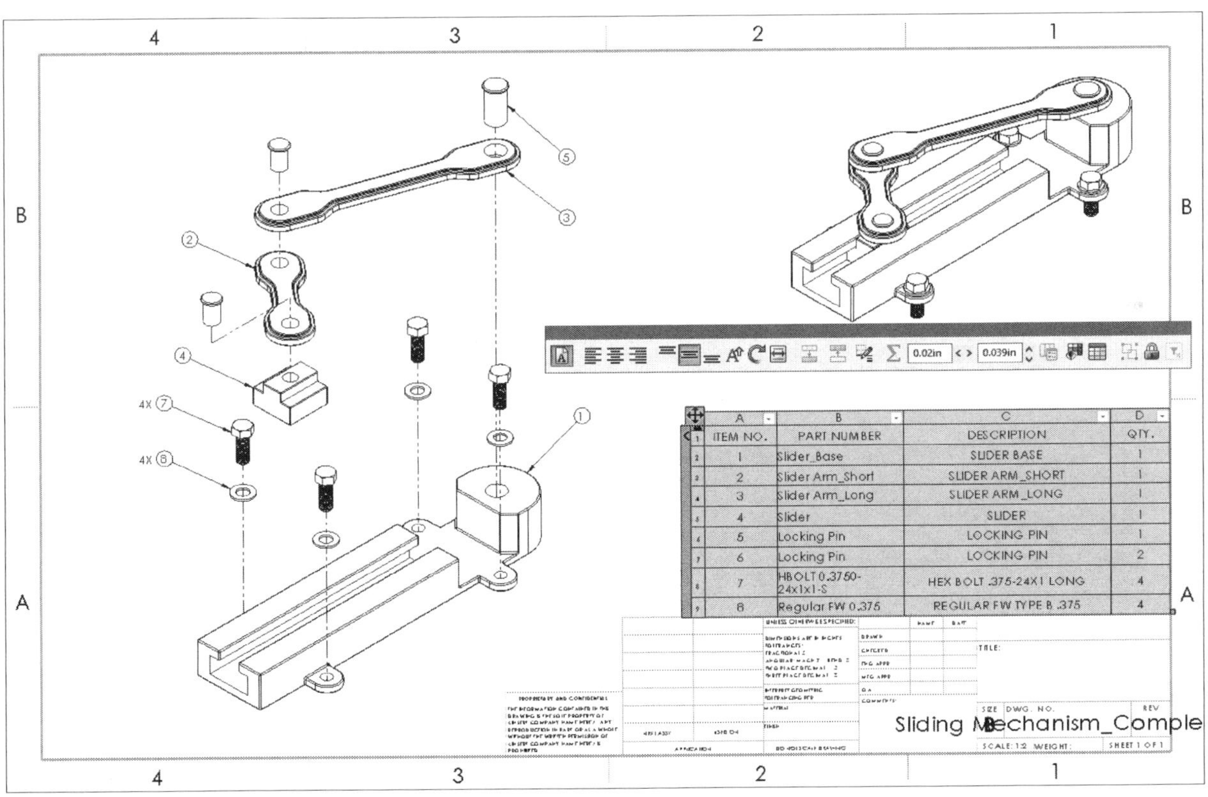

8. Formatting the B.O.M.:

Click anywhere inside the BOM to access the **Formatting** toolbar.

Select the following:

Center Align
Century Gothic

Middle Align
12 Points

Table Header Bottom

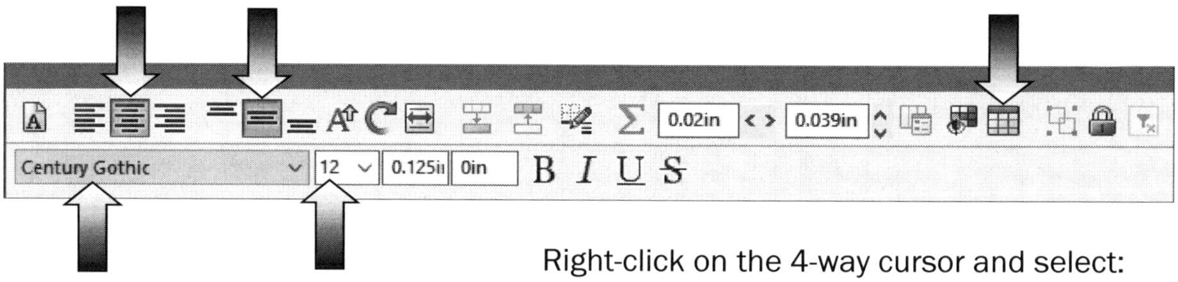

Right-click on the 4-way cursor and select: **Formatting, Row Height.**

Enter **.25in** for the Row Height and click **OK.**

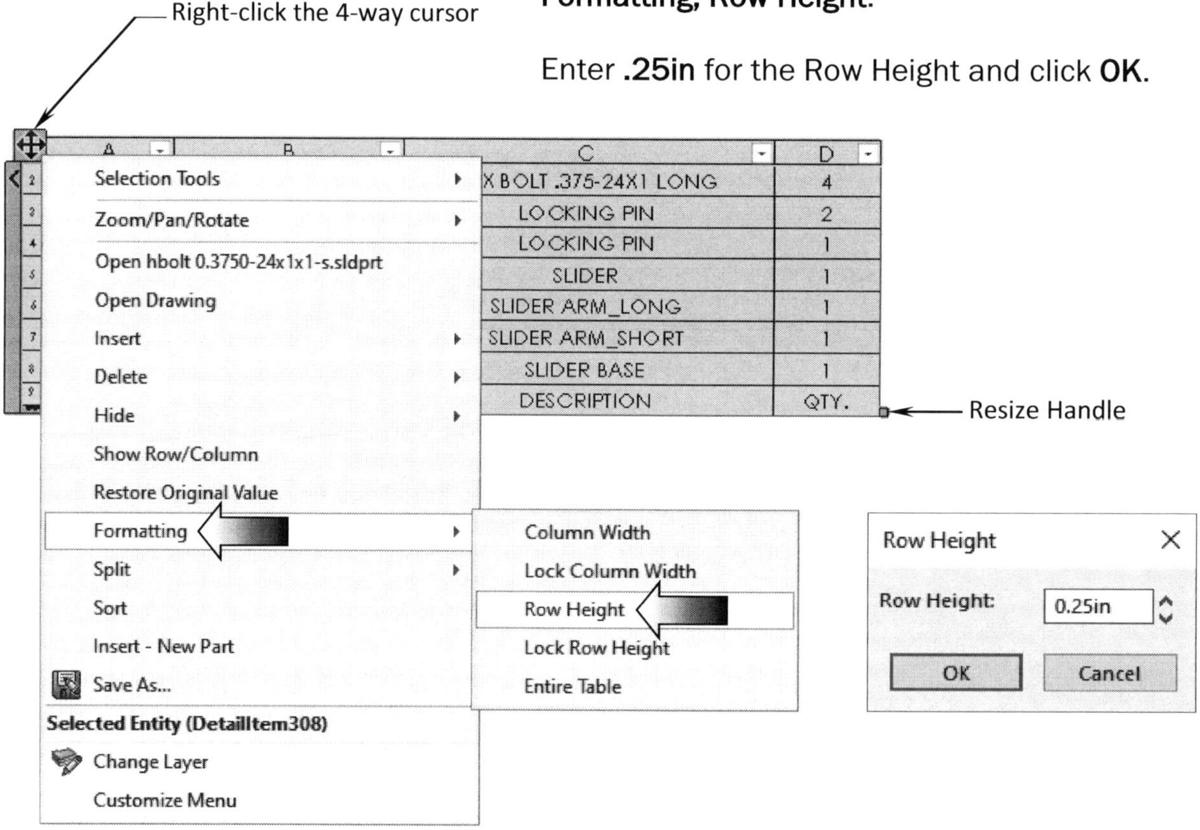

Drag the handle at the lower right corner of the table to adjust the overall size of the BOM table, if needed.

9. Changing the Custom Properties:

The Part Number Column should display the part numbers (numeric) instead of the description. This information can be retrieved quickly if it has been entered in the part document ahead of time.

8	Regular FW 0.375	REGULAR FW TYPE B .375	4
7	HBOLT 0.3750-24x1x1-S	HEX BOLT .375-24X1 LONG	4
6	Locking Pin	LOCKING PIN	2
5	Locking Pin	LOCKING PIN	1
4	Slider	SLIDER	1
3	Slider Arm_Long	SLIDER ARM_LONG	1
2	Slider Arm_Short	SLIDER ARM_SHORT	1
1	Slider_Base	SLIDER BASE	1
ITEM NO.	PART NUMBER	DESCRIPTION	QTY.

Double-click the **column header B** and select the following:

Column Type: **Custom Property** Property Name: **PartNo**

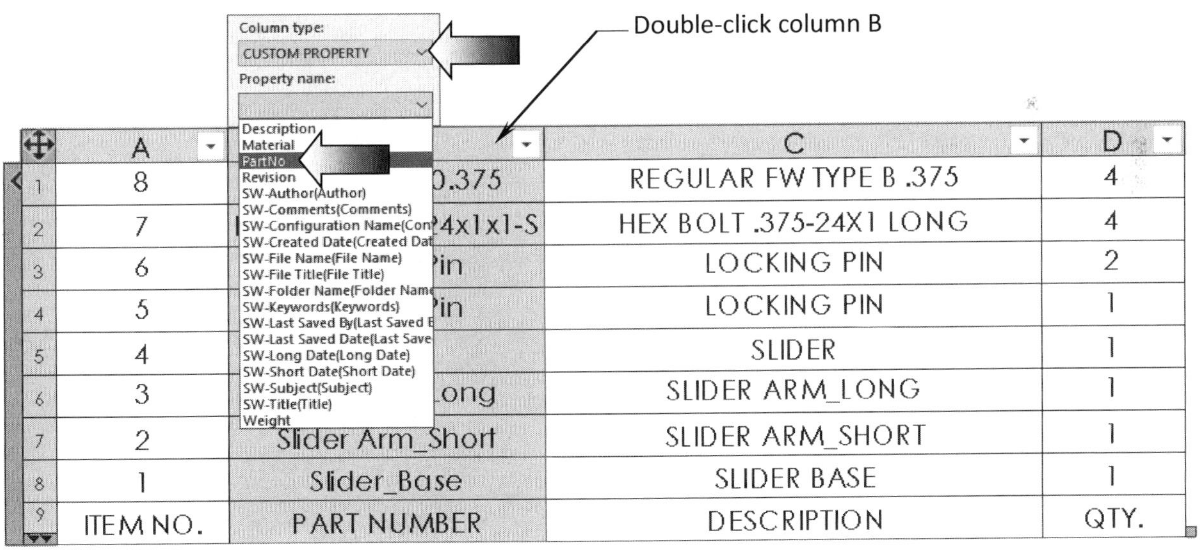

The part numbers that were previously entered in each part are displayed.

Compare your BOM against the table shown below. (Open the part document and select File, Properties to make any corrections needed.)

8	02-10-47467	REGULAR FW TYPE B .375	4
7	02-10-47466	HEX BOLT .375-24X1 LONG	4
6	02-10-47465	LOCKING PIN	2
5	02-10-47465	LOCKING PIN	1
4	02-10-47462	SLIDER	1
3	02-10-47463	SLIDER ARM_LONG	1
2	02-10-47464	SLIDER ARM_SHORT	1
1	02-10-47461	SLIDER BASE	1
ITEM NO.	PartNo	DESCRIPTION	QTY.

The assembly drawing is completed at this time, but we will continue to take a look at other tools that are available for assembly drawings.

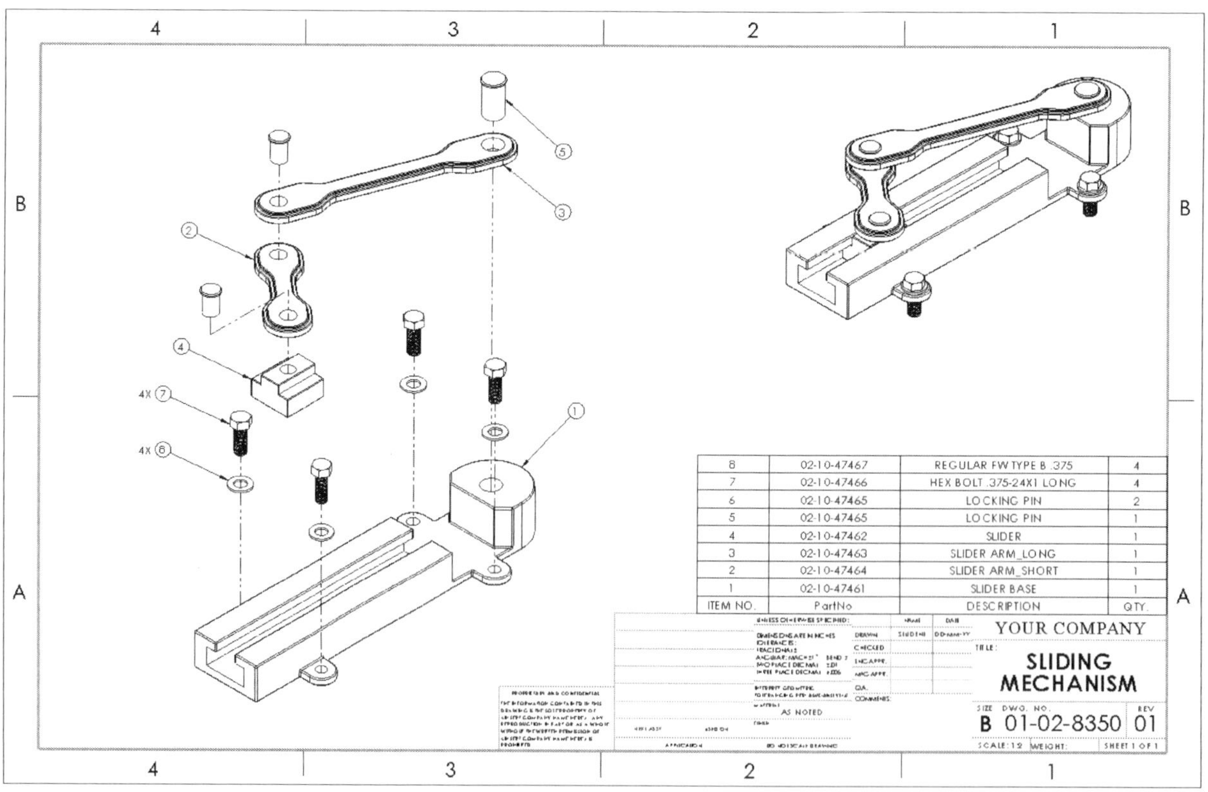

10. Hiding components:

Right-click on the dotted border of the exploded view and select: **Properties**.

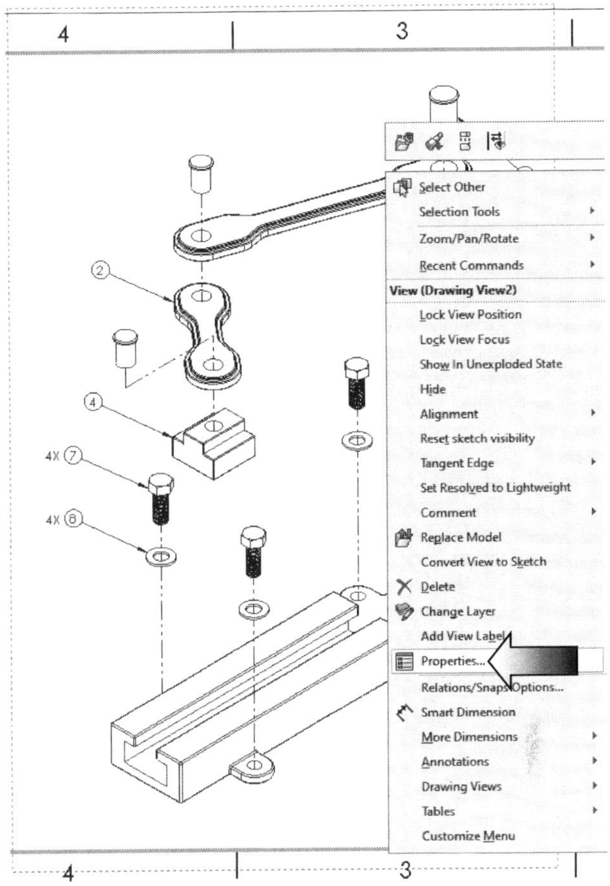

In the Drawing View Properties dialog box, click the **Hide/Show Components** tab.

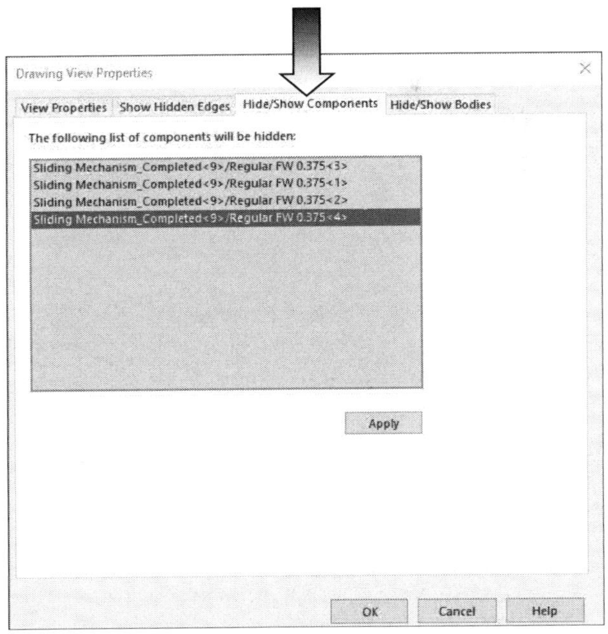

For components to hide, select the <u>4 washers</u> from the graphics area.

Click **Apply** and **OK**.

The 4 selected components are now hidden.

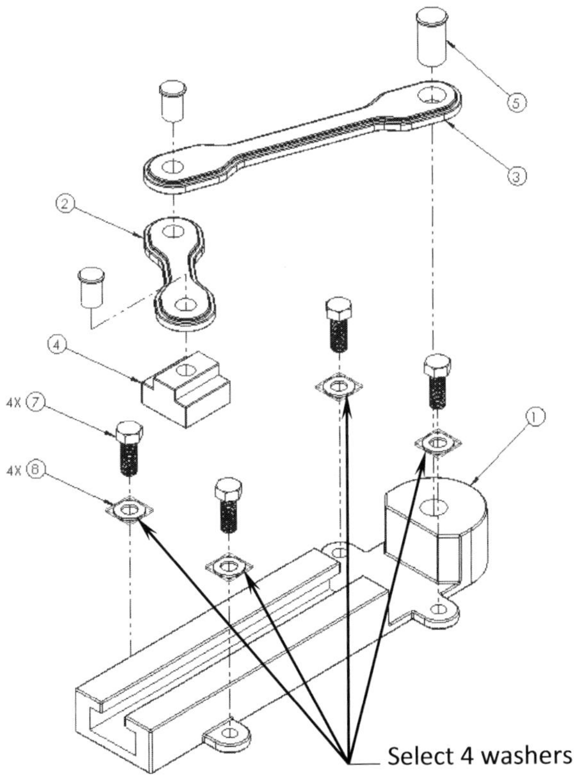

The corresponding components and their balloons should also be removed from the BOM and the drawing view.

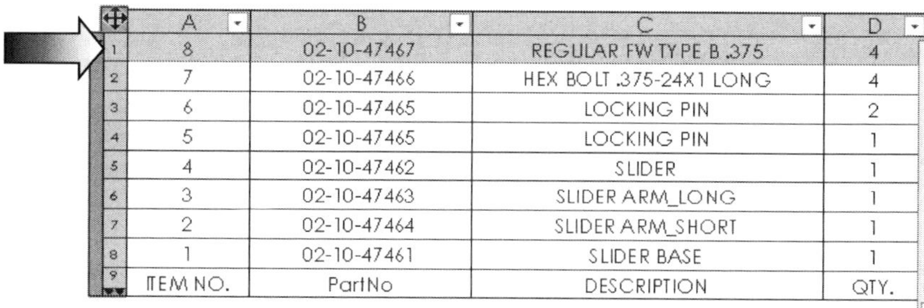

	A	B	C	D
1	8	02-10-47467	REGULAR FW TYPE B .375	4
2	7	02-10-47466	HEX BOLT .375-24X1 LONG	4
3	6	02-10-47465	LOCKING PIN	2
4	5	02-10-47465	LOCKING PIN	1
5	4	02-10-47462	SLIDER	1
6	3	02-10-47463	SLIDER ARM_LONG	1
7	2	02-10-47464	SLIDER ARM_SHORT	1
8	1	02-10-47461	SLIDER BASE	1
9	ITEM NO.	PartNo	DESCRIPTION	QTY.

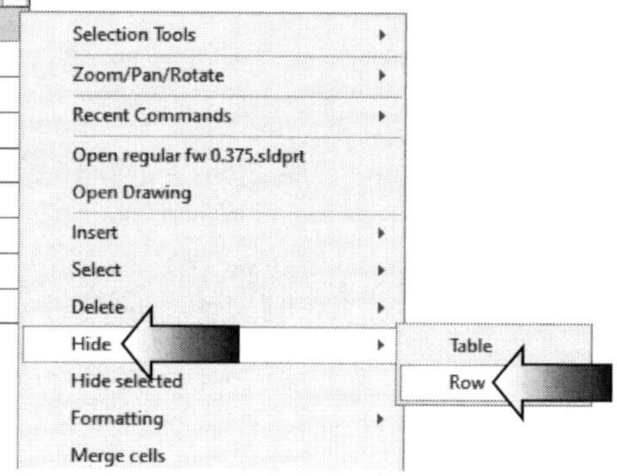

Right-click on **Row-1** and select: **Hide, Row.**

Right-click on **balloon 8** (the washers) and select **Hide.**

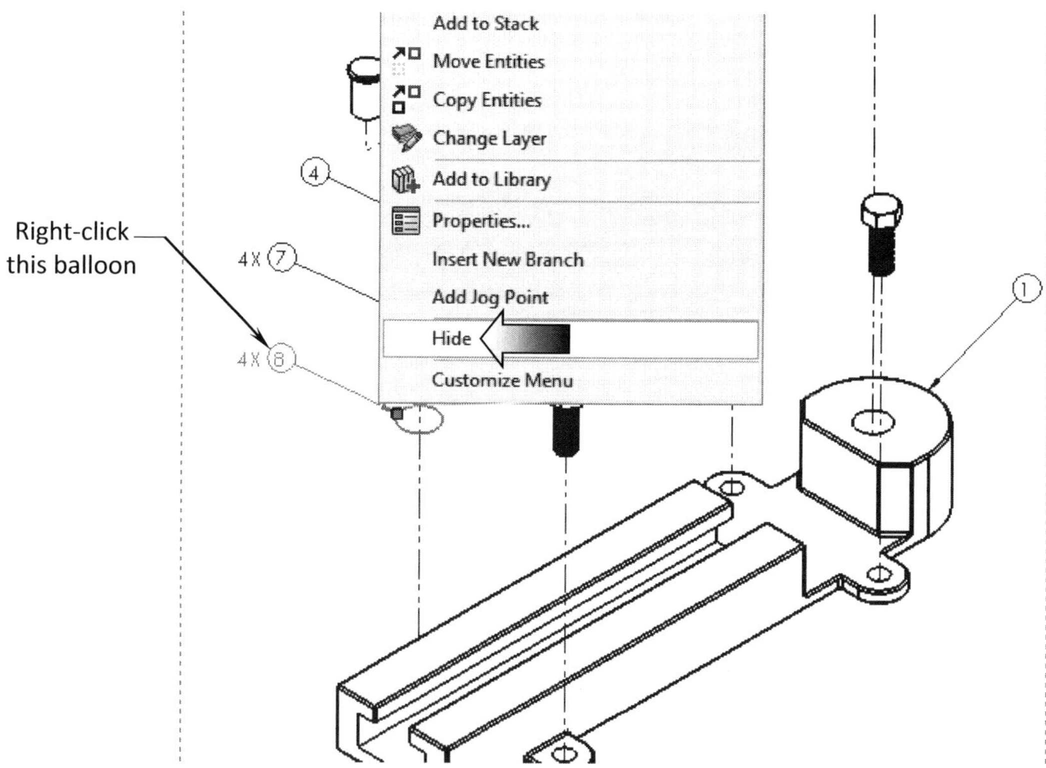

To Unhide the balloons (or any notes and dimensions), select **View, Hide/Show, Annotation,** and click the gray color balloons to unhide them.

11. Filling out the Title Block:

Using the FeatureManager tree, double-click on **Sheet Format1** to activate it.

Fill out the information shown below. Move the lines and adjust the font size to make everything fit correctly, where needed.

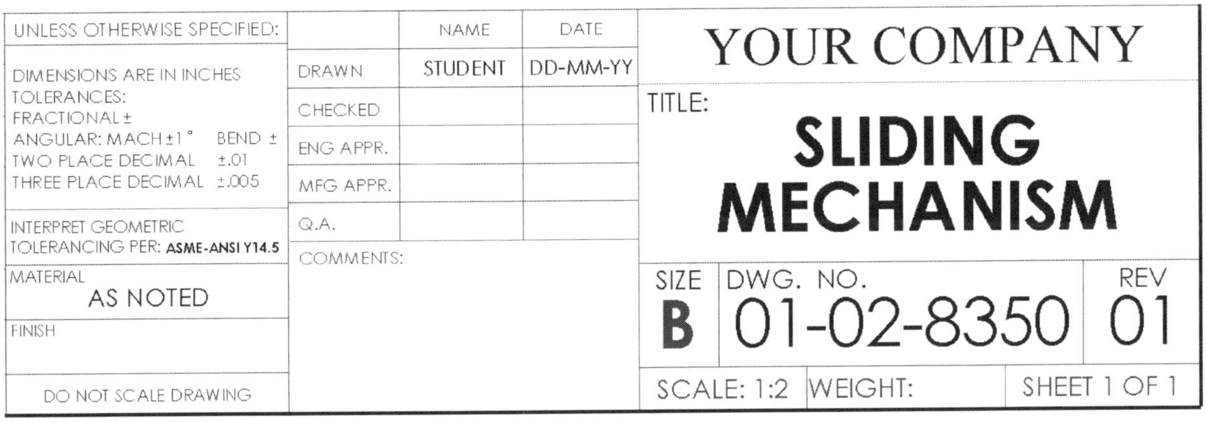

Double-click on **Sheet1** when finished with filling out the Title Block.

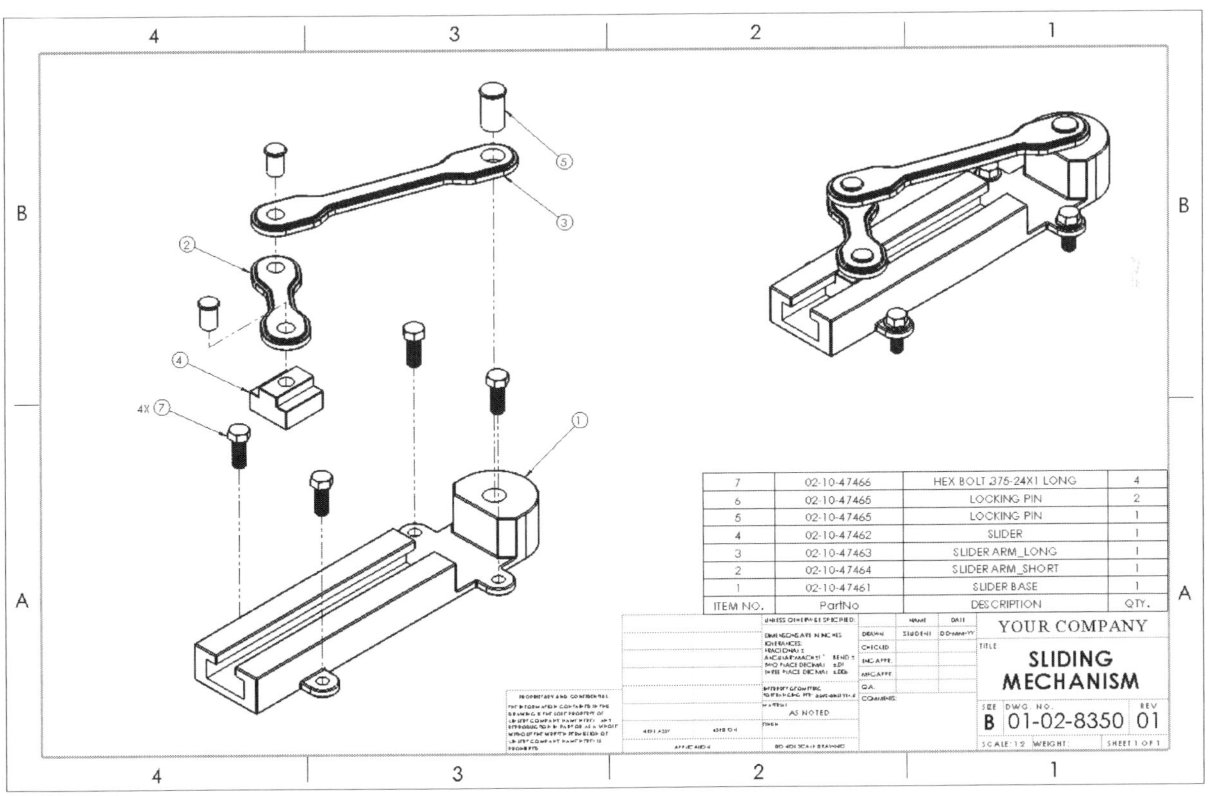

OTHER DISPLAY OPTIONS

Tangent Edges Visible

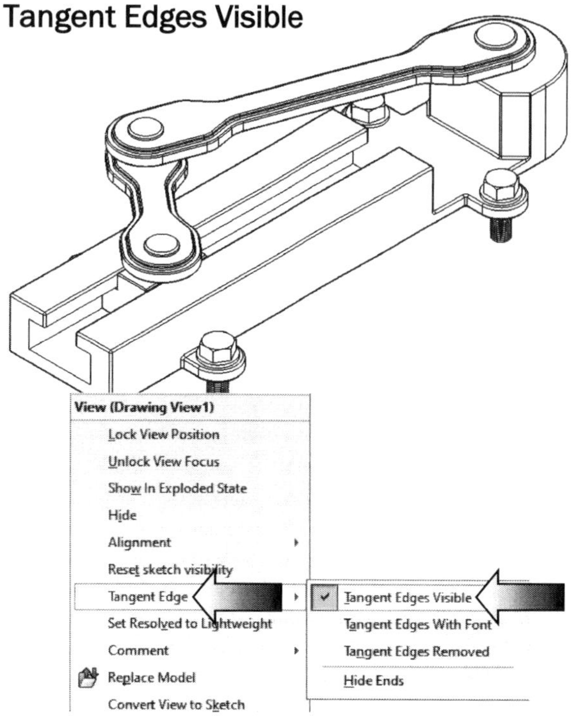

Tangent Edges With Font

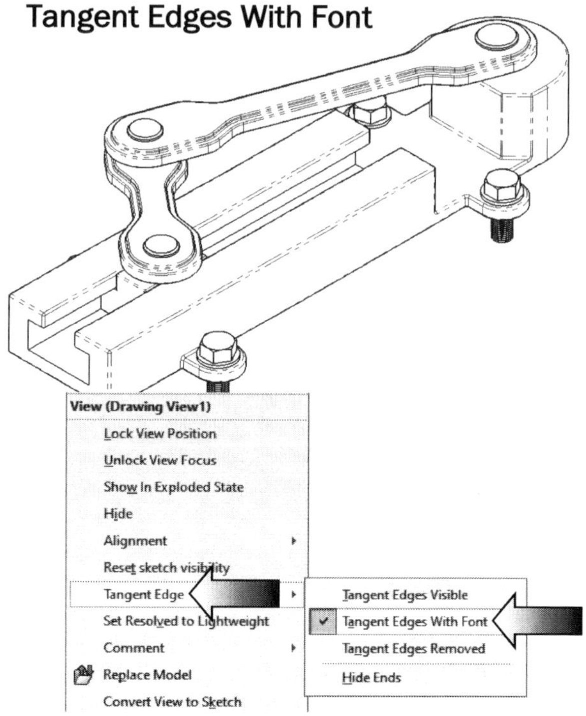

Tangent Edges Removed

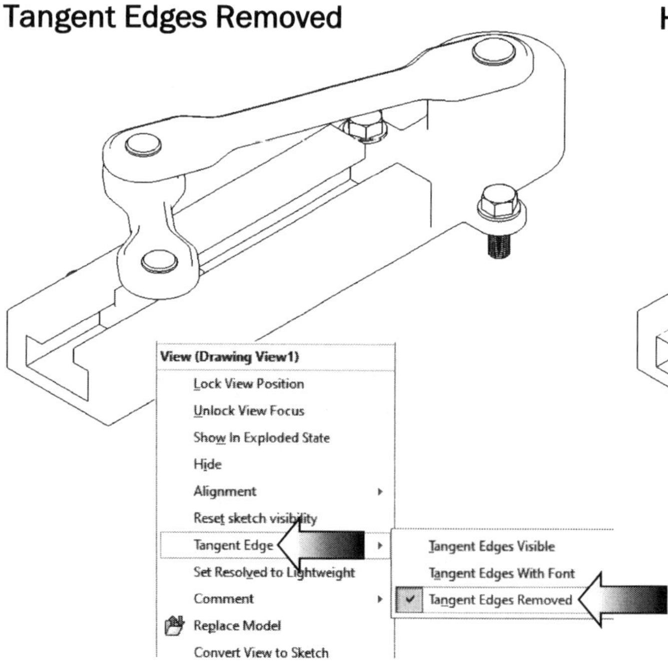

Hidden Lines Visible

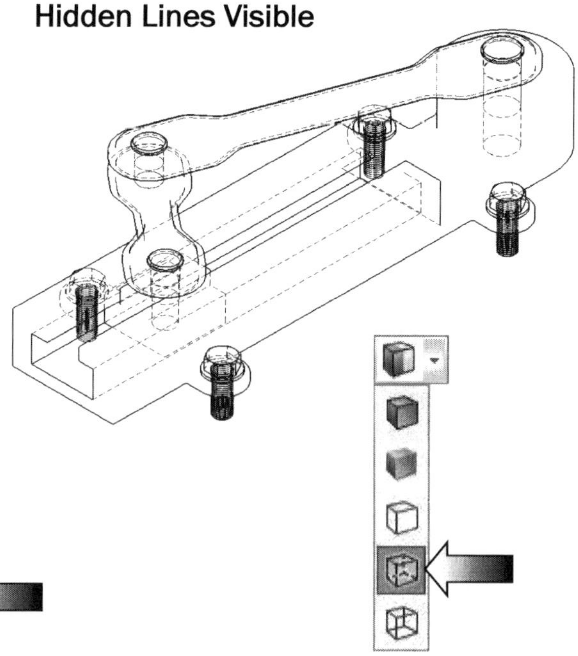

Shaded with Edges

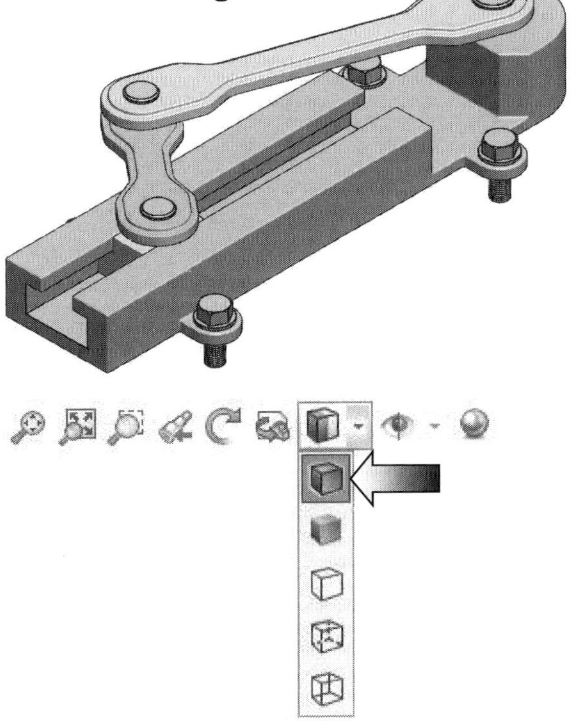

Shaded without Edges

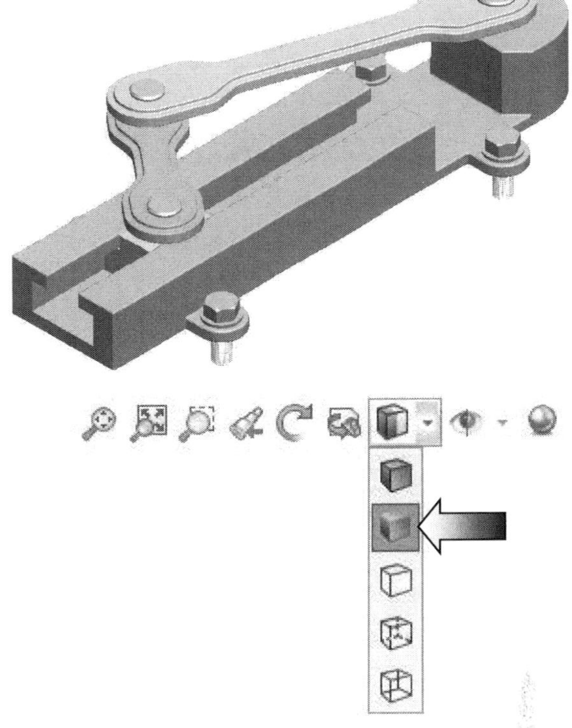

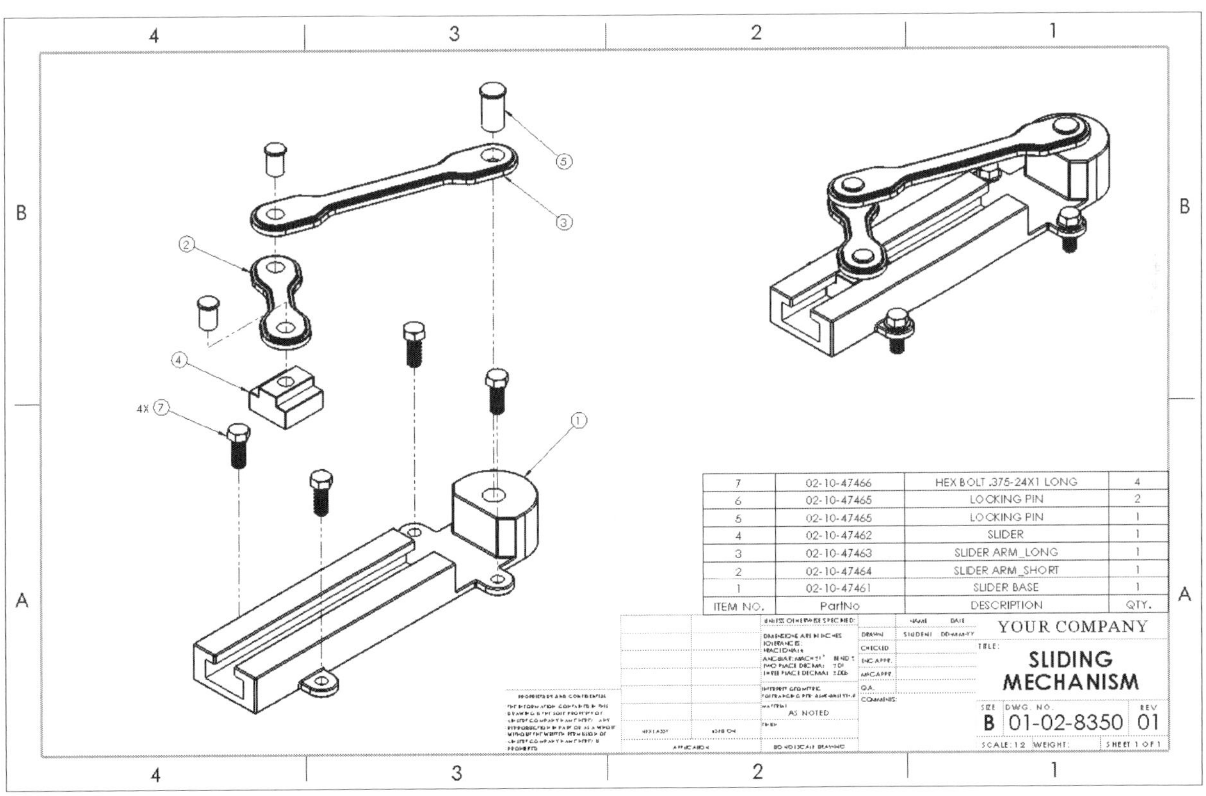

12. Saving your work:

Select **File, Save As.**

Enter: **Sliding Mechanism_Complerted.slddrw** for the file name.

Click **Save.**

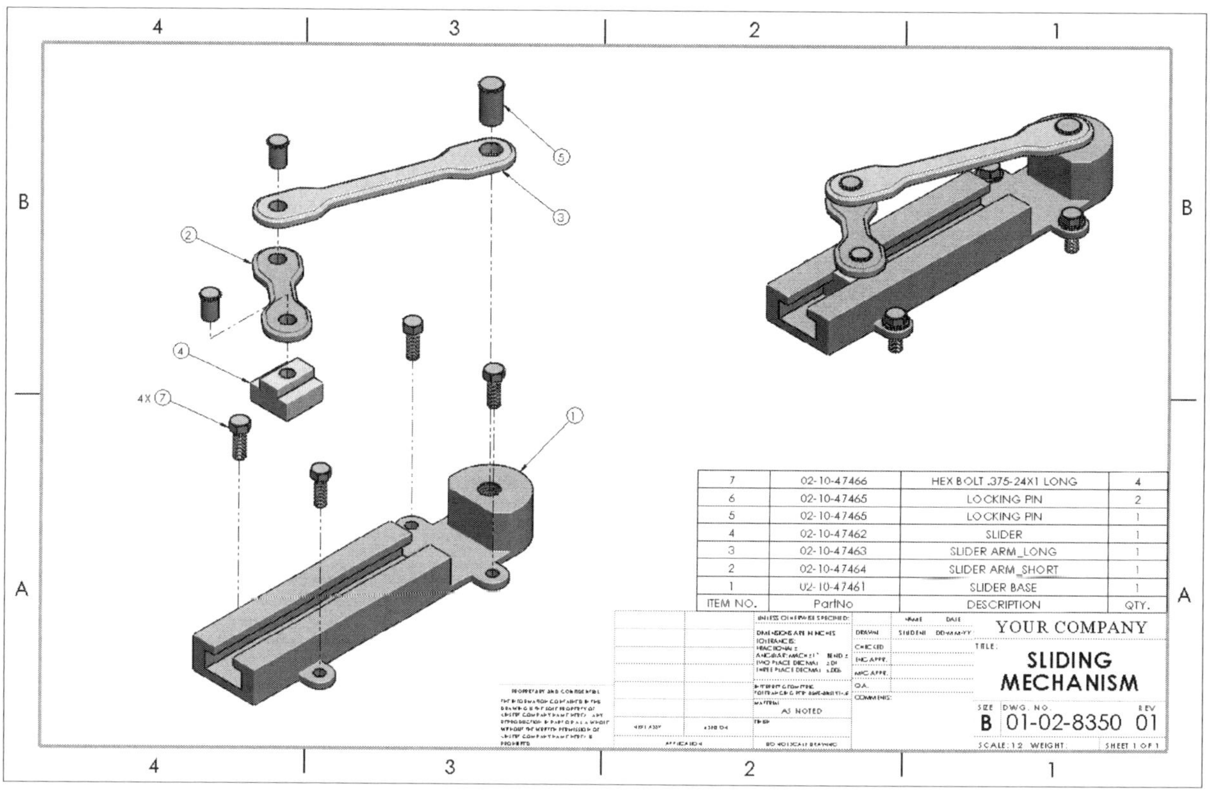

Close all documents.

CHAPTER 12: SOLIDWORKS MBD – PART 1

Model Based Definition – Prismatic Parts

Model-Based Definition (MBD) is the process of defining product & engineering data within a 3D CAD model. With SOLIDWORKS MBD, the model becomes the source that drives all engineering activities such as Design Development, Manufacturing, documentation, and Inspection.

MBD can help:

* Reduce costs, due to the fact that no 2D drawings need to be generated.
* Reduction in scrap and rework, due to misinterpretation of information from the 2D drawings.
* Improved quality, as all the quality requirements can be added directly to the 3D model which is used directly to fabricate the component.

MBD also accelerates the handling and processing of engineering change orders (ECOs) when changes are made after a product has been released into production.

As the model is updated with the appropriate changes, all the associated data automatically gets updated in the master 3D model, thus eliminating the risk of wrong drawings being sent to suppliers or suppliers not updating the drawings for manufacture.

Overall, MBD is a quicker and easier way of disseminating all the vital information required to manufacture products.

This chapter will teach us the tools in SOLIDWORKS MBD to present product and manufacturing information in a model and publish to either 3D PDF or eDrawing for collaborations with others.

1. Opening a part document:

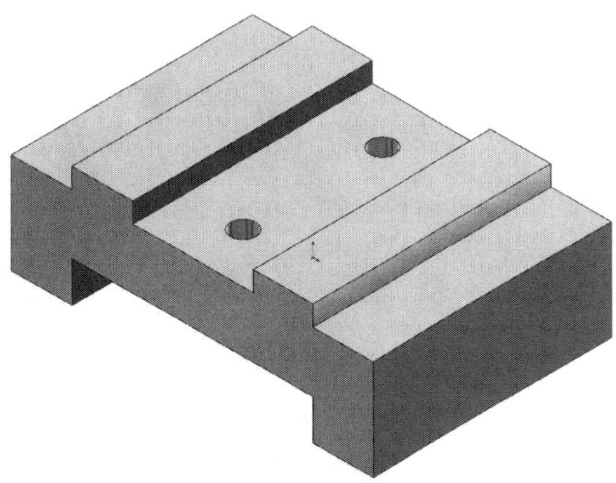

Select **File, Open**.

Navigate to the training folder and open the part document named: **Prismatic Part 1.sldprt**.

The material **AISI 304** has already been assigned to the part.

2. Understanding the types of parts:

Prismatic parts are block or flat shaped and usually comprised of basic features, such as slots, steps, holes, bosses, that may intersect with one another. Prismatic parts are usually made using a milling machine.

Turned parts are cylindrical shaped such as spacers, fittings, contouring, connectors, threaded components and much more. Turned parts are usually made on a turning machine or a lathe machine.

Both Prismatic and Turned parts can be toleranced with MBD.

Prismatic parts

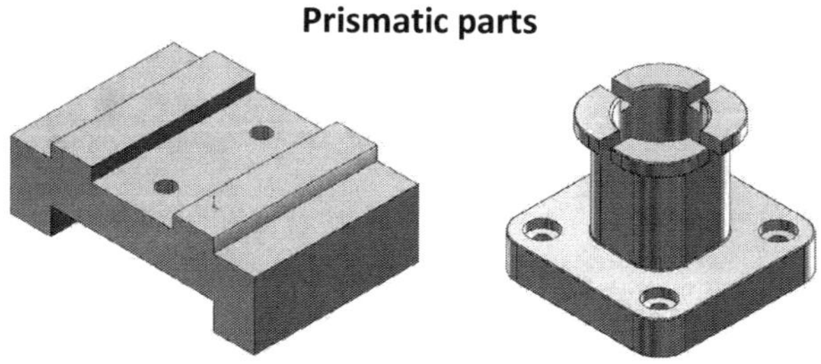

For **Prismatic** parts, when you use Geometric as Tolerance type, DimXpert applies **Position Tolerances** to locate the holes and bosses.

Turned parts

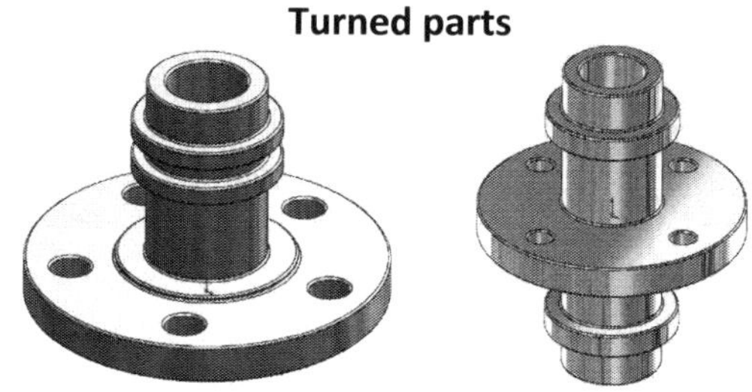

For **Turned** parts, when you use Geometric as Tolerance type, DimXpert applies **Circular Runout Tolerances** to locate the holes and bosses.

3. Understanding the DimXpert tool:

DimXpert is a SOLIDWORKS tool to add tolerances to the geometry of a model. Its associated 3D annotations such as datums, dimensions, and geometric tolerances are also used to define geometry.

DimXpert offers a couple of options such as **Auto-Dimension-Scheme** and **Manual-DimXpert** tools to recognize and define the features in a SOLIDWORKS model. The associated annotations can be added automatically or manually to complete the process.

DimXpert tools create features and annotations such as datum, size and/or **DimXpertManager**.

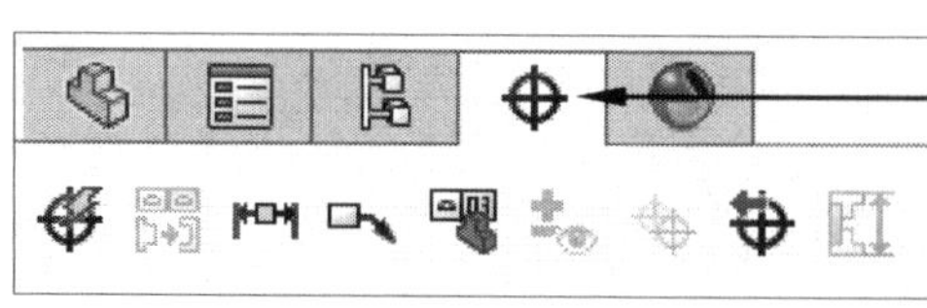

4. Setting up the options for DimXpert:

Click **Options** or select **Tools, Options**.

Select the **Document Properties** tab.

Click the **Drafting Standard** option.

Select **ANSI** under the Overall - Drafting Standard drop-down list.

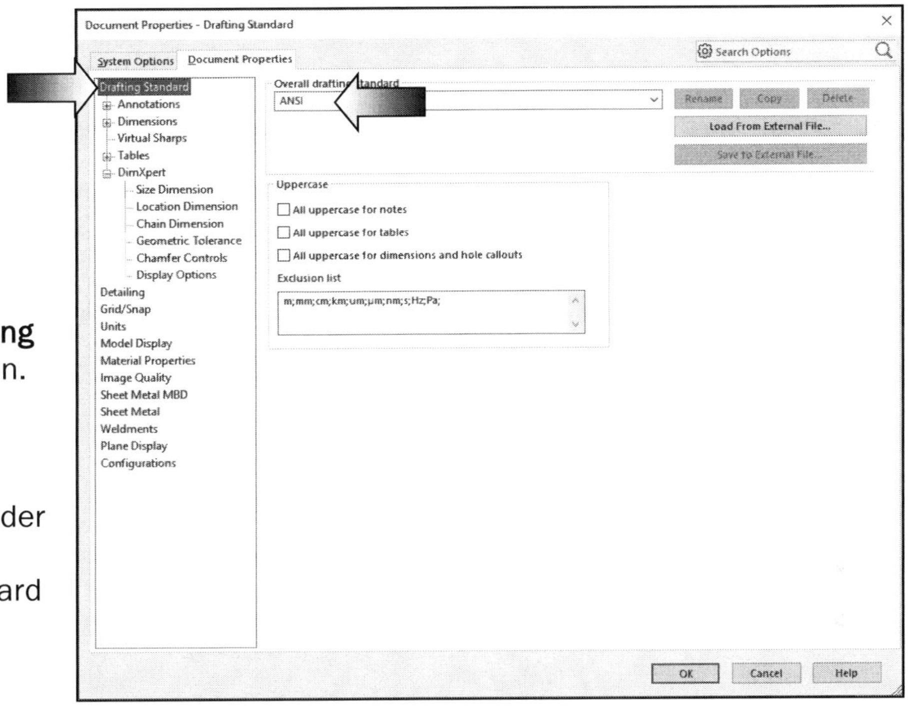

Expand the **DimXpert** option.

Click the **Size-Dimension** option.

Set the tolerances shown in the dialog box. (These tolerances are only for use with this chapter.)

Do not click OK.

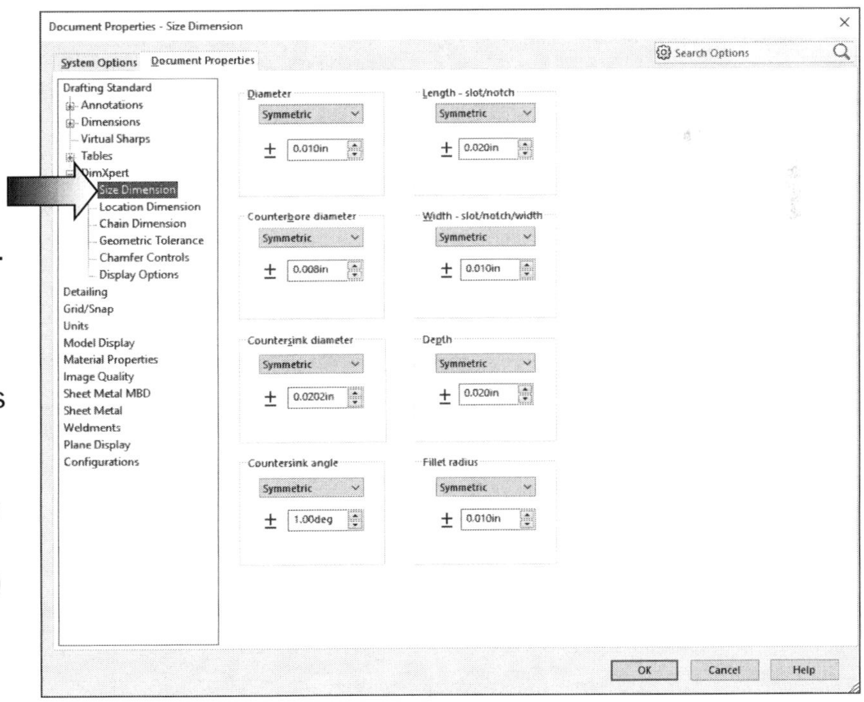

Click the **Location Dimension** option.

Set the tolerances shown here for this option. (Dimensions are in inches.)

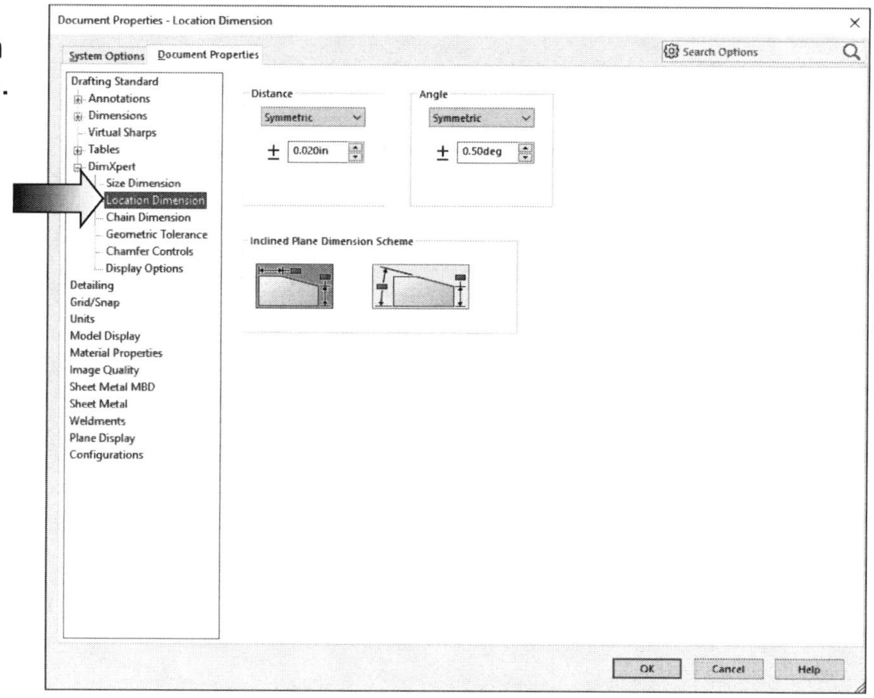

Click the **Geometric Tolerance** option.

Set the tolerances shown in the dialog box to match.

Enable the **Create Basic Dimensions** checkbox.

Leave the options for Display Options at their default settings.

Do not click OK just yet.

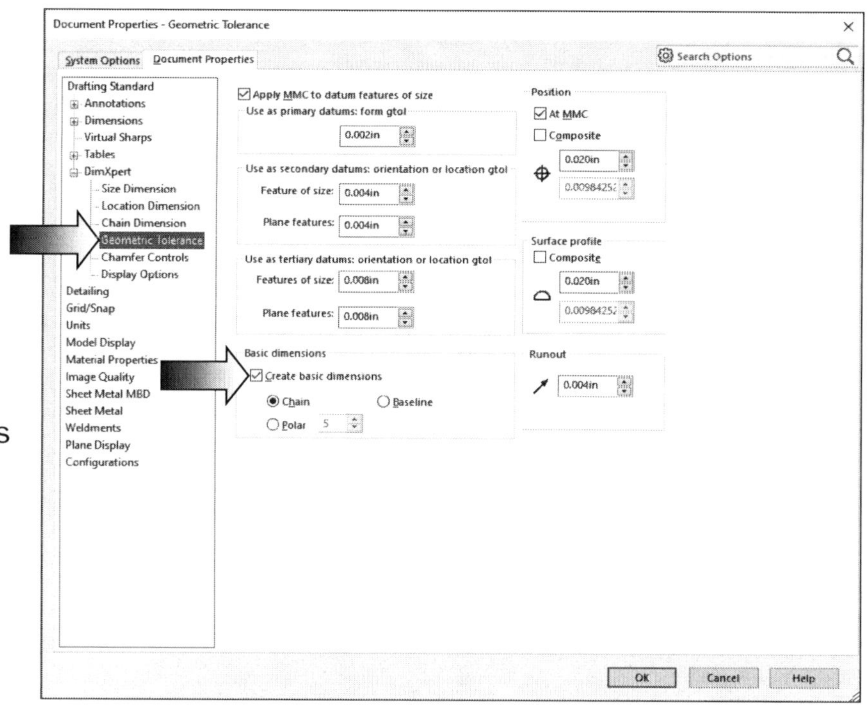

Click the **Display Options.**

Select the <u>1st option</u> for **Slot Dimensions, Hole Callouts, Linear Dimensions GTOL Attachment, Datum GTOL Attachment**, and **Linear Dimension.** Also, enable the checkboxes as shown in the image on the right.

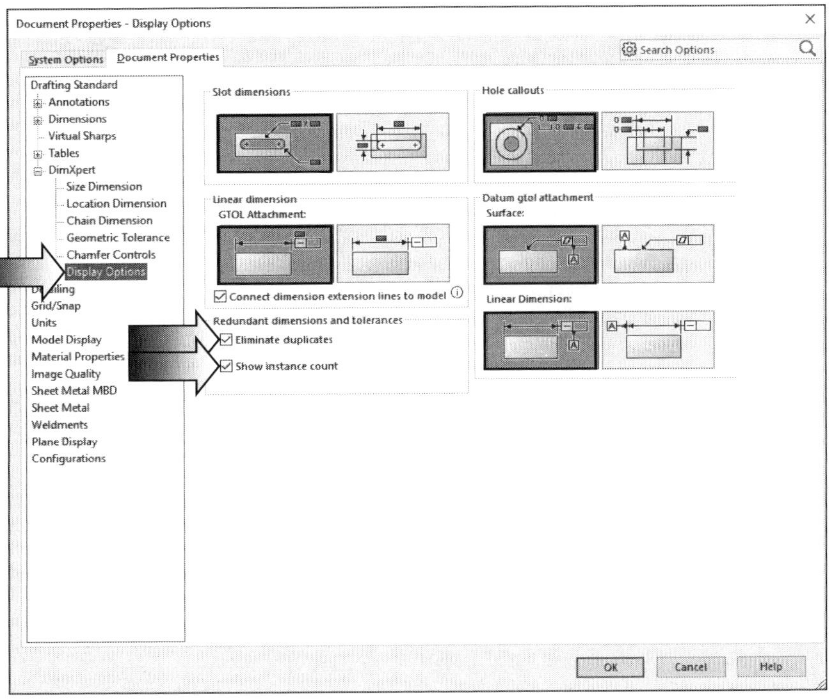

Click **OK** to exit Options.

5. Adding datums:

Auto Dimension Scheme  is one of the quick and easy methods for creating a tolerance scheme.

The user identifies the Primary, Secondary, and Tertiary Datums by selecting the planar or cylindrical faces of the model and Auto Dimension Scheme automatically defines the geometry of the model with the Size Dimensions, Location Dimensions, and Geometric Tolerances.

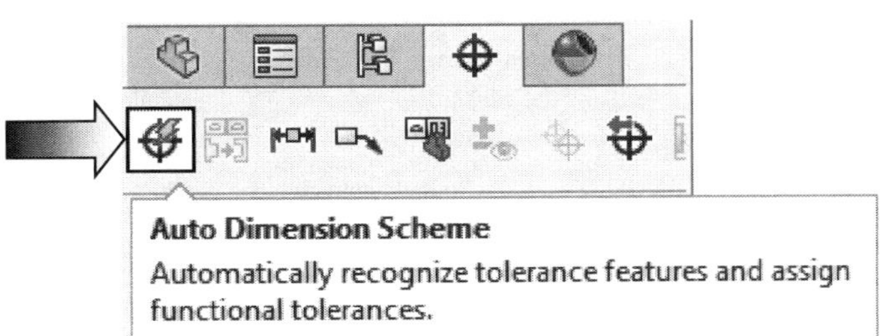

Switch to the **DimXpertManager** tree and click: **Auto Dimension Scheme** .

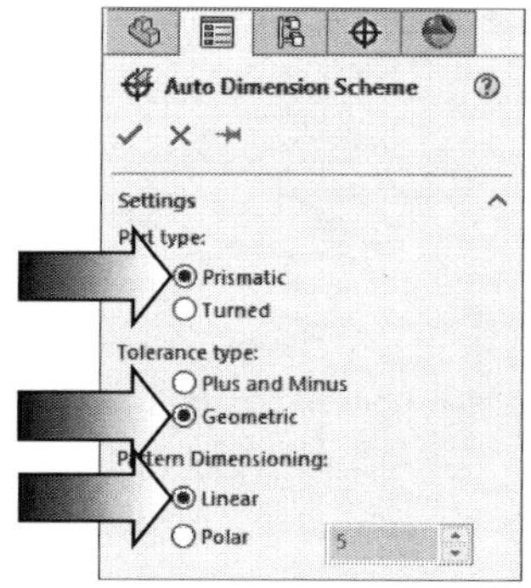

On the **DimXpertManager** tree, in the **Settings** section, select the following:

* **Part Type: Prismatic**

* **Tolerance Type: Geometric**

* **Pattern Dimensioning: Linear**

In the **Datum Selection**, select the following:

* **Primary Datum: Bottom face**

* **Secondary Datum: Right side face**

* **Tertiary Datum: Front face**

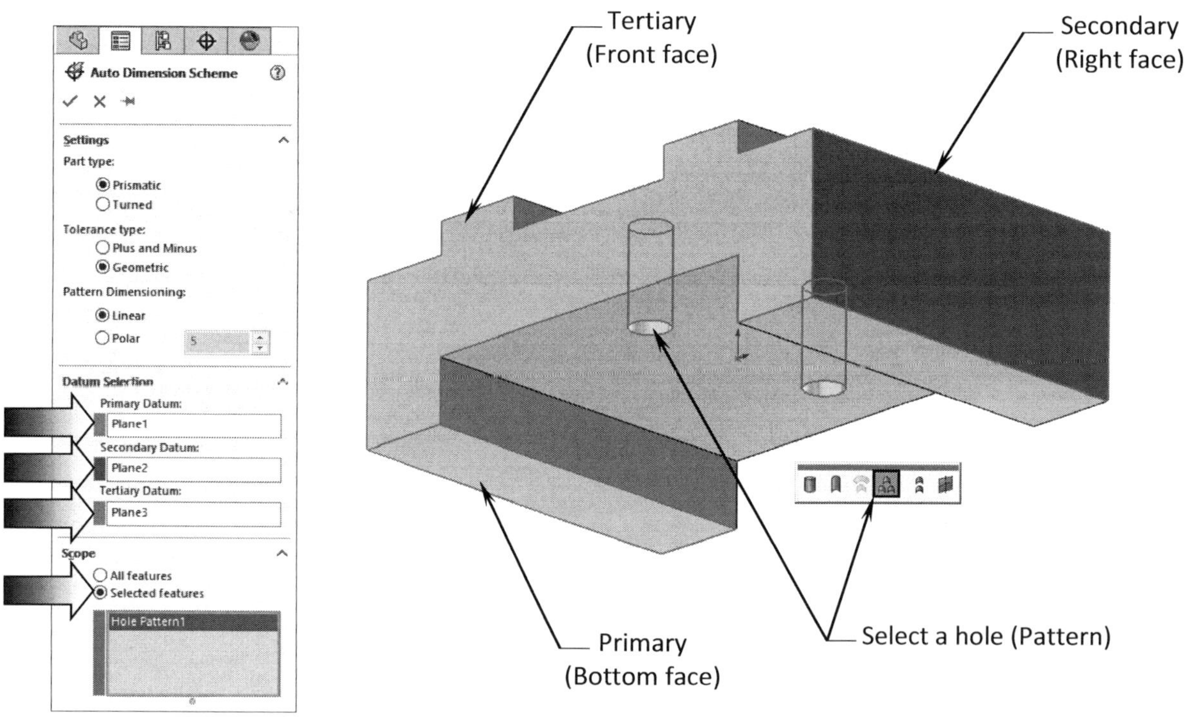

For **Scope**, select one of the <u>holes</u> and click **Pattern** in the pop-up dialog box.

Do <u>not</u> click OK yet.

Additionally, rotate the model and select the **Back face** and the **Left face** of the part to complete the Scope. These 2 faces are used to define the width and depth of the part.

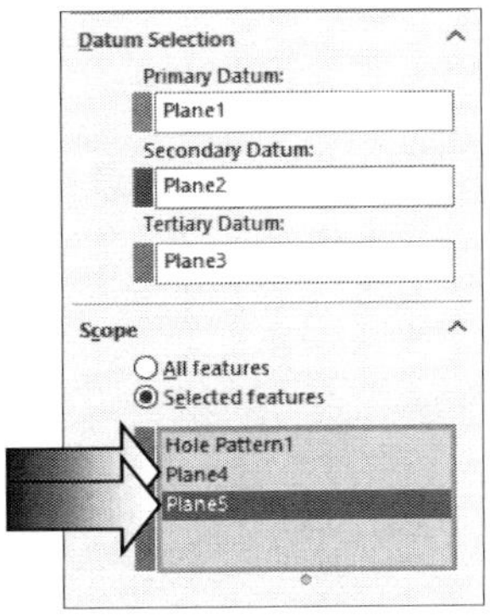

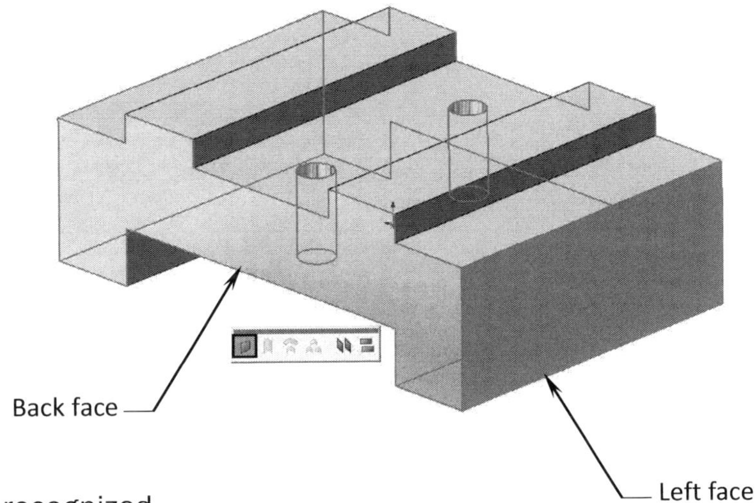

The selected faces are recognized as planes, or planar faces.

Click **OK**.

DimXpert created datums, dimensions, and geometric tolerances to all features in the part.

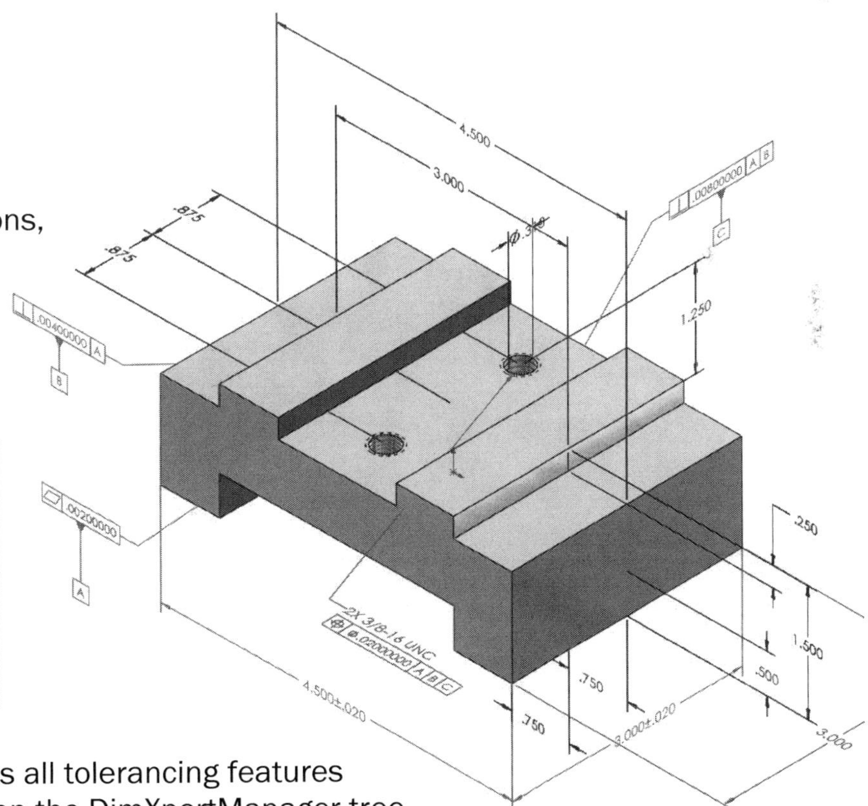

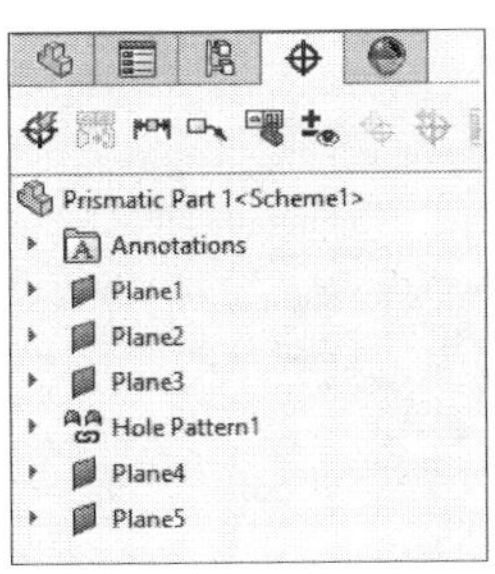

DimXpert also lists all tolerancing features and annotations on the DimXpertManager tree.

6. Showing tolerance status:

The Show Tolerance Status command identifies the manufacturing features that are fully constrained, under constrained, and over constrained from, primarily, a dimensioning and tolerancing perspective.

The MBD tab is needed for the next steps.

Right-click one of the tabs on the Command-Manager and select: **Tabs, MBD.**

Switch to the new **MBD** tab.

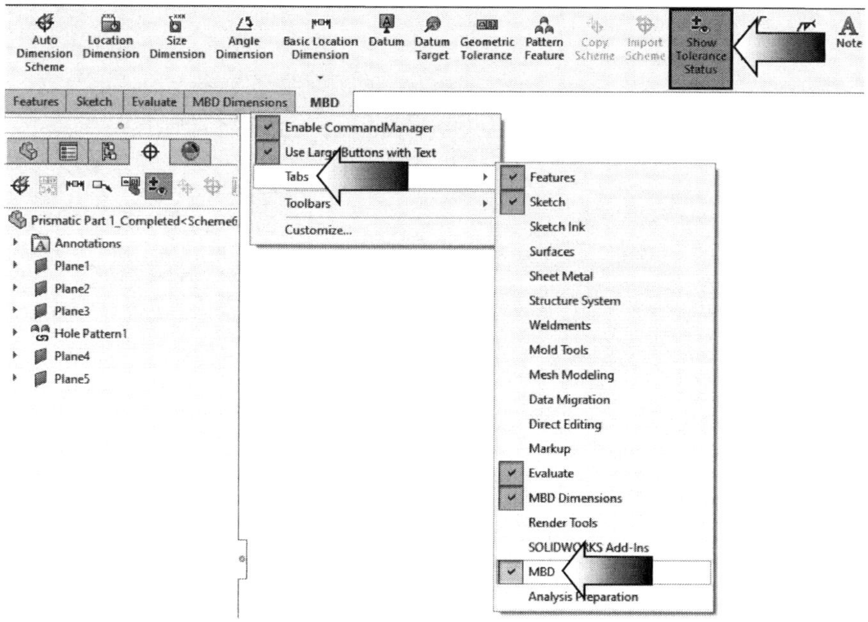

Click **Show Tolerance Status.**

The green color faces represent **Fully Constrained.**

The yellow color faces represent **Under Constrained.**

The red color faces represent **Over Constrained.**

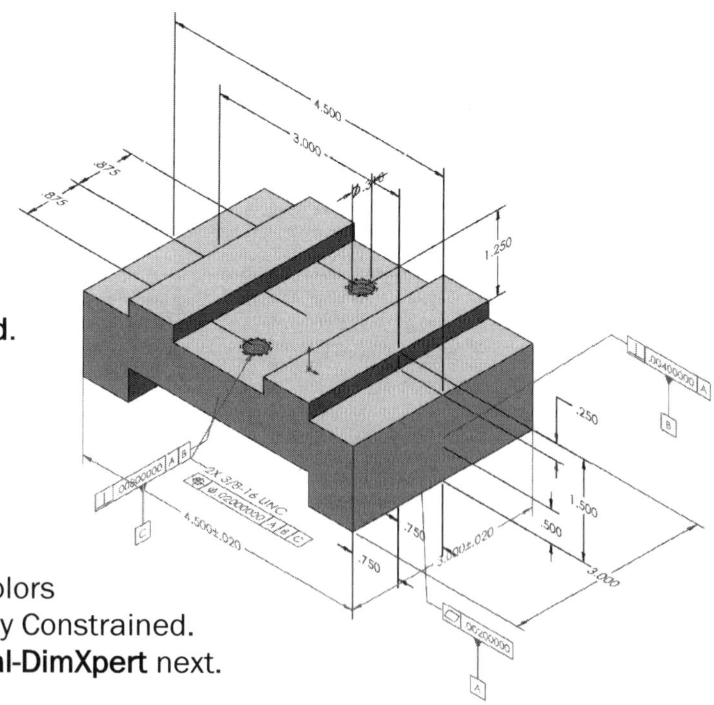

There are no yellow or red colors shown in the model, it is Fully Constrained. We will take a look at **Manual-DimXpert** next.

7. Opening another part document:

Save the previous part document with the name **Prismatic Part 1_Completed.sldprt.**

Select **File, Open.**

Navigate to the training folder and open a part document named: **Prismatic Part 2.sldprt.**

8. Adding datums:

Click **Add Datum** on the **MBD** tab.

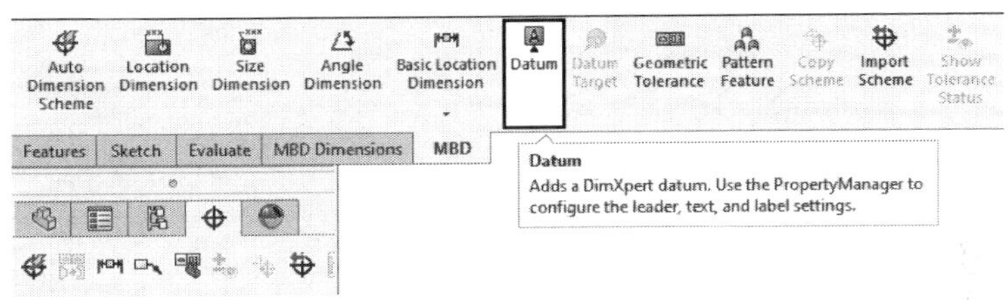

Rotate the model and select the bottom face for **Datum A.**

Select the right-side face for **Datum B.**

Select the front face for **Datum C.**

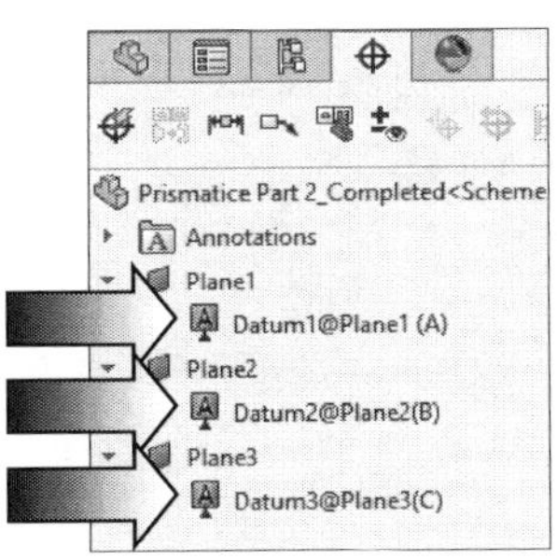

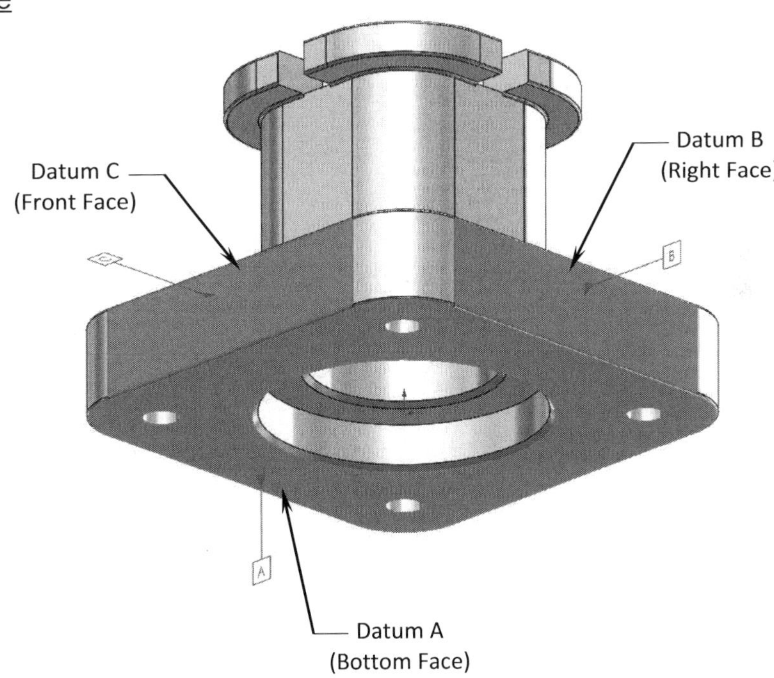

Click **OK.**

DimXpert created 3 datums and displayed them on the DimXpertManager tree.

9. Adding the Size dimensions:

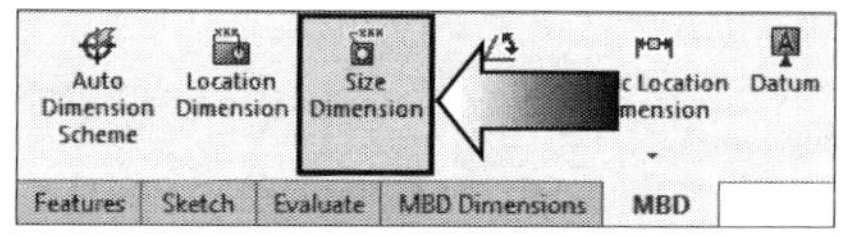

Size Dimensions are for Feature of size (FOS). It is the geometric shape defined by size dimensions such as length, width, and angle. (See Chapter 2, page 3-3 for more information on Feature Of Size.)

Click **Size Dimension**.

Select one of the counterbore holes.

The 4 holes are recognized as a pattern.

Select a hole (pattern)

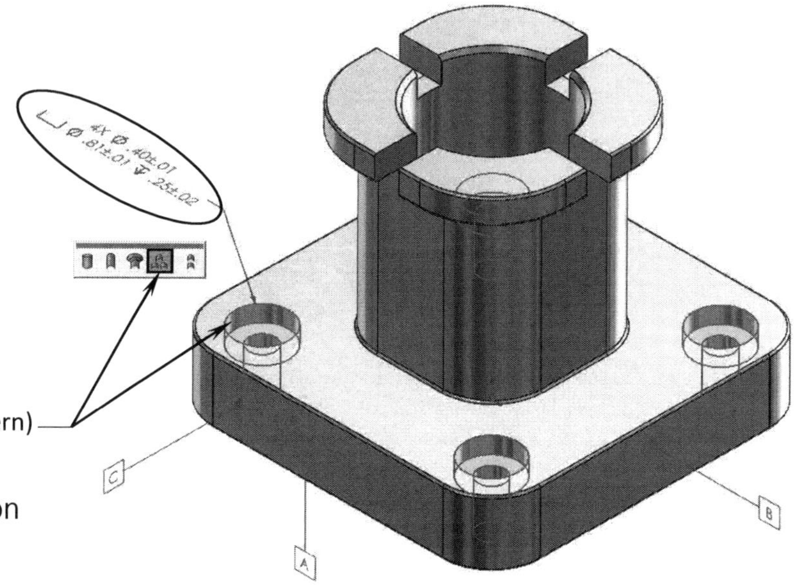

Place the size dimension as circled in the image.

Make sure the Size Dimension command is still selected.

Select a hole (Cylinder)

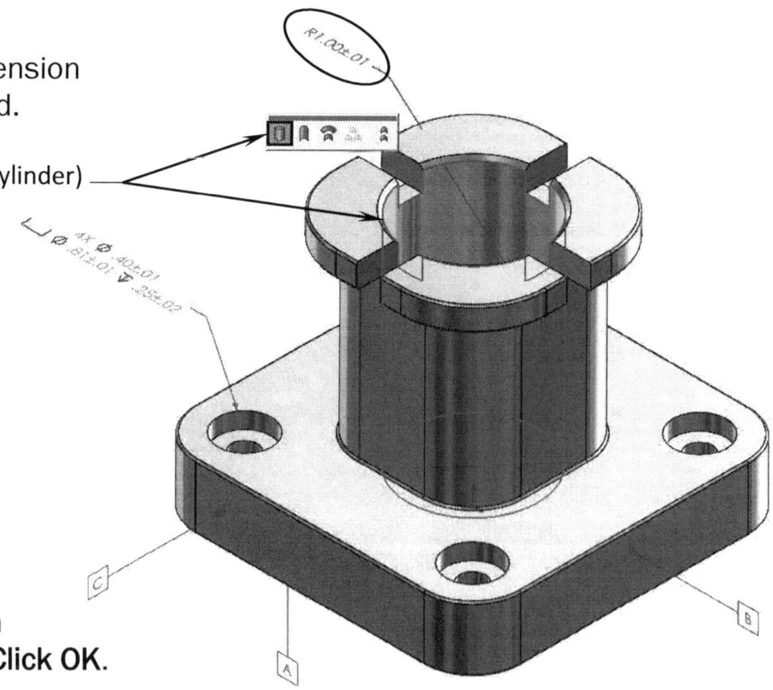

Select the large hole in the middle of the part.

Click the **Cylinder** button on the pop-up toolbar.

Place the size dimension as circled in the image. **Click OK**.

10. Checking the constraint status:

Click **Show Tolerance Status**.

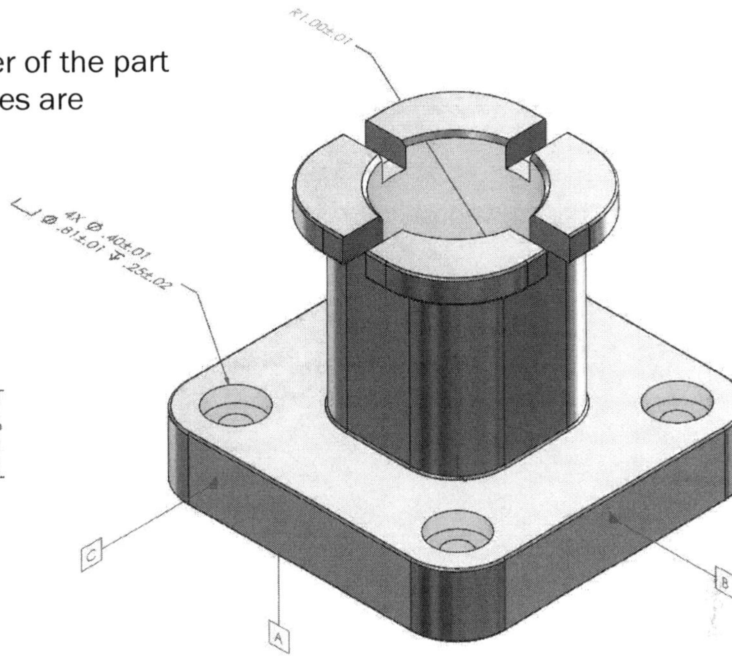

The large hole in the center of the part and the 4 counterbore holes are shown in yellow color.

We will add some more dimensions to further constrain the holes.

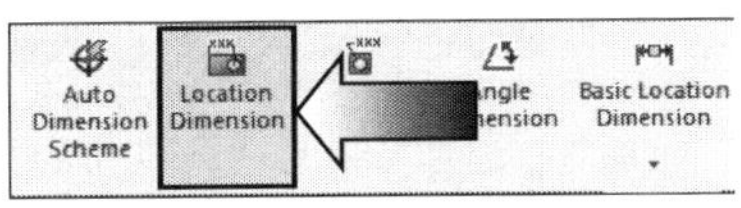

Click **Location Dimension**.

Select the <u>cylindrical face</u> of the large hole and one of the <u>side faces</u> of the square base to create the **2.50** dimension.

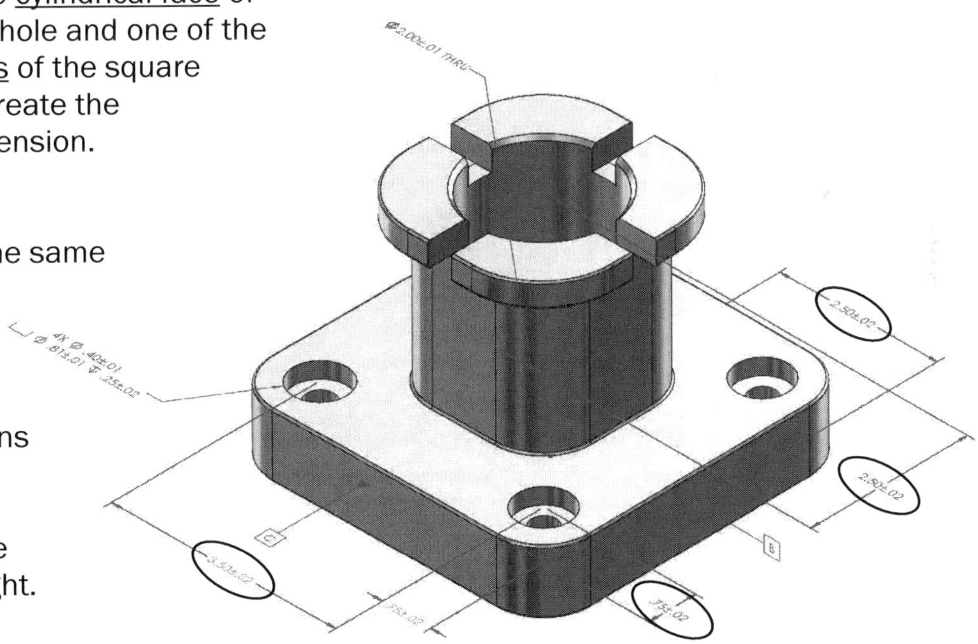

Repeat the same step and add the dimensions that are <u>circled</u> in the image on the right.

It is only necessary to fully constrain those features that require specific tolerances.

11. Showing all annotations:

Most features were defined while designing the model. To avoid over constraining the part, all annotations should be displayed for final inspection.

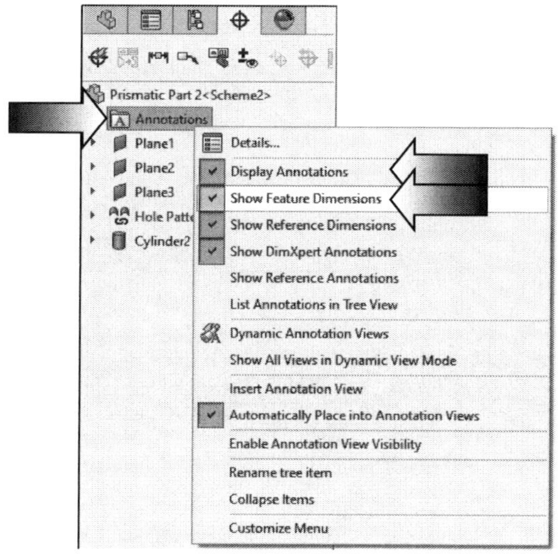

Right-click the **Annotations** folder on the DimXpertManager tree and enable:

* **Display Annotations**

* **Show Feature Dimensions**

Add any missing dimensions and delete any redundant ones.

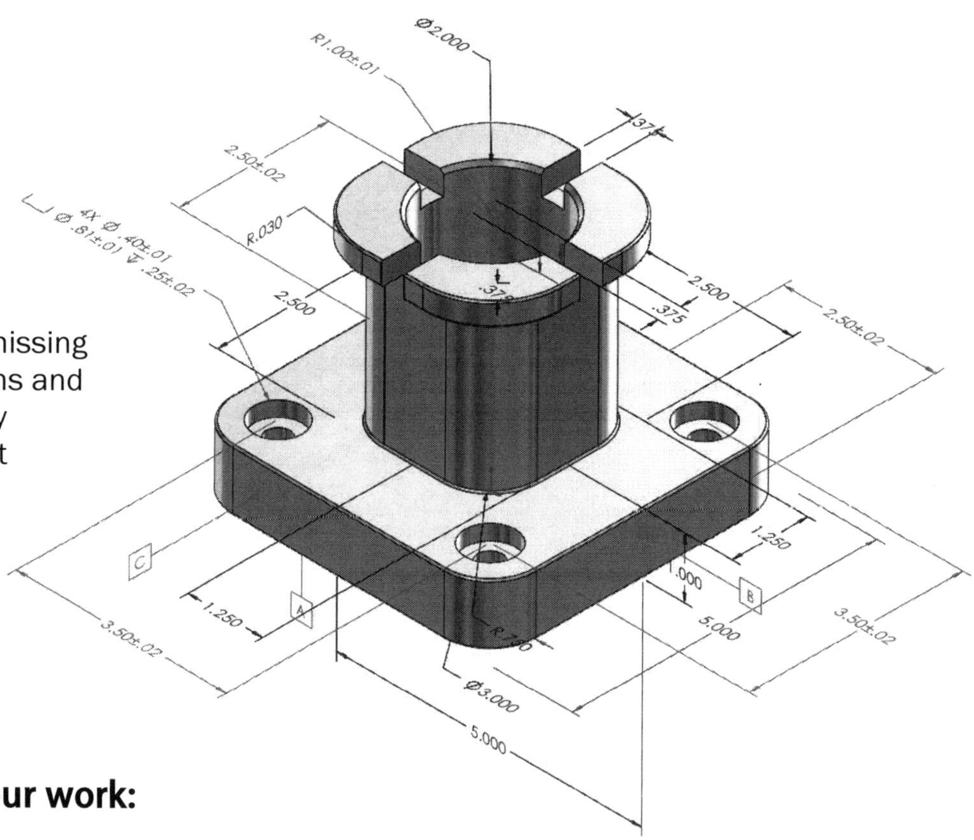

12. Saving your work:

Select **File, Save As.**

Enter **Prismatic Part 2_Completed.sldprt** for the file name.

Click **Save.**

CHAPTER 12: SOLIDWORKS MBD – PART 2

Model Based Definition – Turned Parts

Both Prismatic and Turned parts can be toleranced using SOLIDWORKS Model-Based Definition (MBD).

The Turn option in the Auto Dimension Scheme is used to customize the annotations for a cylindrical type of part (usually made on a lathe machine) with diameter dimensions instead of linear dimensions.

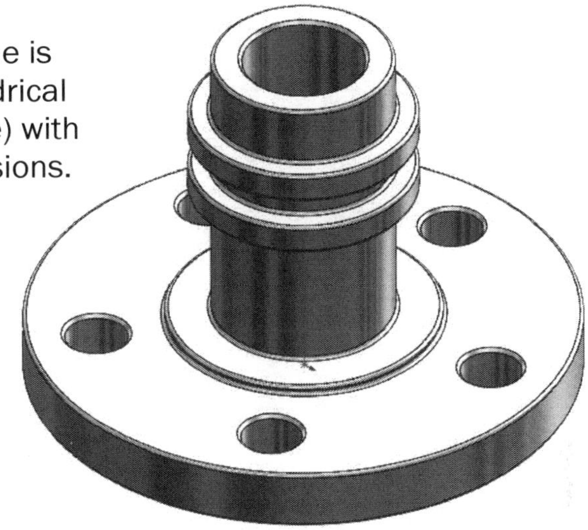

1. Opening a part document:

Select **File, Open**.

Browse to the Training folder and open the part document named: **Turned Part 1.sldprt**.

The material **6061 Alloy** has already been assigned to the part.

The image shown on the right is what we will need to create. It has 2 different colors: the black color dimensions are model dimensions, and the magenta color dimensions are DimXpert dimensions.

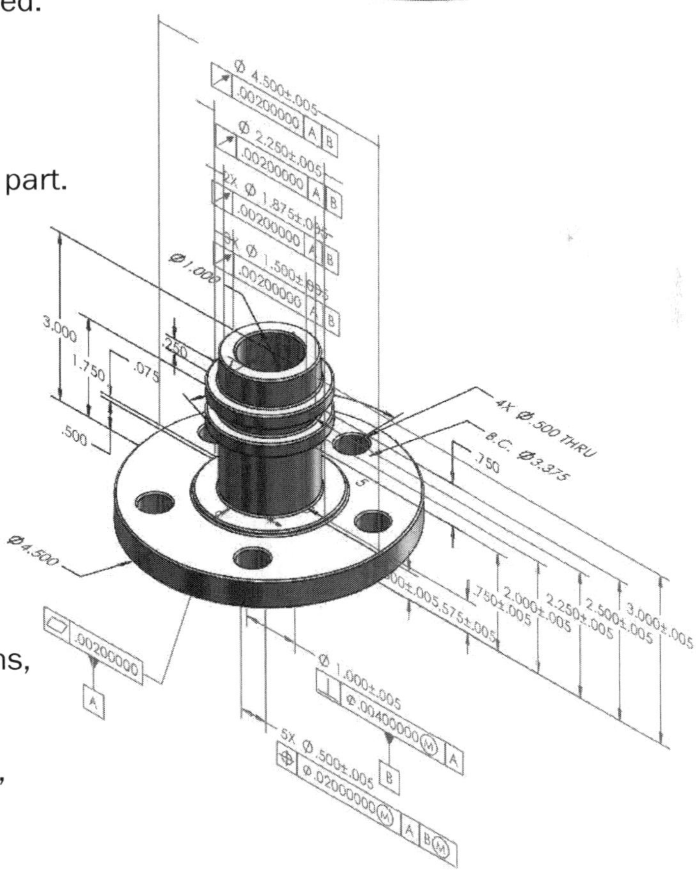

Besides the height dimensions, other dimensions are shown as diameter dimensions including tolerances, datums, and geometric tolerances.

2. Adding datums:

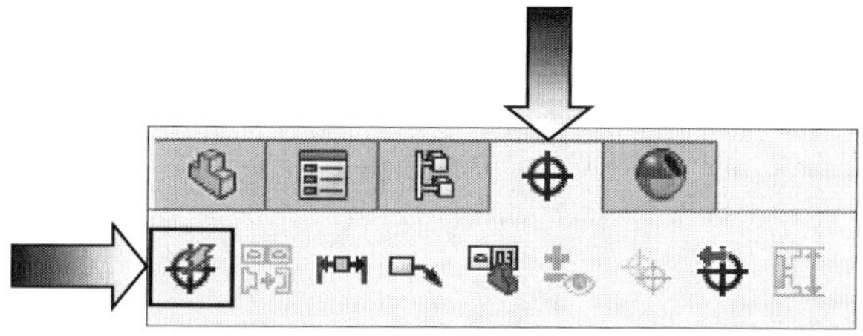

Switch to the **DimXpertManager** tree and click **Auto Dimension Scheme.**

In the **Settings** sections, select the following:

Part Type: Turned

Tolerance Type: Geometric

Pattern Dimensioning: Linear

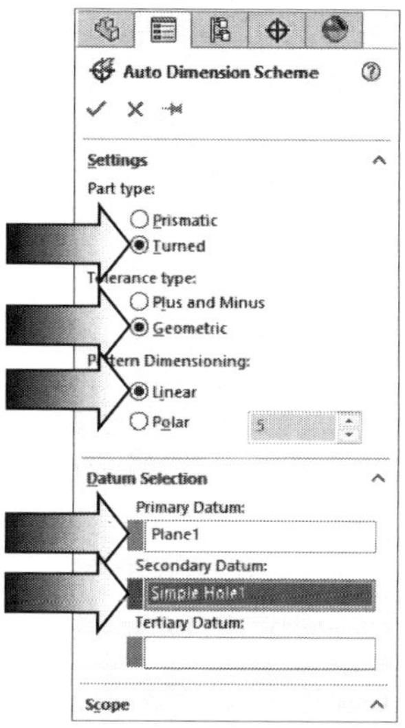

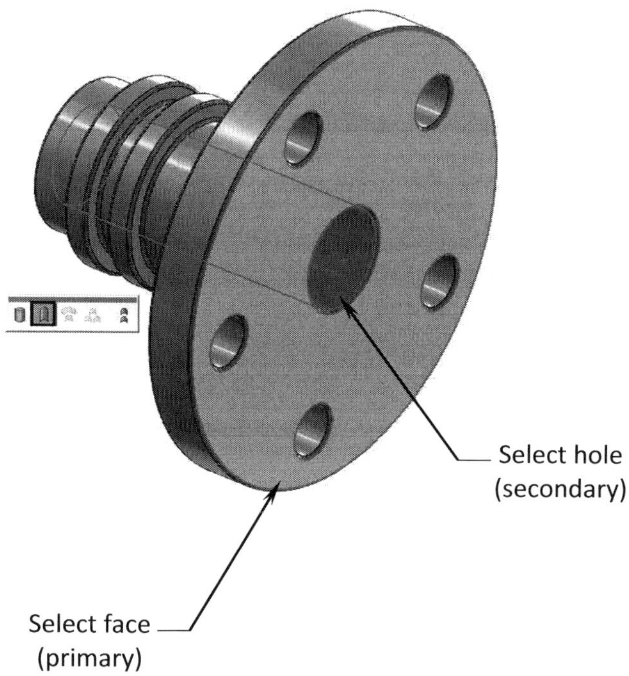

For **Datum Selection**, select the <u>bottom face</u> for **Datum A.**

Select the <u>hole in the center</u> of the part for **Datum B.**

Do not click OK yet.

For **Scope**, click **Selected Features**.

Select all (14) faces of the model, <u>except</u> for the fillets.

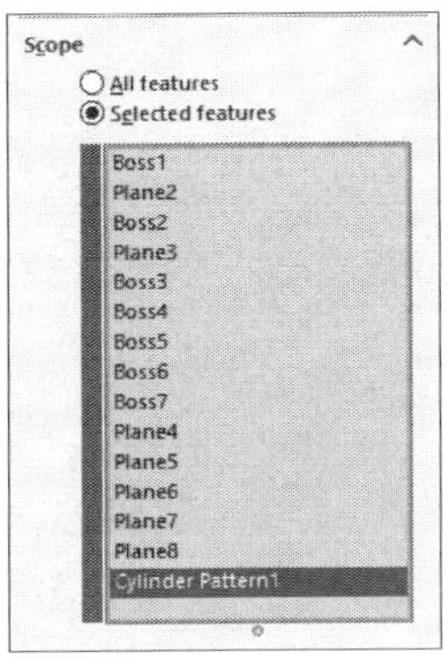

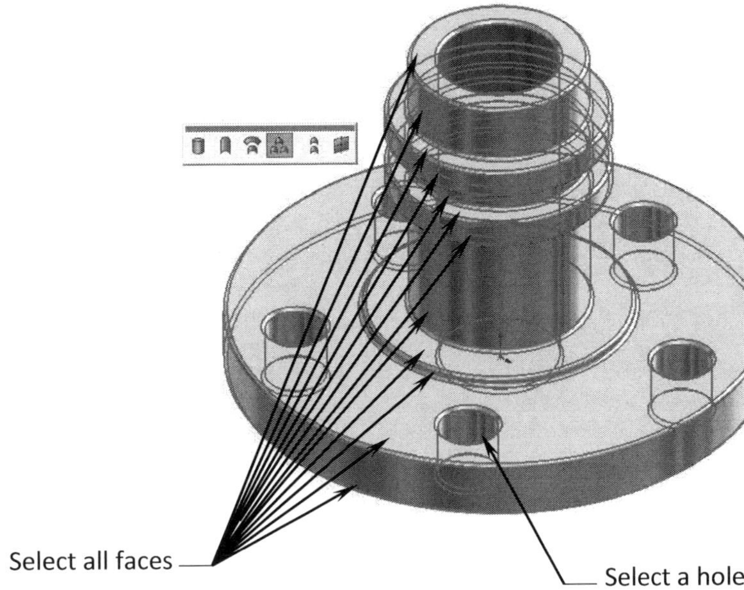

Also select <u>one of the holes</u> on the bottom flange; all 5 holes should be highlighted and selected at the same time.

Click **OK**.

DimXpert added the datums, dimensions, tolerances, and annotations automatically based on the settings specified in the Auto-Dimension-Scheme, and the parameters that were set earlier in the Options for DimXpert.

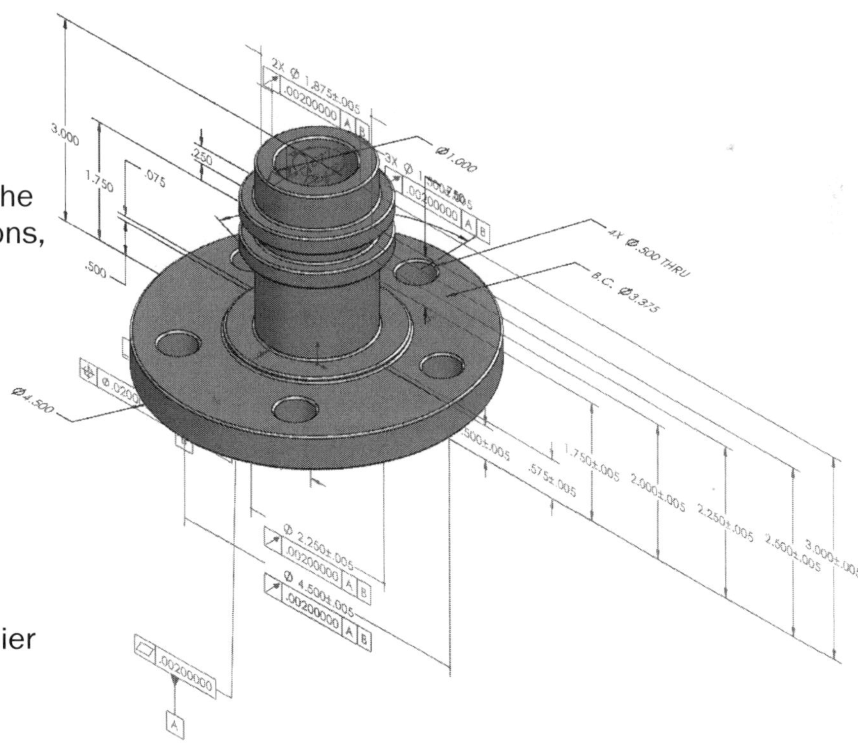

3. Rearranging the annotations:

Using the Isometric view (Control+7), rearrange the dimensions so that they are a little easier to read, similar to the image shown below.

The model dimensions (black color) can be toggled off for clarity. Right-click the **Annotations** folder and clear the **Show Feature Dimensions** checkbox.

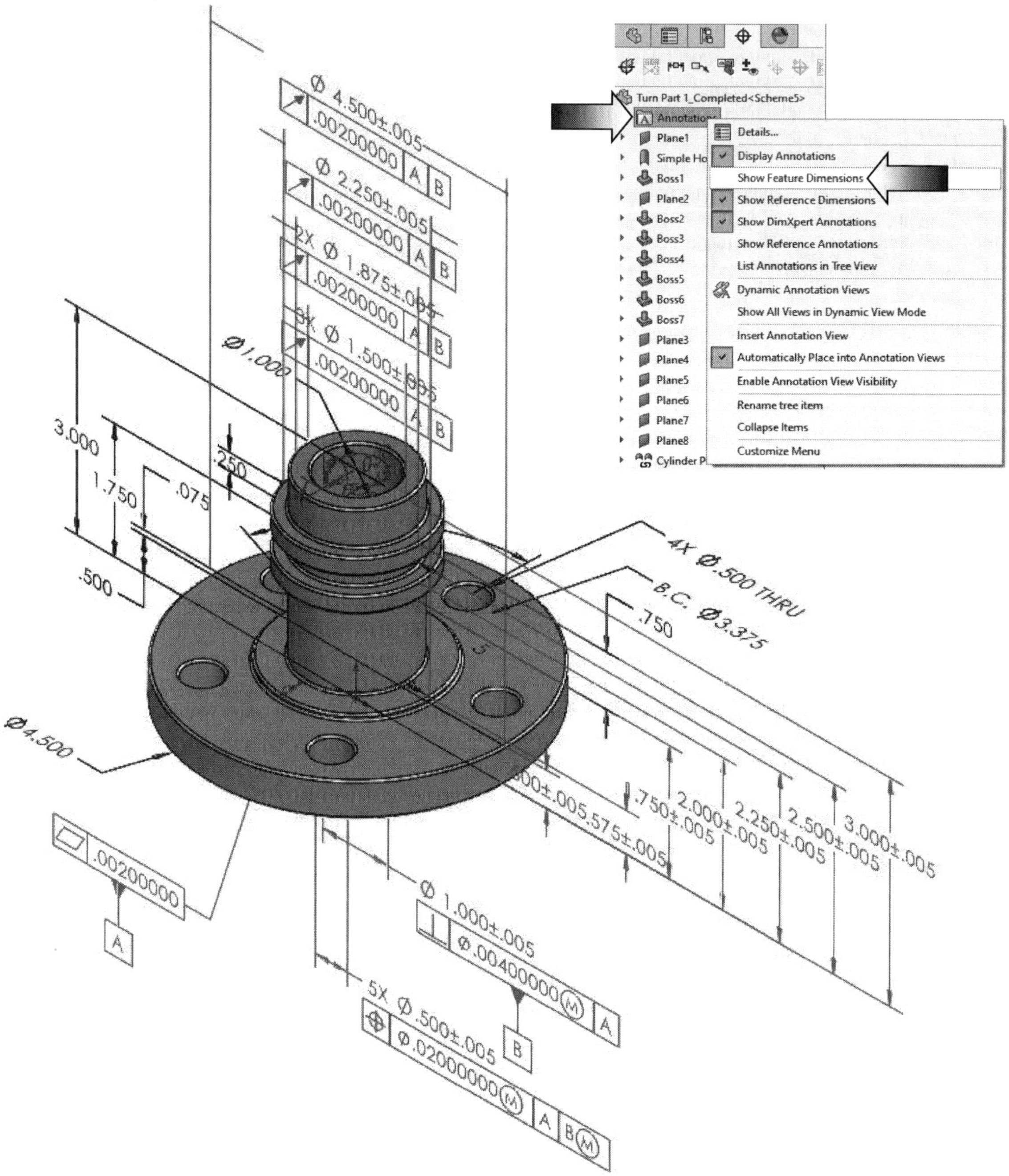

4. Recreating the basic dimensions:

Expand the **Cylinder Pattern1** at the bottom of the DimXpertManager tree, right-click the **Position1** feature and select: **Recreate Basic Dim**.

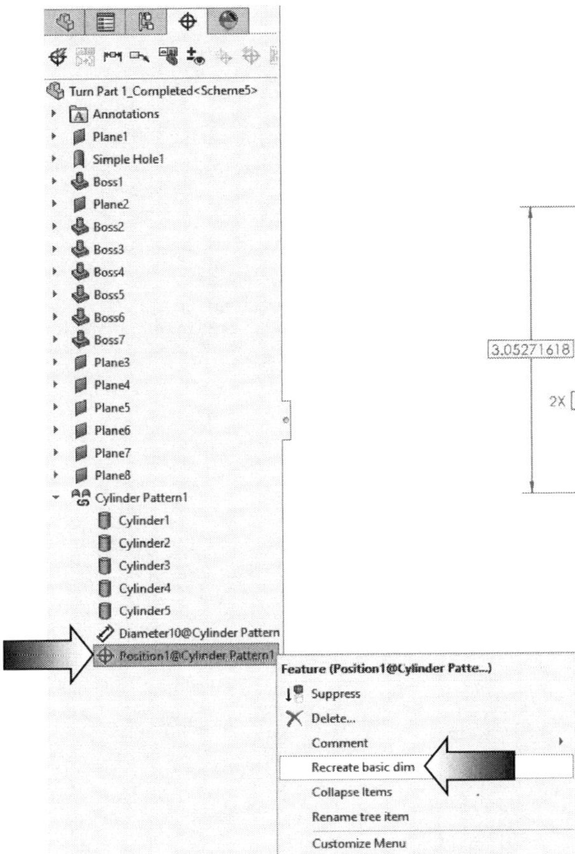

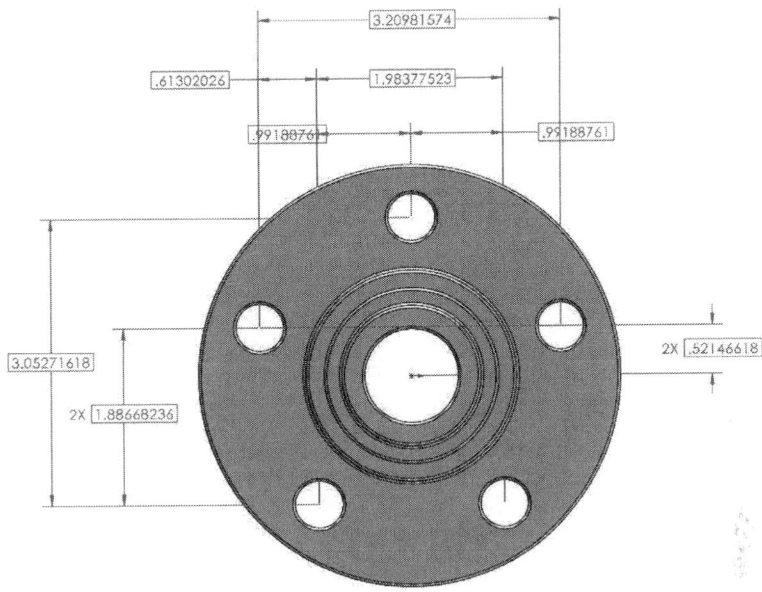

To change the number of decimal places: Hold the **Control** key and select <u>all dimensions</u>.

In the Tolerance / Precision section, select: **.123 (document)** from the drop-down list.

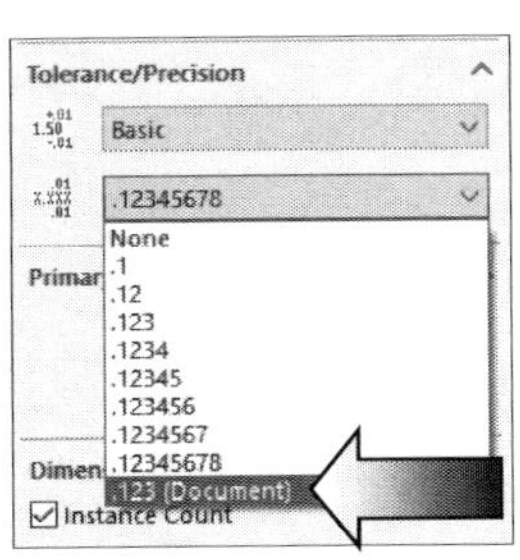

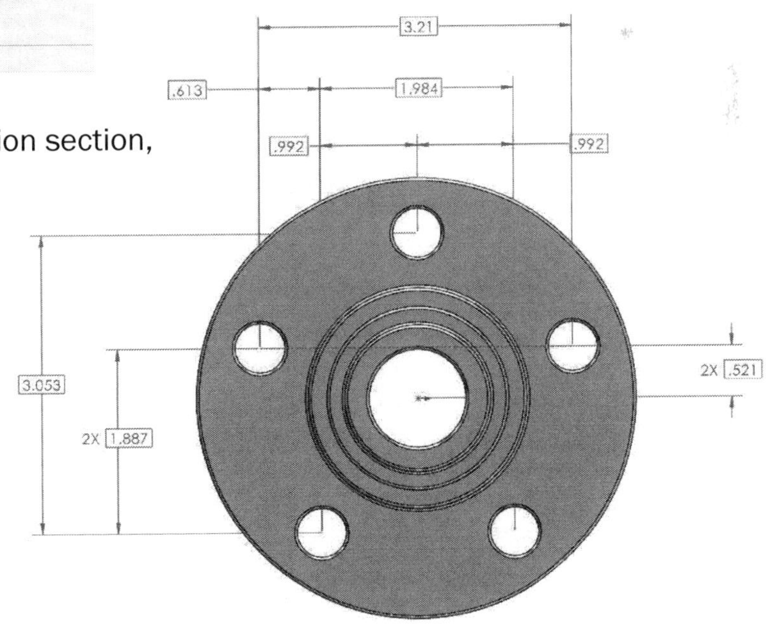

Click **OK**.

5. Saving your work:

In the next exercise, we will take a look at an alternative option called **Plus and Minus** tolerance to constrain a Turned part.

Select **File, Save As**.

Enter **Turned Part 1_Completed.sldprt** for the file name.

Click **Save.**

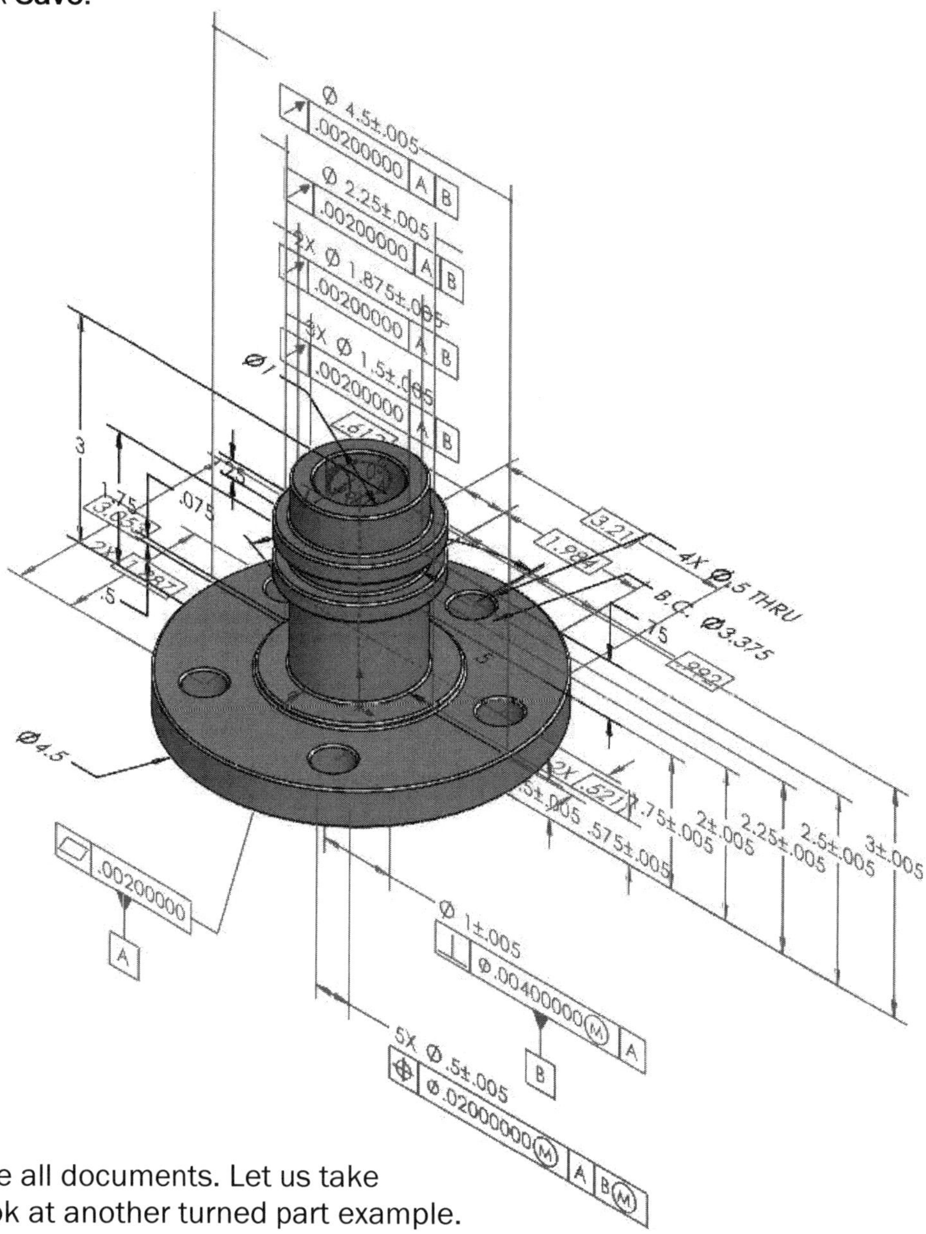

Close all documents. Let us take
a look at another turned part example.

6. Opening another part document:

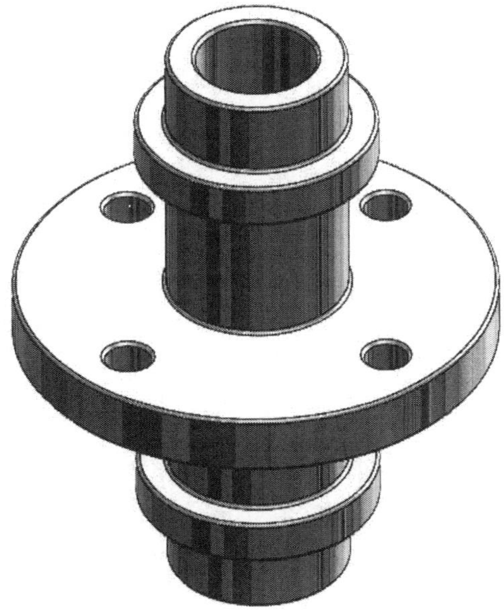

Select **File, Open**.

Browse to the Training Folder and open the part document named: **Turned Part 2.sldprt**.

The material **AISI 304** has already been assigned to the part.

7. Using Plus and Minus Tolerances:

Switch to the **DimXpertManager** tree and click **Auto Dimension Scheme**.

For **Settings**, select the following:

* **Part Type: Turned**
* **Pattern Dimensioning: Linear.**
* **Tolerance Type: Plus and Minus**

For **Reference Features**, select the <u>upper face</u> of the flange for **Datum A** and select the <u>large hole</u> in the middle of the part for **Datum B**.

For **Scope**, click Selected Features and select one of the <u>four holes</u>.

Click **OK**.

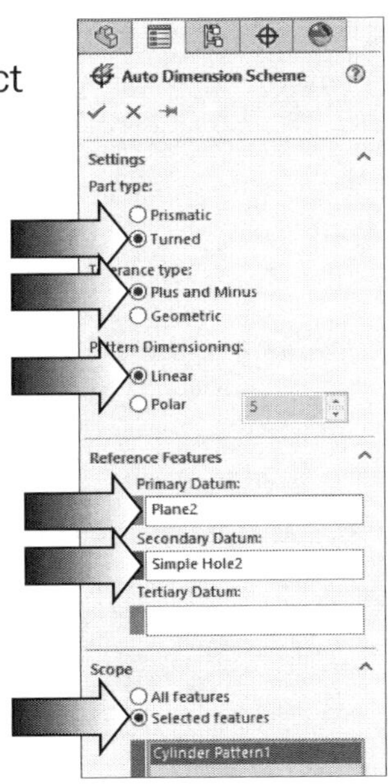

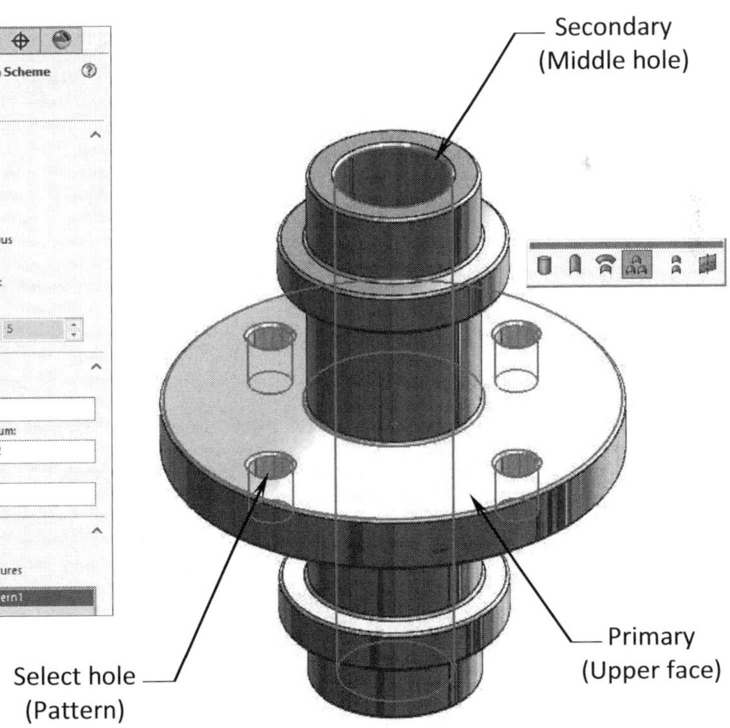

The tolerance Plus and Minus option can be used to create toleranced dimensions without tolerancing.

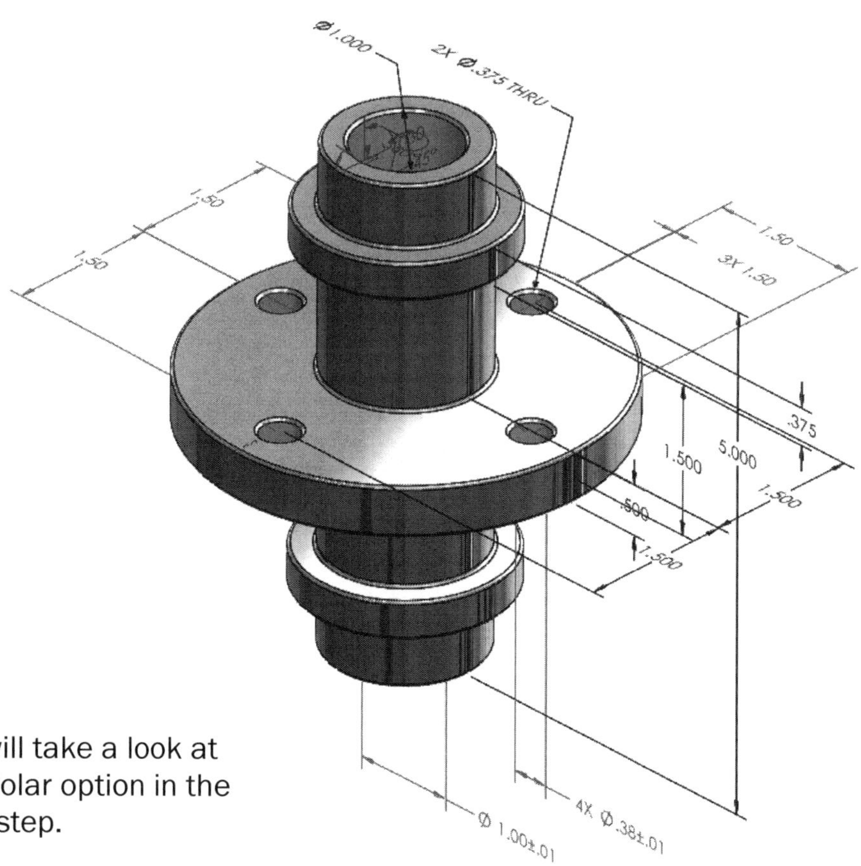

We will take a look at the Polar option in the next step.

8. Using Polar:

On the **DimXpertManager** tree, right-click **Turned Part 2** and select **Delete.**

Click **Yes** to confirm delete.

The dimension scheme and its annotations are deleted.

We can now use the same part and try out the Solar Tolerance option.

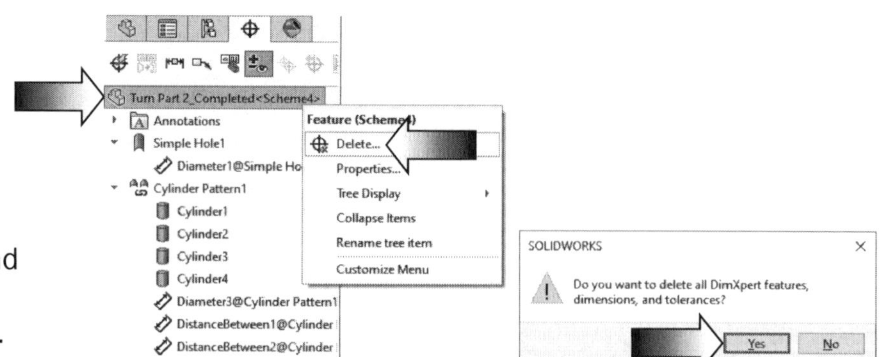

Click **Auto Dimension Scheme** on the DimXpert Manager tree.

For Part Type, select **Turned.**

For Tolerance Type, select **Plus and Minus.**

For Pattern Dimensioning, select **Polar.**

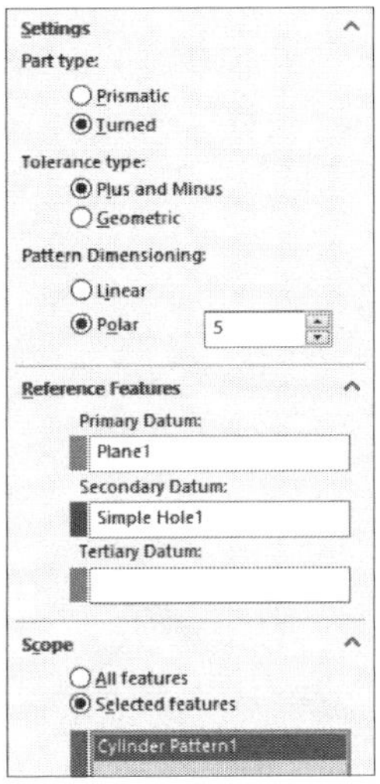

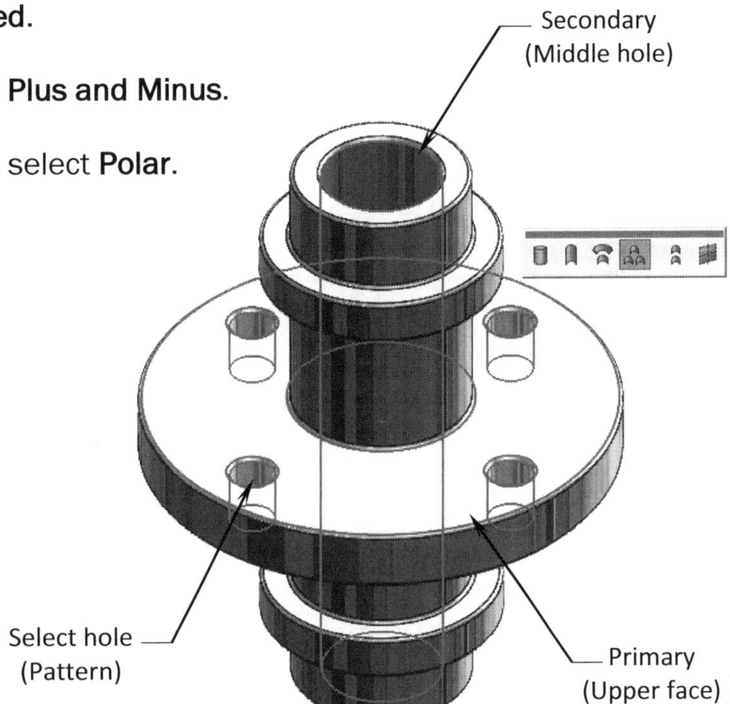

For Scope, click Selected Features and select one of the **4 small holes.**

Click **OK.**

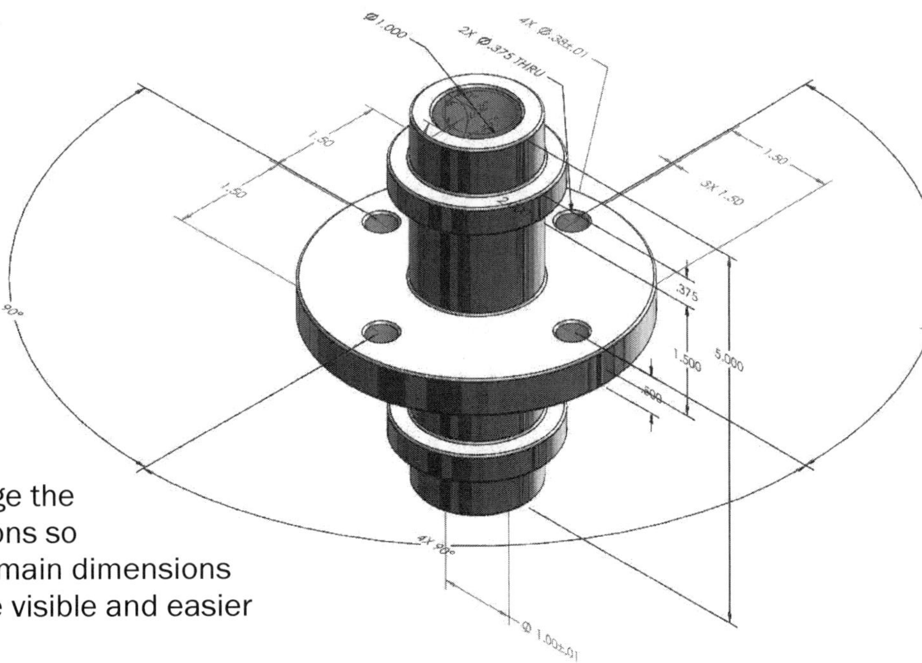

Rearrange the dimensions so that the main dimensions are more visible and easier to read.

CHAPTER 12: SOLIDWORKS MBD – PART 3

Model Based Definition – Capturing 3D Views

The option Capture 3D View is used to capture the Product and Manufacturing Information (PMI) that is needed for reviewing and manufacturing the part.

3D Views are also used to create a 3D-PDF or an eDrawing file. The 3D View tab at the bottom left of the screen is used to create and capture the views needed to publish to PDF or eDrawing.

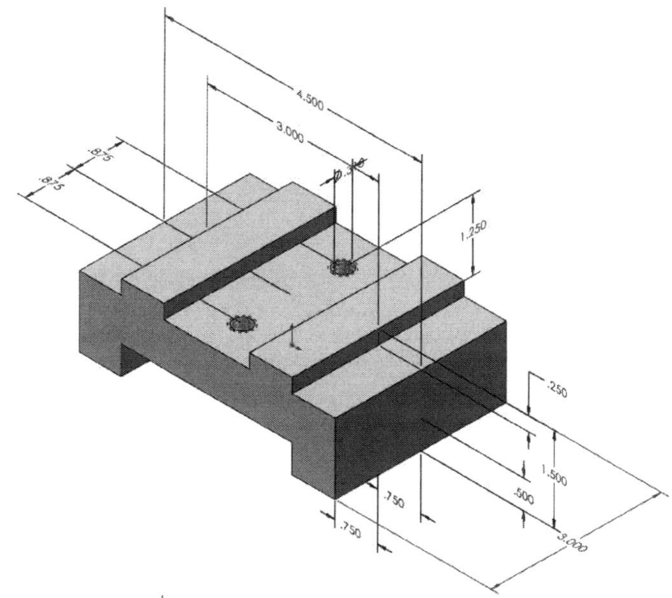

1. Opening a part document:

Open the previous part document named:
Prismatic Part 1 Completed.

If the DimXpert Annotations are not showing, right-click the Annotation folder and enable:
Show DimXpert Annotations.

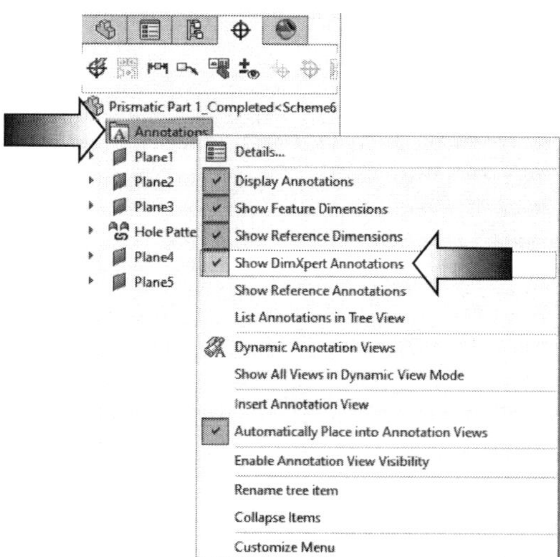

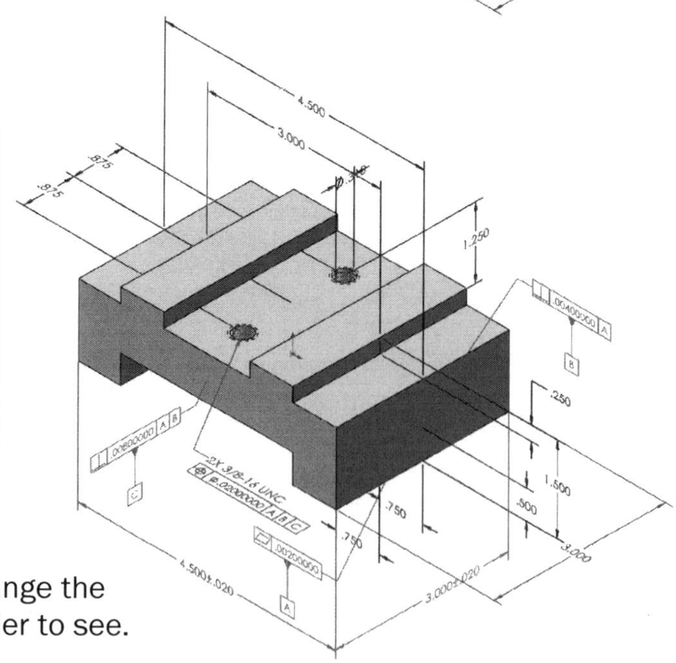

For clarity and readability, rearrange the dimensions so that they are easier to see.

2. Switching to the 3D View tab:

Click the **3D View** tab at the lower left corner of the screen.

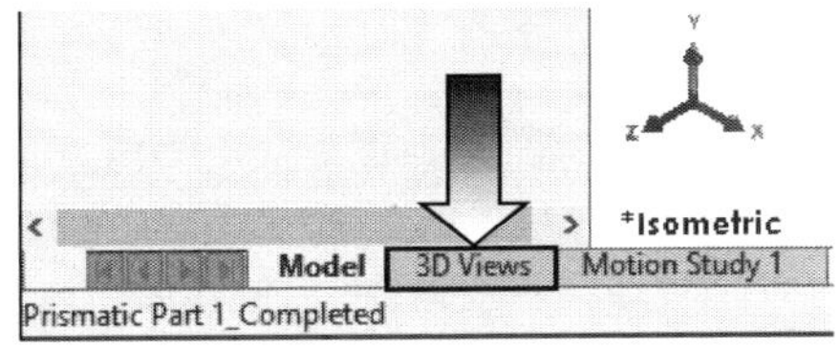

When you capture a 3D View, you are capturing the current image and position of the model in the graphics area, at that exact moment.

Change to the **Isometric** view (Control+ 7). This will be the first 3D View captured with DimXpert Annotations.

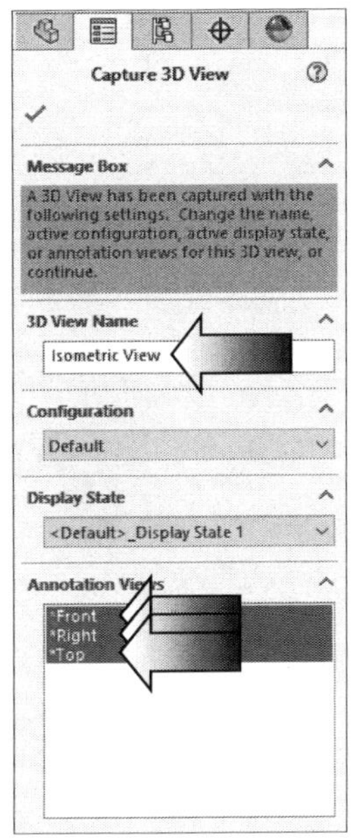

Click **Capture 3D View**  at the lower left corner of the screen.

In the Message Box, under 3D View Name, enter: **Isometric View.**

For Annotation Views, select all <u>3 views</u>, the **Front**, the **Top**, and the **Right** views.

Click **OK.**

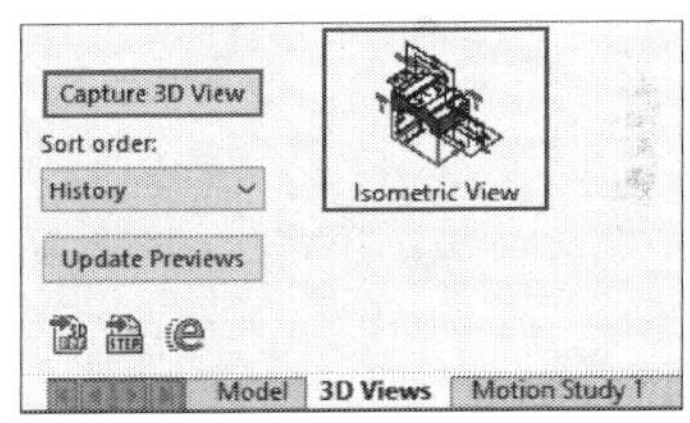

An Isometric view and its annotations are captured and saved in the 3D View pane.

To delete or recapture the 3D View, right-click the Isometric View and select: **Recapture View.**

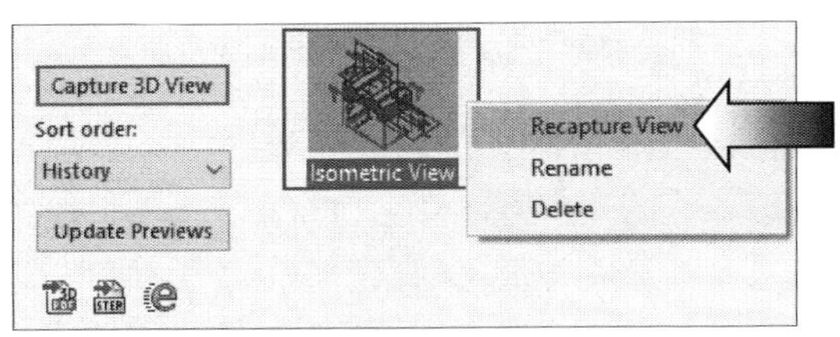

Other 3D views will be created in the next few steps.

3. Capturing the Front views:

Change to the **Front** view orientation (Control +1).

Rearrange the dimensions and annotations to make them easier to read, before capturing the view.

Click **Capture 3D View** .

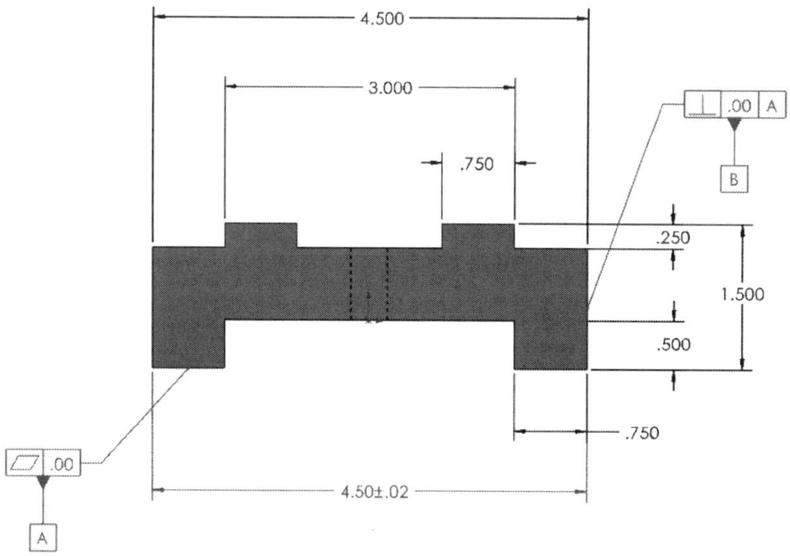

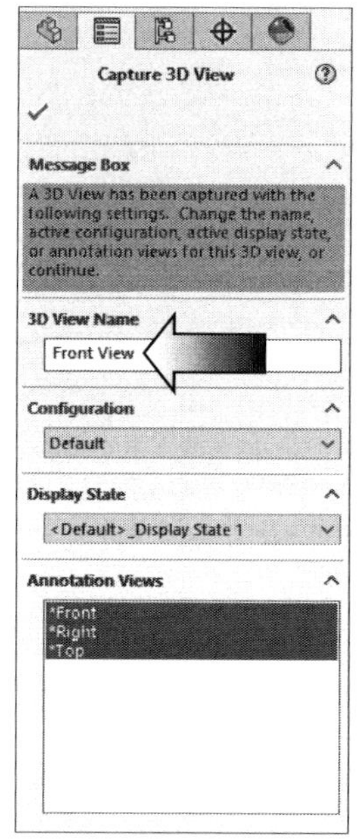

For 3D View Name, enter: **Front View**.

For Annotation Views, select all 3 views, the **Front**, the **Top**, and the **Right** views.

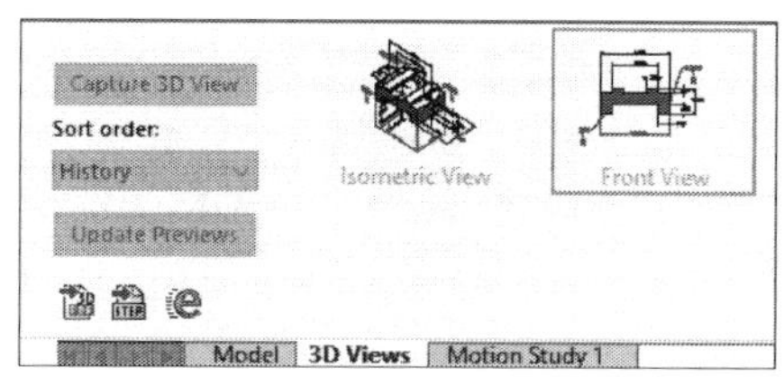

Click **OK.**

The Front view is captured and saved in the 3D View pane.

We will create a few more 3D views and then publish them as 3D-PDF file for reviewing and collaborating with others.

4. Capturing the orthographic views:

The orthographic views make it easier to see the annotations; they can help eliminate some confusion when it comes to reading a busy drawing.

Repeat step 3 and capture the following 3D Views:

Top view (Control+5).

Right view (Control+4).

Remember to rearrange the dimensions and annotations before capturing the views.

Avoid overlapping dimensions. They should be clear and easy to see and understand.

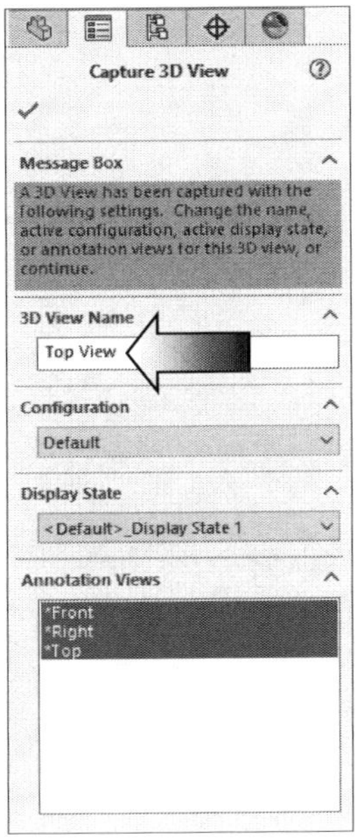

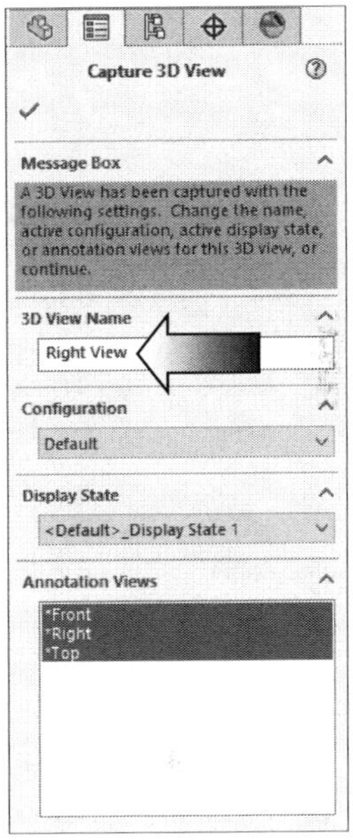

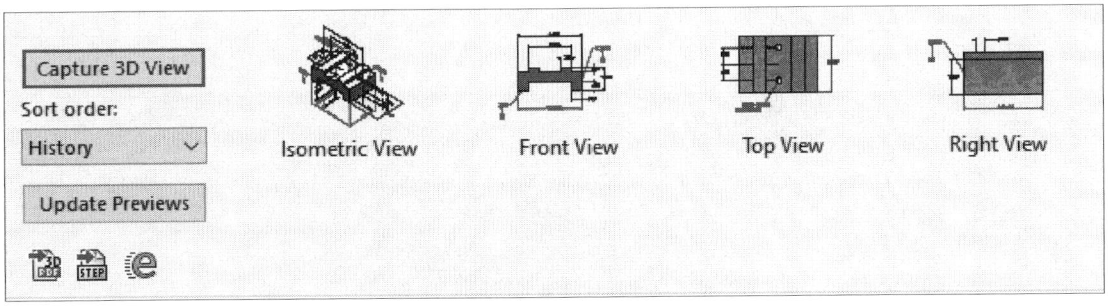

There should be 4 3D-Views in the 3D Views pane at this point.
We will create and capture a Zonal Section view in the next step.

5. Creating a zonal section view:

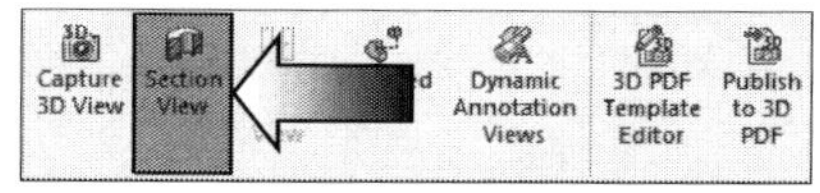

Click **Section View** on the **MBD** tab.

For Section Method, click **Zonal**.

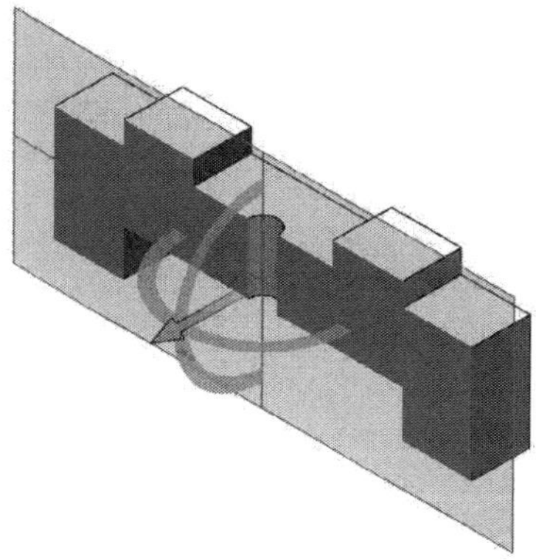

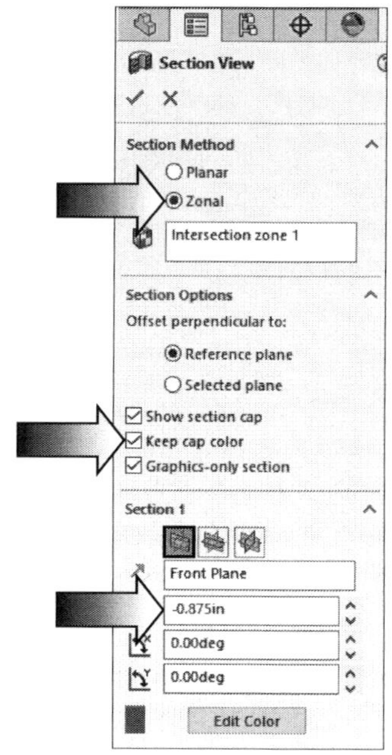

For Section Options, enable checkbox for **Keep Cap Color**.

For Section 1, select the **Front** plane and enter: **-.875in**. for distance.

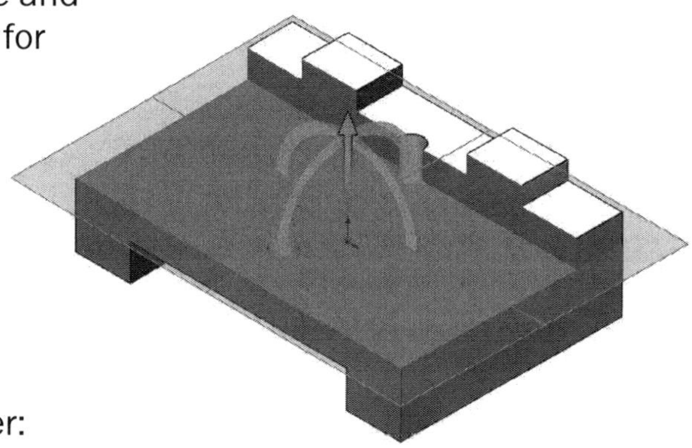

Enable Section 2 checkbox, select the **Top** plane and enter: **.375in**. for distance.

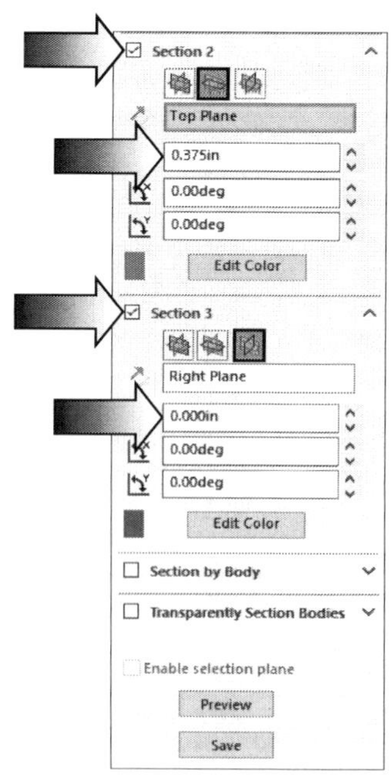

Enable Section 3 checkbox, select the **Right** plane but keep the distance at **zero** (0).

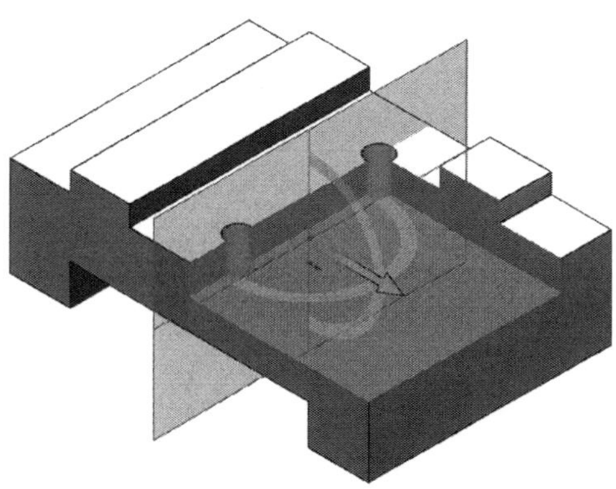

Click **OK**.

6. Capturing the zonal section view:

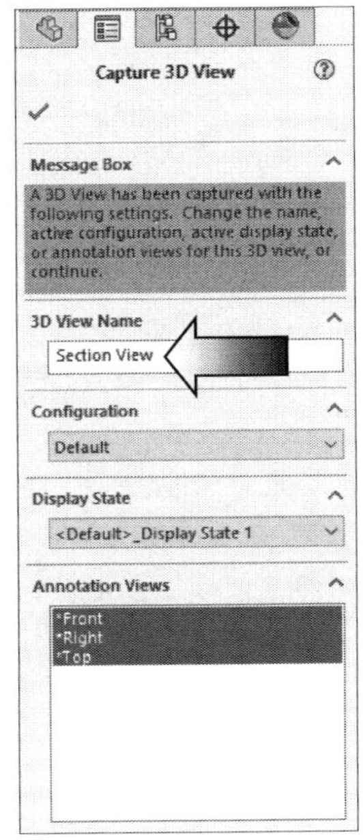

Click **Capture 3D Views** [Capture 3D View].

For 3D View Name. enter: **Section View**.

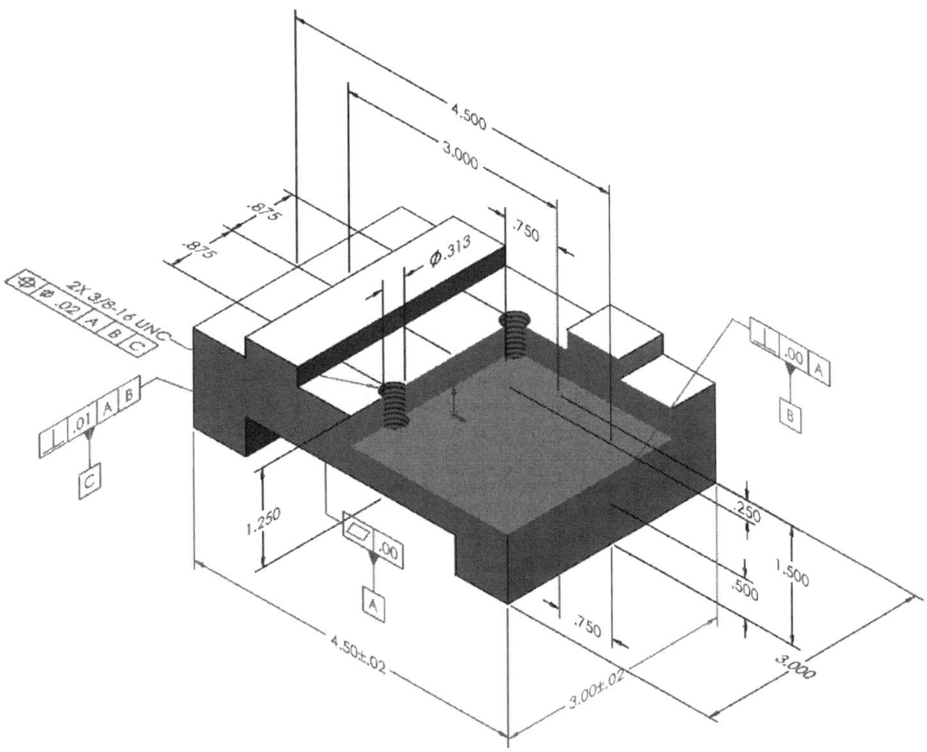

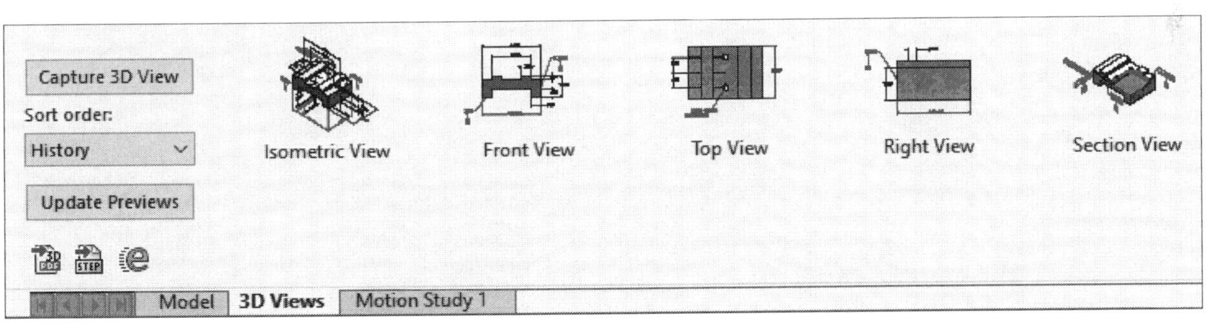

There should be 5 3D-Views in the 3D Views pane at this point.

We need to test out the 3D Views prior to publishing them.

7. Testing the 3D Views:

In the 3D View window, double-click each view to see its annotations. Make any adjustments as needed to make it more readable.

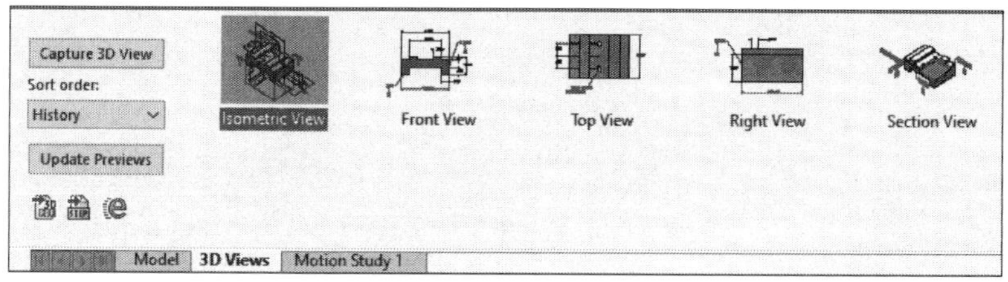

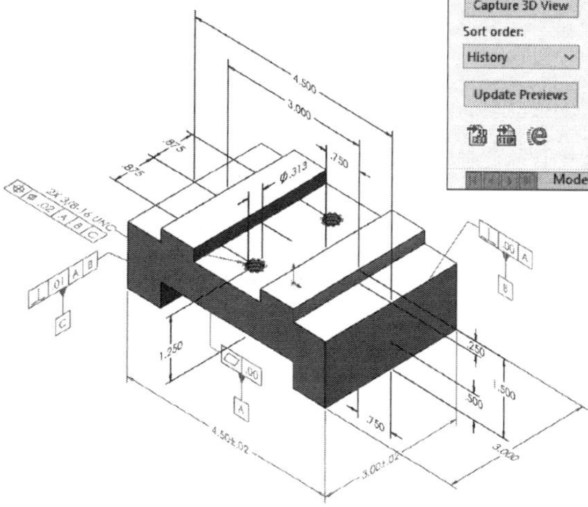

Isometric View

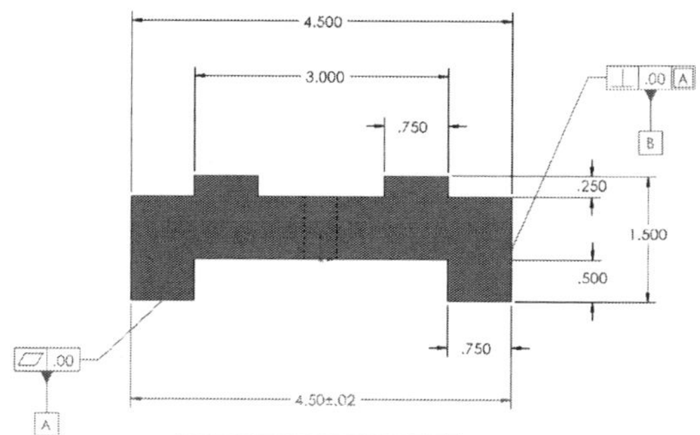

Front View

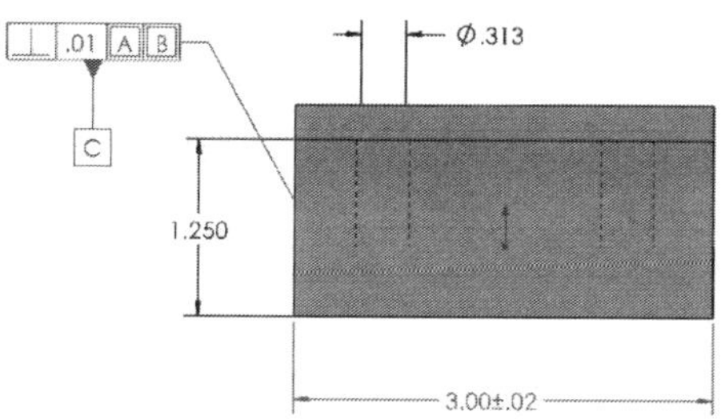

Top View

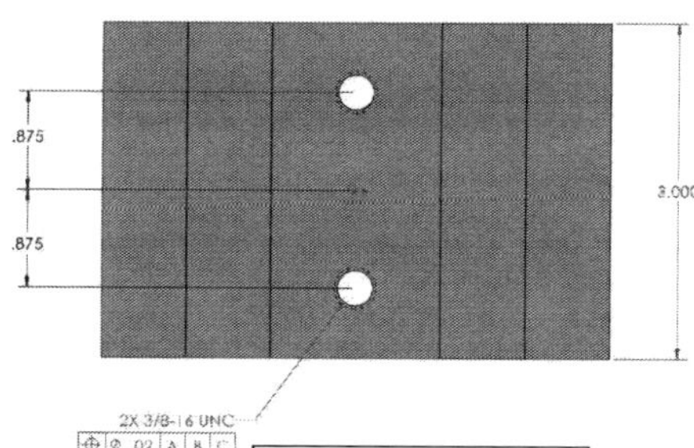

Right View

Everything looks to be in order. We can now publish to both 3D-PDF and eDrawing for reviewing and collaborating with others.

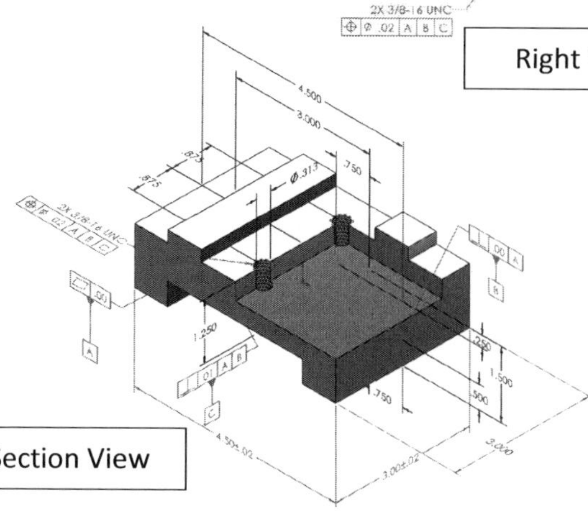

Section View

8. Publishing to 3D-PDF:

Publishing to 3D PDF is the last step in SOLIDWORKS MBD.

You will need to select a 3D-PDF template, and then populate the 3D PDF with items you select, such as 3D views, notes, custom properties, and BOMs if you are publishing an assembly document.

Click **Publish to 3D PDF** on the **MBD** tab.

There are different templates that you can use to create the PDF files with.

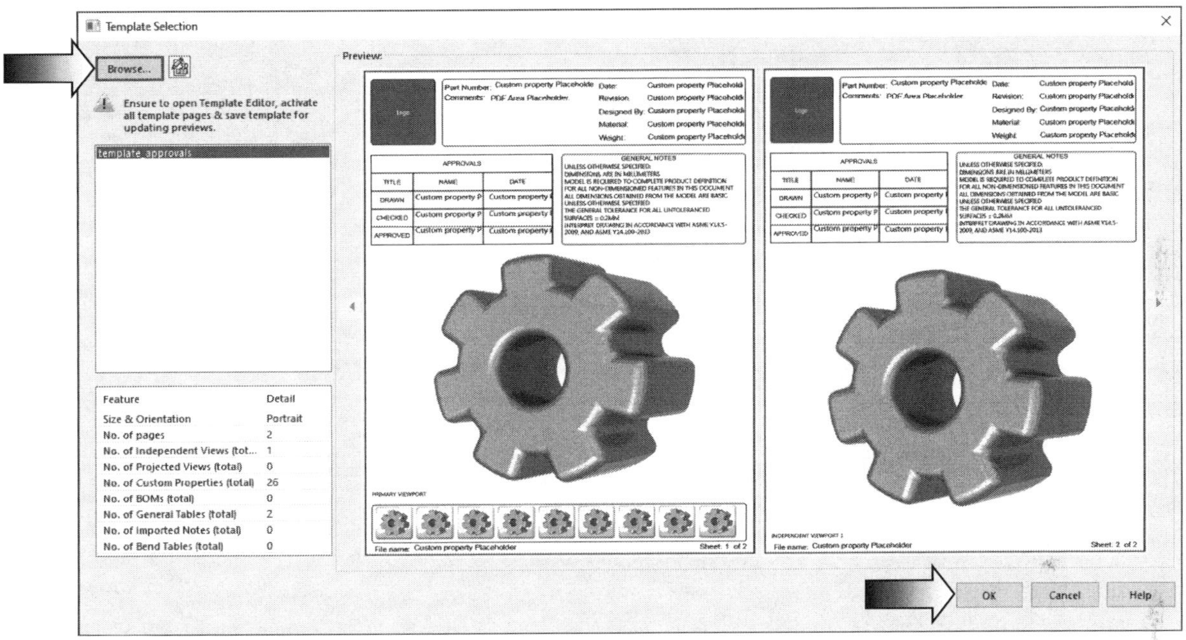

Click **Browse** and select the **Template_ Approvals** from the locations shown in the dialog box.

Click **OK**.

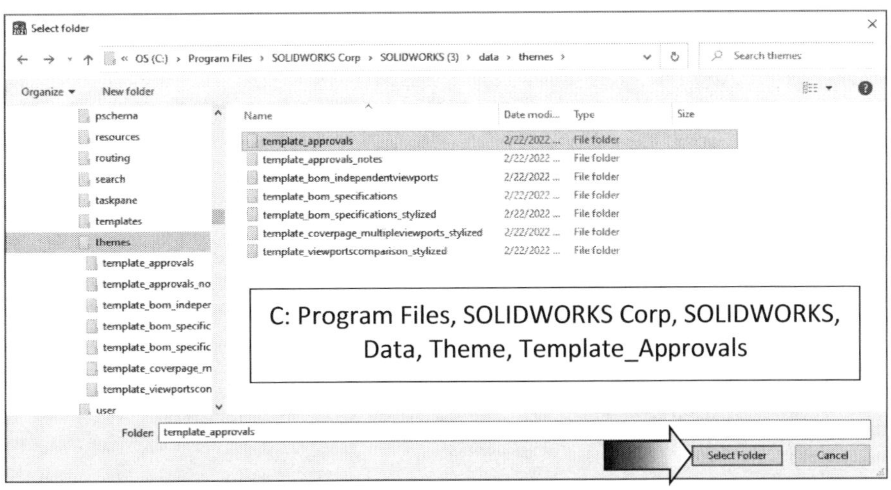

For Sheet 1, select the **Isometric view** and the **Front, Top**, and **Right views** from the 3D View pane.

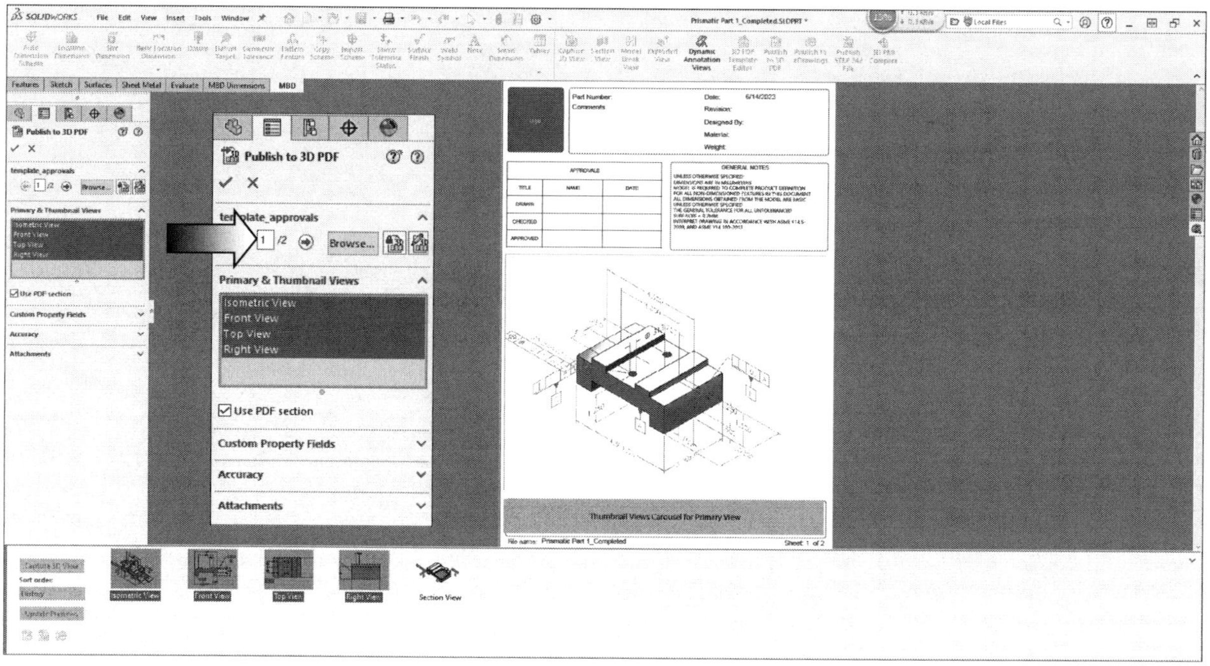

Click **Next** to go to Sheet 2 and select the **Section view** from the 3D View pane.

Click **OK.**

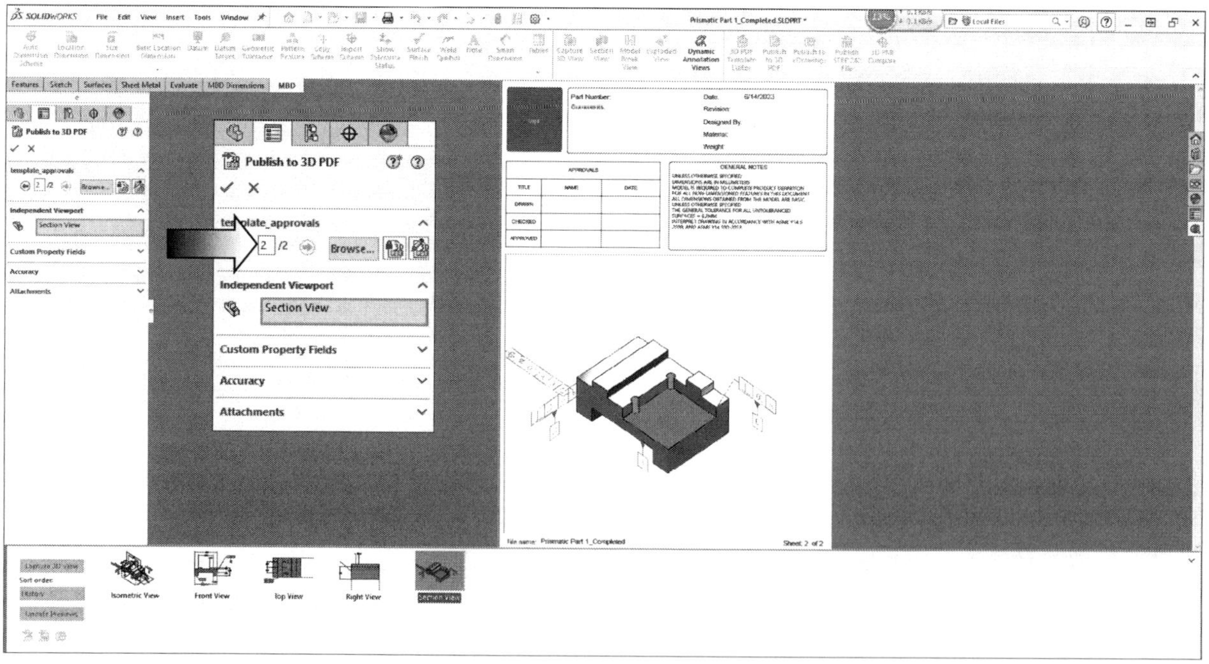

9. Saving the 3D-PDF:

Adobe Reader is required to view the 3D PDF documents.

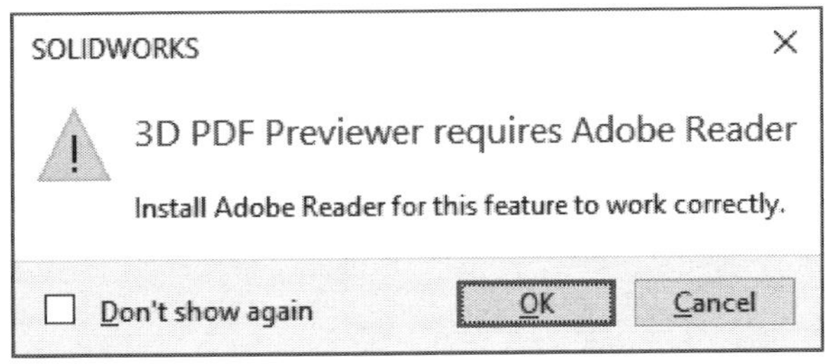

Click **OK** to close the dialog box.

Select a location and folder to save the 3D-PDF file.

For file name, enter: **Prismatic Part 1.pdf**.

Click **Save**.

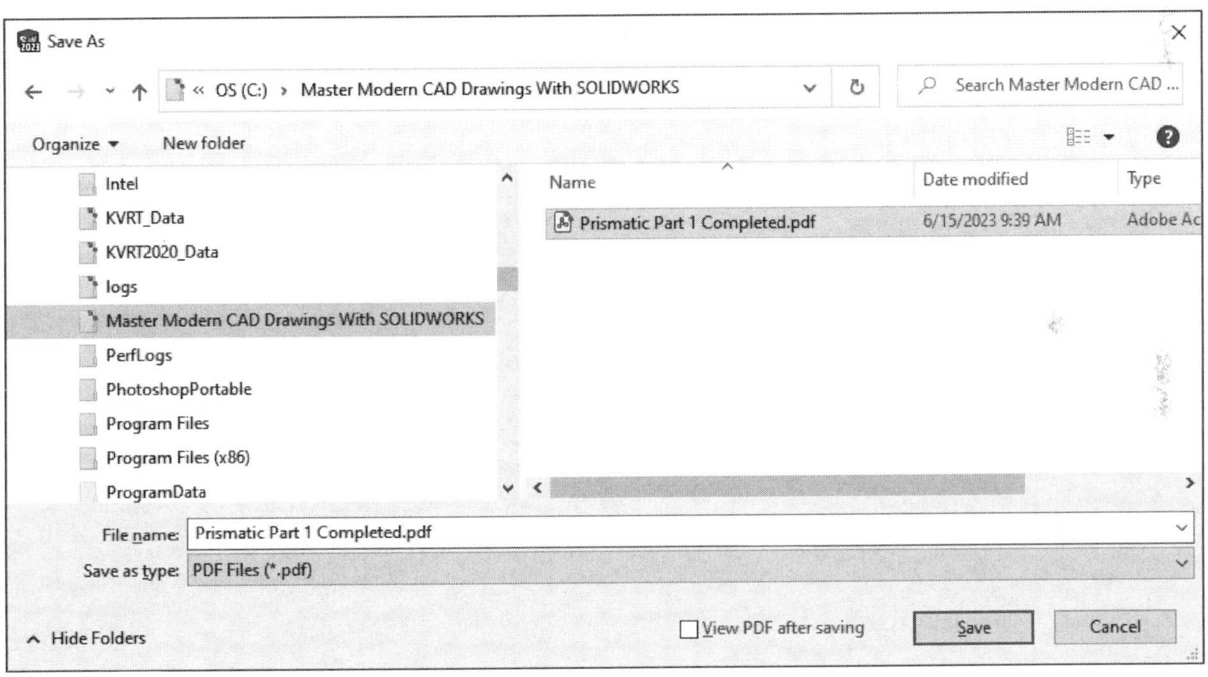

Switch back to SOLIDWORKS.

We will save the same part as an eDrawing next.

10. Publishing to eDrawing:

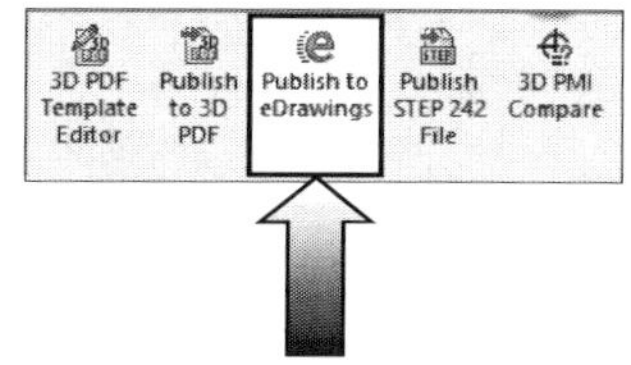

The 3D Views information can be published to an eDrawing file to share your data with others.

The eDrawing documents offer much more manipulation options than a 3D-PDF file, and they are more familiar to most SOLIDWORKS users.

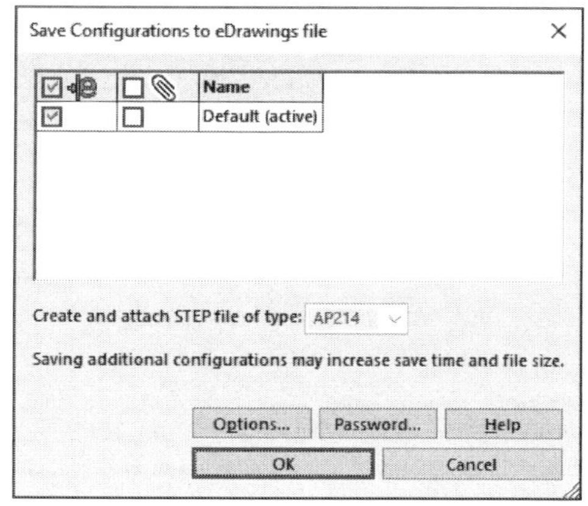

Click **Publish to eDrawings** on the **MBD** tab.

Use the **Default Configuration** and do not assign any password to this document.

Click **OK**.

The eDrawing window is opened.
Click the **3D View** button at the lower right corner of the screen to see the 5 views that were created in the last steps.

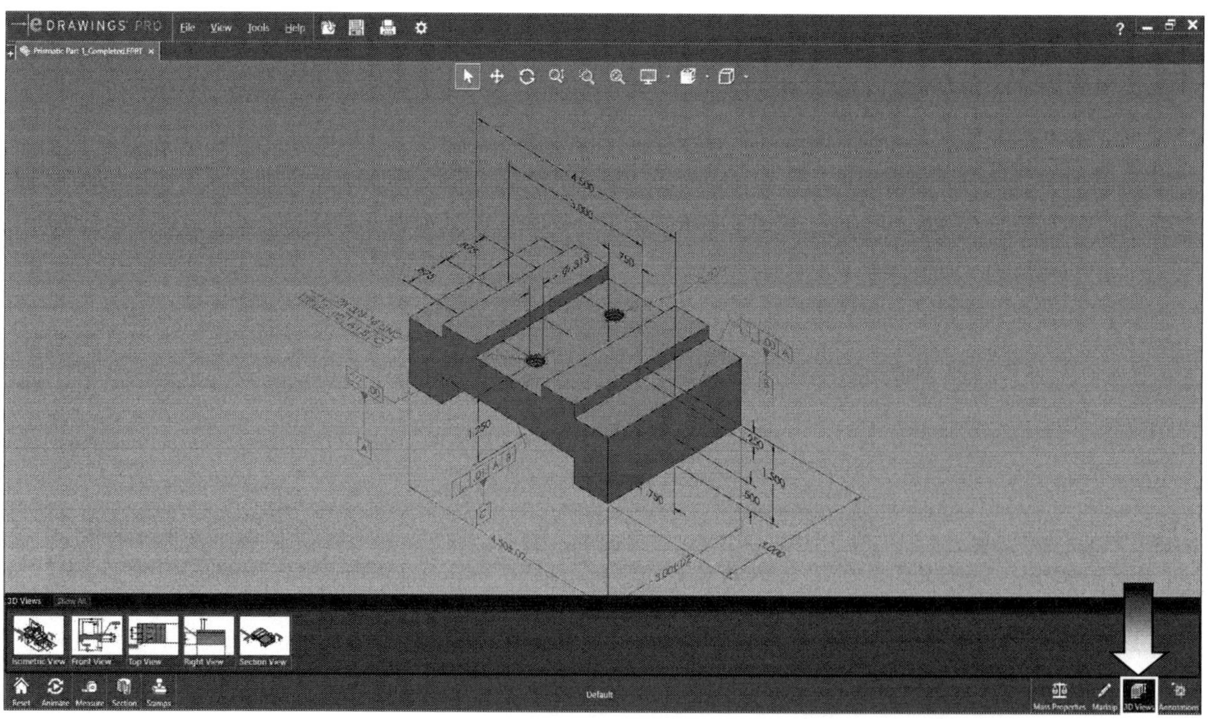

11. Viewing the Animation:

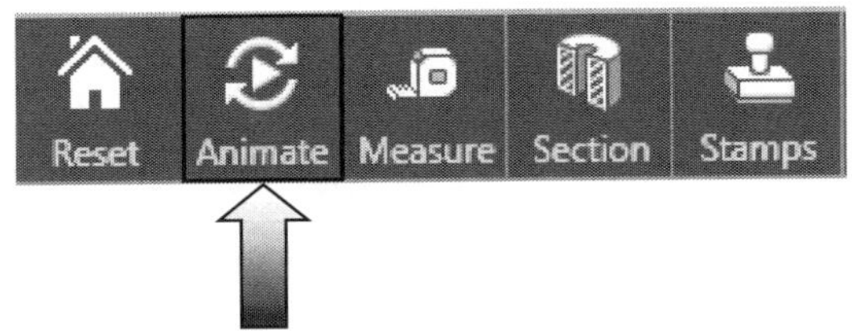

Animations generated in eDrawings. Play through the view orientations or drawing views with shaded data in the order displayed on the Animations pane.

To view the animated 3D Views, click **Animate**.

eDrawing animates the 3D View at 1 second per view.

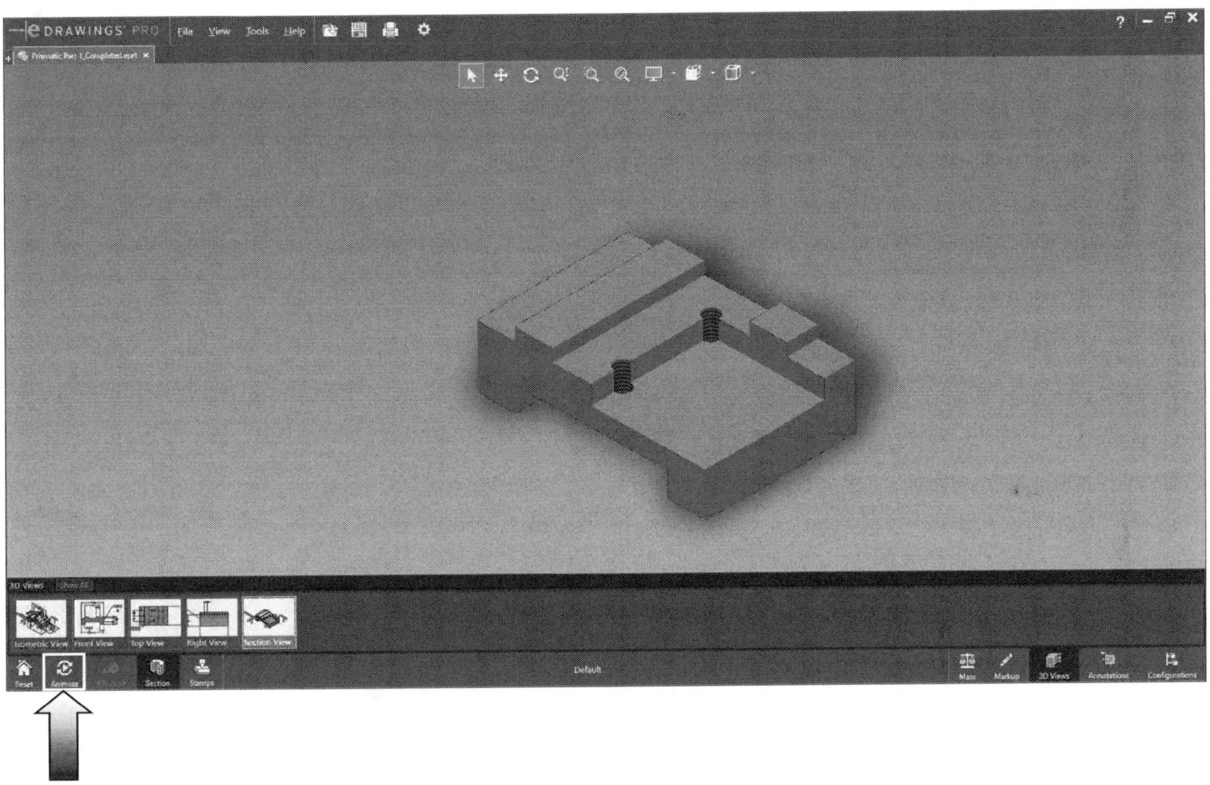

Push **Escape** or click the **Animate** button again to stop the animation.

Click **Reset** to go back to the default Isometric view.

Click **3D View** and double-click each view to display them one at a time.

12. Saving your work:

Save all documents, the SOLIDWORKS part document, the 3D-PDF document, and the eDrawing document.

Close all documents.

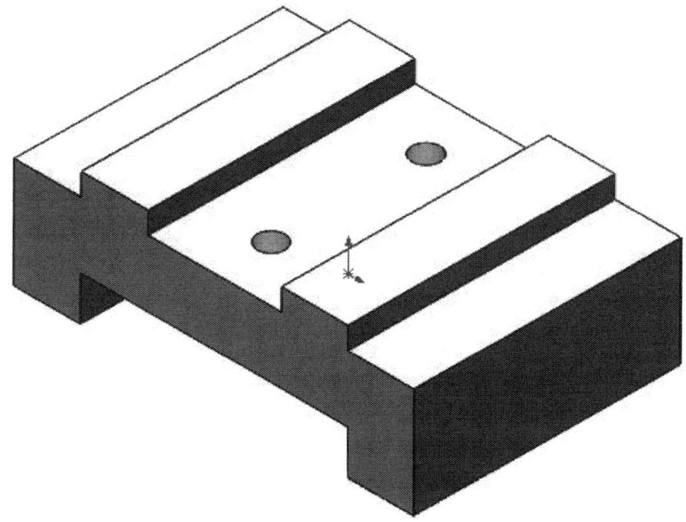

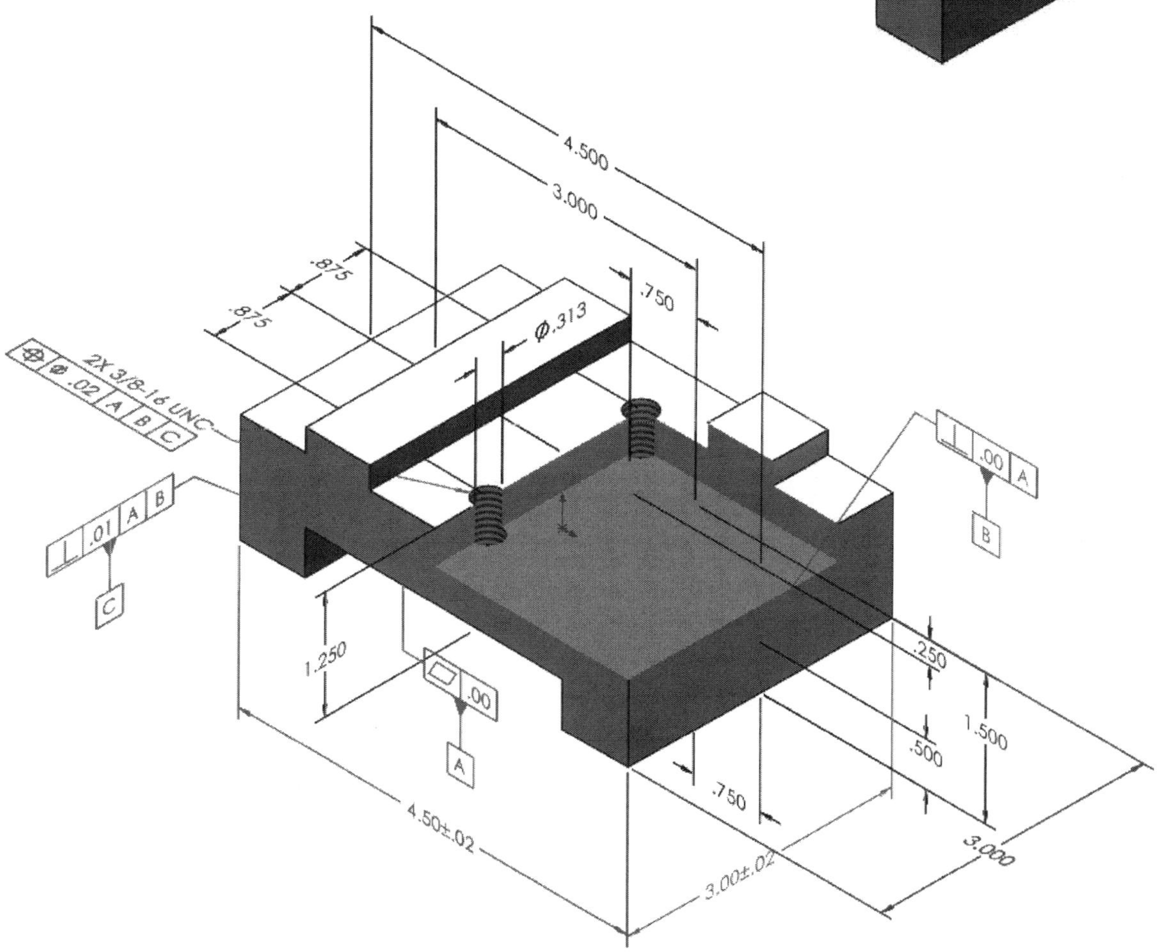

Chapter 13: Certified SOLIDWORKS Professional Drawing Tools (CSWP-DT) Preparation Material

Certified SOLIDWORKS Professional
Drawing Tools Preparation Material

Certified SOLIDWORKS Professional Drawing Tools – CSWP-DT

The completion of the Certified SOLIDWORKS Professional Drawing Tools (CSWP-DT) exam proves that you have successfully demonstrated your ability to use the tools found in the SOLIDWORKS Drawing environment.

Employers can be confident that you understand the tools and functionality found in the SOLIDWORKS Drawing environment.

Note: You must use at least SOLIDWORKS 2019 for this exam. Any use of a previous version will result in the inability to open some of the testing files.

Exam Length: 100 minutes   Minimum Passing grade: 75%

Re-test Policy: There is a minimum 14 day waiting period between every attempt of the CSWP-DT exam. Also, a CSWP-DT exam credit must be purchased for each exam attempt.

All candidates receive electronic certificates and a personal listing on the CSWP directory when they pass.

Exam features hands-on challenges in many of these areas of SOLIDWORKS drawing functionality such as:

Basic View Creation, Section Views, Auxiliary Views, Alternate position Views, Broken Out Sections, Lock View/Sheet Focus, Transferring Sketch Entities from and to Views, Bill of Materials, and Custom Properties.

CHALLENGE 1 – PART DRAWINGS

View Creation & Projected Dimensions

The examples in this exam preparation material are intended to assist you in familiarizing yourself with the structures of the exams and the method in which the questions are asked.

1. Opening an existing drawing:

Select **File, Open**.

Browse to the CSWP-Advanced Drawing Tools Prep folder and open the drawing document named: **Glass.slddrw**.

An Isometric drawing view has been created ahead of time.

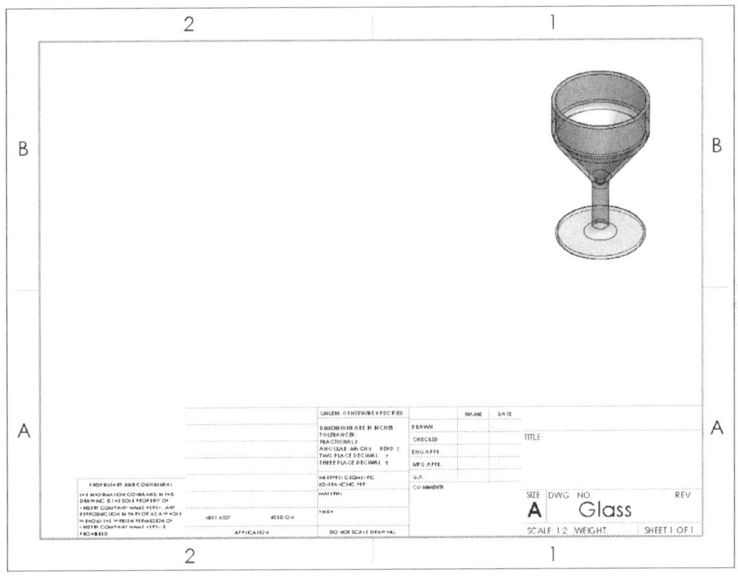

2. Adding the Front drawing view:

Using the **View Palette**, drag & drop the **Front** drawing view into the drawing approximately as shown.

The current view scale is **1:2** (half size).

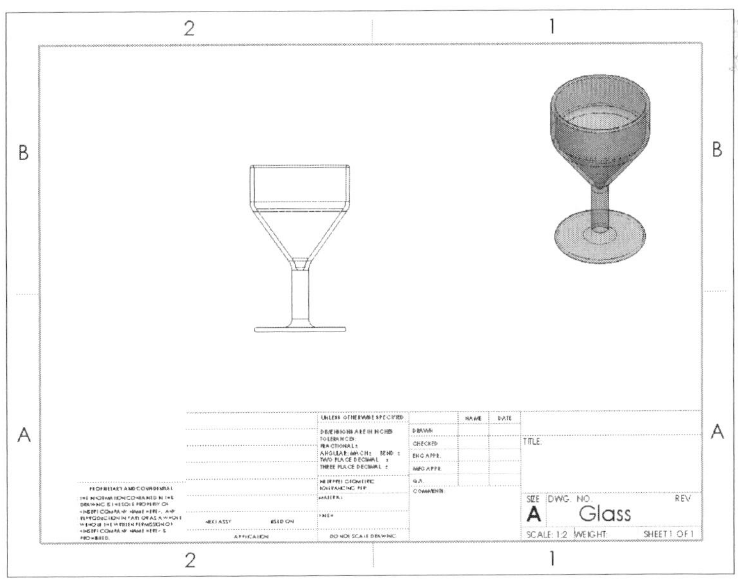

3. Adding dimensions:

SOLIDWORKS specifies **Projected** type dimensions for standard and custom orthogonal views and **True** type dimensions for isometric, dimetric, and trimetric views.

If you create a projected or auxiliary view from another view, the new view uses **Projected** type dimensions, even if the original view used **True** type dimensions.

True Dimension: Accurate model values
Projected Dimensions: 2D dimensions

Using the **Smart Dimension** tool add 2 angular dimensions, 1 to each drawing view.

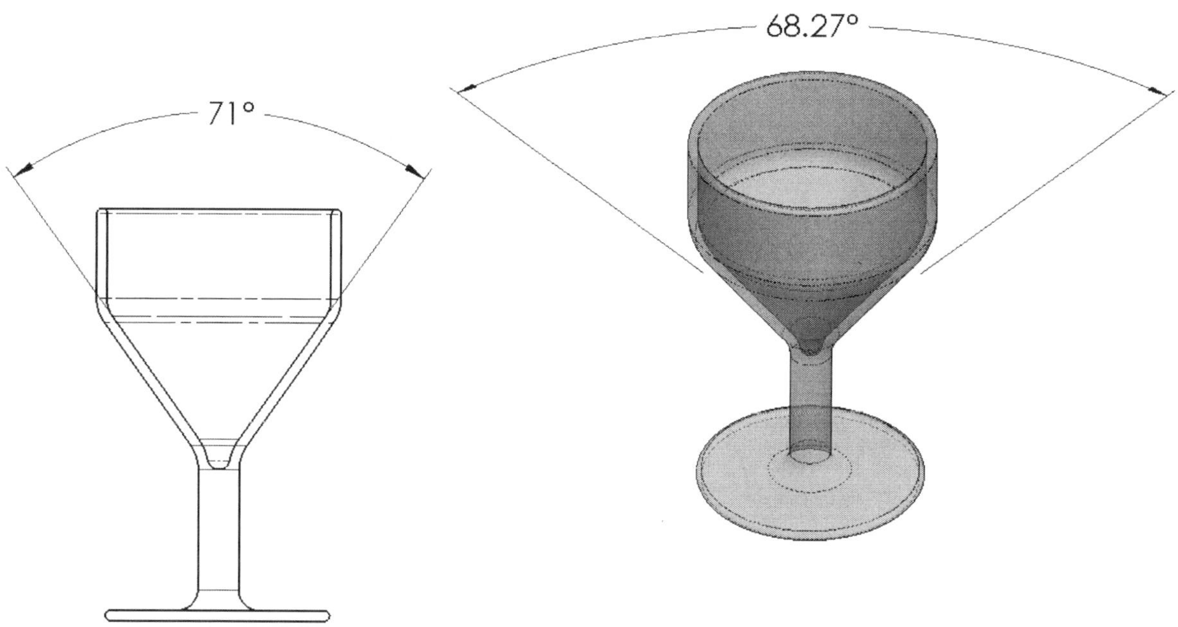

Notice the difference between the 2 values. The dimension in the Front drawing view is **True Dimension** and the one in the Isometric view is **Projected Dimension.**

What is the Projected Dimension of the angle: _________ degrees

4. Creating the 1st section view:

Click the dotted border of the **Front** drawing view to activate it.

Switch to the **Sketch** tab and select the **Line** tool.

Sketch a **vertical line** and add the location dimension shown below.

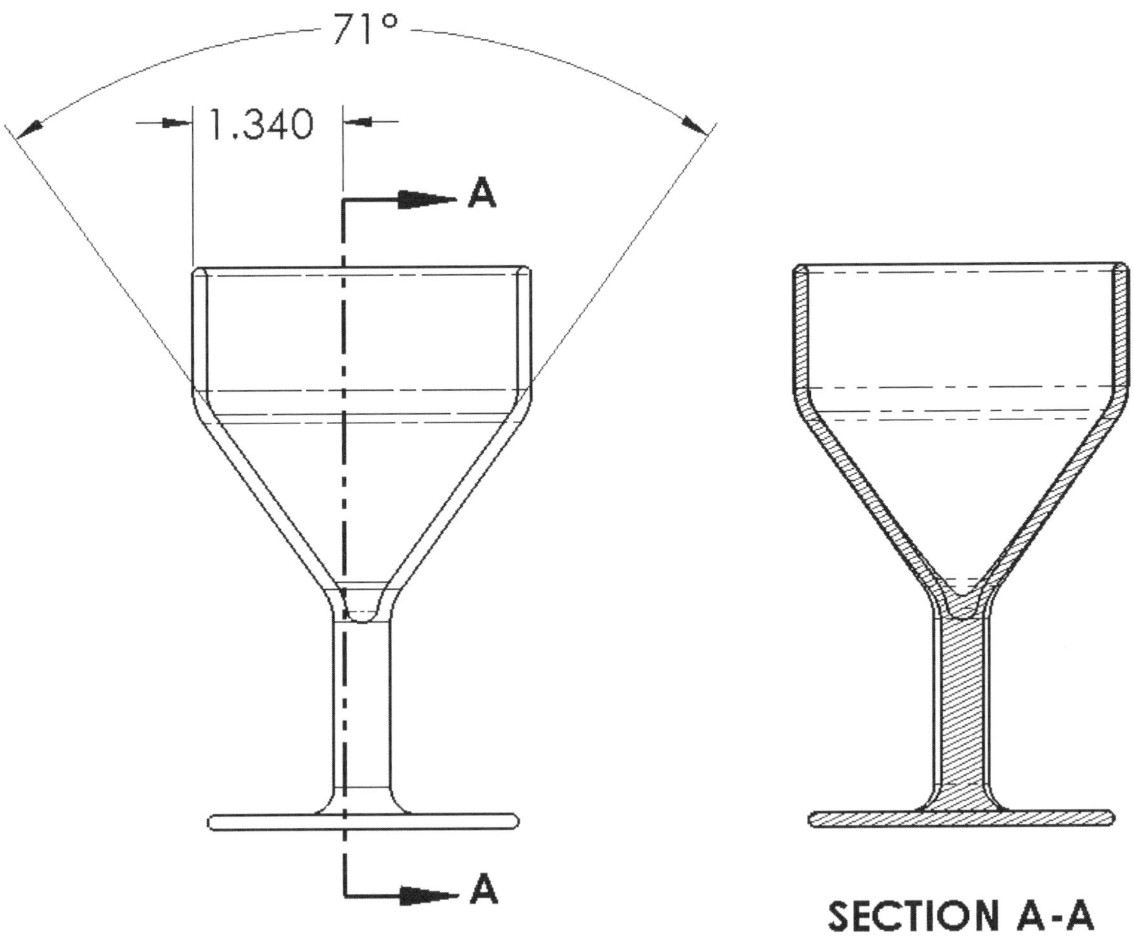

Switch to the **Drawing** tab and click the **Section View** command.

Click **Flip Direction** if needed to point the section arrows to the right.

Place the Section View on the right of the Front drawing view.

5. Measuring the perimeter:

Zoom in closer to the section view.

Switch to the **Evaluation** tab and click **Measure.**

Click inside the **sectioned face** to display the measurements.

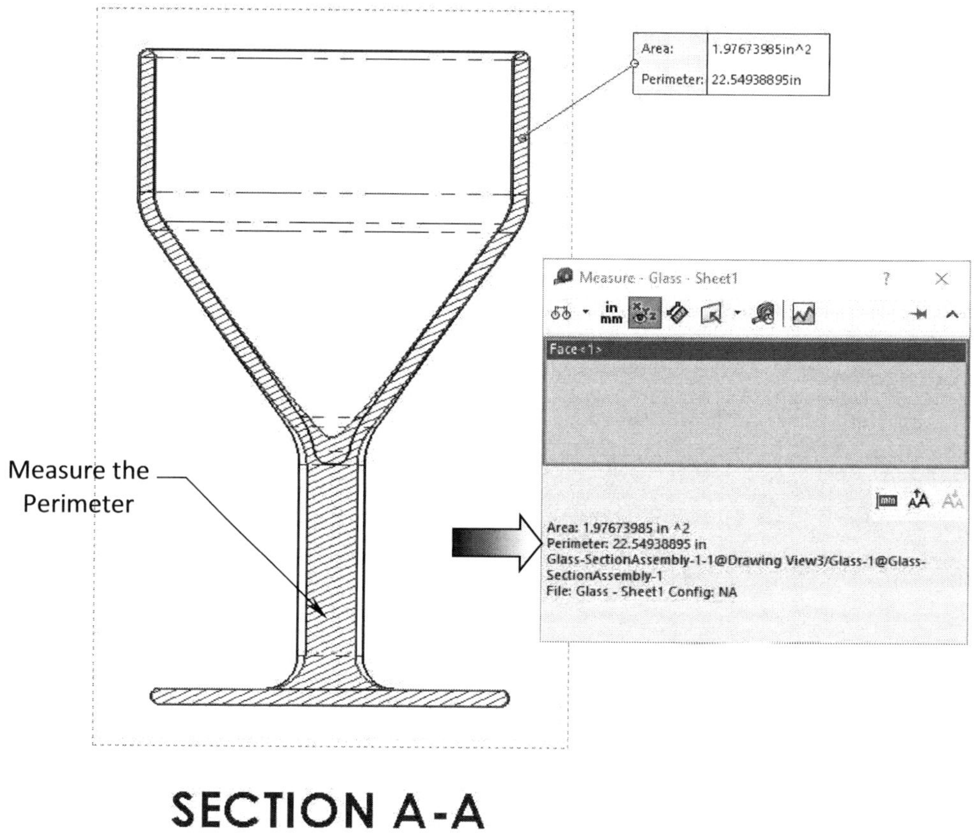

Locate the Perimeter measurement and enter it here:

____________________ in.

6. Creating the 2nd section view:

Click the dotted border of the Front drawing view to activate it.

Switch to the **Sketch** tab and sketch **2 lines** as shown in the image on the right.

Add the 2 location dimensions that are circled below.

Switch to the **Drawing** tab and click the **Section View** command.

Pay close attention to the direction arrows, click Flip Direction if needed.

Place the Section View on the side.

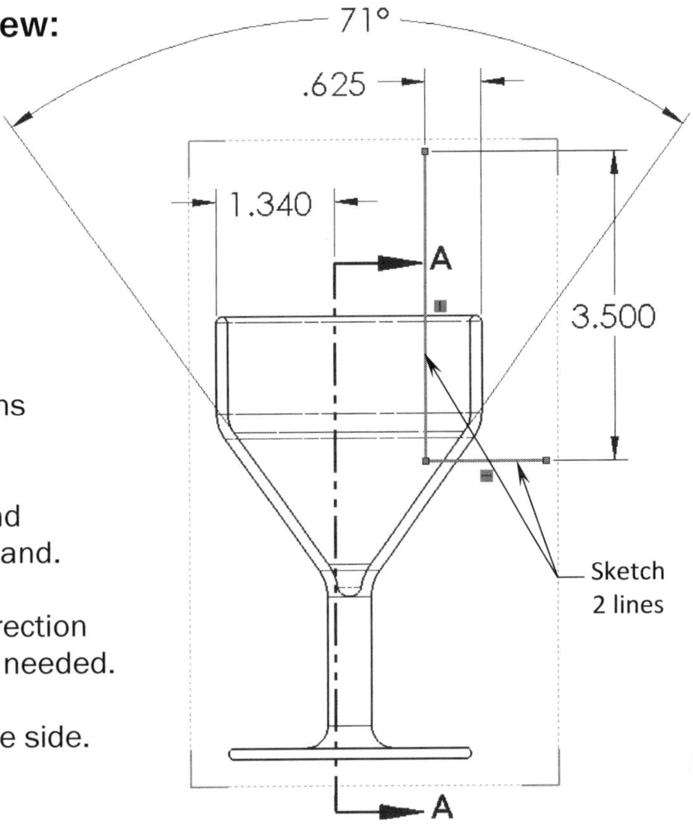

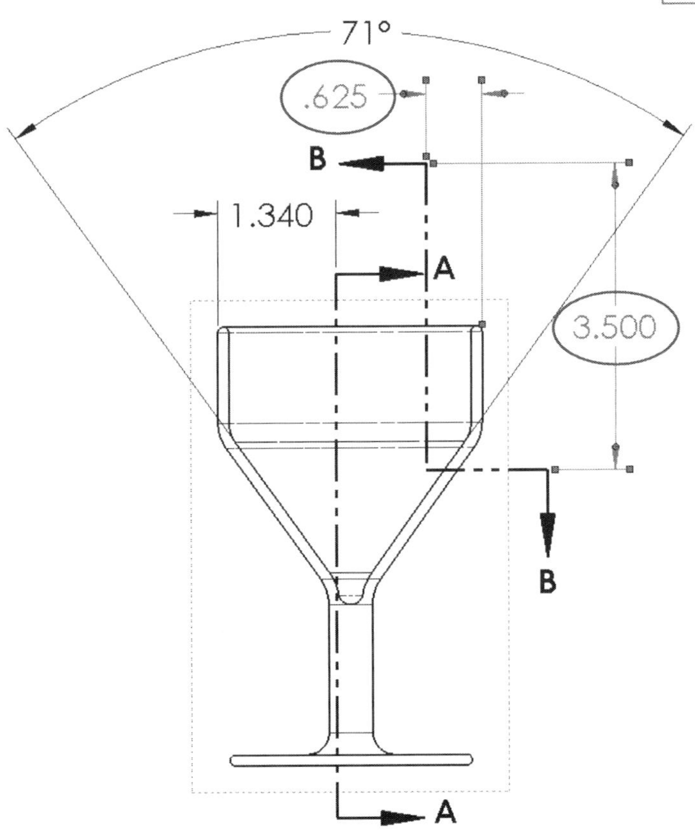

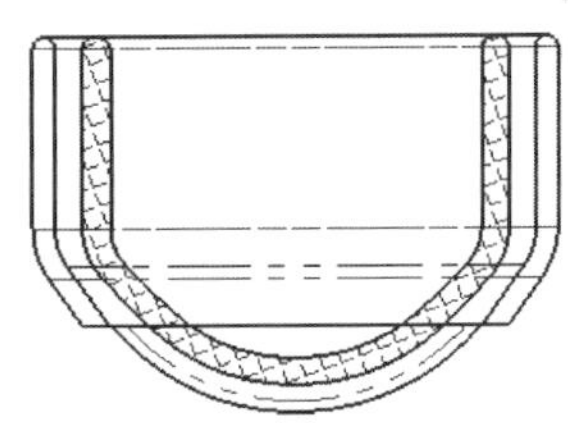

SECTION B-B

7. Measuring the perimeter:

Zoom closer to Section B-B.

Switch to the **Evaluate** tab and click **Measure.**

Click inside the **sectioned face** to display the measurements.

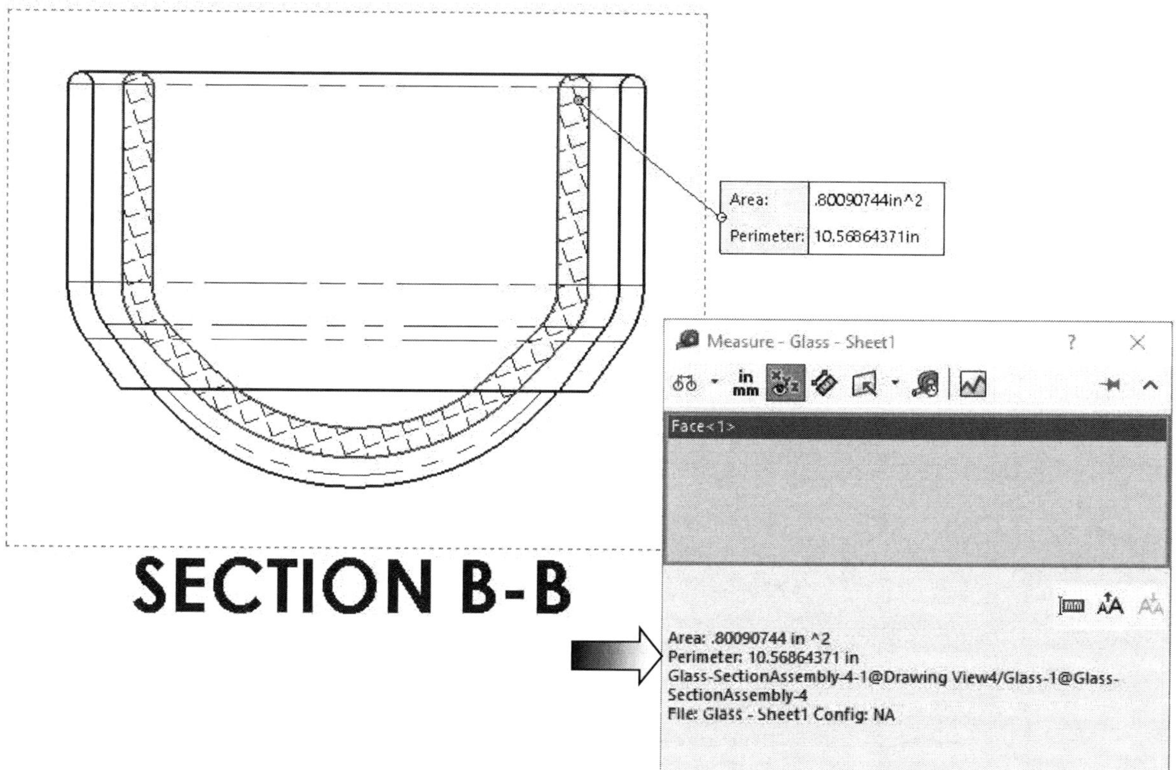

Locate the Perimeter measurement and enter it here:

_________________ in.

8. Saving your work:

Save your drawing as **Glass_completed.slddrw**

Move forward to the next challenge.

CHALLENGE 2 – ASSEMBLY DRAWINGS

View Creation & Measurements

The examples in this exam preparation materials are intended to assist you in familiarizing yourself with the structures of the exams and the method in which the questions are asked.

1. Opening an assembly document:

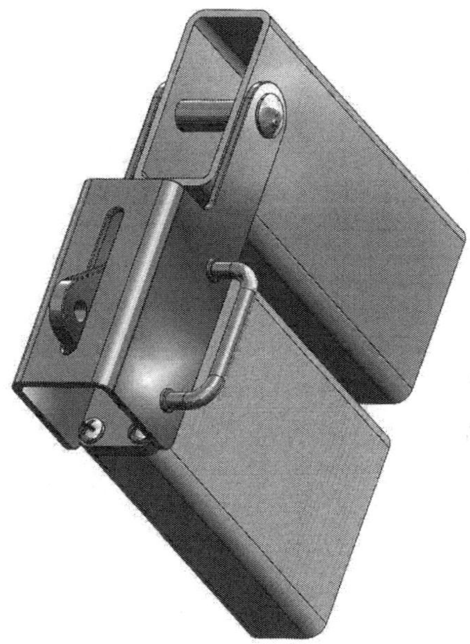

Select **File, Open**.

Locate the Training Folder and open the assembly documents named: **Latch Assembly.sldasm**.

The orientation of this assembly has been changed to an odd angle. We need to find a way to rotate it back to the normal orientation, prior to making a drawing for it.

2. Changing the orientation:

There are a couple of different ways to change the orientation of a model or an assembly document. Let us try the 1st option called: **Update Standard View**.

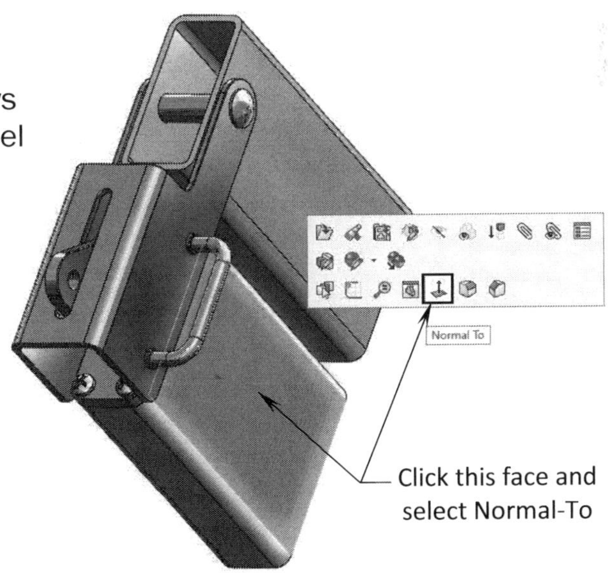

Select the face as indicated on the right and select: **Normal To**.

The assembly rotates normal to you, or flat to screen.

3. Finding the angle:

Select the face indicated below and open a **new sketch.**

Sketch a **horizontal line** and an **angular line** that is Collinear to the bottom edge of the component **Post1.**

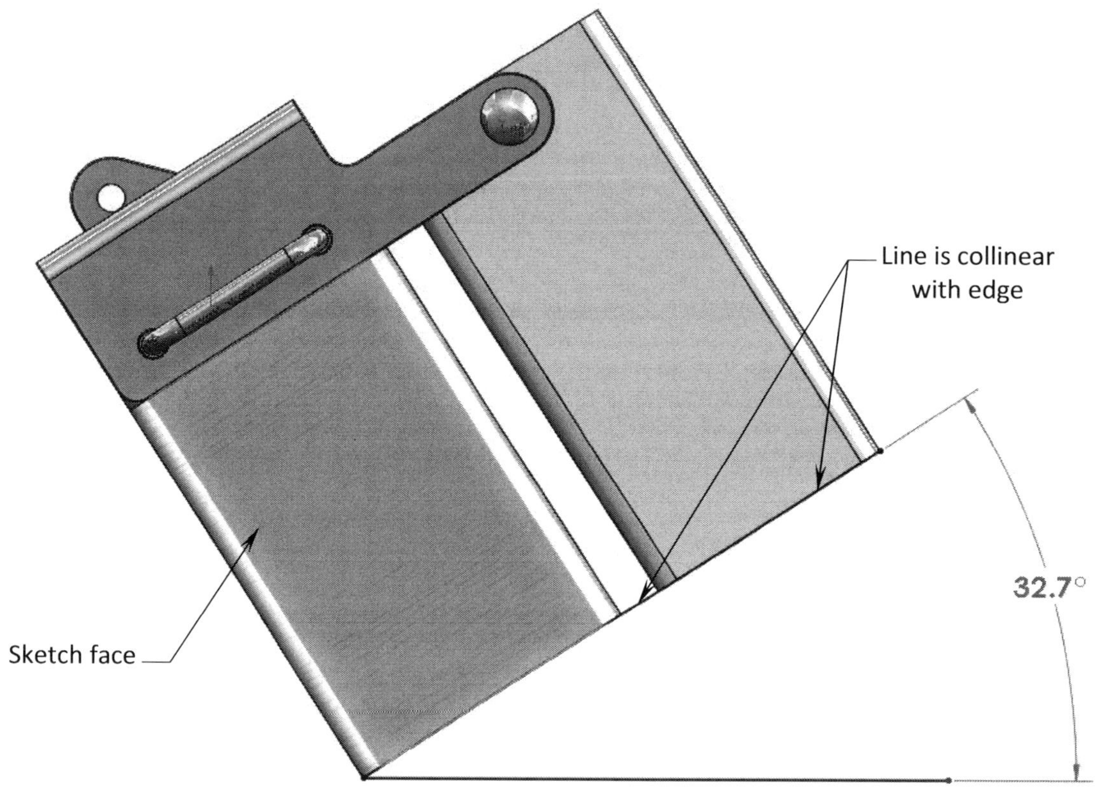

Add the reference angular dimension as shown above.

Look for the angular dimension value on the FeatureManager tree and write it down, up to 5 decimal places.

Exit the sketch. We will need to enter this value into the View Rotation, Arrow Key values in the next step.

4. Entering the angle for Arrow Key rotation:

Select **Tools, Options, System Options.**

Select View and enter the **angle value** that you wrote down in the previous step, use 5 decimal places (32.69960 deg).

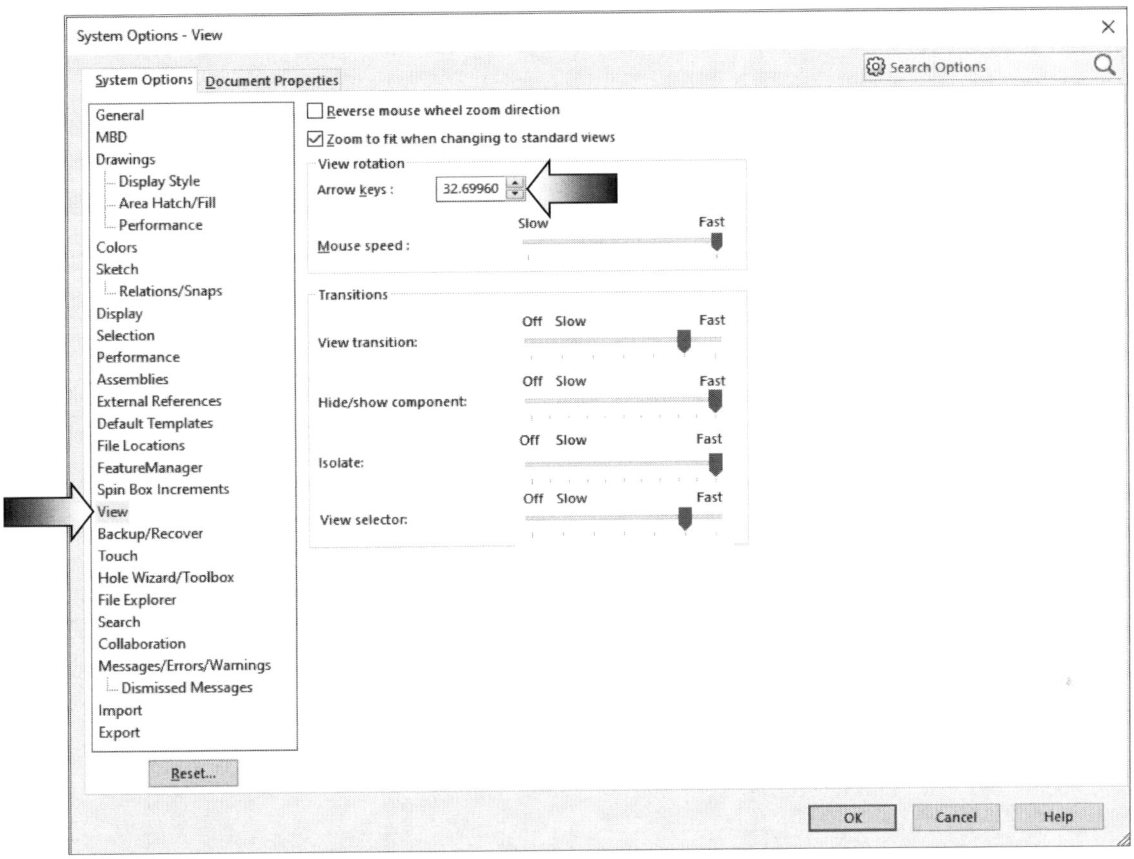

Click **OK** to exit the System Options dialog box.

From this point on, every time you press one of the arrow keys, your model will rotate 32.69960 deg.

The hotkey to rotate the model Normal-To-Screen is Alt + one of the arrow keys.

5. Rotating the model:

Hold down the **ALT** key and press the **LEFT** arrow key once.

The model rotates 32.69960 deg. to the right, resulting in a flat model view.

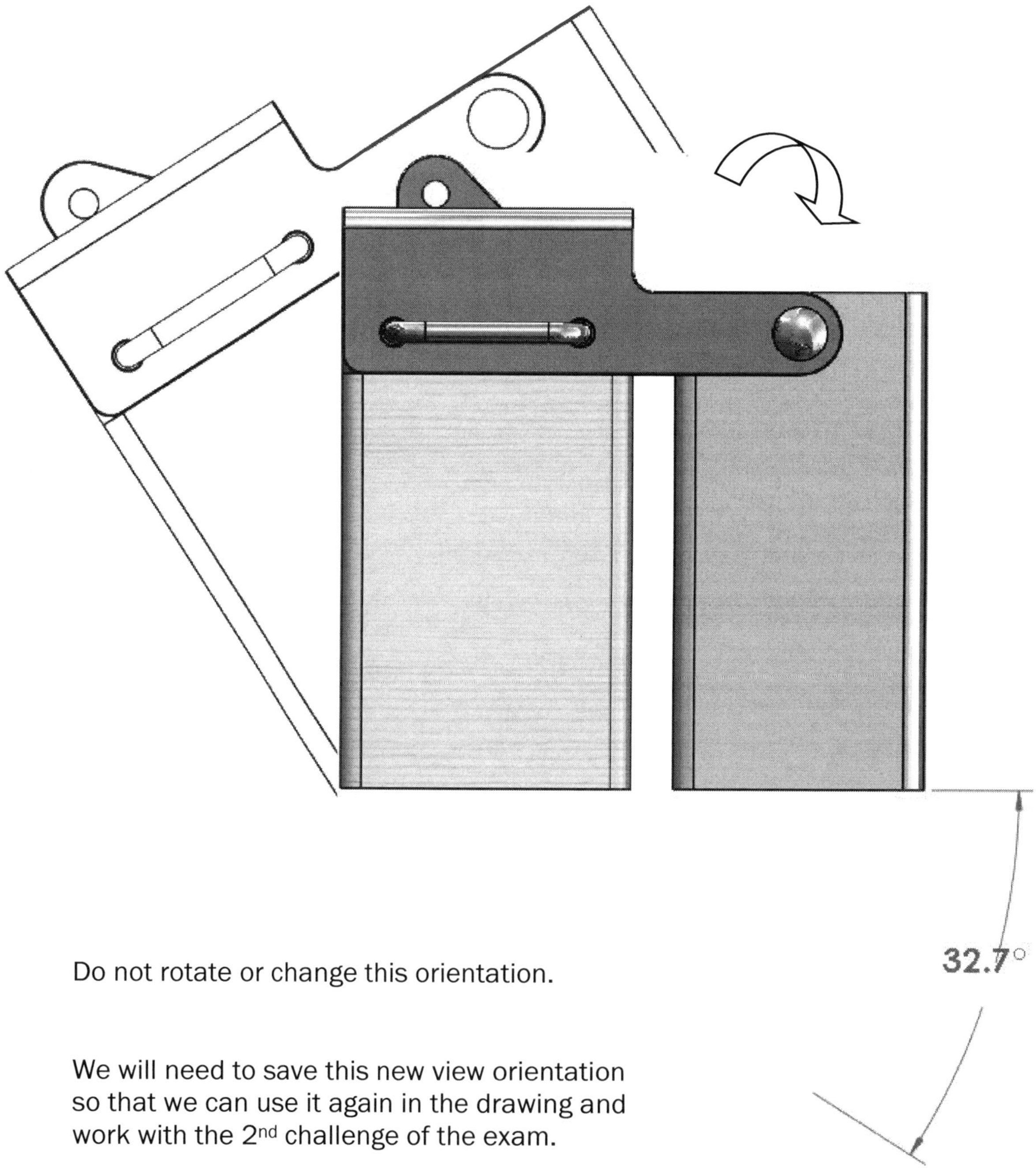

Do not rotate or change this orientation.

We will need to save this new view orientation so that we can use it again in the drawing and work with the 2nd challenge of the exam.

6. Updating the standard views:

Press the **Space-Bar** to display the **View Orientation** dialog box

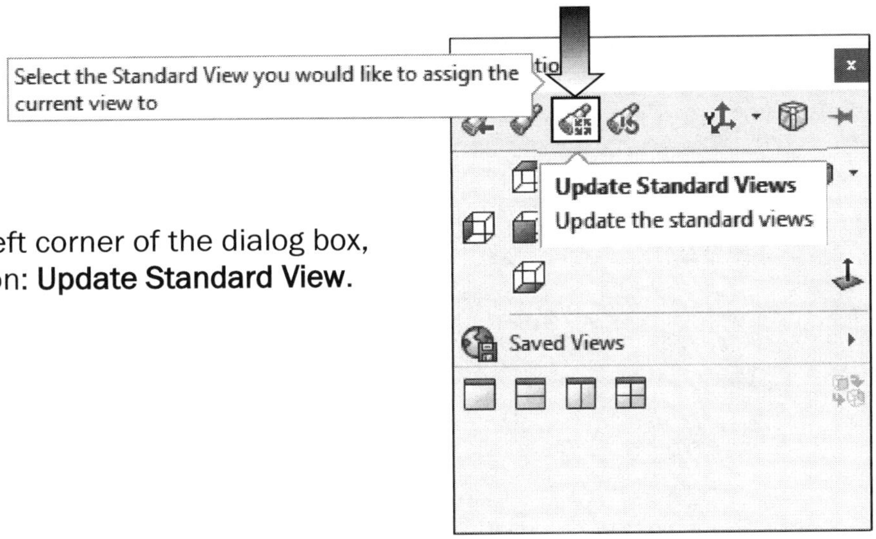

On the upper left corner of the dialog box, click the 3rd icon: **Update Standard View.**

A message pops up asking to select a Standard View to assign the current view to; select the **Front View** icon.

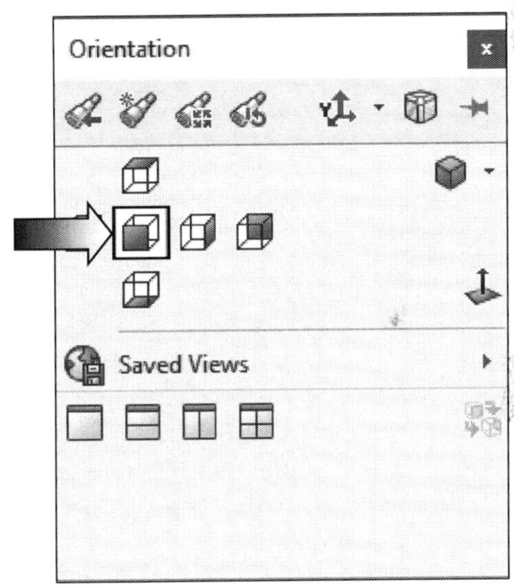

A confirmation dialog box appears; click **Yes** to make the change.

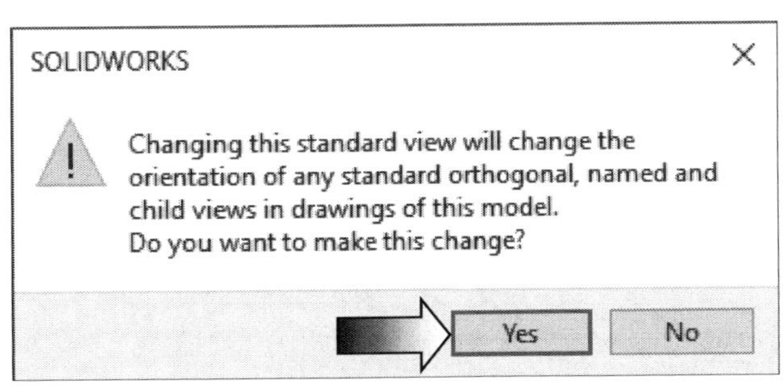

The new view orientation is now confirmed. To revert back to the previous orientation, click the 4th icon: **Reset View Orientation**.

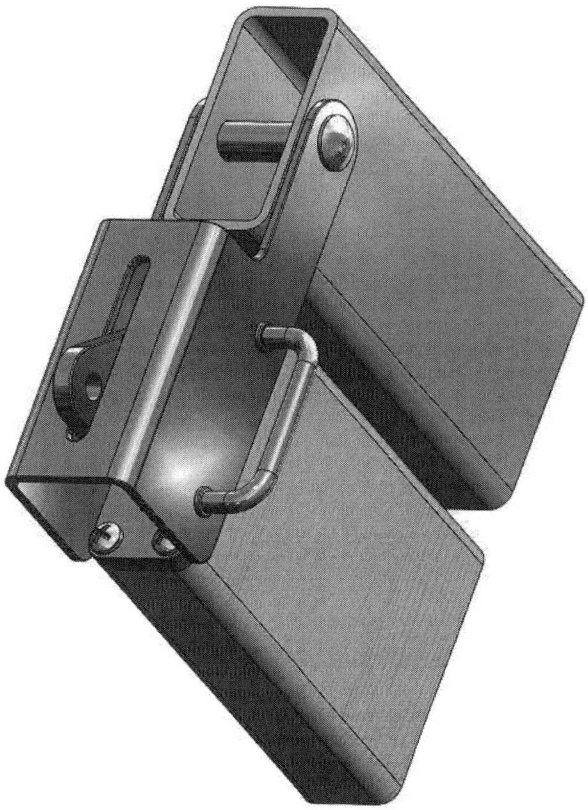

The Isometric view used to look like this when you first open it.

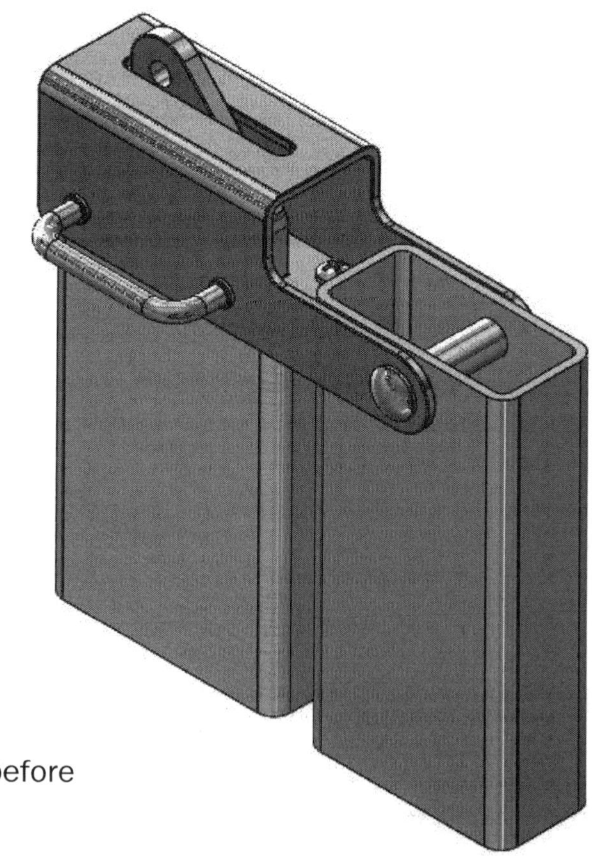

The new Isometric view is now looking like this. It is ready to be transferred to a drawing.

Re-save your assembly document before moving forward to the next step.

7. Making a drawing:

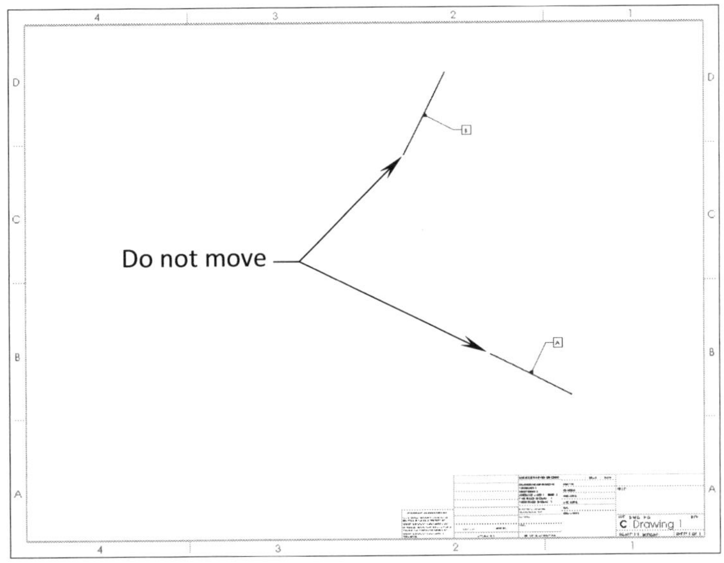

Select **File, Open**.

Browse to the Training folder and open the drawing document named:
Drawing 1.slddrw

This is a C-Size drawing; it has a couple of lines and 2 datum symbols in it.

Do not move the 2 lines or the datum symbols at all times. They need to stay fixed to help locate the other drawing views.

When the **Task Pane** or the **View Palette** is expanded, the lines and the datums are shifted on their own; we will need to solve this issue first.

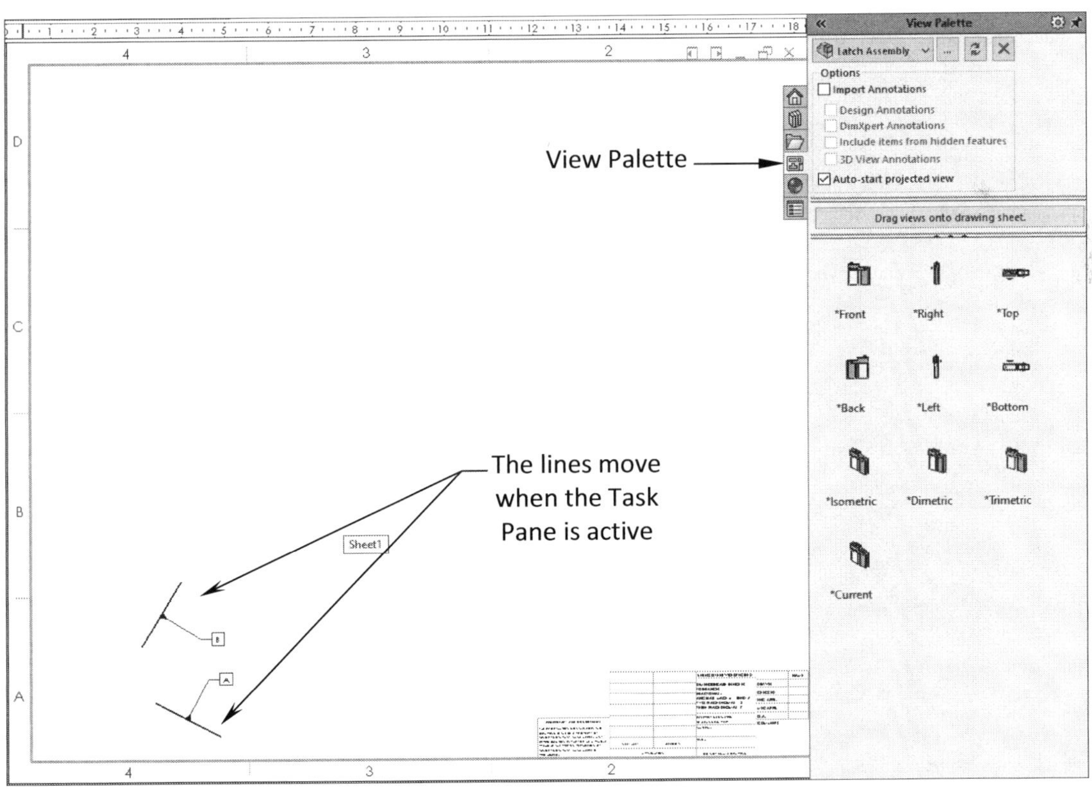

Close the drawing without saving it.

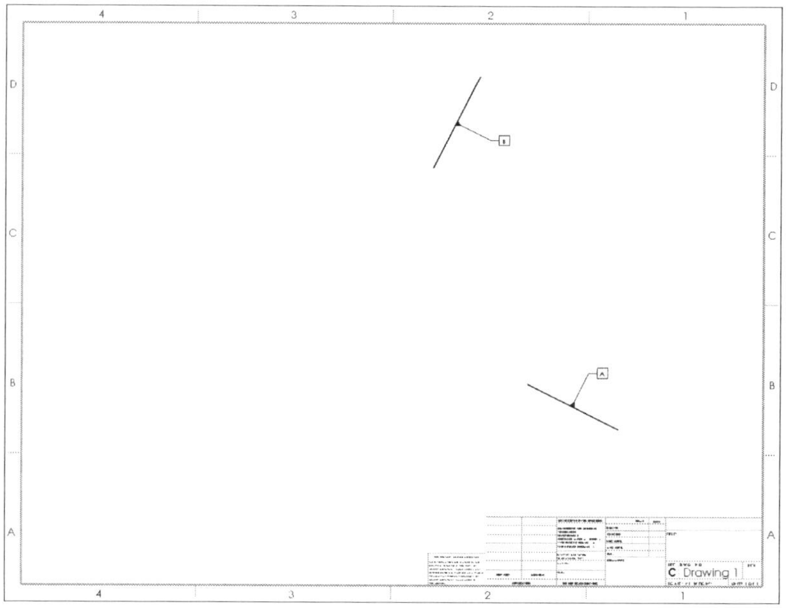

Open the same drawing once again. The 2 lines and the datums must stay where they are.

At the bottom left corner of the screen, click the **Add Sheet** tab to add **Sheet2** to the drawing.

Expand the **Task Pane** by clicking on the View Palette tab (arrow).

We will create the drawing views here on Sheet2, and then move them to Sheet1, that way the lines and datums will not get shifted the way it did last time.

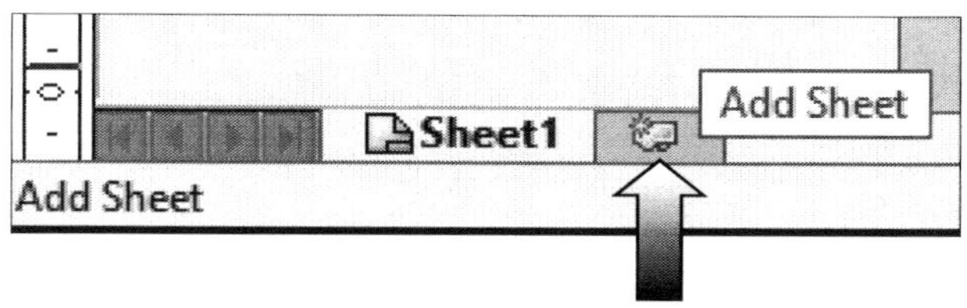

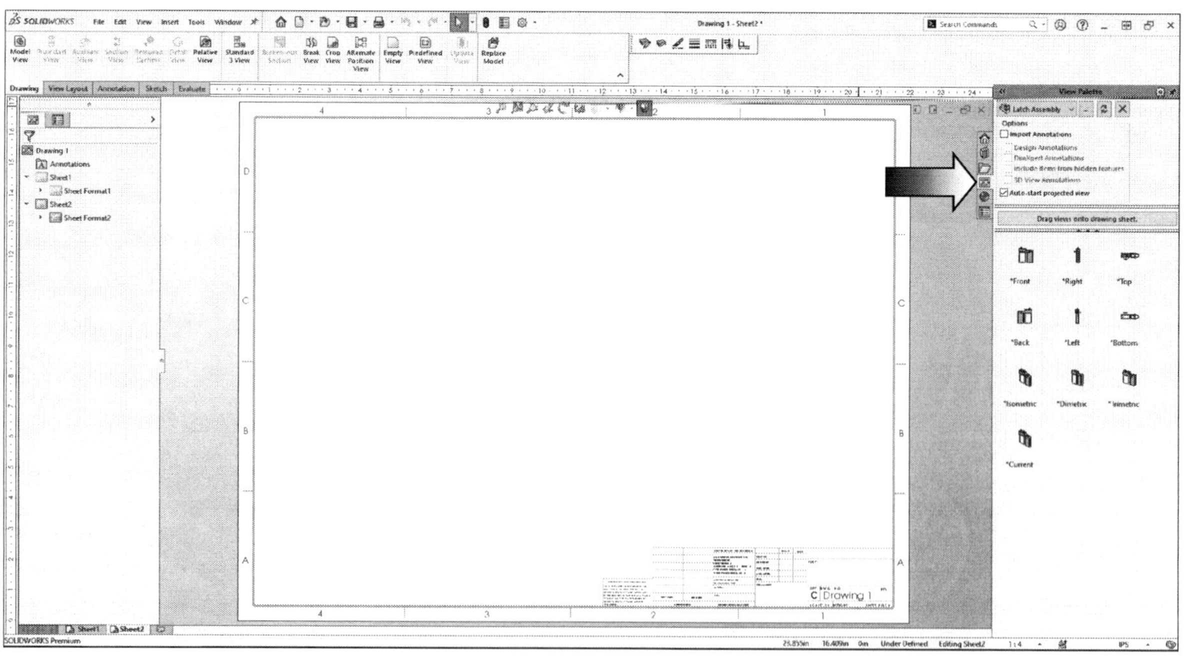

8. Adding a drawing view:

While on Sheet2, expand the **View Palette** and select the **Latch Assembly** document from the drop-down list (arrow).

Clear all checkboxes under **Options**, we will only need to create 1 drawing view without any dimensions at this time.

Locate the **Front** drawing view from the right pane and drag/drop it inside the drawing as shown below.

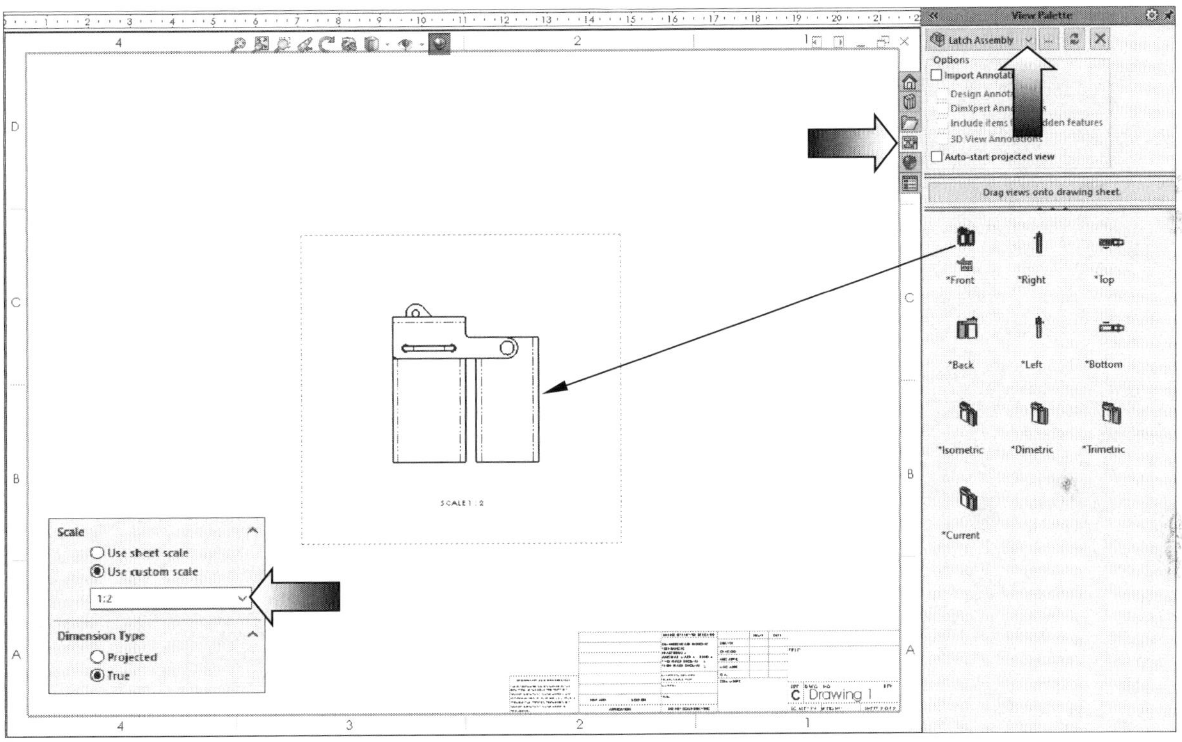

At the lower left side of the FeatureManager tree, locate the **Scale** option and select the scale of **1:2** from the list.

We will move this Front drawing view to Sheet1 by dragging and dropping it from the FeatureManager tree.

9. Moving the drawing view:

Using the FeatureManager tree, locate the **Drawing View1** on Sheet2, drag/drop onto the <u>name</u> **Sheet1**.

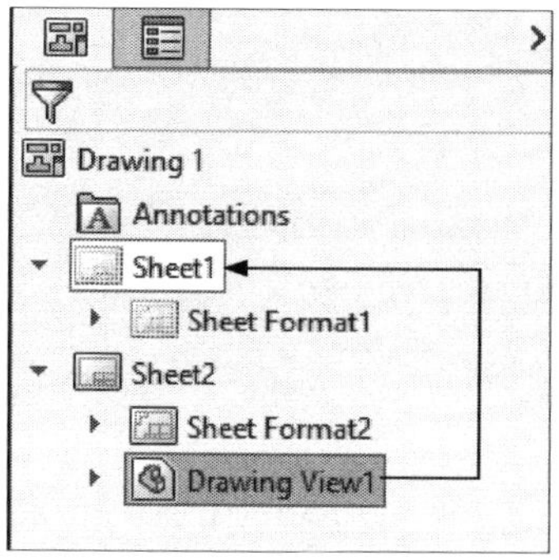

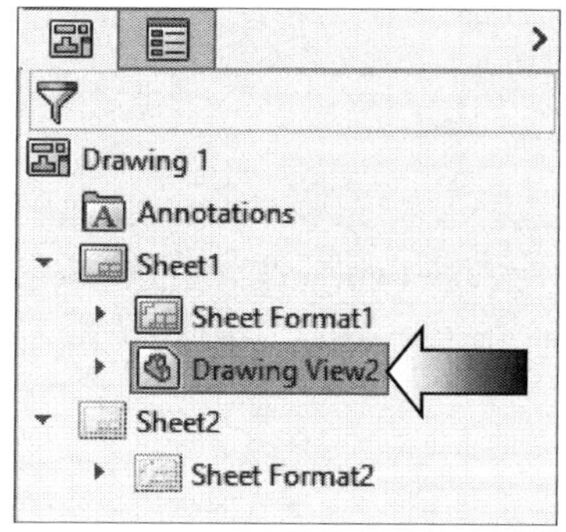

Switch back to **Sheet1** by clicking on the Sheet1 tab at the bottom right of the screen. Notice the 2 lines and the datums did not move.

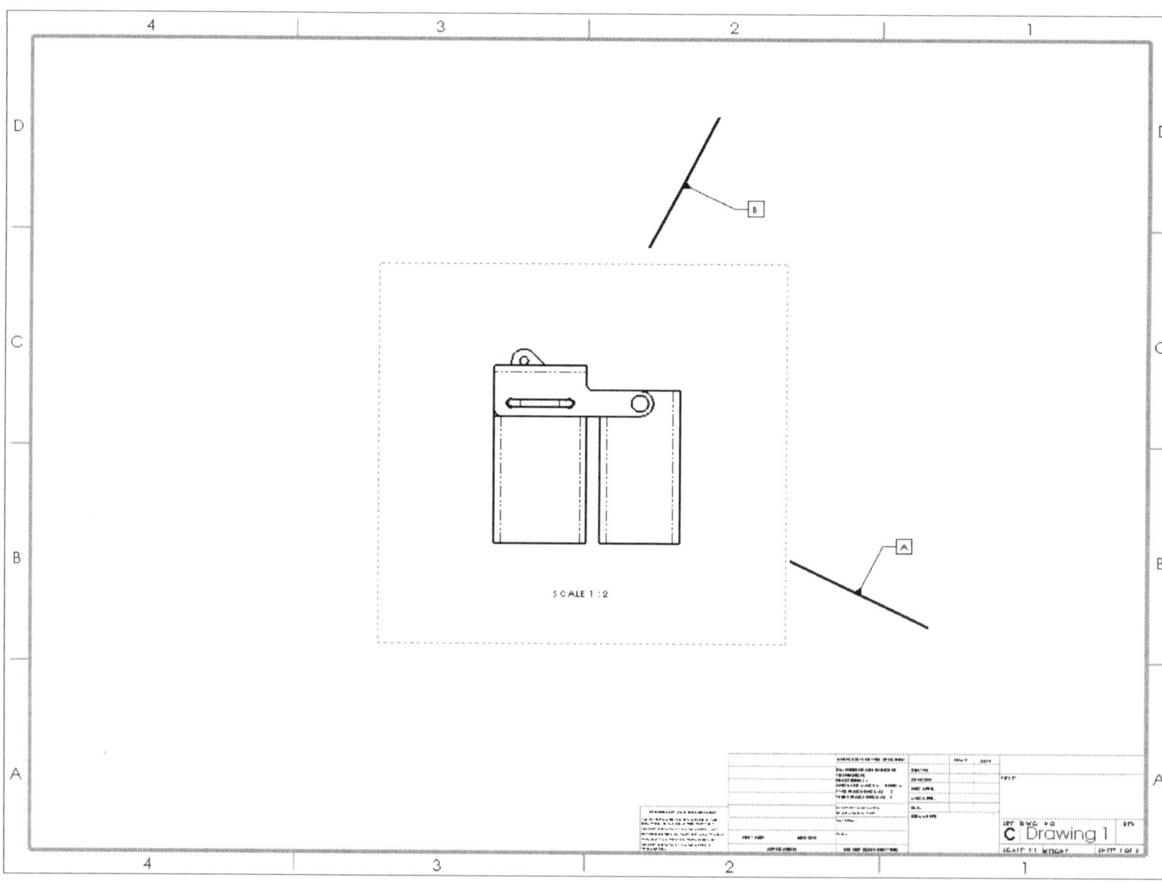

10. Lock View Focus vs. Lock Sheet Focus:

There are 2 options in the drawing mode that allow you to add reference sketch entities for locating and measuring the drawing views; they are Lock View Focus and Lock Sheet Focus.

Lock View Focus: Allows you to add sketch entities to a view, even when the pointer is close to another view. You can be sure that the items you are adding belong to the view you want. You can also double-click a view to lock the focus.

Lock Sheet Focus: Allows you to add sketch entities to the sheet. Otherwise, the sketch entities belong to the view that is closest to where you begin sketching. You can also double-click a sheet to lock the focus. Lock Sheet Focus is available when at least one drawing view is present. When Lock Sheet Focus is enabled, the drawing sheet border is pink.

To measure between a line, which is part of the Sheet, and the Front drawing view, which is part of the View, we will need to Lock Sheet Focus and convert the line in the drawing view, so that this line will be part of the Sheet.

All entities on the sheet can be measured or dimensioned, and the same rule applied to all entities in the drawing views, but entities between the sheet and the drawing views cannot be interchanged or measured when needed.

Right-click inside the drawing and select: **Lock Sheet Focus.**

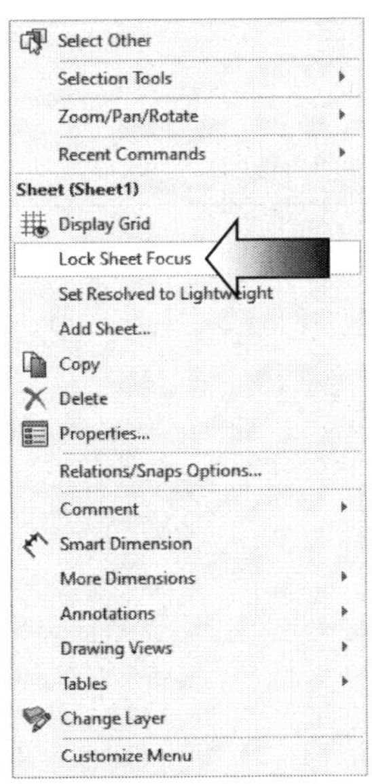

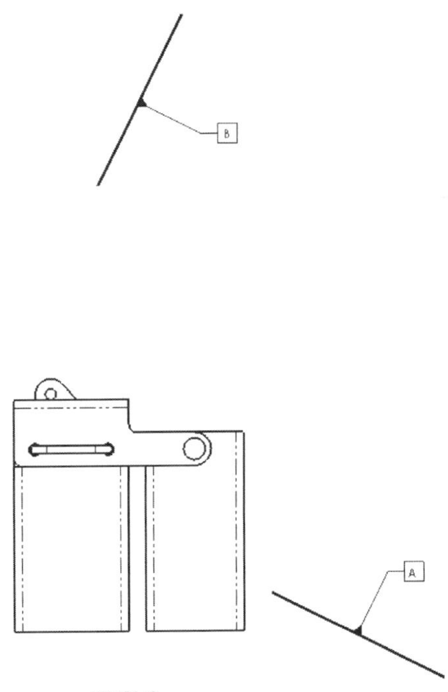

The drawing sheet border is changed to pink color.

Any new entities created at this time will belong to the sheet.

11. Lock Sheet Focus:

While the Sheet Focus is locked (pink sheet border), select the angular edge of the latch as indicated.

Switch to the **Sketch** tab and click: **Convert Entities**.

Move the drawing view away to see the converted line.

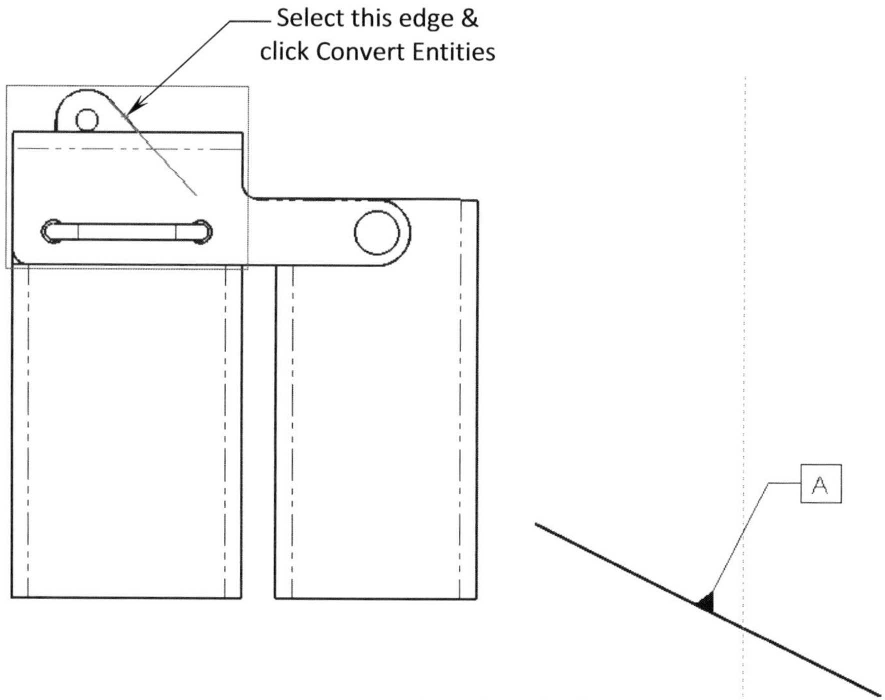

The selected edge is converted to a line.

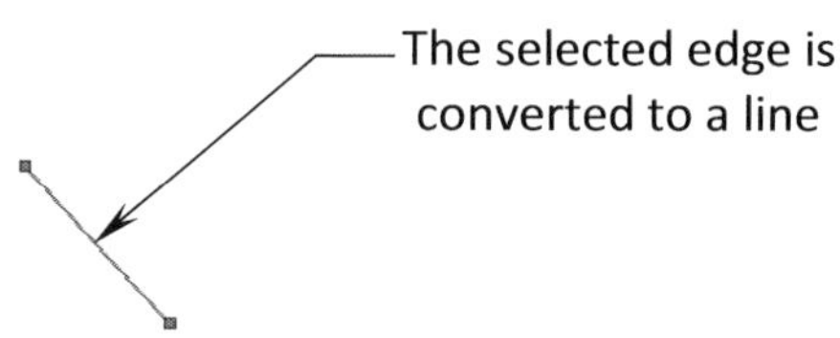

This line is part of the Sheet and the line that has the datum A attached to it is also part of the Sheet; we can now measure between the 2 entities.

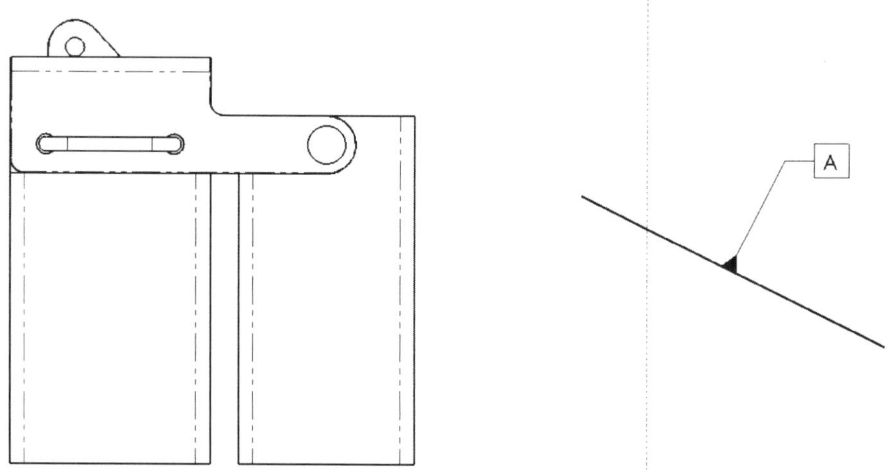

12. Finding the angle:

Create an **angular dimension** between the 2 lines as shown below.

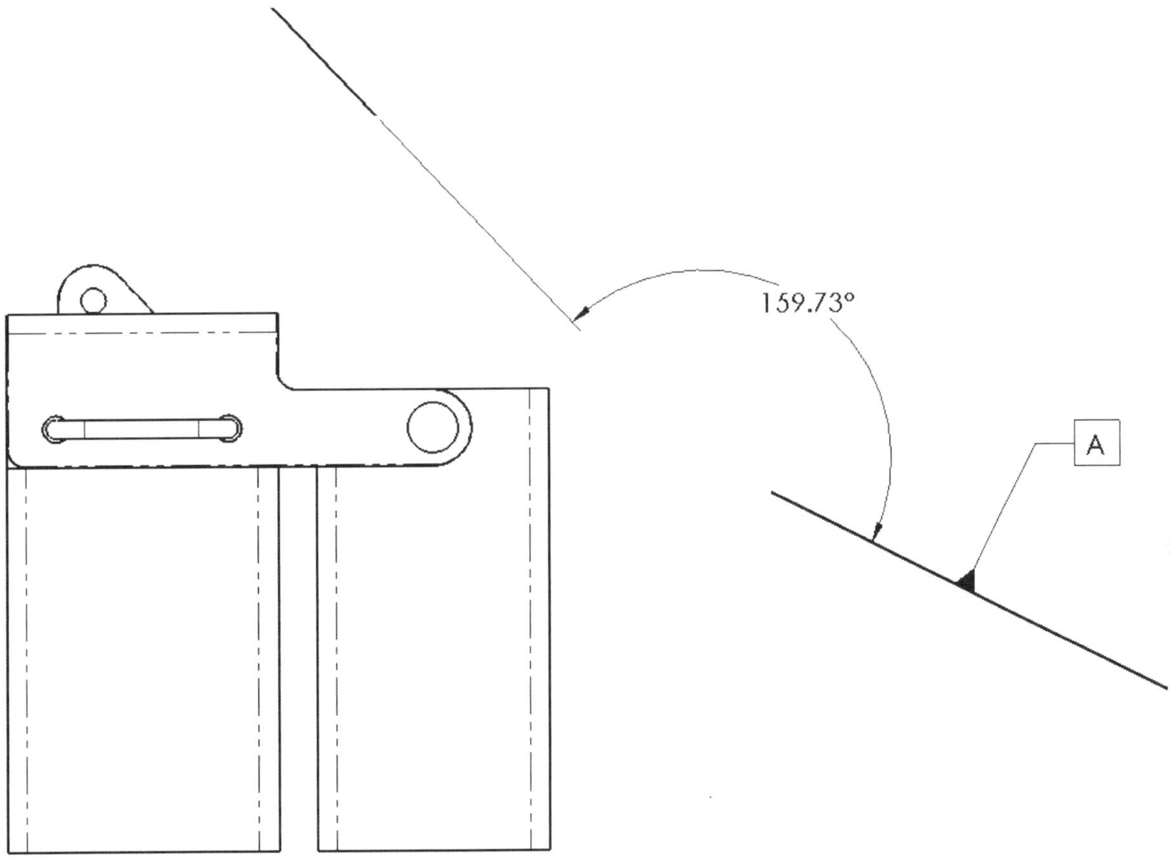

What is the value of the angular dimension (use 2 decimals):

________________ deg.

13. Sketching a reference line:

Zoom closer to the lower right side of the drawing.

Make sure Lock Sheet Focus is still active (pink sheet border).

Sketch a **Line** as shown in the image below and add a **Fix** relation to keep it from moving.

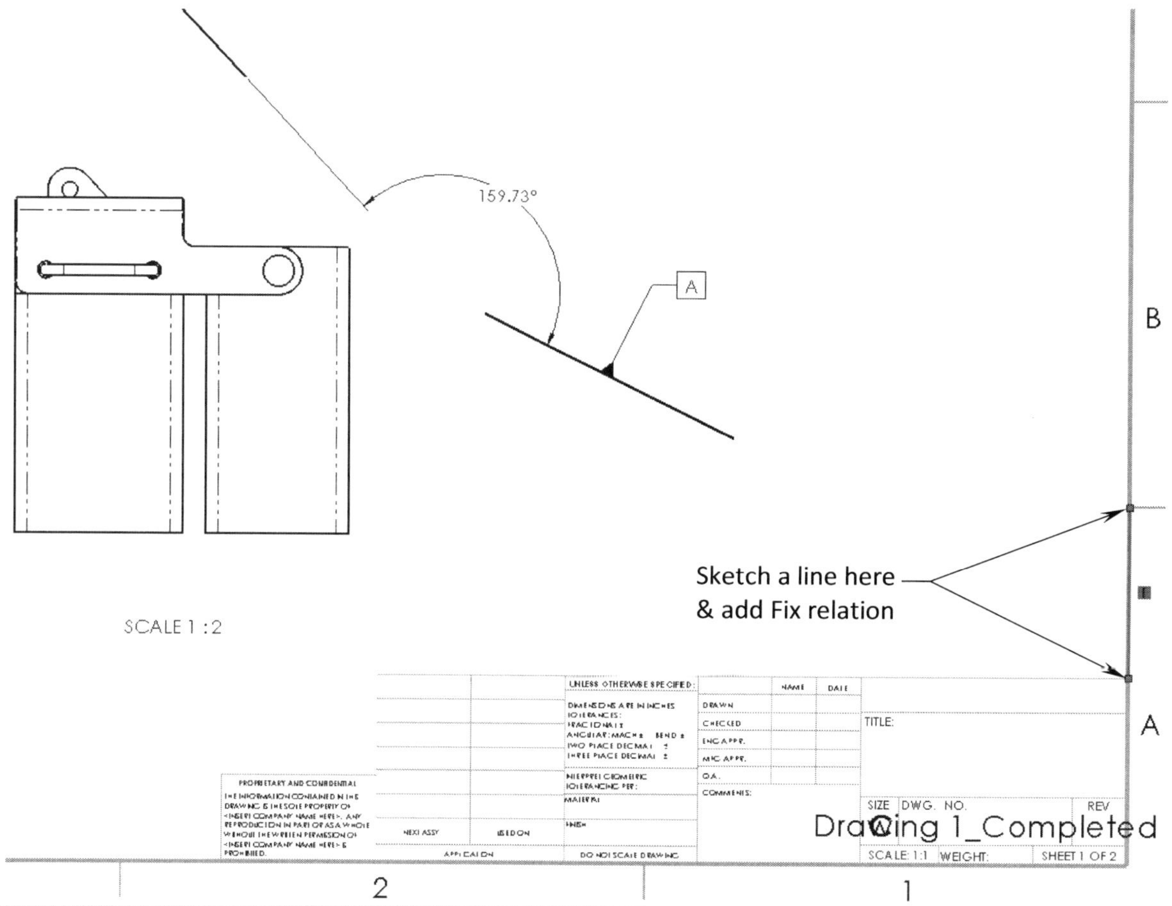

The new line is part of the Sheet; it can be used to measure to any other entities on the Sheet.

We will use it to measure and to locate the Front drawing view.

14. Adding another reference line:

Move the **Front** drawing view back to its original position (it does not need to be exact).

Make sure Lock Sheet Focus is still active (pink sheet border).

Select the vertical edge as noted below and click **Convert Entities** .

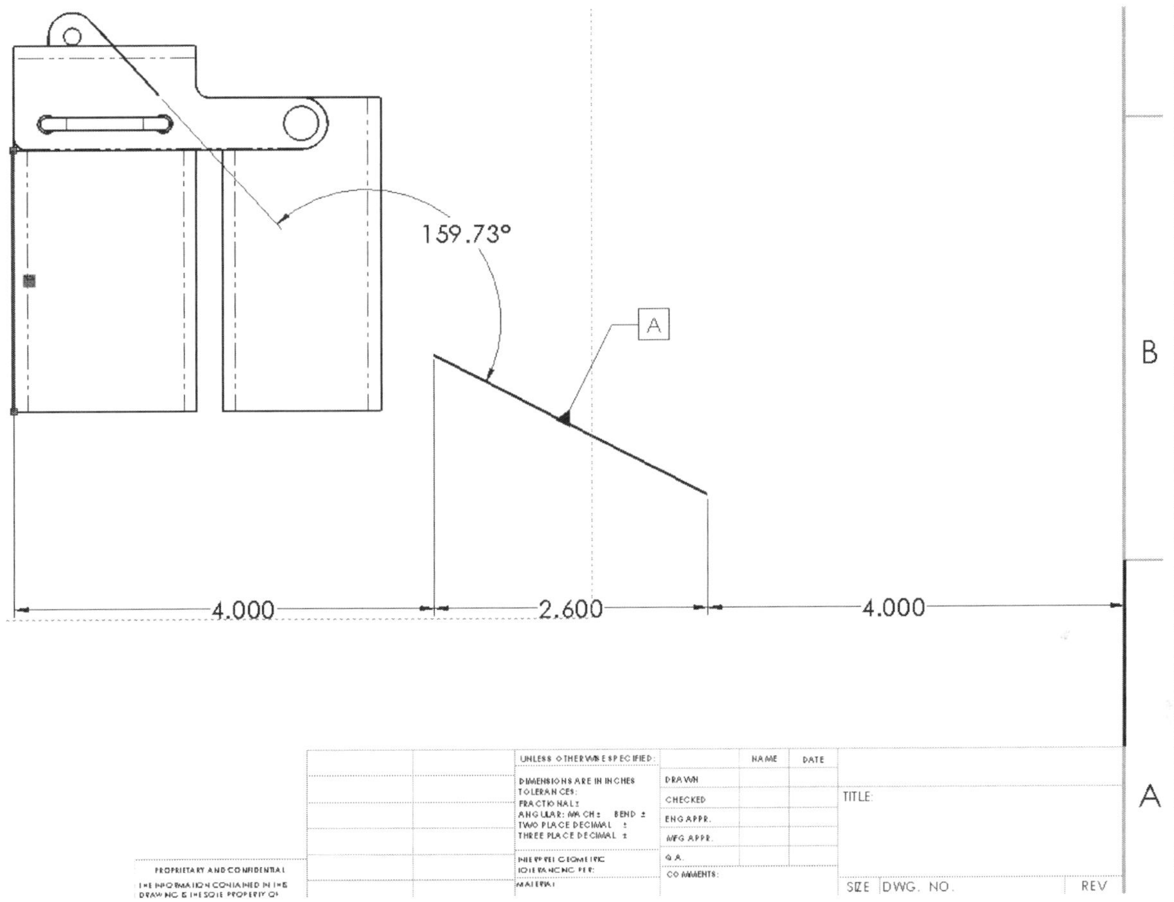

Add the 3 horizontal dimensions shown above.

If the line on the right moves, drag it back to its original location. It is okay to change the length of Line A to match the required dimension.

Next, we will need to find the gap dimension between Line A and the model.

15. Finding the distance:

Repeat the previous step and convert the **right edge** of the model.

Create a reference linear dimension between the **converted edge** and the **left endpoint** of Line A (circled).

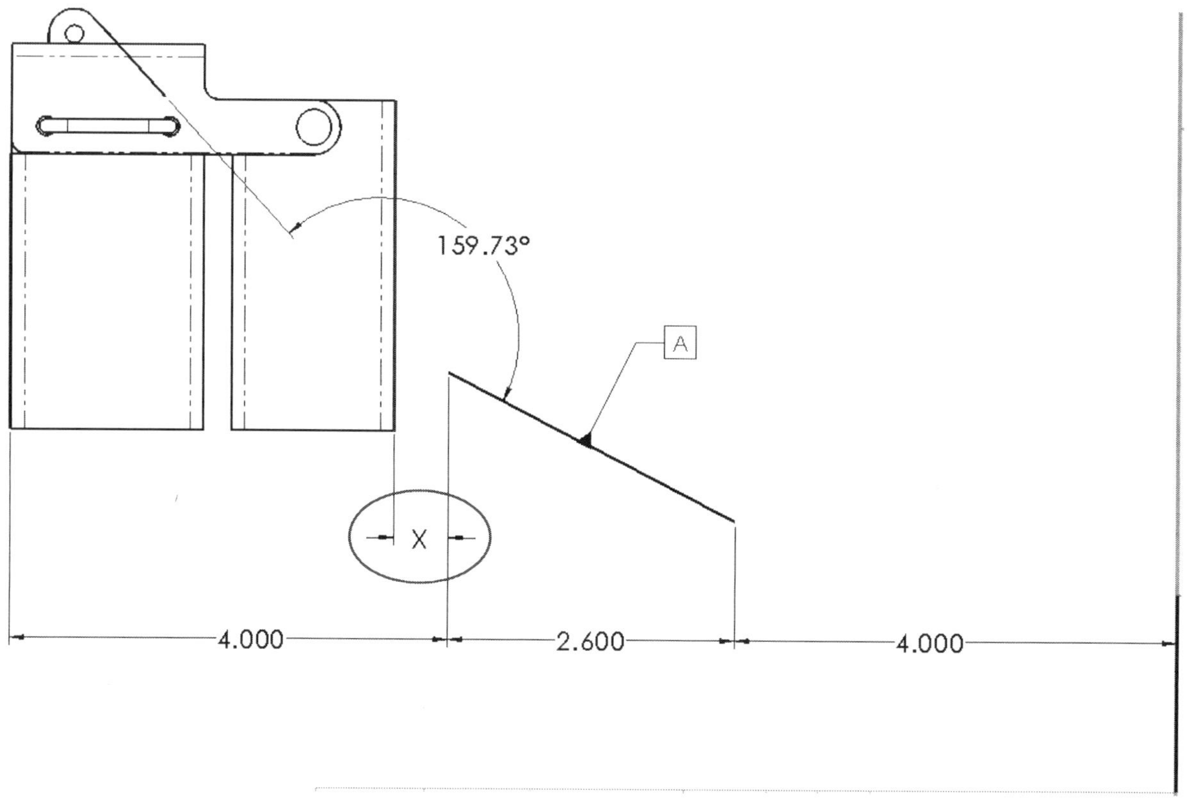

What is the value of dimension X (use 3 decimals):

____________________ in.

Right-click inside the drawing and select: **Unlock View Focus.**

16. Creating an Auxiliary View:

Switch to the Drawing tab and click **Auxiliary View** command [Auxiliary View].

Select the <u>angled edge</u> of the latch as noted below.

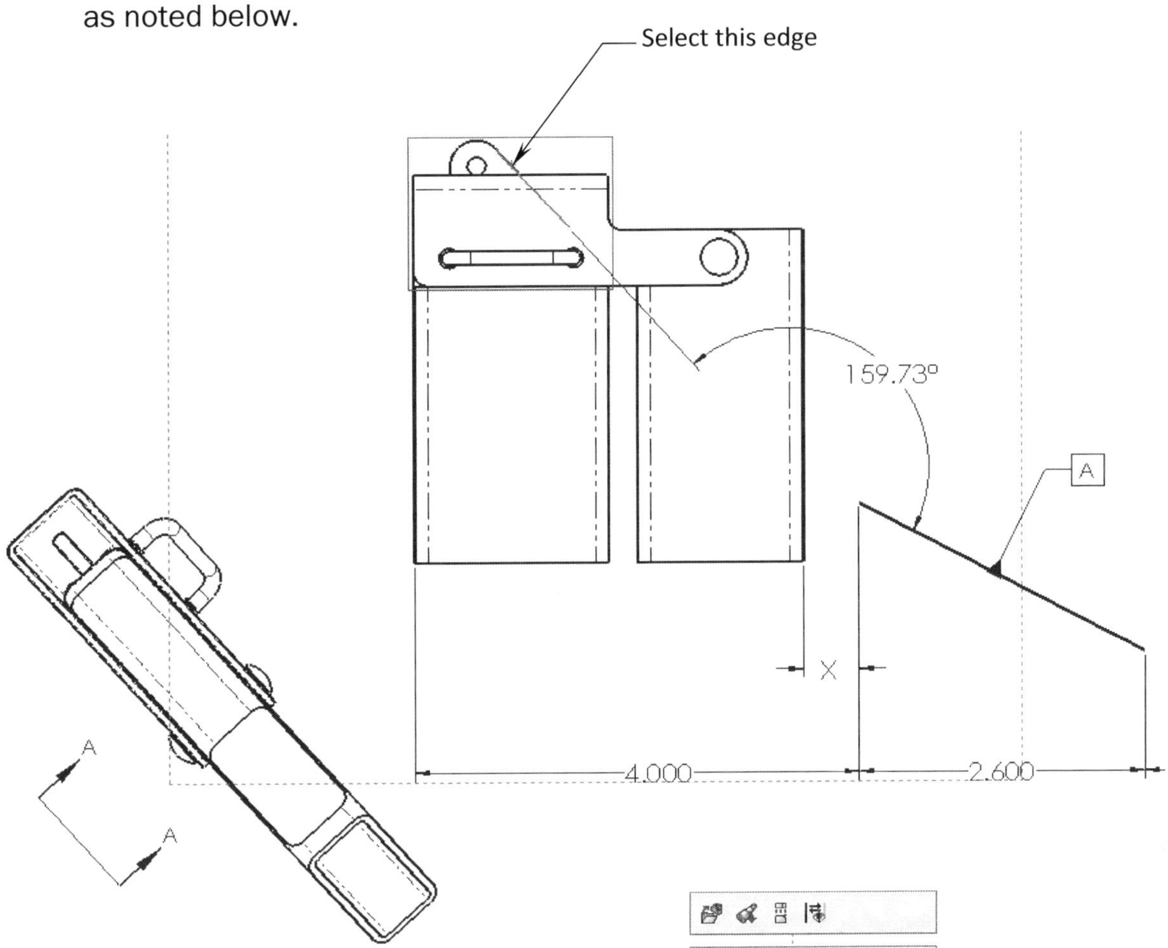

Place the Auxiliary view on the lower left side of the Front drawing view.

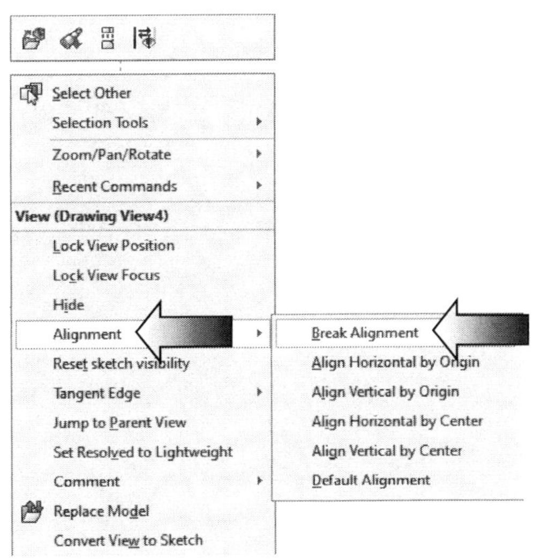

Right-click inside the Auxiliary view and select: **Alignment, Break Alignment**.

We will move the view closer to Line B for the next challenge.

17. Creating an Alternate Position View:

Move the Auxiliary view closer to Line B, approximately as shown below.

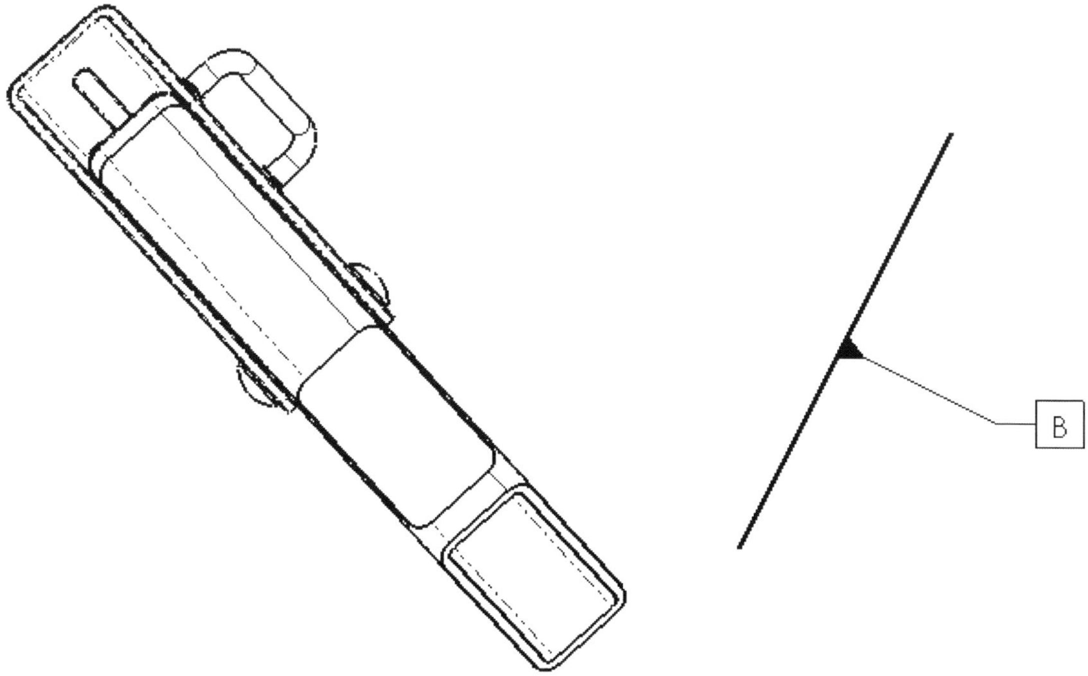

Select the dotted border of the Auxiliary view to activate it.

Click **Alternate Position View** command 

on the Drawing tab.

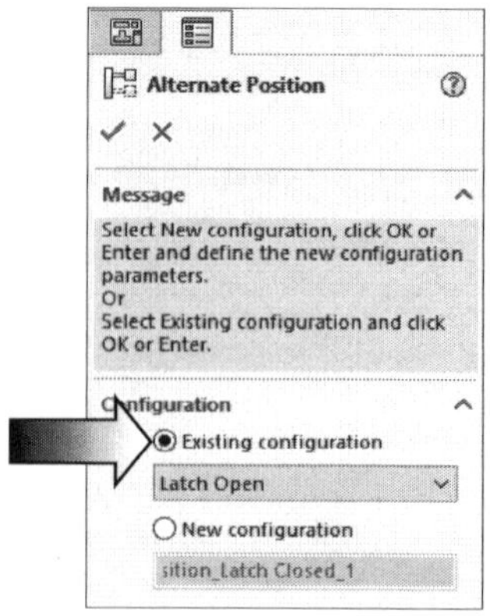

Select **Existing Configuration** from the FeatureManager tree.

The configuration named: Latch Open is selected automatically.

Click **OK**.

Next, we will need to Lock Sheet Focus and convert the edge of the handle, so that we can measure the angle between the handle and Line B.

Right-click inside the drawing and select **Lock Sheet Focus**.

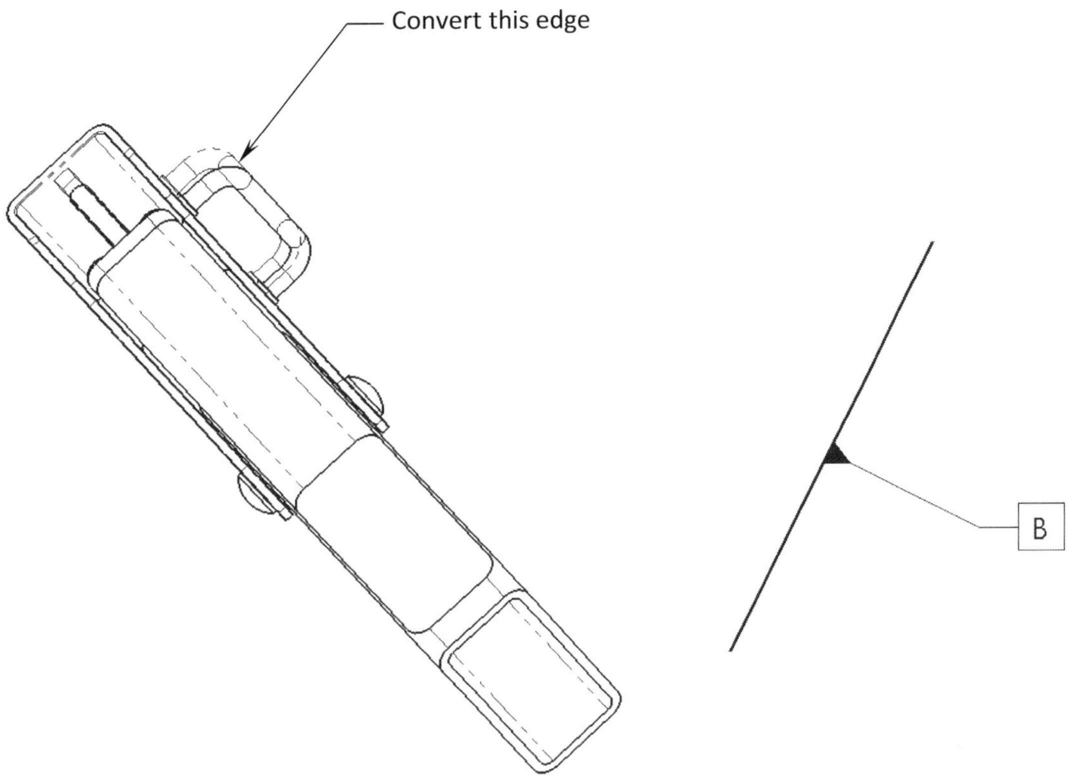

Select the <u>dotted edge</u> of the Handle and click **Convert Entities** on the Sketch toolbar.

Move the Auxiliary View away to see the converted line.

We need to measure the angle between the converted line and Line B.

18. Finding the angle:

Switch to the Annotation tab and select the Smart Dimension tool.

Create a reference **angular dimension** between the converted line and Line B.

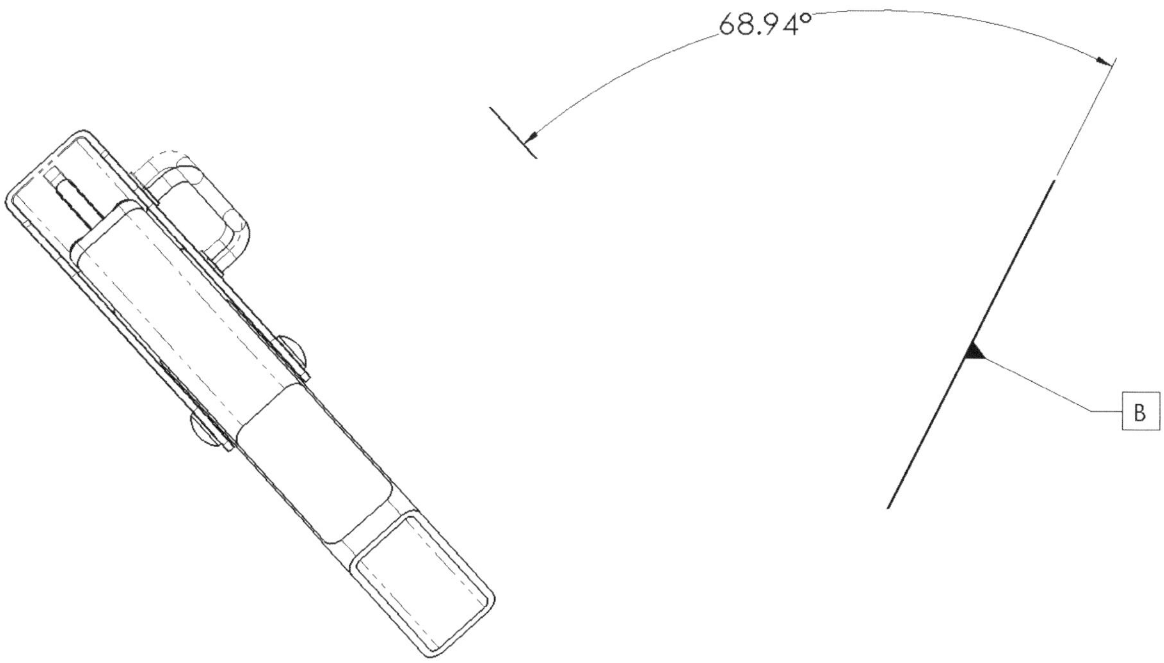

What is the value of the angular dimension (use 2 decimals):

____________________ deg.

19. Saving your work:

Save your drawing as **Drawing1_completed.slddrw**

Move forward to the next challenge.

CHALLENGE 3 – ASSEMBLY DRAWINGS & BOM

Drawing & BOM Creation

The examples in this exam preparation materials are intended to assist you in familiarizing yourself with the structures of the exams and the method in which the questions are asked.

1. Opening an assembly document:

Select **File, Open.**

Go to the Training Folder and open the assembly document named: **Coaster.sldasm**.

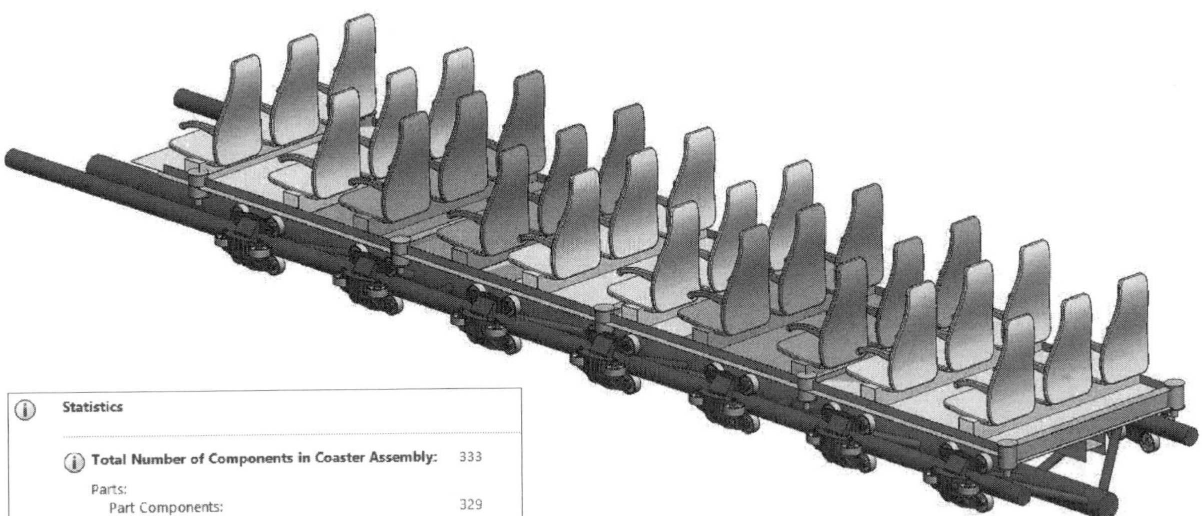

Statistics

Total Number of Components in Coaster Assembly:	333
Parts:	
Part Components:	329
Unique Part Files:	7
Unique Part Configurations:	7
Number Of Bodies:	389
Subassemblies:	
Subassembly Components:	4
Unique Subassembly Configurations:	4
Unique Subassembly Files:	4
Components:	
Resolved Documents:	9
Number Of Top Level Components:	6
Resolved Components:	25
Lightweight Components:	308
Graphics Components:	0
Suppressed Components:	0
Hidden Components:	0
Virtual Components:	0
Envelope Components:	0
Assemblies:	
Maximum Depth:	2
Number Of Total Evaluated Mates:	74
Top Level Mates:	75
Flexible Subassembly Mates:	0

To quickly see how many components, sub-assemblies, and number of mates this assembly has, switch to the **Evaluate** tab and click: **Performance Evaluation**.

Scroll down and look for the Statistic section and view the details of this assembly document.

2. Making a drawing:

Select **File, Make Drawing From Assembly.**

Select the **B-Size (ANSI) Landscape** for this challenge.

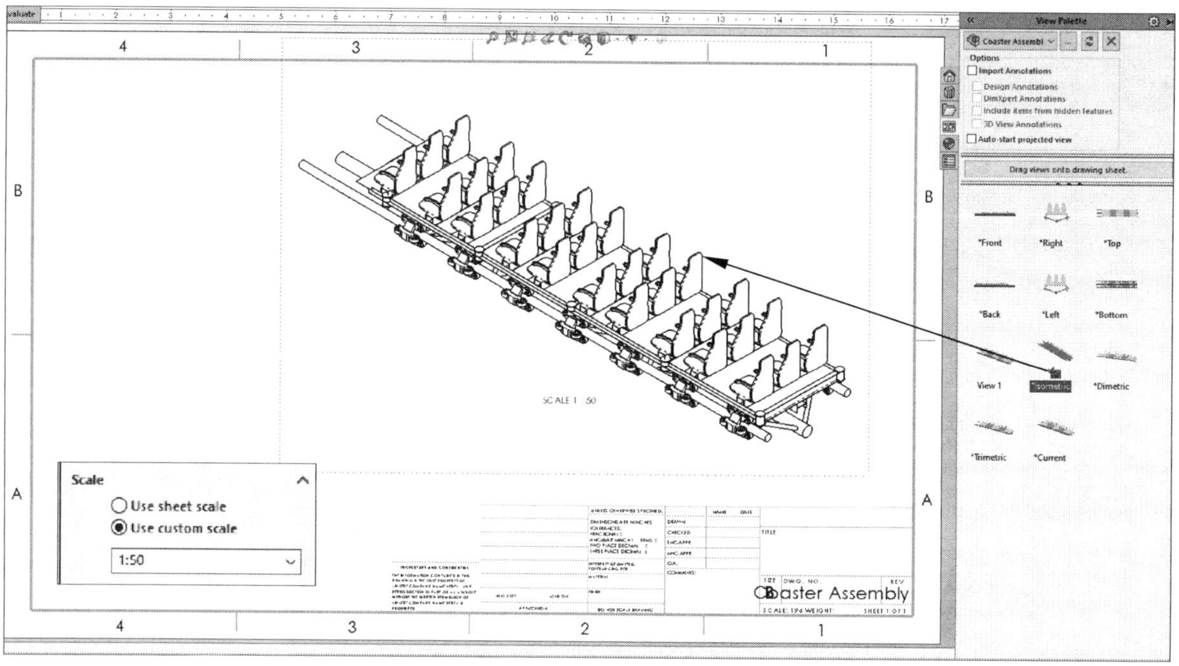

Using the View Palette, drag and drop the **Isometric View** to the drawing.

Set the drawing view scale to **1:50**

<u>Note:</u> This challenge tests your skills on the functionality of the Bill Of Materials. There will be several questions on creating the BOM as well as modifying the BOM to display different details of the assembly document.

Save your drawing after each question under different file names, in case you need to go back to review or make changes to them.

3. Creating a Bill of Materials:

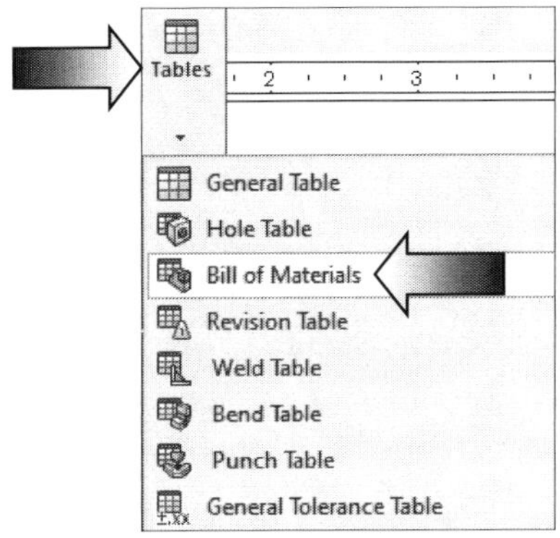

A drawing can contain a table-based Bill of Materials or an Excel-based Bill of Materials, but not both.

A Table Based Bill of Materials is the default one.

Click the dotted border of the isometric view to make it active.

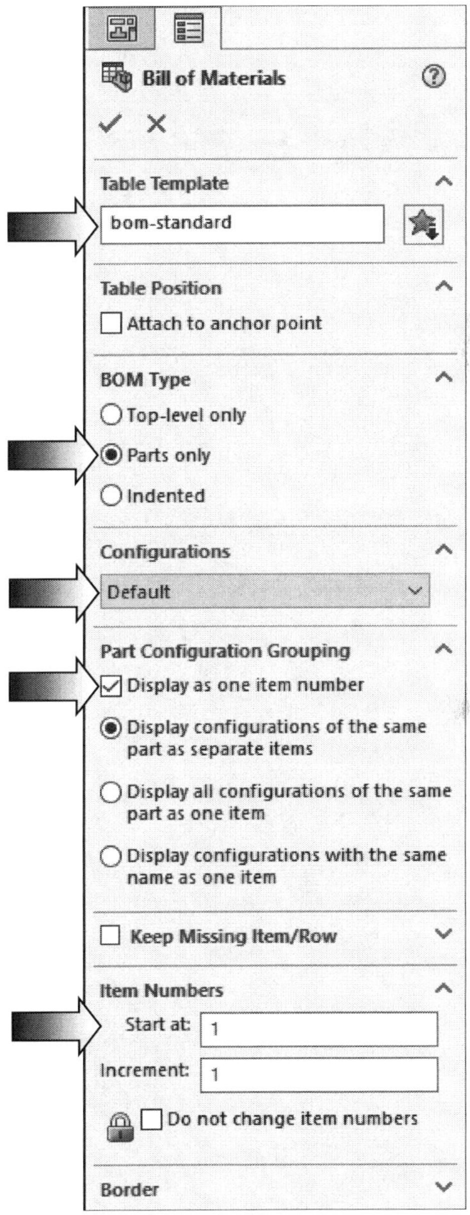

Switch to the **Annotation** tab and select: **Tables, Bill of Materials**.

From the FeatureManager tree, enable or select the following:

*** BOM standard**

*** Parts only**

*** Default Configuration**

*** Display as one item number**

*** Item Numbers Start at 1**

Leave other parameters at their defaults.

Click **OK**.

Place the Bill of Materials anywhere on the left side of the Isometric drawing view.

A Bill of Materials is added to the drawing.

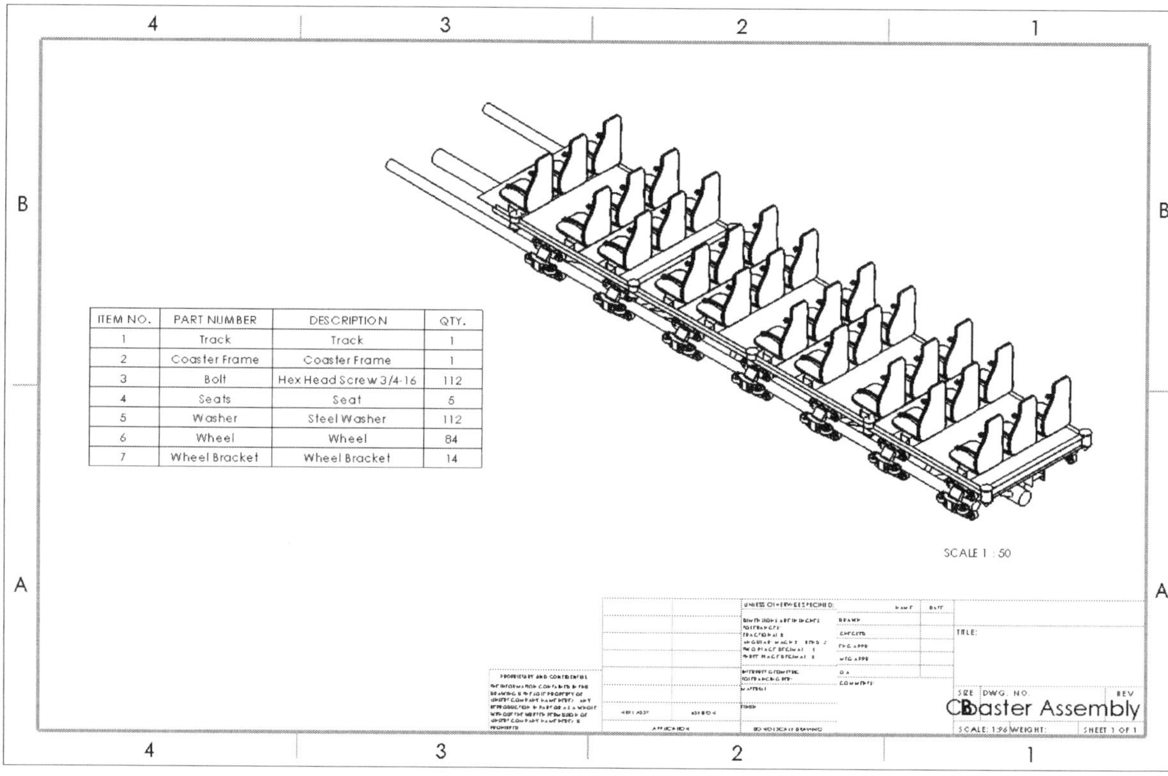

4. Finding the quantity of a component:

The BOM table displays the default information found in the models, some of which needs to be changed to show the correct details such as Part Numbers, Colors, Materials, etc.

ITEM NO.	PART NUMBER	DESCRIPTION	QTY.
1	Track	Track	1
2	Coaster Frame	Coaster Frame	1
3	Bolt	Hex Head Screw 3/4-16	112
4	Seats	Seat	5
5	Washer	Steel Washer	112
6	Wheel	Wheel	84
7	Wheel Bracket	Wheel Bracket	14

Using the BOM table that you have just created, locate the total number of the **Wheel Brackets** in this assembly and **select the correct quantity checkbox** below:

☐ **1** ☐ **112** ☐ **5** ☐ **14** ☐ **84**

5. Switching the Custom Properties:

Column B is currently showing the names of each model, or File Name. We need to change the entire column to a custom property called Part Number, so that the actual Part Number in each model can be called and displayed in column B.

Double-click on the **column header B** and select the following:

Column Type: **CUSTOM PROPERTY**

Property Name: **PART NUMBER**

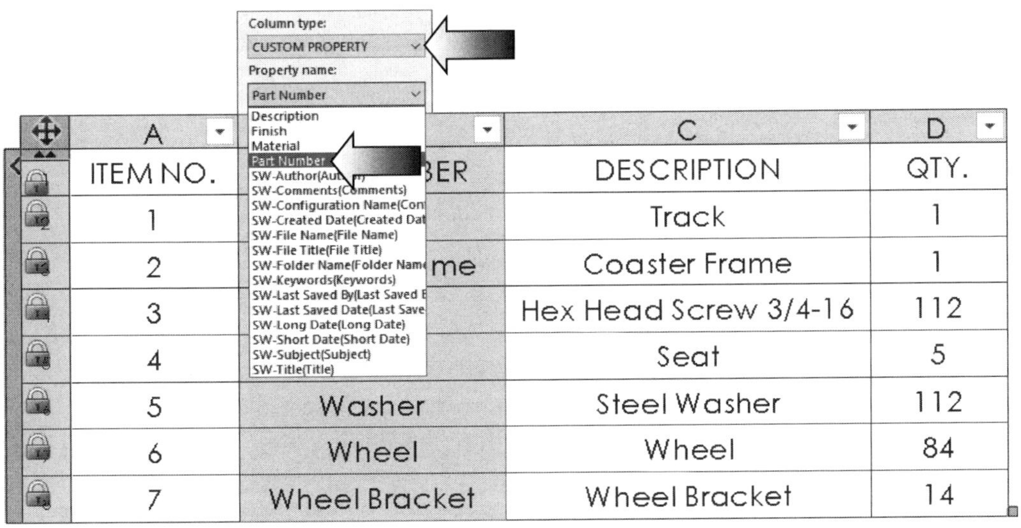

Column B is now displaying the actual Part Number of each component.

ITEM NO.	Part Number	DESCRIPTION	QTY.
1	20-070-0240	Track	1
2	20-070-0241	Coaster Frame	1
3	20-070-0242	Hex Head Screw 3/4-16	112
4	20-070-0244	Seat	5
5	20-070-0243	Steel Washer	112
6	20-070-0246	Wheel	84
7	20-070-0246	Wheel Bracket	14

6. Finding the Item Number of a component:

Zoom in closer to the Isometric drawing view.

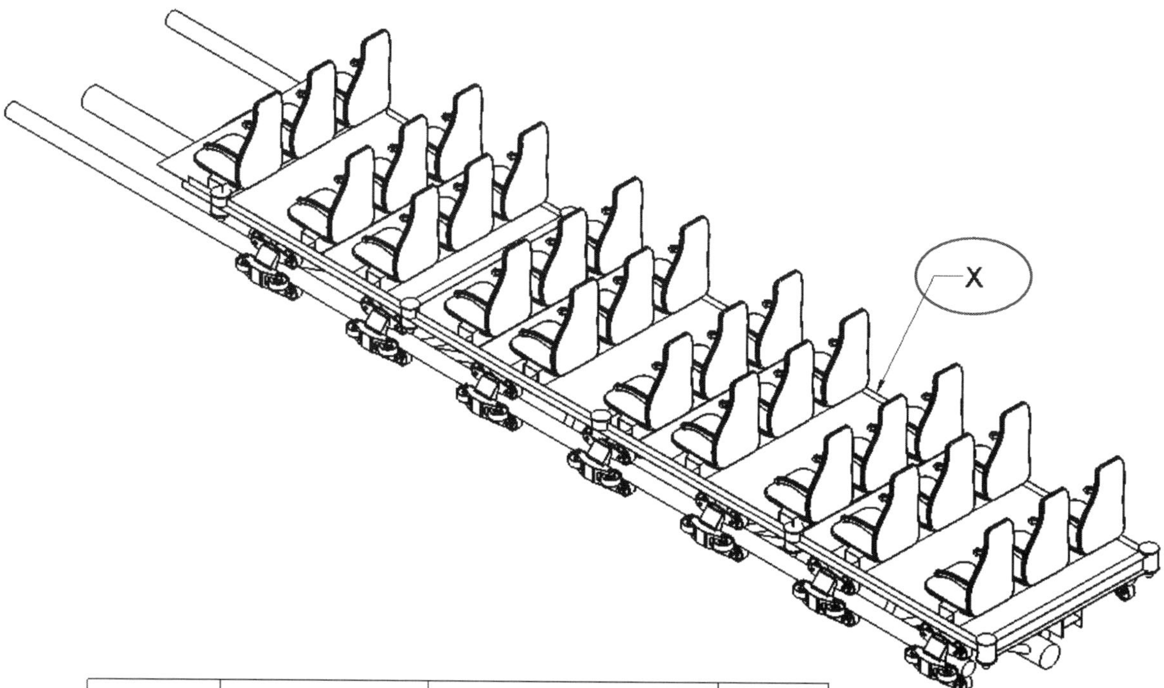

ITEM NO.	Part Number	DESCRIPTION	QTY.
1	20-070-0240	Track	1
2	20-070-0241	Coaster Frame	1
3	20-070-0242	Hex Head Screw 3/4-16	112
4	20-070-0244	Seat	5
5	20-070-0243	Steel Washer	112
6	20-070-0246	Wheel	84
7	20-070-0246	Wheel Bracket	14

Find the Item Number that corresponds to the assembly component identified by the letter **"X"** shown in the image above and mark one of the checkboxes below:

☐ 1 ☐ 2 ☐ 3 ☐ 4

☐ 5 ☐ 6 ☐ 7

7. Switching the BOM Type:

Hover the mouse cursor over the BOM and click the 4-way cursor to access the table options.

Change the BOM Type to: **Indented, No Numbering.**

Click **OK.**

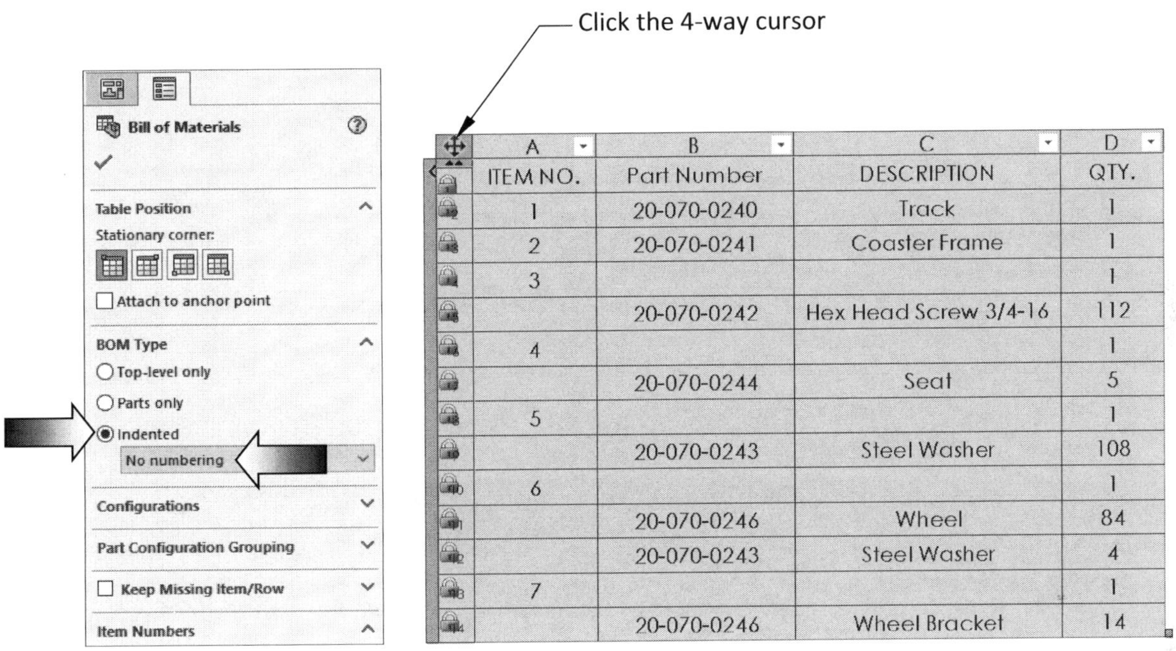

What is the Part Number under which the BOM item file name **"Seat"** appears?

Select one:

- ☐ 20-070-0240
- ☐ 20-070-0241
- ☐ 20-070-0242
- ☐ 20-070-0243
- ☐ 20-070-0244
- ☐ 20-070-0245
- ☐ 20-070-0246

8. Finding the Total Cost:

Click the 4-way cursor and change the BOM Type back to **Parts Only**.

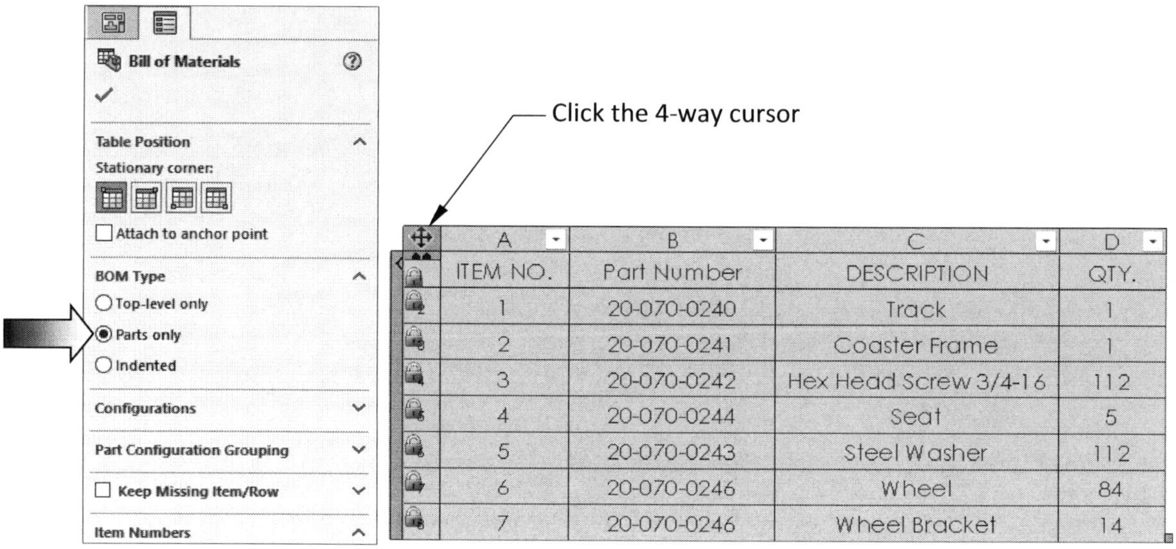

In order to find the Total Cost for this assembly, 2 more columns must be added to the BOM. The 1st one will be the cost of each component, and the 2nd one will be the Total Cost of all components combined.

Right-click on the **column header D** and select: **Insert, Column Right**.

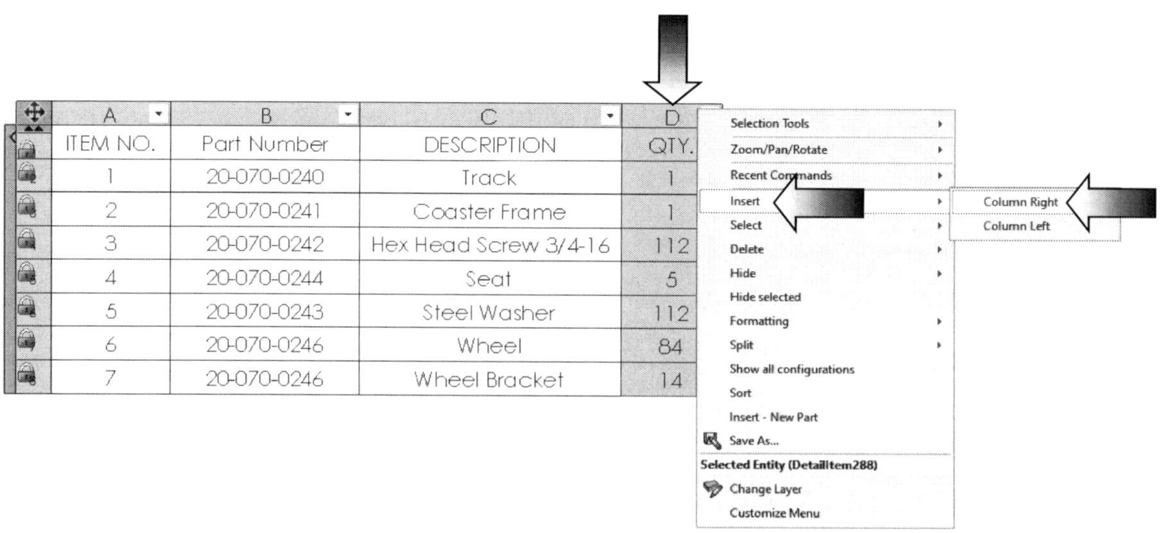

For column E, select the Custom Property **"COST"** as shown below.

The cost of each component is displayed under the column E.

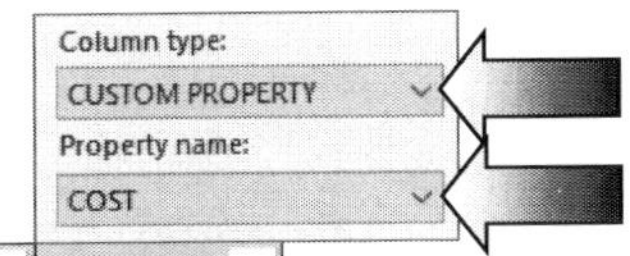

A	B	C	D	E
ITEM NO.	Part Number	DESCRIPTION	QTY.	COST
1	20-070-0240	Track	1	2950
2	20-070-0241	Coaster Frame	1	1750
3	20-070-0242	Hex Head Screw 3/4-16	112	5.50
4	20-070-0244	Seat	5	1600
5	20-070-0243	Steel Washer	112	2.50
6	20-070-0246	Wheel	84	165
7	20-070-0246	Wheel Bracket	14	675

Next, we will add another column for the **Total Cost** and add up the cost of all components using the equation option.

Right-click on the column header E and select:
Insert, Column Right.

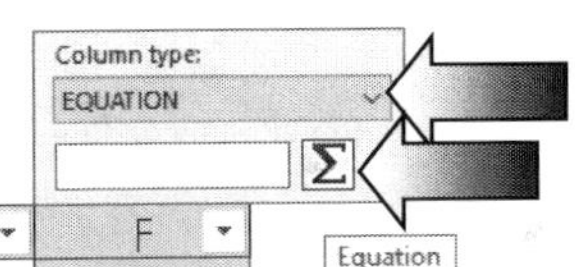

A	B	C	D	E	F
ITEM NO.	Part Number	DESCRIPTION	QTY.	COST	
1	20-070-0240	Track	1	2950	
2	20-070-0241	Coaster Frame	1	1750	
3	20-070-0242	Hex Head Screw 3/4-16	112	5.50	
4	20-070-0244	Seat	5	1600	
5	20-070-0243	Steel Washer	112	2.50	
6	20-070-0246	Wheel	84	165	
7	20-070-0246	Wheel Bracket	14	675	

For column F, change the Column Type to **Equation** (1st arrow), and click the **equation symbol** Σ (2nd arrow).

Start the equation by expanding the Column drop-down list and selecting: **Cost**.

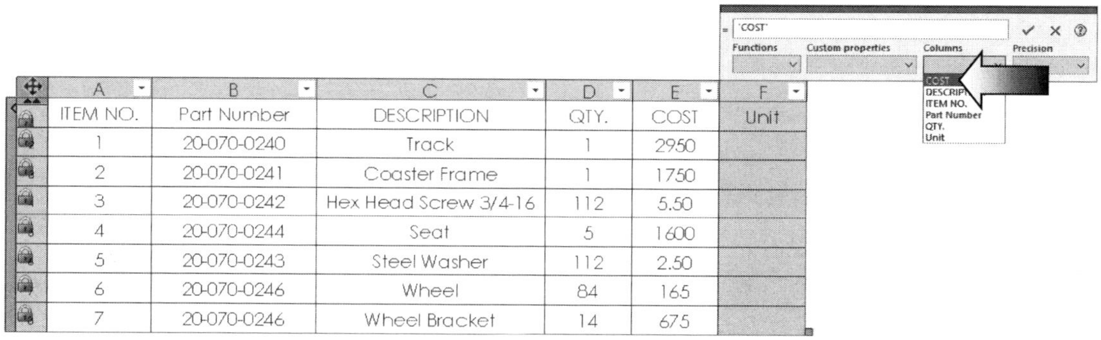

ITEM NO.	Part Number	DESCRIPTION	QTY.	COST	Unit
1	20-070-0240	Track	1	2950	
2	20-070-0241	Coaster Frame	1	1750	
3	20-070-0242	Hex Head Screw 3/4-16	112	5.50	
4	20-070-0244	Seat	5	1600	
5	20-070-0243	Steel Washer	112	2.50	
6	20-070-0246	Wheel	84	165	
7	20-070-0246	Wheel Bracket	14	675	

Type the multiplication symbol * next to Cost.
Expand the Column drop-down list and select: **QTY**.

Enter the symbol * here

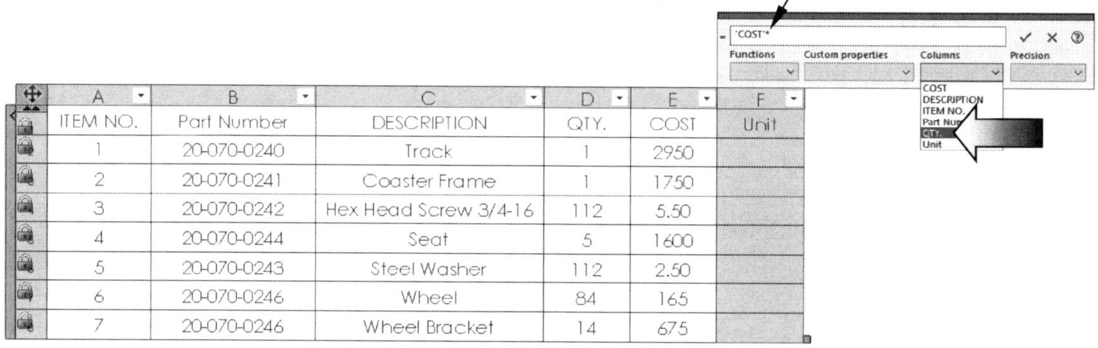

ITEM NO.	Part Number	DESCRIPTION	QTY.	COST	Unit
1	20-070-0240	Track	1	2950	
2	20-070-0241	Coaster Frame	1	1750	
3	20-070-0242	Hex Head Screw 3/4-16	112	5.50	
4	20-070-0244	Seat	5	1600	
5	20-070-0243	Steel Washer	112	2.50	
6	20-070-0246	Wheel	84	165	
7	20-070-0246	Wheel Bracket	14	675	

Lastly, add a new row to sum up the total value.
Right-click on **Row 7** and select: **Insert, Row Below**.

Change the header to Total Cost

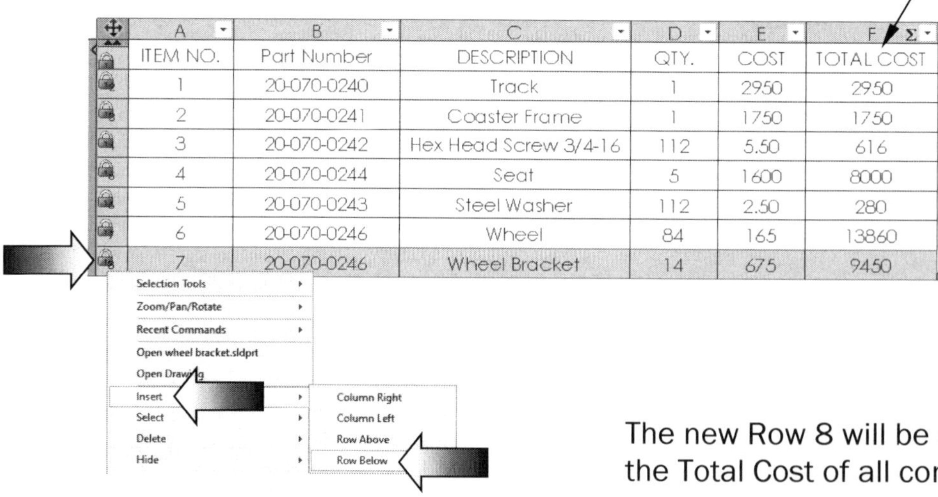

ITEM NO.	Part Number	DESCRIPTION	QTY.	COST	TOTAL COST
1	20-070-0240	Track	1	2950	2950
2	20-070-0241	Coaster Frame	1	1750	1750
3	20-070-0242	Hex Head Screw 3/4-16	112	5.50	616
4	20-070-0244	Seat	5	1600	8000
5	20-070-0243	Steel Washer	112	2.50	280
6	20-070-0246	Wheel	84	165	13860
7	20-070-0246	Wheel Bracket	14	675	9450

The new Row 8 will be used to display the Total Cost of all components.

Select the number **0** (zero) in cell **F8**.

Click the **Equation** symbol Σ on the **Formatting** toolbar.

	A	B	C	D	E	F Σ
1	ITEM NO.	Part Number	DESCRIPTION	QTY.	COST	TOTAL COST
2	1	20-070-0240	Track	1	2950	2950
3	2	20-070-0241	Coaster Frame	1	1750	1750
4	3	20-070-0242	Hex Head Screw 3/4-16	112	5.50	616
5	4	20-070-0244	Seat	5	1600	8000
6	5	20-070-0243	Steel Washer	112	2.50	280
7	6	20-070-0246	Wheel	84	165	13860
8	7	20-070-0246	Wheel Bracket	14	675	9450
9	8					0

Expand the **Function** drop-down list and select: **SUM**.

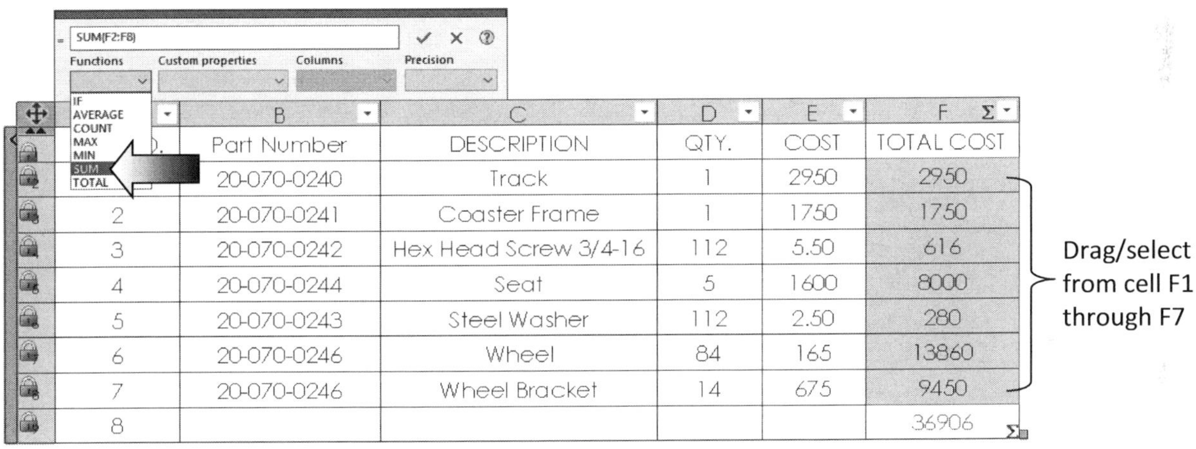

	A	B	C	D	E	F Σ
1	ITEM NO.	Part Number	DESCRIPTION	QTY.	COST	TOTAL COST
2	1	20-070-0240	Track	1	2950	2950
3	2	20-070-0241	Coaster Frame	1	1750	1750
4	3	20-070-0242	Hex Head Screw 3/4-16	112	5.50	616
5	4	20-070-0244	Seat	5	1600	8000
6	5	20-070-0243	Steel Washer	112	2.50	280
7	6	20-070-0246	Wheel	84	165	13860
8	7	20-070-0246	Wheel Bracket	14	675	9450
9	8					36906

Drag/select from cell **F1** through **cell F7.** The **Total Cost** is calculated.

ITEM NO.	Part Number	DESCRIPTION	QTY.	COST	TOTAL COST
1	20-070-0240	Track	1	2950	2950
2	20-070-0241	Coaster Frame	1	1750	1750
3	20-070-0242	Hex Head Screw 3/4-16	112	5.50	616
4	20-070-0244	Seat	5	1600	8000
5	20-070-0243	Steel Washer	112	2.50	280
6	20-070-0246	Wheel	84	165	13860
7	20-070-0246	Wheel Bracket	14	675	9450
8					36906

What is the value of the SUM of the "Total Cost" of all the components:

____

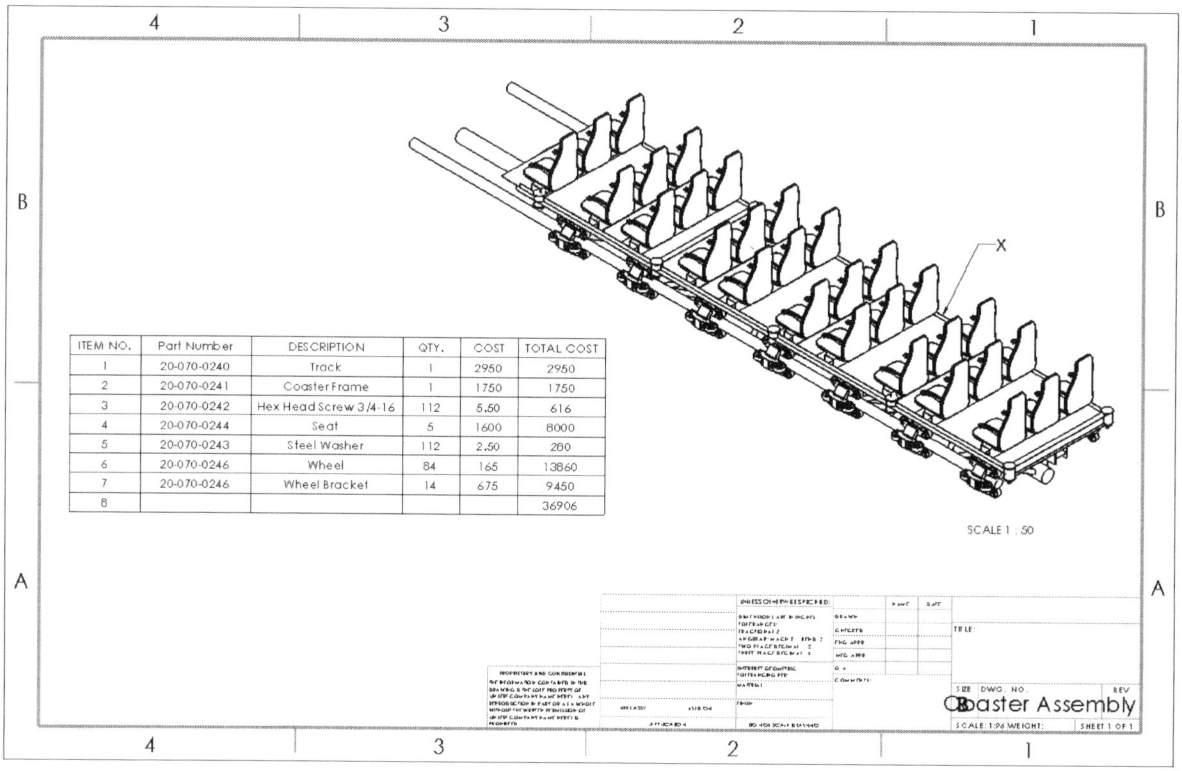

ITEM NO.	Part Number	DESCRIPTION	QTY.	COST	TOTAL COST
1	20-070-0240	Track	1	2950	2950
2	20-070-0241	Coaster Frame	1	1750	1750
3	20-070-0242	Hex Head Screw 3/4-16	112	5.50	616
4	20-070-0244	Seat	5	1600	8000
5	20-070-0243	Steel Washer	112	2.50	280
6	20-070-0246	Wheel	84	165	13860
7	20-070-0246	Wheel Bracket	14	675	9450
8					36906

Remember to save your work every once in a while.

The last question is about linking a Note to a Custom Property that was previously created and saved in the model.

9. Adding a Note:

Insert a **Note** as represented by the letter Y and attach it to the component **Wheel Bracket**.

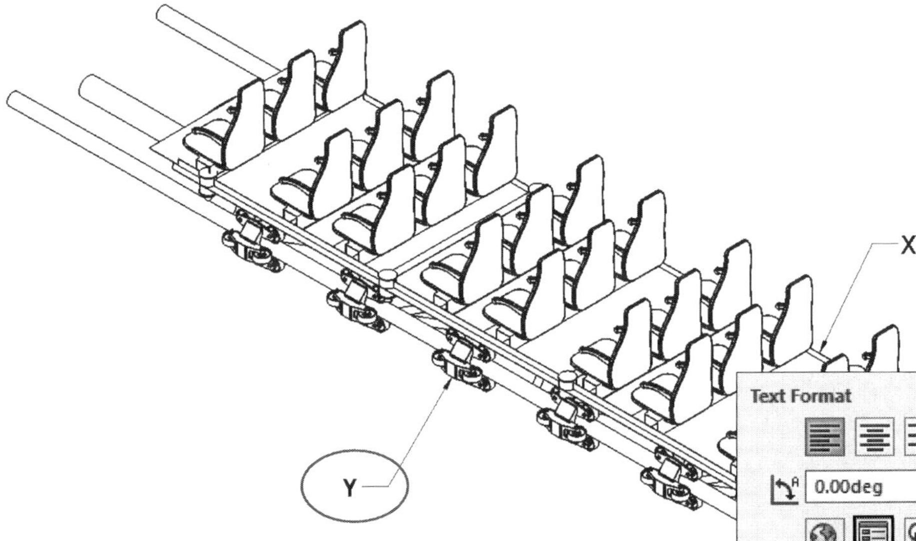

Now, let us link the Note to the Custom Property "Vendor".

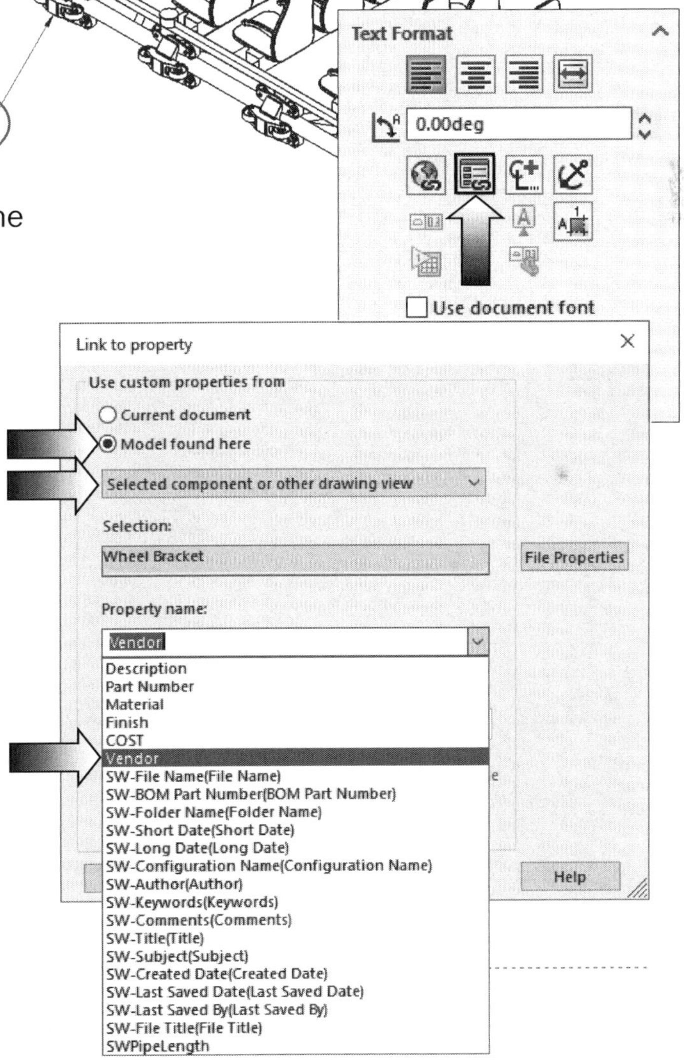

Select the letter **Y** and click **Link To Property** on the FeatureManager tree.

Click **Model Found Here.**

Choose the option: **Select Component or other Drawing View.**

Expand the Property Name section and select: **Vendor.**

Click **OK.**

10. Saving the drawing:

What is the text of the note just created? Check one.

☐ **American Alloys** ☐ **USA Metals** ☐ **ACME**

☐ **Int'l Metals** ☐ **Blank**

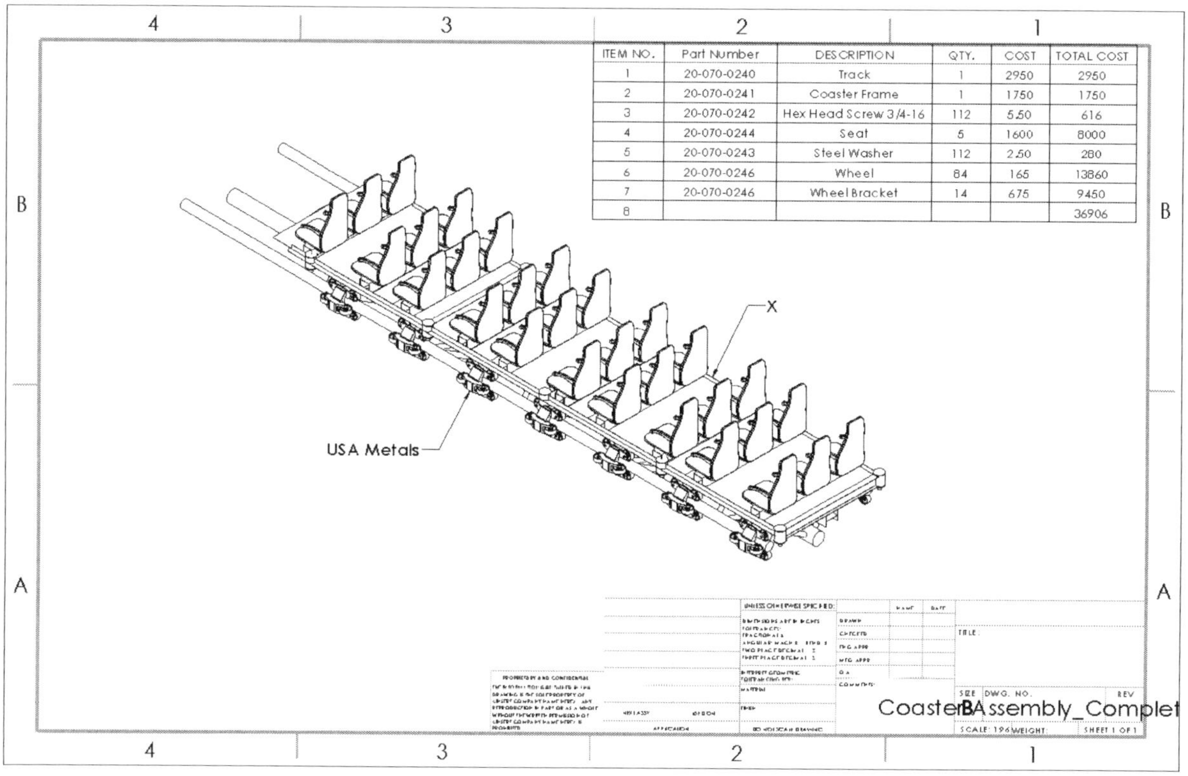

11. Saving the drawing:

Select **File, Save As.**

Enter: **Challenge 3.slddrw** for the file name.

Click **Save.**

Move forward to the next challenge.

CHALLENGE 4 – ASSEMBLY DRAWINGS

Hide and Show Components

The examples in this exam preparation material are intended to assist you in familiarizing yourself with the structures of the exams and the method in which the questions are asked.

1. Opening an assembly document:

Select **File, Open**.

Locate the assembly document named:
Wheel_Sub Assembly.sldasm and open it.

The Exploded View has already been created ahead of time.

This portion of the exam will test your skills on Hiding and Showing components as well as measuring the angle between certain components.

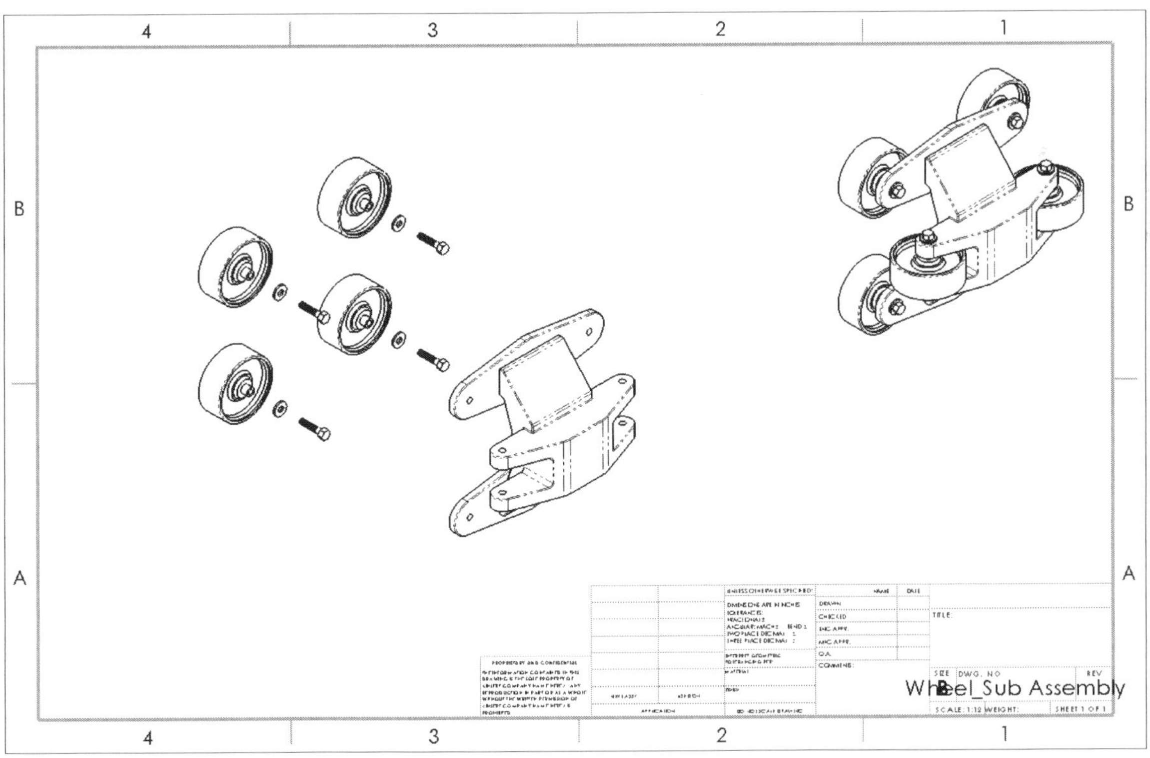

2. Finding the hidden components:

There are some components hidden from the exploded view, determine which ones are hidden.

Right-click on the dotted border of the exploded view and select: **Properties.**

Click the **Hide/Show Components** tab.

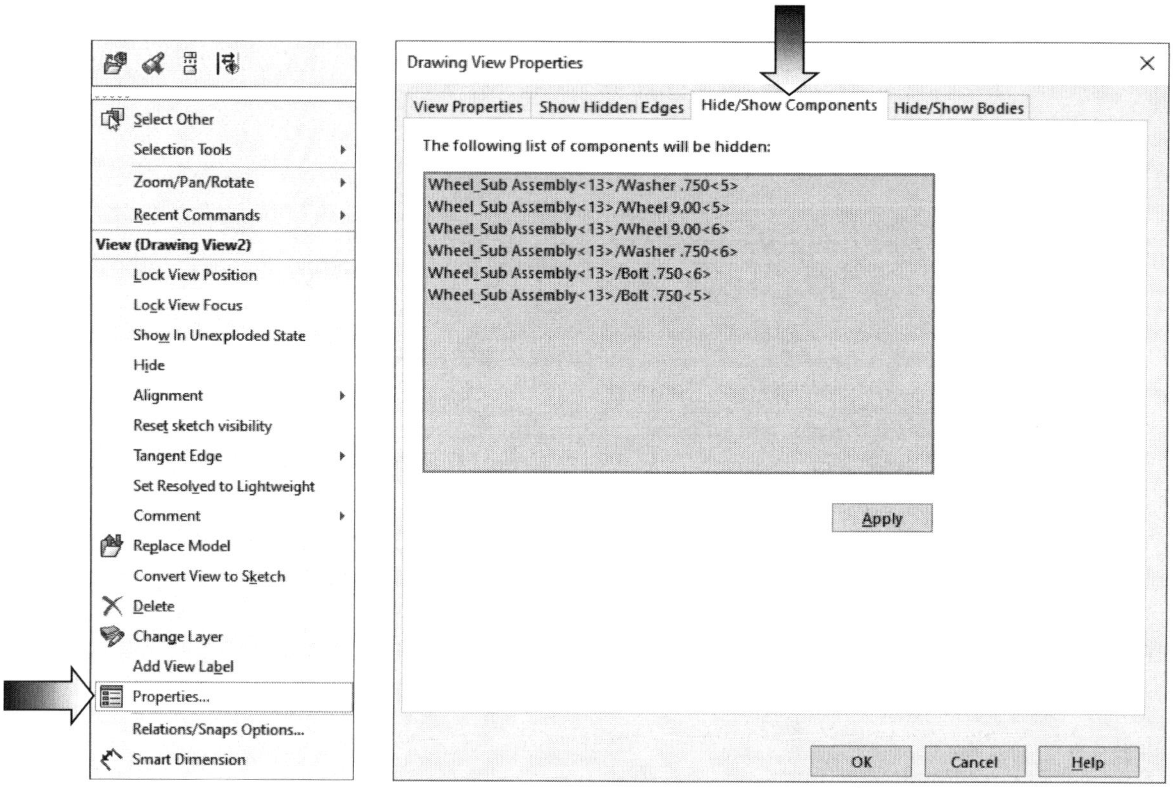

Select all components that are hidden from the exploded view:

- [ ] Wheel_Bracket
- [ ] Washer .750 <5>
- [ ] Wheel 9.00 <5>
- [ ] Wheel 9.00 <6>
- [ ] Washer .750 <6>
- [ ] Track
- [ ] Bolt .750 <5>
- [ ] Coaster Frame
- [ ] Bolt .750 <6>

Delete all components listed in the dialog box to make them visible for the next question.

3. Measuring the angle:

There are a couple of different ways to find the angle between the features.

The 1st method is to measure the angle using the Measure tool.

Switch to the **Evaluate** tab and click **Measure**.

Select the <u>2 edges</u> as indicated.

The angle is **77.06deg**.

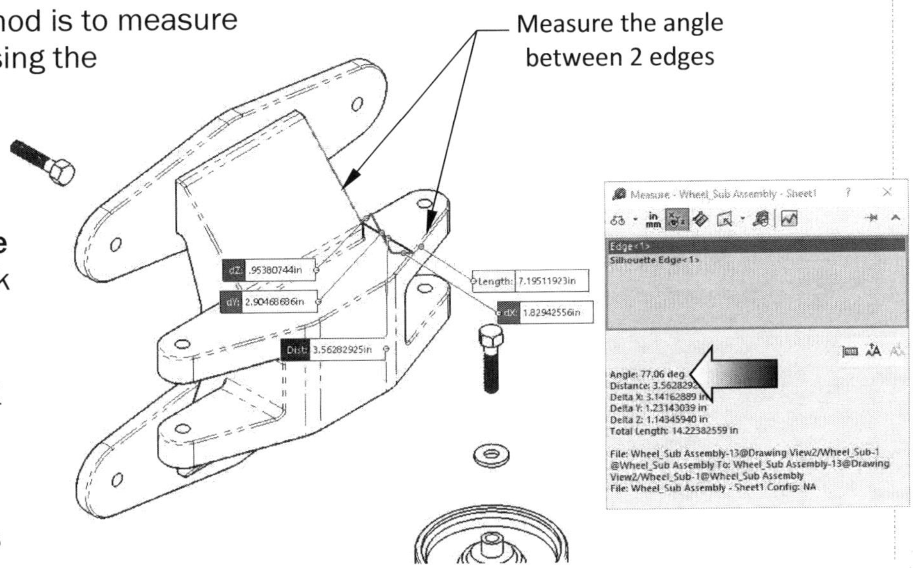

The 2nd method is to Lock Sheet Focus, convert the 2 edges and add dimension.

Right-click inside the drawing and select **Lock Sheet Focus.**

Select the <u>2 edges</u> and click **Convert Entities.**

Add a **dimension** between the 2 converted entities. The Angle is **66.57deg.**

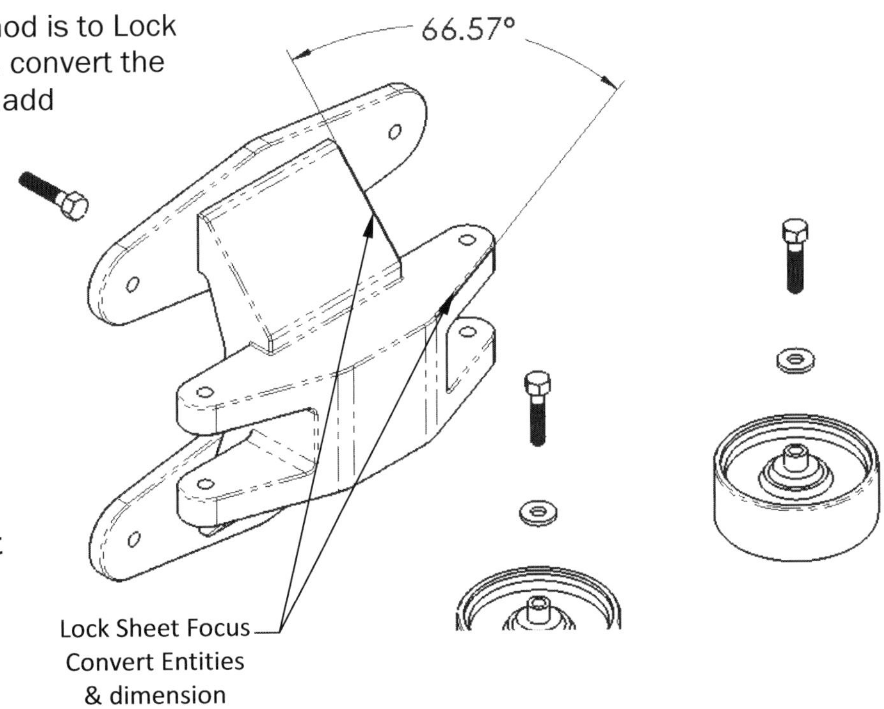

What is the measured angle?

__________________ degrees.

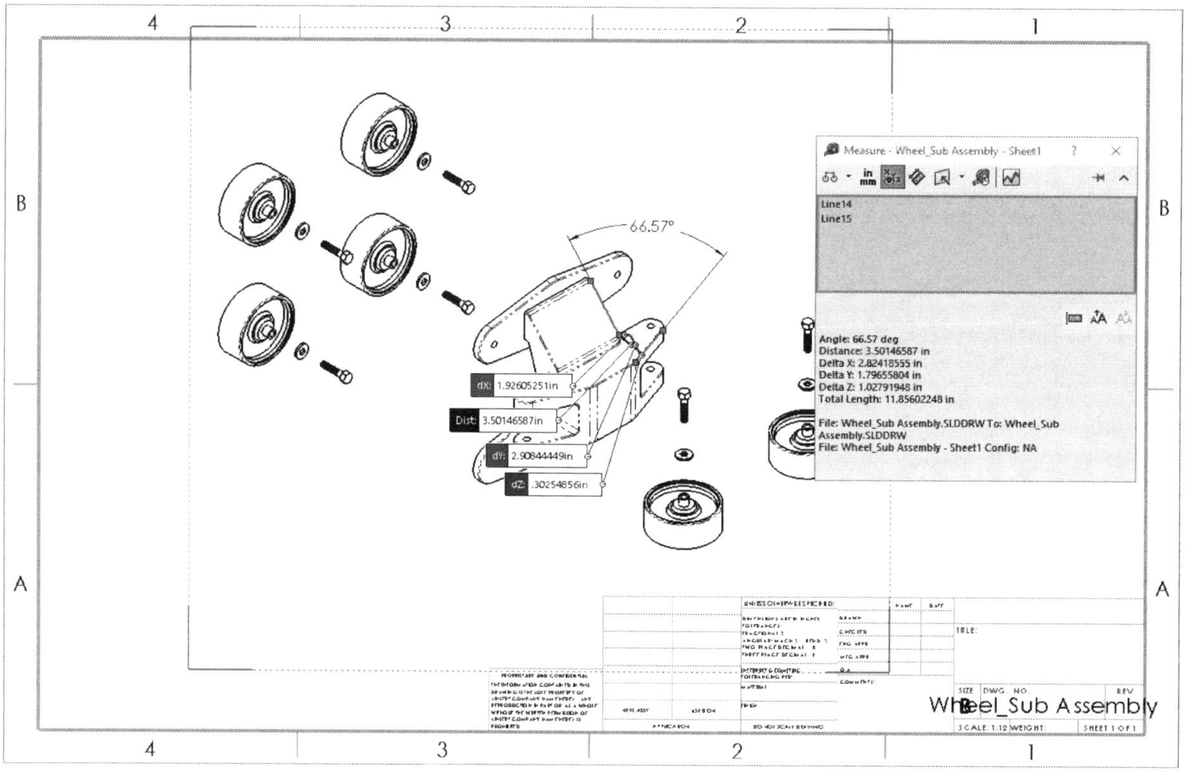

4. Saving the drawing:

Select **File, Save As**.

Enter: **Challenge 4.slddrw** for the file name.

Click **Save**.

Move forward to the next challenge.

CHALLENGE 5 – PART DRAWINGS

Broken Out Section & Insert Model Items

The examples in this exam preparation material are intended to assist you in familiarizing yourself with the structures of the exams and the method in which the questions are asked.

1. Opening a drawing document:

Select **File, Open.**

Locate the drawing document named: **Broken Out Section.slddrw** and open it.

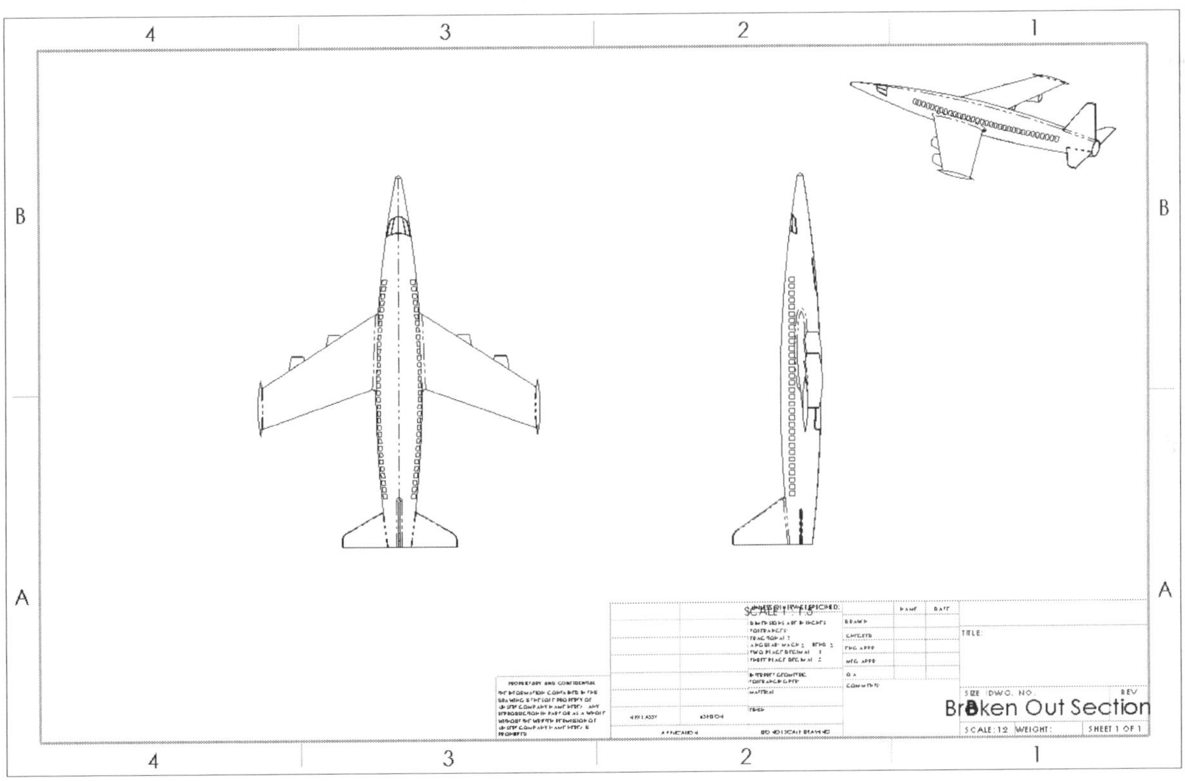

There are 3 drawing views that have already been created for this drawing.

We will need to create a Broken Out Section view and add dimensions to it.

2. Creating a Broken Out Section view:

Switch to the **Sketch** tab and click the **Circle** tool.

Sketch a **circle** and add the **dimensions** shown in the image below.

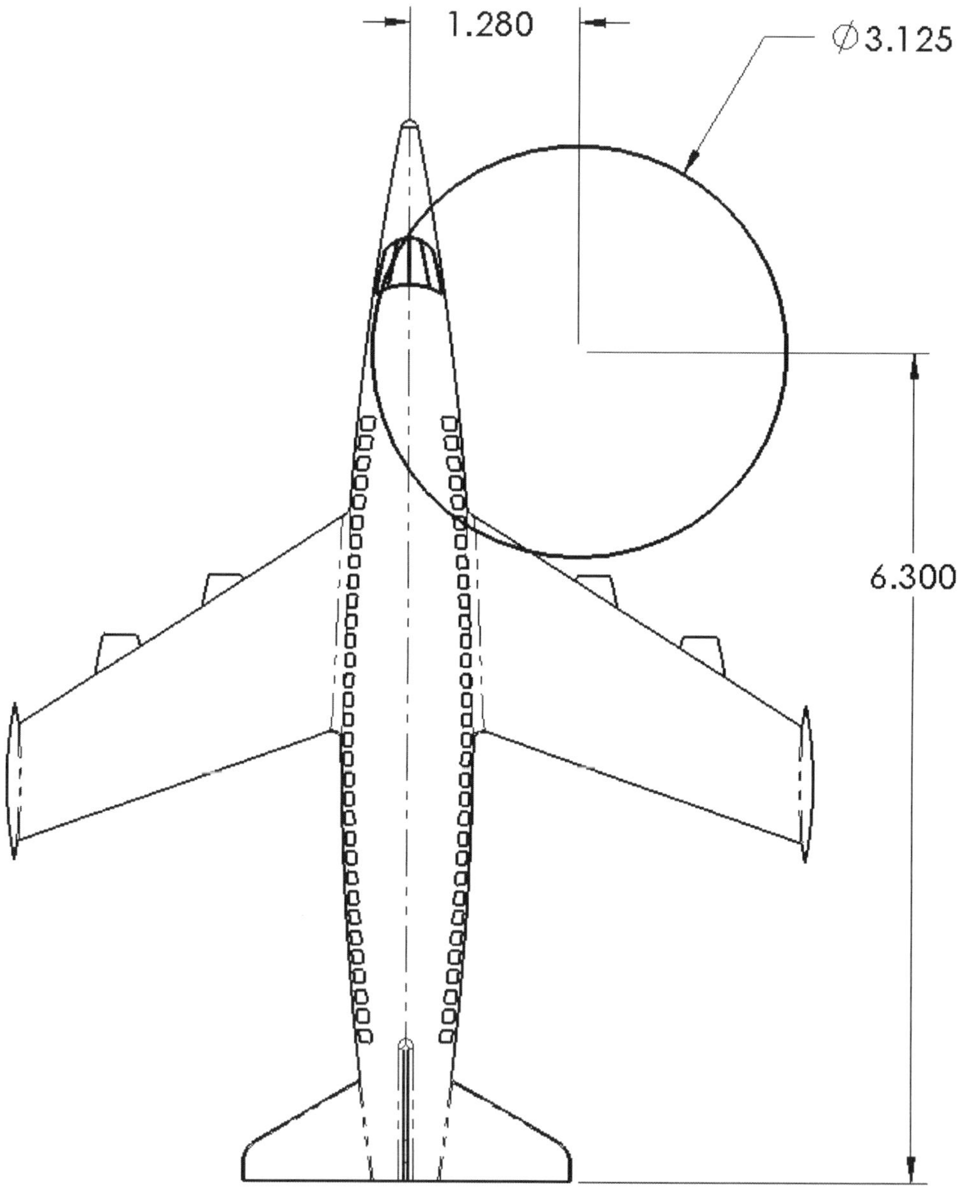

The circle should be black, fully defined at this point.

Zoom in closer to the Right drawing view.

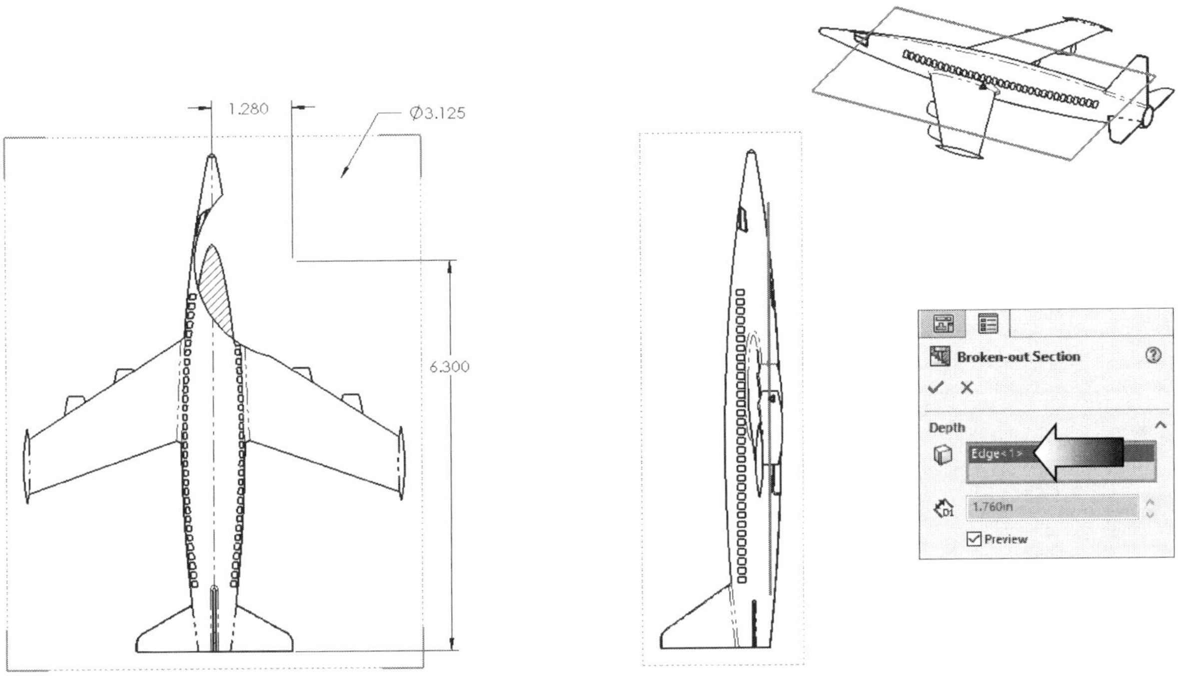

For Depth, select the **upper edge** of the engine (or 1.760in).

Enable the **Preview** checkbox to see the preview of the section cut.

Click **OK**.

The sectioned face will be used to calculate the perimeter of the Broken Out Section view.

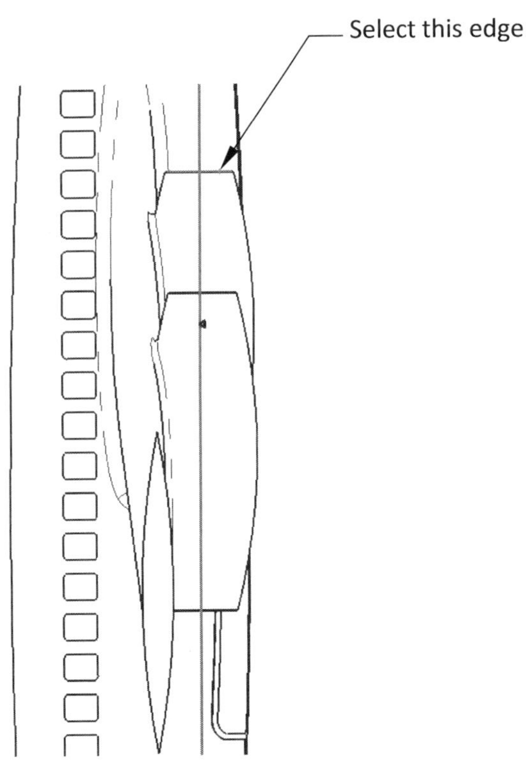

3. Measuring the perimeter:

Zoom closer to the sectioned face where the crosshatch lines are.

Switch to the **Evaluate** tab and click **Measure**.

Click inside the crosshatch area to measure the perimeter.

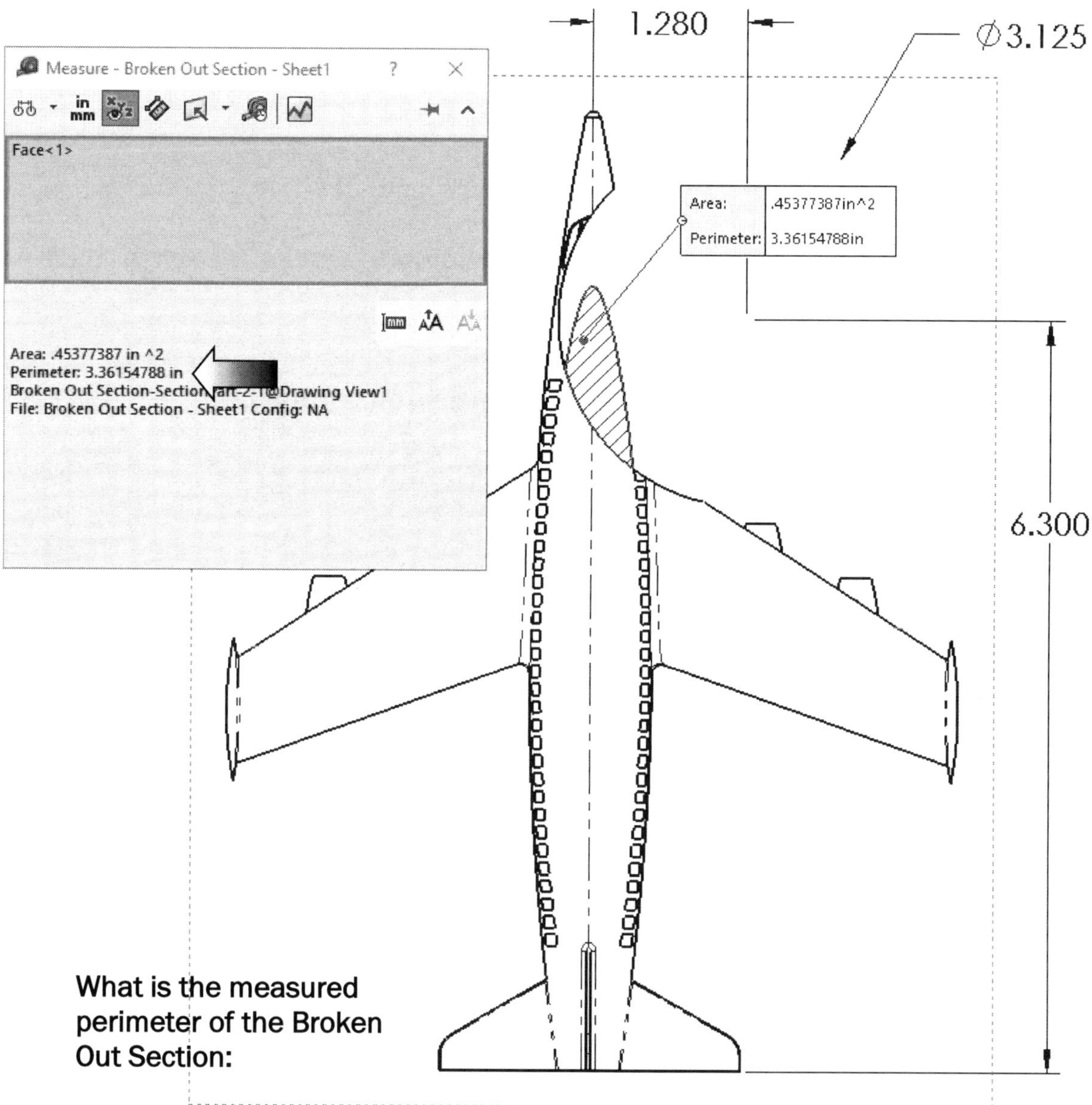

What is the measured perimeter of the Broken Out Section:

__________________ in.

4. Inserting the Model Dimensions:

Switch to the **Annotation** tab and click **Model Items.**

Enable / select the following:

* **Entire Model**
* **Marked for Drawing**
* **Not Marked for drawing**
* **Eliminate Duplicates**

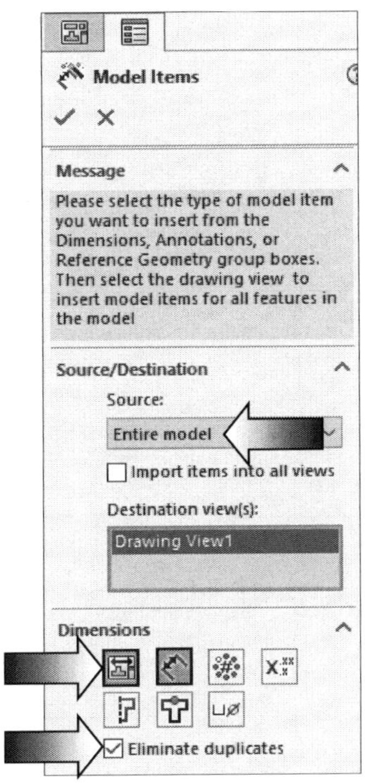

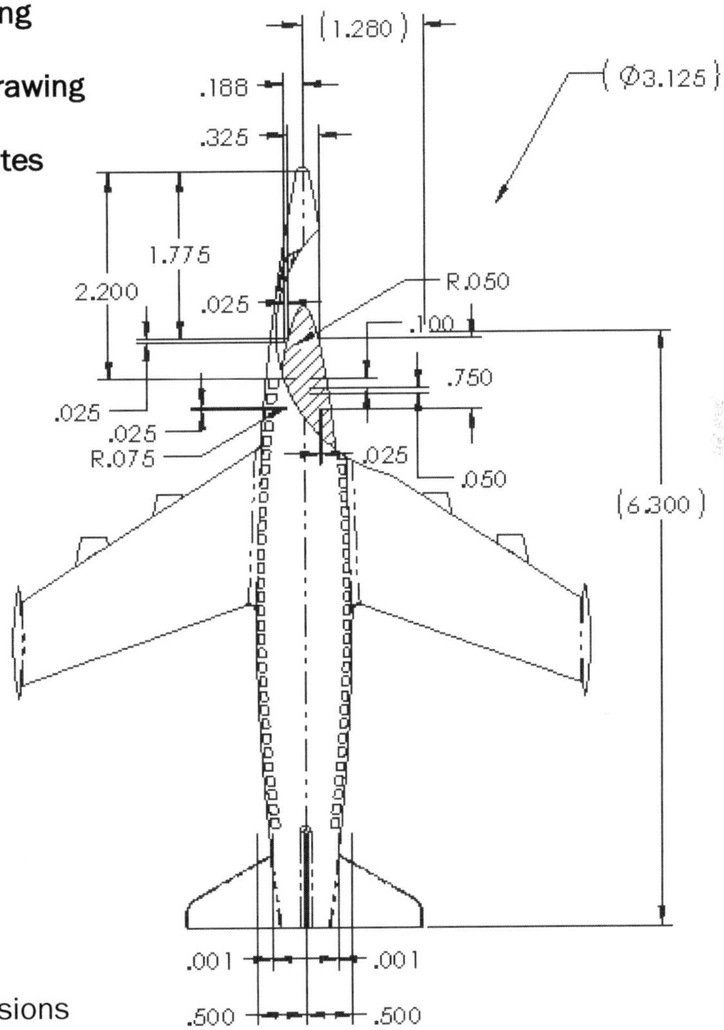

Do not count the 3 dimensions that were created in the previous step (shown in parentheses).

How many dimensions were imported into the Top drawing view? Check one:

☐ 3 ☐ 9 ☐ 12 ☐ 17 ☐ 21

5. Saving the drawing:

Select **File, Save As**.

Enter: **Challenge 5.slddrw** for the file name.

Click **Save.**

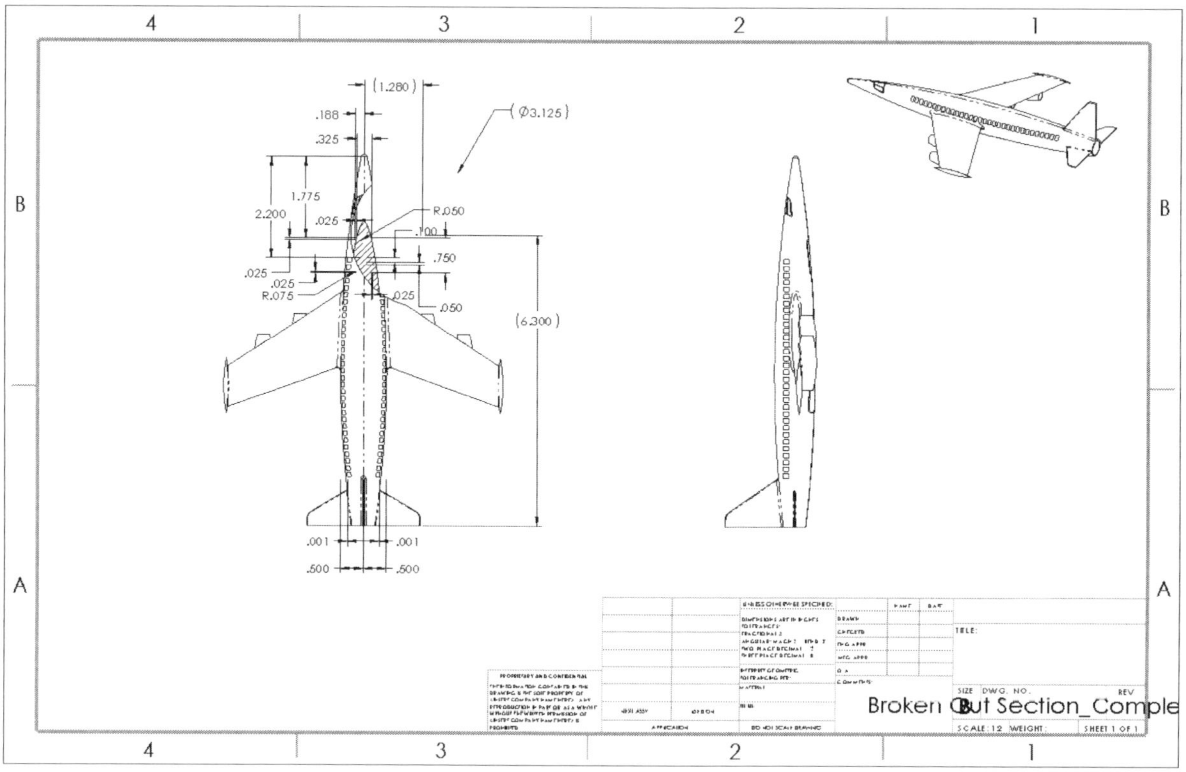

Move forward to the next challenge.

CHALLENGE 6 – PART DRAWINGS

View Creation & Feature Measurement

The examples in this exam preparation material are intended to assist you in familiarizing yourself with the structures of the exams and the method in which the questions are asked.

1. Opening a drawing document:

Select **File, Open**.

Locate the drawing document named: **View Creation.slddrw** and open it.

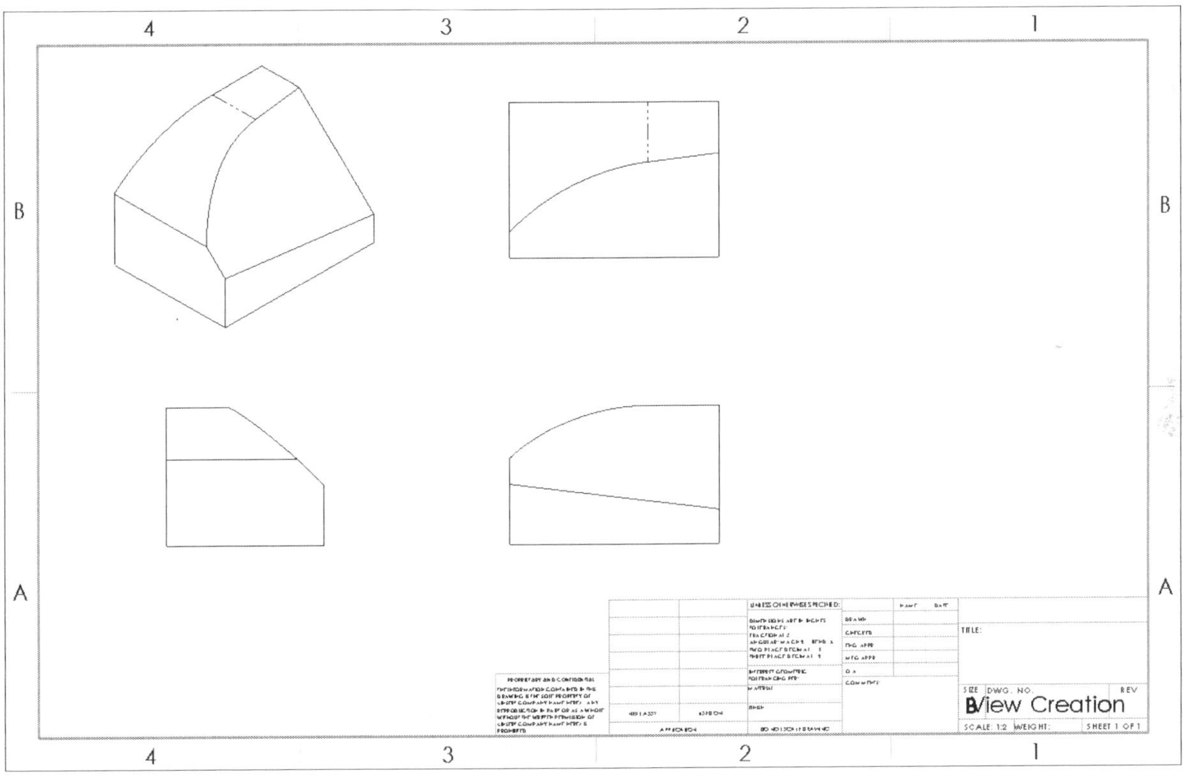

There are 4 standard views that have already been created for this drawing. We will need to create a couple more views and add dimensions to them.

2. Creating a custom drawing view:

The drawing view that is needed for this challenge is quite unique and it must be created and saved in the model.

<u>Open</u> the model named: **View Creation.sldprt**

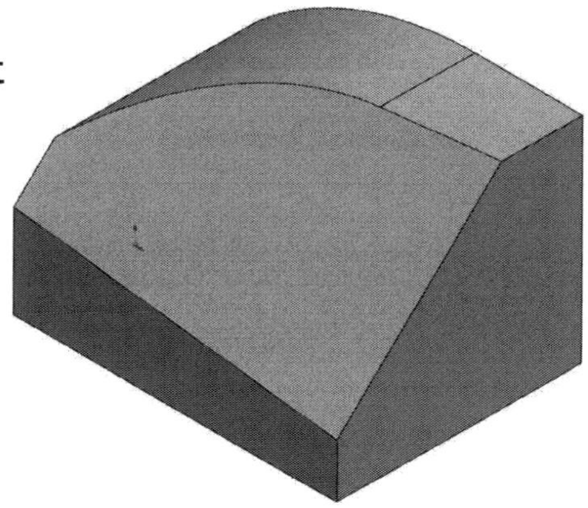

The rotate angle of the arrow keys must be switched back to the default 15deg. for this challenge.

Select **Tools, Options, System Option, View.**

Under View Rotation, change the **Arrow keys** angle to **15deg**.

Click **OK.**

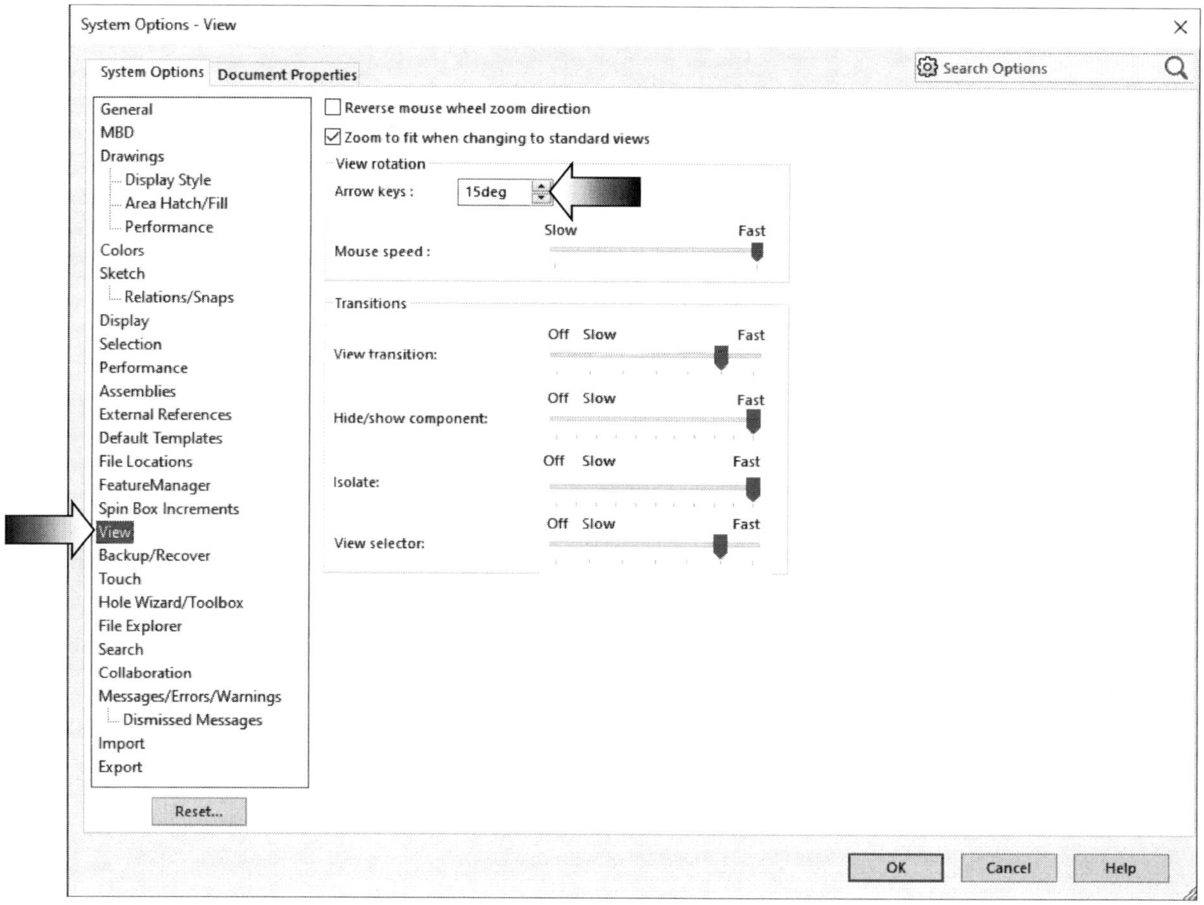

Change the orientation of the model as follows:

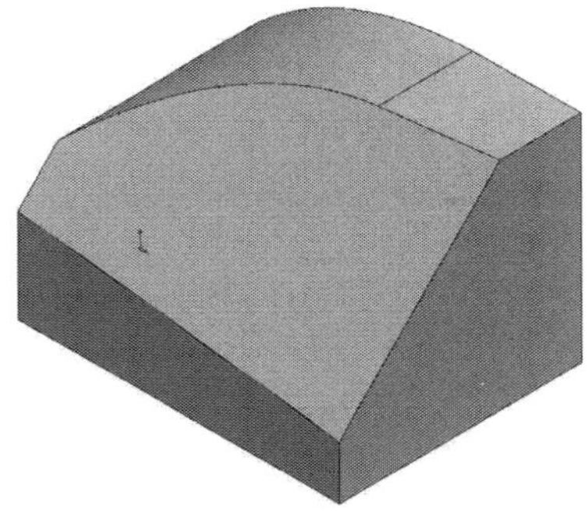

A. Select the face as indicated and click **Normal-To** from the pop-up menu.

(The hotkey Control+8 also works well.)

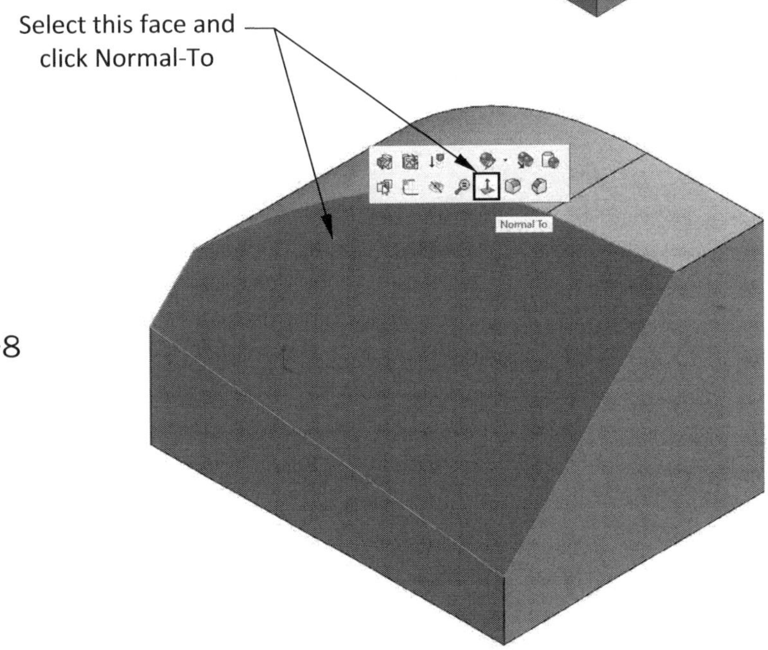

B. Hold down the **ALT** key and press the **RIGHT** arrow key 3 times (45° total).

The custom view is created.

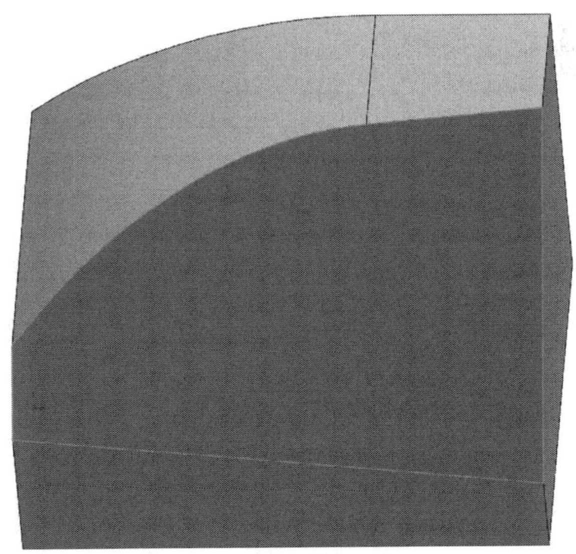

3. Saving the custom view:

The custom view must be saved so that it can be used as a drawing view in the drawing.

Press the **Spacebar** on the keyboard to display the Orientation dialog box.

Click the **New View** icon and enter **Custom View** for the name.

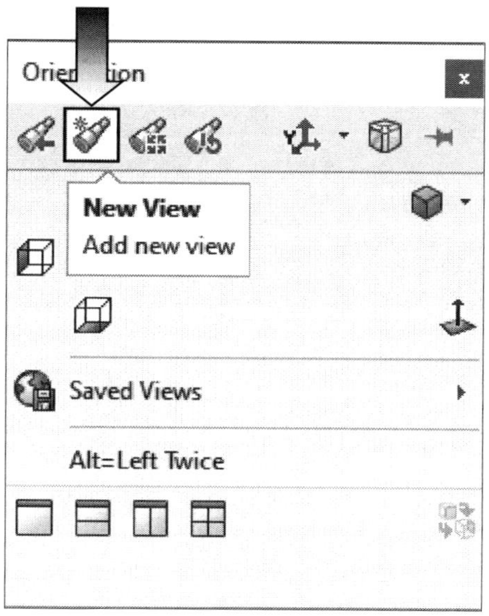

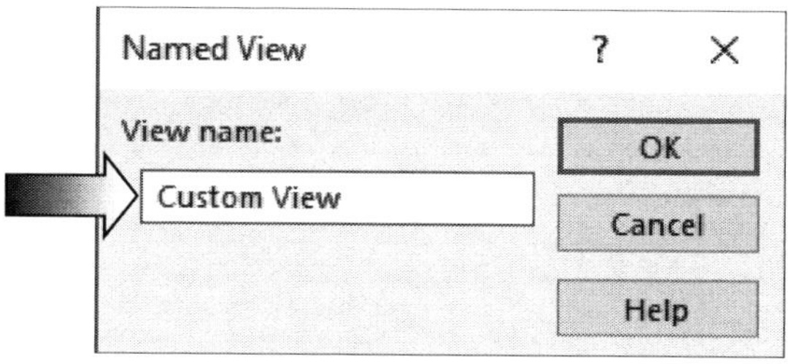

Click **OK**.

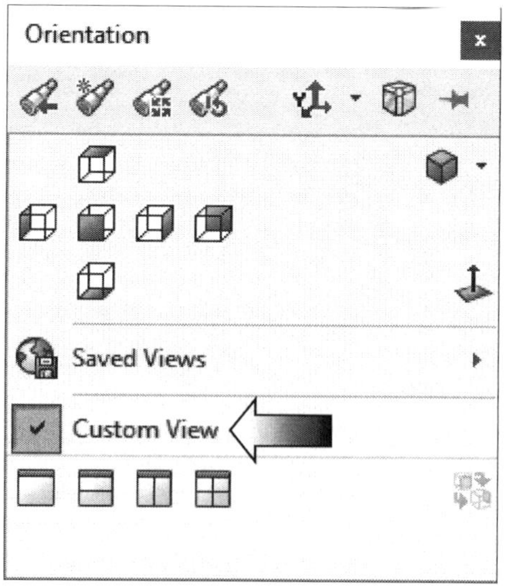

The Custom View is now saved inside the Orientation dialog box. It can be retrieved anytime when pressing the spacebar key.

In the drawing mode, the Custom View will also appear on the View Palette.

Save and **close** the model and return to the drawing.

4. Inserting the custom view:

From the Task Pane, click the **View Palette** tab to see the drawing views. Click the **Refresh** button to reload the drawing views, if needed.

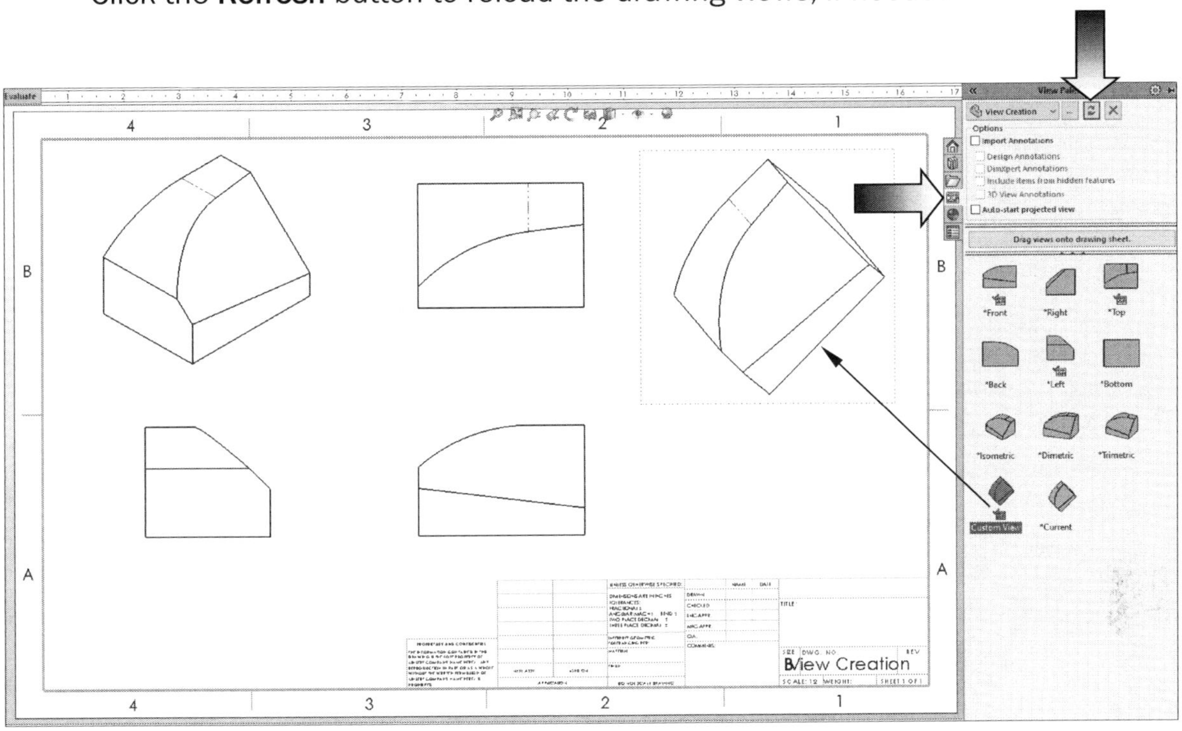

Create a Projected Dimension as shown on the lower right.

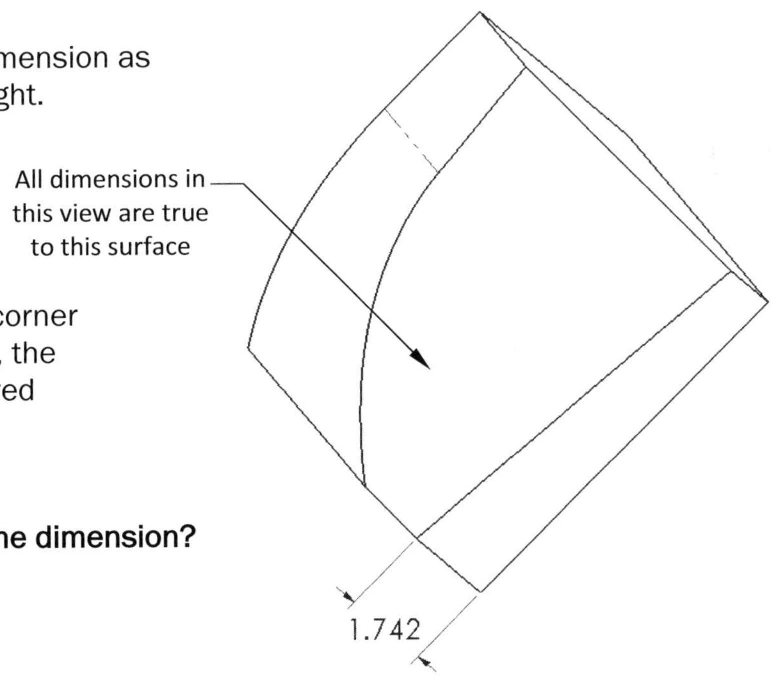

Since the lower right corner is not true to the face, the dimension is considered Projected dimension.

What is the value of the dimension?

______________ in.

5. Creating a section view:

Switch to the **Sketch** tab and draw a **Line** across the Custom View.

Add a **Parallel** relation between the **line** and the **lower right edge** of the drawing view.

Add the dimension **2.500in.** to fully position the line.

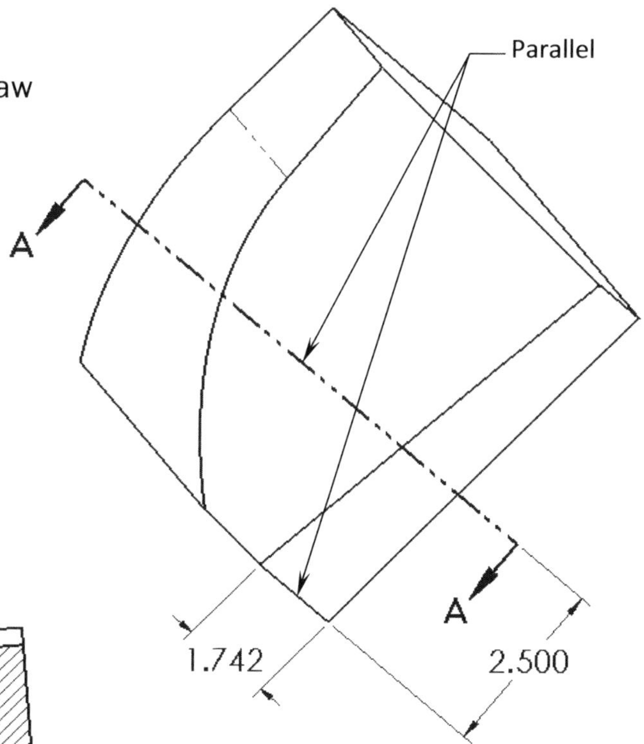

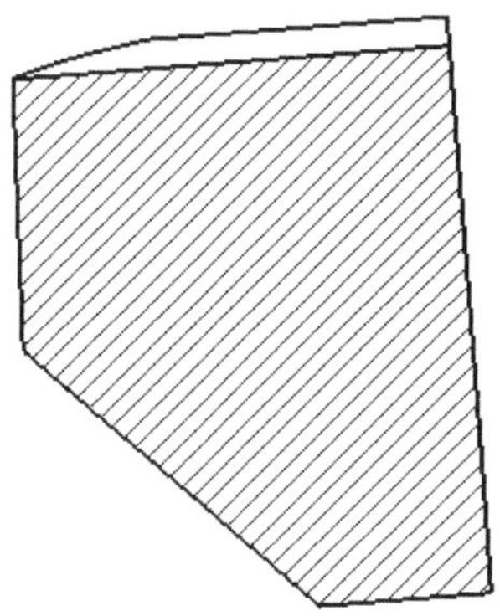

SECTION A-A

Using the new line, create a **Section View** as shown above.

Switch to the **Evaluate** tab and click **Measure.**

Select the sectioned face to display the measurements.

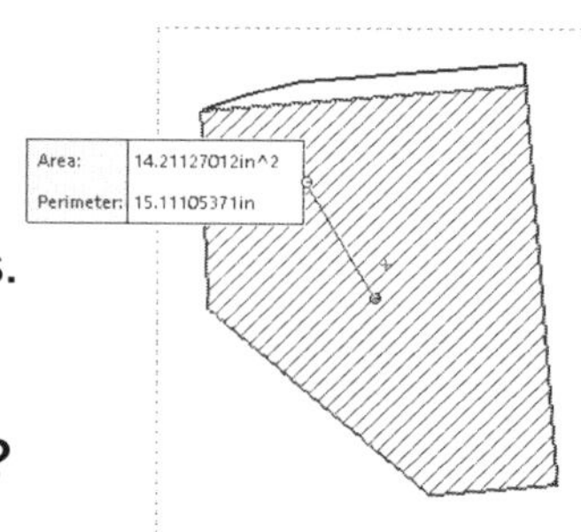

SECTION A-A

What is the measured Perimeter of the sectioned face?

____________________ in.

6. Saving your drawing:

Select **File, Save As**.

Enter: **Challenge 6.slddrw** for the file name.

Click **Save**.

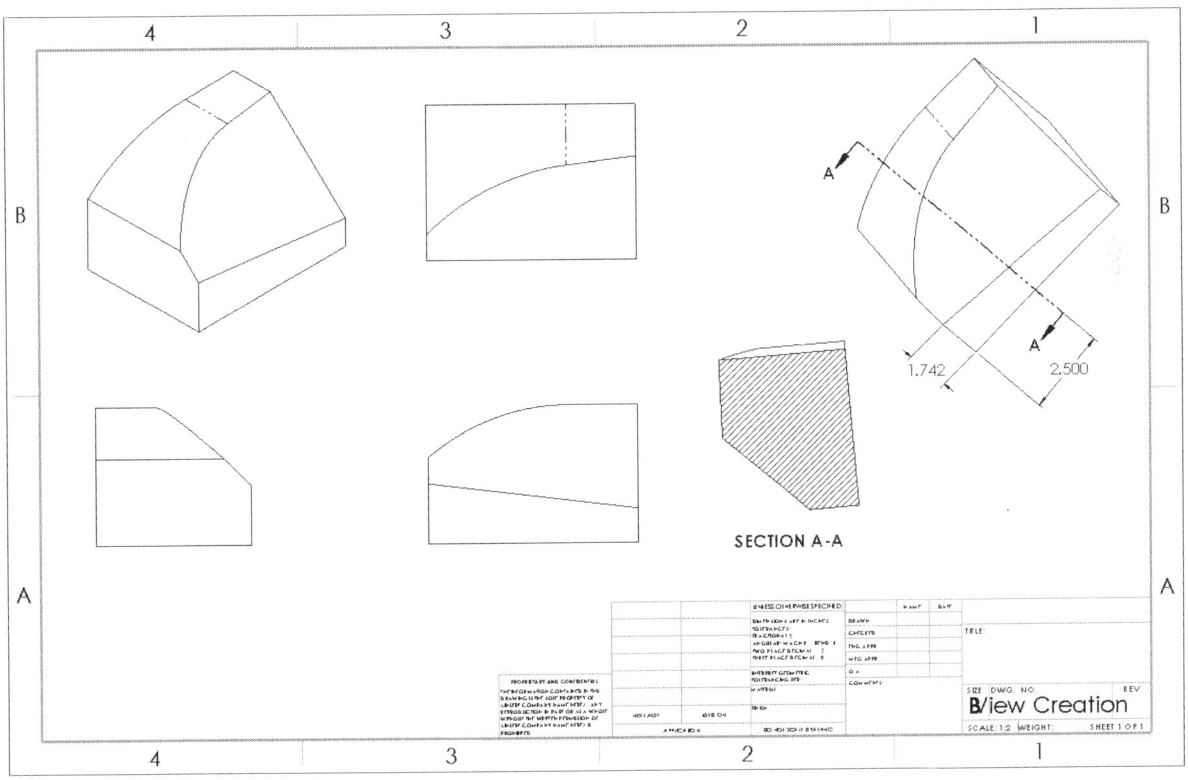

Close all documents.

To register and purchase the exam, go to: **www.solidworks.com/certification**

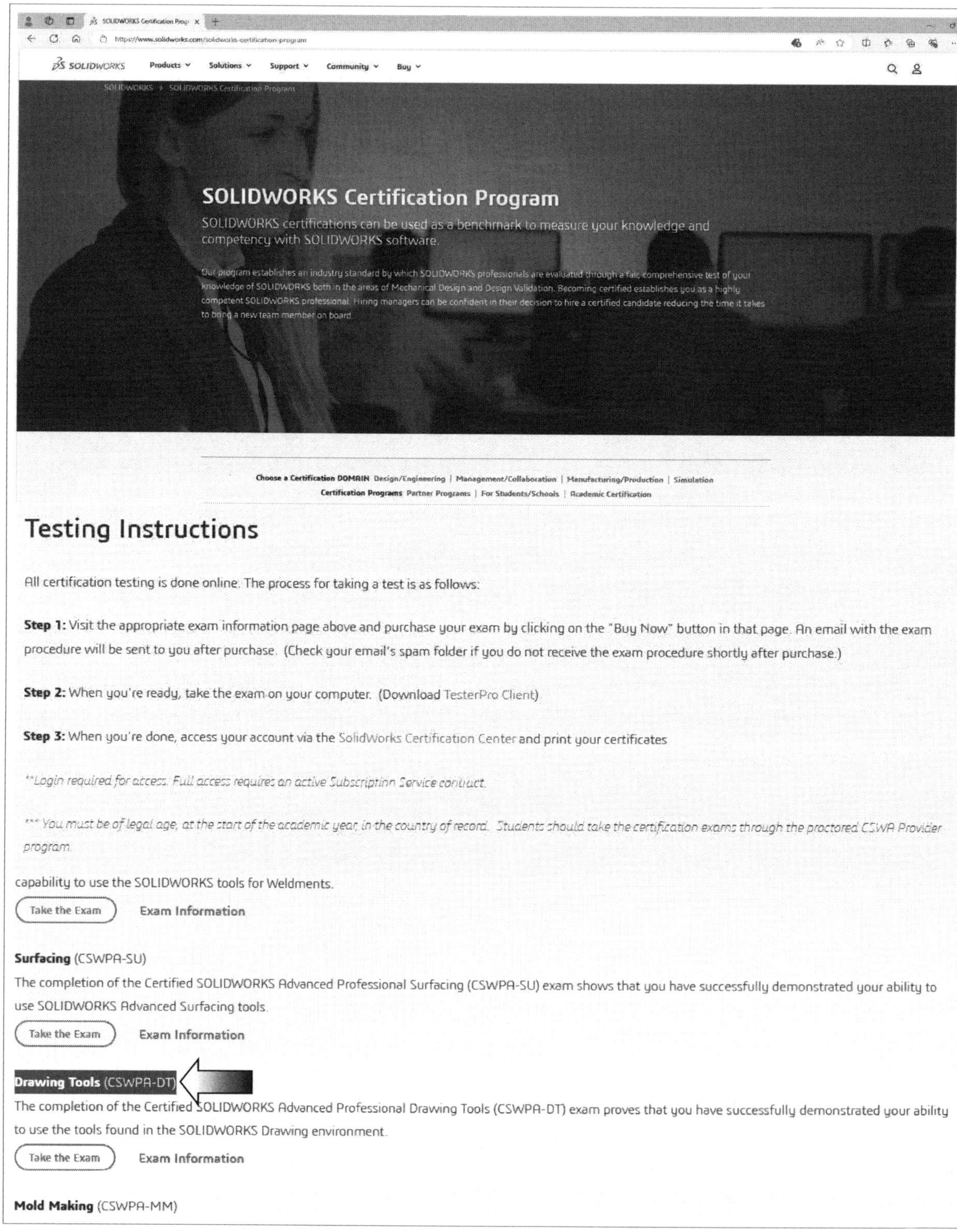

Additional information regarding the CSWP-DT

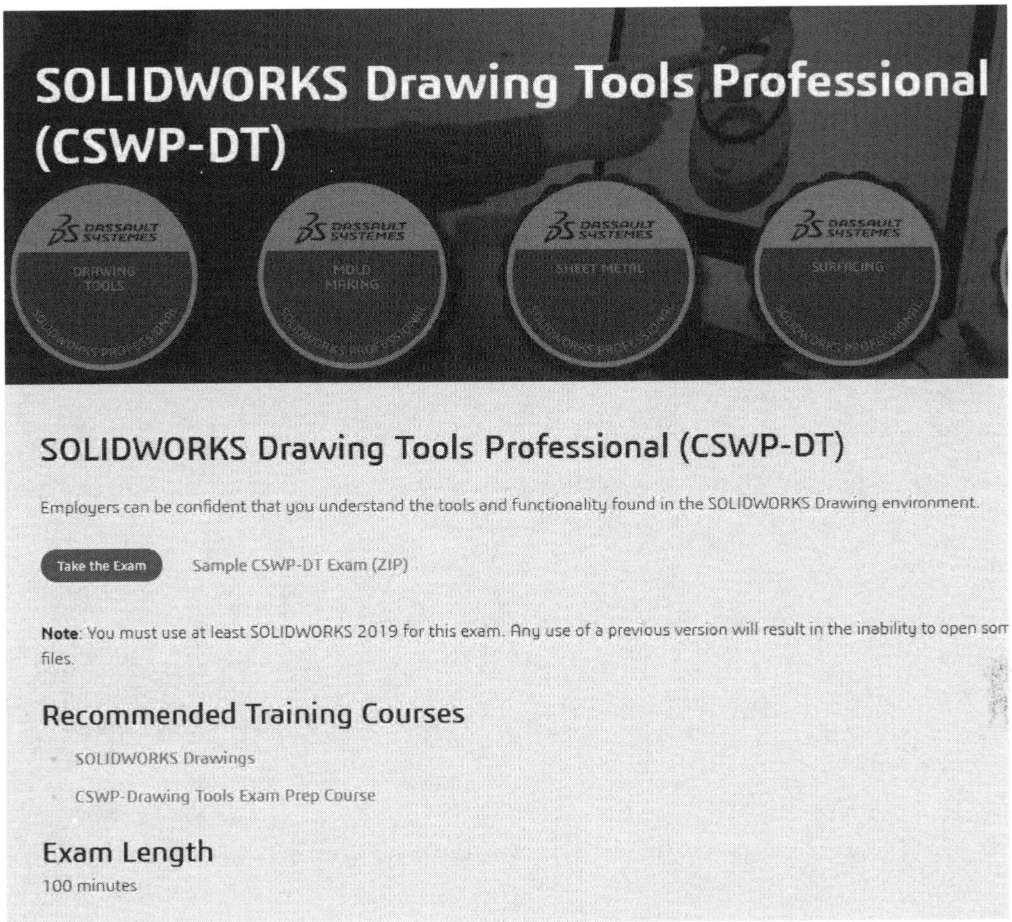
SOLIDWORKS Drawing Tools Professional (CSWP-DT)

SOLIDWORKS Drawing Tools Professional (CSWP-DT)

Employers can be confident that you understand the tools and functionality found in the SOLIDWORKS Drawing environment.

Take the Exam   Sample CSWP-DT Exam (ZIP)

Note: You must use at least SOLIDWORKS 2019 for this exam. Any use of a previous version will result in the inability to open sorr files.

Recommended Training Courses

- SOLIDWORKS Drawings
- CSWP-Drawing Tools Exam Prep Course

Exam Length

100 minutes

The CSWP-DT costs $20.00.

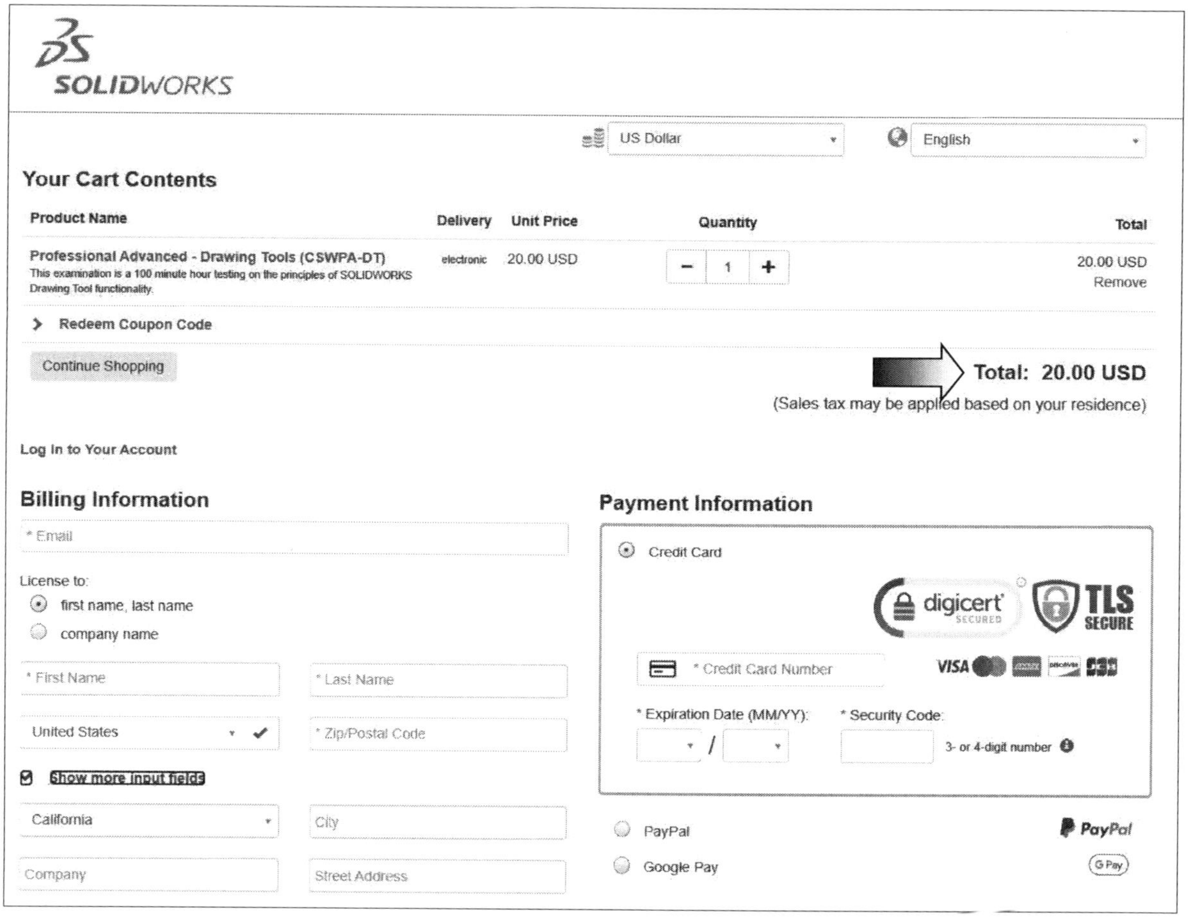

All candidates receive electronic certificates and a personal listing on the CSWP directory when they pass.

Index

1

1 Character, 9-7
1982, 3-3

2

2D CAD, 1-3,
2D drawing, 1-5
2nd sheet, 7-2, 7-3, 7-17

3

3D annotations, 12-2
3D CAD, 1-4, 12-1
3D-PDF, 12-22, 12-24, 12-28, 12-29, 12-31, 12-32, 12-34
3D printed, 2-1
3rd Angle, 4-13, 6-12, 8-2, 8-13, 9-5
3D View pane, 12-24, 12-25, 12-30
3D View tab, 12-22, 12-23
3D Views, 12-22, 12-25, 12-27, 12-28, 12-29, 12-32, 12-33

6

6061 Alloy, 12-13
6061 Aluminum Alloy, 11-25
6061-T6, 4-13, 5-20

A

Acetal, 5-1
Add Datum, 4-9, 4-11, 5-14, 5-15
Adding Datums, 5-14, 7-12, 7-30, 12-5, 12-9, 12-14
Additional Drawing Tools, 11-1, 11-19, 11-23, 11-25
Additions and Removals, 11-21, 11-22
AddRows, 10-9
Add Sheet, 7-3
Add Suffix, 11-24
Add Symbol, 2-19
Aerospace, 1-1, 1-7
AISI 304, 2-1, 12-1, 12-19
Align, 7-26
Aligned Section View, 7-26
Alignment, 5-26, 7-18, 7-20, 8-3, 8-14, 10-12, 11-4
Aluminum Block, 11-25, 11-30
Angular dimension, 5-11, 5-12
Angularity, 3-6, 3-7, 3-9, 3-22
Animate, 12-33
Annotation, 2-10, 2-12, 2-13, 2-14, 2-17, 2-19, 2-20, 2-21, 2-23, 2-24, 2-26, 2-31, 2-33, 4-9, 4-15, 4-17, 4-18, 5-7, 5-8, 5-14, 5-17, 7-4, 7-6, 7-9, 7-10, 7-11, 7-12, 7-21, 7-23, 7-28, 7-30, 7-31, 8-4, 8-8, 8-15, 9-7, 9-8
Annotations folder, 12-12, 12-16
Annotation tab, 10-11, 11-8, 11-9, 11-16
Annotation Views, 12-23, 12-24
ANSI, 1-4, 9-5, 9-12, 9-21, 12-3
ANSI32, 7-21, 7-27, 11-6
ANSI34, 5-5, 5-23
ANSI38 Aluminum, 4-14
Apply Changes Immediately, 5-5, 5-23, 7-21
Approved Date, 4-19
Area Hatch/Fill, 2-9
Arc Ext. Line or Opposite Side, 5-9
Architectural, 1-1, 1-7
Area Hatch/Fill, 5-5, 5-23
Assembly document, 9-1, 11-23
Assembly Drawing, 8-1, 8-13
ASME Y14.5, 4-7
Attach to Anchor Point, 5-17, 8-8
Attributes, 9-14, 9-15, 9-16
Auto Balloons, 8-15, 9-7
Auto Dimension Scheme, 12-5, 12-13, 12-14, 12-19, 12-21
Auto-Start, 2-4
Auto Start Projected View, 5-21, 7-3, 7-25
Auto-Start Projected View, 5-3, 6-3, 7-17, 11-2
Auxiliary, 11-1, 11-3, 11-4, 11-8, 11-14, 11-15, 11-26, 11-28
Auxiliary View, 6-4, 11-1, 11-3, 11-4, 11-8, 11-15, 11-26

B

Balloon Layout, 8-4
Balloons, 8-1, 8-3, 8-4, 8-5, 8-6, 8-14, 8-15, 9-7, 11-38
B (ANSI) Landscape, 5-2, 10-10
B-Landscape, 2-2
B-Size, 4-13, 4-14
B size, 6-2
Basic, 4-5, 4-6, 4-7
Basic dimension, 4-5
Basic Dimensions, 3-4
Bends, 6-1
Bilateral, 4-3, 4-7, 4-16
Bilateral tolerance, 4-3
Bill of Materials, 8-1, 8-3, 8-7, 8-8, 8-16, 8-17, 9-1, 9-4, 9-7, 9-8, 9-9, 9-10, 11-39
Black color, 12-13, 12-16
Blank notes, 7-7
Blind, 9-21
Bolt Circle, 2-18, 4-5, 11-14
BOM, 8-7, 8-8, 8-9, 8-10, 8-14, 8-16, 9-1, 9-2, 9-4, 9-8
Bom Standard, 8-8, 8-16
Bonus Tolerance, 4-10
Break Alignment, 5-26, 7-20, 8-3, 8-14, 11-4
Break-Lines, 2-16
Broken Circle, 5-6
Broken-out section, 11-5
Broken-out section view, 11-1

C

CAD, 1-1, 1-3, 1-4, 1-5, 1-6, 1-7, 1-9, 1-10
Callouts, 2-18, 2-19
Cap Screw, 8-6
Caption, 9-14, 9-15, 9-16, 9-18, 9-19
Capture 3D View, 12-22, 12-23, 12-24
Capturing 3D Views, 12-22
Cast Alloy Steel, 10-18
Casted Part, 7-1, 7-15, 7-16, 7-33
Casting, 2-1
Casting Materials, 7-1
Castings, 7-16
Castings & Forgings, 7-1, 7-16
Cast Stainless Steel, 7-1
Catia, 1-3
Center, 7-4, 7-5, 7-10, 7-20, 7-27
Centerline, 2-10, 4-15, 5-7, 5-11, 5-14, 5-24, 7-10, 7-11, 11-8
Centerlines, 5-7, 7-4, 7-5, 7-20, 7-27, 11-1, 11-8, 11-26
Center Mark, 4-15, 11-8
Center marks, 11-1, 11-8, 11-26
Chamfer, 2-19, 5-10
Changing color, 11-13
Changing the custom properties, 11-41
Circle, 6-5, 11-7, 11-8, 11-14
Circular Arrowhead Handle, 5-9
Circular Split Line, 8-5
Circularity, 3-9, 3-10, 3-14, 3-23
Civil, 1-1, 1-7
Closed profile, 11-5
CMM, 3-11, 3-12, 3-13, 3-14, 3-15, 3-18, 3-19, 3-20, 3-21, 3-22
Collapse, 11-35
Column, 8-7, 8-17, 9-9
Column header, 9-9
Columns, 10-4, 10-9, 10-15, 10-20
Computer Aided Design, 1-3
Computer-aided design, 1-6, 1-10
Concentricity, 3-10, 3-23, 3-26, 4-11
Configuration, 8-7, 8-8
Configure Feature, 10-1
ConfigurationManager, 10-7, 10-9, 10-19
Configurations, 7-1, 7-2, 7-17, 8-1, 8-7, 10-1, 10-2, 10-4, 10-6, 10-7, 10-8, 10-15, 10-18, 10-22
Connected, 5-6
Control frame, 5-14
Control key, 5-10, 9-4
Control + Tab, 9-5, 10-21
Construction circle, 7-22, 7-29
Control, 2-15
Coordinate Measuring Machine, 3-14
Create Basic dimension, 12-4
Create Now, 9-13
Crop view, 5-26, 6-5
Crosshatch, 2-8, 2-9, 4-14, 5-5, 5-22, 5-23, 11-6
C-Size, 2-12

Custom, 9-1, 9-2, 9-3, 9-4, 9-9, 9-12, 9-13, 9-15, 9-16, 9-17, 9-18, 9-19, 9-20, 9-22
Custom Properties, 8-7, 8-10, 8-16, 8-17, 9-1, 9-2, 9-4, 9-9, 9-12, 9-13, 9-15, 9-16, 9-17, 9-19, 9-20, 9-22
Custom tab, 9-2, 9-4
Cutting line, 2-8, 5-4, 5-22, 7-19
Cylinder, 12-10, 12-17
Cylindricity, 3-9, 3-10, 3-15, 3-24, 5-15

D

Dassault Systems, 1-7
Datum, 2-2, 2-21, 3-3, 3-5, 3-8, 3-12, 3-16, 3-17, 3-18, 3-19, 3-20, 3-21, 3-22, 3-23, 3-24, 3-25, 3-26, 3-27, 5-14, 7-12, 7-30
Datum Feature, 4-15, 7-12, 7-30
Datum GTOL, 12-5
Datum Label, 6-2
Datum Selection, 12-6, 12-14
Datums, 2-13, 2-21, 3-11, 3-12, 3-14, 3-15, 3-16, 3-17, 4-16, 7-12, 7-30
Degree symbol, 5-12
Delete, 2-6
Depths, 5-10
Derived Median Plane, 3-13
Derived median points, 3-26, 4-11
Description, 2-24, 2-25, 9-1, 9-2, 9-3, 9-4, 9-18, 9-20, 9-22
Design, 1-3, 1-5, 1-7, 1-9, 1-10
Design Binder, 11-23
Design intents, 3-1, 5-2
Designers, 1-1, 1-3, 1-5, 3-1, 3-28
Design Table, 10-1, 10-2, 10-3, 10-4, 10-5, 10-6, 10-7, 10-8, 10-9, 10-10, 10-11, 10-12, 10-13, 10-15, 10-17, 10-18, 10-19, 10-20
Detached drawings, 11-20
Detailing, 5-1, 5-20
Detail view, 5-6, 5-24, 11-1, 11-7, 11-11
Diagrams, 1-2
Diameter, 4-9, 4-10
Diameter dimensions, 7-29
Differences, 11-21
Dimension, 10-2, 10-3
Dimension scheme, 12-13, 12-14, 12-19, 12-21
Dimension Text, 2-18, 4-5, 4-6, 5-12, 11-28
Dimensions, 4-1, 4-3, 4-5, 4-7, 4-15, 4-16, 4-17, 6-1, 6-4, 6-6, 6-7, 6-14, 6-15, 11-9, 11-10, 11-11, 11-15, 11-27
DimXpert, 12-3, 12-5, 12-6, 12-7, 12-9, 12-12, 12-14, 12-15, 12-21, 12-22, 12-23
DimXpertManager, 12-2, 12-6, 12-7, 12-9, 12-12, 12-14, 12-17, 12-19, 12-20
Display options, 11-46, 12-4, 12-12
DMP, 3-13
Document, 2-2, 2-11, 2-16
Document Font, 5-4, 5-6, 5-22
Document properties, 12-3
Drafter, 1-1, 1-2, 1-3
Drafting, 1-1, 1-2, 1-3, 1-8, 1-10
Drafting standards, 12-3
Draftsperson, 1-1
DrawCompare, 11-19, 11-20, 11-23
Drawing, 2-2, 5-2, 5-3, 5-4, 5-6, 5-7, 5-8, 5-9, 5-10, 5-11, 5-13, 5-14, 5-16, 5-17, 5-20, 5-21, 5-22, 5-25, 5-26, 5-27, 5-28, 5-29, 9-5, 9-12, 9-14, 9-17, 9-21, 11-1, 11-3, 11-5, 11-7, 11-9, 11-10, 11-14, 11-19, 11-20, 11-23, 11-25
Drawing data, 9-14, 9-15, 9-16
DrawingManager, 2-17
Drawing Number, 4-19
Drawing sheet, 2-2, 6-2
Drawing template, 9-5, 10-10
Drawing Title, 4-19
Drawing view, 6-3, 6-4, 6-5, 6-7, 6-10, 6-13, 6-14, 6-15
Drawing views, 4-14, 4-15, 4-19, 6-1, 6-3, 6-7, 6-13, 6-14, 6-15, 8-1, 8-2, 8-3, 8-14, 9-6, 9-7, 9-8, 11-1, 11-2, 11-3, 11-9, 11-10, 11-11, 11-12, 11-17, 11-25, 11-26, 11-28
Drawn By, 9-16
Drawn Date, 4-19, 9-17
DRW Properties, 9-17
Dual coaxial datum, 3-23

E

Edit Document Units, 2-16
eDrawing, 12-1, 12-22, 12-28, 12-31, 12-32, 12-33, 12-34
Electrical, 1-1, 1-4, 1-7
Engineering, 1-1
Engineering drawings, 4-1, 4-17
Engineers, 1-1, 1-5, 1-6
Enlarged scale, 11-7
Entire Model, 2-14, 5-8, 6-6, 11-9
Excel-Based, 8-7
Excel Design Table, 10-3
Exploded drawing view, 8-1, 8-8
Exploded line sketch, 11-32
Exploded view, 9-6
Extruded Boss-Base, 9-21
Extrusion, 2-1

F

F key, 11-12
Factor of Safety, 3-8
Families of models, 10-1
Feature, 3-3, 3-4, 3-5, 3-6, 3-10, 3-13, 3-16, 3-17, 3-18, 3-19, 3-20, 3-21, 3-22
Feature control frame, 3-12, 3-15
FEATURE CONTROL FRAME, 3-4
FeatureManager, 2-7, 2-11, 2-26, 2-27, 4-2, 4-19, 6-9, 6-10, 6-17, 7-7, 7-8, 7-14, 7-24, 7-25, 7-32, 9-10, 10-2, 10-14, 11-3, 11-14, 11-29
FeatureManager tree, 5-7, 5-16, 5-18, 5-29
Feature of Size Rule, 3-3
Features, 9-21
File Properties, 9-2, 9-4, 9-20
File- Properties, 8-10
FIM, 3-23, 3-24
Finish, 4-19, 9-18
Flatness, 3-6, 3-7, 3-9, 3-12, 3-13, 4-16
Flat pattern, 6-10, 6-13
Flat patterns, 6-1, 6-10
Font, 5-4, 5-6, 5-22
Font Size, 2-10, 8-9, 9-8
Forgings, 7-16
Form, 3-4, 3-5, 3-8
Format Cells, 10-12
Form Building blocks, 9-14
Formatting the BOM, 11-40
Formatting Toolbar, 8-9
Form Control Options, 9-13, 9-14
FORM CONTROLS, 3-9
Forms, 6-1
FOS, 3-3, 3-13, 3-18, 3-21
Full indicator movement, 3-23
Full Outline, 11-7
Fully constrained, 12-8
Functional features, 4-1

G

GD&T, 3-1, 3-2, 3-3, 3-4, 3-5, 3-8, 3-9, 3-10, 3-17, 3-25, 3-28, 4-1, 4-11, 4-16
General Notes, 2-13, 2-22, 2-23, 4-17, 5-16, 5-28, 6-8, 6-16, 7-6, 7-23
Geometric Dimensioning & Tolerancing, 3-1, 3-28, 4-1
Geometric Tolerance, 4-9, 4-11, 4-15, 5-14, 5-15, 12-4, 12-6, 12-14
Geometric Tolerances, 7-13, 7-31
Geometry, 3-1, 3-5, 12-2, 12-5
Gray color, 11-10
Green color faces, 12-8
GTOL Attachment, 12-5
Groupbox, 9-14

H

Hatch, 5-5, 5-23
Hatch Pattern, 2-8, 2-9, 5-5, 7-21, 7-27, 11-1, 11-6,
Hex Nut, 8-6, 8-15
Hide, 5-10
Hiding components, 11-43
Hiding dimensions, 5-10
Hole Callout, 5-8, 6-6, 6-14, 7-9, 11-9
Hole Callouts, 12-5
Hole Wizard Locations, 5-8, 6-6, 6-14, 7-9, 11-10
Hollow cavity, 7-1

I

Import Items into All Views, 11-9
Include Drawings, 11-24
Include Suppressed Components, 11-24

Inspectors, 1-1
Instance Call Out, 8-5, 8-6
Instance count, 5-13
Instance counts, 8-15, 11-11, 11-28
Instance/Revolution Counts, 11-9
Iron, 2-1
ISO, 1-1, 1-4
ISO 128, 1-1
ISO Standards, 3-26
Isometric, 2-4, 2-25, 4-14, 8-3, 12-16, 12-23, 12-30, 12-33
Isometric Exploded, 8-3, 8-14, 8-15, 9-6, 9-8
Isometric Flat Pattern, 6-10
Isometric view, 10-10, 10-11, 10-20

J

Jagged Outline, 5-25

K

Keep Link, 8-10

L

Landscape, 2-2, 2-12
Lathe, 2-1
Leaders, 2-16
Least Material Condition, 3-5, 3-7, 3-10
Limit, 4-4
Limit Tolerance, 3-1, 4-4
Line, 5-9, 5-11
Linear Dimension, 12-5
Linear Dimensions, 12-5
Line Color, 11-13
Line Format, 11-13
LMC, 3-3, 3-5, 3-6, 3-7, 3-10, 3-16, 3-17, 3-26
Location, 3-4, 3-5, 3-8
LOCATION CONTROLS, 3-9
Location dimension, 12-4, 12-5, 12-11
Lock Note, 7-23

M

Machined drawing, 7-8, 7-17
Machined parts, 2-1
Machinists, 1-1
Magenta 10-8, 10-19
Magenta color dimensions, 12-13
Make Drawing, 8-2, 8-13
Make Drawing From Assembly, 8-2, 9-5
Make Drawing from Part, 4-13, 5-2, 6-2, 10-10
Manual Configuration, 10-1
Manual Drawing, 1-2
Marked For Drawing, 2-14, 5-8, 6-6, 6-14, 7-9, 11-9
Mass, 9-3, 9-4
Material, 2-1, 2-8, 2-9, 4-9, 4-19, 9-1, 9-2, 9-3, 9-4, 9-18, 9-20, 9-22
Material Condition, 4-9
Material Crosshatch, 2-8, 2-9, 5-5, 5-23, 11-6
Maximum/Minimum variation, 4-2
Max Material Condition, 3-5, 3-11, 3-13, 3-21
MBD, 12-1, 12-2, 12-8, 12-9, 12-13, 12-22, 12-26, 12-29, 12-32
Merge Cell, 10-12
Mid-point, 5-11, 5-22
Mill, 2-1
Missing dimensions, 5-11, 5-27
MMC, 3-3, 3-5, 3-6, 3-7, 3-10, 3-11, 3-13, 3-16, 3-17, 3-26, 4-10, 4-11
Model Based Definition, 12-1, 12-13, 12-22
Model dimensions, 2-13, 2-14, 5-8, 7-4, 7-9, 7-21, 7-28, 11-9, 11-27
Model Items, 2-14, 2-17, 4-15, 5-8, 5-26, 5-27, 7-4, 7-9, 7-10, 7-11, 7-21, 7-28, 11-1, 11-9, 11-15, 11-27
Modifiers, 3-5, 3-6, 3-10
Molding, 2-1
Move dimensions, 5-9
Moving dimensions, 2-15, 11-11
MS-Excel, 10-1, 10-3, 10-12, 10-15, 10-20

N

Name field, 9-15, 9-16
Nested View, 11-24
Notches, 6-1

Note, 4-14, 4-15, 4-17, 7-6, 7-10, 7-23, 11-11, 11-16
Notes, 4-15, 4-17, 4-19
Not marked for Drawing, 5-8, 6-6, 6-14, 7-9, 11-9
Number of instances, 5-26, 5-27

O

Other drawing tools, 11-1
Orientation, 3-4, 3-5, 3-8
ORIENTATION CONTROLS, 3-9
Orthographic views, 12-25
Over constrained, 12-8

P

Pack and Go, 11-23, 11-24
Paper size, 2-12
Parallel, 1-2
Parallelism, 3-6, 3-7, 3-9, 3-18, 3-19, 3-22
Parametric, 1-8
Parametric Notes, 11-1
Part Data, 9-18
PartNo, 9-3, 9-4, 9-9
Part Number, 8-7, 8-16, 8-17, 9-1, 9-2, 9-9
Part Template, 9-18, 9-19, 9-20
Parts List, 8-1
Parts Only, 8-8, 8-16, 9-8
Pattern, 12-6, 12-14, 12-19, 12-21
Pattern Dimensioning, 12-6, 12-14, 12-19, 12-21
Patterned features, 11-1
Pattern instance, 11-17
Pattern instances, 11-15, 11-17
Perpendicular, 3-21, 4-16, 5-14
Perpendicularity, 3-6, 3-7, 3-9, 3-20, 3-21, 3-22, 7-13, 7-31
Per Standard, 5-6, 11-7
Plain Carbon Steel, 6-1, 6-12
Plastic Gear, 5-1, 5-19
Plastic Part, 5-1, 5-20, 5-30
Plus/minus, 4-3
Plus and Minus, 12-21
Plus and Minus Tolerances, 12-19
PMI, 12-22
Polar, 12-20, 12-21
POM Acetal Copolymer, 5-1
Position, 3-6, 3-7, 3-9, 3-18, 3-21, 3-25, 3-26, 3-27, 4-9, 4-10, 4-11, 7-13, 7-31
Precision, 2-1, 2-22, 2-28, 3-1
Preview, 11-5
Primary Datum, 12-6
Primary Value, 10-2
Prismatic Parts, 12-1
Product and manufacturing information, 12-22
PROFILE CONTROLS, 3-9
Profile of a Line, 3-16
Projected View, 2-4, 5-3, 5-21, 5-25
Projection Line, 11-26
Properties, 2-2, 2-7, 2-9, 2-12, 9-2, 9-5, 9-12, 9-17, 9-19, 9-20
Property Name, 8-17
Property Tab Builder, 9-12, 9-22
Property Tab Template, 9-17
Publish to 3D-PDF, 12-29
Publish to eDrawing, 12-32
Punches, 6-1

Q

Quantity, 8-6

R

Radius, 2-20
Rebuild, 10-13, 10-16, 10-21, 11-17
Recapture View, 12-23
Recreate Basic Dim, 12-17
Rectangle, 9-20
Red color faces, 12-8
Reference Configuration, 7-8
Reference features, 12-19
Regardless of Feature Size, 3-3, 3-5, 3-10
Relief, 6-1
Resize, 8-9
Revision, 1-6, 4-18, 4-19, 5-17, 9-1, 9-2, 9-3, 9-4, 9-15
Revision Block, 2-13, 2-22, 2-24, 4-18, 5-17
Revision Table, 2-24, 2-25, 5-17
RFS, 3-3, 3-10
Rib Thickness, 5-27

Rips, 6-1
Router, 2-1
Row Height, 9-8
Rows, 10-4, 10-9
Rules, 3-3
Runout, 3-4, 3-10, 3-23, 3-24, 3-26, 5-15

S

Saving 3D-PDF, 12-31
Scale, 2-2, 2-5, 2-6, 2-7, 2-12, 5-2, 5-5, 5-21, 5-23, 8-14, 9-5, 9-6, 9-11
Scope, 12-66, 12-15, 12-19, 12-21
Secondary Datum, 12-6
Section line, 7-26
Section view, 2-8, 4-9, 4-11, 4-14, 5-4, 5-7, 5-12, 5-15, 5-26, 7-19, 7-20, 7-21, 7-22, 7-26, 7-29, 7-31, 12-26, 12-30
Selected Features, 12-15, 12-21
Select / Replace, 11-24
Settings, 12-6, 12-14, 12-19
Shaded, 9-11
Sheet, 2-2, 2-6, 2-7, 2-12, 2-25, 2-26, 2-27, 10-14
Sheet1, 5-18, 5-29, 6-9, 6-17, 11-29
Sheet Format, 2-2, 2-12, 2-26, 2-27, 4-19, 6-2, 9-5, 10-14, 11-29
Sheet Format1, 5-18, 5-29
Sheet Format/Size, 6-2
Sheet Format Size, 8-2
Sheet metal, 2-1
Sheet metal drawings, 6-1
Sheet Metal Part, 6-1, 6-11, 6-12, 6-18
Sheet Properties, 2-7, 5-2, 6-2, 8-2
Sheet scale, 2-6
Sheet size, 10-10
Shift, 2-15, 2-17
Shift + drag, 11-11, 11-28
Shift key, 5-9, 11-10
Show, 2-17, 11-14
Show Feature Dimensions, 12-12, 12-16
Show in Exploded or Model Break State, 9-6
Showing tolerance status, 12-8
Simulation results, 11-23
Single datum, 3-24
Single Limit Tolerance, 3-2
Size, 3-3, 3-4, 3-5, 3-8, 3-13, 3-18, 3-19, 3-20, 3-21, 3-22
Size dimension, 12-3
Size Dimensions, 12-5, 12-10
Size or Dimensional Tolerance, 3-4
Sketch, 1-1, 1-2, 6-5
Sketch tab, 11-5
SLOF, 3-8
Slot dimension, 12-5
Smart Dimension, 4-15
SOLIDWORKS, 1-3, 1-6, 1-7, 1-8, 1-9, 1-10, 4-13, 5-2, 5-7, 9-5, 9-12, 9-13, 9-16, 9-17, 9-19, 9-20, 10-1, 10-3, 10-5, 10-7, 10-13, 10-21, 11-19, 11-23
SOLIDWORKS MBD, 12-1
Source, 7-4, 7-9, 7-11, 7-21, 7-28
Square, 1-2
Square Pattern, 9-7
Stainless steel, 2-1, 4-1
Standard drawings, 11-20
Standard views, 11-2
State, 10-6
Steel, 2-1, 2-9
Straightness, 3-6, 3-7, 3-9, 3-11
Suppressed, 10-6
Surface, 3-5, 3-10, 3-11, 3-12, 3-16, 3-17, 3-19, 3-20, 3-22
Surface Features, 3-4
Surface Profile, 3-16, 3-17
Symmetric, 5-10
Symmetric tolerance, 4-2, 4-8, 4-16
Symmetry, 3-10, 3-27

T

TAB, 9-4
Table-Based, 8-7
Table Header, 10-12
Tables, 10-3, 10-7, 10-11, 10-18, 10-19, 10-20
Table template, 2-24, 9-8
Tabulated Table, 10-15, 10-16, 10-18, 10-20, 10-21
Tangent Edges, 8-14
Task Pane, 2-3, 9-13, 9-17, 9-20, 11-2
Technical drawings, 1-1
Template approvals, 12-29

Template Preview, 9-13, 9-14
Tertiary Datum, 12-6
Textbox field, 9-15, 9-16, 9-18
Text Format, 7-10
Third Angle, 2-2, 5-2
Title Block, 2-6, 2-13, 2-22, 2-25, 2-26, 2-27, 4-19, 5-18, 5-21, 5-29, 6-9, 6-17, 7-7, 7-14, 7-24, 7-32, 8-9, 8-11, 8-18, 9-8, 9-10, 9-15, 10-14, 11-45
Tolerance, 2-22, 2-28, 3-1, 3-2, 3-4, 3-5, 3-10
Tolerance & Precision, 4-1, 4-12, 4-13
Tolerance/Precision, 4-3, 4-4, 4-5, 4-6
Tolerances, 12-3, 12-4, 12-5, 12-7, 12-11, 12-13, 12-15
Tolerance zone, 3-11, 3-12, 3-13, 3-14, 3-15, 3-16, 3-17, 3-18, 3-19, 3-20, 3-21, 3-22, 3-25, 3-26, 3-27
Toolbars, 2-3
Top Justify, 2-20
Total Runout, 3-10, 3-23
Triangles, 1-2
True Position, 4-9
Turned parts, 12-2, 12-13
T-square, 1-2
Two planes, 3-27
TYP, 5-13, 11-11
Type, 9-8, 9-14, 9-16, 9-17, 9-19
Type-Of-, 5-20

U

Uncropped, 5-25
Under constrained, 12-8
Uniform thickness, 6-1
Unilateral Tolerance, 3-1, 4-7
Unsuppressed, 10-5, 10-6

V

Value / Text Expression, 9-3
Variations, 10-1
Vary, 3-1, 3-18, 3-21
Vendor, 9-1, 9-3, 9-4, 9-19, 9-20
Vertex, 2-19
View alignment, 5-26, 11-4
Viewing Animation, 12-33
Viewing configurations, 10-8
View Label, 6-2
View Palette, 2-3, 4-14, 5-3, 5-21, 6-3, 6-13, 7-3, 7-8, 7-17, 7-25, 8-3, 8-14, 9-6, 9-21, 10-10, 11-2
Visible, 8-14

W

Wall thickness, 2-1
Washer, 8-6, 8-15
Weight, 9-1, 9-3, 9-4
With Leader, 5-6
Worksheet, 10-2, 10-3, 10-18
Wrap Text, 10-12

Y

Y14.5, 3-3, 3-8
Yellow color faces, 12-8

Z

Zonal section view, 12-26
Zone, 3-25, 3-27

Glossary

Absorbed

A feature, sketch, or annotation that is contained in another item (usually a feature) in the FeatureManager design tree. Examples are the profile sketch and profile path in a base-sweep, or a cosmetic thread annotation in a hole.

Align

Tools that assist in lining up annotations and dimensions (left, right, top, bottom, and so on). For aligning parts in an assembly.

Alternate position view

A drawing view in which one or more views are superimposed in phantom lines on the original view. Alternate position views are often used to show range of motion of an assembly.

Anchor point

The end of a leader that attaches to the note, block, or other annotation. Sheet formats contain anchor points for a bill of materials, a hole table, a revision table, and a weldment cut list.

Annotation

A text note or a symbol that adds specific design intent to a part, assembly, or drawing. Specific types of annotations include note, hole callout, surface finish symbol, datum feature symbol, datum target, geometric tolerance symbol, weld symbol, balloon, and stacked balloon. Annotations that apply only to drawings include center mark, annotation centerline, area hatch, and block.

Appearance callouts

Callouts that display the colors and textures of the face, feature, body, and part under the entity selected and are a shortcut to editing colors and textures.

Area hatch

A crosshatch pattern or fill applied to a selected face or to a closed sketch in a drawing.

Assembly

A document in which parts, features, and other assemblies (sub-assemblies) are mated together. The parts and sub-assemblies exist in documents separate from the assembly. For example, in an assembly, a piston can be mated to other parts, such as a connecting rod or cylinder. This new assembly can then be used as a sub-assembly in an assembly of an engine. The extension for a SOLIDWORKS assembly file name is .SLDASM.

Attachment point
The end of a leader that attaches to the model (to an edge, vertex, or face, for example) or to a drawing sheet.

Axis
A straight line that can be used to create model geometry, features, or patterns. An axis can be made in several different ways, including using the intersection of two planes.

Balloon
Labels parts in an assembly, typically including item numbers and quantity. In drawings, the item numbers are related to rows in a bill of materials.

Base
The first solid feature of a part.

Baseline dimensions
Sets of dimensions measured from the same edge or vertex in a drawing.

Bend
A feature in a sheet metal part. A bend generated from a filleted corner, cylindrical face, or conical face is a round bend; a bend generated from sketched straight lines is a sharp bend.

Bill of materials
A table inserted into a drawing to keep a record of the parts used in an assembly.

Block
A user-defined annotation that you can use in parts, assemblies, and drawings. A block can contain text, sketch entities (except points), and area hatch, and it can be saved in a file for later use as, for example, a custom callout or a company logo.

Bottom-up assembly
An assembly modeling technique where you create parts and then insert them into an assembly.

Broken-out section
A drawing view that exposes inner details of a drawing view by removing material from a closed profile, usually a spline.

Cavity
The mold half that holds the cavity feature of the design part.

Center mark
A cross that marks the center of a circle or arc.

Centerline
Centerline marks, in phantom font, an axis of symmetry in a sketch or drawing.

Chamfer
Bevels a selected edge or vertex. You can apply chamfers to both sketches and features.

Child
A dependent feature related to a previously built feature. For example, a chamfer on the edge of a hole is a child of the parent hole.

Click-release
As you sketch, if you click and then release the pointer, you are in click-release mode. Move the pointer and click again to define the next point in the sketch sequence.

Click-drag
As you sketch, if you click and drag the pointer, you are in click-drag mode. When you release the pointer, the sketch entity is complete.

Closed profile
Also called a closed contour, it is a sketch or sketch entity with no exposed endpoints, for example, a circle or polygon.

Collapse
The opposite of explode. The collapse action returns an exploded assembly's parts to their normal positions.

Collision Detection
An assembly function that detects collisions between components when components move or rotate. A collision occurs when an entity on one component coincides with any entity on another component.

Component
Any part or sub-assembly within an assembly.

Configuration
A variation of a part or assembly within a single document. Variations can include different dimensions, features, and properties. For example, a single part such as a bolt can contain different configurations that vary the diameter and length.

ConfigurationManager
Located on the left side of the SOLIDWORKS window, it is a means to create, select, and view the configurations of parts and assemblies.

Constraint
The relations between sketch entities, or between sketch entities and planes, axes, edges, or vertices.

Construction geometry
The characteristic of a sketch entity that is used in creating other geometry but is not itself used in creating features.

Coordinate system
A system of planes used to assign Cartesian coordinates to features, parts, and assemblies. Part and assembly documents contain default coordinate systems; other coordinate systems can be defined with reference geometry. Coordinate systems can be used with measurement tools and for exporting documents to other file formats.

Cosmetic thread
An annotation that represents threads.

Crosshatch
A pattern (or fill) applied to drawing views such as section views and broken-out sections.

Curvature
Curvature is equal to the inverse of the radius of the curve. The curvature can be displayed in different colors according to the local radius (usually of a surface).

Cut
A feature that removes material from a part by such actions as extrude, revolve, loft, sweep, thicken, cavity, and so on.

Dangling
A dimension, relation, or drawing section view that is unresolved. For example, if a piece of geometry is dimensioned, and that geometry is later deleted, the dimension becomes dangling.

Degrees of freedom
Geometry that is not defined by dimensions or relations is free to move. In 2D sketches, there are three degrees of freedom: movement along the X and Y axes, and rotation about the Z axis (the axis normal to the sketch plane). In 3D sketches and in assemblies, there are six degrees of freedom: movement along the X, Y, and Z axes, and rotation about the X, Y, and Z axes.

Derived part
A derived part is a new base, mirror, or component part created directly from an existing

part and linked to the original part such that changes to the original part are reflected in the derived part.

Derived sketch
A copy of a sketch, in either the same part or the same assembly that is connected to the original sketch. Changes in the original sketch are reflected in the derived sketch.

Design Library
Located in the Task Pane, the Design Library provides a central location for reusable elements such as parts, assemblies, and so on.

Design table
An Excel spreadsheet that is used to create multiple configurations in a part or assembly document.

Detached drawing
A drawing format that allows opening and working in a drawing without loading the corresponding models into memory. The models are loaded on an as-needed basis.

Detail view
A portion of a larger view, usually at a larger scale than the original view.

Dimension line
A linear dimension line references the dimension text to extension lines indicating the entity being measured. An angular dimension line references the dimension text directly to the measured object.

DimXpertManager
Located on the left side of the SOLIDWORKS window, it is a means to manage dimensions and tolerances created using DimXpert for parts according to the requirements of the ASME Y.14.41-2003 standard.

DisplayManager
The DisplayManager lists the appearances, decals, lights, scene, and cameras applied to the current model. From the DisplayManager, you can view applied content, and add, edit, or delete items. When PhotoView 360 is added in, the DisplayManager also provides access to PhotoView options.

Document
A file containing a part, assembly, or drawing.

Draft
The degree of taper or angle of a face usually applied to molds or castings.

Drawing
A 2D representation of a 3D part or assembly. The extension for a SOLIDWORKS drawing file name is .SLDDRW.

Drawing sheet
A page in a drawing document.

Driven dimension
Measurements of the model, but they do not drive the model and their values cannot be changed.

Driving dimension
Also referred to as a model dimension, it sets the value for a sketch entity. It can also control distance, thickness, and feature parameters.

Edge
A single outside boundary of a feature.

Edge flange
A sheet metal feature that combines a bend and a tab in a single operation.

Equation
Creates a mathematical relation between sketch dimensions, using dimension names as variables, or between feature parameters, such as the depth of an extruded feature or the instance count in a pattern.

Exploded view
Shows an assembly with its components separated from one another, usually to show how to assemble the mechanism.

Export
Save a SOLIDWORKS document in another format for use in other CAD/CAM, rapid prototyping, web, or graphics software applications.

Extension line
The line extending from the model indicating the point from which a dimension is measured.

Extrude
A feature that linearly projects a sketch to either add material to a part (in a base or boss) or remove material from a part (in a cut or hole).

Face
A selectable area (planar or otherwise) of a model or surface with boundaries that help define the shape of the model or surface. For example, a rectangular solid has six faces.

Fasteners
A SOLIDWORKS Toolbox library that adds fasteners automatically to holes in an assembly.

Feature
An individual shape that, combined with other features, makes up a part or assembly. Some features, such as bosses and cuts, originate as sketches. Other features, such as shells and fillets, modify a feature's geometry. However, not all features have associated geometry. Features are always listed in the FeatureManager design tree.

FeatureManager design tree
Located on the left side of the SOLIDWORKS window, it provides an outline view of the active part, assembly, or drawing.

Fill
A solid area hatch or crosshatch. Fill also applies to patches on surfaces.

Fillet
An internal rounding of a corner or edge in a sketch, or an edge on a surface or solid.

Forming tool
Dies that bend, stretch, or otherwise form sheet metal to create such form features as louvers, lances, flanges, and ribs.

Fully defined
A sketch where all lines and curves in the sketch, and their positions, are described by dimensions or relations, or both, and cannot be moved. Fully defined sketch entities are shown in black.

Geometric tolerance
A set of standard symbols that specify the geometric characteristics and dimensional requirements of a feature.

Graphics area
The area in the SOLIDWORKS window where the part, assembly, or drawing appears.

Guide curve
A 2D or 3D curve is used to guide a sweep or loft.

Handle
An arrow, square, or circle that you can drag to adjust the size or position of an entity (a feature, dimension, or sketch entity, for example).

Helix
A curve defined by pitch, revolutions, and height. A helix can be used, for example, as a path for a swept feature cutting threads in a bolt.

Hem
A sheet metal feature that folds back at the edge of a part. A hem can be open, closed, double, or teardrop.

HLR
(Hidden lines removed) A view mode in which all edges of the model that are not visible from the current view angle are removed from the display.

HLV
(Hidden lines visible) A view mode in which all edges of the model that are not visible from the current view angle are shown gray or dashed.

Import
Open files from other CAD software applications into a SOLIDWORKS document.

In-context feature
A feature with an external reference to the geometry of another component; the in-context feature changes automatically if the geometry of the referenced model or feature changes.

Inference
The system automatically creates (infers) relations between dragged entities (sketched entities, annotations, and components) and other entities and geometry. This is useful when positioning entities relative to one another.

Instance
An item in a pattern or a component in an assembly that occurs more than once. Blocks are inserted into drawings as instances of block definitions.

Interference detection
A tool that displays any interference between selected components in an assembly.

Jog
A sheet metal feature that adds material to a part by creating two bends from a sketched line.

Knit
A tool that combines two or more faces or surfaces into one. The edges of the surfaces must be adjacent and not overlapping, but they cannot ever be planar. There is no difference in the appearance of the face or the surface after knitting.

Layout sketch
A sketch that contains important sketch entities, dimensions, and relations. You reference the entities in the layout sketch when creating new sketches, building new geometry, or positioning components in an assembly. This allows for easier updating of your model because changes you make to the layout sketch propagate to the entire model.

Leader
A solid line from an annotation (note, dimension, and so on) to the referenced feature.

Library feature
A frequently used feature, or combination of features, that is created once and then saved for future use.

Lightweight
A part in an assembly or a drawing has only a subset of its model data loaded into memory. The remaining model data is loaded on an as-needed basis. This improves performance of large and complex assemblies.

Line
A straight sketch entity with two endpoints. A line can be created by projecting an external entity such as an edge, plane, axis, or sketch curve into the sketch.

Loft
A base, boss, cut, or surface feature created by transitions between profiles.

Lofted bend
A sheet metal feature that produces a roll form or a transitional shape from two open profile sketches. Lofted bends often create funnels and chutes.

Mass properties
A tool that evaluates the characteristics of a part or an assembly such as volume, surface area, centroid, and so on.

Mate
A geometric relationship, such as coincident, perpendicular, tangent, and so on, between parts in an assembly.

Mate reference
Specifies one or more entities of a component to use for automatic mating. When you drag a component with a mate reference into an assembly, the software tries to find other combinations of the same mate reference name and mate type.

Mates folder
A collection of mates that are solved together. The order in which the mates appear within the Mates folder does not matter.

Mirror
(a) A mirror feature is a copy of a selected feature, mirrored about a plane or planar face.
(b) A mirror sketch entity is a copy of a selected sketch entity that is mirrored about a centerline.

Miter flange
A sheet metal feature that joins multiple edge flanges together and miters the corner.

Model
3D solid geometry in a part or assembly document. If a part or assembly document contains multiple configurations, each configuration is a separate model.

Model dimension
A dimension specified in a sketch or a feature in a part or assembly document that defines some entity in a 3D model.

Model item
A characteristic or dimension of feature geometry that can be used in detailing drawings.

Model view
A drawing view of a part or assembly.

Mold
A set of manufacturing tooling used to shape molten plastic or other material into a designed part. You design the mold using a sequence of integrated tools that result in cavity and core blocks that are derived parts of the part to be molded.

Motion Study
Motion Studies are graphical simulations of motion and visual properties with assembly models. Analogous to a configuration, they do not actually change the original assembly model or its properties. They display the model as it changes based on simulation elements you add.

Multibody part
A part with separate solid bodies within the same part document. Unlike the components in an assembly, multibody parts are not dynamic.

Native format
DXF and DWG files remain in their original format (are not converted into SOLIDWORKS format) when viewed in SOLIDWORKS drawing sheets (view only).

Open profile
Also called an open contour, it is a sketch or sketch entity with endpoints exposed. For example, a U-shaped profile is open.

Ordinate dimensions
A chain of dimensions measured from a zero ordinate in a drawing or sketch.

Origin
The model origin appears as three gray arrows and represents the (0,0,0) coordinate of the model. When a sketch is active, a sketch origin appears in red and represents the (0,0,0) coordinate of the sketch. Dimensions and relations can be added to the model origin, but not to a sketch origin.

Out-of-context feature
A feature with an external reference to the geometry of another component that is not open.

Over defined
A sketch is over defined when dimensions or relations are either in conflict or redundant.

Parameter
A value used to define a sketch or feature (often a dimension).

Parent
An existing feature upon which other features depend. For example, in a block with a hole, the block is the parent to the child hole feature.

Part
A single 3D object made up of features. A part can become a component in an assembly, and it can be represented in 2D in a drawing. Examples of parts are bolt, pin, plate, and so on. The extension for a SOLIDWORKS part file name is .SLDPRT.

Path
A sketch, edge, or curve used in creating a sweep or loft.

Pattern
A pattern repeats selected sketch entities, features, or components in an array, which can be linear, circular, or sketch driven. If the seed entity is changed, the other instances in the pattern update.

Physical Dynamics
An assembly tool that displays the motion of assembly components in a realistic way. When you drag a component, the component applies a force to other components it touches. Components move only within their degrees of freedom.

Pierce relation
Makes a sketch point coincident to the location at which an axis, edge, line, or spline pierces the sketch plane.

Planar
Entities that can lie on one plane. For example, a circle is planar, but a helix is not.

Plane
Flat construction geometry. Planes can be used for a 2D sketch, section view of a model, a neutral plane in a draft feature, and others.

Point
A singular location in a sketch, or a projection into a sketch at a single location of an external entity (origin, vertex, axis, or point in an external sketch).

Predefined view
A drawing view in which the view position, orientation, and so on can be specificd before a model is inserted. You can save drawing documents with predefined views as templates.

Profile
A sketch entity used to create a feature (such as a loft) or a drawing view (such as a detail view). A profile can be open (such as a U shape or open spline) or closed (such as a circle or closed spline).

Projected dimension
If you dimension entities in an isometric view, projected dimensions are the flat dimensions in 2D.

Projected view
A drawing view projected orthogonally from an existing view.

PropertyManager
Located on the left side of the SOLIDWORKS window, it is used for dynamic editing of sketch entities and most features.

RealView graphics
A hardware (graphics card) support of advanced shading in real time; the rendering applies to the model and is retained as you move or rotate a part.

Rebuild
Tool that updates (or regenerates) the document with any changes made since the last time the model was rebuilt. Rebuild is typically used after changing a model dimension.

Reference dimension
A dimension in a drawing that shows the measurement of an item but cannot drive the model and its value cannot be modified. When model dimensions change, reference dimensions update.

Reference geometry
Includes planes, axes, coordinate systems, and 3D curves. Reference geometry is used to assist in creating features such as lofts, sweeps, drafts, chamfers, and patterns.

Relation
A geometric constraint between sketch entities or between a sketch entity and a plane, axis, edge, or vertex. Relations can be added automatically or manually.

Relative view
A relative (or relative to model) drawing view is created relative to planar surfaces in a part or assembly.

Reload
Refreshes shared documents. For example, if you open a part file for read-only access while another user makes changes to the same part, you can reload the new version, including the changes.

Reorder
Reordering (changing the order of) items is possible in the FeatureManager design tree. In parts, you can change the order in which features are solved. In assemblies, you can control the order in which components appear in a bill of materials.

Replace
Substitutes one or more open instances of a component in an assembly with a different component.

Resolved
A state of an assembly component (in an assembly or drawing document) in which it is fully loaded in memory. All the component's model data is available, so its entities can be selected, referenced, edited, and used in mates, and so on.

Revolve
A feature that creates a base or boss, a revolved cut, or revolved surface by revolving one or more sketched profiles around a centerline.

Rip
A sheet metal feature that removes material at an edge to allow a bend.

Rollback
Suppresses all items below the rollback bar.

Section
Another term for profile in sweeps.

Section line
A line or centerline sketched in a drawing view to create a section view.

Section scope
Specifies the components to be left uncut when you create an assembly drawing section view.

Section view
A section view (or section cut) is (1) a part or assembly view cut by a plane, or (2) a drawing view created by cutting another drawing view with a section line.

Seed
A sketch or an entity (a feature, face, or body) that is the basis for a pattern. If you edit the seed, the other entities in the pattern are updated.

Shaded
Displays a model as a colored solid.

Shared values
Also called linked values; these are named variables that you assign to set the value of two or more dimensions to be equal.

Sheet format
Includes page size and orientation, standard text, borders, title blocks, and so on. Sheet

formats can be customized and saved for future use. Each sheet of a drawing document can have a different format.

Shell
A feature that hollows out a part, leaving open the selected faces and thin walls on the remaining faces. A hollow part is created when no faces are selected to be open.

Sketch
A collection of lines and other 2D objects on a plane or face that forms the basis for a feature such as a base or a boss. A 3D sketch is non-planar and can be used to guide a sweep or loft, for example.

Smart Fasteners
Automatically adds fasteners (bolts and screws) to an assembly using the SOLIDWORKS Toolbox library of fasteners.

SmartMates
An assembly mating relation that is created automatically.

Solid sweep
A cut sweep created by moving a tool body along a path to cut out 3D material from a model.

Spiral
A flat or 2D helix, defined by a circle, pitch, and number of revolutions.

Spline
A sketched 2D or 3D curve defined by a set of control points.

Split line
Projects a sketched curve onto a selected model face, dividing the face into multiple faces so that each can be selected individually. A split line can be used to create draft features, to create face blend fillets, and to radiate surfaces to cut molds.

Stacked balloon
A set of balloons with only one leader. The balloons can be stacked vertically (up or down) or horizontally (left or right).

Standard 3 views
The three orthographic views (front, right, and top) that are often the basis of a drawing.

StereoLithography
The process of creating rapid prototype parts using a faceted mesh representation in STL files.

Sub-assembly
An assembly document that is part of a larger assembly. For example, the steering mechanism of a car is a sub-assembly of the car.

Suppress
Removes an entity from the display and from any calculations in which it is involved. You can suppress features, assembly components, and so on. Suppressing an entity does not delete the entity; you can unsuppressed the entity to restore it.

Surface
A zero-thickness planar or 3D entity with edge boundaries. Surfaces are often used to create solid features. Reference surfaces can be used to modify solid features.

Sweep
Creates a base, boss, cut, or surface feature by moving a profile (section) along a path. For cut sweeps, you can create solid sweeps by moving a tool body along a path.

Tangent arc
An arc that is tangent to another entity, such as a line.

Tangent edge
The transition edge between rounded or filleted faces in hidden lines visible or hidden lines removed modes in drawings.

Task Pane
Located on the right side of the SOLIDWORKS window, the Task Pane contains SOLIDWORKS Resources, the Design Library, and the File Explorer.

Template
A document (part, assembly, or drawing) that forms the basis of a new document. It can include user-defined parameters, annotations, predefined views, geometry, and so on.

Temporary axis
An axis created implicitly for every conical or cylindrical face in a model.

Thin feature
An extruded or revolved feature with constant wall thickness. Sheet metal parts are typically created from thin features.

TolAnalyst
A tolerance analysis application that determines the effects that dimensions and tolerances have on parts and assemblies.

Top-down design
An assembly modeling technique where you create parts in the context of an assembly by referencing the geometry of other components. Changes to the referenced components propagate to the parts that you create in context.

Triad
Three axes with arrows defining the X, Y, and Z directions. A reference triad appears in part and assembly documents to assist in orienting the viewing of models. Triads also assist when moving or rotating components in assemblies.

Under defined
A sketch is under defined when there are not enough dimensions and relations to prevent entities from moving or changing size.

Vertex
A point at which two or more lines or edges intersect. Vertices can be selected for sketching, dimensioning, and many other operations.

Viewports
Windows that display views of models. You can specify one, two, or four viewports. Viewports with orthogonal views can be linked, which links orientation and rotation.

Virtual sharp
A sketch point at the intersection of two entities after the intersection itself has been removed by a feature such as a fillet or chamfer. Dimensions and relations to the virtual sharp are retained even though the actual intersection no longer exists.

Weldment
A multibody part with structural members.

Weldment cut list
A table that tabulates the bodies in a weldment along with descriptions and lengths.

Wireframe
A view mode in which all edges of the part or assembly are displayed.

Zebra stripes
Simulate the reflection of long strips of light on a very shiny surface. They allow you to see small changes in a surface that may be hard to see with a standard display.

Zoom

To simulate movement toward or away from a part or an assembly.

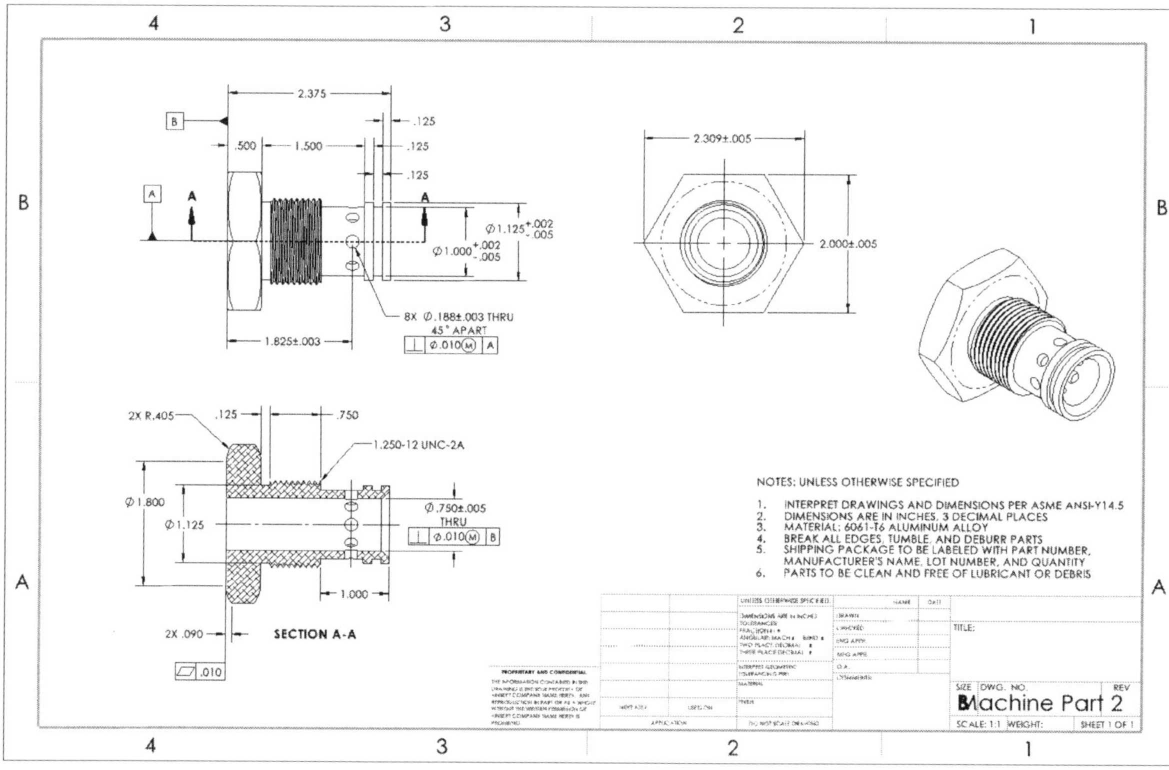

Mastering Surface Modeling with SOLIDWORKS 2026

Model Library

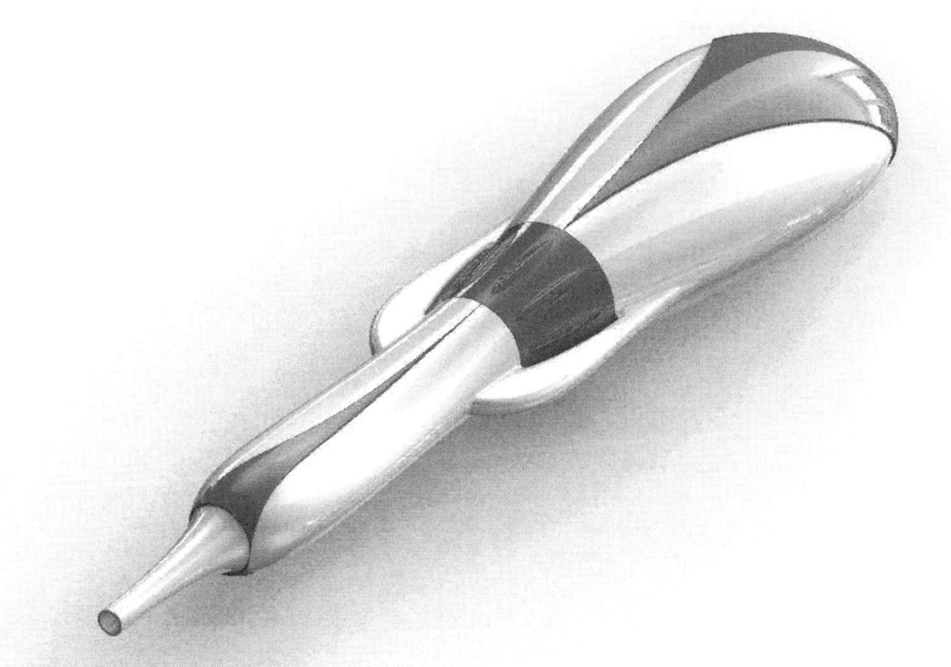

Catheter Handle - Model designed with SOLIDWORKS

Space Station - Model designed with SOLIDWORKS

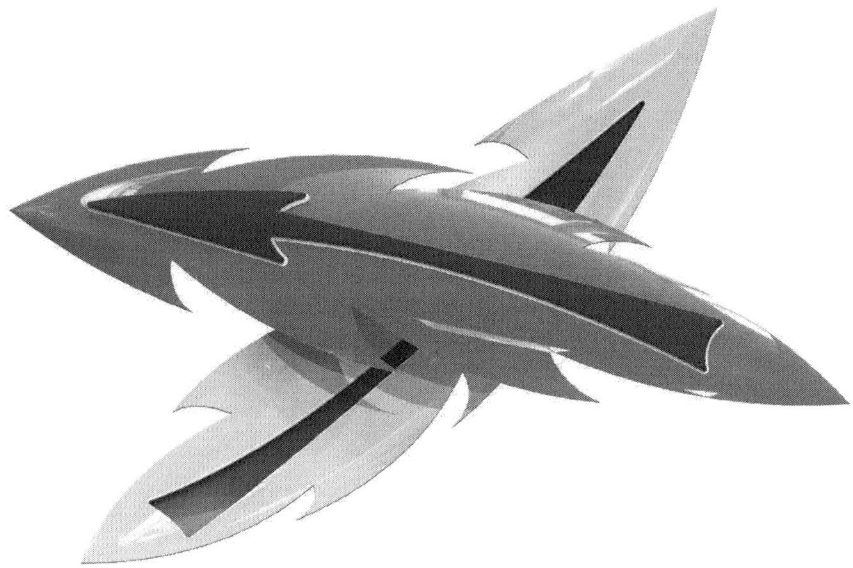

Logo Designs - Model designed with SOLIDWORKS

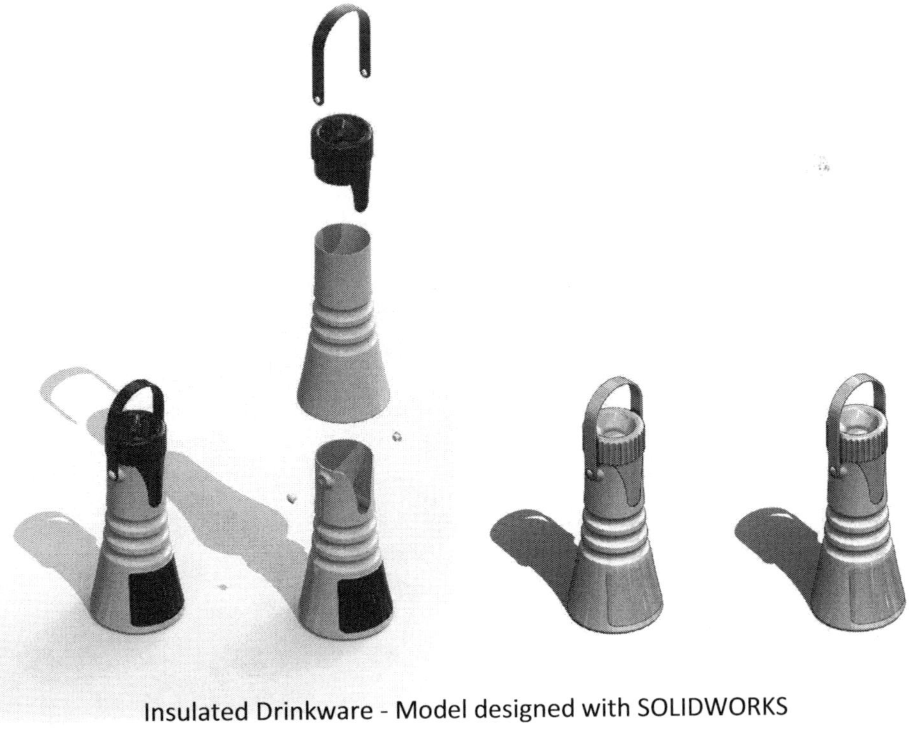

Insulated Drinkware - Model designed with SOLIDWORKS

Bug Bots - Model designed with SOLIDWORKS

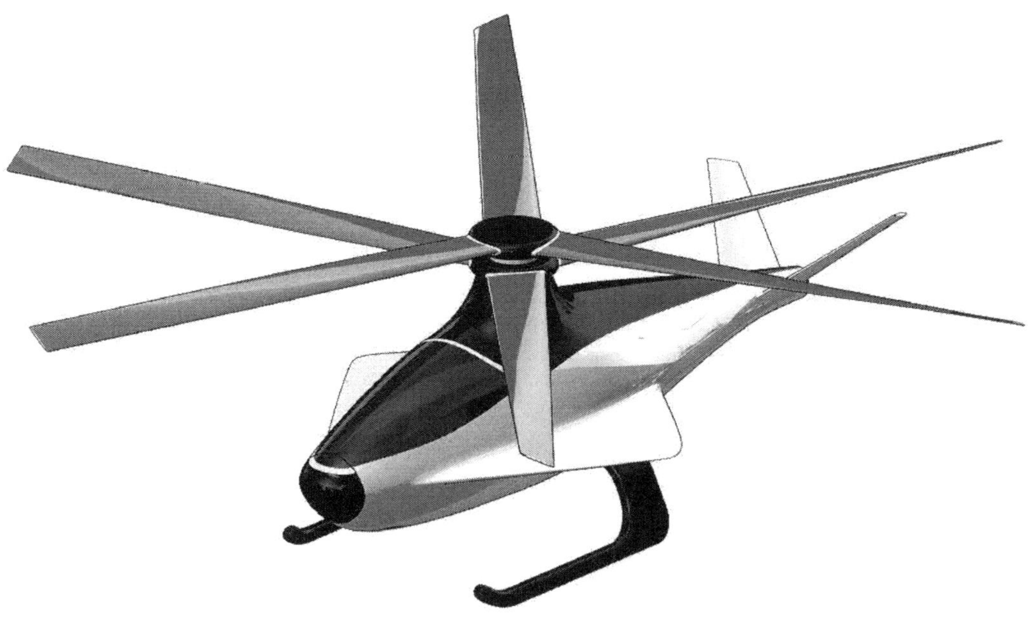

Futuristic Helicopter - Model designed with SOLIDWORKS

Modern Bike - Model designed with SOLIDWORKS

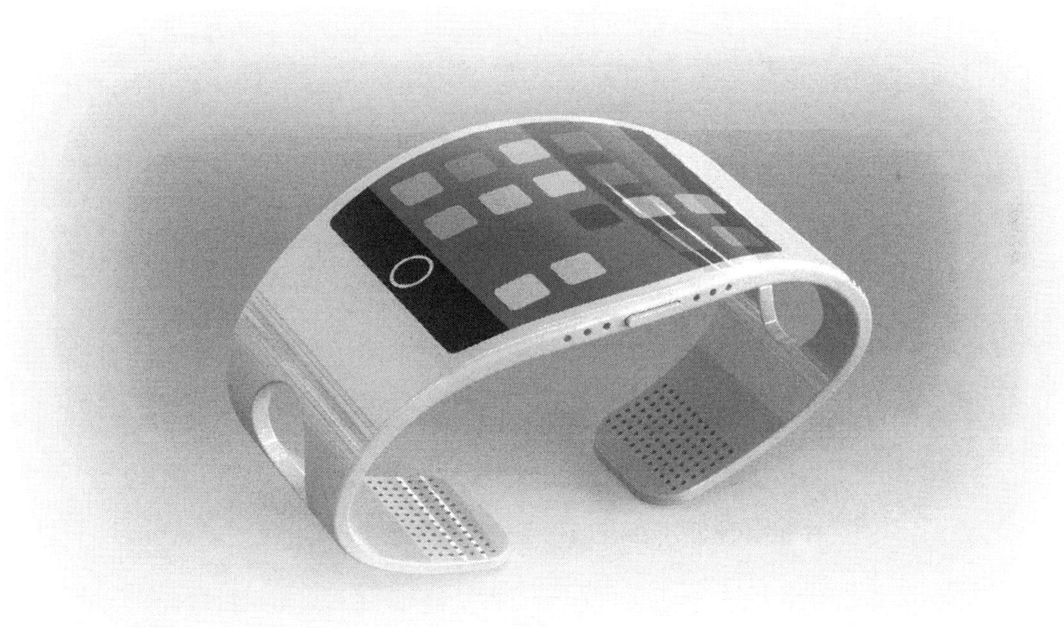

Phone Watch - Model designed with SOLIDWORKS

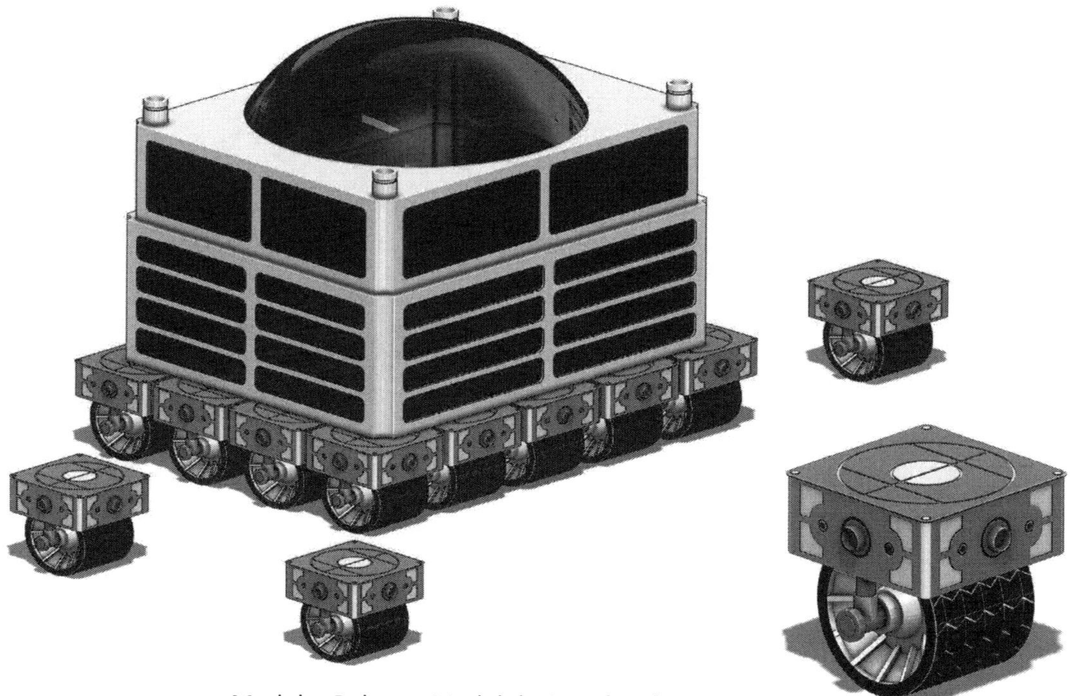

Modular Robots - Model designed with SOLIDWORKS

Car Mouse - Model designed with SOLIDWORKS

Toy Designs - Model designed with SOLIDWORKS

Helipads - Model designed with SOLIDWORKS

Superyacht - Model designed with SOLIDWORKS

MS Robots - Model designed with SOLIDWORKS

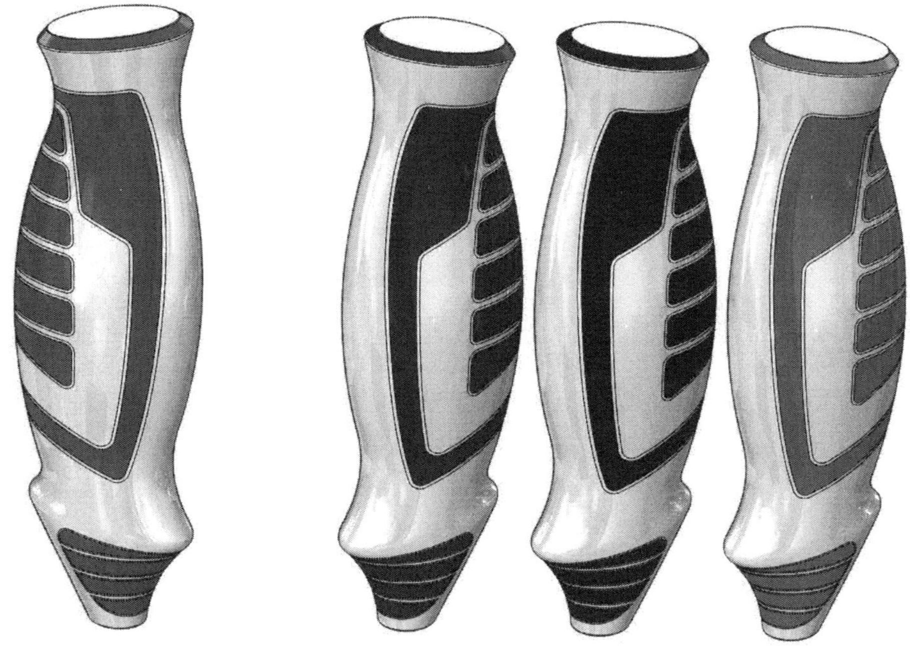

Handle Designs - Model designed with SOLIDWORKS

Helicopter Rotors - Model designed with SOLIDWORKS

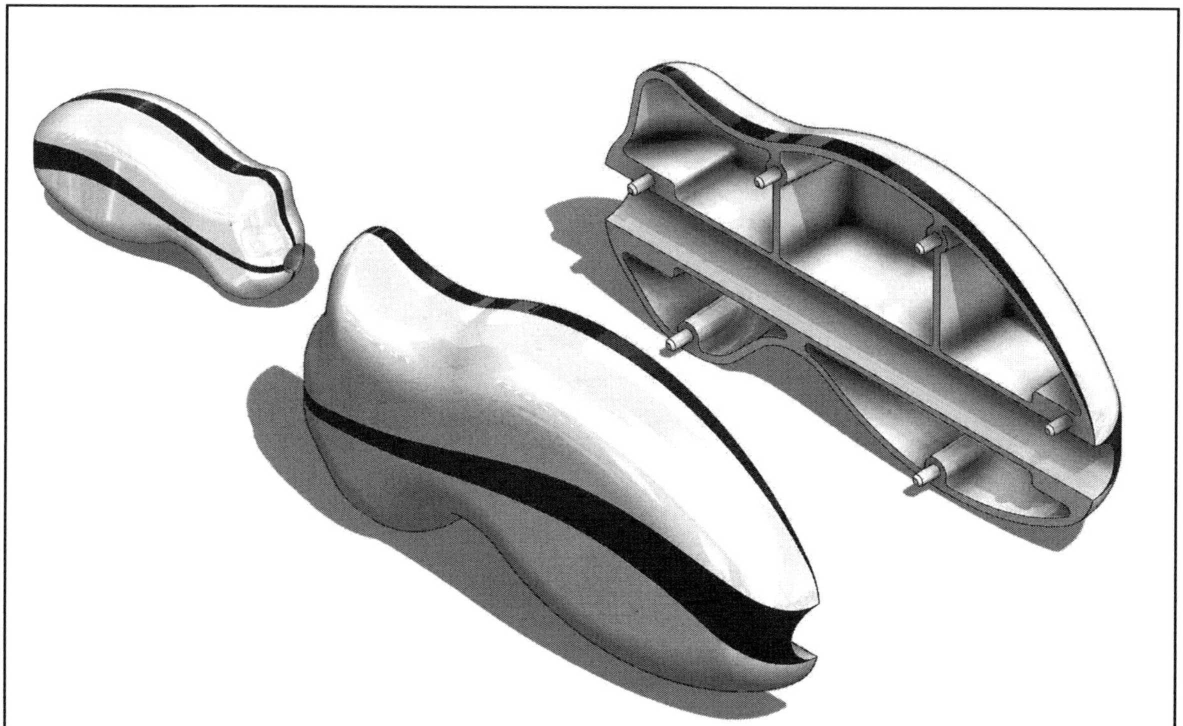

Med-Device Handle - Model designed with SOLIDWORKS

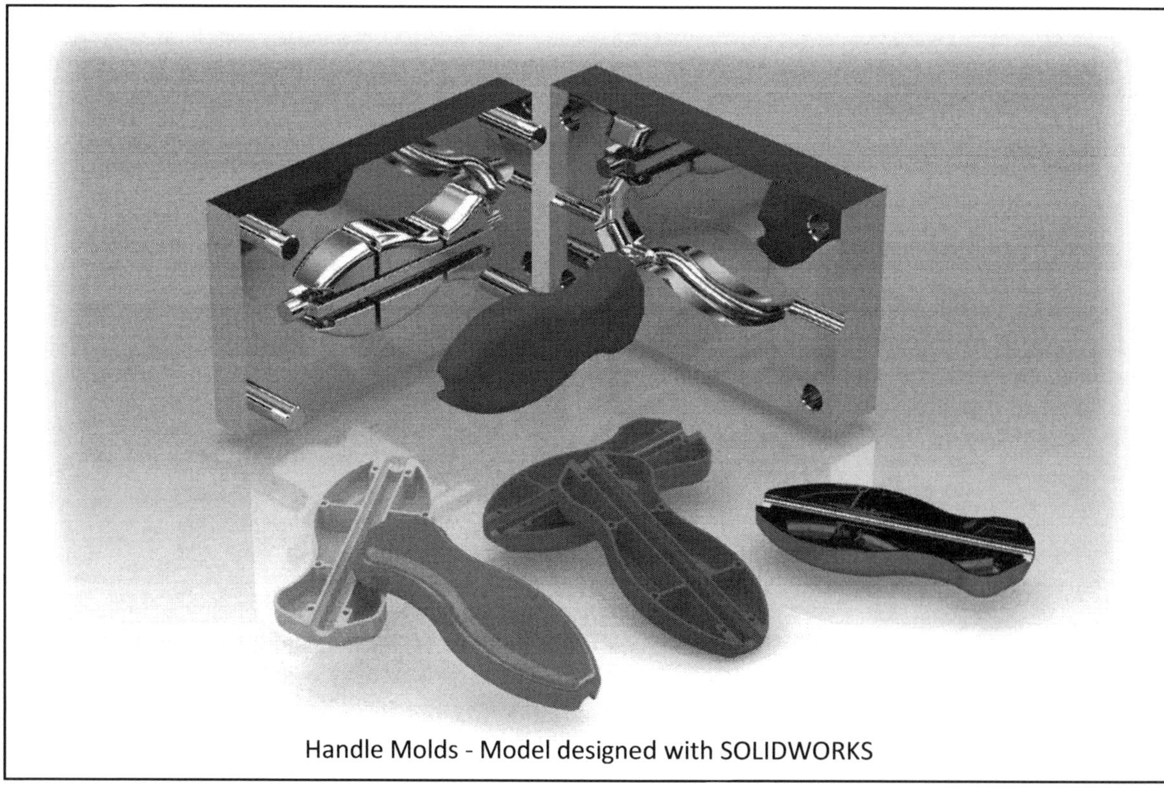

Handle Molds - Model designed with SOLIDWORKS

Ladybug - Model designed with SOLIDWORKS

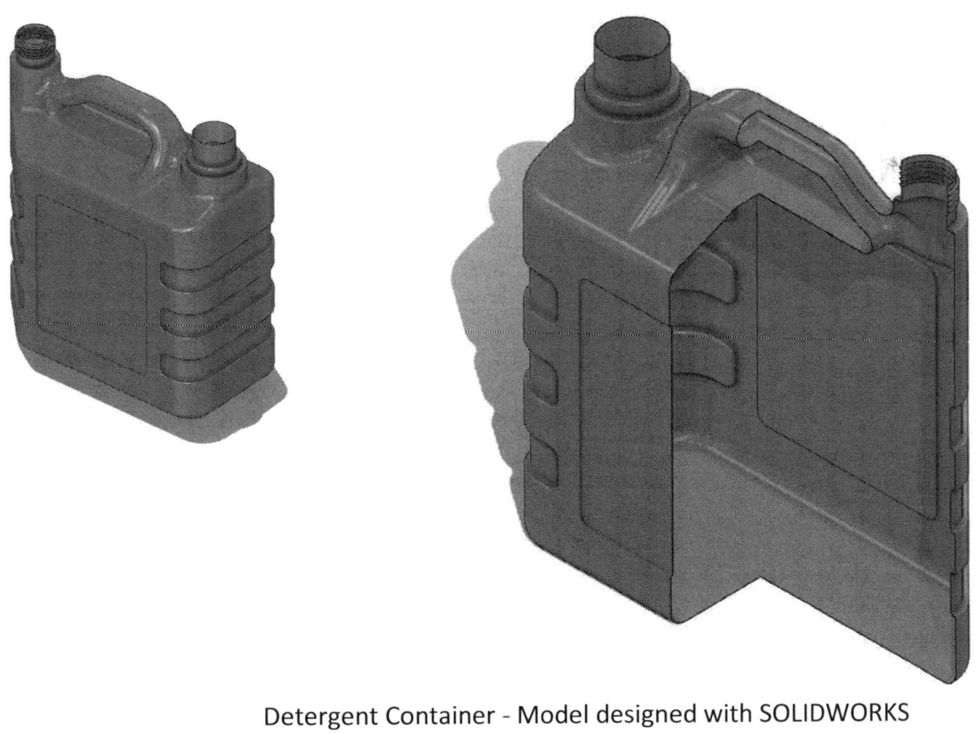

Detergent Container - Model designed with SOLIDWORKS

Blue Angel Aircraft - Model designed with SOLIDWORKS

Helicopter - Model designed with SOLIDWORKS

Concept Car - Model designed with SOLIDWORKS

Concept Car - Model designed with SOLIDWORKS

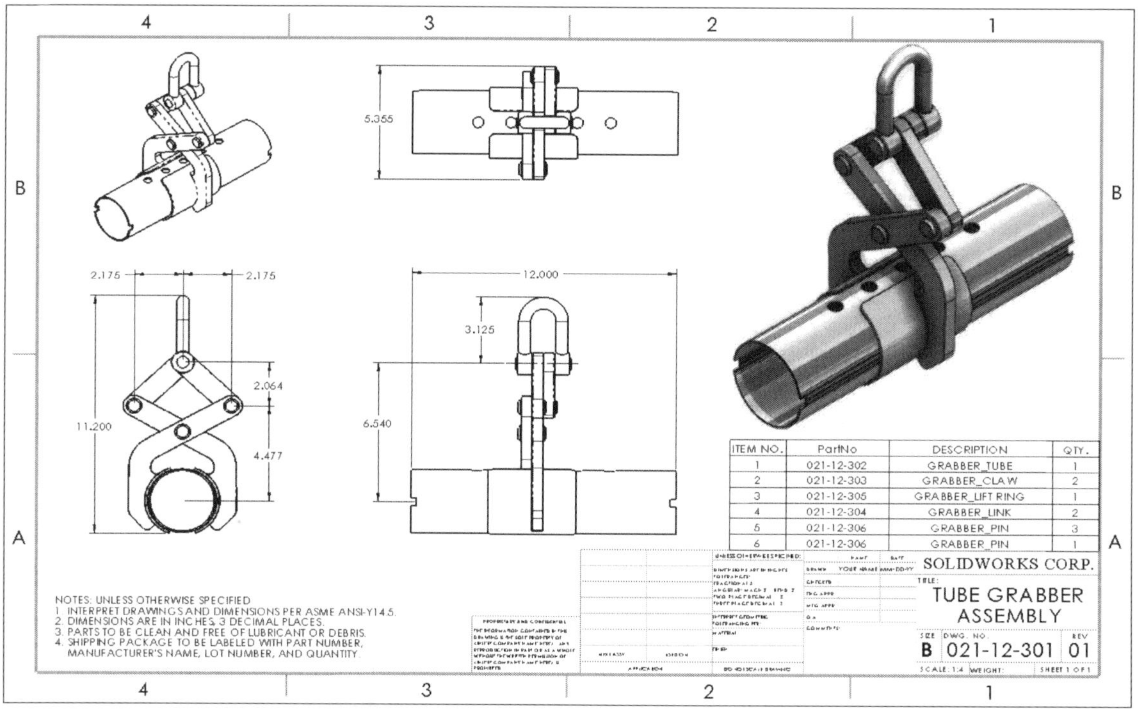

Tube Grabber – Drawing created with SOLIDWORKS

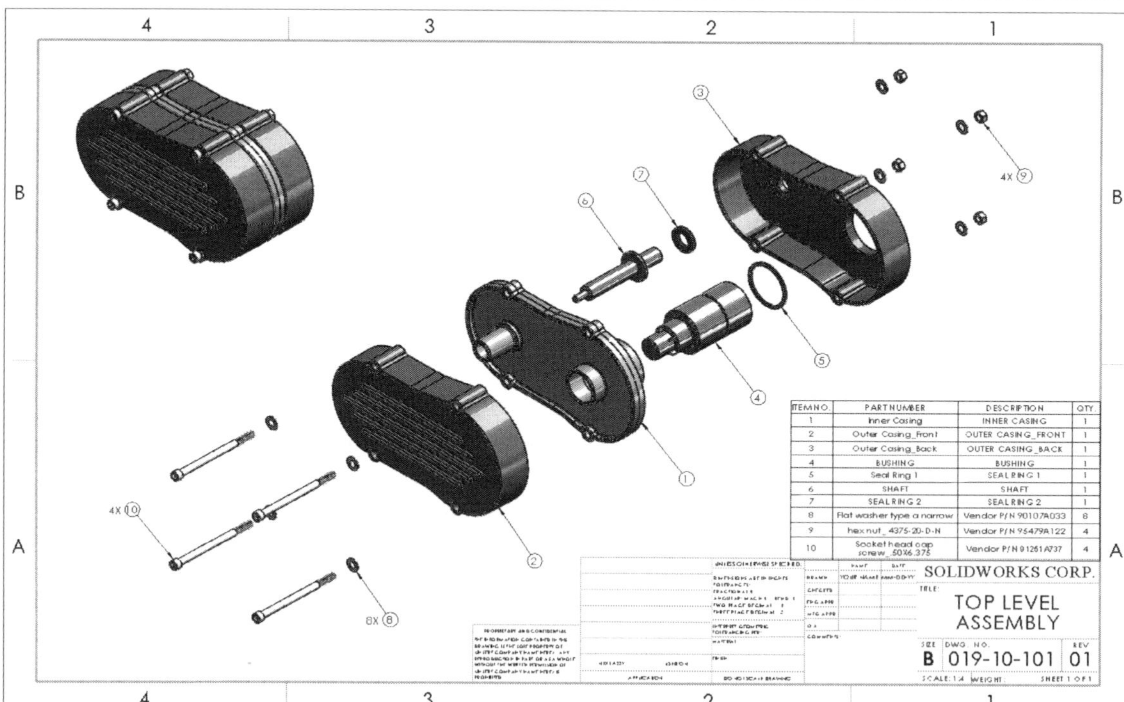

Casted Casing - Drawing created with SOLIDWORKS

Flying Car - Model designed with SOLIDWORKS

Shark Boat - Model designed with SOLIDWORKS

Propeller - Model designed with SOLIDWORKS

3-Way Bracket - Model designed with SOLIDWORKS

CyberBee - Model designed with SOLIDWORKS

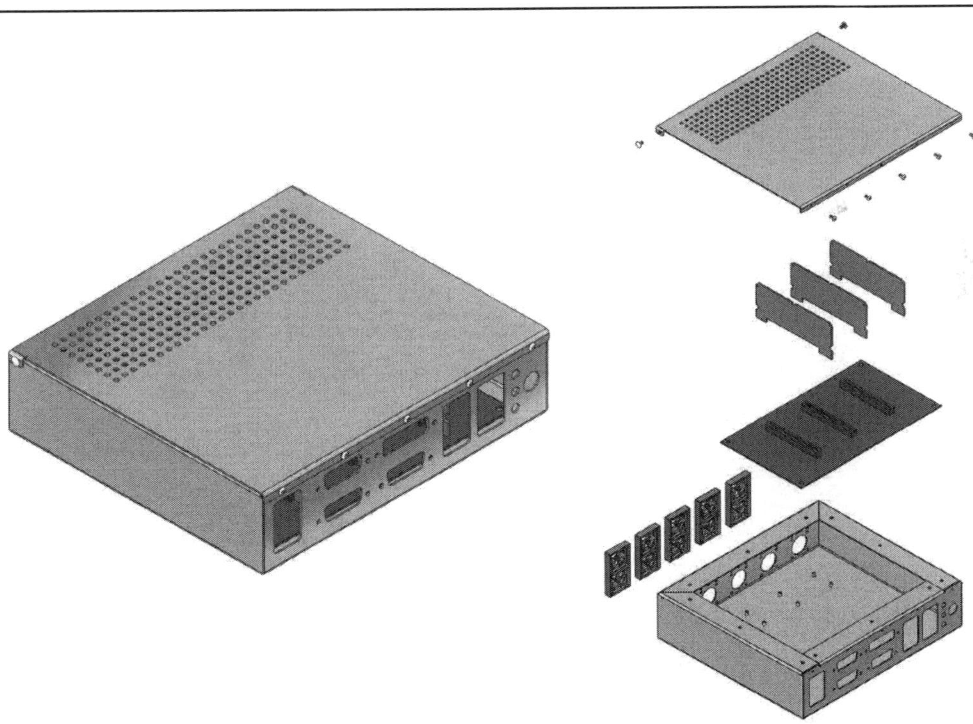

Sheet Metal Chassis - Model designed with SOLIDWORKS

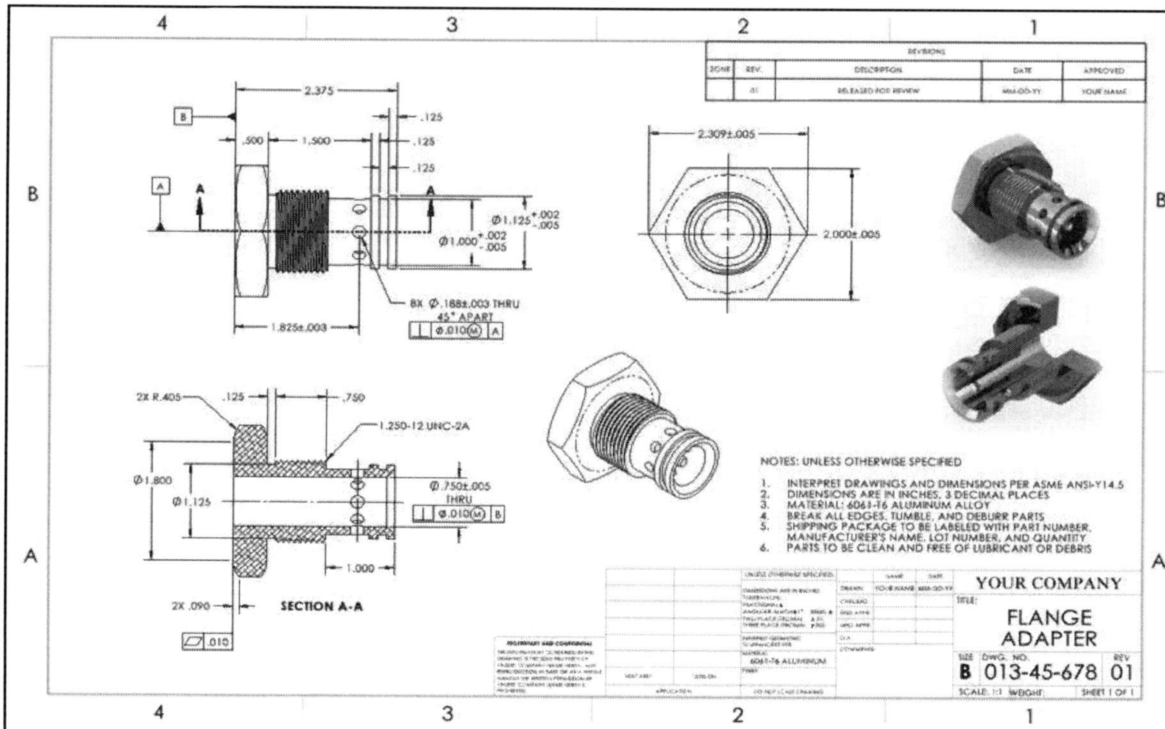

Flange Adapter - Model & Drawing designed with SOLIDWORKS

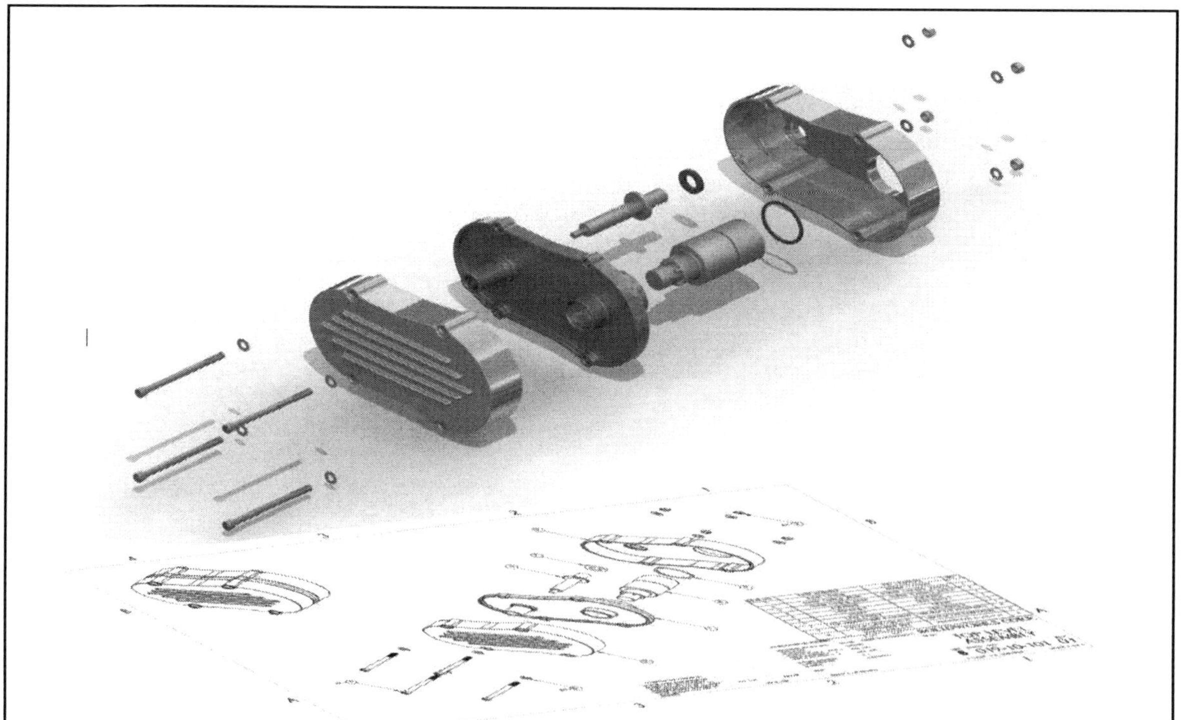

Casing Assembly - Model & Drawing designed with SOLIDWORKS

PGIL2026USA